T0137021

Lecture Notes in Computer Science   12704

More information about this subseries at http://www.springer.com/series/7410

Kenneth G. Paterson (Ed.)

Topics in Cryptology – CT-RSA 2021

Cryptographers' Track at the RSA Conference 2021
Virtual Event, May 17–20, 2021
Proceedings

 Springer

Editor
Kenneth G. Paterson
ETH Zürich
Zürich, Switzerland

ISSN 0302-9743 ISSN 1611-3349 (electronic)
Lecture Notes in Computer Science
ISBN 978-3-030-75538-6 ISBN 978-3-030-75539-3 (eBook)
https://doi.org/10.1007/978-3-030-75539-3

LNCS Sublibrary: SL4 – Security and Cryptology

This Springer imprint is published by the registered company Springer Nature Switzerland AG
The registered company address is: Gewerbestrasse 11, 6330 Cham, Switzerland

Preface

The RSA conference has been a major international event for information security experts since its inception in 1991. It is an annual event that attracts several hundred vendors and over 40,000 participants from industry, government, and academia. Since 2001, the RSA conference has included the Cryptographer's Track (CT-RSA). This track, essentially a sub-conference of the main event, provides a forum for the dissemination of current research in cryptography.

This volume represents the proceedings of the 2021 edition of the RSA Conference Cryptographer's Track. Due to the COVID-19 pandemic, the conference was held online during May 17–20, 2021. The unusual circumstances provided an opportunity to revisit the format of the event and try to integrate it more fully into the main RSA conference. This was done by partnering each presentation session with a more informal, broader discussion session involving the presented papers' authors and invited guests. I am grateful to the authors and guests for engaging with this experimental approach.

A total of 100 submissions were received for review, of which 27 were selected for presentation and publication. The selection process was a difficult task since there were many more high quality submissions than we could accept. The submissions were anonymous, and each submission was assigned to at least three reviewers (four if the paper included a Program Committee member as an author or if it was a "Systemisation of Knowledge" paper). I am thankful to all Program Committee members for producing high-quality reviews and for actively participating in discussions. My appreciation also goes to all external reviewers. I am also grateful to the Program Committee members who acted as shepherds for some of the submissions.

The submission and review process, as well as the editing of these proceedings, were greatly simplified by using the webreview software written by Dr. Shai Halevi, which we used with the permission of the International Association for Cryptologic Research (IACR). My thanks go to Shai. I am also grateful to Prof. Stanislaw Jarecki, my predecessor as Program Chair for CT-RSA. Stas provided a wealth of advice and insights based on his experience. I hope to be able to pass on to my successor as much as I obtained from Stas.

My sincere thanks go also to Dr. Guido Zosimo-Landolfo from Springer Verlag and everyone on the team there for their assistance in preparing and producing these proceedings.

Last, but not least, on behalf of all CT-RSA participants, I would like to thank Tara Jung and Britta Glade who acted as RSA Conference liaison to the Cryptographer's Track. In this capacity, Tara and Britta essentially played the role of General Chairs for

the CT-RSA conference, and I am very grateful to them for all the work they did in
helping to organise the conference and making it run smoothly.

March 2021   Kenneth G. Paterson

Organization

Program Chair

Kenneth G. Paterson   ETH Zürich, Switzerland

Program Committee

Masayuki Abe	NTT Secure Platform Labs, Japan
Shi Bai	Florida Atlantic University, USA
Paulo Barreto	University of Washington, USA
Lejla Batina	Radboud University, The Netherlands
Elif Bilge Kavun	University of Passau, Germany
Olivier Blazy	Université de Limoges, XLim, France
Chris Brzuska	Aalto University, Finland
Céline Chevalier	CRED, Université Paris II Panthéon-Assas, France
Craig Costello	Microsoft Research, USA
Jean Paul Degabriele	TU Darmstadt, Germany
Luca De Feo	IBM Research – Zürich, Switzerland
Ben Fuller	University of Connecticut, USA
Steven Galbraith	University of Auckland, New Zealand
Lydia Garms	Royal Holloway, University of London, UK
Daniel Genkin	University of Michigan, USA
Paul Grubbs	NYU, Cornell Tech, University of Michigan, USA
Goichiro Hanaoka	AIST, Japan
Helena Handschuh	Rambus Cryptography Research, USA
Carmit Hazay	Bar-Ilan University, Israel
Andreas Hülsing	Eindhoven University of Technology, The Netherlands
Takanori Isobe	University of Hyogo, Japan
Marcel Keller	CSIRO's Data61, Australia
Tancrède Lepoint	Google, USA
Benoit Libert	CNRS and ENS de Lyon, France
Brice Minaud	Inria and ENS, France
Tarik Moataz	Aroki Systems, USA
Svetla Nikova	KU Leuven, Belgium
Jiaxin Pan	NTNU Norway, Norway
Charalampos Papamanthou	University of Maryland, USA
Bertram Poettering	IBM Research – Zürich, Switzerland
Bart Preneel	KU Leuven, Belgium
Eyal Ronen	Tel Aviv University, Israel
Andy Rupp	University of Luxembourg, Luxembourg
Alexander Russell	University of Connecticut, USA
Jacob Schuldt	AIST, Japan

Nigel Smart	KU Leuven, Belgium
Juraj Somorovsky	Paderborn University, Germany
Martijn Stam	Simula UiB, Norway
Douglas Stebila	University of Waterloo, Canada
Fernando Virdia	Royal Holloway, University of London, UK
Michael Walter	IST Austria, Austria
Yuval Yarom	University of Adelaide and Data61, Australia

Additional Reviewers

Miguel Ambrona	Gunnar Hartung	Thomas Peters
Benedikt Auerbach	Shoichi Hirose	Chen Qian
Gustavo Banegas	Le Phi Hung	Yuan Quan
Laasya Bangalore	Ilia Iliashenko	Markus Raiber
Subhadeep Banik	Akiko Inoue	Adrian Ranea
Tim Beyne	Samuel Jaques	Simon Rastikian
Rishabh Bhadauria	Saqib A. Kakvi	Krijn Reijnders
Nina Bindel	Vukasin Karadzic	Vincent Rijmen
Estuardo Alpirez Bock	Shuichi Katsumata	Yusuke Sakai
Ryann Rose Carter	Michael Klooss	John Schanck
Shan Chen	Lilia Kraleva	Berry Schoenmakers
Ilaria Chillotti	Kaoru Kurosawa	Madura Shelton
Ana Costache	Gregor Leander	Tjerand Silde
Anamaria Costache	Chaoyun Li	Yongsoo Song
Thomas Debris-Alazard	Fukang Liu	Jessica Sorrell
Ioannis Demertzis	Patrick Longa	Christoph Striecks
Amit Deo	Vadim Lyubashevsky	Younes Talibi
Siemen Dhooghe	Akash Madhusudan	Ida Tucker
Samuel Dobson	Takahiro Matsuda	Qingju Wang
Keita Emura	Alireza Mehrdad	Yunhua Wen
Eiichiro Fujisaki	Nadia El Mrabet	Keita Xagawa
Alonso Gonzalez	Kazuma Ohara	Jianhua Yan
Jérôme Govinden	Satsuya Ohata	Avishay Yanai
Felix Günther	Miyako Ohkubo	Greg Zaverucha
Fabrice Ben Hamouda	Elisabeth Oswald	Lukas Zobernig
Keisuke Hara	Guillermo Pascual Perez	Marcus Brinkmann

Contents

Secure Fast Evaluation of Iterative Methods: With an Application to Secure
PageRank. 1
   Daniele Cozzo, Nigel P. Smart, and Younes Talibi Alaoui

Compilation of Function Representations for Secure
Computing Paradigms 26
   Karim Baghery, Cyprien Delpech de Saint Guilhem, Emmanuela Orsini,
   Nigel P. Smart, and Titouan Tanguy

Oblivious TLS via Multi-party Computation. 51
   Damiano Abram, Ivan Damgård, Peter Scholl, and Sven Trieflinger

Noisy Simon Period Finding. 75
   Alexander May, Lars Schlieper, and Jonathan Schwinger

A Bunch of Broken Schemes: A Simple yet Powerful Linear Approach
to Analyzing Security of Attribute-Based Encryption. 100
   Marloes Venema and Greg Alpár

Zero-Correlation Linear Cryptanalysis with Equal Treatment for Plaintexts
and Tweakeys. 126
   Chao Niu, Muzhou Li, Siwei Sun, and Meiqin Wang

SoK: Game-Based Security Models for Group Key Exchange. 148
   Bertram Poettering, Paul Rösler, Jörg Schwenk, and Douglas Stebila

EPID with Malicious Revocation 177
   Olivier Sanders and Jacques Traoré

Signed Diffie-Hellman Key Exchange with Tight Security 201
   Jiaxin Pan, Chen Qian, and Magnus Ringerud

Lattice-Based Proof of Shuffle and Applications to Electronic Voting 227
   Diego F. Aranha, Carsten Baum, Kristian Gjøsteen, Tjerand Silde,
   and Thor Tunge

More Efficient Shuffle Argument from Unique Factorization 252
   Toomas Krips and Helger Lipmaa

Cryptanalysis of a Dynamic Universal Accumulator over Bilinear Groups . . . 276
   Alex Biryukov, Aleksei Udovenko, and Giuseppe Vitto

FAN: A Lightweight Authenticated Cryptographic Algorithm   299
    Lin Jiao, Dengguo Feng, Yonglin Hao, Xinxin Gong, and Shaoyu Du

Related-Key Analysis of Generalized Feistel Networks with Expanding
Round Functions   326
    Yuqing Zhao, Wenqi Yu, and Chun Guo

The Key-Dependent Message Security of Key-Alternating Feistel Ciphers . . .   351
    Pooya Farshim, Louiza Khati, Yannick Seurin, and Damien Vergnaud

Mesh Messaging in Large-Scale Protests: Breaking Bridgefy   375
    Martin R. Albrecht, Jorge Blasco, Rikke Bjerg Jensen,
    and Lenka Mareková

Inverse-Sybil Attacks in Automated Contact Tracing   399
    Benedikt Auerbach, Suvradip Chakraborty, Karen Klein,
    Guillermo Pascual-Perez, Krzysztof Pietrzak, Michael Walter,
    and Michelle Yeo

On the Effectiveness of Time Travel to Inject COVID-19 Alerts   422
    Vincenzo Iovino, Serge Vaudenay, and Martin Vuagnoux

SoK: How (not) to Design and Implement Post-quantum Cryptography   444
    James Howe, Thomas Prest, and Daniel Apon

Dual Lattice Attacks for Closest Vector Problems (with Preprocessing)   478
    Thijs Laarhoven and Michael Walter

On the Hardness of Module-LWE with Binary Secret   503
    Katharina Boudgoust, Corentin Jeudy, Adeline Roux-Langlois,
    and Weiqiang Wen

Multi-party Revocation in Sovrin: Performance through Distributed Trust . . .   527
    Lukas Helminger, Daniel Kales, Sebastian Ramacher,
    and Roman Walch

Balancing Privacy and Accountability in Blockchain Identity Management . . .   552
    Ivan Damgård, Chaya Ganesh, Hamidreza Khoshakhlagh,
    Claudio Orlandi, and Luisa Siniscalchi

Non-interactive Half-Aggregation of EdDSA and Variants of Schnorr
Signatures   577
    Konstantinos Chalkias, François Garillot, Yashvanth Kondi,
    and Valeria Nikolaenko

A Framework to Optimize Implementations of Matrices   609
    Da Lin, Zejun Xiang, Xiangyong Zeng, and Shasha Zhang

Improvements to RSA Key Generation and CRT on Embedded Devices   633
Mike Hamburg, Mike Tunstall, and Qinglai Xiao

On the Cost of ASIC Hardware Crackers: A SHA-1 Case Study.   657
Anupam Chattopadhyay, Mustafa Khairallah, Gaëtan Leurent,
Zakaria Najm, Thomas Peyrin, and Vesselin Velichkov

Author Index   683

Secure Fast Evaluation of Iterative Methods: With an Application to Secure PageRank

Daniele Cozzo[1], Nigel P. Smart[1,2], and Younes Talibi Alaoui[1]

[1] imec-COSIC, KU Leuven, Leuven, Belgium
{daniele.cozzo,nigel.smart,younes.talibialaoui}@kuleuven.be
[2] University of Bristol, Bristol, UK

Abstract. Iterative methods are a standard technique in many areas of scientific computing. The key idea is that a function is applied repeatedly until the resulting sequence converges to the correct answer. When applying such methods in a secure computation methodology (for example using MPC, FHE, or SGX) one either needs to perform enough steps to ensure convergence irrespective of the input data, or one needs to perform a convergence test within the algorithm, and this itself leads to a leakage of data. Using the Banach Fixed Point theorem, and its extensions, we show that this data-leakage can be quantified. We then apply this to a secure (via MPC) implementation of the PageRank methodology. For PageRank we show that allowing this small amount of data-leakage produces a much more efficient secure implementation, and that for many underlying graphs this 'leakage' is already known to any attacker.

1 Introduction

Iterative methods are a standard technique in scientific computing; indeed a vast array of the problems have traditionally been mapped to iterative methods. Examples include finding roots of systems of equations (e.g. the Newton-Raphson method for polynomials in a single variable), finding eigenvalues and eigenvectors of matrices (and hence performing tasks such as Principal Component Analysis), or of finding solutions to ordinary and partial differential equations. Indeed the solution of many real world problems involve mapping the problem into a mathematical formulation in which an iterative method can be applied.

Leakage From Iterative Methods: At its heart an iterative method involves a map $F : \mathcal{M} \longrightarrow \mathcal{M}$ on a metric space $\mathcal{M}$ for which we want to compute a stationary point, i.e. a value $x \in \mathcal{M}$ s.t. $F(x) = x$. That $\mathcal{M}$ is a metric space implies we have a well defined distance metric $d(x, y)$, and thus a well defined notion of convergence. If $\mathcal{M}$ is a normed vector space with norm $\| \cdot \|$ then this induces the distance $d(x, y) = \|x - y\|$. The iterative method requires one to determine a subset $X \subset A$ containing the desired fixed point x, s.t. if we pick any starting value $x_0 \in X$, then the sequence $x_{i+1} \leftarrow F(x_i)$ will converge to x.

© Springer Nature Switzerland AG 2021
K. G. Paterson (Ed.): CT-RSA 2021, LNCS 12704, pp. 1–25, 2021.
https://doi.org/10.1007/978-3-030-75539-3_1

In applying the iterative method often the most difficult task is the initial choice of the set X.

However, when examined from the point of view of secure computation one has an additional problem. Suppose the function F is itself secret, for example F could be a polynomial of bounded degree whose coefficients are unknown for which it is desired to compute a root, or F could be a matrix operator of a given dimension for which an eigenvector is desired. Apart from the actual computation of the iteration, in the secure domain we need to determine how many iterations we need to perform. This is a problem irrespective of whether we try to perform the secure computation with Multi-Party Computation (MPC), Fully-Homomorphic Encryption (FHE) or using a form of Trusted Execution Environment (TEE) such as Intel's SGX platform.

When operating in the clear the iteration is performed until the difference satisfies $d(x_{i+1}, x_i) \leq \epsilon_{\mathsf{abs}}$, for some fixed tolerance ϵ_{abs}. We could perform such a termination condition in the secure domain, but that would leak information. Thus a tempting solution to this problem is simply to compute the sequence $(x_i)_{i=0}^N$ for a large enough N so that we do not need to leak any information. Clearly, the latter solution is more expensive.

In this paper we examine this 'when to terminate' problem in generality, and relate the information leakage to the classical Banach Fixed Point Theorem (a.k.a. the Contraction Mapping Theorem) which was proved by Banach in 1922. This restricts the function $F : \mathcal{M} \longrightarrow \mathcal{M}$ to a function $F : X \longrightarrow X$ for a subset $X \subset \mathcal{M}$ for which the resulting function is a contraction (see below for the definition). In particular the speed of convergence is related to the Lipschitz constant of the underlying contraction mapping $F : X \longrightarrow X$. Thus the information leakage is the single value giving the number of iterations until convergence. This value itself encodes information about the function F and the set X, as well as the starting position x_0. We answer the question as to what this information actually encodes, specifically with respect to the map F. By quantifying the precise information leakage, the user of the secure computation environment can determine whether this leakage is acceptable or not. In many examples this leakage is indeed totally acceptable.

We focus on what information is leaked about the function F from the number of iterations. Clearly the number of iterations taken also leaks something about the initial starting vector x_0, in particular how close it is to the final solution. For some applications of iterated methods this could itself leak information about F, for example when using a Newton iteration to find a root of a polynomial. Thus the number of iterations leaks information about F and the initial starting point. For the power method to find the dominant eigenvalue one can select x_0 to be a random vector (as long as it has a non-zero component in the direction of the corresponding eigenvector). Hence, for our application to the power method the parties can select x_0 at random, meaning even less information is revealed about F via a single iteration. Of course if one applies the method repeatedly with different random x_0 values, then the contribution from the starting value x_0 can be averaged out. Hence, in what follows one needs to bear in mind that we are considering the best possible case for an attacker. In practice, for a single execution of an iterative method, the ability to extract meaningful information about either x_0 or F is limited.

The Power Method for Matrices: To illustrate this we then go on to discuss one of the most famous applications of iterative methods; namely the power method for matrices used to compute eigenvalues/eigenvectors. In this problem, which forms the basis of many numerical computation problems, one is given an $m \times m$ complex valued matrix $A \in \mathcal{C}^{m \times m}$, and one is asked to compute an eigenvalue/eigenvector, i.e. a solution to the equation $A \cdot \mathbf{x} = \lambda \cdot \mathbf{x}$. If we order the eigenvalues of A as $|\lambda_1| > |\lambda_2| \geq |\lambda_3| \geq \ldots \geq |\lambda_m|$ then the iteration

$$\mathbf{x}_{i+1} \leftarrow \frac{A \cdot \mathbf{x}_i}{\|A \cdot \mathbf{x}_i\|}$$

will converge to an eigenvector $\mathbf{x}$ of A corresponding to the *dominant eigenvalue* λ_1, assuming the starting vector $\mathbf{x}_0$ is has a non-zero component in the direction of eigenvector $\mathbf{x}$.

The advantage of iterative methods for solving the eigenvector problem is that they respect any sparseness of the underlying matrix A. In other words memory is constant. In addition they scale well with the dimension, which the traditional methods used for low dimension matrices do not. Iterative methods are also data oblivious, i.e. apart from the termination test the algorithm requires no data dependent branching or memory access operations.

It is a classical result, found in almost all undergraduate mathematics courses, that the speed of convergence of the power method iteration is *related* to the quotient λ_2/λ_1, called the spectral gap. Thus, revealing the number of iterations required in order to satisfy $\|\mathbf{x}_{i+1} - \mathbf{x}_i\| \leq \epsilon_{\mathsf{abs}}$ reveals something about the quantity $|\lambda_2|/|\lambda_1|$. For large dimensional matrices A revealing this quantity is a small price to pay for the performance improvement of the computation. Note, the number of iterations does not leak the exact value of λ_2, as the exact number of iterations depends on all eigenvalues and the initial starting position. However, the dominant term is dependent on λ_2. Whether revealing something about λ_2 reveals something adversarially interesting about the original input matrix A depends upon the problem one is solving, i.e. from where A originates.

PageRank: PageRank is originally an algorithm devised by Brin and Page, in order to give 'importance' rankings to web-pages [28], which formed the basis of the original Google search algorithm. The algorithm models the Internet as a directed graph G in which the m nodes are web-pages. A node i has an edge towards node j, if web-page i contains a hyper-link to web-page j. The PageRank algorithm aims to simulate a random surfer performing a random walk on the graph of such web-pages. The output of the algorithm is a probability distribution $\boldsymbol{\pi}$ over the set of all web pages (i.e. all elements are in the range $[0, 1]$ and we have $\|\boldsymbol{\pi}\|_1 = 1$). The vector $\boldsymbol{\pi}$ is known as the PageRank vector. The PageRank vector represents the probabilities of our random surfer ending up on a specific web-page. Those probabilities serve as a ranking to web-pages, that is further used to sort the results that will be displayed for a user after a search request. The idea being that a page which the random surfer is more likely to land on is more likely to be important/useful than one which they are less likely to land on.

To run PageRank we first compute the adjacency matrix A of the graph G of the m web-pages. This matrix contains zeros except in entry $a_{i,j}$ when page i has a link to page j, in which case we place a one. We then transform A into a row-stochastic matrix P. To do this we replace each value of one in P by the value of one over the Hamming weight of the corresponding row in A. Thus $p_{i,j}$ equals the probability of a surfer on page i clicking one of the outgoing links with uniform probability.

However, the matrix P has some issues. In particular there are rows which are all zero, which correspond to webpages which have no outgoing links. In the graph such pages are called 'dangling nodes'. The fix for this problem is to add to P a matrix $D = \mathbf{d} \cdot \mathbf{v}^T$, where $d^{(i)} = 1$ if node i is a dangling node, and $\mathbf{v}$ represents a probability distribution, called the *personalization vector*. In 'traditional' PageRank the personalization vector is set as $\mathbf{v}$ with $v^{(i)} = 1/m$. This models the idea that once the random surfer reaches a dangling web-page, he then jumps to a completely random page on the Internet. However, this is purely a choice and other vectors could be selected. For example users might be more likely to jump to Facebook or Google in an Internet application. The resulting matrix $Q = P + D$ is then a row-stochastic matrix.

However, this is yet to model a realistic random surfer, as it supposes that the surfer will be restricted to the links contained in non-dangling web-pages he passes through during the random walk, but we know this not to be true. To take this into account, PageRank has a parameter $\lambda \in [0, 1]$ called the damping factor, which (in classical PageRank) represents the probability that a user does not click on a link on a web-page while moving to the next one, but instead jumps to a random one following the probabilities contained in the personalization vector $\mathbf{v}$. From this we define the matrix $E = \mathbf{e} \cdot \mathbf{v}^T$, where $\mathbf{e}$ denotes the all one m-dimensional column vector, and then compute the final PageRank matrix as

$$M = ((1 - \lambda) \cdot Q + \lambda \cdot E)^\mathsf{T}. \tag{1}$$

The value λ is usually selected to be between 0.1 and 0.2, for reasons we will explain later.

Clearly, by construction, M is a column stochastic matrix, and since it is stochastic the right eigenvalues of M satisfy $\lambda_1 = 1 \geq |\lambda_2| \geq \ldots \geq |\lambda_m| \geq 0$. The solution to the PageRank problem is the eigenvector corresponding to the dominant eigenvalue; i.e. the solution to the problem $M \cdot \boldsymbol{\pi} = \boldsymbol{\pi}$. Thus PageRank is an example of a problem which can be solved via iterative methods. Indeed, iterative methods are preferred since the matrix M is very large.

Note, there is a whole line of work within graph theory which is dedicated to the relationship between the spectra of adjacency matrices and the structure of the underlying graphs [1,2,32]. However, this is only applicable in the case of *undirected* graphs. For directed graphs underlying PageRank, it is known [12,21,22] that if the eigenvalues of Q are given by $\{1, \lambda_2', \ldots, \lambda_n'\}$ then the eigenvalues of M are given by $\{1, (1 - \lambda) \cdot \lambda_2', \ldots, (1 - \lambda) \cdot \lambda_n'\}$. This generalized a result in [16] which showed that if the Markov chain underlying the stochastic matrix Q has at least two irreducible closed subsets then $\lambda_2' = 1$. Thus assuming the underlying directed graph has two irreducible closed subsets, then we already know that the second eigenvalue of the PageRank matrix is equal to $1 - \lambda$. Thus for this *specific* application of the power method to the PageRank matrix leaking a function of the second eigenvalue λ_2 reveals no more information than one already knows.

Why a Secure PageRank?: Graph analysis techniques are nowadays a crucial tool for financial institutions, serving as a means to identify fraudulent bank accounts, or fraudulent or suspicious transactions (such as transactions related to money laundering). See [24] for a discussion on secure computation technologies applied to financial intelligence sharing, or [15] for a specific example of secure graph analysis for financial stress testing. These techniques help to extract features from a large amount of data, consisting of, for example, money movements between bank accounts. Leading to accounts being investigated if anomalies are detected. One of the techniques proposed is the PageRank algorithm, which turns out to be well suited for the financial context.

PageRank can be used in different ways in this direction. One way [27] consists of modeling the bank accounts and transactions taking place between them as a directed graph, where nodes consist of bank accounts, and an edge is set from bank account i to bank account j if i has sent to j a transaction, and then running a random *biased* walk to extract the PageRank vector, where the random walker bias his walk towards acknowledged fraudulent accounts. The bias is introduced by making the personalisation vector zero on all accounts which were not known to be fraudulent, with the same for the starting vector.

Doing this will help determine the bank accounts that are important from the point of view of fraud. See also [35] for similar ideas in the context of social security fraud. In another method explained, in [26], the use of PageRank is to reduce false positive rates in traditional fraud scoring.

In order to obtain reliable results with PageRank, we need many financial institutions to collaborate. In fact, each financial institution I_k can locally only build its own transaction graph G_k, modeling transactions in which the sender or the receiver is a bank account from the set B_k of the bank accounts that I_k manages. While this will cover the full activity of transfers within B_k, data will be missing (for example) from regarding bank accounts that receive transactions from accounts in B_k but which are not in B_k. Such extended transaction graphs are crucial in applications in which one is trying to locate money laundering. Thus the more financial institutions that combine their graphs, the more accurate the results of PageRank will be in detecting fraud; this is explained in more detail in [11].

However, financial institutions are not willing, or able for regulatory reasons, to simply share this information among each other. Therefore, they need to engage in a protocol, where they can perform the computation (the PageRank algorithm) on their respective inputs (G_k), and the only information revealed out of this computation is the output (the rankings of the bank accounts).

Another use case where one would take use of a secure implementation of PageRank is the analysis of social networks. That is, similarly to the Web and to transactions among institutions, social networks such as YouTube, Twitter and Facebook etc., can be modeled as graphs [17] where nodes are users' accounts. Running PageRank within one network on the publicly available data is already deemed to be useful, where PageRank can be used to evaluate the reputation of users [14]. However, addressing a more complicated problem such as understanding the flow of photos or news stories etc. across interconnected networks may require the owners of these social networks to engage in a secure computation of PageRank in order to provide the relevant data.

PageRank and MPC: As already remarked the convergence of fixed point methods is an issue in any secure computation paradigm in relation to the number of steps needed to determine convergence. There has already been some work in looking at MPC as a means of securely evaluating the PageRank algorithm [30], due to the above mentioned applications in fraud detection.

MPC protocols can be divided into two big families with respect to the level of security they can offer; protocols providing passive security, and protocols providing active security. In a passively secure MPC protocol, the adversary is assumed to be honest, but curious. That is, the parties are assumed to follow the exact description of the protocol, however they can use the information they see in order to infer information about inputs of the other parties. In an actively secure MPC protocol, the adversary can deviate from the protocol, and yet the privacy of the parties' inputs must be still maintained.

In [30] the authors presented a *passively* secure MPC protocol for PageRank in the context of fraud detection for bank account transactions. The authors are able to obtain a very fast and scalable protocol due to the fact that they assume all banks with relevant accounts *participate* in the protocol. In particular each bank locally holds their view of the transaction graph, i.e. the movements between accounts which they have sight of. This enables the protocol to be efficiently implemented using partially homomorphic encryption. Note, the work in [30] could be improved using our analysis of termination conditions for the power method.

Roughly speaking in [30], party I_k is in charge of updating the rankings of the nodes of B_k in iteration i, using the encryptions it received of the rankings of the other nodes after iterations $i-1$, by taking use of the fact that the encryption scheme is partially homomorphic and the needed data to update the ranking is held in clear by I_k. Thus only linear operations are needed to be performed.

Apart from being passively secure, the protocol crucially relied on each part of the graph being held in the clear to at least one party. In many situations this may not be feasible. Indeed the protocol is unsuitable for use in a secure outsourcing scenario for precisely this reason. For an outsourcing based approach to be secure, the financial institutions need to provide all their data encrypted, and therefore a partially homomorphic encryption scheme will no longer be sufficient.

To cope with these limitations we provide a 'pure' MPC implementation of the PageRank power iteration. In other words a method in which parts of the graph are hidden from all parties. The protocol will benefit from our early termination procedure. Furthermore, since we are employing general MPC techniques that guarantee active security, the resulting implementation will be inherently actively secure.

Our solution does not require from all the institutions to participate in the computation, but only a subset of them or third parties, which the institutions agree upon. Thus we distinguish here between three different entities, the financial institutions $\{I_1, \ldots, I_u\}$, the computing servers $S = \{S_1, \ldots, S_v\}$ with $v = 2$ or $v = 3$, and the bank accounts $\{b_1, \ldots, b_m\}$ that the institutions manage. The institutions do not need to trust all the servers in S, but they do need to trust at least one party for the case where $v = 2$, and at least two parties not to collude for the case of $v = 3$.

Even though we are unable to cope with the size of graphs reported on in [30], we feel our solution can be applied in other situations where one has a different trade off. In the course of which we provide an optimization to the secure dot-product computation over fixed point numbers at the heart of PageRank which is similar to that introduced in [25]; this results in a number of $N \cdot m^2$ secure additions, $N \cdot (m^2 + m)$ secure multiplications and $N \cdot m$ truncations, where N is the number of the iterations performed. From this it is clear that the computations are mainly algebraic therefore motivating our using of arithmetic modulo p to represent secret shared numbers. Indeed linear secret sharing seems to have an advantage over garbling techniques even for the case of two servers, due to that adding and multiplying large numbers many times is expensive with such techniques.

2 Preliminaries

In many applications, such as ours of securely evaluating the PageRank algorithm, we require to work with approximations to real numbers. One could try to emulate precise IEEE floating point arithmetic, but this is rather expensive. Thus we need to somehow 'encode' the real numbers within the arithmetic of $\mathbb{F}_p$. A common way of doing this is to use a form of fixed point arithmetic, introduced in [6].

To represent a real number e we approximate it as a fixed point number $\bar{e}$, where

$$\bar{e} = e \cdot 2^{-f}.$$

The value f is a fixed public value that defines the precise position of the fixed point, i.e. 2^{-f} is the smallest unit we can represent and the increment between two successive values. The value e is an integer in the range $[-2^{k-1}, \ldots, 2^{k-1}]$, for some public parameter k. The value k determines the total number of binary points of data we can represent, thus the biggest value we can represent is 2^{k-1-f}.

To hold a secret version of this approximation $\bar{e}$ to the real number $\mathfrak{e}$ we simply secret share the integer e above as an element in $\mathbb{F}_p$. In particular this means that we must have $p > 2^k$; and indeed to perform arithmetic we will require an even larger value of p as we shall later see. We write $\langle \bar{e} \rangle$ to represent the sharing of a fixed point value $\bar{e}$, and the mod-p value we actually store we shall denote as $\langle e \rangle$.

If $\langle h \rangle$ is a shared integer in the range $[-2^{k-1-f}, \ldots, 2^{k-1-f}]$ then we can obtain the shared fixed point representation $\langle \bar{g} \rangle$ of the same value h by computing $\langle g \rangle = \langle h \rangle \cdot 2^f$ (and therefore $\bar{g} = g \cdot 2^{-f} = h$), which is a linear operation. Fixed point shared values can also be added by simply adding the underlying shared integer representation.

Multiplying fixed point numbers $\langle \bar{e} \rangle$ and $\langle \bar{g} \rangle$ is however a little more complex. We first multiply the underlying shared integer representations $\langle e \rangle$ and $\langle g \rangle$, to obtain the value $\langle h \rangle \leftarrow \langle e \rangle \cdot \langle g \rangle$ and then we shift and truncate $\langle h \rangle$ by f bits, see Fig. 1. The value h will be an integer in the range $[-2^{2 \cdot k - 2}, \ldots, 2^{2 \cdot k - 2}]$ thus to avoid wrap-around modulo p we will require $2^{2 \cdot k - 2} < p$.

Fixed Point Multiply

Input: $\langle \bar{e} \rangle$, $\langle \bar{g} \rangle$, **Output:** $\langle \bar{h} \rangle = \langle \bar{e} \rangle \cdot \langle \bar{g} \rangle$.
- $\langle v \rangle \leftarrow \langle e \rangle \cdot \langle g \rangle$.
- $\langle h \rangle \leftarrow \mathsf{TruncPr}(\langle v \rangle, 2 \cdot k, f)$.

Fig. 1. Algorithm to multiply two shared fixed point values

The truncation by f-bits is done using a technique from [6]. The algorithm $\mathsf{TruncPr}(\langle x \rangle, t, o)$ takes a shared integer value $\langle x \rangle$ where $x \in [-2^{t-1}, \ldots, 2^{t-1}]$, a value $o \in [1, \ldots, t-1]$ and outputs the value $\langle y \rangle$ where $y = \lfloor x/2^o \rfloor + u$ for an (essentially random) unknown bit $u \in \{0, 1\}$. This probabilistic truncation algorithm turns out to be more efficient in MPC than a method which avoids the random bit u. The method works by opening the value $\langle a + r \rangle$ for some blinding value $r \in [0, \ldots, 2^{t+\kappa}]$ where κ is a statistical security parameter, and then computing the result from the clear value $c = a + r$. In particular we require, to avoid overflows modulo p, that $2^{t+\kappa} < p$. To ensure correctness of the entire procedure we hence require that $2 \cdot k + \kappa < \log_2 p$.

Another computation we will be performing on secret shared fixed-point values is comparison. The protocols implementing comparison that we will be using are also taken from [6], where it is also performed using truncation. That is, comparison is based on the observation that if $a < 0$, then $\lfloor a/2^{k-1} \rfloor = -1$ and if $a \geq 0$ then $\lfloor a/2^{k-1} \rfloor = 0$. Therefore, we can compute the sign of a secret shared value $\langle \bar{a} \rangle$ by truncating it by $k - 1$ bits.

However, truncation here uses a deterministic sub-routine Trunc unlike the sub-routine $\mathsf{TruncPr}$, as we need to round to the correct integer here. While Trunc does not add any extra conditions to the requirements on the parameters for correctness, it is relatively expensive compared to TruncPr. However, we will be performing orders of magnitude more TruncPr's than Trunc operations and so, whilst it is more expensive, the effect of Trunc on the final runtime of the overall algorithm can be ignored.

3 Banach Fixed Point Theorem and the Power Method

Suppose we have a function $F : \mathcal{M} \longrightarrow \mathcal{M}$ on a complete metric space $\mathcal{M}$ with distance $d(x, y)$. The function F we will compute securely, and then repeat the application, thus producing a sequence of values

$$x_{i+1} \leftarrow F(x_i),$$

for some starting value x_0. We assume, for the moment, that this sequence tends to a value $x_i \longrightarrow x$ which is a fixed point of the function F, i.e. $F(x) = x$. Our goal is to securely compute a value x_N such that $d(x_N, x) \leq \epsilon_{\mathsf{abs}}$; indeed it may be that we keep the final value x_N secure and do not release it to the computing parties. But as we are computing this in the secure domain, we have two options:

1. We pick a large value of N, irrespective of the specific value of F and x_0.
2. At each iteration we reveal to the parties the value $d(x_i, x_{i-1})$, or whether $d(x_i, x_{i-1}) \leq \epsilon_{\mathsf{abs}}$ and terminate the iteration if this is less than some given tolerance ϵ_{abs}. Let $N = i$ denote the first instance when this happens.

Clearly the second methodology, irrespective of the underlying secure computation technology (be it MPC, FHE or TEE) potentially reveals more information than the first. The question is; how much? The answer to this question is provided by the Banach Fixed Point Theorem.

To ensure the sequence (x_i) converges we need to make some assumptions about the starting point x_0 and the map F. We first need to restrict the domain/codomain $\mathcal{M}$ to a complete subset $X \subset \mathcal{M}$ on which F is a *contraction mapping*.

Definition 3.1. *A map $F : X \longrightarrow X$ is said to be a contraction mapping on X if there exists a constant $q \in [0, 1)$ such that, for all $x, y \in X$,*

$$d(F(x), F(y)) \leq q \cdot d(x, y).$$

The constant q is called the Lipschitz constant for F and X, it depends on both F and (sometimes) the set X. The following theorem is classical, and proved by Banach in 1922,

Theorem 3.1 (Banach Fixed Point Theorem). *Let (X, d) be a non-empty complete metric space and let $F : X \longrightarrow X$ be a function. If F is a contraction mapping, with constant q, then there is a unique fixed point $x \in X$, i.e. $F(x) = x$. If we pick $x_0 \in X$ and define the sequence $x_{i+1} = F(x_i)$ for $i \geq 0$, then $x_i \longrightarrow x$ as $i \longrightarrow \infty$.*

The speed of convergence is itself controlled by the value q; in particular we have

$$d(x, x_i) \leq \frac{q^i}{1-q} \cdot d(x_1, x_0), \qquad d(x, x_{i+1}) \leq \frac{q}{1-q} \cdot d(x_{i+1}, x_i),$$

$$d(x, x_{i+1}) \leq q \cdot d(x, x_i), \qquad d(x, x_{i+1}) \leq q^i \cdot d(x, x_0).$$

Thus in our second secure computation strategy above if we terminated at step N when $d(x_N, x_{N-1}) \leq \epsilon_{\mathsf{abs}}$ then we have that

$$d(x, x_N) \leq \frac{q}{1-q} \cdot \epsilon_{\mathsf{abs}}.$$

We examine this within the context of the power method, which is the standard example application of the above theorem. Here we aim to find the eigenvector corresponding to the dominant eigenvalue λ_1 for $A \in \mathcal{C}^{m \times m}$, i.e. the solution to $A \cdot \mathbf{x} = \lambda_1 \cdot \mathbf{x}$. The iteration is given by

$$\mathbf{x}_{i+1} \leftarrow \frac{A \cdot \mathbf{x}_i}{\|A \cdot \mathbf{x}_i\|} = \frac{A^i \cdot \mathbf{x}_0}{\|A^i \cdot \mathbf{x}_0\|}$$

for some vector norm $\|\cdot\|$. The norm ensures that $\mathbf{x}_{i+1}$ has norm one. We select $\mathbf{x}_0$ to also have norm one at random, thus we have a mapping F from vectors of norm one to vectors of norm one.

We make the simplifying assumption (for exposition) that A has distinct eigenvalues $\lambda_1, \ldots, \lambda_m$ with corresponding eigenvectors $\mathbf{v}_1, \ldots, \mathbf{v}_m$, with $|\lambda_i| > |\lambda_j|$ for $j > i$, and define F via

$$F(\mathbf{x}) = \frac{A \cdot \mathbf{x}}{\|A \cdot \mathbf{x}\|_1}. \qquad (2)$$

For concreteness in the above we chose the 1-norm, as in the following we will be treating stochastic matrices and vectors. Normalizing the eigenvectors so that $\|\mathbf{v}_i\| = 1$, we can write

$$\mathbf{x}_0 = c_1 \cdot \mathbf{v}_1 + \cdots + c_m \cdot \mathbf{v}_m.$$

Assuming $c_1 \neq 0$ the iteration $\mathbf{x}_i = F(\mathbf{x}_{i-1})$ will converge to the eigenvector corresponding to the dominant eigenvalue since

$$A^i \cdot \mathbf{x}_0 = c_1 \cdot \lambda_1^i \cdot \left(\mathbf{v}_1 + \frac{c_2}{c_1} \left(\frac{\lambda_2}{\lambda_1} \right)^i \cdot \mathbf{v}_2 + \cdots + \frac{c_m}{c_1} \left(\frac{\lambda_m}{\lambda_1} \right)^i \cdot \mathbf{v}_m \right). \qquad (3)$$

Thus the speed of convergence is predominantly determined by the value $|\lambda_2|/|\lambda_1|$, with the precise number of iterations depending on *all* of the eigenvalues and the distance between the starting position $\mathbf{x}_0$ and the final solution.

We would like to iterate until the difference between two successive iterations $\mathbf{x}_{N-1}$ and $\mathbf{x}_N$ is sufficiently close. In other words we will terminate when

$$\|\mathbf{x}_N - \mathbf{x}_{N-1}\|_2^2 \leq \epsilon_{\mathsf{abs}}^2$$

holds for the first time, for some constant ϵ_{abs}. Note, in our experiments we later also use termination using the relative error

$$\|\mathbf{x}_N - \mathbf{x}_{N-1}\|_2^2 \le \epsilon_{\mathsf{rel}}^2 \cdot \|\mathbf{x}_N\|_2^2,$$

for some other constant ϵ_{rel}, as (for large dimension m) the entries in the solution to PageRank behave like $1/m$ for a graph with many links, and thus the relative error allows us to deal with increasing m, without needing to adjust ϵ_{abs} accordingly. Note, for our termination condition we would prefer to use, for computational reasons, the square of the 2-norm, (as performing square roots is expensive in an MPC system).

We make the simplifying assumption that we select our starting set X so that the map *is* indeed a contraction mapping for the 2-norm with Lipschitz constant $q = |\lambda_2|/|\lambda_1|$[1]. With the above simplifying assumption, and for this value of N, we have

$$\|\mathbf{v}_1 - \mathbf{x}_N\|_2 \le \frac{q}{1-q} \cdot \|\mathbf{x}_N - \mathbf{x}_{N-1}\|_2 \le \frac{q}{1-q} \cdot \epsilon_{\mathsf{abs}} = \frac{\lambda_2 \cdot \epsilon_{\mathsf{abs}}}{\lambda_1 - \lambda_2}.$$

So the bigger the difference between λ_2 and λ_1, the smaller the error between where we terminate and the correct solution.

For the iteration before we reach this value of N we have

$$\begin{aligned}
\epsilon_{\mathsf{abs}} &< \|\mathbf{x}_{N-1} - \mathbf{x}_{N-2}\|_2 \\
&\le \|\mathbf{v}_1 - \mathbf{x}_{N-1}\|_2 + \|\mathbf{v}_1 - \mathbf{x}_{N-2}\|_2 \\
&\le \left(\frac{q^{N-1}}{1-q} + \frac{q^{N-2}}{1-q}\right) \cdot \|\mathbf{x}_1 - \mathbf{x}_0\|_2 \\
&\le \frac{q^{N-2} \cdot (q+1)}{1-q} \cdot (\|\mathbf{x}_1\|_2 + \|\mathbf{x}_0\|_2) \\
&= \frac{2 \cdot q^{N-2} \cdot (q+1)}{1-q}.
\end{aligned}$$

Thus revealing N reveals information about q, and thus information about the spectral gap $|\lambda_2|/|\lambda_1|$. In the context of a given application some information about the eigenvalues may have already leaked as part of the problem statement. For example in the PageRank algorithm we already know that $\lambda_1 = 1$ and that λ_2 is $(1 - \lambda)$ times the second eigenvalue of the original stochastic matrix Q. As already remarked, when the underlying graph contains at least two irreducible closed subsets (which holds in practice for the internet graph) we already know that λ_2 is *exactly* equal to $1 - \lambda$.

In conclusion if the mapping is indeed a contraction mapping for the metric used to determine when to terminate an iterative method, then the number of iterations leaked by performing this test leaks information about the Lipschitz

---

[1] This is not quite true, but is true if we modify the metric used to measure convergence. But then the metric depends on the final answer, which is perfect for theoretical considerations, but useless in practice. See Appendix A for more details.

constant and the distance between the starting value and the fixed point. For all mappings for which the power method converges one can find a metric for which it is a contraction mapping, but this metric may not be applicable for use in an algorithm as a convergence test.

For the power method applied to matrices it is known that the speed of convergence is related to the value $q = |\lambda_2|/|\lambda_1|$. For some matrices and sets X this does indeed define a contraction mapping, but not for all. Making the simplifying assumption, for exposition, that the power method is defined from a contraction mapping with this Lipschitz constant, one can from N derive information about q.

Note that whether this is an acceptable leakage or not depends on the application in hand, i.e., from where the map F originates. It is worth recalling that the speed of convergence of an iterative method does not leak the value of q, but only provides *some information* about its distribution, which may be considered as a minor leakage in many cases, or even no leakage at all, such as the case of PageRank over the internet graph.

4   Stability of PageRank

Being a numerical algorithm we need to worry about the stability of the PageRank algorithm. However, as we are computing in the secure domain we not only need to worry about the traditional stability of the algorithm, but we also need to worry about stability caused by the representation of the floating point numbers within the secure computation system. In this section we address these two issues (normal numerical stability and stability within the MPC system).

4.1   Traditional Stability of PageRank

As the value of m is large in applications of PageRank solving for π analytically or via high-school linear algebra is not feasible. Thus in practice the *only* method one can use to solve the PageRank problem is to apply the power method.

Applying the power method on our matrix M requires that we compute in iteration i

$$\mathbf{x}_i = (1 - \lambda) \cdot Q^\mathsf{T} \cdot \mathbf{x}_{i-1} + \lambda \cdot \mathbf{v}$$

Note that here we used the fact that M (from Eq. (1)) is stochastic, and the initial vector $\mathbf{x}_0$ is a probability distribution. Thus all $\mathbf{x}_i$ will be probability distributions, which implies that $\|\mathbf{x}_i\|_1 = 1$ (this explains why $\mathbf{x}_{i-1}$ is dropped from the term $\lambda \cdot \mathbf{v}$ above; since $\lambda \cdot E^\mathsf{T} \cdot \mathbf{x}_{i-1} = \lambda \mathbf{v} \cdot \mathbf{e}^\mathsf{T} \cdot \mathbf{x}_{i-1} = \lambda \cdot \mathbf{v}$). Besides, it also implies that we do not need to normalize $\mathbf{x}_i$ throughout the computation. See Method 1 in Fig. 2 for PageRank in the clear when we iterate over a fixed number N of iterations.

The problem though with the power method is that it could be unstable, i.e. floating point errors in the computation could affect the final outcome. In [7] the authors proved that solving the PageRank problem is equivalent to solving the matrix equation $R \cdot \mathbf{y} = \mathbf{v}$, where $R = I - (1 - \lambda) \cdot P^\mathsf{T}$ and then normalizing y to

---

Three Variants of PageRank

Input: $\lambda, \mathbf{v}, \mathbf{x}_0, \epsilon_{\mathsf{abs}}/\epsilon_{\mathsf{rel}}, Q, N$. For the secure variants Q and $\mathbf{v}$ may be represented in secret shared form.

Output: The PageRank vector $\boldsymbol{\pi}$ of M from equation (1)

Method 1: Using Standard Floating Point (in clear)

1. $C \leftarrow (1 - \lambda) \cdot Q^{\mathsf{T}}$.
2. For i in $1, \ldots, N$
   (a) $\mathbf{x}_i \leftarrow C \cdot \mathbf{x}_{i-1} + \lambda \cdot \mathbf{v}$
3. $\boldsymbol{\pi} \leftarrow \mathbf{x}_N$

Method 2: Using Fixed Point Arithmetic (in MPC or in the clear)

1. $\langle\, \overline{C}\, \rangle \leftarrow (1 - \lambda) \cdot \langle\, \overline{Q}\, \rangle^{\mathsf{T}}$.
2. For i in $1, \ldots, N$
   (a) For l in $1, \ldots, m$
      i. $\langle\, \overline{y_i^{(l)}}\, \rangle \leftarrow \mathsf{dot\text{-}product}(\langle\, \overline{c_l}\, \rangle, \langle\, \overline{\mathbf{x}_{i-1}}\, \rangle)$
      ii. $\langle\, \overline{x_i^{(l)}}\, \rangle \leftarrow \langle\, \overline{y_i^{(l)}}\, \rangle + \lambda \cdot \langle\, \overline{v^{(l)}}\, \rangle$
3. $\langle\, \overline{\boldsymbol{\pi}}\, \rangle \leftarrow (\langle\, \overline{\mathbf{x}^N}\, \rangle)$

Method 3: Using Fixed Point Arithmetic and Loop Truncation (in MPC or in the clear)

1. $\langle\, \overline{C}\, \rangle \leftarrow (1 - \lambda) \cdot \langle\, \overline{Q}\, \rangle^{\mathsf{T}}$.
2. For l in $1, \ldots, N$
   (a) For l in $1, \ldots, m$
      i. Parties compute $\langle\, \overline{y_i^{(l)}}\, \rangle \leftarrow \mathsf{dot\text{-}product}(\langle\, \overline{c_l}\, \rangle, \langle\, \overline{\mathbf{x}_{i-1}}\, \rangle)$
      ii. $\langle\, \overline{x_i^{(l)}}\, \rangle \leftarrow \langle\, \overline{y_i^{(l)}}\, \rangle + \lambda \cdot \langle\, \overline{v^{(l)}}\, \rangle$.
   (b) $\langle g \rangle \leftarrow (\|\langle\, \overline{\mathbf{x}_{i-1}}\, \rangle - \langle\, \overline{\mathbf{x}_i}\, \rangle\|_2^2 < \epsilon_{\mathsf{rel}}^2 \cdot \|\langle\, \overline{\mathbf{x}_{i-1}}\, \rangle\|_2^2$ if using relative error) or
   $\langle g \rangle \leftarrow (\|\langle\, \overline{\mathbf{x}_{i-1}}\, \rangle - \langle\, \overline{\mathbf{x}_i}\, \rangle\|_2^2 < \epsilon_{\mathsf{abs}}^2$ if using absolute error).
   (c) Open $\langle g \rangle$
   (d) If $g = 1$ then break.
3. $\langle\, \overline{\boldsymbol{\pi}}\, \rangle \leftarrow (\langle\, \overline{\mathbf{x}_i}\, \rangle)$ and Open $\boldsymbol{\pi}$ to all parties.

Fig. 2. Our various PageRank algorithms

obtain $\boldsymbol{\pi}$ via $\boldsymbol{\pi} = \mathbf{y}/\|\mathbf{y}\|_1$. The authors of [7] also bound the condition number of R (with respect to the 1-norm)

$$\kappa(R) \le \|R^{-1}\|_1 \cdot \|R\|_1 \le \frac{2 - \lambda}{\lambda},$$

where $\|R\|_1 = \max_{1 \le j \le m} \sum_{i=1}^{m} |r_{i,j}|$. A similar result is given in [19] for the case when the diagonal entries of Q are all null.

The condition number explains how numerical errors in data can propagate after doing computation on it to errors in the result of this computation. Thus as λ approaches zero any algorithm to solve the PageRank problem will likely become unstable; this explains the traditional choice of $0.1 \leq \lambda \leq 0.2$.

4.2   Stability Due to Approximate Computations

MPC systems based on linear secret sharing usually work on values defined in a finite field $\mathbb{F}_p$ of large prime characteristic, e.g. a prime p of size 128 bits. A data item x secret shared among the parties is denoted as $\langle x \rangle$. Calculation is then performed by expressing the computation in terms of additions, multiplications, and openings over $\mathbb{F}_p$. Linear operations on shared values is essentially for free, whereas multiplications typically require some pre-processed data and communication. We extend the notation of secret shared values to vectors of shared values $\langle \mathbf{x} \rangle$ and matrices of shared values $\langle A \rangle$.

In our application to PageRank we will need to compute mainly dot-products between vectors of fixed point values, i.e.

$$\langle \overline{\mathbf{x}} \rangle^{\mathsf{T}} \cdot \langle \overline{\mathbf{y}} \rangle = \sum_{j=1}^{m} \langle \overline{x^{(j)}} \rangle \cdot \langle \overline{y^{(i)}} \rangle.$$

The dot-product is one of the problems which have been previously studied in the MPC literature; see [4] for over the integers, [29] and [25] for over fixed point values, and [18] for over floating point values. For fixed point values recall that addition is cheap, but multiplication is expensive. Indeed the most expensive part of multiplication is the truncation step. In [29], authors used the two-party ABY framework [10], which allows to do conversions between linear secret sharing and garbled circuit. Their strategy consisted of converting to garbled circuit after each multiplication between fixed point numbers, in order to perform the truncation as garbled circuits are well suited for this latter operation. As well as being focused on the two-party passively secure case, this method introduces to the computation the cost of converting to-and-from the secret shared form. In [25], authors proposed a passively secure protocol for fixed point multiplications, for a setting of three-parties assuming an honest majority, and showed how we can use an optimization to perform the dot-product. The core idea of this optimization consists of performing the truncation step only after that all the necessary additions have been calculated. Authors also proposed an actively secure protocol under the same setting for matrix by matrix products. The protocol works by pre-processing matrix triples (U, V, W), s.t. $W = U \cdot V$, using the fixed point multiplication protocol of [25], and use a generalization of [13] to perform matrix by matrix product using the pre-processed matrix triples.

In contrast our work is focused on the many party, actively secure. We perform all computation with linear secret sharing, however, we introduce a similar optimization to [25] into the procedure for executing a dot-product. This optimization is given in Fig. 3 and we refer to the algorithm as dot-product($\langle \overline{\mathbf{x}} \rangle, \langle \overline{\mathbf{y}} \rangle$).

The method works as [25] by delaying the necessary truncation until all additions have been performed. Since truncation is the expensive part of the procedure, this basically produces a $1/m$ performance improvement. Ignoring

---

Optimized Dot-Product

Input: $\langle\,\overline{\mathbf{x}}\,\rangle, \langle\,\overline{\mathbf{y}}\,\rangle$, **Output:** $\langle\,\overline{z}\,\rangle = \sum_{j=1}^{m}\langle\,\overline{x^{(j)}}\,\rangle\cdot\langle\,\overline{y^{(j)}}\,\rangle = \mathsf{dot\text{-}product}(\langle\,\overline{\mathbf{x}}\,\rangle, \langle\,\overline{\mathbf{y}}\,\rangle)$.
  - $\langle s\rangle \leftarrow 0$.
  - For $j \in [1, \ldots, m]$ do
      - $\langle s\rangle \leftarrow \langle s\rangle + \langle x^{(j)}\rangle \cdot \langle y^{(j)}\rangle$.
  - $\langle z\rangle \leftarrow \mathsf{TruncPr}(\langle s\rangle, 2\cdot k, f)$.

Fig. 3. Optimized dot-product of vectors of shared fixed point values

the fact that our truncation procedure can be incorrect by a single bit (which occurs for normal fixed point multiplications in any case), we need to ensure that the output of this procedure is correct. Indeed, as we apply TruncPr less, we will introduce less errors in the truncation procedure overall.

The correctness depends to some extent on our precise application. In the PageRank algorithm using fixed point approximations (Method 2 in Fig. 2) we apply dot-product on vectors $\langle\overline{\mathbf{c}}\rangle$ and $\langle\overline{\mathbf{x}}\rangle$ such that each entry in $\langle\overline{\mathbf{c}}\rangle$ is a positive value bounded by $1 - \lambda$, and each entry in $\langle\overline{\mathbf{x}}\rangle$ is a positive value bounded by one. Thus we can assume that the integers representing the fixed point values satisfy $0 \leq c^{(j)}, x^{(j)} \leq 2^f$, and in fact we have $\|\mathbf{c}\|_\infty \leq 2^f$ and $\|\mathbf{x}\|_1 \leq 2^f$. We then find a bound on s as

$$s = \sum_{j=1}^{m} c^{(j)} \cdot x^{(j)} \leq \|\mathbf{c}\|_\infty \cdot \|\mathbf{x}\|_1 \leq 2^{2\cdot f}.$$

This means that the intermediate sum value s, as an integer, will be at most $2^{2\cdot f}$, thus (since $k > f$) the application of TruncPr, using second parameter of $2 \cdot k$, will be correct assuming we can deal with the expansion needed in TruncPr due to the statistical security parameter κ. Thus, we additionally require $2 \cdot k + \kappa < \log_2 p$, Hence, we require exactly the same correctness requirement as we have for standard multiplication.

The only remaining parameter which needs to be set for our fixed point representation is the value k. It is easily seen that all vectors in the algorithm consist of positive values less than one. Indeed the only place we utilize values outside the range $[0, \ldots, 1]$ is in computing the 2-norms (which we will do in Method 3 to be discussed later), where we utilize values in the range $[-1, \ldots, 1]$. To cope with these negative values we set $k = f + 1$.

Using fixed point representation, instead of floating point representation, hence does not affect the stability of PageRank, as long as the precision chosen is big enough to handle the computation taking place. However, for an expander graph we would expect the final PageRank vector $\boldsymbol{\pi}$ to be uniform, and thus have entries of the form $1/m$ in each coordinate. Thus we need to cope with an output which might have entries all close to $1/m$. To cope with this possibility in fixed point representation we need to make f a function of m. In particular we set $f = 30 + \log_2 m$ so that entries which are around $1/m$ can have around nine decimal digits of 'interesting' data. We can show that this strategy of setting f works through the following experiment, which compares the two first methodologies presented in Fig. 2. We think of operations on values $\langle \overline{x} \rangle$ as being (for the time being) not on secret shared values but on fixed point values with the above representation, i.e. on $\overline{x}$ alone. Take a random graph $G^{m,l}$ of size m and number of links l, and run one hundred iterations of PageRank using floating point representation to obtain $\mathbf{x}_{100}$, and then run one hundred iterations on the same graph using the fixed point representation (in the clear) to obtain $\overline{\mathbf{z}_{100}}$.

We generated graphs for various values of with m between 100 and 10000, and for number of links $l = i \cdot m$ for $i = 2, \ldots, 40$. For each (m, l) considered we generated a set of $T = 100$ graphs $S^{m,l} = \{G_k^{m,l} \text{ for } k \in \{1, \ldots, T\}\}$ using the NetworkX package of python3. We then computed for each set the maximum error observed

$$e_{\max}^m = \max_{G \in \{S^{m,2} \cup \ldots \cup S^{m,40}\}} e_G,$$

where

$$e_G = \|\overline{\mathbf{z}_{100}} - \mathbf{x}_{100}\|_\infty = \max_{j \in \{1, \ldots, m\}} \left| \overline{z_{100}^{(j)}} - x_{100}^{(j)} \right|.$$

with the results given in Table 1. As expected, the error induced by using fixed point representation is negligible, thanks to how we chose f for the experiments.

Table 1. Max error observed for the PageRank vector between fixed point and floating point representations (i.e. comparing Method 1 to Method 2 in Fig. 2).

m	100	500	1000	5000	10000
$e_{\max}^m$	1.1e-10	4.2e-11	1.5e-11	5.7e-12	2.3e-12

5   Effect of Early Termination of PageRank

If we examine Method 3 of Fig. 2 we now terminate the main loop when the error meets a given condition. We use the square of the 2-norm for the terminating conditions as this will be easier to implement securely in our MPC system; since there is no need for costly absolute values as with the 1-norm and no need for costly square roots as with the non-squared 2-norm.

We define two conditions, one defined by an absolute error

$$\|\langle \overline{\mathbf{x}_{i-1}} \rangle - \langle \overline{\mathbf{x}_i} \rangle\|_2^2 < \epsilon_{\text{abs}}^2.$$

and one defined by a relative error

$$\|\langle \overline{\mathbf{x}_{i-1}} \rangle - \langle \overline{\mathbf{x}_i} \rangle\|_2^2 < \epsilon_{\text{rel}}^2 \cdot \|\langle \overline{\mathbf{x}_{i-1}} \rangle\|_2^2$$

Note, that since $\|\mathbf{x}_i\|_1 = 1$ the relative error implies the absolute error bound in the case when $\epsilon_{rel} = \epsilon_{abs}$. However, we will be choosing $\epsilon_{rel} \neq \epsilon_{abs}$ in such a way that

$$\epsilon_{abs}^2 < \epsilon_{rel}^2 \cdot \|\langle \overline{\mathbf{x}_{i-1}} \rangle\|_2^2.$$

This should enable using the relative error to produce almost as accurate a solution, but with fewer iterations.[2]

Recall the speed of the convergence of the power method follows a geometric distribution with ratio $|\lambda_2/\lambda_1|$. Namely if λ_2 is close to λ_1 then the method converges slowly. As we are dealing with stochastic matrices we already know that $\lambda_1 = 1$, i.e. for a given dimension m, thus the number of iterations needed is proportional to $|\lambda_2|$. As remarked earlier, for graphs with at least two irreducible closed subsets one has $|\lambda_2| = 1 - \lambda$ [16]. Recall a closed subset S is one in which if $x \in S$ and y can be reached from x, then y is also in S. A closed set is irreducible if it contains no proper closed subset, i.e. there is a path between each pair of elements in S.

For the traditional PageRank case, i.e. the application to the internet graph, the underlying graph does indeed have at least two irreducible closed subsets [5]. In addition experimentally it has been shown that the power method produces the correct value π (assuming no floating point errors accumulate) for iteration values between 50 and 100 [23].

For graphs generated uniformly at random (called random graphs from now on) $|\lambda_2|$ is not necessarily as big as $1 - \lambda$ (recall λ is between 0.1 and 0.2 and in the case of the original PageRank algorithm $\lambda = 0.15$). Therefore one may need fewer iterations to ensure convergence. By inserting the abort-test into Method 3 we potentially improve the performance of PageRank, but at the same time we leak the number of iterations needed to achieve our level of convergence. See below for experimental validation of this for random graphs. As explained in Sect. 3 the number of iterations N leaked, for the absolute error variant, implies information is leaked about the second eigenvalue λ_2 and $\mathbf{x}_0$.

However, for transaction graphs for bank accounts, one cannot tell whether there are at least two irreducible subsets. In [33], authors studied the topology of the daily graphs, of the interbanks payments transferred between a set of participants (commercial banks) of the Fedwire Funds Service, corresponding to the first quarter of 2004. The structure of the underlying graph observed shows that the degree distribution corresponds to a scale free graph, and from the results they obtained, one can conclude that over at least 50% of the days, there exist at least two irreducible subsets.

For our second set of experiments we generated graphs according to the simulator of transaction graphs from [34]; in what follows we call these banking graphs. This simulator generates scale free graphs, in particular, following the Barabasi-Albert model, with a tweak over the strength of the preferential

---

[2] In practice it is easy to choose ϵ_{abs} and ϵ_{rel} satisfying the above. Observe that the $\| \bullet \|_2$ norm on the hypercube given by equation $\|\mathbf{x}\|_1 = 1$ attains its minimum $\frac{1}{m}$ at the points $(\pm\frac{1}{m}, \ldots, \pm\frac{1}{m})$. Therefore it suffices to choose any $\epsilon_{abs} < \epsilon_{rel}$ such that $\epsilon_{abs}^2 < \epsilon_{rel}^2 \cdot \frac{1}{m}$. This way the choice of the errors will be independent of the sequence.

attachment. The resulting graphs as the experiments will show, do not contain two closed subsets.

To choose the tolerance $\epsilon_{\mathsf{abs}}/\epsilon_{\mathsf{rel}}$, one needs to consider how small the components of $\mathbf{x}$ are, as it may occur that $\|\mathbf{x}_i - \mathbf{x}_{i-1}\|_2^2$ triggers the abort due to the fact that the components of $\mathbf{x}_i$ and $\mathbf{x}_{i-1}$ are small (if the tolerance was not chosen to be small enough) while there could be still room for convergence. As explained earlier if the vector $\boldsymbol{\pi}$ was uniform then we would expect each coordinate to be $1/m$, thus for absolute errors it makes sense to have the tolerance depend on m; just as we made f depend on m in the previous section. An alternative approach, which we examine, is to instead look at relative errors instead of the absolute errors, in which case the effect of small values in $\boldsymbol{\pi}$ is already accounted for by taking relative errors. Thus we always set $\epsilon_{\mathsf{rel}} = 2^{-10}$ irrespective of m, i.e. we want our two final iterations to be within 0.1 percent of each other. For the absolute error we set $\epsilon_{\mathsf{abs}} = 2^{-f/2}$, and thus we terminate when the $\|\langle\overline{\mathbf{x}_{i-1}}\rangle - \langle\overline{\mathbf{x}_i}\rangle\|_2^2$ is identically equal to zero in our fixed point representation.

To verify that the early termination indeed provides an efficiency improvement, and does not affect the overall accuracy of the output compared to nontermination, we compared Method 1 against Method 3 using the same type of experiments, in the clear, as performed in Sect. 4; for both random and our simulated banking graphs. We computed the average number of iterations N needed to obtain the required termination condition (when we set ϵ_{abs} and ϵ_{rel} as above), and compared the result with the values which would have been obtained in the clear. The accuracy was measured according to the metric e_{max}^m from the previous section, the results being given in Table 2.

From the results of these experiments, it is clear that one does not need to run many iterations before obtaining convergence, for both the cases of random graphs and banking graphs. In particular, for a randomly generated graph, we can see that the more links within the graph, the fewer iterations are needed to reach convergence. We can also see that the banking graphs take longer time to process compared to the random graphs the more links we have. Besides, the experiments show that using the absolute error to test convergence, requires running more iterations to obtain convergence than using the relative error. This is due to the fact that the epsilon chosen ϵ_{abs}, implies that convergence is only obtained when $\|\langle\overline{\mathbf{x}_{i-1}}\rangle - \langle\overline{\mathbf{x}_i}\rangle\|_2^2$ is equal to zero as explained earlier, while for the case of the relative error, convergence can happen without necessarily having it. As for the difference between the PageRank vector obtained after convergence, and the PageRank vector obtained after one hundred iterations, we can see that for both cases of using the absolute error and the relative error, the difference is very small. Besides, we can also see that this difference is slightly bigger for the case of the relative error. This would imply that considering a termination condition for the PageRank algorithm, either with an absolute error or a relative error set as specified in this section, would produce a fairly close PageRank vector to the one produced after running one hundred iteration.

Table 2. Iterations needed for convergence and accuracy of the result for the PageRank algorithm using Method 3 on random and banking graphs with absolute and relative errors, with respect to the number of nodes and links in the graphs tested.

m	Error		Number of links									
			Random graphs					Banking graphs				
			$2 \cdot m$	$5 \cdot m$	$10 \cdot m$	$20 \cdot m$	$40 \cdot m$	$2 \cdot m$	$5 \cdot m$	$10 \cdot m$	$20 \cdot m$	$40 \cdot m$
100	abs	N	21	13	9	7	5	16	12	11	9	11
		$e_{\max}^m$	3.1e-6	6.3e-7	1.8e-7	7.3e-8	6.5e-8	6.8e-6	7.2e-6	4.2e-6	5.4e-7	3.3e-7
100	rel	N	15	9	6	5	4	11	8	7	6	7
		$e_{\max}^m$	3.2e-4	1.5e-5	7.6e-6	5.3e-6	5.1e-7	4.5e-4	4.1e-4	2.8e-4	3.6e-5	2.0e-5
500	abs	N	21	13	9	7	5	15	11	9	9	13
		$e_{\max}^m$	3.3e-6	4.3e-7	2.9e-7	5.1e-8	4.8e-8	1.5e-6	9.9e-7	8.3e-7	1.0e-6	2.8e-7
500	rel	N	15	9	6	5	4	10	8	7	7	9
		$e_{\max}^m$	2.9e-4	1.6e-5	3.0e-6	4.9e-7	2.1e-7	3.9e-5	2.8e-5	1.5e-5	1.7e-5	1.2e-5
1000	abs	N	21	13	9	7	6	17	12	10	10	15
		$e_{\max}^m$	4.5e-6	3.6e-7	5.2e-8	8.6e-9	3.4e-9	2.6e-6	2.4e-6	3.3e-7	6.7e-8	8.3e-8
1000	rel	N	15	9	6	5	4	11	8	7	7	10
		$e_{\max}^m$	1.5e-4	9.7e-6	1.0e-6	2.3e-7	1.4e-7	1.8e-4	1.6e-4	1.4e-5	7.2e-6	1.0e-5
5000	abs	N	21	12	8	7	5	15	11	10	10	15
		$e_{\max}^m$	3.9e-6	9.8e-8	3.3e-8	5.1e-9	3.4e-9	2.7e-6	2.7e-7	1.5e-7	3.8e-7	1.0e-7
5000	rel	N	14	9	6	5	4	10	8	7	7	10
		$e_{\max}^m$	9.1e-5	6.2e-7	1.9e-7	8.9e-8	7.8e-8	7.0e-5	6.9e-6	4.5e-6	6.8e-6	6.9e-6
10000	abs	N	21	12	8	6	5	16	12	10	10	16
		$e_{\max}^m$	3.8e-6	8.5e-8	1.2e-8	5.3e-9	3.1e-9	8.1e-7	1.5e-7	5.0e-8	8.5e-8	2.4e-8
10000	rel	N	14	9	6	5	4	11	8	7	7	10
		$e_{\max}^m$	4.5e-5	4.9e-7	1.8e-7	3.7e-8	2.1e-8	5.6e-5	5.0e-6	2.9e-6	2.7e-6	6.4e-6

6   A Multiparty Actively-Secure Protocol for the PageRank Algorithm

Recall our motivating application of using PageRank for financial fraud detection. We discussed earlier how the more institutions which are involved the better the analysis will be. This means that the methodology of [30] which requires all financial institutions which contribute data to be involved in the protocol may not scale to the large number of institutions required in a cross-border analysis of money laundering. Thus we look at a methodology in which a large number of financial institutions $\{I_1, \ldots, I_u\}$ wish to apply PageRank over the bank accounts they maintain. They will do this by securely distributing their data to a smaller set of computing servers $S = \{S_1, \ldots, S_v\}$, with $v = 2$ or $v = 3$. Our solution will allow us to arbitrarily scale u, but it results in us not being able to deal with such a large matrix, i.e. number of accounts, as the prior work did [30], due to the fact that the whole matrix for our case is being secret shared, for reasons described in the introduction. It is interesting none-the-less to see the difference in performance between the two approaches.

The first stage of our algorithm is for each institution I_k to secret share its component of the PageRank matrix to the servers in S. This is simply a data-entry phase which we ignore in our analysis. Thus we start by assuming that the parties in S hold a secret sharing of the initial matrix $\langle \overline{Q} \rangle$ and the personalisation vector $\langle \overline{\mathbf{v}} \rangle$.

Our experiments are performed using Scale-Mamba [3], which is an MPC framework that utilizes the above secret sharing based methodology and in addition already has a number of built in routines for dealing with the above fixed point representation. Scale-Mamba is an actively secure framework with abort, which means that it offers the strong security guarantee that if an adversary deviates from the protocol then it is detected with overwhelming probability.

The system works in an offline-online manner. In particular in the function independent offline phase pre-processed data is generated, such as so-called Beaver triples (random triples shared values $\langle a \rangle$, $\langle b \rangle$, and $\langle c \rangle$ s.t. $c = a \cdot b$) and random bits (shared values $\langle b \rangle$ s.t. $b \in \{0, 1\}$). In the online phase the actual computation takes place, during this phase the pre-processed random data is consumed. The main metric for measuring cost in the online phase is the number of rounds of communication required by an operation. Whilst the online phase is relatively fast, the offline phase can be an order of 10 to 100 times slower.

To summarize the cost of the different operations we need in terms of pre-processed data, we present Table 3; where $h(k)$ is the function $\sum_{i=1}^{\lceil log_2(k) \rceil} g(i)$, for $g(i) = f(i) - 2 \cdot \left(\frac{f(i-1)}{2} \mod 2 \right) - 1$ and $f(i+1) = \frac{f(i)}{2} + \left(\frac{f(i)}{2} \mod 2 \right)$ and $f(0) = 2 \cdot k$ (see [3] for details about the function h). Note that while we provided the rounds of communication required by each operation we need, these can be merged if many operations can be performed in parallel.

Table 3. Costs of Basic Scale-Mamba Operations over Integers

Operation	Open	$\langle a \rangle \cdot \langle b \rangle$	$\langle \overline{a} \rangle \cdot \langle \overline{b} \rangle$	$\langle \overline{a} \rangle < \langle \overline{b} \rangle$	TruncPr($\langle a \rangle, k, f$)	Trunc($\langle a \rangle, k, f$)
No. Triples	0	1	1	$h(k)$	0	$h(k)$
No. Bits	0	0	$2 \cdot k + \kappa$	$k + \kappa$	$k + \kappa$	$k + \kappa$
Rounds	1	1	2	$\lceil \log_2 k \rceil + 1$	1	$\lceil \log_2(k) \rceil + 1$

A key parameter of an MPC system is the number of parties in the system, and the number of 'bad' players which can be tolerated. Scale-Mamba supports various options for these access structures. Each one coming with different advantages and disadvantages. To illustrate our protocol we focus on two cases:

1. Two party protocol with one active corruption. Here the Scale-Mamba system makes use of the SPDZ protocol [8]. The offline phase is roughly 180 times slower than the online phase, but the online phase is very fast.
2. Three party protocol with one active corruption. Here we utilize a secret sharing scheme based on Shamir sharing [31]. In this case Scale-Mamba implements the protocol of [20] to obtain a fast online phase, at the expense of having an offline phase which is roughly 4 times slower.

We implemented PageRank within the Scale-Mamba system and then run various experiments, with different transaction graphs to see how performance behaved. We varied the value of m to range from around $m = 100$ to $m = 10000$. We fixed the initialization vector $\mathbf{x}_0$ and the personalization vector $\mathbf{v}$ to be the vectors with $1/m$ in each entry, although modifying our code to deal with secret shared value $\mathbf{v}$ is trivial. Finally we fixed λ to be 0.15 in the PageRank algorithm itself, modeling the damping factor that the institutions would use, but of course the institutions can choose any value they wish prior to executing PageRank. For our approximation of floating point by fixed point numbers considered earlier we used $f = 30 + \log_2 m$, $k = f + 1$, $\kappa = 40$, and a modulus of $2 \cdot k + \kappa$ bits.

The most expensive part (by a large margin) of the entire procedure is the execution of Step 2a in Method 3 of Fig. 2. For single execution of this step we present our runtimes in Table 4, in addition to the amount of data sent per party. Our experiments were run on Intel i-9900 CPU based machines with 128 GB of RAM, connected by a local network with a ping time around 0.048 ms, connected with a switch of bandwidth 1 Gb. We notice that the case of the two parties is slightly faster than the case of three parties.

Table 4. Average online runtimes in seconds for Step 2a in Method 3 of Fig. 2 for one iteration of the PageRank algorithm for two players and three players with respect to the number of nodes m, as well as the size of data sent by each player in MB.

m	100	500	1000	5000	10000
Two parties	0.03	0.40	2.11	55.23	231.61
Three parties	0.03	0.61	2.42	60.82	245.34
Data sent	1.56	14.50	45.19	1305.93	5014.23

Thus we have the expected time for execution of a single iteration of the PageRank algorithm. To obtain the final runtime we need to multiply this by the expected number of iterations, from Table 2, to obtain Table 5. Here we can see the effect of the terminating condition on the runtime. Without our terminating condition we would need to run for a large number (say 100) of iterations, which is costly. By terminating after a suitable convergence has been reached we save a lot of time, *but* we leak some information. However, as we have explained the information leaked is essentially only information about the spectral gap; which may be considered a minor leakage depending on the application.

Table 5. Average runtimes in seconds for the PageRank algorithm of Fig. 2 for Method 2, as well as Method 3 with absolute and relative errors on random and banking graphs, for two parties and three parties with respect to the number of nodes m.

m	Setting	Runtimes				
		100	Random graphs		Banking graphs	
		iteration	abs	rel	abs	rel
100	Two parties	3	0.6	0.4	0.5	0.3
100	Three parties	3	0.6	0.4	0.5	0.3
500	Two parties	40	8.4	6.0	6.0	4.0
500	Three parties	61	12.8	9.1	9.1	6.1
1000	Two parties	210	44.1	31.5	35.7	23.1
1000	Three parties	242	50.8	36.3	41.1	26.6
5000	Two parties	5500	1161.3	774.2	829.5	553.0
5000	Three parties	6070	1274.7	849.8	910.5	607.0
10000	Two parties	23100	4855.2	3236.8	3699.2	2543.2
10000	Three parties	24530	5151.3	3434.2	3924.8	2698.3

Acknowledgments. The authors would like to thank Dragoş Rotaru and Titouan Tanguy, for suggestions in relation to this paper, and Frederik Vercauteren for the helpul discussions in the early stages of this work. This work was supported in part by CyberSecurity Research Flanders with reference number VR20192203, by ERC Advanced Grant ERC-2015-AdG-IMPaCT, by the Defense Advanced Research Projects Agency (DARPA) and Space and Naval Warfare Systems Center, Pacific (SSC Pacific) under contract No. FA8750-19-C-0502, and by the FWO under an Odysseus project GOH9718N. Any opinions, findings and conclusions or recommendations expressed in this material are those of the author(s) and do not necessarily reflect the views of the ERC, DARPA, the US Government or the FWO. The U.S. Government is authorized to reproduce and distribute reprints for governmental purposes notwithstanding any copyright annotation therein.

A   Converses to Banach's Fixed Point Theorem

To understand the convergence of fixed point iterations of contraction mappings more precisely, we need to appeal to so-called converse to Banach's Theorem. These are results which show that if an iterative method converges for some set X on a metric space with metric d, then there is a (potentially different) metric d' for which the map is a contraction mapping for any Lipschitz constant q. In particular in [9] the following converse theorem is proved.

Theorem A.1 (Theorem 1 of [9]). *Let (X, d) be a complete, proper metric space and $F : X \longrightarrow X$ be continuous with respect to d such that F has a unique fixed point x^*, and the iteration $x_i \leftarrow F(x_{i-1})$ converges to x^* with respect to d, and there exists an open neighbourhood U of x^* such that $F^{(n)}(U) \longrightarrow \{x^*\}$ as $n \longrightarrow \infty$.*

Then, for all $q \in (0,1)$ and $\epsilon > 0$, there is a metric $d_{q,\epsilon}$ which is topologically equivalent to d, such that $(X, d_{c,\epsilon})$ is a complete metric space and

1. $\forall x, y \in X : d_{q,\epsilon}(\ f(x), f(y)\ ) \leq q \cdot d_{q,\epsilon}(\ x.y\ )$.
2. $\forall x, y \in X : d_{q,\epsilon}(\ x, y\ ) \leq \epsilon$ *implies that*

$$\min\{\ d_{q,\epsilon}(\ x^*, x\ ), d_{q,\epsilon}(\ x^*, y\ ), d_{q,\epsilon}(\ x, y\ )\ \} \leq 2 \cdot \epsilon.$$

The second property here is used to bound the number of iterations needed in terms of the constants q, ϵ and the distance $d(\ x_0, x^*\ )$.

The authors of [9] illustate this in terms of the power method for matrices. Indeed in [9][Proposition 1] it is shown that if we restrict to real matrices A (with eigenvalues $|\lambda_1| > |\lambda_2| \geq \ldots \geq |\lambda_m|$) then there is a metric $d(\mathbf{x}, \mathbf{y})$ on $\mathcal{R}^m$ such that the mapping, for any vector norm $\| \cdot \|$,

$$F(\mathbf{x}) = \frac{A \cdot \mathbf{x}}{\|A \cdot \mathbf{x}\|}$$

is a contraction mapping with

$$d(F(\mathbf{x}), F(\mathbf{y})) \leq \frac{|\lambda_2|}{|\lambda_1|} \cdot d(\mathbf{x}, \mathbf{y})$$

for all $\mathbf{x}, \mathbf{y} \in \mathcal{R}^m$. The metric being

$$d(\mathbf{x}, \mathbf{y}) = \left\| \frac{\mathbf{x}}{\mathbf{x}^\mathsf{T} \cdot \mathbf{v}_1} - \frac{\mathbf{y}}{\mathbf{y}^\mathsf{T} \cdot \mathbf{v}_1} \right\|_2.$$

Thus *there is* a metric for which the Lipschitz constant *is* $q = |\lambda_2|/|\lambda_1|$. In addition for any $\mathbf{x}_0 \in \mathcal{R}^n$ which has a nonzero component in the direction of $\mathbf{v}_1$, we have that after

$$N^* = \frac{\log(d(\ \mathbf{x}_0, \mathbf{v}_1\ )/\epsilon)}{\log(|\lambda_1|/|\lambda_2|)}$$

steps we have $\|\mathbf{x}_{N^*} - \mathbf{v}_1\|_2 \leq d(\ \mathbf{x}_{N^*}, \mathbf{v}_1\ ) \leq \epsilon$. This allows us to upperbound the number of iterations needed for a given level of convergence. However, the metic is not suitable to use within the algorithm to determine the first eigenvalue/eigenvector as it depends on the value of the first eigenvector itself.

References

1. Alon, N., Milman, V.: Lambda1, isoperimetric inequalities for graphs, and super-concentrators. J. Comb. Theory Series B **38**(1), 73–88 (1985). http://www.sciencedirect.com/science/article/pii/0095895685900929
2. Alon, N.: Eigenvalues and expanders. Combinatorica **6**(2), 83–96 (1986)
3. Aly, A., et al.: SCALE and MAMBA v1.9: Documentation (2020). https://homes.esat.kuleuven.be/~nsmart/SCALE/Documentation.pdf
4. Bogdanov, D., Laur, S., Willemson, J.: Sharemind: a framework for fast privacy-preserving computations. Cryptology ePrint Archive, Report 2008/289 (2008). http://eprint.iacr.org/2008/289

5. Broder, A., et al.: Graph structure in the web (2000)
6. Catrina, O., Saxena, A.: Secure computation with fixed-point numbers. In: Sion, R. (ed.) FC 2010. LNCS, vol. 6052, pp. 35–50. Springer, Heidelberg (2010). https://doi.org/10.1007/978-3-642-14577-3_6
7. Del Corso, G.M., Gullí, A., Romani, F.: Fast PageRank computation via a sparse linear system (extended abstract). In: Leonardi, S. (ed.) WAW 2004. LNCS, vol. 3243, pp. 118–130. Springer, Heidelberg (2004). https://doi.org/10.1007/978-3-540-30216-2_10
8. Damgård, I., Pastro, V., Smart, N., Zakarias, S.: Multiparty computation from somewhat homomorphic encryption. In: Safavi-Naini, R., Canetti, R. (eds.) CRYPTO 2012. LNCS, vol. 7417, pp. 643–662. Springer, Heidelberg (2012). https://doi.org/10.1007/978-3-642-32009-5_38
9. Daskalakis, C., Tzamos, C., Zampetakis, M.: A converse to Banach's Fixed Point Theorem and its CLS completeness. CoRR abs/1702.07339 (2017). http://arxiv.org/abs/1702.07339
10. Demmler, D., Schneider, T., Zohner, M.: ABY - a framework for efficient mixed-protocol secure two-party computation. In: NDSS 2015. The Internet Society, February 2015
11. Dikland, T.: Added value of combining transaction graphs on fraud detection using the PageRank algorithm. Internship Report, TNO and TU Delft (2018)
12. Elden, L.: A note on the eigenvalues of the Google matrix (2004). http://arxiv.org/abs/math/0401177
13. Furukawa, J., Lindell, Y., Nof, A., Weinstein, O.: High-throughput secure three-party computation for malicious adversaries and an honest majority. In: Coron, J.-S., Nielsen, J.B. (eds.) EUROCRYPT 2017. LNCS, vol. 10211, pp. 225–255. Springer, Cham (2017). https://doi.org/10.1007/978-3-319-56614-6_8
14. Han, Y.-S., Kim, L., Cha, J.-W.: Evaluation of user reputation on YouTube. In: Ozok, A.A., Zaphiris, P. (eds.) OCSC 2009. LNCS, vol. 5621, pp. 346–353. Springer, Heidelberg (2009). https://doi.org/10.1007/978-3-642-02774-1_38
15. Hastings, M., Falk, B.H., Tsoukalas, G.: Privacing preserving network analytics (2020). https://papers.ssrn.com/sol3/papers.cfm?abstract_id=3680000
16. Haveliwala, T., Kamvar, S.: The second eigenvalue of the Google matrix. Technical Report 2003-20, Stanford InfoLab (2003). http://ilpubs.stanford.edu:8090/582/
17. Huynh, T.D.: Extension of PageRank and application to social networks. (Extension de PageRank et application aux réseaux sociaux). Ph.D. thesis, Pierre and Marie Curie University, Paris, France (2015). https://tel.archives-ouvertes.fr/tel-01187929
18. Kamm, L., Willemson, J.: Secure floating-point arithmetic and private satellite collision analysis. Cryptology ePrint Archive, Report 2013/850 (2013). http://eprint.iacr.org/2013/850
19. Kamvar, S., Haveliwala, T.: The condition number of the PageRank problem. Technical report 2003-36, Stanford InfoLab, June 2003. http://ilpubs.stanford.edu:8090/597/
20. Keller, M., Rotaru, D., Smart, N.P., Wood, T.: Reducing communication channels in MPC. In: Catalano, D., De Prisco, R. (eds.) SCN 2018. LNCS, vol. 11035, pp. 181–199. Springer, Cham (2018). https://doi.org/10.1007/978-3-319-98113-0_10
21. Langville, A.N., Meyer, C.D.: Deeper inside PageRank. Technical report, Department of Mathematics, N. Carolina State University (2003)
22. Langville, A.N., Meyer, C.D.: Fiddling with PageRank. Technical report, Department of Mathematics, N. Carolina State University (2003)

23. Langville, A.N., Meyer, C.D.: Survey: Deeper inside PageRank. Internet Math. **1**(3), 335–380 (2003). https://doi.org/10.1080/15427951.2004.10129091

24. Maxwell, N.: Innovation and discussion paper: case studies of the use of privacy preserving analysis to tackle financial crime. Technical report, Royal United Services Institute (2020). https://www.future-fis.com/uploads/3/7/9/4/3794525/ffis_innovation_and_discussion_paper_-_case_studies_of_the_use_of_privacy_preserving_analysis.pdf

25. Mohassel, P., Rindal, P.: ABY^3: a mixed protocol framework for machine learning. In: Lie, D., Mannan, M., Backes, M., Wang, X. (eds.) ACM CCS 2018, pp. 35–52. ACM Press, October 2018

26. Molloy, I., et al.: Graph analytics for real-time scoring of cross-channel transactional fraud. In: Grossklags, J., Preneel, B. (eds.) FC 2016. LNCS, vol. 9603, pp. 22–40. Springer, Heidelberg (2017). https://doi.org/10.1007/978-3-662-54970-4_2

27. Moreau, A.: How to perform fraud detection with personalized PageRank, 9 January 2019. Blog: https://www.sicara.ai/blog/2019-01-09-fraud-detection-personalized-page-rank

28. Page, L., Brin, S., Motwani, R., Winograd, T.: The PageRank citation ranking: bringing order to the web. In: Proceedings of the 7th International World Wide Web Conference, pp. 161–172 (1998)

29. Riazi, M.S., Weinert, C., Tkachenko, O., Songhori, E.M., Schneider, T., Koushanfar, F.: Chameleon: a hybrid secure computation framework for machine learning applications. In: Kim, J., Ahn, G.J., Kim, S., Kim, Y., López, J., Kim, T. (eds.) ASIACCS 2018, pp. 707–721. ACM Press, April 2018

30. Sangers, A., et al.: Secure multiparty PageRank algorithm for collaborative fraud detection. In: Goldberg, I., Moore, T. (eds.) FC 2019. LNCS, vol. 11598, pp. 605–623. Springer, Cham (2019). https://doi.org/10.1007/978-3-030-32101-7_35

31. Shamir, A.: How to share a secret. Commun. Assoc. Comput. Mach. **22**(11), 612–613 (1979)

32. Simić, S.K., Anđelić, M., da Fonseca, C.M., Živković, D.: Notes on the second largest eigenvalue of a graph. Linear Algebra Appl. **465**, 262–274 (2015). http://www.sciencedirect.com/science/article/pii/S002437951400617X

33. Soramaki, K., Bech, M.L., Arnold, J., Glass, R.J., Beyeler, W.E.: The topology of interbank payment flows. Physica A: Stat. Mech. Appl. **379**(1), 317–333 (2007). http://www.sciencedirect.com/science/article/pii/S0378437106013124

34. Soramaki, K., Cook, S.: Sinkrank: an algorithm for identifying systemically important banks in payment systems. Economics Open-Access Open-Assess. E-Journal **7**, 1–27 (2013)

35. Vlasselaer, V.V., Eliassi-Rad, T., Akoglu, L., Snoeck, M., Baesens, B.: GOTCHA! network-based fraud detection for social security fraud. Manag. Sci. **63**(9), 3090–3110 (2017). https://doi.org/10.1287/mnsc.2016.2489

Compilation of Function Representations for Secure Computing Paradigms

Karim Baghery[1], Cyprien Delpech de Saint Guilhem[1],
Emmanuela Orsini[1], Nigel P. Smart[1,2](✉), and Titouan Tanguy[1]

[1] imec-COSIC, KU Leuven, Leuven, Belgium
{karim.baghery,cyprien.delpechdesaintguilhem,emmanuela.orsini,
nigel.smart,titouan.tanguy}@kuleuven.be
[2] University of Bristol, Bristol, UK

Abstract. This paper introduces M-Circuits, a program representation which generalizes arithmetic and binary circuits. This new representation is motivated by the way modern multi-party computation (MPC) systems based on linear secret sharing schemes actually operate. We then show how this representation also allows one to construct zero knowledge proof (ZKP) systems based on the MPC-in-the-head paradigm. The use of the M-Circuit program abstraction then allows for a number of program-specific optimizations to be applied generically. It also allows to separate complexity and security optimizations for program compilation from those for application protocols (MPC or ZKP).

1 Introduction

Secure computation methodologies are becoming more mainstream with multi-party computation (MPC), fully homomorphic encryption (FHE) and zero-know-ledge proofs of knowledge (ZKPoKs) all finding applications at an increasing rate. At their heart all three technologies work with a public function; either to be compute it securely (in the case of MPC or FHE), or to prove the correctness of public outputs under secret inputs (in the case of ZKPoKs). The representation of this function is key to many of the practical realizations. For example: in theoretical MPC papers functions are often represented by arithmetic circuits, in FHE they are often binary circuits, and in ZKPoK papers R1CS representations are often used.

In this work we concentrate on two secure computation technologies: MPC protocols based on linear secret sharing schemes (LSSS) and ZKPoKs based on MPC-in-the-Head (MPCitH). It is common in theoretical treatments of these protocols to assume the input function representation is given as an arithmetic or binary circuit. However, in practice, this is not how functions are represented as input to such protocols. It has been known since Beaver's work [6] that sometimes a more interesting representation is as a set of linear operations, combined with a correlated randomness source. Previous work showed that more efficient representations for LSSS-based MPC can be obtained using

© Springer Nature Switzerland AG 2021
K. G. Paterson (Ed.): CT-RSA 2021, LNCS 12704, pp. 26–50, 2021.
https://doi.org/10.1007/978-3-030-75539-3_2

different sources of correlated randomness, as well as a combination of different finite fields [10,11,16]. This latter idea has been expanded in recent years with the advent of so-called daBit-based protocols for switching between LSSS-based MPC and garbled circuit-based MPC [27]. Thus the standard theoretical assumption of representing the function as a simple arithmetic circuit is at least ten years out of date given the state-of-the-art of LSSS-based MPC protocols.

A similar situation holds for MPCitH protocols. These are a class of zero-knowledge protocols introduced by Ishai et al. in [22], and recently extended in a number of works e.g. [3,5,9,12,21,23] In such protocols, a key aspect is to represent the function as a sequence of linear operations, combined with access to sources of correlated randomness, as in [5,23]. In MPC protocols, the creation of the correlated randomness sources often involves expensive pre-processing, but for MPCitH this can be done essentially for free. Therefore, larger performance improvements for MPCitH could result from expanding the use of correlated randomness sources.

Indeed in both LSSS-based MPC and MPCitH there is no single 'correct' representation of a function, with different representations presenting different performance trade-offs in the final protocol. But it is also case that different representations can also present different security trade-offs as well. Indeed the compilation of the abstract function into a concrete representation can introduce security issues.

Our Contributions and Paper Overview. The first contribution of this paper (in Sect. 2) is a generalized definition of the program input to such LSSS-based MPC and MPCitH protocols, which we call an M-Circuit. It can be considered as a generalization of arithmetic circuits, but tuned for MPC and MPCitH protocols (hence the name). An M-Circuit can make use of linear operations on sensitive variables, correlated randomness sources, as well as objects we call 'gadgets'. A gadget is a function call from the M-Circuit representation of the program which is not necessarily implemented itself as an M-Circuit. Such gadgets allow for specific functions to be implemented in ways which avoid inefficiencies from implementing them using only an M-Circuit definition. Each M-Circuit belongs to a set of classes of M-Circuits, determined by what correlated randomness sources we allow, what finite fields are utilized, and what magic 'gadgets' are used. We can then determine which classes of protocols are best suited for different protocols.

We furthermore examine what it means for a compilation of a function into an M-Circuit to be 'secure'. And we relate this security definition to the security of the resulting MPC/MPCitH protocol when the given M-Circuit representation is used. Some compilation strategies are clearly insecure, some give perfect security and some give statistical security; leading to the same corresponding security of the final protocol in which they are used. Whilst well understood in the practical community, we can find no treatment of the security aspect of program compilation being discussed in the MPC literature before.

After presenting our representation we show how this maps, in Sect. 3, onto common MPC frameworks (such as MP-SPDZ [24] and SCALE-MAMBA [1]), and how the M-Circuit representation is already the underlying one used in practice. This application is now standard and we only sketch it in this work.

In our second contribution in Sect. 4, we show how M-Circuits can be used in MPCitH protocols. We recast the protocols of [5,23] to use our general M-Circuit definition (initially excluding the use of the gadgets). We define the components needed to allow M-Circuits to be used in general MPCitH protocols. We then go on to present a number of optimization strategies which our M-Circuit representation allows one to express easily for MPCitH protocols. The first, in Sect. 5, examines how introducing new correlated randomness sources can produce more efficient proofs. We recall that for MPCitH adding new correlated randomness sources comes at little extra cost and thus this is a resource we can utilize to improve efficiency quite aggressively. The second, in Sect. 6, shows how, for some randomness sources, one can replace cut-and-choose checking with a form of sacrificing (as used in MPC protocols such as SPDZ). This acts as a warm up for our method which introduces the ability to introduce complex gadgets into our MPCitH protocol, given in Sect. 7. Details of standard definitions and proofs of our main results are given in the full version.

2 M-Circuits

Given a function F there are many ways of representing the function: theoreticians may look at binary or arithmetic circuit representations, programmers may think of C, Java, or Haskell, a processor designer may think of an x86 instruction stream. By the Church-Turing thesis all are essentially equivalent. In this section we formalize a way of representing a function for use in LSSS-based MPC and/or MPCitH systems. A key aspect of our definition is that the process of compiling/programming an abstract mathematical function F as a concrete representation involves some form of security analysis, i.e. it is not only the MPC/MPCitH protocol which impacts security but also the input representation of the function being operated upon.

2.1 Defining an M-Circuit

At the heart of our definitions is the idea that a function maps input variables to output variables, but that some of the input variables, and indeed some of the output variables may be sensitive.

Machine State. We start by defining a machine state.

Definition 2.1 (Machine State). *A machine state* state *defined over a set of finite fields* $\mathcal{F} = \{\mathbb{F}_{q_1}, \ldots, \mathbb{F}_{q_f}\}$ *is a collection of variables (or memory addresses). Each variable has a type which is one of the following three forms:*

- $(q_i, -)$, *which refers to a variable which holds a non-sensitive variable in the finite field* $\mathbb{F}_{q_i}$;

- (q_i, s), *which refers to a variable which holds a sensitive variable in the finite field* $\mathbb{F}_{q_i}$;
- $(-, -)$ *which refers to a signed integer variable (i.e. an element of* $\mathbb{Z}$*) in some bounded range (for example a 64-bit integer).*

The machine state can hold these variables in a number of manners, for example as memory locations indexed by integers via stacks. The usage of the signed integer variables are to allow memory access operations and stack operations within the machine. Note, one could extend the definition to finite rings, and not just finite fields, using techniques such as those from SPDZ2k [15], but for now we keep to the simpler case of finite fields.

To ease notation in what follows we let $\{x\}_q$ denote a variable of type $(q, -)$, $\langle x \rangle_q$ denote a variable of type (q, s), and x denote a variable of type $(-, -)$. Also, we make no distinction between the name of the variable and the value it contains. If we want to refer to a type, and are not interested in its sensitivity classification, we refer to the type $(q, *)$, and call it the *base type* of the variable.

We note that variables of the same type can be added, subtracted and multiplied etc. Variables of different types can be combined in the following sense: the operation of a binary arithmetic operator on two variables of type (p_1, s_1) and (p_2, s_2) can be applied if $\gcd(p_1, p_2) \neq 1$, resulting in a type (p_3, s_3) where:

- $p_3 = \gcd(p_1, p_2)$,
- $s_3 = s$ if and only if $s_1 = s$ or $s_2 = s$, otherwise $s_3 = -$. (This means that variables can only become more sensitive, akin to the 'no write down' rule of Bell-LaPadula [7]).

Thus one can form (relatively) arbitrary arithmetic expressions on variables, and one can assign a type to the result of the expression.

Variables of type $(p, -)$, for prime p, can be arbitrarily converted into variables of type $(-, -)$ and vice-versa, using the inclusion $\mathbb{F}_p \longrightarrow [0, \ldots, p-1) \subset \mathbb{Z}$ and the mapping $\mathbb{Z} \longrightarrow \mathbb{F}_p$ given by $x \mapsto x \pmod{p}$.

Correlated Randomness Sources: As well as variables, and the arithmetic expressions we can create from them, there are two additional components for an M-Circuit, namely *correlated randomness sources* and *gadgets*, which we describe in the following.

Definition 2.2 (Correlated Randomness Source). *A correlated randomness source* $\mathbb{S}$ *is defined by a set of variables* $\{v_1, \ldots, v_t\}$ *of any (specific) types* $\{(q_1, *), \ldots, (q_t, *)\}$ *and a predicate* pred *on those variables.*

A correlated randomness source should be thought of as related to the data which is produced in preprocessing phases of MPC protocols such as SPDZ [20]. Thus typical sources would be:

- Triple: This has associated to it three variables, (a, b, c) all of type (p, s), for which the predicate is $\mathsf{pred}(a, b, c) := a \cdot b = c$, with a, b being uniformly randomly chosen from $\mathbb{F}_p$.

- Square: This has associated to it two variables, (a, b), both of type (p, s) for which the predicate is $\mathsf{pred}(a, b) := a \cdot a = b$, with a being uniformly randomly chosen from $\mathbb{F}_p$.
- Bit: This has associated to it a single variable, a, of type (p, s) for which the predicate is $\mathsf{pred}(a) := a \in \{0, 1\}$, and a is uniformly randomly chosen from $\{0, 1\}$.
- daBit: This has associated to it two variables, a, b, one of type (p, s) and one of type $(2, s)$, for which the predicate is $\mathsf{pred}(a, b) := (a = b) \land (a \in \{0, 1\})$, with a uniformly randomly chosen from $\{0, 1\}$.

Gadgets: The second component we introduce now is called a 'gadget'. From a high level point of view these can be arbitrary operations. More formally, they are function calls made by the M-Circuit which we do not necessarily implement using an M-Circuit. This means, for example, that their functionality could be provided by some externally defined protocol. In practice, we will use gadgets to perform very specific operations within specific protocols and also to help to define stages of program transformation within a compilation. Thus gadget's correspond to operations which are done using special protocols, with the idea being that if we can show the special protocol for implementing the gadget is secure and correct, then we can use the gadget as an optimization process within our final protocols.

Definition 2.3 (Gadget). *A gadget* $\mathbb{G}$ *is a mathematical function which takes a set of variables and outputs a set of variables* $(\hat{v}_1, \ldots, \hat{v}_u) \leftarrow \mathbb{G}(v_1, \ldots, v_t)$, *where no assumption is made about how* $\mathbb{G}$ *will be implemented. The types of the input and output variables are assumed to be implicitly defined by the gadget itself.*

Looking ahead, in the context of MPC using a gadget is like calling a protocol to perform a Garbled Circuit operation on some secret shared data over $\mathbb{F}_2$ in a system such as that described by the Zaphod paper [2]. The gadget in this case goes outside the neat confines of LSSS-based MPC, but it is integrated with the LSSS based MPC and is thus able to allow greater functionality at reduced cost. Another example of a gadget could be a multiplication gate, which we do not expand into its Beaver representation if we want to avoid correlated randomness sources.

Instructions and M-Circuits. An M-Circuit is composed of an *ordered* finite list of instructions as follows.

Definition 2.4 (Instruction). *An instruction can be one of the following forms:*

- *A pair* (v, expr), *where* v *is a variable and* expr, *is an arithmetic expression as described above. The type of* v *must correspond to the type of* expr. *As a shorthand we may write* $v \leftarrow \mathsf{expr}$. *We restrict the expressions* expr *to be arbitrary arithmetic expressions, however the* total *degree of the expression in any* sensitive *variables must be one. Thus we can only compute linear functions on sensitive variables.*

- *A tuple* $(\{v_1, \dots, v_t\}, \mathbb{S})$ *where* $\mathbb{S}$ *is a correlated randomness source, and the variables* $\{v_1, \dots, v_t\}$ *have the same types as the variables associated to the source. As a shorthand we may write* $v_1, \dots, v_t \leftarrow \mathbb{S}$.
- *A tuple* $(\{\hat{v}_1, \dots, \hat{v}_u\}, \{v_1, \dots, v_t\}, \mathbb{G})$ *where* $\hat{v}_i$ *and* v_i *are variables and* $\mathbb{G}$ *is a gadget as described above. The types of* v_j *and* $\hat{v}_i$ *must correspond to the input and output types of the Gadget. As a shorthand we may write* $\hat{v}_1, \dots, \hat{v}_u \leftarrow \mathbb{G}(v_1, \dots, v_t)$.
- *A 'declassification' instruction which we write as* $x \leftarrow y.\mathsf{reveal}()$. *This takes a variable* y *of type* (p, s) *and creates a variable* x *of type* $(p, -)$ *which has the same value as* y.
- *A special instruction called* terminate.

Examples, of the first three types of instruction, could include:

$$\langle z \rangle \leftarrow \langle x \rangle_p + \langle y \rangle_p$$

$$\langle x \rangle_p, \langle y \rangle_p, \langle z \rangle_p \leftarrow \mathsf{Triple}$$

$$\{\langle c_i \rangle_2\}_{i=0}^{127} \leftarrow \mathsf{AES}\Big(\{\langle k_i \rangle_2\}_{i=0}^{127}, \{\langle m_i \rangle_2\}_{i=0}^{127} \Big).$$

Finally, we can define what we mean by an M-Circuit.

Definition 2.5. *An M-Circuit is a tuple consisting of an ordered list of instructions* $\mathcal{I}$ *and two sets of variables* $\mathcal{V}_I$ *and* $\mathcal{V}_O$ *(called the input and the output variables).*

A class of M-Circuits $\mathcal{C}_{\{\mathbb{F}_{q_1}, \dots, \mathbb{F}_{q_f}\}}^{(\{\mathbb{S}_1, \dots, \mathbb{S}_s\}, \{\mathbb{G}_1, \dots, \mathbb{G}_g\})}$ is the set of all M-Circuits over the finite fields $\{\mathbb{F}_{q_1}, \dots, \mathbb{F}_{q_f}\}$, which utilize correlated randomness sources $\{\mathbb{S}_1, \dots, \mathbb{S}_s\}$ and gadgets $\{\mathbb{G}_1, \dots, \mathbb{G}_g\}$. If $\mathcal{F}$ and $\mathcal{F}'$ are sets of finite fields, and $\mathcal{S}$ and $\mathcal{S}'$ are sets of correlated randomness sources, and $\mathcal{G}$ and $\mathcal{G}'$ are sets of gadgets then we have $\mathcal{C}_{\mathcal{F}}^{(\mathcal{S}, \mathcal{G})} \subseteq \mathcal{C}_{\mathcal{F}'}^{(\mathcal{S}', \mathcal{G}')}$ if $\mathcal{F} \subseteq \mathcal{F}'$, $\mathcal{S} \subseteq \mathcal{S}'$ and $\mathcal{G} \subseteq \mathcal{G}'$.

2.2   Executing an M-Circuit

An M-Circuit $(\mathcal{I}, \mathcal{V}_I, \mathcal{V}_O)$ operates on a machine state as follows. The machine state state has an initial state consisting of the set of registers $\mathcal{V}_I$ with pre-assigned values given to them (i.e. the inputs to the function). In addition there is a special register of type $(-, -)$, called pc, which is initial set to zero. Then the following operations are repeated until a terminate instruction is met.

- Instruction numbered pc is fetched from the list of instructions $\mathcal{I}$.
- The value of pc is incremented by one.
- The instruction is executed as follows depending on its type
  - (v, expr) is evaluated if all the variables in expr are currently defined, and the result is assigned to variable v. If not all variables are defined then the system aborts.

- $(\{v_1, \ldots, v_t\}, \mathbb{S})$ is evaluated by sampling the variables $\{v_1, \ldots, v_t\}$ according to the source definition.
- $(\{\hat{v}_1, \ldots, \hat{v}_u\}, \{v_1, \ldots, v_t\}, \mathbb{G})$ is evaluated as for (v, expr)
- Declassification instructions do the obvious declassification operation.
- If the instruction is terminate then the M-Circuit terminates.

On termination the M-Circuit outputs the variables in the set $\mathcal{V}_O$, if they are defined. If any are not defined it aborts.

Note, this is a rather general model in a number of senses:

- One can perform a conditional branch on non-sensitive variables by making instructions of the form $(\mathsf{pc}, \mathsf{expr})$, e.g. $\mathsf{pc} \leftarrow b \cdot 100 + (1 - b) \cdot 200$ will either result in a jump to instruction 100 or instruction 200 depending on the value of variable $b \in \{0, 1\}$ of type $(-, -)$.
- Subroutines calls, and hence recursion, can be performed by using creating a stack of type $(-, -)$ in the machine state, and then using this to push/pop the pc variable on or off of it.

The main limitation of the model seems to be that instructions of the form (v, expr) can only contain linear functions of sensitive variables. This is where our gadgets and randomness sources will come in.

There are four different measures of complexity of an M-Circuit, and we name these so as to link them with their analogues when we use M-Circuits for MPC (where analogues exist), as follows.

- The *offline complexity* is the number of calls to the source oracles $\{\mathbb{S}_1, \ldots, \mathbb{S}_s\}$ made by the M-Circuit on a given input.
- The *online communication complexity* is the number of calls to the operation $\mathsf{reveal}()$ made by the M-Circuit on a given input.
- The *online round complexity* is the minimum number of *parallel* calls to the operation $\mathsf{reveal}()$ made by the M-Circuit on a given input.
- The *gadget-complexity* (which has no usual analogue in the MPC domain) is the number of calls to gadgets $\mathbb{G}$ made by the M-Circuit on a given input.

2.3   Compiling M-Circuits

An M-Circuit is created by a process called compilation.

Definition 2.6 (Compilation). *A compilation step is an algorithm which takes an M-Circuit C in a class $\mathcal{C}_{\mathcal{F}}^{(\mathcal{S}, \mathcal{G})}$ and maps it to an M-Circuit C' in a class $\mathcal{C}_{\mathcal{F}'}^{(\mathcal{S}', \mathcal{G}')}$. The algorithm must ensure that the functional behaviour of C and C' are identical, i.e. the input/output behaviour of C and C' are the same.*

Note a compilation says nothing about whether $\mathcal{C}_{\mathcal{F}}^{(\mathcal{S}, \mathcal{G})} \subseteq \mathcal{C}_{\mathcal{F}'}^{(\mathcal{S}', \mathcal{G}')}$ or vice-versa.

Given an arbitrary polynomial time function F, defined over a set of finite fields $\mathcal{F}$ and the integers, there is always an M-Circuit, which we call C_F, which implements F in the class $\mathcal{C}_{\mathcal{F}}^{(\emptyset, \{F\})}$, namely the M-Circuit which uses the gadget $\mathbb{G} = F$. The goal of compilation is to find representations of C_F in simpler classes, in particular a class which can be implemented in either an MPC or MPCitH system. We present three exemplar compilations here to fix ideas:

– **Arithmetic Circuit:** Consider the gadget $\mathbb{G}_M$ for a finite field $\mathbb{F}_p$ which multiples two input values, giving the output value of the same type. Then the standard 'arithmetization' of polynomial time functions F compiles the M-Circuit C_F to an M-Circuit C_F^A in the class $\mathcal{C}_{\mathbb{F}_p}^{(\emptyset, \{\mathbb{G}_M\})}$.

– **Beaver Randomized Circuit:** We can take the M-Circuit C_F^A produces in the previous example and compile it to an M-Circuit C_F^B in the class $\mathcal{C}_{\mathbb{F}_p}^{(\mathsf{Triple}, \{\emptyset\})}$ using Beaver's standard circuit randomization trick, [6].

– **Insecure Circuit:** Here we take F, and create the functionally equivalent function F' which first de-classifies all the sensitive input variables of F. Then it evaluates F on the clear values, using the arithmetic circuit representation of F. Finally, it re-classifies any output variables as sensitive which need to be sensitive, by multiplication by $\langle 1 \rangle_p$. The associated arithmetic circuit $C_{F'}^A$ (which includes reveal() operations as well as the usual arithmetic operations) is an M-Circuit in the class $\mathcal{C}_{\mathbb{F}_p}^{(\emptyset, \{\mathbb{G}_M\})}$.

The last example here hints that compilation can create something which is 'insecure'. To quantify this notion we need to define what we mean by security of an M-Circuit.

2.4   Security of M-Circuits

To define security of an M-Circuit we have to examine the reveal() operations in more detail, since these are the operations which potentially de-classify sensitive information. Informally we require that the reveal() operations never reveal more than an negligible amount of sensitive information about any sensitive inputs to the function.

To each reveal operation of the form $a \leftarrow \langle b \rangle_q$.reveal() we associate a given distribution $\mathcal{R}_b$ on the set $\mathbb{F}_q$. The reader can think of $\mathcal{R}_b$ on first reading as the uniform distribution (which will be true for circuits compiled using the Beaver compilation above, but it is not true in general). To take into account the type of efficient function representations used in say [11] we need to be a little more nuanced.

The distributions $\mathcal{R}_b$ are on the outputs of reveal() are conditioned on the following three things:

– The specific non-sensitive inputs and outputs of the function being evaluated.
– The random execution path taken by the circuit.
– The distributions of the correlated randomness sources.

However, the distributions are not conditioned on sensitive input and output values to the function. For example consider the code fragments in Fig. 1. In fragment (a) the function is b, in which case the distribution $\mathcal{R}_z$ has probability mass of one at the value $b - 1$ and is zero elsewhere, whilst in fragment (b) the distribution $\mathcal{R}_z$ is the set of values in the range $[-B, \ldots, B]$ with an associated binomial distribution.

Code Fragment (a)
```
a = z.reveal()
b = a+1
Output b
```

Code Fragment (b)
```
for i in range(2*B):
    b_i = Bits
z = sum(b[2*i]-b[2*i+1],i in range(B))
a = z.reveal()
```

Code Fragment (c)
```
z=x+y
a=z.reveal()
Output a
```

Code Fragment (d)
```
b=x.reveal()
c=y.reveal()
a=b+c
Output a
```

Fig. 1. Example code fragments

The trace Trace_C of an M-Circuit, on a given input, consists of the set of non-sensitive input variables, the non-sensitive output variables, plus the output of every reveal() operation. A simulated trace Sim_C is the same except that the output of every reveal() operation is replaced by a value chosen via the distributions $\mathcal{R}_b$ above.

Definition 2.7 (Perfectly Secure M-Circuit). *An M-Circuit C is said to perfectly securely implement a function F if the functional behaviour of the M-Circuit C and the M-Circuit C_F are identical, and the distribution of Trace_C and Sim_C are identical for all input values.*

Definition 2.8 (Statistically Secure M-Circuit). *The M-Circuit C is said to securely implement a function F with statistical security sec if the functional behaviour of the M-Circuit C and the function C_F are identical, and the statistical distance between the distribution of Trace_C and Sim_C is bounded by $2^{-\mathsf{sec}}$ for all input values.*

The first question one must ask is if such a definition is vacuous. The celebrated technique of Beaver's Circuit Randomization [6] says no.

Theorem 2.1. *Every polynomial time function F can be perfectly securely implemented by the M-Circuit C_F^B with polynomial complexity (in all four metrics).*

Proof. Using the compilation process above we can compile the M-Circuit C_F^B. It is well known that the reveal() operations this creates are associated with uniform distributions, and thus the reveals are perfectly hiding.

Note, this definition is about the representation of the function i.e. the compilation of the M-Circuit from the function definition. It asks whether the compilation process is itself secure; it makes no claim about how the M-Circuit is then used or evaluated within an MPC or MPCitH system.

Not all compilations will result in secure M-Circuits, as our insecure compilation example illustrates. To see why this compilation violates our security definition, consider the specific function F which takes two sensitive values x

and y, and returns their sum, but as a non-sensitive value. Mathematically one could write $F(\langle x \rangle, \langle y \rangle) = (\langle x \rangle + \langle y \rangle).\mathsf{reveal}()$. A functionally valid M-Circuit for this function is given in code fragment (c) of Fig. 1, whilst another functionally valid M-Circuit for the same function is given in code fragment (d).

Code fragment (c) is a perfectly secure M-Circuit, with the distribution $\mathcal{R}_z$ being the point distribution will all the probability mass at the point a (where a is the public output of the function). Thus the valid transcript Trace_C and Sim_C are identical and equal to $\mathsf{Trace}_C = \mathsf{Sim}_C = \{\emptyset, \{a\}, \{a\}.\}$, i.e. there are no distributions here at all, Trace_C and Sim_C are fixed by the output a. Note, the $\emptyset$ corresponds to the set of non-sensitive input variables, the first $\{a\}$ is the set of non-sensitive output variables, and the second $\{a\}$ is the output of every reveal (resp. the simulated reveals) in the case of the actual trace (resp. the simulated trace).

Code fragment (d) has $\mathcal{R}_x$ being the point distribution on x, with y being the point distribution of $y = a - x$. Thus Trace_C of the second M-Circuit is equal to $\mathsf{Trace}_C = \{\emptyset, \{a\}, \{x, a-x\}\}$ which is a fixed value (for each given input), whereas the simulated trace $\mathcal{S}_C$ is equal to the value given by $\mathcal{S}_C = \{\emptyset, \{a\}, \{r, a - r\}\}$ where r uniformly chosen from $\mathbb{F}_p$. Thus Trace_C and $\mathcal{S}_C$ in the second case can never be statistically close. Thus the second compilation to an M-Circuit is insecure, but functionally correct.

3   M-Circuits for Multi-party Computation

It turns out that our M-Circuit notion lies underneath almost all algorithmic level optimizations of LSSS-based MPC over the last decade (by which we mean optimizations related to the program representation and not the MPC protocol itself). The M-Circuit concept allows us to isolate which optimizations can be utilized by which MPC protocols, since not all MPC protocols can implement all M-Circuit classes.

As remarked earlier, arithmetic circuit representation of a functionality over a finite field $\mathbb{F}_q$ correspond to M-Circuits in the class $\mathcal{C}_{\mathbb{F}_q}^{(\emptyset, \{\mathbb{G}_M\})}$. Thus 'traditional' LSSS based MPC protocols such as [8,13], or modern protocols such as [14], which have specific protocols for the multiplication operation can utilize this M-Circuit representation. However, the security of these protocols is then proved by showing that the implementation of the specific multiplication gadget leaks no information.

Protocols which expand the multiplication gadget via Beaver's trick [6] utilize circuits from the class $\mathcal{C}_{\mathbb{F}_p}^{(\{\mathsf{Triple}\}, \emptyset)}$. The security of the underlying (passively secure) online protocol then follows from the security of the M-Circuit representation; if the M-Circuit is secure then so is the obvious LSSS-based MPC protocol in which one replaces the sensitive variables in the M-Circuit by secret shared values. The problem comes in creating an offline phase to produce the necessary correlated randomness source Triple in a secret shared manner. For honest majority protocols this offline phase is usually performed using hyper-invertible matrices (as in VIFF [17]) or, for dishonest majority protocols using homomorphic encryption (as in SPDZ [20]) or OT (as in MASCOT [26]). In the latter case to prove active security of the underlying MPC protocol one needs to provide a form of authenticated secret sharing, while the privacy of the protocol follows from the security of the M-Circuit representation. For the passive case the security of the online phase we cover in Sect. 4.1 later.

Papers such as [10,11,16] showed that one can obtain greater efficiency by working with M-Circuits in the class $C_{\mathbb{F}_{2^8},\mathbb{F}_q}^{(\emptyset,\{\mathbb{G}_M\})}$, or equivalently $C_{\mathbb{F}_{2^8},\mathbb{F}_q}^{(\{\text{Triple}_{2^8},\text{Triple}_q\},\emptyset)}$; although of course they did not use this language. In these latter works the authors used multiplication to create shared-random bits, whereas if one assumes these as a random source then the protocols become simpler to describe; thus the same work can be cast as corresponding to M-Circuits in the class $C_{\mathbb{F}_q}^{(\{\text{Triple},\text{Bit}\},\emptyset)}$. It is this latter representation which is used in modern LSSS-based systems in the pre-processing model; for example the second generation of the SPDZ protocol [18] utilizes function descriptions which are M-Circuits in the class $C_{\mathbb{F}_p}^{(\{\text{Triple},\text{Square},\text{Bit}\},\emptyset)}$. The papers such as [10,11] also showed one can obtain more efficient representations, in terms of minimizing the various complexity measures we described earlier, by compiling to what we call statistically secure M-Circuits as opposed to perfectly secure M-Circuits.

Systems which make use of daBits [27] to translate between binary and arithmetic fields utilize M-Circuits in the class $C_{\{\mathbb{F}_p,\mathbb{F}_2\}}^{(\{\text{Triple},\text{Square},\text{Bit},\text{daBit}\},\emptyset)}$. Systems such as Zaphod, [2] extend this idea further by allowing gadgets based on garbled circuits to be evaluated within the MPC-computation. Thus they allow M-Circuits in the class $C_{\{\mathbb{F}_p,\mathbb{F}_2\}}^{(\{\text{Triple},\text{Square},\text{Bit},\text{daBit}\},\{\mathbb{G}_1,...,\mathbb{G}_g\})}$ for specific garbled circuit based subprocedures $\mathbb{G}_1,\ldots,\mathbb{G}_g$. As long as the gadget can be securely implemented, then the overall MPC protocol is itself secure.

Obviously compilation methods, and different sources of correlated randomness, will give different M-Circuits with different complexities. This is essentially the engineering challenge of MPC solutions: to pick the compilation strategy and sources of correlated randomness in order to achieve an efficient M-Circuit which can be executed by a given MPC engine.

4   M-Circuits for MPC-in-the-Head

In this section, we present an MPCitH-based Honest Verifier Zero-Knowledge (HVZK) argument of knowledge system for satisfiability of a function (computation) that is compiled to an M-Circuit. Initially we consider M-Circuits with no gadgets, namely we consider the class of M-Circuits $C_{\{\mathbb{F}_{q_1},...,\mathbb{F}_{q_f}\}}^{(\{\mathbb{S}_1,...,\mathbb{S}_s\},\emptyset)}$. Later we shall remove this restriction, at the expense of introducing more rounds of communication.

Our construction extends Katz et al.'s construction [23] for arbitrary finite fields. Since we work with M-Circuits, we do not consider operations such as AND, multiplication or squaring (as in Katz et al.'s presentation), but rather we formalize the protocol in term of generic correlated randomness sources over arbitrary finite fields, along with calls to the reveal() function. As we have already explained, such a representation is universal, and can lead to optimizations (which we will discuss later).

We first describe the specific underlying MPC protocol to securely compute an M-Circuit instance that we will exploit in our MPCitH protocol. Then, we present an MPCitH-based HVZK argument of knowledge based on the input M-Circuit instance. Initially, we present a protocol which checks the correlated randomness sources using the *cut-and-choose* paradigm. This method works for arbitrary sources. In a latter section we present another methodology which works for some specific correlated randomness sources which is based on the *sacrificing* idea used in some actively secure MPC protocols.

4.1 The Underlying MPC Protocol

The MPCitH protocol we utilize will make use of a very simple (passively secure) MPC protocol based on full threshold secret sharing in the pre-processing model. The function F we will be evaluating is assumed to have (some) sensitive input variables, but no sensitive output variables. The N parties in the protocol we will denote by $P_1, \ldots, P_N$.

Offline Phase. We define an ideal functionality for the offline phase, which implements the generation of suitable correlated randomness according to the sources required by the M-Circuit. This is given in Fig. 2.

MPC Offline Functionality $\mathcal{F}^{\mathcal{S}}_{\text{Offline}}$

For every source $\mathbb{S} \in \mathcal{S}$ we define a command which operates as follows:

$\mathbb{S}$:   On input of ($\mathbb{S}$) the functionality proceeds as follows
  1. Generate $(v_1, \ldots, v_t)$ according to the source definition $\mathbb{S}$.
  2. For all variables v_i of type (q_i, s) wait for shares $v_{i,j}$ from the adversary $\mathcal{A}$.
  3. On receiving these shares complete them to a full set of shares $\sum_{j \notin \mathcal{A}} v_{i,j} = v_i - \sum_{j \in \mathcal{A}} v_{i,j}$ and send the relevant $v_{i,j}$ to the honest parties.
  4. Output v_i when it is of type $(q_i, -)$ to all parties.

Fig. 2. Functionality $\mathcal{F}^{\mathcal{S}}_{\text{Offline}}$

Online Phase. We wish to implement the passively MPC/SFE functionality given in Fig. 3, in which we assume the sensitive inputs are assigned to specific parties. This is done using the online phase given in Fig. 4, which is defined in the $\mathcal{F}_{\text{Offline}}$-hybrid model.

Passively Secure MPC/SFE Functionality $\mathcal{F}_{\mathsf{MPC}}$

Given a function F defined over finite fields with input variables V_I and output variables V_O, the functionality proceeds as follows.

1. For each input variable $v \in V_I$:
    (a) If input variable v of type (q, s) is assigned to party P_i then wait for party P_i to enter the value v.
    (b) If input variable v is of type $(q, -)$ then wait for all parties to input the same value v.
2. Compute the function F on $(v_1, \ldots, v_t)$ and output the output variables to all parties (recall we assume F has no sensitive output variables).

Fig. 3. Passively secure MPC/SFE functionality $\mathcal{F}_{\mathsf{MPC}}$

Security. We let $\mathcal{A}$ denote an adversary which statically corrupts a subset of the parties. We abuse notation slightly by referring to $\mathcal{A}$ both as the adversary, and as the set of parties which it has corrupted. We define $\mathsf{view}^{\{\mathcal{A}, \Pi_{\mathsf{MPC}}\}}(C)$ to be the view of $\mathcal{A}$ during the execution of the protocol Π_{MPC} on the function F represented by the M-Circuit C in the $\mathcal{F}_{\mathsf{Offline}}$-hybrid model. This view consists of the inputs of the parties in $\mathcal{A}$, the shares of the correlated randomness the parties in $\mathcal{A}$ receive from $\{\mathbb{S}_1, \ldots, \mathbb{S}_s\}$, and the messages they obtain from the other parties while evaluating the protocol. The security of Π is stated in the following theorem, the proof of which is given in the full version.

Theorem 4.1. *For every subset of parties $\mathcal{A} \subseteq \{P_1, \cdots, P_N\}$, with $|\mathcal{A}| \leq N - 1$, there exists a probabilistic polynomial-time algorithm $\mathcal{S}$, with access to the functionality $\mathcal{F}_{\mathsf{MPC}}$, such that $\{\mathcal{S}(\mathcal{A}, F, v_{\mathcal{A}})\} \equiv \mathsf{view}^{\{\mathcal{A}, \Pi_{\mathsf{MPC}}\}}(C)$, where $v_{\mathcal{A}}$ are the function inputs of the parties in $\mathcal{A}$.*

The equivalence relation is a perfect equivalence if the M-Circuit C is a perfectly secure implementation of the functionality F, and is a statistical equivalence if the M-Circuit is a statistically secure implementation of F.

4.2 Sub-procedures for MPCitH

In this subsection we collect together a number of sub-procedures and algorithms for our general MPCitH protocol for M-Circuits.

Pseudo-Random Generator. We let PRG_q denote a pseudo-random function, which on input of a key seed and an index j outputs a (pseudo-) uniformly random element of the finite field $\mathbb{F}_q$. We let PRF_λ denote an equivalent function which outputs values in $\{0, 1\}^\lambda$.

Passively Secure MPC/SFE Protocol $\Pi_{\mathsf{MPC}}^{(\mathcal{F},\mathcal{S})}(C)$

Given a function F defined over finite fields with input variables V_I and output variables V_O represented as an M-Circuit C in the class $\mathcal{C}_{\mathcal{F}}^{(\mathcal{S},\emptyset)}$, the protocol proceeds as follows.

1. For each input variable $v \in V_I$
   (a) If input variable v of type (q, s) is assigned to party P_i then party P_i shares $v = \sum v_j$ and sends v_j to party P_j.
   (b) If input variable v is of type $(q, -)$ then all parties agree on the value v.
2. Now execute the M-Circuit line by line (as above).
   - For a $x.\mathsf{reveal}()$ command, party P_i sends his share x_i to all parties.
   - For a call to a correlated randomness source $\mathbb{S} \in \mathcal{S}$, make the appropriate call to the functionality $\mathcal{F}_{\mathsf{Offline}}$.
   - For an arithmetic operation, perform the associated operation on the linear secret sharing scheme given above.
3. Finally, for a terminate operation, for each variable $v \in V_O$ the parties output their (necessarily opened) value v as their output.

Fig. 4. Passively secure MPC/SFE protocol $\Pi_{\mathsf{MPC}}^{(\mathcal{F},\mathcal{S})}(C)$

GenAux Function. To a correlated randomness source $\mathbb{S}$ we associate a deterministic algorithm $\mathsf{GenAux}^{\mathbb{S}}$ which on input of a given assignment to the variables $\{v_1, \ldots, v_t\}$ in the source will output a set of variables $\{v_1', \ldots, v_t'\}$ of the same types. The output should satisfy the following equality of distributions, where $v_1 \leftarrow \mathbb{F}_{p_1}$ means sample v_1 uniformly from the field $\mathbb{F}_{p_1}$,

$$\Big\{ (v_1 + v_1', \ldots, v_t + v_t') \; : \; v_i \leftarrow \mathbb{F}_{p_i} \text{ for } i = 1, \ldots, t,$$

$$(v_1', \ldots, v_t') \leftarrow \mathsf{GenAux}^{\mathbb{S}}(v_1, \ldots, v_t) \Big\}$$

$$\equiv \Big\{ (v_1, \ldots, v_t) \; : \; (v_1, \ldots, v_t) \leftarrow \mathbb{S} \Big\}$$

Note, there can be many ways for a given source to define the algorithm GenAux; some are more compact than others. For example take the source Triple which has (at least) the two following definitions for GenAux.

1. $\mathsf{GenAux}^{\mathsf{Triple}}(a, b, c) = (0, 0, a \cdot b - c)$.
2. $\mathsf{GenAux}^{\mathsf{Triple}}(a, b, c) = (x - a, y - b, z - c)$ where x, y are deterministically selected from $\mathbb{F}_p$ by $\mathsf{GenAux}^{\mathsf{Triple}}$ using a PRG with the seed $H(a, b, c)$, for some hash function H, and $z = x \cdot y$.

The first of these is more efficient in our application as the user knows the first two coordinates are always zero, and can therefore drop them from any data transferred. It turns out the first is also better for one of our optimizations we present later.

Sources which require some specific distribution, such as the Bit source from earlier, can be produced by defining $\mathsf{GenAux}^{\mathsf{Bit}}(a) = (a - b)$ where $b = H(a)\&1$ for some hash function H.

GenShares. To each correlated randomness source $\mathbb{S}$, with variables $\{v_1, \ldots, v_t\}$ we associate the following seeds:

1. If v_i is of type $(q_i, -)$ then we associate a single seed $\mathsf{seed}_i^{\mathbb{S}}$.
2. If v_i is of type (q_i, s) then we associate N seeds $\mathsf{seed}_{i,j}^{\mathbb{S}}$ for $j = 1, \ldots, N$.

We also associate a counter $\mathsf{cnt}^{\mathbb{S}}$, which on initialization of the source is set to zero. In the MPCitH protocol below when $\mathbb{S}$ is called we execute an algorithm $\mathsf{GenShares}^{\mathbb{S}}$ (given in Fig. 5) which takes as input the above seeds and the counter $\mathsf{cnt}^{\mathbb{S}}$ and produces a sample from the randomness source presented as a sharing amongst the parties, as well as the correction term. We write $(\{v_i\}_\dagger, \{v_{i,j}\}_*, \mathsf{aux}, \mathsf{cnt}^{\mathbb{S}}) \leftarrow \mathsf{GenShares}^{\mathbb{S}}(\{\mathsf{seed}_i^{\mathbb{S}}\}_\dagger, \{\mathsf{seed}_{i,j}^{\mathbb{S}}\}_*, \mathsf{cnt}^{\mathbb{S}})$.

The GenShares$^{\mathbb{S}}$ Algorithm

1. For all variables v_i output by $\mathbb{S}$ of type $(q, -)$ execute
   (a) $v_i \leftarrow \mathsf{PRG}_{q_i}(\mathsf{seed}_i^{\mathbb{S}}, \mathsf{cnt}^{\mathbb{S}})$
2. For all variables v_i output by $\mathbb{S}$ of type (q, s) execute
   (a) $v_{i,j} \leftarrow \mathsf{PRG}_{q_i}(\mathsf{seed}_{i,j}^{\mathbb{S}}, \mathsf{cnt}^{\mathbb{S}})$ for $j = 1, \ldots, N$.
   (b) $v_i \leftarrow \sum_{j=1}^n v_{i,j}$ for all $i \in 1, \ldots, t$.
3. $\mathsf{cnt}^{\mathbb{S}} \leftarrow \mathsf{cnt}^{\mathbb{S}} + 1$.
4. $\mathsf{aux} = (v_1', \ldots, v_t') \leftarrow \mathsf{GenAux}^{\mathbb{S}}(v_1, \ldots, v_t)$.
5. $v_i \leftarrow v_i + v_i'$ for all i.
6. $v_{i,N} \leftarrow v_{i,N} + v_i'$ for all i such that v_i has type (q_i, s).
7. Output $(\{v_i\}_\dagger, \{v_{i,j}\}_*, \mathsf{aux}, \mathsf{cnt}^{\mathbb{S}})$, where $\dagger$ denotes v_i has type $(q_i, -)$ and $*$ denotes v_i has type (q_i, s).

Fig. 5. The GenShares$^{\mathbb{S}}$ algorithm for a source $\mathbb{S}$

4.3   The Construction of HVZK Argument of Knowledge

We can now present our generalization of the MPCitH protocols of [5,23] to the case of arbitrary M-Circuits. Our initial construction uses the *cut-and-choose* checking paradigm, but later we will also consider the other checking approach, i.e. sacrificing, that we show to be more efficient for particular cases. Recall at this point we assume an M-Circuit C is given in the class $\mathcal{C}_{\{\mathbb{F}_{q_1}, \ldots, \mathbb{F}_{q_f}\}}^{(\{\mathbb{S}_1, \ldots, \mathbb{S}_s\}, \emptyset)}$. The M-Circuit has no sensitive output variables, but there are a set of sensitive input variables, which we denote by $\mathbf{w}$. The prover wishes to show that he knows a witness for these output variables, which by abuse of notation we also call $\mathbf{w}$, such that the M-Circuit produces a given output.

At a high level the proof proceeds by the prover simulating the N-party MPC protocol from Sect. 4.1 in his head and executes it over an additive sharing of $\mathbf{w}$, along with calls to the correlated randomness sources $(\{\mathbb{S}_1, \ldots, \mathbb{S}_s\}, \emptyset)$, which are performed using the algorithm $\mathsf{GenShares}^{\mathbb{S}}$ given above. Clearly, as the secret sharing scheme is executed in prover's head, the prover might try to cheat and convince the verifier about a false statement. To prevent such issues, and hence to obtain a negligible soundness error, the construction allows the verifier to challenge the prover. Namely, at the end of the first round the prover commits (by the above commitment scheme) to the views of N parties in M executions. Then, the verifier (randomly) challenges a subset of executions $E \subset [M]$ of size τ for which all correction terms induced by calls to the correlated randomness sources will be revealed and verified. The verifier also (randomly) challenges a single party $j \in [N]$, such that all parties views are opened to him (bar party j) for all $e \in [M] \setminus E$.

After revealing the secret information for the challenged executions and parties, e.g. the master seeds, the challenged parties' seeds, or the commitments, the verifier recomputes (either using directly the values sent by the Prover, or by using the parties' seeds and correction terms to emulate the secret sharing scheme) and checks the commitments and final output of the M-Circuit.

In the described HVZK argument, intuitively, zero-knowledge is achieved relying on the fact that the M-Circuit is secure (its trace is simulatable) and the revealed data are only random values which are independent of the witness $\mathbf{w}$. Thus the $N - 1$ views that are revealed do not reveal anything as the underlying MPC protocol is passively secure against $N - 1$ semi-honest parties.

In our protocol description, as before, we use $\langle x \rangle_q$ to denote a sensitive variable (associated to an additive sharing $x = \sum_{j \in [N]} x_i$) and $\{x\}_q$ to denote a non-sensitive variable within the M-Circuit. As input to both the protocol and the verifier we have a general M-circuit C in the class $\mathcal{C}_{\mathcal{F}}^{(\mathcal{S}, \emptyset)}$, with the set of finite fields $\mathcal{F} = \{\mathbb{F}_{q_1}, \ldots, \mathbb{F}_{q_f}\}$, a set of Correlated Randomness Sources $\mathcal{S} = \{\mathbb{S}_1, \ldots, \mathbb{S}_s\}$, and no gadget. We assume that the prover and verifier have agreed on the non-sensitive input variables to the M-Circuit, and the prover additionally has an assignment to the *sensitive* input variables (witness) such that the M-Circuit evaluates to a given public output. Due to the similarity with the protocol from [23] we present the specific protocols in the full version.

5   Using Different Correlated Randomness Sources

In the case of MPC protocols if one wants to add a new form of correlated randomness to a protocol then this equates to a more complex and costly offline phase. When using our cut-and-choose methodology for checking the correlated randomness sources in the MPCitH protocol we have already paid the cost of introducing a single source. Thus introducing new sources is essentially 'for free', and can indeed *reduce* complexity of this stage by requiring less data to check, as well as reducing proof complexity (both in time to produce/verify and in terms of size). Thus a new correlated randomness source should aim to reduce the online cost c_{online}, whilst not increasing c_{offline} (and the associated size of the auxiliary data needed for the resource) by a similar amount. We give two examples, one arithmetic and one non-arithmetic.

5.1 Dot-Product Computation

As an example, suppose in an M-Circuit program one is given sensitive vectors $\langle \mathbf{x} \rangle_q$ and $\langle \mathbf{y} \rangle_q$ of size k and one wishes to compute their dot-product. The naive way of doing the dot product would be to call the correlated randomness source for triple generation k times; thus receiving $\{(\langle a_i \rangle_q, \langle b_i \rangle_q, \langle c_i \rangle)_q\}_{i \in [k]}$, and then doing the Beaver multiplication trick k times.

$$\langle z_1 \rangle_q = \langle c_1 \rangle_q - (x_1 - a_1) \cdot \langle b_1 \rangle_q - (y_1 - b_1) \cdot \langle a_1 \rangle_q + (x_1 - a_1) \cdot (y_1 - b_1)$$

$$\cdots \cdots$$

$$\langle z_k \rangle_q = \langle c_k \rangle - (x_k - a_k) \cdot \langle b_k \rangle_q - (y_k - b_k) \cdot \langle a_k \rangle_q + (x_k - a_k) \cdot (y_k - b_k)$$

Finally we obtain $\langle z \rangle_q = \sum_{i \in [k]} \langle z_i \rangle_q$. The k calls to the correlated randomness source, however, require k correction terms to make sure that $\langle c_i \rangle = \langle a_i \cdot b_i \rangle$ for all i. Thus these k terms need to be added to the proof. However, by introducing a different correlated randomness source tailored to this specific operation we can replace these k correction terms with a single term. To see this note that we could also write

$$\langle z \rangle_q = \sum \langle c_i \rangle_q - \sum \Big((x_i - a_i) \cdot \langle b_i \rangle_q - (y_i - b_i) \cdot \langle a_i \rangle_q + (x_i - a_i) \cdot (y_i - b_i) \Big).$$

Therefore, the necessary pre-processing data could be obtained by defining a new correlated source which produces values of the form

$$\langle a_1 \rangle_q, \ldots, \langle a_k \rangle_q, \langle b_1 \rangle_q, \ldots, \langle b_k \rangle_q, \langle c \rangle_q \text{ where } c = \sum_{i \in [k]} c_i = \sum_{i \in [k]} a_i \cdot b_i.$$

Using this source we thus need only one correction term for c, thus saving $(M - \tau) \cdot (k - 1)$ field elements of communication for the pre-processing material when using our cut-and-choose method for source correctness verification.

5.2 Matrix Triples

This is a trick known in the MPC literature that can be easily applied to the setting of MPCitH. Consider $\langle \mathbf{X} \rangle_q$ and $\langle \mathbf{Y} \rangle_q$ two matrices of size $n \cdot m$ and $m \cdot l$ respectively. The naive way of computing $\langle \mathbf{Z} \rangle_q = \langle \mathbf{X} \cdot \mathbf{Y} \rangle_q$ requires $O(n \cdot m \cdot l)$ calls to the correlated randomness source for triple generation. However if one has access to a correlated randomness source for **matrix** triples $(\langle \mathbf{A} \rangle_q, \langle \mathbf{B} \rangle_q, \langle \mathbf{C} \rangle_q)$ such that $\mathbf{C} = \mathbf{A} \cdot \mathbf{B}$ and $\mathbf{A}, \mathbf{B}$ are two matrices of size $n \cdot m$ and $m \cdot l$ respectively, one can perform the matrix multiplication much more efficiently. Indeed, this source only requires $n \cdot l$ auxiliary information and the multiplication protocol is similar to the classic Beaver multiplication, thus requires to reveal one $n \cdot m$ and one $m \cdot l$ matrix.

5.3 Tiny-Tables

Interesting optimizations from the MPC world can be carried over directly to the MPCitH worlds using our abstraction. Consider for example the Tiny-Tables optimization, see [19] as extended by [25]. Suppose we wish, at some point in the computation, to compute a function $y = G(x)$ where $x, y \in \mathbb{F}_q$, for prime q, and x is known to be restricted to come from a small domain $\mathcal{D} \subset \mathbb{F}_q$ of size $d - 1$, with $d < q/2$. For simplicity assume $\mathcal{D} = \{0, \dots, d - 1\}$ in what follows.

We can define the correlated randomness source $\mathbb{S}_G$ which outputs sensitive values $\langle s \rangle, \langle g_0 \rangle, \dots, \langle g_{d-1} \rangle$, subject to the constraints that s is uniformly randomly chosen from $\mathbb{F}_q$ and that

$$g_i = G\Big(\, (s + i \pmod q) \, \pmod d \, \Big).$$

Evaluation of the table on a shared value $\langle x \rangle$, whose value is guaranteed to lie in $\mathcal{D}$, can then be performed by opening the value $\langle h \rangle = \langle x \rangle - \langle s \rangle$, to obtain h (which we reduce into the centred interval $(-q/2, \dots, q/2)$) and then taking the result of the table look up as $\langle g_{h \pmod d} \rangle$.

In the case of MPCitH the size of the output of GenAux will depend on the input domain size d. Thus the Tiny-Table approach will result in a smaller proof if the table size is less than the multiplicative complexity of the function G, assuming the only alternative is to compute G via an arithmetic circuit.

6 Sacrificing

Another trick we can take from the MPC world and apply to the world of MPCitH protocols, directly from our M-Circuit definition, is that of sacrificing. At a high level one can consider the cut-and-choose component of the MPCitH protocol i.e. where the verifier selects the set E and the prover opens all the correlated randomness from the executions in E, as a method to turn a passively secure offline phase into an actively secure offline phase for the underlying MPC protocol. The method of cut-and-choose is very general, and thus applies to any correlated randomness source. However, some correlated randomness sources are arithmetic in nature and thus can be checked using arithmetic means. This is well known in the MPC literature, and is called sacrificing. We note a similar trick was proposed in [5] but not in the generality we present.

We refer to correlated randomness sources for which one can execute a method akin to sacrificing as a *Checkable Correlated Randomness Source*. Using such a check, as opposed to the generic cut-and-choose methodology from earlier, can introduce efficiencies. However, it comes at the cost of needing a five-round, as opposed to a three-round protocol.

The basic idea is to modify the correlated randomness source so that it produces an additional correlation, which is 'sacrificed' so as to check the correctness of the desired correlation. The correctness check makes use of a verifier defined random nonce, which can be fixed across all of the checks. To simplify our presentation we consider the case where all the variables in a randomness source are defined over the same finite field $\mathbb{F}_q$, where q is large; extending to smaller and different finite fields is trivial.

In terms of an M-Circuit definition, suppose we have an initial M-Circuit utilizing a desired source $\mathbb{S}$ which produces correlated variables $\mathbf{x}$. However, to compile it we utilize a related source $\mathbb{S}'$ whose output variables are of the form $(\mathbf{x}, \mathbf{y})$ and which has a function generating auxiliary input $\mathsf{GenAux}^{\mathbb{S}'}$. There is then a procedure $\mathsf{SCheck}^{\mathbb{S}}$ which takes $\mathbf{x}$, $\mathbf{y}$, the output of $\mathsf{GenAux}^{\mathbb{S}'}$ and a challenge value t. The procedure $\mathsf{SCheck}^{\mathbb{S}}$ which outputs a single bit b; if $b = 0$ then the value $\mathbf{x}$ is not from the same distribution as $\mathbb{S}$ and if $b = 1$ then it is. The probability that the bit b is incorrect is bounded by a value $\epsilon^{\mathbb{S}'}$, with the probability being a function of the choice of the challenge value t. We say that such a source $\mathbb{S}'$ is a Checkable Correlated Randomness Source. The required modifications to our MPCitH protocol we give in the full version. Our protocol is similar to the one before, except now the prover cannot commit to the views of the M-Circuit evaluation until it knows the versifier's choice for $\mathbf{t}^{\mathbb{S}'}$ for every $\mathbb{S} \in \mathcal{S}_{\mathsf{check}}$. On the other hand it must commit to the seeds generating the players secret sharings before it knows the value of $\mathbf{t}^{\mathbb{S}'}$. This introduces an extra two rounds of communication, resulting in a total of five rounds of interaction.

We note that to determine how many calls we make to the random sources, we need to know the value of all the variables in the M-circuit. Therefore, the output of all sources (checkable and non-checkable) must be known before receiving the cut-and-choose challenge. An attentive reader may thus point out that if one has to pay the soundness cost of cut-and-choose, then there is no practical reason for adding sacrificing on top of it, as all correlated randomness sources that can be checked by sacrificing can also be checked by cut-and-choose. This is indeed the case, and in the case of an M-Circuit $C \in \mathcal{C}_{\mathcal{F}}^{(\mathcal{S}, \emptyset)}$, one should, in practice, use the sacrificing technique only if $\forall \mathbb{S} \in \mathcal{S}, \mathbb{S} \in \mathcal{S}_{\mathsf{check}}$, and completely ignore the cut-and-choose part of the protocol (set $\tau = 0$).

However the usefulness of our 5-round protocol will be clear once we describe gadgets. Indeed, gadgets will be treated in a similar way as checkable correlated randomness sources, with the exception that, unlike correlated randomness sources, the cut-and-choose technique can not be used to check the correctness of their execution.

Example Checkable Correlated Randomness Sources: Note, the 'program' for the check $\mathsf{SCheck}^{\mathbb{S}}$ can be expressed as an M-Circuit in the class $\mathcal{C}_{\mathbb{F}_q}^{(\emptyset, \emptyset)}$. Thus property of being a checkable correlated randomness source is a function not only of the procedure $\mathsf{SCheck}^{\mathbb{S}}$ existing, but also of the definition of the function $\mathsf{GenAux}^{\mathbb{S}'}$ as we now illustrate.

Triple. Recall the source Triple produces tuples $(\langle a \rangle, \langle b \rangle, \langle c \rangle)$ such that $c = a \cdot b$. Our 'extended' source Triple$'$ produces values $(\langle a \rangle, \langle b \rangle, \langle c \rangle, \langle d \rangle, \langle e \rangle)$ where it is 'claimed' that $c = a \cdot b$ and $e = b \cdot d$. This validity can be verified by the following algorithm which takes as input a public value $t \in \mathbb{F}_q$ (which can be the same for every output of Triple$'$).

1. $\langle \rho \rangle \leftarrow t \cdot \langle a \rangle - \langle d \rangle$.
2. $\rho \leftarrow \langle \rho \rangle.\mathsf{reveal}()$.
3. $\langle r \rangle \leftarrow t \cdot \langle c \rangle - \langle e \rangle - \rho \cdot \langle b \rangle$.
4. $r \leftarrow \langle r \rangle.\mathsf{reveal}()$.
5. Reject if $r \neq 0$.

Note, this algorithm is an M-Circuit in the class $C_{\mathbb{F}_q}^{(\emptyset, \emptyset)}$. Also note that the algorithm reveals no information about the values $\langle a \rangle, \langle b \rangle$ and $\langle c \rangle$. Also note, that for a valid tuple we have $r = t \cdot c - e - \rho \cdot b = t \cdot a \cdot b - b \cdot d - (t \cdot a - d) \cdot b = 0$, and note that if $c \neq a \cdot b$ and $e \neq b \cdot d$ then we have $r = t \cdot (c - a \cdot b) + e + b \cdot d$ which will equal zero with probability $\epsilon^{\mathsf{Triple}'} = 1/q$, when t is chosen independently of the output of Triple'.

However, whilst this verifies that the $(\langle a \rangle, \langle b \rangle, \langle c \rangle)$ variables output by Triple' satisfy the desired multiplicative relationship, it does not on its own demonstrate that the distribution of $(\langle a \rangle, \langle b \rangle, \langle c \rangle)$ is correct; namely that $\langle a \rangle$ and $\langle b \rangle$ are chosen uniformly at random. To ensure this we need to examine how $\mathsf{GenAux}^{\mathsf{Triple}'}$ is defined. Mirroring our two previous instantiations of $\mathsf{GenAux}^{\mathsf{Triple}}$ we have

1. $\mathsf{GenAux}^{\mathsf{Triple}'}(a, b, c, d, e) = (0, 0, a \cdot b - c, b \cdot d - e)$.
2. $\mathsf{GenAux}^{\mathsf{Triple}'}(a, b, c, d, e) = (x - a, y - b, z - c, u - d, w - e)$ where x, y, u are deterministically selected from $\mathbb{F}_p$ by $\mathsf{GenAux}^{\mathsf{Triple}'}$ using a PRG with the seed $H(a, b, c, d, e)$, for some hash function H, $z = x \cdot y$ and $w = y \cdot u$.

The first case produces the correct distribution irrespective of what the prover computes, whereas the second case does not. In the second case a cheating prover can deviate from the protocol and make $\langle a \rangle$ follow any distribution they desire.

Bit. As remarked earlier this is the more interesting correlated randomness source in applications, as it enables far more efficient M-Circuit representations of functions. The source Bit produces a value $\langle b \rangle$ such that b is guaranteed to lie in $\{0, 1\}$. However, whilst in an MPC protocol there is a sacrificing methodology for Bits, this does not translate over to the MPCitH paradigm as one needs a way of verifying the bits are uniformly selected. Thus checking the source Bit seems to require cut-and-choose.

7 Executable Gadgets

Up until now we have considered for our MPCitH protocols only M-Circuits from classes of the form $C_{\mathcal{F}}^{(\mathcal{S}, \emptyset)}$, i.e. M-Circuits with no gadgets. A gadget captures an essential non-linear subroutine within an M-Circuit. By abstracting it away, we simplify the composition of special-purpose protocols for such subroutines within a more generic M-Circuit. Whilst M-Circuits can describe arbitrary gadgets, only special gadgets, which we call *executable gadgets* are able to be supported by the MPCitH protocol.

We proceed to the formal definition of an executable gadget, which we define over a single finite field $\mathbb{F}_q$ of large characteristic for ease of exposition, and then we present two examples of executable gadgets for MPCitH protocols.

Definition 7.1 (Executable Gadget). *An Executable Gadget* $\mathbb{G}$ *is an object defined by*

I. *A function G with (possibly zero) inputs and (at least one) output in $\mathcal{F}$.*

II. *A* $\mathsf{GenAux}^{\mathbb{G}}$ *function that fixes the auxiliary information needed to correct a uniformly random $\mathbf{y}$ to be equal to $G(\mathbf{x})$, i.e.* $\mathsf{GenAux}^{\mathbb{G}}(\mathbf{x}, \mathbf{y}) = G(\mathbf{x}) - \mathbf{y}$.

III. *A* $\mathsf{GCheck}^{\mathbb{G}}$ *M-Circuit in the class* $\mathcal{C}_{\mathcal{F}}^{(\mathcal{S}, \emptyset)}$ *for a set of randomness sources $\mathcal{S}$, the function which takes as input $\mathbf{x}$, $\mathbf{y}$, the output of* $\mathsf{GenAux}^{\mathbb{G}}(\mathbf{x}, \mathbf{y})$ *and a challenge value $t \in \mathcal{F}$. The procedure* $\mathsf{GCheck}^{\mathbb{G}}$ *which outputs a single bit b; if $b = 0$ then the the values are inconsistent, i.e. the purported value of* aux *is not correct, and if $b = 1$ then it is correct. The probability that the bit b is incorrect is bounded by a value $\epsilon^{\mathbb{G}'}$, with the probability being a function of the choice of the challenge value t.*

Thus an executable gadget is very similar to the checkable randomness sources from the previous section. To process the gadget with in the MPCitH protocol we thus proceed just as we did for checkable randomness sources; the initial M-Circuit C is extended to an augmented circuit C' which includes all the necessary $\mathsf{GCheck}^{\mathbb{G}}$ operations. As $\mathsf{GCheck}^{\mathbb{G}}$ itself potentially requires access to correlated randomness sources this might require the addition of addition correlated randomness source. Then the five round protocol is executed, so that the augmented circuit C' can be created (as it depends on the versifier's selection of the challenges t in $\mathsf{GCheck}^{\mathbb{G}}$). The modification to the soundness error is the same as that introduced for checkable randomness sources.

The BitDecomp Gadget: The executable gadget BitDecomp for a given sensitive value $\langle x \rangle_q$ produces the $\lceil \log_2(q) \rceil$ sensitive values $\langle b_i \rangle_q$ such that $b_i \in \{0,1\}$ and $x = \sum_{i=0}^{\lceil \log_2(q) \rceil - 1} b_i \cdot 2^i$. A simple example is the bit decomposition operation $(\langle b_0 \rangle_q, \ldots, \langle b_{\lceil \log_2(q) \rceil - 1} \rangle_q \leftarrow \mathsf{BitDecomp}(\langle x \rangle))$, where $\forall i, b_i \in \{0,1\}$ and $\sum_i b_i 2^i = x$. See Fig. 6 for a formal specification, note this checking procedure requires no random input from the verifier; this is because there is implicitly random input needed to check the (checkable) correlated randomness source Square which it requires.

In the above instantiation of BitDecomp we assumed that our randomness source Square was already checked by either cut-and-choose or sacrificing. However, we can obtain a further efficiency if we merge the checking of the output of Square with the checking of this bits produced in the gadget. To present this we give utilize a correlated randomness source USquare, which represents an unchecked square tuple. Namely, we check the output is correct neither by the sacrificing style check or via cut-and-choose. This allows us to present an more efficient check of the BitDecomp Gadget in Fig. 7, where now we require the verifier to provide a random challenge $t \in \mathbb{F}_q$. At first sight it seems to involve the same number of reveals operations, but we actually save operations as we no longer need reveals to check the output of Square.

The BitDecomp Gadget

I. Function $G : (\langle x \rangle_q) \mapsto (\langle b_0 \rangle_q, \ldots, \langle b_{\lceil \log_2(q) \rceil - 1} \rangle_q)$ such that $b_i \in \{0, 1\}$ and $x = \sum_i b_i \cdot 2^i$

II. $\mathsf{GenAux}^{\mathsf{BitDecomp}}(x, (y_0, \ldots, y_{\lceil \log(q) \rceil - 1})) = (0, b_0 - y_0, \ldots, b_{\lceil \log_2(q) \rceil - 1} - y_{\lceil \log_2(q) \rceil - 1})$

III. $\mathsf{GCheck}^{\mathsf{BitDecomp}} \in \mathcal{C}_{\mathbb{F}_q}^{(\mathsf{Square}, \emptyset)}$: On input of $\langle b_0 \rangle_q, \ldots, \langle b_{\lceil \log_2(q) \rceil - 1} \rangle_q, \langle x \rangle_q$:

   (a) flag $\leftarrow 1$, $\langle s \rangle_q \leftarrow 0$

   (b) For i from $\lceil \log_2(q) \rceil - 1$ to 0 do

      - $\langle a \rangle_q, \langle a^2 \rangle_q \leftarrow \mathsf{Square}$

      - $\langle \alpha \rangle_q \leftarrow \langle b_i \rangle_q - \langle a \rangle_q$

      - $\{\alpha\}_q \leftarrow \langle \alpha \rangle_q.\mathsf{reveal}()$

      - $\langle r \rangle_q \leftarrow \{\alpha\}_q \cdot (\langle b_i \rangle_q + \langle a \rangle_q) + \langle a^2 \rangle_q - \langle b_i \rangle_q$

      - $\{r\}_q \leftarrow \langle r \rangle_q.\mathsf{reveal}()$

      - If $\{r\}_q \neq 0$ then flag $\leftarrow 0$

      - $\langle s \rangle_q \leftarrow 2 \cdot \langle s \rangle_q + \langle b_i \rangle_q$

   (c) $\langle s \rangle_q \leftarrow \langle s \rangle_q - \langle x \rangle_q$

   (d) $\{s\}_q \leftarrow \langle s \rangle_q.\mathsf{reveal}()$

   (e) If $\{s\}_q \neq 0$ then flag $\leftarrow 0$

   (f) Return flag

Fig. 6. The BitDecomp Gadget

The Optimized BitDecomp Gadget

I. Function $G : (\langle x \rangle_q) \mapsto (\langle b_0 \rangle_q, \ldots, \langle b_{\lceil \log_2(q) \rceil - 1} \rangle_q)$ such that $b_i \in \{0, 1\}$ and $x = \sum_i b_i \cdot 2^i$

II. $\mathsf{GenAux}^{\mathsf{BitDecomp}}(x, (y_0, \ldots, y_{\lceil \log(q) \rceil - 1})) = (0, b_0 - y_0, \ldots, b_{\lceil \log_2(q) \rceil - 1} - y_{\lceil \log_2(q) \rceil - 1})$

III. $\mathsf{GCheck}^{\mathsf{BitDecomp}} \in \mathcal{C}_{\mathbb{F}_q}^{(\mathsf{Square}, \emptyset)}$: On input of $\langle b_0 \rangle_q, \ldots, \langle b_{\lceil \log_2(q) \rceil - 1} \rangle_q, \langle x \rangle_q$ and a value t from the verifier:

   (a) flag $\leftarrow 1$, $\langle s \rangle_q \leftarrow 0$

   (b) For i from $\lceil \log_2(q) \rceil - 1$ to 0 do

      - $\langle a \rangle_q, \langle a^2 \rangle_q \leftarrow \mathsf{USquare}$

      - $\langle \rho \rangle_q \leftarrow \langle b_i \rangle_q - t \cdot \langle a \rangle_q$

      - $\{\rho\}_q \leftarrow \langle \rho \rangle_q.\mathsf{reveal}()$

      - $\langle r \rangle_q \leftarrow \langle b_i \rangle_q - \{\rho\}_q \cdot (\langle b_i \rangle_q + t \cdot \langle a \rangle_q) - t^2 \cdot \langle a^2 \rangle_q.$

      - $\{r\}_q \leftarrow \langle r \rangle_q.\mathsf{reveal}()$

      - If $\{r\}_q \neq 0$ then flag $\leftarrow 0$

      - $\langle s \rangle_q \leftarrow 2 \cdot \langle s \rangle_q + \langle b_i \rangle_q$

   (c) $\langle s \rangle_q \leftarrow \langle s \rangle_q - \langle x \rangle_q$

   (d) $\{s\}_q \leftarrow \langle s \rangle_q.\mathsf{reveal}()$

   (e) If $\{s\}_q \neq 0$ then flag $\leftarrow 0$

   (f) Return flag

Fig. 7. The optimized BitDecomp gadget

The RNSDecomp Gadget: If we extend our definitions to rings $\mathbb{Z}_q$ with $q = \prod_{i=1}^{k} p_i$ and p_i primes, an interesting technique which has been widely used in cryptography is to make use of the Chinese Remainder Theorem. In MPCitH it is very easy for the prover to inject the residues of a sensitive variable such that the M-Circuit can operate on those residues. Since CRT reconstruction is a linear operation, it is also trivial to design a GCheck M-Circuit, as it suffice to apply the linear CRT reconstruction algorithm to the residues, and compare the result with the original value. An application of such a technique would then be to use the Tiny-Tables optimization described previously, but for functions with domain $\mathbb{Z}_q$ that can be computed residue-wise. By following the blueprint of [4], one would then create a table of the desired function for all the residues, thus going from a prohibitive size q table to k tables of total size $\sum p_i$. (e.g. exponentiation of a sensitive variable by a non-sensitive variable) (Fig. 8).

The RNSDecomp get

I. Function $G : (\langle x \rangle_q) \mapsto (\langle x_1 \rangle_{p_1}, \ldots, \langle x_k \rangle_{p_k})$ such that $x_i \in \mathbb{F}_{p_i}$ and $x = \mathsf{CRT}([x_1, \ldots, k_k], [p_1, \ldots, p_k])$

II. $\mathsf{GenAux}^{\mathsf{RNSDecomp}}(x, (y_1, \ldots, y_k)) = (0, x_1 - y_1, \ldots, b_k - y_k)$

III. $\mathsf{GCheck}^{\mathsf{RNSDecomp}} \in C_{\mathbb{Z}_q, \mathbb{F}_{p_1}, \ldots, \mathbb{F}_{p_k}}^{(\emptyset, \emptyset)}$: On input of $\langle x_1 \rangle_{p_1}, \ldots, \langle x_k \rangle_{p_k}, \langle x \rangle_q$:

   (a) flag $\leftarrow 1$

   (b) $\langle s \rangle_q \leftarrow \mathsf{CRT}([\langle x_1 \rangle_{p_1}, \ldots, \langle x_k \rangle_{p_k}], [p_1, \ldots, p_k])$ (Local operation)

   (c) $\langle s \rangle_q \leftarrow \langle s \rangle_q - \langle x \rangle_q$

   (d) $\{s\}_q \leftarrow \langle s \rangle_q.\mathsf{reveal}()$

   (e) If $\{s\}_q \neq 0$ then flag $\leftarrow 0$

   (f) Return flag

Fig. 8. Residue number system decomposition

Acknowledgments. This work has been supported in part by ERC Advanced Grant ERC-2015-AdG-IMPaCT, by the Defense Advanced Research Projects Agency (DARPA) and Space and Naval Warfare Systems Center, Pacific (SSC Pacific) under contract No. HR001120C0085 and FA8750-19-C-0502, by the FWO under an Odysseus project GOH9718N, and by CyberSecurity Research Flanders with reference number VR20192203.

References

1. Aly, A., et al.: SCALE and MAMBA documentation, v1.11 (2021). https://homes. esat.kuleuven.be/~nsmart/SCALE/Documentation.pdf
2. Aly, A., Orsini, E., Rotaru, D., Smart, N.P., Wood, T.: Zaphod: efficiently combining LSSS and garbled circuits in SCALE. In: Brenner, M., Lepoint, T., Rohloff, K. (eds.) Proceedings of the 7th ACM Workshop on Encrypted Computing & Applied Homomorphic Cryptography, WAHC@CCS 2019, London, UK, 11–15 November 2019, pp. 33–44. ACM (2019). https://doi.org/10.1145/3338469.3358943

3. Ames, S., Hazay, C., Ishai, Y., Venkitasubramaniam, M.: Ligero: lightweight sublinear arguments without a trusted setup. In: Thuraisingham, B.M., Evans, D., Malkin, T., Xu, D. (eds.) ACM CCS 2017, pp. 2087–2104. ACM Press, October/November 2017

4. Ball, M., Malkin, T., Rosulek, M.: Garbling gadgets for Boolean and arithmetic circuits. In: Weippl, E.R., Katzenbeisser, S., Kruegel, C., Myers, A.C., Halevi, S. (eds.) ACM CCS 2016, pp. 565–577. ACM Press, October 2016

5. Baum, C., Nof, A.: Concretely-efficient zero-knowledge arguments for arithmetic circuits and their application to lattice-based cryptography. In: Kiayias, A., Kohlweiss, M., Wallden, P., Zikas, V. (eds.) PKC 2020. LNCS, vol. 12110, pp. 495–526. Springer, Cham (2020). https://doi.org/10.1007/978-3-030-45374-9_17

6. Beaver, D.: Efficient multiparty protocols using circuit randomization. In: Feigenbaum, J. (ed.) CRYPTO 1991. LNCS, vol. 576, pp. 420–432. Springer, Heidelberg (1992). https://doi.org/10.1007/3-540-46766-1_34

7. Bell, D.E., LaPadula, L.J.: Secure computer systems: mathematical foundations. MITRE Corporation Technical Report 2547 (1973)

8. Ben-Or, M., Goldwasser, S., Wigderson, A.: Completeness theorems for non-cryptographic fault-tolerant distributed computation (extended abstract). In: 20th ACM STOC, pp. 1–10. ACM Press, May 1988

9. Bhadauria, R., Fang, Z., Hazay, C., Venkitasubramaniam, M., Xie, T., Zhang, Y.: Ligero++: a new optimized sublinear IOP. In: Ligatti, J., Ou, X., Katz, J., Vigna, G. (eds.) ACM CCS 2020, pp. 2025–2038. ACM Press, November 2020

10. Catrina, O., de Hoogh, S.: Improved primitives for secure multiparty integer computation. In: Garay, J.A., De Prisco, R. (eds.) SCN 2010. LNCS, vol. 6280, pp. 182–199. Springer, Heidelberg (2010). https://doi.org/10.1007/978-3-642-15317-4_13

11. Catrina, O., Saxena, A.: Secure computation with fixed-point numbers. In: Sion, R. (ed.) FC 2010. LNCS, vol. 6052, pp. 35–50. Springer, Heidelberg (2010). https://doi.org/10.1007/978-3-642-14577-3_6

12. Chase, M., et al.: Post-quantum zero-knowledge and signatures from symmetric-key primitives. In: Thuraisingham, B.M., Evans, D., Malkin, T., Xu, D. (eds.) ACM CCS 2017, pp. 1825–1842. ACM Press, October/Novemebr 2017

13. Chaum, D., Crépeau, C., Damgård, I.: Multiparty unconditionally secure protocols (extended abstract). In: 20th ACM STOC, pp. 11–19. ACM Press, May 1988

14. Chida, K., et al.: Fast large-scale honest-majority MPC for malicious adversaries. In: Shacham, H., Boldyreva, A. (eds.) CRYPTO 2018. LNCS, vol. 10993, pp. 34–64. Springer, Cham (2018). https://doi.org/10.1007/978-3-319-96878-0_2

15. Cramer, R., Damgård, I., Escudero, D., Scholl, P., Xing, C.: SPDZ$_{2^k}$: efficient MPC mod 2^k for dishonest majority. In: Shacham, H., Boldyreva, A. (eds.) CRYPTO 2018. LNCS, vol. 10992, pp. 769–798. Springer, Cham (2018). https://doi.org/10.1007/978-3-319-96881-0_26

16. Damgård, I., Fitzi, M., Kiltz, E., Nielsen, J.B., Toft, T.: Unconditionally secure constant-rounds multi-party computation for equality, comparison, bits and exponentiation. In: Halevi, S., Rabin, T. (eds.) TCC 2006. LNCS, vol. 3876, pp. 285–304. Springer, Heidelberg (2006). https://doi.org/10.1007/11681878_15

17. Damgård, I., Geisler, M., Krøigaard, M., Nielsen, J.B.: Asynchronous multiparty computation: theory and implementation. In: Jarecki, S., Tsudik, G. (eds.) PKC 2009. LNCS, vol. 5443, pp. 160–179. Springer, Heidelberg (2009). https://doi.org/10.1007/978-3-642-00468-1_10

18. Damgård, I., Keller, M., Larraia, E., Pastro, V., Scholl, P., Smart, N.P.: Practical covertly secure MPC for dishonest majority – or: breaking the SPDZ limits. In: Crampton, J., Jajodia, S., Mayes, K. (eds.) ESORICS 2013. LNCS, vol. 8134, pp. 1–18. Springer, Heidelberg (2013). https://doi.org/10.1007/978-3-642-40203-6_1

19. Damgård, I., Nielsen, J.B., Nielsen, M., Ranellucci, S.: The TinyTable protocol for 2-party secure computation, or: gate-scrambling revisited. In: Katz, J., Shacham, H. (eds.) CRYPTO 2017. LNCS, vol. 10401, pp. 167–187. Springer, Cham (2017). https://doi.org/10.1007/978-3-319-63688-7_6

20. Damgård, I., Pastro, V., Smart, N., Zakarias, S.: Multiparty computation from somewhat homomorphic encryption. In: Safavi-Naini, R., Canetti, R. (eds.) CRYPTO 2012. LNCS, vol. 7417, pp. 643–662. Springer, Heidelberg (2012). https://doi.org/10.1007/978-3-642-32009-5_38

21. Giacomelli, I., Madsen, J., Orlandi, C.: ZKBoo: faster zero-knowledge for Boolean circuits. In: Holz, T., Savage, S. (eds.) USENIX Security 2016, pp. 1069–1083. USENIX Association, August 2016

22. Ishai, Y., Kushilevitz, E., Ostrovsky, R., Sahai, A.: Zero-knowledge from secure multiparty computation. In: Johnson, D.S., Feige, U. (eds.) 39th ACM STOC, pp. 21–30. ACM Press, June 2007

23. Katz, J., Kolesnikov, V., Wang, X.: Improved non-interactive zero knowledge with applications to post-quantum signatures. In: Lie, D., Mannan, M., Backes, M., Wang, X. (eds.) ACM CCS 2018, pp. 525–537. ACM Press, October 2018

24. Keller, M.: MP-SPDZ: a versatile framework for multi-party computation. In: Ligatti, J., Ou, X., Katz, J., Vigna, G. (eds.) ACM CCS 2020, pp. 1575–1590. ACM Press, November 2020

25. Keller, M., Orsini, E., Rotaru, D., Scholl, P., Soria-Vazquez, E., Vivek, S.: Faster secure multi-party computation of AES and DES using lookup tables. In: Gollmann, D., Miyaji, A., Kikuchi, H. (eds.) ACNS 2017. LNCS, vol. 10355, pp. 229–249. Springer, Cham (2017). https://doi.org/10.1007/978-3-319-61204-1_12

26. Keller, M., Orsini, E., Scholl, P.: MASCOT: faster malicious arithmetic secure computation with oblivious transfer. In: Weippl, E.R., Katzenbeisser, S., Kruegel, C., Myers, A.C., Halevi, S. (eds.) ACM CCS 2016, pp. 830–842. ACM Press, October 2016

27. Rotaru, D., Wood, T.: MArBled circuits: mixing arithmetic and boolean circuits with active security. In: Hao, F., Ruj, S., Sen Gupta, S. (eds.) INDOCRYPT 2019. LNCS, vol. 11898, pp. 227–249. Springer, Cham (2019). https://doi.org/10.1007/978-3-030-35423-7_12

Oblivious TLS via Multi-party Computation

Damiano Abram[1], Ivan Damgård[1], Peter Scholl[1(✉)], and Sven Trieflinger[2]

[1] Aarhus University, Aarhus, Denmark
peter.scholl@cs.au.dk
[2] Robert Bosch GmbH, Stuttgart, Germany

Abstract. In this paper, we describe Oblivious TLS: an MPC protocol
that we prove UC secure against a majority of actively corrupted parties.
The protocol securely implements TLS 1.3. Thus, any party P who runs
TLS can communicate securely with a set of servers running Oblivious
TLS; P does not need to modify anything, or even be aware that MPC
is used.

Applications of this include communication between servers who offer
MPC services and clients, to allow the clients to easily and securely provide inputs or receive outputs. Also, an organization could use Oblivious
TLS to improve in-house security while seamlessly connecting to external parties.

Our protocol runs in the preprocessing model, and we did a preliminary non-optimized implementation of the on-line phase. In this version,
the hand-shake completes in about 1 s. Based on implementation results
from other work, performance of the record protocol using the standard
AES-GCM can be expected to achieve an online throughput of about
3 MB/s.

1 Introduction

Secure multi-party computation (MPC) allows a group of parties to jointly evaluate a function on private inputs, ensuring that no party learns anything more
than what can be deduced from the output of the function. Developments in
recent years have shown that MPC can be practical for a range of use-cases, and
is starting to see real-world deployments. While the classic scenario for MPC
involves a set of parties who each have a private input, more recent applications
also focus on the setting where a set of *MPC servers*, called an *MPC engine*,
are distributively performing a computation on inputs uploaded by clients and
known to none of the servers. In this client-server setting, the computation may
be outsourced by external parties who initially provided the inputs, or the servers
may be part of a larger system which delegated a private computation to them.
As in the regular MPC setting, there must be some intrinsic motivation or incen-
tive for the parties operating the MPC servers not to collude. For instance, the
servers can be hosted by independent organisations which have interest in protecting the confidentiality of the clients' data against the other parties, perhaps
because some form of representation is implemented.

© Springer Nature Switzerland AG 2021
K. G. Paterson (Ed.): CT-RSA 2021, LNCS 12704, pp. 51–74, 2021.
https://doi.org/10.1007/978-3-030-75539-3_3

The set of clients can be dynamic in such systems and clients should not need to participate in the actual MPC protocol, instead they should be able to send private input to the protocol using standardized algorithms, which is exactly the issue we address. This creates a more flexible overall system that more closely resembles the cloud-based IT system deployments that are common today. For instance, in [8], Damgård et al. describe a concrete instantiation of such a system. They propose a credit rating system that enables banks to benchmark their customers' confidential performance data against a large representative set of confidential performance data from a consultancy house. The authors anticipate that the MPC servers would be run by the consultancy house and the Danish Bankers Association in a commercial setting. Individual banks as clients learn nothing but the computed benchmarking score.

Security is typically maintained as long as not too many of the servers are corrupted; for instance, in the *dishonest majority* setting it is common to allow up to $n - 1$ out of n servers to be corrupted, while the *honest majority setting* relaxes this by assuming that more than half of the servers are honest.

The Transport Layer Security protocol (TLS) is the leading standard for secure communication over the Internet. TLS allows two parties, or *endpoints*, to first run a handshake protocol to establish a common key, and secondly, in the record layer protocol, to securely and authentically transmit information using the key. The latest version of the protocol is TLS 1.3, which has seen major design changes to address vulnerabilities in previous versions.

Contributions. In this work, based on a master's thesis [1], we study the problem of obliviously running one or more endpoints of the TLS 1.3 protocol, *inside an MPC engine*. We refer to this scheme as *Oblivious TLS*. The protocol allows the engine to securely communicate with any endpoint of the Internet that runs TLS, in a completely oblivious manner: the other endpoint does not need to be modified, nor even be aware of the fact that it is interacting with a multi-party computation (and likewise, the *second* endpoint may also be an Oblivious TLS instance, unbeknownst to the first).

The possibilities created by Oblivious TLS are manifold and potentially groundbreaking: Oblivious TLS facilitates the integration of MPC-based components into today's complex IT systems. For example, distributed key management systems based on MPC can be interfaced without time-consuming and sometimes infeasible client-side modifications. Workloads that, despite the impressive performance gains seen in recent years, are still outside the realm of the possible using MPC today, could be securely outsourced to external services protected by comparatively low overhead Trusted Execution Environments by seamlessly integrating with TLS-based remote attestation mechanisms. Another fascinating possibility is the use of Oblivious TLS in conjunction with *Distributed Autonomous Organizations* (DAO) that ensure the confidentiality of data through the use of MPC. In the future, Oblivious TLS may enable DAOs to obliviously use external services to, for example, autonomously manage cloud resources required to conduct their business.

The MPC engine itself can be instantiated with a large class of standard, modern MPC protocols based on secret-sharing with arithmetic operations. We focus on instantiating this with actively secure MPC protocols based on information-theoretic MACs with security against a dishonest majority, such as SPDZ [9,10] and related protocols [19], however, our techniques are also applicable to other settings and honest majority protocols.

TLS 1.3 is notoriously complex, and running this inside MPC presents several technical challenges. We first give an overview of some of these challenges below, and then describe some further motivation for the problem of running TLS in MPC.

Multi-party Diffie-Hellman. For the handshake protocol, we chose to run elliptic-curve Diffie-Hellman, currently the most popular key exchange method. Doing this inside MPC requires an exponentiation between a known public key and a secret exponent, where the output must remain secret. Moreover, the shared key (an elliptic curve point) must be represented in a suitable manner in the MPC engine to allow for further private computations. We present a new method for doing this based on *doubly-authenticated points*, namely, a way of reliably generating random elliptic curve points that are secret-shared both in a standard finite field MPC representation, and simultaneously in a specialized shared elliptic curve representation. This allows for efficient conversions between the two representations, and may be of independent interest.

In the full version of this paper [2], we also present a more efficient variant, which avoids the use of doubly-authenticated points. This comes with the slight downside that we do not manage to securely realise the same key exchange functionality, since a corrupted MPC server in the oblivious endpoint can force the derived key to be shifted by an arbitrary amount. In practice, however, we argue that this weaker version of the functionality suffices to run TLS, since the shift to the key is completely harmless, unless the adversary already happened to know the private key of the other endpoint.

Threshold Signing. To authenticate the endpoints, we additionally need to run a threshold signing protocol. Here, the message to be signed (based on the TLS transcript) is public, so the only information secret-shared in the MPC engine is the signing key and signature randomness. For this, we use EdDSA Schnorr-based signatures, which allow a simple threshold protocol without any expensive MPC operations.

Record Layer Protocol. For the record layer, we need to run authenticated encryption inside MPC. For this, we present an approach based on the standard AES-GCM construction, and only in the full version of this paper [2], a more specialized approach based on a custom MPC-friendly AEAD scheme. AES-GCM is quite well-suited to MPC, because of the linear structure of its Galois field MACs. The second approach is much more efficient, however, since it avoids doing any AES operations inside MPC. This comes at the cost of a small modification to the TLS specification, which also requires the endpoint to know the number of MPC servers involved in the computation.

Motivation and Related Work. As MPC becomes more widespread, it is natural to think not only about designing new and improved MPC protocols, but also about how these can be integrated into existing infrastructure. In particular, an MPC engine will typically not be a standalone piece, but rather a secure component of a larger system.

Whenever some private data passes in or out of the MPC component, this has to be done in a secure manner. With typical MPC protocols based on some form of secret sharing, the natural solution is to simply have the external process secret-share inputs to the MPC servers, and receive shares of outputs to be reconstructed. When active security is required, this is less straightforward since shares can be tampered with, although there are known methods and protocols that allow receiving inputs from, or sending outputs to, an external client in an authentic manner [8].

A drawback of these solutions is that they tend to be tailored to specific MPC protocols, meaning that all the clients and components of the system must be aware of the fact that MPC is taking place. This firstly has the potential security concern that it reveals that an MPC protocol is being carried out in the first place, and secondly, requires highly specialized software to implement.

In [14], this motivated the study of symmetric primitives such as PRFs, which are *MPC-friendly* (either by design, or by chance), meaning that they can be evaluated inside an MPC engine relatively cheaply. This was later extended to build MPC-friendly modes of operation for block ciphers [21].

While these works address the problem of encrypting data inside an MPC engine, they do not immediately lead to solutions for securely communicating with an external party, without either resorting to protocol-specific methods or other assumptions like pre-shared keys. DISE [3] also studied distributed forms of symmetric encryption including authenticated encryption. However, in their setting the message is always known to one party, which is not the case for us.

Finally, the recent and independent work DECO [23] presents a protocol that allows a TLS client to prove provenance of TLS data to a third party. Their solution is essentially based on a 2-party execution of a TLS client, with a very similar approach to the one described in this paper. Oblivious TLS is however applicable to both client and server sides of the connection and generalises to the multiparty case. Moreover, the multiparty Diffie-Hellman procedure presented in this paper is completely actively secure, whereas the solution proposed in [23] allows for influence of the adversary that may cause a Handshake failure.

Roadmap. We begin with some preliminaries in Sect. 2, where we explain notation, give an overview of TLS 1.3, and the MPC building blocks we use. In Sect. 3, we outline our solution, describing the general idea and presenting the main steps of the protocol. Section 4 covers the handshake layer of Oblivious TLS, where we focus on the method for generating doubly-authenticated points, the elliptic-curve Diffie-Hellman protocol and the signature generation. In Sect. 5, we describe the record layer. Then, in Sect. 6, we discuss security and performance of Oblivious TLS.

2 Notation and Preliminaries

We denote the finite field with p elements by $\mathbb{F}_p$, where p is a prime or prime power. Its multiplicative group is $\mathbb{F}_p^\times$. Sometimes, when the cardinality is not important for the discussion, we simply write $\mathbb{F}$. When dealing with groups, we represent the cyclic subgroup generated by an element g with $\langle g \rangle$.

When dealing with bit sequences, we identify the sets $\{0,1\}^k$, $\mathbb{F}_2^k$ and $\mathbb{F}_{2^k}$ as different representations of the finite field with 2^k elements. For this reason, when multiplying two elements $a, b \in \{0,1\}^k$, we mean multiplication in $\mathbb{F}_{2^k}$. The set $\{0,1\}^*$ instead represents $\bigcup_{i=0}^{\infty} \{0,1\}^i$.

The symbol $[m]$ indicates the set $\{1, 2, \ldots, m\}$. Whenever we write $a \leftarrow b$ to assign the value of b to a, and similarly, write $a \xleftarrow{\$} S$, where S is a set, to mean that a is randomly sampled from S. Finally, $\mathbb{P}$ represents a probability measure.

2.1 An Overview of TLS 1.3

TLS 1.3 [20] is the latest version of TLS, one of the most common protocols for secure communications over the Internet. The procedure is composed of two subprotocols: the Handshake and the Record layer. The goal of the first one is to negotiate secure symmetric keys between the two endpoints. The second one instead uses the bargained keys to protect the communications.

The Record Layer. Security is enforced by an AEAD (authenticated encryption with additional data), an encryption algorithm that guarantees privacy and integrity of the plaintext as well as the integrity of the header of the Record layer fragments. In order to encrypt and decrypt, an AEAD needs a different nonce for every fragment. These are deterministically derived from an initial vector (IV) and do not need to be kept secret. Indeed, security is guaranteed as long as the key remains private. The Record layer of TLS 1.3 provides for three types of fragments: Handshake messages, alerts and application data. The first type consists of all the information concerning the standard management of the TLS connection. Alerts are used to notify unexpected and potentially malicious events, whereas application data refers to the actual communication between the two endpoints (i.e. all the information for which they decided to use TLS 1.3).

The Handshake. We use the term "client" to denote the endpoint that initiates the connection, whereas the term "server" indicates the other endpoint. Furthermore, we define the transcript as the concatenation of all the messages exchanged on the connection until the analysed moment. The Handshake can be split into two phases: the key exchange phase, whose goal is to establish the keys and negotiate the cryptographic algorithms used in the connection, and the authentication phase, which has the objective of authenticating the endpoints and provide key confirmation.

The Key Exchange Phase. The protocol is started by the client sending a Client-Hello to the server. This is a message containing a 32-byte nonce (protection against replay attacks), information concerning the cryptographic algorithms supported by the client (signatures, AEADs, Diffie-Hellman groups) and at least one Diffie-Hellman public key. The server replies with a ServerHello, which contains another 32-byte nonce, the cryptographic algorithms selected among those offered by the client and one Diffie-Hellman public key. When the initial exchange is concluded, the two endpoints perform a Diffie-Hellman key exchange using the keys specified in the Hello messages. A key derivation function is then applied on the result. The operation takes as input also the transcript. At the end, the parties obtain two AEAD keys (handshake keys), as well as the related IVs. From that moment, the Record layer protects the client-to-server flow (resp. the serve-to-client flow) using the first key (resp. using the second key). The endpoints obtain also two MAC keys. After that, the server could provide further information concerning the management of the connection through the EncryptedExtensions message.

The Authentication Phase. Starting from the server, the endpoints exchange their certificates (ServerCertificate and ClientCertificate) and a signature on the transcript using the key specified on them (ServerCertificateVerify and ClientCertificateVerify). Finally, they send an HMAC on the transcript using the MAC keys obtained from the key derivation (ServerFinished and ClientFinished). In particular, the client uses the first key, the server uses the second one. In general, only the server is required to authenticate itself, the client is only required to send ClientFinished. Anyway, the server may impose the authentication of the client through a CertificateRequest message. Clearly, the endpoints verify all the signatures and the MAC supplied by the other endpoint. If any check fails, the connection is closed.

Derivation of the Keys. At the end of the Handshake, the endpoints feed the new messages of the transcript into the key derivation function.[1] At the end, the parties obtain two new AEAD keys (application keys), as well as the related new IVs. From that moment, the Record layer protects the client-to-server flow (resp. the serve-to-client flow) with the first new key (resp. with the second new key). The old keys are never used again.

As it was proven in [11], all the values output by the Handshake are computationally independent. Furthermore, slight modifications in the transcripts input in the key derivation function would lead to completely different and unpredictable outputs.

---

[1] The key derivation function maintains an internal state, therefore all its outputs depend on the Diffie-Hellman secret and the Hello messages.

2.2   Multiparty Computation Protocols

Multiparty computation (MPC) deals with techniques that allow a set of parties (sometimes called an MPC engine) to jointly perform computations with security guarantees against external attackers as well as against dishonest parties.

Throughout the work we assume there is a fixed set of n parties, denoted $P_1, \ldots, P_n$. We want to prove security against an active adversary that can corrupt up to $n - 1$ parties, in the static corruption model, so that the set of (indices of) honest parties $\mathcal{H} := \{i \in [n] \mid P_i \text{ is honest}\}$ is fixed and non-empty. We denote the set of corrupted parties $[n] \setminus \mathcal{H}$ with $\mathcal{C}$. Our security proofs are expressed in the universal composability (UC) framework [6].

Authenticated Secret Sharing. We use protocols based on additive secret-sharing schemes over finite fields, specifically, large prime fields, large binary fields and $\mathbb{F}_2$. We say that $x \in \mathbb{F}$ is secret-shared if every party P_i holds a random share $x_i \in \mathbb{F}$ such that $\sum_{i \in [n]} x_i = x$. As long as at least one party keeps its share secret, nobody learns anything about the value of x. If all parties collaborate, x can be reconstructed by revealing all the shares. This operation is called opening. To prevent corrupted parties from opening incorrect values, protocols typically augment the shares with information-theoretic MACs as in the SPDZ protocol [4, 10]. Then, whenever secret-shared values are opened, the MACs can be checked and any tampering is detected with overwhelming probability.

Secret Sharing over Elliptic Curve Groups. Additive secret sharing, as presented above, can be performed over any finite group. Suppose now that E is an elliptic curve. Let G be one of its points with prime order q. In [7], the authors showed that the authenticated secret-sharing scheme of SPDZ over $\mathbb{F}_q$ induces an authenticated secret-sharing scheme over $\langle G \rangle$ which uses the same MAC key. Given a public value $a \in \mathbb{F}_q$ and a secret-shared point $[[Q]] \in \langle G \rangle$, this allows the parties to obtain shares $[[aQ]]$ (over E) without any communication between the parties. Moreover, given a secret-shared $[[a']] \in \mathbb{F}_q$ and a public point $Q' \in \langle G \rangle$, it is possible to non-interactively obtain $[[a'Q']]$ over E.

Arithmetic Black Box Functionality. We work in the arithmetic black box model, which abstracts away the underlying details of secret-sharing by an ideal functionality. The functionality has separate commands for receiving inputs from the parties, performing certain arithmetic operations, and delivering outputs. We write $[[x]]$ to denote that a value $x \in \mathbb{F}$ is stored by the functionality under some public identifier known to all parties.

The specific functionality we use is $\mathcal{F}_{\text{MPC}}$, given in Appendix A of the full version of this paper [2]. It supports computations on different fields, as well as over an elliptic curve as described above. It can also handle conversions between values stored in $\mathbb{F}_2$ and $\mathbb{F}_p$. These operations can be instantiated using protocols such as SPDZ [10] (for computations over large fields), TinyOT [19] or multiparty garbled circuits [15] (for computations over $\mathbb{F}_2$). Conversions between $\mathbb{F}_p$ and $\mathbb{F}_2$ can be done using so-called preprocessed doubly-authenticated bits [22].

In Sect. 4.1, we provide further discussion on how the $\mathcal{F}_{\mathrm{MPC}}$ functionality can be instantiated.

3   Overview of the Solution

Oblivious TLS is a protocol that allows an n-party MPC engine to communicate with a TLS 1.3 endpoint, preserving privacy and correctness of the transmissions against up to $n-1$ corrupted parties. Effectiveness and security are guaranteed when either one or both TLS endpoints are replaced by such an MPC engine. For concreteness, however, in this paper we assume Oblivious TLS is adopted at the server side, which we expect to be the most common scenario.

The Communicating Party. We assume that only one of the parties manages the communication with the client. Supposing this is party P_1, then whenever the MPC engine has to send a message, P_1 is the entity that physically performs the operation. Moreover, when the client sends a message to the engine, P_1 receives it and shares it with the other parties. Clearly, P_1 can always perform a Denial-of-Service attack, by simply dropping the incoming or outgoing communications.

Handshake Modes. The goal of our work was to design the simplest protocol that allowed a set of parties to communicate with a TLS 1.3 endpoint. For this reason, we focused our attention on Diffie-Hellman-based Handshakes without the use of pre-shared keys (see [20, Sect. 2]). We believe that Oblivious TLS can be extended to other Handshake modes. However, it might be the case that the use of pre-shared keys decreases the efficiency of the whole protocol as the key derivation would become more complicated. Since this is an expensive part of Oblivious TLS, opening a new connection might be preferable to resuming an older session.

Privacy of Metadata. Oblivious TLS does not preserve privacy of Handshake messages and alerts against the corrupted parties of the MPC engine, but only against external attackers. This is because the derived handshake keys are revealed to the MPC engine, and the alerts are immediately opened upon receipt. This choice allows a more efficient management of alerts and handshake messages, including verification of signatures and computation of transcripts. On the other hand, if an attacker corrupts any party of the engine, it gains access to the metadata of the connection. We do not believe this to be a huge concern, however, since this type of targeted attack is not typically feasible for, say, a mass surveillance adversary who aims to harvest metadata.

Handshake

The Handshake of Oblivious TLS is a multiparty execution of its original version. In particular, the messages exchanged between the client and the MPC engine are the same as in a traditional TLS 1.3 connection. However, additional security properties are guaranteed, specifically, the protocol protects the privacy of the application keys against up to $n - 1$ corrupted parties and ensures the authenticity of the multiparty endpoint. Both objectives are achieved using multiparty public keys, i.e. key pairs where the private counterpart is secret-shared. We now outline the main steps of the protocol.

Initialisation. To set up an Oblivious TLS server, the parties generate an EdDSA key using Π_{Sign} (see Sect. 4.2) and request a Certificate Authority to issue a certificate that binds the public key to the identity of the MPC engine. The private counterpart is secret-shared, therefore, its value remains secret as long as at least one party is honest. The key will be used to guarantee the authenticity of the communications. The MPC engine also generates a random seed s for a PRG (this can be done using commitment schemes). Every random value inserted in the Handshake messages must be generated using s and the selected PRG.

ClientHello and ServerHello. The two messages are generated following the specification of TLS 1.3. However the 32-byte nonces must be generated using the seed s and the selected PRG. Moreover, the messages must contain a not-necessarily-fresh DH public key which was generated using Π_{DH} (see Sect. 4.1). The private counterpart of such key is secret-shared, therefore, its value is known to nobody as long as at least one party is honest.

Cryptographic Computations - Part I. After sending the Hello messages, the parties perform a multiparty Diffie-Hellman key exchange using Π_{DH}, obtaining a secret-shared output. Then, the key derivation function is applied to the result using the MPC techniques described in Sect. 4. At the end, the Handshake keys[2] and IVs are opened. The MAC keys for ServerFinished and ClientFinished as well as the internal state of the key derivation function are instead kept in shared form.

EncryptedExtensions, CertificateRequest and Certificates. These messages are generated and checked as described in the specification of TLS 1.3. Observe that their encryption and decryption can be computed locally by each party. Indeed, the handshake keys and IVs have been opened in the previous step. Clearly, the parties must send the certificate of the MPC engine.

ServerCertificateVerify and ClientCertificateVerify. Observe that the transcript of the connection is known to all the parties of the engine. Therefore, the verification of ClientCertificateVerify can be performed locally. The signature in ServerCertificateVerify is instead generated using the MPC protocol Π_{Sign} (see Sect. 4.2). Clearly, in order to do that, all the parties must agree on the transcript. In particular, they must check that P_1 generated a fresh nonce using s and the DH key was generated by the whole MPC engine. Since the EdDSA private key is shared, only with the collaboration of the whole engine, it is possible to generate a signature.

---

[2] Using the notation of [20, Sect. 7.1], *client_handshake_traffic_secret* and *server_handshake_traffic_secret* **must not** be opened.

ServerFinished and ClientFinished. The generation of the HMAC in ServerFinished is performed by applying MPC algorithms to the corresponding secret-shared MAC key (see Sect. 4). The verification of the HMAC in ClientFinished instead does not require the use of any multiparty protocol. Indeed, the client MAC key can be opened just after the reception of the message. Each party can then check the MAC locally. It is fundamental that the MAC key is opened after the reception of ClientFinished. Otherwise, the protocol would not guarantee explicit authentication. In any case, opening the MAC keys for the verification does not affect security. Indeed, the opened MAC key is never used afterwards and its value does not leak any information.

Cryptographic Computations - Part II. The second part of the key derivation is performed using the MPC techniques described in Sect. 4. The operation takes as input the full transcript of the connection as well as the internal state of the key derivation function, which is secret-shared. At the end, the new IVs are opened. The remaining outputs must be kept in shared form.

Key Update. TLS 1.3 describes a key update scheme based on the key derivation function of the Handshake (see [20, Sect. 7.2]). Again, we can perform the operations using the MPC techniques presented in Sect. 4. At the end, the new IVs are opened. The remaining outputs must be kept in shared form.

Record Layer

The Record layer of Oblivious TLS is essentially an adaptation of the original protocol to secret-shared keys. As a consequence, the changes do not affect the Handshake messages. Indeed, in that case, the keys as well as the nonces are known to every party. When we switch to the application keys, instead, only the nonces are known. For compatibility, the fragment partition, the additional data, the nonce generation and the padding are performed as in TLS 1.3. Encryptions and decryptions are instead executed using multiparty operations (see Sect. 5). Specifically, the encryption outputs a non-shared ciphertext taking as input a secret-shared plaintext, a secret-shared key and cleartext nonce and additional data. The decryption outputs either $\perp$ (in case of a tampered ciphertext) or a secret-shared plaintext and takes as input a secret-shared key and non-shared nonce, ciphertext and additional data. Upon decryption, the fragment type (which is encoded in the padding) is checked. In case of Alerts and Handshake messages, the plaintext is opened and handled according to TLS.

4   Handshake Operations

The Handshake of TLS 1.3 is based on Diffie-Hellman key exchange. Given the public key of the client, the parties running Oblivious TLS should be able to compute a secret-sharing of the exchanged secret. Notice that if any party P_i learns the exchanged secret, Oblivious TLS would completely lose its purpose as

P_i could compute the symmetric keys and communicate with the client without any restriction. In order to design a multiparty Diffie-Hellman protocol, it is necessary for the parties to have a secret-shared private key. Clearly, the public key does need to be kept secret.

We chose to focus on Diffie-Hellman over elliptic curves, as it is the most popular version of the protocol and allows us to work over smaller finite fields than traditional DH. Specifically, we use the curve *Curve25519* of [5], although with minor changes the protocol could also use other curves of TLS 1.3.

In this section, we will present an actively secure protocol for Diffie-Hellman. In Sect. 4.2 of the full version of this paper [2], we will also describe a more efficient variant that allows some limited influence on the computation to the adversary. The downside of this solution is that it does not permit to directly reduce the security of Oblivious TLS to the security proof of TLS 1.3 [11] without introducing new cryptographic assumptions.

Diffie-Hellman Notation. For the whole section, we assume to work with an elliptic curves E of equation

$$Y^2 = X^3 + AX^2 + BX + C$$

over a prime field of cardinality $p \neq 2$. Furthermore, we assume the Diffie-Hellman group to be $\langle G \rangle$ where $G \in E$ has prime order q such that $q^2 \nmid |E|$. We denote the identity element of the group with ∞. Remember that this is the only non-affine point of the group. In this section, we use the notation $[[\cdot]]_q$, $[[\cdot]]_p$ and $[[\cdot]]_E$ to denote secret-sharings over $\mathbb{F}_q$, $\mathbb{F}_p$ and $\langle G \rangle$ respectively (modelled as values in $\mathcal{F}_{\mathrm{MPC}}$).

For clarity, we assume the elliptic curve Diffie-Hellman key exchange to be the algorithm that, on input a secret key $s \in \mathbb{F}_q^\times$ and a point $Q \in \langle G \rangle \setminus \{\infty\}$, outputs the x-coordinate of sQ. Actually, among all the elliptic curves supported by TLS 1.3, this description applies only to *Curve25519* and *Curve448*. The output of the other algorithms usually depends on both the coordinates of sQ.

Computations over Elliptic Curves. Recall that given two affine points (x_0, y_0) and (x_1, y_1) of the curve E such that $x_0 \neq x_1$, their sum (x_3, y_3) is computed as follows

$$m \leftarrow \frac{y_1 - y_0}{x_1 - x_0}, \qquad x_3 \leftarrow m^2 - A - x_0 - x_1, \qquad y_3 \leftarrow m(x_1 - x_3) - y_1 \qquad (1)$$

We also recall that given an affine point (x_0, y_0) of E, its opposite is $(x_0, -y_0)$. As a consequence, two points P and Q of the curve have the same x-coordinate if and only if $P = Q$ or $P = -Q$.

Actually, there exist multiple ways to compute the addition between elliptic curve points. In traditional computation (i.e. non-multiparty computation), alternative coordinate systems are usually preferred as they permit to perform operations over elliptic curves without divisions. However, for secret-sharing based protocols like SPDZ the cost of a division is roughly twice the cost of a multiplication. All the division-free methods known so far need at least 10 multiplications to perform additions, so in our case, affine coordinates are still the best solution.

Key Derivation, HMAC and Key Updates. After having performed the Diffie-Hellman key exchange, the obtained secret is input into a key derivation function which outputs multiple symmetric keys. In particular, TLS 1.3 uses the HKDF scheme of [18] which is based on hash functions (concretely, *SHA256* or *SHA384*). Since both the exchanged secret and the derived symmetric keys must remain private, the key derivation must be performed in MPC.

Before computing the hash function, we convert the secret from a $[[\cdot]]_p$ sharing into a $[[\cdot]]_2$ sharing, so we can compute the hash function as a binary circuit, using e.g. a garbled circuit-based protocol [15]. Alternatively, we could use a customized MPC-friendly hash function, however, this is non-standard and not supported by endpoints on the Internet.

The same approach can be used also to compute the IVs and the actual encryption keys of the AEAD (see [20, Sect. 7.3]), the HMAC keys and the HMACs used in *ClientFinished* and *ServerFinished* (see [20, Sect. 4.4.4]) and the key updates (see [20, Sect. 7.2]).

Signatures. The last cryptographic operation that the MPC engine needs to perform in the Handshake is the generation and verification of signatures. Since the transcript is known to all the parties of the engine, signatures can always be verified locally. Signing instead is more complex, indeed, the signature must be issued only with the approval of all the parties. We therefore use a threshold Schnorr-style protocol based on EdDSA signatures, given in Sect. 4.2. Since the message being signed is public, we can do this step without any expensive MPC operations.

4.1 Diffie-Hellman

DaPoint. The proposed protocol needs a particular preprocessing phase Π_{daPoint}, which is described in Figs. 1 and 2. The description uses $\mathcal{F}_{\mathrm{MPC}}$ and $\mathcal{F}_{\mathrm{Rand}}$ as resources. The latter is a simple functionality that outputs a random permutation to all the parties.

The protocol Π_{daPoint} has the purpose of generating N doubly-authenticated-point (daPoint) tuples, i.e. random triples of the form $([[R]]_E, [[u]]_p, [[v]]_p)$ such that $R \in \langle G \rangle \setminus \{\infty\}$ and (u, v) are the affine coordinates of R. The algorithm is based on a cut-and-choose style bucketing technique [19].

It is possible to prove that Π_{daPoint} securely implements the functionality $\mathcal{F}_{\mathsf{daPoint}}$ described in Fig. 3.

Theorem 1. *Assuming that*

$$\omega := N \binom{M + N \cdot l}{l}^{-1} \quad and \quad \omega' := \frac{M + N \cdot l}{q}$$

Π_{daPoint}

Let $M, N, l \in \mathbb{N}$ be three security-parameter-dependent values with $M, l \geq 2$.

MPC

The parties can issue queries to $\mathcal{F}_{\text{MPC}}$ but they cannot access the internal values (i.e. everything except the output) of the procedure DaPoint.

DaPoint

On input $(\text{daPoint}, (\text{id}_{i,1}, \text{id}_{i,2}, \text{id}_{i,3})_{i \in [N]})$ the parties compute the following steps:

1. For each $i \in [n]$, the parties generate $M + Nl$ random elements $[[z_{i,1}]]_q, [[z_{i,2}]]_q, \ldots, [[z_{i,M+Nl}]]_q$ in $\mathbb{F}_q$ such that $z_{i,j}$ is known only to P_i for each $j \in [M + Nl]$. This operation is performed using $\mathcal{F}_{\text{MPC}}$.

2. For each $i \in [n]$ and $j \in [M + Nl]$, the parties compute $[[Z_{i,j}]]_E \leftarrow [[z_{i,j}]]_q G$ using $\mathcal{F}_{\text{MPC}}$ and P_i computes $Z_{i,j}$ locally.

3. For each $i \in [n]$ and $j \in [M + Nl]$, party P_i computes $(x_{i,j}, y_{i,j})$, the affine coordinates of $Z_{i,j}$. If this is not possible since $Z_{i,j} = \infty$, the protocol aborts. Otherwise, P_i inputs $x_{i,j}$ and $y_{i,j}$ in $\mathcal{F}_{\text{MPC}}$ with domain $\mathbb{F}_p$.

4. The parties sample a random permutation ψ of $[M + Nl]$ using $\mathcal{F}_{\text{Rand}}$.

5. For each $i \in [n]$ and $j \in [M + Nl] \setminus [Nl]$, the parties open $[[Z_{i,\psi(j)}]]_E$, $[[x_{i,\psi(j)}]]_p$ and $[[y_{i,\psi(j)}]]_p$. If the affine coordinates of the former do not coincide with the latter, the protocol aborts.

6. For each $(i, j) \in [n] \times [Nl]$, the parties set $[[s_{i,\psi(j)}]]_p \leftarrow [[x_{i,\psi(j)}]]_p^2$ and open

$$t_{i,\psi(j)} \leftarrow [[y_{i,\psi(j)}]]_p^2 - [[x_{i,\psi(j)}]]_p \cdot [[s_{i,\psi(j)}]]_p - A \cdot [[s_{i,\psi(j)}]]_p - B \cdot [[x_{i,\psi(j)}]]_p - C.$$

If any of the $t_{i,\psi(j)}$'s is different from zero, the protocol aborts.

7. For each $j \in [Nl]$, the parties set $[[R_{\psi(j)}]]_E \leftarrow \sum_{i \in [n]} [[Z_{i,\psi(j)}]]_E$ and $[[x_{\psi(j)}]]_p \leftarrow [[x_{1,\psi(j)}]]_p$, $[[y_{\psi(j)}]]_p \leftarrow [[y_{1,\psi(j)}]]_p$. Then, for $i \in [n] \setminus \{1\}$,

$$[[m]]_p \leftarrow \frac{[[y_{\psi(j)}]]_p - [[y_{i,\psi(j)}]]_p}{[[x_{\psi(j)}]]_p - [[x_{i,\psi(j)}]]_p}$$

$$[[x_{\psi(j)}]]_p \leftarrow [[m]]_p^2 - A - [[x_{\psi(j)}]]_p - [[x_{i,\psi(j)}]]_p$$

$$[[y_{\psi(j)}]]_p \leftarrow [[m]]_p \cdot ([[x_{i,\psi(j)}]]_p - [[x_{\psi(j)}]]_p) - [[y_{i,\psi(j)}]]_p.$$

If for any i, m cannot be computed due to a zero denominator, the protocol aborts.

8. For each $(i, j) \in [N] \times [l]$, let $[[R_{i,j}]]_E := [[R_{\psi((i-1)l+j)}]]_E$ and

$$[[u_{i,j}]]_p := [[x_{\psi((i-1)l+j)}]]_p, \quad [[v_{i,j}]]_p := [[y_{\psi((i-1)l+j)}]]_p.$$

The sequence $\mathcal{B}_i := (\psi((i-1)l + j - 1))_{j \in [l]}$ is called the i-th bucket. This is equivalent to splitting the first Nl elements of the permuted sequence into blocks of l elements called buckets.

Fig. 1. The daPoint protocol - part 1

are negligible functions in the security parameter, Π_{daPoint} securely implements $\mathcal{F}_{\text{daPoint}}$ in the $(\mathcal{F}_{\text{MPC}}, \mathcal{F}_{\text{Rand}})$-hybrid model.

9. For each $i \in [N]$ and $j \in \{2, 3, \ldots, l\}$, the parties compute and open

$$W_{i,j} \leftarrow [[R_{i,1}]]_E + [[R_{i,j}]]_E$$

$$[[m]]_p \leftarrow \frac{[[v_{i,1}]]_p - [[v_{i,j}]]_p}{[[u_{i,1}]]_p - [[u_{i,j}]]_p}$$

$$w_{i,j} \leftarrow [[m]]_p^2 - A - [[u_{i,j}]]_p - [[u_{1,j}]]_p$$

$$w'_{i,j} \leftarrow [[m]]_p \cdot ([[u_{i,j}]]_p - [[w_{i,j}]]_p) - [[v_{i,j}]]_p$$

If for any j, m cannot be computed due to a zero denominator or the affine coordinates of $W_{i,j}$ do not coincide with $(w_{i,j}, w'_{i,j})$, the protocol aborts. Otherwise, for every $i \in [N]$, the parties store $[[R_{i,1}]]_E$, $[[u_{i,1}]]_p$ and $[[v_{i,1}]]_p$ with identities $\mathrm{id}_{i,1}$, $\mathrm{id}_{i,2}$ and $\mathrm{id}_{i,3}$.

Fig. 2. The daPoint protocol - part 2

$\mathcal{F}_{\mathrm{daPoint}}$

MPC

$\mathcal{F}_{\mathrm{daPoint}}$ replies to the queries as $\mathcal{F}_{\mathrm{MPC}}$ did.

daPoint

After receiving $(\mathrm{daPoint}, (\mathrm{id}_{i,1}, \mathrm{id}_{i,2}, \mathrm{id}_{i,3})_{i \in [N]})$ from every honest party and the adversary, $\mathcal{F}_{\mathrm{daPoint}}$ samples a random point R_i in $\langle G \rangle \setminus \{\infty\}$ for every $i \in [N]$. Let (u_i, v_i) be its affine coordinates. The functionality stores R_i, u_i and v_i with labels $\mathrm{id}_{i,1}$, $\mathrm{id}_{i,2}$ and $\mathrm{id}_{i,3}$.

Fig. 3. The daPoint functionality

We present a sketch of the proof of Theorem 1. The complete version can be found in Appendix B.1 of the full version of this paper [2]. We point out that if the order of the additions in step 7 of Π_{daPoint} is changed, the protocol is probably still secure but our proof does not apply anymore.

Proof (Sketch). Consider the simulator $\mathcal{S}_{\mathrm{daPoint}}$ that runs the protocol with the adversary impersonating the honest parties and sends (Abort) to the functionality if and only if the simulated execution aborts. We show that no PPT adversary can distinguish between Π_{daPoint} and the composition of $\mathcal{F}_{\mathrm{daPoint}}$ with $\mathcal{S}_{\mathrm{daPoint}}$.

For simplicity, we ignore the fact that the addition of elliptic curve points can fail due to a zero-denominator. Each of these operations indeed comes with some leakage, which accumulates throughout the protocol. Showing its negligibility is actually the most complex part of the proof.

When there exist $i \in [n]$ and $j \in [M + Nl]$ such that $(x_{i,j}, y_{i,j}) \notin E$, the protocol always aborts. Indeed, if the incorrect point is opened in step 5, the protocol aborts. Moreover, in the lucky case in which the point passes the check, the protocol aborts in the following step when the equation of the curve is checked on all the non-opened points.

Consider the protocol. For every i and j, we define

$$R_j := \sum_{i \in [n]} Z_{i,j}, \qquad Z'_{i,j} := (x_{i,j}, y_{i,j}), \qquad R'_j := \sum_{i \in [n]} Z'_{i,j}.$$

Observe that the coordinates of $R'_{\psi(j)}$ are $(x_{\psi(j)}, y_{\psi(j)})$ (see step 7 of Π_{daPoint}). Moreover, since at least one of the addends $Z_{i,j}$ is not known to the adversary, R_j is random from the adversary's perspective.

Claim. If there exists any $j \in [M + Nl]$ such that $R'_j \neq R_j$, the protocol aborts with overwhelming probability.

Let $S := \{j \in [M + Nl] \mid R'_j \neq R_j\}$. Observe that if $R'_j \neq R_j$, there exists at least one $i \in [n]$ such that $Z'_{i,j} \neq Z_{i,j}$. Therefore, if there exist more than Nl elements in S, the protocol aborts with probability 1 at step 5.

For each $i \in [N]$ and $j \in [l]$, let $f(i,j) := \psi((i-1)l + j)$. The protocol does not abort only if every bucket is either contained in S or in $S^{\mathbb{C}}$. Indeed, in every bucket $W_{i,j} = R_{f(i,1)} + R_{f(i,j)}$, whereas $(w_{i,j}, w'_{i,j}) = R'_{f(i,1)} + R'_{f(i,j)}$. Therefore, if $|S| > Nl$ or $l \nmid |S|$, the probability of an abortion is 1. We now analyse what is the probability of aborting in the other cases, i.e. when $|S| = rl$ with $0 < r \leq N$.

We consider the possible permutations ψ that would make the protocol succeed. Let their set be Σ. We can represent each permutation as a sequence of $M + Nl$ non-repeated numbers in $[M + Nl]$. The j-th number of the sequence represents the image of j. The i-th bucket is the sequence of elements from position $(i-1)l + 1$ to il. The permutations that cause no abortion have to send all the elements of S in r of the first N buckets. There are $\binom{N}{r}$ ways of choosing these buckets, $(rl)!$ ways of permuting the elements in S and $(M + Nl - rl)!$ ways of permuting the remaining elements. Therefore, the probability of picking any of the permutations that cause no abortion is

$$\mathbb{P}(\psi \in \Sigma) \leq \frac{\binom{N}{r} \cdot (rl)! \cdot (M + Nl - rl)!}{(M + Nl)!} = \binom{N}{r}\binom{M + Nl}{rl}^{-1} \leq \omega.$$

The last inequality was proven in [13, Sect. 5]. The claim follows from the fact that ω is negligible by hypothesis.

Observe that the values opened in step 5 and in the buckets are independent of the final output, that terminates the sketch of the proof. □

Complexity of daPoint. If we implement $\mathcal{F}_{\text{MPC}}$ using SPDZ, the execution of Π_{daPoint} takes $10 + 4(n-1)$ rounds. Each of the generated tuples has the following cost: $2nl - 1$ multiplicative triples in $\mathbb{F}_p$, $nl - 1$ division tuples in $\mathbb{F}_p$, $3nl - 1$ squaring couples in $\mathbb{F}_p$, $2n(l + M/N)$ input masks in $\mathbb{F}_p$, $n(l + M/N)$ input masks over $\mathbb{F}_q$ and the communication of

$$\big(3nM/N + 2M/N + 5l + 11nl - 9\big) \cdot \log(p) + nM/N + l - 1$$

bits for every party.

Multiparty Diffie-Hellman. Given the functionality $\mathcal{F}_{\mathrm{daPoint}}$, it is possible to construct a multiparty protocol for elliptic curve Diffie-Hellman as described in Fig. 5. The following theorem shows that Π_{DH} securely implements the functionality $\mathcal{F}_{\mathrm{DH}}$ presented in Fig. 4.

$$\mathcal{F}_{\mathrm{DH}}$$

MPC

$\mathcal{F}_{\mathrm{DH}}$ replies to the queries as $\mathcal{F}_{\mathrm{daPoint}}$ did.

Key Generation

After receiving (KeyGen, id) from every honest party and the adversary, $\mathcal{F}_{\mathrm{DH}}$ samples a random value $s \xleftarrow{\$} \mathbb{F}_q^{\times}$ and computes $S \leftarrow sG$. Then, it passes S to the adversary and waits for a reply. If the answer is OK, $\mathcal{F}_{\mathrm{DH}}$ outputs S to every honest party and stores s with label id. Otherwise, it aborts.

Diffie-Hellman

After receiving (DH, $\mathrm{id}_1, Q, \mathrm{id}_2$) from the adversary and every honest party, $\mathcal{F}_{\mathrm{DH}}$ retrieves the private key s of label id_1. If $Q = \infty$ or $qQ \neq \infty$, the functionality does nothing. Otherwise, it computes e, the x coordinate of sQ, and stores it with identity id_2.

Fig. 4. The Diffie-Hellman functionality

$$\Pi_{\mathrm{DH}}$$

MPC

The parties can issue queries to $\mathcal{F}_{\mathrm{daPoint}}$ but they cannot access the private keys and the internal values of the key exchange procedure.

Key Generation

On input (KeyGen, id) the parties perform the following steps

1. Sample a random secret value $[[s]]_q \in \mathbb{F}_q$ and set $[[S]]_E \leftarrow [[s]]_q G$.
2. Call $\mathcal{F}_{\mathrm{daPoint}}$ to open $[[S]]_E$. If $S = \infty$, the protocol restarts.
3. Store the secret key $[[s]]_q$ with label id and output the public key S.

Diffie-Hellman

On input (DH, $\mathrm{id}_1, Q, \mathrm{id}_2$) the parties perform the following steps

1. They retrieve the private key $[[s]]_q$ with label id_1. Such key is stored in $\mathcal{F}_{\mathrm{daPoint}}$. If $Q = \infty$ or $qQ \neq \infty$, the protocol stops.
2. They compute $[[Z]]_E \leftarrow [[s]]_q Q$ using $\mathcal{F}_{\mathrm{daPoint}}$.
3. They call $\mathcal{F}_{\mathrm{daPoint}}$ to obtain a random daPoint tuple $([[R]]_E, [[x]]_p, [[y]]_p)$.
4. They compute and open $W \leftarrow [[Z]]_E - [[R]]_E$.
5. Let (u, v) be the affine coordinates of W. If $W = \infty$, the final output is $[[x]]_p$. Otherwise, using $\mathcal{F}_{\mathrm{daPoint}}$, the parties compute the output

$$[[e]]_p \leftarrow \left(\frac{[[y]]_p - v}{[[x]]_p - u} \right)^2 - A - [[x]]_p - u.$$

In case of zero denominator, the protocol aborts. The value of $[[e]]_p$ is stored with label id_2.

Fig. 5. The Diffie-Hellman protocol

Theorem 2. *Assuming q^{-1} to be a negligible sequence in the security parameter, the protocol Π_{DH} securely implements the functionality $\mathcal{F}_{DH}$ in the $\mathcal{F}_{daPoint}$-hybrid model.*

We present a sketch of the proof of theorem 2. The complete version can be found in Appendix B.2 of the full version of this paper [2].

Proof (Sketch). Consider the simulator $\mathcal{S}_{DH}$ that forwards the communications between adversary and functionality in the key generation and simulates Diffie-Hellman by sending a random point in $\langle G \rangle$. We show that no PPT adversary is able to distinguish between Π_{DH} and the composition of $\mathcal{F}_{DH}$ and $\mathcal{S}_{DH}$.

It is easy to see that the no adversary can distinguish between the original key generation and the simulated one. Therefore, we focus on Diffie-Hellman. We recall that $R = (x, y)$ by how $\mathcal{F}_{daPoint}$ is defined. As a consequence, in step 5, we compute the first coordinate of $W + R = Z = sQ$. The relation holds even if $W = \infty$, indeed, in such case $sQ = Z = R$. Observe that in the protocol the value of W is random, as the adversary does not know R. Moreover, the probability that the procedure fails due to a zero denominator is negligible. Indeed, that happens if and only if $R = W = Z - R$ or $R = -W = R - Z$, therefore, if and only if $2R = Z$ or $Z = \infty$. The first case occurs with negligible probability, the second one is just impossible because it would require either $S = \infty$ or $Q = \infty$. That terminates the sketch of the proof. $\square$

Complexity of Diffie-Hellman. If we implement $\mathcal{F}_{MPC}$ using SPDZ, the protocol Π_{DH} takes 4 rounds, 1 division tuple over $\mathbb{F}_p$, 1 squaring couple over $\mathbb{F}_p$, 1 daPoint tuple and the communication of $5\log(p) + 1$ bits for every party. The key generation requires instead just 1 random shared element of $\mathbb{F}_q$ and the communication of $\log(p) + 1$ bits for every party.

Instantiating $\mathcal{F}_{MPC}$ on the Required Fields. In concrete situations, we cannot choose the elliptic curve used by the Diffie-Hellman algorithm. As a matter of fact, TLS 1.3 supports only 5 secure curves. Although, it may be possible to find other secure curves, very few endpoints of the Internet would support them. For this reason, the choice of the fields $\mathbb{F}_p$ and $\mathbb{F}_q$ used by $\mathcal{F}_{MPC}$ is very restricted. If $\mathcal{F}_{MPC}$ is implemented using SPDZ, the Offline phase (i.e. the expensive preprocessing phase which is necessary to perform multiplications and inputs) must be instantiated on these fields. Unfortunately, some of the most efficient solutions (e.g. homomorphic encryption based Offline phases) come with strong constraints, which are usually not satisfied in our case. However, Oblivious Transfer based protocols such as MASCOT [17] just require the field to have cardinality sufficiently close to a power of 2. This condition is satisfied by both $\mathbb{F}_p$ and $\mathbb{F}_q$ for most the elliptic curves proposed by TLS 1.3. A more extensive discussion on the topic can be found in Sect. 4.3 of the full version of this paper [2].

4.2   Signature Generation

The authentication of the TLS connection is essentially based on signatures. Since the identity of the MPC engine consists in the union of all its parties, it is necessary for the private key to be secret-shared, otherwise, an attacker may issue new signatures without having control of all the parties.

In TLS 1.3, the endpoints sign the transcript of the Handshake. Since the latter is known to all the members of the MPC engine, it is sufficient that we design a multiparty protocol that on input a secret-shared key $[[a]]$ and a cleartext message m, outputs a cleartext signature $s \leftarrow \mathrm{Sign}(a, m)$. Clearly, the signing algorithm should be supported by TLS 1.3. We decided to base our protocol on EdDSA. Indeed, Schnorr signatures have interesting homomorphic properties that suit our context.

Schnorr Signatures. We briefly recall how Schnorr signatures are generated. Let $(\langle G \rangle, +)$ be an elliptic curve group of prime order q and suppose that the discrete logarithm problem is hard over $\langle G \rangle$. Let $H : \{0, 1\}^* \longrightarrow \mathbb{F}_q$ be a hash function. A private key is a random element $a \in \mathbb{F}_q$, whereas its public counterpart is defined to be $A := aG$. A signature (R, s) of a message $m \in \{0, 1\}^*$ is generated as follows

$$r \xleftarrow{\$} \mathbb{F}_q, \qquad R \leftarrow rG, \qquad s \leftarrow (r + H(R, A, m) \cdot a) \bmod q$$

The signature can be verified by checking whether $sG = R + H(R, A, m)A$.

$\mathcal{F}_{\mathrm{Sign}}$

Let G be the base point of the curve and let q be its order.
Initialization. Upon receiving (Init) from every party, $\mathcal{F}_{\mathrm{Sign}}$ generates a random pair (a, A) such that $A = aG$. Then, it sends A to the adversary and waits for a reply. If the answer is OK, the functionality outputs A to every honest party and stores (a, A). Otherwise, it aborts.
Sign: Upon receiving (Sign, m) from every party, where m is in $\{0, 1\}^*$, $\mathcal{F}_{\mathrm{Sign}}$ generates a signature (r, R) of m using the stored key. Then, it sends (s, R, m) to the adversary. If the answer is OK, $\mathcal{F}_{\mathrm{Sign}}$ outputs (s, R) to every honest party.
Abort: On input (Abort) from the adversary, the functionality aborts.

Fig. 6. The functionality $\mathcal{F}_{\mathrm{Sign}}$

Multiparty Signature. Using the functionality $\mathcal{F}_{\mathrm{Key}}$ as a resource (see Fig. 7), the parties can generate EdDSA signatures using the protocol Π_{Sign} described in Fig. 8. In practice, $\mathcal{F}_{\mathrm{Key}}$ can be implemented by having each P_i broadcast S_i, and run a zero-knowledge proof of knowledge of the secret s_i. The proof of the following theorem can be found in Appendix D of the full version of this paper [2].

Key

$\mathcal{F}_{\mathsf{Key}}$

On input (Key) from each party, $\mathcal{F}_{\mathsf{Key}}$ samples $s_i \xleftarrow{\$} \mathbb{F}_q$ for each $i \in \mathcal{H}$ and computes $S_i \leftarrow s_i G$. When the adversary provides a pair (s_j, S_j) for every $j \in \mathcal{C}$, the functionality answers with $\{S_i\}_{i \in \mathcal{H}}$ and waits for a reply. If the adversary sends OK, $\mathcal{F}_{\mathsf{Key}}$ checks that $S_j = s_j G$ for each $j \in \mathcal{C}$. In such case, it outputs $(s_i, S_1, S_2, \ldots, S_n)$ to $P_i \ \forall i \in \mathcal{H}$. Otherwise, it sends $\bot$ to each honest party.

Fig. 7. The functionality $\mathcal{F}_{\mathsf{Key}}$

Π_{Sign}

Let G be the base point of the curve and let q be its order.

Initialization. Party P_i sends (Key) to $\mathcal{F}_{\mathsf{KEY}}$. If $\mathcal{F}_{\mathsf{KEY}}$ replies with $(a_i, A_1, A_2, \ldots, A_n)$, P_i outputs $A \leftarrow \sum_{j \in [n]} A_j$ and stores (A, a_i). Otherwise, it aborts.

Sign. Let m be in $\{0,1\}^*$, every party P_i performs the following operations.

1. It sends (Key) to $\mathcal{F}_{\mathsf{KEY}}$. If $\mathcal{F}_{\mathsf{KEY}}$ replies with $(r_i, R_1, R_2, \ldots, R_n)$, P_i computes $R \leftarrow \sum_{j \in [n]} R_j$. Otherwise, it aborts.
2. P_i computes and broadcasts $s_i \leftarrow (r_i + H(R, A, m) \cdot a_i) \bmod q$.
3. P_i waits for s_j from every other party P_j and computes $s \leftarrow \sum_{i \in [n]} s_i \bmod q$. Then, it checks that $sG = R + H(R, A, m) \cdot A$. If this is not true, it aborts. Otherwise, it outputs (R, s).

Fig. 8. The protocol Π_{Sign}

Theorem 3. *The protocol Π_{Sign} securely implements $\mathcal{F}_{Sign}$ in the $\mathcal{F}_{Key}$-hybrid model.*

5 Record Layer Operations

In the Record layer for Oblivious TLS, we need secure protocols that given an AEAD scheme $(\mathcal{E}, \mathcal{D})$ and a secret-shared symmetric key $[[K]]$, allow performing the following operations

- **Encrypt.** On input a cleartext nonce N, cleartext associated data A and a secret-shared plaintext $[[X]]$, output a cleartext string $C = \mathcal{E}(K, N, A, X)$.
- **Decrypt.** On input a cleartext nonce N, cleartext associated data A and a non-shared ciphertext C, output $\bot$ if and only if $\bot = \mathcal{D}(K, N, A, C)$. Otherwise, output a secret-shared value $[[X]]$ where $X = \mathcal{D}(K, N, A, C)$.

The secret-sharing scheme used in this high-level description strongly depends on the AEAD. Observe that in practical situations, there might be a mismatch between the secret-sharing scheme used by the application on top of TLS and the secret-sharing scheme used by the AEAD. In such cases, we assume that suitable conversions were already performed.

Padding. In TLS 1.3, the plaintexts always have a padding. Whereas its application is a simple operation, the removal can be a bit complex. Indeed, using multiparty computation, we need to discover the position of the last non-zero byte and open it. Its value encodes the fragment type (see [20, Section 5.1]). In the case of an alert or Handshake data (key update requests, post Handshake authentication or new session tickets), the plaintext is simply opened and handle according TLS 1.3. In the case of application data, the first part of the plaintext (up to the second last non-zero value) is kept in shared form and is handled following the instructions of the application on top of TLS.

Supported AEADs. Oblivious TLS supports two different AEAD schemes. The first one is AES-GCM, one of the most popular encryption algorithms. The second one is instead a novel AEAD specifically designed by us for Oblivious TLS, and avoids all evaluation of block ciphers inside MPC. The description and the security analysis of the latter can be found in Sect. 5.2 of the full version of this paper [2]. The efficiency of the MPC friendly AEAD is considerably better than AES-GCM, however, the downside is that a custom algorithm is generally not supported by TLS clients. Both solutions rely on MACs to guarantee integrity. For this reason, the associated MAC keys must always be kept in shared form, otherwise a corrupted party would be able to tamper with the communications.

5.1   AES-GCM

We decided to adopt AES-GCM as it seemed to allow the most efficient MPC execution among all the AEADs suggested by TLS 1.3 (see [20, Section B.4]).

Overview of AES-GCM. We briefly recall how the cipher works (for details, see [12]). Let k be the key and let N be a nonce. Let $\text{AES}(k, x)$ denote the encryption of x under the key k using the AES block cipher. The algorithm defines the MAC key $H := \text{AES}(k, O)$ where O is the 128-bit string entirely made of zeros. Figure 9 describes the encryption procedure. The value C_0 is usually called the MAC of the AEAD. Decryptions are performed in a similar way: at the beginning the MAC is regenerated from the ciphertext and the result is compared with the MAC received from the client. If the check fails, the algorithm outputs $\perp$, otherwise the plaintext is retrieved by reversing the operations of the encryption.

---

1. The plaintext is split into 128-bit blocks $X_1, X_2, \ldots, X_L$. Do the same on the associated data to get $A_1, A_2, \ldots, A_{L'}$.
2. From N, $L + 1$ 128-bit nonces $N_0, N_1, N_2, \ldots, N_L$ are derived.
3. Set $C_i \leftarrow X_i \oplus \text{AES}(k, N_i)$ for every $i \in [L]$.
4. Let S be an encoding of L and L' as a 128-bit string.
5. Set $M \leftarrow \bigoplus_{i=1}^{L'} A_i \cdot H^i \oplus \bigoplus_{i=1}^{L} C_i \cdot H^{i+L'} \oplus S \cdot H^{L+L'+1}$.
6. Set $C_0 \leftarrow M \oplus \text{AES}(k, N_0)$ and output $C_0, C_1, \ldots, C_L$.

Fig. 9. AES-GCM encryption

Multiparty AES Evaluation. To run AES-GCM inside MPC, we need many evaluations of AES on cleartext inputs derived from the nonce, under a secret-shared key and with secret-shared output. We consider two methods for evaluating AES:

- The secret-sharing based AES evaluation of [16]. This solution might be preferable when the parties can communicate over fast networks.
- A multi-party garbled circuit protocol such as [15]. This involves evaluating AES as a binary circuit, but obtains a constant round complexity so may be preferable over slow networks.

After the AES evaluations, the parties get $[[C_i]]$ from $[[X_i]]$ (in the encryption) or $[[X_i]]$ from C_i (in the decryption) for every $i \in [L]$. In encryption, $[[C_i]]$ is opened for every $i \in [L]$.

The MAC Generation. It remains to explain how C_0 is generated (or checked in the case of a decryption). Suppose now that we have a secret-sharing of $[[H^i]]$ over $\mathbb{F}_{2^{128}}$ for every $i \in [L+L'+1]$. It is possible to obtain a secret-sharing of the MAC $[[C_0]]$ without communication between the parties. Indeed, the additional data as well as $C_1, C_2, \ldots, C_L$ and S are cleartext information, therefore

$$[[C_0]] = [[\text{AES}(k, N_0)]] \oplus \bigoplus_{i=1}^{L'} A_i \cdot [[H^i]] \oplus \bigoplus_{i=1}^{L} C_i \cdot [[H^{L'+i}]] \oplus S \cdot [[H^{L+L'+1}]].$$

The MAC must be opened only in the case of an encryption, otherwise H might be leaked. When decrypting, the parties must check $[[C_0]]$ for equality with the first 128-bit block of the ciphertext received from the client. The operation must leak no information besides the output bit.

Once and for All Operations. Observe that some operations do not have to be repeated for every encryption or decryption. Specifically, for every symmetric key, the AES key scheduling, the computation of the secret-shared MAC key $[[H]]$ and its powers can be performed only once. Clearly, it is sufficient to compute the first T powers where T is an upper bound on $L+L'+1$. In TLS 1.3, $L+L'+1$ is at most 1026, but depending on the application, it may be smaller.

6 Security and Performance

The Multi-stage Key Exchange Model. We want to prove the security of Oblivious TLS in the Multi-Stage Key Exchange Security Model [11]. The adversary interacts with several endpoints running the protocol and has complete control over the network. In particular, it is allowed to intercept, drop and inject communications. Moreover, it has the ability to corrupt endpoints and request the leakage of established keys. The adversary wins when it succeeds in breaking particular authentication properties (Match Security) or can distinguish a tested key from a random string of the same length (Multi-Stage Security). Since the model was used to prove the security of TLS 1.3 [11], our intention is to reduce the security of Oblivious TLS to the proof of TLS 1.3.

Adaptations to Oblivious TLS. The main difference between our protocol and the traditional version of TLS 1.3 is the use of MPC, therefore, every endpoint of our multi-stage model is actually an MPC engine. We regard them as atomic entities. Observe that we can model the actual MPC protocols for Diffie-Hellman, key derivation, signature generation and encryption and decryption with the corresponding functionalities. We allow the multi-stage adversary the same influence on the multiparty procedures as if it controlled the corrupted parties of the engine. The corruption of an MPC engine in the model corresponds in practice to the corruption of all the associated parties.

We obtain a model that is almost identical to the security model of TLS 1.3. The only differences are the following:

- The Handshake keys are leaked to the multi-stage adversary whenever there exists at least one corrupted party.
- The MAC keys used in ClientFinished and ServerFinished are leaked to the multi-stage adversary upon reception of the corresponding messages.
- The IVs are leaked to the adversary.

Actually, in this model, it would be trivial for the adversary to win. Indeed, it would be sufficient to test a handshake key of an engine with a corrupted party (distinguishing it from random is straightforward as the key is leaked). To fix this problem, we allow the adversary to test handshake keys only if none of the parties of the two endpoints is corrupted.

Security of Oblivious TLS. In [11], the authors proved that in TLS 1.3, the application keys remain secure and authenticated even if the encryption keys are leaked. Moreover, they proved that the MAC keys used in ClientFinished and ServerFinished are computationally independent of all the other keys of the protocol. Since they are used for the last time in the verification of the MACs, the Handshake remains secure as long as they are leaked after the reception of ClientFinished and ServerFinished. Even the IVs are independent of the keys (see [20, Section 7.3]). Therefore, their knowledge does not leak any additional information. Moreover, the security of an AEAD is guaranteed as long as the keys are kept secret. As a consequence, the security proof of [11] applies to Oblivious TLS too, after minor modifications.

6.1   Performance

To estimate the performance of Oblivious TLS, we carried out some benchmarks using the SCALE-MAMBA library[3], based on implementation of the main components in the handshake and record layers, which we believe to be the bottleneck. This does not give a full, standards-compliant implementation of Oblivious TLS, but rather, is intended to obtain some estimates of its expected performance.

---

[3] https://github.com/KULeuven-COSIC/SCALE-MAMBA.

We tested the online phase of the resulting MPC protocol, assuming the necessary input-independent preprocessing (multiplication triples etc.) has been generated. Based on the results, we can expect a Handshake to take around 1 or 2 s. We also tested the throughput of the different multiparty AEADs we considered. The MPC-friendly AEAD showed interesting outcomes with a throughput of around 300 KB/s. The Garbled-Circuit-based version of AES-GCM, instead, proved itself to be rather inefficient (around 1 KB/s). We expect that with the alternative AES evaluation method based on [16] (which is not currently available in SCALE-MAMBA), we could achieve throughputs up to 3 MB/s for AES-GCM, even exceeding our MPC-friendly AEAD. The drawback of this is that the preprocessing material is much more expensive to generate, and also the round complexity is higher. For further information on performance, see Appendix F of the full version [2].

Acknowledgments. We would like to thank Douglas Stebila and the anonymous reviewers for valuable feedback which helped to improve the paper, as well as Roberto Zunino for suggestions and comments on Damiano Abram's master's thesis. The work of Sven Trieflinger and Damiano Abram was funded by Robert Bosch GmbH. Ivan Damgård was supported by the European Research Council (ERC) under the European Unions's Horizon 2020 research and innovation programme under grant agreement No 669255 (MPCPRO). Peter Scholl was supported by a starting grant from the Aarhus University Research Foundation.

References

1. Abram, D.: Oblivious TLS. Master's thesis, Università degli Studi di Trento, March 2020
2. Abram, D., Damgård, I., Scholl, P., Trieflinger, S.: Oblivious TLS via multi-party computation. Cryptology ePrint Archive, Report 2021/318 (2021). https://eprint.iacr.org/2021/318
3. Agrawal, S., Mohassel, P., Mukherjee, P., Rindal, P.: DiSE: distributed symmetric-key encryption. In: ACM CCS 2018. ACM Press, October 2018
4. Bendlin, R., Damgård, I., Orlandi, C., Zakarias, S.: Semi-homomorphic encryption and multiparty computation. In: Paterson, K.G. (ed.) EUROCRYPT 2011. LNCS, vol. 6632, pp. 169–188. Springer, Heidelberg (2011). https://doi.org/10.1007/978-3-642-20465-4_11
5. Bernstein, D.J.: Curve25519: new Diffie-Hellman speed records. In: Yung, M., Dodis, Y., Kiayias, A., Malkin, T. (eds.) PKC 2006. LNCS, vol. 3958, pp. 207–228. Springer, Heidelberg (2006). https://doi.org/10.1007/11745853_14
6. Canetti, R.: Universally composable security: a new paradigm for cryptographic protocols. In: 42nd FOCS. IEEE Computer Society Press, October 2001
7. Dalskov, A., Orlandi, C., Keller, M., Shrishak, K., Shulman, H.: Securing DNSSEC keys via threshold ECDSA from generic MPC. In: Chen, L., Li, N., Liang, K., Schneider, S. (eds.) ESORICS 2020. LNCS, vol. 12309, pp. 654–673. Springer, Cham (2020). https://doi.org/10.1007/978-3-030-59013-0_32
8. Damgård, I., Damgård, K., Nielsen, K., Nordholt, P.S., Toft, T.: Confidential benchmarking based on multiparty computation. In: Grossklags, J., Preneel, B. (eds.) FC 2016. LNCS, vol. 9603, pp. 169–187. Springer, Heidelberg (2017). https://doi.org/10.1007/978-3-662-54970-4_10

9. Damgård, I., Keller, M., Larraia, E., Pastro, V., Scholl, P., Smart, N.P.: Practical covertly secure MPC for dishonest majority – or: breaking the SPDZ limits. In: Crampton, J., Jajodia, S., Mayes, K. (eds.) ESORICS 2013. LNCS, vol. 8134, pp. 1–18. Springer, Heidelberg (2013). https://doi.org/10.1007/978-3-642-40203-6_1

10. Damgård, I., Pastro, V., Smart, N., Zakarias, S.: Multiparty computation from somewhat homomorphic encryption. In: Safavi-Naini, R., Canetti, R. (eds.) CRYPTO 2012. LNCS, vol. 7417, pp. 643–662. Springer, Heidelberg (2012). https://doi.org/10.1007/978-3-642-32009-5_38

11. Dowling, B., Fischlin, M., Günther, F., Stebila, D.: A cryptographic analysis of the TLS 1.3 handshake protocol. Cryptology ePrint Archive, Report 2020/1044 (2020)

12. Dworkin, M.: Recommendation for block cipher modes of operation: galois/counter mode (GCM) and GMAC. Technical report (2007)

13. Furukawa, J., Lindell, Y., Nof, A., Weinstein, O.: High-throughput secure three-party computation for malicious adversaries and an honest majority. In: Coron, J.-S., Nielsen, J.B. (eds.) EUROCRYPT 2017. LNCS, vol. 10211, pp. 225–255. Springer, Cham (2017). https://doi.org/10.1007/978-3-319-56614-6_8

14. Grassi, L., Rechberger, C., Rotaru, D., Scholl, P., Smart, N.P.: MPC-friendly symmetric key primitives. In: ACM CCS 2016. ACM Press, October 2016

15. Hazay, C., Scholl, P., Soria-Vazquez, E.: Low cost constant round MPC combining BMR and oblivious transfer. In: Takagi, T., Peyrin, T. (eds.) ASIACRYPT 2017. LNCS, vol. 10624, pp. 598–628. Springer, Cham (2017). https://doi.org/10.1007/978-3-319-70694-8_21

16. Keller, M., Orsini, E., Rotaru, D., Scholl, P., Soria-Vazquez, E., Vivek, S.: Faster secure multi-party computation of AES and DES using lookup tables. In: Gollmann, D., Miyaji, A., Kikuchi, H. (eds.) ACNS 2017. LNCS, vol. 10355, pp. 229–249. Springer, Cham (2017). https://doi.org/10.1007/978-3-319-61204-1_12

17. Keller, M., Orsini, E., Scholl, P.: MASCOT: faster malicious arithmetic secure computation with oblivious transfer. In: ACM CCS 2016. ACM Press, October 2016

18. Krawczyk, H.: Cryptographic extraction and key derivation: the HKDF scheme. In: Rabin, T. (ed.) CRYPTO 2010. LNCS, vol. 6223, pp. 631–648. Springer, Heidelberg (2010). https://doi.org/10.1007/978-3-642-14623-7_34

19. Nielsen, J.B., Nordholt, P.S., Orlandi, C., Burra, S.S.: A new approach to practical active-secure two-party computation. In: Safavi-Naini, R., Canetti, R. (eds.) CRYPTO 2012. LNCS, vol. 7417, pp. 681–700. Springer, Heidelberg (2012). https://doi.org/10.1007/978-3-642-32009-5_40

20. Rescorla, E.: The transport layer security (TLS) protocol version 1.3. RFC 8446 (2018)

21. Rotaru, D., Smart, N.P., Stam, M.: Modes of operation suitable for computing on encrypted data. IACR Trans. Symm. Cryptol. (3) (2017)

22. Rotaru, D., Smart, N.P., Tanguy, T., Vercauteren, F., Wood, T.: Actively secure setup for SPDZ. Cryptology ePrint Archive, Report 2019/1300 (2019). https://eprint.iacr.org/2019/1300

23. Zhang, F., Maram, D., Malvai, H., Goldfeder, S., Juels, A.: DECO: liberating web data using decentralized Oracles for TLS. In: Proceedings of the 2020 ACM SIGSAC Conference on Computer and Communications Security (2020)

Noisy Simon Period Finding

Alexander May[ID], Lars Schlieper[✉][ID], and Jonathan Schwinger

Horst Görtz Institute for IT Security, Ruhr-University Bochum, Bochum, Germany
{alex.may,lars.schlieper,jonathan.schwinger}@rub.de

Abstract. Let $f : \mathbb{F}_2^n \to \mathbb{F}_2^n$ be a Boolean function with period **s**. It is well-known that Simon's algorithm finds **s** in time polynomial in n on quantum devices that are capable of performing error-correction. However, today's quantum devices are inherently noisy, too limited for error correction, and Simon's algorithm is not error-tolerant.

We show that even noisy quantum period finding computations may lead to speedups in comparison to purely classical computations. To this end, we implemented Simon's quantum period finding circuit on the 15-qubit quantum device IBM Q 16 Melbourne. Our experiments show that with a certain probability $\tau(n)$ we measure erroneous vectors that are not orthogonal to **s**. We propose new, simple, but very effective smoothing techniques to classically mitigate physical noise effects such as e.g. IBM Q's bias towards the 0-qubit.

After smoothing, our noisy quantum device provides us a statistical distribution that we can easily transform into an LPN instance with parameters n and $\tau(n)$. Hence, in the noisy case we may not hope to find periods in time polynomial in n. However, we may still obtain a quantum advantage if the error $\tau(n)$ does not grow too large. This demonstrates that quantum devices may be useful for period finding, even before achieving the level of full error correction capability.

Keywords: Noise-tolerant simon period finding · IBM-Q16 · LPN · Quantum advantage

1 Introduction

The discovery of Shor's quantum algorithm [24] for factoring and computing discrete logarithms in 1994 had a dramatic impact on public-key cryptography, initiating the fast growing field of post-quantum cryptography that studies problems supposed to be hard even on quantum computers, such as e.g. Learning Parity with Noise (LPN) [3] and Learning with Errors (LWE) [21].

For some decades, the common belief was that the impact of quantum algorithms on symmetric crypto is way less dramatic, since the effect of Grover search can easily be handled by doubling the key size. However, starting with

---

See arXiv [19] for a full version.

A. May and L. Schlieper—Funded by DFG under Germany's Excellence Strategy - EXC 2092 CASA - 390781972.

© Springer Nature Switzerland AG 2021
K. G. Paterson (Ed.): CT-RSA 2021, LNCS 12704, pp. 75–99, 2021.
https://doi.org/10.1007/978-3-030-75539-3_4

the initial work of Kuwakado, Morii [17] and followed by Kaplan, Leurent, Leverrier and Naya-Plasencia [15] it was shown that (among others) the well-known Even-Mansour construction can be broken with quantum CPA-attacks [5] in polynomial time using Simon's quantum period finding algorithm [25]. This is especially interesting, because Even and Mansour [12] proved that in the ideal cipher model any classical attack on their construction with n-bit keys requires $\Omega(2^{\frac{n}{2}})$ steps.

These results triggered a whole line of work that studies the impact of Simon's algorithm and its variants for symmetric key cryptography, including e.g. [2, 6–8,14,18,22]. In a nutshell, Simon's quantum circuit produces for a periodic function $f : \mathbb{F}_2^n \to \mathbb{F}_2^n$ with period $\mathbf{s} \in \mathbb{F}_2^n$, i.e. $f(\mathbf{x}) = f(\mathbf{z})$ iff $\mathbf{z} \in \{\mathbf{x}, \mathbf{x} + \mathbf{s}\}$, via quantum measurements uniformly distributed vectors $\mathbf{y}$ that are orthogonal to $\mathbf{s}$. It is not hard to see that from a basis of $\mathbf{y}$'s that spans the subspace orthogonal to $\mathbf{s}$, the period $\mathbf{s}$ can be computed via elementary linear algebra in time polynomial in n. Thus, Simon's algorithm finds the period with a linear number of quantum measurements (and calls to f), and some polynomial time classical post-processing. On any purely classical computer however, finding the period of f requires in general $\Omega(2^{\frac{n}{2}})$ operations [20]. Let us stress again that we consider quantum CPA attacks via Simon, i.e. the attacker has access to a cipher that is implemented quantumly—a very powerful attack model.

Our Contributions. We implemented Simon's algorithm on IBM's freely available Q16 MELBOURNE [1], called IBM-Q16 in the following, that realizes 15-qubit quantum circuits. Since Simon's quantum circuit requires for n-bit periodic functions $2n$ qubits, we were able to implement functions up to $n = 7$ bits. Due to its limited size, IBM-Q16 is not capable of performing full error correction [9] for $n > 1$. However, we show that error correction is no necessary requirement for achieving quantum speedups.

Implementation. Our experiments show that with some (significant) error probability τ, we measure on IBM-Q16 vectors $\mathbf{y}$ that are *not orthogonal* to $\mathbf{s}$. The error probability τ depends on many factors, such as the number of 1- and 2-qubit gates that we use to realize Simon's circuit, IBM-Q16's topology that allows only limited 2-qubit applications, and even the individual qubits that we use. We optimize our Simon implementation to achieve minimal error τ. Since increasing n requires an increasing amount of gates, we discover experimentally that $\tau(n)$ grows as a function of n. For the function f that we implemented, we found τ-values ranging between $\tau(2) = 0.09$ and $\tau(7) = 0.13$. We would like to stress that our choice of f is highly optimized to minimize IBM-Q16's error. Any realistic real-word cryptographic f would at the moment result in outputs close to random noise, i.e. with $\tau(n)$ close to $\frac{1}{2}$.

For our simple f despite the errors we still qualitatively observe the desired quantum effect: Vectors $\mathbf{y}$ orthogonal to $\mathbf{s}$ appear with significant larger probabilities than vectors not orthogonal to $\mathbf{s}$. Similar experimental observations have been achieved in Tame et al. [26].

Smoothing Techniques. In the error free case, Simon's circuit produces vectors that are uniformly distributed. However, on IBM-Q16 this is not the case. First, IBM-Q16's qubits have different noise level, hence different reliability. Second, we experimentally observe vectors with small Hamming weight more frequently, the measured qubits have a bias towards 0.

To mitigite both effects we introduce simple, but effective *smoothing techniques*. First, the quality of qubits can be averaged by introducing permutations that preserve the overall error probability τ. Second, the 0-bias can be removed by suitable addition of vectors, both quantumly and classically. In combination, our smoothing methods are effective in the sense that they provide a distribution where vectors orthogonal to **s** appear uniformly distributed with probability $1 - \tau$, and vectors not orthogonal to **s** appear uniformly distributed with probability τ. Note that our smoothing techniques do not reduce the overall error τ, but smooth the error distribution.

We call the problem of recovering $\mathbf{s} \in \mathbb{F}_2^n$ from such a distribution *Learning Simon with Noise* (LSN) with parameters n and τ. Notice that intuitively it should be hard to distinguish orthogonal vectors from non-orthogonal ones.

Hardness. We show that solving LSN with parameters n, τ is tightly polynomial time equivalent to solving the famous *Learning Parity with Noise* (LPN) problem with the same parameters n, τ. The core of our reduction shows that LSN samples coming from smoothed quantum measurements of Simon's circuit can be turned into perfectly distributed LPN samples, and vice versa. Hence, smoothed quantum measurements of Simon's circuit realize a *physical LPN oracle.*

From an error-tolerance perspective, our LPN-to-LSN reduction may at first sound quite negative, since it is commen belief that we cannot solve LPN (and thus also not LSN) in time polynomial in (n, τ)—not even on a quantum computer.

Error Handling. On the positive side, we may use the converse LSN-to-LPN reduction to handle errors from noisy quantum devices like IBM-Q16 via LPN-solving algorithms. Theoretically, the best algorithm for solving LPN with constant τ is the BKW-algorithm of Blum, Kalai and Wasserman [4] with time complexity $2^{\mathcal{O}\left(\frac{n}{\log(\frac{n}{\tau})}\right)}$. This already improves on the classical time $2^{\frac{n}{2}}$ for period finding.

Practically, the current LPN records with errors $\tau \in [0.09, 0.13]$—as observed in our IBM-Q16 experiments— are solved with variants of the algorithms POOLED GAUSS and WELL-POOLED GAUSS of Esser, Kübler, May [11]. We show that POOLED GAUSS solves LSN for $\tau \leq 0.292$ faster than classical period finding algorithms. WELL-POOLED GAUSS even improves on any classical period finding algorithm for all errors $\tau < \frac{1}{2}$.

WELL-POOLED GAUSS is able to handle errors in time 2^{cn}, where $c < \frac{1}{2}$ is constant for constant τ. For the error-free case $\tau = 0$, we obtain polynomial time as predicted by Simon's analysis. In the noisy case $0 < \tau < \frac{1}{2}$ we achieve exponential run time, yet still improve over purely classical computation. This indicates that we achieve *quantum advantage* for the Simon period finding problem on sufficiently large computers, even in the presence of errors: Our quantum oracle helps us in speeding up computation! But as opposed to the exponential speedup from the (unrealistic) error-free Simon setting $\tau = 0$, we obtain in the practically relevant noisy Simon setting $0 < \tau < \frac{1}{2}$ only a *polynomial speedup* with a polynomial of degree $\frac{1}{2c} > 1$.

Assume that in a possibly far future one could build a quantum device with 486 qubits performing Simon's circuit on a 243-bit *realistic real-world cryptographic* periodic function with error $\tau(486) = \frac{1}{8}$. Then our smoothed techniques could translate the noisy quantum data into an LPN-instance with $(n, \tau) = (243, \frac{1}{8})$. Such an LPN instance was solved in [11] on 64 threads in only 15 days, whereas classically period finding would require 2^{121} steps.

We would like to stress that our introduction of a simple error parameter τ is to indicate at which point in the future quantum devices may help to speed up Simon-based quantum cryptanalysis. We do not give any predictions how $\tau(n)$ behaves for future devices, nor for realistic cryptographic functions. This remains an open problem.

Our paper is organized as follows. In Sect. 2 we recall Simon's original quantum circuit, and already introduce our LSN Error Model. In Sect. 3 we run IBM-Q16 experiments, and show in Sect. 4 how to smooth the results of the quantum computations[1] such that they fit our error model. In Sect. 5 we show the polynomial time equivalence of LSN and LPN. In Sect. 6 we theoretically show that quantum measurements with error τ in combination with LPN-solvers outperform classical period finding for any $\tau < \frac{1}{2}$. Eventually, in Sect. 7 we experimentally extract periods from noisy IBM-Q16 measurements.

2   Simon's Algorithm in the Noisy Case

Notation. All logs in this paper are base 2. Let $\mathbf{x} \in \mathbb{F}_2^n$ denote a binary vector with coordinates $\mathbf{x} = (x_{n-1}, \dots, x_0)$ and Hamming weight $h(\mathbf{x}) = \sum_{i=0}^{n-1} x_i$. Let $\mathbf{0} \in \mathbb{F}_2^n$ be the vector with all-zero coordinates. We denote by $\mathcal{U}$ the uniform distribution over $\mathbb{F}_2$, and by $\mathcal{U}_n$ the uniform distribution over $\mathbb{F}_2^n$. If a random variable X is chosen from distribution $\mathcal{U}$, we write $X \sim \mathcal{U}$. We denote by Ber_τ the Bernoulli distribution for $\mathbb{F}_2$, i.e. a $0, 1$-valued $X \sim \text{Ber}_\tau$ with $\mathbb{P}[X = 1] = \tau$.

Two vectors $\mathbf{x}, \mathbf{y}$ are *orthogonal* if their inner product $\langle \mathbf{x}, \mathbf{y} \rangle :=$ $\sum_{i=0}^{n-1} x_i y_i \mod 2$ is 0, otherwise they are called *non-orthogonal*. Let $\mathbf{s} \in \mathbb{F}_2^n$. Then we denote the subspace of all vectors orthogonal to $\mathbf{s}$ as

$$\mathbf{s}^\perp = \left\{ \mathbf{x} \in \mathbb{F}_2^n \mid \langle \mathbf{x}, \mathbf{s} \rangle = 0 \right\}.$$

Let $Y = \{\mathbf{y}_1, \dots, \mathbf{y}_k\} \subseteq \mathbb{F}_2^n$. Then we define $Y^\perp = \{\mathbf{x} \mid \langle \mathbf{x}, \mathbf{y}_i \rangle = 0 \text{ for all } i\}$.

---

[1] IBM-Q16 data can be found in our supplementary material.

For a Boolean function $f : \mathbb{F}_2^n \rightarrow \mathbb{F}_2^n$ we denote its *universal (quantum) embedding* by

$$U_f : \mathbb{F}_2^{2n} \rightarrow \mathbb{F}_2^{2n} \text{ with } (\mathbf{x}, \mathbf{y}) \mapsto (\mathbf{x}, f(\mathbf{x}) + \mathbf{y}).$$

Notice that $U_f(U_f(\mathbf{x}, \mathbf{y})) = (\mathbf{x}, \mathbf{y})$.

Let $|x\rangle \in \mathbb{C}^2$ with $x \in \mathbb{F}_2$ be a qubit. We denote by H the *Hadamard function*

$$x \mapsto \frac{1}{\sqrt{2}}(|0\rangle + (-1)^x |1\rangle).$$

We briefly write H_n for the n-fold tensor product $H \otimes \ldots \otimes H$. Let $|x\rangle |y\rangle \in \mathbb{C}^4$ be a 2-qubit system. The **cnot** (controlled **not**) function is the universal embedding of the identity function, i.e. $|x\rangle |y\rangle \mapsto |x\rangle |x + y\rangle$. We call the first qubit $|x\rangle$ *control bit*, since we perform a **not** on $|y\rangle$ iff $x = 1$.

A *Simon function* is a periodic $(2 : 1)$-Boolean function defined as follows.

Definition 2.1 (Simon function/problem). *Let* $f : \mathbb{F}_2^n \rightarrow \mathbb{F}_2^n$. *We call* f *a Simon function if there exists some period* $\mathbf{s} \in \mathbb{F}_2^n \setminus \{\mathbf{0}\}$ *such that for all* $\mathbf{x} \neq \mathbf{y} \in \mathbb{F}_2^n$ *we have*

$$f(\mathbf{x}) = f(\mathbf{y}) \Leftrightarrow \mathbf{y} = \mathbf{x} + \mathbf{s}.$$

In Simon's problem *we have to find* $\mathbf{s}$ *given oracle access to* f.

In order to solve Simon's problem classically, we have to find some collision $\mathbf{x} \neq \mathbf{y}$ satisfying $f(\mathbf{x}) = f(\mathbf{y})$. It is well-known that this requires $\Omega(2^{\frac{n}{2}})$ function evaluations.

Simon's quantum algorithm [25], called SIMON (see Algorithm 1), solves Simon's problem with only $\mathcal{O}(n)$ function evaluations on a quantum circuit. It is known that on input $|0^n\rangle \otimes |0^n\rangle$ a measurement of the first n qubits

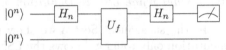

Fig. 1. Quantum circuit Q_f^{SIMON}

of the quantum circuit Q_f^{SIMON} depicted in Fig. 1 yields some $\mathbf{y} \in \mathbb{F}_2^n$ that is orthogonal to $\mathbf{s}$. Moreover, $\mathbf{y} \in \mathbb{F}_2^n$ is uniformly distributed in the subspace $\mathbf{s}^\perp$, i.e. we obtain each $\mathbf{y} \in \mathbf{s}^\perp$ with probability $\frac{1}{2^{n-1}}$. SIMON repeats to measure Q_f^{SIMON} until it has collected $n - 1$ linearly independent vectors $\mathbf{y}_1, \ldots, \mathbf{y}_{n-1}$, from which $\mathbf{s}$ can be computed via linear algebra in polynomial time. It is not hard to see that the collection of $n - 1$ linearly independent vectors requires only $\mathcal{O}(n)$ function evaluations.

At this point we should stress that SIMON only works for *noiseless* quantum computations. Hence we have to ensure that each $\mathbf{y}$ is indeed in $\mathbf{s}^\perp$. Assume that we obtain in line 4 of algorithm SIMON at least a single $\mathbf{y}$ with $\langle \mathbf{y}, \mathbf{s} \rangle = 1$. Then the output of SIMON is always false! Thus, SIMON is not robust against noisy quantum computations.

More precisely, if we obtain in line 4 erroneous $\mathbf{y} \notin \mathbf{s}^\perp$ with probability τ, $0 < \tau \leq \frac{1}{2}$, then SIMON outputs the correct $\mathbf{s}$ only with exponentially small probability success probability $(1-\tau)^n$. This motivates our following quite simple error model.

Algorithm 1: SIMON

Input : Simon function $f : \mathbb{F}_2^n \to \mathbb{F}_2^n$.
Output: Period $\mathbf{s} \in \mathbb{F}_2^n$
1 Set $Y = \emptyset$.
2 **repeat**
3 | Run Q_f^{SIMON} on $|0^n\rangle \otimes |0^n\rangle$.
4 | Let $\mathbf{y} \in \mathbb{F}_2^n$ be the measurement of the first n qubits.
5 | If $\mathbf{y} \notin \text{span}(Y)$, then include $\mathbf{y}$ in Y.
6 **until** $|Y| = n - 1$
7 Compute the unique $\mathbf{s} \in Y^\perp \setminus \{\mathbf{0}\}$.
8 **return** s.

Definition 2.2 (LSN Error Model). *Let $\tau \in \mathbb{R}$ with $0 \leq \tau \leq \frac{1}{2}$. Upon measuring the first n qubits of Q_f^{SIMON}, our quantum device outputs with probability $1 - \tau$ some uniformly random $\mathbf{y} \in \mathbf{s}^\perp$, and with probability τ some uniformly random $\mathbf{y} \in \mathbb{F}_2^n \setminus \mathbf{s}^\perp$. That is, the output distribution is*

$$\mathbb{P}[Q_f^{\text{SIMON}} \text{ outputs } \mathbf{y}] = \begin{cases} \frac{1-\tau}{2^{n-1}} & \text{if } \mathbf{y} \in \mathbf{s}^\perp \\ \frac{\tau}{2^{n-1}} & \text{else} \end{cases} . \tag{1}$$

We call τ the error rate *of our quantum device. We call the problem of computing $\mathbf{s}$ from the distribution in Equation (1) Learning Simon with Noise (LSN). We further refine LSN in Definition 5.2.*

In the subsequent Sect. 3 we show that the results of our IBM-Q16 implementation only roughly follows the LSN Error Model of Definition 2.2. However, we also introduce in Sect. 4 simple smoothing techniques such that the IBM-Q16 measurements can be transformed into almost perfectly matching our error model.

Notice that intuitively there is no efficient way to tell whether $\mathbf{y} \in \mathbf{s}^\perp$. This intuition is confirmed in Sect. 5, where we show that solving LSN is tightly as hard as solving the Learning Parity with Noise (LPN) problem.

3   Quantum Period Finding on IBM-Q16

We ran our experiments on the IBM-Q16 Melbourne device, which (despite its name) realizes 15-qubit circuits. Let us number IBM-Q16's qubits as $0, \ldots, 14$. Our implementation goal was to realize quantum period finding for Simon functions $f : \mathbb{F}_2^n \to \mathbb{F}_2^n$ with error rate as small as possible. To this end we used the following optimization criteria.

Gate Count. IBM-Q16 realizes several 1-qubit gates such as Hadamard and rotations, but only the 2-qubit gate **cnot**. On IBM-Q16, the application of any gates introduces some error, where especially the 2-qubit **cnot** introduces approximately as much error as ten 1-qubit gates (see Fig. 2). Therefore, we introduce a circuit norm that defines a weighted gate count, which we minimize in the following.

Definition 3.1. *Let Q be a quantum circuit with g_1 many 1-qubit gates and g_2 many 2-qubit gates. Then we define Q's circuit-norm as* $CN(Q) := g_1 + 10g_2$.

Topology. IBM-Q16 can only process 2-qubit gates on qubits that are adjacent in its topology graph, see Fig. 2. Let $G = (V, E)$ be the undirected topology graph, where node i denotes qubit i.

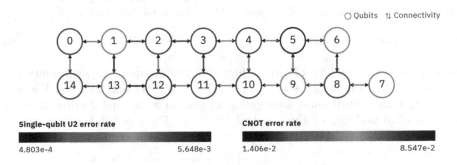

Fig. 2. Topology graph $G(V, E)$ of IBM-Q16.

If $\{u, v\} \in E$ then we can directly implement $\mathbf{cnot}(u, v)$, respectively $\mathbf{cnot}(v, u)$, where u, respectively v, serves as the control bit. Hence, we call qubits u, v *adjacent* iff $\{u, v\} \in E$.

Let us assume that we want to realize $\mathbf{cnot}(1, 3)$ in our algorithm. Since $\{1, 3\} \notin E$ we may first swap the contents of qubits 2 and 3 by realizing a **swap** gate via 3 **cnot**s as depicted in Fig. 3. Thus, with a total of 3 **cnot**s we swap the content of qubit 3 into 2. Since $\{1, 2\} \in E$, we may now apply $\mathbf{cnot}(1, 2)$.

Fig. 3. Realisation of **swap** via 3 **cnot**s.

3.1 Function Choice

Notice that in Definition 2.1 of Simon's problem, we obtain oracle access to a Simon function f. In a quantum-CPA attack we assume that a cryptographic function f is realized via its quantum embedding U_f. An attacker gets black-box access to U_f, i.e. he can query U_f on inputs of his choice in superposition.

We choose the following function $f_{\mathbf{s}}$ whose $U_{f_{\mathbf{s}}}$ is not too expensive to realize on IBM-Q16.

Definition 3.2. *Let* $s \in \mathbb{F}_2^n \setminus \{0\}$, *and let* $i \in [0, n-1]$ *be the smallest* i *with* $s_i = 1$. *We define*

$$f_s : \mathbb{F}_2^n \to \mathbb{F}_2^n, \quad \mathbf{x} \mapsto \mathbf{x} + x_i \cdot \mathbf{s}.$$

Let us first show that f_s is indeed a Simon function as given in Definition 2.1. Moreover, we show that *every* Simon function – no matter whether it is efficiently computable or not – is of the form f_s followed by some permutation.

Lemma 3.1. *Let* $f_s(\mathbf{x}) = \mathbf{x} + x_i \cdot \mathbf{s}$ *as in Definition 3.2. Then the following holds.*

(1) f_s is a Simon function with period $\mathbf{s}$, *i.e. $f_s(\mathbf{x}) = f_s(\mathbf{y})$ iff* $\mathbf{y} \in \{\mathbf{x}, \mathbf{x} + \mathbf{s}\}$.
(2) Any Simon function is of the form $P \circ f_s$ *for some bijection* $P : \mathbb{F}_2^n \to \mathbb{F}_2^n$.

Proof. See full version [19]. □

Instantiation of Function Choice. Throughout the paper, we instantiate our function f_s with the period $\mathbf{s} = (s_{n-1}, \ldots, s_0) = 0^{n-2}11$ and $x_i = x_0$. We may realize f_s with n **cnot**-gates for copying $\mathbf{x}$, and an additional 2 **cnot**-gates for the controlled addition of $\mathbf{s}$ via control bit 0. See Fig. 4 for an implementation of f_s with $n = 3$.

Our function choice has the advantage that it can be implemented with only $n+2$ **cnot** gates (if we are able to avoid **swaps**). In addition, we need $2n$ Hadamards for realizing SIMON. Thus we obtain a small circuit norm $CN = 10(n+2) + 2n$, which in turn implies a relatively small error on IBM-Q16. We perform further circuit norm minimization in Sect. 3.2.

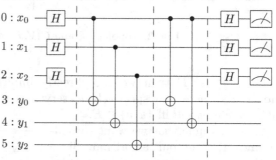

Fig. 4. Simon circuit Q_1 with our realization of f_s and $CN(Q_1) = 56$. The first 3 **cnots** copy $\mathbf{x}$, the remaining two **cnots** add $\mathbf{s} = 110$.

Discussion of our Simple Function Choice. As shown in Lemma 3.1, our function f_s is general in the sense that any Simon function is of the form $g = P \circ f_s(\mathbf{x})$. However, for obtaining small circuit norm we instantiate our Simon function with the simplest choice, where P is the identity function. In general, we could instantiate non-trivial P via some variable-length PRF with fixed key such as SiMeck [27]. This would however result in an explosion of the circuit norm and therefore in an explosion of IBM-Q16's noise rate $\tau(n)$.

Thus, SIMON with a general Simon function could be implemented as depicted in Fig. 5, where the permutation P is quantumly implemented in-place on the last n qubits (with at most one ancilla bit as shown in [23]). But already from Fig. 5 one observes that P does not at all effect the SIMON algorithm. In fact, SIMON outputs the measurement of the first n qubits, which only depend on which arguments $\mathbf{x}, \mathbf{x+s}$ collide under $f_\mathbf{s}$, but *not* which function value $f_\mathbf{s}(\mathbf{x}) = f_\mathbf{s}(\mathbf{x+s})$ they take (which is controlled by P). So, quantumly the choice of a non-trivial P would just unnecessarily increase the error rate τ.

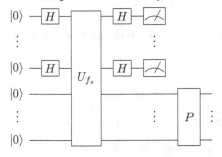

Fig. 5. SIMON with a general Simon function $P \circ f_\mathbf{s}$.

However, we would like to point out that choosing P as the identity function implies that classically extract the period $\mathbf{s}$ is *not hard*. Notice that $f_\mathbf{s}(\mathbf{x}) \in \{\mathbf{x}, \mathbf{x} + \mathbf{s}\}$. Thus, we may compute $f_\mathbf{s}(1^n) + 1^n = \mathbf{s}$. The reason that $f_\mathbf{s}(\mathbf{x})$ classically reveals its period so easily is that the image $\mathbf{x} + \mathbf{s}$ together with the argument $\mathbf{x}$ directly gives us $\mathbf{s}$. This correlation between argument $\mathbf{x}$ and image $\mathbf{x} + \mathbf{s}$ is destroyed by a random P, which explains why in general period finding classically becomes as hard as collision finding.

However, as explained above, SIMON does *not profit* from a trivial P, since SIMON is oblivious to concrete function values.

3.2 Minimizing the Gate Count of $f_\mathbf{s}$

We may implement $f_\mathbf{s}$ on IBM-Q16 directly as the circuit Q_1 from Fig. 4. Since Q_1 uses 6 Hadamard- and 5 **cnot**-gates, we have circuit norm $\mathrm{CN}(Q_1) = 56$, but only when ignoring IBM-Q16's topology. As already discussed, IBM-Q16 only allows **cnots** between adjacent qubits in the topology graph $G = (V, E)$ of Fig. 2.

Thus, IBM-Q16 compiles Q_1 to Q_2 as depicted in Fig. 6. Let us check that Q_2 realizes the same circuit as Q_1, but only acts on adjacent qubits. Let $U_{f_\mathbf{s}} : \mathbb{F}_2^6 \to \mathbb{F}_2^6$ be the universal quantum embedding of $f_\mathbf{s}$ with $(\mathbf{x}, \mathbf{y}) \mapsto (\mathbf{x}, f_\mathbf{s}(\mathbf{x}) + \mathbf{y}) = \mathbf{x} + x_0\mathbf{s} + \mathbf{y}$. In $U_{f_\mathbf{s}}$ we first add each x_i to y_i via **cnots**, see Fig. 4. Thus, we have to make sure that each x_i is adjacent to its y_i. Second, we add $\mathbf{s} = 011$ via **cnots** controlled by x_0. Thus, we have to ensure that x_0 is adjacent to y_0 and y_1.

We denote by $i : j$ that qubit i contains the value j. This allows us to define the starting *configuration* as

$$0 : x_0 \quad 1 : x_1 \quad 2 : x_2 \quad 3 : y_0 \quad 4 : y_1 \quad 5 : y_2.$$

Step 1 of Q_2 (see Fig. 4) performs **swap**$(2, 3)$ and thus results in configuration

$$0 : x_0 \quad 1 : x_1 \quad 2 : y_0 \quad 3 : x_2 \quad 4 : y_1 \quad 5 : y_2.$$

Step 2 of C_2 performs **swap**$(1, 2)$ as well as **swap**$(4, 3)$. This results in configuration

$$0 : x_0 \quad 1 : y_0 \quad 2 : x_1 \quad 3 : y_1 \quad 4 : x_2 \quad 5 : y_2.$$

Since $\{0,1\}, \{2,3\}, \{4,5\} \in E$, in Step 3 we now compute $\mathbf{cnot}(0,1)$, $\mathbf{cnot}(2,3)$ and $\mathbf{cnot}(4,5)$. This realizes the computation of $\mathbf{x} + \mathbf{y}$. Eventually, Step 4 of C_2 performs $\mathbf{swap}(0,1)$ and $\mathbf{swap}(2,3)$ resulting in

$$0 : y_0 \quad 1 : x_0 \quad 2 : y_1 \quad 3 : x_1 \quad 4 : x_2 \quad 5 : y_2.$$

For realizing the addition of $x_i \cdot \mathbf{s} = x_0 \cdot 011$, in Step 5 we compute $\mathbf{cnot}(1,0)$ and $\mathbf{cnot}(1,2)$ using $\{0,1\}, \{1,2\} \in E$.

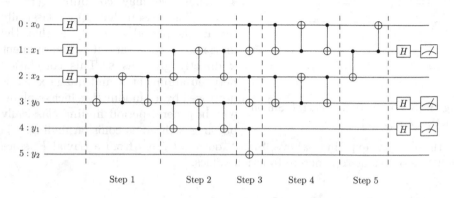

Fig. 6. IBM-Q16 compiles Q_1 to Q_2 with $CN(Q_2) = 206$.

In total Q_2 consumes six 1-bit gates and twenty 2-bit gates and thus has $CN(Q_2) = 206$, as compared to $CN(Q_1) = 56$. In the following, our goal is the construction of a quantum circuit that implements Q_1's functionality with minimal circuit norm on IBM-Q16.

In Fig. 7 we start with circuit Q_3, for which our optimization eventually results in circuit Q_4 (Fig. 10) that can be realized on IBM-Q16 with gate count only $CN(Q_4) = 33$.

From the discussion before, it should not be hard to see that Q_3 realizes $Q_{f_{\mathbf{s}}}^{\text{SIMON}}$, but yet it has to be optimized for IBM-Q16. First of all observe that $\mathbf{cnot}$ is self-inverse, and thus we can eliminate the two $\mathbf{cnot}(2,3)$ gates. Afterwards, we can

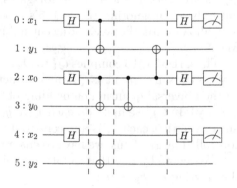

Fig. 7. Circuit Q_3.

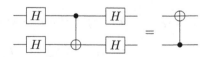

Fig. 8. Control bit change.

safely remove qubit 3. The resulting situation for qubits $0, 1, 2$ is depicted in Fig. 9, where we use a control bit change (see Fig. 8).

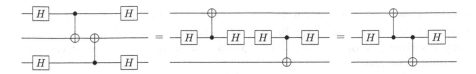

Fig. 9. Optimization of Q_3.

From Fig. 9 we see that the change of control bits from $\mathbf{cnot}(0,1)$, $\mathbf{cnot}(2,1)$ to $\mathbf{cnot}(1,0)$, $\mathbf{cnot}(1,2)$ leads to some cancellation of self-inverse Hadamard gates. Moreover, the second Hadamard of qubit 1 can be eliminated, since it does not influence the measurement. We end up with circuit Q_4 with an optimized gate count of $\mathrm{CN}(Q_4) = 33$.

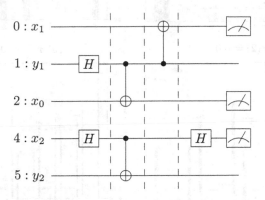

Fig. 10. Optimized circuit Q_4 on IBM-Q16 with $\mathrm{CN}(Q_4) = 33$.

Since $\{0,1\}, \{1,2\}, \{4,5\} \in E$, all three **cnots** of Q_4 can directly be realized on IBM-Q16. Notice that a configuration with optimal circuit norm is in general not unique. For our example, the following configuration yields the same circuit norm as the configuration of Q_4:

$$3 : y_0 \quad 4 : x_0 \quad 5 : y_1 \quad 6 : x_1 \quad 8 : y_2 \quad 9 : x_2.$$

We optimized our IBM-Q16 implementation by choosing among all configurations with minimal circuit norm the one using IBM-Q16's qubits of smallest error rate (see Fig. 2). The choice of our configurations and a complete list of optimized circuits with this configurations can be found in the full version [19].

3.3 Experiments on IBM Q 16

For each dimension $n = 2, \ldots, 7$ we took 8192 measurements on IBM-Q16 of our optimized circuits from the previous section. The resulting relative frequencies are depicted in Fig. 11. For each n, let $S(n)$ denote the set of erroneous measurements in $\mathbb{F}_2^n \setminus \mathbf{s}^\perp$. Then we compute the error rate $\tau(n)$ as $\tau(n) = \frac{|S(n)|}{8192}$. In Fig. 11 we draw horizontal lines $\frac{1-\tau(n)}{2^{n-1}}$, respectively $\frac{\tau(n)}{2^{n-1}}$, for the probability distributions of our LSN Error Model for orthogonal, respectively non-orthogonal, vectors.

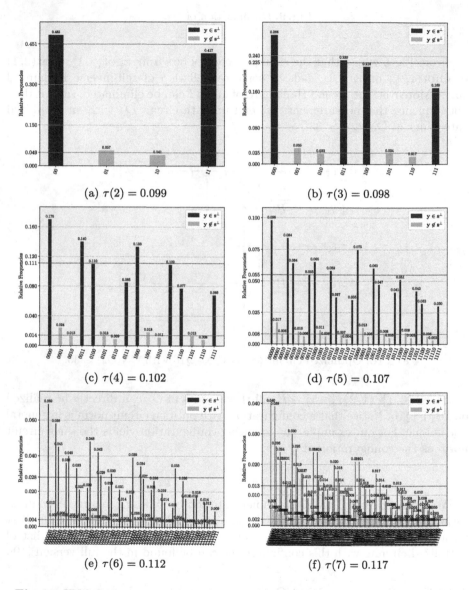

(a) $\tau(2) = 0.099$

(b) $\tau(3) = 0.098$

(c) $\tau(4) = 0.102$

(d) $\tau(5) = 0.107$

(e) $\tau(6) = 0.112$

(f) $\tau(7) = 0.117$

Fig. 11. IBM-Q16 measurements of our optimized circuits (see full version [19]).

On the positive side, we observe that vectors in $\mathbf{s}^\perp$ are much more frequent. Hence, IBM-Q16 is noisy, but in principle works well for period finding. E.g. for $n = 3$, we have $\{\mathbf{s}\}^\perp = \{011\}^\perp = \{000, 011, 100, 111\}$, and we measure one of these vectors with probability $1 - \tau \approx 90\%$.

On the negative side, we observe the following effects.

- **Different Qubit Quality.** We deliberately ordered our qubits by error rate to make the quality effect visible. Using the IBM-Q16 calibration, we choose lowest error rate for the least significant bit x_0 up to highest error rate for the most significant bit x_{n-1} (nevertheless e.g. for $n = 4$ it seems that the qubit for x_2 performed worse than the one for x_3).
- **Bias Towards 0.** In Fig. 11 we ordered our measurements on the x-axis lexicographically. It can be observed that in general measurements with small Hamming weight appear with larger frequencies than large Hamming weight measurements. This indicates a bias towards the $|0\rangle$ qubit, which seems to be a natural physical effect since $|0\rangle$ is a non-activated ground state.
- **Increasing $\tau(n)$.** The error rate $\tau(n)$ is a function increasing in n. This is what we expected, since the circuit norm increases with n, and for larger n we also had to include lower quality qubits.

Remark 3.1. We experimented with different periodic $f_\mathbf{s}$, especially more complex than our choice from Definition 3.2. Qualitatively, we observed similar effects albeit with larger error rates $\tau(n)$.

The effects of *different qubit quality* and *bias towards* 0 obviously violate our LSN Error Model from Definition 2.2, since they destroy the uniform distribution among orthogonal, respectively non-orthogonal, vectors. However, we introduce in the subsequent Sect. 4 simple smoothing technique that (almost perfectly) mitigate both effects.

4 Smoothing Techniques

Let us first introduce a simple permutation technique that mitigates the *different qubit quality*.

Permutation Technique. We already saw in Sect. 3.2 that configurations for some quantum circuit C with minimal circuit norm are not unique. Let M be the set of configurations with minimal circuit norm, including all permutations of qubits. Then we may perform measurements for circuits randomly chosen from M, see Algorithm 2. This approach averages over the qubit quality, while due to its invariant circuit norm preserving the error rate $\tau(n)$.

Algorithm 2: Permutation Technique.

1 Let $M :=$ {Configurations of C with minimal circuit norm}.
2 Evaluate C with configurations chosen randomly from M.

Instantiation of M in Our Experiments. First we chose a set of of highest quality qubits $\{i_1, \ldots, i_{2n-1}\}$ together with a starting configuration with minimal circuit norm. Let this be

$$i_1 : x_0 \quad i_2 : x_1 \quad i_3 : y_1 \quad i_4 : x_2 \quad \ldots \quad i_{2n-2} : x_{n-1} \quad i_{2n-1} : y_{n-1}.$$

We then chose $b \sim \mathcal{U}$ and a random permutations π on $\{2, \ldots, n-1\}$. This gives us circuit-norm preserving configurations

$$i_1 : x_b \quad i_2 : x_{1-b} \quad i_3 : y_1 \quad i_4 : x_{\pi(2)} \quad \ldots \quad i_{2n-2} : x_{\pi(n-1)} \quad i_{2n-1} : y_{\pi(n-1)}.$$

We took 50 circuit-norm preserving configurations, and for each we performed 8192 measurements on IBM-Q16.

The experimental results of our Permuation Technique are illustrated for $n = 5$ in Fig. 13b. In comparison, we have in Fig. 13a the unsmoothed distribution for 8192 measurements of a single optimal configuration (as in Fig. 11). We already see a significant distribution smoothing, especially vectors with the same Hamming weight obtain similar probabilities. But of course, there is still a clear *bias towards 0*, which cannot be mitigated by permutations.

Double-Flip Technique. To mitigate the effect that vectors with small Hamming weight are measured more frequently than vectors with large Hamming weight, we flip in Simon's circuit all bits via NOT-gates X before measurement, see Fig. 12. This flipping inverts the bias towards 0 that comes from the quantum measurement (not from the previous quantum computation). Since after flipping we measure the complement, we have to again flip all bits (classically) after measurement and combine them with the original measurements.

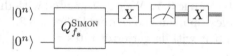

Fig. 12. Double-Flip circuit Q_{DF}. Triple lines represent classical wires.

Experimental Results and Discussion. We performed 8192 measurements with circuit Q_{DF} from Fig. 12, the results are illustrated in Fig. 13c. As expected, we now obtain a bias towards 1. Hence, in the *Double-Flip Technique* we put together the original measurements with 0-bias from Fig. 13a and the flipped measurements with 1-bias from Fig. 13c, resulting in the smoothed distribution from Fig. 13d.

From Fig. 13d we already see that the Double-Flip Technique is quite effective. Moreover, similar to the Permutation Technique, Double-Flip is a general smoothing technique that can be applied for other quantum circuits as well. However, there is also a significant drawback of Double-Flip, since it requires additional (small) quantum circuitry for performing X. Thus, as opposed to the Permutation Technique the Double-Flip does not preserve circuit norm. This implies that it slightly increases the error rate τ, as we will see in Sect. 4.1, where we study more closely the quality of our smoothing techniques.

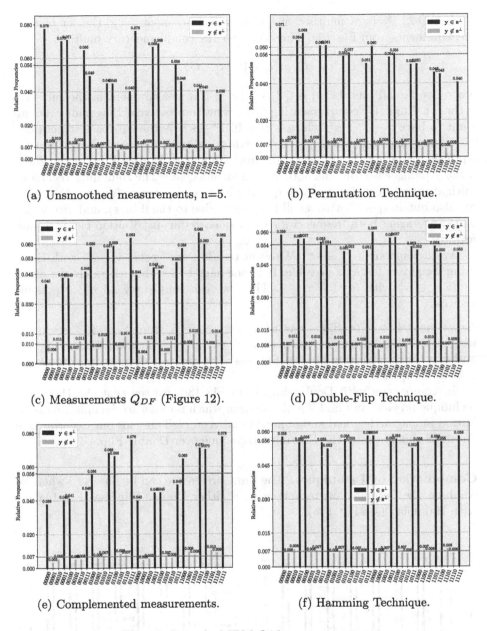

(a) Unsmoothed measurements, n=5.

(b) Permutation Technique.

(c) Measurements Q_{DF} (Figure 12).

(d) Double-Flip Technique.

(e) Complemented measurements.

(f) Hamming Technique.

Fig. 13. Smoothed IBM-Q16 measurements.

Hamming Technique. The Hamming Technique is similar to the Double-Flip Technique, but as opposed to Double-Flip Hamming is specific to Simon-type problems and a purely classical post-processing of data without adding any additional circuitry.

Let $Q \subseteq \mathbb{F}_2^n$ be a multiset of quantum measurements, e.g. the set of 8192 measurements from Fig. 13a. Then consider the complementary multiset

$$\bar{Q} = \{\mathbf{q} + 1^n \mid \mathbf{q} \in Q\},$$

where we flip all bits. Let $\mathbf{q} \in Q \cap \mathbf{s}^\perp$, i.e. $\mathbf{q}$ is a measurement in the subspace orthogonal to $\mathbf{s}$. By complementing Q we want to preserve orthogonality, i.e. we want to have $\mathbf{q} + 1^n \in \mathbf{s}^\perp$ which is true iff $1^n \in \mathbf{s}^\perp$ by the subspace structure.

Thus, complementation preserves orthogonality iff $1^n \in \mathbf{s}^\perp$, which is in turn equivalent to even Hamming weight $h(\mathbf{s})$. Similar to Double-Flip, in the *Hamming Technique* we combine both measurements $Q \cup \bar{Q}$. The Hamming Technique mitigates the effect that for each $\mathbf{q} \in Q$ with large frequency (due to the 0-bias) we also obtain $\mathbf{q} + 1^n$ with small frequency (due to the 0-bias), and vice versa. Thus, averaging both frequencies should smooth our distribution closer to uniformity.

What happens if $1^n \notin \mathbf{s}^\perp$? We want to add some vector $\mathbf{v} \in \mathbb{F}_2^n$ with Hamming weight as large as possible. It is not hard to see that there always exists some $\mathbf{v} \in \mathbf{s}^\perp$ with $h(\mathbf{v}) \geq n - 1$. Thus, we can simply try all $n + 1$ possible vectors.

Experimental Results. Since our instantiation of $f_\mathbf{s}$ from Sect. 3.1 uses even-weight periods $\mathbf{s}$, we can use the multiset $\bar{Q}$ (with 1^n), which was done in Fig. 13e and is a direct mirroring of Q in Fig. 13a. The multiset of measurement $Q \cup \bar{Q}$ is then depicted in Fig. 13f.

In comparison with Double-Flip from Fig. 13d, we see that the Hamming technique provides in Fig. 13f a distribution which is closer to the uniform distribution among orthogonal and non-orthonal vectors. Thus, for our experimental data one should prefer the Hamming technique over Double-Flip.

Combination of Techniques. The same preference can be observed when we combine the Permutation technique with either Double-Flip (see Fig. 14a) or with Hamming (see Fig. 14b).

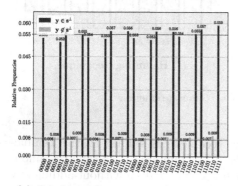 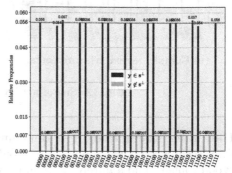

(a) Combined Permutation/Double-Flip   (b) Combined Permutation/Hamming

Fig. 14. Smoothing using a combination of techniques.

The combination Permutation/Hamming seems to outperform Permutation/ Double-Flip, and Permutation/Hamming almost optimally follows our LSN Error Model from Definition 2.2.

4.1 Quality Measures Statistics

Let us introduce a well-known statistical distance that quantitatively measures the effectiveness of our smoothing techniques. Recall that we require error distributions close to our LSN Error Model, in order to justify the proper use of LPN solvers in subsequent sections.

The Kullback-Leibler divergence describes the loss of information when going from a distribution P – e.g. our LSN Error Model distribution – to another distribution Q – e.g. our smoothed IBM-Q16 measurements.

Definition 4.1 (Kullback–Leibler divergence (KL)). *The Kullback-Leibler divergence of two probability distributions P towards Q on $\mathbb{F}_2^n$ is*

$$D_{KL}(P\|Q) := \sum_{y \in \mathbb{F}_2^n} P(Y) \log \left(\frac{P(y)}{Q(y)} \right) .$$

We compute KL and the error rate τ on the data from Figs. 13 and 14. The results are given in Table 1.

Table 1. Kullback–Leibler applied to our Smoothing Techniques.

Smoothing	Measure	
	KL	τ
None	0.04644	0.10730
Permutation	0.01596	0.10954
Double-Flip	0.00600	0.13104
Permutation/Double-Flip	0.00297	0.12044
Hamming	0.00139	0.10730
Permutation/Hamming	0.00011	0.10954

As we would expect for KL, Hamming is more effective than Double-Flip. Also as predicted, Double-Flip increases the error rate τ, whereas the other techniques leave τ (basically) unchanged. In particular, Hamming leaves τ unchanged, since it is only a classical post-processing of our quantum data. We have already seen qualitatively in Fig. 14 that the combination Permutation/Hamming performs best. This is supported also quantitatively in Table 1: KL is very close to zero, indicating that via Permutation/Hamming smoothed IBM-Q16 quantum measurements almost perfectly agree with the LSN Error Model.

The results of applying Permutation/Hamming to all $n = 2, \ldots, 7$ are depicted in Fig. 15.

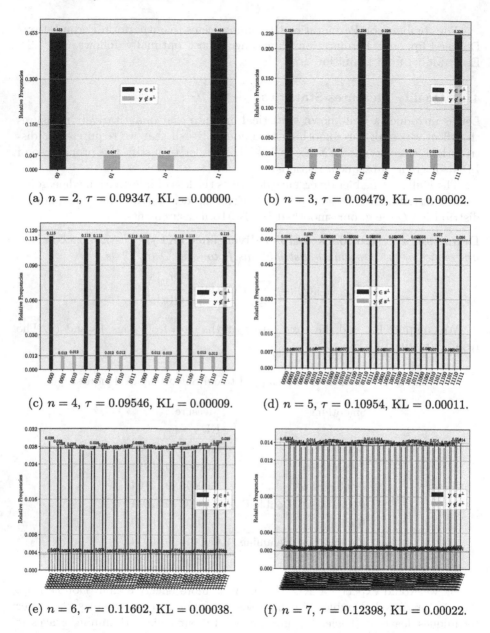

(a) $n = 2$, $\tau = 0.09347$, KL $= 0.00000$.   (b) $n = 3$, $\tau = 0.09479$, KL $= 0.00002$.

(c) $n = 4$, $\tau = 0.09546$, KL $= 0.00009$.   (d) $n = 5$, $\tau = 0.10954$, KL $= 0.00011$.

(e) $n = 6$, $\tau = 0.11602$, KL $= 0.00038$.   (f) $n = 7$, $\tau = 0.12398$, KL $= 0.00022$.

Fig. 15. Via Permutation/Hamming Technique smoothed IBM-Q16 measurements for $n = 2, \ldots, 7$. KL is the Kullback-Leibler divergence to the LSN Error Model distribution.

5   LSN is Polynomial Time Equivalent to LPN

In the previous section, we smoothed our IBM-Q16 experiments to the LSN Error Model (Definition 2.2). Recall that the LSN Error Model states that with probability τ we measure in the quantum circuit $Q_{f_s}^{\text{SIMON}}$ some uniformly distributed $\mathbf{y} \in \mathbb{F}_2^n \setminus \mathbf{s}^\perp$. The question is now whether such erroneous $\mathbf{y}$ as in our error model can easily be handled, i.e. whether LSN can be efficiently solved.

In this section, we answer this question in the negative. Namely, we show that solving LSN is tightly as hard as solving the well-studied LPN problem, which is supposed to be hard even on quantum computers.

Definition 5.1 (LPN-Problem). *Let* $\mathbf{s} \in \mathbb{F}_2^n \setminus \{\mathbf{0}\}$ *be chosen uniformly at random, and let* $\tau \in [0, \frac{1}{2})$. *In the* Learning Parity with Noise *problem, denoted* $LPN_{n,\tau}$, *one obtains access to an oracle* $\mathcal{O}_{LPN}(\mathbf{s})$ *that provides samples* $(\mathbf{a}, \langle \mathbf{a}, \mathbf{s} \rangle + \epsilon)$, *where* $\mathbf{a} \sim \mathcal{U}_n$ *and* $\epsilon \sim \text{Ber}_\tau$. *The goal is to compute* $\mathbf{s}$.

Definition 5.1 explicitly excludes $\mathbf{s} = \mathbf{0}$ in LPN. Notice that the case $\mathbf{s} = \mathbf{0}$ implies that the LPN oracle has distribution $U_n \times \text{Ber}_\tau$, whereas in the case $\mathbf{s} \neq \mathbf{0}$ we have $\mathbb{P}_{\mathbf{a}}[\langle \mathbf{a}, \mathbf{s} \rangle = 0] = \frac{1}{2}$ and therefore $\mathbb{P}_{\mathbf{a}}[\langle \mathbf{a}, \mathbf{s} \rangle + \epsilon = 0] = \frac{1}{2}$. Hence, for $\mathbf{s} \neq \mathbf{0}$ the LPN samples have distribution $U_n \times U$. This allows us to easily distinguish both cases by a majority test, whenever τ is polynomially bounded away from $\frac{1}{2}$. In conclusion, $\mathbf{s} = \mathbf{0}$ is not a hard case for LPN and may wlog be excluded.

Let us now define the related *Learning Simon with Noise* problem that reflects the LSN Error Model.

Definition 5.2 (LSN-Problem). *Let* $\mathbf{s} \in \mathbb{F}_2^n \setminus \{\mathbf{0}\}$ *be chosen uniformly at random, and let* $\tau \in [0, \frac{1}{2})$. *In the* Learning Simon with Noise *problem, denoted* $LSN_{n,\tau}$, *one obtains access to an oracle* $\mathcal{O}_{LSN}(\mathbf{s})$ *that provides samples* $\mathbf{y}$, *where* $\mathbf{y} \in \mathbb{F}_2^n$ *is distributed as in Definition 2.2, i.e.*

$$\mathbb{P}[\mathbf{y}] = \begin{cases} \frac{1-\tau}{2^{n-1}} & , \text{if } y \in \mathbf{s}^\perp \\ \frac{\tau}{2^{n-1}} & , \text{else} \end{cases} \quad \text{and therefore } \mathbb{P}[\langle \mathbf{y}, \mathbf{s} \rangle = 0] = 1 - \tau.$$

The goal is to compute $\mathbf{s}$.

In the following we prove that $LSN_{n,\tau}$ is polynomial time equivalent to $LPN_{n,\tau}$ by showing that we can perfectly mutually simulate $\mathcal{O}_{LPN}(\mathbf{s})$ and $\mathcal{O}_{LSN}(\mathbf{s})$. The purpose of excluding $\mathbf{s} \neq \mathbf{0}$ from $LPN_{n,\tau}$ is to guarantee in the reduction non-trivial periods $\mathbf{s} \neq \mathbf{0}$ in $LSN_{n,\tau}$.

Theorem 5.1 (Equivalence of LPN and LSN). *Let* $\mathcal{A}$ *be an algorithm that solves* $LPN_{n,\tau}$ *(respectively* $LSN_{n,\tau}$*) using* m *oracle queries in time* T *with success probability* $\epsilon_{\mathcal{A}}$. *Then there exists an algorithm* $\mathcal{B}$ *that solves* $LSN_{n,\tau}$ *(respectively* $LPN_{n,\tau}$*) using* m *oracle queries in time* T *with success probability* $\epsilon_{\mathcal{B}} \geq \frac{\epsilon_{\mathcal{A}}}{2}$.

Proof. See full version [19]. □

Theorem 5.1 shows that under the LPN assumption we cannot expect to solve LSN in polynomial time. However, it does not exclude that quantum measurements that lead to an LSN distribution are still useful in the sense that they help us to solve period finding faster than on classical computers. In the following section, we show that LSN distributed quantum outputs indeed lead to speedups even for large error rates τ.

6   Theoretical Error Handling for Simon's Algorithm

It is well-known [20] that period finding for n-bit Simon functions classically requires time $\Omega(2^{\frac{n}{2}})$. So despite the hardness results of Sect. 5 we may still hope that even error-prone quantum measurements lead to period finding speedups. Indeed, it is also known that for any fixed $\tau < \frac{1}{2}$ the BKW algorithm [4] solves

$\mathrm{LPN}_{n,\tau}$—and thus by Theorem 5.1 also $\mathrm{LSN}_{n,\tau}$—in time $2^{\mathcal{O}\left(\frac{n}{\log n}\right)}$. This implies that asymptotically the combination of LSN samples together with a suitable LPN-solver already outperforms classical period finding.

In this work, we focus on the LPN-solvers of Esser, Kübler, May [11] rather than the class of BKW-type solvers [4,10,13,16], since they have a simple description and runtime analysis, are easy to implement, have low memory consumption, are sufficiently powerful for showing quantum advantage even for large errors $\tau < \frac{1}{2}$, and finally they are practically best for the IBM-Q16 error rates $\tau \in [0.09, 0.13]$.

We start with the analysis of the POOLED GAUSS algorithm [11]. POOLED GAUSS solves $\mathrm{LPN}_{n,\tau}$ in time $\tilde{\Theta}\left(2^{\log\left(\frac{1}{1-\tau}\right)\cdot n}\right)$ using $\tilde{\Theta}\left(n^2\right)$ samples.

The following theorem shows that period finding with error-prone quantum samples in combination with POOLED GAUSS is superior to purely classical period finding whenever the error τ is bounded by $\tau \le 0.293$.

Theorem 6.1. *In the LSN Error Model (Definition 2.2),* POOLED GAUSS *finds the period* $\mathbf{s} \in \mathbb{F}_2^n$ *of a Simon function* $f_\mathbf{s}$ *using* $\tilde{\Theta}\left(n^2\right)$ *many* $\mathrm{LSN}_{n,\tau}$-*samples, coming from practical measurements of Simon's circuit* $Q_{f_\mathbf{s}}^{\mathrm{SIMON}}$ *with error rate* τ, *in time* $\tilde{\Theta}\left(2^{\log\left(\frac{1}{1-\tau}\right)\cdot n}\right)$. *This improves over classical period finding for error rates*

$$\tau < 1 - \frac{1}{\sqrt{2}} \approx 0.293.$$

Proof. See full version [19].   □

Theorem 6.1 already shows the usefulness of a quite limited quantum oracle that only allows us polynomially many measurements, whenever its error rate τ is small enough.

If we allow for more quantum measurements, the WELL-POOLED GAUSS algorithm [11] solves $\mathrm{LPN}_{n,\tau}$ in improved time and query complexity $\tilde{\Theta}(2^{f(\tau)n})$, where $f(\tau) = 1 - \frac{1}{1+\log\left(\frac{1}{1-\tau}\right)}$. The following theorem shows that WELL-POOLED GAUSS in combination with error-prone quantum measurements improves on classical period finding for *any* error rate τ.

Theorem 6.2. *In the LSN Error Model (Definition 2.2),* WELL POOLED GAUSS *finds the period* $\mathbf{s} \in \mathbb{F}_2^n$ *of a Simon function* $f_{\mathbf{s}}$ *using* $\tilde{\Theta}(2^{f(\tau)n})$ *many* $LSN_{n,\tau}$*-samples, coming from practical measurements of Simon's circuit* $Q_{f_{\mathbf{s}}}^{\text{SIMON}}$ *with error rate* τ*, in time* $\tilde{\Theta}(2^{f(\tau)n})$*, where*

$$f(\tau) = 1 - \frac{1}{1 + \log(\frac{1}{1-\tau})}.$$

This improves over classical period finding for all *error rates* $\tau < \frac{1}{2}$*.*

Proof. See full version [19]. □

The results of Theorem 6.1 and Theorem 6.2 show that quantum measurements of $Q_{f_{\mathbf{s}}}^{\text{SIMON}}$ help us (asymptotically) even for large error rates τ, provided that our error model is sufficiently accurate.

7 Practical Error Handling for Simon's Algorithm

In this section, we compare the practical runtimes needed to find periods $\mathbf{s}$ with the smoothed experimental data from our IBM-Q16 quantum measurements (see Fig. 15) with purely classical period finding.

Notice that our LPN-solvers incur some polynomial overhead, which makes them for very small n as on IBM-Q16 inferior to purely classical period finding. Moreover, we would like to stress the experimental result of Sect. 3 that IBM-Q16's error rate $\tau(n)$ is a function increasing in n. So even if asymptotically LPN-solvers outperform classical period finding, a fast convergence of $\tau(n)$ towards $\frac{1}{2}$ prevents practical quantum advantage.

Periods Classically. Let us start with the description of an optimal classical period finding algorithm, inspired by [20]. Naively, one may think that it is optimal to query f_s at different random points $\mathbf{x}_i$, until one hits the first collision $f_{\mathbf{s}}(\mathbf{x}_i) = f_{\mathbf{s}}(\mathbf{x}_j)$. However, assume that we have already queried the set of points $P = \{\mathbf{x}_1, \mathbf{x}_2, \mathbf{x}_3\}$, without obtaining a collision. This gives us the information that $\mathbf{s}$ is *not* in set of distances $D = \{\mathbf{x}_1 + \mathbf{x}_2, \mathbf{x}_2 + \mathbf{x}_3, \mathbf{x}_1 + \mathbf{x}_3\}$. This implies that we should not ask $\mathbf{x}_1 + \mathbf{x}_2 + \mathbf{x}_3$, since it lies at distance $\mathbf{x}_1 + \mathbf{x}_2$ of $\mathbf{x}_3$. Hence on optimal algorithm keeps track of the set D of all excluded distances. This is realized in our algorithm PERIOD, see Algorithm 3.

Periods Quantumly. By the result of Sect. 5 we may first transform our quantum measurements into LPN samples, and then use one of the LPN-solvers from Sect. 6. Since the error rates from our *smoothed* IBM-Q16 measurements (Fig. 15) are below $\frac{1}{8}$, according to Theorem 6.1 we may use POOLED GAUSS.

Instead of applying the LSN-to-LPN reduction to our smoothed data, we directly adapt POOLED GAUSS into an LSN-solver, called POOLED LSN (Algorithm 4). POOLED LSN can be considered as a fault-tolerant version of SIMON (Algorithm 1) that iterates until we obtain an error-free set of $n-1$ linearly independent vectors. Notice that error-freeness can be tested, since the resulting potential period $\mathbf{s}'$ is correct iff $f_{\mathbf{s}}(\mathbf{s}')=f_{\mathbf{s}}(\mathbf{0})$.

Algorithm 3: PERIOD

Input : Access to $f_{\mathbf{s}}$.
Output: Secret s.
1 **begin**
2   Set $P = \{(\mathbf{0}, f_{\mathbf{s}}(\mathbf{0}))\}$. $\triangleright$ `Set of queried points.`
3   Set $D = \{\mathbf{0}\}$. $\triangleright$ `Set of distances.`
4   **repeat**
5   Select $\mathbf{x} \in \operatorname{argmax}\{|\{\mathbf{s}' \in D \mid (\mathbf{x}+\mathbf{s}',\cdot) \notin P\}|\}$. $\triangleright$ `Optimal next query.`
6          $P := P \cup (\mathbf{x}, f_{\mathbf{s}}(\mathbf{x}))$ $\triangleright$ `Update queries.`
7   **for** $(\mathbf{x}', f_{\mathbf{s}}(\mathbf{x}')) \in P$ **do**
8              $D := D \cup \{\mathbf{x}+\mathbf{x}'\}$ $\triangleright$ `Update distances.`
9   **end**
10   **until** $\exists \mathbf{x}' \neq \mathbf{x} : (\mathbf{x}', f_{\mathbf{s}}(\mathbf{x})) \in P$ **or** $|D| = 2^n - 1$
11   **if** $|D| = 2^n - 1$ **then return** $\mathbf{s} \in \mathbb{F}_2^n \setminus D$. $\triangleright$ `Only possible period.`
12   **else return** $\mathbf{x}+\mathbf{x}'$. $\triangleright$ `Collision found.`
13 **end**

Algorithm 4: POOLED LSN

Input : Pool $P \subset \mathbb{F}_2^n$ of LSN samples with $|P| \geq n - 1$
Output: Secret s
1 **begin**
2   **repeat**
3   Randomly select a linearly independent set $Y = \{\mathbf{y}_1, \ldots, \mathbf{y}_{n-1}\} \subseteq P$.
4   Compute the unique $\mathbf{s}' \in Y^{\perp} \setminus \{\mathbf{0}\}$.
5   **until** $f_{\mathbf{s}}(\mathbf{s}') \stackrel{?}{=} f_{\mathbf{s}}(\mathbf{0})$
6   **return** $\mathbf{s}'$.
7 **end**

Run Time Comparison. PERIOD and POOLED LSN exponentially often iterate their **repeat**-loops, where each iteration runs in polynomial time (using the right data structure). Hence, asymptotically the number of iterations dominate runtimes for both algorithms. For ease of simplicity, we take as cost measure only the exponential number of loops, ignoring all polynomial factors (the polynomial factors actually dominate in practice for our small dimensions n).

Using this (over-)simplified loop cost measure, we ran 10.000 iterations of PERIOD for $n = 2, \ldots, 7$ and averaged over the runtimes. For the quantum period finding we took as pool P the complete smoothed data of Fig. 15. We then also ran 10.000 iterations of POOLED LSN for $n = 2, \ldots, 7$ and averaged over the runtimes. The resulting log-scaled runtimes are depicted in Fig. 16.

As expected, PERIOD's experimental runtime exponent is $\frac{n}{2}$. For POOLED LSN, we obtain an experimental regression line of roughly $\frac{n}{3}$, where the slope seems to decrease with n. This results in a cut-off point for the loop numbers between $n = 4$ and $n = 5$. Thus, experimentally we obtain quantum advantage, at least for our loop cost measure.

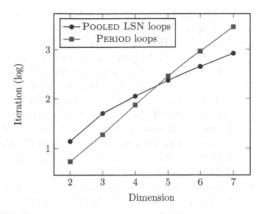

Fig. 16. Log-scaled loop iterations of POOLED LSN and PERIOD, averaged over 10.000 iterations.

References

1. 15-qubit backend: IBM Q team, "IBM Q 16 Melbourne backend specification V2.0.1," (2020). https://quantum-computing.ibm.com. Accessed 14 Jan 2020
2. Alagic, G., Russell, A.: Quantum-secure symmetric-key cryptography based on hidden shifts. In: Coron, J.-S., Nielsen, J.B. (eds.) EUROCRYPT 2017. LNCS, vol. 10212, pp. 65–93. Springer, Cham (2017). https://doi.org/10.1007/978-3-319-56617-7_3
3. Alekhnovich, M.: More on average case vs approximation complexity. In: 44th FOCS, pp. 298–307. IEEE Computer Society Press, October 2003
4. Blum, A., Kalai, A., Wasserman, H.: Noise-tolerant learning, the parity problem, and the statistical query model. In: 32nd ACM STOC, pp. 435–440. ACM Press, May 2000
5. Boneh, D., Zhandry, M.: Secure signatures and chosen ciphertext security in a quantum computing world. In: Canetti, R., Garay, J.A. (eds.) CRYPTO 2013. LNCS, vol. 8043, pp. 361–379. Springer, Heidelberg (2013). https://doi.org/10.1007/978-3-642-40084-1_21
6. Bonnetain, X.: Quantum key-recovery on full AEZ. In: Adams, C., Camenisch, J. (eds.) SAC 2017. LNCS, vol. 10719, pp. 394–406. Springer, Cham (2018). https://doi.org/10.1007/978-3-319-72565-9_20
7. Bonnetain, X., Hosoyamada, A., Naya-Plasencia, M., Sasaki, Yu., Schrottenloher, A.: Quantum attacks without superposition queries: the offline Simon's algorithm. In: Galbraith, S.D., Moriai, S. (eds.) ASIACRYPT 2019. LNCS, vol. 11921, pp. 552–583. Springer, Cham (2019). https://doi.org/10.1007/978-3-030-34578-5_20
8. Bonnetain, X., Naya-Plasencia, M.: Hidden shift quantum cryptanalysis and implications. In: Peyrin, T., Galbraith, S. (eds.) ASIACRYPT 2018, Part I. LNCS, vol. 11272, pp. 560–592. Springer, Heidelberg (2018)

9. Calderbank, A.R., Rains, E.M., Shor, P.W., Sloane, N.J.: Quantum error correction and orthogonal geometry. Phys. Rev. Lett. **78**(3), 405 (1997)

10. Esser, A., Heuer, F., Kübler, R., May, A., Sohler, C.: Dissection-BKW. In: Shacham, H., Boldyreva, A. (eds.) CRYPTO 2018. LNCS, vol. 10992, pp. 638–666. Springer, Cham (2018). https://doi.org/10.1007/978-3-319-96881-0_22

11. Esser, A., Kübler, R., May, A.: LPN decoded. In: Katz, J., Shacham, H. (eds.) CRYPTO 2017. LNCS, vol. 10402, pp. 486–514. Springer, Cham (2017). https://doi.org/10.1007/978-3-319-63715-0_17

12. Even, S., Mansour, Y.: A construction of a cipher from a single pseudorandom permutation. In: Imai, H., Rivest, R.L., Matsumoto, T. (eds.) ASIACRYPT 1991. LNCS, vol. 739, pp. 210–224. Springer, Heidelberg (1993). https://doi.org/10.1007/3-540-57332-1_17

13. Guo, Q., Johansson, T., Löndahl, C.: Solving LPN using covering codes. In: Sarkar, P., Iwata, T. (eds.) ASIACRYPT 2014. LNCS, vol. 8873, pp. 1–20. Springer, Heidelberg (2014). https://doi.org/10.1007/978-3-662-45611-8_1

14. Hosoyamada, A., Sasaki, Yu.: Cryptanalysis against symmetric-key schemes with online classical queries and offline quantum computations. In: Smart, N.P. (ed.) CT-RSA 2018. LNCS, vol. 10808, pp. 198–218. Springer, Cham (2018). https://doi.org/10.1007/978-3-319-76953-0_11

15. Kaplan, M., Leurent, G., Leverrier, A., Naya-Plasencia, M.: Breaking symmetric cryptosystems using quantum period finding. In: Robshaw, M., Katz, J. (eds.) CRYPTO 2016. LNCS, vol. 9815, pp. 207–237. Springer, Heidelberg (2016). https://doi.org/10.1007/978-3-662-53008-5_8

16. Kirchner, P., Fouque, P.-A.: An improved BKW algorithm for LWE with applications to cryptography and lattices. In: Gennaro, R., Robshaw, M. (eds.) CRYPTO 2015. LNCS, vol. 9215, pp. 43–62. Springer, Heidelberg (2015). https://doi.org/10.1007/978-3-662-47989-6_3

17. Kuwakado, H., Morii, M.: Security on the quantum-type even-mansour cipher. In: Proceedings of the International Symposium on Information Theory and its Applications, ISITA 2012, Honolulu, HI, USA, 28–31 October 2012, pp. 312–316 (2012). http://ieeexplore.ieee.org/document/6400943/

18. Leander, G., May, A.: Grover meets Simon–quantumly attacking the FX-construction. In: Takagi, T., Peyrin, T. (eds.) ASIACRYPT 2017. LNCS, vol. 10625, pp. 161–178. Springer, Cham (2017). https://doi.org/10.1007/978-3-319-70697-9_6

19. May, A., Schlieper, L., Schwinger, J.: Noisy simon period finding (2020). https://arxiv.org/abs/1910.00802

20. Montanaro, A., de Wolf, R.: A survey of quantum property testing. Theor. Comput. Grad. Surv. **7**, 1–81 (2016). https://doi.org/10.4086/toc.gs.2016.007

21. Regev, O.: On lattices, learning with errors, random linear codes, and cryptography. In: Gabow, H.N., Fagin, R. (eds.) 37th ACM STOC, pp. 84–93. ACM Press, May 2005

22. Santoli, T., Schaffner, C.: Using Simon's algorithm to attack symmetric-key cryptographic primitives. Quant. Inf. Comput. **17**(1&2), 65–78 (2017). http://www.rintonpress.com/xxqic17/qic-17-12/0065-0078.pdf

23. Shende, V.V., Prasad, A.K., Markov, I.L., Hayes, J.P.: Synthesis of reversible logic circuits. IEEE Trans. CAD Integr. Circ. Syst. **22**(6), 710–722 (2003). https://doi.org/10.1109/TCAD.2003.811448

24. Shor, P.W.: Algorithms for quantum computation: Discrete logarithms and factoring. In: 35th FOCS, pp. 124–134. IEEE Computer Society Press, November 1994

25. Simon, D.R.: On the power of quantum computation. In: 35th FOCS, pp. 116–123. IEEE Computer Society Press, November 1994
26. Tame, M.S., Bell, B.A., Di Franco, C., Wadsworth, W.J., Rarity, J.G.: Experimental realization of a one-way quantum computer algorithm solving Simon's problem. Phys. Rev. Lett. **113**, 200501, November 2014. https://link.aps.org/doi/10.1103/PhysRevLett.113.200501
27. Yang, G., Zhu, B., Suder, V., Aagaard, M.D., Gong, G.: The simeck family of lightweight block ciphers. In: Güneysu, T., Handschuh, H. (eds.) CHES 2015. LNCS, vol. 9293, pp. 307–329. Springer, Heidelberg (Sep (2015)

A Bunch of Broken Schemes: A Simple yet Powerful Linear Approach to Analyzing Security of Attribute-Based Encryption

Marloes Venema[1(✉)] and Greg Alpár[1,2]

[1] Radboud University, Nijmegen, The Netherlands
{m.venema,g.alpar}@cs.ru.nl
[2] Open University of the Netherlands, Heerlen, The Netherlands

Abstract. Verifying security of advanced cryptographic primitives such as attribute-based encryption (ABE) is often difficult. In this work, we show how to break eleven schemes: two single-authority and nine multi-authority (MA) ABE schemes. Notably, we break DAC-MACS, a highly-cited multi-authority scheme, published at TIFS. This suggests that, indeed, verifying security of complex schemes is complicated, and may require simpler tools. The multi-authority attacks also illustrate that mistakes are made in transforming single-authority schemes into multi-authority ones. To simplify verifying security, we systematize our methods to a linear approach to analyzing generic security of ABE. Our approach is not only useful in analyzing existing schemes, but can also be applied during the design and reviewing of new schemes. As such, it can prevent the employment of insecure (MA-)ABE schemes in the future.

Keywords: Attribute-based encryption · Cryptanalysis · Multi-authority attribute-based encryption · Attacks

1 Introduction

Attribute-based encryption (ABE) [30] is an advanced type of public-key encryption. Ciphertext-policy (CP) ABE [5] naturally implements a fine-grained access control mechanism, and is therefore often considered in applications involving e.g. cloud environments [22,23,26,37,38,40] or medical settings [25,27,29]. These applications of ABE allow the storage of data to be outsourced to potentially untrusted providers whilst ensuring that data owners can securely manage access to their data. Many such works use the multi-authority (MA) variant [8], which employs multiple authorities to generate and issue secret keys. These authorities can be associated with different organizations, e.g. hospitals, insurance companies or universities. This allows data owners, e.g. patients, to securely share their data with other users from various domains, e.g. doctors, actuaries or medical

© Springer Nature Switzerland AG 2021
K. G. Paterson (Ed.): CT-RSA 2021, LNCS 12704, pp. 100–125, 2021.
https://doi.org/10.1007/978-3-030-75539-3_5

researchers. Many new schemes are designed for specific real-world applications, that cannot be sufficiently addressed with existing schemes.

Unfortunately, proving and verifying security of new schemes are difficult, and, perhaps unsurprisingly, several schemes turn out to be broken. Some schemes were shown to be generically broken with respect to the basic functionality, and are therefore insecure. Others were only broken with respect to additional functionality. Table 1 shows that many of these schemes have been published at venues that include cryptography in their scope. This suggests that, even for cryptographers, it is difficult to verify security of ABE. In addition, many of these schemes are highly cited due to their focus on practical applications. This popularity shows that the claimed properties of these schemes are high in demand. It is thus important to simplify security analysis.

Table 1. Attacks on existing schemes. For each scheme, we list in which work it was broken, which functionality was attacked, and whether it was later fixed. Also, we provide the venue and number of citations for these schemes according to Google Scholar. These measures were taken on 18 November 2020.

Scheme	Broken in	Attacked functionality	Fixed?	Venue	Cit.
LRZW09 [21]	LHC+11 [20]	Private access policies	[20]	ISC	203
ZCL+13 [41]	CDM15 [9]			AsiaCCS	104
XFZ+14 [36]				NC	46
HSMY12 [12]	GZZ+13 [11]	Basic	U	NC	176
YJR+13 [40]	HXL15 [15]	Revocation	[35]	TIFS	474
	WJB17 [35]				
HSM+14 [13]	WZC15 [32]	Basic	U	ESORICS	30
HSM+15 [14]				TIFS	128
JLWW15 [17]	MZY16 [24]	Distributed key generation	[18]	TIFS	161

NC = non-crypto venue/journal; U = unknown

To simplify the design and analysis of complex primitives such as ABE, frameworks have been introduced [1,3,34] based on the common structure of many schemes. These frameworks allow for the analysis of the exponent space of the schemes—called *pair encoding*—with respect to simpler security notions. Interestingly, Agrawal and Chase [1] show that fully secure schemes can be constructed from pair encodings that are provably symbolically secure. Using this, they show that any scheme that is not trivially broken implies a fully secure scheme. Later, Ambrona et al. [2] expand their framework to a broader class of schemes, and devise automated tools to prove symbolic security, subsequently yielding provably secure schemes in the generic bilinear group model [6,7]. However, operating these tools still requires a considerable expertise (and in a different field). Additionally, these frameworks do not support practical extensions of ABE such as multi-authority ABE (MA-ABE).

In any case, these works illustrate that proving generic security of a scheme provides a meaningful first step in the analysis of a new scheme, and may even imply stronger notions of security. Conversely, showing that a scheme is *not* generically secure provides overwhelming evidence that a scheme is insecure, regardless of the underlying group structure or accompanying security proofs. As such, devising *manual* tools and heuristics to effectively analyze the generic (in)security of schemes may further contribute to these frameworks. That is, finding a generic attack—assuming that one exists—is often much simpler than verifying the correctness of a security proof. In fact, it is often the first step that an experienced cryptographer takes when designing a new scheme.

1.1   Our Contribution

We focus on simplifying the search for generic attacks (provided that they exist). In a broader context, our goal is not necessarily to attack existing schemes, but to propose a framework that simplifies the analysis—and by extension, design— of secure ABE schemes. We do this by systematizing a simple heuristic approach to finding attacks. Our contribution in this endeavor is twofold. First, we show that eleven schemes are vulnerable to generic attacks, rendering them (partially) insecure. Five of these are insecure in the basic security model. The other six are insecure in the multi-authority security model—which also allows for the corruption of one or more authorities—but are possibly secure if all authorities are assumed to be honest. Essentially, these six schemes provide a comparable level of security as single-authority schemes. Second, we systematize our methods to a linear approach to generic security analysis of ABE based on the common structure of many schemes. Similarly as the aforementioned frameworks, we consider the pair encodings of the schemes. To this end, we also formalize such pair encodings for multi-authority schemes. Furthermore, we describe three types of attacks, which model the implicit security requirements on the keys and ciphertexts, and simplify the search for generic attacks. They model whether the master-key of the/an authority can be recovered, or whether users can collude and decrypt ciphertexts that they cannot individually decrypt. In the multi-authority setting, we also model the notion of corruption.

1.2   Technical Details

Ciphertext-Policy ABE. In CP-ABE, ciphertexts are associated with access policies, and secret keys are associated with sets of attributes. A secret key is authorized to decrypt a ciphertext if its access structure is satisfied by the associated set. These secret keys are generated by a key generation authority (KGA) from a master-key, which can be used to decrypt any ciphertext. Users with keys for different sets of attributes should not be able to collude in collectively decrypting a ciphertext that they are individually not able to decrypt. Therefore, these keys need to be secure in two ways. First, the master-key needs to be sufficiently hidden in the secret keys. Second, combining the secret keys of different users should not result in more decryption capabilities.

A Brief Overview of the Attack Models. We propose three types of attacks, which all imply attacks on the security model for ABE. This model considers chosen-plaintext attacks (CPA) and collusion of users. Two of our attack models only consider the secret keys issued in the first key query phase of the security model, while the third model also considers the challenge ciphertext. Informally, the attacks are:

- **Master-key attack (MK):** The attacker can extract the KGA's master-key, which can be used to decrypt any ciphertext.
- **Attribute-key attack (AK):** The attacker can generate a secret key for a set $\mathcal{S}'$ that is strictly larger than each set $\mathcal{S}_i$ associated with an issued key.
- **Decryption attack (D):** The attacker can decrypt a ciphertext for which no authorized key was generated.

In addition, we distinguish complete from conditional decryption attacks. Conditional attacks can only be performed when the collective set of attributes possessed by the colluding users satisfies the access structure. In contrast, complete attacks allow any ciphertext to be decrypted. Figure 1 illustrates the relationship between the attacks, and how the attacks relate to the security model. We consider the first key query phase and the challenge phase, which output the secret keys for a polynomial number of sets of attributes, and a ciphertext associated with an access structure such that all keys are unauthorized, respectively.

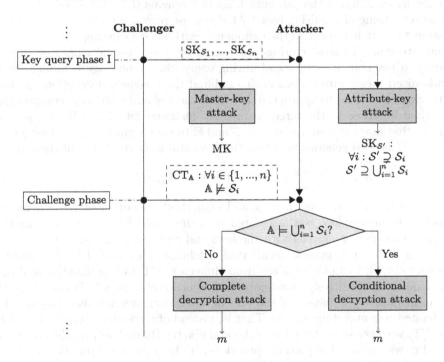

Fig. 1. The general attacks and how they relate to one another.

The security models in the multi-authority setting are similar, but include the notion of corruption. The attacker is allowed to corrupt one or more authorities in an attack, which should not yield sufficient power to enable an attack against the honest authorities. Sometimes, schemes employ a central authority (CA) in addition to employing multiple attribute authorities. This CA is assumed to perform the algorithms as expected, though sometimes, it may be corruptable. In this work, we show how to model the corruption of attribute authorities and corruptable CAs, and how the additional knowledge (e.g. the master secret keys) gained from corrupting an authority can be included in the attacks.

Finally, we observe that sometimes it is unclear whether a multi-authority scheme is supposed to provide security against corruption. Initially, multi-authority ABE was designed to be secure against corruption [8,19]. Not only does this protect honest authorities from corrupt authorities, but it also increases security from the perspective of the users. Conversely, not allowing corruption in the security model provides a comparable level of security as single-authority ABE. In some cases, the informal description of a scheme is ambiguous on whether it protects against corruption. For instance, schemes are compared with other multi-authority schemes that are secure against corruption, while the proposed scheme is not, even though this is not explicitly mentioned [23,27].

Finding Attacks, Generically. We evaluate the generic (in)security of a scheme by considering the pair encodings of a scheme [1,2]. Intuitively, the pair encoding scheme of a pairing-based ABE scheme provides an abstraction of the scheme to what happens "in the exponent", without considering the underlying group structure. In most pairing-based schemes, the keys and ciphertexts exist mainly in two source groups, and during encryption, a message is blinded by a randomized target group element. To unblind the message, decryption consists of pairing operations to appropriately match the key and ciphertext components and then lift these to the target group. For instance, let $e \colon \mathbb{G} \times \mathbb{H} \to \mathbb{G}_T$ be a pairing that maps two source groups $\mathbb{G}$ and $\mathbb{H}$ to target group $\mathbb{G}_T$, and let $g \in \mathbb{G}$ and $h \in \mathbb{H}$ be two generators. Then, the keys and ciphertexts are of the form:

$$\mathrm{SK} = h^{\mathbf{k}(\alpha, \mathbf{r}, \mathbf{b})}, \qquad \mathrm{CT} = (m \cdot e(g, h)^{\alpha s}, g^{\mathbf{c}(\mathbf{s}, \mathbf{b})}),$$

such that $\mathbf{k}$ and $\mathbf{c}$ denote the key and ciphertext encodings of the scheme, α denotes the master-key, $\mathbf{b}$ is associated with the public key and $\mathbf{r}$ and $\mathbf{s}$ are the random variables associated with the keys and ciphertexts, respectively.

On a high level, generic security of a scheme is evaluated by considering whether $e(g, h)^{\alpha s}$ can be retrieved from ciphertext CT and an unauthorized key SK. Due to the additively homomorphic properties of groups $\mathbb{G}, \mathbb{H}$ and $\mathbb{G}_T$, and the multiplicative behavior of the pairing operation, we can also consider the associated pair encoding scheme. That is, instead of retrieving $e(g, g)^{\alpha s}$ from SK and CT, we retrieve αs from $\mathbf{k}(\alpha, \mathbf{r}, \mathbf{b})$ and $\mathbf{c}(\mathbf{s}, \mathbf{b})$. By multiplying the entries of $\mathbf{k}$ and $\mathbf{c}$, we emulate the pairing operations. By linearly combining the resulting values (for which we require additions), we emulate the other available group operations. As a result, such a "combination" of a key and ciphertext encoding can be denoted by a matrix multiplication, i.e. $\mathbf{E}$ for which $\mathbf{kEc}^{\mathsf{T}} = \alpha s$.

Pair encoding schemes allow us to evaluate the generic security of any scheme that satisfies this structure, regardless of the underlying group structure. Unfortunately, the structure of most multi-authority schemes differs from this structure. Therefore, we extend the existing definitions to additionally support these multi-authority schemes. Furthermore, we split the key and ciphertext encodings in two parts, so we can separately evaluate the stronger attacks, i.e. master-key and complete decryption attacks, and the weaker attacks, i.e. attribute-key and conditional decryption attacks. This further simplifies the analysis of schemes.

Table 2. The schemes for which we provide attacks. For each scheme, we indicate on which scheme it is based, which type of attack we apply to it and whether it is complete, whether it uses collusion or corruption, whether the attack explicitly contradicts the model in which the scheme is claimed to be secure. We also list the conference or journal in which the scheme was published and how many times the paper is cited according to Google Scholar. These measures were taken on 18 November 2020.

	Scheme	Based on	CD	Att.	Col.	Cor.	Con.	Venue	Cit.
	ZH10 [42,43]	–	✗	AK	2	–	✓	NC	112
	ZHW13 [44]							NC	123
	NDCW15 [26]	Wat11 [33]	✓	D	–	–	✓	ESORICS	46
	YJ12 [37]	–	✓	MK	–	$\mathcal{A}$	✓	NC	155
	YJR+13 [39,40]	–	✓	D	–	–	✓	NC, TIFS	474
	WJB17 [35]							NC	28
Multi-authority ABE	JLWW13 [16]	BSW07 [5]	✗	AK	2	–	✓	NC	174
	JLWW15 [17]							TIFS	161
	QLZ13 [28]	–	✓	MK	–	–	✓	ICICS	42
	YJ14 [38]	–	✓	D	–	$\mathcal{A}$	✓	NC	240
	CM14 [10]	–	✓	D	–	$\mathcal{A}$	U	NC	42
	LXXH16 [22]	Wat11 [33]	✓	MK	–	CA	✓	NC	110
	MST17 [25]						U	AsiaCCS	25
	PO17 [27]	–	✓	D	–	$\mathcal{A}$	U	SACMAT	16
	MGZ19 I [23]	LW11 [19]	✓	MK	–	CA	U	Inscrypt	4

CD = complete decryption attack, Att = attack, MK = master-key attack, AK = attribute-key attack, D = decryption attack; Col = collusion, Cor = corruption, Con = contradicts proposed security model, U = unclear, NC = not published at peer-reviewed crypto venue/journal

The Attacked Schemes. Table 2 lists the schemes for which we have found attacks. Many of these schemes are published at venues that include cryptography in their scope, or have been highly cited. Hence, even though many researchers have studied these schemes, mistakes in the security proofs have gone unnoticed. These attacks also illustrate that systematizing any generic attacks may actually have merit. Not only does it provide designers with simple tools to test their own schemes with respect to generic attacks, but also reviewers and practitioners. Because most schemes are broken with respect to the strongest attacks, i.e. master-key and complete decryption attacks, formalizing these models—which are stronger but easier to verify—simplifies the search for generic attacks as well.

2   Preliminaries

Notations. If an element is chosen uniformly at random from some finite set S, we write $x \in_R S$. If an element x is generated by running algorithm Alg, we write $x \leftarrow$ Alg. We use boldfaced variables for vectors $\mathbf{x}$ and matrices $\mathbf{M}$, where $\mathbf{x}$ denotes a row vector and $\mathbf{y}^\mathsf{T}$ denotes a column vector. Furthermore, x_i denotes the i-th entry of $\mathbf{x}$. If the vector size is unknown, $\mathbf{v} \in_R S$ indicates that for each entry: $v_i \in_R S$. Finally, $\mathbf{x}(y_1, y_2, ...)$ denotes a vector, where the entries are polynomials over variables $y_1, y_2, ...$, with coefficients in some specified field. However, for conciseness, we often only write $\mathbf{x}$. We refer to a polynomial with only one term, or alternatively one term of the polynomial, as a monomial.

Access Structures. We consider monotone access structures (see the full version [31] for a formal definition) [4]. If a set S satisfies access structure $\mathbb{A}$, we denote this as $\mathbb{A} \models S$. For monotone access structures, it holds that if $S \supseteq S'$ and $\mathbb{A} \models S'$, then $\mathbb{A} \models S$. We denote the i-th attribute in the access structure as $\mathrm{att}_i \sim \mathbb{A}$.

Pairings. We define a pairing to be an efficiently computable map e on three groups $\mathbb{G}, \mathbb{H}$ and $\mathbb{G}_T$ of order p, such that $e \colon \mathbb{G} \times \mathbb{H} \to \mathbb{G}_T$, with generators $g \in \mathbb{G}, h \in \mathbb{H}$ such that for all $a, b \in \mathbb{Z}_p$, it holds that $e(g^a, h^b) = e(g, h)^{ab}$ (bilinearity), and for $g^a \neq 1_{\mathbb{G}}, h^b \neq 1_{\mathbb{H}}$, it holds that $e(g^a, h^b) \neq 1_{\mathbb{G}_T}$, where $1_{\mathbb{G}'}$ denotes the unique identity element of the associated group $\mathbb{G}'$ (non-degeneracy).

2.1   Formal Definition of (Multi-authority) Ciphertext-Policy ABE

We slightly adjust the more traditional definition of CP-ABE [5] and its multi-authority variant [19]. Specifically, we split the generation of the keys in two parts: the part that is dependent on an attribute and the part that is not. These are relevant distinctions in the definitions of various attack models.

Definition 1 (Ciphertext-policy ABE). *A CP-ABE scheme with some authorities $\mathcal{A}_1, ..., \mathcal{A}_n$ (where $n \in \mathbb{N}$) such that each $\mathcal{A}_i$ manages universe $\mathcal{U}_i$, users and a universe of attributes $\mathcal{U} = \bigcup_{i=1}^n \mathcal{U}_i$ consists of the following algorithms.*

- GlobalSetup(λ) $\to$ GP: *The global setup is a randomized algorithm that takes as input the security parameter λ, and outputs the public global system parameters* GP *(independent of any attributes).*
- MKSetup(GP) $\to$ (GP, MK): *The master-key setup is a randomized algorithm that takes as input the global parameters* GP, *and outputs the (secret) master-key* MK *(independent of any attributes) and updates the global parameters by adding the public key associated with* MK.
- AttSetup(att, MK, GP) $\to$ (MSK$_{\mathrm{att}}$, MPK$_{\mathrm{att}}$): *The attribute-key setup is a randomized algorithm that takes as input an attribute, possibly the master-key and the global parameters, and outputs a master secret* MSK$_{\mathrm{att}}$ *and public key* MPK$_{\mathrm{att}}$ *associated with attribute* att.

- UKeyGen(id, MK, GP) → SK$_{id}$: *The user-key generation is a randomized algorithm that takes as input the identifier* id, *the master-key* MK *and the global parameters* GP, *and outputs the secret key* SK$_{id}$ *associated with* id.
- AttKeyGen($\mathcal{S}$, GP, MK, SK$_{id}$, {MSK$_{att}$}$_{att \in \mathcal{S}}$) → SK$_{id,att}$: *The attribute-key generation is a randomized algorithm that takes as input an attribute* att *possessed by some user with identifier* id, *and the global parameters, the master-key* MK, *the secret key* SK$_{id}$ *and master secret key* MSK$_{att}$, *and outputs a user-specific secret key* SK$_{id,att}$.
- Encrypt(m, $\mathbb{A}$, GP, {MPK$_{att}$}$_{att \sim \mathbb{A}}$) → CT$_{\mathbb{A}}$: *This randomized algorithm is run by any encrypting user and takes as input a message* m, *access structure* $\mathbb{A}$ *and the relevant public keys. It outputs the ciphertext* CT$_{\mathbb{A}}$.
- Decrypt(SK$_{id,\mathcal{S}}$, CT$_{\mathbb{A}}$) → m: *This deterministic algorithm takes as input a ciphertext* CT$_{\mathbb{A}}$ *and secret key* SK$_{id,\mathcal{S}}$ = {SK$_{id}$, SK$_{id,att}$}$_{att \in \mathcal{S}}$ *associated with an authorized set* $\mathcal{S}$, *and outputs plaintext* m. *Otherwise, it aborts.*
- MKDecrypt(MK, CT) → m: *This deterministic algorithm takes as input a ciphertext* CT *and the master-key* MK, *and outputs plaintext* m.

The scheme is called correct if decryption outputs the correct message for a secret key associated with a set of attributes that satisfies the access structure.

In the single-authority setting (i.e. where $n = 1$), the GlobalSetup, MKSetup and AttSetup are described in one Setup, and the UKeyGen and AttKeyGen have to be run in one KeyGen. In the multi-authority setting (i.e. where $n > 1$), the GlobalSetup is run either jointly or by some $\mathcal{CA}$. MKSetup can either be run distributively or independently by each $\mathcal{A}_i$. AttSetup can be run distributively or individually by $\mathcal{A}_i$ for the managed attributes $\mathcal{U}_i$. UKeyGen is run either distributively, individually for each $\mathcal{A}_i$, or implicitly (e.g. by using a hash). AttKeyGen is run by the $\mathcal{A}_i$ managing the set of attributes.

2.2 The Security Model and Our Attack Models

Definition 2 (Full CPA-security for CP-ABE [5]). *Let $\mathfrak{C}$ = (GlobalSetup, ..., MKDecrypt) be a CP-ABE scheme for authorities $\mathcal{A}_1, ..., \mathcal{A}_n$ conform Definition 1. We define the game between challenger and attacker as follows.*

- ***Initialization phase:*** *The attacker corrupts a set $\mathcal{I} \subsetneq \{1, ..., n\}$ of authorities, and sends $\mathcal{I}$ to the challenger. In the selective security game, the attacker also commits to an access structure $\mathbb{A}$.*
- ***Setup phase:*** *The challenger runs the GlobalSetup, MKSetup for all authorities, and AttSetup for all attributes. It sends the global parameters GP, master public keys {MPK$_{att}$}$_{att \in \mathcal{U}}$, and corrupted master secret keys {MSK$_{att}$}$_{att \in \mathcal{U}_{\mathcal{I}}}$ to the attacker, where $\mathcal{U}_{\mathcal{I}} = \bigcup_{i \in \mathcal{I}} \mathcal{U}_i$.*
- ***Key query phase I:*** *The attacker queries secret keys for sets of attributes $(id_1, \mathcal{S}_1), ..., (id_{n_1}, \mathcal{S}_{n_1})$. The challenger runs UKeyGen and AttKeyGen for each $(id_j, \mathcal{S}_j)$ and sends SK$_{id_1, \mathcal{S}_1}$, ..., SK$_{id_{n_1}, \mathcal{S}_{n_1}}$ to the attacker.*
- ***Challenge phase:*** *The attacker generates two messages m_0 and m_1 of equal length, together with an access structure $\mathbb{A}$ such that $\mathcal{S}_j \cup \mathcal{U}_{\mathcal{I}}$ does not satisfy $\mathbb{A}$ for all j. The challenger flips a coin $\beta \in_R \{0, 1\}$ and encrypts m_β under $\mathbb{A}$. It sends the resulting challenge ciphertext CT$_{\mathbb{A}}$ to the attacker.*

- **Key query phase II:** *The same as the first key query phase, with the restriction that the queried sets* $S_{n_1+1}, ..., S_{n_2}$ *are such that* $\mathbb{A} \not\models S_j \cup \mathcal{U}_{\mathcal{I}}$.
- **Decision phase:** *The attacker outputs a guess* β' *for* β.

The advantage of the attacker is defined as $|\Pr[\beta' = \beta] - \frac{1}{2}|$. A ciphertext-policy attribute-based encryption scheme is fully secure (against static corruption) if all polynomial-time attackers have at most a negligible advantage in this security game.

We formally define our attack models in line with the chosen-plaintext attack model above and Fig. 1, such that CPA-security also implies security against these attacks. Conversely, the ability to find such attacks implies insecurity in this model. While this follows intuitively, we prove this in the full version [31].

Definition 3 (Master-key attacks (MKA)). *We define the game between challenger and attacker as follows. First, the initialization, setup and first key query phases are run as in Definition 2. Then:*

- **Decision phase:** *The attacker outputs* MK'.

The attacker wins the game if for all messages m, *decryption of ciphertext* $\text{CT} \leftarrow \text{Encrypt}(m, ...)$ *yields* $m' \leftarrow \text{MKDecrypt}(\text{MK}', \text{CT})$ *such that* $m = m'$.

Definition 4 (Attribute-key attacks (AKA)). *We define the game between challenger and attacker as follows. First, the initialization, setup and first key query phases are run as in Definition 2. Then:*

- **Decision phase:** *The attacker outputs* $\text{SK}_{S'}$, *where* $S' \supsetneq S_j$ *for all* $j \in \{1, ..., n_1\}$, *and* $S' \supseteq \bigcup_{j=1}^{n_1} S_j$.

The attacker wins the game if $\text{SK}_{\text{id}', S'}$ *is a valid secret key for some arbitrary identifier* id' *and set* S'.

Definition 5 (Decryption attacks (DA)). *We define the game between challenger and attacker as follows. First, the initialization, setup, first key query and challenge phases are run as in Definition 2. Then:*

- **Decision phase:** *The attacker outputs plaintext* m'.

The attacker wins the game if $m' = m$. *A decryption attack is* **conditional** *if* $\mathbb{A} \models \bigcup_{j=1}^{n_1} S_j$. *Otherwise, it is* **complete.**

3   Warm-Up: Attacking DAC-MACS (YJR+13 [39,40])

We first give an example of how an attack can be found effectively by attacking the YJR+13 [39, 40] scheme, also known as DAC-MACS. DAC-MACS is a popular multi-authority scheme that supports key revocation. This functionality was already broken in [15, 35], but a fix for its revocation functionality was proposed in [35]. We show that even the basic scheme—which matches the "fixed version"

[35]—is vulnerable to a complete decryption attack. We review a stripped-down version of the global and master-key setups, the user-key generation and encryption. In particular, we consider only the parts that are not dependent on any attributes. Also note that we use a slightly different notation for the variables: $(a, \alpha_k, \beta_k, z_j, u_j, t_{j,k}) \mapsto (b, \alpha_i, b_i, x_1, x_2, r_i)$.

- GlobalSetup: The central authority generates pairing $e \colon \mathbb{G} \times \mathbb{G} \to \mathbb{G}_T$ over groups $\mathbb{G}$ and $\mathbb{G}_T$ of prime order p with generator $g \in \mathbb{G}$, chooses random integer $b \in_R \mathbb{Z}_p$ and publishes as global parameters $\mathrm{GP} = (p, e, \mathbb{G}, \mathbb{G}_T, g, g^b)$;
- MKSetup: Authority $\mathcal{A}_i$ chooses random $\alpha_i, b_i \in_R \mathbb{Z}_p$, and outputs master secret key $\mathrm{MSK}_i = (\alpha_i, b_i)$ and master public key $\mathrm{MPK}_i = (e(g,g)^{\alpha_i}, g^{1/b_i})$;
- UKeyGen: Upon registration, the user receives partial secret key $\mathrm{SK} = (x_1, g^{x_2})$ from the central authority, with a certificate that additionally includes x_2. To request a key from authority $\mathcal{A}_i$, the user sends this certificate. The attribute-independent part of a user's secret key provided by authority $\mathcal{A}_i$ is $\mathrm{SK}'_i = (g^{\alpha_i/x_1+x_2 b+r_i b/b_i}, g^{r_i b_i/x_1}, g^{r_i b})$, where $r_i \in_R \mathbb{Z}_p$;
- Encrypt: A message m is encrypted by picking random $s \in_R \mathbb{Z}_p$ and computing: $\mathrm{CT} = (m \cdot (\prod_i e(g,g)^{\alpha_i})^s, g^s, g^{s/b_i}, ...)$.

Note that an authority $\mathcal{A}_i$ can individually generate $g^{\alpha_i/x_1+x_2 b+r_i b/b_i}$, if x_2 is known to the authority. In the specification of DAC-MACS, the central authority generates a certificate containing x_2 and the identifier of the user, such that these are linked. In the conference version [39], this certificate is encrypted, and can be decrypted only by the authorities. However, in the journal version [40], this certificate is not explicitly defined to be hidden from the user. We assume that x_2 is therefore also known to the user. Then, after receiving the certificate from the user, x_2 is used by the authority $\mathcal{A}_i$ to link the secret keys to this particular user. However, we show that knowing exponents x_1, x_2 enables an attack. That is, any decrypting user is trivially able to decrypt any ciphertext, without even needing to consider the attribute-dependent part of the keys and ciphertexts. First, we show that we cannot perform a master-key attack, i.e. retrieve α_i. In particular, the partial secret keys are of the form $\mathrm{SK} = (x_1, g^{x_2}, x_2, g^{\alpha_i/x_1+x_2 b+r_i b/b_i}, g^{r_i b_i/x_1}, g^{r_i b})$. We observe that master-key α_i only occurs in $g^{\alpha_i/x_1+x_2 b+r_i b/b_i}$. Now, we can cancel out $g^{x_2 b}$, because x_2 is known and g^b is a global parameter. Unfortunately, we cannot cancel out $g^{r_i b/b_i}$.

Subsequently, we show that it is possible to perform a decryption attack. For this, we also consider $\mathrm{CT} = (m \cdot e(g,g)^{\alpha_i s}, g^s, g^{s/b_i}, ...)$. To retrieve $e(g,g)^{\alpha_i s}$, we start by pairing $g^{\alpha_i/x_1+x_2 b+r_i b/b_i}$ and g^s, and compute

$$e(g^{\alpha_i/x_1+x_2 b+r_i b/b_i}, g^s)^{x_1} = \underbrace{e(g,g)^{\alpha_i s}}_{\text{Blinding value}} + \overbrace{e(g,g)^{x_1 x_2 s b + x_1 r_i s b/b_i}}^{\text{to cancel}}$$

$$\underbrace{e(g^b, g^s)^{x_1 x_2}}_{} \quad \underbrace{e(g^{r_i b}, g^{s/b_i})^{x_1}}_{}$$

Hence, $e(g,g)^{\alpha_i s}$ can be retrieved and thus the ciphertext can be decrypted. Resisting this attack is not trivial. The main issue is that x_2 is known to the user, because x_2 needs to be known by the authority to generate $g^{\alpha_i/x_1+x_2 b+r_i b/b_i}$. Otherwise, it cannot generate $g^{x_2 b}$. To avoid the attack, the CA could encrypt the certificate containing x_2—like in the conference version [39]—so only the authorities $\mathcal{A}_i$ can decrypt it, and the user does not learn x_2. The attacker can however corrupt any authority, learn x_2 and perform the attack. This still breaks the scheme, because of its claimed security against corruption of authorities $\mathcal{A}_i$.

This attack illustrates two things. First, it shows the simplicity of finding a master-key or complete decryption attack—the two strongest attacks—provided that one exists. In particular, in the analysis, we only have to consider the parts of the keys that are not related to the attributes or additional functionality. This strips away a significantly more complicated part of the scheme. Second, we can systematically focus on the the the goal of retrieving g^{α_i} or $e(g,g)^{\alpha_i s}$. Due to the structure of the scheme, we can directly analyze the exponent space of the key and ciphertext components. The pairing operation effectively allows us to compute products of these values "in the exponent". Therefore, we do not have to consider the underlying group structure. Instead, we can attempt to retrieve $\alpha_i s$ by linearly combining the products of the exponent spaces of the key and ciphertext components. In addition, we can use the explicit knowledge of certain variables "in the exponent" by using these variables in the coefficients.

Not only is finding such a generic attack simpler than verifying a security proof, it may also help finding the mistake in the proof. As shown, the main reason that our attack works is that x_2 is known to the user. We use this observation to find the mistake in the security proof in the journal version [40], which is loosely based on the selective security proof by Waters [33]. In the proof, the challenger and attacker play the security game in Definition 2. The attacker is assumed to be able to break the scheme with non-negligible advantage. The challenger uses this to break the complexity assumption by using the inputs to the assumption in the simulation of the keys and challenge ciphertext. Roughly, the challenger embeds the element that needs to be distinguished from a random element in the complexity assumption in the challenge ciphertext component $e(g,g)^{\alpha_i s}$. To ensure that $e(g,g)^{\alpha_i s}$ cannot be generated trivially from e.g. g^{α_i} and g^s, the challenger cannot simulate the master secret key g^{α_i}. To simulate the key $g^{\alpha_i/x_1+x_2 b+r_i b/b_i}$, the part with g^{α_i} is canceled out by the $g^{x_2 b}$ part. By extension, the challenger cannot fully simulate $g^{x_2 b}$. Because g^b needs to be simulated (as it is part of the public key), it is not possible to simulate the secret in x_2. In [40], the authors attempt to solve this issue by generating x_2 randomly, and by implicitly writing it as the sum of the non-simulatable secret and another random integer x_2' (which is thus unknown to the challenger). While this allows the simulation of x_2, this causes an issue in the simulation of $g^{\alpha_i/x_1+x_2 b}$. Because the secret part in x_2 is meant to cancel out the non-simulatable part, $g^{\alpha_i/x_1+x_2 b}$ needs to be simulated by computing $g^{x_2' b}$. This is not possible, since x_2' is unknown to the challenger.

4 Systematizing Our Methodology

Our methodology consists of a systemized approach to finding attacks. It consists of a more concise notation implied by the common structure of many ABE schemes (Sect. 4.1). We model how learning explicit values "in the exponent", e.g. by corrupting an authority, can be used in the attacks (Sect. 4.2). We give our attack models in the concise notation (Sects. 4.3, 4.4). Finally, we describe a heuristic approach that simplifies the effort of finding attacks (Sect. 4.5).

4.1 The Common Structure Implies a More Concise Notation

Many schemes have a similar structure, captured in frameworks that analyze the exponent space through pair encodings [3,34]. We adapt their definitions of pair encoding schemes to match our definition of CP-ABE (Definition 1), which also covers the multi-authority setting. Pair encodings facilitate a shorter notation.

Definition 6 (Extended pair encoding implied by CP-ABE). *Let authorities $\mathcal{A}_1,...,\mathcal{A}_n$ manage universes $\mathcal{U}_i$ for each i, and set $\mathcal{U} = \bigcup_{i=1}^{n}\mathcal{U}_i$ as the collective universe.*

- GlobalSetup(λ): *This algorithm generates three groups $\mathbb{G}, \mathbb{H}, \mathbb{G}_T$ of order p with generators $g \in \mathbb{G}, h \in \mathbb{H}$, and a pairing $e\colon \mathbb{G} \times \mathbb{H} \to \mathbb{G}_T$. It may also select **common variables** $\mathbf{b} \in_R \mathbb{Z}_p$. It publishes the global parameters*

$$GP = (p, \mathbb{G}, \mathbb{H}, \mathbb{G}_T, g, h, \mathcal{U}, g^{\mathbf{gp}(\mathbf{b})}),$$

*where we refer to **gp** as the **global parameter encoding**.*
- MKSetup(GP): *This algorithm selects $\alpha \in_R \mathbb{Z}_p$, sets master-key MK $= \alpha$ and publishes master public key MPK $= \{e(g,h)^{\alpha}\}$.*
- AttSetup(att, MK, GP): *This algorithm selects integers $\mathbf{b}_{\mathrm{att}} \in_R \mathbb{Z}_p$ as secret* **MSK**$_{\mathrm{att}} = \mathbf{b}_{\mathrm{att}}$, *and publishes*

$$\mathbf{MPK}_{\mathrm{att}} = g^{\mathbf{mpk}_a(\mathbf{b}_{\mathrm{att}},\mathbf{b})},$$

*where we refer to $\mathbf{mpk}_a$ as the **master attribute-key encoding**.*
- UKeyGen(id, MK, GP): *This algorithm selects user-specific random integers $\mathbf{r}_u \in_R \mathbb{Z}_p$ and computes partial user-key*

$$SK_{\mathrm{id}} = h^{\mathbf{k}_u(\mathrm{id},\alpha,\mathbf{r}_u,\mathbf{b})},$$

*where we refer to $\mathbf{k}_u$ as the **user-key encoding**.*
- AttKeyGen($\mathcal{S}$, GP, MK, SK$_{\mathrm{id}}$, $\{$MSK$_{\mathrm{att}}\}_{\mathrm{att}\in\mathcal{S}}$): *Let* SK$_{\mathrm{id}} = (h_{\mathrm{id},1}, h_{\mathrm{id},2}, ...)$. *This algorithm selects user-specific random integers $\mathbf{r}_a \in_R \mathbb{Z}_p$ and computes a key* SK$_{\mathrm{id},\mathcal{S}} = \{SK_{\mathrm{id},\mathrm{att}}\}_{\mathrm{att}\in\mathcal{S}}$, *such that for all att $\in \mathcal{S}$*

$$SK_{\mathrm{id},\mathrm{att}} = (h_{\mathrm{id},1}^{\mathbf{k}_{a,1}(\mathrm{att},\mathbf{r}_a,\mathbf{b},\mathbf{b}_{\mathrm{att}})}, h_{\mathrm{id},2}^{\mathbf{k}_{a,2}(\mathrm{att},\mathbf{r}_a,\mathbf{b},\mathbf{b}_{\mathrm{att}})}, ...),$$

*where we refer to $\mathbf{k}_{a,i}$ as the **user-specific attribute-key encodings**.*

- Encrypt$(m, \mathbb{A}, \mathrm{GP}, \{\mathrm{MPK}_{\mathrm{att}}\}_{\mathrm{att}\sim\mathbb{A}})$: *This algorithm picks ciphertext-specific randoms* $\mathbf{s} = (s, s_1, s_2, ...) \in_R \mathbb{Z}_p$ *and outputs the ciphertext*

$$\mathrm{CT}_{\mathbb{A}} = (\mathbb{A}, m \cdot e(g, h)^{\alpha s}, g^{\mathbf{c}(\mathbb{A}, \mathbf{s}, \mathbf{b})}, g^{\mathbf{c}_a(\mathbb{A}, \mathbf{s}, \mathbf{b}, \{\mathbf{b}_{\mathrm{att}}\}_{\mathrm{att}\sim\mathbb{A}})}),$$

where we refer to $\mathbf{c}$ *as the* **attribute-independent ciphertext encoding,** *and* $\mathbf{c}_a$ *the* **attribute-dependent ciphertext encoding.**
- Decrypt$((\mathrm{SK}_{\mathrm{id}}, \mathrm{SK}_{\mathrm{id},\mathcal{S}}), \mathrm{CT}_{\mathbb{A}})$: *Let* $\mathrm{SK}_{\mathrm{id}} = h^{\mathbf{k}_u(\mathrm{id}, \alpha, \mathbf{r}_u, \mathbf{b})} = (h_{\mathrm{id},1}, h_{\mathrm{id},2}, ...)$, $\mathrm{SK}_{\mathrm{id},\mathcal{S}} = \{(h_{\mathrm{id},1}^{\mathbf{k}_{a,1}(\mathrm{att}, \mathbf{r}_{a,i}, \mathbf{b}, \mathbf{b}_{\mathrm{att}})}, h_{\mathrm{id},2}^{\mathbf{k}_{a,2}(\mathrm{att}, \mathbf{r}_{a,i}, \mathbf{b}, \mathbf{b}_{\mathrm{att}})}, ...)\}_{i \in \{1,...,n\}, \mathrm{att} \in \mathcal{S} \cap \mathcal{U}_i}$, *and* $\mathrm{CT}_{\mathbb{A}} = (\mathbb{A}, C = m \cdot e(g, h)^{\alpha s}, \mathbf{C} = g^{\mathbf{c}(\mathbb{A}, \mathbf{s}, \mathbf{b})}, \mathbf{C}_a = g^{\mathbf{c}_a(\mathbb{A}, \mathbf{s}, \mathbf{b}, \{\mathbf{b}_{\mathrm{att}}\}_{\mathrm{att}\sim\mathbb{A}})})$. *Define* $\mathcal{S}_{\mathbb{A}} = \{\mathrm{att} \sim \mathbb{A} \mid \mathrm{att} \in \mathcal{S}\}$, *and matrices* $\mathbf{E}$, $\mathbf{E}_{\mathrm{att},\mathcal{S},\mathbb{A}}$ *for each* $\mathrm{att} \in \mathcal{S}$ *such that*

$$\mathbf{c}\mathbf{E}\mathbf{k}_u^{\mathsf{T}} + \sum_{\mathrm{att} \in \mathcal{S}_{\mathbb{A}}} (\mathbf{c} \mid \mathbf{c}_a)\mathbf{E}_{\mathrm{att},\mathcal{S},\mathbb{A}}(\mathbf{k}_u \mid \mathbf{k}_a)^{\mathsf{T}} = \alpha s.$$

Then, the plaintext m *can be retrieved by recovering* $e(g, h)^{\alpha s}$ *from* $\mathbf{C}, \mathbf{C}_a$ *and* $\mathrm{SK}_{\mathrm{id}}, \mathrm{SK}_{\mathrm{id},\mathcal{S}}$, *and* $m = C/e(g, h)^{\alpha s}$.
- MKDecrypt$(\mathrm{MK}, \mathrm{CT})$: *Let* $\mathrm{MK} = \alpha$, $\mathrm{MK}' = h^{\mathrm{mk}(\alpha, \mathbf{b})}$ *and* $\mathrm{CT} = (C = m \cdot e(g, h)^{\alpha s}, \mathbf{C} = g^{\mathbf{c}(\mathbb{A}, \mathbf{s}, \mathbf{b})}, \mathbf{C}_a = g^{\mathbf{c}_a(\mathbb{A}, \mathbf{s}, \mathbf{b}, \{\mathbf{b}_{\mathrm{att}}\}_{\mathrm{att}\sim\mathbb{A}})})$. *Define vector* $\mathbf{e}$ *such that* $\mathbf{c}\mathbf{e}^{\mathsf{T}}\mathbf{mk} = \alpha s$. *Then,* m *can be retrieved by computing*

$$C/\prod_{\ell} e(C_{\ell}, \mathrm{MK}')^{\mathbf{e}_{\ell}},$$

where C_{ℓ} *and* $\mathbf{e}_{\ell}$ *denote the* ℓ-*th entry of* $\mathbf{C}$ *and* $\mathbf{e}$, *respectively.*

Each encoding **enc**(var) *denotes a vector of polynomials over variables* var. *Generators constructed by hash functions [5] are covered by this definition by assuming that* $\mathcal{H}(\mathrm{att}) = g^{b_{\mathrm{att}}}$ *for some implicit* b_{att}. *Depending on the scheme,* MKSetup *may be run distributively or by a single CA (in which case there is only one public key* $e(g, h)^{\alpha}$ *associated with the master-keys), or independently and individually by multiple authorities* $\mathcal{A}_i$ *(in which case there are multiple public keys* $e(g, h)^{\alpha_i}$, *and we replace the blinding value* $e(g, h)^{\alpha s}$ *by* $e(g, h)^{\sum_{i \in \mathcal{I}} \alpha_i s}$).

4.2   Modeling Knowledge of Exponents – Extending $\mathbb{Z}_p$

The previously defined notation describes the relationship between the various variables "in the exponent" of the keys and ciphertexts. The explicit values of most variables are unknown to the attacker. In multi-authority ABE, authorities provide the inputs to some encodings, and therefore know these values, as well as their (part of the) master-key. Hence, corruption of authorities results in the knowledge of some explicit values "in the exponent". If the values provided by honest authorities are not well-hidden, it might enable an attack on them.

We model the "knowledge of exponents" in attacks by extending the space from which the entries of $\mathbf{E}$ and $\mathbf{E}_{\mathrm{att},\mathcal{S},\mathbb{A}}$ are chosen: $\mathbb{Z}_p$ (or some extension with variables associated with $\mathcal{S}$ and $\mathbb{A}$). In fact, the entries of these matrices may be any fraction of polynomials over $\mathbb{Z}_p$ and the known exponents. Let $\mathfrak{K}$ be the set of known exponents, then the extended field of rational fractions is defined as

$$\mathbb{Z}_p(\mathfrak{K}) = \{ab^{-1} \pmod{p} \mid a, b \in \mathbb{Z}_p[\mathfrak{K}]\},$$

where $\mathbb{Z}_p[\mathfrak{K}]$ denotes the polynomial ring of variables $\mathfrak{K}$.

4.3 Formal Definitions of the Attacks in the Concise Notations

We formally define our attack models (conform Definitions 7–9, depicted in Fig. 1) in the concise notation. For each attack, $\mathfrak{K} \subseteq \{x, x_1, x_2, ...\}$ denotes the set of known variables. We use the following shorthand for a key encoding for a user id with set $\mathcal{S}$ and for a ciphertext encoding for access structure $\mathbb{A}$:

$$\mathbf{k}_{\mathrm{id},\mathcal{S}} := (\mathbf{gp}(\mathbf{b}), \mathbf{mpk}_a(b_{\mathrm{att}}, \mathbf{b}), \mathbf{k}_u(\mathrm{id}, \alpha, \mathbf{r}_u, \mathbf{b}) \mid \mathbf{k}_{a,1}(\mathrm{att}, \mathbf{r}_a, \mathbf{b}, b_{\mathrm{att}}) \mid ...),$$
$$\mathbf{c}_{\mathbb{A}} := (\mathbf{gp}(\mathbf{b}), \mathbf{mpk}_a(b_{\mathrm{att}}, \mathbf{b}), \mathbf{c}(\mathbb{A}, \mathbf{s}, \mathbf{b}) \mid \mathbf{c}_a(\mathbb{A}, \mathbf{s}, \mathbf{b}, \{b_{\mathrm{att}}\}_{\mathrm{att}\sim\mathbb{A}})).$$

We first define the master-key attacks. In these attacks, the attacker has to retrieve master-key $\mathrm{mk}(\alpha, \mathbf{b})$, so any ciphertext can be decrypted conform MKDecrypt. In many schemes, it holds that master-key mk is α (i.e. h^α), though in others, recovering e.g. $\mathrm{mk}_i = \alpha_i/b_i$ for authorities $\mathcal{A}_i$ is required to decrypt all ciphertexts. This is because ciphertext encoding $\mathbf{c}$ often contains s or sb_i.

Definition 7 (Master-key attacks). *A scheme is vulnerable to a master-key attack if there exist* $(\mathrm{id}_1, \mathcal{S}_1), ..., (\mathrm{id}_{n_1}, \mathcal{S}_{n_1})$ *and the associated key encodings* $\mathbf{k}_{\mathrm{id}_i, \mathcal{S}_i}$, *and there exist* $\mathbf{e}_i \in \mathbb{Z}_p(\mathfrak{K})^{\ell_i}$, *where* $\ell_i = |\mathbf{k}_{\mathrm{id}_i, \mathcal{S}_i}|$ *denotes the length of the i-th key encoding, such that* $\sum_i \mathbf{k}_i \mathbf{e}_i^\mathsf{T} = \mathrm{mk}(\alpha, \mathbf{b}) \in \mathbb{Z}_p(\alpha, \mathbf{b})$. *Then, it holds that for all attribute-independent ciphertext encodings* $\mathbf{c}$ *there exists* $\mathbf{e}' \in \mathbb{Z}_p^{\ell'}$ *(with* $|\mathbf{c}| = \ell'$ *) such that* $\mathrm{mk}\mathbf{e}'\mathbf{c}^\mathsf{T} = \alpha s$.

We formally define attribute-key attacks. In an attribute-key attack, the attacker has to generate a secret key associated with a set $\mathcal{S}'$ that is strictly larger than any of the sets $\mathcal{S}_i$ associated with the issued keys.

Definition 8 (Attribute-key attacks). *A scheme is vulnerable to an attribute-key attack if there exist* $(\mathrm{id}_1, \mathcal{S}_1), ..., (\mathrm{id}_{n_1}, \mathcal{S}_{n_1})$ *such that for the key encodings* $\mathbf{k}_{\mathrm{id}_i, \mathcal{S}_i}$, *it holds that a valid key* $\overline{\mathbf{k}}_{\mathrm{id}', \mathcal{S}'}$ *(with user-specific randoms* $\overline{\mathbf{r}}_u$ *and* $\overline{\mathbf{r}}_a$ *constructed linearly from the other user-specific randoms) can be computed such that* $\bigcup_{i=1}^{n_1} \mathcal{S}_i \subseteq \mathcal{S}'$ *and* $\mathcal{S}_i \subsetneq \mathcal{S}'$ *for all* $i \in \{1, ..., n_1\}$. *We say that* $\overline{\mathbf{k}}_{\mathrm{id}', \mathcal{S}'}$ *can be computed, if there exist* $\mathbf{E}_i \in \mathbb{Z}_p(\mathfrak{K})^{\ell_i \times \overline{\ell}}$, *where* $\overline{\ell} = |\overline{\mathbf{k}}_{\mathrm{id}', \mathcal{S}'}|$ *and* $\ell_i = |\mathbf{k}_{\mathrm{id}_i, \mathcal{S}_i}|$, *for all* $\mathcal{S}_i$ *such that* $\overline{\mathbf{k}}_{\mathrm{id}', \mathcal{S}'} = \sum_i \mathbf{k}_{\mathrm{id}_i, \mathcal{S}_i} \mathbf{E}_i$.

We formally define the complete and conditional decryption attacks. In a decryption attack, the attacker decrypts a ciphertext for which it only has unauthorized keys. The attack is conditional if the collective set of attributes satisfies the access structure associated with the ciphertext. Otherwise, it is complete.

Definition 9 (Complete/conditional decryption attacks). *A scheme is vulnerable to a decryption attack if there exist* $(\mathrm{id}_1, \mathcal{S}_1), ..., (\mathrm{id}_{n_1}, \mathcal{S}_{n_1})$ *and* $\mathbb{A}$ *such that* $\mathbb{A} \not\models \mathcal{S}_i$ *for all* i, *associated ciphertext encoding* $\mathbf{c}_\mathbb{A}$ *and key encodings* $\mathbf{k}_{\mathrm{id}_i, \mathcal{S}_i}$, *for which there exist* $\mathbf{E}_i \in \mathbb{Z}_p(\mathfrak{K})^{\ell_i \times \ell'}$, *where* $\ell_i = |\mathbf{k}_{\mathrm{id}_i, \mathcal{S}_i}|$ *and* $\ell' = |\mathbf{c}_\mathbb{A}|$, *such that* $\sum_i \mathbf{k}_{\mathrm{id}_i, \mathcal{S}_i} \mathbf{E}_i \mathbf{c}_\mathbb{A}^\mathsf{T} = \alpha s$. *The attack is conditional if it holds that* $\mathbb{A} \models \bigcup_i \mathcal{S}_i$. *Otherwise, it is complete.*

It readily follows that master-key and attribute-key attacks imply decryption attacks. Specifically, master-key attacks and attribute-key attacks for which $\bigcup_{i=1}^{n_1} \mathcal{S}_i \subsetneq \mathcal{S}'$ holds imply complete decryption attacks.

4.4 Definitions of Multi-authority-specific Attacks

The multi-authority setting yields two additional difficulties in the design of secure schemes. First, the corruption of authorities yields extra knowledge about the exponent space. Second, the distributed nature of the master-key may enable new attacks. Formally, we define attacks under corruption as follows.

Definition 10 (Attacks under corruption). *A scheme is vulnerable to attacks under corruption if an attacker can corrupt a subset* $\mathcal{I} \subsetneq \{1, ..., n\}$ *of authorities* $\mathcal{A}_1, ..., \mathcal{A}_n$ *and thus obtain knowledge of variables* $\mathfrak{K}$ *consisting of all variables and (partial) encodings generated by the corrupt authorities, enabling an attack conform Definitions 7, 8 or 9.*

Oftentimes, the master-key is generated distributively by the authorities. Hence, the blinding value is of a distributed form, e.g. $e(g, h)^{\alpha s} = e(g, h)^{\sum_i \alpha_i s}$. If each partial blinding value e.g. $e(g, h)^{\alpha_i s}$ can be recovered independently of the user's randomness, then the scheme is vulnerable to a multi-authority-specific decryption attack under collusion. For instance, suppose the blinding value is defined as $(\alpha_1 + \alpha_2)s$. If one user can recover $\alpha_1 s$ (but not $\alpha_2 s$) and another user can recover $\alpha_2 s$ (but not $\alpha_1 s$), then the scheme is vulnerable to a multi-authority-specific decryption attack. They can collectively recover $(\alpha_1 + \alpha_2)s$, while clearly, they cannot do this individually. This type of attack was also performed by Wang et al. [32] on the HSM+14 [13] and HSM+15 [14] schemes.

Definition 11 (Multi-authority-specific (MAS) decryption attacks). *Suppose the blinding value of the message is of the form* $\sum_i \mathrm{bv}_i(\alpha_i, \mathbf{s}, \mathbf{b})$, *where* α_i *denotes the master-key of authority* $\mathcal{A}_i$, *and* bv_i *represent elements in* $\mathbb{G}_T$. *A scheme is vulnerable to a MAS-decryption attack if there exist a ciphertext encoding* $\mathbf{c}_\mathbb{A}$ *and sets* $\mathcal{S}_i \subseteq \mathcal{U}_i$ *with key encodings* $\mathbf{k}_{\mathrm{id}_i, \mathcal{S}_i}$ *for which there exist* $\mathbf{E}_i \in \mathbb{Z}_p(\mathfrak{K})^{\ell_i \times \ell'}$, *where* $\ell_i = |\mathbf{k}_{\mathrm{id}_i, \mathcal{S}_i}|$ *and* $\ell' = |\mathbf{c}_\mathbb{A}|$, *such that* $\mathbf{k}_{\mathrm{id}_i, \mathcal{S}_i} \mathbf{E}_i \mathbf{c}_\mathbb{A}^\mathsf{T} = \mathrm{bv}_i$.

A MAS-decryption attack is also a decryption attack conform Definition 9. The blinding value can be retrieved, while the individual sets are not authorized to decrypt the ciphertext. Conversely, because such attacks do not exist in the single-authority setting, they are weaker than regular decryption attacks.

4.5   Our Heuristic Approach

We devise a targeted approach, which can be applied manually (or automatically), to finding attacks. As the definitions in the previous section imply, finding an attack is equivalent to finding a suitable linear combination—where the linear coefficients are the entries of $\mathbf{e}$ or $\mathbf{E}$—of all products of the key and ciphertext entries. While finding such coefficients is relatively simple, we note that finding suitable inputs to the attacks may be more difficult. In particular, the number of colluding users and the number of attributes associated with the keys and ciphertexts are effectively unbounded. However, we observe that it often suffices to consider a limited number of inputs, and that for some attacks, only the user-key and attribute-independent ciphertext entries need to be considered. Specifically, Table 3 describes these inputs in terms of encodings, the sets of attributes, and the access policy. Depending on the maximum number of monomials consisting of common variables in any key entry, the attacker might need multiple secret keys for the same set of attributes to recover certain coefficients. For instance, suppose the attacker wants to retrieve α from $\alpha + r_1 b_{\mathrm{att}_1} + r_1' b_{\mathrm{att}_1}'$, where r_1 and r_1' are known, user-specific random variables, and b_{att_1} and b_{att_1}' denote the common variables associated with attribute att_1. Because of the three unknown, linearly independent monomials, this can only be done if the attacker has three distinct keys for attribute att_1. In general, the maximum number of keys with the same set of attributes can be determined in this way, i.e. by counting the maximum number of linearly independent monomials for each entry.

Table 3. The inputs of the attacks, and which encodings are needed.

Attack	Secret keys			Ciphertexts		
	UK	AK	$\mathcal{S}$	AI	AD	$\mathbb{A}$
Master-key	✓	✗	–	✗	✗	–
Attribute-key	✓	✓	$\mathcal{S}_1 = \{\mathrm{att}_1\}, \mathcal{S}_2 = \{\mathrm{att}_2\}$	✗	✗	–
Complete decryption	✓	✗	–	✓	✗	–
Conditional decryption	✓	✓	$\mathcal{S}_1 = \{\mathrm{att}_1\}, \mathcal{S}_2 = \{\mathrm{att}_2\}$	✓	✓	$\mathbb{A} = \mathrm{att}_1 \wedge \mathrm{att}_2$

UK, AK = user-, attribute-key; AI, AD = attribute-independent, -dependent

Similarly, the inputs to multi-authority specific attacks can be limited. First, we consider the attacks under corruption. Corruption of any number of authorities results in the additional knowledge of some otherwise hidden exponents, i.e. the master keys and any random variables generated by these authorities. For most schemes, it should be sufficient to consider one corrupted and one honest authority in the attacks, though depending on how e.g. the master-key α is shared, the number of corrupted authorities may need to be increased. Further, we use the same descriptions of the inputs to the attacks as in the single-authority setting, with the additional requirement that the input attributes are managed by the honest authority. Second, we consider multi-authority specific (MAS) decryption attacks. Corruption is not necessary in this setting, so we assume that all authorities are honest. Additionally, we require at least two honest authorities as input to finding any attack, so we let each authority manage one attribute. Table 4 summarizes the additional inputs to the attacks in Table 3. Finally, it may be possible that a corruptable central authority (CA) is part of the scheme, in which case we also consider whether corruption of this CA enables an attack.

Table 4. The number of required honest authorities n and the attribute universes $\mathcal{U}_1$ and $\mathcal{U}_2$ managed by authorities $\mathcal{A}_1$ and $\mathcal{A}_2$, respectively, in the multi-authority setting.

Attack	n	$\mathcal{U}_1$	$\mathcal{U}_2$
Master-key	1	✗	✗
Attribute-key	1	$\{att_1, att_2\}$	✗
Complete decryption	1	✗	✗
Conditional decryption	1	$\{att_1, att_2\}$	✗
MAS-decryption	2	$\{att_1\}$	$\{att_2\}$

We describe a more targeted approach to finding an attack, i.e. the linear coefficients $\mathbf{e}$ and $\mathbf{E}$, given the input encodings. The approach to finding an attack is linear, as we attempt to retrieve the desired output (conform Definitions 7, 8 and 9) by making linear combinations of products of encodings. The simplest attacks are the master-key and complete decryption attacks, as we only need to consider the attribute-independent parts of the keys and ciphertexts. For these attacks, the goal is to retrieve master-key α, or blinding value αs. Typically, α occurs only in one entry of the keys, while s occurs only in one entry of the ciphertext. Instead of trying all combinations of the key entries with the ciphertext, we formulate a more targeted approach. First, consider the monomials to be canceled, and then which combinations of the key and ciphertext entries can make these monomials. In canceling the previous monomials, it might be that new monomials are added, meaning that these in turn also need to be canceled. This process repeats until all monomials are canceled, and α or αs remains, unless such an attack does not exist. For attribute-key attacks, this effort is considerably more difficult, as the target is less clear. However, it often suffices to consider whether the same monomial occurs more than once in the key encoding. For conciseness, we will only provide the non-zero coefficients in an attack.

5   Examples of Our Attacks Demonstrating the Approach

Using examples of attacks that we have found, we illustrate the way in which our heuristic approach can be applied. In particular, this suggests the simplicity of only considering the exponent space rather than also considering the underlying group structure. Furthermore, in our strongest attack models (i.e. master-key and complete decryption), we often only need to consider the attribute-independent variables, which strips away a large and significantly more difficult part of the scheme. Because many schemes are broken in these models, we assert that it has merit to manually analyze schemes with respect to these models.

5.1 Example Without Corruption: The YJR+13 [39,40] scheme

We perform the attack on YJR+13 in Sect. 3 in the concise notations.

- **Type of attack:** Complete decryption attack;
- **Global parameters: gp** $= (\mathrm{gp}_1, ...) = (b, ...)$;
- **Master keys** $\mathcal{A}_i$**:** $\mathrm{mpk}_i = b_i$;
- **User-key:** $\mathbf{k}_u(\alpha, \mathbf{r}, \mathbf{b}) = (\alpha_i/x_1 + x_2 b + r_i b/b_i, r_i b_i/x_1, r_i b)$;
- **Attribute-independent ciphertext:** $\mathbf{c}(\mathbf{s}, \mathbf{b}) = (s, s/b_i)$;
- **Blinding value:** $\alpha_i s$;
- **Known exponents:** $\mathfrak{K} = \{x_1, x_2\}$ (by definition);

Note that this notation is not only more concise, it is also more structured. In particular, it is clearly denoted what the goal is (i.e. retrieve the blinding value), and what the relevant keys and ciphertexts look like without considering any information about the underlying groups or attribute-dependent variables. Furthermore, this allows us to strip away any additional functionality that further complicates the structure—and by extension, the analysis—of the scheme.

Due to the concise notations, the previous attack can also be found more simply than before. First, we sample a user-key $(k_1, k_2, k_3) \leftarrow \mathbf{k}_u(\alpha, \mathbf{r}, \mathbf{b})$, and ciphertext $(c_1, c_2) \leftarrow \mathbf{c}(\mathbf{s}, \mathbf{b})$. To retrieve $\alpha_i s$, we start by pairing k_1 with c_1:

$$
\underset{\substack{\uparrow \\ \text{Blinding value}}}{} \qquad \overbrace{}^{\text{to cancel}}
$$

$$
x_1 k_1 c_1 = \alpha_i s + \underset{\underset{x_1 x_2 \mathrm{gp}_1 c_1 \quad x_1 k_3 c_2}{\uparrow \qquad\qquad \uparrow}}{x_1 x_2 sb + x_1 r_i sb/b_i},
$$

which yields two monomials to cancel. Subsequently, we can combine the other components and our explicit knowledge of x_1 and x_2 in such a way that these monomials can be canceled. This attack can be formulated in matrix notations:

$$
\alpha_i s = \underbrace{(k_1, k_2, k_3, \mathrm{gp}_1)}_{\mathbf{k}_u} \underbrace{\begin{pmatrix} x_1 & 0 & 0 \\ 0 & 0 & 0 \\ 0 & -x_1 & 0 \\ -x_1 x_2 & 0 & 0 \end{pmatrix}}_{\mathbf{E}} \underbrace{\begin{pmatrix} c_1 \\ c_2 \\ \mathrm{gp}_1 \end{pmatrix}}_{\mathbf{c}}
$$

$$
= x_1 k_1 c_1 - x_1 k_3 c_2 - x_1 x_2 \mathrm{gp}_1 c_1.
$$

Because most of the entries of $\mathbf{E}$ are zero, we will only write the non-zero entries of $\mathbf{E}$ in further attacks. Note that attacks found in the concise notations also translate back to the original description, e.g. compare this attack with that in Sect. 3. More generally, computing $\mathbf{k}_j \mathbf{E}_{i,j} \mathbf{c}_i$ in terms of pair encodings corresponds to computing $e(g^{\mathbf{c}_i}, h^{\mathbf{k}_j})^{\mathbf{E}_{i,j}}$ in the original description of the scheme.

5.2   Example with Corruption: The YJ14 [38] scheme

The YJ14 [38] scheme is somewhat similar to the YJR+13 [40] scheme in the secret keys. However, the decrypting user knows fewer exponents: instead of sharing x_2 in YJR+13 with the user, it is shared with the authorities $\mathcal{A}_i$. Regardless, corruption of one authority leads to the knowledge of x_2, and thus enables an attack. We define the encodings and attack as follows.

– **Type of attack:** Complete decryption attack, under corruption of one $\mathcal{A}_i$;
– **Global parameters:** $\mathsf{gp} = (b, b')$;
– **Master secret key** $\mathcal{A}_i$: $\mathsf{msk}_i = (\alpha_i, x)$;
– **User-key:** $\mathbf{k}_u(\alpha_i, \mathbf{r}, \mathbf{b}) = (\alpha_i + xb + rb', r)$;
– **Attribute-independent ciphertext:** $\mathbf{c}(\mathbf{s}, \mathbf{b}) = (s, sb', ...)$;
– **Blinding value:** $(\sum_i \alpha_i)s$;
– **Known variables:** $\mathfrak{K} = \{x\}$ (by corrupting $\mathcal{A}'$);
– **The goal:** Recover $\alpha_i s$ from $(k_{1,i}, k_{2,i}) \leftarrow \mathbf{k}_u(\alpha_i, \mathbf{r}, \mathbf{b})$, $(c_1, c_2) \leftarrow \mathbf{c}(\mathbf{s}, \mathbf{b})$;
– **The attack:** $\alpha_i s = k_{1,i} c_1 - k_{2,i} c_2 - x \mathsf{mpk}_1 c_1$.   □

5.3   Example Without Corruption: The JLWW13 [16] scheme

We also give an example of a conditional attribute-key attack enabled by two colluding users. This illustrates the increased difficulty of executing more general attacks, as they require us to evaluate the entire key. An additional difficulty of executing an attribute-key attack is in finding an appropriate target key encoding. However, our possibilities as an attacker are considerably limited, as we can only linearly combine the key components, and not multiply them. In fact, as Table 2 shows, we could only find attribute-key attacks if a key consists of recurring monomials. While it is difficult to prove that an attribute-key attack does not exist, it is easy to verify whether a key consists of recurring monomials.

We attack the JLWW13 [16] and JLWW15 [17] schemes—also known as AnonyControl—which have the same key generation. The JLWW15 [17] scheme is different from JLWW13 in the encryption. It is however incorrect, because a value of a single user's secret key is used. The encodings are defined as follows.

– **Type of attack:** Conditional attribute-key attack, collusion of two users;
– **Global parameters:** $\mathsf{gp} = (b, b')$, $\mathsf{mpk}_a(\mathsf{att}_i) = b_{\mathsf{att}_i}$;
– **Secret keys:** $\mathbf{k}_u(\alpha, r, \mathbf{b}) = (\alpha + r)$, $\mathbf{k}_a(\mathsf{att}_i, r, r_i, \mathbf{b}) = (r_i b_{\mathsf{att}_i} + r, r_i)$;

We show that the recurrence of r as a monomial in the user-key and attribute-key encoding enables an attack. While it is relatively simple to show that this cannot be exploited in a single-user setting, we show that sampling two keys for two different sets of attributes $S_1 = \{att_1\}$ and $S_2 = \{att_2\}$ (as in Table 3) enables the generation of a third key for both attributes, i.e. $S_3 = \{att_1, att_2\}$. For $S_1 = \{att_1\}$, we sample $k \leftarrow \mathbf{k}_u(\alpha, r, \mathbf{b})$, and $(k_1, k_2) \leftarrow \mathbf{k}_a(att_1, r, r_1, \mathbf{b})$. For $S_2 = \{att_2\}$, we sample $k' \leftarrow \mathbf{k}_u(\alpha, r', \mathbf{b})$, and $(k'_1, k'_2) \leftarrow \mathbf{k}_a(att_2, r', r_2, \mathbf{b})$.

The goal is to compute a key for set $S_3 = \{att_1, att_2\}$. We aim to generate attribute-keys for the user-key associated with S_1, i.e. k, which links the keys together with r. As such, to create a key for S_3, we need to generate an attribute-key for att_2. We do this by computing: $\mathbf{k}_a(att_2, r, r_2, \mathbf{b}) = (k'_1 + k - k', k'_2)$. □

6 More Attacks, on Several Other Schemes

We present attacks on several existing schemes. For each scheme, we describe the secret keys, and possibly the global parameters and master keys, the ciphertext, and the form of the blinding value in the concise notation introduced in Sect. 4.1. Furthermore, we show whether collusion between users and corruption of any entities are required for the attack. Such corruption results in extra knowledge of exponents, so $\mathbb{Z}_p$ is extended with the known variables conform Sect. 4.2.

6.1 Single-Authority ABE

The ZH10 [42] and ZHW13 [44] Schemes. In these schemes, three generators are defined for each attribute att: a positive (att), a negative (¬att) and a dummy *att value. For each user, the secret key consists of a part associated with the positive or negative attribute and the dummy value.

- **Type of attack:** Conditional attribute-key attack, collusion of two users;
- **Global parameters:** $\mathbf{gp} = (b)$, $\mathbf{mpk}_a(att_i) = (b_{att_i}, b_{\neg att_i}, b_{*att_i})$;
- **Secret keys:** Define $\overline{att} = att$ if $att \in S$ and otherwise $\overline{att} = \neg att$, $\mathbf{k}_u(\sum r_i, b) = ((\sum_{att_i \in \mathcal{U}} r_i)b)$, and $\mathbf{k}_a(\overline{att}_i, r_i, \mathbf{b}) = (r_i b + b b_{\overline{att}_i}, r_i b + b b_{*att_i})$;
- **Input:** $S_1 = \{att_1, \neg att_2\}$, $k_u \leftarrow \mathbf{k}_u(r_1 + r_2, b)$, $(k_{1,i}, k_{2,i}) \leftarrow \mathbf{k}_{a,1}(\overline{att}_i, r_i, \mathbf{b})$, $S_2 = \{\neg att_1, att_2\}$, with $k'_u \leftarrow \mathbf{k}_u(r'_1 + r'_2, b)$, $(k'_{1,i}, k'_{2,i}) \leftarrow \mathbf{k}_a(\overline{att}_i, r'_i, \mathbf{b})$;
- **The goal:** Generate a key for $S_3 = \{att_1, att_2\}$;
- **The attack:** $\mathbf{k}_u(r'_1 + r'_2, \mathbf{b}) = k'_u$, $\mathbf{k}_a(\overline{att}_1, r'_1, \mathbf{b}) = (k_{1,1} + k'_{2,1} - k_{2,1}, k'_{2,1})$, and $\mathbf{k}_a(\overline{att}_2, r'_2, \mathbf{b}) = (k'_{1,2}, k'_{2,2})$. □

The NDCW15 [26] Scheme. This scheme implements a tracing algorithm, allowing the KGA to trace misbehaving users. To this end, some exponents are known to the user. The keys considered below correspond to those given in the second step of the key generation in [26] (which the user can compute).

- **Type of attack:** Complete decryption attack;
- **Global parameters:** $\mathbf{gp} = (b_1, b_2)$;
- **User-key:** $\mathbf{k}_u(\alpha, \mathbf{b}) = (\frac{\alpha}{b_1 + x_3} + x_2 \frac{b_2}{b_1 + x_3}, x_1, x_1 b_1)$;
- **Attribute-independent ciphertext:** $\mathbf{c}(\mathbf{s}, \mathbf{b}) = (s, sb_1, sb_2)$;
- **Known variables:** $\mathfrak{K} = \{x_1, x_2, x_3\}$ (by definition);
- **The goal:** Recover αs from $(k_1, k_2, k_3) \leftarrow \mathbf{k}_u(\alpha, \mathbf{b})$, $(c_1, c_2, c_3) \leftarrow \mathbf{c}(\mathbf{s}, \mathbf{b})$;
- **The attack:** $\alpha s = x_3 k_1 c_1 + k_1 c_2 - x_2 c_3$. □

6.2   Multi-authority ABE

The YJ12 [37] Scheme. This scheme employs a certificate authority (CA), assumed to be fully trusted, and (corruptable) attribute authorities ($\mathcal{A}_i$), responsible for the generation of the secret keys. For the key encodings, we assume that the master public keys are generated as $\mathcal{H}(\mathrm{att})^{\alpha_i}$ rather than as it was originally proposed in [37]: $g^{\alpha_i \mathcal{H}'(\mathrm{att})}$. The latter trivially enables complete attribute-key attacks (because $\mathcal{H}'$ is public), while the former ensures that $\mathcal{H}(\mathrm{att})^{\alpha_i} = g^{\alpha_i b_{\mathrm{att}}}$ is such that b_{att} is unknown to everyone and thus protects against these attacks.

- **Type of attack:** Complete master-key attack, corruption of one $\mathcal{A}$;
- **Global parameters:** $\mathbf{gp} = (b', 1/b')$;
- **Master secret key** $\mathcal{A}_i$: $\mathfrak{msk}_i = (\alpha_i, b/b')$;
- **User-key:** $\mathbf{k}(\alpha_i, \mathbf{r}, \mathbf{b}) = (r, rb/b' + \alpha_i/b')$;
- **Attribute-independent ciphertext:** $\mathbf{c}(\mathbf{s}, \mathbf{b}) = (sb')$;
- **Blinding value:** $(\sum_i \alpha_i)s$, so $\mathrm{mk}(\alpha_i, \mathbf{b}) = \alpha_i/b'$;
- **Known exponents:** $\mathfrak{K} = \{\alpha', b/b'\}$ (by corrupting $\mathcal{A}'$);
- **The goal:** Recover $\mathrm{mk}(\alpha_i, \mathbf{b})$ from $(k_{1,i}, k_{2,i}) \leftarrow \mathbf{k}(\alpha_i, \mathbf{r}, \mathbf{b})$;
- **The attack:** $\mathrm{mk}(\alpha_i, \mathbf{b}) = k_{2,i} - b/b' k_{1,i}$. ☐

The QLZ13 [28] Scheme. This scheme supports hidden access structures and a blind key generation. However, the secret keys trivially leak the master-keys.

- **Type of attack:** Complete master-key attack;
- **Global parameters:** $\mathbf{gp} = (b, b_1, b', ...)$;
- **User-key:** $\mathbf{k}_u(\alpha, \mathbf{r}, \mathbf{b}) = (\alpha + rb + \frac{b_1}{x+b'}, rb - r'b_1, (r' + \frac{1}{x+b'})b_1)$;
- **Known variables:** $\mathfrak{K} = \{x\}$ (by definition);
- **The goal:** Recover α from $(k_1, k_2, k_3) \leftarrow \mathbf{k}_u(\alpha, \mathbf{r}, \mathbf{b})$;
- **The attack:** $\alpha = k_1 - k_2 + k_3$. ☐

The CM14 [10] Scheme. This scheme is a multi-authority version of [33].

- **Type of attack:** Complete decryption attack, under corruption of one $\mathcal{A}$;
- **Master key pair of** $\mathcal{A}_i$: $\mathbf{mpk}_i = (b_i)$, $\mathfrak{msk}_i = (b_i)$;
- **User-key:** $\mathbf{k}_u(\alpha_i, \mathbf{r}, \mathbf{b}) = (\frac{\alpha_i + r}{b_i}, r)$;
- **Attribute-independent ciphertext:** $\mathbf{c}(\mathbf{s}, \mathbf{b}) = (sb_i)$;
- **Blinding value:** $(\sum_i \alpha_i)s$;
- **Known variables:** $\mathfrak{K} = \{b_1\}$ (by corrupting $\mathcal{A}_1$);
- **The goal:** Recover $\alpha_i s$ from $(k_{1,i}, k_{2,i}) \leftarrow \mathbf{k}_u(\alpha_i, \mathbf{r}, \mathbf{b})$, $c_1 \leftarrow \mathbf{c}(\mathbf{s}, \mathbf{b})$;
- **The attack:** $\alpha_i s = k_{1,i} c_1 - 1/b_1 k_{2,i} c_1$ such that $i \neq 1$. ☐

The LXXH16 [22] and MST17 [25] Schemes. These schemes are similar. The LXXH16 scheme employs a corruptable CA to run the global setup. In the MST17 scheme, it is unclear which entity runs it and thus generates the b below.

- **Type of attack:** Complete master-key attack, under corruption of CA;
- **Global parameters:** $\mathbf{gp} = (b)$;
- **User-key:** $\mathbf{k}_u(\alpha, \mathbf{r}, \mathbf{b}) = (\alpha + rb, r)$;

- **Known variables:** $\mathfrak{K} = \{b\}$ (by corrupting CA, and thus the global setup);
- **The goal:** Recover α from $(k_1, k_2) \leftarrow \mathbf{k}_u(\alpha, \mathbf{r}, \mathbf{b})$;
- **The attack:** $\alpha = k_1 - bk_2$.   □

The PO17 [27] Scheme. This scheme was proposed to address an issue of the Cha07 [8] scheme, which requires that a user receives a key from each authority. However, unlike Cha07, the PO17 scheme does not protect against corruption. Thus, in terms of security, it is closer to any single-authority scheme.

- **Type of attack:** Complete decryption attack under corruption of one $\mathcal{A}$;
- **Master key pair of $\mathcal{A}_i$:** $\mathbf{mpk}_i = (b_i)$, $\mathbf{msk}_i = (b_i)$;
- **User-key:** $\mathbf{k}_u(\alpha_i, \mathbf{r}, \mathbf{b}) = (\frac{\alpha_i - r}{b_i}, r)$;
- **Attribute-independent ciphertext:** $\mathbf{c}(\mathbf{s}, \mathbf{b}) = (sb_i)$;
- **Blinding value:** $(\sum_i \alpha_i)s$;
- **Known variables:** b_1 (by corrupting $\mathcal{A}_1$);
- **The goal:** Recover $\alpha_i s$ from $(k_{1,i}, k_{2,i}) \leftarrow \mathbf{k}_u(\alpha_i, \mathbf{r}, \mathbf{b})$, $c_1 \leftarrow \mathbf{c}(\mathbf{s}, \mathbf{b})$;
- **The attack:** $\alpha_i s = k_{1,i}c_1 + 1/b_1 k_{2,i}c_1$.   □

The First MGZ19 [23] Scheme. This scheme employs multiple "central authorities"—to remove the random oracle from [19]—and attribute authorities (AA). The security model considers corruption of the AAs but not the CAs. The description of the scheme does not require the attribute authorities to be aware of the CAs. However, we show that all CAs need to be trusted to ensure security. In particular, we show that corruption of one of the CAs enables an attack.

- **Type of attack:** Complete master-key attack, under corruption of one CA;
- **Master key pair $\mathcal{A}_i$:** $\mathbf{mpk}_{a,i}(\mathrm{att}_j) = (b_{\mathrm{att}_j})$, $\mathbf{msk}_i(\mathrm{att}_j) = (\alpha_i, b_{\mathrm{att}_j})$;
- **CA_i generates:** r;

Table 5. The schemes for which we found attacks, and the consequences of these. For each scheme, we list whether a scheme is insecure in the basic (CPA-)security model, or only under corruption of the central authority (CA) or attribute authorities ($\mathcal{A}$).

	Scheme	Problem	CPA-security
	ZH10 [42,43], ZHW13 [44]	Recurring monomials	✗
	NDCW15 [26]	Known-exponent exploits	✗
	YJ12 [37]	Known-exponent exploits	✗$_\mathcal{A}$
	YJR+13 [39,40], WJB17 [35]	Known-exponent exploits	✗
MA-ABE	JLWW13 [16], JLWW15 [17]	Recurring monomials	✗
	QLZ13 [28]	Recurring monomials	✗
	YJ14 [38]	Known-exponent exploits	✗$_\mathcal{A}$
	CM14 [10]	Known-exponent exploits	✗$_\mathcal{A}$
	LXXH16 [22], MST17 [25]	Known-exponent exploits	✗$_{CA}$
	PO17 [27]	Known-exponent exploits	✗$_\mathcal{A}$
	MGZ19 I [23]	Known-exponent exploits	✗$_{CA}$

✗$_\mathcal{A}$, ✗$_{CA}$ = none under corruption of $\mathcal{A}$, CA

- **Secret key:** $\mathbf{k}_u(\alpha_i, \mathbf{r}, \mathbf{b}) = (r)$, $\mathbf{k}_a(\text{att}_j, \alpha_i, \mathbf{r}, \mathbf{b}) = (\alpha_i + rb_{\text{att}_j})$;
- **Known variables:** $\mathfrak{K} = \{r\}$ (by corrupting one CA);
- **The goal:** Recover α_i from $k_{i,j} \leftarrow \mathbf{k}_a(\text{att}_j, \alpha_i, \mathbf{r}, \mathbf{b})$, $\text{mpk}_{i,j} \leftarrow \mathbf{mpk}_{a,i}(\text{att}_j)$;
- **The attack:** $\alpha_i = k_{i,j} - r\text{mpk}_{i,j}$. □

7   Discussion

We have presented a linear, heuristic approach to analyzing security—consisting of a more concise notation—and applied it to existing schemes. This approach simplifies manually finding generic attacks provided that they exist. For future work, it would be valuable to extend the approach to be provably exhaustive, such that it follows with [2] that the scheme also implies a provably secure scheme. In addition, it would be valuable to automatize finding attacks for the multi-authority encodings like [2] does in the single-authority setting. To demonstrate the effectiveness of our approach, we have shown that several existing schemes are vulnerable to our attacks, either rendering them fully or partially insecure. Most of the attacks are similar in that they either exploit that one monomial occurs more than once in the keys, or known exponents yield sufficient knowledge to enable an attack. Table 5 lists each attacked scheme and the associated fundamental problem that enables the attack. In general, schemes for which we found an attack without requiring corruption are structurally more complicated than the single-authority schemes on which they are (loosely) based. Schemes that are insecure against corruption are generally closer to their (provably secure) single-authority variants, but knowing certain exponents enables an attack. Possibly, distributively generating these exponents may prevent this. For future work, it may be interesting to consider whether this yields secure schemes.

Acknowledgments. The authors would like to thank the anonymous reviewers for their helpful comments and suggestions.

References

1. Agrawal, S., Chase, M.: Simplifying design and analysis of complex predicate encryption schemes. In: Coron, J.-S., Nielsen, J.B. (eds.) EUROCRYPT 2017. LNCS, vol. 10210, pp. 627–656. Springer, Cham (2017). https://doi.org/10.1007/978-3-319-56620-7_22
2. Ambrona, M., Barthe, G., Gay, R., Wee, H.: Attribute-based encryption in the generic group model: automated proofs and new constructions. In: CCS, pp. 647–664. ACM (2017)
3. Attrapadung, N.: Dual system encryption via doubly selective security: framework, fully secure functional encryption for regular languages, and more. In: Nguyen, P.Q., Oswald, E. (eds.) EUROCRYPT 2014. LNCS, vol. 8441, pp. 557–577. Springer, Heidelberg (2014). https://doi.org/10.1007/978-3-642-55220-5_31
4. Beimel, A.: Secure schemes for secret sharing and key distribution (1996)
5. Bethencourt, J., Sahai, A., Waters, B.: Ciphertext-policy attribute-based encryption. In: S&P, pp. 321–334. IEEE (2007)

6. Boneh, D., Boyen, X., Goh, E.-J.: Hierarchical identity based encryption with constant size ciphertext. In: Cramer, R. (ed.) EUROCRYPT 2005. LNCS, vol. 3494, pp. 440–456. Springer, Heidelberg (2005). https://doi.org/10.1007/11426639_26

7. Boyen, X.: The uber-assumption family. In: Galbraith, S.D., Paterson, K.G. (eds.) Pairing 2008. LNCS, vol. 5209, pp. 39–56. Springer, Heidelberg (2008). https://doi.org/10.1007/978-3-540-85538-5_3

8. Chase, M.: Multi-authority attribute based encryption. In: Vadhan, S.P. (ed.) TCC 2007. LNCS, vol. 4392, pp. 515–534. Springer, Heidelberg (2007). https://doi.org/10.1007/978-3-540-70936-7_28

9. Chaudhari, P., Das, M.L., Mathuria, A.: On anonymous attribute based encryption. In: Jajodia, S., Mazumdar, C. (eds.) ICISS 2015. LNCS, vol. 9478, pp. 378–392. Springer, Cham (2015). https://doi.org/10.1007/978-3-319-26961-0_23

10. Chen, J., Ma, H.: Efficient decentralized attribute-based access control for cloud storage with user revocation. In: ICC, pp. 3782–3787. IEEE (2014)

11. Ge, A., Zhang, J., Zhang, R., Ma, C., Zhang, Z.: Security analysis of a privacy-preserving decentralized key-policy attribute-based encryption scheme. IEEE TPDS 24(11), 2319–2321 (2013)

12. Han, J., Susilo, W., Mu, Y., Yan, J.: Privacy-preserving decentralized key-policy attribute-based encryption. IEEE TPDS 23(11), 2150–2162 (2012)

13. Han, J., Susilo, W., Mu, Y., Zhou, J., Au, M.H.: PPDCP-ABE: privacy-preserving decentralized ciphertext-policy attribute-based encryption. In: Kutyłowski, M., Vaidya, J. (eds.) ESORICS 2014. LNCS, vol. 8713, pp. 73–90. Springer, Cham (2014). https://doi.org/10.1007/978-3-319-11212-1_5

14. Han, J., Susilo, W., Mu, Y., Zhou, J., Au, M.H.A.: Improving privacy and security in decentralized ciphertext-policy attribute-based encryption. IEEE TIFS 10(3), 665–678 (2015)

15. Hong, J., Xue, K., Li, W.: Comments on DAC-MACS: Effective data access control for multiauthority cloud storage systems/security analysis of attribute revocation in multiauthority data access control for cloud storage systems. IEEE TIFS 10(6), 1315–1317 (2015)

16. Jung, T., Li, X.Y., Wan, Z., Wan, M.: Privacy preserving cloud data access with multi-authorities. In: INFOCOM, pp. 2625–2633. IEEE (2013)

17. Jung, T., Li, X.Y., Wan, Z., Wan, M.: Control cloud data access privilege and anonymity with fully anonymous attribute-based encryption. IEEE TIFS 10(1), 190–199 (2015)

18. Jung, T., Li, X.Y., Wan, Z., Wan, M.: Rebuttal to Comments on Control cloud data access privilege and anonymity with fully anonymous attribute-based encryption. IEEE TIFS 10(4), 868 (2016)

19. Lewko, A., Waters, B.: Decentralizing attribute-based encryption. In: EUROCRYPT. pp. 568–588. Springer (2011)

20. Li, J., Huang, Q., Chen, X., Chow, S.S.M., Wong, D.S., Xie, D.: Multi-authority ciphertext-policy attribute-based encryption with accountability. In: AsiaCCS, pp. 386–390. ACM (2011)

21. Li, J., Ren, K., Zhu, B., Wan, Z.: Privacy-aware attribute-based encryption with user accountability. In: Samarati, P., Yung, M., Martinelli, F., Ardagna, C.A. (eds.) ISC 2009. LNCS, vol. 5735, pp. 347–362. Springer, Heidelberg (2009). https://doi.org/10.1007/978-3-642-04474-8_28

22. Li, W., Xue, K., Xue, Y., Hong, J.: TMACS: a robust and verifiable threshold multi-authority access control system in public cloud storage. IEEE TPDS 27(5), 1484–1496 (2016)

23. Ma, C., Ge, A., Zhang, J.: Fully secure decentralized ciphertext-policy attribute-based encryption in standard model. In: Guo, F., Huang, X., Yung, M. (eds.) Inscrypt 2018. LNCS, vol. 11449, pp. 427–447. Springer, Cham (2019). https://doi.org/10.1007/978-3-030-14234-6_23

24. Ma, H., Zhang, R., Yuan, W.: Comments on Control cloud data access privilege and anonymity with fully anonymous attribute-based encryption. IEEE TIFS **11**(4), 866–867 (2016)

25. Malluhi, Q.M., Shikfa, A., Trinh, V.C.: Ciphertext-policy attribute-based encryption scheme with optimized ciphertext size and fast decryption. In: AsiaCCS, pp. 230–240. ACM (2017)

26. Ning, J., Dong, X., Cao, Z., Wei, L.: Accountable authority ciphertext-policy attribute-based encryption with white-box traceability and public auditing in the cloud. In: ESORICS. pp. 270–289. Springer (2015)

27. Pussewalage, H.S.G., Oleshchuk, V.A.: A distributed multi-authority attribute based encryption scheme for secure sharing of personal health records. In: SAC-MAT, pp. 255–262. ACM (2017)

28. Qian, H., Li, J., Zhang, Y.: Privacy-preserving decentralized ciphertext-policy attribute-based encryption with fully hidden access structure. In: Qing, S., Zhou, J., Liu, D. (eds.) ICICS 2013. LNCS, vol. 8233, pp. 363–372. Springer, Cham (2013). https://doi.org/10.1007/978-3-319-02726-5_26

29. Qian, H., Li, J., Zhang, Y., Han, J.: Privacy-preserving personal health record using multi-authority attribute-based encryption with revocation. Int. J. Inf. Security **14**(6), 487–497 (2014). https://doi.org/10.1007/s10207-014-0270-9

30. Sahai, A., Waters, B.: Fuzzy identity-based encryption. In: Cramer, R. (ed.) EURO-CRYPT 2005. LNCS, vol. 3494, pp. 457–473. Springer, Heidelberg (2005). https://doi.org/10.1007/11426639_27

31. Venema, M., Alpár, G.: A bunch of broken schemes: A simple yet powerful linear approach to analyzing security of attribute-based encryption. Cryptology ePrint Archive, Report 2020/460 (2020)

32. Wang, M., Zhang, Z., Chen, C.: Security analysis of a privacy-preserving decentralized ciphertext-policy attribute-based encryption scheme. Concurrency and Computation **28**(4), 1237–1245 (2015)

33. Waters, B.: Ciphertext-policy attribute-based encryption: an expressive, efficient, and provably secure realization. In: Catalano, D., Fazio, N., Gennaro, R., Nicolosi, A. (eds.) PKC 2011. LNCS, vol. 6571, pp. 53–70. Springer, Heidelberg (2011). https://doi.org/10.1007/978-3-642-19379-8_4

34. Wee, H.: Dual system encryption via predicate encodings. In: Lindell, Y. (ed.) TCC 2014. LNCS, vol. 8349, pp. 616–637. Springer, Heidelberg (2014). https://doi.org/10.1007/978-3-642-54242-8_26

35. Wu, X., Jiang, R., Bhargava, B.: On the security of data access control for multiauthority cloud storage systems. IEEE Trans. Serv. Comput. **10**(2), 258–272 (2017)

36. Xhafa, F., Feng, J., Zhang, Y., Chen, X., Li, J.: Privacy-aware attribute-based phr sharing with user accountability in cloud computing. J. Supercomput. **71**, 1607–1619 (2014)

37. Yang, K., Jia, X.: Attribute-based access control for multi-authority systems in cloud storage. In: IEEE Distributed Computing Systems, pp. 536–545. IEEE Computer Society (2012)

38. Yang, K., Jia, X.: Expressive, efficient, and revocable data access control for multi-authority cloud storage. IEEE TPDS **25**(7), 1735–1744 (2014)

39. Yang, K., Jia, X., Ren, K., Zhang, B.: DAC-MACS: effective data access control for multiauthority cloud storage systems. In: INFOCOM, pp. 2895–2903. IEEE (2013)

40. Yang, K., Jia, X., Ren, K., Zhang, B., Xie, R.: DAC-MACS: effective data access control for multiauthority cloud storage systems. IEEE TIFS **8**(11), 1790–1801 (2013)
41. Zhang, Y., Chen, X., Li, J., Wong, D., Li, H.: Anonymous attribute-based encryption supporting efficient decryption test. In: AsiaCCS, pp. 511–516. ACM (2013)
42. Zhou, Z., Huang, D.: On efficient ciphertext-policy attribute based encryption and broadcast encryption. In: CCS (poster), pp. 753–755. ACM (2010)
43. Zhou, Z., Huang, D.: On efficient ciphertext-policy attribute based encryption and broadcast encryption. Cryptology ePrint Archive, Report 2010/395 (2010)
44. Zhou, Z., Huang, D., Wang, Z.: Efficient privacy-preserving ciphertext-policy attribute based-encryption and broadcast encryption. IEEE Trans. Comput. **64**(1), 126–138 (2015)

Zero-Correlation Linear Cryptanalysis with Equal Treatment for Plaintexts and Tweakeys

Chao Niu[1,2], Muzhou Li[1,2], Siwei Sun[3,4], and Meiqin Wang[1,2(✉)]

[1] School of Cyber Science and Technology, Shandong University,
Qingdao 266237, Shandong, China
{niuchao,limuzhou}@mail.sdu.edu.cn
[2] Key Laboratory of Cryptologic Technology and Information Security
of Ministry of Education, Shandong University, Qingdao 266237, Shandong, China
mqwang@sdu.edu.cn
[3] State Key Laboratory of Information Security, Institute of Information
Engineering, Chinese Academy of Sciences, Beijing, China
[4] University of Chinese Academy of Sciences, Beijing, China

Abstract. The original zero-correlation linear attack on a tweakable block cipher $E_{K,T}$ ($E_{K,T}$ is an ordinary block cipher when $|T| = 0$) with key K and tweak T exploits linear approximations $\langle \alpha, x \rangle \oplus \langle \beta, E_{K,T}(x) \rangle$ with correlation zero for any *fixed* K and T, where the correlation is computed over all possible plaintexts x. Obviously, the plaintexts, keys, and tweaks are not treated equally. In this work, we regard the tweakable block cipher as a vectorial Boolean function $F : \mathbb{F}_2^{n+m+l} \to \mathbb{F}_2^n$ mapping $(x, K, T) \in \mathbb{F}_2^{n+m+l}$ to $E_{K,T}(x) \in \mathbb{F}_2^n$, and try to find zero-correlation linear approximations of F of the form

$$\langle \alpha, x \rangle \oplus \langle \gamma, K \rangle \oplus \langle \lambda, T \rangle \oplus \langle \beta, F(K, T, x) \rangle,$$

where the correlation is computed over all possible (x, K, T)'s. Standard tools based on SAT and SMT can be employed to search for this type of zero-correlation linear approximations under a unified framework of which Ankele *et al.*'s work on zero-correlation analysis at ToSC 2019 by taking tweaks into account can be seen as a special case with linear tweak schedules and $\gamma = 0$. Due to the links between zero-correlation linear approximations and integral distinguishers, we can convert the new type of zero-correlation linear distinguishers into related-tweakey integral distinguishers. We apply our method to TWINE, LBlock, and SKINNY with both linear and nonlinear tweakey schedules. As a result, we obtain the longest distinguishers for TWINE and longer zero-correlation linear distinguishers for LBlock and SKINNY when considering key/tweak schedule. The correctness of our method is verified by recovering the results of Ankele *et al.* and experiments on a toy cipher.

Keywords: Zero-correlation linear cryptanalysis · SAT · SMT · Tweakable block ciphers · TWINE · LBlock · SKINNY

© Springer Nature Switzerland AG 2021
K. G. Paterson (Ed.): CT-RSA 2021, LNCS 12704, pp. 126–147, 2021.
https://doi.org/10.1007/978-3-030-75539-3_6

1 Introduction

Linear cryptanalysis [17] is one of the most important techniques for analyzing block ciphers, from which many cryptanalytic techniques have been derived, including the linear hull effect [20], multiple linear cryptanalysis [12], multidimensional linear cryptanalysis [10], etc. Basically, these techniques rely on linear approximations of the targets with relatively high absolute correlations. In 2014, a variant of linear cryptanalysis named as zero-correlation linear cryptanalysis exploiting linear hulls with absolute zero correlation was proposed by Bogdanov and Rijmen [5]. The main drawback of this technique in its infancy stage is that it requires almost the whole codebook to execute the attack. This limitation in terms of data complexity of zero-correlation linear cryptanalysis was overcome at FSE 2012, where multiple linear approximations of the target with correlation zero (MPZC) are exploited [6]. However, the assumption in MPZC distinguisher that all involved zero-correlation linear approximations are independent restricts its application. At ASIACRYPT 2012 [4], a new distinguisher called multidimensional zero-correlation (MDZC) distinguisher was constructed, which removed the assumption in MPZC distinguisher. Subsequently, the fundamental links between zero-correlation linear approximations and integral distinguishers [4,22] allows us to observe an integral property in the data-path.

Another interesting development of the zero-correlation linear cryptanalysis discussing the effect of the tweakeys was initiated at ToSC 2019 [1]. In this work, Ankele *et al.* show that it is possible to find zero-correlation linear approximations involving the bits of plaintexts, tweaks, and ciphertexts, sometimes leading to distinguishers covering more rounds of the target. Note that such improvements are only possible in the context of zero-correlation linear cryptanalysis, since Kranz, Leander, and Wiemer showed that the addition of a tweak using a linear tweak schedule does not introduce new valid linear characteristics [15]. However, Ankele *et al.*'s approach only applies to ciphers with linear tweakey schedule algorithms and at the word level, and thus may miss some bit-level distinguishers.

Our Contributions. We generalize Ankele *et al.*'s idea [1] by considering zero-correlation linear approximations of a (tweakable) block cipher involving the bits of plaintexts, keys, and tweaks, where the correlation is computed over all possible plaintexts, keys, and tweaks. Under this framework, the public and secret inputs of the target ciphers are treated equally.

Then we show that such zero-correlation linear approximations can be found with automatic tools based on SAT or SMT. The only difference between the new models and the traditional ones [5] for zero-correlation linear analysis is that in our models we also need to describe the behavior of the linear characteristics propagating through the key schedule algorithms. Compared with Ankele *et al.*'s work (which can be regarded as a special case of ours), the new approach is much more straightforward and applies to ciphers with both linear and nonlinear tweakey schedule algorithms and it works at the bit level.

Since the zero-correlation linear approximations are taken over all possible inputs including the secret keys, it is difficult to use them by following the approach of traditional zero-correlation linear cryptanalysis. To actually use these zero-correlation linear approximations in attacks, we can convert them into related-tweakey integral distinguishers according to the links between zero-correlation linear approximations and integral distinguishers.

We apply our method to TWINE [13], LBlock [28], and SKINNY [2] with both linear and nonlinear tweakey schedules. As a result, we obtain the longest distinguishers for TWINE and longer zero-correlation linear distinguishers for LBlock and SKINNY when considering key/tweak schedule. A summary of the results on block cipher with nonlinear key schedule can be found in Table 1. Using our new method, we can find distinguisher for SKINNY that is one round longer than Ankele et al.'s work, one can refer to Table 2. In addition, to confirm the correctness of our model, we try to automatically recover the results of Ankele et al. and perform full experiments on a toy cipher. The source code is available at https://github.com/zero-cryptanalysis/Experiment-on-TC.

Table 1. A comparison of our results and previous results on TWINE, LBlock, where ZC, ID, RK, and KDIB stand for zero correlation, impossible differential, related-key, and key difference invariant bias, respectively. #keys : the number of different keys used; CP: chosen plaintext; KP: known plaintext.

Cipher	Distinguisher	Data per Key	#keys	Attack type	Ref.
TWINE-80	14	$2^{62.1}$KP	1	ZC	[25]
TWINE-80	15	$2^{61.42}$CP	2	RK-ID	[26]
TWINE-80	**17**	2^{64}**KP**	**16**	**ZC/Integral**	Sect. 4.1
TWINE-128	14	$2^{52.21}$CP	1	ID	[13]
TWINE-128	17	$2^{62.29}$KP	32	KDIB	[3]
TWINE-128	**18**	2^{64}**KP**	**16**	**ZC/Integral**	Sect. 4.1
LBlock-80	14	$2^{62.3}$KP	1	ZC	[29]
LBlock-80	**15**	2^{64}**KP**	**16**	**ZC/Integral**	Sect. 4.2
LBlock-80	16	$2^{61.4}$CP	4	RK-ID	[27]
LBlock-80	16	$2^{62.29}$KP	32	KDIB	[3]

Table 2. A comparison of our results and previous results on SKINNY, where ZC stands for zero correlation. #tks: the number of different tweaks used; KP: known plaintext.

Cipher	Distinguisher	Data per Tweaks	#tks	Attack type	Ref.
SKINNY-64/128	13	2^{68}KP	2^8	ZC/Integral	[1]
SKINNY-64/128	**14**	2^{68}**KP**	2^8	**ZC/Integral**	Sect. 4.3
SKINNY-64/192	15	2^{72}KP	2^{12}	ZC/Integral	[1]
SKINNY-64/192	**16**	2^{72}**KP**	2^{12}	**ZC/Integral**	Sect. 4.3

Related Work. Most symmetric-key cryptanalytic techniques such as impossible differential cryptanalysis and zero-correlation cryptanalysis are originally proposed in the single-key setting. These years, lots of cryptanalysts are trying to make use of the key schedule in their attack model which means in this kind of attack scenario related keys should be taken into account. Related-key impossible differential cryptanalysis of TWINE [26,30] and LBlock [27] exploit the key schedule of a block cipher by involving difference into both data path and key expansion data path which can get a longer distinguisher. Worth mentioning, the property of linear hulls with invariant bias under a related-key difference was proposed by Bogdanov *et al.* in [3]. Their cryptanalytic method is effective with the application on TWINE and LBlock. Our zero-correlation linear approximation considering key/tweak schedule also makes use of the construction of the key/tweak schedule and gets a longer distinguisher on TWINE. Different from the key schedule of TWINE, a bit-level rotation in the key schedule of LBlock has a strong diffusion. This may be the reason we can not get a longer distinguisher of LBlock than the above two cryptanalytic methods. Our method exploited the slow diffusion property of the key schedule which is different from the above two cryptanalytic methods.

Outline. In Sect. 2, we briefly recall the basic zero-correlation linear cryptanalysis and a variant of it where the linear approximations also involve tweak bits. In Sect. 3 we consider a new type of zero-correlation linear approximations where the plaintext, keys, and tweaks are treated equally. Then we present a SAT-based automatic method for finding such zero-correlation linear approximations. Finally, we show that these new zero-correlation linear approximations can be translated into related-tweakey integral distinguishers. We apply our method to TWINE, LBlock, and SKINNY in Sect. 4. Section 5 concludes the paper.

2 Preliminaries

In this section, we briefly recall the zero-correlation linear cryptanalysis on an n-bit tweakable block cipher $E_{K,T}$ with key $K \in \mathbb{F}_2^m$ and tweak $T \in \mathbb{F}_2^l$. When $l = 0$, it turns into an ordinary block cipher with no tweaks. Alternatively, a block cipher can be regarded as a vectorial Boolean function:

$$F : \mathbb{F}_2^m \times \mathbb{F}_2^l \times \mathbb{F}_2^n \to \mathbb{F}_2^n,$$

which maps (K, T, x) to $E_{K,T}(x)$, i.e., $F(K, T, x) = E_{K,T}(x)$.

Let α and β be n-bit vectors in $\mathbb{F}_2^n$. The correlation

$$\mathrm{cor}_{F(K,T,\cdot)}(\alpha, \beta) = \mathrm{cor}_{E_{K,T}(\cdot)}(\alpha, \beta)$$

of $F(K, T, \cdot) = E_{K,T}(\cdot)$ with a given $(K, T) \in \mathbb{F}_2^{m+l}$ is defined as

$$\frac{\#\{x \in \mathbb{F}_2^n : \langle \alpha, x \rangle \oplus \langle \beta, E_{K,T}(x) \rangle = 0\} - \#\{x \in \mathbb{F}_2^n : \langle \alpha, x \rangle \oplus \langle \beta, E_{K,T}(x) \rangle = 1\}}{2^n}, \quad (1)$$

where $\langle u, v \rangle$ denotes the inner product of two bit vectors of the same length. The orignal zero-correlation linear cryptanalysis exploits linear approximations with input and output linear masks α and β such that $\mathrm{cor}_{E_{K,T}(\cdot)}(\alpha, \beta) = 0$ for any K and T. Such an (α, β) is called a zero-correlation linear approximation of $E_{K,T}$. Given a single zero-correlation linear approximation of $E_{K,T}$, one can distinguish $E_{K,T}$ by using almost the whole codebook [5]. In [4], Andrey *et al.* showed that it is possible to distinguish $E_{K,T}$ with data complexity $\mathcal{O}(2^n/\sqrt{s})$ by using s zero-correlation linear approximations.

At ToSC 2019, Ankele *et al.* proposed to consider a new type of zero-correlation linear cryptanalysis where the linear masks for tweaks can be nonzero [1]. We formally describe their idea in the following.

Let $\mathcal{L}_{F(K,\cdot,\cdot)}^{((\lambda,\alpha),\beta)}(T, x) = \langle \lambda, T \rangle \oplus \langle \alpha, x \rangle \oplus \langle \beta, F(K, T, x) \rangle$. The correlation

$$\mathrm{cor}_{F(K,\cdot,\cdot)}((\lambda, \alpha), \beta)$$

of $F(K, \cdot, \cdot)$ for any fixed key K is defined as

$$\frac{\#\{(T, x) \in \mathbb{F}_2^{l+n} : \mathcal{L}_{F(K,\cdot,\cdot)}^{((\lambda,\alpha),\beta)}(T, x) = 0\} - \#\{(T, x) \in \mathbb{F}_2^{l+n} : \mathcal{L}_{F(K,\cdot,\cdot)}^{((\lambda,\alpha),\beta)}(T, x) = 1\}}{2^{l+n}}, \quad (2)$$

i.e., the correlation is computed over all possible plaintexts and tweaks. To search for such zero-correlation linear approximations involving also tweak bits, Ankele *et al.* adopted the following strategy, which is only applicable to ciphers with linear tweakey expansions.

First, fix the linear masks for plaintext and ciphertext to α and β. Then derive all linear characteristics with nonzero correlation whose masks for plaintext and ciphertext are α and β, from which the set $\mathbb{S}$ of all possible λ such that $\mathrm{cor}_{F(K,\cdot,\cdot)}((\lambda, \alpha), \beta) \neq 0$ is computed. Finally, pick a $\lambda' \notin \mathbb{S}$, and we have $\mathrm{cor}_{F(K,\cdot,\cdot)}((\lambda', \alpha), \beta) = 0$. We note that the derivation of $\mathbb{S}$ heavily relies on the linearity and simplicity of the tweak expansion. Moreover, since Ankele *et al.*'s method is performed manually and works at the word level, it only applies to ciphers with linear tweak expansions and may miss some zero-correlation linear approximations.

3 Zero-Correlation Linear Cryptanalysis with Equal Treatment for Plaintexts, Keys, and Tweaks

Taking Ankele *et al.*'s idea one step further, we treat all the public and secret inputs of the block cipher E equally, and consider linear approximations involving plaintexts, keys, tweaks, and ciphertexts. Moreover, the output of the key/tweak schedule is not available to us. To find this kind of new linear approximation, we set the mask on the output of the key/tweak schedule equal to zero.

Denote $((\gamma, \lambda, \alpha), \beta)$ be the linear mask on key, tweak, plaintext, and ciphertext respectively. Let $\Lambda = ((\gamma, \lambda, \alpha), \beta) \in \mathbb{F}_2^{m+l+2n}$. The linear approximation $\mathcal{L}_F^\Lambda(K, T, x)$ is defined as

$$\langle \gamma, K \rangle \oplus \langle \lambda, T \rangle \oplus \langle \alpha, x \rangle \oplus \langle \beta, F(K, T, x) \rangle, \quad (3)$$

and the correlation $\text{cor}_F((\gamma, \lambda, \alpha), \beta)$ of the linear approximation is defined as

$$\frac{\#\{(K, T, x) \in \mathbb{F}_2^{m+l+n} : \mathcal{L}_F^{\Lambda}(K, T, x) = 0\} - \#\{(K, T, x) \in \mathbb{F}_2^{m+l+n} : \mathcal{L}_F^{\Lambda}(K, T, x) = 1\}}{2^{m+l+n}}. \quad (4)$$

From the above definition, we can see that the correlation is computed over all possible plaintexts, keys, and tweaks. Therefore, due to the involvement of the keys, it is unknown how to carry out a key-recovery attack based on such zero-correlation linear approximations. To exploit this type of zero-correlation linear approximations, we show how to translate them into related-tweakey integral distinguishers in the following.

The links between the original zero-correlation linear approximations and integral distinguishers facilitating the conversions between them are established in [4, 22]. The most relevant theorem in our context is rephrased as follows.

Theorem 1 ([22]). *Let $F : \mathbb{F}_2^n \to \mathbb{F}_2^n$ be a vectorial Boolean function, and A be a subspace of $\mathbb{F}_2^n$ and $\beta \in \mathbb{F}_2^n \backslash \{0\}$. Suppose that (α, β) is a zero correlation linear approximation for any $\alpha \in A$, then for any $\lambda \in \mathbb{F}_2^n, \langle \beta, F(x \oplus \lambda) \rangle$ is balanced on $A^{\perp} = \{x \in \mathbb{F}_2^n : \langle \alpha, x \rangle = 0, \alpha \in A\}$.*

Theorem 1 can be adapted into the following form to serve our purpose, and the same strategy for proving Theorem 1 can be applied to its new form.

Corollary 1. *Let $F : \mathbb{F}_2^m \times \mathbb{F}_2^l \times \mathbb{F}_2^n \to \mathbb{F}_2^n$ be a vectorial Boolean function, and A be a subspace of $\mathbb{F}_2^{m+l+n}$ and $\beta \in \mathbb{F}_2^n \backslash \{0\}$. Suppose that $\Lambda = ((\gamma, \lambda, \alpha), \beta) \in \mathbb{F}_2^{m+l+2n}$ is a zero correlation linear approximation for any $(\gamma, \lambda, \alpha) \in A$, then for any $u \in \mathbb{F}_2^{m+l+n}, \langle \beta, F(x \oplus u) \rangle$ is balanced on*

$$A^{\perp} = \left\{ x \in \mathbb{F}_2^{m+l+n} : \langle (\gamma, \lambda, \alpha), x \rangle = 0, (\gamma, \lambda, \alpha) \in A \right\}.$$

Corollary 1 tells us that if we can find a family of linear approximations $\Lambda = ((\gamma, \lambda, \alpha), \beta) \in \mathbb{F}_2^{m+l+2n}$ which are zero correlation for any $(\gamma, \lambda, \alpha)$ in a d-dimensional linear subspace $A \subseteq \mathbb{F}_2^{m+l+n}$, then we can construct an integral distinguisher with data complexity $2^{m+l+n-d}$, and the set of chosen inputs of F is

$$A^{\perp} \oplus u = \left\{ x \oplus u \in \mathbb{F}_2^{m+l+n} : \langle (\gamma, \lambda, \alpha), x \rangle = 0, (\gamma, \lambda, \alpha) \in A \right\}$$

for any fixed $u \in \mathbb{F}_2^{m+l+n}$.

Automatic Search Tools. To search for linear approximations of the form given in Equation (3) with correlation zero, we can employ the constraint-based approach presented in [16, 21]. Note that in the original models [6], the keys and thus the subkeys as well as the tweaks are regarded as constants. Therefore, the original models only model the propagations of the linear masks in the encryption data path without considering the tweakey schedule algorithms, for which no variables and constraints are introduced. In our model, since we treat $E_{K,T}(x)$ as a function $F(K, T, x)$ from $\mathbb{F}_2^{m+l+n}$ to $\mathbb{F}_2^n$, the propagation of the input linear masks for plaintexts, keys, and tweaks through F, including both

---

Algorithm 1: Search for Zero-Correlation Linear Approximations

---

Input: A cipher $E_{K,T}(\cdot)$ with $F(K,T,x) = E_{K,T}(x)$
Output: Zero-correlation linear approximations of F

1 Let $\mathcal{X}$ be some predefined subset of $\mathbb{F}_2^{m+l+2n}$
2 **for** $((\gamma, \lambda, \alpha), \beta) \in \mathcal{X} \subseteq \mathbb{F}_2^{m+l+2n}$ **do**
3 | $\mathcal{M} \leftarrow$ `GenerateLinearModel`(F)
4 | Add the following constraints to $\mathcal{M}$:
5 | ▷ Fix the linear mask of (K, T, x) to $(\gamma, \lambda, \alpha)$
6 | ▷ Fix the linear mask of the ciphertext to β
7 | **if** $\mathcal{M}$ *has no solution* **then**
8 | └ Output $((\gamma, \lambda, \alpha), \beta)$ as a zero-correlation linear approximation of F

---

the encryption data path and tweakey schedule data path has to be modeled. The general framework of the search algorithm is described in Algorithm 1.

In Algorithm 1, $\mathcal{X}$ is defined heuristically by the cryptanalysts, since it is impossible to enumerate all patterns in $\mathbb{F}_2^{m+l+2n}$. Typically, $\mathcal{X}$ is chosen to be the set of patterns with relatively low Hamming weights. The subroutine `GenerateLinearModel()` generates a mathematical model containing the variables representing the linear characteristics of F, and the constraints imposed on these variables according to the propagation rules of the linear characteristics. Therefore, after the execution of

$$\mathcal{M} \leftarrow \texttt{GenerateLinearModel}(F),$$

the solution space of the mathematical model $\mathcal{M}$ is the set of all nonzero-correlation linear characteristics of F. Moreover, after we fixing the linear masks of (K, T, x) and the ciphertext, the solution space of $\mathcal{M}$ is the set of all nonzero-correlation linear characteristics of F with input mask $(\gamma, \lambda, \alpha)$ and output mask β. Consequently, if the solution space of M is an empty set at this point, we know that the linear approximation $((\gamma, \lambda, \alpha), \beta)$ must be zero-correlation. Since all of our targets contain only the four types of basic operations, including XOR, branch, linear transformations, and S-boxes, we only specify the mathematical constraints imposed on these basic operations, and the full model $\mathcal{M}$ can be assembled from the constraints of these basic operations.

- **XOR**([16]). The XOR operation maps $(x, y) \in \mathbb{F}_2^n$ to $z = x \oplus y$. Let a and b denote linear masks of the two input bits, and c denote the output mask. Then the linear approximation of XOR due to (a, b, c) is of nonzero-correlation if and only if it fulfills $a = b = c$.
- **Branch**([16]). The branch operation maps $x \in \mathbb{F}_2^n$ to $(y, z) \in \mathbb{F}_2^{2n}$ with $x = y = z$. Let (a, b, c) be the linear mask of (x, y, z), then the linear approximation of the branch operation due to (a, b, c) is of nonzero-correlation if and only if $c = a \oplus b$.

- **Linear transformation([16]).** A linear transformation with matrix representation M maps a column vector $\boldsymbol{x}$ to $\boldsymbol{y} = M\boldsymbol{x}$. Let $(\boldsymbol{a}, \boldsymbol{b})$ be the linear mask of $(\boldsymbol{x}, \boldsymbol{y})$. Then the linear approximation of the linear transformation M due to $(\boldsymbol{a}, \boldsymbol{b})$ is of nonzero-correlation if and only if $\boldsymbol{a} = M^T \boldsymbol{b}$.
- **S-box([16]).** Let S be an S-box with a linear approximation table LAT. Let θ_{in} and θ_{out} be the input and output linear masks, respectively. Then the correlation of the linear approximation of S due to $(\theta_{in}, \theta_{\mathrm{out}})$ is nonzero if and only if LAT $(\theta_{in}, \theta_{\mathrm{out}}) \neq 0$.

In practice, the mathematical model can be constructed with the languages of CP [8,23], SAT/SMT [14,18], or MILP [19,24]. In this work, we choose the SAT/SMT based approach and use the well-known STP solver [7].

Experimental Verifications. Since our models are strictly generalizations of previous models, to partly confirm the correctness of our model, we try to recover the results of Ankele *et al.* [1] and Hosein *et al.* [9] automatically with our technique. Taking Ankele *et al.*'s result on SKINNY for example, we first set up the model describing the linear approximations of SKINNY involving both the encryption and tweakey-schedule data paths. Then we add the constraints fixing the linear masks of the master key to zero, and the masks of the plaintext, tweak, and ciphertext to the values given by the zero-correlation linear approximations found in [1]. Finally, we solve the model with STP and indeed there is no solution for the model, meaning that the predefined linear approximations are indeed zero correlation in our model.

Besides, our model is fully verified on a toy cipher based on the Type-II GFS structure (see Fig. 1). The block size and key size of the toy cipher are both 16-bit. Using our method, we obtain a family of 10-round zero-correlation linear approximations of the toy cipher shown in Fig. 1. Firstly, we can verify the zero-correlation property by going over all the 2^{32} input plaintext and key combinations. Then we convert the zero-correlation linear approximations into a related-key integral distinguisher, which can be verified with about 2^{16} calls to the toy cipher. Due to inaccuracy of manual derivation, the confliction that leads to the zero-correlation property can not be found in Fig. 1, where white nibbles and the nibbles marked by red T are traversed positions in our integral distinguisher. The code for the experiments is available at https://github.com/zero-cryptanalysis/Experiment-on-TC.

4 Applications

In this section, we apply our method to TWINE, LBlock, and SKINNY. We will visualize the conflictions leading to the zero-correlation property whenever it is possible.

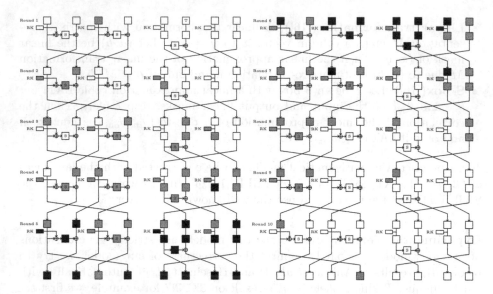

Fig. 1. Zero-correlation linear approximations of the 10-round toy cipher, where the S-boxes are borrowed from TWINE

4.1　Application to TWINE

TWINE is a family of 64-bit lightweight block ciphers with the generalized Feistel structure designed by Suzaki *et al.* [13]. There are two members TWINE-80 and TWINE-128 in the family supporting 80-bit and 128-bit keys respectively. The round function of the TWINE and the key schedule algorithms for TWINE-80 and TWINE-128 are visualized in Figs. 2, 5, and 3. We refer the reader to [13] for more details of the cipher.

Results for TWINE-80. We identify a family of 17-round zero-correlation linear approximations for TWINE-80 shown in Table 3. To illustrate the contradiction making it zero-correlation we depict the propagation of the linear masks through both the encryption data path and key schedule data path in Figs. 4 and 5, respectively. Given the mask (α, γ, β) that we found in our zero-correlation linear approximations, we can manually derive the confliction in the key schedule. The mask propagation is characterized by three kinds of active states of the mask, where white nibble, gray nibble, and black nibble denote inactive mask, active mask, and any mask, respectively.

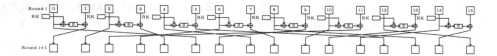

Fig. 2. Round function of TWINE block cipher

Table 3. Zero-correlation linear approximations for 17-round `TWINE-80`, where * can be any 4-bit value and c is an arbitrary 4-bit nonzero value.

Domain	Mask for	Value
$\alpha \in \mathbb{F}_2^{64}$	Plaintext	*000 0000 0000 0000
$\gamma \in \mathbb{F}_2^{80}$	Key	***0 **** **** **** ****
$\beta \in \mathbb{F}_2^{64}$	Ciphertext	0000 0000 0000 0c00

Table 4. Integral distinguisher for 17-round `TWINE-80`, where c is a 4-bit constant nibble, a is a 4-bit active nibble, b is a 4-bit balanced nibble, and ? is a 4-bit unknown nibble.

Pattern on	Value
Plaintext	caaa aaaa aaaa aaaa
Key	ccca cccc cccc cccc cccc
Ciphertext	???? ???? ???? ?b??

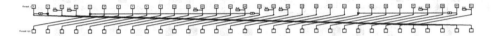

Fig. 3. Key schedule of `TWINE-128`

Then, according to Corollary 1, the family of zero-correlation linear approximations can be converted to an integral distinguisher given in Table 4. The integral distinguisher requires to encrypt a set of plaintexts enumerating the values of 15 nibbles over 2^4 different master keys, and the sum of the corresponding ciphertext bits is balanced. Since the attack needs 2^4 different keys, we regard it as a related-key integral attack.

Table 5. Zero-correlation linear approximations for two 18-round `TWINE-128`, where * can be any 4-bit value and c is an arbitrary 4-bit nonzero value.

Domain	Mask for	Value
$\alpha \in \mathbb{F}_2^{64}$	Plaintext	00*0 0000 0000 0000
$\gamma \in \mathbb{F}_2^{128}$	Key	**** *0** **** **** **** **** **** ****
$\beta \in \mathbb{F}_2^{64}$	Ciphertext	0c00 0000 0000 0000
$\alpha \in \mathbb{F}_2^{64}$	Plaintext	0000 00*0 0000 0000
$\gamma \in \mathbb{F}_2^{128}$	Key	**** *0** **** **** **** **** **** ****
$\beta \in \mathbb{F}_2^{64}$	Ciphertext	0c00 0000 0000 0000

Results for `TWINE-128`. We identify two families of 18-round zero-correlation linear approximations for `TWINE-128` shown in Table 5, and their corresponding

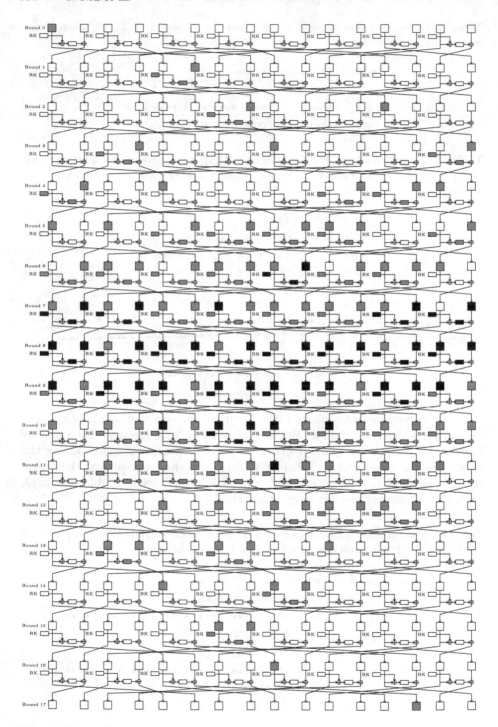

Fig. 4. The propagation of the linear masks through the encryption data path of 17-round TWINE-80

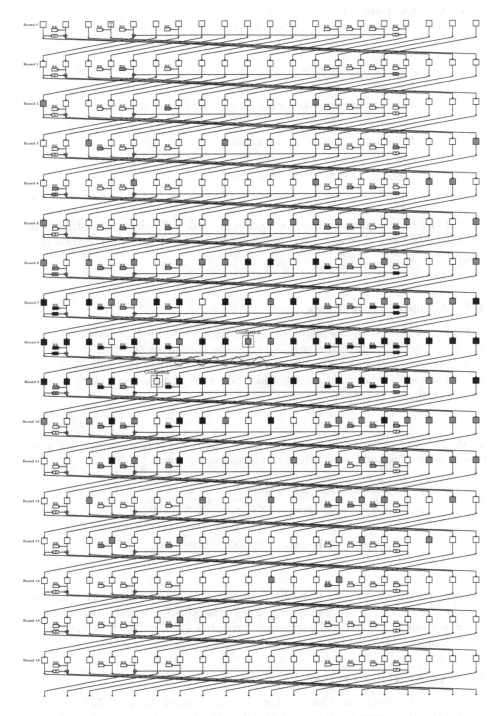

Fig. 5. Mask propagation in the key schedule of TWINE-80

Table 6. Integral distinguisher for 18-round TWINE-128, where c is a 4-bit constant nibble, a is a 4-bit active nibble, b is a 4-bit balanced nibble, and ? is a 4-bit unknown nibble.

Pattern on	Value
Plaintext	aaca aaaa aaaa aaaa
Key	cccc cacc cccc cccc cccc cccc cccc cccc
Ciphertext	?b?? ???? ???? ????
Plaintext	aaaa aaca aaaa aaaa
Key	cccc cacc cccc cccc cccc cccc cccc cccc
Ciphertext	?b?? ???? ???? ????

related-key integral distinguishers are given in Table 6 The integral distinguisher requires $2^{15\times4} = 2^{60}$ chosen plaintexts over 2^4 master keys, and the total data complexity is $2^{60+4} = 2^{64}$.

4.2 Application to LBlock

LBlock is a lightweight 64-bit block cipher with an 80-bit key designed by Wu *et al.* in 2011 [28]. It is designed based on a variant of the Feistel structure and contains 32 rounds. The round function and the key schedule algorithms for LBlock are visualized in Figs. 6 and 7. We refer the readers to [28] for more details of the cipher.

Table 7. Zero-correlation linear approximations for 15-round LBlock-80, where * can be any 4-bit value and c is an arbitrary 4-bit nonzero value.

Domain	Mask for	Value
$\alpha \in \mathbb{F}_2^{64}$	Plaintext	0000 *000 0000 0000
$\gamma \in \mathbb{F}_2^{80}$	Key	**** **** **** **** ***0
$\beta \in \mathbb{F}_2^{64}$	Ciphertext	0000 0000 0000 c000

We identify a family of 15-round zero-correlation linear approximations for LBlock shown in Table 7. its corresponding related-key integral distinguisher is given in Table 8. The integral distinguisher requires $2^{15\times4} = 2^{60}$ chosen plaintexts over 2^4 master keys, and the total data complexity is $2^{60+4} = 2^{64}$.

4.3 Application to SKINNY

SKINNY [2] is a family of block ciphers designed based on the TWEAKEY framework [11]. In this work, we focus on SKINNY-64/t, where $t \in \{64, 128, 192\}$ denotes the tweakey size. We refer the reader to [2] for more details of the design.

Table 8. Integral distinguisher for 15-round `LBlock-80`, where c is a 4-bit constant nibble, a is a 4-bit active nibble, b is a 4-bit balanced nibble, and ? is a 4-bit unknown nibble.

Pattern on	Value
Plaintext	aaaa caaa aaaa aaaa
Key	cccc cccc cccc cccc ccca
Ciphertext	???? ???? ???? b???

Round i

SB, LN

$\lll 8$

SK

Round $i + 1$

Fig. 6. Round function of `LBlock`

Zero-Correlation Linear Hull on STK with TK-p.

Using our method, we can recover the results of Ankele *et al.* for `SKINNY`. Moreover, we also get longer distinguisher for `SKINNY-64/128` and `SKINNY-64/192`. To confirm the correctness of our results, Ankele *et al.*'s method for checking the zero-correlation property can be employed. In the tweakey expansion algorithm of `SKINNY`, the c-bit nibbles are independent of each other. One can focus on the updating of one nibble in the tweak schedule to find contradictions. To this end, Ankele *et al.* proposed the definition of Γ sequence.

Definition 1 (Γ sequence [1]). *The forward and backward propagations with probability one are evaluated from the given input linear mask Γ_0 and output linear mask Γ_r, respectively. Then, for any i, the Γ sequence is defined by the*

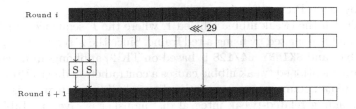

Round i

$\lll 29$

S S

Round $i + 1$

Fig. 7. Key schedule of `LBlock`

$(R + 1)$ *sequence, where whether* $\Gamma_r [h'^r (i)]$ *is active, inactive, or any is stored in the r-th element.*

When the Γ sequence is inactive for any i, it causes a contradiction when the i-th nibble of master tweak $\Lambda[i]$ is an active mask, since the master tweak can be obtained by XORing all the values in the Γ sequence. Moreover, when there is only one active value in the Γ sequence, it also causes a contradiction when $\Lambda[i]$ is the zero mask.

Ankele *et al.* proved that tweakable block cipher based on STK structure with TK-p has the zero-correlation linear hull as follows.

Proposition 1. *If there is a pair of linear masks* (Γ_0, Γ_r) *and the nibble position* i *such that the* Γ *sequence has at most p linearly active values, the tweakable block cipher has a non-trivial zero-correlation linear hull.*

Proposition 1 is proven in [1]. It shows that if the number of active nibbles in the Γ sequence is not more than the number of parallel tweakey schedule in the STK structure, applying an inactive mask to the master tweak nibble causes contradiction.

Table 9. Zero-correlation linear approximations for two 14-round SKINNY-64/128, where * can be any 4-bit value and c is an arbitrary 4-bit nonzero value.

Domain	Mask for	Value
$\alpha \in \mathbb{F}_2^{64}$	Plaintext	0000 0000 0000 **00
$\lambda \in \mathbb{F}_2^{2 \times 64}$	$TK1 \parallel TK2$	*0** **** **** **** *0** **** **** ****
$\beta \in \mathbb{F}_2^{64}$	Ciphertext	0000 000c 0000 0000
$\alpha \in \mathbb{F}_2^{64}$	Plaintext	0000 0000 0000 **00
$\lambda \in \mathbb{F}_2^{2 \times 64}$	$TK1 \parallel TK2$	*0** **** **** **** *0** **** **** ****
$\beta \in \mathbb{F}_2^{64}$	Ciphertext	0000 0000 000c 0000

Results for SKINNY-64/128. We identify a family of 14-round zero-correlation linear approximations for SKINNY-64/128 shown in Table 9. To illustrate the contradiction that leads to zero correlation we depict the propagation of the linear masks through both the encryption data path and tweakey schedule data path in Fig. 8. Then, we can manually derive the contradiction in the tweakey schedule by using Proposition 1.

We focus on the tweak nibble labeled 1, where the Γ sequence which defined in Definition 1 is depicted by using a red frame. Since the Γ sequence has just two active nibbles and SKINNY-64/128 is based on TK-2, applying an inactive mask to the before mentioned tweak nibble causes a contradiction due to Proposition 1.

Then, we can connect zero-correlation linear hull to a integral distinguisher. Its corresponding related-tweak integral distinguisher is given in Table 10. The integral distinguisher requires $2^{14 \times 4} = 2^{56}$ chosen plaintexts over 2^8 master tweaks, and the total data complexity is $2^{56+8} = 2^{64}$.

Table 10. Integral distinguisher for two 14-round `SKINNY-64/128`, where c is a 4-bit constant nibble, a is a 4-bit active nibble, b is a 4-bit balanced nibble, and ? is a 4-bit unknown nibble.

Pattern on	Value
Plaintext	`aaaa aaaa aaaa ccaa`
$TK1 \parallel TK2$	`cacc cccc cccc cccc cacc cccc cccc cccc`
Ciphertext	`???? ???b ???? ????`
Plaintext	`aaaa aaaa aaaa ccaa`
$TK1 \parallel TK2$	`cacc cccc cccc cccc cacc cccc cccc cccc`
Ciphertext	`???? ???? ???b ????`

Table 11. Zero-correlation linear approximations for two 16-round `SKINNY-64/192`, where * can be any 4-bit value and c is an arbitrary 4-bit nonzero value.

Domain	Mask for	Value
$\alpha \in \mathbb{F}_2^{64}$	Plaintext	`*000 0000 0000 0000`
$\lambda \in \mathbb{F}_2^{3 \times 64}$	$TK1 \parallel TK2 \parallel TK3$	`**** ***0 **** **** **** ***0 **** ****`
		`**** ***0 **** ****`
$\beta \in \mathbb{F}_2^{64}$	Ciphertext	`0000 000c 0000 0000`
$\alpha \in \mathbb{F}_2^{64}$	Plaintext	`*000 0000 0000 0000`
$\lambda \in \mathbb{F}_2^{3 \times 64}$	$TK1 \parallel TK2 \parallel TK3$	`**** ***0 **** **** **** ***0 **** ****`
		`**** ***0 **** ****`
$\beta \in \mathbb{F}_2^{64}$	Ciphertext	`0000 0000 000c 0000`

Table 12. Integral distinguisher for two 16-round `SKINNY-64/192`, where c is a 4-bit constant nibble, a is a 4-bit active nibble, b is a 4-bit balanced nibble, and ? is a 4-bit unknown nibble.

Pattern on	Value
Plaintext	`caaa aaaa aaaa aaaa`
$TK1 \parallel TK2 \parallel TK3$	`cccc ccca cccc cccc cccc ccca cccc cccc`
	`cccc ccca cccc cccc`
Ciphertext	`???? ???b ???? ????`
Plaintext	`caaa aaaa aaaa aaaa`
$TK1 \parallel TK2 \parallel TK3$	`cccc ccca cccc cccc cccc ccca cccc cccc`
	`cccc ccca cccc cccc`
Ciphertext	`???? ???? ???b ????`

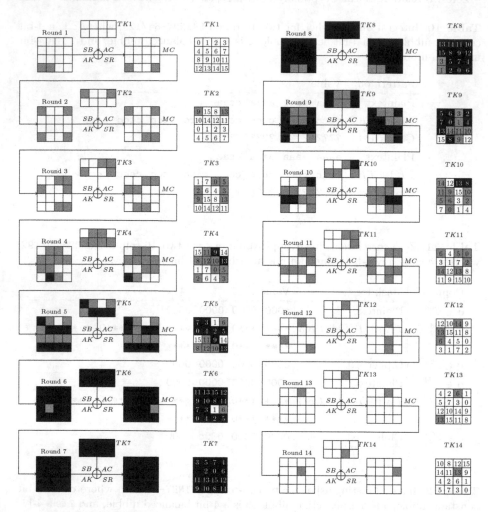

Fig. 8. 14-round zero-correlation linear hulls for SKINNY-64/128

Results for SKINNY-64/192. We identify a family of 16-round zero-correlation linear approximations for SKINNY-64/192 shown in Table 11. Its related-tweak integral distinguisher is given in Table 12. The integral distinguisher requires $2^{15 \times 4} = 2^{60}$ chosen plaintexts over 2^{12} master tweaks, and the total data complexity is $2^{60+12} = 2^{72}$. One can refer to Appendix A for the 16 round zero-correlation distinguisher (Fig. 9).

5 Conclusion

In this paper, we generalize Ankele *et al.*'s work [1] by treating plaintexts, keys, and tweaks equally in zero-correlation linear cryptanalysis. To make our zero-correlation linear approximations apply to practical attack scenarios, we proposed a unified linear mask setting on key/tweak schedule. Using our new linear mask setting, we can convert obtained zero-correlation linear approximations into related tweakey integral distinguishers which can be used for key recovery attacks. We also show that such zero-correlation linear approximations can be found by standard automatic tools based on SAT and SMT, which is much more straightforward than Ankele *et al.*'s approach and applies to both linear and nonlinear tweak-key schedule algorithms. We apply the method to TWINE, LBlock, and SKINNY and obtain improved results. To confirm the correctness of our method, we recover the results of Ankele *et al.* automatically and run a full experiment on a toy cipher.

Compared to related-key impossible differential and key difference invariant bias cryptanalysis, our method exploits the different property of the key schedule. After comparing the result of TWINE and LBlock, we get an observation that our method is suited for block ciphers with a slow diffusion in the key/tweak schedules. It is noteworthy that the inner connection of these three cryptanalytic methods is not yet known.

Acknowledgements. We thank the anonymous reviewers for their valuable comments and suggestions to improve the quality of the paper. Siwei Sun is funded by the National Key Research and Development Program of China (Grant No. 2018YFA0704704), the Chinese Major Program of National Cryptography Development Foundation (Grant No. MMJJ20180102), and the National Natural Science Foundation of China (Grant No. 62032014, Grant No. 61772519). This work is supported by the National Natural Science Foundation of China (Grant No. 62002201, Grant No. 62032014), the National Key Research and Development Program of China (Grant No. 2018YFA0704702), the Major Scientific and Technological Innovation Project of Shandong Province, China (Grant No. 2019JZZY010133), the Major Basic Research Project of Natural Science Foundation of Shandong Province, China (Grant No. ZR202010220025).

A   Zero-Correlation Linear Hulls for SKINNY-64/192

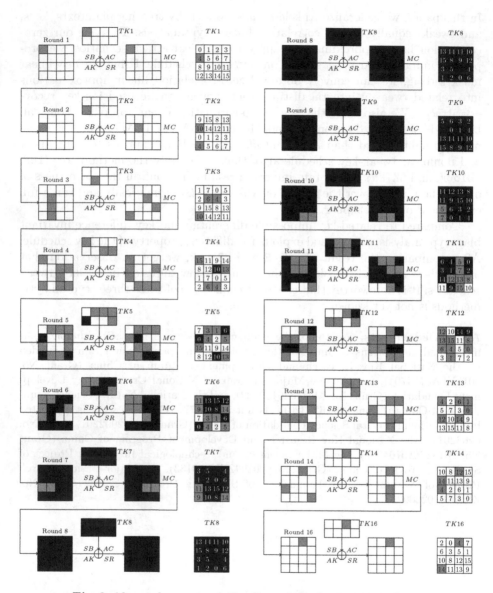

Fig. 9. 16-round zero-correlation linear hulls for SKINNY-64/192.

References

1. Ankele, R., Dobraunig, C., Guo, J., Lambooij, E., Leander, G., Todo, Y.: Zero-correlation attacks on tweakable block ciphers with linear tweakey expansion. IACR Trans. Symmetric Cryptol. **2019**(1), 192–235 (2019). https://doi.org/10.13154/tosc.v2019.i1.192-235
2. Beierle, C., et al.: The SKINNY family of block ciphers and its low-latency variant MANTIS. In: Robshaw, M., Katz, J. (eds.) CRYPTO 2016. LNCS, vol. 9815, pp. 123–153. Springer, Heidelberg (2016). https://doi.org/10.1007/978-3-662-53008-5_5
3. Bogdanov, A., Boura, C., Rijmen, V., Wang, M., Wen, L., Zhao, J.: Key difference invariant bias in block ciphers. In: Sako, K., Sarkar, P. (eds.) ASIACRYPT 2013. LNCS, vol. 8269, pp. 357–376. Springer, Heidelberg (2013). https://doi.org/10.1007/978-3-642-42033-7_19
4. Bogdanov, A., Leander, G., Nyberg, K., Wang, M.: Integral and multidimensional linear distinguishers with correlation zero. In: Wang, X., Sako, K. (eds.) ASIACRYPT 2012. LNCS, vol. 7658, pp. 244–261. Springer, Heidelberg (2012). https://doi.org/10.1007/978-3-642-34961-4_16
5. Bogdanov, A., Rijmen, V.: Linear hulls with correlation zero and linear cryptanalysis of block ciphers. Designs, Codes Cryptogr. **70**(3), 369–383 (2012). https://doi.org/10.1007/s10623-012-9697-z
6. Bogdanov, A., Wang, M.: Zero correlation linear cryptanalysis with reduced data complexity. In: Canteaut, A. (ed.) FSE 2012. LNCS, vol. 7549, pp. 29–48. Springer, Heidelberg (2012). https://doi.org/10.1007/978-3-642-34047-5_3
7. Ganesh, V., Hansen, T., Soos, M., Liew, D., Govostes, R.: STP (2014). https://stp.github.io/
8. Gerault, D., Minier, M., Solnon, C.: Constraint programming models for chosen key differential cryptanalysis. In: Principles and Practice of Constraint Programming - 22nd International Conference, CP 2016, Toulouse, France, September 5–9, 2016, Proceedings. pp. 584–601 (2016). https://doi.org/10.1007/978-3-319-44953-1_37
9. Hadipour, H., Sadeghi, S., Niknam, M.M., Song, L., Bagheri, N.: Comprehensive security analysis of CRAFT. IACR Trans. Symmetric Cryptol. **2019**(4), 290–317 (2019). https://doi.org/10.13154/tosc.v2019.i4.290-317
10. Hermelin, M., Cho, J.Y., Nyberg, K.: Multidimensional linear cryptanalysis of reduced round serpent. In: Mu, Y., Susilo, W., Seberry, J. (eds.) ACISP 2008. LNCS, vol. 5107, pp. 203–215. Springer, Heidelberg (2008). https://doi.org/10.1007/978-3-540-70500-0_15
11. Jean, J., Nikolić, I., Peyrin, T.: Tweaks and keys for block ciphers: the TWEAKEY framework. In: Sarkar, P., Iwata, T. (eds.) ASIACRYPT 2014. LNCS, vol. 8874, pp. 274–288. Springer, Heidelberg (2014). https://doi.org/10.1007/978-3-662-45608-8_15
12. Kaliski, Burton S.., Robshaw, M.. J.. B..: Linear cryptanalysis using multiple approximations and FEAL. In: Preneel, Bart (ed.) FSE 1994. LNCS, vol. 1008, pp. 249–264. Springer, Heidelberg (1995). https://doi.org/10.1007/3-540-60590-8_19
13. Kobayashi, E., Suzaki, T., Minematsu, K., Morioka, S.: Twine: a lightweight block cipher for multiple platforms. In: The Conference on Selected Areas in Cryptography (2012). https://doi.org/10.1007/978-3-642-35999-6_22

14. Kölbl, S., Leander, G., Tiessen, T.: Observations on the SIMON block cipher family. In: Gennaro, R., Robshaw, M. (eds.) CRYPTO 2015. LNCS, vol. 9215, pp. 161–185. Springer, Heidelberg (2015). https://doi.org/10.1007/978-3-662-47989-6_8

15. Kranz, T., Leander, G., Wiemer, F.: Linear cryptanalysis: key schedules and tweakable block ciphers. IACR Trans. Symmetric Cryptol. **2017**(1), 474–505 (2017). https://doi.org/10.13154/tosc.v2017.i1.474-505

16. Liu, Y., et al.: STP models of optimal differential and linear trail for s-box based ciphers. IACR Cryptol. ePrint Arch. **2019**, 25 (2019)

17. Matsui, M.: Linear cryptanalysis method for DES cipher. In: Helleseth, T. (ed.) EUROCRYPT 1993. LNCS, vol. 765, pp. 386–397. Springer, Heidelberg (1994). https://doi.org/10.1007/3-540-48285-7_33

18. Mouha, N., Preneel, B.: Towards finding optimal differential characteristics for ARX: application to salsa20. Cryptology ePrint Archive, Report 2013/328 (2013). https://eprint.iacr.org/2013/328

19. Mouha, N., Wang, Q., Gu, D., Preneel, B.: Differential and linear cryptanalysis using mixed-integer linear programming. In: Information Security and Cryptology - 7th International Conference, Inscrypt 2011, Beijing, China, November 30–December 3, 2011, pp. 57–76. Revised Selected Papers (2011). https://doi.org/10.1007/978-3-642-34704-7_5

20. Nyberg, K.: Linear approximation of block ciphers. In: De Santis, A. (ed.) EUROCRYPT 1994. LNCS, vol. 950, pp. 439–444. Springer, Heidelberg (1995). https://doi.org/10.1007/BFb0053460

21. Sasaki, Yu., Todo, Y.: New impossible differential search tool from design and cryptanalysis aspects. In: Coron, J.-S., Nielsen, J.B. (eds.) EUROCRYPT 2017. LNCS, vol. 10212, pp. 185–215. Springer, Cham (2017). https://doi.org/10.1007/978-3-319-56617-7_7

22. Sun, B., et al.: Links among impossible differential, integral and zero correlation linear cryptanalysis. In: Gennaro, R., Robshaw, M. (eds.) CRYPTO 2015. LNCS, vol. 9215, pp. 95–115. Springer, Heidelberg (2015). https://doi.org/10.1007/978-3-662-47989-6_5

23. Sun, S., Gérault, D., Lafourcade, P., Yang, Q., Todo, Y., Qiao, K., Hu, L.: Analysis of AES, skinny, and others with constraint programming. IACR Trans. Symmetric Cryptol. **2017**(1), 281–306 (2017). https://doi.org/10.13154/tosc.v2017.i1.281-306

24. Sun, S., Hu, L., Wang, P., Qiao, K., Ma, X., Song, L.: Automatic security evaluation and (related-key) differential characteristic search: application to SIMON, PRESENT, LBlock, DES(L) and other bit-oriented block ciphers. In: Sarkar, P., Iwata, T. (eds.) ASIACRYPT 2014. LNCS, vol. 8873, pp. 158–178. Springer, Heidelberg (2014). https://doi.org/10.1007/978-3-662-45611-8_9

25. Wang, Y., Wu, W.: Improved multidimensional zero-correlation linear cryptanalysis and applications to LBlock and TWINE. In: Susilo, W., Mu, Y. (eds.) ACISP 2014. LNCS, vol. 8544, pp. 1–16. Springer, Cham (2014). https://doi.org/10.1007/978-3-319-08344-5_1

26. Wei, Y., Xu, P., Rong, Y.: Related-key impossible differential cryptanalysis on lightweight cipher TWINE. J. Ambient Intell. Hum. Comput. **10**(2), 509–517 (2018). https://doi.org/10.1007/s12652-017-0675-1

27. Wen, L., Wang, M., Zhao, J.: Related-key impossible differential attack on reduced-round LBlock. J. Comput. Sci. Technol. **29**(1), 165–176 (2014). https://doi.org/10.1007/s11390-014-1419-8

28. Wu, W., Zhang, L.: LBlock: a lightweight block cipher. In: Lopez, J., Tsudik, G. (eds.) ACNS 2011. LNCS, vol. 6715, pp. 327–344. Springer, Heidelberg (2011). https://doi.org/10.1007/978-3-642-21554-4_19

29. Xu, H., Jia, P., Huang, G., Lai, X.: Multidimensional zero-correlation linear cryptanalysis on 23-round LBlock-s. In: Qing, S., Okamoto, E., Kim, K., Liu, D. (eds.) ICICS 2015. LNCS, vol. 9543, pp. 97–108. Springer, Cham (2016). https://doi.org/10.1007/978-3-319-29814-6_9

30. Zheng, X., Jia, K.: Impossible differential attack on reduced-round TWINE. In: Lee, H.-S., Han, D.-G. (eds.) ICISC 2013. LNCS, vol. 8565, pp. 123–143. Springer, Cham (2014). https://doi.org/10.1007/978-3-319-12160-4_8

SoK: Game-Based Security Models
for Group Key Exchange

Bertram Poettering[1][iD], Paul Rösler[2][(⊠)][iD], Jörg Schwenk[3][iD],
and Douglas Stebila[4][iD]

[1] IBM Research – Zurich, Rüschlikon, Switzerland
poe@zurich.ibm.com
[2] TU Darmstadt, Darmstadt, Germany
paul.roesler@tu-darmstadt.de
[3] Ruhr University Bochum, Bochum, Germany
joerg.schwenk@rub.de
[4] University of Waterloo, Waterloo, Canada
dstebila@uwaterloo.ca

Abstract. *Group key exchange* (GKE) protocols let a group of users
jointly establish fresh and secure key material. Many flavors of GKE have
been proposed, differentiated by, among others, whether group membership is static or dynamic, whether a single key or a continuous stream of
keys is established, and whether security is provided in the presence of
state corruptions (forward and post-compromise security). In all cases,
an indispensable ingredient to the rigorous analysis of a candidate solution is a corresponding formal security model. We observe, however, that
most GKE-related publications are more focused on building new constructions that have more functionality or are more efficient than prior
proposals, while leaving the job of identifying and working out the details
of adequate security models a subordinate task.

In this systematization of knowledge we bring the formal modeling of
GKE security to the fore by revisiting the intuitive goals of GKE, criti-
cally evaluating how these goals are reflected (or not) in the established
models, and how they would be best considered in new models. We classify and compare characteristics of a large selection of *game-based* GKE
models that appear in the academic literature, including those proposed
for GKE with post-compromise security. We observe a range of shortcomings in some of the studied models, such as dependencies on overly
restrictive syntactical constrains, unrealistic adversarial capabilities, or
simply incomplete definitions. Our systematization enables us to identify a coherent suite of desirable characteristics that we believe should
be represented in all general purpose GKE models. To demonstrate the
feasibility of covering all these desirable characteristics simultaneously
in one concise definition, we conclude with proposing a new generic reference model for GKE.

The full version [PRSS21] of this article is available as entry 2021/305 in the IACR
eprint archive.

K. G. Paterson (Ed.): CT-RSA 2021, LNCS 12704, pp. 148–176, 2021.
https://doi.org/10.1007/978-3-030-75539-3_7

Keywords: Group key exchange · Key agreement · Key
establishment · Security model · Multi-user protocol

1 Introduction

The group key exchange (GKE) primitive was first considered about four decades
ago. The aim of early publications on the topic [ITW82, BD95] was to generalize
the (two-party) Diffie–Hellman protocol to groups of three or more participants,
i.e., to construct a basic cryptographic primitive that allows a fixed set of anonymous participants to establish secure key material in the presence of a passive
adversary. Later research identified a set of additional features that would be
desirable for GKE, for instance the support of participant authentication, the
support of dynamic groups (where the set of participants is not fixed but members can join and leave the group at will), the support of groups where one
or many members might temporarily be unresponsive (asynchronous mode of
operation), or a maximum resilience against adversaries that can obtain read-
access to the states of participants for a limited amount of time (forward and
post-compromise security).

Standard applications that require a GKE protocol as a building block
include online audio-video conference systems and instant messaging [RMS18].
Indeed, in an ongoing standardization effort the IETF's Messaging Layer Security (MLS) initiative [BBM+20] tests employing GKE protocols for the protection of instant messaging in asynchronous settings.

While, intuitively, most of the GKE protocols proposed in the literature can
serve as a building block for such applications, it turns out that effectively no two
security analyses of such protocols were conducted in the same formal model,
meaning that there is effectively no modularity: For every GKE candidate that
is used in some application protocol, a new security evaluation of the overall
construction has to be conducted. In fact, as will become clear in the course
of this article, the GKE literature has neither managed to agree on a common
unified syntax of the primitive, nor on a common approach for developing and
expressing corresponding security definitions. In our view, the lack of a common
reference framework for GKE, including its security, and the implied lack of
modularity and interoperability, imposes an unnecessary obstacle on the way to
secure conference and messaging solutions.

1.1 Systemizing Group Key Exchange Models

With the goal of developing a general reference formalization of the GKE primitive, we have a fresh look at how it should be modeled such that it simultaneously provides sufficient functionality and sufficient security. More precisely,
we are looking for a formalization that is versatile enough to practically fit and
protect generic applications like the envisioned video conferencing. To achieve
this, we need to consider questions like the following: What features does an
application expect of GKE? What type of underlying infrastructure (network

services, authentication services, . . .) can a GKE primitive assume to exist? What types of adversaries should be considered? To obtain a satisfactory reference formalization, our model should be as generic as possible when meeting the requirements of applications, should make minimal assumptions on its environment, and should tolerate a wide class of adversaries.

After identifying the right questions to ask, we derive a taxonomy in which existing models for GKE can be evaluated to determine whether they provide answers to these questions. If they don't, we explore the consequences of this. As a side product, our taxonomy also sheds light on how the research domain of GKE has evolved over time, and how models in the literature relate to each other. It also informs us towards our goal to develop a versatile and uniform model for GKE.

We organize our taxonomy and investigations with respect to four property categories of GKE models:

1. the syntax of GKE (Sect. 2),
2. the definition of partnering (Sect. 3.1),
3. the definition of correctness (due to space restriction only in the full version [PRSS21]), and
4. the definition of security (Sect. 4).

While syntax, correctness, and security are properties generally formalized for all kinds of cryptographic primitives, the partnering notion is specific to the domain of key exchange. In a nutshell, partnering captures the conditions under which remote parties compute the same session key.

For each of these four categories, we discuss their purposes and central features, and classify the literature with respect to them. Having both considered the literature and revisited GKE with a fresh view, we identify a set of desirable characteristics in each of the four categories, from the perspective of generality of use and minimality of assumptions on the context in which GKE takes place. Based on these findings, we see how individual definitional approaches and, to some extent, subparadigms of GKE, do not fully satisfy the needs of GKE analysis. We are further able to synthesize a coherent set of desirable properties into a single, generic model (Sects. 2.5, 3.2, and 4.1), demonstrating that it is possible to design a model that simultaneously incorporates all these characteristics.

Choice of Literature. Most of the literature in the domain of GKE revolves around the exposition of a new construction (accompanied either with formal or only heuristic security arguments; see, e.g., [ITW82,BD95]). When selecting prior publications to survey in this SoK article, we focused on those that were developed with respect to a *formal computational game-based security model*. Our comparison covers all publications on GKE with this type of model that appeared in cryptographic "tier-one" proceedings[1] [BCP01,BCPQ01, BCP02a,BCP02b,KY03,KLL04,KS05,CCG+18,ACDT19]. Beyond that, we

---

[1] CRYPTO, Eurocrypt, Asiacrypt, CCS, S&P, Usenix Security, and the Journal of Cryptology.

browsed through the proceedings of all relevant "tier-two" conferences[2] and selected publications that explicitly promise to enhance the formal modeling of GKE [GBG09, YKLH18].[3] We also include three recently published articles on GKE with post-compromise security (aka. group ratcheting or continuous GKE), one of which is yet only available as a preprint [CCG+18, ACDT19, ACC+19]. [4] As computational simulation-based (UC) and symbolic modeling approaches are essentially incomparable with computational game-based notions, we exclude these type of models from our systematization.

Tables 1, 2, and 3 summarize and compare the common features that we identified in the surveyed models. The models reflected in these tables are arranged into three clusters. Leftmost: GKE in static groups [BCPQ01, BCP02b, KY03, KS05, GBG09, CCG+18]; centered: GKE with regular, post-compromise secure key material updates (aka. ratcheting) [CCG+18, ACDT19, ACC+19]; and rightmost: GKE in dynamic groups [ACDT19, ACC+19, BCP01, BCP02a, KLL04, YKLH18]. Within each cluster, models are, where possible, ordered chronologically by publication date. Naturally, works are historically related, did influence each other, and use intuitively similar notations across these clusters (e.g., due to overlapping sets of authors). Our results, however, show that these "soft" properties are almost independent of the factual features according to which we systematized the models. We correspondingly refrain from introducing further "clustering-axes" with respect to historic relations between the considered works as this may mislead more than it supports comprehensibility. Nevertheless, we refer the interested reader to the extended version [PRSS21] for a short overview of the historic context of the chosen literature and the purposes of each selected article.

We use symbols ●, ◉, ◑, ◐, ○, -, and others to condense the details of the considered model definitions in our systematizing tables, and accompany them with textual explanations. Not surprisingly, this small set of symbols can hardly reflect all details encoded in the models but makes "losses due to abstraction" unavoidable. We optimized the selection of classification criteria such that the amount of information loss due to simplifications is minimized.

Relation to Two-Party Key Exchange. While the focus of this article is on GKE, many of the notions that we discuss are relevant also in the domain of two-party key exchange. In our comparisons, we indicate which properties are specific to the setting of GKE, and which apply to key exchange in general. Given the large amount of two-party key exchange literature, we do not attempt to provide more direct comparisons between group and two-party key exchange.

---

[2] TCC, PKC, CT-RSA, ACNS, ESORICS, CANS, ARES, ProvSec, FC.

[3] We appreciate that many more publications introduce other GKE constructions (e.g., [BC04, ABCP06, JKT07, JL07, Man09, NS11, XHZ15, BDR20]). However, we did not identify that they contribute new insights to the modeling of GKE.

[4] Since our analysis started before [ACDT20] was submitted to CRYPTO 2020, we consider a fixed preprint version [ACDT19] here. Note that the two follow-up works [ACJM20, AJM20] use simulation-based security models.

Proposed Model. Since none of the models that we survey achieves all the desirable properties that we identify, we conclude this article with proposing a simple and generic GKE model that achieves all these properties. The components of this model are introduced gradually at the end of each systematization section. We emphasize that it is not necessarily our goal to guide all future research efforts to a unified GKE model. Some modeling design decisions are not universal and cannot be reduced to objective criteria, so we are neither under the illusion that a perfectly unified model exists, nor that the research community will any time soon agree on a single formalization. Our primary goal when writing down a model was rather to demonstrate the relative compatibility of the desirable properties. That said, as our systematization reveals undesirable shortcomings even in very recent GKE models for ratcheting—shortcomings that partially seem inherited from older work—we believe that proposing a better alternative is long overdue.

Although our model can be used for analyzing GKE protocols with various realistic, so far disregarded properties, achieving these properties is not mandatory but optional for covered GKE protocols. For example, dynamic GKE protocols with multi-device support that can handle fully asynchronous interaction can be analyzed by our model as well as static GKE protocols in which the interaction between the participating instances follows a fixed schedule. We consider these properties as implementation details of the protocols to which our model is carefully defined indifferent. The only mandatory property that our model demands is the secrecy of keys in the presence of either active or passive adversaries, which demonstrates the generality and versatility of our proposal.

1.2   Basic Notions in Group Key Exchange

A group key exchange scheme is a tuple of algorithms executed by a group of participants with the minimal outcome that one or multiple (shared) symmetric keys are computed.

Terminology of GKE. A **global session** is a joint execution of a GKE protocol. By joint execution we mean the distributed invocation of GKE algorithms by participants that influence each other through communication over a network, eventually computing (joint) keys. Each *local* execution of algorithms by a participant is called a **local instance**. Each local instance computes one or more symmetric keys, referred to as **group keys**. Each group key computed by a single local instance during a global session has a distinct **context**, which may consist of: the set of designated participants, the history of previously computed group keys, the algorithm invocation by which its computation was initiated, etc. Participants of global sessions, represented by their local instances, are called **parties**.[5] If the set of participants in a global session can be modified during the lifetime of the session, this is an example of **dynamic** GKE; otherwise the GKE is **static**.

---

[5] We further clarify on the relation between local instances and parties and their participation in sessions in the full version [PRSS21].

There are many alternative terms used in the GKE literature for these ideas: local instances are sometimes called *processes*, local *sessions*, or (misleadingly) *oracles*; group keys are sometimes called *session keys*; and parties are sometimes called *users*.

Security Models for GKE. As it is common in game-based key exchange models, an adversary against the security of a GKE scheme plays a game with a challenger that simulates multiple parallel real global sessions of the GKE scheme. The challenge that the adversary is required to solve is to distinguish whether a **challenge key** is a real group key established in one of the simulated global sessions or is a random key. In order to solve this challenge, the adversary is allowed to obtain (through a **key reveal** oracle) group keys that were computed independently, to obtain (through a **state exposure** oracle) ephemeral local secret states of instances that do not enable the trivial solution of the challenge, and to obtain (through a **corruption** oracle) static party secrets that do not trivially invalidate the challenge either. While the GKE literature agrees on these high-level concepts, the crucial details are implemented in various incompatible ways in these articles.

2   Syntax Definitions

Modeling a cryptographic primitive starts with fixing its syntax: the set of algorithms that are available, the inputs they take and the outputs they generate. We categorized the GKE models we consider according to the most important classes of syntactical design choices. In particular, the GKE syntax may reflect (1) imposed limits on the number of supported parties, sessions, and instances; (2) assumptions made on the available infrastructure (e.g., the existence of a PKI); (3) the type of operations that the protocols implement (adding users, removing users, refreshing keys, ...); and (4) the information that the protocols provide to the invoking application (set of group members, session identifiers, ...). We compile the results of our studies in Table 1. If for some models an unambiguous mapping to our categories is not immediate, we report the result that comes closest to what we believe the authors intended. Independently, if in any of the categories one option is clearly more attractive than the other options, we indicate this in the **Desirable** column. (We leave the cells of that column empty if no clearly best option exists.) The **Our model** column indicates the profile of our own GKE model; see also Sect. 2.5. Note that no two models in the table have identical profiles.[6]

The upcoming paragraphs introduce our categories in detail.

2.1   Quantities

All models we consider assume a universe of parties that are potential candidates for participating in GKE sessions. **Instances per party:** While most

---

[6] Surprisingly, this holds even for models that appeared in close succession in publications of the same authors.

Table 1. Syntax definitions. Notation: n: many; **F**: fixed; **V**: variable; **D**: dynamic; ●: yes; ◉: implicitly; ◑: partially; ○: no; -: not applicable; (blank): no option clearly superior/desirable; **SK**: symmetric key; **PW**: password; **PK**: public key; **G**: global; **L**: local.

Syntax	GKE-specific	[BCPQ01]	[BCP02b]	[KY03]	[KS05]	[GBG09]	[CCG+18]	[ACDT19]	[ACC+19]	[BCP01]	[BCP02a]	[KLL04]	[YKLH18]	Desirable	Our model
Quantities															
Instances per party	○	n	n	n	n	n	n	1	(1)	1	n	n	n	n	n
Parties per session	●	F	F	V	V	V	V	D	D	D	D	D	D	D	D
Multi-participation	●	○	○	○	○	○	○	○	○	○	○	○	○	●	●
Setup assumptions															
Authentication by ...	○	SK	PW	PK	PK	PK	PK	PK	(PK)	SK	PK	PK	PK		any
PKI	○	-	-	●*	●*	◉	◉	●*	◉	-	◉	●*	●		-
Online administrator	●	-	-	-	-	-	-	◉	◑	●	●	◉	○	○	○
Operations															
Level of specification	○	○	G	○	○	○	L	L	L	G	G	G	◑	L	L
Algo: Setup	○	○	●	○	○	○	●	●	●	●	●	●	○		-
Algo: Add	●	○	○	○	○	○	○	●	●	●	●	●	●		-
Algo: Remove	●	○	○	○	○	○	○	●	●	●	●	●	●		-
Algo: Refresh/Ratchet	○	○	○	○	○	○	◉	●	●	○	○	○	○		-
Abstract interface	○	○	○	○	○	○	●	○	○	○	○	○	○	●	●
Return values															
Group key	○	●	●	●	●	●	●	●	●	●	●	●	●	●	●
Ref. for session	●	○	○	◉	●	◉	○	○	○	○	○	○	◉	●	○
Ref. for group key	○	○	○	◉	◉	◉	○	○	○	○	○	○	◉	○	●
Designated members	●	◉	◉	◉	●	●	●	○	◉	◉	○	◉	◉	●	○
Ongoing operation	○	-	◉	-	-	-	○	○	●	○	○	○	◉	●	○
Status of instance	○	○	○	◉	○	◉	◉	◉	◉	○	○	○	◉	●	◉

models assume that each party can participate—using independent instances—in an unlimited number of sessions, three models impose a limit to a single instance per party.[7] In Table 1 we distinguish these cases with the symbols n and 1, respectively. **Parties per session:** While some models prescribe a fixed number of parties that participate in each GKE session, other models are more flexible and assume either that the number of parties is in principle variable yet bound to a static value when a session is created, or even allow that the number of parties changes dynamically over the lifetime of a session (accommodating parties being added/removed). In the table we encode the three cases with the symbols **F,V,D**, respectively. **Multi-participation:** In principle it is plausible that parties participate multiple times in parallel in the same session (through different, independent instances, e.g., from their laptop and smartphone). We note however that all of the assessed models exclude this and don't allow for more than one participation per party. We encode this in the table by placing the symbol ○ in the whole row. Despite no model supporting it, we argue that a multi-participation feature might be useful in certain cases.

Discussion. We note that security reductions of early ring-based GKE protocols [BD95] require that the number of participants in sessions always be even [BD05]. We take this as an example that clarifies a crucial difference between the **F** and **V** types in the Parties-per-session category, as [BD95] fits into the **F** regime but not into the **V** regime.

---

[7] The case of [ACC+19] is somewhat special: While their syntax in principle allows that parties operate multiple instances, their security definition reduces this to strictly one instance per party. For their application (secure instant messaging) this is not a limitation as parties are short-lived and created ad-hoc to participate in only a single session.

2.2   Setup Assumptions

Security models are formulated with respect to a set of properties that are assumed to hold for the environment in which the modeled primitive is operated. We consider three classes of such assumptions. The classes are related to the pre-distribution of key material that is to be used for authentication, the availability of a centralized party that leads the group communication, and the type of service that is expected to be provided by the underlying communication infrastructure. **Authentication by ...**: If a GKE protocol provides key agreement with authentication, its syntax has to reflect that the latter is achievable only if some kind of cryptographic setup is established before the protocol session is executed. For instance, depending on the type of authentication, artifacts related to accessing pre-shared symmetric keys, passwords, or authentic copies of the peers' public keys, will have to emerge in the syntax. In the table we encode these cases with the symbols **SK,PW,PK**, respectively.[8] **PKI:** In the case of public-key authentication we studied what the models say about how public keys are distributed, in particular whether a public key infrastructure (PKI) is explicitly or implicitly assumed. In the table we indicate this with the symbols ● and ◉. We further specially mark with ●* the cases of "closed PKIs" that service exclusively potential protocol participants, i.e., PKIs with which non-participants (e.g., an adversary) cannot register their keys. **Online administrator:** The number of participants in a GKE session can be very large, and, by consequence, properly orchestrating the interactions between them can represent a considerable technical challenge.[9] Two of the models we consider resolve this by requiring that groups be managed by a distinguished always-honest leader (either being a group member or an external delivery service) who decides which operations happen in which order, and another two models assume the same but without making it explicit. The model of [ACC+19] is slightly different in that a leader is still required, but it does not have to behave honestly. The model of [YKLH18] does not assume orchestration: Here, protocols proceed execution as long as possible, even if concurrent operations of participants are not compatible with each other. This is argued to be sufficient if security properties ensure that the resulting group keys are sufficiently independent. The remaining models are so simple that they do not require any type of administration.

Discussion. While the authentication component that is incorporated into GKE protocols necessarily requires the pre-distribution of some kind of key material, the impact of this component on the GKE model should be minimal; in particular, details of PKI-related operations should not play a role. It is even less desirable to assume closed PKIs to which outsiders cannot register their keys.

---

[8] In continuation of Footnote 7: The case of [ACC+19] is special in that the requirement is an *ephemeral asymmetric key*, that is, a public key that is ad-hoc generated and used only once.

[9] Consider, for instance, that situations stemming from participants concurrently performing conflicting operations might have to be resolved, as have to be cases where participants become temporarily unavailable without notice.

As we have seen, some models require an online administrator where others do not. If an online administrator is available, tasks like ensuring that all participants in a session have the same view on the communication and group membership list become easy. However, in many settings an online administrator is just not available. For instance, instant messaging protocols are expected to tolerate that participants, including any administrator, might go offline without notice. Unfortunately, if no administrator is available, seemingly simple tasks like agreeing on a common group membership list become hard to solve as, at least implicitly, they require solving a Byzantine Consensus instance. On the other hand, strictly speaking, achieving key security in GKE protocols is possible without reaching consensus.

2.3   Operations

In this category we compare the GKE models with respect to the algorithms that parties have available for controlling how they engage in sessions. **Level of specification:** While precisely fixing the APIs of these algorithms seems a necessity for both formalizing security and allowing applications to generically use the protocols, we found that very few models are clear about API details: Four models leave the syntax of the algorithms fully undefined.[10] Another four models describe operations only as global operations, i.e., specify how the overall state of sessions shall evolve without being precise about which steps the individual participants shall conduct. Only three models fix a local syntax, i.e., specify precisely which participant algorithms exist and which inputs and outputs they take and generate. In the table, we indicate the three levels of specification with the symbols O, **G**, and **L**, encoding the terms "missing", "global", and "local", respectively. The model of [YKLH18] sits somewhere between **G** and **L**, and is marked with ◑. **Algo:** The main operations executed by participants are session initialization (either of an empty group or of a predefined set of parties), the addition of participants to a group, the removal of participants from a group, and in some cases a key refresh (which establishes a new key without affecting the set of group members). In the table we indicate which model supports which of these operations. Note that the correlation between the Add/Remove rows and symbol **D** in Quantities/Parties-per-Session is as expected. Only very recent models that emerged in the context of group ratcheting support the key refresh operation. **Abstract interface:** While the above classes Add/Remove/Refresh are the most important operations of GKE, other options are possible, including Merge and Split operations that join two established groups or split them into partitions, respectively. In principle, each additional operation could explicitly appear in the form of an algorithm in the syntax definition of the GKE model, but a downside of this would be that the models of any two protocols with slightly different feature sets would become, for purely syntactic reasons,

---

[10] In some cases, however, it seems feasible to reverse-engineer some information about an assumed syntax from the security reductions also contained in the corresponding works.

formally incomparable. An alternative is to use only a single algorithm for all group-related operations, which can be directed to perform any supported operation by instructing it with corresponding commands. While we believe that this flexible approach towards defining APIs to group operations has quite desirable advantages, we have to note that only one of the considered models supports it.

Discussion. Instance-centric ('**L**-level') specifications of algorithms are vital for achieving both practical implementability and meaningful security definitions. To see the latter, consider that the only way for adversaries to attack (global) sessions is by exposing (local) instances to their attacks.

2.4 Return Values

The main outcome of a successful GKE protocol execution is the group key itself. In addition, protocol executions might establish further information that can be relevant for the invoking application. We categorize the GKE models by the type of information contained in the protocol outcome. **Group key:** We confirm that all models that we consider have a syntactical mechanism for delivering established keys. **Reference for session:** By a session reference we understand a string that serves as an unambiguous handle to a session, i.e., a value that uniquely identifies a distributed execution of the scheme algorithms. Some of the models we consider require that such a string be established as part of the protocol execution, but not necessarily they prescribe that it be communicated to the invoking application along with the key. (Instead the value is used to define key security.) In Table 1, we indicate with symbols ● and ◉ whether the models require the explicit or implicit derivation and communication of a session reference. We mark models with ○ if no such value appears in the model. **Reference for group key:** A key reference is similar to a session reference but instead of referring to a session it refers to an established key. While references to sessions and keys are interchangeable in some cases, in general they are not. The latter is the case, for instance, for protocols that establish multiple keys per execution. Further, if communication is not authentic, session references of protocol instances can be matching while key references (and keys) are not. In the table we indicate with symbols ● and ◉ if the models consider explicit or implicit key references. **Designated members:** Once a GKE execution succeeds with establishing a shared key, the corresponding participants should learn who their partners are, i.e., with whom they share the key. In some models this communication step is made explicit, in others, in particular if the set of partners is *input* to the execution, this step is implicit. A third class of models does not communicate the set of group members at all. In the table we indicate the cases with symbols ●, ◉, ○, respectively. **Ongoing operation:** In GKE sessions, keys are established as a result of various types of actions, particularly including the addition/removal of participants, and the explicit refresh of key material. We document for each considered model whether it communicates for established group keys through which operation they were established. **Status of instance:** Instances can attain different protocol-dependent internal states.

Common such states are that instances can be in an accepted or rejected state, meaning that they consider a protocol execution successful or have given up on it, respectively. In this category we indicate whether the models we consider communicate this status information to the invoking application.

Discussion. In settings where parties concurrently execute multiple sessions of the same protocol, explicit references to sessions and/or keys are vital for maintaining clarity about which key belongs to which execution. (Consider attacks where an adversary substitutes all protocol messages of one session with the messages of another session, and vice versa, with the result that a party develops a wrong understanding of the context in which it established a key.) We feel that in many academic works the relevance of such references could be more clearly appreciated. The formal version of our observation is that session or key references are a prerequisite of sound composition results (as in [BFWW11]). Sound composition with other protocols plays a pivotal role also in the Universal Composability (UC) framework [Can01]. Indeed, not surprisingly, the concept of a session reference emerges most clearly in the UC-related model of [KS05].

Also related to composition is the requirement of explicitly (and publicly) communicating session and key references, member lists, and information like the instance status: If a security model does not make this information readily available to an adversary, a reductionist security argument cannot use such information without becoming formally, and in many cases also effectively, invalid.

Finally, we emphasize that some GKE protocols allow for the concurrent execution of incompatible group operations (e.g., the concurrent addition and removal of a participant) so that different participants might derive keys with different understandings of whom they share it with. This indicates that the **Designated members** category in Table 1 is quite important.

2.5 Our Syntax Proposal

We turn to our syntax proposal that achieves all desirable properties from the above comparison. It is important to note that, in contrast to our *party-centric* perspective in the comparative systematization of this article, we design our model with an *instance-centric* view. That means, we here consider *instances* as the active entities in group key exchange and *parties* as only the passive key-storage in authenticated GKE to which distinct groups of instances have joint access. We discuss the perspectives on the relation between instances and parties in more detail in the full version of this article [PRSS21].

A GKE protocol is a quadruple GKE = (gen, init, exec, proc) of algorithms that generate authentication values, initialize an instance, execute operations according to protocol-dependent commands, and process incoming ciphertexts received from other instances. In order to highlight simplifications that are possible for unauthenticated GKE, we indicate parts of the definition with gray marked boxes that are only applicable to the authenticated case of GKE.

We define GKE protocol GKE over sets $\mathcal{PAU}, \mathcal{SAU}, \mathcal{IID}, \mathcal{ST}, \mathcal{CMD}, \mathcal{C}, \mathcal{K}, \mathcal{KID}$ where $\mathcal{PAU}$ and $\mathcal{SAU}$ are the public and secret authenticator spaces (e.g., verification and signing key spaces, or public group identifier and symmetric pre-shared group secret spaces), $\mathcal{IID}$ is the space of instance identifiers, $\mathcal{ST}$ is the space of instances' local secret states, $\mathcal{CMD}$ is the space of protocol-specific commands (that may include references from $\mathcal{IID}$ to other instances) to initiate operations in a session (such as adding users, etc.), $\mathcal{C}$ is the space of protocol ciphertexts that can be exchanged between instances, $\mathcal{K}$ is the space of group keys, and $\mathcal{KID}$ is the space of key identifiers that refer to computed group keys. The GKE algorithms are defined as follows:

- gen $\xrightarrow{out}$ $\mathcal{PAU} \times \mathcal{SAU}$. This algorithm takes no input and outputs a pair of public and secret authenticator.
- $\mathcal{IID} \xrightarrow{in}$ init $\xrightarrow{out}$ $\mathcal{ST}$. This algorithm initializes an instance's secret state.[11]
- $\mathcal{SAU} \times \mathcal{ST} \times \mathcal{CMD} \xrightarrow{in}$ exec $\xrightarrow{out}$ $\mathcal{ST}$. This algorithm initiates the execution of an operation in a group, e.g., the adding/joining/leaving/removing of instances; affected instances' identifiers can be encoded in the command parameter $cmd \in \mathcal{CMD}$.
- $\mathcal{SAU} \times \mathcal{ST} \times \mathcal{C} \xrightarrow{in}$ proc $\xrightarrow{out}$ $\mathcal{ST} \cup \{\bot\}$. This algorithm processes a received ciphertext. Return value $\bot$ signals rejection of the input ciphertext.

Interfaces for Algorithms. In contrast to previous works, we model communication to upper layer applications and to the underlying network infrastructure via interfaces that are provided by the environment in which a protocol runs rather than via direct return values. Each of the above algorithms can call the following interfaces (to send ciphertexts and report keys, respectively):

- $\mathcal{IID} \times \mathcal{C} \xrightarrow{in}$ snd. This interface takes a ciphertext (and the calling instance's identifier) and hands it over to the network which is expected to deliver it to other instances for processing. (The receiving instances are encoded in the ciphertext, see below.)
- $\mathcal{IID} \times \mathcal{KID} \times \mathcal{K} \xrightarrow{in}$ key. This interface takes a key identifier and the associated key (and the calling instance's identifier) and delivers them to the upper layer protocol.

Information Encoded in Objects. We assume that certain context information like paired protocol instances and public authenticators is encoded in objects like key identifiers, ciphertexts, and instance identifiers. More precisely, we assume three 'getter functions' mem, rec, pau as follows:

- Function $\mathcal{KID} \xrightarrow{in}$ mem $\xrightarrow{out}$ $\mathcal{P}(\mathcal{IID})$ extracts from a key identifier the list of identifiers of the instances that are expected to be able to compute the same key.[12]

---

[11] Although exec and proc could implicitly initialize the state internally, we treat the state initialization explicitly for reasons of clarity.

[12] $\mathcal{P}(\mathcal{X})$ denotes the powerset of $\mathcal{X}$.

- Function $\mathcal{C} \xrightarrow{in} \mathsf{rec} \xrightarrow{out} \mathcal{P}(\mathcal{IID})$ extracts the identifiers of the instances that are expected to receive the indicated ciphertext.
- Function $\mathcal{IID} \xrightarrow{in} \mathsf{pau} \xrightarrow{out} \mathcal{PAU}$, in the authenticated setting, extracts the public authenticator of an instance from its identifier.

While this notation is non-standard, it has a number of advantages over alternatives. One advantage has to do with clarity. For instance, function mem is precise about the fact that the list of peers with whom a key is shared is a function of the key itself, represented by its key identifier, and not of the session that established it. Indeed, the latter could establish also further keys with different sets of peers. A second advantage has to do with compactness of description. (This will be discussed in more detail in Sect. 3.1.) For instance, the notation of the proc algorithm would be more involved if the set of recipient instances of the ciphertext would have to be made explicit as well.

The properties of this syntax proposal are presented in the rightmost column of Table 1. Note that some properties are implied only by the use of this syntax in our partnering, correctness, and security definitions. For example, the flexible consideration of authentication mechanisms and the dispensability of online administrators are due to the game definition in our security notion of Sect. 4.1. We clarify on the advantages of our model at the end of Sect. 4.1.

3 Communication Models

The high flexibility in communication (i.e., interaction among participants) in a GKE protocol execution creates various challenges for modeling and defining security of GKE. Firstly, tracing participants of a single global session is a crucial yet typically complex task. Nearly all considered GKE models trace communication partners differently and, in the two-party key exchange literature, there exists an even wider variety of *partnering predicates* (aka. matching mechanisms) for this task. Secondly, normatively defining valid executions of a GKE protocol (versus invalid ones) in order to derive correctness requirements for them is not trivial for a generic consideration of GKE protocols. We note that only five out of the twelve considered models define correctness. In the following, we discuss partnering notions of the analyzed models. Due to space limits we systematize their correctness definitions in the full version [PRSS21].

3.1 Partnering

Generally, a partnering predicate identifies instances with related, similar, or even equal contexts of their protocol execution. However, partnering has served many different, somewhat related and somewhat independent purposes in (group) key exchange security models. We distinguish four subtly distinct purposes of partnering.

1. *Forbid trivial key reveals.* In security experiments where an adversary trying to break a challenge key can also reveal "independently" established keys,

partnering is used to restrict the adversary's ability to learn a challenge instance's key by revealing partner instances' keys. Here, the partnering predicate must include *at least* those instances that necessarily computed the same key (e.g., group members), but it could be extended to further instances to artificially weaken the adversary (as this restricts its ability to reveal keys), for example, in order to allow for more efficient GKE constructions.

2. *Detect authentication attacks.* In some explicitly authenticated GKE security definitions, partnering is used to identify successful authentication attacks when one instance completes without there existing partner instances at every designated group member. Here, the partnering predicate must include *at least* those instances belonging to designated members of a computed key, otherwise it is trivial to break authentication. But in this use, compared to use (1) above, the predicate should not be extended to further instances, as actual attacks against authentication might go undetected, if partnering is used for this purpose.

3. *Define correctness.* Partnering is sometimes used to identify instances expected to compute the same key for correctness purposes. In this case, the partnering predicate must include *at most* those instances that are required to compute the same key.

4. *Enabling generic composability.* Partnering also plays a crucial role in the generic composability of (group) key exchange with other primitives: Brzuska et al. [BFWW11] show that a publicly computable partnering predicate is sufficient and (in some cases) even necessary for proving secure the composition of a symmetric key application with keys from an AKE protocol. (Although they consider two-party key exchange, the intuition is applicable to group key exchange as well.)

Even though the first three purposes share some similarities, there are also subtle differences, and defining them via one unified notion can lead to problems.[13]

Our Consideration of Partnering Predicates. We consider the forbidding trivial key attacks ((1) above) as the core purpose of the partnering predicate. If the predicate is defined precisely (i.e., it exactly catches the set of same keys that result from a common global session) and is publicly derivable, it also allows for generic compositions of group key exchange with other primitives ((4) above), which we also consider indispensable.

Thereby, it is important to overcome a historic misconception of partnering: for either of the two above mentioned purposes (detection of key reveals and

---

[13] During the research for this article, we found two recent papers' security definitions for two-party authenticated key exchange that, due to reusing the partnering definition for multiple purposes, cannot be fulfilled: Li and Schäge [LS17] and Cohn-Gordon et al. [CCG+19] both require in their papers' proceedings version for authentication that an instance only computes a key if there exists a partner instance that also computed the key (which is impossible as not all/both participants compute the key simultaneously). Still, the underlying partnering concept suffices for detecting reveals and challenges of the same key (between partnered instances).

Table 2. Partnering definitions. Notation: ●: yes, ◉: implicitly, ◕: almost, ◑: partially, ○: no, -: not applicable; (blank): no option clearly superior/desirable.

Partnering/Matching/...	GKE-specific	[BCPQ01]	[BCP02b]	[KY03]	[KS05]	[GBG09]	[CCG+18]	[ACDT19]	[ACC+19]	[BCP01]	[BCP02a]	[KLL04]	[YKLH18]	Desirable	Our model
Defined?	○	●	●	●	●	●	●	◉	○	●	○	◕	●	●	●
Generic ● or protocol-specific ○	○	●	○	●	●	●	●	●		●		●	●	●	●
Normative/Precise/Retrospect. Variable	○	N		N	N	N	N	N	-	N	-	V	V	P	P
↳ Tight ● (vs. loose ○)	○	●	-	●	○	○	○	●	-	●	-	●	-	-	●
Publicly derivable	○	○	●	◉	○	◉	○	●	-	○	-	○	○	●	●
Components included in partnering predicate:															
Transcript															
Matching transcripts	○	◉	◉	●	○	○	○	●	-	◉	-	○	○	○	○
Sequence of matching transcripts	●	●	◉	○	○	○	○	○	-	●	-	○	○	○	○
Identifiers															
Group identifier	●	○	○	◉	◉	●	○	○	-	○	-	●*	●		○
Key identifier	○	○	○	○	○	○	○	○	-	○	-	●*	○		●
Externally input identifier	○	○	○	○	●	○	○	○	-	○	-	○	○		○
Group key															
Whether partners computed a key	○	●	○	◕	●	●	○	○	-	●	-	○	○	◉	◉
Whether group computed a key	●	◕	○	○	○	○	○	○	-	◕	-	○	○	○	○
Whether partners computed same key	○	○	○	○	○	○	●	○	-	○	-	○	○	●	◉
Members of the group	●	○	○	●	●	●	○	○	-	○	-	●	●	●	◉

use of established keys in compositions), not the *instances* (that compute keys) are central for the partnering predicate but the *keys themselves* and the *contexts* in which they are computed are. As a result, a partnering definition ideally determines the relation between established keys and their contexts instead of the relation between interacting instances. We elaborate on this in the following: In two-party key exchange, the context of a key is defined by its global session which itself is defined by its two participating instances. In multi-stage key exchange, keys are computed in consecutive stages of a protocol execution. Hence, the context can be determined by the two participating instances in combination with the current (consecutive) stage number. However, in group key exchange—especially if we consider dynamic membership changes—the context of a key is not defined consecutively anymore: due to parallel, potentially conflicting changes of the member set in a protocol execution, it is not necessary that all instances, computing multiple keys, perform these computations in the same order. Consequently, partnering is not a linear, *monotone predicate* defined for instances but an *individual predicate* for each computed group key that reflects its individual context. This context can be protocol-dependent and may include the set of designated member instances, a record of operation by which its computation was initiated, etc. We treat the context information of group keys as an explicit output of the protocol execution also for supporting the use of these keys in upper layer applications (see Table 1).

Models Without Partnering Definitions. Three models do not **define** a partnering predicate at all. In one of these, [ACDT19], a partnering predicate is implicit within their correctness definition. Two of these have no need of partnering since they restrict to (quasi-)passive adversaries [ACDT19] or do not offer adversaries a dedicated access to group keys [ACC+19], however by not defining a partnering predicate, they do not allow for generic composition with symmetric applications. [BCP02a] seemingly rely on an undefined partnering predicate, using the term 'partner' in their security definition but not defining it in the paper. [KLL04] define a partnering predicate of which two crucial components (group and key identifier; see the asterisk marked items in Table 2) are neither defined generically nor defined for the specific protocol that is analyzed in it.

Generality of Predicates. A partnering predicate can be **generic** or **protocol-specific**. From the considered models, only one has a predicate explicitly tailored to the analyzed GKE construction. But many of the generic partnering predicates involve values that are not necessarily part of all GKE schemes (e.g., group identifiers, externally input identifiers, etc.); a sufficiently generic partnering predicate should be able to cover a large class of constructions.

Character of Predicates. Generic partnering predicates can be **normative, precise**, or **retrospectively variable**.

Normative predicates define objective, static conditions under which contexts of keys are declared partnered independent of whether a particular protocol, analyzed with it, computes equal keys under these conditions. This has normative character because protocols analyzed under these predicates must implement measures to let contexts that are—according to the predicate—declared unpartnered result in the computation of independent (or no) keys. As almost all security experiments allow adversaries to reveal keys that are not partnered with a challenge key (see Sect. 4), protocols that do not adhere to a specified normative predicate are automatically declared insecure (because solving the key challenge thereby becomes trivial). These predicates can hence be considered as (hidden) parts of the security definition.

The class of normative predicates can further be divided into **tight** and **loose** ones. **Tight** predicates define only those contexts partnered that result from a joint protocol execution when not attacked by active adversaries. This corresponds to the idea of *matching conversations* being the first tight predicate from the seminal work on key exchange by Bellare and Rogaway [BR94]. Two instances have matching conversations if each of them received a non-empty prefix of, or exactly the same, ciphertexts that their peer instances sent over the network—resulting in partnered contexts at the end of their session. Matching conversations are problematic for the GKE setting for two reasons. First, achieving security under matching conversations necessitates *strongly unforgeable* signatures or message authentication codes when being used to authenticate the communication transcript.[14] Second, lifting matching conversations directly and incautiously to the group setting, as in [KY03], requires all communication in a global session to be broadcast among all group members so each can compute the same transcript—inducing impractical inefficiency for real-world deployment. If the model's syntax generically allows to (partially) reveal ciphertexts' receivers, as in [ACDT19], pairwise transcript comparison does not require all ciphertexts to be broadcast but the strong unforgeability for authenticating signatures or MACs remains unnecessarily required. Several models [BCPQ01, BCP01] circumvent the necessity of broadcasting all group communication in a matching conversation-like predicate, although their syntax does not reveal receivers of

---

[14] Note that every manipulated bit in the transcript (including signatures or MAC tags themselves) dissolves partnering.

ciphertext: they define two instances and their contexts as partnered if there exists a sequence of instances between them such that any consecutive instances in this sequence have partnered contexts according to matching conversations. (This still needs strongly unforgeable signatures and MACs, however.)

A **loose** partnering predicate is still static but declares more contexts partnered than those that inevitably result in the same key due to a joint, unimpeded protocol execution. This may include contexts of instances that actually did not participate in the same global session, or that did not compute the same (or any) key. An example for loose partnering predicates is *key partnering* [CCG+18] which declares the context of a key as the value of the key itself, regardless of whether it is computed due to participation in the same global session. Clearly, two instances that participated in two independent global sessions (e.g., one global session terminated before the other one begun) should intuitively not compute keys with partnered contexts even if these keys equal. Forbidding the reveal of group keys of intuitively unpartnered contexts results in security definitions that declare protocols 'secure' that may be intuitively insecure. On the other hand, partnering predicates that involve the comparison of a protocol-dependent [GBG09] or externally input [KS05] group identifier are loose because equality of this identifier means being partnered but does not imply the computation of an equal (or any) key.

A **precise** partnering predicate exactly declares those contexts as partnered that refer to equal keys computed *due to* the participation in the same global session. Hence, the conditions for being partnered are not static but depend on the respectively analyzed protocol. As a response to the disadvantages of normative partnering (and in particular tight matching conversations), Li and Schäge [LS17] proposed *original-key partnering* as a precise predicate for two-party key exchange: two instances have partnered contexts if they computed the same key, due to participating in a global session, that they would also have computed (when using the same random coins) in the absence of an adversary. As of yet, there exists no use of original-key partnering for the group setting in the literature, and we discuss drawbacks of this form of precise predicate with respect to the purpose of partnering below.

Variable predicates are parameterized by a customizable input that can be post-specified individually for each use of the model in which they are defined. Hence, these predicates are neither statically fixed nor determined for each protocol (individually) by their model, but can be specified ad hoc instead. As a result, a cryptographer, using a model with a variable predicate (e.g., when proving a construction secure in it), can define the exact partnering conditions for this predicate at will. The main drawback is that different instantiations of the same variable predicate in the same security model can produce different security statements for the same construction. We consider this ambiguity undesirable. Both group identifier and key identifier are left undefined in [KLL04] so they are effectively variable; in [YKLH18] the group ID is outsourced and thus left effectively variable.

Public Derivability of Predicates. A partnering predicate can and—in order to allow for generic compositions—should be **publicly derivable**. That is, the set of partnered contexts should be deducible from the adversarial interaction with the security experiment (or, according to Brzuska et al. [BFWW11], from the communication transcript of all instances in the environment). Only four models considered achieve this as listed in Table 2; ⊙ here refers to the implicit ability to observe whether group keys are computed. Partnering in all remaining models involves private values in instances' secret states. We remark that original-key partnering [LS17] (for two-party key exchange) is the only known precise predicate but it is not publicly computable as it depends on secret random coins.

Components of Predicates. The lower part of Table 2 lists the various parameters on which partnering predicates we consider are defined. These parameters include: the **transcript** of communications, protocol-specific **identifiers**, **external inputs**, the computed **group key**, the set of **group members**, etc.

The two main purposes of partnering ((1) forbidding trivial attacks and (4) allowing for generic composition) use the partnering predicate to determine which keys computed during a protocol execution are meant to be the same and in fact equal (i.e., whether they share the same context). Consequently, an ideal partnering predicate should depend on the context that describes the circumstances under which (and if) the group key is computed. As only for few protocols (e.g., optimal secure ones; cf. [PR18a, PR18b, JS18]) it is reasonable that the entire communicated transcript primarily determines the circumstances (i.e., the context) under which a key is computed, we consider it unsuitable to define partnering based on the transcript generally.

We conclude that it is not the task of the partnering predicate to define security (as normative predicates do). Neither should the variability of partnering predicates lead to ambiguous security notions. Hence, we consider generic, precise, and publicly derivable partnering predicates desirable. With our proposed partnering predicate from Sect. 3.2, we demonstrate that the problems of the yet only known precise partnering predicate [LS17] can be solved.

3.2 Our Partnering Proposal

Our partnering predicate defines keys with the same explicitly (and publicly; see Sect. 4.1) output context *kid* partnered:

Definition 1 (Partnering). *Two keys k_1, k_2 computed by instances id_1 and id_2 and output as tuples (id_1, kid_1, k_1) and (id_2, kid_2, k_2) via their* **key** *interface are partnered iff $kid_1 = kid_2$.*

4 Security Definitions

Although the actual definition of security is the core of a security model, there is no unified notion of "security" nor agreement on how strong or weak "security" should be—in part because different scenarios demand different strengths.

Thus we do not aim to compare the strength of models' security definitions, but do review clearly their comparable properties. We focus on the desired security goals, adversarial power in controlling the victims' protocol execution, and adversarial access to victims' secret information. We do not compare the conditions under which adversaries win the respective security experiments (aka. "freshness predicates", "adversarial restrictions", etc.) as this relates to the models' "strength", but we do report on characteristics such as forward-secrecy or post-compromise security.

Table 3. Security definitions. Notation: ●: yes, ◉: implicitly, ◑: almost, ◐: partially, ○: no, -: not applicable; (blank): no option clearly superior/desirable.

Security	GKE-specific	[BCPQ01]	[BCP02b]	[KY03]	[K805]	[GBG09]	[CCG+18]	[ACDT19]	[ACC+19]	[BCP01]	[BCP02a]	[KLL04]	[YKLH18]	Desirable	Our model
Security goals															
Key indistinguishability	○	●	●	●	●	●	●	●	●	●	●	●	●	●	●
∟ Multiple challenges	○	○	○	○	○	○	○	●	○	○	○	○	○	●	●
Explicit authentication	○	●	○	○	●	●	○	○	○	●	○	◐	○		○
Adversarial protocol execution															
All algorithms	○	●	●	●	●	●	●	●	◑	●	●	●	●	●	●
Instance specific	●	●	●	●	●	●	●	●	●	◑	◑	◑	●	●	●
Concurrent invocations	●	●	●	●	●	●	●	◑	●	○	○	○	●	●	●
Active communication manipulation	○	●	●	●	●	●	◑	○	◑	●	●	●	●	●	●
Adversarial access to secrets															
Corruption of involved parties' secrets	○	●	○	●	●	●	●	-	●	○	●	●	●	●	●
∟ After key exchange	○	●	-	●	●	●	●	-	-	-	●	●	◑	●	●
∟ Before key exchange	○	○	-	○	○	●	●	-	-	○	○	○	●	●	●
Corruption of independent parties' secrets	○	●	○	●	●	●	●	-	●	○	●	●	●	●	●
∟ Always	○	●	-	●	●	●	●	-	-	○	○	●	●	●	●
Exposure of involved instances' states	○	○	○	○	●	●	●	◑	●	●	○	●	○	●	●
∟ After key exchange	○	-	-	-	-	●	●	◑	●	●	●	-	●	-	●
∟ Before key exchange	○	-	-	-	○	○	●	●	●	●	-	○	-	○	○
Exposure of independent instances' states	○	○	○	○	-	●	●	●	●	●	○	●	○	●	●
∟ Always	○	-	-	-	●	●	●	●	●	●	-	○	-	○	●
Reveal of independent group keys	○	●	●	●	●	●	●	●	●	◉	●	◑	◑	●	●
∟ Always	○	●	●	●	●	●	●	●	●	◉	◑	◑	○	●	●

Security Goals. The analyzed models primarily consider two independent security goals: secrecy of keys and authentication of participants.

Secrecy of keys is in all models realized as **indistinguishability** of actually established **keys** from random values, within the context of an experiment in which the adversary controls protocol executions. During the experiment, the adversary can query a challenge oracle that outputs either the real key for a particular context or a random key; a protocol is *secure* if the adversary cannot dinistinguish between these two. Only one model allows adversaries to query the **challenge** oracle **multiple** times; all others allow only one query to the challenge oracle, resulting in an unnecessary and undesirable tightness loss in reduction-based proofs of composition results.

Key indistinguishability against active adversaries already implies *implicit authentication* of participants. That means keys computed in a session must diverge in case of active attacks that modify communications. Some models require **explicit authentication**: that the protocol explicitly rejects when there was an active attack. ([KLL04] only provide a very specialized notion thereof.) However, the value of explicit authentication in GKE, or even authenticated key exchange broadly, has long been unclear [Sho99]: GKE is never a standalone application but only a building block for some other purpose, providing keys that are implicitly authenticated and thus known only to the intended participants. If the subsequent application aims for explicit authentication of its payload, the diverging of keys due to implicit authentication can be used accordingly.

Adversarial Protocol Execution. To model the most general attacks by an adversary, the security experiment should allow adversaries to setup the experiment and control **all** victims' invocations of protocol **algorithms** and operations; all models considered do so. However, in two models the adversary can setup only one group during the entire security experiment (❷); this again introduces a tightness loss in the number of groups for composition results, and means that the use of long-term keys by parties across different sessions, as defined by [ACC+19], cannot be proven secure in the respective model.

Most models allow for **instance-specific** scheduling of invocations. This means that the adversary can let each instance execute the protocol algorithms individually instead of, for example, being restricted to only initiate batched protocol executions (e.g., of all instances involved in a group together). Three models (❸) indeed require that the adversary schedules algorithm and operation invocations that change group membership for all affected instances at once (and not individually); hence, diverging and concurrent operations (e.g., fractions of the group process different actions) cannot be scheduled in these three models. In practice this restriction means that some form of consensus is required (e.g., a central delivery server). While algorithms and operations can be **invoked concurrently** in [ACDT19], this model allows only one of the resulting concurrently sent ciphertexts to be delivered to and processed by the other participants of the same session; this similarly requires some consensus mechanism.

An **active** adversary who **modifies communication** between instances is permitted in almost all models. However, [CCG+18] forbid active attacks during the first communication round, [ACC+19] only allow adversaries to inconsistently forward ciphertexts but not manipulate them, and [ACDT19] require honest delivery of the communication. For the deployment of protocols secure according to the latter two models, active adversaries must be considered impractical or authentication mechanisms must be added.

Adversarial Access to Secrets. GKE models allow the adversary to learn certain secrets used by simulated participants during the security experiment. Below we discuss the different secrets that can be learned and the conditions under which this is allowed. We neglect adversarial access to algorithm invocations' random coins in our systematization as only three models consider this threat in their security experiments [CCG+18, ACDT19, ACC+19].

Corruption of party secrets models a natural threat scenario where parties use static secrets to authenticate themselves over a long period. Corruption is also necessary to model adversarial participation in environments with closed public key infrastructure (see Sect. 2), allowing the adversary to impersonate some party. Table 3 shows which models allow for corruptions of party secrets *after* and *before* the exchange of a secure group key (i.e., *forward-secrecy* and *post-compromise security*, respectively), and corruptions of independent parties anytime. In [ACDT19] parties do not maintain static secrets so corruption is irrelevant. Two other models do have parties with static secrets but do not provide an oracle for the adversary to corrupt them.[15] Due to imprecise definitions, [KLL04] partially forbids corruptions of involved parties even after a secure key was established, and two other models even forbid corruptions of independent parties before an (independent) secure group key is established. Only three models treat authentication as the sole purpose of party secrets, defining precise conditions that allow corruptions before and after the establishment of a secure group key. As secrecy of a group key should never depend solely on secrecy of independent parties' long-term secrets and *forward-secrecy* is today considered a minimum standard, we deem security despite later corruption of long-term secrets desirable.

Exposure of instance states is especially important in GKE because single sessions may be quite long-lived—such as months- or years-long chats—so local states may become as persistent as party secrets. In most security experiments that provide adversarial access to instance states, their exposure is not permitted before the establishment of a secure group key. Some of these models further restrict the exposure of independent instances' states (e.g., because they were involved in earlier stages of the same session). The three papers that consider *ratcheting* of state secrets allow adversarial access to these states shortly before and after the establishment of a secure group key. [CCG+18] model state expose through the reveal of random coins, which means an exposure at a particular moment reveals only newly generated secrets in the current state, not old state secrets. We consider the ability to expose states independent of and after the establishment of a group key desirable, and leave state exposure before establishment—post-compromise security—as a bonus feature.[16]

The **reveal** of established **group keys** in the security experiment is important to show that different group keys are indeed independent. One motivation for this is that use of keys in weak applications should not hurt secure applications that use different keys from the same GKE protocol. The reveal of keys is furthermore necessary to prove implicit authentication of group keys. Reveals should also be possible to permit composition of key exchange with a generic symmetric key protocol [BFWW11]. Almost all models allow the reveal of different (i.e., unpartnered) group keys unlimitedly. As [BCP02a] and [KLL04] do not define partnering adequately (see Sect. 3.1), it cannot be assessed which group keys are declared *unpartnered* in their models. The adversary in [ACC+19] is not equipped with a dedicated reveal oracle but since the security in this model is strong enough, the exposure of instance states suffices to obtain all keys without affecting unpartnered keys. [YKLH18] forbid the reveal of earlier group keys in

---

[15] Moreover, in [BCP02b, ACC+19], party secrets cannot be derived via state exposures. Although [ACC+19] allow the exposure of instance states, their syntax, strictly speaking, does not have a method for *using* party secrets in the protocol execution, even though their construction makes use of them (violating the syntax definition).

[16] Note, for example, that post-compromise security is rather irrelevant for short-lived static GKE protocols.

the same session. As unpartnered keys should always be independent we consider it desirable to allow their unrestricted reveal.

4.1 Our Security Proposal

We define security of GKE schemes via a game in which adversaries can interact with these schemes via oracles: For each algorithm of the GKE scheme (see Sect. 2.5), adversaries can query a corresponding oracle—Init, Execute, Process in the unauthenticated setting and additionally Gen in the authenticated setting—and thereby choose the respective public input parameters. The public outputs, produced by the respective internal algorithm invocations of these oracles, are given to adversaries via the interfaces snd and key. Adversaries can also query oracles Expose, Reveal and in the authenticated setting additionally Corrupt to obtain instances' secret states, established group keys, and parties' authentication secrets, respectively. By querying oracle Challenge, adversaries obtain challenge group keys and win the game if they correctly determine whether these keys were actually established by simulated instances during the game or randomly sampled.

We provide the formal pseudo-code description of this game in Fig. 1. The majority of lines of code in this figure only realizes the sound simulation of the game and, therefore, equally appears in our correctness definition that we provide in the full version of this article [PRSS21]. Below we textually describe the remaining parts that constitute restrictions of the adversary and the definition of security.

Table 4. Variables in Fig. 1.

K	Array of computed group keys
ST	Array of instance states
SAU	Array of secret authenticators
CR	Set of corrupted or external authenticators
WK	Set of weak group keys
CH	Set of keys challenged for A
CP	Set of keys already computed by an instance
TR	Transcript as queue of ciphertexts sent among instances

To prevent the trivial solving of challenges, the game forbids the adversary to conduct the following attacks.

1. A group key must not be both revealed via oracle Reveal and queried as a challenge via oracle Challenge (lines 37,42,05).
2. After an instance's local state is exposed via oracle Expose, all keys that can be computed by this instance according to their key identifier are declared *weak*

Game $\mathrm{KIND}^b_{\mathrm{GKE}}(\mathcal{A})$
```
00   K[·] ← ⊥; ST[·] ← ⊥
01   SAU[·] ← ⊥; CR ← PAU
02   WK ← ∅; CH ← ∅
03   CP[·] ← ∅; TR[·][·] ← ⊥
04   b' ←$ A()
05 · Require WK ∩ CH = ∅
06   Stop with b'
```

Oracle Gen
```
07   (pau, sau) ←$ gen
08   SAU[pau] ← sau
09 · CR ← CR \ {pau}
10   Return pau
```

Oracle Init(*iid*)
```
11   Require iid ∈ IID
12   Require SAU[pau(iid)] ≠ ⊥
13   Require ST[iid] = ⊥
14   st ←$ init(iid)
15   ST[iid] ← st
16   Return
```

Oracle Execute(*iid, cmd*)
```
17   Require ST[iid] ≠ ⊥
18   sau ← SAU[pau(iid)]; st ← ST[iid]
19   st ←$ exec( sau, st, cmd)
20   ST[iid] ← st
21   Return
```

Oracle Process(*iid, c*)
```
22   Require ST[iid] ≠ ⊥
23   sau ← SAU[pau(iid)]; st ← ST[iid]
24   st ←$ proc( sau, st, c)
25 · If ∄iid_s : c = TR[iid_s][iid].peek()
         ∧st ≠ ⊥:
26 ·    WK ⟵∪ {kid ∈ KID \ CP[iid] :
               ∃iid_cr : {iid, iid_cr} ⊆ mem(kid)
                 ∧ pau(iid_cr) ∈ CR}
27   Else: TR[iid_s][iid].dequeue()
28   ST[iid] ← st
29   Return
```

Proc snd$_{iid}$(*c*)
```
30 · For all iid_r ∈ rec(c):
31 ·    TR[iid][iid_r].enqueue(c)
32   Give c to A
```

Proc key$_{iid}$(*kid, k*)
```
33   K[kid] ← k
34 · CP[iid] ⟵∪ {kid}
35   Give kid to A
```

Oracle Reveal(*kid*)
```
36   Require K[kid] ≠ ⊥
37 · WK ⟵∪ kid
38   Return K[kid]
```

Oracle Challenge(*kid*)
```
39   Require K[kid] ≠ ⊥ ∧ kid ∉ CH
40   k_0 ← K[kid]
41   k_1 ←$ K
42 · CH ⟵∪ kid
43   Return k_b
```

Oracle Expose(*iid*)
```
44   Require ST[iid] ≠ ⊥
45 · WK ⟵∪ {kid ∈ KID \ CP[iid] :
               iid ∈ mem(kid)}
46   Return ST[iid]
```

Oracle Corrupt(*pau*)
```
47   Require SAU[pau] ≠ ⊥
48 · CR ⟵∪ {pau}
49   Return SAU[pau]
```

Fig. 1. KIND game of GKE modeling unauthenticated or authenticated group key exchange. '·' at the margin highlight mechanisms to restrict the adversary (e.g., to forbid trivial attacks). Almost all remaining code equally appears in our correctness definition (see the full version [PRSS21]) and is less important for understanding the security definition. The used variables are explained in Table 4. Line 27 uses iid_s from line 25.

(i.e., known to the adversary), if these keys have not already been computed by this exposed instance before (lines 45,34).

As weak keys cannot be challenged but non-weak keys can, we require forward-secrecy—previously computed keys are required to stay secure after an exposure—but not post-compromise security—all future keys of this instance are declared insecure after an exposure. We sketch how to add post-compromise security requirements to this notion below but we consider this weaker security definition sufficient for our demonstration purposes.

Finally, the treatment of active impersonation attacks against the communication in the unauthenticated setting is as follows:

3a) If a ciphertext from an unknown sender (or from a known sender in the wrong order) is processed by an instance without being rejected (lines 30–31, 25), then all keys that can be computed by this processing instance according to their key identifier are declared weak, if they have not already been computed by this processing instance before (lines 26, 34).

This reflects that in the unauthenticated setting every adversarially generated ciphertext that is accepted as valid by an instance can be considered a successful impersonation of another (honest) instance. Hence, future keys computed by the accepting receiver are potentially known to the adversary.

In the authenticated setting, the set of keys that are declared weak is reduced based on the set of corrupted authenticators. Authenticators are considered *corrupted* if they have not been generated by the challenger (lines 01, 09; because thereby they are potentially adversarially generated) or if they have been honestly generated first but then corrupted via oracle Corrupt (lines 01, 09, 48). As the impersonation of instances with uncorrupted authenticators should be hard in the authenticated setting, active attacks against the communication between instances are treated as follows:

3b) If a ciphertext from an unknown sender (or from a known sender in the wrong order) is processed by an instance without being rejected (lines 30–31, 25), then all keys that can be computed by this processing instance according to their key identifier are declared weak, if they have not already been computed by this processing instance before (lines 26, 34) *and, according to their key identifier, they are also computable by an instance with a corrupted authenticator* (lines 26, 01, 09, 48).

Definition 2 (Adversarial Advantage). *The advantage of an adversary $\mathcal{A}$ in winning game KIND from Fig. 1 is* $\mathrm{Adv}_{\mathrm{GKE}}^{\mathrm{kind}}(\mathcal{A}) := |\Pr[\mathrm{KIND}_{\mathrm{GKE}}^{1}(\mathcal{A}) = 1] - \Pr[\mathrm{KIND}_{\mathrm{GKE}}^{0}(\mathcal{A}) = 1]|$.

Intuitively, a GKE scheme is secure if all realistic adversaries have negligible advantage in winning this game.

Discussion of the Model. With our proposed model we only want to provide an example definition of security. As mentioned before, we believe that optimal security for GKE is often too strong for practical demands (and hence undesired), and we are not under the illusion that there exists a unified definition of security on which the literature should or aims to agree on. Our contribution is instead that we provide a simple, compact, and precise framework that generically captures GKE and in which the restriction of the adversary (which essentially models the required security) can easily be adjusted. The provided instance of this framework achieves all properties that we identified as desirable in our systematization of knowledge. To name only some advantages of our model: 1. it allows for participation of multiple instances per party per session, 2. it covers unauthenticated, symmetric-key authenticated, and public-key authenticated settings, 3. it imposes no form of key distribution mechanism on GKE constructions and their environment, 4. neither does it impose a consensus mechanism for unifying all session participants' views on the session (although they can be implemented on top), 5. it permits any variant of protocol-specific membership operations, 6. it bases on natural generic interfaces, 7. it outputs the context of group keys along with the group keys themselves to upper-layer applications, 8. it allows for actual asynchronous protocol executions in which not all participants need to agree upon the same order of group key computations,9. it defines partnering naturally via the context that the protocol itself declares for each group key, 10. it illustrates how a generic model can allow for protocol-dependent definitions of contexts for group keys, 11. it respects the requirements of composition results [BFWW11], 12. it naturally gives adversaries in the security experiment full power in executing the protocol algorithms and determining their public inputs, 13. and it can easily express different strengths of security (see the next paragraph). At the same time, none of the newly captured properties are required to be achieved by analyzed protocols since our model is designed to be *indifferent* to them. We conclude that this model fulfills its main purpose: demonstrating that the desired properties from our systematization framework do not conflict and can hence be achieved simultaneously.

Adding Post-Compromise Security. Extending our proposed security definition to also require secrecy of group keys *after* an involved instance's state was exposed is, due to our flexible key identifiers, straight forward. Intuitively, an instance can recover from a state exposure by contributing new (public) key material to the group. The period between two such contributions by an instance is sometimes called "epoch" (cf. [PR18b, ACDT20]). By encoding in the key identifier of each group key the current epoch of each involved instance, the set of keys that are declared weak due to a state exposure can be reduced accordingly: Instead of declaring all keys weak that an instance can compute in the future after its state was exposed (see item 2 and line 45), only those keys that can be computed by this instance in the current epoch are declared weak. This has the effect that group keys of future epochs are required to be secure again.

5   Concluding Remarks and Open Problems

Our systematization of knowledge reveals some shortcomings in the GKE literature, stemming from a tendency to design a security model hand-in-hand with a protocol to be proven; such a model tends to be less generic, making specific assumptions about characteristics of the protocols it can be used for or the application environment with which it interacts. Sometimes the application environment appeared to be fully neglected. We revisit the underlying concepts of GKE and take into account the broad spectrum of requirements that may arise from the context in which a GKE protocol may be used, such as the type and distribution of authentication credentials of parties, how groups are formed and administered, and whether parties can have multiple devices in the same group. The goal is not to develop a single unified model of group key exchange security, but to support the development of models within the GKE literature that are well-informed by the principle requirements of GKE. Our prototype model demonstrates that these desirable properties of GKE can be satisfied within one generic model, with reduced complexity, increased precision and without restricting its applicability and coverage.

Looking forward, group key exchange is on track for increasing complexity. There now exist prominent applications requiring group key exchange—group instant messaging, videoconferencing—and using a cryptographic protocol in a real-world setting invariably leads to greater complexity in modeling and design. Moreover, the desire for novel properties such as highly dynamic groups and post-compromise security using ratcheting, manifested in proposed standards such as MLS, make it all the more important to have a clear approach to modeling the security of group key exchange.

Among others, our work leaves a number of challenges as open problems. As noted, our model should be seen as a general framework from which versions dedicated to specific use cases can be derived by restricting certain components. Identifying a palette of such submodels that are simultaneously useful and general is challenging, and left for future research. Independently, appropriately integrating the consideration of weakened randomness sources or low entropy password-based authentication into our model remains an open task. Finally, our work contributes a new model that, so far, has not been tested by analyzing the security of a concrete real-world GKE construction.

Acknowledgments. We thank the reviewers of CT-RSA 2021 for their detailed and helpful comments. B.P. was supported by the European Union's Horizon 2020 Research and Innovation Programme under Grant Agreement No. 786725 – OLYMPUS. P.R. was supported by the research training group "Human Centered Systems Security" (NERD.NRW) sponsored by the state of North-Rhine Westphalia. D.S. was supported by Natural Sciences and Engineering Research Council of Canada (NSERC) Discovery grant RGPIN-2016-05146 and NSERC Discovery Accelerator Supplement grant RGPIN-2016-05146.

References

[ABCP06] Abdalla, M., Bresson, E., Chevassut, O., Pointcheval, D.: Password-based group key exchange in a constant number of rounds. In: Yung, M., Dodis, Y., Kiayias, A., Malkin, T. (eds.) PKC 2006. LNCS, vol. 3958, pp. 427–442. Springer, Heidelberg (2006). https://doi.org/10.1007/11745853_28

[ACC+19] Alwen, J., et al.: Keep the dirt: tainted TreeKEM, an efficient and provably secure continuous group key agreement protocol. Cryptology ePrint Archive, Report 2019/1489 (2019). https://eprint.iacr.org/2019/1489. Accessed 13 Feb 2020

[ACDT19] Alwen, J., Coretti, S., Dodis, Y., Tselekounis, Y.: Security analysis and improvements for the IETF MLS standard for group messaging. Cryptology ePrint Archive, Report 2019/1189 (2019). https://eprint.iacr.org/2019/1189. Accessed 13 Feb 2020

[ACDT20] Alwen, J., Coretti, S., Dodis, Y., Tselekounis, Y.: Security analysis and improvements for the IETF MLS standard for group messaging. In: Micciancio, D., Ristenpart, T. (eds.) CRYPTO 2020, Part I. LNCS, vol. 12170, pp. 248–277. Springer, Cham (2020). https://doi.org/10.1007/978-3-030-56784-2_9

[ACJM20] Alwen, J., Coretti, S., Jost, D., Mularczyk, M.: Continuous group key agreement with active security. Cryptology ePrint Archive, Report 2020/752 (2020). https://eprint.iacr.org/2020/752

[AJM20] Alwen, J., Jost, D., Mularczyk, M.: On the insider security of MLS. Cryptology ePrint Archive, Report 2020/1327 (2020). https://eprint.iacr.org/2020/1327

[BBM+20] Barnes, R., Beurdouche, B., Millican, J., Omara, E., Cohn-Gordon, K., Robert, R.: The messaging layer security (MLS) protocol. Technical report (2020). https://datatracker.ietf.org/doc/draft-ietf-mls-protocol/

[BC04] Bresson, E., Catalano, D.: Constant round authenticated group key agreement via distributed computation. In: Bao, F., Deng, R., Zhou, J. (eds.) PKC 2004. LNCS, vol. 2947, pp. 115–129. Springer, Heidelberg (2004). https://doi.org/10.1007/978-3-540-24632-9_9

[BCP01] Bresson, E., Chevassut, O., Pointcheval, D.: Provably authenticated group Diffie-Hellman key exchange — the dynamic case. In: Boyd, C. (ed.) ASIACRYPT 2001. LNCS, vol. 2248, pp. 290–309. Springer, Heidelberg (2001). https://doi.org/10.1007/3-540-45682-1_18

[BCP02a] Bresson, E., Chevassut, O., Pointcheval, D.: Dynamic group Diffie-Hellman key exchange under standard assumptions. In: Knudsen, L.R. (ed.) EUROCRYPT 2002. LNCS, vol. 2332, pp. 321–336. Springer, Heidelberg (2002). https://doi.org/10.1007/3-540-46035-7_21

[BCP02b] Bresson, E., Chevassut, O., Pointcheval, D.: Group Diffie-Hellman key exchange secure against dictionary attacks. In: Zheng, Y. (ed.) ASIACRYPT 2002. LNCS, vol. 2501, pp. 497–514. Springer, Heidelberg (2002). https://doi.org/10.1007/3-540-36178-2_31

[BCPQ01] Bresson, E., Chevassut, O., Pointcheval, D., Quisquater, J.-J.: Provably authenticated group Diffie-Hellman key exchange. In: Reiter, M.K., Samarati, P. (eds.) ACM CCS 2001, pp. 255–264. ACM Press, November 2001

[BD95] Burmester, M., Desmedt, Y.: A secure and efficient conference key distribution system. In: De Santis, A. (ed.) EUROCRYPT 1994. LNCS, vol. 950, pp. 275–286. Springer, Heidelberg (1995). https://doi.org/10.1007/BFb0053443

[BD05] Burmester, M., Desmedt, Y.: A secure and scalable group key exchange system. Inf. Process. Lett. **94**(3), 137–143 (2005)

[BDR20] Bienstock, A., Dodis, Y., Rösler, P.: On the price of concurrency in group ratcheting protocols. In: Pass, R., Pietrzak, K. (eds.) TCC 2020, Part II. LNCS, vol. 12551, pp. 198–228. Springer, Cham (2020). https://doi.org/10.1007/978-3-030-64378-2_8

[BFWW11] Brzuska, C., Fischlin, M., Warinschi, B., Williams, S.C.: Composability of Bellare-Rogaway key exchange protocols. In: Chen, Y., Danezis, G., Shmatikov, V. (eds.) ACM CCS 2011, pp. 51–62. ACM Press, October 2011

[BR94] Bellare, M., Rogaway, P.: Entity authentication and key distribution. In: Stinson, D.R. (ed.) CRYPTO 1993. LNCS, vol. 773, pp. 232–249. Springer, Heidelberg (1994). https://doi.org/10.1007/3-540-48329-2_21

[Can01] Canetti, R.: Universally composable security: a new paradigm for cryptographic protocols. In: 42nd FOCS, pp. 136–145. IEEE Computer Society Press, October 2001

[CCG+18] Cohn-Gordon, K., Cremers, C., Garratt, L., Millican, J., Milner, K.: On ends-to-ends encryption: asynchronous group messaging with strong security guarantees. In: Lie, D., Mannan, M., Backes, M., Wang, X. (eds.) ACM CCS 2018, pp. 1802–1819. ACM Press, October 2018

[CCG+19] Cohn-Gordon, K., Cremers, C., Gjøsteen, K., Jacobsen, H., Jager, T.: Highly efficient key exchange protocols with optimal tightness. In: Boldyreva, A., Micciancio, D. (eds.) CRYPTO 2019, Part III. LNCS, vol. 11694, pp. 767–797. Springer, Cham (2019). https://doi.org/10.1007/978-3-030-26954-8_25

[GBG09] Gorantla, M.C., Boyd, C., González Nieto, J.M.: Modeling key compromise impersonation attacks on group key exchange protocols. In: Jarecki, S., Tsudik, G. (eds.) PKC 2009. LNCS, vol. 5443, pp. 105–123. Springer, Heidelberg (2009). https://doi.org/10.1007/978-3-642-00468-1_7

[ITW82] Ingemarsson, I., Tang, D., Wong, C.: A conference key distribution system. IEEE Trans. Inf. Theory **28**(5), 714–720 (1982)

[JKT07] Jarecki, S., Kim, J., Tsudik, G.: Group secret handshakes or affiliation-hiding authenticated group key agreement. In: Abe, M. (ed.) CT-RSA 2007. LNCS, vol. 4377, pp. 287–308. Springer, Heidelberg (2006). https://doi.org/10.1007/11967668_19

[JL07] Jarecki, S., Liu, X.: Unlinkable secret handshakes and key-private group key management schemes. In: Katz, J., Yung, M. (eds.) ACNS 2007. LNCS, vol. 4521, pp. 270–287. Springer, Heidelberg (2007). https://doi.org/10.1007/978-3-540-72738-5_18

[JS18] Jaeger, J., Stepanovs, I.: Optimal channel security against fine-grained state compromise: the safety of messaging. In: Shacham, H., Boldyreva, A. (eds.) CRYPTO 2018, Part I. LNCS, vol. 10991, pp. 33–62. Springer, Cham (2018). https://doi.org/10.1007/978-3-319-96884-1_2

[KLL04] Kim, H.-J., Lee, S.-M., Lee, D.H.: Constant-round authenticated group key exchange for dynamic groups. In: Lee, P.J. (ed.) ASIACRYPT 2004. LNCS, vol. 3329, pp. 245–259. Springer, Heidelberg (2004). https://doi.org/10.1007/978-3-540-30539-2_18

[KS05] Katz, J., Shin, J.S.: Modeling insider attacks on group key-exchange protocols. In: Atluri, V., Meadows, C., Juels, A. (eds.) ACM CCS 2005, pp. 180–189. ACM Press, November 2005

[KY03]   Katz, J., Yung, M.: Scalable protocols for authenticated group key exchange. In: Boneh, D. (ed.) CRYPTO 2003. LNCS, vol. 2729, pp. 110–125. Springer, Heidelberg (2003). https://doi.org/10.1007/978-3-540-45146-4_7

[LS17]   Li, Y., Schäge, S.: No-match attacks and robust partnering definitions: defining trivial attacks for security protocols is not trivial. In: Thuraisingham, B.M., Evans, D., Malkin, T., Xu, D. (eds.) ACM CCS 2017, pp. 1343–1360. ACM Press, October/November 2017

[Man09]   Manulis, M.: Group key exchange enabling on-demand derivation of peer-to-peer keys. In: Abdalla, M., Pointcheval, D., Fouque, P.-A., Vergnaud, D. (eds.) ACNS 2009. LNCS, vol. 5536, pp. 1–19. Springer, Heidelberg (2009). https://doi.org/10.1007/978-3-642-01957-9_1

[NS11]   Neupane, K., Steinwandt, R.: Communication-efficient 2-round group key establishment from pairings. In: Kiayias, A. (ed.) CT-RSA 2011. LNCS, vol. 6558, pp. 65–76. Springer, Heidelberg (2011). https://doi.org/10.1007/978-3-642-19074-2_5

[PR18a]   Poettering, B., Rösler, P.: Asynchronous ratcheted key exchange. Cryptology ePrint Archive, Report 2018/296 (2018). https://eprint.iacr.org/2018/296

[PR18b]   Poettering, B., Rösler, P.: Towards bidirectional ratcheted key exchange. In: Shacham, H., Boldyreva, A. (eds.) CRYPTO 2018, Part I. LNCS, vol. 10991, pp. 3–32. Springer, Cham (2018). https://doi.org/10.1007/978-3-319-96884-1_1

[PRSS21] Poettering, B., Rösler, P., Schwenk, J., Stebila, D.: SoK: game-based security models for group key exchange. Cryptology ePrint Archive, Report 2021/305 (2021). https://eprint.iacr.org/2021/305

[RMS18]   Rösler, P., Mainka, C., Schwenk, J.: More is less: on the end-to-end security of group chats in Signal, WhatsApp, and Threema. In: 2018 IEEE European Symposium on Security and Privacy (EuroS&P), pp. 415–429. IEEE (2018)

[Sho99]   Shoup, V.: On formal models for secure key exchange. Technical report RZ 3120, IBM (1999)

[XHZ15]   Xu, J., Hu, X.-X., Zhang, Z.-F.: Round-optimal password-based group key exchange protocols in the standard model. In: Malkin, T., Kolesnikov, V., Lewko, A.B., Polychronakis, M. (eds.) ACNS 2015. LNCS, vol. 9092, pp. 42–61. Springer, Cham (2015). https://doi.org/10.1007/978-3-319-28166-7_3

[YKLH18] Yang, Z., Khan, M., Liu, W., He, J.: On security analysis of generic dynamic authenticated group key exchange. In: Gruschka, N. (ed.) NordSec 2018. LNCS, vol. 11252, pp. 121–137. Springer, Cham (2018). https://doi.org/10.1007/978-3-030-03638-6_8

EPID with Malicious Revocation

Olivier Sanders[1]([✉]) and Jacques Traoré[2]

[1] Orange Labs, Applied Crypto Group, Cesson-Sévigné, France
olivier.sanders@orange.com
[2] Orange Labs, Applied Crypto Group, Caen, France

Abstract. EPID systems are anonymous authentication protocols where a device can be revoked by including one of its signatures in a revocation list. Such protocols are today included in the ISO/IEC 20008-2 standard and are embedded in billions of chips, which make them a flagship of advanced cryptographic tools. Yet, their security analysis is based on a model that suffers from several important limitations, which either questions the security assurances EPID can provide in the real world or prevents such systems from achieving their full impact. The most prominent example is the one of revocation lists. Although they could be managed locally by verifiers, which would be natural in most use-cases, the security model assumes that they are managed by a trusted entity, a requirement that is not easily met in practice and that is thus tempting to ignore, as illustrated in the corresponding standard.

In this paper, we propose to revisit the security model of EPID, by removing some limitations of previous works but mostly by answering the following question: what can we achieve when revocation lists are generated by a malicious entity?

Surprisingly, even in this disadvantageous context, we show that it is possible to retain strong properties that we believe to better capture the spirit of EPID systems. Moreover, we show that we can construct very efficient schemes resisting such powerful adversaries by essentially tweaking previous approaches. In particular, our constructions do not require to perform any significant test on the revocation lists during the signature generation process. These constructions constitute the second contribution of this paper.

1 Introduction

1.1 Related Works

Direct Anonymous Attestation (DAA) was introduced by Brickell, Camenisch and Chen [10] as an anonymous authentication mechanism with some controlled linkability features. In such systems, platforms can issue anonymous signatures after being enrolled by an issuer, in a way akin to group signatures [16]. A few years later, Brickell and Li [11] proposed a variant with enhanced revocation features under the name of Enhanced Privacy ID (EPID). Indeed, EPID additionally allows to revoke a platform $\mathcal{P}$ by adding one of its signature to a so-called

© Springer Nature Switzerland AG 2021
K. G. Paterson (Ed.): CT-RSA 2021, LNCS 12704, pp. 177–200, 2021.
https://doi.org/10.1007/978-3-030-75539-3_8

signature revocation list SRL. In such a case, $\mathcal{P}$ will not be able to produce new (valid) signatures on input SRL but we stress, to avoid confusion, that signatures issued by $\mathcal{P}$ with different revocation lists remain anonymous and unrevoked.

Both DAA and EPID systems are among the few advanced[1] cryptographic mechanisms that are widely deployed today. They are indeed embedded in billion of devices [23,31] and have been included in standards, such as ISO/IEC 20008-2 [25].

Surprisingly, the real-world popularity of these mechanisms did not extend to cryptographic literature as only a few papers have been published on these topics. This stands in sharp contrast with a sibling primitive, group signature, that has been extensively studied by the cryptographic community.

Actually, this relatedness with group signature probably explains the lack of academic interest for DAA and EPID schemes. It is indeed tempting to see a DAA or an EPID system as a simple variant of group signature, which lessens the appeal for any contribution in this area. More concretely, a DAA can be seen as a group signature where the opening feature is discarded and replaced by a linking feature that is rather easy to implement. EPID replaces the latter feature by a more intricate revocation mechanism that is nevertheless rather simple to add modularly.

From the algorithmic standpoint, constructing a DAA or an EPID system from a group signature might therefore look trivial. However, from the security model standpoint, removing the opening feature has huge consequences and makes the formalization of security properties much more difficult. In the particular case of EPID, the revocation feature creates additional problems as it is more complex to control in this context. This explains in part the somewhat chaotic history of DAA and EPID security models that we briefly recall here.

The original security model [11] for EPID was based on simulation. Back then, it was a natural choice as DAA [10] also considered simulation-based models. Unfortunately, the security model of [10] was not correct and several attempts [17–19] to fix it failed (see [5] for a discussion on these issues). This probably explains the shift to game-based models for DAA that was followed by EPID in [12]. The latter paper, enhanced with some remarks from [5], is a good starting point to study the security of EPID but unfortunately the resulting model still suffers from several problems that limit the practical assurances it provides in the real world. More recently, a new simulation-based model was proposed by Camenisch et al. [13] for DAA and later extended to EPID in [26]. Although it implies a cleaner definition of unforgeability, it imposes in practice the same kind of restrictions to the constructions as in [12]. Moreover, [26] suffers from the same limitations regarding anonymity as previous models of EPID, which has important consequences in the real world. All these issues are discussed in details below.

Concretely this means that, as of today, the security assurances provided by mechanisms deployed in billion of devices are not well understood and sometimes

---

[1] By "advanced" we here mean asymmetric mechanisms that go beyond standard signature, encryption and key exchange.

rely on some assumptions that seem questionable. This is particularly true in the context of EPID as the revocation mechanism imposes very strong constraints on the whole system, which has been underestimated in previous works. In this paper, we will then focus on the case of EPID as it is the most complex one but we note that many of our remarks also apply to standard DAA schemes.

1.2 Our Contributions

The contribution of our paper is actually twofold. First, we propose a security model for EPID with new unforgeability and anonymity definitions that we believe to better capture what we expect from such systems. In particular, we are the first (to our knowledge) to consider the case where revocation lists are not generated by a trusted entity. Such a trusted entity is indeed very convenient from the theoretical standpoint but its existence is not obvious and the way it will proceed to decide in practice which signature should be added to revocation lists is far from clear. To deal with malicious revocation lists is a very challenging task but we argue it is a realistic scenario and it is thus important to understand what we can retain in this case and how to construct schemes that still resist such powerful adversaries. We extensively discuss the issues of previous models in the following paragraphs as it is necessary to understand the rationale behind our new definitions. We choose a game-based approach as we believe it is better suited for complex primitives such as EPID. In particular, we hope that separate experiments will lead to a better understanding of what an EPID system can achieve in our model. Our second contribution consists of two efficient constructions that achieve our new security properties. They share many similarities with existing constructions but also present some differences that we comment at the end of this section.

Issues with Previous Unforgeability Notions. The problems regarding unforgeability (called traceability in [5]) concern both DAA and EPID models and we believe they all find root in the difficulty to properly define what is a valid forgery in this context. Indeed, any model must provide to the adversary $\mathcal{A}$ the ability to own some signing keys (that are called *corrupt*), which inevitably allows $\mathcal{A}$ to issue signatures. We can't therefore rely on something akin to unforgeability for standard digital signature. The idea that seems to be behind previous models is then to mimic security notions of group signatures, but this does not work well in this setting. Indeed, group signature provides an opening algorithm that allows to trace back any group signature to its issuer. Dealing with corrupt keys is then simple, as we have a way to detect if the adversary's forgery is *trivial* (that is, it has been generated using corrupt keys) or not (the signature cannot be linked to a corrupt key). In a DAA or an EPID scheme there is no counterpart of the opening algorithm but one can test if a signature has been generated by a given platform if one knows its secret key. This has led to the following two cases.

In game-based models [5,12], the experiment assumes that the adversary provides all its signing keys, which enables "opening" of signatures issued with corrupt keys and so to rule out trivial wins by the adversary. In the context of EPID, this constraint can be partially relaxed by alternatively requiring a signature from each malicious platform that has not yet revealed its secret key (see [12]). More concretely, existing game-based EPID models consider a set $\mathcal{U}$ of malicious platforms and requires, for each $i \in \mathcal{U}$, either the signing key sk_i or a signature issued by i. If we set aside the problem of identifying in the real world the set $\mathcal{U}$ of malicious platforms without an opening procedure, it remains to explain why the adversary would ever agree to 1) reveal some of its secret keys and/or 2) return a signature generated with sk_i for every unrevealed key sk_i. The assumption 1) is clearly questionable. The plausibility of the second assumption is not much more obvious because the challenger is not able to determine if the signatures returned by the adversary fulfil the corresponding requirement (the adversary could have generated all the returned signatures using the same key) unless it knows the corresponding secret keys, which brings us back to the first problem. Put differently, this defines a success condition for the adversary that the challenger is not able to verify. To sum up, current game-based security models define an unforgeability experiment that either makes an unrealistic assumption on the adversary behaviour or whose output (success or failure) cannot be computed.

The problem 1) was actually already pointed out in [13] who addressed it by introducing a new simulation-based model taken up in [26]. The authors of these works indeed assume that their ideal functionality knows the secret keys of all corrupt platforms, which solves the problems mentioned above. This is theoretically cleaner as the model no longer expects the adversary to hand over its keys willingly. However, this implies that every construction realising their ideal functionality must provide a way to recover all platforms keys in the security proof (including corrupt ones), which in practice does not seem that different from what happens in game-based models. In particular this suggests the use of zero-knowledge proofs of the platform secret key during Join, which either limits the number of concurrent Join sessions (if one uses rewinding techniques) or requires additional features such as online-extractability [20], which negatively impacts performance.

Our Unforgeability Notion. At the heart of the problems we discuss in both cases, there are thus the attempts to identify the signing key that was used to generate the "forgery". In our security model, we therefore try to avoid these identification issues and favour a different reasoning that seems more pragmatic. Concretely, if an adversary owns n signing keys sk_i, then we should not focus on whether its forgeries has been generated using sk_0, sk_1, etc. since it necessary leads to the issues we discuss above. What we can do is to successively revoke each of the adversary signing keys by adding every signature it generates to SRL, thus ensuring that it will not be able to produce $n + 1$ successive signatures. In practice, it means that if a user with sk is revoked via the inclusion of one of his signatures σ in the revocation list, then he cannot produce a new signature σ' unless he gets a new signing key sk'. In the latter case, contrarily to previous models, we do not care if σ' is produced using sk or sk' because this is uncheckable without the knowledge of these keys. All we ensure is that this user will not be able to produce a third signature, regardless of the key it used to produce σ'. We believe this captures what is expected from EPID without making assumptions on the ability to recover adversary's keys.

Issues with Previous Anonymity Notions. The last problem regarding existing models is related to anonymity and is very specific to EPID (not DAA) systems. It concerns the signature revocation list that every model (game-based [12] or simulation-based [26]) assumes to be honestly generated without discussing the plausibility and the concrete consequences of this assumption. More concretely, they all assume that these revocation lists only contain valid signatures, which is enforced in [12,26] by appointing a trusted entity, called the *revocation manager* that will perform these verifications. We see several problems with this solution.

Firstly, we note that the existence of such trusted entity is far from insignificant as all anonymity assurances would be lost if the revocation manager did not correctly carry out its task. In some way, the revocation manager can be compared to the opening authority of a group signature as anonymity of the whole system relies on his honesty. There is indeed a link between revocation and the ability to trace users as noted in [8] although the case of EPID is more subtle.

Secondly, it implies a very centralized system where each service manager would not be able to directly revoke a platform which misbehaved based on its signature but would have to first contact the central revocation manager. As central revocation must not be treated lightly, this is likely to imply a regulated procedure and the grounds on which the revocation manager will decide the legitimacy of the demand are not clear.

Thirdly, it means that any platform must be aware of the current (and authentic) version of the revocation list SRL at the time of signing, which may be problematic in some use-cases. In particular, privacy can no longer be ensured if the verifier sends its own revocation list SRL. An alternative solution could be to shift the burden of verifying the elements of SRL to the platform when generating the signature but this would clearly result in an inefficient signing protocol.

Finally, this requirement is somewhat inconsistent with the ISO/IEC 20008-2 [25] standard. Indeed, the specifications of the EPID system called "Mechanism 3" in [25] clearly states that signature revocation can be *local*, which, according to ISO/IEC 20008-1 [24], means that the signature revocation list may be managed by the verifier itself. However, the same specifications contain the following note:

"To preserve anonymity, it is recommended to have a trusted entity for updating the signature revocation list. If a malicious entity controls the signature revocation list, the anonymity of the signer can be reduced."

The wording is surprising for a standard as it does not sound like a requirement but it yet threatens unspecified problems regarding anonymity if one does not comply with this informal instruction. This results in a blurry situation that is indicative of an EPID paradox. On the one hand, there is a revocation mechanism that is inherently decentralized as any verifier is able to revoke a signature by placing it in its own revocation list. This is clearly the most natural and convenient solution for most use-cases. On the other hand, there are security models that all require a central and trusted entity to manage revocation lists, with the consequences discussed above. In this context, it is extremely tempting to ignore this requirement in practice and, to say the least, even the ISO/IEC recommendation above does not deter us very forcefully from doing so.

We therefore believe it would be better to remove all restrictions on SRL and to rather consider a model where the adversary $\mathcal{A}$ has a total control on the elements of the revocation lists and where the platform does not have to check any property of SRL beyond the one that it can correctly be parsed. This will offer much more flexibility to EPID systems by removing the need for a central trusted revocation entity and thus allow decentralized services managing their own revocation lists.

Our first remark is that current proofs strategies no longer work in this new setting. Indeed let us consider the quite standard approach of EPID systems (e.g. [11,12]) where each signature μ contains a pair (h, h^x) where $h \in \mathbb{G}$ is random and x is the platform secret key, leading to an anonymity proof under the DDH assumption. If μ is added to SRL, then any platform generating a signature with this revocation list will have to include a proof that they did not generate (h, h^x). In security proofs of existing models, the challenger does not know x (otherwise DDH is trivial) but it can recognize (h, h^x) from its previous signatures and so correctly simulate the proof. Now, in our model where we allow the adversary to generate SRL, it could replace (h, h^x) by $(h^r, (h^x)^r)$ for any $r \in \mathbb{Z}_p$. In this case, the challenger will be unable to recognize if this pair was generated using x (unless it can itself solve DDH) and so will not be able to correctly answer a signature query, leading to an incorrect simulation.

This example highlights the fact that removing restrictions on SRL is not just a formalization issue and that it has important consequences on EPID systems. In particular, it gives to any verifier (and so to the adversary) the power of a revocation authority, which is very unusual in privacy-preserving protocols. This leads to a new anonymity experiment that we believe to better capture the security assurances we can retain in the real world.

Our Anonymity Notion. In our security experiment, we give the adversary a total control on the elements of this list. In return, we need to completely redefine the notion of anonymity we can really achieve without these restrictions. Indeed, we note that nothing now prevents the adversary from testing if a signature σ was issued by a given platform i. It can simply add σ (or some part of it in practice) in SRL and then query a signature from i with SRL: if a valid signature is returned then σ was not produced by i; else, i will return a failure message or will abort. The main consequence is that our model cannot provide the adversary with an access to a signing oracle that takes as input an identifier i and returns a signature on behalf of this platform. This is not a restriction of our model as it only reflects the real-world situation of EPID where any verifier suspecting a signer to be the issuer of a previous signature can proceed as we have explained to identify it. This is actually the very goal of EPID.

We then need to be much more careful when defining the signing oracle and the success conditions of the adversary in our new experiment. The first novelty is the absence of a user identifier in the inputs of the signing oracle as it prevents any meaningful definition as we explained. Our oracle will instead return a signature using one of the honest keys that are not implicitly revoked by SRL. As the adversary is now oblivious of the users' identifiers we can't expect it to return the identifier of the issuer of some signature. We will instead ask it to link two signatures in a game where it will select two signatures μ_0 and μ_1 and then ask for a new signature μ^* from the issuer of μ_b. It will succeed if it can guess the value of b with probability different from $\frac{1}{2}$, that is, if it can link two signatures with non-trivial probability.

Our Constructions. Our new security model has two important consequences in practice. Firstly, we no longer need to extract all platforms secret keys thanks to our new unforgeability experiment. This allows us to define simple Join protocols where a platform simply receives a certificate without needing to prove knowledge of its secret key or to use alternative solutions that would enable extraction of this key. Secondly, we now need to deal with malicious revocation lists SRL without performing any test on them. As we explain above, this invalidates the strategy of previous constructions as the adversary is now able to place in SRL elements that were not part of valid signatures. Surprisingly, we can deal with this problem very efficiently by defining a signature algorithm where the platform generates a proof of non-revocation with respect to the hash of (some of) the elements in SRL, instead of the elements themselves. Intuitively, the use of a hash function will prevent the re-randomization strategy of the adversary described above and leads to one of the following two situations. Either the elements of SRL were indeed included in a valid signature or they were generated by the adversary. In the former case, it is easy to know which platforms are revoked, which allows to correctly answer signing queries in the security proof. In the latter case, we show that the forged elements are unlikely to revoke an honest user under the computational Diffie-Hellman assumption. Our first construction reflects these changes and proves that our new security properties can be efficiently achieved. Our second construction is a simple variant of the first one where we further reduce the size of the EPID signatures by using a different building block, at the cost of reintroducing proofs of knowledge in the Join protocol.

2   Preliminaries

Bilinear Groups. Our constructions require bilinear groups which are constituted of a set of three groups $\mathbb{G}_1$, $\mathbb{G}_2$, and $\mathbb{G}_T$ of order p along with a map, called pairing, $e : \mathbb{G}_1 \times \mathbb{G}_2 \to \mathbb{G}_T$ that is

1. bilinear: for any $g \in \mathbb{G}_1, \widetilde{g} \in \mathbb{G}_2$, and $a, b \in \mathbb{Z}_p$, $e(g^a, \widetilde{g}^b) = e(g, \widetilde{g})^{ab}$;
2. non-degenerate: for any $g \in \mathbb{G}_1^*$ and $\widetilde{g} \in \mathbb{G}_2^*$, $e(g, \widetilde{g}) \neq 1_{\mathbb{G}_T}$;
3. efficient: for any $g \in \mathbb{G}_1$ and $\widetilde{g} \in \mathbb{G}_2$, $e(g, \widetilde{g})$ can be efficiently computed.

As most recent cryptographic papers, we only consider bilinear groups of prime order with *type 3* pairings [22], meaning that no efficiently computable homomorphism is known between $\mathbb{G}_1$ and $\mathbb{G}_2$.

Computational Assumptions. The security analysis of our protocols will make use of the following assumptions.

- DL assumption: Given $(g, g^x) \in \mathbb{G}^2$, this assumption states that it is hard to recover x.
- DDH assumption: Given $(g, g^x, g^y, g^z) \in \mathbb{G}^4$, the DDH assumption in the group $\mathbb{G}$ states that it is hard to decide whether $z = x \cdot y$ or z is random.
- CDH assumption: Given $(g, g^x, g^y, \widetilde{g}, \widetilde{g}^x, \widetilde{g}^y)$, the CDH assumption (extended to type 3 bilinear groups) states that it is hard to compute $g^{x \cdot y}$.

3   Specification of EPID

3.1   Syntax

Our EPID system considers three types of entities, an issuer $\mathcal{I}$, platforms $\mathcal{P}$ and verifiers $\mathcal{V}$. When comparing our model with the one of group signature, we will sometimes use the term *user* instead of *platform* to match the terminology of this primitive.

- Setup(1^k): on input a security parameter 1^k, this algorithm returns the public parameters pp of the system.
- GKeygen(pp): on input the public parameters pp, this algorithm generates the issuer's key pair (isk, ipk). We assume that ipk contains pp and so we remove pp from the inputs of all following algorithms.
- Join: this is an interactive protocol between a platform $\mathcal{P}$, taking as inputs ipk, and the issuer $\mathcal{I}$ owning isk. At the end of the protocol, the platform returns either $\perp$ or a signing key sk whereas the issuer does not return anything.
- KeyRevoke($\{sk_i\}_{i=1}^m$): this algorithm takes as input a set of m platform secret keys sk_i and returns a corresponding key revocation list KRL containing m elements that will be denoted as KRL[i], for $i \in [1, m]$.
- SigRevoke($\{(\mu_i)\}_{i=1}^n$): this algorithm takes as input a set of n EPID signatures $\{(\mu_i)\}_{i=1}^n$ and returns a corresponding signature revocation list SRL containing n elements that will be denoted as SRL[i], for $i \in [1, n]$.
- Sign(ipk, sk, m, SRL): this algorithm takes as input the issuer's public key ipk, a platform secret key sk a message m and a signature revocation list SRL and returns an EPID signature μ.

- Identify(sk, t): given a platform secret key and an element t from a revocation list SRL (*i.e.* there exists some i such that $t = $ SRL$[i]$), this algorithm returns either 1 (t was generated using sk) or 0.
- Verify(ipk, KRL, SRL, μ, m): given an issuer public key ipk, a key revocation list KRL, a signature revocation list SRL, a signature μ and a message m, this algorithms returns 1 (the signature is valid on m for the corresponding revocation lists) or 0.

Remark 1. We note that our definition of SigRevoke implicitly assumes that no verification is performed on the purported signatures μ_i since this algorithm does not take as input the elements that would be necessary to run Verify (such as the issuer's public key, the message m and the corresponding revocation list). We indeed do not see which security assurances could be provided by such verifications in our context where we do not assume the existence of a trusted entity managing the lists SRL and therefore choose this simpler definition. In practice, it will then be up to each verifier (even a malicious one) to decide how to construct the revocation lists. This will be captured by our security model and our constructions will be secure even in this very strong model.

3.2 Security Model

As in [12], we expect an EPID system to be correct, unforgeable and anonymous. However, the comparison stops here as our definitions of unforgeability and anonymity strongly differ from the ones of previous works. We refer to Sect. 1.2 for a discussion on this matter and here only formalize the intuition provided in our introduction.

Correctness. Here, we essentially follow [12] and require that a signature generated with a platform signing key sk will be considered as valid by the Verify algorithm as long as sk was not revoked, either explicitly using KRL or implicitly using SRL. However, we note a minor problem in the correctness definition of [12] because the latter assumes that SRL contains signatures whereas it only contains parts of signatures in their concrete constructions. To match reality, we do not assume anything regarding the elements placed in SRL but instead use in our formal definition of correctness the Identify algorithm that tests whether an element SRL$[i]$ was generated using a given signing key or not. Additional requirements on this Identify algorithm will be specified by our other security properties. This leads to the following formal requirement: for all signing key sk_i generated using Join, KRL generated using KeyRevoke and SRL generated using SigRevoke:

$$\text{Verify(ipk, KRL, SRL, Sign(ipk, sk}_i, m, \text{SRL}), m) = 1$$
$$\Leftrightarrow sk_i \notin \text{KRL} \wedge \forall j : \text{Identify(sk}_i, \text{SRL}[j]) = 0$$

Unforgeability. Our unforgeability experiment is defined in Fig. 1, where c (resp. d) is a counter indicating the number of corrupt users created by $\mathcal{A}$ (resp. of signatures issued by the adversary $\mathcal{A}$) at the current time and where $\mathcal{A}$ may query the following oracles:

- $\mathcal{O}\text{Add}(k)$ is an oracle that is used by the adversary to add a new honest platform k. A signing key sk_k is then generated for this platform using the Join protocol but nothing is returned to $\mathcal{A}$.
- $\mathcal{O}\text{Join}_{cor}()$ is an oracle playing the issuer's side of the Join protocol. It is used by $\mathcal{A}$ to add a new corrupt platform. Each call to this oracle increases by 1 the current value of c ($c = c + 1$).
- $\mathcal{O}\text{Cor}(k)$ is an oracle that returns the signing key sk_k of an honest platform k and also adds it to a list $\mathcal{K}$ that is initially set as empty.
- $\mathcal{O}\text{Sign}(k, \text{SRL}, m)$ is an oracle that is used by $\mathcal{A}$ to query a signature from the platform k on a message m with a signature revocation list SRL. We define $\mathcal{S}$ as the set of all signatures returned by this oracle.

$\text{Exp}_{\mathcal{A}}^{unf}(1^k)$ – Unforgeability Security Game
1. $c, d \leftarrow 0$
2. $\mathcal{S}_\mathcal{A} \leftarrow \emptyset$
3. $pp \leftarrow \text{Setup}(1^k)$
4. $(\text{isk}, \text{ipk}) \leftarrow \text{GKeygen}(pp)$
5. **while** $d \leq c$:
    – $\text{SRL} \leftarrow \text{SigRevoke}(\mathcal{S}_\mathcal{A})$
    – $(\mu, m) \leftarrow \mathcal{A}^{\mathcal{O}\text{Add}, \mathcal{O}\text{Join}_{cor}, \mathcal{O}\text{Cor}, \mathcal{O}\text{Sign}}(\text{SRL}, \text{ipk})$
    – $\text{KRL} \leftarrow \text{KeyRevoke}(\mathcal{K})$
    – **if** $1 = \text{Verify}(\text{ipk}, \text{KRL}, \text{SRL}, \mu, m) \wedge \mu \notin \mathcal{S}_\mathcal{A} \cup \mathcal{S}$
      then $d = d + 1 \wedge \mathcal{S}_\mathcal{A} \leftarrow \mathcal{S}_\mathcal{A} \cup \{\mu\}$
6. **Return** 1

Fig. 1. Unforgeability Game for EPID Signature

An EPID system is unforgeable if $\text{Adv}^{unf}(\mathcal{A}) = \Pr[\text{Exp}_{\mathcal{A}}^{unf}(1^k) = 1]$ is negligible for any $\mathcal{A}$. Concretely, an adversary owning $d - 1$ corrupt keys succeeds if it has generated d valid (and distinct) signatures despite systematic revocation of the signatures it has previously issued. For sake of simplicity, we chose to place each key corrupted through a $\mathcal{O}\text{Cor}$ query on a key revocation list KRL. We could proceed differently by offering to the adversary the ability to decide which one should be revoked with KRL but we believe that it would only introduce unnecessary complexity to our model. We also implicitly assume that our while loop aborts after some polynomial number of iterations, in which case the experiment returns 0.

Anonymity. Our formal anonymity experiment described in Fig. 2 makes use of the following oracles. An EPID system is anonymous if $\text{Adv}^{an}(\mathcal{A}) = |\Pr[\text{Exp}_{\mathcal{A}}^{an-1}(1^k) = 1] - \Pr[\text{Exp}_{\mathcal{A}}^{an-0}(1^k) = 1]|$ is negligible for any $\mathcal{A}$.

- $\mathcal{O}\text{Join}_{hon}()$ is an oracle playing the user's side of the Join protocol and is then used by $\mathcal{A}$, playing the issuer, to add a new honest platform. Each call generates a platform secret key sk that is kept secret by the challenger.
- $\mathcal{O}\text{Sign}^*(\text{SRL}, m)$ is an oracle used by $\mathcal{A}$ to query a signature on m from an honest platform that is not implicitly revoked by SRL. The challenger of the experiment randomly selects a signing key sk among those that are not revoked by SRL (that is, the secret keys sk_i such that $\text{Identify}(\text{sk}_i, \text{SRL}[j]) = 0$ for every element $\text{SRL}[j]$ of SRL) and then return the output of $\text{Sign}(\text{ipk}, \text{sk}, m, \text{SRL})$. We define $\mathcal{S}$ as the set of all signatures returned by this oracle concatenated with the key sk used to generate them.
- $\mathcal{O}\text{Cor}^*(\mu)$ is an oracle that returns the signing key sk_k used to generate the signature μ if there is some pair $(\mu\|\text{sk}_k)$ in $\mathcal{S}$. Else, it returns $\bot$. Once the adversary has returned the two challenge signatures μ_0 and μ_1 (step 3 of the anonymity game), we slightly modify the behaviour of this oracle to prevent unintentional failure of the adversary. Indeed, the adversary could inadvertently query $\mathcal{O}\text{Cor}^*$ on a signature μ generated using the same key as μ_0 or μ_1, making it lose the game at step 8. After step 3, this oracle therefore returns $\bot$ if queried on a signature μ generated using sk_i, for $i \in \{0, 1\}$. We note that we nevertheless still need the success condition of step 8 as the adversary could have queried $\mathcal{O}\text{Cor}^*$ on such a signature μ before outputting μ_0 and μ_1. However, in such a case, the adversary knows that μ_0 and μ_1 are illicit choices before returning them and its failure will then no longer be unintended.

$\text{Exp}_{\mathcal{A}}^{an-b}(1^k)$ – Anonymity Security Game
1. $pp \leftarrow \text{Setup}(1^k)$
2. $(\text{isk}, \text{ipk}) \leftarrow \text{GKeygen}(pp)$
3. $(\mu_0, \mu_1, m, \text{SRL}) \leftarrow \mathcal{A}^{\mathcal{O}\text{Join}_{hon}, \mathcal{O}\text{Cor}^*, \mathcal{O}\text{Sign}^*}(\text{isk})$
4. if no entry (μ_i, sk_i) in $\mathcal{S}$ for $i \in \{0, 1\}$, then return 0
5. if $\exists j$ and $i \in \{0, 1\}$: $\text{Identify}(\text{sk}_i, \text{SRL}[j]) = 1$, then return 0
6. $\mu^* \leftarrow \text{Sign}(\text{ipk}, \text{sk}_b, m, \text{SRL})$
7. $b' \leftarrow \mathcal{A}^{\mathcal{O}\text{Join}_{hon}, \mathcal{O}\text{Cor}^*, \mathcal{O}\text{Sign}^*}(\text{isk}, \mu^*)$
8. if $\exists i \in \{0, 1\}$: sk_i leaked during a $\mathcal{O}\text{Cor}^*$ query, then return 0
9. Return $(b = b')$

Fig. 2. Anonymity Game for EPID Signature

4 Our First Construction

4.1 Description

Intuition. The goal of our first construction is to highlight the fact that security in our strong model can be achieved quite efficiently with a few tweaks to previous approaches. Indeed, a platform producing an EPID signature essentially does two things. Firstly, it proves that it is a legitimate platform that has been correctly enrolled by the issuer during a Join protocol. Secondly, it proves that it has not generated any of the signatures in the revocation list SRL.

The first part is common to many privacy-preserving signatures such as group signature [3], DAA [10], EPID [11], multi-show anonymous credentials [21], etc. It essentially consists in proving knowledge of a signature issued by $\mathcal{I}$ on a secret value s generated by the platform. In bilinear groups, there are many signature schemes [6,14,27] that have been specifically designed for this purpose but we will not use them in our first construction for a purely technical reason. Indeed, a benefit of our new model over previous works is that we do not inherently need a way to extract all platform secrets. In particular, we do not need zero-knowledge proofs of s during Join and thus to limit the number of concurrent Join sessions. Using one of the signature schemes cited above would however force us to reintroduce zero-knowledge proofs as we would need, in the security proof, knowledge of the secret scalars to query the signing oracle of the corresponding EUF-CMA experiment. To avoid this problem, we will instead use a signature scheme able of signing group elements (in $\mathbb{G}_1$), and more specifically the one from [21] which is particularly well suited for anonymous constructions. We nevertheless stress that this choice is only driven by our will to highlight the differences between our model and the previous ones. In particular, the scheme from [21] can be replaced by one from [6,14,27] in the following construction as we will show in Sect. 5.

For the second part, we will here follow an approach very similar to the one from [12] but with some adjustments that are made necessary by the absence of a trusted entity to construct revocation lists SRL. As in [12], we indeed implicitly include a pair (h, h^s) to each signature generated with a secret s to enable efficient proof of non-revocation. The latter will be implemented with the protocol from [15]. However, as we explain in Sect. 1, we cannot just add the pair (h, h^s) to the revocation list as it will prevent us in the security proof from correctly simulating the answers from honest platforms. For the latter, we need a way to detect such elements without knowing s or $\tilde{g}^s \in \mathbb{G}_2$. In our scheme, this will be done by constructing $h \in \mathbb{G}_1$ as a hash output $H(\texttt{str})$ for some random string $\texttt{str}$ and so by replacing (h, h^s) by $(\texttt{str}, h^s)$. This way, our security reduction faces two cases for each element $(\texttt{str}, h^s)$ in SRL. Either $\texttt{str}$ was used in a previous signing query or the reduction never used it before. In the first case, the reduction knows that the key s is revoked if and only if the corresponding entry in SRL is exactly the pair $(\texttt{str}, h^s)$ used in a previous signature. In the second case, the reduction knows that the key s is not revoked unless the adversary managed to forge a BLS signature [7] and thus to break the CDH assumption.

In all cases, this means that we can prove anonymity under DDH without performing any verification on SRL nor making any assumption on the way SRL is constructed.

We provide the formal description of our scheme below but first recall some elements on the signature on equivalence classes from [21].

FHS Signature. In [21], Fuchsbauer, Hanser and Slamanig introduce a signature on equivalence classes for the following equivalence relation on tuples in $\mathbb{G}_1^n$: $(M_1, \ldots, M_n)$ is in the same equivalence class as $(N_1, \ldots, N_n)$ if there exists a scalar a such that $N_i = M_i^a$ for all $i \in [1, n]$. The point of their signature is that anyone, given a signature τ on some $(M_1, \ldots, M_n)$, can derive a signature τ' on a new representative $(N_1, \ldots, N_n)$ of this class. By correctly computing the latter values, one can ensure that $(\tau, (M_1, \ldots, M_n))$ and $(\tau', (N_1, \ldots, N_n))$ are unlinkable under the DDH assumption. In this paper, we will only need the case $n = 2$.

- Setup(1^λ): outputs parameters pp containing the description of type-3 bilinear groups $(\mathbb{G}_1, \mathbb{G}_2, \mathbb{G}_T, e)$, with generators $(g, \widetilde{g}) \in \mathbb{G}_1 \times \mathbb{G}_2$.
- Keygen(pp): generates two random scalars x_1 and x_2 and sets sk as (x_1, x_2) and pk as $(\widetilde{A}_1, \widetilde{A}_2) = (\widetilde{g}^{x_1}, \widetilde{g}^{x_2})$.
- Sign(sk, (M_1, M_2)): selects a random scalar t and computes the signature $(\tau_1, \tau_2, \widetilde{\tau}) \leftarrow ((M_1^{x_1} M_2^{x_2})^t, g^{1/t}, \widetilde{g}^{1/t})$ on the representative $(M_1, M_2) \in \mathbb{G}_1^2$.
- Verify(pk, $(M_1, M_2), (\tau_1, \tau_2, \widetilde{\tau})$): accepts $(\tau_1, \tau_2, \widetilde{\tau}) \in \mathbb{G}_1^2 \times \mathbb{G}_2$, a signature on $(M_1, M_2) \neq (1, 1)$, if $e(\tau_1, \widetilde{\tau}) = e(M_1, \widetilde{A}_1) \cdot e(M_2, \widetilde{A}_2)$ and $e(\tau_2, \widetilde{g}) = e(g, \widetilde{\tau})$ hold.

One can note that if $(\tau_1, \tau_2, \widetilde{\tau})$ is valid on (M_1, M_2), then $(\tau_1^{r \cdot t'}, \tau_2^{1/t'}, \widetilde{\tau}^{1/t'})$ is valid on (M_1^r, M_2^r) for all pairs $(r, t') \in \mathbb{Z}_p^2$.

Construction.

- Setup(1^k): this algorithm returns the public parameters pp containing the description of a bilinear group $(e, \mathbb{G}_1, \mathbb{G}_2, \mathbb{G}_T)$ along with two generators $g \in \mathbb{G}_1$ and $\widetilde{g} \in \mathbb{G}_2$ and two hash functions $H : \{0, 1\} \rightarrow \mathbb{Z}_p$ and $H' : \{0, 1\} \rightarrow \mathbb{G}_1$.
- GKeygen(pp): this algorithm generates a key pair isk $\leftarrow (x_1, x_2)$ and ipk $\leftarrow (\widetilde{A}_1, \widetilde{A}_2)$ for the FHS signature.
- Join: this protocol starts when a platform sends g^s to the issuer for some random secret s. $\mathcal{I}$ then generates a FHS signature $\tau \leftarrow (\tau_1, \tau_2, \widetilde{\tau})$ on the pair (g, g^s) and returns τ to the platform. The latter can then verify τ using ipk and store sk $\leftarrow (s, \tau)$ (if τ is valid) or return $\perp$.
- KeyRevoke($\{sk_i\}_{i=1}^m$): this algorithm takes as input a set of m platform secret keys $sk_i = (s^{(i)}, \tau^{(i)})$ and returns a corresponding key revocation list KRL with KRL[i] = sk_i, for $i \in [1, m]$.
- SigRevoke($\{(\mu_i)\}_{i=1}^n$): this algorithm takes as input a set of n EPID signatures $\{(\mu_i)\}_{i=1}^n$ and parses each of them as $((\tau_1^{(i)}, \tau_2^{(i)}, \widetilde{\tau}^{(i)}), (M_1^{(i)}, M_2^{(i)}), h_2^{(i)}, \pi^{(i)})$. It then returns a signature revocation list SRL such that SRL[i] = $(M_1^{(i)}, h_2^{(i)})$, for $i \in [1, n]$.

- Sign(ipk, sk, m, SRL): to issue a signature on a message m with a revocation list SRL, a platform owning a secret key $(s, (\tau_1, \tau_2, \widetilde{\tau}))$ proceeds as follows:
  1. it first re-randomizes its FHS signature by selecting two random scalars (r, t) and computing $(\tau_1', \tau_2', \widetilde{\tau}') \leftarrow (\tau_1^{r \cdot t}, \tau_2^{1/t}, \widetilde{\tau}^{1/t})$ along with a new representative $(M_1, M_2) = (g^r, g^{r \cdot s})$ of (g, g^s);
  2. it computes $(h_1, h_2) \leftarrow (H'(g^r), h_1^s)$;
  3. for all $i \in [1, n]$, it parses SRL$[i]$ as $(M_1^{(i)}, h_2^{(i)})$ and computes $h_1^{(i)} \leftarrow H'(M_1^{(i)})$;
  4. it generates a proof π of knowledge of s such that $M_2 = M_1^s$ and $h_2 = h_1^s$ and that $(h_1^{(i)})^s \neq h_2^{(i)}$ for all $i \in [1, n]$ using the protocol from [15]. More specifically, it selects random scalars r_i and computes $C_i = ((h_1^{(i)})^s / h_2^{(i)})^{r_i}$. If $\exists i \in [1, n]$ such that $C_i = 1$, then it returns $\perp$. Else, it selects $k, \{k_{i,1}, k_{i,2}\}_{i=1}^n \overset{\$}{\leftarrow} \mathbb{Z}_p^{2n+1}$ and computes $(K_{0,1}, K_{0,2}) \leftarrow (M_1^k, h_1^k)$ along with $(K_{i,1}, K_{i,2}) \leftarrow ((h_1^{(i)})^{k_{i,1}} \cdot (1/(h_2^{(i)})^{k_{i,2}}, h_1^{k_{i,1}} \cdot (1/h_2)^{k_{i,2}})$. It then computes

  $$c = H(\tau_1', \tau_2', \widetilde{\tau}', M_1, M_2, h_1, h_2, \{C_i\}_{i=1}^n, \{K_{i,1}, K_{i,2}\}_{i=0}^n, \mathsf{m}).$$

  along with $z = k + c \cdot s$ and $(z_{i,1}, z_{i,2}) = (k_{i,1} + c \cdot s \cdot r_i, k_{i,2} + c \cdot r_i)$. The proof π is then set as $(\{C_i\}_{i=1}^n, c, z, \{z_{i,1}, z_{i,2}\}_{i=1}^n)$;
  5. it returns the signature $\mu = ((\tau_1, \tau_2, \widetilde{\tau}), (M_1, M_2), h_2, \pi)$.
- Identify(sk, t): this algorithm parses sk as $(s, (\tau_1, \tau_2, \widetilde{\tau}))$ and t as (M_1, h_2), and returns 1 if $h_2 = H'(M_1)^s$ and 0 otherwise.
- Verify(ipk, KRL, SRL, μ, m): This algorithm parses μ as $((\tau_1, \tau_2, \widetilde{\tau}), (M_1, M_2), h_2, \pi)$, each KRL$[i]$ as $(s^{(i)}, (\tau_1^{(i)}, \tau_2^{(i)}, \widetilde{\tau}^{(i)}))$ for $i \in [1, m]$ and each SRL$[i]$ as $(M_1^{(i)}, h_2^{(i)})$ for $i \in [1, n]$. It then returns 1 if all the following conditions hold and 0 otherwise.
  1. $e(\tau_1, \widetilde{\tau}) = e(M_1, \widetilde{A}_1) \cdot e(M_2, \widetilde{A}_2) \wedge e(\tau_2, \widetilde{g}) = e(g, \widetilde{\tau})$;
  2. $\forall i \in [1, m]$, Identify(KRL$[i]$, (M_1, h_2)) $= 0$;
  3. $\forall i \in [1, n]$, $C_i \neq 1$;
  4. $c = H(\tau_1, \tau_2, \widetilde{\tau}, M_1, M_2, h_1, h_2, \{C_i\}_{i=1}^n, \{K_{i,1}, K_{i,2}\}_{i=0}^n, \mathsf{m})$, where $h_1 \leftarrow H'(M_1)$, $(K_{0,1}, K_{0,2}) \leftarrow (M_1^z \cdot M_2^{-c}, h_1^z \cdot h_2^{-c})$ and $(K_{i,1}, K_{i,2}) \leftarrow (C_i^{-c} \cdot [(h_1^{(i)})^{z_{i,1}} / (h_2^{(i)})^{z_{i,2}}], h_1^{z_{i,1}} / (h_2^{z_{i,2}}))$ with $h_1^{(i)} = H'(M_1^{(i)})$.

Correctness. The first step of the verification protocol checks that $(\tau_1, \tau_2, \widetilde{\tau})$ is a valid FHS signature on the representative (M_1, M_2). The second step checks that the issuer of μ is not revoked by KRL. It is easy to verify that this step fails if μ was generated using a secret s in KRL. The third step checks that s has not been used to generate one of the elements in SRL. By construction, we would necessarily have $C_i = 1$ in this case. The last step checks the validity of π. The proof is a simple combination of the Schnorr's protocol [30] and the Camenisch's and Shoup's one [15]. For a valid signature μ, one can indeed see that

$$- M_1^z \cdot M_2^{-c} = M_1^{k+c \cdot s} \cdot M_2^{-c} = M_1^k,$$
$$- h_1^z \cdot h_2^{-c} = h_1^{k+c \cdot s} \cdot h_2^{-c} = h_1^k,$$
$$- K_{i,1} = \frac{(h_1^{(i)})^{z_{i,1}}}{(h_2^{(i)})^{z_{i,2}}} \cdot C_i^{-c} = \frac{(h_1^{(i)})^{k_{i,1}+c \cdot s \cdot r_i}}{(h_2^{(i)})^{k_{i,2}+c \cdot r_i}} \cdot \frac{(h_1^{(i)})^{-c \cdot s \cdot r_i}}{(h_2^{(i)})^{-c \cdot r_i}} = \frac{(h_1^{(i)})^{k_{i,1}}}{(h_2^{(i)})^{k_{i,2}}},$$
$$- K_{i,2} = \frac{h_1^{z_{i,1}}}{h_2^{z_{i,2}}} = \frac{h_1^{k_{i,1}+c \cdot s \cdot r_i}}{h_2^{k_{i,2}+c \cdot r_i}} = \frac{h_1^{k_{i,1}}}{h_2^{k_{i,2}}},$$

which ensures that the last condition is satisfied.

Remark 2. As we explain at the beginning of this section, we need to generate h_1 as some hash output. We could use any random string str but the latter would then have to be added to μ. As several elements of μ are already random, we arbitrarily choose to derive h_1 from one of them. We selected M_1 that is simply considered as a bitstring by the hash function H' but most other elements of μ (or combinations of them) would work.

Theorem 1. *In the random oracle model, our EPID system is*

- *unforgeable under the* DL *assumption, the* CDH *assumption and the EUF-CMA security of the FHS signature if π is a sound zero-knowledge proof system.*
- *anonymous under the* CDH *and* DDH *assumptions if π is a zero-knowledge proof system.*

4.2 Security Proofs

Unforgeability. Let $\mathcal{A}$ be an adversary succeeding against the unforgeability of our scheme with probability ϵ. We recall that $\mathcal{A}$ succeeds if it can issue $c + 1$ valid signatures $\{\mu_i\}_{i=1}^{c+1}$ despite systematic revocation of its previous signatures, where c is the number of corrupted keys it has created. In this proof, an *honest* key refers to a key that was generated during a $\mathcal{O}\text{Add}$ query and that has never been involved in a $\mathcal{O}\text{Cor}$ query. We distinguish the following three types of forgeries:

- (type 1) $\mathcal{A}$ has queried $\mathcal{O}\text{Sign}$ with a revocation list SRL such that $\exists i :$ Identify(sk, SRL[i]) $= 1$ for some honest key sk and yet none of the previous signatures returned by $\mathcal{O}\text{Sign}$ contains the pair in SRL[i];
- (type 2) the previous case does not occur and $\exists i \in [1, c+1]$ such that μ_i can be parsed as $((\tau_1^{(i)}, \tau_2^{(i)}, \tilde{\tau}^{(i)}), (M_1^{(i)}, M_2^{(i)}), h_2^{(i)}, \pi^{(i)})$ with Identify(sk, $(M_1^{(i)}, h_2^{(i)})$) $= 1$ for some honest key sk;
- (type 3) none of the previous cases occur.

The first case intuitively deals with malicious verifiers that would introduce illicit elements in SRL, that is, elements that were not part of a previous EPID signature and that can yet be associated with some honest user. We show that this case implies an attack against the CDH assumption.

The second case is an attack against what would be called non-frameability in a group signature [4] paper, that is, $\mathcal{A}$ has managed to produce a signature that can be "traced back" to some honest user. We show in lemma 2 that $\mathcal{A}$ can be used against the DL assumption in such case.

Else, we will show that $\mathcal{A}$ has necessarily produced a signature on a new class of equivalences and has thus broken the security of FHS signatures.

Lemma 1. *Let $q_{H'}$ (resp. q_a) be a bound on the number of oracle queries to H' (resp. $\mathcal{O}\mathrm{Add}$) made by the adversary $\mathcal{A}$. Then any type 1 adversary succeeding with probability ϵ can be converted into an adversary against the CDH assumption succeeding with probability at least $\frac{\epsilon}{q_{H'} \cdot q_a}$.*

Proof. Let $(g, g^x, g^y, \widetilde{g}, \widetilde{g}^x, \widetilde{g}^y)$ be a CDH challenge, we construct a reduction $\mathcal{R}$ using $\mathcal{A}$ to compute g^{xy}. In our proof, $\mathcal{A}$ will submit a set of $n < q_{H'}$ different strings $\{\mathtt{str}_i\}_{i=1}^n$ to the hash oracle H'. $\mathcal{R}$ then selects a random index $i^* \in [1, q_{H'}]$ and proceeds as follows to answer such queries. First it checks if $\mathtt{str}_i$ has already been queried in which case it returns the same answer as previously. Else, it selects and stores a random $r \xleftarrow{\$} \mathbb{Z}_p$ and returns g^r if $i \neq i^*$ and g^y if $i = i^*$. In the experiment, $\mathcal{R}$ makes a guess on the identifier $k^* \in [1, q_a]$ of the platform illicitly revoked by the adversary's revocation list SRL and generates the issuer's key pair as usual. Upon receiving a query on k to $\mathcal{O}\mathrm{Add}$, it proceeds as usual except if $k = k^*$, in which case it implicitly sets the platform secret value as x. Thanks to isk, it can then handle any $\mathcal{O}\mathrm{Add}$ and $\mathcal{O}\mathrm{Join}_{cor}$ query. $\mathcal{R}$ can also handle any $\mathcal{O}\mathrm{Cor}$ query except the one on k^* in which case it aborts.

To answer a signing query with revocation list SRL, $\mathcal{R}$ first uses its knowledge of $\widetilde{g}^x$ to test whether SRL contains a pair (h_0, h_2) with $e(H'(h_0), \widetilde{g}^x) = e(h_2, \widetilde{g})$. If no such pair is found, then $\mathcal{R}$ answers a signing query for k^* as follows (the case $k \neq k^*$ is trivial). $\mathcal{R}$ re-randomizes the FHS certificate and the representative (M_1, M_2) as usual. In the very unlikely event where $M_1 = \mathtt{str}_{i^*}$, it simply chooses a different representative of (M_1, M_2). This means that it knows in all cases the scalar r such that $H'(M_1) = g^r$ and can thus compute $h_2 = (g^x)^r$. It then simulates the zero-knowledge proof π and returns the resulting EPID signature μ. Now let us assume that SRL contains a pair (h_0, h_2) with $e(H'(h_0), \widetilde{g}^x) = e(h_2, \widetilde{g})$. This event occurs if the guess on k^* was right as we assume type 1 adversary. Moreover, we also know that this pair has never been used by $\mathcal{R}$ to answer a $\mathcal{O}\mathrm{Sign}$ query. This means that h_0 has never been used by $\mathcal{R}$ as h_2 is deterministically computed from it. The value h_0 has then been queried by $\mathcal{A}$ to H' and there are two cases. Either $\mathcal{R}$ returned g^y, which means that $h_2 = g^{x \cdot y}$, or $\mathcal{R}$ returned some element g^r for a random r and it aborts.

In the former case, $\mathcal{R}$ has thus broken the CDH assumption. This occurs if both the guess on k^* and the one on i^* are correct and so with probability at least $\frac{\epsilon}{q_{H'} \cdot q_a}$.

Lemma 2. *Let q_a be a bound on the number of $\mathcal{O}\mathrm{Add}$ queries made by $\mathcal{A}$. Then, any type 2 adversary succeeding with probability ϵ can be converted into an adversary against the DL assumption succeeding with probability at least $\frac{\epsilon}{q_a \cdot (c+1)}$.*

Proof. Let (g, g^x) be a DL instance, we construct a reduction $\mathcal{R}$ using $\mathcal{A}$ to recover x. First, $\mathcal{R}$ makes a guess on the identifier k^* of the honest platform that will be associated with the adversary's forgery and on the index i^* of the forgery. It then generates the issuer's key pair (isk, ipk) and is thus able to answer any Join query. It answers any oracle query on a string str to the hash function H' by generating (and storing) a random scalar r and returning g^r, unless str has already been queried in which case it returns the original answer. Upon receiving a $\mathcal{O}$Add query on k, it proceeds as usual except when $k = k^*$. In this case, it acts as if the platform secret were x. Note that this is not a problem as the issuer generates a signature τ directly on (g, g^x) instead of x. Regarding $\mathcal{O}$Cor queries, it simply forwards the secret key except if $k = k^*$, in which case $\mathcal{R}$ aborts. However, the latter case does not occur if $\mathcal{R}$ guess on k^* is valid.

Let SRL be the revocation list associated with some $\mathcal{O}$Sign query on k^*. Since we here consider type 2 adversary we know that, $\forall i \in [1, n]$, either SRL$[i]$ is a part of a signature previously issued by $\mathcal{R}$ or that it does not revoke one of the honest platforms. In the former case, $\mathcal{R}$ checks if SRL$[i]$ was used to issue a signature on behalf of k^* in which case it returns $\bot$. Else, it knows that k^* can produce a signature. To generate μ, it re-randomizes the certificate τ into τ' along with the representative (g, g^x) into (M_1, M_2). It then defines $H'(M_1) = g^r$ for some random r unless in the very unlikely event where H' has already been queried on M_1, in which case $\mathcal{R}$ simply recovers the corresponding scalar r. In all cases, $\mathcal{R}$ is able to compute a valid $h_2 = (g^x)^r$. It then only remains to simulate the proof π and to return the resulting signature μ.

Now $\mathcal{R}$ extracts from the proof of knowledge contained in μ_{i^*} the secret key s^* used by the adversary to generate this signature (recall that μ_{i^*} must differ from the signatures issued by $\mathcal{R}$). If the guesses on both k^* and i^* are correct, then $s^* = x$ thanks to the soundness of the proof. $\mathcal{R}$ can thus solve the DL problem with probability at least $\frac{1}{q_a \cdot (c+1)}$.

Lemma 3. *Any type 3 adversary succeeding with probability ϵ can be converted into an adversary against the EUF-CMA security of FHS signatures succeeding with probability at least $\frac{\epsilon}{c+1}$.*

Proof. Our reduction $\mathcal{R}$ receives a FHS public key from the challenger of the EUF-CMA security and sets it as the issuer's public key ipk. $\mathcal{R}$ generates as usual the secret values for honest platforms and is thus able to handle any $\mathcal{O}$Sign or $\mathcal{O}$Cor query. It can also use its FHS signing oracle to address any $\mathcal{O}$Add and $\mathcal{O}$Join query. The simulation is then perfect and $\mathcal{A}$ eventually outputs, with probability ϵ, $c+1$ EPID signatures μ_i fulfilling the type 3 requirements. Each of them contains a FHS signature $\tau^{(i)}$ on some representative $(M_1^{(i)}, M_2^{(i)})$. The fact that all keys returned by $\mathcal{O}$Cor are revoked and that none of the EPID signature satisfies the condition Identify(sk, $(M_1^{(i)}, h_2^{(i)})) = 1$ for honest keys sk means that $(M_1^{(i)}, M_2^{(i)})$ is not in the equivalence class of (g, g^{s_j}) for all $i \in [1, c+1]$ and (g, g^{s_j}) generated during a $\mathcal{O}$Add query. Moreover, as μ_i is produced while taking as input a revocation list SRL containing $\mu_1, \ldots, \mu_{i-1}$, we know, thanks to the soundness of π, that $(M_1^{(i)}, M_2^{(i)})$ is not in the equivalence class of $(M_1^{(j)}, M_2^{(j)})$ $\forall i \neq j \in [1, c+1]$. Therefore, the $c+1$ signatures $\tau^{(i)}$ are valid on $c+1$ different equivalence classes. As the adversary only received c FHS signatures and as it did not use one associated with a honest platform (otherwise $\mathcal{A}$ would be a type 2 adversary), $\exists i^* \in [1, c+1]$ such that $\tau^{(i^*)}$ is valid on an equivalence class that was never submitted to the FHS signing oracle. $\mathcal{R}$ then makes a guess on i^* and returns $\tau^{(i^*)}$ along with $(M_1^{(i^*)}, M_2^{(i^*)})$ to the challenger of the EUF-CMA security experiment. It then succeeds with probability at least $\frac{\epsilon}{c+1}$.

Anonymity. We here proceed through a sequence of games where Game $1, b$ is exactly the experiment $\mathsf{Exp}_{\mathcal{A}}^{an-b}$ defined in Sect. 3.2. For each i, we define Adv_i as the advantage of $\mathcal{A}$ playing Game $i, 0$ and Game $i, 1$. As Game $i, 0$ and Game $i, 1$ are virtually identical (the only difference is the parameter b), we will abuse notation and omit b in what follows. We set ϵ as the advantage of $\mathcal{A}$ playing Game 1 and define $\mathsf{Adv}_{\mathsf{CDH}}$ (resp. $\mathsf{Adv}_{\mathsf{DDH}}$) as the advantage against the CDH (resp. DDH) assumption.

Game 1. Here, the reduction generates normally all the platform secrets and is thus able to answer any oracle query by the adversary. By definition, $\mathsf{Adv}_1 = \epsilon$.

Game 2. In this second game, $\mathcal{R}$ randomly selects $k_0, k_1 \in [1, q_a]$ where q_a is a bound on the number of $\mathcal{O}\mathsf{Join}_{hon}$ queries. If the signatures μ_0 and μ_1 returned by the adversary in the experiment were not issued by the platforms k_0 and k_1, then $\mathcal{R}$ aborts. We then have $\mathsf{Adv}_2 = \frac{\epsilon}{q_a^2}$. The conditions we define in Fig. 2 then ensure that no successful adversary can receive sk_{k_0} and sk_{k_1} through $\mathcal{O}\mathsf{Cor}^*$ oracle queries.

Game 3. In this third game, $\mathcal{R}$ proceeds as in Game 2 but parses each signature revocation list SRL used by $\mathcal{A}$ in $\mathcal{O}\mathsf{Sign}$ queries. If one of these lists contains a pair (h_0, h_2) that can be linked back to an honest secret key (that is, a key that has not leaked through a $\mathcal{O}\mathsf{Cor}^*$ query) and yet $\mathcal{R}$ never used this pair to answer a previous $\mathcal{O}\mathsf{Sign}$ query, then $\mathcal{R}$ aborts. We show below that $\mathsf{Adv}_3 \geq \mathsf{Adv}_2 - \mathsf{Adv}_{\mathsf{CDH}}$.

Game 4. In this fourth game, $\mathcal{R}$ proceeds as in Game 3 except that it now simulates the proof of knowledge π included in signatures it generates. We then have $\mathsf{Adv}_4 \geq \mathsf{Adv}_3 - \mathsf{Adv}_{ZK}$, where Adv_{ZK} is the advantage of an adversary against the zero-knowledge property of the proof system used to generate π.

Game (5, i). In this game, defined for $i \in [1, q_S]$ with q_S a bound on the number of $\mathcal{O}\mathsf{Sign}$ queries, $\mathcal{R}$ proceeds as in Game 4 but answers the i first $\mathcal{O}\mathsf{Sign}$ queries as follows. For $j \in [1, i]$, let SRL_j be the signature revocation list involved in the j-th query to $\mathcal{O}\mathsf{Sign}$ and $\mathcal{H}_j$ the set of honest keys that are not revoked by SRL_j. Since Game 3, $\mathcal{R}$ is indeed perfectly able to identify the set $\mathcal{H}_j$ corresponding to SRL_j. $\mathcal{R}$ selects a random key $\mathsf{sk} \in \mathcal{H}_j$ and proceeds as usual if $\mathsf{sk} \notin \{\mathsf{sk}_{k_0}, \mathsf{sk}_{k_1}\}$. Else, it replaces in the generated signature the elements (M_1, M_2) and h_2 by ones generated using a fresh random secret key and the FHS signature τ by one valid on (M_1, M_2). We show below that $\mathsf{Adv}_{(5,i)} \geq \mathsf{Adv}_{(5,i-1)} - \mathsf{Adv}_{\mathsf{DDH}}$ if we define $\mathsf{Adv}_{(5,0)} = \mathsf{Adv}_4$.

Game 6. In this sixth game, $\mathcal{R}$ replaces in μ^* the elements (M_1, M_2) and h_2 by ones generated using a fresh random secret key and the FHS signature τ by one valid on (M_1, M_2). We show below that $\mathtt{Adv}_6 \geq \mathtt{Adv}_5 - \mathtt{Adv}_{\mathsf{DDH}}$.

In the end we then get

$$\mathtt{Adv}_6 \geq \frac{\epsilon}{q_a^2} - \mathtt{Adv}_{\mathsf{CDH}} - \mathtt{Adv}_{ZK} - (q_S + 1)\mathtt{Adv}_{\mathsf{DDH}}.$$

As all the signatures in Game 6 (including μ^*) are generated with keys independent of sk_{k_0} and sk_{k_1}, the adversary can only succeed with negligible probability, which concludes our proof.

It then remains to prove the inequalities (1) $\mathtt{Adv}_3 \geq \mathtt{Adv}_2 - \mathtt{Adv}_{\mathsf{CDH}}$, (2) $\mathtt{Adv}_{(5,i)} \geq \mathtt{Adv}_{(5,i-1)} - \mathtt{Adv}_{\mathsf{DDH}}$ and (3) $\mathtt{Adv}_6 \geq \mathtt{Adv}_5 - \mathtt{Adv}_{\mathsf{DDH}}$. Regarding (1), we note that this is exactly what we prove in Lemma 1. We now focus on (2).

Let (g, g^x, g^y, g^z) be a DDH instance, we show that if $\mathcal{A}$ can distinguish Game $(5, i)$ from Game $(5, i-1)$, then it can be used to decide whether $z = x \cdot y$.

$\mathcal{R}$ implicitly sets the signing keys of k_0 and k_1 as $x \cdot u_0$ and $x \cdot u_1$, respectively, for random $u_0, u_1 \in \mathbb{Z}_p$, when it receives the corresponding $\mathcal{O}\mathsf{Join}_{hon}$ queries. Using g^x, it can indeed receive, for $d \in \{0, 1\}$, a FHS signature τ on $(g, g^{x \cdot u_d})$ that it stores for further uses.

Upon receiving the j-th $\mathcal{O}\mathsf{Sign}^*$ query, $\mathcal{R}$ proceeds as follows. If $j < i$, then it proceeds as defined in Game $(5, i-1)$. If $j > i$, it randomly selects a platform k that is not revoked by SRL. If $k \notin \{k_0, k_1\}$, then it generates the signature as usual. Else, $k = k_d$ for some $d \in \{0, 1\}$ and $\mathcal{R}$ re-rerandomizes τ together with $(g, g^{x \cdot u_d})$ and thus gets a FHS signature τ' valid on a new representative (M_1, M_2). It then sets $h_1 = H'(M_1) = g^r$ for some random r and is then able to compute $h_2 = (g^{x \cdot u_d})^r$. As π is simulated since Game 4, it can then return a valid EPID signature μ.

If $j = i$, we distinguish two cases depending on the value of $\mathsf{sk} \in \mathcal{H}_j$, the key selected by $\mathcal{R}$ to answer this query. If $\mathsf{sk} \notin \{\mathsf{sk}_{k_0}, \mathsf{sk}_{k_1}\}$, then $\mathcal{R}$ generates normally the signature and we clearly have $\mathtt{Adv}_{(5,i)} = \mathtt{Adv}_{(5,i-1)}$. Else, let d be such that $\mathsf{sk} = \mathsf{sk}_{k_d}$. $\mathcal{R}$ selects a random $r \in \mathbb{Z}_p$, defines $M_1 = g^{y \cdot r}$ and $M_2 = g^{z \cdot r \cdot u_d}$, programs $h_1 = H'(M_1) = g^y$ (in the unlikely event where M_1 has already been queried, then $\mathcal{R}$ starts over with a new random value r) and then sets $h_2 = (g^z)^{u_d}$. Using its knowledge of isk, it can then generate a valid FHS signature on (M_1, M_2) and returns the resulting signature μ (the proof π is simulated since Game 4). In the case where $z = x \cdot y$, this is a valid signature issued by k_d and we are playing Game $(5, i-1)$. Else, this is exactly Game $(5, i)$. Any adversary able to distinguish these two games in this case can thus be used to solve the DDH problem. In all cases, we have $\mathtt{Adv}_{(5,i)} \geq \mathtt{Adv}_{(5,i-1)} - \mathtt{Adv}_{\mathsf{DDH}}$.

The proof regarding the point (3) is essentially the same, which proves anonymity of our construction.

Remark 3. A reader familiar with security proofs of group signature schemes might be surprised by our Games $5, i$ for $i \in [1, q_S]$. Indeed, with group signatures, the game 6 would be enough as it ensures that the elements constituting the challenge signature μ^* are independent of the bit b. This reasoning does not seem to apply for EPID schemes because even a fully random μ^* remains implicitly associated with sk_{k_b}, which has consequences on subsequent $\mathcal{O}\mathtt{Sign}^*$ queries. Indeed, we recall that $\mathcal{O}\mathtt{Sign}^*$ normally uses an honest key that is not implicitly revoked by SRL to generate a signature. An adversary querying the genuine $\mathcal{O}\mathtt{Sign}^*$ oracle with empty revocation lists SRL could then expect to receive from time to time signatures generated with either sk_{k_0} or sk_{k_1}. Conversely, among these two keys, only $\mathsf{sk}_{k_{\overline{b}}}$ (with $\overline{b} + b = 1$) has a chance to be used to answer $\mathcal{O}\mathtt{Sign}^*$ queries with a revocation list containing elements from the random μ^*. With standard $\mathcal{O}\mathtt{Sign}^*$ answers, it therefore seems unreasonable to claim that a random μ^* will necessarily lead to a negligible advantage for $\mathcal{A}$ as the distribution of elements returned by $\mathcal{R}$ still depends on $\mathsf{sk}_{k_{\overline{b}}}$ (and so on b). Fortunately, this problem can easily be solved by tweaking the behaviour of $\mathcal{O}\mathtt{Sign}^*$, as we do in Games $5, i$ for $i \in [1, q_S]$. Once all signatures involving k_0 or k_1 are generated with fresh random keys, we can indeed assure that our reduction in Game 6 is perfectly independent of the bit b that $\mathcal{A}$ must guess.

5   An Efficient Variant with Limited Concurrent Enrolments

5.1   Description

In the previous scheme, an EPID signature issued on an empty revocation list SRL contains 2 scalars, 5 elements of $\mathbb{G}_1$ and 1 of $\mathbb{G}_2$. We can do even better and construct EPID signatures with only 2 scalars and 4 elements of $\mathbb{G}_1$ (non-revocation proof excluded) using Pointcheval-Sanders (PS) signatures [27,28]. Using the BLS12 curve from [9] to provide a common metric, this means a reduction of 36 % of the bit size of the signature. Moreover, this avoids to implement the complex arithmetic of $\mathbb{G}_2$ (that is usually defined over a non-prime field) on the signer's side, which is particularly important when the signer is a constrained device. Apart from this, this new variant is very similar to the previous one and is mostly presented here for completeness. But first, we need to recall some elements on PS signatures.

PS Signature. In [27], Pointcheval and Sanders constructed re-randomizable signatures σ consisting of only 2 elements of $\mathbb{G}_1$, no matter the size n of the signed vector $(\mathsf{m}_1, \ldots, \mathsf{m}_n)$. Here, re-randomizability means that one can publicly derive a new signature σ' from σ by simply raising each element to the same random power. The point is that σ and σ' are unlinkable (under the DDH assumption in $\mathbb{G}_1$) for anyone that does not know the full signed vector.

We will here focus on the case where $n = 1$ as it is sufficient for our construction. The scheme described below is actually a slight variant of the original scheme that uses some folklore techniques (see *e.g.* [1,2,5]) to reduce the verification complexity at the cost of an additional element in the signature.

- Setup(1^λ): Outputs the parameters pp containing the description of type-3 bilinear groups $(\mathbb{G}_1, \mathbb{G}_2, \mathbb{G}_T, e)$ along with a set of generators $(g, \widetilde{g}) \in \mathbb{G}_1 \times \mathbb{G}_2$.
- Keygen(pp): Generates two random scalars x and y and sets sk as (x, y) and pk as $(\widetilde{X} = \widetilde{g}^x, \widetilde{Y} = \widetilde{g}^y)$.
- Sign(sk, m): On message m, generates a signature $(\sigma_1, \sigma_2, \sigma_3)$ $\leftarrow$ $(g^r, g^{r(x+y \cdot m)}, g^{r \cdot m})$ for some random scalar r.
- Verify(pk, m, $(\sigma_1, \sigma_2, \sigma_3)$): Accepts the signature on m if $\sigma_3 = \sigma_1^m$ and if the following equality holds: $e(\sigma_1, \widetilde{X}) \cdot e(\sigma_3, \widetilde{Y}) = e(\sigma_2, \widetilde{g})$.

With this variant, m is no longer involved in the pairing equation of Verify, which will dramatically reduce the cost of related zero-knowledge proofs. The price is the additional element σ_3, which seems reasonable in our context. If one needs instead to optimise the EPID size, then one can simply use the original PS signature and adapt the following construction. One can note that the EUF-CMA security of this variant is trivially implied by the one of the original scheme.

Construction

- Setup(1^k): this algorithm returns the public parameters pp containing the description of a bilinear group $(e, \mathbb{G}_1, \mathbb{G}_2, \mathbb{G}_T)$ along with two generators $g \in \mathbb{G}_1$ and $\widetilde{g} \in \mathbb{G}_2$ and two hash functions $H : \{0,1\} \rightarrow \mathbb{Z}_p$ and $H' : \{0,1\} \rightarrow \mathbb{G}_1$.
- GKeygen(pp): this algorithm generates a key pair (isk, ipk) for the PS signature scheme by setting isk $= (x, y) \xleftarrow{\$} \mathbb{Z}_p^2$ and ipk $= (pp, \widetilde{X}, \widetilde{Y}) \leftarrow (\widetilde{g}^x, \widetilde{g}^y)$.
- Join: this protocol starts when a platform $\mathcal{P}$, taking as inputs ipk, contacts the issuer $\mathcal{I}$ for enrolment. It first generates a random $s \xleftarrow{\$} \mathbb{Z}_p$ and sends g^s to $\mathcal{I}$ who owns isk. $\mathcal{P}$ then engages in an interactive proof of knowledge of s with $\mathcal{I}$, using the Schnorr's protocol [30]. Once the latter is complete, $\mathcal{I}$ selects a random $r \xleftarrow{\$} \mathbb{Z}_p$ and computes a PS signature $\sigma = (\sigma_1, \sigma_2, \sigma_3) \leftarrow (g^r, g^{r \cdot x} \cdot (g^s)^{r \cdot y}, (g^s)^r)$ on s that it returns to $\mathcal{P}$. The platform then stores (s, σ) as its secret key sk.
- KeyRevoke($\{sk_i\}_{i=1}^m$): this algorithm takes as input a set of m platform secret keys $sk_i = (s^{(i)}, \sigma^{(i)})$ and returns a corresponding key revocation list KRL with KRL$[i] = sk_i$, for $i \in [1, m]$.
- SigRevoke($\{(\mu_i)\}_{i=1}^n$): this algorithm takes as input a set of n EPID signatures $\{(\mu_i)\}_{i=1}^n$ and parses each of them as $((\sigma_1^{(i)}, \sigma_2^{(i)}, \sigma_3^{(i)}), h_2^{(i)}, \pi^{(i)})$. It then returns a signature revocation list SRL such that SRL$[i] = (\sigma_1^{(i)}, h_2^{(i)})$, for $i \in [1, n]$.
- Sign(ipk, SRL, sk, m): To sign a message m while proving that it has not been implicitly revoked by SRL, a platform $\mathcal{P}$ owning sk $= (s, (\sigma_1, \sigma_2, \sigma_3))$ generates a random $r \xleftarrow{\$} \mathbb{Z}_p^*$ and
  1. re-randomizes the PS signature $(\sigma_1', \sigma_2', \sigma_3') \leftarrow (\sigma_1^r, \sigma_2^r, \sigma_3^r)$;
  2. computes $(h_1, h_2) \leftarrow (H'(\sigma_1'), h_1^s)$;
  3. for all $i \in [1, n]$, it parses SRL$[i]$ as $(\sigma_1^{(i)}, h_2^{(i)})$ and computes $h_1^{(i)} \leftarrow H'(\sigma_1^{(i)})$;

4. it generates a proof π of knowledge of s such that $\sigma_3 = \sigma_1^s$ and $h_2 = h_1^s$ and that $(h_1^{(i)})^s \neq h_2^{(i)}$ for all $i \in [1, n]$ using the protocol from [15]. More specifically, it selects random scalars r_i and computes $C_i = ((h_1^{(i)})^s / h_2^{(i)})^{r_i}$. If $\exists i \in [1, n]$ such that $C_i = 1$, then it returns $\bot$. Else, it selects $k, \{k_{i,1}, k_{i,2}\}_{i=1}^n \xleftarrow{\$} \mathbb{Z}_p^{2n+1}$ and computes $(K_{0,1}, K_{0,2}) \leftarrow (\sigma_1^k, h_1^k)$ along with $(K_{i,1}, K_{i,2}) \leftarrow ((h_1^{(i)})^{k_{i,1}} \cdot (1/(h_2^{(i)}))^{k_{i,2}}, h_1^{k_{i,1}} \cdot (1/h_2)^{k_{i,2}})$. It then computes

$$c = H(\sigma_1', \sigma_2', \sigma_3', h_1, h_2, \{C_i\}_{i=1}^n, \{K_{i,1}, K_{i,2}\}_{i=0}^n, \mathsf{m}).$$

along with $z = k + c \cdot s$ and $(z_{i,1}, z_{i,2}) = (k_{i,1} + c \cdot s \cdot r_i, k_{i,2} + c \cdot r_i)$. The proof π is then set as $(\{C_i\}_{i=1}^n, c, z, \{z_{i,1}, z_{i,2}\}_{i=1}^n)$;
5. it returns the signature $\mu = ((\sigma_1', \sigma_2', \sigma_3'), h_2, \pi)$.
- Identify(sk, t): this algorithm parses sk as $(s, (\sigma_1, \sigma_2, \sigma_3))$ and t as (σ_1, h_2), and returns 1 if $h_2 = H'(\sigma_1)^s$ and 0 otherwise.
- Verify(ipk, SRL, KRL, μ, m): to verify an EPID signature μ, the verifier parses it as $((\sigma_1', \sigma_2', \sigma_3'), h_2, \pi)$, each KRL[$i$] as $(s^{(i)}, (\sigma_1^{(i)}, \sigma_2^{(i)}, \sigma_3^{(i)}))$ for $i \in [1, m]$ and each SRL[i] as $(\sigma_1^{(i)}, h_2^{(i)})$ for $i \in [1, n]$. It then returns 1 if all the following conditions hold and 0 otherwise.
  1. $\sigma_1 \neq 1_{\mathbb{G}_1} \wedge e(\sigma_1, \widetilde{X}) \cdot e(\sigma_3, \widetilde{Y}) = e(\sigma_2, \widetilde{g})$;
  2. $\forall i \in [1, m]$, Identify(KRL[i], (σ_1, h_2)) = 0;
  3. $\forall i \in [1, n]$, $C_i \neq 1$;
  4. $c = H(\sigma_1, \sigma_2, \sigma_3, h_1, h_2, \{C_i\}_{i=1}^n, \{K_{i,1}, K_{i,2}\}_{i=0}^n, \mathsf{m})$, where $h_1 \leftarrow H'(\sigma_1)$, $(K_{0,1}, K_{0,2}) \leftarrow (\sigma_1^z \cdot \sigma_3^{-c}, h_1^z \cdot h_2^{-c})$ and $(K_{i,1}, K_{i,2}) \leftarrow ([(h_1^{(i)})^{z_{i,1}} / (h_2^{(i)})^{z_{i,2}}] \cdot C_i^{-c}, h_1^{z_{i,1}} / (h_2^{z_{i,2}}))$ with $h_1^{(i)} = H'(\sigma_1^{(i)})$.

The correctness of this variant essentially follows from the one of the previous scheme, the main difference being located in Step 1 of the Verify algorithm where the verification of a FHS signature is here replaced by a verification of a PS signature. Similarly, the security proofs from the previous section readily adapt to this variant, except for some subtleties that we discuss in the full version [29] of this paper.

6   Conclusion

In this paper, we have introduced a new security model for EPID, a cryptographic primitive embedded in billions of chips [23], which has important consequences in practice. Firstly, our new unforgeability property addresses the problems of previous models and in particular removes the need to extract all platforms' secret keys. This makes enrolment of new platforms simpler while allowing concurrent Join. Secondly, our new anonymity property allows decentralized management of revocation lists, which better captures the spirit of EPID. We have in particular showed that we can retain a strong anonymity notion even in presence of powerful adversaries with unlimited control of the revocation lists. All this leads to a better understanding of what an EPID system can truly ensure in what we believe to be the most realistic usage scenario.

Another result of our paper is that such strong properties can actually be achieved by very efficient constructions that we describe. Perhaps the most surprising feature of the latter is that they do not require to perform any significant test on the malicious revocation lists. This is particularly important as it proves that we are not simply shifting the burden of the revocation manager to each platform. The latter can indeed issue signatures with essentially the same complexity as in existing systems that require a trusted revocation manager.

Acknowledgements. The authors are grateful for the support of the ANR through project ANR-18-CE-39-0019-02 MobiS5.

References

1. Ateniese, G., Camenisch, J., Hohenberger, S., de Medeiros, B.: Practical group signatures without random oracles. IACR Cryptol. ePrint Arch (2005)
2. Barki, A., Desmoulins, N., Gharout, S., Traoré, J.: Anonymous attestations made practical. ACM WISEC (2017)
3. Bellare, M., Micciancio, D., Warinschi, B.: Foundations of group signatures: formal definitions, simplified requirements, and a construction based on general assumptions. In: Biham, E. (ed.) EUROCRYPT 2003. LNCS, vol. 2656, pp. 614–629. Springer, Heidelberg (2003)
4. Bellare, M., Shi, H., Zhang, C.: Foundations of group signatures: the case of dynamic groups. In: Menezes, A. (ed.) CT-RSA 2005. LNCS, vol. 3376, pp. 136–153. Springer, Heidelberg (2005)
5. Bernhard, D., Fuchsbauer, G., Ghadafi, E., Smart, N.P., Warinschi, B.: Anonymous attestation with user-controlled linkability. Int. J. Inf. Sec. (2013)
6. Boneh, D., Boyen, X.: Short signatures without random oracles and the SDH assumption in bilinear groups. J. Cryptol. **21**(2), 149–177 (2008)
7. Boneh, D., Lynn, B., Shacham, H.: Short signatures from the Weil pairing. In: Boyd, C. (ed.) ASIACRYPT 2001. LNCS, vol. 2248, pp. 514–532. Springer, Heidelberg (2001)
8. Boneh, D., Shacham, H.: Group signatures with verifier-local revocation. In: Vijayalakshmi, A., Pfitzmann, B., McDaniel, P., (eds.), ACM CCS 2004, pp. 168–177. ACM Press, October 2004
9. Bowe, S.: BLS12-381: New zk-SNARK Elliptic Curve Construction (2017). https://electriccoin.co/blog/new-snark-curve/
10. Brickell, E.F., Camenisch, J., Chen, L.: Direct anonymous attestation. In Vijayalakshmi, A., Pfitzmann, B., McDaniel, P., (eds) ACM CCS 2004, pp. 132–145. ACM Press, October 2004
11. Brickell, E., Li, J.: Enhanced privacy id: a direct anonymous attestation scheme with enhanced revocation capabilities. In WPES 2007 (2007)
12. Brickell, E., Li, J.: Enhanced privacy ID from bilinear pairing for hardware authentication and attestation. In: Elmagarmid, A.K., Agrawal, D., (eds.) IEEE Conference on Social Computing, SocialCom (2010)
13. Camenisch, J., Drijvers, M., Lehmann, A.: Universally composable direct anonymous attestation. In: Cheng, C.-M., Chung, K.-M., Persiano, G., Yang, B.-Y. (eds.) PKC 2016. Part II, volume 9615 of LNCS, pp. 234–264. Springer, Heidelberg (2016)

14. Camenisch, J., Lysyanskaya, A.: Signature schemes and anonymous credentials from bilinear maps. In: Franklin, M. (ed.) CRYPTO 2004. LNCS, vol. 3152, pp. 56–72. Springer, Heidelberg (2004)

15. Camenisch, J., Shoup, V.: Practical verifiable encryption and decryption of discrete logarithms. In: Boneh, D. (ed.) CRYPTO 2003. LNCS, vol. 2729, pp. 126–144. Springer, Heidelberg (2003)

16. Chaum, D., van Heyst, E.: Group signatures. In: Davies, D.W. (ed.) EUROCRYPT 1991. LNCS, vol. 547, pp. 257–265. Springer, Heidelberg (1991)

17. Chen, L., Morrissey, P., Smart, N.P.: DAA: fixing the pairing based protocols. IACR Cryptol. ePrint Arch. 198 (2009)

18. Chen, L., Morrissey, P., Smart, N.P.: On proofs of security for DAA schemes. In: ProvSec 2008 (2008)

19. Chen, L., Morrissey, P., Smart, N.P.: Pairings in trusted computing. In: Pairing 2008 (2008)

20. Fischlin, M.: Communication-efficient non-interactive proofs of knowledge with online extractors. In: Shoup, V. (ed.) CRYPTO 2005. LNCS, vol. 3621, pp. 152–168. Springer, Heidelberg (2005)

21. Fuchsbauer, G., Hanser, C., Slamanig, D.: Structure-preserving signatures on equivalence classes and constant-size anonymous credentials. J. Cryptol. $32(2)$, 498–546 (2019)

22. Galbraith, S.D., Paterson, K.G., Smart, N.P.: Pairings for cryptographers. Discret. Appl. Math. (2008)

23. Intel. A cost-effective foundation for end-to-end IOT security, white paper (2016). https://www.intel.in/content/www/in/en/internet-of-things/white-papers/iot-identity-intel-epid-iot-security-white-paper.html

24. ISO/IEC. ISO/IEC 20008–1:2013 information technology - security techniques - anonymous digital signatures - part 1: General (2013). https://www.iso.org/standard/57018.html

25. ISO/IEC. ISO/IEC 20008–2:2013 information technology - security techniques - anonymous digital signatures - part 2: Mechanisms using a group public key (2013). https://www.iso.org/standard/56916.html

26. El Kassem, N., Fiolhais, L., Martins, P., Chen, L., Sousa, L.: A lattice-based enhanced privacy ID. In: WISTP 2019 (2019)

27. Pointcheval, D., Sanders, O.: Short randomizable signatures. In: Sako, K. (ed.) CT-RSA 2016. LNCS, vol. 9610, pp. 111–126. Springer, Cham (2016). https://doi.org/10.1007/978-3-319-29485-8_7

28. Pointcheval, D., Sanders, O.: Reassessing security of randomizable signatures. In: Smart, N.P. (ed.) CT-RSA 2018. LNCS, vol. 10808, pp. 319–338. Springer, Heidelberg (2018)

29. Sanders, O., Traoré, J.: EPID with malicious revocation (full version). IACR Cryptol. ePrint Arch., 1498 (2020)

30. Schnorr, C.-P.: Efficient identification and signatures for smart cards. In: Brassard, G. (ed.) CRYPTO 1989. LNCS, vol. 435, pp. 239–252. Springer, Heidelberg (1990)

31. TCG (2015). https://trustedcomputinggroup.org/authentication/

Signed Diffie-Hellman Key Exchange with Tight Security

Jiaxin Pan[(✉)], Chen Qian, and Magnus Ringerud

Department of Mathematical Sciences,
NTNU – Norwegian University of Science and Technology, Trondheim, Norway
{jiaxin.pan,chen.qian,magnus.ringerud}@ntnu.no

Abstract. We propose the first tight security proof for the ordinary two-message signed Diffie-Hellman key exchange protocol in the random oracle model. Our proof is based on the strong computational Diffie-Hellman assumption and the multi-user security of a digital signature scheme. With our security proof, the signed DH protocol can be deployed with optimal parameters, independent of the number of users or sessions, without the need to compensate any security loss. We abstract our approach with a new notion called verifiable key exchange.

In contrast to a known tight three-message variant of the signed Diffie-Hellman protocol (Gjøsteen and Jager, CRYPTO 2018), we do not require any modification to the original protocol, and our tightness result is proven in the "Single-Bit-Guess" model which we known can be tightly composed with symmetric cryptographic primitives to establish a secure channel.

Keywords: Authenticated key exchange · Signed Diffie-Hellman · Tight security

1 Introduction

Authenticated key exchange (AKE) protocols are protocols where two users can securely share a session key in the presence of active adversaries. Beyond passively observing, adversaries against an AKE protocol can modify messages and adaptively corrupt users' long-term keys or the established session key between users. Hence, it is very challenging to construct a secure AKE protocol.

The signed Diffie-Hellman (DH) key exchange protocol is a classical AKE protocol. It is a two-message (namely, two message-moves or one-round) protocol and can be viewed as a generic method to transform a passively secure Diffie-Hellman key exchange protocol [14] into a secure AKE protocol using digital signatures. Figure 1 visualizes the protocol. The origin of signed DH is unclear to us, but its idea has been used in and serves as a solid foundation for many well-known AKE protocols, including the Station-to-Station protocol [15], IKE protocol [19], the one in TLS 1.3 [32], and many others [7,18,22,23,25].

© Springer Nature Switzerland AG 2021
K. G. Paterson (Ed.): CT-RSA 2021, LNCS 12704, pp. 201–226, 2021.
https://doi.org/10.1007/978-3-030-75539-3_9

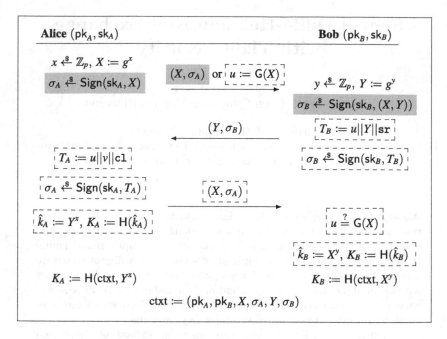

Fig. 1. Our signed Diffie-Hellman key exchange protocol and the tight variant of Gjøsteen and Jager [18]. The functions H and G are hash functions. Operations marked with a gray box are for our signed DH protocol, and dashed boxes are for Gjøsteen and Jager's. Operations without a box are performed by both protocols. All signatures are verified upon arrival with the corresponding messages, and the protocol aborts if any verification fails.

TIGHT SECURITY. Security of a cryptographic scheme is usually proven by constructing a reduction. Asymptotically, a reduction reduces any efficient adversary $\mathcal{A}$ against the scheme into an adversary $\mathcal{R}$ against the underlying computational problem. Concretely, a reduction provides a security bound for the scheme, $\varepsilon_{\mathcal{A}} \le \ell \cdot \varepsilon_{\mathcal{R}}$, where $\varepsilon_{\mathcal{A}}$ is the success probability of $\mathcal{A}$ and $\varepsilon_{\mathcal{R}}$ is that of $\mathcal{R}$. We say a reduction is *tight* if ℓ is a small constant and the running time of $\mathcal{A}$ is approximately the same as that of $\mathcal{R}$. For the same scheme, it is more desirable to have a tight security proof than a non-tight one, since a tight security proof enables implementations without the need to compensate a security loss with increased parameters.

MULTI-CHALLENGE SECURITY FOR AKE. An adversary against an AKE protocol has full control of the communication channel and, additionally, it can adaptively corrupt users' long-term keys and reveal session keys. The goal of an adversary is to distinguish between a (non-revealed) session key and a random bit-string of the same length, which is captured by the TEST query. We follow the Bellare-Rogaway (BR) model [5] to capture these capabilities, but formalize it with the game-based style of [21]. Instead of weak perfect forward secrecy, our model captures the (full) perfect forward secrecy.

Unlike the BR model, our model captures multi-challenge security, where an adversary can make T many TEST queries which are answered with a single random bit. This is a standard and well-established multi-challenge notion, and [21] called it "Single-Bit-Guess" (SBG) security. Another multi-challenge notion is the "Multi-Bit-Guess" (MBG) security where each TEST query is answered with a different random bit. Although several tightly secure AKE protocols [2,18,28,35] are proven in the MBG model, we stress that the SBG model is well-established and allows tight composition of the AKE with symmetric cryptographic primitives, which is not the case for the non-standard MBG model. Thus, the SBG multi-challenge model is more desirable than the MBG model. More details about this have been provided by Jager et al.[21, Introduction] and Cohn-Gordon et al. [10, Section 3].

THE NON-TIGHT SECURITY OF SIGNED DH. Many existing security proofs of signed DH-like protocols [7,22,23] lose a quadratic factor, $O(\mu^2 S^2)$, where μ and S are the maximum numbers of users and sessions. In the SBG model with T many TEST queries, these proofs also lose an additional multiplicative factor T.

At CRYPTO 2018, Gjøsteen and Jager [18] proposed a tightly secure variant of it by introducing an additional message move into the ordinary signed DH protocol. They showed that if the signature scheme is tightly secure in the multi-user setting then their protocol is tightly secure. They required the underlying signature scheme to be strongly unforgeable against adaptive Corruption and Chosen-Message Attacks (StCorrCMA) which is a notion in the multi-user setting and an adversary can adaptively corrupt some of the honest users to see their secret keys. Moreover, they constructed a tightly multi-user secure signature scheme based on the Decisional Diffie-Hellman (DDH) assumption in the random oracle model [4]. Combining these two results, they gave a practical three message fully tight AKE. We note that their tight security is proven in the less desirable MBG model, and, to the best of our knowledge, the MBG security can only non-tightly imply the SBG security [21]. Due to the "commitment problem", the additional message is crucial for the tightness of their protocol. In particular, the "commitment problem" seems to be the reason why most security proofs for AKEs are non-tight.

1.1 Our Contribution

In this paper, we propose a new tight security proof of the ordinary two-message signed Diffie-Hellman key exchange protocol in the random oracle model. More precisely, we prove the security of the signed DH protocol *tightly* based on the multi-user security of the underlying signature scheme in the random oracle model. Our proof improves upon the work of Gjøsteen and Jager [18] in the sense that we do not require any modification to the signed DH protocol and our tight multi-challenge security is in the SBG model. This implies that our analysis supports the optimal implementation of the ordinary signed DH protocol with theoretically sound security in a meaningful model.

Our technique is a new approach to resolve the "commitment problem". At the core of it is a new notion called *verifiable key exchange protocols*. We first briefly recall the "commitment problem" and give an overview of our approach.

TECHNICAL DIFFICULTY: THE "COMMITMENT PROBLEM". As explained in [18], this problem is the reason why almost all proofs of classical AKE protocols are non-tight. In a security proof of an AKE protocol, the reduction needs to embed a hard problem instance into the protocol messages of TEST sessions so that in the end the reduction can extract a solution to the hard problem from the adversary $\mathcal{A}$. After the instance is embedded, $\mathcal{A}$ has not committed itself to which sessions it will query to TEST yet, and, for instance, $\mathcal{A}$ can ask the reduction for REVEAL queries on sessions with a problem instance embedded to get the corresponding session keys. At this point, the reduction cannot respond to these REVEAL queries. A natural way to resolve this is to guess which sessions $\mathcal{A}$ will query TEST on, and to embed a hard problem instance in those sessions only. However, this introduces an extremely large security loss. To resolve this "commitment problem", a tight reduction should be able to answer both TEST and REVEAL for every session without any guessing. Gjøsteen and Jager achieved this for the signed DH by adding an additional message.

In this paper, we show that this additional message is not necessary for tight security.

OUR APPROACH: VERIFIABLE KEY EXCHANGE. In this work we, for simplicity, use the signed Diffie-Hellman protocol based on the plain Diffie-Hellman protocol [14] (as described in Fig. 1) to explain our approach. In the technical part, we abstract and present our idea with a new notion called verifiable key exchange protocols. Our approach is motivated by the two-message non-tight AKE in [10].

Let $\mathbb{G} := \langle g \rangle$ be a cyclic group of prime-order p where the computational Diffie-Hellman (CDH) problem is hard. Let (g^α, g^β) (where $\alpha, \beta \xleftarrow{\$} \mathbb{Z}_p$) be an instance of the CDH problem. By its random self-reducibility, we can efficiently randomize it to multiple independent instances $(g^{\alpha_i}, g^{\beta_i})$, and, given a $g^{\alpha_i \beta_i}$, we can extract the solution $g^{\alpha\beta}$.

For preparation, we assume that a TEST session does not contain any forgeries. This can be tightly justified by the StCorrCMA security of the underlying signature scheme which can be implemented tightly by the recent scheme in [12].

After that, our reduction embeds the randomized instance $(g^{\alpha_i}, g^{\beta_i})$ into each session. Now it seems we can answer neither TEST nor REVEAL queries: The answer has the form $K := \mathsf{H}(\mathrm{ctxt}, g^{xy})$, but the term g^{xy} cannot be computed by the reduction, since g^x is from either adversary $\mathcal{A}$ or the CDH problem challenge. However, our reduction can answer this by simulating the random oracle H. More precisely, we answer TEST and REVEAL queries with a random K, and we carefully program the random oracle H so that adversary $\mathcal{A}$ cannot detect this change. To achieve this, when we receive a random oracle query $\mathsf{H}(\mathrm{ctxt}, Z)$, we answer it consistently if the secret element Z corresponds to the context ctxt and ctxt belongs to one of the TEST or REVEAL queries. This check can be efficiently done by using the strong DH oracle [1].

The approach described above can be abstract by a notion called verifiable key exchange (VKE) protocols. Roughly speaking, a VKE protocol is firstly passively secure, namely, a passive observer cannot compute the secret session key. Additionally, a VKE allows an adversary to check whether a session key belongs to some honestly generated session, and to forward honestly generated transcripts in a different order to create non-matching sessions. This VKE notion gives rise to a tight security proof of the signed DH protocol. We believe this is of independent interest.

ON THE STRONG CDH ASSUMPTION. Our techniques require the Strong CDH assumption [1] for the security of our VKE protocol. We refer to [11, Appendix B] for a detailed analysis of this assumption in the Generic Group Model (GGM). Without using the GGM, we can use the twinning technique [9] to remove this strong assumption and base the VKE security tightly on the (standard) CDH assumption. This approach will double the number of group elements. Alternatively, we can use the group of signed Quadratic Residues (QR) [20] to instantiate our VKE protocol, and then the VKE security is tightly based on the factoring assumption (by [20, Theorem 2]).

REAL-WORLD IMPACTS. As mentioned earlier, the signed DH protocol serves as a solid foundation for many real-world protocols, including the one in TLS 1.3 [32], IKE [19], and the Station-to-Station [15] protocols. We believe our approach can naturally be extended to tighten the security proofs of these protocols. In particular, our notion of VKE protocols can abstract some crucial steps in a recent tight proof of TLS 1.3 [11].

Another practical benefit of our tight security proof is that, even if we implement the underlying signature with a standardized, non-tight scheme (such as Ed25519 [8] or RSA-PKCS #1 v1.5 [31]), our implementation does not need to lose the additional factor that is linear in the number of sessions. In today's Internet, there can be easily 2^{60} sessions per year.

1.2 Protocol Comparison

We compare the instantiation of signed DH according to our tight proof with the existing explicitly authenticated key exchange protocols in Fig. 2. For complete tightness, all these protocols require tight multi-user security of their underlying signature scheme. We implement the signature scheme in all protocols with the recent efficient scheme from Diemert et al. [12] whose signatures contain 3 $\mathbb{Z}_p$ elements, and whose security is based on the DDH assumption. The implementation of TLS is according to the recent tight proofs in [11,13], and we instantiate the underlying signature scheme with the same DDH-based scheme from [12].

We note that the non-tight protocol from Cohn-Gorden et al. [10], whose security loss is linear in the number of users, has better communication efficiency $(2,0,0)$. However, its security is weaker than all protocols listed in Fig. 2, since their protocol is only implicitly authenticated and achieves weak perfect forward secrecy.

Protocol	Comm. $(\mathbb{G}, \{0,1\}^\lambda, \mathbb{Z}_p)$	#Msg.	Assumption	Auth.	Model	State Reveal	Security loss
TLS* [11,13]	$(2,4,6)$	3	StCDH + DDH	expl.	SBG	no	$O(1)$
GJ [18]	$(2,1,6)$	3	DDH	expl.	MBG	no	$O(1)$
LLGW [28]	$(3,0,6)$	2	DDH	expl.	MBG	no	$O(1)$
JKRS [21]	$(5,1,3)$	2	DDH	expl.	SBG	yes	$O(1)$
This work	$(2,0,6)$	2	StCDH + DDH	expl.	SBG	no	$O(1)$

Fig. 2. Comparison of AKE protocols. We denote **Comm.** as the communication complexity of the protocols in terms of the number of group elements, hashes and $\mathbb{Z}_p$ elements (which is due to the use of the signature scheme in [12]). The column **Model** lists the AKE security model and distinguishes between multi-bit guessing (MBG) and the single-bit-guessing (SBG) security.

We detail the comparison with JKRS [21]. Using the DDH-based signature scheme in [12], the communication complexity of our signed DH protocol is $(2,0,6)$, while that of JKRS is $(5,1,3)$. We suppose the efficiency of our protocol is comparable to JKRS.

Our main weakness is that our security model is weaker that of JKRS. Namely, ours does not allow adversaries to corrupt any internal secret state. We highlight that our proof does not inherently rely on any decisional assumption. In particular, if there is a tightly multi-user secure signature scheme based on only search assumptions, our proof directly gives a tightly secure AKE based on search assumptions only, which is not the case for [21].

OPEN PROBLEMS. We do not know of any tightly multi-user secure signature schemes with corruptions based on a search assumption, and the schemes in [30] based on search assumptions do not allow any corruption. It is therefore insufficient for our purpose, and we leave constructing a tightly secure AKE based purely on search assumptions as an open problem.

2   Preliminaries

For $n \in \mathbb{N}$, let $[n] = \{1, \ldots, n\}$. For a finite set $\mathcal{S}$, we denote the sampling of a uniform random element x by $x \xleftarrow{\$} \mathcal{S}$. By $[\![B]\!]$ we denote the bit that is 1 if the evaluation of the Boolean statement B is **true** and 0 otherwise.

ALGORITHMS. For an algorithm $\mathcal{A}$ which takes x as input, we denote its computation by $y \leftarrow \mathcal{A}(x)$ if $\mathcal{A}$ is deterministic, and $y \xleftarrow{\$} \mathcal{A}(x)$ if $\mathcal{A}$ is probabilistic. We assume all the algorithms (including adversaries) in this paper to be probabilistic unless we state it. We denote an algorithm $\mathcal{A}$ with access to an oracle O by $\mathcal{A}^O$.

GAMES. We use code-based games [6] to present our definitions and proofs. We implicitly assume all Boolean flags to be initialized to 0 (**false**), numerical variables to 0, sets to $\varnothing$ and strings to $\bot$. We make the convention that a procedure terminates once it has returned an output. $G^{\mathcal{A}} \Rightarrow b$ denotes the final (Boolean) output b of game G running adversary $\mathcal{A}$, and if $b = 1$ we say $\mathcal{A}$ wins G. The randomness in $\Pr[G^{\mathcal{A}} \Rightarrow 1]$ is over all the random coins in game G. Within a procedure, "**abort** " means that we terminate the run of an adversary $\mathcal{A}$.

DIGITAL SIGNATURES. We recall the syntax and security of a digital signature scheme. Let par be some system parameters shared among all participants.

Definition 1 (Digital Signature). *A digital signature scheme* SIG := (Gen, Sign, Ver) *is defined as follows.*

- *The key generation algorithm* Gen(par) *returns a public key and a secret key* (pk, sk). *We assume that* pk *implicitly defines a message space* $\mathcal{M}$ *and a signature space* Σ.
- *The signing algorithm* Sign(sk, $m \in \mathcal{M}$) *returns a signature* $\sigma \in \Sigma$ *on* m.
- *The deterministic verification algorithm* Ver(pk, m, σ) *returns 1 (accept) or 0 (reject).*

SIG *is perfectly correct, if for all* (pk, sk) $\in$ Gen(par) *and all messages* $m \in \mathcal{M}$, Ver(pk, m, Sign(sk, m)) = 1.

In addition, we say that SIG *has* α *bits of (public) key min-entropy if an honestly generated public key* pk *is chosen from a distribution with at least* α *bits min-entropy. Formally, for all bit-strings* pk' *we have* $\Pr[\text{pk} = \text{pk}' : (\text{pk}, \text{sk}) \xleftarrow{\$} \text{Gen(par)}] \leq 2^{-\alpha}$.

Definition 2 (StCorrCMA Security [12,18]). *A digital signature scheme* SIG *is* $(t, \varepsilon, \mu, Q_s, Q_{\text{COR}})$-StCorrCMA *secure* (<u>St</u>rong unforgeability against <u>Cor</u>ruption *and* <u>C</u>hosen <u>M</u>essage <u>A</u>ttacks), *if for all adversaries* $\mathcal{A}$ *running in time at most* t, *interacting with* μ *users, making at most* Q_s *queries to the signing oracle* SIGN, *and at most* Q_{COR} $(Q_{\text{COR}} < \mu)$ *queries to the corruption oracle* CORR *as in Fig. 3, we have*

$$\Pr[\text{StCorrCMA}^{\mathcal{A}} \Rightarrow 1] \leq \varepsilon.$$

GAME StCorrCMA:	SIGN(i, m):	CORR(i):
01 **for** $i \in [\mu]$: (pk$_i$, sk$_i$) $\xleftarrow{\$}$ Gen(par)	04 $\sigma := $ Sign(sk$_i$, m)	07 $\mathcal{L}_C := \mathcal{L}_C \cup \{i\}$
02 $(i^*, m^*, \sigma^*) \xleftarrow{\$} \mathcal{A}^O(\{\text{pk}_i\}_{i \in [\mu]})$	05 $\mathcal{L}_S := \mathcal{L}_S \cup \{(i, m, \sigma)\}$	08 **return** sk$_i$
03 **return** $[\![\text{Ver}(\text{pk}_{i^*}, m^*, \sigma^*)]\!]$	06 **return** σ	
$\quad \wedge [\![(i^*, m^*, \sigma^*) \notin \mathcal{L}_S]\!] \wedge [\![i^* \notin \mathcal{L}_C]\!]$		

Fig. 3. StCorrCMA security game for a signature scheme SIG. $\mathcal{A}$ has access to the oracles O := {SIGN, CORR}.

SECURITY IN THE RANDOM ORACLE MODEL. A common approach to analyze the security of signature schemes that involve a hash function is to use the random oracle model [4] where hash queries are answered by an oracle H, where H is defined as follows: On input x, it first checks whether $H(x)$ has previously been defined. If so, it returns $H(x)$. Otherwise, it sets $H(x)$ to a uniformly random value in the range of H and then returns $H(x)$. We parameterize the maximum number of hash queries in our security notions. For instance, we define $(t, \varepsilon, \mu, Q_s, Q_{\mathrm{COR}}, Q_H)$-StCorrCMA as security against any adversary that makes at most Q_H queries to H in the StCorrCMA game. Furthermore, we make the standard convention that any random oracle query that is asked as a result of a query to the signing oracle in the StCorrCMA game is also counted as a query to the random oracle. This implies that $Q_s \leq Q_H$.

SIGNATURE SCHEMES. The tight security of our authenticated key exchange (AKE) protocols are established based on the StCorrCMA security of the underlying signature schemes. To obtain a completely tight AKE, we use the recent signature scheme from [12] to implement our protocols.

By adapting the non-tight proof in [17], the standard unforgeability against chosen-message attacks (UF-CMA) notion for signature schemes implies the StCorrCMA security of the same scheme non-tightly (with security loss μ). Thus, many widely used signature schemes (such as the Schnorr [33], Ed25519 [8] and RSA-PKCS #1 v1.5 [31] signature schemes) are non-tightly StCorrCMA secure. We do not know any better reductions for these schemes. We leave proving the StCorrCMA security of these schemes without losing a linear factor of μ as a future direction. However, our tight proof for the signed DH protocol strongly indicates that the aforementioned non-tight reduction is optimal for these practical schemes. This is because if we can prove these schemes tightly secure, we can combine them with our tight proof to obtain a tightly secure AKE with unique and verifiable private keys, which may contradict the impossibility result from [10].

For the Schnorr signature, we analyze its StCorrCMA security in the generic group model (GGM) [29,34]. We recall the Schnorr signature scheme below and show the GGM bound of its StCorrCMA security in Theorem 1.

Let $\mathsf{par} = (p, g, \mathbb{G})$, where $\mathbb{G} = \langle g \rangle$ is a cyclic group of prime order p with a hard discrete logarithm problem. Let $G : \{0,1\}^* \to \mathbb{Z}_p$ be a hash function. Schnorr's signature scheme, $\mathsf{Schnorr} := (\mathsf{Gen}, \mathsf{Sign}, \mathsf{Ver})$, is defined as follows:

Gen(par):	Sign(sk, m):	Ver(pk, m, σ):
01 $x \overset{\$}{\leftarrow} \mathbb{Z}_p$	06 **parse** $x =:$ sk	11 **parse** $(h, s) =: \sigma$
02 $X := g^x$	07 $r \overset{\$}{\leftarrow} \mathbb{Z}_p$; $R := g^r$	12 **parse** $X =:$ pk
03 pk $:= X$	08 $h := G(\mathsf{pk}, R, m)$	13 $R = g^s \cdot X^{-h}$
04 sk $:= x$	09 $s := r + x \cdot h$	14 **return** $[\![G(R, m) = h]\!]$
05 **return** (pk, sk)	10 **return** (h, s)	

Theorem 1 (StCorrCMA Security of Schnorr in the GGM). *Schnorr's signature* SIG *is* $(t, \varepsilon, \mu, Q_s, Q_{\mathrm{COR}}, Q_G)$-*StCorrCMA-secure in the GGM and in the programmable random oracle model, where*

$$\varepsilon \leq \frac{(Q_G + \mu + 1)^2}{2p} + \frac{(\mu - Q_{\mathrm{COR}})}{p} + \frac{Q_G Q_s + 1}{p}, \quad and \quad t' \approx t.$$

Here, $Q_{\mathbb{G}}$ is the number of group operations queried by the adversary.

The proof of Theorem 1 is following the approach in [3,24]: We first define an algebraic interactive assumption, CorrIDLOG, which is tightly equivalent to the StCorrCMA security of Schnorr, and then we analyze the hardness of CorrIDLOG in the GGM. CorrIDLOG stands for Interactive Discrete Logarithm with Corruption. It is motivated by the IDLOG (Interactive Discrete Logarithm) assumption in [24]. CorrIDLOG is a stronger assumption than IDLOG in the sense that it allows an adversary to corrupt the secret exponents of some public keys. Due to space limit, we leave the detailed proof of Theorem 1 in our full version.

3 Security Model for Two-Message Authenticated Key Exchange

In this section, we use the security model in [21] to define the security of two-message authenticated key exchange protocols. This section is almost verbatim to Sect. 4 of [21]. We highlight the difference we make for our protocol: Since our protocols do not have security against (ephemeral) state reveal attacks (as in the extended Canetti-Krawczyk (eCK) model [26]), we do not consider state reveals in our model.

A two-message key exchange protocol $\mathsf{AKE} := (\mathsf{Gen}_{\mathsf{AKE}}, \mathsf{Init}_I, \mathsf{Der}_R, \mathsf{Der}_I)$ consists of four algorithms which are executed interactively by two parties as shown in Fig. 4. We denote the party which initiates the session by P_i and the party which responds to the session by P_r. The key generation algorithm $\mathsf{Gen}_{\mathsf{AKE}}$ outputs a key pair $(\mathsf{pk}, \mathsf{sk})$ for one party. The initialization algorithm Init_I inputs the initiator's long-term secret key sk_i and the responder's long-term public key pk_r, and outputs a message m_i and a state st. The responder's derivation algorithm Der_R takes as input the responder's long-term secret key, the initiator's public key pk_i and a message m_i. It computes a message m_r and a session key K. The initiator's derivation algorithm Der_I inputs the initiator's long term key sk_i, the responder's long term public key pk_r, the responder's message m_r and the state st. Note that the responder is not required to save any internal state information besides the session key K.

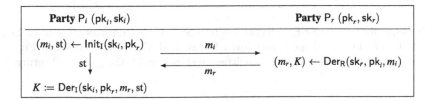

Fig. 4. Running an authenticated key exchange protocol between two parties.

We give a security game written in pseudocode. We define a model for *explicit authenticated* protocols achieving (full) forward secrecy instead of weak forward secrecy. Namely, an adversary in our model can be active and corrupt the user who owns the TEST session sID*, and the only restriction is that if there is no matching session to sID*, then the peer of sID* must not be corrupted before the session finishes.

Here explicit authentication means entity authentication in the sense that a party can explicitly confirm that he is talking to the actual owner of the recipient's public key. The key confirmation property is only implicit [16], where a party is assured that the other identified party can compute the same session key. The game IND-FS is given in Figs. 5 and 6.

GAME IND-FS	$\text{SESSION}_I((i, r) \in [\mu]^2)$
00 **for** $n \in [\mu]$	24 cnt_S ++
01 $(\text{pk}_n, \text{sk}_n) \leftarrow \text{Gen}_{\text{AKE}}$	25 $\text{sID} := \text{cnt}_S$
02 $b \xleftarrow{\$} \{0, 1\}$	26 $(\text{init}[\text{sID}], \text{resp}[\text{sID}]) := (i, r)$
03 $b' \leftarrow \mathcal{A}^O(\text{pk}_1, \cdots, \text{pk}_\mu)$	27 $\text{type}[\text{sID}] := \text{"In"}$
04 **for** $\text{sID}^* \in \mathcal{S}$	28 $(m_i, \text{st}) \leftarrow \text{Init}_I(\text{sk}_i, \text{pk}_r)$
05 **if** $\text{FRESH}(\text{sID}^*) = \textbf{false}$	29 $(I[\text{sID}], \text{state}[\text{sID}]) := (m_i, \text{st})$
06 **return** b // session not fresh	30 **return** (sID, m_i)
07 **if** $\text{VALID}(\text{sID}^*) = \textbf{false}$	
08 **return** b // no valid attack	$\text{DER}_I(\text{sID} \in [\text{cnt}_S], m_r)$
09 **return** $[\![b = b']\!]$	31 **if** $\text{sKey}[\text{sID}] \neq \perp$ **or** $\text{type}[\text{sID}] \neq \text{"In"}$
	32 **return** $\perp$ // no re-use
$\text{SESSION}_R((i, r) \in [\mu]^2, m_i)$	33 $(i, r) := (\text{init}[\text{sID}], \text{resp}[\text{sID}])$
10 cnt_S ++	34 $\text{st} := \text{state}[\text{sID}]$
11 $\text{sID} := \text{cnt}_S$	35 $\text{peerCorrupted}[\text{sID}] := \text{corrupted}[r]$
12 $(\text{init}[\text{sID}], \text{resp}[\text{sID}]) := (i, r)$	36 $K := \text{Der}_I(\text{sk}_i, \text{pk}_r, m_r, \text{st})$
13 $\text{type}[\text{sID}] := \text{"Re"}$	37 $(R[\text{sID}], \text{sKey}[\text{sID}]) := (m_r, K)$
14 $\text{peerCorrupted}[\text{sID}] := \text{corrupted}[i]$	38 **return** ϵ
15 $(m_r, K) \leftarrow \text{Der}_R(\text{sk}_r, \text{pk}_i, m_i)$	
16 $(I[\text{sID}], R[\text{sID}], \text{sKey}[\text{sID}]) := (m_i, m_r, K)$	$\text{REVEAL}(\text{sID})$
17 **return** (sID, m_r)	39 $\text{revealed}[\text{sID}] := \textbf{true}$
	40 **return** $\text{sKey}[\text{sID}]$
$\text{TEST}(\text{sID})$	
18 **if** $\text{sID} \in \mathcal{S}$ **return** $\perp$ // already tested	$\text{CORR}(n \in [\mu])$
19 **if** $\text{sKey}[\text{sID}] = \perp$ **return** $\perp$	41 $\text{corrupted}[n] := \textbf{true}$
20 $\mathcal{S} := \mathcal{S} \cup \{\text{sID}\}$	42 **return** sk_n
21 $K_0^* := \text{sKey}[\text{sID}]$	
22 $K_1^* \xleftarrow{\$} \mathcal{K}$	
23 **return** K_b^*	

Fig. 5. Game IND-FS for AKE. $\mathcal{A}$ has access to oracles $O := \{\text{SESSION}_I, \text{SESSION}_R, \text{DER}_I,$ REVEAL, CORR, TEST$\}$. Helper procedures FRESH and VALID are defined in Fig. 6. If there exists any test session which is neither fresh nor valid, the game will return b.

EXECUTION ENVIRONMENT. We consider μ parties $\text{P}_1, \ldots, \text{P}_\mu$ with long-term key pairs $(\text{pk}_n, \text{sk}_n)$, $n \in [\mu]$. Each session between two parties has a unique identification number sID and variables which are defined relative to sID:

- $\text{init}[\text{sID}] \in [\mu]$ denotes the initiator of the session.
- $\text{resp}[\text{sID}] \in [\mu]$ denotes the responder of the session.

```
FRESH(sID*)
00  (i*, r*) := (init[sID*], resp[sID*])
01  𝔐(sID*) := {sID | (init[sID], resp[sID]) = (i*, r*) ∧ (I[sID], R[sID]) =
                    (I[sID*], R[sID*]) ∧ type[sID] ≠ type[sID*]}        //matching sessions
02  if revealed[sID*] or (∃sID ∈ 𝔐(sID*) : revealed[sID] = true)
03      return false                                    //A trivially learned the test session's key
04  if ∃sID ∈ 𝔐(sID*) s.t. sID ∈ S
05      return false                                    //A also tested a matching session
06  return true

VALID(sID*)
07  (i*, r*) := (init[sID*], resp[sID*])
08  𝔐(sID*) := {sID | (init[sID], resp[sID]) = (i*, r*) ∧ (I[sID], R[sID]) =
                    (I[sID*], R[sID*]) ∧ type[sID] ≠ type[sID*]}        //matching sessions
09  for attack ∈ Table 1
10      if attack = true return true
11  return false
```

Fig. 6. Helper procedures FRESH and VALID for game IND-FS defined in Fig. 5. Procedure FRESH checks if the adversary performed some trivial attack. In procedure VALID, each attack is evaluated by the set of variables shown in Table 1 and checks if an allowed attack was performed. If the values of the variables are set as in the corresponding row, the attack was performed, i.e. attack = **true**, and thus the session is valid.

- type[sID] ∈ { "In", "Re"} denotes the session's view, i.e. whether the initiator or the responder computes the session key.
- I[sID] denotes the message that was computed by the initiator.
- R[sID] denotes the message that was computed by the responder.
- state[sID] denotes the (secret) state information, i.e. ephemeral secret keys.
- sKey[sID] denotes the session key.

To establish a session between two parties, the adversary is given access to oracles SESSION$_I$ and SESSION$_R$, where the first one starts a session of type "In" and the second one of type "Re". The SESSION$_R$ oracle also runs the Der$_R$ algorithm to compute it's session key and complete the session, as it has access to all the required variables. In order to complete the initiator's session, the oracle DER$_I$ has to be queried.

Following [21], we do not allow the adversary to register adversarially controlled parties by providing long-term public keys, as the registered keys would be treated no differently than regular corrupted keys. If we would include the key registration oracle, then our proof requires a stronger notion of signature schemes in the sense that our signature challenger can generate the system parameters with some trapdoor. With the trapdoor, the challenger can simulate a valid signature under the adversarially registered public keys. This is the case for the Schnorr signature and the tight scheme in [12], since they are honest-verifier zero-knowledge and the aforementioned property can be achieved by programming the random oracles. However, for readability, we treat the registered keys as corrupted keys.

Finally, the adversary has access to oracles CORR and REVEAL to obtain secret information. We use the following boolean values to keep track of which queries the adversary made:

- corrupted[n] denotes whether the long-term secret key of party P_n was given to the adversary.
- revealed[sID] denotes whether the session key was given to the adversary.
- peerCorrupted[sID] denotes whether the peer of the session was corrupted and its long-term key was given to the adversary at the time the session key is computed, which is important for forward security.

The adversary can forward messages between sessions or modify them. By that, we can define the relationship between two sessions:

- **Matching Session:** Two sessions sID and sID' *match* if the same parties are involved (init[sID] = init[sID'] and resp[sID] = resp[sID']), the messages sent and received are the same (I[sID] = I[sID'] and R[sID] = R[sID']) and they are of different types (type[sID] $\neq$ type[sID']).

Our protocols use signatures to preserve integrity so that any successful no-match attacks described in [27] will lead to a signature forgery and thus can be excluded.

Finally, the adversary is given access to oracle TEST, which can be queried multiple times and which will return either the session key of the specified session or a uniformly random key. We use one bit b for all test queries, and store test sessions in a set S. The adversary can obtain information on the interactions between two parties by querying the long-term secret keys and the session key. However, for each test session, we require that the adversary does not issue queries such that the session key can be trivially computed. We define the properties of freshness and validity which all test sessions have to satisfy:

- **Freshness:** A (test) session is called *fresh* if the session key was not revealed. Furthermore, if there exists a matching session, we require that this session's key is not revealed and that this session is not also a test session.
- **Validity:** A (test) session is called *valid* if it is fresh and the adversary performed any attack which is defined in the security model. We capture this with attack Table 1.

ATTACK TABLES. We define validity of different attack strategies. All attacks are defined using variables to indicate which queries the adversary may (not) make. We consider three dimensions:

- whether the test session is on the initiator's (type[sID*] = "In") or the responder's side (type[sID*] = "Re"),
- all combinations of long-term secret key reveals, taking into account when a corruption happened (corrupted and peerCorrupted variables),
- whether the adversary acted passively (matching session) or actively (no matching session).

Table 1. Distilled table of attacks for adversaries against explicitly authenticated two-message protocols without ephemeral state reveals. An attack is regarded as an AND conjunction of variables with specified values as shown in the each line, where "–" means that this variable can take arbitrary value and **F** means "false".

$\mathcal{A}$ gets (Initiator, Responder)	corrupted$[i^*]$	corrupted$[r^*]$	peerCorrupted$[\mathrm{sID}^*]$	type$[\mathrm{sID}^*]$	$|\mathfrak{M}(\mathrm{sID}^*)|$
0. **multiple matching sessions**	–	–	–	–	>1
1.+2. **(long-term, long-term)**	–	–	–	–	1
5.+6. **(long-term, long-term)**	–	–	**F**	–	0

This way, we capture all kind of combinations which are possible. From the 6 attacks in total presented in Table 2, two are trivial wins for the adversary and can thus be excluded:

– Attack (3.)+(4.): If there is no matching session, and the peer is corrupted, the adversary will trivially win, as he can forge a signature on any message of his choice, and then compute the session key.

Other attacks covered in our model capture *forward secrecy* (FS) and *key compromise impersonation* (KCI) attacks. An attack was performed if the variables are set to the corresponding values in the table.

However, if the protocol does not use appropriate randomness, it should not be considered secure. Thus, if the adversary is able to create more than one matching session to a test session, he may also run a trivial attack. We model this in row (0.) of Table 2.

Note that we do not include reflection attacks, where the adversary makes a party run the protocol with himself. For the KE$_{\mathsf{DH}}$ protocol, we could include these and create an additional reduction to the square Diffie-Hellman assumption (given g^x, to compute g^{x^2}), but for simplicity of our presentation we will not consider reflection attacks in this paper.

HOW TO READ THE TABLES. As an example, we choose row (5.) of Table 2. Then, if the test session is an initiating session (namely, type$[\mathrm{sID}^*]$ = "In"), the responder is not corrupted when the key is computed, and there does not exist a matching session (namely, $|\mathfrak{M}(\mathrm{sID}^*)| = 0$), this row will evaluate to true. In this scenario, the adversary is allowed to query both long-term secret keys. Note that row (6.) denotes a similar attack against a responder session. Since the session's type does not change the queries the adversary is allowed to make in this case, we merge these rows in Table 1. For the same reason, we also merge lines (1.) and (2.).

Table 2. Full table of attacks for adversaries against explicitly authenticated two-message protocols. The trivial attacks where the session's peer is corrupted when the key is derived, and the corresponding variables are set to **T**, are marked with gray . The ⊥ symbol indicates that the adversary cannot query anything from this party, as he already possesses the long-term key.

$\mathcal{A}$ gets (Initiator, Responder)	corrupted[i^*]	corrupted[r^*]	peerCorrupted[sID*]	type[sID*]	|$\mathfrak{M}$(sID*)|
0. **multiple matching sessions**	–	–	–	–	>1
1. **(long-term, long-term)**	–	–	–	"In"	1
2. **(long-term, long-term)**	–	–	–	"Re"	1
3. **(long-term, ⊥)**	–	**T**	**T**	"In"	0
4. **(⊥, long-term)**	**T**	–	**T**	"Re"	0
5. **(long-term, long-term)**	–	–	**F**	"In"	0
6. **(long-term, long-term)**	–	–	**F**	"Re"	0

The purpose of these tables are to make our proofs precise, by listing all the possible attacks. We note that while in our case it would have been possible to simply write out the attacks, the number of possible combinations get too large if state-reveals are considered. As we adopt our model from [21], which does include state-reveals, we stuck to their notation.

For all test sessions, at least one attack has to evaluate to true. Then, the adversary wins if he distinguishes the session keys from uniformly random keys which he obtains through queries to the TEST oracle.

Definition 3 (Key Indistinguishability of AKE). *We define game* IND-FS *as in Figs. 5 and 6. A protocol* AKE *is* $(t, \varepsilon, \mu, S, T, Q_{\text{COR}})$*-*IND-FS*-secure if for all adversaries* $\mathcal{A}$ *attacking the protocol in time* t *with* μ *users,* S *sessions,* T *test queries and* Q_{COR} *corruptions, we have*

$$\left| \Pr[\text{IND-FS}^{\mathcal{A}} \Rightarrow 1] - \frac{1}{2} \right| \leq \varepsilon.$$

Note that if there exists a session which is neither fresh nor valid, the game outputs the bit b, which implies that $\Pr[\text{IND-FS}^{\mathcal{A}} \Rightarrow 1] = 1/2$, giving the adversary an advantage equal to 0. This captures that an adversary will not gain any advantage by performing a trivial attack.

4 Verifiable Key Exchange Protocols

A key exchange protocol $\mathsf{KE} := (\mathsf{Init_I}, \mathsf{Der_R}, \mathsf{Der_I})$ can be run between two (unauthenticated) parties i and r, and can be visualized as in Fig. 4, but with differences where (1): parties does not hold any public key or private key, and (2): public and private keys in algorithms $\mathsf{Init_I}, \mathsf{Der_R}, \mathsf{Der_I}$ are replaced with the corresponding users' (public) identities.

The standard signed Diffie-Hellman (DH) protocol can be viewed as a generic way to transform a passively secure key exchange protocol to an actively secure AKE protocol using digital signatures. Our tight transformation does not modify the construction of the signed DH protocol, but requires a security notion (i.e. One-Wayness against Honest and key Verification attacks, or OW-HV) that is (slightly) stronger than passive security: Namely, in addition to passive attacks, an adversary is allowed to check if a key corresponds to some honestly generated transcripts and to forward transcripts in a different order to create non-matching sessions. Here we require that all the involved transcripts must be honestly generated by the security game and not by the adversary. This is formally defined by Definition 4 with security game OW-HV as in Fig. 7.

```
GAME OW-HV                                    SESSIONᵢ((i,r) ∈ [μ]²)                    //i ≠ r
01  (sID*, K*) ←$ A^O(μ)                      16  cnts ++
02  if sID* > cnts                            17  sID := cnts
03     return 0                               18  (init[sID], resp[sID]) := (i, r)
04  else                                      19  type[sID] := "In"
05     return KVER(sID*, K*)                  20  (X, st) ←$ Initᵢ(i, r)
                                              21  (I[sID], state[sID]) := (X, st)
KVER(sID, K)                                  22  return (sID, X)
06  return ⟦sKey[sID] = K⟧
                                              SESSIONᵣ((i,r) ∈ [μ]², X)                //i ≠ r
DERᵢ(sID, Y)                                  23  if ∀sID ∈ [cnts] : I[sID] ≠ X
07  if sKey[sID] ≠ ⊥ or type[sID] ≠ "In"      24     return ⊥           //X is not honest
08     return ⊥                               25  cnts ++
09  if ∀sID' ∈ [cnts] : R[sID'] ≠ Y           26  sID' := cnts
10     return ⊥        //Y is not honest      27  (init[sID'], resp[sID']) := (i, r)
11  (i, r) := (init[sID], resp[sID])          28  type[sID'] := "Re"
12  st := state[sID]                          29  I[sID'] := X
13  K := Derᵢ(i, r, Y, st)                    30  (Y, K') ←$ Derᵣ(r, i, X)
14  (R[sID], sKey[sID]) := (Y, K)             31  R[sID'] := Y
15  return ε                                  32  sKey[sID'] := K'
                                              33  return (sID', Y)
```

Fig. 7. Game OW-HV for KE. $\mathcal{A}$ has access to oracles $\mathsf{O} := \{\mathrm{SESSION_I}, \mathrm{SESSION_R}, \mathrm{DER_I}, \mathrm{KVER}\}$.

Definition 4 (One-Wayness against Honest and key Verification attacks (OW-HV)). *A key exchange protocol* KE *is* $(t, \varepsilon, \mu, S, Q_V)$-OW-HV *secure, where* μ *is the number of users,* S *is the number of sessions and* Q_V

is the number of calls to KVER, *if for all adversaries* $\mathcal{A}$ *attacking the protocol in time at most* t, *we have*

$$\Pr[\text{OW-HV}^{\mathcal{A}} \Rightarrow 1] \leq \varepsilon.$$

We require that a key exchange protocol KE has α *bits of min-entropy*, i.e. that for all messages m' we have $\Pr[m = m'] \leq 2^{-\alpha}$, where m is output by either Init_I or Der_R.

4.1 Example: Plain Diffie-Hellman Protocol

We show that the plain Diffie-Hellman (DH) protocol over prime-order group [14] is a OW-HV-secure key exchange under the strong computational DH (StCDH) assumption [1]. We use our syntax to recall the original DH protocol KE_DH in Fig. 8.

Let $\text{par} = (p, g, \mathbb{G})$ be a set of system parameters, where $\mathbb{G} := \langle g \rangle$ is a cyclic group of prime order p.

Definition 5 (Strong CDH Assumption). *The strong CDH (StCDH) assumption is said to be* $(t, \varepsilon, Q_{\text{DH}})$-*hard in* $\text{par} = (p, g, \mathbb{G})$, *if for all adversaries* $\mathcal{A}$ *running in time at most* t *and making at most* Q_{DH} *queries to the DH predicate oracle* DH_a, *we have:*

$$\Pr\left[Z = B^a \middle| \begin{array}{l} a, b \xleftarrow{\$} \mathbb{Z}_p; \ A := g^a \ B := g^b \\ Z \xleftarrow{\$} \mathcal{A}^{\text{DH}_a}(A, B) \end{array} \right] \leq \varepsilon,$$

where the DH predicate oracle $\text{DH}_a(C, D)$ *outputs 1 if* $D = C^a$ *and 0 otherwise.*

$\text{Init}_\text{I}(i, r)$:	$\text{Der}_\text{R}(r, i, X \in \mathbb{G})$	$\text{Der}_\text{I}(i, r, Y \in \mathbb{G}, \text{st} \in \mathbb{Z}_p)$
01 $\text{st} := x \xleftarrow{\$} \mathbb{Z}_p$	04 $y \xleftarrow{\$} \mathbb{Z}_p$	08 $K := Y^{\text{st}}$
02 $X := g^x$	05 $Y := g^y$	09 **return** K
03 **return** (X, st)	06 $K := X^y$	
	07 **return** (Y, K)	

Fig. 8. The Diffie-Hellman key exchange protocol, KE_DH, in our syntax definition.

Lemma 1. *Let* KE_DH *be the DH key exchange protocol as in Fig. 8. Then* KE_DH *has* $\alpha = \log_2 p$ *bits of min-entropy, and for every adversary* $\mathcal{A}$ *that breaks the* $(t, \varepsilon, \mu, S, Q_V)$-*OW-HV-security of* KE_DH, *there is an adversary* $\mathcal{B}$ *that breaks the* $(t', \varepsilon', Q_{\text{DH}})$-*StCDH assumption with*

$$\varepsilon' = \varepsilon, \quad t' \approx t, \quad \text{and} \quad Q_{\text{DH}} = Q_V + 1. \tag{1}$$

Proof. The min-entropy assertion is straightforward, as the DH protocol generates messages by drawing exponents $x, y \xleftarrow{\$} \mathbb{Z}_p$ uniformly as random.

We prove the rest of the lemma by constructing a reduction $\mathcal{B}$ which inputs the StCDH challenge (A, B) and is given access to the decisional oracle DH_a. $\mathcal{B}$ simulates the OW-HV security game for the adversary $\mathcal{A}$, namely, answers $\mathcal{A}$'s oracle access as in Fig. 9. More precisely, $\mathcal{B}$ uses the random self-reducibility of StCDH to simulate the whole security game, instead of using the Init_I and Der_R algorithms. The most relevant codes are highlighted with **bold** line numbers.

$\mathcal{B}^{\mathrm{DH}_a}(A, B)$	$\mathrm{SESSION}_I((i, r) \in [\mu]^2)$ $/\!/ i \neq r$
01 $(\mathrm{sID}^*, K^*) \xleftarrow{\$} \mathcal{A}^O(\mu)$	21 cnt$_S$ ++
02 **if** sID* > cnt$_S$ **or** $\mathrm{KVER}(\mathrm{sID}^*, K^*) = 0$	22 sID := cnt$_S$
03 **return** 0	23 $(\mathrm{init}[\mathrm{sID}], \mathrm{resp}[\mathrm{sID}]) := (i, r)$
04 **else**	24 type[sID] := "In"
05 $(X, Y) := (I[\mathrm{sID}^*], R[\mathrm{sID}^*])$	25 $\alpha[\mathrm{sID}] \xleftarrow{\$} \mathbb{Z}_p$
06 **fetch** sID$_1$ s.t. type[sID$_1$] = "In" and $I[\mathrm{sID}_1] = X$	**26** $X := A \cdot g^{\alpha[\mathrm{sID}]}$
07 **fetch** sID$_1$ s.t. type[sID$_2$] = "Re" and $R[\mathrm{sID}_2] = Y$	27 $(I[\mathrm{sID}], \mathrm{state}[\mathrm{sID}]) := (X, \bot)$
08 $Z := K^* / (Y^{\alpha[\mathrm{sID}_1]} \cdot A^{\alpha[\mathrm{sID}_2]})$	28 **return** (sID, X)
09 **return** $[\![Z \in \mathrm{Win}_{\mathrm{StCDH}}]\!]$ //break StCDH	
	$\mathrm{SESSION}_R((i, r) \in [\mu]^2, X)$ $/\!/ i \neq r$
	29 **if** $\forall \mathrm{sID} \in [\mathrm{cnt}_S] : I[\mathrm{sID}] \neq X$
$\mathrm{KVER}(\mathrm{sID}, K)$	30 **return** $\bot$ $/\!/X$ is not honest
10 $(X, Y) := (I[\mathrm{sID}], R[\mathrm{sID}])$	31 cnt$_S$ ++
11 fetch sID$_1$ s.t. type[sID$_1$] = "In" and $I[\mathrm{sID}_1] = X$	32 sID$'$:= cnt$_S$
12 fetch sID$_1$ s.t. type[sID$_2$] = "Re" and $R[\mathrm{sID}_2] = Y$	33 $(\mathrm{init}[\mathrm{sID}'], \mathrm{resp}[\mathrm{sID}']) := (i, r)$
13 if sID$_1 = \bot$ **or** sID$_2 = \bot$	34 type[sID$'$] := "Re"
14 **return** $\bot$	35 $I[\mathrm{sID}'] := X$
15 return $\mathrm{DH}_a(Y, K / Y^{\alpha[\mathrm{sID}_1]})$	**36** $\alpha[\mathrm{sID}'] \xleftarrow{\$} \mathbb{Z}_p$
	37 $Y := B \cdot g^{\alpha[\mathrm{sID}']}$
$\mathrm{DER}_I(\mathrm{sID}, Y)$	38 $R[\mathrm{sID}'] := Y$
16 **if** sKey[sID] $\neq \bot$ **or** type[sID] $\neq$ "In"	39 **return** (sID$'$, Y)
17 **return** $\bot$	
18 **if** $\forall \mathrm{sID}' \in [\mathrm{cnt}_S] : R[\mathrm{sID}'] \neq Y$	
19 **return** $\bot$ //Y is not honest	
20 **return** ϵ	

Fig. 9. Reduction $\mathcal{B}$ that breaks the StCDH assumption and simulates the OW-HV game for $\mathcal{A}$, when $A = g^a$ and $B = g^b$ for some unknown a and b.

We show that $\mathcal{B}$ simulates the OW-HV game for $\mathcal{A}$ perfectly:

- Since X generated in line 26 and Y generated in line 37 are uniformly random, the outputs of $\mathrm{SESSION}_I$ and $\mathrm{SESSION}_R$ are distributed as in the real protocol. Note that the output of DER_I does not get modified.
- For $\mathrm{KVER}(\mathrm{sID}, K)$, if K is a valid key that corresponds to session sID, then there must exist sessions sID$_1$ and sID$_2$ such that type[sID$_1$] = "In" (defined in line 24) and type[sID$_2$] = "Re" (defined in line 34) and

$$K = (B \cdot g^{\alpha[\mathrm{sID}_2]})^{(a+\alpha[\mathrm{sID}_1])} = Y^a \cdot Y^{\alpha[\mathrm{sID}_1]}. \tag{2}$$

where $I[\text{sID}] = I[\text{sID}_1] = A \cdot g^{\alpha[\text{sID}_1]}$ (defined in line 26) and $R[\text{sID}] = R[\text{sID}_2] = Y := B \cdot g^{\alpha[\text{sID}_2]}$ (defined in line 37). Thus, the output of $\text{KVER}(\text{sID}, K)$ is the same as that of $\text{DH}_a(Y, K/Y^{\alpha[\text{sID}_1]})$.

Finally, $\mathcal{A}$ returns $\text{sID}^* \in [\text{cnt}_S]$ and a key K^*. If $\mathcal{A}$ wins, then $\text{KVER}(\text{sID}^*, K^*) = 1$ which means that there exists sessions sID_1 and sID_2 such that $\text{type}[\text{sID}_1] = \text{"In"}$, $\text{type}[\text{sID}_2] = \text{"Re"}$ and

$$K^* = g^{(a+\alpha[\text{sID}_1])(b+\alpha[\text{sID}_2])} = g^{ab} \cdot A^{\alpha[\text{sID}_2]} \cdot B^{\alpha[\text{sID}_1]} g^{\alpha[\text{sID}_1]\alpha[\text{sID}_2]} = g^{ab} \cdot A^{\alpha[\text{sID}_2]} \cdot Y^{\alpha[\text{sID}_1]},$$

where $Y = R[\text{sID}_2] = B \cdot g^{\alpha[\text{sID}_2]}$. This means $\mathcal{B}$ breaks the StCDH with $g^{ab} = K^*/(Y^{\alpha[\text{sID}_1]} \cdot A^{\alpha[\text{sID}_2]})$ as in line 08, if $\mathcal{A}$ break the OW-HV of KE_{DH}. Hence, $\varepsilon = \varepsilon'$. The running time of $\mathcal{B}$ is the running time of $\mathcal{A}$ plus one exponentiation for every call to SESSION_I and SESSION_R, so we get $t \approx t'$. The number of calls to DH_a is the number of calls to KVER, plus one additional call to verify the adversary's forgery, and hence $Q_{\text{DH}} = Q_V + 1$.

Group of Signed Quadratic Residues. Our construction of a key exchange protocol in Fig. 8 is based on the StCDH assumption over a prime order group. Alternatively, we can instantiate our VKE portocol in a group of signed quadratic residues QR_N^+ [20]. As the StCDH assumption in QR_N^+ groups is tightly implied by the factoring assumption (by [20, Theorem 2]), our VKE protocol is secure based on the classical factoring assumption.

5   Signed Diffie-Hellman, Revisited

Following the definition in Sect. 3, we want to construct a IND-FS-secure authenticated key exchange protocol $\text{AKE} = (\text{Gen}_{\text{AKE}}, \text{Init}_I, \text{Der}_I, \text{Der}_R)$ by combining a StCorrCMA-secure signature scheme $\text{SIG} = (\text{Gen}, \text{Sign}, \text{Ver})$, a OW-HV-secure key exchange protocol $\text{KE} = (\text{Init}_I', \text{Der}_I', \text{Der}_R')$, and a random oracle H. The construction is given in Fig. 10, and follow the execution order from Fig. 4.

$\text{Gen}_{\text{AKE}}(\text{par})$:	$\text{Init}_I(\text{sk}_i, \text{pk}_r)$:
01 $(\text{pk}, \text{sk}) \xleftarrow{\$} \text{Gen}(\text{par})$	10 $(X, \text{st}) \xleftarrow{\$} \text{Init}_I'(i, r)$
02 **return** (pk, sk)	11 $\sigma_i \xleftarrow{\$} \text{Sign}(\text{sk}_i, X)$
	12 **return** (X, st, σ_i)
$\text{Der}_R(\text{sk}_r, \text{pk}_i, X, \sigma_i)$	
03 **if** $\text{Ver}(\text{pk}_i, X, \sigma_i) = 0$	$\text{Der}_I(\text{sk}_i, \text{pk}_r, Y, \sigma_r, \text{st})$
04 **return** $\perp$	13 **if** $\text{Ver}(\text{pk}_r, (X, Y), \sigma_r) = 0$
05 $(Y, K^*) \leftarrow \text{Der}_R'(r, i, X)$	14 **return** $\perp$
06 $\sigma_r \xleftarrow{\$} \text{Sign}(\text{sk}_r, (X, Y))$	15 $K^* := \text{Der}_I'(i, r, Y, \text{st})$
07 $\text{ctxt} := (\text{pk}_i, \text{pk}_r, X, \sigma_i, Y, \sigma_r)$	16 $\text{ctxt} := (\text{pk}_i, \text{pk}_r, X, \sigma_i, Y, \sigma_r)$
08 $K := \text{H}(\text{ctxt}, K^*)$	17 $K := \text{H}(\text{ctxt}, K^*)$
09 **return** $((Y, \sigma_r), K)$	18 **return** K

Fig. 10. Generic construction of AKE from SIG, KE and a random oracle H.

We now prove that this construction is in fact a secure AKE protocol.

Theorem 2. *For every adversary $\mathcal{A}$ that breaks the $(t, \varepsilon, \mu, ST, Q_H,, Q_{COR})$-IND-FS-security of a protocol AKE constructed as in Fig. 10, we can construct an adversary $\mathcal{B}$ against the $(t', \varepsilon', \mu, Q_s, Q'_{COR})$-StCorrCMA-security of a signature scheme SIG with α bits of key min-entropy, and an adversary $\mathcal{C}$ against the $(t'', \varepsilon'', \mu, S', Q_V)$-OW-HV security of a key exchange protocol KE with β bits of min-entropy, such that*

$$\varepsilon \leq 2\varepsilon' + \frac{\varepsilon''}{2} + \frac{\mu^2}{2^{\alpha+1}} + \frac{S^2}{2^{\beta+1}}$$

$$t' \approx t, \quad Q_s \leq S, \quad Q'_{COR} = Q_{COR}$$

$$t'' \approx t, \quad S' = S, \quad Q_V \leq Q_H.$$

Proof. We will prove this by using the following hybrid games, which are illustrated in Fig. 11.

GAME G_0: This is the IND-FS security game for the protocol AKE. We assume that all long term keys, and all messages output by $\mathsf{Init_I}$ and $\mathsf{Der_R}$ are distinct. If a collision happens, the game aborts. To bound the probability of this happening, we use that SIG has α bits of key min-entropy, and KE has β bits of min-entropy. We can upper bound the probability of a collision happening in the keys as $\mu^2/2^{\alpha+1}$ for μ parties, and the probability of a collision happening in the messages as $S^2/2^{\beta+1}$ for S sessions, as each session computes one message. Thus we have

$$\Pr[\mathsf{IND\text{-}FS}^{\mathcal{A}} \Rightarrow 1] = \Pr[G_0^{\mathcal{A}} \Rightarrow 1] + \frac{\mu^2}{2^{\alpha+1}} + \frac{S^2}{2^{\beta+1}}. \tag{3}$$

GAME G_1: In this game, when the oracles $\mathsf{DER_I}$ and $\mathsf{SESSION_R}$ try to derive a session key, they will abort if the input message does not correspond to a previously sent message, and the corresponding signature is valid *w.r.t.* an uncorrupted party (namely, $\mathcal{A}$ generates the message itself).

This is the preparation step for reducing an IND-FS adversary of AKE to an OW-HV adversary of KE. Note that in this game we do not exclude all the non-matching TEST sessions, but it is already enough for the "IND-FS-to-OW-HV" reduction. For instance, $\mathcal{A}$ can still force some responder session to be non-matching by reusing some of the previous initiator messages to query $\mathsf{SESSION_R}$, and then $\mathcal{A}$ uses the non-matching responder session to query TEST.

The only way to distinguish G_0 and G_1 is to trigger the new abort event in either line 19 (i.e. $\mathsf{AbortDer_R}$) or line 39 (i.e. $\mathsf{AbortDer_I}$) of Fig. 11. We define the event $\mathsf{AbortDer} := \mathsf{AbortDer_I} \vee \mathsf{AbortDer_R}$ and have that

$$|\Pr[G_0^{\mathcal{A}} \Rightarrow 1] - \Pr[G_1^{\mathcal{A}} \Rightarrow 1]| \leq \Pr[\mathsf{AbortDer}].$$

To bound this probability, we construct an adversary $\mathcal{B}$ against the $(t', \varepsilon', \mu, Q_s, Q'_{COR})$-StCorrCMA-security of SIG in Fig. 12.

We note that AbortDer is **true** only if $\mathcal{A}$ performs attacks $5+6$ in Table 1 which may lead to a session without any matching session. If AbortDer = **true**

```
GAMES G₀-G₂                                    SESSIONᵢ((i, r) ∈ [μ]²)
01  cnt_S := 0            // session counter    24  cnt_S ++
02  for n ∈ [μ]                                 25  sID := cnt_S
03     (pk_n, sk_n) ⇐$ Gen_AKE                  26  (init[sID], resp[sID]) := (i, r)
04  b ⇐$ {0,1}                                  27  type[sID] := "In"
05  b' ⇐$ A^O(pk₁,···,pk_μ)                     28  (X, st, σᵢ) ⇐$ Init_I(sk_i, pk_r)
06  for sID* ∈ S                                29  (I[sID], state[sID]) := ((X, σᵢ), st)
07     if FRESH(sID*) = false                   30  return (sID, (X, σᵢ))
08         return b
09     if VALID(sID*) = false                   DERᵢ(sID, (Y, σ_r))
10         return b                             31  if sKey[sID] ≠ ⊥ or type[sID] ≠ "In"
11  return [[b = b']]                           32      return ⊥              // no re-use
                                                33  (i, r) := (init[sID], resp[sID])
                                                34  st := state[sID]
SESSIONᵣ((i, r) ∈ [μ]², (X, σᵢ))               35  peerCorrupted[sID] := corrupted[r]
12  cnt_S ++                                     36  K := Derᵢ(sk_i, pk_r, Y, σ_r, st)
13  sID := cnt_S                                 37  (X, σᵢ) := I[sID]
14  (init[sID], resp[sID]) := (i, r)            38  if peerCorrupted[sID] = false and
15  type[sID] := "Re"                               ∄sID' : (resp[sID'], type[sID'], I[sID'], R[sID'])
16  peerCorrupted[sID] := corrupted[i]              = (r, "Re", (X, σᵢ), (Y, σ_r))        // G₁₋₂
17  ((Y, σ_r), K) ⇐$ Der_R(sk_r, pk_i, (X, σᵢ)) 39      AbortDerᵢ := true                   // G₁₋₂
18  if peerCorrupted[sID] = false and          40      abort                                // G₁₋₂
    ∄sID' : (init[sID'], type[sID'], I[sID'])  41  (R[sID], sKey[sID]) := ((Y, σ_r), K)
    = (i, "In", (X, σᵢ))          // G₁₋₂       42  return ε
19      AbortDer_R := true         // G₁₋₂
20      abort                      // G₁₋₂      TEST(sID)
21  (I[sID], R[sID]) := ((X, σᵢ), (Y, σ_r))     43  if sID ∈ S return ⊥         // already tested
22  sKey[sID] := K                              44  if sKey[sID] = ⊥ return ⊥
23  return (sID, (Y, σ_r))                      45  S := S ∪ {sID}
                                                46  K₀* := sKey[sID]            // G₀₋₁
                                                47  K₀* ⇐$ K                    // G₂
                                                48  K₁* ⇐$ K
                                                49  return K_b*
```

Fig. 11. Games G_0-G_2. $\mathcal{A}$ has access to oracles $O := \{\text{SESSION}_I, \text{SESSION}_R, \text{DER}_I, \text{REVEAL}, \text{CORR}, \text{TEST}\}$, where REVEAL and CORR are simulated as in the original IND-FS game in Fig. 5. Game G_0 implicitly assumes that there is no collision between long term keys or messages output by the experiment.

then Σ is defined in lines 26 and 42 of Fig. 12 and Σ is a valid StCorrCMA forge for SIG. We only show that for the case when $\text{AbortDer}_R = \textbf{true}$ here, and the argument is similar for the case when $\text{AbortDer}_I = \textbf{true}$. Given that AbortDer_R happens, we have that $\text{Ver}(pk_i, X, \sigma_i) = 1$ and $\text{peerCorrupted}[sID] = \textbf{false}$. Due to the criteria in line 40, the pair (X, σ_i) has not been output by SESSION_I on input (i, r) for any r, and hence (i, X) has never been queried to the SIGN' oracle. Therefore, $\mathcal{B}$ aborts $\mathcal{A}$ in the IND-FS game and returns (i, X, σ_i) to the StCorrCMA challenger to win the StCorrCMA game. Therefore, we have

$$\Pr[\text{AbortDer}_R] \leq \varepsilon', \tag{4}$$

$\mathcal{B}^{\text{Corr}', \text{Sign}'}(\text{pk}_1, \ldots, \text{pk}_\mu)$	$\text{Session}_\text{R}((i, r) \in [\mu]^2, (X, \sigma_i))$
01 $b \xleftarrow{\$} \{0, 1\}$	33 cnt_S ++
02 $b' \leftarrow \mathcal{A}^O(\text{pk}_1, \ldots, \text{pk}_\mu)$	34 $\text{sID} := \text{cnt}_\text{S}$
03 for $\text{sID}^* \in \mathcal{S}$	35 $(\text{init}[\text{sID}], \text{resp}[\text{sID}]) := (i, r)$
04 if $\text{Fresh}(\text{sID}^*) = \textbf{false}$	36 $\text{type}[\text{sID}] := \text{"Re"}$
05 return b	37 $\text{peerCorrupted}[\text{sID}] := \text{corrupted}[i]$
06 if $\text{Valid}(\text{sID}^*) = \textbf{false}$	38 if $\text{Ver}(\text{pk}_i, X, \sigma_i) = 0$
07 return b	39 return $\bot$
08 return $[\![\Sigma \in \text{Win}_{\text{StCorrCMA}}]\!]$ //break	40 if $\text{peerCorrupted}[\text{sID}] = \textbf{false}$ and
StCorrCMA	$\nexists \text{sID}': (\text{init}[\text{sID}'], \text{type}[\text{sID}'], I[\text{sID}'])$
	$= (i, \text{"In"}, (X, \sigma_i))$
$\text{Session}_\text{I}((i, r) \in [\mu]^2)$	41 $\text{AbortDer}_\text{R} := \textbf{true}$
09 cnt_S ++	**42** $\Sigma := (i, X, \sigma_i)$ //valid forgery
10 $\text{sID} := \text{cnt}_\text{S}$	43 **abort**
11 $(\text{init}[\text{sID}], \text{resp}[\text{sID}]) := (i, r)$	44 $(Y, K^*) \xleftarrow{\$} \text{Der}_\text{R}'(r, i, X)$
12 $\text{type}[\text{sID}] := \text{"In"}$	**45** $\sigma_r \xleftarrow{\$} \text{Sign}'(\text{pk}_r, (X, Y))$
13 $(X, \text{st}) \xleftarrow{\$} \text{Init}_\text{I}'(i, r)$	46 $\text{ctxt} := (\text{pk}_i, \text{pk}_r, X, \sigma_i, Y, \sigma_r)$
14 $\sigma_i \xleftarrow{\$} \text{Sign}'(\text{pk}_i, X)$	47 $K := \text{H}(\text{ctxt}, K^*)$
15 $(I[\text{sID}], \text{state}[\text{sID}]) := ((X, \sigma_i), \text{st})$	48 $(I[\text{sID}], R[\text{sID}]) := ((X, \sigma_i), (Y, \sigma_r))$
16 return $(\text{sID}, (X, \sigma_i))$	49 $\text{sKey}[\text{sID}] := K$
	50 return $(\text{sID}, (Y, \sigma_r))$
$\text{Der}_\text{I}(\text{sID}, (Y, \sigma_r))$	
17 if $\text{sKey}[\text{sID}] \neq \bot$ or $\text{type}[\text{sID}] \neq \text{"In"}$	$\text{Corr}(n \in [\mu])$
18 return $\bot$ //no re-use	51 $\text{corrupted}[n] := \textbf{true}$
19 $(i, r) := (\text{init}[\text{sID}], \text{resp}[\text{sID}])$	**52** $\text{sk}_n \leftarrow \text{Corr}'(n)$
20 $\text{st} := \text{state}[\text{sID}]$	53 return sk_n
21 $\text{peerCorrupted}[\text{sID}] := \text{corrupted}[r]$	
22 if $\text{Ver}(\text{pk}_r, (X, Y), \sigma_r) = 0$	$\text{H}(\text{pk}_i, \text{pk}_r, X, Y, K^*)$
23 return $\bot$	54 $\text{ctxt} := (\text{pk}_i, \text{pk}_r, X, Y)$
24 if $\text{peerCorrupted}[\text{sID}] = \textbf{false}$ and	55 if $\text{H}[\text{ctxt}, K^*] = K$
$\nexists \text{sID}': (\text{resp}[\text{sID}'], \text{type}[\text{sID}'], I[\text{sID}'], R[\text{sID}'])$	56 return K
$= (r, \text{"Re"}, (X, \sigma_i), (Y, \sigma_r))$	57 $K \xleftarrow{\$} \mathcal{K}$
25 $\text{AbortDer}_\text{I} := \textbf{true}$	58 $\text{H}[\text{ctxt}, K^*] := K$
26 $\Sigma := (r, (X, Y), \sigma_r)$ //valid forgery	59 return K
27 **abort**	
28 $K^* := \text{Der}_\text{I}'(i, r, Y, \text{st})$	
29 $\text{ctxt} := (\text{pk}_i, \text{pk}_r, X, \sigma_i, Y, \sigma_r)$	
30 $K := \text{H}(\text{ctxt}, K^*)$	
31 $(R[\text{sID}], \text{sKey}[\text{sID}]) := ((Y, \sigma_r), K)$	
32 return ϵ	

Fig. 12. Adversary $\mathcal{B}$ against the $(t', \varepsilon', \mu, Q_s, Q'_{\text{COR}})$-StCorrCMA-security of SIG. The StCorrCMA game provides oracles Sign', Corr'. The adversary $\mathcal{A}$ has access to oracles $O := \{\text{Session}_\text{I}, \text{Session}_\text{R}, \text{Der}_\text{I}, \text{Reveal}, \text{Corr}, \text{Test}, \text{H}\}$, where Reveal and Test remain the same as in Fig. 4. We highlight the most relevant codes with **bold** line numbers.

which implies that

$$\left| \Pr[G_0^\mathcal{A} \Rightarrow 1] - \Pr[G_1^\mathcal{A} \Rightarrow 1] \right| \leq \Pr[\text{AbortDer}_\text{I}] + \Pr[\text{AbortDer}_\text{R}] \leq 2\varepsilon'. \tag{5}$$

The running time of $\mathcal{B}$ is the same as that of $\mathcal{A}$, plus the time used to run the key exchange algorithms Init_I', Der_R', Der_I' and the signature verification algorithm

VER. This gives $t' \approx t$. For the number of signature queries we have $Q_s \leq S$, since SESSION$_R$ can abort before it queries the signature oracle, and the adversary can reuse messages output by SESSION$_I$. For the number of corruptions, we have $Q'_{COR} = Q_{COR}$.

GAME G_2: The TEST oracle always returns a uniformly random key, independent on the bit b.

Since we have excluded collisions in the messages output by the experiment, it is impossible to create two sessions of the same type that compute the same session key. Hence, an adversary must query the random oracle H on the correct input of a test session to detect the change between G_1 and G_2 (which is only in case $b = 0$). More precisely, we have $\Pr[G_2^{\mathcal{A}} \Rightarrow 1 \mid b = 1] = \Pr[G_1^{\mathcal{A}} \Rightarrow 1 \mid b = 1]$ and

$$
\begin{aligned}
\left|\Pr[G_2^{\mathcal{A}} \Rightarrow 1] - \Pr[G_1^{\mathcal{A}} \Rightarrow 1]\right| &= \frac{1}{2} \left| \Pr[G_2^{\mathcal{A}} \Rightarrow 1 \mid b = 0] + \Pr[G_2^{\mathcal{A}} \Rightarrow 1 \mid b = 1] \right. \\
&\quad \left. - \Pr[G_1^{\mathcal{A}} \Rightarrow 1 \mid b = 0] - \Pr[G_1^{\mathcal{A}} \Rightarrow 1 \mid b = 1] \right| \\
&= \frac{1}{2} \left| \Pr[G_2^{\mathcal{A}} \Rightarrow 1 \mid b = 0] - \Pr[G_1^{\mathcal{A}} \Rightarrow 1 \mid b = 0] \right|.
\end{aligned}
\tag{6}
$$

To bound Eq. (6), we construct an adversary $\mathcal{C}$ to $(t'', \varepsilon'', \mu, S', Q_V)$-break the OW-HV security of KE. The input to $\mathcal{C}$ is the number of parties μ, and system parameters par. In addition, $\mathcal{C}$ has access to oracles SESSION$'_I$, SESSION$'_R$, DER$'_I$ and KVER.

We firstly show that the outputs of SESSION$_I$, SESSION$_R$ and DER$_I$ (simulated by $\mathcal{C}$) are distributed the same as in G_1. Due to the abort conditions introduced in G_1, for all sessions that has finished computing a key without making the game abort, their messages are honestly generated, although they may be in a different order and there are non-matching sessions. Hence, SESSION$_I$, SESSION$_R$ and DER$_I$ can be perfectly simulated using SESSION$'_I$, SESSION$'_R$ and DER$'_I$ of the OW-HV game and the signing key.

It is also easy to see that the random oracle H simulated by $\mathcal{C}$ has the same output distribution as in G_1. We stress that if line 66 is executed then adversary $\mathcal{A}$ may use the sID to distinguish G_2 and G_1 for $b = 0$, which is the only case for $\mathcal{A}$ to see the difference. At the same time, we obtain a valid attack $\Sigma := (\text{sID}, K^*)$ for the OW-HV security. Thus, we have

$$
\left| \Pr[G_2^{\mathcal{A}} \Rightarrow 1 \mid b = 0] - \Pr[G_1^{\mathcal{A}} \Rightarrow 1 \mid b = 0] \right| \leq \varepsilon''.
$$

As before, the running time of $\mathcal{C}$ is that of $\mathcal{A}$, plus generating and verifying signatures, and we have $t'' \approx t$. Furthermore, $S' = S$, as the counter for the OW-HV game increases once for every call to SESSION$_I$ and SESSION$_R$.

$\mathcal{C}^{O'}(\mu)$

01 **for** $n \in [\mu]$
02     $(\mathrm{pk}_n, \mathrm{sk}_n) \xleftarrow{\$} \mathsf{Gen}(\mathrm{par})$
03     $b \xleftarrow{\$} \{0, 1\}$
04 $b' \leftarrow \mathcal{A}^O(\mathrm{pk}_1, \ldots, \mathrm{pk}_\mu)$
05 **for** $\mathrm{sID}^* \in \mathcal{S}$
06   **if** $\mathrm{FRESH}(\mathrm{sID}^*) = \mathbf{false}$
07   **return** b
08   **if** $\mathrm{VALID}(\mathrm{sID}^*) = \mathbf{false}$
09   **return** b
10 **return** $[\![\Sigma \in \mathrm{Win}_{\mathsf{OW\text{-}HV}}]\!]$

$\mathrm{SESSION_I}((i, r) \in [\mu]^2)$

11 $(\mathrm{sID}, X) \xleftarrow{\$} \mathrm{SESSION_I}'(i, r)$
12 $\mathrm{cnt_S}{+}{+}$
13 $(\mathrm{init}[\mathrm{sID}], \mathrm{resp}[\mathrm{sID}]) := (i, r)$
14 $\mathrm{type}[\mathrm{sID}] := \text{"In"}$
15 $\sigma_i \xleftarrow{\$} \mathsf{Sign}(\mathrm{sk}_i, X)$
16 $I[\mathrm{sID}] := (X, \sigma_i)$
17 **return** $(\mathrm{sID}, (X, \sigma_i))$

$\mathrm{DER_I}(\mathrm{sID}, (Y, \sigma_r))$

18 **if** $\mathrm{sKey}[\mathrm{sID}] \neq \bot$ **or** $\mathrm{type}[\mathrm{sID}] \neq \text{"In"}$
19   **return** $\bot$ // no re-use
20 $(i, r) := (\mathrm{init}[\mathrm{sID}], \mathrm{resp}[\mathrm{sID}])$
21 $\mathrm{peerCorrupted}[\mathrm{sID}] := \mathrm{corrupted}[r]$
22 $(X, \sigma_i) := I[\mathrm{sID}]$
23 **if** $\mathsf{Ver}(\mathrm{pk}_r, (X, Y), \sigma_r) = 0$
24   **return** $\bot$
25 **if** $\mathrm{peerCorrupted}[\mathrm{sID}] = \mathbf{false}$ **and**
    $\nexists \mathrm{sID}' : (\mathrm{resp}[\mathrm{sID}'], \mathrm{type}[\mathrm{sID}'], I[\mathrm{sID}'], R[\mathrm{sID}'])$
    $= (r, \text{"Re"}, (X, \sigma_i), (Y, \sigma_r))$
26   **abort**
27 $\mathrm{ctxt} := (\mathrm{pk}_i, \mathrm{pk}_r, X, \sigma_i, Y, \sigma_r)$
28 $\mathrm{DER_I}'(\mathrm{sID}, Y)$
29 **if** $\exists K^* : \mathsf{H}[\mathrm{ctxt}, K^*, 1] = K$
30 $\mathrm{sKey}[\mathrm{sID}] := K$
31 **elseif** $\mathsf{H}[\mathrm{ctxt}, \bot, \bot] = K$
32 $\mathrm{sKey}[\mathrm{sID}] := K$
33 **else** $K \xleftarrow{\$} \mathcal{K}$
34 $\mathsf{H}[\mathrm{ctxt}, \bot, \bot] := K$
35 $\mathrm{sKey}[\mathrm{sID}] := K$
36 $R[\mathrm{sID}] := (Y, \sigma_r)$
37 **return** ϵ

$\mathrm{SESSION_R}((i, r) \in [\mu]^2, (X, \sigma_i))$

38 **if** $\mathsf{Ver}(\mathrm{pk}_i, X, \sigma_i) = 0$
39   **return** $\bot$
40 $(\mathrm{sID}, Y) \xleftarrow{\$} \mathrm{SESSION_R}'(i, r, X)$
41 $\mathrm{cnt_S}{+}{+}$
42 $\mathrm{peerCorrupted}[\mathrm{sID}] := \mathrm{corrupted}[i]$
43 **if** $\mathrm{peerCorrupted}[\mathrm{sID}] = \mathbf{false}$ **and**
    $\nexists \mathrm{sID}' : (\mathrm{init}[\mathrm{sID}'], \mathrm{type}[\mathrm{sID}'], I[\mathrm{sID}'])$
    $= (i, \text{"In"}, (X, \sigma_i))$
44   **abort**
45 $(\mathrm{init}[\mathrm{sID}], \mathrm{resp}[\mathrm{sID}]) := (i, r)$
46 $\mathrm{type}[\mathrm{sID}] := \text{"Re"}$
47 $I[\mathrm{sID}] := (X, \sigma_i)$
48 $\sigma_r \xleftarrow{\$} \mathsf{Sign}(\mathrm{sk}_r, (X, Y))$
49 $R[\mathrm{sID}] := (Y, \sigma_r)$
50 $\mathrm{ctxt} := (\mathrm{pk}_i, \mathrm{pk}_r, X, \sigma_i, Y, \sigma_r)$
51 **if** $\exists K^* : \mathsf{H}[\mathrm{ctxt}, K^*, 1] = K$
52 $\mathrm{sKey}[\mathrm{sID}] := K$
53 **elseif** $\mathsf{H}[\mathrm{ctxt}, \bot, \bot] = K$
54 $\mathrm{sKey}[\mathrm{sID}] := K$
55 **else** $K \xleftarrow{\$} \mathcal{K}$
56 $\mathsf{H}[\mathrm{ctxt}, \bot, \bot] := K$
57 $\mathrm{sKey}[\mathrm{sID}] := K$
58 **return** (Y, σ_r)

$\mathsf{H}(\mathrm{pk}_i, \mathrm{pk}_r, X, \sigma_i, Y, \sigma_r, K^*)$

59 $\mathrm{ctxt} := (\mathrm{pk}_i, \mathrm{pk}_r, X, \sigma_i, Y, \sigma_r)$
60 **if** $\mathsf{H}[\mathrm{ctxt}, K^*, \cdot] = K$
61   **return** K
62 $h := \bot$
63 **if** $\mathsf{H}[\mathrm{ctxt}, \bot, \bot] = K$ **and** $\exists \mathrm{sID} :$
    $(I[\mathrm{sID}], R[\mathrm{sID}]) = ((X, \sigma_i), (Y, \sigma_r))$
64 $\mathrm{DER_I}'(\mathrm{sID}, Y)$
65   **if** $\mathrm{KVER}(\mathrm{sID}, K^*) = 1$
66 $\Sigma := (\mathrm{sID}, K^*)$ // attack for OW-HV

67   replace $(\bot, \bot)$ in $\mathsf{H}[\mathrm{ctxt}, \bot, \bot]$
           with $(K^*, 1)$
68   **return** K
69   **else** $h := 0$
70 $K \xleftarrow{\$} \mathcal{K}$
71 $\mathsf{H}[\mathrm{ctxt}, K^*, h] := K$
72 **return** K

Fig. 13. Reduction $\mathcal{C}$ against the $(t'', \varepsilon'', \mu, S', Q_V)$-OW-HV-security of KE. The OW-HV game provides oracles $\mathrm{O}' := \{\mathrm{SESSION_I'}, \mathrm{SESSION_R'}, \mathrm{DER_I'}, \mathrm{KVER}\}$. The adversary $\mathcal{A}$ has access to oracles $\mathrm{O} := \{\mathrm{SESSION_I}, \mathrm{SESSION_R}, \mathrm{DER_I}, \mathrm{REVEAL}, \mathrm{CORR}, \mathrm{TEST}, \mathsf{H}\}$, where $\mathrm{REVEAL}, \mathrm{CORR}$ and TEST are defined as in G_2 of Fig. 11. We highlight the most relevant codes with **bold** line numbers. The center dot '$\cdot$' in this figure means arbitrary value.

At last, for game G_2 we have $\Pr[G_2^{\mathcal{A}} \Rightarrow 1] = \frac{1}{2}$, as the response from the TEST oracle is independent of the bit b. Summing up all the equations, we obtain

$$\varepsilon \leq \left| \Pr[\mathsf{IND\text{-}FS}^{\mathcal{A}} \Rightarrow 1] - \frac{1}{2} \right|$$

$$= \left| \Pr[G_0^{\mathcal{A}} \Rightarrow 1] + \frac{\mu^2}{2^{\alpha+1}} + \frac{S^2}{2^{\beta+1}} - \Pr[G_2^{\mathcal{A}} \Rightarrow 1] \right|$$

$$= \left| \Pr[G_0^{\mathcal{A}} \Rightarrow 1] - \Pr[G_1^{\mathcal{A}} \Rightarrow 1] + \Pr[G_1^{\mathcal{A}} \Rightarrow 1] - \Pr[G_2^{\mathcal{A}} \Rightarrow 1] + \frac{\mu^2}{2^{\alpha+1}} + \frac{S^2}{2^{\beta+1}} \right|$$

$$\leq \left| \Pr[G_0^{\mathcal{A}} \Rightarrow 1] - \Pr[G_1^{\mathcal{A}} \Rightarrow 1] \right| + \left| \Pr[G_1^{\mathcal{A}} \Rightarrow 1] - \Pr[G_2^{\mathcal{A}} \Rightarrow 1] \right| + \frac{\mu^2}{2^{\alpha+1}} + \frac{S^2}{2^{\beta+1}}$$

$$\leq 2\varepsilon' + \frac{\varepsilon''}{2} + \frac{\mu^2}{2^{\alpha+1}} + \frac{S^2}{2^{\beta+1}},$$

and $t' \approx t$, $Q_s \leq S$, $Q'_{\mathrm{COR}} = Q_{\mathrm{COR}}$, $t'' \approx t$, $S' = S$, $Q_V \leq Q_{\mathsf{H}}$.

Acknowledgement. We thank the anonymous reviewers for their many insightful suggestions to improve our paper.

References

1. Abdalla, M., Bellare, M., Rogaway, P.: The oracle Diffie-Hellman assumptions and an analysis of DHIES. In: Naccache, D. (ed.) CT-RSA 2001. LNCS, vol. 2020, pp. 143–158. Springer, Heidelberg (2001). https://doi.org/10.1007/3-540-45353-9_12
2. Bader, C., Hofheinz, D., Jager, T., Kiltz, E., Li, Y.: Tightly-secure authenticated key exchange. In: Dodis, Y., Nielsen, J.B. (eds.) TCC 2015, Part I. LNCS, vol. 9014, pp. 629–658. Springer, Heidelberg (2015). https://doi.org/10.1007/978-3-662-46494-6_26
3. Bellare, M., Dai, W.: The multi-base discrete logarithm problem: tight reductions and non-rewinding proofs for Schnorr identification and signatures. Cryptology ePrint Archive, Report 2020/416 (2020). https://eprint.iacr.org/2020/416
4. Bellare, M., Rogaway, P.: Random oracles are practical: a paradigm for designing efficient protocols. In: Denning, D.E., Pyle, R., Ganesan, R., Sandhu, R.S., Ashby, V. (eds.) ACM CCS 1993, pp. 62–73. ACM Press, November 1993
5. Bellare, M., Rogaway, P.: Entity authentication and key distribution. In: Stinson, D.R. (ed.) CRYPTO 1993. LNCS, vol. 773, pp. 232–249. Springer, Heidelberg (1994). https://doi.org/10.1007/3-540-48329-2_21
6. Bellare, M., Rogaway, P.: The security of triple encryption and a framework for code-based game playing proofs. In: Vaudenay, S. (ed.) EUROCRYPT 2006. LNCS, vol. 4004, pp. 409–426. Springer, Heidelberg (2006). https://doi.org/10.1007/11761679_25
7. Bergsma, F., Jager, T., Schwenk, J.: One-round key exchange with strong security: an efficient and generic construction in the standard model. In: Katz, J. (ed.) PKC 2015. LNCS, vol. 9020, pp. 477–494. Springer, Heidelberg (2015). https://doi.org/10.1007/978-3-662-46447-2_21
8. Bernstein, D.J., Duif, N., Lange, T., Schwabe, P., Yang, B.-Y.: High-speed high-security signatures. In: Preneel, B., Takagi, T. (eds.) CHES 2011. LNCS, vol. 6917, pp. 124–142. Springer, Heidelberg (2011). https://doi.org/10.1007/978-3-642-23951-9_9

9. Cash, D., Kiltz, E., Shoup, V.: The twin Diffie-Hellman problem and applications. In: Smart, N. (ed.) EUROCRYPT 2008. LNCS, vol. 4965, pp. 127–145. Springer, Heidelberg (2008). https://doi.org/10.1007/978-3-540-78967-3_8
10. Cohn-Gordon, K., Cremers, C., Gjøsteen, K., Jacobsen, H., Jager, T.: Highly efficient key exchange protocols with optimal tightness. In: Boldyreva, A., Micciancio, D. (eds.) CRYPTO 2019, Part III. LNCS, vol. 11694, pp. 767–797. Springer, Cham (2019). https://doi.org/10.1007/978-3-030-26954-8_25
11. Davis, H., Günther, F.: Tighter proofs for the SIGMA and TLS 1.3 key exchange protocols. ACNS 2021 (2021). https://eprint.iacr.org/2020/1029
12. Diemert, D., Gellert, K., Jager, T., Lyu, L.: More efficient digital signatures with tight multi-user security. In: PKC 2021 (2021). https://ia.cr/2021/235
13. Diemert, D., Jager, T.: On the tight security of TLS 1.3: theoretically-sound cryptographic parameters for real-world deployments. J. Cryptol. (2020). https://eprint.iacr.org/2020/726
14. Diffie, W., Hellman, M.E.: New directions in cryptography. IEEE Trans. Inf. Theory **22**(6), 644–654 (1976)
15. Diffie, W., van Oorschot, P.C., Wiener, M.J.: Authentication and authenticated key exchanges. Des. Codes Crypt. **2**(2), 107–125 (1992)
16. Fischlin, M., Günther, F., Schmidt, B., Warinschi, B.: Key confirmation in key exchange: a formal treatment and implications for TLS 1.3. In: 2016 IEEE Symposium on Security and Privacy, pp. 452–469. IEEE Computer Society Press, May 2016
17. Galbraith, S.D., Malone-Lee, J., Smart, N.P.: Public key signatures in the multiuser setting. Inf. Process. Lett. **83**(5), 263–266 (2002). https://doi.org/10.1016/S0020-0190(01)00338-6
18. Gjøsteen, K., Jager, T.: Practical and tightly-secure digital signatures and authenticated key exchange. In: Shacham, H., Boldyreva, A. (eds.) CRYPTO 2018, Part II. LNCS, vol. 10992, pp. 95–125. Springer, Cham (2018). https://doi.org/10.1007/978-3-319-96881-0_4
19. Harkins, D., Carrel, D.: The internet key exchange (IKE). RFC 2409 (1998). https://www.ietf.org/rfc/rfc2409.txt
20. Hofheinz, D., Kiltz, E.: The group of signed quadratic residues and applications. In: Halevi, S. (ed.) CRYPTO 2009. LNCS, vol. 5677, pp. 637–653. Springer, Heidelberg (2009). https://doi.org/10.1007/978-3-642-03356-8_37
21. Jager, T., Kiltz, E., Riepel, D., Schäge, S.: Tightly-secure authenticated key exchange, revisited. In: EUROCRYPT 2021 (2021). https://ia.cr/2020/1279
22. Jager, T., Kohlar, F., Schäge, S., Schwenk, J.: On the security of TLS-DHE in the standard model. In: Safavi-Naini, R., Canetti, R. (eds.) CRYPTO 2012. LNCS, vol. 7417, pp. 273–293. Springer, Heidelberg (2012). https://doi.org/10.1007/978-3-642-32009-5_17
23. Jager, T., Kohlar, F., Schäge, S., Schwenk, J.: Authenticated confidential channel establishment and the security of TLS-DHE. J. Cryptol. **30**(4), 1276–1324 (2017)
24. Kiltz, E., Masny, D., Pan, J.: Optimal security proofs for signatures from identification schemes. In: Robshaw, M., Katz, J. (eds.) CRYPTO 2016, Part II. LNCS, vol. 9815, pp. 33–61. Springer, Heidelberg (2016). https://doi.org/10.1007/978-3-662-53008-5_2
25. Krawczyk, H.: SIGMA: the "SIGn-and-MAc" approach to authenticated Diffie-Hellman and its use in the IKE protocols. In: Boneh, D. (ed.) CRYPTO 2003. LNCS, vol. 2729, pp. 400–425. Springer, Heidelberg (2003). https://doi.org/10.1007/978-3-540-45146-4_24

26. LaMacchia, B., Lauter, K., Mityagin, A.: Stronger security of authenticated key exchange. In: Susilo, W., Liu, J.K., Mu, Y. (eds.) ProvSec 2007. LNCS, vol. 4784, pp. 1–16. Springer, Heidelberg (2007). https://doi.org/10.1007/978-3-540-75670-5_1

27. Li, Y., Schäge, S.: No-match attacks and robust partnering definitions: defining trivial attacks for security protocols is not trivial. In: Thuraisingham, B.M., Evans, D., Malkin, T., Xu, D. (eds.) ACM CCS 2017, pp. 1343–1360. ACM Press, October–November 2017

28. Liu, X., Liu, S., Gu, D., Weng, J.: Two-pass authenticated key exchange with explicit authentication and tight security. In: ASIACRYPT 2020 (2020). https://ia.cr/2020/1088

29. Maurer, U.: Abstract models of computation in cryptography (invited paper). In: Smart, N.P. (ed.) Cryptography and Coding 2005. LNCS, vol. 3796, pp. 1–12. Springer, Heidelberg (2005). https://doi.org/10.1007/11586821_1

30. Pan, J., Ringerud, M.: Signatures with tight multi-user security from search assumptions. In: Chen, L., Li, N., Liang, K., Schneider, S. (eds.) ESORICS 2020, Part II. LNCS, vol. 12309, pp. 485–504. Springer, Cham (2020). https://doi.org/10.1007/978-3-030-59013-0_24

31. PKCS #1: RSA Cryptography Standard. RSA Data Security, Inc., June 1991

32. Rescorla, E.: The Transport Layer Security (TLS) Protocol Version 1.3. RFC 8446 (Proposed Standard (2018). https://tools.ietf.org/html/rfc8446

33. Schnorr, C.P.: Efficient signature generation by smart cards. J. Cryptol. 4(3), 161–174 (1991)

34. Shoup, V.: Lower bounds for discrete logarithms and related problems. In: Fumy, W. (ed.) EUROCRYPT 1997. LNCS, vol. 1233, pp. 256–266. Springer, Heidelberg (1997). https://doi.org/10.1007/3-540-69053-0_18

35. Xiao, Y., Zhang, R., Ma, H.: Tightly secure two-pass authenticated key exchange protocol in the CK model. In: Jarecki, S. (ed.) CT-RSA 2020. LNCS, vol. 12006, pp. 171–198. Springer, Cham (2020). https://doi.org/10.1007/978-3-030-40186-3_9

Lattice-Based Proof of Shuffle
and Applications to Electronic Voting

Diego F. Aranha[1] , Carsten Baum[1] , Kristian Gjøsteen[2] ,
Tjerand Silde[2(✉)] , and Thor Tunge[2]

[1] Aarhus University, Aarhus, Denmark
{dfaranha,cbaum}@cs.au.dk
[2] Norwegian University of Science and Technology, Trondheim, Norway
{kristian.gjosteen,tjerand.silde}@ntnu.no

Abstract. A verifiable shuffle of known values is a method for proving that a collection of commitments opens to a given collection of known messages, without revealing a correspondence between commitments and messages. We propose the first practical verifiable shuffle of known values for lattice-based commitments.

Shuffles of known values have many applications in cryptography, and in particular in electronic voting. We use our verifiable shuffle of known values to build a practical lattice-based cryptographic voting system that supports complex ballots. Our scheme is also the first construction from candidate post-quantum secure assumptions to defend against compromise of the voter's computer using return codes.

We implemented our protocol and present benchmarks of its computational runtime. The size of the verifiable shuffle is 17τ KB and takes time 33τ ms for τ voters. This is around 5 times faster and at least 50% smaller per vote than the lattice-based voting scheme by del Pino et al. (ACM CCS 2017), which can only handle yes/no-elections.

Keywords: Lattice-based cryptography · Proof of shuffle · Verifiable encryption · Return codes · Electronic voting · Implementation

1 Introduction

A *verifiable shuffle of known values* is a method for proving that a collection of commitments opens to a given collection of known messages, without revealing exactly which commitment corresponds to which message.

One well-known approach is due to Neff [25]: Define two polynomials, one that has the known messages as its roots and another that has the values committed to as its roots. Since polynomials are stable under permutation of their roots, it

C. Baum–This work was funded by the European Research Council (ERC) under the European Unions' Horizon 2020 research and innovation programme under grant agreement No. 669255 (MPCPRO). Part of this work was done while visiting NTNU in Trondheim.

ⓒ Springer Nature Switzerland AG 2021
K. G. Paterson (Ed.): CT-RSA 2021, LNCS 12704, pp. 227–251, 2021.
https://doi.org/10.1007/978-3-030-75539-3_10

is sufficient to prove that these two polynomials have the same evaluation at a randomly chosen point.

Proving that the second polynomial has a given evaluation at a given point could be done using multiplication and addition proofs on the commitments. Usually multiplication proofs for committed values are quite expensive, while it is somewhat cheap to do proofs of linear combinations of committed values with public coefficients. Following the idea of Neff, the determinant of a particular band matrix is the difference of the two polynomials, and we show that the polynomials are equal by showing that the columns of the matrix are linearly dependent.

1.1 Our Contribution

Verifiable Shuffle of Known Values. Our main contribution is a verifiable shuffle of known values for lattice-based commitments. This is the first efficient construction from a candidate post-quantum secure assumption of such a primitive. As discussed above, our construction is based on techniques originating with Neff [25], although there are a number of obstacles with this approach in the lattice-based setting, where we use the commitments of Baum *et al.* [5].

First of all, many group-homomorphic commitment schemes allow either direct or very simple verification of arbitrary linear relations. No known commitment scheme secure under an assumption considered as post-quantum secure has a similar structure, which means that we must use adaptations of existing proofs for linear relations. Secondly, the underlying algebraic structure is a ring, not a field. Since we need certain elements to be invertible, we need to choose challenges from special sets of invertible elements, and carefully adapt the proof so that the correctness of the shuffle is guaranteed.

In order to make our construction practical, we use the Fiat-Shamir transform to make the underlying Zero-Knowledge proofs non-interactive. We want to stress that our proof of security only holds in the conventional Random Oracle Model, which is not a sound model when considering quantum adversaries. Constructing a post-quantum secure verifiable shuffle of known values is an interesting open problem.

Voting from Lattices. Our second contribution is the first construction of a practical voting system that is suitable for more general ballots (such as various forms of ranked choice voting, perhaps in various non-trivial combinations with party lists and candidate slates) and that is secure under lattice-based assumptions.

We adopt an architecture very similar to deployed cryptographic voting systems [13, 17]. The protocol works as follows:

- The voter's computer commits to the voter's ballot and encrypts an opening of the ballot. The commitment and ciphertext are sent to a ballot box.
- When counting starts, the ballot box removes any identifying material from the ciphertext and sends this to the shuffle server.

- The shuffle server decrypts the openings, verifies the commitments and outputs the ballots. It uses our verifiable shuffle of known values to prove that the ballots are consistent with the commitments.
- One or more auditors inspect the ballot box and the shuffle server.

For this to work, the voter's ciphertext must contain a valid opening of the voter's commitment. To achieve this, we use the verifiable encryption scheme of Lyubashevsky and Neven [22].

This architecture seems to be an acceptable trade-off between security and practicality. It achieves privacy for voters under the usual threat models, it provides cast-as-intended verification via return codes, it achieves coercion-resistance via revoting, and it achieves integrity as long as at least one auditor is honest. However, the architecture makes it difficult to simultaneously achieve privacy and universal verifiability. (We cannot simply publish the ballot box, the decrypted ballots and the shuffle proofs, because the shuffle server then learns who submitted which ballot, breaking privacy.) This is often not a significant problem, because coercion resistance requires keeping the decrypted ballots secret when so-called Italian attacks apply, and it is usually quite expensive to achieve universal verifiability without publishing the decrypted ballots. If Italian attacks do not apply or coercion resistance is otherwise not an issue, if one is willing to pay the price, it would be possible to distribute the decryption among two (or more) players by using nested encryption and nested commitments, after which everything could be published and universal verifiability is achieved. The cost is significant, though. Limited verifiability can be achieved in cheaper ways.

Voting with Return Codes. Our third contribution is the first construction of a voting system that supports so-called return codes for verifying that ballots have been cast as intended and that is based on a candidate post-quantum assumption.

One of the major challenges in using computers for voting is that computers can be compromised. Countermeasures such as Benaloh challenges do not work very well in practice, since they are hard to understand[1]. Return codes can provide integrity for voters with a fairly high rate of fraud detection [14]. Return codes do not work well with complex ballots, but our scheme could be modified to use return codes only for parts of a complex ballot.

We again use the commitments and verifiable encryption. The voter's computer commits to a pre-code and proves that this pre-code has been correctly computed from the ballot and some key material. It also verifiably encrypts an opening of this commitment. The pre-code is later decrypted and turned into a return code, which the voter can inspect.

Implementation of Our Voting Scheme. Our fourth contribution is a concrete choice of parameters for the system along with a prototype implementation, demonstrating that the scheme is fully practical. We choose parameters in such

---

[1] Very few members of the International Association for Cryptologic Research use Benaloh challenges when casting ballots in their elections.

a way that arithmetic in the used algebraic structures can be efficiently implemented. This gives a fairly low computational cost for the scheme, so the limiting factor seems to be the size of the proofs. For elections with millions of voters, the total proof size will be measured in gigabytes, while systems based on discrete logarithms would produce much smaller proofs. Since we do not try to achieve universal verifiability, which means that proofs in our architecture are only handled by well-resourced infrastructure players, the proof size is unlikely to matter much. (If ordinary voters were to verify all the shuffle proofs, this would still not be infeasible, but it would be more of an issue.)

1.2 Related Work

Verifiable Shuffles. The idea for a verifiable shuffle of known values that we use was introduced by Neff [25]. Since [25], there has been a huge body of work improving verifiable shuffles of ciphertexts, but not for constructions that use post-quantum assumptions.

Costa *et al.* [10] use ZK proofs for lattice commitments to show a correct shuffle and re-randomization of a collection of ciphertexts. They also adopt some of the techniques from Neff, but instead of using a linear algebra argument they use multiplication proofs. This is conceptually simpler than our approach, but turns out to be less efficient even with the newer, improved multiplication proofs of [3]. A related concept to the verifiable shuffle of known values is the decrypting mix-net [8], which proves that the decryption of a collection of ciphertexts equals a given collection of messages. Decryption mix-nets can be very fast [6], but these constructions provide guarantees of correct decryption only if at least one participant in the mix-net is honest at the time of decryption, unlike our approach which provides proper soundness even if both the ballot box and shuffle server are compromised at the time of decryption.

Candidate Post-quantum Cryptographic Voting Systems. There is a large body of academic work on cryptographic voting systems, and several systems have been deployed in practice in Europe in e.g. Estonia [17] and Norway [13,17], while Switzerland [19] also planned to use an e-voting system. All of these systems make significant efforts to provide so-called cast-as-intended verification, to defend against compromise of the voter's computer. For lower-stakes elections, Helios [1] has seen significant use. All of these systems have roughly the same architecture, and offer varying levels of verifiability. None of these systems are secure against quantum computers.

Many real-world political elections have ballots that are essentially very simple, such as a single yes/no question, or a t-out-of-n structure (even though many such races can be combined to form a visually and cognitively complex ballot). However, real-world voting systems can also have more complicated ballots that cannot be decomposed to a series of simple, independent races. For example, the Australian parliamentary ballot may encode a total order on all candidates in a district, and transferable votes make counting quite complex. While work has been done on homomorphic counting for such elections, the usual approach is to recover cleartext ballots and count them.

While it is a simple exercise to use existing theoretical constructions to build a candidate quantum-safe voting system similar to the above deployed systems, the problem is that these constructions are practically inefficient, either because they are too computationally expensive or the proofs used are too large to make verification of many such proofs practical.

del Pino et al. [11] gives a feasible construction that uses homomorphic counting, but it is only applicable to yes/no-elections (though it can be extended to 1 out of n elections, at some cost). The scheme also does not try to defend against compromise of the voter's computer, limiting its applicability. Chillotti et al. [9] proposed a system based on homomorphic counting, but using fully homomorphic encryption. Again, this only supports 1 out of n elections, and practical efficiency is unclear. Gjøsteen and Strand [15] proposed a method for counting a complex ballot using homomorphic encryption. However, their scheme is not complete and the size of the circuit makes the system barely practical.

As discussed above, existing verifiable shuffles for candidate post-quantum secure cryptosystems could be used for generic constructions. Costa et al. [10] uses certain ZK proofs for lattice commitments to show a correct shuffle and re-randomization of a collection of ciphertexts. The bottleneck of their approach are the underlying rather inefficient ZK proofs. The faster construct by Strand [27] is too restrictive in the choice of plaintext domain. Even given that shuffle, these schemes still require a verifiable (distributed) decryption for lattice-based constructions. These, currently, do not exist.

2   Preliminaries

If $\varPhi$ is a probability distribution, then $z \xleftarrow{\$} \varPhi$ denotes that z was sampled according to $\varPhi$. If S is a finite set, then $s \xleftarrow{\$} S$ denotes that s was sampled uniformly from the set S. The expressions $z \leftarrow xy$ and $z \leftarrow \mathtt{Func}(x)$ denote that z is assigned the product of x and y and the value of the function $\mathtt{Func}$ evaluated on x, respectively.

For two matrices $A \in S^{\alpha \times \beta}, B \in S^{\gamma \times \delta}$ over an arbitrary ring S, we denote by $A \otimes B \in S^{(\alpha \cdot \gamma) \times (\beta \cdot \delta)}$ their tensor product, i.e. the matrix

$$
B = \begin{pmatrix} b_{1,1} \cdots b_{1,\delta} \\ \vdots \ddots \vdots \\ b_{\gamma,1} \cdots b_{\gamma,\delta} \end{pmatrix}, \qquad A \otimes B := \begin{pmatrix} b_{1,1} \cdot A \cdots b_{1,\delta} \cdot A \\ \vdots \ddots \vdots \\ b_{\gamma,1} \cdot A \cdots b_{\gamma,\delta} \cdot A \end{pmatrix}.
$$

2.1   The Rings R and R_p

Let $p, r \in \mathbb{N}^+$ and $N = 2^r$. Then we define the rings $R = \mathbb{Z}[X]/\langle X^N + 1 \rangle$ and $R_p = R/\langle p \rangle$, that is, R_p is the ring of polynomials modulo $X^N + 1$ with integer coefficients modulo a prime p. If p is congruent to $1 \bmod 2\delta$, for $N \geq \delta > 1$ a power of 2, then $X^N + 1$ splits into δ irreducible factors.

We define the norms of elements $f(X) = \sum \alpha_i X^i \in R$ to be the norms of the coefficient vector as a vector in $\mathbb{Z}^N$:

$$\|f\|_1 = \sum |\alpha_i| \qquad \|f\|_2 = \left(\sum \alpha_i^2\right)^{1/2} \qquad \|f\|_\infty = \max_{i \in \{1,\dots,N\}} \{|\alpha_i|\}.$$

For an element $\bar{f} \in R_p$ we choose coefficients as the representatives in $\left[-\frac{p-1}{2}, \frac{p-1}{2}\right]$, and then compute the norms as if $\bar{f}$ is an element in R. For vectors $\boldsymbol{a} = (a_1, \dots, a_k) \in R^k$ we define the 2-norm to be $\|\boldsymbol{a}\|_2 = \sqrt{\sum \|a_i\|^2}$, and analogously for the ∞-norm. We omit the subscript in the case of the 2-norm.

One can show that sufficiently short elements in the ring R_p (with respect to the aforementioned norms) are invertible.

Lemma 1 ([24], Corollary 1.2). *Let $N \geq \delta > 1$ be powers of 2 and p a prime congruent to $2\delta + 1 \bmod 4\delta$. Then $X^N + 1$ factors into δ irreducible factors $X^{N/\delta} + r_j$, for some r_j's in R_p. Additionally, any non-zero y such that*

$$\|y\|_\infty < p^{1/\delta}/\sqrt{\delta} \quad \text{or} \quad \|y\| < p^{1/\delta}$$

is invertible in R_p.

For the remaining part of this paper we will assume that the parameters p, δ and N are chosen such that Lemma 1 is satisfied. We define a set of short elements

$$D_{\beta_\infty} = \{x \in R_p \mid \|x\|_\infty \leq \beta_\infty\}.$$

We furthermore define

$$\mathcal{C} = \{c \in R_p \mid \|c\|_\infty = 1, \|c\|_1 = \nu\},$$

which consists of all elements in R_p that have trinary coefficients and are non-zero in exactly ν positions, and we denote by

$$\bar{\mathcal{C}} = \{c - c' \mid c \neq c' \in \mathcal{C}\}$$

the set of differences of distinct elements in $\mathcal{C}$. The size of $\mathcal{C}$ is $2^\nu \binom{N}{\nu}$. It can be seen from Lemma 1 that, for a suitable choice of parameters, we can ensure that all non-zero elements from the three sets are invertible.

We need a bound on how many roots a polynomial can have over the ring R_p. The total number of elements in the ring is $|R_p| = p^N$.

Lemma 2. *Let $N \geq \delta \geq 1$ be powers of 2, p a prime congruent to $2\delta + 1 \bmod 4\delta$ and $T \subseteq R_p$. Let $g \in R_p[X]$ be a polynomial of degree τ. Then, g has at most τ^δ roots in T, and $\Pr[g(\rho) = 0 | \rho \xleftarrow{\$} T] \leq \tau^\delta/|T|$.*

Proof. First, by Lemma 1, we divide $X^N + 1$ into δ irreducible factors $X^{N/\delta} + r_j$. Each of the irreducible factors contributes at most τ roots to a polynomial $g \in R_p[X]$ of degree τ. Using the Chinese remainder theorem to combine the roots, we get that g has at most τ^δ roots in R_p. If we choose $\rho \xleftarrow{\$} R_p$ uniformly at random, the probability that this is a root of g is the total number of roots divided by the size of the ring. Since T is a subset of R_p, it can contain at most as many roots as R_p itself. $\qquad\square$

2.2   The Discrete Gaussian Distribution

The continuous normal distribution over $\mathbb{R}^k$ centered at $v \in \mathbb{R}^k$ with standard deviation σ is given by

$$\rho(x)_{v,\sigma}^N = \frac{1}{\sqrt{2\pi}\sigma} \exp\left(\frac{-||x - v||^2}{2\sigma^2}\right).$$

When sampling randomness for our lattice-based commitment and encryption schemes, we'll need samples from the *discrete Gaussian distribution*. This distribution is achieved by normalizing the continuous distribution over R^k by letting

$$\mathcal{N}_{v,\sigma}^k(x) = \frac{\rho_{v,\sigma}^{kN}(x)}{\rho_\sigma^{kN}(R^k)} \text{ where } x \in R^k \text{ and } \rho_\sigma^{kN}(R^k) = \sum_{x \in R^k} \rho_\sigma^{kN}(x).$$

When $\sigma = 1$ or $v = 0$, they are omitted.

3   Lattice-Background: Commitments and ZK Proofs

We first introduce the commitments of Baum et al. [5], and continue with a zero-knowledge proof protocol of linear relation over the ring R_p using these commitments. The protocol is implicitly mentioned in [5].

3.1   Lattice-Based Commitments

Algorithms. The scheme consists of three algorithms: KeyGen_C, Com, and Open for key generation, commitments and verifying an opening, respectively. We describe these algorithms for committing to one message, and refer to [5] for more details.

KeyGen_C outputs a public matrix B over R_p of the form

$$B_1 = \begin{bmatrix} I_n & B_1' \end{bmatrix} \qquad \text{where } B_1' \xleftarrow{\$} R_p^{n \times (k-n)}$$
$$b_2 = \begin{bmatrix} 0^n & 1 & b_2' \end{bmatrix} \qquad \text{where } (b_2')^\top \xleftarrow{\$} R_p^{(k-n-1)},$$

for width k and height $n + 1$ of the public key $\mathsf{pk} := B = \begin{bmatrix} B_1 \\ b_2 \end{bmatrix}$.

Com commits to messages $m \in R_p$ by sampling an $r_m \xleftarrow{\$} D_{\beta_\infty}^k$ and computing

$$\mathsf{Com}(m; r_m) = B \cdot r_m + \begin{bmatrix} 0 \\ m \end{bmatrix} = \begin{bmatrix} c_1 \\ c_2 \end{bmatrix} = [\![m]\!].$$

Com outputs $[\![m]\!]$ and $d = (m; r_m, 1)$.

Open verifies whether an opening $(m; \boldsymbol{r}_m, f)$ with $f \in \bar{C}$ is a valid opening of $\boldsymbol{c}_1, \boldsymbol{c}_2$ by checking if

$$f \cdot \begin{bmatrix} \boldsymbol{c}_1 \\ \boldsymbol{c}_2 \end{bmatrix} \stackrel{?}{=} \boldsymbol{B} \cdot \boldsymbol{r}_m + f \cdot \begin{bmatrix} \boldsymbol{0} \\ m \end{bmatrix},$$

and that $\|\boldsymbol{r}_m[i]\| \leq 4\sigma_C \sqrt{N}$ for $i \in [k]$ with $\sigma_C = 11 \cdot \beta_\infty \cdot \nu \cdot \sqrt{kN}$. Open outputs 1 if all these conditions hold, and 0 otherwise.

Baum et al. [5] proved the security properties of the commitment scheme with respect to knapsack problems (which in turn are versions of standard Module-SIS/Module-LWE problems). More concretely, they showed that any algorithm $\mathcal{A}$ that efficiently solves the hiding property can be turned into an algorithm $\mathcal{A}'$ solving $\mathsf{DKS}^\infty_{n+1,k,\beta_\infty}$ with essentially the same runtime and success probability. Furthermore, any algorithm $\mathcal{A}$ that efficiently solves the binding problem can be turned into an algorithm $\mathcal{A}''$ solving $\mathsf{SKS}^2_{n,k,16\sigma_C\sqrt{\nu N}}$ with the same success probability. We provide formal definitions of these assumptions in the full version.

The commitments [5] have a weak additively homomorphic property:

Proposition 1. *Let $\boldsymbol{z}_0 = \mathsf{Com}(m; \boldsymbol{r}_m)$ be a commitment with opening $(m; \boldsymbol{r}_m, f)$ and let $\boldsymbol{z}_1 = \mathsf{Com}(\rho; \boldsymbol{0})$. Then $\boldsymbol{z}_0 - \boldsymbol{z}_1$ is a commitment with opening $(m - \rho; \boldsymbol{r}_m, f)$.*

The proof follows from the linearity of the verification algorithm.

3.2   Zero-Knowledge Proof of Linear Relations

Let $[\![x]\!], [\![x']\!]$ be commitments as above such that $x' = \alpha x + \beta$ for some public $\alpha, \beta \in R_p$. Then Π_{Lin} in Fig. 1 shows a zero-knowledge proof of knowledge (ZKPoK) of this fact (it is an adapted version of the linearity proof in [5]). The proof is a Σ protocol that aborts[2] with a certain probability to achieve the zero-knowledge property. For the protocol in Fig. 1 we define

$$[\![x]\!] = \mathsf{Com}(x; \boldsymbol{r}) = \begin{bmatrix} \boldsymbol{c}_1 \\ \boldsymbol{c}_2 \end{bmatrix}, \quad [\![x']\!] = \mathsf{Com}(x'; \boldsymbol{r}') = \begin{bmatrix} \boldsymbol{c}'_1 \\ \boldsymbol{c}'_2 \end{bmatrix}.$$

In [5] the authors show that a version of Π_{Lin} is a Honest-Verifier Zero-Knowledge Proof of Knowledge for the aforementioned commitment scheme. This can directly be generalized to relations of the form $\alpha \cdot \tilde{x} + \beta$ as follows:

Lemma 3. *Let $\alpha, \beta, [\![x]\!], [\![x']\!]$ be defined as above. Then Π_{Lin} is a HVZK proof of the relation*

$$R_{\mathrm{Lin}} = \left\{ (s, w) \middle| \begin{array}{l} s = (\alpha, \beta, [\![x]\!], [\![x']\!], \boldsymbol{B}_1, \boldsymbol{b}_2), w = (\tilde{x}, \tilde{\boldsymbol{r}}, \tilde{\boldsymbol{r}}', f), \\ \mathsf{Open}([\![x]\!], \tilde{x}, \tilde{\boldsymbol{r}}, f) = \mathsf{Open}([\![x']\!], \alpha \cdot \tilde{x} + \beta, \tilde{\boldsymbol{r}}', f) = 1 \end{array} \right\}$$

---

[2] This approach is usually referred to as *Fiat Shamir with Aborts* (see e.g. [20,21] for a detailed description). If the proof is compiled with a random oracle into a NIZK, then these aborts only increase the prover time by a constant factor.

Prover $\mathcal{P}$ Verifier $\mathcal{V}$

$y, y' \overset{\$}{\leftarrow} \mathcal{N}_{\sigma_C}^k$

$t \leftarrow B_1 y, t' \leftarrow B_1 y'$

$u \leftarrow \alpha \langle b_2, y \rangle - \langle b_2, y' \rangle$ $\xrightarrow{\quad t, t', u \quad}$

                                    $\xleftarrow{\quad d \quad}$ $d \overset{\$}{\leftarrow} \mathcal{C}$

$z \leftarrow y + dr$

$z' \leftarrow y' + dr'$

Continue with probability:

$\displaystyle\prod_{(a,b) \in \{(r,z),(r',z')\}} \min\left(1, \frac{\mathcal{N}_{\sigma_C}^k(b)}{M \cdot \mathcal{N}_{da,\sigma_C}^k(b)}\right)$ $\xrightarrow{\quad z, z' \quad}$

                                         return Accept iff

                                     1 : $\|z[i]\|, \|z'[i]\| \leq 2\sigma_C \sqrt{N}, \; i \in [k]$

                                     2 : $B_1 z \overset{?}{=} t + d c_1$

                                     3 : $B_1 z' \overset{?}{=} t' + d c_1'$

                                     4 : $\alpha \langle b_2, z \rangle - \langle b_2, z' \rangle \overset{?}{=} (\alpha c_2 + \beta - c_2')d + u$

Fig. 1. Protocol Π_{Lin} is a Sigma-protocol to prove the relation $x' = \alpha x + \beta$, given the commitments $[\![x]\!], [\![x']\!]$ and the scalars α, β.

The proof for this is exactly the same as in [5], and we do only sketch it now: Assume that we can rewind an efficient poly-time prover and obtain two accepting transcripts with the same first message t, t', u but differing $d, \overline{d}$ (as well as responses $z, z', \overline{z}, \overline{z}'$). Then one can extract valid openings $(\tilde{x}; \tilde{r}, f)$ and $(\alpha\tilde{x} + \beta; \tilde{r}', f)$ for $[\![x]\!], [\![x']\!]$ respectively as follows: From the two accepting transcripts and the equations checked by the verifier we can set $f = d - \overline{d}, \tilde{r} = z - \overline{z}, \tilde{r}' = z' - \overline{z}'$ where it must hold that

$$\alpha \langle b_2, \tilde{r} \rangle - \langle b_2, \tilde{r}' \rangle \overset{?}{=} f(\alpha c_2 + \beta - c_2').$$

By setting $\tilde{x} = c_2 - f^{-1}\langle b_2, \tilde{r} \rangle$ and $\tilde{x}' = c_2' - f^{-1}\langle b_2, \tilde{r}' \rangle$, we then have that $\alpha x + \beta = x'$ by the aforementioned equation. The validity and bounds of the opening follow from the same arguments as in [5].

Compression. Using the techniques from [4,16], as already mentioned in [5, Section 5.3], allows to compress the non-interactive version of the aforementioned zero-knowledge proof. The main idea is that the prover only hashes the parts of the proof that got multiplied by the uniformly sampled part B_1' of B_1, and that the verifier only checks an approximate equality with these when recomputing the challenge. We do the following changes to the protocol.

The prover samples vectors y, y' of dimension $k - n$ according to σ_C, then computes $t = B_1' y$ and $t' = B_1' y'$. Note that u is computed as before, as the n first values of b_2 are zero. Then z and z' are computed as earlier, but are of dimension $k - n$ instead of k. The prover computes the challenge d as

$$d = \text{H}(B, [\![x]\!], [\![x']\!], \alpha, \beta, u, \lfloor t \rceil_\gamma, \lfloor t' \rceil_\gamma)$$

where $\gamma \in \mathbb{N}$ and $\lfloor \cdot \rceil_\gamma$ denotes rounding off the least γ bits.

To make sure that the non-interactive proof can be verified, we must ensure that d can be re-computed from the public information. Let $\hat{t} = B_1' z - dc_1$ and $\hat{t}' = B_1' z' - dc_1'$ and observe that $\hat{t}[i] - t[i] = dr[i]$, for each coordinate $i \in [n]$, and similar for $\hat{t}'$ and t'. For honestly generated randomness, for each $i \in [k]$, we have that $\|r[i]\| \le \beta_\infty \sqrt{N}$, and since $d \in \bar{C}$, we have that $\|d\| = \sqrt{\nu}$. It follows that $\|dr[i]\|_\infty \le \beta_\infty \sqrt{\nu N}$, and similar for $dr'[i]$. When hashing t and t' to get the challenge d, we then remove the $\gamma = \lceil \log \beta_\infty \sqrt{\nu N} \rceil$ lower bits of each coordinate first, to ensure that both the prover and the verifier compute on the same value. Hence, before outputting the proof, the prover will also test that

$$d' = \mathtt{H}(B, [\![x]\!], [\![x']\!], \alpha, \beta, \hat{u}, \lfloor B_1' z - dc_1 \rceil_\gamma, \lfloor B_1' z' - dc_1' \rceil_\gamma), \text{ where}$$
$$\hat{u} = \alpha \langle [1 \quad b_2'], z \rangle - \langle [1 \quad b_2'], z' \rangle - (\alpha c_2 + \beta - c_2')d.$$

The prover then outputs the proof (d, z, z') if $d = d'$ and $\|z[i]\|, \|z'[i]\| \le 2\sigma_C \sqrt{N}$ (when setting up the check as in [4,16], then the test will fail with probability at most $1/2$), and the verifier will make the same checks to validate it. The proof size is reduced from k to $k - n$ Gaussian-distributed ring-elements.

4   Protocol: Zero-Knowledge Proof of Correct Shuffle

In this section we present the shuffle protocol for openings of commitments. We construct a public-coin $4 + 3\tau$-move protocol[3] such that the commit-challenge-response stages require the prover to solve a system of linear equations in order to prove a correct shuffle. Our construction extends Neff's construction [25] to the realm of post-quantum assumptions.

The proof of shuffle protocol will use the commitments defined in Sect. 3. For the shuffle proof to work, the prover $\mathcal{P}$ and verifier $\mathcal{V}$ receive commitments $\{[\![m_i]\!]\}_{i=1}^\tau$. $\mathcal{P}$ also receives the set of openings $\{(m_i, r_i)\}_{i=1}^\tau$ as well as a permutation $\pi \in S_\tau$. Additionally, both parties also obtain $\{\hat{m}_i\}_{i=1}^\tau$.

The goal is to ensure that the following relation R_{Shuffle} holds:

$$R_{\text{Shuffle}} = \left\{ (s, w) \left| \begin{array}{l} s = ([\![m_1]\!], \ldots, [\![m_\tau]\!], \hat{m}_1, \ldots, \hat{m}_\tau, \hat{m}_i \in R_p), \\ w = (\pi, f_1, \ldots, f_\tau, r_1, \ldots, r_\tau), \pi \in S_\tau, \\ \forall i \in [\tau] : \mathtt{Open}([\![m_{\pi^{-1}(i)}]\!], \hat{m}_i, r_i, f_i) = 1 \end{array} \right. \right\}$$

To use the idea of Neff, all $\hat{m}_i$ messages involved have to be invertible. However, this may not be the case for arbitrary ring elements. We start by showing that if $\mathcal{V}$ samples a random ρ in R_p then all $\hat{m}_i - \rho$ will be invertible with high probability:

Proposition 2. *Let $N \ge \delta \ge 1$ be powers of 2, p a prime congruent to $2\delta + 1 \bmod 4\delta$. Then*

$$\Pr_{x_1, \ldots, x_\tau \in R_p} [x_1 - \rho, \ldots, x_\tau - \rho \text{ invertible in } R_p \mid \rho \xleftarrow{\$} R_p] \le 1 - \max(1, \tau \cdot (1 - e^{-\delta/p})).$$

---

[3] This is only a theoretical problem as the protocol is public-coin and can therefore directly be transformed into NIZKs using the Fiat-Shamir transform.

Plugging in realistic parameters ($p = 2^{32}, \delta = 2, \tau = 1,000,000$) we see that the probability of all $\hat{m}_i - \rho$ being simultaneously invertible is essentially 1. The proof for Proposition 2 can be found in the full version.

Therefore, the first step for our shuffle protocol will be that $\mathcal{V}$ picks a random appropriate $\rho \xleftarrow{\$} R_p$ and sends ρ to $\mathcal{P}$. $\mathcal{P}$ and $\mathcal{V}$ then locally compute the values $\hat{M}_i, M_i$ by setting $M_i = m_i - \rho$, $\hat{M}_i = \hat{m}_i - \rho$. The proof, on a high level, then shows that $\prod_i M_i = \prod_i \hat{M}_i$. This is in fact sufficient, as the $m_i, \hat{m}_i$ can be considered as roots of polynomials of degree τ. By subtracting ρ from each such entry and multiplying the results we obtain the evaluation of these implicit polynomials in the point ρ, and if the $\hat{m}_i$ are not a permutation of the m_i then these implicit polynomials will be different. At the same time, the number of points on which both polynomials can agree is upper-bounded as shown in Lemma 2.

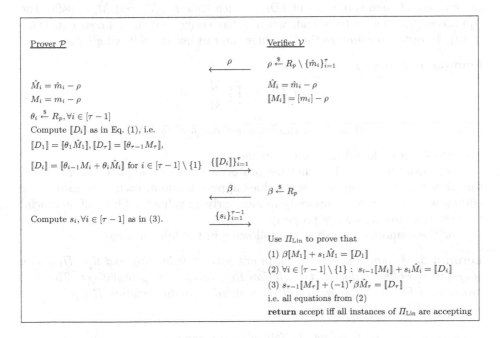

Fig. 2. The public-coin zero-knowledge protocol of correct shuffle Π_{Shuffle}.

Our public-coin zero-knowledge protocol proves this identity of evaluations of these two polynomials by showing that a particular set of linear relations (2) is satisfied (we will show later how it is related to the aforementioned product of M_i and $\hat{M}_i$).

As a first step, $\mathcal{P}$ draws $\theta_i \xleftarrow{\$} R_p$ uniformly at random for each $i \in \{1, \dots, \tau\}$, and computes the commitments

$$[\![D_1]\!] = [\![\theta_1 \hat{M}_1]\!]$$
$$\forall j \in \{2, \ldots, \tau - 1\} : \quad [\![D_j]\!] = [\![\theta_{j-1} M_j + \theta_j \hat{M}_j]\!] \tag{1}$$
$$[\![D_\tau]\!] = [\![\theta_{\tau-1} M_\tau]\!].$$

$\mathcal{P}$ then sends these commitments $\{[\![D_i]\!]\}_{i=1}^{\tau}$ to the verifier[4] $\mathcal{V}$, which in turn chooses a challenge $\beta \in R_p$, whereupon $\mathcal{P}$ computes $s_i \in R_q$ such that the following equations are satisfied:

$$\beta M_1 + s_1 \hat{M}_1 = \theta_1 \hat{M}_1$$
$$\forall j \in \{2, \ldots, \tau - 1\} : \quad s_{j-1} M_j + s_j \hat{M}_j = \theta_{j-1} M_j + \theta_j \hat{M}_j \tag{2}$$
$$s_{\tau-1} M_\tau + (-1)^\tau \beta \hat{M}_\tau = \theta_{\tau-1} M_\tau.$$

To verify the relations, $\mathcal{P}$ uses the protocol Π_{Lin} from Sect. 3 to prove that the content of each commitment $[\![D_i]\!]$ is such that D_i, M_i and $\hat{M}_i$ satisfies the equations (2). The protocol ends when $\mathcal{V}$ has verified all the τ linear equations in (2). In order to compute the s_i values, we can use the following fact:

Lemma 4. *Choosing*

$$s_j = (-1)^j \cdot \beta \prod_{i=1}^{j} \frac{M_i}{\hat{M}_i} + \theta_j \tag{3}$$

for all $j \in 1, \ldots, \tau - 1$ *yields a valid assignment for Eq. (2).*

The proof can be found in the full version.

From Lemma 4 it is clear that the protocol is indeed complete. Interestingly, this choice of s_j also makes these values appear random: each s_j is formed by adding a fixed term to a uniformly random private value θ_j. This will be crucial to show the zero-knowledge property.

For the soundness, we show the following in the full version:

Lemma 5. *Assume that the commitment scheme is binding and that* Π_{Lin} *is a sound proof of knowledge for the relation* R_{Lin} *except with probability* t. *Then the protocol in Fig. 2 is a sound proof of knowledge for the relation* R_{Shuffle} *except with probability* $\epsilon \leq \frac{\tau^\delta + 1}{|R_p|} + 4\tau t$.

From Lemmas 4 and 5 we get the following theorem:

Theorem 1. *Assume that* $(\mathrm{KeyGen}_{\mathrm{C}}, \mathrm{Com}, \mathrm{Open})$ *is a secure commitment scheme with* Π_{Lin} *as a HVZK Proof of Knowledge of the relation* R_{Lin} *with soundness error* t. *Then the protocol* Π_{Shuffle} *is an HVZK Proof of Knowledge for the relation* R_{Shuffle} *with soundness error* $(\tau^\delta + 1)/|R_p| + 4\tau t$.

The proof can be found in the full version.

---

[4] $\mathcal{P}$ does not show that these commitments are well-formed, this will not be necessary.

5   Applications to Electronic Voting

We now construct an e-voting protocol by combining the shuffle protocol from Sect. 4 with a verifiable encryption scheme and a return code mechanism.

Towards this end, consider the shuffled openings of commitments as the outcome of the election, meaning that each commitment will contain a vote. Commitments are not sufficient for a voting system, and we also need encryptions of the actual ballots and these must be tied to the commitments, so that the shuffling server can open the commitments without anyone else being able to. We use a version of the verifiable encryption scheme by Lyubashevsky and Neven [22] to verifiably encrypt openings under a public key that belongs to the shuffle server. We also reuse the verifiable encryption to get a system for return codes. The return code computation is done in two stages, where the first stage is done on the voter's computer, and the second stage is done by an infrastructure player. The voter's computer commits to its result and verifiably encrypts an opening of that commitment for the infrastructure player. Then it proves that the commitment contains the correct value.

We will now describe the verifiable encryption scheme that we use as well as the return code mechanism in more detail, before explaining how to construct the full e-voting protocol.

5.1   Verifiable Encryption

In a *verifiable encryption scheme*, anyone can verify that the encrypted plaintext has certain properties. We use a version of [22] where we use a generalization of the [7,23] encryption system. The reason is that in [22] the public key only consists of single polynomials of degree N, requiring that the plaintext vector must also be a multiple of N - which might not always be the case as in our setting. This section only describes the algorithms of the generalized scheme here, while we argue its security in the full version.

In our setting, the goal is to show that the plaintext is a value $\boldsymbol{\mu} \in D_{\beta_\infty}^\kappa$ such that

$$T\boldsymbol{\mu} = \boldsymbol{u} \bmod p, \tag{4}$$

for some fixed $T, \boldsymbol{u}$ and where $T \in R_p^{\lambda \times \kappa}$. Using the construction of [22], one can show a weaker version of the statement, namely that decryption yields a small $\bar{\boldsymbol{\mu}}$ and $\bar{c} \in \bar{C}$ over R_p such that

$$T\bar{\boldsymbol{\mu}} = \bar{c}\boldsymbol{u} \bmod p. \tag{5}$$

We will see that this will be sufficient for our voting scheme[5].

The verifiable encryption scheme consists of 4 algorithms: Key generation KeyGen_V, encryption Enc, verification Ver and decryption Dec. To generate a

---

[5] Recently, [3] showed a more efficient HVZKPoK for the respective relation. Unfortunately, their proof cannot guarantee that $\bar{c}$ is invertible, which is crucial for the verifiability of the encryption scheme. Their optimization can therefore not be applied in our setting.

public key $(\boldsymbol{A}, \boldsymbol{t})$ for the verifiable encryption scheme one samples $\boldsymbol{A} \leftarrow R_q^{\ell \times \ell}$ uniformly at random as well as $\boldsymbol{s}_1, \boldsymbol{s}_2 \leftarrow D_1^\ell$, sets $\boldsymbol{t} \leftarrow \boldsymbol{A}\boldsymbol{s}_1 + \boldsymbol{s}_2$ and outputs $(\boldsymbol{A}, \boldsymbol{t})$ as public key as well as $\boldsymbol{s}_1$ as private key. The encryption, verification and decryption algorithms are described in Figs. 3, 4 and 5 respectively. Here, encryption follows [7,23] but additionally computes a NIZK that the plaintext is a valid preimage of Eq. 4 and also bounded. Ver validates the NIZK, while Dec decrypts to a short plaintext that is valid under Eq. 5.

There are multiple parameter restrictions in [22] in order to achieve security. These also apply to our setting:

1. The underlying encryption scheme must safely be able to encrypt and decrypt messages from R_p^κ. For this, we obviously need that message and noise, upon decryption, do not "overflow" $\mod q$ while the noise at the same time must be large enough such that the underlying MLWE-problem is hard. For concrete parameters, the latter can be established by e.g. using the LWE Estimator [2]. For correctness of the decryption alone, we require that the decryption of a correct encryption must yield[6] a value $< q/2$. This also means that the decryption algorithm will always terminate for $\bar{c} = 1$ in case the encryptor is honest.
2. The NIZK requires "quasi-unique responses", which (as the authors of [22] argue) it will have with overwhelming probability over the choice of $\boldsymbol{A}$ as long as $24\sigma_E^2 < q$.

Encrypting Openings of Commitments. We want to make sure that the voter actually knows his vote, and that the commitment and the opening of the commitment are well-formed. We also want to ensure that the ciphertext actually contains a valid opening of the commitment. This can be achieved if the voter creates a proof that the underlying plaintext is an opening of the commitment. Then the ballot box can ensure that the shuffle server will be able to decrypt the vote and use it in the shuffle protocol. Note that the voter may send a well-formed but invalid vote, but then the shuffle server can publicly discard that vote later, and everyone can check that the vote indeed was invalid.

Recall that the commitment is of the form

$$\mathrm{Com}(m; \boldsymbol{r}_m) = \begin{bmatrix} c_1 \\ c_2 \end{bmatrix} = \begin{bmatrix} \boldsymbol{B}_1 \\ \boldsymbol{b}_2 \end{bmatrix} \cdot \boldsymbol{r}_m + \begin{bmatrix} \boldsymbol{0} \\ m \end{bmatrix}.$$

The value c_1 serves to bind the committer to a single choice of $\boldsymbol{r}_m$, while c_2 hides the actual message using the unique $\boldsymbol{r}_m$. Fixing $\boldsymbol{r}_m$ fixes m uniquely, and m can indeed be recovered using $\boldsymbol{r}_m$ only. The idea is to use the verifiable encryption scheme to encrypt the opening $\boldsymbol{r}_m$, and prove that the voter knows a witness for the relation $c_1 = \boldsymbol{B}_1\boldsymbol{r}_m \mod p$ where $\boldsymbol{r}_m$ is bounded. Any such randomness could then be used to uniquely open the commitment.

---

[6] This translates into the requirement that $q > 2p(2\ell \cdot N^2 \cdot \beta_\infty^2 + N + 1)$.

Input: Public key $\mathrm{pk} = (\boldsymbol{A}, \boldsymbol{t}, p, q)$, pair $(\boldsymbol{T}, \boldsymbol{u}), \boldsymbol{\mu} \in D_\beta^\kappa$ such that
$\boldsymbol{T\mu} = \boldsymbol{u}$, hash function $H : \{0,1\}^* \to \mathcal{C}$,
$$\sigma_E = 11 \cdot \max_{c \in \mathcal{C}} \|c\| \cdot \sqrt{\kappa N(3+\beta)}$$
Output: ciphertext $(\boldsymbol{v}, \boldsymbol{w}, c, \boldsymbol{z}) \in R_q^{\ell \cdot \kappa} \times R_q^\kappa \times \mathcal{C} \times R^{(2\ell+2)\kappa}$

1: $\boldsymbol{r}, \boldsymbol{e} \stackrel{\$}{\leftarrow} D_1^{\ell \cdot \kappa}, \boldsymbol{e}' \stackrel{\$}{\leftarrow} D_1^\kappa$

2: $\begin{bmatrix} \boldsymbol{v} \\ \boldsymbol{w} \end{bmatrix} \leftarrow \begin{bmatrix} \boldsymbol{A}^\top \otimes (p\boldsymbol{I}_\kappa) & p\boldsymbol{I}_{\ell \cdot \kappa} & \boldsymbol{0}^{(\ell \cdot \kappa) \times \kappa} & \boldsymbol{0}^{(\ell \cdot \kappa) \times \kappa} \\ \boldsymbol{t}^\top \otimes (p\boldsymbol{I}_\kappa) & \boldsymbol{0}^{\kappa \times (\ell \cdot \kappa)} & p\boldsymbol{I}_\kappa & \boldsymbol{I}_\kappa \end{bmatrix} \begin{bmatrix} \boldsymbol{r} & \boldsymbol{e} & \boldsymbol{e}' & \boldsymbol{\mu} \end{bmatrix}^\top$

3: $\boldsymbol{y} \leftarrow \begin{bmatrix} \boldsymbol{y}_r & \boldsymbol{y}_e & \boldsymbol{y}_{e'} & \boldsymbol{y}_\mu \end{bmatrix}^\top \stackrel{\$}{\leftarrow} D_{R^{(2\ell+2)\kappa}, 0, \sigma_E}$

4: $\boldsymbol{Y} \leftarrow \begin{bmatrix} \boldsymbol{A}^\top \otimes (p\boldsymbol{I}_\kappa) & p\boldsymbol{I}_{\ell \cdot \kappa} & \boldsymbol{0}^{(\ell \cdot \kappa) \times \kappa} & \boldsymbol{0}^{(\ell \cdot \kappa) \times \kappa} \\ \boldsymbol{t}^\top \otimes (p\boldsymbol{I}_\kappa) & \boldsymbol{0}^{\kappa \times (\ell \cdot \kappa)} & p\boldsymbol{I}_\kappa & \boldsymbol{I}_\kappa \\ \boldsymbol{0}^{\lambda \times (\ell \cdot \kappa)} & \boldsymbol{0}^{\lambda \times (\ell \cdot \kappa)} & \boldsymbol{0}^{\lambda \times \kappa} & \boldsymbol{T} \end{bmatrix} \begin{bmatrix} \boldsymbol{y}_r & \boldsymbol{y}_e & \boldsymbol{y}_{e'} & \boldsymbol{y}_\mu \end{bmatrix}^\top \begin{matrix} \mod q \\ \mod q \\ \mod p \end{matrix}$

5: $c \leftarrow H \left(\begin{bmatrix} \boldsymbol{A}^\top \otimes (p\boldsymbol{I}_\kappa) & p\boldsymbol{I}_{\ell \cdot \kappa} & \boldsymbol{0}^{(\ell \cdot \kappa) \times \kappa} & \boldsymbol{0}^{(\ell \cdot \kappa) \times \kappa} \\ \boldsymbol{t}^\top \otimes (p\boldsymbol{I}_\kappa) & \boldsymbol{0}^{\kappa \times (\ell \cdot \kappa)} & p\boldsymbol{I}_\kappa & \boldsymbol{I}_\kappa \\ \boldsymbol{0}^{\lambda \times (\ell \cdot \kappa)} & \boldsymbol{0}^{\lambda \times (\ell \cdot \kappa)} & \boldsymbol{0}^{\lambda \times \kappa} & \boldsymbol{T} \end{bmatrix}, \begin{bmatrix} \boldsymbol{v} \\ \boldsymbol{w} \\ \boldsymbol{u} \end{bmatrix}, \boldsymbol{Y} \right)$

6: $\boldsymbol{s} \leftarrow \begin{bmatrix} \boldsymbol{r} & \boldsymbol{e} & \boldsymbol{e}' & \boldsymbol{\mu} \end{bmatrix}^\top c$

7: $\boldsymbol{z} \leftarrow \boldsymbol{s} + \boldsymbol{y}$

8: With probability $1 - \min \left(1, \dfrac{D_{R^{(2\ell+2)\kappa}, 0, \sigma_E}(\boldsymbol{z})}{3 \cdot D_{R^{(2\ell+2)\kappa}, \boldsymbol{s}, \sigma_E}(\boldsymbol{z})} \right)$ goto 3

9: if $\|\boldsymbol{z}\|_\infty \geq 6\sigma_E$ goto 3, **else return** $\boldsymbol{e} = (\boldsymbol{v}, \boldsymbol{w}, c, \boldsymbol{z})$

Fig. 3. The verifiable encryption algorithm Enc.

Input: Secret key $\mathrm{sk} = (\boldsymbol{s}_1)$, pair $x = (\boldsymbol{T}, \boldsymbol{u})$,
ciphertext $t = (\boldsymbol{v}, \boldsymbol{w}, c, \boldsymbol{z}), C = \max_{c \in \overline{C}} \|c\|_\infty$

1: **if** Ver$(t, x, \mathrm{pk}) = 1$ **then**

2:     **while**

3:        $c' \stackrel{\$}{\leftarrow} \mathcal{C}$

4:        $\overline{c} \leftarrow c - c'$

5:        $\overline{\boldsymbol{m}}[i] \leftarrow (\boldsymbol{w} - \langle \boldsymbol{s}_1, \boldsymbol{v}_i \rangle)\overline{c} \mod q$ for all $i \in [\kappa]$

6:        **if** $\|\overline{\boldsymbol{m}}\|_\infty \leq q/2C$ and $\|\overline{\boldsymbol{m}} \mod p\|_\infty < 12\sigma_E$ **then**

7:          **return** $(\overline{\boldsymbol{m}} \mod p, \overline{c})$

Fig. 4. Algorithm Dec for decryption of a ciphertext.

Input: ciphertext $t = (\boldsymbol{v}, \boldsymbol{w}, c, \boldsymbol{z}) \in R_q^{\ell \cdot \kappa} \times R_q^\kappa \times R_q \times R^{(2\ell+2)\kappa}$, language element $x = (\boldsymbol{T}, \boldsymbol{u})$,
public key $\mathrm{pk} = (\boldsymbol{A}, \boldsymbol{t}, p, q)$

1: **if** $\|\boldsymbol{z}\|_\infty > 6 \cdot \sigma_E$ **then return** 0

2: $\boldsymbol{Z} \leftarrow \begin{bmatrix} \boldsymbol{A}^\top \otimes (p\boldsymbol{I}_\kappa) & p\boldsymbol{I}_{\ell \cdot \kappa} & \boldsymbol{0}^{(\ell \cdot \kappa) \times \kappa} & \boldsymbol{0}^{(\ell \cdot \kappa) \times \kappa} \\ \boldsymbol{t}^\top \otimes (p\boldsymbol{I}_\kappa) & \boldsymbol{0}^{\kappa \times (\ell \cdot \kappa)} & p\boldsymbol{I}_\kappa & \boldsymbol{I}_\kappa \\ \boldsymbol{0}^{\lambda \times (\ell \cdot \kappa)} & \boldsymbol{0}^{\lambda \times (\ell \cdot \kappa)} & \boldsymbol{0}^{\lambda \times \kappa} & \boldsymbol{T} \end{bmatrix} \boldsymbol{z} - c \begin{bmatrix} \boldsymbol{v} \\ \boldsymbol{w} \\ \boldsymbol{u} \end{bmatrix} \begin{matrix} \mod q \\ \mod q \\ \mod p \end{matrix}$

3: **if** $c \neq \mathrm{H} \left(\begin{bmatrix} \boldsymbol{A}^\top \otimes (p\boldsymbol{I}_\kappa) & p\boldsymbol{I}_{\ell \cdot \kappa} & \boldsymbol{0}^{(\ell \cdot \kappa) \times \kappa} & \boldsymbol{0}^{(\ell \cdot \kappa) \times \kappa} \\ \boldsymbol{t}^\top \otimes (p\boldsymbol{I}_\kappa) & \boldsymbol{0}^{\kappa \times (\ell \cdot \kappa)} & p\boldsymbol{I}_\kappa & \boldsymbol{I}_\kappa \\ \boldsymbol{0}^{\lambda \times (\ell \cdot \kappa)} & \boldsymbol{0}^{\lambda \times (\ell \cdot \kappa)} & \boldsymbol{0}^{\lambda \times \kappa} & \boldsymbol{T} \end{bmatrix}, \begin{bmatrix} \boldsymbol{v} \\ \boldsymbol{w} \\ \boldsymbol{u} \end{bmatrix}, \boldsymbol{Z} \right)$ **then return** 0

4: **return** 1

Fig. 5. Algorithm Ver for verification of a ciphertext.

To encrypt the opening r_m verifiably, Step 4 in Fig. 3 is now the system

$$\begin{bmatrix} v \\ w \\ c_1 \end{bmatrix} = \begin{bmatrix} A^\top \otimes (pI_\kappa) & pI_{\ell \cdot \kappa} & 0^{(\ell \cdot \kappa) \times \kappa} & 0^{(\ell \cdot \kappa) \times \kappa} \\ t^\top \otimes (pI_\kappa) & 0^{\kappa \times (\ell \cdot \kappa)} & pI_\kappa & I_\kappa \\ 0^{\lambda \times (\ell \cdot \kappa)} & 0^{\lambda \times (\ell \cdot \kappa)} & 0^{\lambda \times \kappa} & B_1 \end{bmatrix} \cdot \begin{bmatrix} r \\ e \\ e' \\ r_m \end{bmatrix} .$$

5.2   Return Codes

In the case of a malicious computer, we need to make sure that the voter can detect if the encrypted vote being sent to the ballot box is not an encryption of the correct ballot. We achieve this by giving the voter a pre-computed table of return codes which he can use for verification. The return codes are generated per voter, using a voter-unique blinding-key and a system-wide PRF-key.

A commitment to the blinding key is made public. The computer gets the blinding-key and must create a pre-code by blinding the ballot with the blinding-key. The computer also generates commitments to the ballot and the pre-code, along with a proof that the pre-code has been generated correctly. Anyone with an opening of the pre-code commitment and the PRF-key can now generate the correct return code without learning anything about the ballot.

Defining the Return Code. Assume that the voters have ω different options in the election. Let $\hat{v}_1, \hat{v}_2, \ldots, \hat{v}_\omega \in R_p$ be ballots, let $a_j \in R_p$ be a blinding-key for a voter V_j and let $\mathsf{PRF}_k : \{0,1\}^* \times R_p \to \{0,1\}^n$ be a pseudo-random function, instantiated with a PRF-key k, from pairs of binary strings and elements from R_p to the set of binary strings of length n. The *pre-code* $\hat{r}_{ij}$ corresponding to the ballot $\hat{v}_i$ is $\hat{r}_{ij} = a_j + \hat{v}_i \mod p$. The *return code* r_{ij} corresponding to the ballot $\hat{v}_i$ is $r_{ij} = \mathsf{PRF}_k(V_j, \hat{r}_{ij})$.

Let c_{a_j}, c_j and $c_{\hat{r}_j}$ be commitments to the blinding key a_j, the ballot $v_j \in \{\hat{v}_1, \ldots, \hat{v}_\omega\}$ and the pre-code $\hat{r}_j = a_j + v_j \mod p$. It is now clear that we can prove that a given $\hat{r}_j$ value has been correctly computed by giving a proof of linearity that $a_j + v_j = \hat{r}_j$. This can be done either by adding the commitments c_{a_j} and c_j together directly to get a commitment $c_{a_j+v_j}$ with larger randomness (if the choice of parameters allows for the sum of the randomness to be a valid opening of the commitment) and then prove the equality of the committed messages, or to extend the proof of linearity to handle three terms. Our return code construction is now straight-forward:

A commitment c_{a_j} to voter V_j's voter-unique blinding key a_j is public. The voter V_j's *computer* will get the voter-unique blinding-key a_j together with the randomness used to create c_{a_j}. It has already created a commitment c_j to the ballot v_j. It will compute the pre-code $\hat{r}_j = a_j + v_j$, a commitment $c_{\hat{r}_j}$ to $\hat{r}_j$ and a proof $\Pi_{\hat{r}_j}$ of knowledge of the opening of that sum. Finally, it will verifiably encrypt as $e_{\hat{r}_j}$ the opening of $c_{\hat{r}_j}$ with the return code generator's public key.

The *return code generator* receives V_j, $c_{\hat{r}_j}$, c_j, $e_{\hat{r}_j}$ and $\Pi_{\hat{r}_j}$. It verifies the proof and the encryption, and then decrypts the ciphertext to get $\hat{r}_j$. It computes the return code as $r_j = \mathsf{PRF}_k(V_j, \hat{r}_j)$.

Note that if a voter re-votes (such as when exposed to coercion), the return code generator would be able to learn something about the ballots involved. We give a return code mechanism for re-voting in the full version of the paper.

5.3 The Voting Scheme

We get our e-voting protocol by combining the shuffle protocol with the verifiable encryption scheme and the return code construction. A complete description of this protocol can be found in Fig. 6 and we elaborate more on it in the full version. All communication happens over secure channels. We discuss the *privacy*, *integrity* and *coercion resistance* of the voting scheme in detail in the full version.

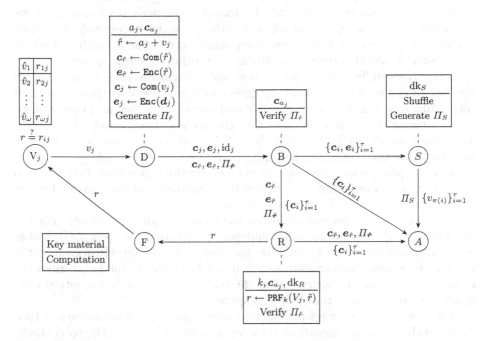

Fig. 6. Complete voting protocol. A voter V_j gives a vote v_j to their computer D. The value d_j is the opening of the commitment c_j. The public keys for commitments and encryption are assumed known to all parties. Signatures are omitted: D signs the vote to be verified by the ballot box B and the return code server R, while R signs the incoming votes and sends the signature in return, via B, to D to confirm that the vote is received. Both B and R sends the commitments of the votes to authorities A to verify consistent views. After all votes are cast, B forwards them to the shuffle server S, stripping away the voters id's and signatures.

Registration Phase. The only thing that happens in this phase is key generation. Every player generates their own key material and publishes the public keys and any other commitments.

The voter's computer, the return code generator and a *trusted printer* then use a multi-party computation protocol[7] to compute the ballot-return code pairs for the voter, such that only the trusted printer learns the pairs. The trusted printer then sends these pairs to the voter through a secure channel. We emphasize that for many voters, the registration phase likely requires significant computational resources for the return code generator and the trusted printer. In practice, the voter's computer will usually play a minor role in this key generation.

Casting a Ballot. The voter begins the ballot casting by giving the ballot v_j to the voter's computer.

The voter's computer has the per-voter secret key material, and gets the ballot v_j to be cast from the voter. It computes the pre-code $\hat{r}$ and generates commitments c_j and $c_{\hat{r}}$ to the ballot and the pre-code, respectively. It creates a proof $\Pi_{\hat{r}}$ that the pre-code has been correctly computed (with respect to the commitments). It creates a verifiable encryption e_j of an opening of c_j to v_j under the shuffle server's public key, and a verifiable encryption $e_{\hat{r}}$ of an opening of $c_{\hat{r}}$ under the return code generator's public key. It then signs all of these values, together with its identity and every public key and commitment used to create the proofs. We note that the voter's identity and relevant keys and commitments are included in the proofs used. (This is not an artefact of making the security proof work, but it prevents real-world attacks.)

The computer sends the commitments, encryptions, proofs and signature to the ballot box. The ballot box verifies the signature and the proofs. Then it sends everything to the return code generator.

The return code generator verifies the signature and the proofs. Then it decrypts the opening of $e_{\hat{r}}$ and computes the return code from $\hat{r}$. It hashes everything and creates a signature on the hash. It sends the return code to the voter's phone and the signature to the ballot box. The ballot box verifies the return code generator's signature on the hash. Then it sends the return code generator's signature to the voter's computer.

The voter's computer verifies the return code generator's signature and then shows the hash and the signature to the voter as the transcript. The voter checks that the computer accepts the ballot as cast. When the phone displays the return code r, the voter accepts the ballot as cast if (v_j, r) is in the return code table.

Tallying. When the tally phase begins, the ballot box sends everything from every successful ballot casting to the auditors. It extracts the commitments to the ballots and the encrypted openings (without any proofs), organizes them into a sorted list of commitment-ciphertext pairs and sends the sorted list to the shuffle server. The return code generator sends everything from every successful ballot

---

[7] Since this happens before the election, speed is no longer essential. Even so, for the computations involved here, ordinary MPC is sufficiently practical. In a practical deployment, the voter's computer is unlikely to be part of this computation. It would instead be delegated to a set of trusted key generation players.

casting to the auditors. The shuffle server receives a sorted list of commitment-ciphertext pairs from the ballot box. It hashes the list and sends a hash to the auditors. The shuffle server waits for the auditors to accept provisionally.

An auditor receives data from the ballot box and the return code generator, and a hash from the shuffle server. If the data from the ballot box and the return code generator agree, the auditor extracts the sorted commitment-ciphertext pairs from the data, hashes it and compares the result with the hash from the shuffle server. If it matches, the auditor provisionally accepts.

When the shuffle server receives the provisional accept, it decrypts the commitment openings and verifies that the openings are valid. For any invalid opening, it sends the commitment-ciphertext pair and the opening to the auditors. It then sorts the ballots and creates a shuffle proof for the ballots and the commitments. It then counts the ballots to get the election result and sends the ballots, the shuffle proof and the result to the auditors.

An auditor receives the ballots, the shuffle proof and the result from the shuffle server. It verifies the proof and that the election result is correct. It extracts the hashes (but not the signatures) signed by the return code generator from the ballot box data and creates a sorted list of hashes. It signs the hash list and the result and send both signature and hash list to the shuffle server. Once the shuffle server has received signatures and hash lists from every auditor, it verifies that the hash lists are identical and that the signatures verify. It then outputs the result, the hash list and the auditors' signatures as the transcript.

Verification. The voter has the transcript output by the voter's computer and the transcript output by the shuffle server. It first verifies that the hash from the computer's transcript is present in the shuffle server's hash list. Then it verifies all the signatures. If everything checks out, the voter accepts.

6   Performance

As outlined in our construction, we are nesting the commitment scheme of [5] into the encryption scheme of [22]. To determine secure while not enormously big parameters for our scheme, we need to first make sure that we have sufficiently large parameters to ensure both binding and hiding of the commitments for which we will use the "optimal" parameter set of [5] (but with twice the standard deviation to keep the probability of abort in the rejection sampling down to 3 trials for the proofs of linearity) which is both computationally binding and hiding (see Table 2). The LWE-estimator [2] estimates at least 100 bits of security with these parameters. We then instantiate the verifiable encryption scheme with compatible parameters, which is possible due to our generalization of [22]. The verifiable encryption scheme will then yield decryptions with an ∞-norm that is way below the bound for which the commitment scheme is binding, so any valid decryption which differs from the original vote would break the binding of the commitment scheme. In general, the instantiation of the encryption scheme offers much higher security than the commitment scheme, but the

Table 1. Parameters for the commitment and verifiable encryption schemes.

Parameter	Explanation	Constraints
N, δ	Degree of polynomial $X^N + 1$ in R	$N \geq \delta \geq 1$, where N, δ powers of two
p	Modulus for commitments	Prime $p = 2\delta + 1 \mod 4\delta$
β_∞	∞-norm bound of certain elements	Choose β_∞ such that $\beta_\infty < p^{1/\delta}/\sqrt{\delta}$
σ_C	Standard deviation of discrete Gaussians	Chosen to be $\sigma_C = 22 \cdot \nu \cdot \beta_\infty \cdot \sqrt{kN}$
k	Width (over R_p) of commitment matrix	
n	Height (over R_p) of commitment matrix	
ν	Maximum l_1-norm of elements in $\mathcal{C}$	
$\mathcal{C}$	Challenge space	$\mathcal{C} = \{c \in R_p \mid \|c\|_\infty = 1, \|c\|_1 = \nu\}$
$\bar{\mathcal{C}}$	The set of differences $\mathcal{C} - \mathcal{C}$ excluding 0	$\bar{\mathcal{C}} = \{c - c' \mid c \neq c' \in \mathcal{C}\}$
D_{β_∞}	Set of elements of ∞-norm at most β_∞	$D_{\beta_\infty} = \{x \in R_p \mid \|x\|_\infty \leq \beta_\infty\}$
σ_E	Standard deviation of discrete Gaussians	Chosen to be $\sigma_E = 11 \cdot \nu \cdot \sqrt{\kappa N(3 + \beta_\infty)}$
κ	Dimension of message space in encryption	Equal to the length of randomness k
ℓ	Dimension the encryption matrix	Equal to the size of the commitments $k - n$
λ	Dimension of public $\boldsymbol{u}$ in $T\mu = \boldsymbol{u}$	Equal to the height $n + 1$ of the commitment matrix
q	Modulus for encryption	Must choose prime q such that $q > 24\sigma_E^2$ and $q > 2p(2\ell \cdot N^2 \cdot {\beta_\infty}^2 + N + 1)$ and $q = 2\delta + 1 \mod 4\delta$
τ	Total number of votes	For soundness we need $(\tau^\delta + 1)/|R_p| < 2^{-128}$

choice of parameters are restricted by the constraints from combining it with the commitments (Table 2).

6.1 Size

Size of the Votes. Note that each ciphertext $\boldsymbol{e}$ includes both the encrypted opening $(\boldsymbol{v}, \boldsymbol{w})$ and the proof of valid opening $(\boldsymbol{c}, \boldsymbol{z})$. Using a lattice based signature scheme like Falcon-768 [26], we have signatures of size $\approx 1\,\mathrm{KB}$. The voter verifiability protocol requires a commitment, an encryption + proof, and a proof of linearity. It follows that a vote $(\boldsymbol{c}_j, \boldsymbol{e}_j, \boldsymbol{c}_{\hat{r}}, \boldsymbol{e}_{\hat{r}}, \Pi_{\hat{r}})$ is of total size $\approx 235\,\mathrm{KB}$, which means that, for τ voters, the ballot box $\mathcal{B}$ receives $235\tau\,\mathrm{KB}$ of data.

Size of the Shuffle Proof. Our shuffle protocol is a $4 + 3\tau$-move protocol with elements from R_p. Each element in R_p has at most N coefficients of size at most p, and hence, each R_p-element has size at most $N \log p$ bits. For every R_p-vector that follows a Gaussian distribution with standard deviation σ we assume that we can represent the element using $N \cdot \log(6\sigma)$ bits. Every element from $\mathcal{C}$ will be assumed to be representable using at most $2N$ bits.

We analyze how much data we have to include in each step of the shuffling protocol in Fig. 2. Using the Fiat-Shamir transform [12], we can ignore the challenge-messages from the verifier. The prover ends up sending 1 commitment, 1 ring-element and 1 proof of linearity per vote. Using the parameters from Table 2, we get that the shuffle proof is of total size $\approx 17\tau\,\mathrm{KB}$.

6.2 Timings

We collected performance figures from our prototype implementation written in C to estimate the runtime of our scheme. Estimates are based on Table 2 and the implementation was benchmarked on an Intel Skylake Core i7-6700K CPU running at 4 GHz without TurboBoost using `clang` 12.0 and FLINT 2.7.1 [18]. Timings are available in Table 3, and the source code can be found on GitHub[8].

Table 2. Parameters for the commitments by Baum et al. [5] and verifiable encryption scheme by Lyubashevsky and Neven [22].

Parameter	Commitment (I)	Encryption (III)
N	1024	1024
p	$\approx 2^{32}$	$\approx 2^{32}$
q	-	$\approx 2^{56}$
β_∞	1	1
σ	$\sigma_C \approx 54000$	$\sigma_E \approx 54000$
ν	36	36
δ	2	2
k	3	-
n	1	-
ℓ	-	2
κ	-	3
λ	-	2
Proof	4.7 KB	42.4 KB
Primitive	8.2 KB	64.5 KB

Table 3. Timings for cryptographic operations. Numbers were obtained by computing the average of 10^4 consecutive executions of an operation measured using the cycle counter available in the platform.

Our scheme:	Commit	Open	Encrypt	Verify	Decrypt	Shuffle
Time	1.1 ms	1.2 ms	208 ms	39 ms	6 ms	27τ ms

Elementary Operations. Multiplication in R_p and R_q is usually implemented when $p \equiv q \equiv 1 \bmod (2N)$ and $X^N + 1$ splits in N linear factors, for which the Number-Theoretic Transform is available. Unfortunately, Lemma 1 restricts parameters and we instead adopt $p \equiv q \equiv 5 \bmod 8$ [22]. In this case, $X^N + 1$ splits in two $N/2$-degree irreducible polynomials $(X^{N/2} \pm r)$ for r a modular square root of -1. This gives an efficient representation for $a = a_1 X^{N/2} + a_0$ using the

---

[8] https://github.com/dfaranha/lattice-voting-ctrsa21.

Chinese Remainder Theorem: $CRT(a) = (a \pmod{X^{N/2} - r}, a \pmod{X^{N/2} + r})$. Even though the conversions are efficient due to the choice of polynomials, we sample ring elements directly in this representation whenever possible. As in [24], we implement the base case for degree $N/2$ using FLINT for polynomial arithmetic [18]. We use SHA256 for hashing to generate challenges.

Commitment. A commitment is generated by multiplying the matrix $\boldsymbol{B}$ by a vector $\boldsymbol{r}_m$ over R_p and finally adding the message m to the second component in the CRT domain. Computing and opening a commitment takes 0.9 ms and 1.2 ms, respectively, and sampling randomness $\boldsymbol{r}_m$ takes only 0.2 ms.

Verifiable Encryption. Verifiable encryption needs to sample vectors according to a discrete Gaussian distribution. For an R_q element with standard deviation $\sigma_E \approx 2^{15.7}$ (for the encryption scheme), the implementation from COSAC [28] made available for $\sigma = 2^{17}$ samples 1024 integers in 0.12 ms using very small precomputation tables. Each encryption iteration takes 69 ms and, because we expect to need 3 attempts to generate one valid encryption (line 8 in Fig. 3), the total time of encryption is around 208 ms. For verification, 39 ms are necessary to execute a test; and 6 ms are required for the actual decryption.

Shuffle Proof. The shuffle proof operates over R_p and is thus more efficient. Sampling uses the same approach as above for σ_C from the commitment scheme. Benchmarking includes all samplings required inside the protocol, the commitment, the proof of linearity and, because we expect to need 3 attempts to generate each of the proofs of linearity to the cost of 7.5 ms, amounts to 27τ ms for the entire proof, omitting the communication cost.

6.3   Comparison

We briefly compare our scheme with the scheme by del Pino et al. [11] from CCS 2017 in Table 4. We note that the scheme in [11] requires at least $\xi \geq 2$ authorities to ensure ballot privacy, where at least one authority must be honest. The authorities run the proof protocol in parallel, and the time they need to process each vote is ≈ 5 times slower per vote than in our scheme. We only need one party to compute the shuffle proof, where we first decrypt all votes and then shuffle. Our proof size is at least 19 KB smaller per vote when $\xi = 2$, that is, a saving of more than 50%, and otherwise much smaller in comparison for $\xi \geq 3$. We further note that both implementations partially rely on FLINT for polynomial arithmetic and were benchmarked on Intel Skylake processors. A significant speedup persists after correcting for clock frequency differences.

Table 4. Comparing our scheme with the yes/no voting scheme in [11]

Comparison	Vote size	Voter time	Proof size	Prover time
Our scheme:	115 KB	209 ms	17τ KB	33τ ms
CCS 2017 [11]:	20ξ KB	9 ms	$18\xi\tau$ KB	150τ ms

For a fair comparison, we only included the size and timings of the commitment of the vote and the encrypted openings from our scheme. In practice, the size and timings of the voter will be twice of what it is in the table, because of the return code mechanism, which is not a part of [11]. This has no impact on the decryption and shuffle done by the prover. The work done by the voter is still practical. For [11] to be used in a real world election, they would need to include an additional mechanism for providing voter verifiability, like the one we have constructed.

Finally, we note that [11] can be extended from yes/no voting to votes consisting of strings of bits. However, the size and timings of such an extension will be linear in the length of the bit-strings, and our scheme would do even better in comparison, as we can handle votes encoded as arbitrary ring-elements.

Thanks

We thank Andreas Hülsing and the anonymous reviewers for their helpful comments.

References

1. Adida, B.: Helios: web-based open-audit voting. In: USENIX Security 2008. USENIX Association, July–August 2008
2. Albrecht, M.R., Player, R., Scott, S.: On the concrete hardness of learning with errors. J. Math. Cryptol. **9**(3), 169–203 (2015)
3. Attema, T., Lyubashevsky, V., Seiler, G.: Practical product proofs for lattice commitments. In: Micciancio, D., Ristenpart, T. (eds.) CRYPTO 2020, Part II. LNCS, vol. 12171, pp. 470–499. Springer, Cham (2020). https://doi.org/10.1007/978-3-030-56880-1_17
4. Bai, S., Galbraith, S.D.: An improved compression technique for signatures based on learning with errors. In: Benaloh, J. (ed.) CT-RSA 2014. LNCS, vol. 8366, pp. 28–47. Springer, Cham (2014). https://doi.org/10.1007/978-3-319-04852-9_2
5. Baum, C., Damgård, I., Lyubashevsky, V., Oechsner, S., Peikert, C.: More efficient commitments from structured lattice assumptions. In: Catalano, D., De Prisco, R. (eds.) SCN 2018. LNCS, vol. 11035, pp. 368–385. Springer, Cham (2018). https://doi.org/10.1007/978-3-319-98113-0_20
6. Boyen, X., Haines, T., Müller, J.: A verifiable and practical lattice-based decryption mix net with external auditing. In: Chen, L., Li, N., Liang, K., Schneider, S. (eds.) ESORICS 2020, Part II. LNCS, vol. 12309, pp. 336–356. Springer, Cham (2020). https://doi.org/10.1007/978-3-030-59013-0_17

7. Brakerski, Z., Gentry, C., Vaikuntanathan, V.: (Leveled) fully homomorphic encryption without bootstrapping. In: ITCS 2012. ACM, January 2012
8. Chaum, D.: Untraceable electronic mail, return addresses, and digital pseudonyms. Commun. ACM **24**(2), 84–88 (1981)
9. Chillotti, I., Gama, N., Georgieva, M., Izabachène, M.: A homomorphic LWE based e-voting scheme. In: Takagi, T. (ed.) PQCrypto 2016. LNCS, vol. 9606, pp. 245–265. Springer, Cham (2016). https://doi.org/10.1007/978-3-319-29360-8_16
10. Costa, N., Martínez, R., Morillo, P.: Lattice-based proof of a shuffle. In: Bracciali, A., Clark, J., Pintore, F., Rønne, P.B., Sala, M. (eds.) FC 2019 Workshops. LNCS, vol. 11599, pp. 330–346. Springer, Cham (2020). https://doi.org/10.1007/978-3-030-43725-1_23
11. del Pino, R., Lyubashevsky, V., Neven, G., Seiler, G.: Practical quantum-safe voting from lattices. In: ACM CCS 2017. ACM Press, October–November 2017
12. Fiat, A., Shamir, A.: How to prove yourself: practical solutions to identification and signature problems. In: Odlyzko, A.M. (ed.) CRYPTO 1986. LNCS, vol. 263, pp. 186–194. Springer, Heidelberg (1987). https://doi.org/10.1007/3-540-47721-7_12
13. Gjøsteen, K.: The Norwegian internet voting protocol. In: E-Voting and Identity - Third International Conference, VoteID 2011, pp. 1–18 (2011)
14. Gjøsteen, K., Lund, A.S.: An experiment on the security of the Norwegian electronic voting protocol. Ann. Telecommun. 1–9 (2016
15. Gjøsteen, K., Strand, M.: A roadmap to fully homomorphic elections: stronger security, better verifiability. In: Brenner, M., et al. (eds.) FC 2017 Workshops. LNCS, vol. 10323, pp. 404–418. Springer, Cham (2017). https://doi.org/10.1007/978-3-319-70278-0_25
16. Güneysu, T., Lyubashevsky, V., Pöppelmann, T.: Practical lattice-based cryptography: a signature scheme for embedded systems. In: Prouff, E., Schaumont, P. (eds.) CHES 2012. LNCS, vol. 7428, pp. 530–547. Springer, Heidelberg (2012). https://doi.org/10.1007/978-3-642-33027-8_31
17. Hao, F., Ryan, P.Y.A. (eds.): Real-World Electronic Voting: Design, Analysis and Deployment. CRC Press, Boca Raton (2016)
18. Hart, W., Johansson, F., Pancratz, S.: FLINT: fast library for number theory (2013). Version 2.4.0, http://flintlib.org
19. Lewis, S.J., Pereira, O., Teague, V.: Trapdoor commitments in the SwissPost e-voting shuffle proof (2019)
20. Lyubashevsky, V.: Fiat-Shamir with aborts: applications to lattice and factoring-based signatures. In: Matsui, M. (ed.) ASIACRYPT 2009. LNCS, vol. 5912, pp. 598–616. Springer, Heidelberg (2009). https://doi.org/10.1007/978-3-642-10366-7_35
21. Lyubashevsky, V.: Lattice signatures without trapdoors. In: Pointcheval, D., Johansson, T. (eds.) EUROCRYPT 2012. LNCS, vol. 7237, pp. 738–755. Springer, Heidelberg (2012). https://doi.org/10.1007/978-3-642-29011-4_43
22. Lyubashevsky, V., Neven, G.: One-shot verifiable encryption from lattices. In: Coron, J.-S., Nielsen, J.B. (eds.) EUROCRYPT 2017, Part I. LNCS, vol. 10210, pp. 293–323. Springer, Cham (2017). https://doi.org/10.1007/978-3-319-56620-7_11
23. Lyubashevsky, V., Peikert, C., Regev, O.: A toolkit for ring-lwe cryptography. In: Johansson, T., Nguyen, P.Q. (eds.) EUROCRYPT 2013. LNCS, vol. 7881, pp. 35–54. Springer, Heidelberg (2013). https://doi.org/10.1007/978-3-642-38348-9_3
24. Lyubashevsky, V., Seiler, G.: Short, invertible elements in partially splitting cyclotomic rings and applications to lattice-based zero-knowledge proofs. In: Nielsen, J.B., Rijmen, V. (eds.) EUROCRYPT 2018, Part I. LNCS, vol. 10820, pp. 204–224. Springer, Cham (2018). https://doi.org/10.1007/978-3-319-78381-9_8

25. Neff, C.A.: A verifiable secret shuffle and its application to e-voting. In: ACM CCS 2001. ACM Press, November 2001
26. Prest, T., et al.: FALCON. Technical report, National Institute of Standards and Technology (2017). https://csrc.nist.gov/projects/post-quantum-cryptography/round-1-submissions
27. Strand, M.: A verifiable shuffle for the GSW cryptosystem. In: Zohar, A., et al. (eds.) FC 2018 Workshops. LNCS, vol. 10958, pp. 165–180. Springer, Heidelberg (2019). https://doi.org/10.1007/978-3-662-58820-8_12
28. Zhao, R.K., Steinfeld, R., Sakzad, A.: COSAC: COmpact and scalable arbitrary-centered discrete Gaussian sampling over integers. In: Ding, J., Tillich, J.-P. (eds.) PQCrypto 2020. LNCS, vol. 12100, pp. 284–303. Springer, Cham (2020). https://doi.org/10.1007/978-3-030-44223-1_16

More Efficient Shuffle Argument from Unique Factorization

Toomas Krips[1] and Helger Lipmaa[1,2(✉)]

[1] University of Tartu, Tartu, Estonia
[2] Simula UiB, Bergen, Norway

Abstract. Efficient shuffle arguments are essential in mixnet-based e-voting solutions. Terelius and Wikström (TW) proposed a 5-round shuffle argument based on unique factorization in polynomial rings. Their argument is available as the `Verificatum` software solution for real-world developers, and has been used in real-world elections. It is also the fastest non-patented shuffle argument. We will use the same basic idea as TW but significantly optimize their approach. We generalize the TW characterization of permutation matrices; this enables us to reduce the communication without adding too much to the computation. We make the TW shuffle argument computationally more efficient by using Groth's coefficient-product argument (JOC 2010). Additionally, we use batching techniques. The resulting shuffle argument is the fastest known ≤5-message shuffle argument, and, depending on the implementation, can be faster than Groth's argument (the fastest 7-message shuffle argument).

Keywords: Mix-net · Shuffle argument · Unique factorization

1 Introduction

A (zero knowledge [20]) shuffle argument enables a prover to convince a verifier that given two lists of ciphertexts (encrypted by using a suitable homomorphic, blindable public-key cryptosystem like Elgamal [11]) $[\boldsymbol{w}] = ([\boldsymbol{w}_1], \ldots, [\boldsymbol{w}_N])$ and $[\widehat{\boldsymbol{w}}] = ([\widehat{\boldsymbol{w}}_1], \ldots, [\widehat{\boldsymbol{w}}_N])$, she knows a permutation $\pi \in S_N$ and a vector of randomizers $\boldsymbol{s} = (s_1, \ldots, s_N)$, such that $[\widehat{\boldsymbol{w}}_i] = [\boldsymbol{w}_{\pi^{-1}(i)}] + \mathsf{Enc}_{\mathsf{pk}}(0; s_{\pi^{-1}(i)})$ for $i = 1, \ldots, N$.[1] On top of satisfying the intuitively clear soundness requirement, it is required that the verifier obtains no additional information except the truth of the statement; that is, a shuffle argument should be zero knowledge [20]. In particular, shuffle arguments are important in e-voting applications, [9], allowing one to anonymize encrypted ballots while preventing one from cheating, e.g., by

---

[1] Here, the computation is done in an *additive* cyclic group $\mathbb{G}$ of prime order q, and for a fixed generator $P = [1]$ of $\mathbb{G}$, we denote $xP = x[1]$ by $[x]$. We generalize this notation to matrices as in $([a_{ij}]) = [(a_{ij})] = (a_{ij}P)$. Nevertheless, when discussing efficiency, we use multiplicative terminology by (say) computing the number of exponentiations instead of the number of scalar multiplications. Finally, recall that an Elgamal encryption belongs to $\mathbb{G}^2$.

© Springer Nature Switzerland AG 2021
K. G. Paterson (Ed.): CT-RSA 2021, LNCS 12704, pp. 252–275, 2021.
https://doi.org/10.1007/978-3-030-75539-3_11

changing some of the ballots. Shuffle arguments and mix-nets have several other prominent applications, see [25] for further references. As an important recent emerging application, shuffle arguments have become popular in cryptocurrencies, [15].

Since the prover may not know any of the corresponding plaintexts, the construction of efficient shuffle arguments is nontrivial. While contemporary shuffle arguments are relatively efficient, they are conceptually quite complicated, often relying on (say) a novel characterization of permutation matrices. In particular, computationally most efficient shuffle arguments either offer less security (for example, the argument of [18] is not zero-knowledge) or rely on the CRS-model [6] and require a large number of rounds (unless one relies on the random oracle model [4] to make the argument non-interactive by using the Fiat-Shamir heuristic [16]). On the other hand, the proposed random oracle-less CRS-model non-interactive shuffle arguments [12–14, 23, 27] are computationally considerably less efficient. While the random oracle model and the Fiat-Shamir heuristic are dubious from the security viewpoint [8, 19], there are no known attacks on random oracle-model shuffle arguments. Moreover, the most efficient random oracle-less shuffle arguments [12–14, 27] are only proven to be sound in the generic group model that is also known to be problematic. For the sake of efficiency, we only consider interactive shuffle arguments with the implicit understanding that they can be made non-interactive by using the Fiat-Shamir heuristic. Nevertheless, it is preferable to minimize the number of rounds.

We recall three main paradigms used in the known *computationally* most efficient shuffle arguments. Other approaches are known, but they have, up to now, resulted in significantly less computation-efficient shuffle arguments. For example, an orthogonal direction is to minimize the communication and the verifier's computation at the cost of possibly larger prover's computation and the number of rounds; see [1].

First, the approach of Furukawa and Sako [18] relies on a specific characterization of permutation matrices. Namely, a matrix M is a permutation matrix if $\langle M^{(i)}, M^{(j)} \rangle = \delta_{ij}$ and $\langle M^{(i)}, M^{(j)} \odot M^{(k)} \rangle = \delta_{ijk}$, where $M^{(i)}$ is the ith column vector of M, $\delta_{ij} = [i = j]$ is the Kronecker delta, $\delta_{ijk} = \delta_{ij}\delta_{ik}$, $\odot$ denotes the element-wise multiplication, and $\langle, \rangle$ denotes the scalar product. The Furukawa-Sako argument satisfies a privacy requirement that is weaker than zero knowledge. Later, Furukawa [17] made it more efficient and zero-knowledge. Importantly, shuffle arguments of this approach have only 3 messages.

Second, the approach of Neff [28] uses the fact that permuting the roots of polynomial results in the same polynomial. Groth [21] optimized Neff's argument, and the resulting argument is the most computationally efficient known shuffle argument. Unfortunately, the arguments that follow Neff's approach require 7 messages.

Terelius and Wikström (TW [32]) proposed the third approach that uses the fact that $\mathbb{Z}_q[X]$ is a unique factorization domain. This approach is based on another characterization of permutation matrices: namely, $M \in \mathbb{Z}_q^{N \times N}$ is a permutation matrix iff

(a) $\prod_{i=1}^{N}\langle M^{(i)}, X_i\rangle = \prod_{i=1}^{N} X_i$, where X_i are independent random variables, and

(b) $M \cdot 1_N = 1_N$.

The TW approach results in shuffle arguments of the intermediate number of messages (namely, 5). However, up to now, it has resulted in somewhat higher computational complexity than the first two approaches; see Table 1 for an efficiency comparison.

Notably, the TW approach has some benefits that are important in practical applications. First, the first two approaches are patented, while the TW approach is not. Second, the TW approach is backed up by an available open-source software package[2] that has been used in several real-life electronic elections. Therefore, we see it as an important open problem to optimize the TW approach to the level of the first two approaches, if not above.

Our Contributions. We propose a more efficient version of the shuffle argument of Terelius and Wikström [32] (that is, the TW approach). It provides better computational and communication complexity than the argument of Terelius and Wikström as described in [32,34], due to the new characterization of permutation matrices, the use of Groth's coefficient-product argument, and more precise security analysis. Computationally, the resulting shuffle argument is the most efficient known ≤5-message shuffle argument, and comparable to the most efficient 7-message shuffle argument by Groth [21], see Table 1.

We also note that [32] only has a sketch of the security proof (although their main reduction is precise), while [34] lacks any security proofs. Thus, for the first time, we give full security proof of a unique-factorization-based shuffle argument.

In some aspects, the new argument is very similar to the 7-message argument of Groth [21] that corresponds to the second approach. A precise efficiency comparison between the new argument and Groth's argument is up to implementation since we replaced some multi-exponentiations with the same number of fixed-base exponentiations. See Table 1 for an efficiency comparison.

The new shuffle argument is broadly based on the TW shuffle argument, with three main technical changes that range from a generalization of the TW's characterization of permutation matrices to using a protocol from Groth's shuffle argument to using batch verification techniques.

First. In Sect. 4, we generalize the permutation matrix characterization of Terelius-Wikström. Namely, we call a family of non-zero polynomials $\psi_i(X)$, $1 \leq i \leq N$, *PM-evidential*, iff neither any non-linear sum of ψ_i nor any ψ_i^2 divides their product. Generalizing a result from [32], we prove that $M \in \mathbb{Z}_q^{N \times N}$ is a permutation matrix iff the following holds:

(i) $\prod_{i=1}^{N}\langle M^{(i)}, \psi_i(X)\rangle = \prod_{i=1}^{N} \psi_i(X)$ for some PM-evidential polynomial family ψ_i, and

---

[2] http://www.verificatum.org.

Table 1. The complexity of some known interactive shuffle arguments, sorted by the number of rounds. Multi-exponentiations and fixed-based exponentiations are much more efficient than usual exponentiations.

	Prover			Verifier			Prover + Ver.			♯round
	#(N-wide m.e.)	$\frac{\#\text{exp.}}{N}$	#(N-wide f.b.e.)	#(N-wide m.e.)	$\frac{\#\text{exp.}}{N}$	#(N-wide f.b.e.)	#(N-wide m.e.)	$\frac{\#\text{exp.}}{N}$	#(N-wide f.b.e.)	
Furukawa [17]	3	1	5	6	—	—	9	1	6	3
Verificatum [34]	9	1	—	9	—	—	18	1	—	5
Current paper	5	—	1	6	—	—	11	—	1	5
Groth [21]	6	—	—	6	—	—	12	—	—	7

(ii) $M \cdot \mathbf{1}_N = \mathbf{1}_N$.

In particular, we show that one can choose $\psi_i(X_1, X_2) = X_1^i + X_2$. The use of the novel characterization allows us to minimize communication: in one round of the communication, the TW shuffle verifier returns N new random variables X_i. In our case, 2 variables suffice.[3]

Second. In a *coefficient-product argument*, the prover proves that the product of the coefficients of a committed vector is equal to a publicly known integer. Almost all (non-multi-)exponentiations in the TW shuffle argument are executed during the coefficient-product argument. Instead of the coefficient-product argument of [32], we use a more efficient coefficient-product argument by Groth [21]. Together with batch verification techniques [2], this is the main technique that helps us to decrease the *computational* complexity of the TW argument.

Third. We use batch verification techniques to speed up the verifier. Intuitively, batch verification means that instead of checking two (or more) verification equations, one checks whether a random linear combination of them holds. Depending on the equations, this allows us to save some verifier's computation.

Discussion. We compare efficiency in Table 1, see Sect. 6 for more information. Note that Table 1 is not completely precise since many of the single exponentiations come as part of (say) 2-wide multi-exponentiations. In the new shuffle

---

[3] We note that one can use a PRG to generate N random variables from a random seed, and thus if this method is applicable, one does not have to use our optimization. However, there might be situations where one does not want to or cannot rely on a PRG.

argument, the prover executes four ($\approx N$)-wide multi-exponentiations and in addition approximately N fixed-base exponentiations. Since an N-wide multi-exponentiation is much more efficient than N (non fixed-base) exponentiations, the new argument is significantly faster than the arguments of the first approach or the argument of Terelius and Wikström [32].

The comparison of the new shuffle argument with the best arguments following Neff's approach like [21] is more complicated. Since Neff's approach does not use permutation matrices, it only uses multi-exponentiations. However, in the new shuffle argument, the only non-multi exponentiations are fixed-base exponentiations, and the prover has only to execute N of them. By using a version Straus's algorithm [31], the computation of N fixed-base exponentiations requires one to execute approximately $2N \log_2 q / \log_2(N \log_2 q)$ squarings or multiplications. This is comparable to the time required by Straus's multi-exponentiation algorithm, where one has to use approximately the same number of multiplications.

However, when one uses a parallel computation model (like a modern GPU), an N-wide multi-exponentiation induces a latency (at least $\Theta(\log N)$, to combine all N individual exponentiations) while N fixed-base exponentiations can be computed independently. Hence, a precise comparison depends on the used hardware platform. Moreover, the bit complexity of (multi-)exponentiations depends heavily on the bit-length of exponents. In the current paper, we provide a precise analysis of the size of exponents; such analysis in the case of the Groth's argument from [21] is still missing.

2 Preliminaries

Let q be a large prime. All arithmetic expressions with integers (for example, Eqs. (1)–(3)) are in $\mathbb{Z}_q$ by default, while commitments and ciphertexts belong to an order q cyclic additive group $\mathbb{G}$ of order q. For a fixed generator $P = [1]$ of $\mathbb{G}$, we denote $xP = x[1]$ by $[x]$. We generalize this notation to matrices as in $([a_{ij}]) = [(a_{ij})] = (a_{ij}P)$; e.g., $[a, b] = ([a], [b])$. We assume that $\mathsf{p} \leftarrow (\mathbb{G}, q, [1])$ is generated by a public algorithm $\mathsf{Pgen}(1^\lambda)$.

Implicitly, all vectors are column vectors. For a vector $\boldsymbol{a}$, let $wt(\boldsymbol{a})$ be the number of its non-zero coefficients. The dimension of all vectors is by default N. Let $\langle \boldsymbol{a}, \mathbf{b} \rangle = \sum_{i=1}^N a_i b_i$ be the scalar product of vectors $\boldsymbol{a}$ and $\mathbf{b}$ (in $\mathbb{Z}_q$, as usual). We denote the vertical concatenation of two vectors $\boldsymbol{a}$ and $\mathbf{b}$ by $\boldsymbol{a} \mathbin{/\!/} \mathbf{b}$. Let $\boldsymbol{e}_i$ be the ith unit vector. For a matrix $\boldsymbol{M} = (M_{ij})_{ij} \in \mathbb{Z}_q^{N \times N}$, let $\boldsymbol{M}_i$ be its ith row vector, and $\boldsymbol{M}^{(j)}$ be its jth column vector. Let S_N be the symmetric group of N elements. For a permutation $\pi \in S_N$, the corresponding permutation matrix $\boldsymbol{M} = \boldsymbol{M}_\pi \in \mathbb{Z}_2^{N \times N}$ is defined by $M_{ij} = 1$ iff $i = \pi(j)$. Thus, a Boolean matrix $\boldsymbol{M}$ is a permutation matrix if it has a single 1 in every row and column. When $\mathcal{A}$ is a randomized algorithm, we denote by $a \leftarrow \mathcal{A}(\mathtt{inp}; r)$ the output of A on input $\mathtt{inp}$ given the random tape r.

Let λ be a security parameter; the complexity of algorithms is computed as a function of λ. Let $\mathsf{poly}(\lambda)/\mathsf{negl}(\lambda)$ be an arbitrary polynomial/negligible function, and let $f(X) \approx_c g(X)$ iff $|f(X) - g(X)| = \mathsf{negl}(\lambda)$.

Lemma 1 (Schwartz-Zippel [30,35]**).** *Let* $f \in \mathbb{F}[X_1, \dots, X_n]$ *be a non-zero polynomial of total degree* $d \geq 0$ *over a field* $\mathbb{F}$. *Let* S *be a finite subset of* $\mathbb{F}$, *and let* $x_1, \dots, x_n$ *be selected at random independently and uniformly from* S. *Then* $\Pr[f(x_1, \dots, x_n) = 0] \leq d/|S|$.

Cryptography. Let λ be the security parameter. For two distributions $\mathcal{D}_1$ and $\mathcal{D}_2$, $\mathcal{D}_1 \approx_c \mathcal{D}_2$ means that they are computationally indistinguishable by any non-uniform probabilistic polynomial-time adversary.

In the CRS model [6], a trusted third party generates a CRS crs together with a trapdoor. The CRS is published and given to all participants. The trapdoor is however kept secret, and only used in the proof of zero-knowledge to generate a simulated transcript of the protocol.

Commitment Schemes. A commitment scheme $\Gamma = (\mathsf{Pgen}, \mathsf{KGen}, \mathsf{Com})$ in the CRS model consists of a key generation algorithm KGen, that generates a commitment key ck (the CRS), and a commitment algorithm $\mathsf{Com}_{\mathsf{ck}}(a; \cdot)$ that first samples a random r and then uses it to commit to a message a. We also assume that ck implicitly contains p. Γ is *perfectly hiding* if a random commitment is statistically independent from the message. Γ is (T, ε)-*binding*, if for any probabilistic T-time adversary $\mathcal{A}$, $\mathsf{Adv}_{\Gamma,\mathcal{A}}^{\mathsf{binding}}(\lambda) \leq \varepsilon$, where

$$\mathsf{Adv}_{\Gamma,\mathcal{A}}^{\mathsf{binding}}(\lambda) := \Pr \left[\begin{array}{l} \mathsf{p} \leftarrow \mathsf{Pgen}(1^\lambda); \mathsf{ck} \leftarrow \mathsf{KGen}(\mathsf{p}); (a_0, a_1, r_0, r_1) \leftarrow \mathcal{A}(\mathsf{ck}); \\ \mathsf{Com}_{\mathsf{ck}}(a_0; r_0) = \mathsf{Com}_{\mathsf{ck}}(a_1; r_1) \wedge a_0 \neq a_1 \end{array} \right] .$$

We say that Γ is computationally binding if it is $(\mathsf{poly}(\lambda), \mathsf{negl}(\lambda))$-binding.

The extended Pedersen commitment scheme Γ_p [29] is defined as follows. Let $\mathsf{p} = (\mathbb{G}, q, [1])$. KGen samples $\mathsf{ck} = ([h_1], \dots, [h_N]) \leftarrow_s \mathbb{G}^N$ uniformly at random. For $a \in \mathbb{Z}_q^N$, let $\mathsf{Com}_{\mathsf{ck}}(a; r) := r[1] + \langle a, [h] \rangle = r[1] + \sum_{i=1}^N a_i[h_i]$. Γ_p is computationally binding under the discrete logarithm assumption [7]. It is perfectly hiding since the distribution of $\mathsf{Com}_{\mathsf{ck}}(a; r)$, $r \leftarrow_s \mathbb{Z}_q$, is uniform in $\mathbb{G}$.

The extended Pedersen commitment scheme is additively homomorphic, $\mathsf{Com}_{\mathsf{ck}}(a_0 + a_1; r_0 + r_1) = \mathsf{Com}_{\mathsf{ck}}(a_0; r_0) + \mathsf{Com}_{\mathsf{ck}}(a_1; r_1)$. Clearly, from this it follows that for any integer n, $\mathsf{Com}_{\mathsf{ck}}(na; nr) = n \cdot \mathsf{Com}_{\mathsf{ck}}(a; r)$.

Cryptosystems. An public-key cryptosystem $\Pi = (\mathsf{Pgen}, \mathsf{KGen}, \mathsf{Enc}, \mathsf{Dec})$ consists of a key generation algorithm KGen, that generates a public key pk and a secret key sk, an encryption algorithm $[w] \leftarrow \mathsf{Enc}_{\mathsf{pk}}(a; \cdot)$ that first samples a random r and then uses it to encrypt a message a, and a decryption algorithm $\mathsf{Dec}_{\mathsf{ck}}([w])$ that uses sk to decrypt $[w]$. Obviously, it is required that for $(\mathsf{pk}, \mathsf{sk}) \leftarrow \mathsf{KGen}(\mathsf{p})$, $\mathsf{Dec}_{\mathsf{sk}}(\mathsf{Enc}_{\mathsf{pk}}(a; r)) = a$ for any a, r.

In the Elgamal cryptosystem [11], one samples $\mathsf{sk} \leftarrow_\$ \mathbb{Z}_q$ and then defines the public key as $\mathsf{pk} = \left[\begin{smallmatrix} 1 \\ h \end{smallmatrix}\right]$, where $[h] \leftarrow \mathsf{sk} \cdot [1]$. Let $\mathsf{Enc}_{\mathsf{pk}}([m]; r) = \left[\begin{smallmatrix} c_1 \\ c_2 \end{smallmatrix}\right] = \left(\begin{smallmatrix} [m] + r[h] \\ r[1] \end{smallmatrix}\right)$. To decrypt a ciphertext, one computes $[c_1] - \mathsf{sk}[c_2] = [m]$. The Elgamal cryptosystem is IND-CPA secure, assuming that the Decisional Diffie-Hellman problem is hard. It is group-homomorphic, with $\mathsf{Enc}_{\mathsf{pk}}([m]; r) + \mathsf{Enc}_{\mathsf{pk}}([m]'; r') = \mathsf{Enc}_{\mathsf{pk}}([m] + [m]'; r + r')$.

In the lifted Elgamal, the plaintext m belongs to $\mathbb{Z}_q$, and the ciphertext is $\left(\begin{smallmatrix} m[1] + r[h] \\ r[1] \end{smallmatrix}\right)$. Lifted Elgamal is $\mathbb{Z}_q$-homomorphic, with $\mathsf{Enc}_{\mathsf{pk}}(m; r) + \mathsf{Enc}_{\mathsf{pk}}(m'; r') = \mathsf{Enc}_{\mathsf{pk}}(m + m'; r + r')$.

The new shuffle argument allows to use both lifted and non-lifted Elgamal. Moreover, it allows one to work with a tuple of plaintexts $[\boldsymbol{m}] = ([m_1], \ldots, [m_M])^\top$, for some $M \geq 1$, that is encrypted as $\mathsf{Enc}_{\mathsf{pk}}([\boldsymbol{m}]; \boldsymbol{r}) = (\mathsf{Enc}_{\mathsf{pk}}([m_1]; r_1) // \ldots // \mathsf{Enc}_{\mathsf{pk}}([m_M]; r_M))$. For the sake of simplicity, we concentrate the exposition on the case of (non-lifted) Elgamal and $M = 1$. However, the case $M > 1$ is important in practice, e.g., in the case of complicated ballots.

Arguments. Let $\mathcal{R} = \{(\mathtt{inp}, \mathtt{wit})\}$, with $|\mathtt{wit}| = \mathsf{poly}(|\mathtt{inp}|)$, be a polynomial-time verifiable relation. Let $\mathcal{L}_{\mathcal{R}} = \{\mathtt{inp} : \exists \mathtt{wit}, (\mathtt{inp}, \mathtt{wit}) \in \mathcal{R}\}$. We allow $\mathcal{R}$ and $\mathcal{L}$ to depend on the common reference string (CRS) crs that is generated by a trusted third party by using an algorithm KGen; crs can say contain the description p of a group and the commitment key $\mathsf{ck} = [\{h_i\}]$ of the extended Pedersen commitment scheme. In this case, we denote $\mathcal{R}$ by $\mathcal{R}_{\mathsf{crs}}$ and $\mathcal{L}_{\mathcal{R}}$ by $\mathcal{L}_{\mathcal{R}:\mathsf{crs}}$. Thus, $(\mathsf{crs}, \mathtt{inp}, \mathtt{wit}) \in \mathcal{R}$ iff $(\mathtt{inp}, \mathtt{wit}) \in \mathcal{R}_{\mathsf{crs}}$.

For a randomized two-party protocol $(\mathsf{KGen}, \mathsf{P}, \mathsf{V})$ between the prover P and the verifier V in the CRS model, let σ_p be the number of random choices the prover can make (thus, $\lceil \log_2 \sigma_p \rceil$ is the bit-length of the prover's random tape) and σ_v the number of random choices the verifier can make (thus, $\lceil \log_2 \sigma_v \rceil$ is the bit-length of the verifier's random tape). We require the protocol to be public-coin, at the end of which the verifier will either accept (outputs acc) or reject (outputs rej). We allow the acceptance to be probabilistic, and assume that the verifier does also output the coins he used to decide acceptance. For a protocol between prover P and verifier V in the CRS model, let $\langle \mathsf{P}(\mathsf{crs}, \mathtt{inp}, \mathtt{wit}), \mathsf{V}(\mathsf{crs}, \mathtt{inp}) \rangle$ be the whole transcript between P and V, given crs, common input $\mathtt{inp}$ and prover's private input (witness) $\mathtt{wit}$. We sometimes write $\langle \mathsf{P}(\mathsf{crs}, \mathtt{inp}, \mathtt{wit}), \mathsf{V}(\mathsf{crs}, \mathtt{inp}) \rangle = \mathsf{acc}$ to denote that the verifier accepts, and rej if V rejects. The concrete meaning will be clear from the context.

Then, $(\mathsf{Pgen}, \mathsf{KGen}, \mathsf{P}, \mathsf{V})$ is an *argument* for relation $\mathcal{R}$ if for all non-uniform probabilistic polynomial-time stateful adversaries $\mathcal{A}$,

Completeness: $\Pr[\mathsf{p} \leftarrow \mathsf{Pgen}(1^\lambda); \mathsf{crs} \leftarrow \mathsf{KGen}(\mathsf{p}); (\mathtt{inp}, \mathtt{wit}) \leftarrow \mathcal{A}(\mathsf{crs}) :$
    $(\mathtt{inp}, \mathtt{wit}) \notin \mathcal{R}_{\mathsf{crs}} \vee \langle \mathsf{P}(\mathsf{crs}, \mathtt{inp}, \mathtt{wit}), \mathsf{V}(\mathsf{crs}, \mathtt{inp}) \rangle = \mathsf{acc}] \approx_c 1$.

Soundness: $\Pr[\mathsf{p} \leftarrow \mathsf{Pgen}(1^\lambda); \mathsf{crs} \leftarrow \mathsf{KGen}(\mathsf{p}); \mathtt{inp} \leftarrow \mathcal{A}(\mathsf{crs}) : \mathtt{inp} \notin \mathcal{L}_{\mathcal{R}:\mathsf{crs}} \wedge$
    $\langle \mathcal{A}(\mathsf{crs}, \mathtt{inp}), \mathsf{V}(\mathsf{crs}, \mathtt{inp}) \rangle = \mathsf{acc}] \approx_c 0$.

We call $(\mathsf{KGen}, \mathsf{P}, \mathsf{V})$ a *proof* if soundness holds against unbounded adversaries. An argument is *public coin* if the verifier's subsequent messages correspond to subsequent bit-strings from her random tape. In particular, they do not depend on the prover's messages.

As noted in [21], the standard definition of a proof of knowledge [3] does not work in such a setting since the adversary may have non-zero probability of computing some trapdoor pertaining to the common reference string and use that information in the argument. In this case, it is possible that there exists a prover with 100% probability of making a convincing argument, where we nonetheless cannot extract a witness. We prove security by using witness-extended emulation [26], the CRS-model version of which was defined by Groth [21]. Intuitively, an argument has witness-extended emulation, if for every prover P there exists an emulator Emul, such that if P makes V accept, then almost always Emul makes V accept *and* outputs P*'s witness.

Definition 1. *A public-coin argument* $\Pi = (\mathsf{Pgen}, \mathsf{KGen}, \mathsf{P}, \mathsf{V})$ *has witness-extended emulation if for all deterministic polynomial-time provers* P^* *there exists an expected polynomial-time emulator* Emul, *such that for all non-uniform probabilistic polynomial-time adversaries* $\mathcal{A}$, $\mathsf{Adv}_{\Pi,\mathcal{A}}^{\mathrm{sound}}(\lambda) \approx_c \mathsf{Adv}_{\Pi,\mathcal{A},\mathsf{Emul}}^{\mathrm{emul}}(\lambda)$, *where*

$$\mathsf{Adv}_{\Pi,\mathcal{A}}^{\mathrm{sound}}(\lambda) := \Pr \left[\begin{array}{l} \mathsf{p} \leftarrow \mathsf{Pgen}(1^\lambda); \mathsf{crs} \leftarrow \mathsf{KGen}(\mathsf{p}); \omega_\mathsf{P} \leftarrow_\$ R; (\mathsf{inp}, \mathsf{st}) \leftarrow \mathcal{A}(\mathsf{crs}; \omega_\mathsf{P}); \\ \mathsf{tr} \leftarrow \langle \mathsf{P}^*(\mathsf{crs}, \mathsf{inp}; \mathsf{st}), \mathsf{V}(\mathsf{crs}, \mathsf{inp}) \rangle : \mathcal{A}(\mathsf{tr}) = \mathsf{acc} \end{array} \right] ,$$

$$\mathsf{Adv}_{\Pi,\mathcal{A},\mathsf{Emul}}^{\mathrm{emul}}(\lambda) := \Pr \left[\begin{array}{l} \mathsf{p} \leftarrow \mathsf{Pgen}(1^\lambda); \mathsf{crs} \leftarrow \mathsf{KGen}(\mathsf{p}); \omega_\mathsf{P} \leftarrow_\$ R; (\mathsf{inp}, \mathsf{st}) \leftarrow \mathcal{A}(\mathsf{crs}; \omega_\mathsf{P}); \\ (\mathsf{tr}, \mathsf{wit}) \leftarrow \mathsf{Emul}^{\langle \mathsf{P}^*(\mathsf{crs}, \mathsf{inp}; \mathsf{st}), \mathsf{V}(\mathsf{crs}, \mathsf{inp}) \rangle}(\mathsf{crs}, \mathsf{inp}) : \\ \mathcal{A}(\mathsf{tr}) = \mathsf{acc} \wedge (\mathsf{tr} \text{ is accepting} \Rightarrow (\mathsf{inp}, \mathsf{wit}) \in \mathcal{R}_{\mathsf{crs}}) \end{array} \right] .$$

Here, Emul *can rewind the transcript oracle* $\langle \mathsf{P}^*(\mathsf{crs}, \mathsf{inp}; \mathsf{st}), \mathsf{V}(\mathsf{crs}, \mathsf{inp}) \rangle$ *to any particular round with the verifier choosing fresh random coins,* R *is the space of the random coins for* $\mathcal{A}$, ω_P *is the random tape of* $\mathcal{A}$, *and* st *is the state of* P^* *that also contains his random coins (*P *is deterministic in inputs* $(\mathsf{crs}, \mathsf{inp}, \mathsf{st})$*).*

The verifier's randomness is a part of the transcript (we recall that this includes also the random coins used to probabilistically accept the transcript), while P^* is a deterministic function of $(\mathsf{crs}, \mathsf{inp}; \mathsf{st})$. Thus combining $(\mathsf{crs}, \mathsf{inp}; \mathsf{st})$ with the emulated transcript gives us the view of both the prover and the verifier, and at the same time gives us the witness.

Then, we have an argument of knowledge in the sense that the emulator is able to extract the witness whenever P^* makes a convincing argument. Hence, this definition implies soundness.

Honest-Verifier Zero Knowledge (HVZK, [10]). An argument $\Pi = (\mathsf{Pgen}, \mathsf{KGen}, \mathsf{P}, \mathsf{V})$ is *honest-verifier zero knowledge* if there exists a probabilistic polynomial-time simulator Sim, such that for any non-uniform probabilistic polynomial-time adversary $\mathcal{A}$,

$$\Pr\begin{bmatrix} \mathsf{p} \leftarrow \mathsf{Pgen}(1^\lambda); \mathsf{crs} \leftarrow \mathsf{KGen}(\mathsf{p}); (\mathsf{inp}, \mathsf{wit}, \omega_V) \leftarrow \mathcal{A}(\mathsf{crs}); \\ \mathsf{tr} \leftarrow \langle \mathsf{P}(\mathsf{crs}, \mathsf{inp}, \mathsf{wit}), \mathsf{V}(\mathsf{crs}, \mathsf{inp}; \omega_V) \rangle : (\mathsf{inp}, \mathsf{wit}) \in \mathcal{R}_{\mathsf{crs}} \wedge \mathcal{A}(\mathsf{tr}) = \mathsf{acc} \end{bmatrix}$$

$$\approx_c \Pr\begin{bmatrix} \mathsf{p} \leftarrow \mathsf{Pgen}(1^\lambda); \mathsf{crs} \leftarrow \mathsf{KGen}(\mathsf{p}); (\mathsf{inp}, \mathsf{wit}, \omega_V) \leftarrow \mathcal{A}(\mathsf{crs}); \\ \mathsf{tr} \leftarrow \mathsf{Sim}(\mathsf{crs}, \mathsf{inp}; \omega_V) : (\mathsf{inp}, \mathsf{wit}) \in \mathcal{R}_{\mathsf{crs}} \wedge \mathcal{A}(\mathsf{tr}) = \mathsf{acc} \end{bmatrix} .$$

That is, given that the verifier is honest, there exists a simulator that can simulate the view of the prover without knowing the witness. To compensate for this, Sim is allowed to create the messages of the transcript out-of-order.

3   Coefficient-Product Argument

In the shuffle argument, we need a *coefficient-product* argument, where the prover P shows that given a CRS $\mathsf{ck} = ([h_1], \ldots, [h_N])$ (ck for the Pedersen commitment scheme), a public commitment $[c_t] \in \mathbb{G}$ and a public value $\gamma \in \mathbb{Z}_q$, he knows how to open $[c_t]$ to a vector $\mathbf{t}$, $[c_t] = \mathsf{Com}_{\mathsf{ck}}(\mathbf{t}; r_t)$, so that $\prod_{i=1}^N t_i = \gamma$. Formally, it is an argument for the ck-dependent relation

$$\mathcal{R}_{\mathsf{ck}}^{cpa} := \left\{ (([c_t], \gamma), (\mathbf{t}, r_t)) : [c_t] = \mathsf{Com}_{\mathsf{ck}}(\mathbf{t}; r_t) \wedge \prod_{i=1}^N t_i = \gamma \right\} .$$

Next, we outline the coefficient-product argument that is closely based on the coefficient-product argument from [21]. (More precisely, in [21] it was used as a subargument of a shuffle of known contents. See, for example, [22] for another prior implicit use of the following argument.) We give a formulation of this argument as a separate argument of its own worth.

In the coefficient-product argument, P first proves he knows the message in the commitment $[c_t] = \mathsf{Com}_{\mathsf{ck}}(\mathbf{t}; r_t)$, by using the following standard Σ-protocol. Here, the verifier's message comes from a set of σ_y elements for some $\sigma_y \geq 2^\lambda$.

---

1. The prover samples $\boldsymbol{\tau} \leftarrow_{\$} \mathbb{Z}_q^N$, $\varrho_t \leftarrow_{\$} \mathbb{Z}_q$, and sends $[c_\tau] \leftarrow \mathsf{Com}_{\mathsf{ck}}(\boldsymbol{\tau}; \varrho_t)$ to the verifier.
2. The verifier samples $y \leftarrow_{\$} \{1, \ldots, \sigma_y\}$ and sends it to the prover.
3. The prover sends
$$\mathbf{t}^* \leftarrow y\mathbf{t} + \boldsymbol{\tau} \tag{1}$$
and $r_t^* \leftarrow y r_t + \varrho_t$ to the verifier.
4. The verifier accepts iff $y[c_t] + [c_\tau] =^? \mathsf{Com}_{\mathsf{ck}}(\mathbf{t}^*; r_t^*)$.

(As always, the prover's third message elements are computed modulo q.)

Note that $\prod_{i=1}^N t_i^* = \prod_{i=1}^N (y t_i + \tau_i) = y^N \prod_{i=1}^N t_i + p(y)$, where $p(Y)$ is some degree $\leq N - 1$ polynomial. To finish up the coefficient-vector argument, the prover now only has to demonstrate the knowledge of $p(y)$, for some degree $\leq N - 1$ polynomial $p(Y)$, such that $\prod_{i=1}^N t_i^* - p(y) = y^N \gamma$.

For this, using a technique from [21], the prover does the following. Let

$$Q_i \leftarrow y \prod_{j=1}^{i} t_j + \Delta_i \ , \tag{2}$$

and Δ_i were chosen before y was sent. (Thus, Δ_i does not depend on y and Q_i is a linear polynomial on y.) In particular, set $Q_1 \leftarrow t_1^* = yt_1 + \tau_1$; thus, $\Delta_1 = \tau_1$. Also, choose $\Delta_N \leftarrow 0$, thus

$$Q_N = y \prod_{i=1}^{N} t_i = y\gamma \ , \tag{3}$$

which can be tested by the verifier. (The verifier can recompute Q_N, as we will see shortly.) The prover samples the rest of $\Delta_i \leftarrow_\$ \mathbb{Z}_q$ randomly. Now,

$$y(Q_{i+1} - \Delta_{i+1}) \overset{(2)}{=} yt_{i+1}(Q_i - \Delta_i) \overset{(1)}{=} t_{i+1}^* Q_i - \tau_{i+1}Q_i - yt_{i+1}\Delta_i$$
$$\overset{(2)}{=} t_{i+1}^* Q_i - \tau_{i+1} \left(y \prod_{j=1}^{i} t_j + \Delta_i \right) - yt_{i+1}\Delta_i$$
$$= t_{i+1}^* Q_i - y \left(t_{i+1}\Delta_i + \tau_{i+1} \prod_{j=1}^{i} t_j \right) - \tau_{i+1}\Delta_i \ .$$

Define $b_i \leftarrow \Delta_{i+1} - t_{i+1}\Delta_i - \tau_{i+1} \prod_{j=1}^{i} t_j$, $\beta_i \leftarrow -\tau_{i+1}\Delta_i$, and $b_i^* \leftarrow yb_i + \beta_i$ as on Fig. 1. Thus, for $i = 1, \ldots, N-1$,

$$yQ_{i+1} = t_{i+1}^* Q_i + yb_i + \beta_i = t_{i+1}^* Q_i + b_i^* \ . \tag{4}$$

The verifier can recompute Q_i by using the definition of Q_1, and Eq. (4), see Fig. 1.

Since b_i^* is linear in y,

$$y^N \gamma \overset{(3)}{=} y^{N-1} Q_N \overset{(4)}{=} y^{N-2}(t_N^* Q_{N-1} + b_{N-1}^*) \overset{(4)}{=} \cdots \overset{(4)}{=} \prod_{i=1}^{N} t_i^* + p(y)$$
$$= y^N \prod_{i=1}^{N} t_i + p'(y) \ , \tag{5}$$

where $p(X)$ and $p'(X)$ are degree $\leq N-1$ polynomials. This is equivalent to $y^N(\gamma - \prod_{i=1}^{N} t_i) + p'(y) = 0$. As y was chosen randomly, due to Schwartz-Zippel lemma Eq. (6), with overwhelming probability this implies that $y^N(\gamma - \prod_{i=1}^{N} t_i) + p'(y)$ is a zero polynomial and thus $\gamma = \prod_{i=1}^{N} t_i$. Hence, we are done.

Construction. The full coefficient-product argument Π_{cpa} is depicted by Fig. 1. Note that the verifier chooses $y \neq 0$ to avoid division by 0 on the penultimate line of Fig. 1.

Security. We prove that this argument is perfectly complete, has witness-extended emulation, and is perfectly special honest-verifier zero knowledge. We state the security of Π_{cpa} in Theorem 1. Π_{cpa} is essentially the same as a sub-argument in [21]; it only includes batch verification as an additional step of optimization, and moreover, [21] did not formalize it as a separate argument.

CRS: crs = ck = $([h_1], \ldots, [h_N])$ as in the extended Pedersen.
Common inputs: inp = $([c_t] = \mathsf{Com}_{ck}(\mathbf{t}; r_t), \gamma)$.
Witness: wit = $(\mathbf{t}, r_t)$.

1. The prover $\mathsf{P}(\mathsf{crs}, \mathsf{inp}, \mathsf{wit})$ does:
   (a) Sample $\boldsymbol{\tau} \leftarrow_{\$} \mathbb{Z}_q^N$.
   (b) Let $\Delta_1 \leftarrow \tau_1$ and $\Delta_N \leftarrow 0$.
   (c) For $i = 2, \ldots, N-1$: sample $\Delta_i \leftarrow_{\$} \mathbb{Z}_q$.
   (d) $X_0 \leftarrow 1$; For $i = 1, \ldots, N-1$:
       − Set $X_i \leftarrow X_{i-1} t_i$, $b_i \leftarrow \Delta_{i+1} - t_{i+1}\Delta_i - \tau_{i+1}X_i$, $\beta_i \leftarrow -\tau_{i+1}\Delta_i$.
   (e) Denote $\mathbf{b} = (b_1, \ldots, b_{N-1})^\top$, $\boldsymbol{\beta} = (\beta_1, \ldots, \beta_{N-1})^\top$.
   (f) Sample $\varrho_t, r_b, \varrho_b \leftarrow_{\$} \mathbb{Z}_q$.
   (g) $[c_\tau] \leftarrow \boxed{\mathsf{Com}_{ck}(\boldsymbol{\tau}; \varrho_t)}$; $[c_b] \leftarrow \boxed{\mathsf{Com}_{ck}(\mathbf{b} /\!\!/ 0; r_b)}$;
   (h) $[c_\beta] \leftarrow \boxed{\mathsf{Com}_{ck}(\boldsymbol{\beta} /\!\!/ 0; \varrho_b)}$;
   Send $[c_\tau, c_b, c_\beta]$ to the verifier.
2. The verifier samples $\mathsf{y} \leftarrow_{\$} \{1, \ldots, \sigma_y\}$, and sends y to the prover.
3. Prover does:
   (a) Set $\mathbf{t}^* \leftarrow \mathsf{y}\mathbf{t} + \boldsymbol{\tau}$, $r_t^* \leftarrow \mathsf{y}r_t + \varrho_t$, $\mathbf{b}^* \leftarrow \mathsf{y}\mathbf{b} + \boldsymbol{\beta} \in \mathbb{Z}_q^{N-1}$, $r_b^* \leftarrow \mathsf{y}r_b + \varrho_b$.
   (b) Send $(\mathbf{t}^*, r_t^*, \mathbf{b}^*, r_b^*)$ to the verifier.
4. The verifier samples $\mathsf{z} \leftarrow_{\$} \{0, \ldots, \sigma_z - 1\}$. He checks that

$$\mathsf{y}[c_t] + [c_\tau] + \mathsf{z}(\mathsf{y}[c_b] + [c_\beta]) =^? \boxed{\mathsf{Com}_{ck}(\mathbf{t}^* + \mathsf{z}(\mathbf{b}^* /\!\!/ 0); r_t^* + \mathsf{z}r_b^*)} . \quad (6)$$

Set $Q_1 \leftarrow t_1^*$, $Q_2 \leftarrow (t_2^*Q_1 + b_1^*)/\mathsf{y}$, $\ldots$, $Q_N \leftarrow (t_N^*Q_{N-1} + b_{N-1}^*)/\mathsf{y}$. Check that $Q_N =^? \mathsf{y}\gamma$.
The verifier outputs $(\mathsf{acc}, \mathsf{z})$ iff both checks succeed, and $(\mathsf{rej}, \mathsf{z})$ otherwise.

Fig. 1. The coefficient-product argument. $\boxed{\text{Dotted}}$ formulas correspond to expensive (that is, $\Omega(N)$) computations.

First, note that if either of the following equations does not hold,

$$\mathsf{y}[c_t] + [c_\tau] =^? \mathsf{Com}_{ck}(\mathbf{t}^*; r_t^*) \ , \mathsf{y}[c_b] + [c_\beta] =^? \mathsf{Com}_{ck}(\mathbf{b}^* /\!\!/ 0; r_b^*) \ , \quad (7)$$

then according to Schwartz-Zippel lemma, Eq. (6) holds for a random z at most with probability $1/\sigma_z$. To simplify the proofs of both following theorem, we define another coefficient-product argument Π'_{cpa} that differs from Π_{cpa} only by removing the batch verification: namely, the verifier checks Eq. (7) instead of Eq. (6). Clearly, if an adversary succeeds with probability ε against Π_{cpa}, then it succeeds with probability not larger than ε', $\varepsilon \geq \varepsilon' \geq \varepsilon - 1/\sigma_z$, against Π'_{cpa}.

Fix $\mathsf{p} \leftarrow \mathsf{Pgen}(1^\lambda)$ and $\mathsf{crs} \leftarrow \mathsf{KGen}(\mathsf{p})$. Let us denote with ω_P the random coins of the adversary and with ω_V the random coins of the verifier in Π'_{cpa}. Since Π'_{cpa} is a public-coin protocol, each ω_V corresponds to a different value verifier's challenge y. Let $\boldsymbol{V} = \boldsymbol{V}_{\mathsf{crs}}$ be a crs-dependent matrix with an entry $\boldsymbol{V}_{\omega_\mathsf{P}, \omega_\mathsf{V}} = \boldsymbol{V}(\omega_\mathsf{P}, \omega_\mathsf{V}) = 1$ if for $(\mathsf{inp}, \mathsf{st}) \leftarrow \mathcal{A}(\mathsf{crs}; \omega_\mathsf{P})$, $\langle \mathsf{P}^*(\mathsf{crs}, \mathsf{inp}; \mathsf{st}), \mathsf{V}(\mathsf{crs}, \mathsf{inp}; \omega_\mathsf{V}) \rangle = \mathsf{acc}$ and $\boldsymbol{V}(\omega_\mathsf{P}, \omega_\mathsf{V}) = 0$ otherwise.

Theorem 1. Π_{cpa} *is a three-message public-coin argument for* $[c_t]$ *being a commitment to a message* **t** *such that* $\prod_{i=1}^{N} t_i = \gamma$. *It is perfectly complete and perfectly HVZK. It has witness-extended emulation, assuming the commitment scheme is binding.*

Proof. COMPLETENESS: obvious.

WITNESS-EXTENDED EMULATION: Fix $p \leftarrow \mathsf{Pgen}(1^{\lambda})$ and $\mathsf{crs} \leftarrow \mathsf{KGen}(p)$. Let V' be the verifier of Π'_{cpa}. Let P^* be a prover that makes V' to accept a false statement with some non-negligible probability ε'_{crs}.

To extract a witness, Emul rewinds a runs $\langle P^*, V' \rangle$ on the same challenge x until it gets another acceptable argument. Let $tr_j = (\mathsf{inp}; [c_\tau, c_b, c_\beta]; y_j; \mathbf{t}_j^*, r_{t:j}^*, \mathbf{b}_j^*, r_{b:j}^*)$, $j \in \{1,2\}$, be the two acceptable arguments. Emul uses the last two transcripts to open the commitments. Since $y_1 \neq y_2$ and Eq. (7) holds, from Eq. (7) (left) it follows that $[c_t] = \mathsf{Com}_{ck}(\mathbf{t}; r_t)$, where $\mathbf{t} \leftarrow (\mathbf{t}_1^* - \mathbf{t}_2^*)/(y_1 - y_2)$ and $r_t \leftarrow (r_{t:1}^* - r_{t:2}^*)/(y_1 - y_2)$. Thus, Emul has succeeded in extracting an opening of $[c_t]$.

Following Theorem 1 in [21], we can argue that Emul runs in expected polynomial time. If we are in a situation where P^* can make the verifier to accept with probability $\varepsilon > 0$ on challenge x, then the expected number of rewindings to get an acceptable transcript is $1/\varepsilon$. If P^* fails then we do not have to rewind at all, and thus the number of expected queries to $\langle P^*, V' \rangle$ is 2. Since Emul does an expected polynomial number of queries, there is only negligible probability of ending in a run where $y = y'$ or some other unlikely event (e.g., breaking the binding of the commitment scheme) occurs. Hence, with an overwhelming probability, either P^* did not succeed or Emul succeeded in extraction.

Next, we argue that the probability for extracting an opening of $[c_t]$, such that $\prod_{i=1}^{N} t_i \neq \gamma$, is negligible. Assume that P^* has a non-negligible success probability $1/f(\lambda)$, for a polynomial $f(X)$, to produce an acceptable argument. We now run P^* and rewind to get three random challenges y_1, y_2, y_3. With probability at least $1/f(\lambda)^3$, P^* succeeds in creating accepting arguments for all three challenges. Since $y_1 \neq y_2$, with an overwhelming probability, and Eq. (7) holds, Emul can open the following commitments from the first two transcripts (with an overwhelming probability).

(1) From Eq. (7) (left) it follows that $[c_t] = \mathsf{Com}_{ck}(\mathbf{t}; r_t)$, where $\mathbf{t} \leftarrow (\mathbf{t}_1^* - \mathbf{t}_2^*)/(y_1 - y_2)$; $r_t \leftarrow (r_{t:1}^* - r_{t:2}^*)/(y_1 - y_2)$.
(2) Since it knows $\mathbf{t}_1^*$, $\mathbf{t}$, $r_{t:1}^*$ and r_t, Emul can compute $\tau \leftarrow \mathbf{t}_1^* - y_1\mathbf{t}$; $\varrho_t \leftarrow r_{t:1}^* - y_1 r_t$; thus $[c_\tau] = \mathsf{Com}_{ck}(\tau; \varrho_t)$.
(3) From Eq. (7) (right) it follows that $[c_b] = \mathsf{Com}_{ck}(\mathbf{b} /\!/ 0; r_b)$, where $\mathbf{b} \leftarrow (\mathbf{b}_1^* - \mathbf{b}_2^*)/(y_1 - y_2)$; $r_b \leftarrow (r_{b:1}^* - r_{b:2}^*)/(y_1 - y_2)$.
(4) Since it knows $\mathbf{b}_1^*$, $\mathbf{b}$, $r_{b:1}^*$ and r_b, Emul can compute $\beta \leftarrow \mathbf{b}_1^* - y_1\mathbf{b}$; $\varrho_b \leftarrow r_{b:1}^* - y_1 r_b$; thus $[c_\beta] = \mathsf{Com}_{ck}(\beta /\!/ 0; \varrho_b)$.

Thus, Emul has extracted $\mathbf{t}, r_t, \tau, \varrho_t, \mathbf{b}, r_b, \beta, \varrho_b$, and thus also $\mathbf{t}^* \leftarrow y\mathbf{t} + \tau$ and $\mathbf{b}^* \leftarrow y\mathbf{b} + \beta$.

Consider now the third transcript with y_3. Since $Q_N = y\gamma$, we obtain from Eq. (5) that $P(y_3) := y_3^N(\gamma - \prod_{i=1}^{N} t_i) - p'(y_3) = 0$, where $p'(Y)$ is some degree

$\leq N-1$ polynomial. Since the emulator knows $\mathbf{t}^*$ and $\mathbf{b}^*$, it knows $P(Y)$. Since a non-zero degree-$(\leq N)$ polynomial $P(Y)$ has $\leq N$ roots, then the probability that $P(\mathsf{y}_3) = 0$ and $P(Y) \neq 0$ is at most N/σ_y. Since $P(Y) = 0$ implies that $\gamma = \prod_{i=1}^{N} \mathsf{t}_i$, Emul has retrieved a witness $\mathtt{wit} = (\mathbf{t}, r_\mathsf{t})$, such that $[c_\mathsf{t}] = \mathsf{Com}_{\mathsf{ck}}(\mathbf{t}; r_\mathsf{t})$ and $\gamma = \prod_{i=1}^{N} \mathsf{t}_i$, with an overwhelming probability. Thus, this argument has witness-extended emulation.

PERFECT SHVZK: We construct the following simulator Sim. (This part of the proof follows [21] quite closely.) The simulator is depicted in Fig. 2. Since Sim's output does not depend on $\mathbf{t}$ or r_t, it reveals no information about the witness. Clearly, Sim's output will be accepted by the verifier.

Sample $\mathbf{t}^* \leftarrow_\$ \mathbb{Z}_q^N$, $r_\mathsf{t}^* \leftarrow_\$ \mathbb{Z}_q$;
Set $[c_\tau] \leftarrow \mathsf{Com}_{\mathsf{ck}}(\mathbf{t}^*; r_\mathsf{t}^*) - \mathsf{y}[c_\mathsf{t}]$;
Set $Q_1 \leftarrow \mathsf{t}_1^*$, $Q_i \leftarrow_\$ \mathbb{Z}_q$ for $i \in \{2, \ldots, N-1\}$, and $Q_N \leftarrow \mathsf{y}\gamma$;
Sample $r_\mathsf{b} \leftarrow_\$ \mathbb{Z}_q$;

1   Set $[c_b] \leftarrow \mathsf{Com}_{\mathsf{ck}}(\mathbf{0}_N; r_\mathsf{b})$;
Set $\mathsf{b}_1^* \leftarrow \mathsf{y}Q_2 - \mathsf{t}_2^* Q_1, \ldots, \mathsf{b}_{N-1}^* \leftarrow \mathsf{y}Q_N - \mathsf{t}_N^* Q_{N-1}$;
Sample $r_\mathsf{b}^* \leftarrow_\$ \mathbb{Z}_q$;
Set $[c_\beta] \leftarrow \mathsf{Com}_{\mathsf{ck}}(\mathbf{b}^* /\!/ 0; r_\mathsf{b}^*) - \mathsf{y}[c_b]$;
Return $([c_\tau, c_b, c_\beta]; \mathsf{y}; \mathbf{t}^*, r_\mathsf{t}^*, \mathbf{b}^*, r_\mathsf{b}^*; \mathsf{acc}, \mathsf{z})$;

Fig. 2. Simulator $\mathsf{Sim}(\mathsf{ck}, \mathtt{inp}, (\mathsf{y}, \mathsf{z}))$ of the coefficient-product argument

We use the same idea as [21] to show that this simulator provides output from the correct distribution. First, consider the following simulator Sim_t that otherwise outputs the same thing as Sim, except that it uses the knowledge of $\mathbf{t}$ and r_b to construct $[c_b]$ as $[c_b] \leftarrow \mathsf{Com}_{\mathsf{ck}}(\mathbf{b} /\!/ 0; r_\mathsf{b})$. More precisely, it works as Sim, except that Line 1 in Fig. 2 is replaced with the following three steps:

---

for $i \in [1 \mathinner{.\,.} N]$ **do** $\Delta_i \leftarrow Q_i - \mathsf{y} \prod_{j=1}^{i} \mathsf{t}_i$
for $i \in [1 \mathinner{.\,.} N-1]$ **do** $\mathsf{b}_i \leftarrow \Delta_{i+1} - \mathsf{t}_{i+1}\Delta_i - \tau_{i+1} \prod_{j=1}^{i} \mathsf{t}_j$
$[c_b] \leftarrow \mathsf{Com}_{\mathsf{ck}}(\mathbf{b} /\!/ 0; r_\mathsf{b})$;

Clearly, the output of Sim_t comes from the same distribution as the output of Sim, but it has constructed $[c_b]$ as needed due to the knowledge of $\mathbf{t}$ and r_t.

Finally, clearly Sim_t chooses the values from the same distribution as the real prover (given that y and z are chosen randomly), but in a different order. $\square$

Complexity. Clearly, the prover's computational complexity is dominated by three $\approx N$-wide multi-exponentiations, while the verifier's computational complexity is dominated by one $\approx N$-wide multi-exponentiation. The communication complexity is dominated by $\approx 2N$ elements of $\mathbb{Z}_q$.

4   A Characterization of Permutation Matrices

Next, we prove the following theorem that generalizes a result from [32]. Namely, [32] let the verifier to choose N random values $X_1, \ldots, X_N$. To reduce communication (by avoiding sending all N variables to the prover), they used a pseudo-random number generator to obtain N values X_i out of a short seed X_0. Our result shows that the pseudo-random number generator can be replaced by a what we call *PM-evidential* family of multivariate polynomials. On top of the efficiency aspect, we obtain a novel mathematical characterization of permutation matrices of independent interest.

Definition 2 (PM-evidential). *Let $\mathbb{F}$ be a field. A family of N-degree ν-variate polynomials $\{\psi_i(\boldsymbol{X})\}_{i=1}^N$, $\psi_i \in \mathbb{F}[X_1, \ldots, X_\nu]$, is PM-evidential over $\mathbb{F}$, if for $\Psi(\boldsymbol{X}) := \prod_{i=1}^N \psi_i(\boldsymbol{X})$,*

(i) $\psi_i(\boldsymbol{X}) \neq 0$ for each i,

(ii) for each $\boldsymbol{a} \in \mathbb{F}^n$ with $wt(\boldsymbol{a}) > 1$, $\left(\sum_{i=1}^N a_i \psi_i(\boldsymbol{X}) \right) \nmid \Psi(\boldsymbol{X})$, and

(iii) $(\psi_i(\boldsymbol{X}))^2 \nmid \Psi(\boldsymbol{X})$ for each i.

One can use PM-evidential polynomials to efficiently check whether a matrix is a permutation matrix, as explained by the following result.

Lemma 2. *Let $\mathbb{F}$ be a field. Let $\boldsymbol{M}$ be an $N \times N$ matrix over $\mathbb{F}$, let $\boldsymbol{X} = (X_1, \ldots, X_\nu)$ be a vector of $\nu \leq N$ indeterminates, and let $\{\psi_i(\boldsymbol{X})\}_{i=1}^N$ be PM-evidential over $\mathbb{F}$. Let $\boldsymbol{\psi}(\boldsymbol{X}) := (\psi_1(\boldsymbol{X}), \ldots, \psi_N(\boldsymbol{X}))^\top$, $\Psi_{\boldsymbol{M}}(\boldsymbol{X}) := \prod_{i=1}^N \langle \boldsymbol{M}_i^\top, \boldsymbol{\psi}(\boldsymbol{X}) \rangle$, and $\Psi(\boldsymbol{X}) := \prod_{i=1}^N \psi_i(\boldsymbol{X})$ in $\mathbb{F}[\boldsymbol{X}]$. Then $\boldsymbol{M}$ is a permutation matrix iff $\Psi_{\boldsymbol{M}}(\boldsymbol{X}) = \Psi(\boldsymbol{X})$ and $\boldsymbol{M} \cdot \boldsymbol{1}_N = \boldsymbol{1}_N$.*

Proof. ($\Rightarrow$) Assume $\boldsymbol{M}$ is a permutation matrix. Then clearly, $\Psi_{\boldsymbol{M}}(\boldsymbol{X}) = \Psi(\boldsymbol{X})$ (since then $\Psi_{\boldsymbol{M}}(\boldsymbol{X})$ is a product of ψ_i-s in a permuted order) and $\boldsymbol{M} \cdot \boldsymbol{1}_N = \boldsymbol{1}_N$.

($\Leftarrow$) Assume that $\Psi_{\boldsymbol{M}}(\boldsymbol{X}) = \Psi(\boldsymbol{X})$. Consider the following three cases. First, if some row $\boldsymbol{M}_i$ is a zero vector, then $\Psi_{\boldsymbol{M}}$ is a zero polynomial, and thus $\Psi(\boldsymbol{X}) = 0$, a contradiction to Item i in Definition 2. Second, if the ith row $\boldsymbol{M}_i$ contains more than one non-zero element, then $(\sum M_{ij} \psi_j(\boldsymbol{X})) \mid \Psi_{\boldsymbol{M}}(\boldsymbol{X})$, where $wt(\boldsymbol{M}_i) > 1$. A contradiction with Item ii in Definition 2. Third, if the jth column $\boldsymbol{M}^{(j)}$ contains more than one non-zero element, then—since each row contains exactly one non-zero element—$\psi_j^2(\boldsymbol{X}) \mid \Psi_{\boldsymbol{M}}(\boldsymbol{X})$, contradicting Item iii in Definition 2).

Hence, each row and column of $\boldsymbol{M}$ have exactly one non-zero element. Finally, since $\boldsymbol{M} \cdot \boldsymbol{1}_N = \boldsymbol{1}_N$, the non-zero elements of $\boldsymbol{M}$ must equal one. $\square$

Intuitively, Terelius and Wikström proved that the family $\{\psi_i(\boldsymbol{X}) = X_i\}$ is PM-evidential. Next, we construct a simple family of PM-evidential polynomials, where the number of indeterminates is just two. More precisely, we show that the family of polynomials $\{\psi_k(X, Y) = X^k + Y\}_{k=0}^N$ in $\mathbb{F}[X, Y]$ is PM-evidential.

Lemma 3. *The family of polynomials $\{\psi_k\}_{k=1}^N$, where $\psi_k(X, Y) = X^{k-1} + Y$, is PM-evidential.*

To prove Lemma 3, we need to show that the polynomials $X^k + Y$ are irreducible. For the latter, we will use the well-known Eisenstein's criterion.

Proposition 1 (Eisenstein's Criterion [24]). *Let $\mathbb{V}$ be a unique factorization domain. Let $p(X) = \sum_{i=0}^{k} a_i X^i \in \mathbb{V}[X]$. Then $p(X)$ is irreducible in $\mathbb{V}[X]$ if there exists an irreducible element $s \in \mathbb{V}$ such that the following three conditions hold:*

(i) $s \mid a_i$ for every $i \in [0 .. k - 1]$,
(ii) $s \nmid a_k$,
(iii) $s^2 \nmid a_0$

Proof (Proof of Lemma 3). Items i of Definition 2 holds trivially.

To show that Items ii and iii hold, we first use Eisenstein's criterion to show $X^k + Y$ is irreducible, for $k \in [0 .. N - 1]$. Think of $X^k + Y$ as a polynomial in $\mathbb{V}[X]$, where $\mathbb{V} = \mathbb{F}[Y]$. Then, $a_0 = Y$, $a_i = 0$ for $i \in [1 .. k - 1]$ and $a_k = 1$. Taking $s = Y$, it is easy to see that the three conditions of the Eisenstein's criterion are satisfied. Thus, $X^k + Y$ is irreducible.

To see that Item ii holds, suppose that

$$\sum_{i=1}^{N-1} a_i \psi_i(X, Y) = L(X, Y) , \tag{8}$$

where $L(X, Y) \mid \Psi(X, Y)$. Since $\mathbb{F}[X, Y]$ is a unique factorization domain and ψ_k are all irreducible, we get that $L(X, Y)$ is a product of some of ψ_i. Since on the left hand side of Eq. (8), the degree of Y is 1, then also also the degree of Y on the right hand is also 1. Thus, $L(X, Y) = \psi_j(X, Y)$ for some j, and hence, $\sum_{i=1}^{N-1} a_i \psi_i(X, Y) = \psi_j(X, Y)$. Because they have distinct degrees, $\psi_i(X, Y)$ are linearly independent. Thus we get that $a_i = 0$ if $i \neq j$ and $a_j = 1$. Thus, $wt(a) = 1$ and Item ii holds.

Finally, Item iii follows from the fact that $\psi_i(X, Y)$ are irreducible and distinct. $\square$

While we believe that the proposed solution is close to optimal, we leave it as an open question of whether some other families give even better communication and computational complexity for the final shuffle argument.

Additionally, in the proof of the new shuffle argument of Sect. 5, we will need to invert a certain matrix $(\psi_i(x_j))_{i,j}$ obtained by rewinding the argument. We need to show that the probability that this matrix is invertible is overwhelming. For that analysis, we give the following definition.

Definition 3. *Define*

$$\mathsf{ni}(\psi, \sigma_\mathsf{x}, q) := \max_{x_0, \ldots, x_{N-2}} \left\{ \Pr_{x_{N-1}} [(\psi_i(x_j))_{i,j} \text{ is not invertible}] \mid \begin{array}{c} x_{0,i}, \ldots, x_{N-1,i} \text{ are} \\ \text{pairwise different} \\ \text{for every } i \end{array} \right\} .$$

Here, we assume that $x_0, \ldots, x_{N-1} \in \{0, \ldots, \sigma_\mathsf{x} - 1\}^\nu$.

For good values in the proof, we want to make this value as small as possible.

Lemma 4. *Let* $x_1, \ldots, x_N$ *be distinct random elements of* $\{0, \ldots, \sigma_x - 1\}$, *and let* $y_1, \ldots, y_N$ *be distinct random elements of* $\{0, \ldots, \sigma_x - 1\}$. *Let* M *be the matrix with elements* $(x_i^{j-1} + y_i)_{i,j=1}^N$ *in* $\mathbb{Z}_q$. *Then,* $\det(M) = 0$ *with probability at most* $1/q$. *Additionally, for fixed distinct* $x_1, \ldots, x_N$ *and fixed distinct* $y_1, \ldots, y_{N-1}$, *there exists at most one* y_N, *such that* M *is not invertible.*

Proof. Let the determinant of M be D. Denote $\boldsymbol{x} = (x_1, \ldots, x_N)$ and $S := [1 .. N]$. For a subset $S' \subseteq S$, let M_S be the matrix, where the ith row is $(x_i^{j-1})_{j=1}^N$, if $i \in S'$, and $(y_i)_{j=1}^N$, if $i \notin S'$. Since $\det\left(\begin{smallmatrix} A \\ b + c \\ D \end{smallmatrix}\right) = \det\left(\begin{smallmatrix} A \\ b \\ D \end{smallmatrix}\right) + \det\left(\begin{smallmatrix} A \\ c \\ D \end{smallmatrix}\right)$, we get by induction that $D = \sum_{S' \subseteq S} \det(M_{S'})$.

Moreover, if $|S'| < N - 1$, then $\det(M_{S'}) = 0$. Really, in this case, there exist at least two rows i and j, where the elements are just y_i and y_j. The determinant of every 2×2-submatrix from these two rows is 0. Thus, by the cofactor expansion of a determinant, $\det(M_{S'}) = 0$. Thus, $D = \det(M_S) + \sum_{i=1}^N \det(M_{S \setminus \{i\}})$. Now, M_S is a Vandermonde matrix and thus $\det(M_S) = \prod_{1 \le i < j \le N} (x_j - x_i) \ne 0$.

On the other hand, observe that $\det(M_{S \setminus \{i\}})$ is equal to y_i times $P_i(\boldsymbol{x})$ for some polynomial P_i. There are two possible cases. Either $P_i(\boldsymbol{x}) = 0$, for all i, or at least one $P_i(\boldsymbol{x})$ is nonzero. In the first case, $D = \det(M_S) \ne 0$. Note that then, there exists no y_I such that $\det(M_S) = 0$. In the second case, say $P_I(\boldsymbol{x}) \ne 0$ holds for a concrete I. Then, $D = 0$ iff $y_I = -(\det(M_S) + \sum_{i \ne I} y_i P_i(\boldsymbol{x}))/P_I(\boldsymbol{x})$, which is true for precisely one value of y_I.

Thus, presuming that $x_1, \ldots, x_N$ are pairwise different and taking the probability over the choice y_N,

$$\Pr[D = 0] = 0 \cdot \Pr[\forall i \in S, P_i(\boldsymbol{x}) = 0] + \tfrac{1}{q} \cdot (1 - \Pr[\forall i \in S, P_i(\boldsymbol{x}) = 0]) \le \tfrac{1}{q} .$$

This proves the claim. $\square$

5   Shuffle Argument

Let N be the number of shuffled ciphertexts, let $[\boldsymbol{w}]$ and $[\widehat{\boldsymbol{w}}]$ be two tuples of the ciphertexts. Assume that pk is the public key of an additively homomorphic (in our case, the lifted Elgamal [11]) cryptosystem. In a *shuffle argument*, the prover aims to convince the verifier that, for a fixed pk, he knows a permutation $\pi \in S_N$ and a vector of randomizers $\boldsymbol{s} \in \mathbb{Z}_q^N$, such that $[\widehat{\boldsymbol{w}}_i] = [\boldsymbol{w}_{\pi^{-1}(i)}] + \mathsf{Enc}_{\mathsf{pk}}(0; s_{\pi^{-1}(i)})$. Formally, it is an argument for the relation

$$\mathcal{R}_{\mathsf{pk}} := \left\{ \begin{array}{l} (([\boldsymbol{w}], [\widehat{\boldsymbol{w}}]), (\pi, \boldsymbol{s}) \in S_N \times \mathbb{Z}_q^N) : \\ \forall i \in [1 .. N], [\widehat{\boldsymbol{w}}_i] = [\boldsymbol{w}_{\pi^{-1}(i)}] + \mathsf{Enc}_{\mathsf{pk}}(0; s_{\pi^{-1}(i)}) \end{array} \right\} .$$

Before going on, we recall that if for some matrix $M \in \mathbb{Z}_q^{N \times N}$, $[u_i] = \mathsf{Com}_{\mathsf{ck}}(M^{(i)}; \hat{r}_i)$, then for any $\mathbf{t} \in \mathbb{Z}_q^N$,

$$\langle[\boldsymbol{u}],\mathbf{t}\rangle = \sum_{i=1}^{N} \mathbf{t}_i[u_i] = \mathsf{Com}_{\mathsf{ck}}\left(\sum_{i=1}^{N} \boldsymbol{M}^{(i)}\mathbf{t}_i; \sum_{i=1}^{N} \hat{r}_i\mathbf{t}_i\right) = \mathsf{Com}_{\mathsf{ck}}(\boldsymbol{M}\mathbf{t}; \langle\hat{\boldsymbol{r}},\mathbf{t}\rangle) \ . \quad (9)$$

Next, we will give a short explanation of the argument on Fig. 3. The prover P and the verifier V do the following:

(1) P commits to the permutation matrix $\boldsymbol{M}$, where $[u_i]$ is a commitment to $\boldsymbol{M}^{(i)}$ for $i < N$, and $[u_N]$ is homomorphically computed as a commitment to $\mathbf{1}_N - \sum_{i=1}^{N-1} \boldsymbol{M}^{(i)}$. (This guarantees that $\sum_{i=1}^{N} \boldsymbol{M}^{(i)} = \mathbf{1}_N$.)

(2) V chooses $\mathbf{x}$ after P committed to $\boldsymbol{M}$. Let $\mathbf{t} = \psi(\mathbf{x})$. Both parties compute a permuted vector $\hat{\mathbf{t}}$, $\hat{\mathbf{t}}_i = \mathbf{t}_{\pi^{-1}(i)}$, of the vector $\mathbf{t}$.

(3) P proves that he knows how to open $\langle\mathbf{t},[\boldsymbol{u}]\rangle$ as a commitment of $\boldsymbol{M}\mathbf{t}$.

(4) P proves, by using the coefficient-product argument, that $\prod_{i=1}^{N} \hat{\mathbf{t}}_i = \prod_{i=1}^{N} \mathbf{t}_i$. Hence, the verifier is convinced (via Lemma 2) that $\boldsymbol{M}$ is a permutation matrix. Thus, $\hat{\mathbf{t}}$ is a permutation of $\mathbf{t}$.

The coefficient-product argument is interleaved with the main argument for efficiency reasons. For easier readability, we have added the symbol($) to the lines in Fig. 3 that contain the coefficient-product argument.

(5) Finally, P proves that he used the same matrix $\boldsymbol{M}$ (together with some additional randomness) to form $[\widehat{\boldsymbol{w}}]$ from $[\boldsymbol{w}]$. Since $\boldsymbol{M}$ is a permutation matrix, the shuffle argument is sound (more precisely, has witness-extended emulation).

Construction. The new shuffle argument Π_{sh} is depicted by Fig. 3. Here, we assume $\sigma_{\mathsf{x}}, \sigma_{\mathsf{y}}, \sigma_{\mathsf{z}} \geq 2^{\lambda}$, $\mathbb{G}$ is a group of order q, and N is the number of ciphertexts with $N < 2^{0.5\lambda}$ Fix a family of PM-evidential polynomials $\psi_i \in \mathbb{Z}[X_1, \ldots, X_\nu]$ for some $\nu \leq N$, such that $\mathsf{ni}(\psi, \sigma_{\mathsf{x}}, q)$ is negligible. The common inputs of the prover and the verifier are the ciphertext tuples $[\boldsymbol{w}] = ([\boldsymbol{w}_1], \ldots, [\boldsymbol{w}_N])$ and $[\widehat{\boldsymbol{w}}] = ([\widehat{\boldsymbol{w}}_1], \ldots, [\widehat{\boldsymbol{w}}_N])$, with $[\widehat{\boldsymbol{w}}_i] = [\boldsymbol{w}_{\pi^{-1}(i)}] + \mathsf{Enc}_{\mathsf{pk}}(0; s_{\pi^{-1}(i)})$. The prover's witness is $(\pi, \boldsymbol{s}) \in S_N \times \mathbb{Z}_q^N$. The CRS consists of $\mathsf{pk} = [1 /\!/ h]$, and $\mathsf{ck} = [h_1, \ldots, h_N]$ as in the extended Pedersen.

We will use the terms and algorithms from the coefficient-product argument and we will add a subscript G to them to distinguish them from the analogous terms in the main argument.

Theorem 2 (Security of the shuffle argument). Π_{sh} *is perfectly complete and perfectly SHVZK. If the commitment scheme is computationally binding then this shuffle argument has witness-extended emulation. More precisely, let* $d = \max_i \deg \psi_i(\boldsymbol{X})$ *and* $d_{sum} = \sum_{i=1}^{N} \deg \psi_i(\boldsymbol{X})$. *Let* $\varepsilon \geq \zeta + 1/\sigma_{\mathsf{z}}$ *be the success probability of* P* *to make* V *to accept,* $\varepsilon \geq \varepsilon' \geq \varepsilon - 1/\sigma_{\mathsf{z}}$, *and* $\zeta = \mathsf{ni} + \frac{N(N-1)}{2\sigma_{\mathsf{x}}^\nu} + \frac{N}{\sigma_{\mathsf{y}}}$. *The emulator either recovers the witness or breaks the binding property of the commitment scheme with probability at least* $1 - d_{sum}/\sigma_{\mathsf{x}} - N/\sigma_{\mathsf{y}} - 1/\sigma_{\mathsf{z}}$ *and makes* $\leq (2N+1)/(\varepsilon' - \zeta)$ *queries to* $\boldsymbol{V}$, *where* ζ *is defined as above.*

1. The prover $\mathsf{P}(\mathsf{crs}, ([\boldsymbol{w}], [\widehat{\boldsymbol{w}}]), (\pi, \boldsymbol{s}))$ does:
   (a) For $i \in [1 .. N-1]$: $r_i \leftarrow_\$ \mathbb{Z}_q$; $[u_i] \leftarrow \mathsf{Com}_{\mathsf{ck}}(\boldsymbol{e}_{\pi(i)}; r_{\pi(i)}) /\!\!/ := [h_{\pi(i)}] + r_\pi(i)[1]$
   (b) $[u_N] \leftarrow \mathsf{Com}_{\mathsf{ck}}(\mathbf{1}_N; 0) - \sum_{i=1}^{N-1}[u_i]$.
   (c) Sample $\boldsymbol{\tau} \leftarrow_\$ \mathbb{Z}_q^N$, $\varrho_t \leftarrow_\$ \mathbb{Z}_q$, $\varrho_f \leftarrow_\$ \mathbb{Z}_q.$ (\$)
   (d) Set $[c_\tau] \leftarrow \mathsf{Com}_{\mathsf{ck}}(\boldsymbol{\tau}; \varrho_t)$. (\$)
   (e) Set $\Delta_1 \leftarrow \tau_1$, $\Delta_N \leftarrow 0$. For $i \in [2 .. N-1]$: sample $\Delta_i \leftarrow_\$ \mathbb{Z}_q.$(\$)
   (f) For $i \in [1 .. N-1]$: set $\beta_i \leftarrow -\tau_{i+1}\Delta_i.$(\$)
   (g) Sample $\varrho_b \leftarrow_\$ \mathbb{Z}_q$. Denote $\boldsymbol{\beta} = (\beta_1, \ldots, \beta_{N-1})^\top$.
   (h) Compute $[c_\beta] \leftarrow \mathsf{Com}_{\mathsf{ck}}(\boldsymbol{\beta} /\!/ 0; \varrho_b)$.(\$)
   (i) Set $[\boldsymbol{F_\omega}] \leftarrow \sum_{i=1}^N \tau_i[\widehat{\boldsymbol{w}}_i] + \mathsf{Enc}_{\mathsf{pk}}(0; -\varrho_f).$ $/\!/$ The only online step
   (j) Send $([u_1], \ldots, [u_{N-1}], [c_\tau], [c_\beta], [\boldsymbol{F_\omega}])$ to the verifier.
2. The verifier generates random $\mathsf{x} \leftarrow \{0, \ldots, \sigma_{\mathsf{x}} - 1\}^\nu$. He sends x to the prover. For $i \in [1 .. N]$: set $\mathsf{t}_i \leftarrow \psi_i(\mathsf{x})$.
3. The prover does the following:
   (a) For $i \in [1 .. N]$: set $\mathsf{t}_i \leftarrow \psi_i(\mathsf{x})$.
   (b) For $i \in [1 .. N]$: set $\hat{\mathsf{t}}_i \leftarrow \mathsf{t}_{\pi^{-1}(i)}$.
   (c) $X_0 \leftarrow 1$. For $i = [1 .. N-1]$: $X_i \leftarrow X_{i-1}\hat{\mathsf{t}}_i$, $\mathsf{b}_i \leftarrow \Delta_{i+1} - \hat{\mathsf{t}}_{i+1}\Delta_i - \tau_{i+1}X_i.$(\$)
   (d) Let $\mathbf{b} := (\mathsf{b}_1, \ldots, \mathsf{b}_{N-1})^\top$. Sample $r_b \leftarrow_\$ \mathbb{Z}_q$. Set $[c_b] \leftarrow \mathsf{Com}_{\mathsf{ck}}(\mathbf{b} /\!/ 0; r_b)$.
   (e) Send $[c_b]$ to the verifier.
4. The verifier generates random $\mathsf{y} \leftarrow \{1, \ldots, \sigma_{\mathsf{y}}\}$. He sends y to the prover.
5. The prover does:
   (a) Set $r_t \leftarrow \langle \hat{\mathbf{t}}, \boldsymbol{r} \rangle$, $r_f \leftarrow \langle \mathbf{t}, \boldsymbol{s} \rangle$.
   (b) Compute $\mathbf{t}^* \leftarrow \mathsf{y}\hat{\mathbf{t}} + \boldsymbol{\tau}$, $r_t^* \leftarrow \mathsf{y}r_t + \varrho_t$, $r_f^* \leftarrow \mathsf{y}r_f + \varrho_f.$(\$)
   (c) Set $\mathbf{b}^* \leftarrow \mathsf{y}\mathbf{b} + \boldsymbol{\beta} \in \mathbb{Z}_q^{N-1}$, $r_b^* \leftarrow \mathsf{y}r_b + \varrho_b.$(\$)
   (d) Send $(\mathbf{t}^*, r_t^*, r_f^*, \mathbf{b}^*, r_b^*)$ to the verifier.
6. The verifier sets $\gamma \leftarrow \prod_{i=1}^N \mathsf{t}_i$, $[u_N] \leftarrow \mathsf{Com}_{\mathsf{ck}}(\mathbf{1}_N; 0) - \sum_{i=1}^{N-1}[u_i]$,

$$[\hat{c}_t] \leftarrow \langle \mathbf{t}, [\boldsymbol{u}] \rangle \ , \quad [\boldsymbol{F}] \leftarrow \langle \mathbf{t}, [\boldsymbol{w}] \rangle \ . \tag{10}$$

He generates a random $\mathsf{z} \leftarrow \{0, \ldots, \sigma_{\mathsf{z}} - 1\}$ for batch verification. He checks:

$$\mathsf{y}[\boldsymbol{F}] + [\boldsymbol{F_\omega}] =^? \sum_{i=1}^N \mathsf{t}_i^*[\widehat{\boldsymbol{w}}_i] + \mathsf{Enc}_{\mathsf{pk}}(0; -r_f^*) \ , \tag{11}$$

$$\mathsf{y}[\hat{c}_t] + [c_\tau] + \mathsf{z}(\mathsf{y}[c_b] + [c_\beta]) =^? \mathsf{Com}_{\mathsf{ck}}(\mathbf{t}^* + \mathsf{z}(\mathbf{b}^* /\!/ 0); r_t^* + \mathsf{z}r_b^*) \ . (\$) \tag{12}$$

Set $Q_1 \leftarrow \mathsf{t}_1^*$, $Q_2 \leftarrow (\mathsf{t}_2^*Q_1 + \mathsf{b}_1^*)/\mathsf{y}, \ldots, Q_N \leftarrow (\mathsf{t}_N^*Q_{N-1} + \mathsf{b}_{N-1}^*)/\mathsf{y}$. He checks that $Q_N =^? \mathsf{y}\gamma.$(\$)
Return $(\mathsf{acc}, \mathsf{z})$ iff all checks accept. Otherwise, return $(\mathsf{rej}, \mathsf{z})$.

Fig. 3. The new shuffle argument Π_{sh}. Dashed/Dotted formulas correspond to expensive ($\approx N$ fixed-base/multi exponentiations) computations only. A twice boxed formula signifies $\approx 2N$ operations.

Proof. First, if $[u_i]$ are honestly generated, then from Eq. (9) we get that $[\hat{c}_t] = \langle[u], t\rangle = \mathsf{Com}_{\mathsf{ck}}(\sum_{i=1}^{N} t_i e_{\pi(i)}; \sum_{i=1}^{N} t_i r_{\pi(i)}) = \mathsf{Com}_{\mathsf{ck}}(\sum t_{\pi^{-1}(i)} e_i; \sum t_i r_{\pi(i)}) = \mathsf{Com}_{\mathsf{ck}}(\hat{t}; r_t)$ for $\hat{t}, r_t$ defined as in Items 3b and 5a in Fig. 3.

COMPLETENESS: assume that $[w_i] = \mathsf{Enc}_{\mathsf{pk}}(m_i; R_i)$ and $[\hat{w}_i] = \mathsf{Enc}_{\mathsf{pk}}(m_{\pi^{-1}(i)}; R_{\pi^{-1}(i)} + s_{\pi^{-1}(i)})$ for some (possibly unknown) m_i, R_i, and s_i. According to Eq. (10), $[F] = \langle t, [w]\rangle = \mathsf{Enc}_{\mathsf{pk}}(\langle t, m\rangle; \langle t, R\rangle)$, and according to Item 1i,

$$[F_\omega] = \sum_{i=1}^{N} \tau_i[\hat{w}_i] + \mathsf{Enc}_{\mathsf{pk}}(0; -\varrho_f)$$
$$= \sum_{i=1}^{N} \tau_i \cdot \mathsf{Enc}_{\mathsf{pk}}(m_{\pi^{-1}(i)}; R_{\pi^{-1}(i)} + s_{\pi^{-1}(i)}) + \mathsf{Enc}_{\mathsf{pk}}(0; -\varrho_f)$$
$$= \mathsf{Enc}_{\mathsf{pk}}(\langle\tau, \hat{m}\rangle; \langle\tau, \hat{R} + \hat{s}\rangle - \varrho_f) ,$$

where $\hat{s}_i = s_{\pi^{-1}(i)}$ and $\hat{R}_i = R_{\pi^{-1}(i)}$. Denoting $\hat{m}_i = m_{\pi^{-1}(i)}$, $y[F] + [F_\omega] + \mathsf{Enc}_{\mathsf{pk}}(0; r_f^*) = \mathsf{Enc}_{\mathsf{pk}}(y\langle t, m\rangle + \langle\tau, \hat{m}\rangle; y\langle t, R\rangle + \langle\tau, \hat{R} + \hat{s}\rangle - \varrho_f + \varrho_f) = \mathsf{Enc}_{\mathsf{pk}}(\langle t^*, \hat{m}\rangle; \langle t^*, \hat{R} + \hat{s}\rangle)$, which is equal to $\langle t^*, [\hat{w}]\rangle$ as required by Eq. (11).

Next, if M is the permutation matrix corresponding to the permutation π, then $M_{ij} = 1$ iff $i = \pi(j)$. Hence, $M^{(j)} = e_{\pi(j)}$ and $[u_i] = \mathsf{Com}_{\mathsf{ck}}(e_{\pi(i)}; \hat{r}_i) = \mathsf{Com}_{\mathsf{ck}}(M^{(i)}; \hat{r}_i)$. According to Eq. (10), $[\hat{c}_t] = \langle t, [u]\rangle = \mathsf{Com}_{\mathsf{ck}}(Mt; \langle\hat{r}, t\rangle) = \mathsf{Com}_{\mathsf{ck}}(\hat{t}; \langle\hat{r}, t\rangle)$, where $\hat{t}_i = t_{\pi^{-1}(i)}$. According to Items 1d and 5b, $y[\hat{c}_t] + [c_\tau] = \mathsf{Com}_{\mathsf{ck}}(y\hat{t} + \tau; yr_t + \varrho_t) = \mathsf{Com}_{\mathsf{ck}}(t^*; r_t^*)$. According to Items 1h, 3d and 5c, $y[c_b] + [c_\beta] = \mathsf{Com}_{\mathsf{ck}}((yb + \beta) /\!/ 0; yr_b + \varrho_b) = \mathsf{Com}_{\mathsf{ck}}(b^* /\!/ 0; r_b^*)$. Thus, $y[\hat{c}_t] + [c_\tau] + z(y[c_b] + [c_\beta]) = \mathsf{Com}_{\mathsf{ck}}(t^* + z(b^* /\!/ 0); r_t^* + zr_b^*)$. Hence, Eq. (12) holds.

PERFECT HVZK: Assume that we are given t and y. For fixed t, y, z, the simulator is depicted in Fig. 4. Clearly, the verifier of Fig. 3 will accept the simulated proof (this is taken care of by Lines 2, 3 and 5, together with the definition of b_i^* and Q_N).

Similarly to the proof of Theorem 1, we can argue that the output of the simulator Sim follows the correct distribution (we first change Line 4, obtaining a hybrid simulator Sim_t, and then argue that the outputs of Sim and Sim_t come from the same distribution, and the output of Sim_t and the real protocol come from the same distribution). Thus, we get a simulator for the shuffle argument.

WITNESS-EXTENDED EMULATION: As in the proof of Theorem 1, from Eq. (12) it follows—since this is a standard batch verification, [2]—that with probability $1 - 1/\sigma_z$, Eq. (7) holds. Hence, as in the case of the coefficient-product argument, we define another shuffle argument Π'_{sh} that is exactly the same as Π_{sh}, except that the verifier accepts not when Eq. (12) holds but Eq. (7) holds (that is, we do not use batch verification.) It is clear that if an adversary succeeds with probability ε against Π_{sh}, then it succeeds with probability not larger than ε', $\varepsilon \geq \varepsilon' \geq \varepsilon - 1/\sigma_z$, against Π'_{sh}. Let V' be the verifier of Π'_{sh}.

Let P^* be a prover that makes V' to accept with probability ε'. We first run the argument and obtain one accepting transcript tr. If P^* fails to produce an acceptable transcript, then we reject. Assume now that the transcript is acceptable. In this case we need to extract a witness (π, s) that $([\hat{w}_i])$ is a shuffle

Compute $(\mathbf{x}, \mathbf{y}, \mathbf{z})$ from ω_V;
Set $\mathbf{t}_i \leftarrow \psi_i(\mathbf{x})$; $\gamma \leftarrow \prod_{i=1}^{N} \mathbf{t}_i$;
for $i \in [1 .. N-1]$ do sample $r_i \leftarrow_\$ \mathbb{Z}_q$; set $[u_i] \leftarrow \mathsf{Com}_{\mathsf{ck}}(e_i; r_i)$;
Set $[u_N] \leftarrow \mathsf{Com}_{\mathsf{ck}}(\mathbf{1}_N; 0) - \sum_{i=1}^{N-1} [u_i]$; Set $[\hat{c}_t] \leftarrow \langle \mathbf{t}, [u] \rangle$;
Sample $\mathbf{t}^* \leftarrow_\$ \mathbb{Z}_q^N$, $r_t^* \leftarrow_\$ \mathbb{Z}_q$;

2 | Set $[c_\tau] \leftarrow \mathsf{Com}_{\mathsf{ck}}(\mathbf{t}^*; r_t^*) - \mathbf{y}[\hat{c}_t]$; // need: $\mathbf{y}[\hat{c}_t] + [c_\tau] =^? \mathsf{Com}_{\mathsf{ck}}(\mathbf{t}^*; r_t^*)$

Set $[F] \leftarrow \langle \mathbf{t}, [w] \rangle$; Sample $r_f^* \leftarrow_\$ \mathbb{Z}_q$;

3 | Set $[F_\omega] \leftarrow \langle \mathbf{t}^*, [\hat{w}] \rangle + \mathsf{Enc}_{\mathsf{pk}}(0; -r_f^*) - \mathbf{y}[F]$;
// need: $\mathbf{y}[F] + [F_\omega] =^? \langle \mathbf{t}^*, [\hat{w}] \rangle + \mathsf{Enc}_{\mathsf{pk}}(0; -r_f^*)$;

Set $Q_1 \leftarrow \mathbf{t}_1^*$, $Q_i \leftarrow_\$ \mathbb{Z}_q$ for $i \in \{2, \ldots, N-1\}$, and $Q_N \leftarrow \mathbf{y}\gamma$;
Sample $b_1^* \leftarrow_\$ \mathbb{Z}_q$; Set $b_2^* \leftarrow \mathbf{y}Q_2 - \mathbf{t}_2^*Q_1, \ldots, b_N^* \leftarrow \mathbf{y}Q_N - \mathbf{t}_N^*Q_{N-1}$;
Sample $r_b^* \leftarrow_\$ \mathbb{Z}_q$; Sample $r_b \leftarrow_\$ \mathbb{Z}_q$;

4 | Set $[c_b] \leftarrow \mathsf{Com}_{\mathsf{ck}}(\mathbf{0}_N; r_b)$;

5 | Set $[c_\beta] \leftarrow \mathsf{Com}_{\mathsf{ck}}(\mathbf{b}^* /\!/ 0; r_b^*) - \mathbf{y}[c_b]$ // need: $\mathbf{y}[c_b] + [c_\beta] =^? \mathsf{Com}_{\mathsf{ck}}(\mathbf{b}^* /\!/ 0; r_b^*)$;

Return $([u_1], \ldots, [u_{N-1}], [c_\tau], [c_\beta], [F_\omega]; \mathbf{x}; [c_b]; \mathbf{y}; \mathbf{t}^*, r_t^*, r_f^*, \mathbf{b}^*, r_b^*; \mathsf{acc}, \mathbf{z})$;

Fig. 4. The simulator $\mathsf{Sim}(\mathsf{crs}, \mathtt{inp} = ([w], [\hat{w}]); \omega_V)$ in the proof of Theorem 2.

of $([w_i])$. For this, we rewind the argument to get more transcripts with randomly chosen challenges $\mathbf{x}, \mathbf{y}$, and use the witness-extended emulator of Π'_{cpa} to get openings of $[c_t]$. We repeat this until we obtain $N + 1$ acceptable transcripts. Let $tr_1 = tr$, and let the additional transcripts be $tr_j, j > 1$, where $tr_j =$

$$(([w, \hat{w}])_{i=1}^{N}; ([u_i])_{i=1}^{N-1}; [c_\tau, c_\beta, F_\omega]; \mathbf{x}_j; [c_{b:j}]; \mathbf{y}_j; \mathbf{t}_j^*, r_{t:j}^*, r_{f:j}^*, \mathbf{b}_j^*, r_{b:j}^*; \mathsf{acc}, \mathbf{z}_j) \ .$$

Clearly, the expected number of rewindings for this is N/ε. However, since we only need to extract a witness when the transcript is acceptable, the expected number of rewindings is only N. (As in [21], one can argue that combining expected polynomial-time algorithms results in an expected polynomial-time argument.) Since the emulator uses an expected polynomial number of rewindings, with an overwhelming probability it is the case that either (1) the argument is not acceptable, or (2) the argument is acceptable, but no event with negligible probability (like breaking the binding property of the commitment scheme or having collisions among randomly chosen challenges) occurs. Assume from now on that either (2) holds.

Let us show that Emul obtains the witness. Let $\mathbf{t}_j = \psi(\mathbf{x}_j)$ and $[\hat{c}_{t:j}] = \langle \mathbf{t}_j, [u] \rangle$. From Eq. (7) (left) and the jth transcript, we get

$$\mathbf{y}_j \mathbf{t}_j^\top [u] + [c_\tau] = \mathbf{y}_j \langle \mathbf{t}_j, [u] \rangle + [c_\tau] = \mathbf{y}_j [\hat{c}_{t:j}] + [c_\tau] = \langle \mathbf{t}_j^*, [h] \rangle + r_{t:j}^*[1] \ .$$

Hence,

$$(\mathbf{y}_j \mathbf{t}_j^\top - \mathbf{y}_1 \mathbf{t}_1^\top)[u] = \langle \mathbf{t}_j^*, [h] \rangle + r_{t:j}^*[1] \ .$$

Denote $\mathbf{T}_\mathbf{y} = (\mathbf{y}_2 \mathbf{t}_2 - \mathbf{y}_1 \mathbf{t}_1 \| \ldots \| \mathbf{y}_{N+1} \mathbf{t}_{N+1} - \mathbf{y}_1 \mathbf{t}_1)^\top$ and $\mathbf{T}^* = (\mathbf{y}_2 \mathbf{t}_2^* - \mathbf{y}_1 \mathbf{t}_1^* \| \ldots \| \mathbf{y}_{N+1} \mathbf{t}_{N+1}^* - \mathbf{y}_1 \mathbf{t}_1^*)^\top$. Since $\mathbf{T} = (\mathbf{t}_1 \| \ldots \| \mathbf{t}_N)$ is invertible with (this follows from Lemma 4), then also $\mathbf{T}_\mathbf{y}$ is invertible with overwhelming probability. Define $\mathbf{M} := \mathbf{T}_\mathbf{y}^{-1} \mathbf{T}^*$. Thus, $\mathbf{T}_\mathbf{y}[u] = \mathbf{T}^*[h] + (r_t^* - r_1^* \mathbf{1}_N)[1]$, and thus

$$[u] = \mathbf{M}[h] + \mathbf{T}_\mathbf{y}^{-1}(r_t^* - r_1^* \mathbf{1}_N)[1] \ .$$

Denote $[E_j] := \mathsf{Enc_{pk}}(0; r^*_{f:j})$. From Eq. (11) (left), we have $\mathsf{y}_j \mathbf{t}_j^\top [\boldsymbol{w}] + [F_\omega] = (\mathbf{t}_j^*)^\top [\widehat{\boldsymbol{w}}] + [E_j]$, and thus $(\mathsf{y}_j \mathbf{t}_j - \mathsf{y}_1 \mathbf{t}_j)^\top [\boldsymbol{w}] = (\mathbf{t}_j^* - \mathbf{t}_1^*)^\top [\widehat{\boldsymbol{w}}] + [E_j - E_1]$. Thus, $\boldsymbol{T}_\mathsf{y}[\boldsymbol{w}] = \boldsymbol{T}^*[\widehat{\boldsymbol{w}}] + [E] - \mathbf{1}_N[E_1]$ and thus

$$[\boldsymbol{w}] = \boldsymbol{M}[\widehat{\boldsymbol{w}}] + \boldsymbol{T}_\mathsf{y}^{-1}([E] - \mathbf{1}_N[E_1]) \ .$$

Hence, assuming $\boldsymbol{M}$ is a permutation matrix, we have recovered a permutation π and a randomness $\boldsymbol{s}$, such that $[\widehat{\boldsymbol{w}}_i] = [\boldsymbol{w}_{\pi^{-1}(i)}] + \mathsf{Enc_{pk}}(0; s_{\pi^{-1}(i)})$.

Next, we argue that $\boldsymbol{M}$ is a permutation matrix. Assume that P^* has a non-negligible success probability $1/f(\lambda)$, for a polynomial $f(X)$, to produce an acceptable argument. We run P^* and rewind to get $N + 2$ random challenges. We extract $\boldsymbol{M}$ and other values from the first $N + 1$ transcripts as above.

Consider the $(N + 2)$th argument. Define $\hat{\mathbf{t}}_{N+2} := \boldsymbol{M}^\top \mathbf{t}_{N+2}$. Thus, $\prod_{i=1}^N \langle \boldsymbol{M}^{(i)}, \boldsymbol{\psi}(\boldsymbol{x}_{N+2}) \rangle = \prod_{i=1}^N \langle \boldsymbol{M}^{(i)}, \mathbf{t}_{N+2} \rangle = \prod_{i=1}^N \hat{\mathbf{t}}_{N+2:i}$. Since $\varPi_\mathsf{cpa}$ has witness-extended emulation, then its emulator returns an opening of $[\hat{c}_{\mathsf{t}:N+2}]$ whose coefficient-product is equal to $\gamma_{N+2} := \prod_{i=1}^N \mathbf{t}_{N+2:i}$. Since the commitment scheme is binding and $[\hat{c}_{\mathsf{t}:N+2}] = \mathbf{t}_{N+2}^\top[\boldsymbol{u}]$, the opening is equal to $\boldsymbol{M}^\top \mathbf{t}_{N+2} = \hat{\mathbf{t}}_{N+2}$. Thus, by the soundness of the coefficient-product emulation, $\prod_{i=1}^N \hat{\mathbf{t}}_{N+2:i} = \prod_{i=1}^N \mathbf{t}_{N+2:i}$. Hence, $\prod_{i=1}^N \langle \boldsymbol{M}^{(i)}, \boldsymbol{\psi}(\boldsymbol{x}_{N+2}) \rangle = \prod_{i=1}^N \mathbf{t}_{N+2:i} = \prod_{i=1}^N \psi_i(\boldsymbol{x}_{N+2:i})$. Due to the Schwartz-Zippel lemma, from this it follows with an overwhelming probability that $\prod_{i=1}^N \langle \boldsymbol{M}^{(i)}, \boldsymbol{\psi}(\boldsymbol{X}_{N+2}) \rangle = \prod_{i=1}^N \psi_i(\boldsymbol{X}_{N+2:i})$ as a polynomial.

The ith row of $\boldsymbol{M} \cdot \mathbf{1}_N$ is $\sum_{j=1}^N M_{ij} = 1$ due to the choice of $[u_N]$, and thus $\hat{\boldsymbol{M}} \cdot \mathbf{1}_N = \mathbf{1}_N$. It follows now from Lemma 2 that $\hat{\boldsymbol{M}}$ is a permutation matrix. Thus, with an overwhelming probability, the emulator has extracted $\pi \in S_N$, the permutation corresponding to $\hat{\boldsymbol{M}}$, such that $\hat{\mathbf{t}}_i = \mathbf{t}_{\pi^{-1}(i)}$. $\square$

6   Efficiency

Recall that one N-wide multi-exponentiation and N fixed-base exponentiations by ℓ-bit exponent can be done significantly faster than N arbitrary exponentiations. Importantly, in the new shuffle argument, neither the prover or the verifier has to execute the latter.

Clearly, the prover's computation in the shuffle argument of Fig. 3 is dominated by four ($\approx N$)-wide multi-exponentiations and N fixed-base exponentiations. The verifier's computation is dominated by six $\approx N$-wide multi-exponentiations. The communication is dominated by $([u_1], \ldots, [u_{N-1}], \mathbf{b}^*)$, that is, by $(\ell_\mathbb{G} + \log q)N + O(\lambda)$ bits, where $\ell_\mathbb{G}$ is the number of bits it takes to represent an element of $\mathbb{G}$. In practice, we can assume $\log q = 128$ and $\ell_\mathbb{G} = 256$, in this case the communication is dominated by $388N$ bits. (Note that in the introduction, we already gave an extensive comparison with other shuffles.)

Online Computation. As remarked in [33], online computational complexity (i.e., computation done after the input data—in this case, the ciphertexts—has arrived) is an important separate measure of the shuffle arguments. In the online phase of the protocol on Fig. 3, the prover's computation is dominated by two ($\approx N$)-wide multi-exponentiations (computation of $[F_\omega]$), and the verifier's computation is dominated by four ($\approx N$)-wide multi-exponentiations (the computation of $[F]$ and the verification of $[F_\omega]$).

The Case of Larger Ciphertexts. We assumed that each ciphertext $[w_i]/[\widehat{w}_i]$ corresponds to one Elgamal ciphertext. However, in practice it might be the case—say, if the ballot is complex—that each $[w_i]/[\widehat{w}_i]$ corresponds to $m > 1$ Elgamal ciphertexts. This only changes the "type" of $[w_i]/[\widehat{w}_i]$ in Fig. 3. Efficiency-wise, the prover then has to perform $2\,m + 2$ ($\approx N$)-wide multi-exponentiations and N fixed-base exponentiations, while the verifier has to perform $4\,m + 2$ ($\approx N$)-wide multi-exponentiations.

7 Discussions

Comparison to Bayer-Groth. All shuffle arguments mentioned in Table 1 have linear argument size. Bayer and Groth [1] proposed a shuffle argument that achieves sublinear argument size but pays with higher computation. While sublinear argument size is an excellent property to have, its influence is decreased because the storage of ciphertexts makes the communication and storage requirements linear anyhow. Computation-wise, Bayer and Groth [1] include a comparison with Verificatum [32], claiming that the total computation of the prover and the verifier in Verificatum is $20N$ exponentiations, and in Bayer-Groth it is $16N$ exponentiations. [1] does not distinguish fixed-base exponentiations, multi-exponentiations, and "usual" exponentiations, Hence, we expect it to be slower than both [21] and the new shuffle, especially since the latter shuffles do not include any "usual" exponentiations. Finally, the optimized version of the Bayer and Groth shuffle takes nine rounds, compared to the five rounds in the new shuffle.

PM-Evidential Polynomials and Random Oracle Model. In practice, one would use the Fiat-Shamir heuristic to modify the shuffle argument to be non-interactive, which results in the security proof being in the random oracle model. A natural question that may arise is the necessity of minimizing the verifier's communication in that case since one would use a random oracle to generate the verifier's response. In a setting like in [32], the standard approach is to generate N random strings by applying the random oracle N times. In the new shuffle, one only has to apply the random oracle twice instead of N times.

Bellare and Rogaway [5] argue that it is better to rely less on random oracles. Quoting [5],

> But there may remain some lingering fear that the concrete hash function instantiates the random oracle differs from a random function in some significant way. So it is good to try to limit reliance on random oracles.

We refer to [5] for more discussion.

Acknowledgments. We thank Douglas Wikström and Janno Siim for helpful discussions. The authors were partially supported by the Estonian Research Council grant (PRG49).

References

1. Bayer, S., Groth, J.: Efficient zero-knowledge argument for correctness of a shuffle. In: EUROCRYPT 2012. LNCS, vol. 7237, pp. 263–280 (2012)
2. Bellare, M., Garay, J.A., Rabin, T.: Batch verification with applications to cryptography and checking. In: LATIN 1998. LNCS, vol. 1380, pp. 170–191 (1998)
3. Bellare, M., Goldreich, O.: On defining proofs of knowledge. In: CRYPTO'92. LNCS, vol. 740, pp. 390–420 (1992)
4. Bellare, M., Rogaway, P.: Random oracles are practical: a paradigm for designing efficient protocols. In: ACM CCS 93, pp. 62–73 (1993)
5. Bellare, M., Rogaway, P.: Minimizing the use of random oracles in authenticated encryption schemes. In: ICICS 97. LNCS, vol. 1334, pp. 1–16 (1997)
6. Blum, M., Feldman, P., Micali, S.: Non-interactive zero-knowledge and its applications (extended abstract). In: 20th ACM STOC, pp. 103–112 (1986)
7. Brands, S.: Rapid demonstration of linear relations connected by Boolean operators. In: EUROCRYPT'97. LNCS, vol. 1233, pp. 318–333 (1997)
8. Canetti, R., Goldreich, O., Halevi, S.: The random oracle methodology, revisited (preliminary version). In: 30th ACM STOC, pp. 209–218 (1988)
9. Chaum, D.: Untraceable electronic mail, return addresses, and digital pseudonyms. Commun. ACM **24**(2), 84–88 (1981)
10. Cramer, R., Damgård, I., Schoenmakers, B.: Proofs of partial knowledge and simplified design of witness hiding protocols. In: CRYPTO'94. LNCS, vol. 839, pp. 174–187 (1994)
11. ElGamal, T.: A public key cryptosystem and a signature scheme based on discrete logarithms. In: CRYPTO'84. LNCS, vol. 196, pp. 10–18 (1984)
12. Fauzi, P., Lipmaa, H.: Efficient culpably sound NIZK shuffle argument without random oracles. In: CT-RSA 2016. LNCS, vol. 9610, pp. 200–216 (2016)
13. Fauzi, P., Lipmaa, H., Siim, J., Zajac, M.: An efficient pairing-based shuffle argument. In: ASIACRYPT 2017, Part II. LNCS, vol. 10625, pp. 97–127 (2017)
14. Fauzi, P., Lipmaa, H., Zajac, M.: A shuffle argument secure in the generic model. In: ASIACRYPT 2016, Part II. LNCS, vol. 10032, pp. 841–872 (2016)
15. Fauzi, P., Meiklejohn, S., Mercer, R., Orlandi, C.: Quisquis: A new design for anonymous cryptocurrencies. In: ASIACRYPT 2019, Part I. LNCS, vol. 11921, pp. 649–678 (2019)
16. Fiat, A., Shamir, A.: How to prove yourself: Practical solutions to identification and signature problems. In: CRYPTO'86. LNCS, vol. 263, pp. 186–194 (1986)
17. Furukawa, J.: Efficient and verifiable shuffling and shuffle-decryption. IEICE Trans. **88**-A(1), 172–188 (2005)
18. Furukawa, J., Sako, K.: An efficient scheme for proving a shuffle. In: CRYPTO 2001. LNCS, vol. 2139, pp. 368–387 (2001)
19. Goldwasser, S., Kalai, Y.T.: On the (in)security of the Fiat-Shamir paradigm. In: 44th FOCS, pp. 102–115 (2003)
20. Goldwasser, S., Micali, S., Rackoff, C.: The knowledge complexity of interactive proof-systems (extended abstract). In: 17th ACM STOC, pp. 291–304 (1983)
21. Groth, J.: A verifiable secret shuffle of homomorphic encryptions. J. Cryptol. **23**(4), 546–579 (2010)

22. Groth, J., Kohlweiss, M.: One-out-of-many proofs: Or how to leak a secret and spend a coin. In: EUROCRYPT 2015, Part II. LNCS, vol. 9057, pp. 253–280 (2015)
23. Groth, J., Lu, S.: A non-interactive shuffle with pairing based verifiability. In: ASIACRYPT 2007. LNCS, vol. 4833, pp. 51–67 (2007)
24. Hungerford, T.W.: Algebra. 8 edn. Graduate Texts in Mathematics, vol. 73. Springer, New York (1980)
25. Khazaei, S., Moran, T., Wikström, D.: A mix-net from any CCA2 secure cryptosystem. In: ASIACRYPT 2012. LNCS, vol. 7658, pp. 607–625 (2012)
26. Lindell, Y.: Parallel coin-tossing and constant-round secure two-party computation. In: CRYPTO 2001. LNCS, vol. 2139, pp. 171–189 (2001)
27. Lipmaa, H., Zhang, B.: A more efficient computationally sound non-interactive zero-knowledge shuffle argument. In: SCN 12. LNCS, vol. 7485, pp. 477–502 (2012)
28. Neff, C.A.: A verifiable secret shuffle and its application to e-voting. In: ACM CCS 2001, pp. 116–125 (2001)
29. Pedersen, T.P.: Non-interactive and information-theoretic secure verifiable secret sharing. In: CRYPTO'91. LNCS, vol. 576, pp. 129–140 (1991)
30. Schwartz, J.T.: Fast probabilistic algorithms for verification of polynomial identities. J. ACM **27**(4), 701–717 (1980)
31. Straus, E.G.: Addition chains of vectors. Amer. Math. Monthly **70**, 806–808 (1964)
32. Terelius, B., Wikström, D.: Proofs of restricted shuffles. In: AFRICACRYPT 10. LNCS, vol. 6055, pp. 100–113 (2010)
33. Wikström, D.: A commitment-consistent proof of a shuffle. In: ACISP 2009. LNCS, vol. 5594, pp. 4007–421 (2009)
34. Wikström, D.: How to Implement a Stand-alone Verifier for the Verificatum Mix-Net. Version 1.4.1 (2015). http://www.verificatum.org
35. Zippel, R.: Probabilistic Algorithms for Sparse Polynomials. In: EUROSM 1979. LNCS, vol. 72, pp. 216–226 (1979)

Cryptanalysis of a Dynamic Universal Accumulator over Bilinear Groups

Alex Biryukov[1], Aleksei Udovenko[2], and Giuseppe Vitto[1(✉)]

[1] DCS&SnT, University of Luxembourg, Esch-sur-Alzette, Luxembourg
{alex.biryukov,giuseppe.vitto}@uni.lu
[2] CryptoExperts, Paris, France
aleksei@affine.group

Abstract. In this paper we cryptanalyse the two accumulator variants proposed by Au et al. [1], which we call the α-*based* construction and the common reference string-based ($\mathcal{CRS}$-*based*) construction. We show that if non-membership witnesses are issued according to the α-based construction, an attacker that has access to multiple witnesses is able to efficiently recover the secret accumulator parameter α and completely break its security. More precisely, if p is the order of the underlying bilinear group, the knowledge of $O(\log p \log \log p)$ non-membership witnesses permits to successfully recover α. Further optimizations and different attack scenarios allow to reduce the number of required witnesses to $O(\log p)$, together with practical attack complexity. Moreover, we show that accumulator's collision resistance can be broken if just one of these non-membership witnesses is known to the attacker. We then show how all these attacks for the α-based construction can be easily prevented by using instead a corrected expression for witnesses.

Although outside the original security model assumed by Au et al. but motivated by some possible concrete application of the scheme where the Manager must have exclusive rights for issuing witnesses (e.g. white/black list based authentication mechanisms), we show that if non-membership witnesses are issued using the $\mathcal{CRS}$-based construction and the $\mathcal{CRS}$ is kept secret by the Manager, an attacker accessing multiple witnesses can reconstruct the $\mathcal{CRS}$ and compute witnesses for arbitrary new elements. In particular, if the accumulator is initialized by adding m secret elements, the knowledge of m non-membership witnesses allows to succeed in such attack.

Keywords: Accumulator · Universal · Dynamic · Cryptanalysis · Anonymous credentials

This work was supported by the Luxembourg National Research Fund (FNR) project FinCrypt (C17/IS/11684537).

K. G. Paterson (Ed.): CT-RSA 2021, LNCS 12704, pp. 276–298, 2021.
https://doi.org/10.1007/978-3-030-75539-3_12

1   Introduction

A cryptographic accumulator scheme permits to aggregate values of a possibly very large set into a short digest, which is commonly referred to as the *accumulator value*. Unlike hash functions, where, similarly, (arbitrary) long data is mapped into a fixed length digest, accumulator schemes permit to additionally show whenever an element is accumulated or not, thanks to special values called *witnesses*. Depending on the accumulator design, we can have two kinds of witnesses: *membership witnesses*, which permit to show that an element is included into the accumulator, and *non-membership witnesses*, which, on the contrary, permit to show that an element is not included. Accumulator schemes which support both are called *universal* and the possibility to dynamically add and delete elements, give them the name of *dynamic accumulators*.

The first accumulator scheme was formalized by Benaloh and De Mare [3] in 1993 as a time-stamping protocol. Since then, many other accumulator schemes have been proposed and they play an important role in various protocols from set membership, authentication to (anonymous) credentials systems and cryptocurrency ledgers. However, there is only a small set of underlying cryptographic assumptions on which such accumulator primitives are based. Currently, three main families of accumulators can be distinguished in literature: schemes designed in groups of unknown order [2,3,6,10,14,15,19], schemes designed in groups of known order [1,11,12,18] and hash-based constructions [5,7–9,16]. Relevant to this paper are the schemes belonging to the second of these families, where the considered group is a prime order bilinear group. Moreover, when it comes to Dynamic Universal Accumulators (namely those that support dynamic addition and deletion of members and can maintain both membership and non-membership witnesses) we are down to just a few schemes.

In this paper we cryptanalyse one of these universal scheme proposed for bilinear groups, namely the Dynamic Universal Accumulator by Au et al. [1], which is zero-knowledge friendly and stood unscathed for 10 years of public scrutiny. This scheme comes in two variants which we called the *α-based construction* and the *CRS-based construction*, respectively. For the first one, we show that the non-membership mechanism, designed to allow for more efficiency on the accumulator manager side, has a subtle cryptographic flaw which enables the adversary to efficiently recover the secret of the accumulator manager given just several hundred to few thousand non-membership witnesses (regardless of the number of accumulated elements).

As a consequence, the attacker can fully break the security of the scheme. Moreover, we show that given only *one* non-membership witness generated with this flawed mechanism, it is possible to efficiently invalidate the assumed collision resistance property of the accumulator by creating a membership witness for a non-accumulated element. Despite the presence of a valid security proof, this is possible because the provided security reduction covers the non-membership mechanism of the *CRS*-based construction only and it doesn't take into account non-membership definition given for the α-based construction, which, in fact, resulted to be weak.

The second part of the paper investigates the $\mathcal{CRS}$-based variant: motivated by some concrete applications of the scheme where the Manager must have exclusive rights for issuing witnesses (e.g. white-/black-list based authentication mechanisms), we show that an adversary having access to a sufficient amount of witnesses is able to compute valid witnesses for unauthorized elements even when the Accumulator manager keeps secret all the information needed to compute such witnesses, i.e. the $\mathcal{CRS}$. In particular, if the accumulator is initialized by adding m secret elements, an attacker that has access to m non-membership witnesses would succeed in reconstructing the $\mathcal{CRS}$ and will then become able to issue membership and non-membership witnesses for any accumulated and non-accumulated elements, respectively.

In Sect. 2 we recall both variants of Au et al. accumulator scheme along with the security model and our attack scenarios. In Sect. 3 we detail how collision resistance does not hold when non-membership witnesses are issued accordingly to the α-based construction, while in Sect. 4 we present our first attack for the α-based construction which allows to fully recover the accumulator's secret α. In Sect. 4.3 we provide a complexity analysis in terms of time and non-membership witnesses needed and in Sect. 5 we discuss some further improvements to the α-recovery attack which lead, under different hypothesis, to two new attacks: a *random-y sieving attack* and a *chosen-y sieving attack*, described in Sects. 5.1 and 5.2, respectively. We implemented all these attacks and we compare, in Sect. 6, their success probability as a function of the total number of known witnesses needed. We further report another minor design vulnerability for the α-based construction in Sect. 7. Finally, in Sect. 8 we investigate the security of the $\mathcal{CRS}$-construction under some concrete attack scenarios and we present, in Sect. 8.2, the *Witness Forgery Attack* as well as possible countermeasures. A summary of our main contributions can be found in Table 1.

Table 1. Time and non-membership witnesses required in our attacks on the Au et al. accumulator scheme for both α-based and $\mathcal{CRS}$-based construction. In this table, p denotes the order of the underlying bilinear group, m denotes the number of (secret) elements with which the accumulator is initialized, ℓ denotes the number of accumulations occurred in between the issues of non-membership witnesses. In the $\mathcal{CRS}$-based construction the $\mathcal{CRS}$ is unknown to the attacker.

Construction	Ref.	Scenario	Witnesses	Time	Attack result
	Sect. 4	Random-y	$\mathcal{O}(\log p \log \log p)$	$O(\log^2 p)$	Recovery of α
	Sect. 5.1	Random-y	$\mathcal{O}(\log p \log \log p)$	$O((1 + \ell/\log\log p)\log^2 p)$	Recovery of α
α-based	Sect. 5.2	Chosen-y	$\mathcal{O}(\log p)$	$O(\ell \log^2 p/\log\log p)$	Recovery of α
	Sect. 3	Random-y	1	$\mathcal{O}(1)$	Break collision Resistance
$\mathcal{CRS}$-based	Sect. 8.2	Random-y	m	$\mathcal{O}(m^2)$	Issue witnesses

2   Au et al. Dynamic Universal Accumulator

In their paper, Au and coauthors propose two different constructions for their Dynamic Universal Accumulator, depending on whether information is made available to the accumulator managers. The first requires the accumulator's secret parameter α and is suitable for a centralized entity which efficiently updates the accumulator value and issues witnesses to the users. The second instead, requires a common reference string $\mathcal{CRS}$ and allows to update the accumulator value and to issue witnesses without learning α, but less efficiently. We will refer to the first one as the α-*based* construction, while we will refer to the latter as the $\mathcal{CRS}$-*based* construction.

These two are interchangeable, in the sense that witnesses can be issued from time to time with one or the other construction. Moreover, we note that all operations done with the common reference string $\mathcal{CRS}$, can be done more efficiently by using α directly: hence, if the authority which generates α coincides with the Accumulator Manager, it is more convenient for the latter to always use the secret parameter α to perform operations and thus we will refer to the two constructions mainly to indicate the different defining equations for witnesses (in particular, non-membership witnesses).

We now detail a concrete instance of Au et al. accumulator scheme by using Type-I elliptic curves[1]. Where not explicitly stated, each operation refers to both the α-*based* and $\mathcal{CRS}$-*based* constructions.

Generation. Let E be an elliptic curve of embedding degree k over $\mathbb{F}_q$, which is provided with a symmetric bilinear group $\mathbb{G} = (p, G_1, G_T, P, e)$ such that $e : G_1 \times G_1 \to G_T$ is a non-degenerate bilinear map, G_1 is a subgroup of E generated by P, G_T is a subgroup of $(\mathbb{F}_{q^k})^*$ and $|G_1| = |G_T| = p$ is prime. The secret accumulator parameter α is randomly chosen from $\mathbb{Z}/p\mathbb{Z}^*$. The set of accumulatable elements is $\mathcal{ACC} = \mathbb{Z}/p\mathbb{Z} \setminus \{-\alpha\}$.

- $\mathcal{CRS}$-*based construction.* Let t be the maximum number of accumulatable elements. Then the common reference string $\mathcal{CRS}$ is computed as

$$\mathcal{CRS} = \{ P, \alpha P, \alpha^2 P, \ldots, \alpha^t P \}$$

Accumulator Updates

- α-*based construction.* For any given set $\mathcal{Y}_V \subseteq \mathcal{ACC}$ let $f_V(x) \in \mathbb{Z}/p\mathbb{Z}[x]$ represent the polynomial

$$f_V(x) = \prod_{y \in \mathcal{Y}_V} (y + x)$$

Given the secret accumulator parameter α, we say that an accumulator value $V \in G_1$ accumulates the elements in $\mathcal{Y}_V$ if $V = f_V(\alpha)P$.

---

[1] We note that Au et al. accumulator scheme and our attacks as well can be defined to work with any bilinear group.

An element $y \in \mathcal{ACC} \backslash \mathcal{Y}_V$ is added to the accumulator value V, by computing $V' = (y + \alpha)V$ and letting $\mathcal{Y}_{V'} = \mathcal{Y}_V \cup \{y\}$. Similarly, an element $y \in \mathcal{Y}_V$ is removed from the accumulator value V, by computing $V' = \frac{1}{(y+\alpha)}V$ and letting $\mathcal{Y}_{V'} = \mathcal{Y}_V \backslash \{y\}$.

- **CRS-based construction.** For any given set $\mathcal{Y}_V \subseteq \mathcal{ACC}$ such that $|\mathcal{Y}_V| \leq t$, let $f_V(x) \in \mathbb{Z}/p\mathbb{Z}[x]$ represent the polynomial

$$f_V(x) = \prod_{y \in \mathcal{Y}_V} (y + x) = \sum_{i=0}^{|\mathcal{Y}_V|} c_i x^i$$

Then, the accumulator value V which accumulates the elements in $\mathcal{Y}_V$ is computed using the $\mathcal{CRS}$ as $V = \sum_{i=0}^{|\mathcal{Y}_V|} c_i \cdot \alpha^i P$.

Witnesses Issuing

- **α-based construction.** Given an element $y \in \mathcal{Y}_V$, the *membership witness* $w_{y,V} = C \in G_1$ with respect to the accumulator value V is issued as

$$C = \frac{1}{y + \alpha} V$$

Given an element $y \in \mathcal{ACC} \backslash \mathcal{Y}_V$, the *non-membership witness* $\bar{w}_{y,V} = (C, d) \in G_1 \times \mathbb{Z}/p\mathbb{Z}$ with respect to the accumulator value V is issued[2] as

$$d = \left(f_V(\alpha) \bmod (y + \alpha) \right) \bmod p, \qquad C = \frac{f_V(\alpha) - d}{y + \alpha} P$$

- **CRS-based construction.** Given an element $y \in \mathcal{Y}_V$, let $c(x) \in \mathbb{Z}/p\mathbb{Z}[x]$ be the polynomial such that $f_V(x) = c(x)(y + x)$. Then, the *membership witness* $w_{y,V}$ for y with respect to the accumulator value V is computed using the $\mathcal{CRS}$ as $w_{y,V} = c(\alpha)P$.
  Given an element $y \in \mathcal{ACC} \backslash \mathcal{Y}_V$, apply the Euclidean Algorithm to get the polynomial $c(x) \in \mathbb{Z}/p\mathbb{Z}[x]$ and the scalar $d \in \mathbb{Z}/p\mathbb{Z}$ such that $f_V(x) = c(x)(y + x) + d$. Then, the *non-membership witness* $\bar{w}_{y,V}$ for y with respect to the accumulator value V is computed from the $\mathcal{CRS}$ as $w_{y,V} = (c(\alpha)P, d)$.

Witness Update. When the accumulator value changes, users' witnesses are updated accordingly to the following operations:

---

[2] We assume that here $f_V(\alpha) = \prod_{y \in \mathcal{Y}_V} (y + \alpha)$ is computed over $\mathbb{Z}$. Alternatively, if this computation is done modulo p, then d would be equal to $f_V(\alpha) \bmod p$ for a large fraction of elements $y \in \mathcal{ACC} \backslash \mathcal{Y}_V$ and α can be easily recovered by factoring $f_V(x) - d$ over $\mathbb{Z}/p\mathbb{Z}[x]$.

- **On Addition**: suppose that a certain $y' \in \mathcal{ACC} \setminus \mathcal{Y}_V$ is added into V. Hence the new accumulator value is $V' = (y' + \alpha)V$ and $\mathcal{Y}_{V'} = \mathcal{Y}_V \cup \{y'\}$.
Then, for any $y \in \mathcal{Y}_V$, $w_{y,V} = C$ is updated with respect to V' by computing

$$C' = (y' - y)C + V$$

and letting $w_{y,V'} = C'$.
If, instead, $y \in \mathcal{ACC} \setminus \mathcal{Y}_V$ with $y \neq y'$, its non-membership witness $\bar{w}_{y,V} = (C, d)$ is updated to $\bar{w}_{y,V'} = (C', d \cdot (y' - y))$, where C' is computed in the same way as in the case of membership witnesses.
- **On Deletion**: suppose that a certain $y' \in \mathcal{Y}_V$ is deleted from V. Hence the new accumulator value is $V' = \frac{1}{y'+\alpha}V$ and $\mathcal{Y}_{V'} = \mathcal{Y}_V \setminus \{y'\}$.
Then, for any $y \in \mathcal{Y}_V$, $w_{y,V} = C$ is updated with respect to V' by computing

$$C' = \frac{1}{y' - y}C - \frac{1}{y' - y}V'$$

and letting $w_{y,V'} = C'$.
If, instead, $y \in \mathcal{ACC} \setminus \mathcal{Y}_V$, its witness $\bar{w}_{y,V} = (C, d)$ is updated to $\bar{w}_{y,V'} = (C', d \cdot \frac{1}{y'-y}$, where C' is computed in the same way as in the case of membership witnesses.

We note that in both cases the added or removed element y' has to be public in order to enable other users to update their witnesses.

Verification. A membership witness $w_{y,V} = C$ with respect to the accumulator value V is valid if it verifies the pairing equation $e(C, yP + \alpha P) = e(V, P)$. Similarly, a non-membership witness $\bar{w}_{y,V} = (C, d)$ is valid with respect to V if it verifies $e(C, yP + \alpha P)e(P, P)^d = e(V, P)$.

2.1 Security Model and Attack Scenarios

The security of the above accumulator scheme is intended in terms of *collision resistance*: in [1], this security property is shown under the t-SDH assumption [4]. Informally, collision resistance ensures that an adversary has negligible probability in forging a valid membership witness for a not-accumulated element and, respectively, a non-membership witness for an already accumulated element. In the following, we briefly recall its formal definition due to Derler et al. and we refer to [13] for more details:

Definition 1. (Collision Freeness [13]) *A cryptographic dynamic universal accumulator is collision-free if for any probabilistic polynomial time adversary $\mathcal{A}$ the following probability*

$$\mathbb{P} \left(\begin{array}{c} (sk_{acc}, pk_{acc}) \leftarrow Gen(1^\lambda) \;,\; (y, w_y, \bar{w}_y, \mathcal{Y}, V_{\mathcal{Y}}) \leftarrow \mathcal{A}^{\mathcal{O}}(pk_{acc}) : \\ (\; \text{Verify}(pk_{acc}, V_{\mathcal{Y}}, w_y, y, \texttt{IsMembWit}) = \texttt{true} \quad \wedge \; y \notin \mathcal{Y}\;) \vee \\ (\; \text{Verify}(pk_{acc}, V_{\mathcal{Y}}, \bar{w}_y, y, \texttt{IsNonMembWit}) = \texttt{true} \; \wedge \; y \in \mathcal{Y}\;) \end{array} \right)$$

is a negligible function in the security parameter λ and $\mathcal{O}$ is an oracle returning

- the accumulator value $V_{\mathcal{Y}}$ resulting from the accumulation of elements of any given input set $\mathcal{Y}$,
- the membership witnesses w_{y^*} for any accumulated element y^*,
- the non-membership witnesses $\bar{w}_{y^*}$ for any freely chosen non accumulated element y^*.

By using a secret and public accumulator key pair (sk_{acc}, pk_{acc}), this definition captures the trapdoor nature of Au et al. constructions: in fact, the secret accumulator parameter α corresponds to the formal accumulator secret key sk_{acc}, while pk_{acc} represents the public information, i.e. the bilinear group definition and the group elements needed for public witness verification. Furthermore, due to a result of Vitto and Biryukov [20, Lemma 1], the possibility to arbitrary query the above oracle $\mathcal{O}$ is equivalent to the knowledge of the common reference string $\mathcal{CRS}$, hence both variants can be restated in terms of the above definition and are substantially equivalent in terms of information the attacker has access to.

In next Sections we will show that the non-membership witness definition of the α-based construction is flawed and allows a probabilistic polynomial time attacker to recover the secret accumulator parameter α and thus break collision resistance. This flaw is not present in the non-membership witness definition of the $\mathcal{CRS}$-based construction −which, in fact, fully satisfy the security reduction under the t–SDH assumption− and hence the α-based construction can be easily fixed by using, instead, the non-membership witness defining equation of the other $\mathcal{CRS}$–based variant. In other words, a "fixed" α-based construction will correspond to a slightly more time-efficient (but asymptotically equivalent) version of the $\mathcal{CRS}$–based construction, where the $\mathcal{CRS}$ is not directly given to the attacker but can be computed in polynomial time [20, Lemma 1].

Motivated by this observation and by concrete applications of the scheme where the attacker cannot arbitrarily query an oracle returning witnesses for any freely chosen element, we show, in Sect. 8, that even when the Accumulator Manager keeps the $\mathcal{CRS}$ secret, the attacker is be able to efficiently recover it by accessing few non-membership witnesses, thus making him able to issue membership and non-membership witnesses accordingly to the $\mathcal{CRS}$–based defining equations, but not able to break collision resistance for this variant. We remark that this scenario is outside Au et al. security model −where such $\mathcal{CRS}$ is always available to the attacker which can further obtain witnesses from the oracle− but becomes relevant in all those concrete scenarios where the Manager wishes to have exclusive rights for issuing witnesses (and thus keeps the $\mathcal{CRS}$ secret), such us authentication mechanisms where witnesses are used as black-/white-list authentication tokens.

3   Breaking Collision Resistance in the α-Based Construction

In the α-based construction, the knowledge of a single non-membership witness is enough to break the (assumed) collision resistance property of the accumulator scheme when the polynomial $f_V(x) \in \mathbb{Z}/p\mathbb{Z}[x]$ is fully known or, equivalently, the set of all accumulated elements is publicly known (which is typically the case).

In the security reduction provided in [1], it is required that given a non-accumulated element $y \in \mathcal{ACC} \setminus \mathcal{Y}_V$ and its non-membership witness $\bar{w}_{y,V} = (C_y, d_y)$ with respect to the accumulator value V, the element $\tilde{d}_y \in \mathbb{Z}/p\mathbb{Z}$ verifies

$$\left(f_V(x) - \tilde{d}_y \bmod (y + x)\right) \equiv 0 \pmod p$$

which in turn corresponds to $\tilde{d}_y \equiv f_V(-y) \pmod p$, a condition enforced by the $\mathcal{CRS}$–based construction non-membership witness definition.

By using, instead, the defining equation for d_y provided in the α-based construction, the partial non-membership witness for y equals $d_y = \left(f_V(\alpha) \bmod (y + \alpha)\right) \bmod p$ and thus

$$d_y \equiv \tilde{d}_y \pmod p \quad \Rightarrow \quad \left(f_V(-y) \bmod (y + \alpha)\right) \equiv f_V(-y) \pmod p$$

holds only when $f_V(-y) < y + \alpha$, i.e. with negligible probability if V accumulates more than one element chosen uniformly at random from $\mathbb{Z}/p\mathbb{Z}$.

Now, if $d_y \not\equiv \tilde{d}_y \bmod p$, we have $f_V(x) - d_y \not\equiv 0 \bmod (y + x)$, and we can use Euclidean algorithm to find a polynomial $c(x) \in \mathbb{Z}/p\mathbb{Z}[x]$ and $r \in \mathbb{Z}/p\mathbb{Z}$ such that $f_V(x) - d_y = c(x)(y + x) + r$ in $\mathbb{Z}/p\mathbb{Z}[x]$. Then, by recalling that $C_y = \frac{f_V(\alpha) - d_y}{y + \alpha} P$, under the t–SDH assumption, the attacker uses the available $\mathcal{CRS} = \{P, \alpha P, \ldots, \alpha^t P\}$ to compute $c(\alpha)P$ and obtains a membership witness with respect to V for an arbitrary non accumulated element y as

$$C_y + \frac{d_y}{r}\left(C_y - c(\alpha)P\right) = C_y + \frac{d_y}{r}\left(C_y - C_y - \frac{r}{y + \alpha}P\right) = \frac{f_V(\alpha)}{y + \alpha}P = \frac{1}{y + \alpha}V$$

thus breaking the assumed collision resistance property. We note that this result doesn't invalidate the security proof provided by Au et al. in [1]: indeed, the reduction to the t-SDH assumption is shown for (non-membership) witnesses generated accordingly to the $\mathcal{CRS}$-based construction only, and thus, collision resistance can be guaranteed only for this latter construction.

We speculate that this flaw comes from the wrong assumption that

$$\left(f_V(x) \bmod (y + x)\right) \equiv \left(f_V(\alpha) \bmod (y + \alpha)\right) \pmod p$$

which, if true, would have implied security of non-membership witnesses issued accordingly to the α-based construction as well. The authors also declare [1, Sect. 2.2] that by using the secret accumulator value α, the Accumulator Manager can compute membership and non-membership witnesses in $O(1)$ time: this clearly cannot be true, since, regardless of the variant considered, the evaluation of the polynomial $f_V(x)$ and its reduction modulo a $\sim \log p$-bits integer requires (at least) $O(\deg f_V)$ time.

In the next Sections we will show that within the α-based construction, an attacker can efficiently recover the secret accumulator parameter α by accessing multiple non-membership witnesses, thus making him able to break collision resistance by computing membership witnesses for non-accumulated elements similarly as above, but also non-membership witnesses for accumulated elements.

4   The α-Recovery Attack for the α-Based Construction

From now on, we assume the secret parameter α and the accumulator value V along with the set of currently accumulated elements $\mathcal{Y}_V$ to be fixed.

The following attack on the α-based construction consists of two phases: the retrieval of the value $f_V(\alpha) \in \mathbb{Z}$ used to compute non-membership witnesses modulo many small primes and the full recovery of the accumulator secret parameter α.

4.1   Recovering $f_V(\alpha)$

Let $d_y = \big(f_V(\alpha) \bmod (y+\alpha) \big) \bmod p$ be a partial non-membership witness with respect to V for a certain element $y \in \mathcal{ACC} \setminus \mathcal{Y}_V$, and let $\tilde{d}_y$ denote the integer $f_V(\alpha) \bmod (y+\alpha)$. We then have $d_y = \tilde{d}_y \bmod p$, and we are interested in how often d_y equals $\tilde{d}_y$ as integers. Attacker benefits from the cases when $y + \alpha < p$, since the reduction modulo p does nothing and $d_y = \tilde{d}_y$ for all y.

The worst case happens when α is maximal, i.e. $\alpha = p - 1$. Indeed, in this case, if $y = 0$ then $y + \alpha < p$ and $d_y = \tilde{d}_y$ with probability 1; if instead $y > 0$ and $y \neq p - \alpha = 1$ the probability that $d_y = \tilde{d}_y$ is $\frac{p}{y+\alpha}$ and, hence, is minimal when compared to smaller values of α. Thus, with $\alpha = p - 1$ the probability that d_y equals $\tilde{d}_y$ as integers ranges from 1 (when $y = 0$) to almost $1/2$ (when $y = p - 1$). Assuming that y is sampled uniformly at random, we can obtain the following lower bound on the probability (for arbitrary α):

$$
\mathop{\mathbb{P}}_{\substack{y \in \{0,\ldots,p-1\} \\ y \neq p-\alpha \\ f_V(\alpha) \in \mathbb{Z}}} (d_y = \tilde{d}_y) \geq \frac{1}{p-1}\left(1 + p \sum_{\tilde{y}=2}^{p-1} \frac{1}{\tilde{y} + p - 1} \right)
$$

$$
= \frac{p}{p-1}\left(\sum_{i=1}^{2p-2} \frac{1}{i} - \sum_{i=1}^{p-1} \frac{1}{i} \right) = \frac{p}{p-1}\left(H_{2p-2} - H_{p-1} \right)
$$

$$
= \left(1 + \frac{1}{p-1} \right) \cdot \left(\ln 2 - \frac{1}{4(p-1)} + o\left(p^{-1}\right) \right)
$$

$$
= \ln 2 + \frac{4\ln 2 - 1}{4(p-1)} + o(p^{-1})
$$

$$
> \ln 2. \tag{1}
$$

where H_n denotes the n-th Harmonic number, and the last inequality holds for all values of p used in practice.

Assume that $q | (y + \alpha)$ for a small prime $q \in \mathbb{Z}$ such that $q \ll y + \alpha$. If $d_y = \tilde{d}_y$ we have $f_V(\alpha) \equiv d_y \pmod{q}$ with probability 1, otherwise it happens with probability 0 since then $f_V(\alpha) \equiv d_y + p \pmod{q}$. If instead $q \nmid (y + \alpha)$, we assume $d_y \mod q$ to be random in $\mathbb{Z}/q\mathbb{Z}$ and thus $f_V(\alpha) \equiv d_y \pmod{q}$ happens with probability close to $\frac{1}{q}$.

More precisely,

$$\mathbb{P}\big(f_V(\alpha) \equiv d_y \pmod{q} \big) > \ln 2 \cdot \frac{1}{q} + \frac{q-1}{q^2} = \frac{(\ln 2 + 1)q - 1}{q^2}$$

while for any other $c \in \mathbb{Z}/q\mathbb{Z}$ such that $c \not\equiv d_y \pmod{q}$ we have

$$\mathbb{P}\big(f_V(\alpha) \equiv c \pmod{q} \big) < (1 - \ln 2) \cdot \frac{1}{q} + \frac{q-1}{q^2} = \frac{(2 - \ln 2)q - 1}{q^2}$$

In other words, the value $d_y \mod q$ has a higher chance to be equal to $f_V(\alpha) \mod q$ compared to any other value in $\mathbb{Z}/q\mathbb{Z}$.

We will use this fact to deduce $f_V(\alpha)$ modulo many different small primes. More precisely, suppose that an attacker has access to the elements $y_1, \ldots, y_n$ together with the respective partial non-membership witnesses

$$d_{y_i} \equiv \big(f_V(\alpha) \mod (y_i + \alpha) \big) \mod p$$

If q is a small prime and n is sufficiently large (see Sect. 4.3 for the analysis), $f_V(\alpha) \mod q$ can be deduced by simply looking at the most frequent value among

$$d_{y_1} \mod q, \ \ldots \ , \ d_{y_n} \mod q$$

Once we compute $f_V(\alpha)$ modulo many different small primes $q_1, \ldots, q_k$ such that $q_1 \cdot \ldots \cdot q_k > p$, we can proceed with the next phase of the attack: the full recovery of the secret parameter α.

4.2 Recovering α

If the discrete logarithm of any accumulator value is successfully retrieved modulo many different small primes whose product is greater than p, α can be recovered with (virtually) no additional partial non-membership witnesses. The main observation we will exploit is the following:

Observation 1. *Let q be an integer and let $y \in \mathcal{ACC} \setminus \mathcal{Y}_V$ be a non-accumulated element such that its partial non-membership witness with respect to V satisfies $d_y = \tilde{d}_y$. Then $d_y \not\equiv f_V(\alpha) \pmod{q}$ implies that $q \nmid (y + \alpha)$, or, equivalently, $\alpha \not\equiv -y \pmod{q}$.*

From (1) it follows that for any given $q \in \mathbb{Z}$ and non-accumulated element y such that $(f_V(\alpha) - d_y) \not\equiv 0 \pmod{q}$, we have

$$\mathbb{P}\big(\alpha \not\equiv -y \pmod{q} \mid f_V(\alpha) \not\equiv d_y \pmod{q} \big) > 1 - \frac{(1 - \ln 2)q}{q^2 - (1 + \ln 2)q + 1} \approx 1 - \frac{1 - \ln 2}{q}$$

By considering all available non-membership witnesses, if q is small and n is sufficiently larger than q (see Sect. 4.3), we can deduce $\alpha \bmod q$ as the element in $\mathbb{Z}/q\mathbb{Z}$ which is the least frequent −or not occurring at all− among the residues

$$-y_{i_1} \bmod q , \quad \ldots \quad , -y_{i_j} \bmod q$$

such that $(f_V(\alpha) - d_{y_{i_k}}) \not\equiv 0 \bmod q$ for all $k = 1, \ldots, j$.

It follows that, if $q_1, \ldots, q_k$ are small primes such that $q_1 \cdot \ldots \cdot q_k > p$, from the values $f_V(\alpha) \bmod q_i$ −computed according to Sect. 4.1− and the values $\alpha \bmod q_i$, with $i \in [1, k]$, $\alpha \in \mathbb{Z}$ can be obtained by using the Chinese Remainder Theorem.

4.3   Estimating the Minimum Number of Witnesses Needed

We now give an asymptotic estimate of the minimum number of non-membership witnesses needed so that both phases of the above attack succeed with high probability. We will use the multiplicative Chernoff bound, which we briefly recall.

Theorem 2. (Chernoff Bound) *Let $X_1, \ldots, X_n$ be independent random variables taking values in $\{0, 1\}$ and let $X = X_1 + \ldots + X_n$. Then, for any $\delta > 0$*

$$\mathbb{P}\big(X \leq (1 - \delta)\mathbb{E}[X] \big) \leq e^{-\frac{\delta^2 \mu}{2}} \qquad 0 \leq \delta \leq 1$$

$$\mathbb{P}\big(X \geq (1 + \delta)\mathbb{E}[X] \big) \leq e^{-\frac{\delta^2 \mu}{2+\delta}} \qquad 0 \leq \delta$$

Proof. See [17, Theorem 4.4, Theorem 4.5].   □

Our analysis will proceed as follows: first, we introduce two random variables to model, for a given small prime q, the behaviour of the values $f_V(\alpha) \bmod q$. Then, we will use Chernoff bound to first estimate the probability of wrongly guessing $f_V(\alpha) \bmod q$, and then deduce a value for n so that such probability is minimized for all primes q considered in the attack.

Let $q \in \mathbb{Z}$ be a fixed prime and let X_g be a random variable which counts the number of times $f_V(\alpha) \bmod q$ is among the values $d_1 \bmod q, \ldots, d_n \bmod q$. Similarly, let X_b be a random variable which counts the number of times a certain residue $t \in \mathbb{Z}/q\mathbb{Z}$ not equal to $f_V(\alpha) \bmod q$ is among the values $d_1 \bmod q, \ldots, d_n \bmod q$. Then

$$\mathbb{E}[X_g] = n \cdot \frac{(\ln 2 + 1)q - 1}{q^2} \approx (\ln 2 + 1)\frac{n}{q}$$

$$\mathbb{E}[X_b] = n \cdot \frac{(2 - \ln 2)q - 1}{q^2} \approx (2 - \ln 2)\frac{n}{q}$$

By applying Theorem 2, we can estimate the probability that X_g and X_b crosses $\frac{\mathbb{E}[X_g]+\mathbb{E}[X_b]}{2} = \frac{3n}{2q}$ as

$$\mathbb{P}\left(X_g \leq \frac{3n}{2q} \right) = \mathbb{P}\left(X_g \leq \left(1 - \frac{2\ln 2 - 1}{2\ln 2 + 2} \right) \mathbb{E}[X_g] \right) < e^{-\frac{n}{91q}} \doteq e_{q,g}$$

$$\mathbb{P}\left(X_b \geq \frac{3n}{2q}\right) = \mathbb{P}\left(X_b \geq \left(1 + \frac{2\ln 2 - 1}{4 - 2\ln 2}\right)\mathbb{E}[X_b]\right) < e^{-\frac{n}{76q}} \doteq e_{q,b}$$

and we minimize these inequalities by requiring that

$$1 - (1 - e_{q,g})(1 - e_{q,b})^{q-1} \approx e_{q,g} + (q-1)e_{q,b} \doteq s_q$$

is small for each prime q considered in this attack phase. Thus, if $q = max(q_1, \ldots, q_k)$, we can bound the sum

$$\sum_{i=1}^{k} s_{q_i} \leq qs_q = q(e^{-\frac{n}{91q}} + (q-1)e^{-\frac{n}{76q}}) \approx e^{-\frac{n}{91q} + \log q} + e^{-\frac{n}{76q} + 2\log q}$$

and we make it small by taking $n = O(q \log q)$.

In order to apply the Chinese Remainder Theorem for the full recovery of α we need that $q_1 \cdot \ldots \cdot q_k > p$. If $q_1, \ldots, q_k$ are chosen to be the first k primes, we can use an estimation for the first Chebyshev function growth rate to obtain $\ln(q_1 \cdot \ldots \cdot q_k) = (1 + o(1)) \cdot k \ln k \sim q_k$ by Prime Number Theorem and thus $q_k > \ln p$. We then conclude that

$$n = O(\log p \log \log p)$$

non-membership witnesses are enough to recover $f_V(\alpha) \bmod q_1 \cdot \ldots \cdot q_k$ with high probability.

We note that by using Chernoff bound in order to estimate the minimum number of witnesses needed to recover α, it can be shown, similarly as done above for $f_V(\alpha)$, that $O(\log p \log \log p)$ non-membership witnesses are enough to identify with high probability $\alpha \bmod q_1 \cdot \ldots \cdot q_k = \alpha$.

The time complexity is dominated by

$$(\text{\# primes } q) \times (\text{\# witnesses}) = O\left(\frac{\log p}{\log \log p}\right) \times O(\log p \log \log p)$$

which is equal to $O(\log^2 p)$.

5   Improving the α-Recovery Attack

We will now improve the α-Recovery Attack outlined in Sect. 4 by giving some variants under two different attack scenarios, depending on whether the attacker has access to non-membership witnesses for *random-y* or *chosen-y*.[3] These improvements will further reduce the number of non-membership witnesses needed to fully recover the secret accumulator parameter α to a small multiple of $\log p$.

The main idea behind the improved attack is to keep removing wrong candidates for $\alpha \bmod q$ for small primes q (*sieving*), until only the correct one is left. As in the previous attack, full value of α is then reconstructed using the Chinese Remainder Theorem.

---

[3] We observe that according to Definition 1, the attacker has access to an oracle which returns witnesses for any *chosen-y*. However, in concrete instances of the accumulator scheme, an attacker might have access only to witnesses for *random* values y.

Collecting Witnesses Issued at Different States. In the α-Recovery Attack described in Sect. 4, $O(\log p \log \log p)$ non-membership witnesses issued with respect to the same accumulator value V are needed in order to fully recover α. In the following attacks we drop this condition and allow non-membership witnesses to be issued with respect to different accumulator values $f_1(\alpha)P = V_1$, ..., $f_\ell(\alpha)P = V_\ell$, but we require that no deletions occur between the accumulator states V_1 and V_ℓ. In this case, since the sequence of elements added must be public to permit witness updates, we have that the polynomial functions $g_{i,j}(x) \in \mathbb{Z}/p\mathbb{Z}$ such that $f_j(\alpha) = g_{i,j}(\alpha)f_i(\alpha)$ for any $\alpha \in \mathbb{Z}/p\mathbb{Z}$, can be publicly computed for any $i, j \in [1, \ell]$. It follows that, given a small prime q, once $\alpha \bmod q$ and $f_i(\alpha) \bmod q$ for some $i \in [1, \ell]$ are correctly computed, $f_j(\alpha) \bmod q$ can be computed as $g_{i,j}(\alpha)f_i(\alpha) \bmod q$ for any $j \in [1, \ell]$ such that $j > i$.

The requirement that no deletion operation should occur if the collected witnesses were issued at different states, comes from the fact that the accumulator can be initialized by accumulating some values which are kept secret by the Accumulator Manager.

It follows that, whenever the polynomial $f_1(x) \in \mathbb{Z}/p\mathbb{Z}$ is publicly known (or, equivalently, the set of all accumulated elements $\mathcal{Y}_{V_1}$) for a certain accumulator value V_1, we can remove the condition that no later deletion operations occur during attack execution, since the knowledge of $\alpha \bmod q$ is enough to compute $f_i(\alpha) \bmod q$ for any $i \in [1, \ell]$. Thus any non-membership witnesses issued from V_1 on can be used to recover α.

Removing Reduction Modulo p. We show that, under some practical assumptions, it is possible to eliminate with high probability the noise given by the reduction modulo p performed by the Accumulator Manager when he issues a non-membership witness. That is, we recover $\tilde{d}_{y_i} = f_{V_j}(\alpha) \bmod (y_i + \alpha)$ for a large fraction of pairs (y_i, V_j), given the partial non-membership witnesses $d_{y_i} = (f_{V_j}(\alpha) \bmod (y_i + \alpha)) \bmod p$ collected with respect to different accumulator values V_j with $j > 1$.

Aiming at this, we first observe that from the fact that $0 \leq y, \alpha < p$ for any given $y \in \mathcal{ACC} \setminus \mathcal{Y}_V$, the partial non-membership witness d_y for y with respect to V can be expressed in terms of $\tilde{d}_y$ in one of the following way:

(1) $d_y = f_V(\alpha) \bmod (y + \alpha) = \tilde{d}_y$,
(2) $d_y = (f_V(\alpha) \bmod (y + \alpha)) - p = \tilde{d}_y - p$.

Since p is odd, whenever $y + \alpha$ is even, these two cases can be easily distinguished modulo 2: indeed, in the first case $d_y \equiv f_V(\alpha) \pmod 2$, while in the second case $d_y \not\equiv f_V(\alpha) \pmod 2$.

This observation effectively allows to correctly compute $\tilde{d}_y$ half of the times given a correct guess for $\alpha \bmod 2$ and $f_V(\alpha) \bmod 2$. Indeed, given a set of partial non-membership witnesses $d_{y_1}, \ldots, d_{y_n}$ with respect to V, each guess of $\alpha \bmod 2$ and $f_V(\alpha) \bmod 2$ will split the witnesses in two subsets, namely one where the corresponding elements y_i satisfy $y_i + \alpha \equiv 0 \pmod 2$ (and thus $\tilde{d}_{y_i}$ can be correctly recovered), and the other where this doesn't happen.

Checking if $\alpha \bmod 2$ and $f_V(\alpha) \bmod 2$ were actually correct guesses can be done observing how the attacks described in Sects. 5.1 and 5.2 (or in Sect. 4 if witnesses are issued with respect to the same accumulator value) behaves with respect to the subset of witnesses that permitted to recover the values $\tilde{d}_{y_i}$. In case of a wrong guess, indeed, it will not possible to distinguish α and $f_{V_i}(\alpha)$ modulo some different small primes q: in this case the attack can be stopped and a new guess should be considered. On the other hand, a correct guess will permit to correctly recover α and $f_{V_i}(\alpha)$ modulo few more primes q greater than 2. Since, whenever $\alpha \bmod q$ and $f_V(\alpha) \bmod q$ are known, $\tilde{d}_y$ can be correctly recovered, analogously to the modulo 2 case, for all those y such that $y + \alpha$ is divisible by q, this implies that it is possible to iteratively recover more and more correct values $\tilde{d}_{y_i}$ given the initial set of considered witnesses.

Repeating this procedure for small primes q up to r, it allows to recover $\tilde{d}_{y_i}$ for those y_i that are divisible by at least one prime not exceeding r. This fraction tends to $1 - \varphi(r\#)/(r\#)$ as y_i tend to infinity, where φ is the Euler's totient function and $r\#$ denotes the product of all primes not exceeding r. For example, setting $r = 101$ allows to recover $\tilde{d}_{y_i}$ for about 88% of all available witnesses. We conclude that $\tilde{d}_{y_i}$ can be recovered for practically all $i \in [1, n]$.

In the case where witnesses are issued with respect to different accumulator values $V_1, \ldots, V_\ell$, as remarked above, the knowledge of $\alpha \bmod q$ and $f_{V_1}(\alpha) \bmod q$ allows to compute $f_{V_j}(\alpha) \bmod q$ for all V_j with $j > 1$, so the modulo p noise reduction can be easily performed independently on when the witnesses are issued.

5.1   The Random-y Sieving Attack

In this scenario we assume that all elements y_i for which the partial non-membership witnesses d_{y_i} are available to the adversary, are sampled uniformly at random from $\mathbb{Z}/p\mathbb{Z}$. Furthermore these witnesses are pre-processed accordingly to the method described above, in order to eliminate the noise given by reduction modulo p.

Recovering $\alpha \bmod q$. Let q be a small prime, i.e. $q = O(\log p)$, and let $\mathcal{Y}_\alpha$ be the set containing all pairs $(y_i, \tilde{d}_{y_i})$ such that $y_i + \alpha \equiv 0 \pmod{q}$ for a certain guess $\alpha \bmod q$. If the latter is guessed wrongly, then the values $\tilde{d}_{y_i}$ modulo q are distributed uniformly and independently from the values $f_{V_i}(\alpha) \bmod q$. On the other hand, if the guess is correct, then $\tilde{d}_{y_i} \equiv f_{V_i}(\alpha) \pmod{q}$.

Even in the case when $f_{V_1}(\alpha) \bmod q$ is unknown, $f_{V_i}(\alpha) \bmod q$ can be recovered from the first occurrence of y_i in the set $\mathcal{Y}_\alpha$ and verified at all further occurrences, since all $f_{V_j}(\alpha) \bmod q$ can be computed for any $j \geq i$. It follows that we can easily distinguish if a guess for $\alpha \bmod q$ is either correct or not.

The attack succeeds if for every wrong guess $\alpha^\times$ of $\alpha \bmod q$ we observe a contradiction within the pairs in $\mathcal{Y}_{\alpha^\times}$. It's easy to see that if $|\mathcal{Y}_{\alpha^\times}| = t$, the probability to observe at least one contradiction is $1 - 1/q^{t-1}$. Thus, by ensuring a constant number t of elements in $\mathcal{Y}_{\alpha^\times}$ given each $\alpha^\times \neq \alpha \bmod q$ is sufficient to make the probability of false positives negligible. This requires availability of $O(q \log q)$ witnesses in total.

Recovering α. The final step is the same as in the previous attacks: the secret value α is recovered by repeating the process for different small primes q and then by applying the Chinese Remainder Theorem. Furthermore, if for some primes q there are multiple candidates of α mod q, such primes can be simply omitted from the application of the Chinese Remainder Theorem. In this case, in order to fully recover $\alpha \in \mathbb{Z}$, the maximum prime q that has to be considered must be larger than $\ln p$ by a constant factor. We conclude that $O(q \log q) = O(\log p \log \log p)$ witnesses are sufficient for full recovery of α with overwhelming probability.

The time complexity of the attack is dominated by guessing α mod q for each q considered. Note that for a wrong guess of α mod q, we can expect on average a constant amount of witnesses to check before an inconsistency is observed; this amount is thus enough to identify the correct value. For each such guess, nearly all accumulator states in the history have to be considered in order to take into account all additions to the accumulator. However, the non-membership witnesses issued in each state can be classified by guesses of α mod q in a single scan for each prime q.

We conclude that the time complexity is dominated by

$$(\# \text{ primes } q) \times (q \text{ guesses of } \alpha \text{ mod } q) \times (\# \text{ of accumulator states})$$

and by classifying all non-membership witnesses for each prime q

$$(\# \text{ primes } q) \times (\# \text{ witnesses})$$

The final complexity is $O((1 + \ell/\log \log p) \log^2 p)$.

5.2   The Chosen-y Sieving Attack

If the adversary is allowed to choose the elements y_i for which the partial non-membership witnesses are issued, no matter with respect to which accumulator state, the amount of required witnesses can be further reduced by a $\log \log p$ factor.

First, we assume that the adversary chooses the elements y_i non-adaptively, i.e. before the accumulator is initialized. The idea is simply to use consecutive values, that is $y_0 = r$, $y_1 = r + 1, \ldots, y_i = r + i$, $\ldots$, for some $r \in \mathbb{Z}/p\mathbb{Z}$. This choice fills equally all sets $\mathcal{Y}_{\tilde{\alpha}}$ for all $\tilde{\alpha} \in \mathbb{Z}/q\mathbb{Z}$ and small q, where $\tilde{\alpha}$ represents either a correct guess for α mod q or a wrong guess $\alpha^{\times}$. As a result, $t = O(q)$ elements are enough to make the size of each set $\mathcal{Y}_{\tilde{\alpha}}$ at least equal to t. The full total number of required non-membership witnesses is then reduced to $O(q) = O(\log p)$. The time complexity then is improved by a factor $\log \log p$ in the case when ℓ is small: $O(\ell \log^2 p / \log \log p)$.

We now consider the case when the adversary can adaptively chose the elements y_i. Note that, on average, we need only $2 + 1/(q-1)$ elements in each set $Y_{\alpha^\times}$ to discard the wrong guess of $\alpha \mod q$, for all q. The adaptive choice allows to choose y_i such that $(y_i + \alpha^\times) \equiv 0 \pmod{q}$ specifically for those $\alpha^\times$ which are not discarded yet. Furthermore, the Chinese Remainder Theorem allows us to combine such adaptive queries for all chosen primes q simultaneously. As a result, approximately $2 \ln p$ witnesses for adaptively chosen elements are sufficient for the full recovery of α. This improves the constant factor of the non-adaptive attack in term of number of non-membership witnesses required.

Remark 1. As described at the beginning of this Section, non-membership witnesses can be issued with respect to different successive accumulator values $V_1, \ldots, V_\ell$, within which no deletion operation occurs. If the value $f_{V_1}(x) \in \mathbb{Z}[x]$ is known to the adversary (or equivalently the set of all accumulated elements in V_1), only $\ln p$ non-membership witnesses issued for adaptively chosen elements are sufficient to recover α. In this case, indeed, instead of verifying uniqueness of elements in the set $\mathcal{Y}_{\alpha^\times}$, we can directly compare our guess to the value $f_{V_j}(\alpha) \mod q$ given from $f_{V_1}(\alpha)$, thus requiring $1 + 1/(q-1)$ elements on average.

6   Experimental Results

We implemented the α-*Recovery Attack* from Sect. 4 and both the *random-y* and the *non-adaptive chosen-y sieving* attacks from Sects. 5.1 and 5.2.

For the verification purpose we used a random 512-bit prime p. We measured the success rate of the attacks with respect to the number of available non-membership witnesses. The α-Recovery Attack applies to a single accumulator state, and for the sieving attacks, the number of state changes of the accumulator was 10 times less than the number of issued witnesses. The initial state of the accumulator in all attacks was assumed to be secret. Each attack was executed 100 times per each analyzed number of available non-membership witnesses. The sieving attacks were considered successful if at most 2^{10} candidates for α were obtained and the correct α was among them. The results are illustrated in Fig. 1.

The α-Recovery Attack, while being simple, requires a significant amount of witnesses to achieve a high success rate, more than $20000 \approx 10 \ln p \ln \ln p$ witnesses and finishes in less than 5 s. The random-y sieving attack achieves almost full success rate with about $6000 \approx 3 \ln p \ln \ln p$ available witnesses and completes in less than 10 s. The chosen-y sieving attack requires less than $2000 \approx 4 \ln p$ witnesses to achieve almost perfect success rate and completes in less than 4 s. All timings include the generation of witnesses. The experiments were performed on a laptop with Linux Mint 19.3 OS and an Intel Core i5-10210U CPU clocked at 1.60 GHz.

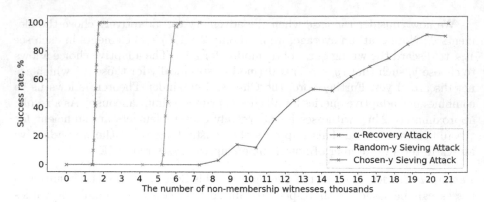

Fig. 1. Attacks experimental success rate as a function of the total number of available witnesses.

7   Weak Non-membership Witnesses

In the α-based construction, non-membership witness definition is affected by another minor design vulnerability: given a non-membership witness $\bar{w}_{y,V} = (C_y, d_y)$ with respect to an accumulator value V, if $d_y \equiv f_V(\alpha) \bmod p$, then $C_y = O$.

Those *"weak non-membership witnesses"* are issued with non-negligible probability in the security parameter λ when only one element is accumulated. Assume, indeed, that $V = (y' + \alpha)P$ for a certain element $y' \in \mathcal{ACC}$. Then, for any element $y \in \mathcal{ACC}$ such that $y' < y$, the corresponding non-membership witness $\bar{w}_{y,V}$ with respect to V is issued as

$$d_y = \big(y' + \alpha \bmod (y + \alpha)\big) \bmod p = (y' + \alpha) \bmod p$$

and thus $C_y = O$. In this case, as soon as the element y' becomes public (e.g. is removed), the accumulator secret parameter can be easily obtained as $\alpha = (d_y - y') \bmod p$.

8   Preventing Witness Forgery in the $\mathcal{CRS}$-Based Construction

All the attacks we have presented so far are ineffective when witnesses (more precisely, non-membership witnesses) are issued according to the defining equations given for the $\mathcal{CRS}$-based construction.

We note that the knowledge of the $\mathcal{CRS}$ is functionally equivalent to the knowledge of α when the set of currently accumulated elements is fully known: indeed, besides accumulator updates, the $\mathcal{CRS}$ permits to issue both membership and non-membership witnesses for arbitrary elements, with the difference that the knowledge of α permits to break collision-resistance, while the knowledge of the $\mathcal{CRS}$ does not. Furthermore, despite what we saw in Sect. 3, witnesses definition in the $\mathcal{CRS}$-based construction satisfy the hypothesis for the t–SDH security reduction provided by Au et al., i.e. collision-resistance is enforced when the $\mathcal{CRS}$ is used to issue witnesses.

Depending on the use-case application of the accumulator scheme, the possibility to publicly issue witnesses for arbitrary elements could be undesirable: for example, this is relevant when the accumulator scheme is used as a privacy-preserving authorization mechanism, i.e. an Anonymous Credential System. Suppose, indeed, that in this scenario the accumulator value V accumulates revoked users' identities and the non-revoked ones authenticate themselves showing the possession of a valid non-membership witness $\bar{w}_{y,V}$ for an identity y, both issued by a trusted Authentication Authority. If an attacker has access to the $\mathcal{CRS}$, he will be able to forge a random pair of credentials $(y', w_{y',V})$ and then he could authenticate himself, even if the Authentication Authority never issued the identity y' nor the corresponding witness. This is especially the case when a zero knowledge protocol is instantiated during users' credentials verification since it is impossible to distinguish between a zero knowledge proof for an authorized identity y and a proof for the never issued, but valid, identity y'.

In the following we will investigate the $\mathcal{CRS}$-based construction under this scenario, i.e. assuming the Accumulator Manager to be the only authority allowed to issue witnesses. We stress that resistance to witness forgeries is outside the security model provided by Au et al. where the attacker can generate as many witnesses as he wishes, and the attacks described in the following do not break any security properties assumed for the $\mathcal{CRS}$–based construction by the respective authors.

In the next two Sections, we will discuss how witness forgery for never-authorized elements can be prevented, namely: a) the manager constructs the set $\mathcal{Y}_V$ of currently accumulated elements in such a way that it is infeasible to fully reconstruct it; b) the common reference string $\mathcal{CRS}$ is not published and an attacker cannot reconstruct it.

8.1   How to Ensure Some Accumulated Elements Remain Unknown

Given an accumulator value V, assume $\mathcal{Y}_V$ is the union of the disjoint sets $\mathcal{Y}_{V_0}$, whose elements are used exclusively to initialize the accumulator value from P to V_0, and $\mathcal{Y}_{id} = \mathcal{Y}_V \setminus \mathcal{Y}_{V_0}$, the set of currently accumulated elements for which a membership witness have been issued.

Since the elements in $\mathcal{Y}_{id}$ must be public to enable users to update their witnesses[4], the reconstruction of $\mathcal{Y}_V = \mathcal{Y}_{V_0} \cup \mathcal{Y}_{id}$ can be prevented only if $\mathcal{Y}_{V_0}$ remains, at least partially, unknown.

---

[4] The very first element for which a membership witness is issued can remain unknown if there are no other users which need to update their witnesses. In this case, we assume that this elements belongs to $\mathcal{Y}_0$.

From $\mathcal{Y}_V = \mathcal{Y}_{V_0} \cup \mathcal{Y}_{id}$ and $\mathcal{Y}_{V_0} \cap \mathcal{Y}_{id} = \emptyset$, it follows that the polynomial $f_V(x)$ can be written as

$$f_V(x) = f_0(x) \cdot f_{id}(x) = \prod_{y_i \in \mathcal{Y}_{V_0}} (y_i + x) \prod_{y_j \in \mathcal{Y}_{id}} (y_j + x)$$

When non-membership witnesses are generated according to the $\mathcal{CRS}$-construction, as soon as an attacker has access to $deg(f_{id}) \geq deg(f_0)$, $|\mathcal{Y}_{V_0}|$ partial non-membership witnesses for the elements $y_1, \ldots, y_{|\mathcal{Y}_{V_0}|}$, i.e.

$$d_{y_i} \equiv f_V(-y_i) \equiv f_0(-y_i) \cdot f_{id}(-y_i) \pmod{p}$$

he will be able to reconstruct the unknown set $\mathcal{Y}_{V_0}$. Indeed, with the knowledge of $\mathcal{Y}_{id}$, the polynomial $f_{id}(x)$ can be easily obtained and it is then possible to compute the $|\mathcal{Y}_{V_0}|$ pairs

$$\left(-y_i, f_0(-y_i) \right) = \left(-y_i, \frac{d_{y_i}}{f_{id}(-y_i)} \right)$$

With these pairs, the attacker is able to uniquely interpolate, using for example Lagrange interpolation, the monic polynomial $f_0(x) \mod p$ whose roots are the elements in $\mathcal{Y}_{V_0}$.[5]

The reconstruction of the set $\mathcal{Y}_V$ can be prevented by initializing the accumulator with a number of random elements which is greater than the total number of issuable non-membership witnesses: this clearly avoids the possibility to interpolate $f_0(x)$, even in the case when the attacker has access to all issued non-membership witnesses.

We note, however, that this approach has some disadvantages. First of all, the maximum number of issuable non-membership witnesses has to be set at generation time and cannot be increased once the first witness is issued, since all further accumulated elements will be public to allow witness updates. When this number is reasonable big, let's say 1 billion, the Accumulator Manager needs to evaluate at least a 1-billion degree polynomial when issuing any new non-membership witnesses, an operation that becomes more and more expensive as the number of accumulated elements increases. On the other hand, by decreasing it, the Accumulator Manager can issue the non-membership witnesses in a less expensive way, but only to a smaller set of users.

8.2   Recovering the $\mathcal{CRS}$

Alternatively to the countermeasure proposed in Sect. 8.1, it's natural to wonder if unauthorized witness forgery can be prevented by just keeping the $\mathcal{CRS}$ secret from the attacker.

We will now show that by executing what we will refer to as *The Witness Forgery Attack*, an attacker that has access to multiple witnesses can successfully recover the $\mathcal{CRS}$, even if the Accumulator Manager keeps it secret.

---

[5] Since $f_0(x)$ is monic, only $deg(f_0)$ evaluations are needed to uniquely interpolate it.

The main observation on which this attack is based on is that given any partial witness C_y (no matter if it is a membership or a non-membership one) for an element y with respect to the accumulator value V, it can be expressed as $C_y = g_y(\alpha)P$ for a polynomial $g_y(x) \in \mathbb{Z}/p\mathbb{Z}[x]$ which depends on y and $f_V(x)$ (i.e. $f_V(x) = g_y(x)(y + x) + d_y$ for some $d_y \in \mathbb{Z}/p\mathbb{Z}$).

Assume the attacker has access to $n \geq |\mathcal{Y}_V| = m$ partial non-membership witnesses

$$C_{y_1} = g_1(\alpha)P, \ldots, C_{y_n} = g_n(\alpha)P$$

with respect to V. From Sect. 8.1, we know that he is able to fully recover the polynomial $f_V(x)$ and so he can explicitly compute from the elements $y_1, \ldots, y_n$ the n polynomials $g_1(x), \ldots, g_n(x)$ in $\mathbb{Z}/p\mathbb{Z}[x]$, each of degree $m - 1$. We note that by randomly choosing m out of these n polynomials, they will be linearly independent with probability

$$\frac{1}{p^{m^2}} \cdot \prod_{k=0}^{m-1} (p^m - p^k) = \prod_{k=1}^{m} \left(1 - \frac{1}{p^k}\right) \approx 1$$

and so we assume, without loss of generality, that $g_1(x), \ldots, g_m(x)$ are independent. It follows that for any fixed $i \in [0, \ldots, m - 1]$, there exist computable not-all-zero coefficients $a_1, \ldots, a_m \in \mathbb{Z}/p\mathbb{Z}$ such that

$$x^i = a_1 g_1(x) + \ldots + a_m g_m(x)$$

and so

$$\alpha^i P = a_1 C_{y_1} + \ldots + a_m C_{y_m}$$

In other words, the partial common reference string

$$\mathcal{CRS}_m \doteq \{P, \alpha P, \ldots, \alpha^{m-1} P\}$$

can be obtained from these witnesses and this will enable the attacker to compute membership and non-membership witnesses with respect to V for any accumulated and non-accumulated element, respectively.

We note that it is more convenient to execute the above attack with respect to the accumulator value V_0 and the polynomial $f_{V_0}(x)$: in fact, any non-membership witness for a never added element which is issued with respect to a later accumulator value than V_0, can be iteratively transformed back to a non-membership witness with respect to V_0 by just inverting the non-membership witness update formula outlined in Sect. 2. Once both $f_{V_0}(x)$ and $\mathcal{CRS}_{|\mathcal{Y}_{V_0}|}$ are computed, the attacker can issue witnesses with respect to V_0 for elements in and not in $\mathcal{Y}_{V_0}$ and update them with respect to the latest accumulator value as usual. Clearly, since it is possible to issue many different non-membership witnesses with respect to V_0, this implies that by updating them, these non-membership witnesses can be used to iteratively expand the previously computed partial common reference string $\mathcal{CRS}_{|\mathcal{Y}_{V_0}|}$.

Attack 1: The Witness Forgery Attack

Input   : $n \geq |\mathcal{Y}_{V_0}|$ non-membership witnesses for never accumulated elements,
       the accumulator history (accumulator values and added/removed
       elements)

Output: a non-membership witness for a non-accumulated element or a
       membership witness for an accumulated one with respect to V

1 *Un-update* all non-membership witnesses with respect to V_0 inverting witness
   update formula and using accumulator history.
2 Interpolate the polynomial $f_{V_0}(x) = \prod_{y_i \in \mathcal{Y}_{V_0}}(y_i + x)$ from witnesses.
3 Use Euclidean Algorithm to find $g_i(x)$ and d_{y_i} such that
   $f_{V_0}(x) = g_i(x)(y_i + x) + d_{y_i}$ for every element y_i, $i = 1, \ldots, n$
4 Use linear algebra to write x^j as a linear combinations of $g_1(x), \ldots, g_n(x)$ for
   any $j = 0, \ldots, |\mathcal{Y}_{V_0}| - 1$
5 Obtain $CRS_{|\mathcal{Y}_{V_0}|}$ from witnesses.
6 Use $CRS_{|\mathcal{Y}_{V_0}|}$ and $f_{V_0}(x)$ to issue many different non-membership witnesses
   with respect to V_0.
7 Use the additional non-membership witnesses issued to expand the common
   reference string to $CRS_{|\mathcal{Y}_V|}$.
8 Issue membership and non-membership witnesses with respect to the
   accumulator value V.

More precisely, given an accumulator value V we know that

$$V = \left(\prod_{y_i \in \mathcal{Y}_V \setminus \mathcal{Y}_{V_0}} (y + \alpha) \right) V_0 = f_V(\alpha)P$$

where $f_V(x)$ can be publicly computed from the published witness update information if the monic polynomial $f_{V_0}(x)$ is recovered by the attacker through
interpolation, as outlined in Sect. 8.1.

Once the attacker successfully computes $CRS_{|\mathcal{Y}_{V_0}|}$, they use it to issue (a
multiple of) $|\mathcal{Y}_V| - |\mathcal{Y}_{V_0}|$ additional non-membership witnesses for random ele-
ments with respect to V_0, he updates them with respect to V and expands its
starting set of elements and witnesses. Then, for each element y_i in this bigger set, he computes the corresponding polynomial $g_i(x)$ of degree $deg(f_V) - 1$
such that $f_V(x) = g_i(x)(y_i + x) + d_{y_i}$. At this point and similarly as before, the
attacker can explicitly write a linear combinations of computable polynomials
which equals x^i for any i such that $deg(f_{V_0}) - 1 < i \leq deg(f_V) - 1$, and thus can
expand the previously computed $CRS_{deg(f_{V_0})}$ to $CRS_{deg(f_V)}$. In conclusion, an
attacker would be able to forge witnesses with respect to the latest accumulator
value by accessing only $|\mathcal{Y}_{V_0}|$ non-membership witnesses. The whole attack is
summarized in Attack 1.

Similarly as discussed in Sect. 8.1, this attack can be prevented if the total
number of issued non-membership witnesses is less than $|\mathcal{Y}_{V_0}|$.

9   Conclusions

In this paper, we cryptanalysed the Dynamic Universal Accumulator scheme proposed by Au et al. [1], investigating the security of the two constructions proposed, to which we refer as the α-*based* and the $\mathcal{CRS}$-*based* construction.

For the first construction we have shown several attacks which allow to recover the accumulator secret parameter α and thus break its collision resistance. More precisely, if p is the order of the underlying bilinear group, an attacker that has access to $O(\log p \log \log p)$ non-membership witnesses for random elements will be able to fully recover α, no matter how many elements are accumulated. If instead the elements can be chosen by the attacker, the number of required witnesses reduces down to just $O(\log p)$, thus making the attack linear in the size of the accumulator secret α. Furthermore, we showed how accumulator collision resistance can be broken in the α-based construction given *one* non-membership witness and we described also another minor design flaw.

For the second, i.e. the $\mathcal{CRS}$-based construction, we investigated resistance to witness forgeries under the hypothesis that the Accumulator Manager has the exclusive right to issue witnesses (as in authentication mechanisms) and thus keeps the $\mathcal{CRS}$ private. We have shown that an attacker that has access to multiple witnesses is able to reconstruct the Accumulator Manager $\mathcal{CRS}$, which would then enable him to compute witnesses for arbitrary elements. In particular, if the accumulator is initialized by accumulating m secret elements, m witnesses suffices to recover the secret $\mathcal{CRS}$.

Countermeasures We have shown that the α-based construction of Au et al. Dynamic Universal Accumulator is insecure, however one still use the witness defining equations provided in the alternative $\mathcal{CRS}$-based construction, which is collision-resistant under the t-SDH assumption. There is one caveat: knowledge of $\mathcal{CRS}$ will enable an attacker to issue witnesses for arbitrary elements. If this needs to be avoided (ex. in authentication mechanisms), then $\mathcal{CRS}$ should be kept secret and the accumulator properly initialized. Namely, the accumulator manager needs to define an upper limit m to the total number of issuable non-membership witnesses and has to initialize the accumulator by adding $m + 1$ secret elements in order to prevent Attack 1.

Acknowledgements. We thank the anonymous reviewers for their helpful comments and suggestions. This work was supported by the Luxembourg National Research Fund (FNR) project FinCrypt (C17/IS/11684537).

References

1. Au, M.H., Tsang, P.P., Susilo, W., Mu, Y.: Dynamic universal accumulators for ddh groups and their application to attribute-based anonymous credential systems. In: CT-RSA, Springer LNCS, vol. 5473, pp. 295–308 (2009)
2. Baric, N., Pfitzmann, B.: Collision-free accumulators and fail-stop signature schemes without trees. In: EUROCRYPT, pp. 480–494 (1997)

3. Benaloh, J., de Mare, M.: One-way accumulators: a decentralized alternative to digital signatures. In: EUROCRYPT, pp. 274–285 (1993)
4. Boneh, D., Boyen, X.: Short signatures without random oracles and the SDH assumption in bilinear groups. J. Cryptol. **21**(2), 149–177 (2008)
5. Boneh, D., Corrigan-Gibbs, H.: Bivariate polynomials modulo composites and their applications. In: International Conference on the Theory and Application of Cryptology and Information Security, pp. 42–62 (2014)
6. Boneh, D., Bünz, B., Fisch, B.: Batching techniques for accumulators with applications to IOPs and stateless blockchains. Cryptology ePrint Archive, Report 2018/1188 (2018)
7. Buldas, A., Laud, P., Lipmaa, H.: Accountable certificate management using undeniable attestations. In: ACM CCS, vol. 9–17 (2000)
8. Buldas, A., Laud, P., Lipmaa, H.: Eliminating counterevidence with applications to accountable certificate management. J. Comput. Secur. **10**, 2002 (2002)
9. Camacho, P., Hevia, A., Kiwi, M.A., Opazo, R.: Strong accumulators from collision-resistant hashing. In: ISC, Springer LNCS, vol. 4222, pp. 471–486 (2008)
10. Camenisch, J., Lysyanskaya, A.: Dynamic accumulators and application to efficient revocation of anonymous credentials. In: CRYPTO, pp. 61–76 (2002)
11. Camenisch, J., Soriente, C.: An accumulator based on bilinear maps and efficient revocation for anonymous credentials. In: PKC 2009, Springer LNCS, vol. 5443, pp. 481–500 (2009)
12. Damgård, I., Triandopoulos, N.: Supporting non-membership proofs with bilinear-map accumulators. IACR Cryptology ePrint Archive, vol. 538 (2008)
13. Derler, D., Hanser, C., Slamanig, D.: Revisiting cryptographic accumulators, additional properties and relations to other primitives. In: CT-RSA 2015, pp. 127–144 (2015)
14. Li, J., Li, N., Xue, R.: Universal accumulators with efficient nonmembership proofs. In: ACNS, Springer LNCS, vol. 4521, pp. 253–269 (2007)
15. Lipmaa, H.: Secure Accumulators from euclidean rings without trusted setup. In: ACNS, Springer LNCS, vol. 7341, pp. 224–240 (2012)
16. Merkle, R.C.: A certified digital signature. In: Advances in Cryptology - CRYPTO 1989, pp. 218–238 (1989)
17. Mitzenmacher, M., Upfal, E.: Probability and Computing: Randomized Algorithms and Probabilistic Analysis. Cambridge University Press, Cambridge(2005)
18. Nguyen, L.: Accumulators from bilinear pairings and applications. In: CT-RSA, Springer LNCS, vol. 3376, pp. 275–292 (2005)
19. Sander, T.: Efficient accumulators without trapdoor. In: ICICS, pp. 252–262 (1999)
20. Vitto, G., Biryukov, A.: Dynamic universal accumulator with batch update over bilinear groups. In: IACR Cryptology ePrint Archive, vol. 777 (2020)

FAN: A Lightweight Authenticated Cryptographic Algorithm

Lin Jiao[1]($\boxtimes$) ⓘ, Dengguo Feng[1,2], Yonglin Hao[1], Xinxin Gong[1], and Shaoyu Du[1]

[1] State Key Laboratory of Cryptology, Beijing 100878, China
[2] State Key Laboratory of Computer Science, ISCAS, Beijing, China

Abstract. The wide application of the low-end embedded devices has largely stimulated the development of lightweight ciphers. In this paper, we propose a new lightweight authenticated encryption with additional data (AEAD) algorithm, named as FAN, which is based on a first non-Grain-like small-state stream cipher that adopts a novel block-wise structure, inspired by the 4-blade daily electric fan. It takes a 128-bit key, a 64-bit initial vector (IV), and a 192-bit state, promising 128-bit security and up to 72-bit authentication tag with the IV-respecting restriction. It consists of a nonlinear spindle, four linear blades and an accumulator, and updates by constant mutual feedbacks between the linear and nonlinear parts, which rapidly provides highly confused level by parallel diffusing the fastest-changing state of spindle. The key is used both in the initialization and generation phases as part of input and state respectively, making FAN suitable for resource-constrained scenarios with internal state diminishment but no security loss. A thorough security evaluation of the entire AEAD mode is provided, which shows that FAN can achieve enough security margin against known attacks. Furthermore, FAN can be implemented efficiently not only in hardware environments but also in software platforms, whose operations are carefully chosen for bit-slice technique, especially the S-box is newly designed efficiently implemented by logic circuit. The hardware implementation requires about 2327 GE on 90 nm technology with a throughput of 9.6 Gbps. The software implementation runs about 8.0 cycle/byte.

Keywords: Lightweight design · Authenticated encryption · Stream cipher · Small-state · Implementation efficiency

1 Introduction

There are several emerging areas (e.g. Radio Frequency Identification, sensor networks, distributed control systems, and Internet of Things etc.) progressing rapidly, in which highly-constrained devices are interconnected, typically communicating wirelessly with one another, and working in concert to accomplish

Supported by the National Natural Science Foundation of China (No. 61902030, 62002024, 62022018).

K. G. Paterson (Ed.): CT-RSA 2021, LNCS 12704, pp. 299–325, 2021.
https://doi.org/10.1007/978-3-030-75539-3_13

some task. These new cryptography scenarios have similar features as extremely limited area size, power or energy, but needs to maintain enough high secure level and efficient communication between networked smart objects. Therefore, the majority of current cryptographic algorithms that were designed for desktop/server environments do not fit any more, and it is necessary to research on lightweight ciphers suited for resource-constraint applications.

Lightweight block ciphers have already possessed many successful designs, such as LED, SIMON, SPECK, PRESENT and etc., while lightweight stream ciphers hit a bottleneck of large internal state size to resist time-memory-data tradeoff (TMDTO) attacks [5]. Then there comes a solution that using the cipher key stored in non-volatile memory of devices not only for initialization phase but during the encryption process as well. This helps to save resources against certain TMDTO, and also allows for a stronger key involvement to achieve higher security. It has been investigated from a view of practical engineering, and resulted in that it is better to access and involve the key from all types of non-volatile memory continuously [18]. Here, this design principle is named as CKU (Continuous-Key-Use) for simplicity. However, the immediate CKU-based designs, such as Sprout, Fruitv2 and Plantlet [3,4,18] are all adopting the Grain-like structure [12], which has recently been reported vulnerable to the correlation attack [21]. Thus, we are motivated to design a new and first CKU-based lightweight stream cipher with entirely different structure, and support integrated encryption and authentication functionality.

Firstly, we adopt byte-wise operations intending to offer a balanced performance in software and hardware implementations. Secondly, we propose a novel structure inspired by the shape of electric fan, which consists of a nonlinear spindle, four linear blades and an accumulator, and updates by constant mutual feedbacks between the linear and nonlinear parts rapidly providing highly confused level in parallelly diffusing manner. Thirdly, the use of underlying components, such as S-box layer and L-layer, all represent the trade-off between security and performance, especially the S-box is newly designed efficiently implemented by logic circuit for small area requirements. In addition, we import the idea of FP(1)-mode [11], a recently suggested principle for initialization phase of stream ciphers, to protect the security of authentication from internal state collision. A counter is used for dividing different work phases and providing round constants. The cipher key is injected into the internal state proportionally and continually in the encryption phase. Thus, it results the new lightweight authenticated encryption with additional data (AEAD) algorithm, named as FAN. It is a CKU-based lightweight cipher, which takes a 128-bit key, a 64-bit initial vector (IV), and a 192-bit state, promising 128-bit security and up to 72-bit authentication tag with the IV-respecting restriction. A thorough security analysis of the entire AEAD mode is provided, which shows that FAN can achieve enough security margin against known attacks, such as cube attack, correlation attack, guess-and-determine attack, time-memory-data tradeoffs and related-key attacks etc. It offers efficient implementations not only in hardware environments but also in software platforms, which requires 2327 GE on 90 nm technology with a throughput of 9.6 Gbps, and runs 8.0 cycle/byte using Intel Haswell processor.

This paper is organized as follow. The specification is introduced in Sect. 2. The design rationale is given in Sect. 3. The security is discussed in Sect. 4. The performance is given in Sect. 5. A conclusion is provided in Sect. 6.

2   Specification of FAN

FAN supports 128-bit key, 64-bit IV, up to 72-bit authentication tag. It is expected to maintain security as long as the IV is unique (not repeated under the same key). FAN has two work modes: self-synchronizing stream cipher and AEAD algorithm[1]. The maximum amount of inputs (plaintext, associated data) that can be securely encrypted under the same key-IV pair is 2^{64} bits. If verification fails, the new tag and the decrypted ciphertext should not be given as output. The security goal of FAN is 128-bit confidentiality and $\leq$ 72-bit integrity.

The specification of FAN consists of three parts: a list view of notations, a description of state and update functions, a full process of initialization, processing associated data, encryption and finalization.

2.1   Notations

Operations used in FAN:

$\oplus$: bit-wise exclusive OR   &: bit-wise AND

|: bit-wise OR   NAND: bit-wise NAND

||: concatenation   mod: modulo operation

$\lll$ ($\ggg$): rotation to the left (right) $\ll$ ($\gg$): shift to the left (right)

$\lceil\ \rceil$: ceiling operation $|x|$: the bit length of a string x

#{ }: the cardinality of a set   GF( ): finite field

$\mathbb{F}_2^n$: n-dimension binary vector space $\mathbb{B}_n$: n-variate boolean functions

---

[1] Since the self-synchronizing stream cipher mode can be seen as part of the AEAD mode, we do not describe this work mode separately in the following text.

Variables used in FAN^2:

0^n (1^n): n-bit 0 (n-bit 1) rc: 8-bit state of the counter

t: the round number x^t: variable x at t-th round

b: four 4-byte states of the blades b_i: 4-byte state of the blade i

a: 4-byte state of the accumulator s: 4-byte state of the spindle

P: the plaintext N_p: number of padded plaintext blocks

AD: the associated data N_{ad}: number of padded associated data blocks

p^t: 24-bit plaintext block at t ad^t: 24-bit associated data block at t

z^t: 24-bit keystream block at t c^t: 24-bit ciphertext block at t

m^t: 24-bit message block at t T: authentication tag

K: 16-byte key $(K_{15}, \ldots, K_1, K_0)$ k^t: 24-bit subkey at t

IV: 8-byte IV $(IV_7, \ldots, IV_1, IV_0)$ S: the S-box permutation

L: the L-layer transformation

ω, μ, ν: three 32-bit intermediate states for S-P-S used in algebraic attack.

2.2   State and Functions

FAN has 192-bit internal state, which is composed of three parts: four blades, one accumulator and one spindle. Let these four blades be $b = (b_3, b_2, b_1, b_0)$, where each blade consists of four bytes, denoted as $b_i = (b_{i,3}\|b_{i,2}\|b_{i,1}\|b_{i,0})$, $i = 0, 1, 2, 3$. The accumulator consists of four bytes, denoted as $a = (a_3\|a_2\|a_1\|a_0)$. The state of the spindle contains four bytes, denoted as $s = (s_3\|s_2\|s_1\|s_0)$, where $s_i = (s_{i,7}\|s_{i,6}\|s_{i,5}\|s_{i,4}\|s_{i,3}\|s_{i,2}\|s_{i,1}\|s_{i,0})$ and $s_{i,0}$ is the least significant bit. Besides, there is one-byte counter in FAN, denoted as[3] $rc = (rc_7\|rc_6\|rc_5\|rc_4\|rc_3\|rc_2\|rc_1\|rc_0)$.

A complete description of the main functions in FAN is given by the following pseudo-code, where $m^t = (m_2^t\|m_1^t\|m_0^t)$ is a 24-bit message block injected at t-th round, $z^t = (z_2^t\|z_1^t\|z_0^t)$ is the corresponding 24-bit keystream block, and $k^t = (k_2^t, k_1^t, k_0^t)$ denotes the round key at t-th round:

KeystreamOutput(s, a)

/ ∗ output keystream block ∗ /

$z_2 \leftarrow s_3 \oplus s_2 \oplus a_3$; $z_1 \leftarrow s_1 \oplus s_0 \oplus a_2$; $z_0 \leftarrow s_0 \oplus a_1 \oplus a_0$; $z^t \leftarrow z_2\|z_1\|z_0$; output z^t.

StateUpdate(b, a, s, rc, m^t, k^t)

---

[2] m^t can be ad^t, p^t or some padding constant given in the following description.

[3] rc_7 is used as an initialization/encryption indicator.

/ * update the internal state * /

$b_{i,(i+1)\bmod 4} \leftarrow b_{i,(i+1)\bmod 4} \oplus s_i, \ i = 0,1,2,3;$

$b_{i,(i+2)\bmod 4} \leftarrow \left(b_{i,(i+2)\bmod 4} \oplus a_i\right)_{\lll(2i+1)}, \ i = 0,1,2,3;$

$a_i \leftarrow a_i \oplus b_{i,(i+3)\bmod 4}, \ i = 0,1,2,3;$

$s_3 \leftarrow s_3 \oplus b_{3,3} \oplus rc, \ s_i \leftarrow s_i \oplus b_{i,i} \oplus m_i^t \oplus k_i^t, \ i = 0,1,2;$

$s_i \leftarrow S[s_i], \ i = 0,1,2,3; (s_3\|s_2\|s_1\|s_0) \leftarrow L(s_3\|s_2\|s_1\|s_0); s_i \leftarrow S[s_i], \ i = 0,1,2,3;$

$(b_3,b_2,b_1,b_0) \leftarrow (b_0,b_3,b_2,b_1).$

/ * update the counter * /

if $rc_6 = 0, (rc_5\|rc_4\|rc_3\|rc_2\|rc_1\|rc_0) \leftarrow (rc_4\|rc_3\|rc_2\|rc_1\|rc_0\|rc_5 \oplus rc_0);$

$\qquad rc_6 \leftarrow rc_5 \& rc_4 \& rc_3 \& rc_2 \& rc_1 \& rc_0;$

else $\qquad (rc_6\|rc_5\|rc_4\|rc_3\|rc_2\|rc_1\|rc_0) \leftarrow (1^7);$

Specifically, the components used above are defined as follows.

(1) L-layer. L: 4 bytes $\rightarrow$ 4 bytes
The input is transformed using the MDS matrix adopted in the `MixColumn` operation of AES [19] given by $L(x_3\|x_2\|x_1\|x_0) = (y_3\|y_2\|y_1\|y_0)$:

$$\begin{bmatrix} y_3 \\ y_2 \\ y_1 \\ y_0 \end{bmatrix} = \begin{bmatrix} 2 & 3 & 1 & 1 \\ 1 & 2 & 3 & 1 \\ 1 & 1 & 2 & 3 \\ 3 & 1 & 1 & 2 \end{bmatrix} \begin{bmatrix} x_3 \\ x_2 \\ x_1 \\ x_0 \end{bmatrix},$$

where each byte represents an element from $GF(2^8)$ with the following polynomial for field multiplication $X^8 + X^4 + X^3 + X + 1$.

(2) S-box. S: 8 bits $\rightarrow$ 8 bits

$\{01, 02, 0d, f3, 31, 73, 2f, df, c1, ec, 89, 4f, bb, d6, e5, 2c,$
$03, 00, 0e, b4, 72, 30, 6d, d8, c7, aa, 8e, 4c, fd, d0, a2, 6e,$
$69, 2a, 76, 92, 09, 0b, 05, ee, a6, 9b, f9, 74, 8d, f0, c5, 46,$
$9c, e1, 37, bf, b7, 8a, 44, c3, 68, 2b, 94, 35, 08, 0a, a8, 07,$
$9a, a7, d5, 5c, f1, 8c, e9, 7e, 11, 12, 1e, fe, 21, 63, 7d, 82,$
$62, 20, 3f, 84, 13, 10, 1d, b8, b6, 8b, af, 3c, 9d, e0, d3, 5f,$
$79, 3a, 25, cf, 19, 1b, 17, e3, ed, c0, f5, 27, d7, ba, 99, 54,$
$18, 1a, a4, 15, 78, 3b, c8, 66, fc, d1, 56, 9e, c6, ab, 64, b2,$
$41, 38, 4d, 8f, 6b, 52, 75, f8, 81, 86, c9, 67, a1, e7, ff, 1f,$
$87, 80, ce, 24, e6, a0, b9, 1c, 43, 7a, 4e, 88, 29, 50, 36, be,$
$16, e2, fa, bd, 3e, 85, cb, cd, e4, 2d, 5b, 32, c2, 45, 60, 49,$
$a5, 14, fb, bc, 83, 7c, ca, cc, 6f, a3, 71, 58, 47, c4, 4a, 23,$
$96, 91, 2e, de, f7, b1, 06, a9, 33, 5a, 98, 55, 48, 61, ae, 3d,$
$7f, e8, 22, 4b, 57, 9f, 59, 70, ef, 04, f6, b0, d9, 6c, 97, 90,$
$b5, 0f, ad, ea, 93, 77, dd, db, 65, b3, 39, 40, 5d, d4, 53, 6a,$
$da, dc, 95, 34, eb, ac, f2, 0c, 51, 28, 5e, d2, 7b, 42, 26, f4\}$

(3) Counter. The counter updates in the control of its indicative bit rc_6. If rc_6 equals 0, the last six bits of counter update as a linear feedback shift register:

$(rc_5\|rc_4\|rc_3\|rc_2\|rc_1\|rc_0)$ are shifted one bit to the left with the new value to rc_0 being computed as $rc_5 \oplus rc_0$ at each round, which corresponds to a minimum generate polynomial of $GF(2^6)$: $X^6 + X^5 + 1$, then they are ANDed together to update rc_6. Once rc_6 arrives at 1, $(rc_6\|rc_5\| \ldots \|rc_0)$ do not change any more and fix at (1^7). It means that, rc_6 can indicate the end of initialization rounds. In addition, the counter state is always added to the first byte of spindle as a round constant. Here, rc_7 is additionally defined as follows to separate the processing associated data and encryption phases, that is, to prevent using part of the associated data as plaintext/ciphertext,

$$rc_7 \leftarrow \begin{cases} 0\,, \texttt{before encryption;} \\ 1\,, \texttt{from the beginning of encryption.} \end{cases}$$

(4) Constant mutual feedback structure.
   - The four bytes of each blade are updated as: one adds a feedback from the accumulator and rotates with some parameter, one adds a feedback from the spindle; the other two are invariant. Finally these four blades run a wholly blade-wise right rotation.
   - The accumulator concentrates the confused properties from the entire state and disseminates back to the state for fast diffusion, by linearly accumulating one of the invariant bytes from each blade on different units. The output function linearly extracts three bytes of the spindle and accumulator for each output byte, which maintain a highly confused level.
   - The spindle provides the only nonlinear operations to the whole cipher. The other invariant byte from each blade is added back to the spindle separately on different units. The update function of spindle takes a Substitution-Permutation-Substitution network (S-P-S) with the S-box and L-layer.
   - The subkey sequence and the message blocks are defined different in each process and take part in the state update by adding to the last three bytes of spindle.

2.3   Initialization

Divide the 64-bit IV into 8 bytes, $IV = IV_7\| \ldots \|IV_1\|IV_0$, and divide the 128-bit key into 16 bytes $K = K_{15}\| \ldots \|K_1\|K_0$. The initialization phase in FAN works as the following pseudo-code:

```
/ * load key and IV into internal state at t = −52 * /
b_{i,j} ← K_{4i+j},  i = 0, 1, 2, 3,  j = 0, 1, 2, 3; a_i ← IV_{4+i},  i = 0, 1, 2, 3; s_i ← IV_i,  i = 0, 1, 2, 3;
/ * initialize the counter * /
rc ← (00110011);
for t = −52 to − 1 do
/ * update the internal state and counter * /
     StateUpdate(b, a, s, rc, m^t, k^t);
end for
```

We briefly illustrate the initialization phase here.

- It loads the key and IV into the internal state first, and then updates 52 rounds and generates the initial internal state of FAN without output.
- The last six bits of counter are initialized to (110011). After 52 rounds update, these six bits run to (111111), and the indicative bit rc_6 arrives at 1 at the first time, which indicates the end of initialization. Here, rc_7 is initialized to 0 and remains 0.
- Let $m^t = 0^{24}, t = -52, -51, \ldots, -1$, and $k^t = 0^{24}, t = -52, -51, \ldots, -1$. That is, neither subkey sequence nor message blocks take part in the state update in this phase.

The state update functions in initialization is shown in Fig. 1.

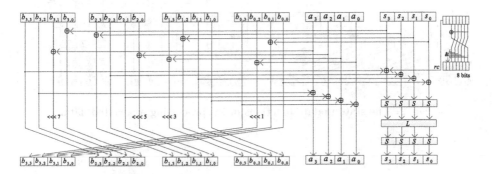

Fig. 1. The state update functions in the initialization.

2.4   Processing Associated Data

After the initialization, FAN is ready to process the associated data as the following pseudo-code:

> **for** $t = 0$ **to** $N_{ad} - 1$ **do**
> /∗ update the internal state and counter ∗/
>   StateUpdate(b, a, s, rc, m^t, k^t);
> **end for**

We briefly illustrate the processing associated data phase here.

- FAN processes the associated data in block of 24 bits. It appends a single 1 and the smallest number of 0s to the end of AD to obtain a multiple of 24 bits and split it into N_{ad} blocks of 24 bits. In case the associated data is empty, no padding is applied and $N_{ad} = 0$.

$$ad^0, ad^1, \ldots, ad^{N_{ad}-1} \leftarrow \begin{cases} \text{24-bit block of } AD\|1\|0^{24-1-(|AD|\bmod 24)} & \text{, if } |AD| > 0; \\ \emptyset & \text{, if } |AD| = 0. \end{cases}$$

- Let $m^t = ad^t$, $t = 0, 1, \ldots, N_{ad}-1$ and $k^t = 0^{24}$, $t = 0, 1, \ldots, N_{ad}-1$. That
  is, only the associated data takes part in the state update in this phase but
  not the subkey.
- The state of counter fix at (01111111) in this phase.

The state update functions in processing associated data phase is shown in Fig. 2.

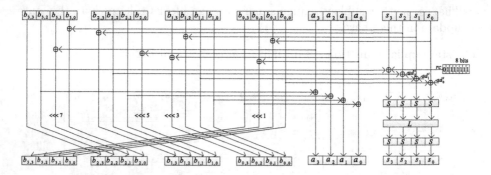

Fig. 2. The state update functions in the processing associated data.

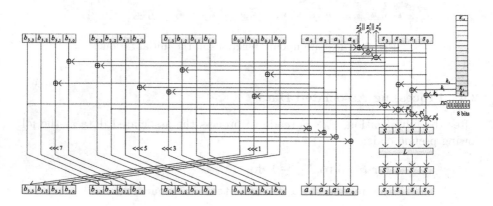

Fig. 3. The state update functions in the encryption/decryption.

2.5   Encryption

Next, FAN processes the plaintext and generates the keystream according to the
pseudo-code as follows:

```
/ * change the separated bit of counter * /
rc7 ← 1;
for t = Nad to Nad + Np − 1 do
/ * output keystream block * /
    KeystreamOutput(s, a);
/ * encrypt plaintext block into ciphertext block * /
    ct ← pt ⊕ zt;
/ * update the internal state and counter * /
    StateUpdate(b, a, s, rc, mt, kt);
end for
```

We briefly illustrate the encryption phase here.

– FAN processes the plaintext in blocks of 24 bits. The padding process appends a single 1 and the smallest number of 0s to P until the padded length is 16 mod 24. The last byte of the padded plaintext is used to record the length of authentication tag to be generated in big-endian binary. That is

$$P\|1\|\underbrace{0\ldots0}_{\sigma}\|(\text{one byte for } |T|), \text{ where } (plen + 1 + \sigma + 8) \bmod 24 = 0.$$

The resulting padded plaintext is with the length of a multiple of 24 bits, and split into N_p blocks of 24 bits as

$$p^0, p^1, \ldots, p^{N_p-1} \leftarrow 24\text{-bit block of } P\|1\|0\ldots0\|(\text{one byte for } |T|).$$

– Let $m^t = p^{t-N_{ad}}$, $t = N_{ad}, N_{ad}+1, \ldots, N_{ad}+N_p-1$,
  and $k_i^t = K_{(3\times(t-N_{ad})+i)\bmod 16}$, $i = 0, 1, 2$, $t = N_{ad}, N_{ad}+1, \ldots, N_{ad}+N_p-1$,
  where the subkeys are simply cyclically selected as the next three consecutive bytes of the cipher key. That is the 128-bit key affect the internal state proportionally and continually, and the subkeys circulate in a period of 16 rounds in this phase.
– Each round in this phase generates a keystream block using KeystreamOutput function, and then generates the ciphertext block using this keystream block.
– Next, update the internal state. Both the plaintext blocks and subkeys join in the update of spindle in this phase.
– The state of counter remains (11111111) in this phase, where rc_7 is changed to 1 for separating the associated data and plaintext.

The state update functions in encryption is shown in Fig. 3. To make differences of all phases more clear, we present a comparison diagram in Appendix 3.

2.6 Finalization

After encrypting all the plaintext blocks, FAN generates the authentication tag by the following pseudo-code:

> / * reload (add) key-IV pair to the internal state * /
> $b_{i,j} \leftarrow b_{i,j} \oplus k_{4i+j}, \ i = 0, 1, 2, 3, \ j = 0, 1, 2, 3;$
> $a_i \leftarrow a_i \oplus IV_{4+i}, \ i = 0, 1, 2, 3; s_i \leftarrow s_i \oplus IV_i, \ i = 0, 1, 2, 3;$
> / * do the re-initialization phase * /
> $rc \leftarrow (10001011)$
> for $t = N_{ad} + N_p$ to $N_{ad} + N_p + 28 - 1$, do
>   StateUpdate(b, a, s, rc, m^t, k^t);
> end for
> / * generate the authentication tag * /
> for $t = N_{ad} + N_p + 28$ to $N_{ad} + N_p + 28 + \lceil |T|/24 \rceil - 1$ do
>   KeystreamOutput(s, a); StateUpdate(b, a, s, rc, m^t, k^t);
> end for
> $$T \leftarrow \left(z^{N_{ad}+N_p+28} \| \cdots \| z^{N_{ad}+N_p+28+\lceil |T|/24 \rceil - 1} \right)_{\text{trunc by } |T|};$$

We briefly illustrate the finalization phase here.

- In the finalization, the key-IV is re-XORed to the internal state at first. Then the internal state is updated 28 rounds using the iteration in the initialization. The counter is re-initialized with (10001011). After 28 rounds update, the last seven bits of counter run to (1111111) one more time, which indicates that FAN is ready to generate the authentication tag.
- Next, FAN generates the authentication tag using the iteration in keystream generation, and finally truncates the keystream blocks according to the length of authentication tag required. In this part, the state of counter remains (11111111).
- Let $m^t = 0^{24}$, $t = N_{ad} + N_p, \ldots, N_{ad} + N_p + 28 + \lceil |T|/24 \rceil - 1$, $k_i^t = 0^{24}$, $t = N_{ad} + N_p, \ldots, N_{ad} + N_p + 28 - 1$, and $k_i^t = K_{(3 \times (t - N_{ad} - 28) + i) \mathrm{mod} 16}, i = 0, 1, 2, \ t = N_{ad} + N_p + 28, \ldots, N_{ad} + N_p + 28 + \lceil |T|/24 \rceil - 1.$

It means that no message blocks take part in the update of internal state in this phase. The subkeys only join in the update part when to generate the authentication tag, and are picked in the subsequence to the last selection of the cipher key bytes in the encryption phase.

2.7 Decryption and Verification

The exact values of key, IV, and tag length should be known to the decryption and verification processes. The decryption-orientation starts with the initialization and processing of associated data. Then the ciphertext is decrypted as

$p^t = c^t \oplus z^t$, since the keystream block z^t is generated without the influence of the plaintext block p^t in the same round, thus it is able to decrypt the ciphertext into the plaintext in the sequence block by block. The update function in the decryption is the same as that in the encryption.

The finalization in the decryption-orientation is the same as that in the encryption-orientation. It needs to emphasize that if the verification fails, the ciphertext and the newly generated authentication tag should not be given as output; otherwise, the state of FAN is vulnerable to known-plaintext or chosen-ciphertext attacks (using a fixed IV).

The overall workflow and test vectors are shown in Fig. 4 and Appendix 1.

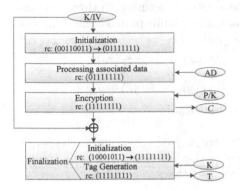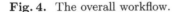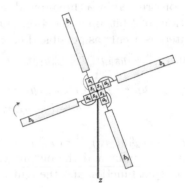

Fig. 4. The overall workflow.   **Fig. 5.** Design prototype

3   Design Rationale

The main goal of FAN is to achieve high performance and strong security.

3.1   Structure

To resist the traditional attacks (correlation attacks and algebraic attacks) on stream ciphers, the internal state of FAN is wholly updated in a nonlinear way, and every state byte affects the whole state quickly. The structure of FAN is inspired by the shape of electric fan (Fig. 5), which aims to be a simple but efficient design that rapidly provides highly confused level by parallel constant mutual feedbacks between the nonlinear spindle and each linear blade. Here, the spindle updates by an S-P-S network, which rotates fastest of the whole state and provides the only nonlinear transformation, considered both good cryptographic properties and low cost; the four blades clockwise rotate without interactions, which is in order to diffuse synchronously with the spindle (accumulator); the accumulator generates the output just with the spindle, which act as a barretter that maintain the confused level of the keystream blocks. The taps are chosen carefully for sufficient diffusions of different components after a few rounds. To offer a balanced performance in software and hardware implementations, FAN adopts byte-wise operations like the ISO standard lightweight stream cipher Enocoro[4] [14]. To implement efficient in hardware, operations are carefully chosen as XOR, rotation, S-box and L-layer as follows.

3.2 S-Box

Since FAN is byte oriented, it naturally takes identical 8×8 S-boxes. In the pursuit of hardware efficiency and especially with a focus on the area, we newly design and exploit a logic circuit based 8×8 S-box with relatively good properties. It is constructed by a three-round balanced-Feistel structure with three different functions of 4-bit input and 4-bit output, and a bit shuffle to make the terms distributed as evenly as possible. Let $x = (x_L \| x_R) = (x_7 \| x_6 \| x_5 \| x_4 \| x_3 \| x_2 \| x_1 \| x_0)$. Then, $(y_7 \| y_6 \| y_5 \| y_4 \| y_3 \| y_2 \| y_1 \| y_0) \xleftarrow{S} (x_7 \| x_6 \| x_5 \| x_4 \| x_3 \| x_2 \| x_1 \| x_0)$:

$$y_R \leftarrow f_0(x_L) \oplus x_R; y_L \leftarrow f_1(y_R) \oplus x_L; y_R \leftarrow f_2(y_L) \oplus y_R;$$
$$y \leftarrow (y_7 \| y_3 \| y_6 \| y_2 \| y_5 \| y_1 \| y_4 \| y_0).$$

Here, $(v_3 \| v_2 \| v_1 \| v_0) \xleftarrow{f} (u_3 \| u_2 \| u_1 \| u_0)$, where $u_3 \| u_2 \| u_1 \| u_0$ and $v_3 \| v_2 \| v_1 \| v_0$ denote the input and the output variables of the function f, and the component output function and the truth table are as follows

f_0:	f_1:	f_2:
$v_2 \leftarrow u_0 \& u_2 \oplus u_1 \oplus u_2;$	$v_3 \leftarrow u_1 \& u_0 \oplus u_3;$	$v_3 \leftarrow u_3 \& u_1 \oplus (u_2 \& (u_1 \oplus u_0));$
$v_3 \leftarrow (v_2 \oplus u_3) \& (u_0 \oplus u_2 \oplus u_3);$	$v_2 \leftarrow v_3 \& u_0 \oplus u_2;$	$v_2 \leftarrow u_2 \& (u_3 \oplus u_1);$
$v_1 \leftarrow (u_0 \& u_2 \oplus u_1) \& u_3;$	$v_1 \leftarrow v_3 \& v_2 \oplus u_1;$	$v_1 \leftarrow u_3 \& (u_1 \oplus u_0);$
$v_0 \leftarrow (u_0 \oplus u_3) \& v_2,$	$v_0 \leftarrow v_2 \& v_1 \oplus u_0,$	$v_0 \leftarrow (u_0 \text{ NAND } (u_2 \oplus u_1)),$
i.e. $\{0, 0, 4, 13, 12, 0, 0, 5,$	i.e. $\{0, 1, 2, 13, 4, 5, 7, 11,$	i.e. $\{1, 1, 1, 0, 1, 8, 13, 5,$
$8, 0, 7, 6, 5, 10, 2, 4\}.$	$14, 10, 3, 15, 9, 12, 6\}.$	$1, 3, 11, 8, 5, 14, 3, 9\}.$

Here f_0 and f_2 are almost perfect nonlinear (APN) functions. f_0 and f_1 are referred to [7], while f_2 is newly introduced.   The properties of the newly constructed S-box are

- Maximum differential probability: $p = \max\limits_{a \neq 0, b} \frac{\#\{x \in \mathbb{F}_2^n | S(x) \oplus S(x \oplus a) = b\}}{2^n} = 2^{-5}$;

- Maximum linear probability: $q = \max\limits_{\Gamma_a, \Gamma_b \neq 0} \left(\frac{\#\{x \in \mathbb{F}_2^n | \Gamma_a \cdot x = \Gamma_b \cdot S(x)\}}{2^{n-1}} - 1 \right)^2 = 2^{-4}$;

- Algebraic degree for the components: (4, 5, 4 ,5, 5, 5, 5, 6);

---

[4] FAN's structure is fundamentally different from Enocoro's, rather than incremental push. FAN divides the buffer in Enocoro into four blades to confuse entire state rapidly by parallel constant mutual feedbacks between nonlinear and linear parts; FAN adds a new component-accumulator to concentrate and maintain the properties from entire state, further disseminate back and participate in keystream generation; FAN's spindle updates by S-P-S network rather than the S-XOR mode in Enocoro; FAN is a CKU cipher. Above all, to provide same security level but much better performance, FAN's state is 196-bit, much smaller than Enocoro128v2's 272-bit.

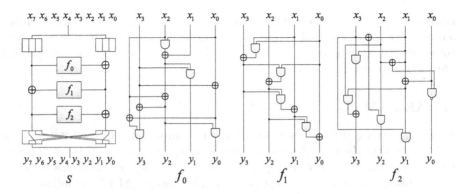

Fig. 6. S-box for FAN

- Algebraic immunity: $AI(S) = 2, NU(S) = 19$, where $AI(F) = \min\{\deg g \mid 0 \neq g \in \mathbb{B}_n, g(gr(F)) = 0\}$ and $gr(F) = \{(x, F(x)) \mid x \in \mathbb{F}^n\} \subseteq \mathbb{F}^{2n}$, $NU(F)$ is the number of linear independent gs with the degree of $AI(F)$.

The above properties are not the best, but provide a trade-off between security, area cost and speed.

For hardware implementation, the digital circuit of the S-box used in FAN is shown in Fig. 6, which totally calls for 12 AND2 gates, 25 XOR2 gates, 1 NAND2 gate, equivalent to 79 GE on 90 nm CMOS technology[5]. For software implementation, the S-box used in FAN can be operated as a table lookup, or bit-slice for case that many independent blocks needed to be processed simultaneously, which simulates a hardware implementation in software as a sequence of logical operations.

3.3 L-Layer

In the aspect of security requirement and to achieve enough active S-boxes in smallest initial rounds, we choose the 4×4 byte-wise permutation with the maximum differential and linear branch numbers of 5. Two kinds of such permutations have been detected, one is SM4-like that is implemented by 128 rotational-XOR gates, while another is the 4×4 MDS matrix in AES, which has a compact implementation with 92 XOR gates (i.e. 230 GE) and depth 6 referred to [17]. The specific implementation is given in Appendix 2.[6] In addition, the 4×4 MDS matrix in AES has standardized implementation on the lastest Intel and AMD microprocessors as AES-NI instructions. Thus for the sake of low memory footprint in hardware and high efficiency in software, we choose the well-analyzed

---

[5] S-box of AES is not used in FAN for its large area requirement of 195 GE on 90 nm CMOS technology to implement its core operation - the inverse function.

[6] AES-NI implements full AES rounds in a single instruction. Here, we use only the linear layer of AES, but not the S-box layer, hence we cannot simply use an AES-NI instruction by itself. However, combining AESENC and AESDECLAST yields the MixColumns layer. This still provides a large performance boost: in our experiments, the cost of one AES-NI instruction is similar to three simple XORs.

primitive in AES. Moreover, since it takes S-P-S network in the spindle for fast confusion, it is the optimal choice to use two layers of S-boxes of sub-optimal properties but less cost, and one L-layer of best properties with acceptable cost here by overall consideration.

3.4   AEAD Mode

To achieve strong initialization security, we ensure that the internal state is randomized after the initialization rounds. Firstly, we consider IV-key differences propagation and check the resistance by the probability of differentially active S-boxes using mixed integer linear programming model (MILP) as follows:

1. Objective function: minimize the number of differentially active S-boxes.
2. For $x \oplus y = z$, it has $\Delta x + \Delta y + \Delta z \geq 2d$, $\Delta x \leq d$, $\Delta y \leq d$, $\Delta z \leq d$.
   For $x = y = z$, it has $\Delta x == \Delta y$, $\Delta y == \Delta z$.
   For $(y_0, y_1, y_2, y_3) = L(x_0, x_1, x_2, x_3)$, it has

$$\sum_{i=0}^{3} \Delta x_i + \sum_{i=0}^{3} \Delta y_i \geq 5h; \Delta x_i \leq h, i = 0, 1, 2, 3; \Delta y_i \leq\leq h, i = 0, 1, 2, 3;$$

3. Assumption of input differences (chosen IV related key): $\sum_{i=0}^{15} \Delta k_i + \sum_{i=0}^{7} \Delta IV_i \geq 1$.

It derives that there are at least 32 active S-box in 26 initialization rounds by Gurobi, where the differential probability of a possible differential path is not bigger than 2^{-160}. To achieve enough generous security margin, we set the initialization rounds by double 26 to 52 rounds. Secondly, in the aspect of linear bias, we test FAN for probability of linearly active S-boxes using the MILP dually similar with that above.

1. Objective function: minimize the number of linearly active S-boxes.
2. For $x = y = z$, it has $\Gamma_x + \Gamma_y + \Gamma_z \geq 2d$, $\Gamma_x \leq d$, $\Gamma_y \leq d$, $\Gamma_z \leq d$.
   For $x \oplus y = z$, it has $\Gamma_x == \Gamma_y$, $\Gamma_y == \Gamma_z$.
   For $(y_0, y_1, y_2, y_3) = L(x_0, x_1, x_2, x_3)$, it has

$$\sum_{i=0}^{3} \Gamma x_i + \sum_{i=0}^{3} \Gamma y_i \geq 5h; \Gamma x_i \leq h, i = 0, 1, 2, 3; \Gamma y_i \leq\leq h, i = 0, 1, 2, 3;$$

3. Assumption of input maskings (chosen IV related key): $\sum_{i=0}^{15} \Gamma_{k_i} + \sum_{i=0}^{7} \Gamma_{IV_i} \geq 1$.

It also derives that there are at least 32 active S-box in 26 initialization rounds by Gurobi, where the probability of possible linear path is not bigger than 2^{-128}. In FAN, there are 26 more initialization rounds in the initialization. Thus, we expect the initialization of FAN is strong.

FAN injects message into the state so that it could obtain authentication security almost for free. In order to divide different work phases, a counter is set: it provides changed round constant in the initialization to prevent the sliding of the states, and indicates the end of initialization; it separates the processing of associated data and plaintext by setting as different unchange constants. In addition, we import the idea of FP(1)-mode [11], a recently suggested construction principle for the state initialization of stream ciphers, which has three main steps referred as Loading-Mixing-Hardening, to protect the security of authentication from internal state collision.

To achieve strong encryption security and exploit 192-bit internal state to resist to TMDTO attacks on 128-bit key, the cipher key also participates in the output generation phases. It is the first time to design an authenticated encryption cipher with the small-state method, and also a CKU stream cipher with non-Grain-like structure.

4   Security Analysis

We analyze the security of the initialization at first.

4.1   Related Key Chosen IV Attack

For the trivium differential attack using both IV-key differences as the threat to the initialization of FAN, a difference would eventually propagate into the ciphertexts, and thus it may be possible to apply a differential attack against FAN. As derived in Sect. 3.4 that there are at least 32 active S-box in 26 initialization rounds, where the differential probability of possible differential path is not bigger than 2^{-160}. In FAN, there are 26 more initialization rounds in the initialization. We expect that a differential attack against the initialization would be more expensive than exhaustive key search. It is also hard to control and eliminate the difference to the keystream by associated data or plaintext.

For the linear cryptanalysis of FAN in the initialization, it may lead to a bias of the ciphertexts. As mentioned in Sect. 3.4, there are at least 32 active S-box in 26 initialization rounds, where the probability of possible linear path is not bigger than 2^{-128}. Actually, it is hard to find an available linear path reached the probability. In FAN, there are 26 more initialization rounds in the initialization. We expect that a linear attack against the initialization would be more expensive than exhaustive key search.

For the sliding attack against FAN, we expect it is invulnerable for two reasons: Firstly, we attach a changed counter to the update function in the initialization, which is a simple and efficient countermeasure; Secondly, the different work phases are separated by different constants, and whether reusing the key as part of the state update.

4.2   Cube Attack

Cube attack is a general cryptanalytic technique, whose main idea is to compress the initialization functions $f(\boldsymbol{k}, \boldsymbol{v})$ to a low-degree or linear polynomial about the key in set J by selecting appropriate IV set I [8]. Recently, cube attack based on division property has got a lot of attention. Unlike the traditional experimental cube attack, it explores the internal trails of integral property according to propagation rules for different operations expressed with some (in)equalities, and models the attacks as MILP problems solving by optimization tools, such as Gurobi and Cplex [20,23].

Here, we use the method in [23], which introduces the "flag" to capture effects of non-cube IV bits and "degree evaluation" to upper bound the algebraic degree d, to evaluate the resistance of FAN against cube attacks as follows:

1. Build MILP model:
   $\mathcal{M}.con \leftarrow v_i = 1, v_i.F = \delta, i \in I;$
   $\mathcal{M}.con \leftarrow v_i = 0, v_i.F = 1_c (\text{if } \boldsymbol{IV}[i] = 1),$
   $\qquad\qquad \text{or } 0_c (\text{if } \boldsymbol{IV}[i] = 0), \ i \in (\{1, 2, \ldots, |IV|\} - I).$
   $\mathcal{M}.con \leftarrow \sum_{i=1}^{n} x_i = 1, x_i.F = \delta, \ i \in \{1, \ldots, |K|\}.$

2. For $a \xrightarrow{\text{COPY}} (b_1, b_2, \ldots, b_m)$, it has
   $\mathcal{M}.var \leftarrow a.val, b_1.val, \ldots, b_m.val$ as binary.
   $\mathcal{M}.con \leftarrow a.val = b_1.val + \cdots + b_m.val$
   $a.F = b_1.F = \ldots = b_m.F$

3. For $(a_1, a_2, \ldots, a_m) \xrightarrow{\text{XOR}} b$, it has
   $\mathcal{M}.var \leftarrow a_1.val, \ldots, a_m.val, b.val$ as binary.
   $\mathcal{M}.con \leftarrow a_1.val + \cdots + a_m.val = b.val$
   $b.F = a_1.F \oplus a_2.F \oplus \cdots \oplus a_m.F$

4. For $(a_1, a_2, \ldots, a_m) \xrightarrow{\text{AND}} b$, it has
   $\mathcal{M}.var \leftarrow a_1.val, \ldots, a_m.val, b.val$ as binary.
   $\mathcal{M}.con \leftarrow b.val \geq a_i.val$ for all $i \in \{1, 2, \ldots, m\}$
   $b.F = a_1.F \times a_2.F \times \cdots a_m.F$
   $\mathcal{M}.con \leftarrow b.val = 0 \quad \text{if } b.F = 0_c$

5. Solve MILP model $\mathcal{M}$ *until it is unfeasible, return J*:
   Pick index $j \in \{1, 2, \ldots, |K|\} s.t. x_j = 1, J = J \cup \{j\}; \ \mathcal{M}.con \leftarrow x_j = 0.$

With J, I and d, the superpoly, usually containing 1 bit of secret-key-related information, can be recovered with complexity $2^{|I|} \times \binom{|J|}{\leq d}$. The MILP model for R-round FAN is constructed, and the parameters of our evaluations are listed in Table 1. According to our evaluation, for $R < 4$, the cube summations are constantly 0. For $R \geq 4$, the superpoly becomes extremely complicated with all 128 key bits involved and superpoly degrees larger than 52. The superpoly-recovery attacks have complexities much larger than 2^{128} which means the key-recovery cube attacks are computationally infeasible. Therefore, 52 initialization rounds are quite sufficient for FAN to resist division property based cube attacks.

Next, we evaluate the security of encryption process.

Table 1. Cube attacks on R-round FAN

Round R	≤ 3	4	5	6
Cube size $|I|$	64	64	64	64
Degree d	0	52	81	128
Involved key size $|J|$	0	128	128	128
Time complexity	–	$2^{250.4141}$	$2^{255.9987}$	2^{256}

4.3 Randomness Test

FAN has passed the randomness test of keystream, such as frequency test, runs test, binary matrix rank test, etc., with two samples size of 10^{10} keystream bits (1.16 GB) generated by $IV = 0^{64}$, $k = 0^{128}$, $P = 0^{10000000000}$, and $IV = 1^{64}$, $k = 1^{128}$, $P = 1^{10000000000}$.

4.4 Guess-and-Determine Attack

In a guess-and-determine attack, the attacker guesses part of the internal state and aims to recover the remaining parts by combining with the state relations and keystream with an overall effort lower than brute force. To estimate the resistance of FAN to this attack, we conduct a byte-oriented heuristic guess-and-determine attack (HGD) [2] on FAN.

Specifically, we describe FAN with its state update function and output function of multiple times at first. Denote the intermediate variables as

$$u_3^t = S[b_{3,3}^t \oplus s_3^t \oplus rc], u_i^t = S[b_{i,i}^t \oplus s_i^t \oplus k_i^t \oplus p_i^t], i = 0, 1, 2$$
$$(v_3^t, v_2^t, v_1^t, v_0^t) = L(u_3^t, u_2^t, u_1^t, u_0^t).$$

Next, we index the variables shown up in the equation system and transform the system into indices table. An index can be removed only if it is guessed or it is uniquely determined by some function with remaining known variables. A basis is identified if it removes all indices in the indices table, or it recovers the 128-bit key. The priority criteria is defined as to maximize the number of removed indices in the indices table for one guess. Finally, we represent all the indices as nodes in a trellis diagram, and run for guessing path step by step.

The best result we derived is that for 7 24-bit keystream words, it needs to guess 21 bytes according to the guessing path (shown in Table 1) to recover the whole internal state (take the 128-bit key as part of unknown state).

Although the guess-and-determine attack derived in this way cannot imply the best, its complexity remains a redundancy more than 2^{40} compared with the 128-bit security bound.

4.5 Time-Memory-Data Tradeoff Attack

It is well known that the cipher is weak to TMDTO attack if the size of its internal state is not at least twice of the security level. Similar to Sprout,

Table 2. Guess-and-determine path for FAN

No.	G.	D.	No.	G.	D.
1	$b_{0,2}^4, b_{1,2}^5$	$a_0^4, b_{2,2}^6$	17	k_9	$u_0^3, u_1^3, u_2^3, u_3^3, v_6^3, k_{11}, b_{3,3}^3, s_2^4,$
2	$b_{1,2}^1$	$b_{2,2}^2, b_{3,2}^3, s_3^3, v_7^2$			$b_{2,3}^2, b_{0,3}^4, a_3^4, k_{14}, a_2^2, b_{1,3}^1, b_{1,3}^5,$
3	a_0^5	$b_{0,1}^4, b_{1,1}^5, b_{2,1}^6$			$b_{3,0}^3, b_{3,0}^4, a_2^1, b_{2,3}^6, b_{2,0}^2, b_{0,0}^4,$
4	$b_{3,1}^3$	a_3^3, s_2^3, v_6^2			$b_{0,0}^4, b_{2,0}^3, b_{0,0}^5, b_{1,0}^2, k_{12}, b_{1,0}^5,$
5	v_6^1	$s_2^2, b_{2,1}^2, b_{1,1}^1, b_{0,1}^0$			$b_{1,0}^6, b_{2,0}^6$
6	v_7^1	$s_3^2, a_3^2, b_{3,0}^2, b_{0,0}^3, b_{1,0}^4$	18	k_{10}	$b_{1,1}^3, b_{0,1}^2, b_{2,1}^1, b_{2,1}^4, a_0^2, b_{3,1}^5, s_0^2, b_{0,2}^2,$
7	$b_{3,1}^2$	$b_{0,1}^3, a_0^3, b_{1,1}^4, b_{2,1}^5$			$b_{0,1}^6, s_1^2, v_4^1, b_{0,3}^2, v_5^1, b_{1,0}^2, b_{3,3}^1,$
8	k_8	u_2^3			$u_0^1, u_1^1, u_2^1, u_3^1, b_{0,0}^1, b_{2,3}^0, s_3^1,$
9	v_4^2	$s_3^3, u_0^3, u_1^2, u_3^3, v_5^2, a_1^3, b_{3,3}^2, s_1^3, b_{2,3}^1, b_{0,3}^3,$			$b_{3,0}^0, a_2^0, v_7^0, b_{3,2}^1, b_{2,2}^0$
		$a_2^3, b_{1,3}^4$	19	k_3	$s_0^1, s_1^1, a_0^1, v_4^0, b_{0,3}^1, k_4, v_5^0, b_{1,0}^1,$
10	$b_{1,2}^3$	$a_1^4, b_{2,2}^4, s_0^4, b_{2,3}^5, b_{3,2}^3, v_4^3, b_{3,3}^6$			$a_0^0, b_{0,1}^1, b_{0,2}^1, b_{3,3}^0, b_{0,0}^0, s_0^0, b_{0,2}^0,$
11	$b_{2,0}^5$	$s_1^4, a_2^4, v_5^3, b_{2,3}^3, b_{3,3}^4, b_{0,3}^5$			$b_{1,1}^2, s_1^0, b_{0,3}^0, k_7, b_{2,1}^1, b_{1,0}^0, b_{3,1}^1,$
12	u_1^4	k_{13}			$b_{0,1}^5, a_0^6, b_{1,1}^6, s_0^6, s_1^6, v_4^5, v_5^5$
13	$b_{1,2}^0$	$b_{2,2}^1, b_{3,2}^2, b_{0,2}^3, b_{1,2}^4, a_1^5, b_{2,2}^5, s_0^5, a_1^6, b_{3,2}^6,$	20	k_0	$u_0^0, u_1^5, u_1^0, u_2^0, u_3^0, v_6^0, u_0^5, u_2^5,$
		$v_4^4, b_{1,3}^6$			$v_6^5, v_7^5, s_3^5, s_2^1, k_{15}, k_1, s_2^6, s_3^6,$
14	v_5^4	$s_1^5, a_2^5, b_{2,3}^4, a_3^6, b_{3,0}^6, b_{1,3}^3, b_{3,3}^5, b_{0,3}^6$			$b_{3,2}^5, a_3^1, k_5, b_{2,1}^6, b_{1,1}^0, a_3^6, a_3^0,$
15	v_7^4	$s_3^5, u_0^4, u_2^4, u_3^4, v_6^4, u_3^5, b_{0,2}^6, s_3^4, s_2^5,$			$b_{3,0}^1, b_{3,1}^1, b_{3,0}^5, s_2^0, b_{3,1}^0, b_{2,0}^0,$
		$v_7^3, a_3^5, b_{3,1}^6$			$b_{0,0}^2, b_{2,0}^4, b_{0,0}^6, k_2, b_{2,1}^0, k_6, b_{1,0}^3$
16	$b_{0,2}^5$	$b_{1,2}^6, b_{3,2}^4, b_{2,2}^3, b_{1,2}^2, a_1^2, a_1^1, b_{1,3}^2, a_1^0, b_{1,3}^0$			

Fruit-v2 and Plantlet, FAN benefits the key as part of internal state in the state update of encryption phase. The effective internal states are 320 bits, which exceeds the lower bound of internal state size of 256 bits. Another necessary condition of such stream cipher to be resistant to TMDTO attack is that the key should affect the internal state proportionally and continually as the other internal state. Since 24 key bits are involved in the state update in each round orderly, and the 128-bit key is injected into the internal state circularly, hence propagates to the keystream, we do not see a possibility for these attacks similar to Sprout to be still effective [9, 24].

4.6 Differential Attack

Under the security claim that each key-IV pair should be used to protect only one message, it is impossible to conduct classic differential attacks on FAN in the encryption phase. Considering the near-collision attack, since every state bit affects the whole state in at most 8 rounds and the S-boxes are used as nonlinear components, any internal state difference will propagate quickly and become complicated. Thus it is hard to statistics analyze the relation between keystream difference and internal state difference, and finally recover the internal state with low-degree equation system.

4.7 Correlation Attack

The traditional correlation attacks [21] against stream ciphers almost exploit the linear update function which at least independently operate on partial internal state in stream ciphers. The state of FAN is totally updated in a nonlinear way, so we expect FAN is strong against those powerful correlation attacks on stream ciphers.

Moreover, it is difficult to apply a linear approximation attack to recover the secret state, since the S-P-S network used in the update function makes the approximation bias extremely small, and the dependency of internal state variables makes it hard to eliminate the nonlinear part.

4.8 Algebraic Attack

The general idea of algebraic attacks is to establish low degree over-defined system of multivariate algebraic equations of the key or internal states and keystream at certain time interval, and then solve the equation system to obtain the key or internal state using some traditional methods, like linearization, Gröbner basis, XL method.

We first present the low degree description of the S-box. The algebraic immunity of S-box is 2, and the number of independent implicit equations in input and output variables with the degree of 2 is 19. The independent implicit equations fully describe the S-box, and totally contain 38 quadratic items.

Next, we present the algebraic structure of FAN. It initially has 320 binary variables, which is composed of 192-bit internal and 128-bit keys, where the key bytes are gradually injected into the internal state. To keep the degree of algebraic system without growth, and reduce the number of items, we have to introduce some intermediate binary variables in each round. The algebraic system is as follows by rounds:

1. The output function generates 24 linear equations:
   $$z_2^t = s_3^t \oplus s_2^t \oplus a_3^t; z_1^t = s_1^t \oplus s_0^t \oplus a_2^t; z_0^t = a_1^t \oplus a_0^t \oplus s_0^t;$$

2. We introduce 32 intermediate binary variables denoted by $\omega_{,}^t$, and generates 32 linear equations: $\omega_{,3}^t = b_{3,3}^t \oplus s_3^t \oplus rc; \omega_{,2}^t = b_{2,2}^t \oplus s_2^t \oplus k_2^t; \omega_{,1}^t = b_{1,1}^t \oplus s_1^t \oplus k_1^t \oplus p_1^t;$
   $$\omega_{,0}^t = b_{0,0}^t \oplus s_0^t \oplus k_0^t \oplus p_0^t.$$

3. One S-box layer introduces 32 intermediate binary variables denoted by μ^t (s^{t+1}), and generates 76 quadratic equations and 152 quadratic items:
   $$\mu_i^t = S[\omega_{,i}^t], \ i = 0, 1, 2, 3. \ (s_i^{t+1} = S[\nu_i^t], \ i = 0, 1, 2, 3.)$$

4. The L-layer introduces 32 intermediate binary variables denoted by ν^t, and generates 32 linear equations: $(\nu_3^t \| \nu_2^t \| \nu_1^t \| \nu_0^t) = L(\mu_3^t \| \mu_2^t \| \mu_1^t \| \mu_0^t).$

We analyze the increasing trend of the number of variables and equations. From Table 3, we can see that at time $t = 3$, the number of total equations is over the number of variables in the equations. For solving m boolean multivariate quadratic equations in n variables when $n = m$, [10] presents a Las-Vegas quantum algorithm that requires $O(2^{0.462n})$ quantum gates on average, which is claimed the fastest algorithm now. It calls for a complexity of at least 2^{300}. Moreover, at this moment, the number of variables and quadratic equations is more than 1500, and the coefficient matrix of equations is not in any special mode. According to the XL algorithm, it is still hard to solve the equations in the complexity under the security bound. Besides, we consider in the linearization of

Table 3. Algebraic structure of Fan

t		0	1	2	3	4	5	6	7	8	9	10
Item	mono.	192	344	496	648	800	952	1088	1216	1344	1472	1600
	quad.	0	304	608	912	1216	1520	1824	2128	2432	2736	3040
	total	192	648	1104	1560	2016	2472	2912	3344	3776	4208	4640
Equa.	linear.	0	88	176	264	352	440	528	616	704	792	880
	quad.	0	152	304	456	608	760	912	1064	1216	1368	1520
	total	0	240	480	720	960	1200	1440	1680	1920	2160	2400

quadratic items. The number of variables expands more quickly than the number of equations by introducing more intervals, which leads to non-deterministic solution. In summary, we expect that algebraic attack on this system is very unlikely to be faster than an exhaustive search for the key.

4.9   Side-Channel Attack

Side-channel analysis is an important issue for the security of embedded cryptographic devices. It is expected that bitslice implementation offers resistance to side channel attacks such as cache timing attacks and cross-VM attacks in a multi-tenant cloud environment. Since the only nonlinear components S-boxes in Fan can be computed using bit-logical instructions rather than table lookups, Fan shows the great potential in fast and timing-attack resistant software implementations.

Finally, we present the security analysis of message authentication. To analyze the authentication of the Fan, we will compute the probability that a forged message would bypass the verification.

4.10   Internal State Collision

Construction of internal state collision is a typical method used in attacking the message authentication. Here we only consider the case that the tag length is 72-bit since it implies the security of the cases with shorter tag length. For Fan, since the key takes part in the tag generation, it is necessary to consider the internal state collision under the single key. Moreover, since IV should not be reused without changing the key, for one fixed key, the queries of IV and plaintext pairs are no more than 2^{64}. Any internal collision through birthday attack requires 2^{96} encryptions, for the internal state size is 192-bit. Thus it cannot be fulfilled, and Fan is resistant to the trivial birthday attack.

Another method to construct an internal state collision is to inject a message difference at a certain step and cancel it at a later step. A simple description of our analysis is given below. We notice that the first difference being injected into the message cannot be fully eliminated in up to 6 rounds; it would pass through 7 rounds before the difference of overall internal state eliminated, and there are at least 25 active S-boxes being involved; it could pass through 12 rounds or more before the difference of overall internal state eliminated, and there are at least 20 active S-boxes being involved. If we consider only a single differential path, the probability of the difference cancellation in the state is less than $2^{-5\times20} = 2^{-100}$. Thus generating a state collision in the verification process requires at least 2^{100} modifications to the ciphertext. Multiple differential paths would not have a significant effect on the forgery attack here, since each differential path has to cancel its own differences being left in the state. It shows that FAN is strong against forgery attack when the ciphertext or tag gets modified.

4.11 Attacks on the Finalization

In addition to the internal state collision, it also needs to consider the situation that there is a difference in the internal state before the finalization. Thus we redo the initialization phase here. It involves 15 active S-boxes in 14 rounds, and the differential probability must be far less than 2^{-75} after the double rounds, i.e. the given 28 rounds. Hence, the difference of the tag is unpredictable.

Moreover, the authentication tag length is padded in the message block, that is able to invent the forge of an authentication tag based on a known authentication tag of smaller length for a same plaintext.

5 Performance

5.1 Software Performance

For some resource-constraint environments, such as smart card and sensor networking system, the embedded CPU is usually 8-bit oriented microcontroller, which is just fit to use the byte-based design of FAN in such software platform.

In addition, for the parallel design of FAN, its internal state can be rearranged in 32-bit unit and equivalent to the structure in Fig. 7. Accordingly, it can be implemented by 32-bit unit. Moreover, the S-P-S permutation in the round function can be combined together and realized as lookup tables.

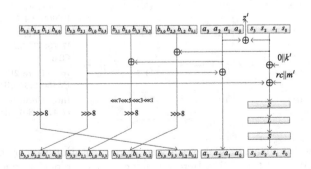

Fig. 7. The equivalent structure of FAN

For further optimization, it can be accelerated by bitslice technique using AVX instruction set and AES-NI instructions introduced in Haswell microarchitecture, since the only nonlinear S-box is designed by logic circuit and the L-layer is chosen from AES round function, which is in the prediction of 4–8× speedup.

We implemented FAN in C code, and tested the speed on Intel Core i7-4790 3.6 GHz processor running 32-bit Windows 7 with VS2010, without any optimizations for fair comparison conventionally. It takes about 8.0 cycle/byte for encryption. We present a software performance comparison of FAN and mainly standard lightweight stream ciphers in Table 4, with comparable implemented platforms[7].

5.2 Hardware Performance

We implemented FAN in Verilog and synthesized it on 90 nm CMOS technology to check for its hardware complexity. In this implementation, we implement the eight S-boxes of round function in parallel. It occupies about 2327 Gate-Equivalent(GE) and the speed is 9.6 Gbps. Table 5 compares the hardware performances of FAN with other lightweight stream ciphers.

In the above implementation for FAN, the area requirement is according to the 90 nm Digital Standard Cell Library referred to [22] (Specifically illustrate in Appendix 4). We do not consider any costs for storing the non-volatile key because we assume that it has to be provided by the device anyway, independent of whether it needs to load the key only once for initialization or requires constant access during the encryption as discussed in [18]. Due to the fact that FAN sequentially accesses and simply reads out the key bytes, it is reasonable to reuse

Table 4. Software performance comparison

Cipher	Security (bits)	Authentication	Performance (cycles/byte)	Platform	Reference
Trivium	80	No	5.1	2017 Intel Core i7-7567U 3.5 GHz	[1]
Enocoro-128v2	128	No	17.4	Intel Core 2Duo E6600 2.4 GHz	[14]
Acornv3	128	Yes	6.0	2017 Intel Core i7-7567U 3.5 GHz	[1]
Grain-128a	128	Yes	11.7	Intel Core 2Duo E6550 2.35 GHz	[16]
FAN	128	Yes	8.0	Intel Core i7-4790 3.6 GHz	This

---

[7] We normalize the measurement of software implementation rate by cycles/byte to reduce the impact of the CPUs. Here we only consider the performance of confidentiality without integrity for uniform comparison with other stream ciphers.

Table 5. Hardware performance comparison

Cipher	Security (bits)	Area (kGE)	Bits/cycle	Throughput (Gbps)	Throughput/ area	Technology (nm)	Lib.	Ref.
Trivium	80	2.599	1	1.95	0.75	130	Std	[6]
Enocoro-128v2	128	4.100	8	3.52	0.86	90	Std	[14]
Acornv3	128	2.412	8	9.09	3.77	65	Std	[15]
Grain-128AEAD	128	4.017	2	1.18	0.29	65	Std	[13]
FAN	128	2.327	24	9.64	4.13	90	Std	This

the existing mechanisms for no needs of multiplexers for selecting the subkeys, and to achieve a high throughput.

From Table 5, we can find that FAN has the best value of Throughput/Area, which is an important parameter no matter what technology is taken. Compared with Acorn, FAN's internal state is more than 100 bits smaller, which is much lighter for the highly-constrained devices. For the differences in technology, using a newer technology such as 65 nm NANGATE open-source library could have been better speed for FAN, which makes it more competitive. Here, we conservatively used 90 nm Digital Standard Cell Library as the contrast.

Hence, FAN can achieve competitive hardware and software performances compared with other known lightweight stream ciphers.

6   Conclusion

In this paper we propose a new AEAD algorithm FAN, which takes a 128-bit key, a 64-bit IV, and a 192-bit state, promising 128-bit security and up to 72-bit authentication tag with the IV-respecting restriction. Our design goal is to provide cryptography security for resource-constraint environments. Moreover, compared with other lightweight stream ciphers, the proposal achieves better hardware performance and also have good software efficiency. Therefore, in the design of FAN, we employ a novel byte-wise structure, inspired by the 4-blade daily electric fan. It is the first non-Grain-like small-state stream cipher and also the first small-state cipher with authentication function. Furthermore, the components are designed with the consideration of both security and implementation efficiency in mind. Especially, we present a new appropriate low-area 8×8 S-box design. Our hardware implementation of FAN requires about 2327 GE on 90 nm technology with a throughput of 9.6 Gbps, which satisfies the regular limitation of 3000 GE in lightweight applications, and the software implementation runs about 8.0 cycle/byte. We also evaluate the security of FAN and our cryptanalytic results show that FAN achieves enough security margin against known attacks. In the end, we strongly encourage helpful comments to the new design with CKU method. We expect our work can push forwards such small-state designs to a wider and multiple perspectives, and inspire further research or in-depth exploration.

7   Appendix 1: Test Vector

Test vectors for FAN are shown in hexadecimal notation as follows:

1. For K_i = 0x00 for i = 0, 1, ..., 15, IV_i = 0x00 for i = 0, 1, ..., 7, AD = 0x00, ..., 0x00 with the length of 1000 bits, and P = 0x00, ..., 0x00 with the length of 1000 bits, the 43 ciphertext blocks are
e29535, b2b2ea, 50e2ef, 1b5efa, c60360, cb0f96, 8befa5, a0320e, 7aebab, 487cb6, 3c1b7f, c59257, 9dfb14, b11fec, 6a5d00, 0d9e2d, e90c43, d764f5, aeeeb8, 16d92b, dbef72, b18a89, 5f3c53, 63458e, c5598a, 05192d, 60a802, eaf8af, 23cd9d, dfd45e, d5861c, 351acc, 2c65ce, 42ceed, 4c6bf9, a1d5a7, 9bca1a, 76eeaf, f57e22, dc6a35, 982ede, 9be801, 4f4359, and the 72-bit tag is 3a4003, dfd872, 051da1.
2. For K_i = 0xff for i = 0, 1, ..., 15, IV_i = 0xff for i = 0, 1, ..., 7, AD = 0xff, ..., 0xff with the length of 1000 bits, and P = 0xff, ..., 0xff with the length of 1000 bits, the 43 ciphertext blocks are
2ee752, 8fc727, 71e76c, 8ef6f2, 35ba5d, 766f7b, 950166, f57fa4, aecc81, e8ec28, 1c5146, a5a477, 9ad473, 835004, 169666, 1fd55d, 3e2df9, 866f6a, 744317, 99f6c8, 083573, 9cbb54, 6a3003, e16638, f67cb5, 3ec873, ea2220, dab472, f8fdeb, 9dba39, 88f6d6, 784c90, 9f1875, 34b40d, 8547b1, 9cc976, 12d5b5, a43ed9, f62af8, 160427, b0cdd1, b71eff, c3761e, and the 72-bit tag is a8255a, f41333, 05928c.

8   Appendix 2: AES MixColumn with 92 XOR Gates

The compact implementation of AES MixColumn with 92 XOR gates and depth 6 [17] is shown as follows.

t0 = x0 ^ x8	t18 = x24 ^ t0	y18 = t4 ^ t30	y13 = t41 ^ t42	t51 = x22 ^ t46
t1 = x16 ^ x24	y16 = t14 ^ t18	t31 = x9 ^ x25	y29 = t39 ^ t42	y30 = t11 ^ t51
t2 = x1 ^ x9	t19 = t1 ^ y16	t32 = t25 ^ t31	t43 = x15 ^ t12	t52 = x19 ^ t28
t3 = x17 ^ x25	t24 = t17 ^ t19	y10 = t30 ^ t32	y7 = t14 ^ t43	y20 = x28 ^ t52
t4 = x2 ^ x10	t20 = x27 ^ t14	y26 = t29 ^ t32	t44 = x14 ^ t37	t53 = x3 ^ t27
t5 = x18 ^ x26	t21 = t0 ^ y0	t33 = x1 ^ t18	y31 = t43 ^ t44	y4 = x12 ^ t53
t6 = x3 ^ x11	y8 = t17 ^ t21	t34 = x30 ^ t11	t45 = x31 ^ t13	t54 = t3 ^ t33
t7 = x19 ^ x27	t22 = t5 ^ t20	y22 = t12 ^ t34	y15 = t44 ^ t45	y9 = y8 ^ t54
t8 = x4 ^ x12	t19 = t6 ^ t22	t35 = x14 ^ t13	t23 = t15 ^ t45	t55 = t21 ^ t31
t9 = x20 ^ x28	t23 = x11 ^ t15	y6 = t10 ^ t35	t46 = t12 ^ t36	y1 = t38 ^ t55
t10 = x5 ^ x13	t24 = t7 ^ t23	t36 = x5 ^ x21	y14 = y6 ^ t46	t56 = x4 ^ t17
t11 = x21 ^ x29	y3 = t4 ^ t24	t37 = x30 ^ t17	t47 = t31 ^ t33	t57 = x19 ^ t56
t12 = x6 ^ x14	t25 = x2 ^ x18	t38 = x17 ^ t16	y17 = t19 ^ t47	y12 = t27 ^ t57
t13 = x22 ^ x30	t26 = t17 ^ t25	t39 = x13 ^ t8	t48 = t6 ^ y3	t58 = x3 ^ t28
t14 = x23 ^ x31	t27 = t9 ^ t23	y5 = t11 ^ t39	y11 = t26 ^ t48	t59 = x17 ^ t58
t15 = x7 ^ x15	t28 = t8 ^ t20	t40 = x12 ^ t36	t49 = t2 ^ t38	y28 = x20 ^ t59
t16 = x8 ^ t1	t29 = x10 ^ t2	t41 = x29 ^ t9	y25 = y24 ^ t49	
y0 = t15 ^ t16	y2 = t5 ^ t29	y21 = t10 ^ t41	t50 = t7 ^ y19	
t17 = x7 ^ x23	t30 = x26 ^ t3	t42 = x28 ^ t40	y27 = t26 ^ t50	

9   Appendix 3: Comparison Outline Diagram for Different Phases

To show the differences for all phases, we focus on the spindle shown in Fig. 8, since the blades and accumulator update part are not differing much from each other.

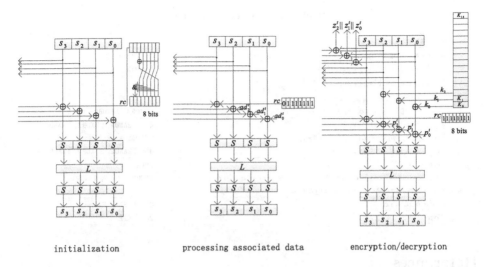

initialization   processing associated data   encryption/decryption

Fig. 8. The main difference: state update function of the spindle in different phases.

10   Appendix 4: Gate Count for FAN

For the hardware implementation of FAN, the area requirement is occupied as shown in Table 7, according to the 90 nm Digital Standard Cell Library given in Table 6 referred to [22].

Table 6. Reference of 90 nm digital standard cell library

GATE	NAND	AND2	AND3	XOR2	XOR3	MUX	DFF
Area (μm^2)	2.8224	3.528	4.2336	5.6448	13.4064	6.3504	15.5232
GE	1	1.25	1.5	2	4.75	2.25	5.5

[1] Gate-Equivalent (GE) is measured with NAND as the unit.
[2] OPERATION2/3 denotes a two/three-input bit-wise operation.
[3] MUX is a bit-control multiplexer; D-Flip Flop (DFF) applies for bit-wise storage.

Table 7. Gate count for FAN

Function	Gate
$z_2 \leftarrow s_3 \oplus s_2 \oplus a_3; z_1 \leftarrow s_1 \oplus s_0 \oplus a_2; z_0 \leftarrow a_1 \oplus a_0 \oplus s_0;$	24XOR3
$b_{i,(i+1)\mathrm{mod}4} \leftarrow b_{i,(i+1)\mathrm{mod}4} \oplus s_i;$	96XOR2
$b_{i,(i+2)\mathrm{mod}4} \leftarrow \left(b_{i,(i+2)\mathrm{mod}4} \oplus a_i\right)_{\lll(2i+1)};$	
$a_i \leftarrow a_i \oplus b_{i,(i+3)\mathrm{mod}4}, \quad i = 0,1,2,3;$	
$s_3 \leftarrow s_3 \oplus b_{3,3} \oplus rc, \quad s_i \leftarrow s_i \oplus b_{i,i} \oplus m_i^t \oplus k_i^t, \quad i = 0,1,2;$	32XOR3, 24XOR2
$s_i \leftarrow S[s_i], i = 0,1,2,3;$	4×(12AND2, 25XOR2, 1NAND)
$(s_3\|s_2\|s_1\|s_0) \leftarrow L(s_3\|s_2\|s_1\|s_0);$	92XOR2
$s_i \leftarrow S[s_i], i = 0,1,2,3;$	4×(12AND2, 25XOR2, 1NAND)
if $rc_6 = 0,$	1MUX
$(rc_5\|rc_4\|rc_3\|rc_2\|rc_1\|rc_0) \leftarrow (rc_4\|rc_3\|rc_2\|rc_1\|rc_0\|rc_5 \oplus rc_0);$	1XOR2, 2AND3, 1AND2
$rc_6 \leftarrow rc_5 \& rc_4 \& rc_3 \& rc_2 \& rc_1 \& rc_0;$	
store b, a, s, rc	200 D-Flip Flop
Total	2327 GE

References

1. ebacs: Ecrypt benchmarking of cryptographic systems. https://bench.cr.yp.to/results-stream.html
2. Ahmadi, H., Eghlidos, T.: Heuristic guess-and-determine attacks on stream ciphers. IET Inf. Secur. **3**(2), 66–73 (2009). https://doi.org/10.1049/iet-ifs.2008.0013
3. Aminghafari, V., Hu, H.: Fruit: ultra-lightweight stream cipher with shorter internal state. IACR Cryptology ePrint Archive 2016, 355 (2016). http://eprint.iacr.org/2016/355
4. Armknecht, F., Mikhalev, V.: On lightweight stream ciphers with shorter internal states. In: Fast Software Encryption - 22nd International Workshop, FSE 2015, Istanbul, Turkey, 8–11 March 2015, Revised Selected Papers, pp. 451–470 (2015). https://doi.org/10.1007/978-3-662-48116-5_22
5. Biryukov, A., Shamir, A.: Cryptanalytic time/memory/data tradeoffs for stream ciphers. In: Okamoto, T. (ed.) ASIACRYPT 2000. LNCS, vol. 1976, pp. 1–13. Springer, Heidelberg (2000). https://doi.org/10.1007/3-540-44448-3_1
6. Canniere, C.D., Preneel, B.: Trivium specifications. eSTREAM, ECRYPT Stream Cipher Project, Citeseer (2005)
7. Canteaut, A., Duval, S., Leurent, G.: Construction of lightweight s-boxes using Feistel and MISTY structures. In: Dunkelman, O., Keliher, L. (eds.) SAC 2015. LNCS, vol. 9566, pp. 373–393. Springer, Cham (2016). https://doi.org/10.1007/978-3-319-31301-6_22
8. Dinur, I., Shamir, A.: Cube attacks on Tweakable black box polynomials. In: Joux, A. (ed.) EUROCRYPT 2009. LNCS, vol. 5479, pp. 278–299. Springer, Heidelberg (2009). https://doi.org/10.1007/978-3-642-01001-9_16
9. Esgin, M.F., Kara, O.: Practical cryptanalysis of full sprout with TMD tradeoff attacks. In: Dunkelman, O., Keliher, L. (eds.) SAC 2015. LNCS, vol. 9566, pp. 67–85. Springer, Cham (2016). https://doi.org/10.1007/978-3-319-31301-6_4
10. Faugère, J., Horan, K., Kahrobaei, D., Kaplan, M., Kashefi, E., Perret, L.: Fast quantum algorithm for solving multivariate quadratic equations. CoRR abs/1712.07211 (2017). http://arxiv.org/abs/1712.07211
11. Hamann, M., Krause, M.: On stream ciphers with provable beyond-the-birthday-bound security against time-memory-data tradeoff attacks. Cryptogr. Commun. **10**(5), 959–1012 (2018). https://doi.org/10.1007/s12095-018-0294-5

12. Hell, M., Johansson, T., Maximov, A., Meier, W.: The grain family of stream ciphers. In: New Stream Cipher Designs - The eSTREAM Finalists, pp. 179–190 (2008). https://doi.org/10.1007/978-3-540-68351-3_14
13. Hell, M., Johansson, T., Meier, W., Sönnerup, J., Yoshida, H.: An AEAD variant of the grain stream cipher. In: Carlet, C., Guilley, S., Nitaj, A., Souidi, E.M. (eds.) C2SI 2019. LNCS, vol. 11445, pp. 55–71. Springer, Cham (2019). https://doi.org/10.1007/978-3-030-16458-4_5
14. Hitachi, L.: Stream cipher Enocoro specification ver. 2.0 and evaluation report. CRYPTREC submission package (2010). http://www.hitachi.com/rd/yrl/crypto/enocoro/
15. Kumar, S., Haj-Yihia, J., Khairallah, M., Chattopadhyay, A.: A comprehensive performance analysis of hardware implementations of CAESAR candidates. IACR Cryptol. ePrint Arch. 2017, 1261 (2017). http://eprint.iacr.org/2017/1261
16. Robshaw, M., Billet, O. (eds.): New Stream Cipher Designs. The eSTREAM Finalists. LNCS, vol. 4986. Springer, Heidelberg (2008). https://doi.org/10.1007/978-3-540-68351-3
17. Maximov, A.: AES mixcolumn with 92 XOR gates. Cryptology ePrint Archive, Report 2019/833 (2019). https://eprint.iacr.org/2019/833
18. Mikhalev, V., Armknecht, F., Müller, C.: On ciphers that continuously access the non-volatile key. IACR Transactions on Symmetric Cryptology 2016(2), 52–79 (2016). https://doi.org/10.13154/tosc.v2016.i2.52-79
19. National Institute of Standards and Technology: Advanced encryption standard. NIST FIPS PUB 197 (2001)
20. Todo, Y., Isobe, T., Hao, Y., Meier, W.: Cube attacks on non-blackbox polynomials based on division property. In: Katz, J., Shacham, H. (eds.) CRYPTO 2017. LNCS, vol. 10403, pp. 250–279. Springer, Cham (2017). https://doi.org/10.1007/978-3-319-63697-9_9
21. Todo, Y., Isobe, T., Meier, W., Aoki, K., Zhang, B.: Fast correlation attack revisited: cryptanalysis on full grain-128a, grain-128, and grain-v1. In: Shacham, H., Boldyreva, A. (eds.) CRYPTO 2018. LNCS, vol. 10992, pp. 129–159. Springer, Cham (2018). https://doi.org/10.1007/978-3-319-96881-0_5
22. TSMC: TSMC 90nm cln90g process sage-xtm v3.0 standard cell library databook (March 2005 Release 11)
23. Wang, Q., et al.: Improved division property based cube attacks exploiting algebraic properties of superpoly. In: Shacham, H., Boldyreva, A. (eds.) CRYPTO 2018. LNCS, vol. 10991, pp. 275–305. Springer, Cham (2018). https://doi.org/10.1007/978-3-319-96884-1_10
24. Zhang, B., Gong, X.: Another tradeoff attack on sprout-like stream ciphers. In: Iwata, T., Cheon, J.H. (eds.) ASIACRYPT 2015. LNCS, vol. 9453, pp. 561–585. Springer, Heidelberg (2015). https://doi.org/10.1007/978-3-662-48800-3_23

Related-Key Analysis of Generalized Feistel Networks with Expanding Round Functions

Yuqing Zhao[1,2], Wenqi Yu[1,2], and Chun Guo[1,2,3(✉)]

[1] School of Cyber Science and Technology, Shandong University, Qingdao, Shandong, China
{yqzhao,wenqiyu}@mail.sdu.edu.cn
[2] Key Laboratory of Cryptologic Technology and Information Security of Ministry of Education, Shandong University, Qingdao 266237, Shandong, China
chun.guo@sdu.edu.cn
[3] State Key Laboratory of Information Security, Institute of Information Engineering, Chinese Academy of Sciences, Beijing 100093, China

Abstract. We extend the prior provable related-key security analysis of (generalized) Feistel networks (Barbosa and Farshim, FSE 2014; Yu et al., Inscrypt 2020) to the setting of *expanding round functions*, i.e., n-bit to m-bit round functions with $n < m$. This includes *Expanding Feistel Networks(EFNs)* that purely rely on such expanding round functions, and *Alternating Feistel Networks(AFNs)* that alternate expanding and contracting round functions. We show that, when two independent keys K_1, K_2 are alternatively used in each round, (a) $2\lceil \frac{m}{n} \rceil + 2$ rounds are sufficient for related-key security of EFNs, and (b) a constant number of 4 rounds are sufficient for related-key security of AFNs. Our results complete the picture of provable related-key security of GFNs, and provide additional theoretical support for the AFN-based NIST format preserving encryption standards FF1 and FF3.

Keywords: Blockcipher · Expanding Feistel Networks · Alternating Feistel Networks · Related-key attack · CCA-security · H-coefficient technique

1 Introduction

Generalized Feistel Networks. The well-known Feistel blockciphers, including the Data Encryption Standard (DES) [25], rely on the Feistel permutation $\Psi^F(A, B) := (B, A \oplus F(B))$, where $F : \{0,1\}^n \to \{0,1\}^n$ is a domain-preserving round function. This structure has been generalized along multiple axes, providing much more choices for the involved parameters and possibilities of applications. In particular, the so-called *Contracting Feistel Networks*

Y. Zhao and W. Yu—are co-first authors of the article.

K. G. Paterson (Ed.): CT-RSA 2021, LNCS 12704, pp. 326–350, 2021.
https://doi.org/10.1007/978-3-030-75539-3_14

(CFNs) employ *contracting round functions* $G : \{0,1\}^m \to \{0,1\}^n$, $m > n$ [44], while *Expanding Feistel Networks* (EFNs) employ the opposite *expanding round functions* $F : \{0,1\}^n \to \{0,1\}^m$ [44]. In some cases, the two sorts of round functions are executed in a alternating manner [2,33], yielding *Alternating Feistel Networks* (AFNs). Following [28], these are now known as *generalized Feistel networks*. Well-known blockciphers that follow these Feistel variants include the Chinese standard SMS4 [19] (contracting) and BEAR/LION/LIONESS [2] (alternating). Besides, CFNs have supported full-domain secure encryption schemes [35], while AFNs have been proposed as blockcipher modes-of-operation for format-preserving encryption (FPE) [8,13,14] and adopted by the NIST format-preserving encryption standard FFX [23], in order to encrypt non-binary alphabet [23] or database records [18] into ciphertexts of the same format.

Provable security of Feistel networks and their variants was initiated by Luby and Rackoff [32]. The approach is to model the round functions as pseudorandom functions (PRFs). Via a generic standard-to-ideal reduction, the schemes are turned into networks using secret random round functions, for which *information theoretic indistinguishability* is provable, i.e., no *distinguisher* is able to distinguish the Feistel network from a random permutation on $2n$-bit strings. With this model, Luby and Rackoff proved CCA security for 4-round balanced Feistel networks, and subsequent works extended this direction to refined results [28,37,39,43] or to cover the aforementioned generalized Feistel networks [2,8,13,28,33,35,38,41,48]. It has been proved that CFNs, EFNs, and AFNs could all achieve CCA security up to nearly $2^{(n+m)}$ adversarial queries [28,45], at the cost of a logarithmic number of rounds.

Related-Key Security. The above PRF or secret random function-based security argument assumed the network using a fixed secret key. We will henceforth refer to this as the *Single-Key (SK) setting*. The adversarial model, however, usually violates this assumption. In particular, the *Related-Key Attacks* (RKAs), first identified by Biham [9] and Knudsen [30], consider a setting where an adversary might be able to run a cryptosystem on multiple keys satisfying known or chose relations (due to key update [24,29] or fault injection [3]). Compared to the classical "single-key" setting, the increased adversarial power enables much more effective attacks against quite a number of blockciphers [10,21].

On the other hand, security against RKAs has become a desirable goal, particularly for blockciphers, as it increases the robustness of the primitive and eases its use. In this respect, Bellare and Kohno [7] initiated the theoretical treatment of security under related-key attacks by proposing definitions for RKA secure pseudorandom functions (PRFs) and pseudorandom permutations (PRPs), formalizing the adversarial goal as distinguishing the cipher oracles with related-keys from independent random functions or permutations, and presenting possibility and impossibility results. Since then, follow up works have established various important positive results for provably RKA secure constructions of complicated cryptographic primitives [1,5,6,26]. In particular, Barbosa and Farshim established RKA security for 4 rounds balanced Feistel networks with two master keys K_1 and K_2 alternatively used in each round [5], and Guo established RKA security for the so-called Feistel-2 or key-alternating Feistel ciphers [26].

RKA Security of GFNs. GFNs remain far less understood in the RKA model. To our knowledge, this was only partly addressed in [47], which established RKA security for contracting Feistel networks using two keys alternatively. In contrast, the generalized Feistel variants using *expanding round functions* have never been analyzed w.r.t. RKAs. This includes expanding EFNs and alternating AFNs.

As already observed [33,36], expanding round functions are attractive in theory, in the sense that the amount of randomness needed to define an ideal expanding function is less than that of the contracting ones.[1] The shortage is that, information theoretic security is limited by the input size n of the round function, and turns vanishing for small n (8 bits for example). Though, even in this case, provable security is usually viewed as theoretical support for the structure (see e.g., [16]).[2] As such, expanding round functions are still used in practice. For example, EFNs can be made practical via storing truly random expanding functions for small input size n (e.g., 8 bits), as done in the hash function CRUNCH [31]. Meanwhile, as mentioned before, AFNs have been the structure of the NIST format-preserving encryption standards [23]. The contracting round functions are built from AES-CBC, while the expanding are from AES-CTR.

Regarding provable security, the landscape is very subtle. For EFNs, it was shown that $2\lceil \frac{m}{n}\rceil + 4$ rounds suffice for the classical SK CCA security up to $2^{n/2}$ queries (generic attacks have been exhibited in [42,46]). For AFNs, it was shown that $12\lceil \frac{m}{n}\rceil + 6$ rounds suffice for SK CCA security up to $2^{m/2}$ queries, which is birthday bound of the parameter m (m is larger than n). With fewer rounds, provable results were restricted to weaker models such as CPA security (3 rounds [33]) or key recovery security (4 rounds [33,34]).[3] In all, for EFNs and AFNs, while asymptotically optimal bounds have been proved, it remains unclear what's the minimal number of rounds necessary for CCA security.

Our Results. As mentioned before, in the regime of RKA security, GFNs with contracting round functions have been studied in [47]. This paper aims to investigate GFNs with expanding round functions to complete the picture.

RKA SECURITY OF $2\lceil \frac{m}{n}\rceil + 2$-ROUND EFN. In detail, we first consider expanding Feistel networks using a keyed round function $F : \mathcal{K} \times \{0,1\}^n \rightarrow \{0,1\}^m$, where $m > n$. We first pinpoint the number of rounds that appear sufficient. In this respect, we note that the proof framework for balanced Feistel, contracting Feistel, and Naor-Reingold views the scheme as several middle rounds sandwiched by a number of outer rounds: the outer rounds ensure some sort of full diffusion, while the middle rounds ensure pseudorandomness of the final

---

[1] It consumes $n \cdot 2^m$ bits to describe the table of a contracting random function from $\{0,1\}^m$ to $\{0,1\}^n$, while $m \cdot 2^n$ bits for an expanding one from $\{0,1\}^n$ to $\{0,1\}^m$.

[2] For AFN-based modes we might have $n = 128$, and the bound would be meaningful. We hope to see concrete designs.

[3] Although many have mentioned the possibility of CCA security on 4 rounds [33].

outputs. This framework has also been used for the RKA security of 3-round Even-Mansour cipher [17]. Following this idea, we identify that the number of expanding Feistel rounds sufficient for full diffusion is $\lceil \frac{m}{n} \rceil$. We also observe that two middle rounds are sufficient as the randomness source. Therefore, we pinpoint $2\lceil \frac{m}{n} \rceil + 2$ as the number of rounds plausible for CCA security. This improves upon the aforementioned *SK CCA* result with $2\lceil \frac{m}{n} \rceil + 4$ rounds [28]. The improvement stems from the fine-grained H-coefficient-based analysis rather than the NCPA(Non-adaptive CPA)-to-CCA transformation used in [28].

The next step is to pinpoint a plausible correlated key assignment—as observed in the context of balanced Feistel networks [5,7], independent round keys actually admit related-key attacks. A natural idea is to alternate two independent keys $K_1, K_2 \in \mathcal{K}$ in each round, as in [5] and in some practical block-ciphers [4,27]. Note that an odd number of Feistel rounds with such alternating key assignment yields an (insecure) involution.[4]

Fortunately, the aforementioned number of rounds $2\lceil \frac{m}{n} \rceil + 2$ is *even*. Therefore, we focus on this alternating key assignment, and prove that the $2\lceil \frac{m}{n} \rceil + 2$ rounds are sufficient for the classical birthday security, i.e., for RKA security up to $2^{n/2}$ adversarial queries.

RKA SECURITY OF 4-ROUND AFN. We then consider alternating Feistel networks, in which the odd rounds use contracting $G : \mathcal{K} \times \{0,1\}^m \rightarrow \{0,1\}^n$ while the even rounds use expanding $F : \mathcal{K} \times \{0,1\}^n \rightarrow \{0,1\}^m$. Somewhat interestingly,—and in contrast to contracting and expanding Feistel networks (see [47] for discussion on the former),—the number of rounds suffice for CCA security in an AFN is always 4, *independent of the ratio m/n*. Briefly, the reason is that AFNs actually behave quite similarly to the classical balanced Feistel networks, except that the domain and range of the round functions are different.

To achieve RKA security, again we have to resort to non-independent key assignments. We consider again the aforementioned key assignment. With the above, we prove that the 4-round AFN (Fig. 1) using round keys (K_1, K_2, K_1, K_2) is RKA secure up to $2^{n/2}$ queries, which is the birthday bound with respect to the parameter n.

For AFN there is another interesting property, i.e., if all the round keys are identical, then an odd number of rounds constitutes an involution (*not CCA secure*), while an even number of rounds is not. As we are trying to establish security for 4 rounds, it seems appealing to employ such identical round keys. Unfortunately, another subtle issue hinders this attempt. In detail, technically, the classical generic standard-to-ideal reduction is unable to handle *two different keyed functions using the same secret key*: the reduction is just unable to simulate the other primitive with the target secret key. On the positive side, this issue can be overcame by using a *tweakable keyed function* that behaves as contracting for tweak input 0 while expanding for tweak 1. For the AFN using

---

[4] By this, even number of rounds are likely vulnerable to recent advanced slide attacks [20]. Though, we remark that slide attacks typically require *at least* $2^{n/2}$ complexities [11,12,20,22], and thus do not violate our birthday provable bounds. Seeking for beyond-birthday provable bounds is a promising future direction.

such a tweakable keyed function as the round function, the reduction is able to handle the case of identical round keys (it just idealizes all round functions "once for all'). Interestingly, this model appears closer to FF1 and FF3. Our analysis is easily adapted to this 4-round **AFN** variant, indicating RKA CCA security up to $2^{n/2}$ queries. For clearness, we summarize our new results and relevant existing results in Table 1.

As mentioned before, our results complete the picture of RKA security of generalized Feistel networks. They also provide additional theoretical support for the NIST standards FF1 and FF3. However, we remark important caveats. The concrete parameters involved in FF1 and FF3 are rather small, and our provable bounds (in fact, *any* information theoretic provable bounds) are too weak to be meaningful. FF1 and FF3 are intended to resist attacks with complexity far beyond the information theoretic upper bound. Therefore, the number of rounds have to be determined by cryptanalytic results rather than the provable ones. In fact, recently, FF1 and FF3 have been found insufficient.

We also mention that the blockcipher LIONESS of Anderson and Biham uses 4 independent keys in its two calls to a stream cipher and two calls to a hash function [2]. Our result can be applied to *halve* the amount of keys while *boosting* provable security (i.e., boosting birthday-bound CCA security to birthday-bound RKA CCA security).

Table 1. Provable security results on expanding and alternating Feistel networks. The scheme AFN* is the aforementioned tweakable function-based AFN. The second column lists the security models, where SK is the abbreviation of *Single-Key*. The third column list the number of rounds required by the provable results. The fourth column list the key assignment in use: **Independent** means independent round keys, **Alternating** means (our) alternating two keys, and **Identical** means identical round keys. Parameter $m > n$, m is the output length of the expanding function and the input length of the contracting function. Parameter n is the input length of the expanding function and the output length of the contracting function. The parameter t is an integer and determines the number of rounds.

Scheme	Model	Rounds	Round keys	Security	Ref.
EFN	SK CCA	$2\lceil \frac{m}{n} \rceil + 4$	Independent	$n/2$	[28,45]
EFN	SK CCA	$4t + 2\lceil \frac{m}{n} \rceil + 1$	Independent	$tn/(t+1)$	[45]
EFN	**RKA CCA**	$2\lceil \frac{m}{n} \rceil + 2$	Alternating	$n/2$	Theorem 1
AFN	Key recovery	3	–	–	[33,34]
AFN	SK CPA	3	Independent	$n/2$	[33]
AFN	SK CCA	$12\lceil \frac{m}{n} \rceil + 6$	Independent	$m/2$	[28]
AFN	SK CCA	$(12\lceil \frac{m}{n} \rceil + 2)t + 5$	Independent	$tm/(t+1)$	[45]
AFN	**RKA CCA**	4	Alternating	$n/2$	Theorem 2
AFN*	**RKA CCA**	4	Identical	$n/2$	Corollary 1

Organization. We serve necessary notations and definitions in Sect. 2. After that, we serve the RKA security analysis for EFN in Sect. 3. In the full version, we serve the analysis of the simplest setting of 6-round EFN as an instructive example. We then present the analysis for 4-round AFN in Sect. 4. We finally conclude in Sect. 5.

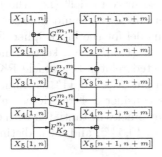 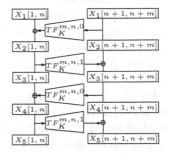

Fig. 1. (Left) The 4-round alternating Feistel network $\mathsf{AFN}^{G^{m,n},F^{n,m},4}$ using a contracting round function $G^{m,n}$ and an expanding round function $F^{n,m}$ and two keys K_1, K_2. (Right) The 4-round alternating Feistel network $\mathsf{AFN}^{TF^{m,n},4}$ using a tweakable round function $TF^{m,n}$ and a single key K.

2 Preliminaries

For two bit strings X, Y of any length, we denote by $X\|Y$ their concatenation. For $X \in \{0,1\}^m$, we denote by $X[a,b]$ the string consisting of the $b - a + 1$ bits between the a-th position and the b-th position. This means $X = X[1,i]\|X[i+1,m]$ for any $i \in \{1, ..., m-1\}$. For example, if $X = \text{0xA5A5}$ (in hexadecimal form), then $X[1,3] = \text{0x5}$, while $X[4,16] = \text{0x05A5}$.

Two of our three results focus on using two independent keys K_1, K_2 in the round functions. In this respect, we denote the master key of the network by $\mathbf{K} = (K_1, K_2) \in \mathcal{K}^2$, i.e., a vector of dimension 2. We denote by $\mathbf{K}[i]$ its i-th coordinate, where $i = 1$ or 2. We further denote by

$$\mathsf{KA}(\mathbf{K}) = (K_{i_1}, ..., K_{i_t})$$

the round key assignment of the network, where $i_1, ..., i_t$ are fixed indices in $\{1, 2\}$. For such a vector of round keys $\mathsf{KA}(\mathbf{K})$, we denote by $\mathsf{KA}(\mathbf{K})[j]$ the j-th round key K_{i_j}. Thereby, a related-key derivation function ϕ maps a certain master key $\mathbf{K} = (K_1, K_2)$ to a new master key $\mathbf{K}' = (K_1', K_2')$. We will write $\mathsf{EFN}_{\mathsf{KA}(\mathbf{K})}$ and $\mathsf{AFN}_{\mathsf{KA}(\mathbf{K})}$ for the corresponding construction using the master key $\mathbf{K}$ and the key assignment KA.

For the case $\mathbf{K} = (K_1, K_2)$, we will specially pay attention to the alternating key assignment $\mathsf{Alter}(\mathbf{K}) = (K_1, K_2, K_1, K_2, ...)$. Formally, $\mathsf{Alter}(\mathbf{K}) := (K_{i_1}, ..., K_{i_t})$, where $i_j = 1$ for j odd and $i_j = 2$ for j even.

2.1 (Multi-user) RKA Security

The RKA security notion is parameterized by the so-called related-key deriving (RKD) sets. Formally, an ν-ary RKD set Φ consists of RKD functions ϕ mapping a ν-tuple of keys $(K_1, ..., K_\nu)$ in some key space $\mathcal{K}^\nu$ to a new ν-tuple of key in $\mathcal{K}^\nu$, i.e., $\phi : \mathcal{K}^\nu \to \mathcal{K}^\nu$.

We need to formalize the multi-user RKA security model[5] (i.e., the model involving multiple independent secret keys) for the keyed round functions and the classical (single-user) RKA CCA security model for the blockcipher/Feistel networks. For the former, let $F : \mathcal{K} \times \{0,1\}^n \to \{0,1\}^m$ be a keyed function, and fix a key $K \in \mathcal{K}$. We define the Φ-restricted related-key oracle $\mathsf{RK}[F_K]$, which takes a RKD function $\phi \in \Phi$ and an input $X \in \{0,1\}^n$ as input, and returns $\mathsf{RK}[F_K](\phi, X) := F_{\phi(K)}(X)$. Then, we consider a Φ-restricted related-key adversary D which has access to u related-key oracles instantiated with either F or an ideal keyed function $\mathsf{RF} : \mathcal{K} \times \{0,1\}^n \to \{0,1\}^m$, and must distinguish between two worlds as follows:

- the "real" world, where it interacts with $\mathsf{RK}[F_{K_1}], ..., \mathsf{RK}[F_{K_u}]$, and $K_1, ..., K_u$ are randomly and independently drawn from $\mathcal{K}$;
- the "ideal" world, where it interacts with $\mathsf{RK}[\mathsf{RF}_{K_1}], ..., \mathsf{RK}[\mathsf{RF}_{K_u}]$, and $K_1,..., K_u$ are randomly and independently drawn from $\mathcal{K}$.

The adversary is adaptive. Note that in the ideal world, each oracle $\mathsf{RK}[\mathsf{RF}_{K_i}]$ essentially implements an independent random function for each related-key $\phi(K_i)$. Formally, D's distinguishing advantage on F is defined as

$$\mathbf{Adv}_F^{\Phi\text{-rka}[u]}(D) := \Big| \ \mathrm{Pr}_{\mathsf{RF}, K_1, ..., K_u}\big[D^{\mathsf{RK}[\mathsf{RF}_{K_1}], \mathsf{RK}[\mathsf{RF}_{K_1}]^{-1}, ..., \mathsf{RK}[\mathsf{RF}_{K_u}], \mathsf{RK}[\mathsf{RF}_{K_u}]^{-1}} = 1\big]$$
$$- \mathrm{Pr}_{K_1, ..., K_u}\big[D^{\mathsf{RK}[F_{K_1}], \mathsf{RK}[F_{K_1}]^{-1}, ..., \mathsf{RK}[F_{K_u}], \mathsf{RK}[F_{K_u}]^{-1}} = 1\big] \ \Big| \ .$$

It was proved that, under some natural restrictions on RKD sets, the single-user and multi-user RKA notions are equivalent up to a factor of u. Moreover, our subsequent sections mainly focus on the case of $u = 2$. We refer to [5] for details.

Similarly, a blockcipher $E : \mathcal{K}^\nu \times \{0,1\}^m \to \{0,1\}^m$ shall be comparable with an ideal cipher. Formally, D's distinguishing advantage on E is defined as

$$\mathbf{Adv}_E^{\Phi\text{-rka}[1]}(D) := \Big| \ \mathrm{Pr}_{\mathsf{IC}, \mathbf{K}}\big[D^{\mathsf{RK}[\mathsf{IC}_\mathbf{K}], \mathsf{RK}[\mathsf{IC}_\mathbf{K}]^{-1}} = 1\big] - \mathrm{Pr}_\mathbf{K}\big[D^{\mathsf{RK}[E_\mathbf{K}], \mathsf{RK}[E_\mathbf{K}]^{-1}} = 1\big] \ \Big|,$$

where $\mathsf{RK}[E_\mathbf{K}]^{-1}(\phi, Y) := E_{\phi(\mathbf{K})}^{-1}(Y)$.

As already noticed in [7], Φ-RKA security is achievable only if the RKD set Φ satisfies certain conditions that exclude trivial attacks. For this, we follow [5] and

---

[5] This was termed *multi-key RKA security* in [5]. As we refer to the classical security model with a single "static" secret key as "single-key (CCA) model", we use the terms *single-user and multi-user* here for distinction.

characterize three properties. Firstly, the *output unpredictability (UP)* advantage of an adversary $\mathcal{A}$ against an RKD set Φ is

$$\mathbf{Adv}_{\Phi}^{\mathsf{up}}(\mathcal{A}) := \Pr\big[\exists(\phi, \mathbf{K}^*) \in \mathsf{L}_1 \times \mathsf{L}_2 \quad \text{s.t.} \quad \phi(\mathbf{K}) = \mathbf{K}^* : \mathbf{K} \leftarrow_{\$} \mathcal{K}; \ (\mathsf{L}_1, \mathsf{L}_2) \leftarrow \mathcal{A}\big].$$

Secondly, the *claw-freeness* (CF) advantage of an adversary $\mathcal{A}$ against an RKD set Φ is

$$\mathbf{Adv}_{\Phi}^{\mathsf{cf}}(\mathcal{A}) := \Pr\big[\exists \phi_1, \phi_2 \in \mathsf{L} \quad \text{s.t.} \quad \phi_1(\mathbf{K}) = \phi_2(\mathbf{K}) \wedge \phi_1 \neq \phi_2 : \mathbf{K} \leftarrow_{\$} \mathcal{K}; \ \mathsf{L} \leftarrow \mathcal{A}\big].$$

Finally, when the master key is the aforementioned vector $\mathbf{K} = (K_1, K_2)$, the *switch-freeness* (SF) advantage of an adversary $\mathcal{A}$ against an RKD set Φ is

$$\mathbf{Adv}_{\Phi}^{\mathsf{sf}}(\mathcal{A}) := \Pr\big[(\exists \phi_1, \phi_2 \in \mathsf{L})(\exists i \neq j \in \{1, 2\}) \quad \text{s.t.} \quad \phi_1(\mathbf{K})[i] = \phi_2(\mathbf{K})[j] :$$
$$\mathbf{K} \leftarrow_{\$} \mathcal{K}; \ \mathsf{L} \leftarrow \mathcal{A}\big].$$

We require the three advantages to be sufficiently small. The necessity of UP and CF has already been noticed in [7]: if $\mathcal{A}$ is able to figure out $\phi \in \Phi$ such that $\phi(\mathbf{K}) = c$ for some constant c or $\phi(\mathbf{K}) = \phi'(\mathbf{K})$ for some $\phi' \neq \phi$, then distinguishing is always possible by comparing $\mathsf{RK}[E_{\mathbf{K}}](\phi, X)$ with $E_c(X)$ or with $\mathsf{RK}[E_{\mathbf{K}}](\phi', X)$ respectively. On the other hand, the SF property aims to ensure a definitive distinction between the round functions using K_1 and those using K_2. I.e., once a master key $\mathbf{K} = (K_1, K_2)$ is fixed, a round function using K_1 will never use K_2 for some RKD function ϕ.

2.2   The H-Coefficient Technique

The core step of our proofs consists of analyzing information theoretic indistinguishability of EFNs and AFNs built upon ideal keyed functions, which will employ the H-coefficient technique [15,40]. To this end, we assume a deterministic distinguisher that has unbounded computation power, and we summarize the information gathered by the distinguisher in a tuple

$$\mathcal{Q} = \big((\phi_1, X_1, Y_1), \ldots, (\phi_q, X_q, Y_q)\big)$$

called the *transcript*, meaning that the j-th query was either a forward query (ϕ_j, X_j) with answer Y_j, or a backward query (ϕ_j, Y_j) with answer X_j.

To simplify the definition of "bad transcripts", we reveal the key $\mathbf{K}$ to the distinguisher at the end of the interaction. This is wlog since D is free to ignore this additional information to compute its output bit. Formally, we append $\mathbf{K}$ to τ and obtain what we call the *transcript* $\tau = (\mathcal{Q}, \mathbf{K})$ of the attack. With respect to some fixed distinguisher D, a transcript τ is said *attainable*, if there exists oracles IC such that the interaction of D with the ideal world $\mathsf{RK}[\mathsf{IC}_{\mathbf{K}}]$ yields $\mathcal{Q}$. We denote $\mathcal{T}$ the set of attainable transcripts. In all the following, we denote T_{re}, resp. T_{id}, the probability distribution of the transcript τ induced by the real world, resp. the ideal world (note that these two probability distributions depend on the distinguisher). By extension, we use the same notation for a random variable distributed according to each distribution.

With the above, the main lemma of H-coefficient technique is: (see [15]).

Lemma 1. *Fix a distinguisher D. Let $\mathcal{T} = \mathcal{T}_{\text{good}} \cup \mathcal{T}_{\text{bad}}$ be a partition of the set of attainable transcripts $\mathcal{T}$. Assume that there exists ε_1 such that for any $\tau \in \mathcal{T}_{\text{good}}$, one has*

$$\frac{\Pr[T_{\text{re}} = \tau]}{\Pr[T_{\text{id}} = \tau]} \geq 1 - \varepsilon_1,$$

and that there exists ε_2 such that $\Pr[T_{\text{id}} \in \mathcal{T}_{\text{bad}}] \leq \varepsilon_2$. Then $\mathbf{Adv}(D) \leq \varepsilon_1 + \varepsilon_2$.

Given a transcript $\mathcal{Q}$, a blockcipher E, and a key $\mathcal{K} \in \mathcal{K}^\nu$, we say the related-key oracle $\mathsf{RK}[E_{\mathbf{K}}]$ *extends* $\mathcal{Q}$, denoted $\mathsf{RK}[E_{\mathbf{K}}] \vdash \mathcal{Q}$, if $E_{\phi(\mathbf{K})}(X) = Y$ for all $(\phi, X, Y) \in \mathcal{Q}$. It is easy to see that for any attainable transcript $\tau = (\mathcal{Q}, \mathbf{K})$, the interaction of the distinguisher with oracles $\mathsf{RK}[E_{\mathbf{K}}]$ produces $(\mathcal{Q}, \mathbf{K})$ if and only if $\mathbf{K}$ is sampled in the interaction and $\mathsf{RK}[E_{\mathbf{K}}] \vdash \tau$. We refer to [15] for a formal argument. With these, it is not hard to see that,

$$\Pr[T_{\text{id}} = \tau] = \Pr[\mathbf{K}] \cdot \Pr[\mathsf{RK}[\mathsf{IC}_{\mathbf{K}}] \vdash \mathcal{Q}] \leq \Pr[\mathbf{K}] \cdot \left(\frac{1}{2^{n+m} - q}\right)^q, \quad (1)$$

where $n + m$ is the block size of the resulting $(n + m)$-bit generalized Feistel network, and $\Pr[\mathbf{K}] = \Pr_{\mathbf{K}^*}[\mathbf{K}^* = \mathbf{K}]$. Similarly,

$$\Pr[T_{\text{re}} = \tau] = \Pr[\mathbf{K}] \cdot \Pr[\mathsf{RK}[E_{\mathbf{K}}] \vdash \mathcal{Q}], \quad (2)$$

and the analysis of $\Pr[\mathsf{RK}[E_{\mathbf{K}}] \vdash \mathcal{Q}]$ will constitute the core of the subsequent proofs.

3   Security Analysis of Expanding Feistel Networks

Let m and n be positive integers such that $m > n$. In this section, we consider the t-round $\mathsf{EFN}_{\mathsf{KA}(\mathbf{K})}^{F^{n,m},t}$ using an expanding round function $F^{n,m}$. Formally, for $X \in \{0,1\}^{n+m}$ and $i \in \{1, ..., t\}$, the ith round of the EFN uses the round key K_i, and is defined as

$$\Psi^{F_{K_i}^{n,m}}(X) := F_{K_i}^{n,m}\big(X[1,n]\big) \oplus X[n+1, n+m] \;\|\; X[1,n].$$

The t-round $\mathsf{EFN}_{\mathsf{KA}(\mathbf{K})}^{F^{n,m}, 2\lceil \frac{m}{n} \rceil + 2}$ using the key assignment $\mathsf{KA}(\mathbf{K}) = (K_1, ..., K_t)$ is a composition of t such rounds, i.e.,

$$\mathsf{EFN}_{\mathsf{KA}(\mathbf{K})}^{F^{n,m}, t}(X) := \Psi^{F_{K_t}^{n,m}} \circ ... \circ \Psi^{F_{K_1}^{n,m}}(X).$$

As mentioned in the Introduction, for such EFNs, $2\lceil \frac{m}{n} \rceil + 2$ rounds and the alternating key assignment $\mathsf{Alter}(\mathbf{K}) = (K_1, K_2, K_1, K_2, ...)$ would ensure RKA security.

Theorem 1. *For any distinguisher D making at most q queries to the oracles* $\mathsf{RK}[\mathsf{EFN}_{\mathsf{Alter}(\mathbf{K})}^{F^{n,m},2\lceil\frac{m}{n}\rceil+2}]$ *and* $\mathsf{RK}[\mathsf{EFN}_{\mathsf{Alter}(\mathbf{K})}^{F^{n,m},2\lceil\frac{m}{n}\rceil+2}]^{-1}$ *in total, it holds*

$$\mathbf{Adv}_{\mathsf{EFN}_{\mathsf{Alter}(\mathbf{K})}^{F^{n,m},2\lceil\frac{m}{n}\rceil+2}}^{\Phi\text{-rka}[1]}(D) \leq \mathbf{Adv}_{F^{n,m}}^{\Phi\text{-rka}[2]}(D) + \mathbf{Adv}_{\Phi}^{\mathsf{cf}}(D) + \mathbf{Adv}_{\Phi}^{\mathsf{sf}}(D)$$

$$+ \frac{(\lceil\frac{m}{n}\rceil+1)^2 q^2}{2^n} + \frac{q^2}{2^{n+m}}. \tag{3}$$

The bound appears independent of the unpredictability advantage $\mathbf{Adv}_{\Phi}^{\mathsf{up}}(D)$. Though, $\mathbf{Adv}_{\Phi}^{\mathsf{up}}(D)$ shall be small in order to ensure that $\mathbf{Adv}_{F^{n,m}}^{\Phi\text{-rka}[2]}(D)$ is sufficiently small.

The proof starts with a generic standard-to-ideal reduction, which replaces the keyed expanding round function $F^{n,m}$ with an ideal keyed expanding function $\mathsf{RF}^{n,m} : \mathcal{K} \times \{0,1\}^n \rightarrow \{0,1\}^m$. Clearly (see [5, Theorem 2] for a more detailed formalism),

$$\left| \mathbf{Adv}_{\mathsf{EFN}_{\mathsf{Alter}(\mathbf{K})}^{\mathsf{RF}^{n,m},2\lceil\frac{m}{n}\rceil+2}}^{\Phi\text{-rka}[1]}(D) - \mathbf{Adv}_{\mathsf{EFN}_{\mathsf{Alter}(\mathbf{K})}^{F^{n,m},2\lceil\frac{m}{n}\rceil+2}}^{\Phi\text{-rka}[1]}(D) \right| \leq \mathbf{Adv}_{F^{n,m}}^{\Phi\text{-rka}[2]}(D),$$

and we could focus on analyzing $\mathbf{Adv}_{\mathsf{EFN}_{\mathsf{Alter}(\mathbf{K})}^{\mathsf{RF}^{n,m},2\lceil\frac{m}{n}\rceil+2}}^{\Phi\text{-rka}[1]}(D)$ for the idealized EFN. We'll employ the H-coefficient technique, define and analyze bad transcripts, and show that the probabilities to obtain any good transcript in the real world and the ideal world are sufficiently close.

3.1 Bad Transcripts

Definition 1. *An attainable transcript $\tau = (\mathcal{Q}, \mathbf{K})$ is bad, if either of the following conditions is fulfilled:*

(B-1) Claw in τ: there exist two triples (ϕ_1, X_1, Y_1) and (ϕ_2, X_2, Y_2) in $\mathcal{Q}$ such that $\phi_1 \neq \phi_2$, while $\phi_1(\mathbf{K}) = \phi_2(\mathbf{K})$;
(B-2) Switch in τ: there exist two triples (ϕ_1, X_1, Y_1) and (ϕ_2, X_2, Y_2) in $\mathcal{Q}$ and two distinct indices $i,j \in \{1,2\}$ such that $\phi_1(\mathbf{K})[i] = \phi_2(\mathbf{K})[j]$.

Otherwise we say τ is good.

It is clear that $\Pr[(\text{B-1})] \leq \mathbf{Adv}_{\Phi}^{\mathsf{cf}}(D)$: an adversary against the claw-freeness of the RKD set Φ could simulate the related-key oracle with Φ against the distinguisher D, collecting D's transcript of queries and responses, and use the records in $\mathcal{Q}$ to break the claw-freeness of Φ. Similarly, $\Pr[(\text{B-2})] \leq \mathbf{Adv}_{\Phi}^{\mathsf{sf}}(D)$, and thus

$$\Pr[T_{\mathsf{id}} \in \mathcal{T}_{\mathsf{bad}}] = \Pr[(\text{B-1}) \vee (\text{B-2})] \leq \mathbf{Adv}_{\Phi}^{\mathsf{cf}}(D) + \mathbf{Adv}_{\Phi}^{\mathsf{sf}}(D). \tag{4}$$

3.2 Analyzing Good Transcripts

Fix a good transcript τ. The ideal world probability simply follows from Eq. (1), and it remains to analyze $\Pr\left[\mathsf{RK}[\mathsf{EFN}_{\mathsf{Alter(K)}}^{\mathsf{RF}^{n,m},2\lceil\frac{m}{n}\rceil+2}] \vdash \mathcal{Q}\right]$, i.e., an ideal keyed function $\mathsf{RF}^{n,m}$ satisfying $\mathsf{RK}[\mathsf{EFN}_{\mathsf{Alter(K)}}^{\mathsf{RF}^{n,m},2\lceil\frac{m}{n}\rceil+2}] \vdash \mathcal{Q}$. We proceed in two steps. First, given an ideal keyed function $\mathsf{RF}^{n,m}$, it is possible to derive the $(\lceil\frac{m}{n}\rceil+1)$ th and $(\lceil\frac{m}{n}\rceil + 2)$ th round intermediate values involved during evaluating the queries in τ. We thus define a "bad predicate" $\mathsf{BadF}(\mathsf{RF}^{n,m})$ on $\mathsf{RF}^{n,m}$, such that once $\mathsf{BadF}(\mathsf{RF}^{n,m})$ is not fulfilled, the event $T_{\mathrm{re}} = \tau$ is equivalent to $\mathsf{RF}^{n,m}$ satisfying $2q$ distinct equations on these intermediate values, the probability of which is close to the ideal world probability. The bound then follows from some simple probabilistic arguments.

Formally, given an ideal keyed function $\mathsf{RF}^{n,m}$, for every $(\phi_i, X_i, Y_i) \in \tau$, we define the induced intermediate values in a "meet-in-the-middle" manner. In detail, we first define $X_{1,i} := X_i$, and

$$X_{\ell,i} := \mathsf{RF}_{\mathsf{Alter}(\phi_i(\mathbf{K}))[\ell-1]}^{n,m}\big(X_{\ell-1,i}[1,n]\big) \oplus X_{\ell-1,i}[n+1,n+m] \;\|\; X_{\ell-1,i}[1,n] \tag{5}$$

for $\ell = 2, ..., \lceil\frac{m}{n}\rceil + 1$. We then define $X_{2\lceil\frac{m}{n}\rceil+3,i} := Y_i$, and

$$\begin{aligned} X_{\ell,i} := \;& X_{\ell+1,i}[m+1, n+m] \\ & \| \; \mathsf{RF}_{\mathsf{Alter}(\phi_i(\mathbf{K}))[\ell]}^{n,m}\big(X_{\ell+1,i}[m+1, n+m]\big) \oplus X_{\ell+1,i}[1, m] \end{aligned} \tag{6}$$

for $\ell = 2\lceil\frac{m}{n}\rceil + 2, 2\lceil\frac{m}{n}\rceil + 1, ..., \lceil\frac{m}{n}\rceil + 3$.

Bad Predicate. Informally, the conditions capture "unnecessary" collisions among calls to the round function $\mathsf{RF}^{n,m}$ during evaluating the q queries.

Definition 2. *Given a function $\mathsf{RF}^{n,m}$, the predicate $\mathsf{BadF}(\mathsf{RF}^{n,m})$ is fulfilled, if any of the following $\lceil\frac{m}{n}\rceil + 3$ conditions is fulfilled.*

- **(C-[ℓ])** *For $\ell = 1, ..., \lceil\frac{m}{n}\rceil$, the ℓ th condition addresses the $\ell + 1$ th and $2\lceil\frac{m}{n}\rceil + 2 - \ell$ th round function "inputs": there exists two indices $i, j \in \{1, ..., q\}$ such that*
  - *there exists $\ell' \in \{1, ..., \ell\}$ such that $\big(\mathsf{Alter}(\phi_i(\mathbf{K}))[\ell+1], X_{\ell+1,i}[1,n]\big) = \big(\mathsf{Alter}(\phi_j(\mathbf{K}))[\ell'], X_{\ell',j}[1,n]\big)$; or*
  - *there exists $\ell' \in \{2\lceil\frac{m}{n}\rceil + 3 - \ell, ..., 2\lceil\frac{m}{n}\rceil + 3\}$ such that $\big(\mathsf{Alter}(\phi_i(\mathbf{K}))[\ell+1], X_{\ell+1,i}[1,n]\big) = \big(\mathsf{Alter}(\phi_j(\mathbf{K}))[\ell'-1], X_{\ell',j}[m+1, n+m]\big)$; or*
  - *there exists an index $\ell' \in \{1, ..., \ell+1\}$ such that $\big(\mathsf{Alter}(\phi_i(\mathbf{K}))[2\lceil\frac{m}{n}\rceil + 2 - \ell], X_{2\lceil\frac{m}{n}\rceil+3-\ell,i}[m+1, n+m]\big) = \big(\mathsf{Alter}(\phi_j(\mathbf{K}))[\ell'], X_{\ell',j}[1,n]\big)$; or*
  - *there exists $\ell' \in \{2\lceil\frac{m}{n}\rceil + 4 - \ell, ..., 2\lceil\frac{m}{n}\rceil + 3\}$ such that $\big(\mathsf{Alter}(\phi_i(\mathbf{K}))[2\lceil\frac{m}{n}\rceil+2-\ell], X_{2\lceil\frac{m}{n}\rceil+3-\ell,i}[m+1, n+m]\big) = \big(\mathsf{Alter}(\phi_j(\mathbf{K}))[\ell'-1], X_{\ell',j}[m+1, n+m]\big)$.*

- (C-$[\lceil \frac{m}{n} \rceil + 1]$) *There exists distinct* $i, j \in \{1, ..., q\}$ *and* $\ell \in \{1, ..., \lceil \frac{m}{n} \rceil\}$ *such that* $\left(\mathsf{Alter}(\phi_i(\mathbf{K}))[\ell], X_{\ell,i}[1, n]\right) \neq \left(\mathsf{Alter}(\phi_j(\mathbf{K}))[\ell], X_{\ell,j}[1, n]\right)$, *while* $X_{\ell+1,i}[1, n] = X_{\ell+1,j}[1, n]$;
- (C-$[\lceil \frac{m}{n} \rceil + 2]$) *There exists two distinct indices* $i, j \in \{1, ..., q\}$ *and an index* $\ell \in \{\lceil \frac{m}{n} \rceil + 4, ..., 2\lceil \frac{m}{n} \rceil + 3\}$ *such that* $\left(\mathsf{Alter}(\phi_i(\mathbf{K}))[\ell - 1], X_{\ell,i}[m + 1, n + m]\right) \neq \left(\mathsf{Alter}(\phi_j(\mathbf{K}))[\ell - 1], X_{\ell,j}[m + 1, n + m]\right)$, *yet* $X_{\ell-1,i}[m + 1, n + m] = X_{\ell-1,j}[m + 1, n + m]$;
- (C-$[\lceil \frac{m}{n} \rceil + 3]$) *There exists two distinct indices* $i, j \in \{1, ..., q\}$ *such that either* $\left(\mathsf{Alter}(\phi_i(\mathbf{K}))[\lceil \frac{m}{n} \rceil + 1], X_{\lceil \frac{m}{n} \rceil + 1,i}[1, n]\right) = \left(\mathsf{Alter}(\phi_j(\mathbf{K}))[\lceil \frac{m}{n} \rceil + 1], X_{\lceil \frac{m}{n} \rceil + 1,j}[1, n]\right)$, *or* $\left(\mathsf{Alter}(\phi_i(\mathbf{K}))[\lceil \frac{m}{n} \rceil + 2], X_{\lceil \frac{m}{n} \rceil + 3,i}[m + 1, n + m]\right) = \left(\mathsf{Alter}(\phi_j(\mathbf{K}))[\lceil \frac{m}{n} \rceil + 2], X_{\lceil \frac{m}{n} \rceil + 3,j}[m + 1, n + m]\right)$.

To bound $\Pr[\mathsf{BadF}(\mathsf{RF}^{n,m})]$, we consider the conditions in turn.

Condition (C-$[\ell]$), $\ell = 1, ..., \lceil \frac{m}{n} \rceil$. Consider any such two indices $i, j \in \{1, ..., q\}$. We distinguish two cases.

Case 1 : ℓ is odd. In this case, the $\ell+1$ th round function uses the keys $\phi_i(\mathbf{K})[2]$ and $\phi_j(\mathbf{K})[2]$, while the $2\lceil \frac{m}{n} \rceil + 2 - \ell$ th uses $\phi_i(\mathbf{K})[1]$ and $\phi_j(\mathbf{K})[1]$. Note that for $\ell' \neq \ell + 1$, $\left(\mathsf{Alter}(\phi_i(\mathbf{K}))[\ell + 1], X_{\ell+1,i}[1, n]\right) = \left(\mathsf{Alter}(\phi_j(\mathbf{K}))[\ell'], X_{\ell',j}[1, n]\right)$ only if ℓ' is even (so that $\mathsf{Alter}(\phi_i(\mathbf{K}))[\ell+1] = \mathsf{Alter}(\phi_j(\mathbf{K}))[\ell']$ means $\phi_i(\mathbf{K})[2] = \phi_j(\mathbf{K})[2]$), as otherwise the condition (B-2) is fulfilled and τ is not good. By this, the 1st subcondition is simplified as

$$X_{\ell+1,i}[1, n] \in \left\{X_{2,j}[1, n], X_{4,j}[1, n], ..., X_{\ell-1,j}[1, n]\right\}.$$

This is yet another composed condition. In this respect, we first consider the probability to have $X_{\ell+1,i}[1, n] = X_{2,j}[1, n]$. By construction, this means

$$\left(\mathsf{RF}^{n,m}_{\phi_i(\mathbf{K})[1]}\left(X_{\ell,i}[1, n]\right) \oplus X_{\ell,i}[n + 1, n + m]\right)[1, n]$$
$$= \left(\mathsf{RF}^{n,m}_{\phi_j(\mathbf{K})[1]}\left(X_{1,j}[1, n]\right) \oplus X_{1,j}[n + 1, n + m]\right)[1, n],$$

where $\left(X_{\ell,i}[n + 1, n + m]\right)[1, n]$ further depends some function values in the set

$$\mathcal{S}_{\ell,1} := \left\{\mathsf{RF}^{n,m}_{\phi_j(\mathbf{K})[1]}\left(X_{1,j}[1, n]\right), \mathsf{RF}^{n,m}_{\phi_j(\mathbf{K})[1]}\left(X_{3,j}[1, n]\right), ..., \mathsf{RF}^{n,m}_{\phi_i(\mathbf{K})[1]}\left(X_{\ell-2,i}[1, n]\right)\right\}.$$

Conditioned on $\neg$(C-$[\ell - 1]$), it holds $X_{\ell,i}[1, n] \notin \{X_{1,j}[1, n], X_{3,j}[1, n], ..., X_{\ell-2,i}[1, n]\}$. By this, $\left(\mathsf{RF}^{n,m}_{\phi_i(\mathbf{K})[\ell]}\left(X_{\ell,i}[1, n]\right)\right)[1, n]$ is independent of the function values in $\mathcal{S}_{\ell,1}$, and is uniformly distributed in $\{0, 1\}^n$. Therefore, the probability to have $X_{\ell+1,i}[1, n] = X_{2,j}[1, n]$ is $1/2^n$.

We then consider the next equality $X_{\ell+1,i}[1, n] = X_{4,j}[1, n]$, which means

$$\left(\mathsf{RF}^{n,m}_{\phi_i(\mathbf{K})[1]}\left(X_{\ell,i}[1, n]\right) \oplus X_{\ell,i}[n + 1, n + m]\right)[1, n]$$
$$= \left(\mathsf{RF}^{n,m}_{\phi_j(\mathbf{K})[1]}\left(X_{3,j}[1, n]\right) \oplus X_{3,j}[n + 1, n + m]\right)[1, n].$$

where $\left(X_{\ell,i}[n+1, n+m]\right)[1, n]$ and $\left(X_{3,j}[n+1, n+m]\right)[1, n]$ further depend on some function values in the set $\mathcal{S}_{\ell,1}$ defined as before. Again, conditioned on $\neg(\text{C-}[\ell-1])$, $\left(\text{RF}^{n,m}_{\phi_i(\mathbf{K})[\ell]}(X_{\ell,i}[1, n])\right)[1, n]$ is independent of the function values in $\mathcal{S}_{\ell,1}$, and is uniform in $\{0,1\}^n$. Therefore, the probability to have $X_{\ell+1,i}[1, n] = X_{4,j}[1, n]$ is $1/2^n$. Similar reasoning holds for the next $(\ell-1)/2 - 2$ equations $X_{\ell+1,i}[1, n] = X_{6,j}[1, n], ..., X_{\ell+1,i}[1, n] = X_{\ell-1,j}[1, n]$, and thus

$$\Pr\left[X_{\ell+1,i}[1, n] \in \{X_{2,j}[1, n], X_{4,j}[1, n], ..., X_{\ell-1,j}[1, n]\}\right] = \frac{(\ell-1)}{2^{n+1}}.$$

We then consider the equality $X_{\ell+1,i}[1, n] = X_{2\lceil \frac{m}{n}\rceil + 4 - \ell, j}[m+1, n+m]$ due to the 2nd subcondition, which means

$$\left(\text{RF}^{n,m}_{\phi_i(\mathbf{K})[1]}(X_{\ell,i}[1, n]) \oplus X_{\ell,i}[n+1, n+m]\right)[1, n]$$
$$= \left(\text{RF}^{n,m}_{\phi_j(\mathbf{K})[1]}(X_{2\lceil \frac{m}{n}\rceil + 5 - \ell, j}[m+1, n+m]) \oplus X_{2\lceil \frac{m}{n}\rceil + 5 - \ell, j}[1, m]\right)[m-n+1, m].$$

Again, $X_{\ell,i}[1, n] \neq X_{2\lceil \frac{m}{n}\rceil + 5 - \ell, i}[1, n]$ conditioned on $\neg(\text{C-}[\ell-1])$, and thus the values $\left(\text{RF}^{n,m}_{\phi_i(\mathbf{K})[1]}(X_{\ell,i}[1, n])\right)[1, n]$ and $\left(\text{RF}^{n,m}_{\phi_j(\mathbf{K})[1]}(X_{2\lceil \frac{m}{n}\rceil + 5 - \ell, j}[1, n])\right)[m - n + 1, m]$ are independent and uniform. Therefore, the probability of $X_{\ell+1,i}[1, n] = X_{2\lceil \frac{m}{n}\rceil + 4 - \ell, j}[m+1, n+m]$ is $1/2^n$.

Similar reasoning holds for the next $(\ell-1)/2$ equations, except for the last one $X_{\ell+1,i}[1, n] = X_{2\lceil \frac{m}{n}\rceil + 3, j}[m+1, n+m]$, which translates into

$$\left(\text{RF}^{n,m}_{\phi_i(\mathbf{K})[1]}(X_{\ell,i}[1, n]) \oplus X_{\ell,i}[n+1, n+m]\right)[1, n] = X_{2\lceil \frac{m}{n}\rceil + 3, j}[m+1, n+m],$$

and which is clearly $1/2^n$ due to the independence between $\text{RF}^{n,m}_{\phi_i(\mathbf{K})[1]}(X_{\ell,i}[1, n])$ and $X_{2\lceil \frac{m}{n}\rceil + 3, j}[m+1, n+m]$. Summing over the $(\ell+1)/2$ equations, it can be seen that the probability of the 2nd subcondition is $\frac{(\ell+1)}{2^{n+1}}$.

The analyses for the 3rd and 4th subconditions are similar by symmetry, and also give rise to probabilities $\frac{(\ell+1)}{2^{n+1}}$ and $\frac{(\ell-1)}{2^{n+1}}$ resp. By the above, we eventually reach the union bound $2(\ell-1)/2^{n+1} + 2(\ell+1)/2^{n+1} \leq 2\ell/2^n$.

Case 2 : ℓ is even. While being different in details, this case is in general similar to Case 1 by symmetry.

With all the above discussion, the probability that one of the four types of collisions occur with respect to a certain pair of indices (i, j) is at most $2\ell/2^n$. Since the number of such pairs is at most q^2, we have

$$\Pr\left[(\text{C-}[\ell]) \mid \neg(\text{C-}[\ell-1])\right] \leq \frac{2\ell q^2}{2^n}. \tag{7}$$

Conditions (C-$[\lceil \frac{m}{n}\rceil + 1]$) and (C-$[\lceil \frac{m}{n}\rceil + 2]$). Consider (C-$[\lceil \frac{m}{n}\rceil + 1]$) first, and consider any such three indices $i, j \in \{1, ..., q\}$ and $\ell \in \{1, ..., \lceil \frac{m}{n}\rceil\}$. The equality $X_{\ell+1,i}[1, n] = X_{\ell+1,j}[1, n]$ translates into

$$\left(\mathsf{RF}^{n,m}_{\mathsf{Alter}(\phi_i(\mathbf{K}))[\ell]}(X_{\ell,i}[1,n]) \oplus X_{\ell,i}[n+1,n+m]\right)[1,n]$$
$$= \left(\mathsf{RF}^{n,m}_{\mathsf{Alter}(\phi_j(\mathbf{K}))[\ell]}(X_{\ell,j}[1,n]) \oplus X_{\ell,j}[n+1,n+m]\right)[1,n].$$

Since $\left(\mathsf{Alter}(\phi_i(\mathbf{K}))[\ell], X_{\ell,i}[1,n]\right) \neq \left(\mathsf{Alter}(\phi_j(\mathbf{K}))[\ell], X_{\ell,j}[1,n]\right)$, the two values $\mathsf{RF}^{n,m}_{\mathsf{Alter}(\phi_i(\mathbf{K}))[\ell]}(X_{\ell,i}[1,n])$ and $\mathsf{RF}^{n,m}_{\mathsf{Alter}(\phi_j(\mathbf{K}))[\ell]}(X_{\ell,j}[1,n])$ are uniform in $\{0,1\}^m$ and independent. Therefore, the probability to have $X_{\ell+1,i}[1,n] = X_{\ell+1,j}[1,n]$ is $1/2^n$. Summing over the $\binom{q}{2} \cdot \lceil \frac{m}{n} \rceil \leq \frac{q^2}{2} \lceil \frac{m}{n} \rceil$ choices of i, j, ℓ, we reach

$$\Pr\left[(\text{C-}[\lceil \frac{m}{n} \rceil + 1])\right] \leq \frac{\lceil \frac{m}{n} \rceil q^2}{2^{n+1}}. \tag{8}$$

The analysis for $(\text{C-}[\lceil \frac{m}{n} \rceil + 2])$ is similar by symmetry, yielding

$$\Pr\left[(\text{C-}[\lceil \frac{m}{n} \rceil + 2])\right] \leq \frac{\lceil \frac{m}{n} \rceil q^2}{2^{n+1}}. \tag{9}$$

Condition $(\text{C-}[\lceil \frac{m}{n} \rceil + 3])$. Consider any distinct $(\phi_i, X_i, Y_i), (\phi_j, X_j, Y_j) \in \mathcal{Q}$.

We consider the probability to have $\left(\mathsf{Alter}(\phi_i(\mathbf{K}))[\lceil \frac{m}{n} \rceil + 1], X_{\lceil \frac{m}{n} \rceil + 1, i}[1,n]\right) = \left(\mathsf{Alter}(\phi_j(\mathbf{K}))[\lceil \frac{m}{n} \rceil + 1], X_{\lceil \frac{m}{n} \rceil + 1, j}[1,n]\right)$ first. Wlog, assume that $\lceil \frac{m}{n} \rceil$ is even, as the case of $\lceil \frac{m}{n} \rceil$ odd exhibits no essential difference (as shown before). In this case, we have $\mathsf{Alter}(\phi_i(\mathbf{K}))[\lceil \frac{m}{n} \rceil + 1] = \phi_i(\mathbf{K})[1]$ and $\mathsf{Alter}(\phi_j(\mathbf{K}))[\lceil \frac{m}{n} \rceil + 1] = \phi_j(\mathbf{K})[1]$, and the condition is fulfilled only if $\phi_i(\mathbf{K})[1] = \phi_j(\mathbf{K})[1]$. With this in mind, we distinguish two cases.

Case 1 : $\phi_i \neq \phi_j$. Then since τ is good and is claw-free, it holds $\phi_i(\mathbf{K}) \neq \phi_j(\mathbf{K})$, which further implies $\phi_i(\mathbf{K})[2] \neq \phi_j(\mathbf{K})[2]$. By this, the probability to have $X_{\lceil \frac{m}{n} \rceil + 1, i}[1,n] = X_{\lceil \frac{m}{n} \rceil + 1, j}[1,n]$, or to have

$$\left(X_{\lceil \frac{m}{n} \rceil, i}[n+1, n+m] \oplus \mathsf{RF}^{n,m}_{\phi_i(\mathbf{K})[2]}(X_{\lceil \frac{m}{n} \rceil, i}[1,n])\right)[1,n]$$
$$= \left(X_{\lceil \frac{m}{n} \rceil, j}[n+1, n+m] \oplus \mathsf{RF}^{n,m}_{\phi_j(\mathbf{K})[2]}(X_{\lceil \frac{m}{n} \rceil, j}[1,n])\right)[1,n], \tag{10}$$

is $1/2^n$, since $\mathsf{RF}^{n,m}_{\phi_i(\mathbf{K})[2]}$ and $\mathsf{RF}^{n,m}_{\phi_j(\mathbf{K})[2]}$ can be viewed as two independent random functions from $\{0,1\}^n$ to $\{0,1\}^m$.

Case 2 : $\phi_i = \phi_j$. For clearness we let $\phi = \phi_i = \phi_j$. Let $\Delta_1 := X_{1,i} \oplus X_{1,j}$. Since D does not make redundant queries, it has to be $\Delta_1 \neq 0$. We further distinguish two subcases.

- Subcase 2.1: $\Delta_1[1, \lceil \frac{m}{n} \rceil \cdot n] \neq 0$. Then, let $\ell \in \{0, ..., \lceil \frac{m}{n} \rceil - 1\}$ be the smallest index such that $\Delta_1[\ell n + 1, (\ell+1)n] \neq 0$. By construction, this means $X_{\ell+1,i}[1,n] \neq X_{\ell+1,j}[1,n]$. Conditioned on $\neg(\text{C-}[\lceil \frac{m}{n} \rceil + 1])$, this further implies $X_{\ell+2,i}[1,n] \neq X_{\ell+2,j}[1,n], ...,$ and eventually $X_{\lceil \frac{m}{n} \rceil + 1, i}[1,n] \neq X_{\lceil \frac{m}{n} \rceil + 1, j}[1,n]$.

- Subcase 2.2: $\Delta_1[1, \lceil \frac{m}{n} \rceil \cdot n] = 0$. Then it has to be $\Delta_1[\lceil \frac{m}{n} \rceil \cdot n + 1, n + m] \neq 0$, which necessarily implies $X_{\lceil \frac{m}{n} \rceil + 1, i}[1, n] \neq X_{\lceil \frac{m}{n} \rceil + 1, j}[1, n]$ by construction.

Therefore, conditioned on $\neg(\text{C-}[\lceil \frac{m}{n} \rceil + 1])$, it is not possible to have $X_{\lceil \frac{m}{n} \rceil + 1, i}[1, n] = X_{\lceil \frac{m}{n} \rceil + 1, j}[1, n]$ for any two distinct indices (i, j).

The analysis for $(\text{Alter}(\phi_i(\mathbf{K}))[\lceil \frac{m}{n} \rceil + 2], X_{\lceil \frac{m}{n} \rceil + 3, i}[m + 1, n + m]) = (\text{Alter}(\phi_j(\mathbf{K}))[\lceil \frac{m}{n} \rceil + 2], X_{\lceil \frac{m}{n} \rceil + 3, j}[m + 1, n + m])$ is similar by symmetry. More concretely, for any such two triples $(\phi_i, X_i, Y_i), (\phi_j, X_j, Y_j)$ such that $\phi_i(\mathbf{K})[2] = \phi_j(\mathbf{K})[2]$, we have:

- If $\phi_i \neq \phi_j$, then it holds $\phi_i(\mathbf{K})[1] \neq \phi_j(\mathbf{K})[1]$ by the claw-freeness and by $\phi_i(\mathbf{K})[2] = \phi_j(\mathbf{K})[2]$, and thus the probability to have $X_{\lceil \frac{m}{n} \rceil + 3, i}[m + 1, n + m] = X_{\lceil \frac{m}{n} \rceil + 3, j}[m + 1, n + m]$ or

$$\left(X_{\lceil \frac{m}{n} \rceil + 4, i}[1, m] \oplus \text{RF}^{n,m}_{\phi_i(\mathbf{K})[1]}(X_{\lceil \frac{m}{n} \rceil + 4, i}[m + 1, n + m]) \right)[m - n + 1, m]$$
$$= \left(X_{\lceil \frac{m}{n} \rceil + 4, j}[1, m] \oplus \text{RF}^{n,m}_{\phi_j(\mathbf{K})[1]}(X_{\lceil \frac{m}{n} \rceil + 4, j}[m + 1, n + m]) \right)[m - n + 1, m] \quad (11)$$

is $1/2^n$ due to the independence between $\text{RF}^{n,m}_{\phi_i(\mathbf{K})[1]}$ and $\text{RF}^{n,m}_{\phi_j(\mathbf{K})[1]}$.
- If $\phi_i = \phi_j$, then it is not possible to have $X_{\lceil \frac{m}{n} \rceil + 3, i}[m + 1, n + m] = X_{\lceil \frac{m}{n} \rceil + 3, j}[m + 1, n + m]$ conditioned on $\neg(\text{C-}[\lceil \frac{m}{n} \rceil + 2])$.

In all, for each pair (i, j) of distinct indices, the probability to have $X_{\lceil \frac{m}{n} \rceil + 1, i}[1, n] = X_{\lceil \frac{m}{n} \rceil + 1, j}[1, n]$ or $X_{\lceil \frac{m}{n} \rceil + 3, i}[m + 1, n + m] = X_{\lceil \frac{m}{n} \rceil + 3, j}[m + 1, n + m]$ is no larger than $2/2^n$. Taking a union bound for the $\binom{q}{2} \leq q^2/2$ choices of (i, j) yields

$$\Pr\left[(\text{C-}[\lceil \frac{m}{n} \rceil + 3]) \mid \neg(\text{C-}[1]) \wedge \ldots \wedge \neg(\text{C-}[\lceil \frac{m}{n} \rceil + 2]) \right] \leq \frac{q^2}{2^n}. \quad (12)$$

Gathering Eqs. (7), (8), (9), and (12), we reach

$$\Pr\left[\text{BadF}(\text{RF}^{n,m}) \right]$$
$$\leq \left(\sum_{\ell = 1, \ldots, \lceil \frac{m}{n} \rceil} \Pr\left[(\text{C-}[\ell]) \mid \neg(\text{C-}[\ell - 1]) \right] \right) + \Pr\left[(\text{C-}[\lceil \frac{m}{n} \rceil + 1]) \right] + \Pr\left[(\text{C-}[\lceil \frac{m}{n} \rceil + 2]) \right]$$
$$+ \Pr\left[(\text{C-}[\lceil \frac{m}{n} \rceil + 3]) \mid \neg(\text{C-}[1]) \wedge \ldots \wedge \neg(\text{C-}[\lceil \frac{m}{n} \rceil + 2]) \right]$$
$$\leq \left(\sum_{\ell = 1, \ldots, \lceil \frac{m}{n} \rceil} \frac{2\ell q^2}{2^n} \right) + \frac{\lceil \frac{m}{n} \rceil q^2}{2^{n+1}} + \frac{\lceil \frac{m}{n} \rceil q^2}{2^{n+1}} + \frac{q^2}{2^n} \leq \frac{(\lceil \frac{m}{n} \rceil + 1)^2 q^2}{2^n}. \quad (13)$$

Completing the Proof. Consider any good transcript $\tau = (\mathcal{Q}, \mathbf{K})$, where $\mathcal{Q} = ((\phi_1, X_1, Y_1), \ldots, (\phi_q, X_q, Y_q))$. With the values defined in Eqs. (5) and (6), it can be seen that, the event $\mathsf{RK}[\mathsf{EFN}_{\mathsf{Alter}(\mathbf{K})}^{\mathsf{RF}^{n,m},2\lceil\frac{m}{n}\rceil+2}] \vdash \mathcal{Q}$ is equivalent to $2q$ equations as follows.

$$\mathsf{RF}_{\phi_i(\mathbf{K})[b_1]}^{n,m}\big(X_{\lceil\frac{m}{n}\rceil+1,i}[1,n]\big) = \Big(X_{\lceil\frac{m}{n}\rceil+1,i}[n+1,2n] \oplus X_{\lceil\frac{m}{n}\rceil+3,i}[m+1,n+m]\Big)$$

$$\Big\| \ \big(X_{\lceil\frac{m}{n}\rceil+1,i}[2n+1,n+m] \oplus X_{\lceil\frac{m}{n}\rceil+3,i}[1,m-n]$$

$$\oplus \ \mathsf{RF}_{\phi_i(\mathbf{K})[b_2]}^{n,m}\big(X_{\lceil\frac{m}{n}\rceil+3,i}[m+1,n+m]\big)[1,m-n]\Big) \quad \text{for} \quad i=1,...,q,$$
$$(14)$$

$$\mathsf{RF}_{\phi_i(\mathbf{K})[b_2]}^{n,m}\big(X_{\lceil\frac{m}{n}\rceil+3,i}[m+1,n+m]\big)[m-n+1,m]$$

$$= \Big(X_{\lceil\frac{m}{n}\rceil+1,i}[1,n] \oplus X_{\lceil\frac{m}{n}\rceil+3,i}[m-n+1,m]\Big) \quad \text{for} \quad i=1,...,q, \qquad (15)$$

where $b_1 = 2, b_2 = 1$ when $\lceil\frac{m}{n}\rceil$ is odd, and $b_1 = 1, b_2 = 2$ when $\lceil\frac{m}{n}\rceil$ is even. We refer to Fig. 2 for illustration.

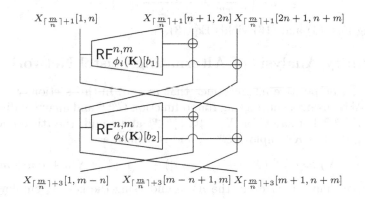

Fig. 2. The middle $\lceil\frac{m}{n}\rceil+1$ th and $\lceil\frac{m}{n}\rceil+2$ th rounds of $\mathsf{EFN}_{\mathsf{Alter}(\mathbf{K})}^{\mathsf{RF}^{n,m},2\lceil\frac{m}{n}\rceil+2}$.

We remark that, the equation on $\mathsf{RF}_{\phi_i(\mathbf{K})[b_1]}^{n,m}\big(X_{\lceil\frac{m}{n}\rceil+1,i}[1,n]\big)$ depends on the $m-n$ output bits $\mathsf{RF}_{\phi_i(\mathbf{K})[b_2]}^{n,m}\big(X_{\lceil\frac{m}{n}\rceil+3,i}[m+1,n+m]\big)[1,m-n]$. Since the first $m-n$ bits and the last n bits of the random function value $\mathsf{RF}_{\phi_i(\mathbf{K})[b_2]}^{n,m}\big(X_{\lceil\frac{m}{n}\rceil+3,i}[m+1,n+m]\big)$ are independent, the probability to have Eqs. (14) and (15) is $\frac{1}{2^m} \times \frac{1}{2^n} = \frac{1}{2^{n+m}}$ for every $i \in \{1,...,q\}$.

Then, for any $\mathsf{RF}^{n,m}$, as long as $\mathsf{BadF}(\mathsf{RF}^{n,m})$ is not fulfilled, the above random variables $\{\mathsf{RF}_{\phi_i(\mathbf{K})[b_1]}^{n,m}\big(X_{\lceil\frac{m}{n}\rceil+1,i}[1,n]\big)\}_{i=1,...,q}$ and $\{\mathsf{RF}_{\phi_i(\mathbf{K})[b_2]}^{n,m}\big(X_{\lceil\frac{m}{n}\rceil+3,i}[m+1,n+m]\big)[m-n+1,m]\}_{i=1,...,q}$ are $2q$ distinct and independent ones, as otherwise (C-$[\lceil\frac{m}{n}\rceil+3]$) is fulfilled. Furthermore, these random variables are not affected by the randomness in $\mathsf{RF}^{n,m}$ that determines the satisfiability of $\mathsf{BadF}(\mathsf{RF}^{n,m})$ (i.e., the values $\{\mathsf{RF}_{\mathsf{Alter}(\phi_i(\mathbf{K}))[\ell]}^{n,m}\big(X_{\ell,i}[1,n]\big)\}_{i\in\{1,...,q\},\ell\in\{1,...,\lceil\frac{m}{n}\rceil,\lceil\frac{m}{n}\rceil+3,...,2\lceil\frac{m}{n}\rceil+2\}}$), as otherwise (C-$[\lceil\frac{m}{n}\rceil]$) is fulfilled. Therefore, by Eq. (13), the real world probability has

$$\Pr\left[\mathrm{RK}[\mathrm{EFN}_{\mathsf{Alter}(\mathbf{K})}^{\mathsf{RF}^{n,m},2\lceil\frac{m}{n}\rceil+2}] \vdash \mathcal{Q}\right]$$

$$\geq \Pr\left[\mathrm{RK}[\mathrm{EFN}_{\mathsf{Alter}(\mathbf{K})}^{\mathsf{RF}^{n,m},2\lceil\frac{m}{n}\rceil+2}] \vdash \mathcal{Q} \wedge \neg\mathsf{BadF}(\mathsf{RF}^{n,m})\right]$$

$$= \Pr\left[\mathrm{RK}[\mathrm{EFN}_{\mathsf{Alter}(\mathbf{K})}^{\mathsf{RF}^{n,m},2\lceil\frac{m}{n}\rceil+2}] \vdash \mathcal{Q} \mid \neg\mathsf{BadF}(\mathsf{RF}^{n,m})\right] \cdot \left(1 - \Pr\left[\mathsf{BadF}(\mathsf{RF}^{n,m})\right]\right)$$

$$\geq \left(1 - \frac{(\lceil\frac{m}{n}\rceil+1)^2 q^2}{2^n}\right) \cdot \left(\frac{1}{2^{n+m}}\right)^q$$

In all, we have the probability

$$\frac{\Pr\left[T_{\mathrm{re}} = \tau\right]}{\Pr\left[T_{\mathrm{id}} = \tau\right]} \geq \left(1 - \frac{(\lceil\frac{m}{n}\rceil+1)^2 q^2}{2^n}\right) \cdot \left(\frac{1}{2^{n+m}}\right)^q \Big/ \left(\frac{1}{2^{n+m}-q}\right)^q$$

$$\geq \left(1 - \frac{q}{2^{n+m}}\right)^q \cdot \left(1 - \frac{(\lceil\frac{m}{n}\rceil+1)^2 q^2}{2^n}\right)$$

$$\geq 1 - \left(\frac{q^2}{2^{n+m}} + \frac{(\lceil\frac{m}{n}\rceil+1)^2 q^2}{2^n}\right). \tag{16}$$

Gathering Eqs. (4) and (16) yields Eq. (3).

4   Security Analysis of Alternating Feistel Networks

Let m and n be positive integers such that $m \geq n$. In this section, we will first consider AFNs using a contracting round function $G^{m,n}$ and an expanding round function $F^{n,m}$.[6] Formally, for $X \in \{0,1\}^{n+m}$ and i odd, the ith round of the AFN using the key K_i employs $G^{m,n}$, and is defined as

$$\Psi^{G_{K_i}^{m,n}}(X) := G_{K_i}^{m,n}\big(X[n+1,n+m]\big) \oplus X[1,n] \parallel X[n+1,n+m].$$

On the other hand, for i even, the ith round using the key K_i employs $F^{n,m}$, and is defined as

$$\Psi^{F_{K_i}^{n,m}}(X) := X[1,n] \parallel F_{K_i}^{n,m}\big(X[1,n]\big) \oplus X[n+1,n+m].$$

Then, the t-round AFN is a composition of such t rounds.

As mentioned in the introduction, 4-round AFN with the alternating key assignment Alter is always RKA secure, regardless of the ratio m/n. Formally,

Theorem 2. *For any distinguisher D making at most q queries to the oracles* $\mathrm{RK}[\mathrm{AFN}_{\mathsf{Alter}(\mathbf{K})}^{G^{m,n},F^{n,m},4}]$ *and* $\mathrm{RK}[\mathrm{AFN}_{\mathsf{Alter}(\mathbf{K})}^{G^{m,n},F^{n,m},4}]^{-1}$ *in total, it holds*

$$\mathbf{Adv}_{\mathrm{AFN}_{\mathsf{Alter}(\mathbf{K})}^{G^{m,n},F^{n,m},4}}^{\Phi\text{-rka}[1]}(D) \leq \mathbf{Adv}_{G^{m,n}}^{\Phi\text{-rka}[1]}(D) + \mathbf{Adv}_{F^{n,m}}^{\Phi\text{-rka}[1]}(D) + \mathbf{Adv}_{\Phi}^{cf}(D)$$

$$+ \frac{q^2}{2^{n+m}} + \frac{3q^2}{2^n}. \tag{17}$$

---

[6] We stress that $G^{m,n}$ and $F^{n,m}$ must be "independent", in the sense that $(G_{K_1}^{m,n}, F_{K_2}^{n,m})$ using independent keys K_1, K_2 is indistinguishable from a pair of independent ideal keyed functions $(\mathsf{RG}^{m,n}, \mathsf{RF}^{n,m})$. For example, $G^{m,n}$ and $F^{n,m}$ cannot be built from the same primitive such as the AES.

The proof flow is similar to Theorem 1. We also start with a generic two-step standard-to-ideal reduction. In the first step, we replace the keyed contracting round function $G^{m,n}$ with an ideal keyed contracting function $\mathsf{RG}^{m,n} : \mathcal{K} \times \{0,1\}^m \to \{0,1\}^n$. This clearly introduces a gap of at most $\mathbf{Adv}_{G^{m,n}}^{\Phi\text{-rka}[1]}(D)$. We then replace the expanding round function $F^{n,m}$ with the ideal $\mathsf{RF}^{n,m} : \mathcal{K} \times \{0,1\}^n \to \{0,1\}^m$, with an additional gap of $\mathbf{Adv}_{F^{n,m}}^{\Phi\text{-rka}[1]}(D)$. As discussed in the introduction, the independence between the two involved keys K_1 and K_2 is crucial for this reduction.

Then, we focus on analyzing $\mathbf{Adv}_{\mathsf{AFN}_{\mathsf{Alter}(\mathbf{K})}^{\mathsf{RG}^{m,n},\mathsf{RF}^{n,m},4}}^{\Phi\text{-rka}[1]}(D)$ for the idealized AFN. We also use the H-coefficient technique, and follow the same (though simpler) flow as Theorem 1.

4.1 Bad Transcripts

An attainable transcript $\tau = (\mathcal{Q}, \mathbf{K})$ is *bad*, if a claw exists τ, i.e., there exist two triples (ϕ_1, X_1, Y_1) and (ϕ_2, X_2, Y_2) in $\mathcal{Q}$ such that $\phi_1 \neq \phi_2$, while $\phi_1(\mathbf{K}) = \phi_2(\mathbf{K})$. Otherwise we say τ is *good*. And it holds

$$\Pr[T_{\mathrm{id}} \in \mathcal{T}_{\mathrm{bad}}] \leq \mathbf{Adv}_\Phi^{\mathsf{cf}}(D). \tag{18}$$

Compared with Sect. 3.1, it is natural to ask why switch-freeness turns useless here. Informally, switch-freeness prevents collisions between keys used in different rounds, i.e., $\phi_i(\mathbf{K})[1] = \phi_j(\mathbf{K})[2]$ for some (ϕ_i, X_i, Y_i) and (ϕ_j, X_j, Y_j). But such a collision is harmless here due to the *different* round functions in use.

4.2 Analyzing Good Transcripts

Fix a good transcript τ. The ideal world probability simply follows from Eq. (1), and it remains to analyze $\Pr[\mathsf{RK}[\mathsf{AFN}_{\mathsf{Alter}(\mathbf{K})}^{\mathsf{RG}^{m,n},\mathsf{RF}^{n,m},4}] \vdash \mathcal{Q}]$. Similarly to Sect. 3.2, we define a "bad predicate" $\mathsf{BadF}(\mathsf{RG}^{m,n}, \mathsf{RF}^{n,m})$ on $\mathsf{RG}^{m,n}$ and $\mathsf{RF}^{n,m}$, such that once $\mathsf{BadF}(\mathsf{RG}^{m,n}, \mathsf{RF}^{n,m})$ is not fulfilled, the event $T_{\mathrm{re}} = \tau$ is equivalent to $\mathsf{RG}^{m,n}$ and $\mathsf{RF}^{n,m}$ satisfying $2q$ distinct equations, the probability of which is close to the ideal world probability. This will enable the argument.

In detail, given a pair of ideal keyed functions $(\mathsf{RG}^{m,n}, \mathsf{RF}^{n,m})$, for every $(\phi_i, X_i, Y_i) \in \tau$, define

$$X_{1,i} := X_i, \quad X_{5,i} := Y_i,$$
$$X_{2,i} := X_{1,i}[1,n] \oplus \mathsf{RG}_{\phi_i(\mathbf{K})[1]}^{m,n}\big(X_{1,i}[n+1, m+n]\big) \,\|\, X_{1,i}[n+1, m+n],$$
$$X_{4,i} := X_{5,i}[1,n] \,\|\, X_{5,i}[n+1, m+n] \oplus \mathsf{RF}_{\phi_i(\mathbf{K})[2]}^{n,m}\big(X_{5,i}[1,n]\big). \tag{19}$$

Bad Predicate. Informally, the conditions capture "unnecessary" collisions among calls to the round functions $\mathsf{RG}^{m,n}$ and $\mathsf{RF}^{n,m}$ while evaluating the q queries.

Definition 3. *Given a pair of random functions* $(\mathsf{RG}^{m,n}, \mathsf{RF}^{n,m})$, *the predicate* $\mathsf{BadF}(\mathsf{RG}^{m,n}, \mathsf{RF}^{n,m})$ *is fulfilled, if any of the following four conditions is fulfilled.*

(C-1) There exists two indices $i, j \in \{1, ..., q\}$ *such that*
$$(\phi_i(\mathbf{K})[2], X_{2,i}[1, n]) = (\phi_j(\mathbf{K})[2], X_{5,j}[1, n]).$$
(C-2) There exists two indices $i, j \in \{1, ..., q\}$ *such that*
$$(\phi_i(\mathbf{K})[1], X_{4,i}[n + 1, n + m]) = (\phi_j(\mathbf{K})[1], X_{1,j}[n + 1, n + m]).$$
(C-3) There exists two distinct indices $i, j \in \{1, ..., q\}$ *such that*
$$(\phi_i(\mathbf{K})[2], X_{2,i}[1, n]) = (\phi_j(\mathbf{K})[2], X_{2,j}[1, n]).$$
(C-4) There exists two distinct indices $i, j \in \{1, ..., q\}$ *such that*
$$(\phi_i(\mathbf{K})[1], X_{4,i}[n + 1, n + m] = (\phi_j(\mathbf{K})[1], X_{4,j}[n + 1, n + m]).$$

Consider the conditions in turn. First, for (C-1), note that $X_{2,i}[1, n] = X_{1,i}[1, n] \oplus \mathsf{RG}^{m,n}_{\phi_i(\mathbf{K})[1]}(X_{1,i}[n + 1, m + n])$, where $\mathsf{RG}^{m,n}_{\phi_i(\mathbf{K})[1]}(X_{1,i}[n + 1, m + n])$ is uniformly distributed and independent of $X_{5,j}[1, n]$ which is specified in τ. Therefore, the probability to have $X_{2,i}[1, n] = X_{5,j}[1, n]$ for any i, j is $1/2^n$, and thus $\Pr[(\text{C-1})] \leq q^2/2^n$. Similarly by symmetry, $X_{4,i}[n + 1, n + m] = X_{5,i}[n + 1, m + n] \oplus \mathsf{RF}^{n,m}_{\phi_i(\mathbf{K})[2]}(X_{5,i}[1, n])$, which means the probability to have $X_{4,i}[n + 1, n + m] = X_{1,j}[n + 1, n + m]$ is $1/2^m$, and further $\Pr[(\text{C-2})] \leq q^2/2^m$.

The condition (C-3) is slightly more cumbersome. Consider any such two triples $(\phi_i, X_i, Y_i), (\phi_j, X_j, Y_j) \in \mathcal{Q}$. The condition is fulfilled only if $\phi_i(\mathbf{K})[2] = \phi_j(\mathbf{K})[2]$. With this in mind, we distinguish two cases.

Case 1 : $\phi_i \neq \phi_j$. Then since τ is good and is claw-free, it holds $\phi_i(\mathbf{K}) \neq \phi_j(\mathbf{K})$, which further implies $\phi_i(\mathbf{K})[1] \neq \phi_j(\mathbf{K})[1]$. By this, the probability to have $X_{2,i}[1, n] = X_{2,j}[1, n]$, or to have

$$X_{1,i}[1, n] \oplus \mathsf{RG}^{m,n}_{\phi_i(\mathbf{K})[1]}(X_{1,i}[n + 1, m + n])$$
$$= X_{1,j}[1, n] \oplus \mathsf{RG}^{m,n}_{\phi_j(\mathbf{K})[1]}(X_{1,j}[n + 1, m + n]), \tag{20}$$

is $1/2^n$, since $\mathsf{RG}^{m,n}_{\phi_i(\mathbf{K})[1]}$ and $\mathsf{RG}^{m,n}_{\phi_j(\mathbf{K})[1]}$ can be viewed as two independent random functions from $\{0, 1\}^m$ to $\{0, 1\}^n$.

Case 2 : $\phi_i = \phi_j$. For clearness we let $\phi = \phi_i = \phi_j$. Then we further distinguish two subcases.

- Subcase 2.1: $X_{1,i}[n + 1, m + n] \neq X_{1,j}[n + 1, m + n]$. Then the probability to have $X_{2,i}[1, n] = X_{2,j}[1, n]$, or to have Eq. (20), is $1/2^n$, since $\mathsf{RG}^{m,n}_{\phi(\mathbf{K})[1]}(X_{1,i}[n + 1, m + n])$ and $\mathsf{RG}^{m,n}_{\phi(\mathbf{K})[1]}(X_{1,j}[n + 1, m + n])$ are independent and uniform in $\{0, 1\}^n$;
- Subcase 2.2: $X_{1,i}[n+1, m+n] = X_{1,j}[n+1, m+n]$. Then since the distinguisher does not make redundant queries, it has to be $X_{1,i}[1, n] \neq X_{1,j}[1, n]$, which means it is impossible to have $X_{2,i}[1, n] = X_{2,j}[1, n]$ or Eq. (20).

Therefore, for each pair (i, j) of indices, the probability to have $X_{2,i}[1, n] = X_{2,j}[1, n]$ is no larger than $1/2^n$. Summing over the $\binom{q}{2} \leq q^2/2$ choices, we reach $\Pr[(\text{C-3})] \leq q^2/2^{n+1}$.

The analysis for (C-4) is similar by symmetry, yielding $\Pr[(\text{C-4})] \leq q^2/2^{m+1}$. Summing over the four probabilities and using $n \leq m$, we reach

$$\Pr\left[\mathsf{BadF}(\mathsf{RG}^{m,n}, \mathsf{RF}^{n,m})\right] \leq \frac{q^2}{2^n} + \frac{q^2}{2^m} + \frac{q^2}{2^{n+1}} + \frac{q^2}{2^{m+1}} \leq \frac{3q^2}{2^n}. \tag{21}$$

Completing the Proof. Consider any good transcript $\tau = (\mathcal{Q}, \mathbf{K})$, where $\mathcal{Q} = ((\phi_1, X_1, Y_1), ..., (\phi_q, X_q, Y_q))$. With the values defined in Eq. (19), it can be seen that, the event $\mathsf{RK}[\mathsf{AFN}_{\mathsf{Alter}(\mathbf{K})}^{\mathsf{RG}^{m,n}, \mathsf{RF}^{n,m}, 4}] \vdash \mathcal{Q}$ is equivalent to $2q$ equations as follows.

$$\mathsf{RF}_{\phi_i(\mathbf{K})[2]}^{n,m}(X_{2,i}[1, n]) = X_{2,i}[n+1, n+m] \oplus X_{4,i}[n+1, n+m] \text{ for } i = 1, ..., q,$$
$$\mathsf{RG}_{\phi_i(\mathbf{K})[1]}^{m,n}(X_{4,i}[n+1, n+m]) = X_{2,i}[1, n] \oplus X_{4,i}[1, n] \text{ for } i = 1, ..., q.$$

For any $\mathsf{RG}^{m,n}$ and $\mathsf{RF}^{n,m}$, as long as $\mathsf{BadF}(\mathsf{RG}^{m,n}, \mathsf{RF}^{n,m})$ is not fulfilled, the above random variables $\{\mathsf{RF}_{\phi_i(\mathbf{K})[2]}^{n,m}(X_{2,i}[1, n])\}_{i=1,...,q}$ are q distinct ones, and $\{\mathsf{RG}_{\phi_i(\mathbf{K})[1]}^{m,n}(X_{4,i}[n+1, n+m])\}_{i=1,...,q}$ are also distinct, as otherwise either (C-3) or (C-4) will be fulfilled. Moreover, these random variables are not affected by the randomness in $\mathsf{RG}^{m,n}$ and $\mathsf{RF}^{n,m}$ that determines the satisfiability of $\mathsf{BadF}(\mathsf{RG}^{m,n}, \mathsf{RF}^{n,m})$ (i.e., the values $\{\mathsf{RG}_{\phi_i(\mathbf{K})[1]}^{m,n}(X_{1,i}[n+1, n+m])\}_{i=1,...,q}$ and $\{\mathsf{RF}_{\phi_i(\mathbf{K})[2]}^{n,m}(X_{5,i}[1, n])\}_{i=1,...,q}$), as otherwise either (C-1) or (C-2) will be fulfilled. Therefore, by Eq. (21), we have

$$\Pr\left[\mathsf{RK}[\mathsf{AFN}_{\mathsf{Alter}(\mathbf{K})}^{\mathsf{RG}^{m,n}, \mathsf{RF}^{n,m}, 4}] \vdash \mathcal{Q}\right]$$
$$\geq \Pr\left[\mathsf{RK}[\mathsf{AFN}_{\mathsf{Alter}(\mathbf{K})}^{\mathsf{RG}^{m,n}, \mathsf{RF}^{n,m}, 4}] \vdash \mathcal{Q} \mid \neg\mathsf{BadF}(\mathsf{RG}^{m,n}, \mathsf{RF}^{n,m})\right]$$
$$\cdot \left(1 - \Pr\left[\mathsf{BadF}(\mathsf{RG}^{m,n}, \mathsf{RF}^{n,m})\right]\right)$$
$$\geq \left(\frac{1}{2^{n+m}}\right)^q \cdot \left(1 - \frac{3q^2}{2^n}\right).$$

With this, and further using Eqs. (1) and (2), we reach

$$\frac{\Pr[T_{\mathrm{re}} = \tau]}{\Pr[T_{\mathrm{id}} = \tau]} \geq \left(\frac{1}{2^{n+m}}\right)^q \cdot \left(1 - \frac{3q^2}{2^n}\right) \Big/ \left(\frac{1}{2^{n+m} - q}\right)^q$$
$$\geq \left(1 - \frac{q}{2^{n+m}}\right)^q \cdot \left(1 - \frac{3q^2}{2^n}\right) \geq 1 - \left(\frac{q^2}{2^{n+m}} + \frac{3q^2}{2^n}\right). \tag{22}$$

Gathering Eqs. (18) and (22) yields Eq. (17).

4.3 AFN Using a Tweakable Round Function and Single Key

While the standard-to-ideal reduction couldn't handle two different functions that use the same secret key, the situation could be remedied by using a *tweakable round function*. In detail, consider a tweakable round function $TF^{m,n}$ that has a tweak input of 1 bit, such that $TF^{m,n}(0, \cdot)$ maps $(K, x) \in \mathcal{K} \times \{0,1\}^m$ to $x \in \{0,1\}^n$ and $TF^{m,n}(1, \cdot)$ maps $(K, x) \in \mathcal{K} \times \{0,1\}^n$ to $x \in \{0,1\}^m$. This is quite different from the standard notion of tweakable blockciphers, as the domain of the standard formalism typically don't vary with the tweak. Here, however, depending on whether the tweak input is 0 or 1, the round function varies between contracting and expanding.

The security of such tweakable round function $TF^{m,n}$ shall be measured by its deviation from the ideal counterpart $\mathsf{RTF}^{m,n}$ that is uniformly picked from all the functions that have exactly the same signature as $TF^{m,n}$. Note that this means $\mathsf{RTF}^{m,n}(0, \cdot)$ and $\mathsf{RTF}^{m,n}(1, \cdot)$ are *independent* ideal keyed functions. Further define

$$\mathsf{Iden}(K) = (K_{i_1}, ..., K_{i_t}), \text{ where } K_{i_1} = ... = K_{i_t} = K.$$

Now, for the 4-round AFN using $TF^{m,n}$ as the round function and identical round key, a RKA security proof is possible.

Corollary 1. *For any distinguisher D making at most q queries to* $\mathsf{RK}[\mathsf{AFN}_{\mathsf{Iden}(K)}^{TF^{m,n},4}]$ *and* $\mathsf{RK}[\mathsf{AFN}_{\mathsf{Iden}(K)}^{TF^{m,n},4}]^{-1}$ *in total, it holds*

$$\mathbf{Adv}_{\mathsf{AFN}_{\mathsf{Iden}(K)}^{TF^{m,n},4}}^{\Phi\text{-rka}[1]}(D) \leq \mathbf{Adv}_{TF^{m,n}}^{\Phi\text{-rka}[1]}(D) + \mathbf{Adv}_{\Phi}^{cf}(D) + \frac{q^2}{2^{n+m}} + \frac{3q^2}{2^n}, \quad (23)$$

where $\mathbf{Adv}_{TF^{m,n}}^{\Phi\text{-rka}[1]}(D) =$

$$\left| \Pr_K \left[D^{\mathsf{RK}[TF_K^{m,n}], \mathsf{RK}[\mathsf{RTF}_K^{m,n}]^{-1}} = 1 \right] - \Pr_{K,\mathsf{RTF}} \left[D^{\mathsf{RK}[\mathsf{RTF}_K^{m,n}], \mathsf{RK}[\mathsf{RTF}_K^{m,n}]^{-1}} = 1 \right] \right|.$$

Proof (Sketch). The proof turns possible simply because a single standard-to-ideal reduction already suffices to turn $\mathsf{AFN}_{\mathsf{Iden}(K)}^{TF^{m,n},4}$ into the ideal $\mathsf{AFN}_{\mathsf{Iden}(K)}^{\mathsf{RTF}^{m,n},4}$. The subsequent analysis for $\mathbf{Adv}_{\mathsf{AFN}_{\mathsf{Iden}(K)}^{\mathsf{RTF}^{m,n},4}}^{\Phi\text{-rka}[1]}(D)$ basically follows the previous for $\mathbf{Adv}_{\mathsf{AFN}_{\mathsf{Iden}(K)}^{\mathsf{RG}^{m,n},\mathsf{RF}^{n,m},4}}^{\Phi\text{-rka}[1]}(D)$, and we sketch the crucial points below. Concretely, the definition and probability of bad transcripts here are the same as Sect. 4.1.

Whereas the definition of $\mathsf{BadF}(\mathsf{RTF}^{m,n})$ is a slight modification of Definition 3 as follows.

Definition 4. *Given a tweakable function $\mathsf{RTF}^{m,n}$, the predicate $\mathsf{BadF}(\mathsf{RTF}^{m,n})$ is fulfilled, if any of the following four conditions is fulfilled.*

(C-1) There exists two indices $i, j \in \{1, ..., q\}$ such that
  $(\phi_i(K), X_{2,i}[1, n]) = (\phi_j(K), X_{5,j}[1, n]).$

(C-2) There exists two indices $i, j \in \{1, ..., q\}$ such that
$$(\phi_i(K), X_{4,i}[n + 1, n + m]) = (\phi_j(K), X_{1,j}[n + 1, n + m]).$$
(C-3) There exists two distinct indices $i, j \in \{1, ..., q\}$ such that
$$(\phi_i(K), X_{2,i}[1, n]) = (\phi_j(K), X_{2,j}[1, n]).$$
(C-4) There exists two distinct indices $i, j \in \{1, ..., q\}$ such that
$$(\phi_i(K), X_{4,i}[n + 1, n + m] = (\phi_j(K), X_{4,j}[n + 1, n + m]).$$

The analyses for the conditions simply exclude the case of $\phi_i \neq \phi_j$, which implies $\phi_i(K) \neq \phi_j(K)$ due to claw-freeness and excludes the possibility of collisions. Anyway, the bound $\Pr[\mathsf{BadF}(\mathsf{RTF}^{m,n})] \leq 3q^2/2^n$ remains, and the subsequent analysis just follows. $\qquad\square$

5 Conclusion

We study provable related-key security (RKA security) of expanding Feistel networks and alternating Feistel networks. For the former built upon a round function $F : \mathcal{K} \times \{0,1\}^n \to \{0,1\}^m$, we prove that $2\lceil \frac{m}{n} \rceil + 2$ rounds with the alternating key assignment suffice for RKA security; for the latter that alternate round functions $F : \mathcal{K} \times \{0,1\}^n \to \{0,1\}^m$ and $G : \mathcal{K} \times \{0,1\}^m \to \{0,1\}^n$, we prove that 4 rounds with the alternating key assignment suffice. These complete the picture of provable RKA security of generalized Feistel networks, and provide further insights into the NIST standards FF1 and FF3.

Provable security of EFNs is limited by the input size of F. On the other hand, provable security of AFNs is upper bounded by G. We thus leave beyond n-bit RKA security of AFNs as an open question.

Acknowledgments. This work was partly supported by the Program of Qilu Young Scholars (Grant No. 61580089963177) of Shandong University, the National Natural Science Foundation of China (Grant No. 62002202), the National Key Research and Development Project under Grant No.2018YFA0704702, and the Shandong Nature Science Foundation of China (Grant No. ZR2020ZD02, ZR2020MF053).

References

1. Abdalla, M., Benhamouda, F., Passelègue, A., Paterson, K.G.: Related-key security for pseudorandom functions beyond the linear barrier. In: Garay, J.A., Gennaro, R. (eds.) CRYPTO 2014. LNCS, vol. 8616, pp. 77–94. Springer, Heidelberg (2014). https://doi.org/10.1007/978-3-662-44371-2_5
2. Anderson, R., Biham, E.: Two practical and provably secure block ciphers: BEAR and LION. In: Gollmann, D. (ed.) FSE 1996. LNCS, vol. 1039, pp. 113–120. Springer, Heidelberg (1996). https://doi.org/10.1007/3-540-60865-6_48
3. Anderson, R.J., Kuhn, M.G.: Low cost attacks on tamper resistant devices. In: Security Protocols, 5th International Workshop, Paris, France, April 7–9, 1997, Proceedings, pp. 125–136 (1997). https://doi.org/10.1007/BFb0028165
4. Banik, S., et al.: Midori: a block cipher for low energy. In: Iwata, T., Cheon, J.H. (eds.) ASIACRYPT 2015. LNCS, vol. 9453, pp. 411–436. Springer, Heidelberg (2015). https://doi.org/10.1007/978-3-662-48800-3_17

5. Barbosa, M., Farshim, P.: The related-key analysis of Feistel constructions. In: Cid, C., Rechberger, C. (eds.) FSE 2014. LNCS, vol. 8540, pp. 265–284. Springer, Heidelberg (2015). https://doi.org/10.1007/978-3-662-46706-0_14

6. Bellare, M., Cash, D.: Pseudorandom functions and permutations provably secure against related-key attacks. In: Rabin, T. (ed.) CRYPTO 2010. LNCS, vol. 6223, pp. 666–684. Springer, Heidelberg (2010). https://doi.org/10.1007/978-3-642-14623-7_36

7. Bellare, M., Kohno, T.: A theoretical treatment of related-key attacks: RKA-PRPs, RKA-PRFs, and applications. In: Biham, E. (ed.) EUROCRYPT 2003. LNCS, vol. 2656, pp. 491–506. Springer, Heidelberg (2003). https://doi.org/10.1007/3-540-39200-9_31

8. Bellare, M., Ristenpart, T., Rogaway, P., Stegers, T.: Format-preserving encryption. In: Jacobson, M.J., Rijmen, V., Safavi-Naini, R. (eds.) SAC 2009. LNCS, vol. 5867, pp. 295–312. Springer, Heidelberg (2009). https://doi.org/10.1007/978-3-642-05445-7_19

9. Biham, E.: New types of cryptanalytic attacks using related keys. J. Cryptol. **7**(4), 229–246 (1994). https://doi.org/10.1007/BF00203965

10. Biryukov, A., Dunkelman, O., Keller, N., Khovratovich, D., Shamir, A.: Key recovery attacks of practical complexity on AES-256 variants with up to 10 rounds. In: Gilbert, H. (ed.) EUROCRYPT 2010. LNCS, vol. 6110, pp. 299–319. Springer, Heidelberg (2010). https://doi.org/10.1007/978-3-642-13190-5_15

11. Biryukov, A., Wagner, D.: Slide attacks. In: Knudsen, L. (ed.) FSE 1999. LNCS, vol. 1636, pp. 245–259. Springer, Heidelberg (1999). https://doi.org/10.1007/3-540-48519-8_18

12. Biryukov, A., Wagner, D.: Advanced slide attacks. In: Preneel, B. (ed.) EURO-CRYPT 2000. LNCS, vol. 1807, pp. 589–606. Springer, Heidelberg (2000). https://doi.org/10.1007/3-540-45539-6_41

13. Black, J., Rogaway, P.: Ciphers with arbitrary finite domains. In: Preneel, B. (ed.) CT-RSA 2002. LNCS, vol. 2271, pp. 114–130. Springer, Heidelberg (2002). https://doi.org/10.1007/3-540-45760-7_9

14. Brightwell, M., Smith, H.: Using datatype-preserving encryption to enhance data warehouse security. In: 20th NISSC Proceedings (1997). http://csrc.nist.gov/nissc/1997

15. Chen, S., Steinberger, J.: Tight security bounds for key-alternating ciphers. In: Nguyen, P.Q., Oswald, E. (eds.) EUROCRYPT 2014. LNCS, vol. 8441, pp. 327–350. Springer, Heidelberg (2014). https://doi.org/10.1007/978-3-642-55220-5_19

16. Cogliati, B., et al.: Provable security of (tweakable) block ciphers based on substitution-permutation networks. In: Shacham, H., Boldyreva, A. (eds.) CRYPTO 2018. LNCS, vol. 10991, pp. 722–753. Springer, Cham (2018). https://doi.org/10.1007/978-3-319-96884-1_24

17. Cogliati, B., Seurin, Y.: On the provable security of the iterated even-Mansour cipher against related-key and chosen-key attacks. In: Oswald, E., Fischlin, M. (eds.) EUROCRYPT 2015. LNCS, vol. 9056, pp. 584–613. Springer, Heidelberg (2015). https://doi.org/10.1007/978-3-662-46800-5_23

18. Council, P.S.S.: Payment card industry (PCI) data security standard: requirements and security assessment procedures, version 1.2.1. (2009). www.pcisecuritystandards.org

19. Diffie, W., (translators), G.L.: SMS4 encryption algorithm for wireless networks. Cryptology ePrint Archive, Report 2008/329 (2008). http://eprint.iacr.org/2008/329

20. Dunkelman, O., Keller, N., Lasry, N., Shamir, A.: New slide attacks on almost self-similar ciphers. In: Canteaut, A., Ishai, Y. (eds.) EUROCRYPT 2020. LNCS, vol. 12105, pp. 250–279. Springer, Cham (2020). https://doi.org/10.1007/978-3-030-45721-1_10

21. Dunkelman, O., Keller, N., Shamir, A.: A practical-time related-key attack on the KASUMI cryptosystem used in GSM and 3G telephony. J. Cryptol. **27**(4), 824–849 (2014)

22. Dunkelman, O., Keller, N., Shamir, A.: Slidex attacks on the even-Mansour encryption scheme. J. Cryptol. **28**(1), 1–28 (2015)

23. Dworkin, M.: Recommendation for block cipher modes of operation: methods for format-preserving encryption. NIST Special Publication 800-38G (2016). https://doi.org/10.6028/NIST.SP.800-38G

24. EMVCo: EMV Integrated Circuit Card Specifications for Payment Systems, Book 2, Security and Key Management (2008). Version 4.2

25. Feistel, H., Notz, W.A., Smith, J.L.: Some cryptographic techniques for machine-to-machine data communications. Proc. IEEE **63**(11), 1545–1554 (1975)

26. Guo, C.: Understanding the related-key security of Feistel ciphers from a provable perspective. IEEE Trans. Inf. Theor. **65**(8), 5260–5280 (2019). https://doi.org/10.1109/TIT.2019.2903796

27. Guo, J., Peyrin, T., Poschmann, A., Robshaw, M.: The LED block cipher. In: Preneel, B., Takagi, T. (eds.) CHES 2011. LNCS, vol. 6917, pp. 326–341. Springer, Heidelberg (2011). https://doi.org/10.1007/978-3-642-23951-9_22

28. Hoang, V.T., Rogaway, P.: On generalized Feistel networks. In: Rabin, T. (ed.) CRYPTO 2010. LNCS, vol. 6223, pp. 613–630. Springer, Heidelberg (2010). https://doi.org/10.1007/978-3-642-14623-7_33

29. Iwata, T., Kohno, T.: New security proofs for the 3GPP confidentiality and integrity algorithms. In: Roy, B., Meier, W. (eds.) FSE 2004. LNCS, vol. 3017, pp. 427–445. Springer, Heidelberg (2004). https://doi.org/10.1007/978-3-540-25937-4_27

30. Knudsen, L.R.: Cryptanalysis of LOKI91. In: Seberry, J., Zheng, Y. (eds.) AUSCRYPT 1992. LNCS, vol. 718, pp. 196–208. Springer, Heidelberg (Dec (1993). https://doi.org/10.1007/3-540-57220-1_62

31. Goubin, L., et al.: Crunch. Submission to NIST (2008)

32. Luby, M., Rackoff, C.: How to construct pseudorandom permutations from pseudorandom functions. SIAM J. Comput. **17**(2), 373–386 (1988)

33. Lucks, S.: Faster Luby-Rackoff ciphers. In: Gollmann, D. (ed.) FSE 1996. LNCS, vol. 1039, pp. 189–203. Springer, Heidelberg (1996). https://doi.org/10.1007/3-540-60865-6_53

34. Maines, L., Piva, M., Rimoldi, A., Sala, M.: On the provable security of BEAR and LION schemes. Appl. Algebra Eng. Commun. Comput. **22**(5–6), 413–423 (2011). https://doi.org/10.1007/s00200-011-0159-z

35. Morris, B., Rogaway, P., Stegers, T.: How to encipher messages on a small domain. In: Halevi, S. (ed.) CRYPTO 2009. LNCS, vol. 5677, pp. 286–302. Springer, Heidelberg (2009). https://doi.org/10.1007/978-3-642-03356-8_17

36. Nachef, V., Patarin, J., Volte, E.: Feistel Ciphers - Security Proofs and Cryptanalysis. Cryptology, Springer, Cham (2017)

37. Nandi, M.: On the optimality of non-linear computations of length-preserving encryption schemes. In: Iwata, T., Cheon, J.H. (eds.) ASIACRYPT 2015. LNCS, vol. 9453, pp. 113–133. Springer, Heidelberg (2015). https://doi.org/10.1007/978-3-662-48800-3_5

38. Naor, M., Reingold, O.: On the construction of pseudorandom permutations: Luby-Rackoff revisited. J. Cryptol. **12**(1), 29–66 (1999)
39. Patarin, J.: Security of Random Feistel Schemes with 5 or More Rounds. In: Franklin, M. (ed.) CRYPTO 2004. LNCS, vol. 3152, pp. 106–122. Springer, Heidelberg (2004). https://doi.org/10.1007/978-3-540-28628-8_7
40. Patarin, J.: The "coefficients H" technique (invited talk). In: Avanzi, R.M., Keliher, L., Sica, F. (eds.) SAC 2008. LNCS, vol. 5381, pp. 328–345. Springer, Heidelberg (2009). https://doi.org/10.1007/978-3-642-04159-4
41. Patarin, J.: Security of balanced and unbalanced Feistel schemes with linear non equalities. Cryptology ePrint Archive, Report 2010/293 (2010). http://eprint.iacr.org/2010/293
42. Patarin, J., Nachef, V., Berbain, C.: Generic attacks on unbalanced Feistel schemes with expanding functions. In: Kurosawa, K. (ed.) ASIACRYPT 2007. LNCS, vol. 4833, pp. 325–341. Springer, Heidelberg (2007). https://doi.org/10.1007/978-3-540-76900-2_20
43. Sadeghiyan, B., Pieprzyk, J.: A construction for super pseudorandom permutations from a single pseudorandom function. In: Rueppel, R.A. (ed.) EUROCRYPT 1992. LNCS, vol. 658, pp. 267–284. Springer, Heidelberg (1993). https://doi.org/10.1007/3-540-47555-9_23
44. Schneier, B., Kelsey, J.: Unbalanced Feistel networks and block cipher design. In: Gollmann, D. (ed.) FSE 1996. LNCS, vol. 1039, pp. 121–144. Springer, Heidelberg (1996). https://doi.org/10.1007/3-540-60865-6_49
45. Shen, Y., Guo, C., Wang, L.: Improved security bounds for generalized Feistel networks. IACR Trans. Symm. Cryptol. **2020**(1), 425–457 (2020)
46. Volte, E., Nachef, V., Patarin, J.: Improved generic attacks on unbalanced Feistel schemes with expanding functions. In: Abe, M. (ed.) ASIACRYPT 2010. LNCS, vol. 6477, pp. 94–111. Springer, Heidelberg (2010). https://doi.org/10.1007/978-3-642-17373-8_6
47. Yu, W., Zhao, Y., Guo, C.: Provable Related-key Security of Contracting Feistel Networks. In: Inscrypt 2020 (to appear, 2020)
48. Zheng, Y., Matsumoto, T., Imai, H.: On the construction of block ciphers provably secure and not relying on any unproved hypotheses. In: Brassard, G. (ed.) CRYPTO 1989. LNCS, vol. 435, pp. 461–480. Springer, New York (1990). https://doi.org/10.1007/0-387-34805-0_42

The Key-Dependent Message Security of Key-Alternating Feistel Ciphers

Pooya Farshim[1], Louiza Khati[2], Yannick Seurin[2], and Damien Vergnaud[3(✉)]

[1] Department of Computer Science, University of York, York, UK
[2] ANSSI, Paris, France
[3] Sorbonne Université, LIP6 and Institut de France, Paris, France
damien.vergnaud@lip6.fr

Abstract. Key-Alternating Feistel (KAF) ciphers are a popular variant of Feistel ciphers whereby the round functions are defined as $x \mapsto \mathsf{F}(k_i \oplus x)$, where k_i are the round keys and F is a public random function. Most Feistel ciphers, such as DES, indeed have such a structure. However, the security of this construction has only been studied in the classical CPA/CCA models. We provide the first security analysis of KAF ciphers in the key-dependent message (KDM) attack model, where plaintexts can be related to the private key. This model is motivated by cryptographic schemes used within application scenarios such as full-disk encryption or anonymous credential systems.

We show that the four-round KAF cipher, with a single function F reused across the rounds, provides KDM security for a non-trivial set of KDM functions. To do so, we develop a generic proof methodology, based on the H-coefficient technique, that can ease the analysis of other block ciphers in such strong models of security.

1   Introduction

The notion of key-dependent message (KDM) security for block ciphers was introduced by Black, Rogaway, and Shrimpton [5]. It guarantees strong confidentiality of communicated ciphertexts, i.e., the infeasibility of learning anything about plaintexts from the ciphertexts, even if an adversary has access to encryptions of messages that may depend on the secret key. This model captures practical settings where possibly adversarial correlations between the secret key and encrypted data exist, as is for example the case in anonymous credential and disk encryption systems; see [2,5,13,18] and references therein.

Typically, block ciphers are based on well-known iterative structures such as substitution-permutation or Feistel networks. The Feistel network, introduced in the seminal Luby–Rackoff paper [20], is a construction that builds an $(n_1 + n_2)$-bit pseudorandom permutation family from a smaller random function family that takes n_1-bit inputs and gives n_2-bit outputs. The general network is a repetition of a simple network (the one-round Feistel network as shown in Fig. 1) based on pseudorandom functions, which can be the same or different for different rounds. Starting from the Luby–Rackoff result that the 3-round Feistel scheme is

© Springer Nature Switzerland AG 2021
K. G. Paterson (Ed.): CT-RSA 2021, LNCS 12704, pp. 351–374, 2021.
https://doi.org/10.1007/978-3-030-75539-3_15

a pseudorandom permutation [20], Patarin [24] proved that four rounds is indistinguishable from a strong pseudorandom permutation, where chosen-ciphertext attacks (CCAs) are considered. Other analyses gave better bounds for r rounds with $r \geq 4$; see for example [22,23,26]. Dai and Steinberger [10] proved that the 8-round Feistel network is indifferentiable from a random permutation, and Barbosa and Farshim gave an analysis in the related-key attack model [3].

Some Feistel networks are *balanced* in that the input is split into two equal-length values L and R and use an n-bit to n-bit round function. For instance, DES and Simon [4] are balanced. Other designs, notably BEAR, LION [1], MISTY [21] and RC6 [17], are unbalanced [16]. Usually, the round functions of a practical block cipher are instantiated with a single public random function and a round key as shown in Fig. 1. This design is known as the key-alternating Feistel (KAF) cipher [19] and is of interest due to its practical use cases. For instance, DES is a 16-round balanced KAF where all round functions are identical and where each round key is derived from a master key.

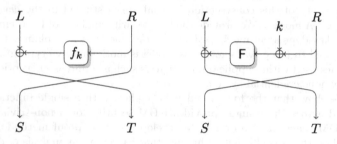

Fig. 1. Round functions of the Feistel network (left) and the KAF network (right).

More formally, a KAF cipher is a Feistel network where the i-th round function F_i is instantiated by $F_i(k_i, x) = f_i(k_i \oplus x)$ where the round functions f_i are public. The KAF construction is said to be idealized when the public functions f_i are modelled as random functions. Lampe and Seurin [19] analyzed the indistinguishability of this construction and proved a security bound up to $2^{\frac{rn}{r+1}}$ for $6r$ rounds using the coupling technique. In these settings the adversary has to distinguish two systems $(\mathsf{KAF}, f_1, \ldots, f_r)$ and $(\mathsf{P}, f_1, \ldots, f_r)$ where f_i are the public random functions and P is a random permutation. They also observed that two rounds of a KAF can be seen as a singly keyed Even–Mansour cipher. Guo and Lin [14] proved that the 21-round KAF* construction, a variant of KAF whereby the key k_i is xored *after* the application of the functions f_i, is indifferentiable from a random permutation. A recent work [15] analyzes the KAF construction with respect to short keys and in a multi-user setting. In the following, we consider only balanced KAFs.

KEY-DEPENDENT MESSAGE (KDM) SECURITY. As mentioned above, the KDM model gives the adversary the possibility of asking for encryptions of functions ϕ of the encryption key k (without knowing this key). An encryption scheme is said to be KDM secure with respect to some set Φ of functions ϕ mapping keys to messages, if it is secure against an adversary that can obtain encryption of $\phi(k)$ for any function $\phi \in \Phi$. KDM security for symmetric encryption was defined by Black, Rogaway and Shrimpton [5] and subsequently analyses for both symmetric and asymmetric constructions were done in this model; see, e.g., [2, 5–7, 13].

The KDM security of the ideal cipher and the Even–Mansour construction [11] were recently analyzed by Farshim, Khati, and Vergnaud [13]. They showed that the ideal cipher is KDM secure with respect to a set Φ of *claw-free* functions, i.e., a set where distinct functions have distinct outputs with high probability when run on a random input. The Even–Mansour (EM) is an iterated block cipher based on public n-bit permutation. Farshim et al. proved that the 1-round EM construction already achieves KDM security under chosen-ciphertext attacks if the set of functions available to the attacker is both claw-free and *offset-free*. The latter property requires that functions do not offset the key by a constant. On the other hand, the 2-round EM construction achieves KDM security if the set of functions available to the attacker is only claw-free (as long as two different permutations are used). To achieve these results, Farshim et al. introduced a so-called *"splitting and forgetting"* technique which is general enough to be applied to other symmetric constructions and/or other security models. Unfortunately, the analysis of KAF with $r \geq 4$ rounds and a unique round function makes this technique difficult to use.

CONTRIBUTIONS. In this paper, we provide the first analysis of the KAF in the key-dependent message attack model. To do so, we develop a generic proof strategy, based on the H-coefficient technique of Patarin [9, 24, 25, 28], to analyze the KDM security of block ciphers. We show how to adapt the H-coefficient technique to take KDM queries into account. We show that the 4-round KAF, where the internal functions are reused, is KDM secure for KDM sets Φ that are claw-free, offset-free, and *offset-xor free*. The latter property requires that functions do not offset the xor of two round keys by a constant. Although our security proofs are somewhat intricate, they still simplify the *"splitting and forgetting"* technique of [13].

In order to allow a convenient application of the H-coefficient technique when proving the KDM security of a block cipher, we introduce an intermediate world (in addition to the classical ideal world and real world), that we call the perfect world (pw) which dispenses with the key. We believe this technique (whose game-based analogues appear in [13]) might be of independent interest and can potentially be applied in other settings. In particular, using our techniques we give an arguably simpler proof of the KDM-security of the 1-round EM construction (which was analyzed in [13]) with respect to claw-free and offset-free functions (see the paper full version [12]).

Moreover, we show in Sect. 5 that if the adversary is only constrained to claw-free functions, it can indeed break the KDM indistinguishability game. We also give sliding KDM attacks on the basic KAF configuration with a single internal public function and either a single or two intervening keys, that *recovers* the key(s) and is adaptable for *any* number of rounds.

2   Preliminaries

NOTATION. Given an integer $n \geq 1$, the set of all functions from $\{0,1\}^n$ to $\{0,1\}^n$ is denoted $\mathsf{Func}(n)$. We let $\mathbb{N} := \{0, 1, \dots\}$ denote the set of non-negative integers, and $\{0,1\}^*$ denote the set of all finite-length bit strings. For two bit strings X and Y, $X|Y$ (or simply XY when no confusion is possible) denotes their concatenation and (X,Y) denotes a uniquely decodable encoding of X and Y. By $x \twoheadleftarrow S$ we mean sampling x uniformly from a finite set S. The cardinality of the set S, i.e., the number of elements in the set S, is denoted $|S|$. We let $L \leftarrow [\,]$ denote initializing a list to empty and $L : X$ denote appending element X to list L. A table T is a list of pairs (x, y), and we write $T(x) \leftarrow y$ to mean that the pair (x, y) is appended to the table. We let $\mathsf{Dom}(T)$ denote the set of values x such that $(x, y) \in T$ for some y and $\mathsf{Rng}(T)$ denote the set of values y such that $(x, y) \in T$ for some x. Given a function F, we let $\mathsf{F}^i(x) := \mathsf{F} \circ \cdots \circ \mathsf{F}(x)$ denote the i-th iterate of F. For integers $1 \leq b \leq a$, we will write $(a)_b := a(a-1)\cdots(a-b+1)$ and $(a)_0 := 1$ by convention. Note that the probability that a random permutation P on $\{0,1\}^n$ satisfies q equations $P(x_i) = y_i$ for distinct x_i's and distinct y_i's is exactly $1/(2^n)_q$.

BLOCK CIPHERS. Given two non-empty subsets $\mathcal{K}$ and $\mathcal{M}$ of $\{0,1\}^*$, called the key space and the message space respectively, we let $\mathsf{Block}(\mathcal{K}, \mathcal{M})$ denote the set of all functions $\mathsf{E} : \mathcal{K} \times \mathcal{M} \to \mathcal{M}$ such that for each $k \in \mathcal{K}$ the map $\mathsf{E}(k, \cdot)$ is (1) a permutation on $\mathcal{M}$ and (2) length preserving in the sense that for all $p \in \mathcal{M}$ we have that $|\mathsf{E}(k, p)| = |p|$. Such an E uniquely defines its inverse $\mathsf{D} : \mathcal{K} \times \mathcal{M} \to \mathcal{M}$. A block cipher for key space $\mathcal{K}$ and message space $\mathcal{M}$ is a triple of efficient algorithms $\mathsf{BC} := (\mathsf{K}, \mathsf{E}, \mathsf{D})$ such that $\mathsf{E} \in \mathsf{Block}(\mathcal{K}, \mathcal{M})$ and its inverse is D. In more detail, K is the randomized key-generation algorithm which returns a key $\mathbf{k} \in \mathcal{K}$. Typically $\mathcal{K} = \{0,1\}^k$ for some $k \in \mathbb{N}$ called the key length, and K endows it with the uniform distribution. Algorithm E is the deterministic enciphering algorithm with signature $\mathsf{E} : \mathcal{K} \times \mathcal{M} \to \mathcal{M}$. Typically $\mathcal{M} = \{0,1\}^n$ for some $n \in \mathbb{N}$ called the block length. (3) D is the deterministic deciphering algorithm with signature $\mathsf{D} : \mathcal{K} \times \mathcal{M} \to \mathcal{M}$. A block cipher is correct in the sense that for all $k \in \mathcal{K}$ and all $p \in \mathcal{M}$ we have that $\mathsf{D}(k, \mathsf{E}(k, p)) = p$. A permutation on $\mathcal{M}$ is simply a block cipher with key space $\mathcal{K} = \{\varepsilon\}$. We denote a permutation with P and its inverse with P^-. A permutation can be trivially obtained from a block cipher (by fixing the key). For a block cipher $\mathsf{BC} := (\mathsf{K}, \mathsf{E}, \mathsf{D})$, notation $\mathcal{A}^{\mathsf{BC}}$ denotes oracle access to both E and D for $\mathcal{A}$. We abbreviate $\mathsf{Block}(\{0,1\}^k, \{0,1\}^n)$ by $\mathsf{Block}(k, n)$ and $\mathsf{Block}(\{\varepsilon\}, \{0,1\}^n)$ by $\mathsf{Perm}(n)$.

KEY-ALTERNATING FEISTEL (KAF) CIPHERS. For a given public function $\mathsf{F} \in \mathsf{Func}(n)$ and a key $k \in \{0,1\}^n$, the one-round KAF is the permutation $\mathsf{P} \in \mathsf{Func}(2n)$ defined via

$$\mathsf{P}_k^{\mathsf{F}}(LR) := R|\mathsf{F}(k \oplus R) \oplus L \ .$$

The values L and R are respectively the left and right n-bit halves of the input. The left and right n-bit halves of the output are usually denoted S and T respectively. Given r public functions $\mathsf{F}_1, \mathsf{F}_2, \ldots, \mathsf{F}_r$ and r keys $k_1, k_2, \ldots, k_r$, the r-round KAF is defined as

$$\mathsf{KAF}^{\mathsf{F}_1, \mathsf{F}_2, \ldots, \mathsf{F}_r}_{k_1, k_2, \ldots, k_r}(LR) := \mathsf{P}^{\mathsf{F}_r}_{k_r} \circ \cdots \circ \mathsf{P}^{\mathsf{F}_1}_{k_1}(LR) .$$

In the following, we write keys $k_1, k_2, \ldots, k_r$ as a key vector $\mathbf{k} = (k_1, k_2, \ldots, k_r)$. When a single public function F is used we write r-round KAF as $\mathsf{KAF}^{\mathsf{F}}_{\mathbf{k}}$.

H-COEFFICIENT. The H-coefficient technique [28] was introduced by Patarin and is widely used to prove the security of block cipher constructions such as the Even–Mansour cipher [8] or Feistel schemes [27]. Consider a deterministic adversary $\mathcal{A}$ that takes no input, interacts with a set of oracles w (informally called a *world* or a *game*), and returns a bit b. We write this interaction as $\mathcal{A}^{\mathsf{w}} \Rightarrow b$. Given two worlds w_0 and w_1, offering the same interfaces, the advantage of $\mathcal{A}$ in distinguishing w_0 and w_1 is defined as

$$\mathbf{Adv}_{\mathsf{w}_0, \mathsf{w}_1}(\mathcal{A}) := |\Pr[\mathcal{A}^{\mathsf{w}_0} \Rightarrow 1] - \Pr[\mathcal{A}^{\mathsf{w}_1} \Rightarrow 1]| .$$

A transcript τ consists of the list of all query/answer pairs respectively made by the adversary and returned by the oracles. Let $X_{\mathcal{A}, \mathsf{w}}$ be the random variable distributed as the transcript resulting from the interaction of $\mathcal{A}$ with world w. A transcript τ is said to be *attainable for $\mathcal{A}$ and* w if this transcript can be the result of the interaction of $\mathcal{A}$ with world w, i.e., when $\Pr[X_{\mathcal{A}, \mathsf{w}} = \tau] > 0$.

Lemma 2.1 (H-coefficient). *Let w_0 and w_1 be two worlds and $\mathcal{A}$ be a distinguisher. Let $\mathcal{T}$ be the set of attainable transcripts for $\mathcal{A}$ in w_0, and let $\mathcal{T}_{\mathrm{good}}$ and $\mathcal{T}_{\mathrm{bad}}$ be a partition of $\mathcal{T}$ such that $\mathcal{T} = \mathcal{T}_{\mathrm{good}} \cup \mathcal{T}_{\mathrm{bad}}$. Then if for some $\varepsilon_{\mathrm{bad}}$*

$$\Pr[X_{\mathcal{A}, \mathsf{w}_0} \in \mathcal{T}_{\mathrm{bad}}] \leq \varepsilon_{\mathrm{bad}} ,$$

and for some $\varepsilon_{\mathrm{good}}$ we have that for all $\tau \in \mathcal{T}_{\mathrm{good}}$

$$\frac{\Pr[X_{\mathcal{A}, \mathsf{w}_1} = \tau]}{\Pr[X_{\mathcal{A}, \mathsf{w}_0} = \tau]} \geq 1 - \varepsilon_{\mathrm{good}} ,$$

then $\mathbf{Adv}_{\mathsf{w}_0, \mathsf{w}_1}(\mathcal{A}) \leq \varepsilon_{\mathrm{good}} + \varepsilon_{\mathrm{bad}}$.

For a given transcript $\mathcal{Q}_{\mathsf{F}}$ and a function F, we say that F extends $\mathcal{Q}_{\mathsf{F}}$ and write $\mathsf{F} \vdash \mathcal{Q}_{\mathsf{F}}$ if $v = \mathsf{F}(u)$ for all $(u, v) \in \mathcal{Q}_{\mathsf{F}}$.

3 KDM Security and a Generic Lemma

3.1 Definitions

KDM FUNCTIONS. A key-dependent-message (KDM) function for key space $\mathcal{K}$ and message space $\mathcal{M}$ is a function $\phi : \mathcal{K} \to \mathcal{M}$ computed by a deterministic and stateless circuit. A KDM set Φ is a set of KDM functions ϕ on the same key and message spaces. We let $\Phi_{\mathcal{M}}$ denote the set of all constant KDM functions, i.e., KDM functions ϕ such that for some $x \in \mathcal{M}$ and $\forall\, k \in \mathcal{K}, \phi : k \mapsto x$. We denote such functions by $\phi : k \mapsto x$ and assume that the constant value x can be read-off from (the description of) ϕ. We also assume membership in KDM sets can be efficiently decided. In what follows, even though we work in an idealized model of computation where all parties have access to some oracle O, we do not consider KDM functions computed by circuits with O-oracle gates. We start by defining the following three properties for KDM sets.

Definition 3.1 (Claw-freeness). *Let Φ be a KDM set for key space $\mathcal{K}$ and message space $\mathcal{M}$. The claw-freeness of Φ is defined as*

$$\mathbf{cf}(\Phi) := \max_{\phi_1 \neq \phi_2 \in \Phi} \Pr[k \twoheadleftarrow \mathcal{K} : \phi_1(k) = \phi_2(k)] .$$

Definition 3.2 (Offset-freeness). *Fix integers $n, \ell > 0$. Let Φ be a KDM set for key space $\mathcal{K} = (\{0,1\}^n)^{\ell}$ and message space $\mathcal{M} = \{0,1\}^n$. The offset-freeness of Φ is defined as*

$$\mathbf{of}(\Phi) := \max_{\substack{i \in \{1,\ldots,\ell\} \\ \phi \in \Phi,\, x \in \{0,1\}^n}} \Pr[(k_1,\ldots,k_{\ell}) \twoheadleftarrow \mathcal{K} : \phi(k_1,\ldots,k_{\ell}) = k_i \oplus x] .$$

Definition 3.3 (Offset-xor-freeness). *Fix integers $n, \ell > 0$. Let Φ be a KDM set for key space $\mathcal{K} = (\{0,1\}^n)^{\ell}$ and message space $\mathcal{M} = \{0,1\}^n$. The offset-xor-freeness of Φ is defined as*

$$\mathbf{oxf}(\Phi) := \max_{\substack{i \neq j \in \{1,\ldots,\ell\} \\ \phi \in \Phi,\, x \in \{0,1\}^n}} \Pr[(k_1,\ldots,k_{\ell}) \twoheadleftarrow \mathcal{K} : \phi(k_1,\ldots,k_{\ell}) = k_i \oplus k_j \oplus x] .$$

EXAMPLE KDM SET. One may ask whether or not there are any KDM sets that satisfy the above three conditions. Suppose $\mathcal{K} = \{0,1\}^k$. Let Φ_d be the sets of all functions mapping $(k_1,\ldots,k_{\ell})$ to $P(k_1,\ldots,k_{\ell})$ where P is a multi-variate polynomial over $\mathrm{GF}(2^k)$ of total degree at most d, with $\oplus$ being field addition and multiplication defined modulo a fixed irreducible polynomial. We consider a subset of Φ_d consisting of all P such that $P(k_1,\ldots,k_{\ell}) \oplus k_i$ and $P(k_1,\ldots,k_{\ell}) \oplus k_i \oplus k_j$ are non-constant for any distinct i and j. Then a direct application of the (multi-variate) Schwartz-Zippel lemma [29] shows that this KDM set satisfies the above three properties, with all advantages upper bounded by $d/2^k$, where d is the total degree of P. Note that this term is negligible for total degree up to $d = 2^{k-\omega(\log k)}$.

KDM SECURITY. Consider a block cipher $\mathrm{BC}^O := (\mathrm{K}, \mathrm{E}^O, \mathrm{D}^O)$ with key space $\mathcal{K}$ and message space $\mathcal{M}$ based on some ideal primitive O sampled from some oracle space OSp. We formalize security under key-dependent message and chosen-ciphertext attacks (KDM-CCA) as a distinguishing game between two worlds that we call the *real* and *ideal* worlds. Given a KDM set Φ, the adversary $\mathcal{A}$ has access to a KDM encryption oracle KDENC which takes as input a function

$\phi \in \Phi$ and returns a ciphertext $y \in \mathcal{M}$, a decryption oracle DEC which takes as input a ciphertext $y \in \mathcal{M}$ and returns a plaintext $x \in \mathcal{M}$, and the oracle O. We do not allow the adversary to ask for decryption of key-dependent ciphertexts as we are not aware of any use cases where such an oracle is available. In the real world, a key k is drawn uniformly at random from $\mathcal{K}$ and KDENC(ϕ) returns $\mathsf{E}^{\mathsf{O}}(k, \phi(k))$ while DEC(y) returns $\mathsf{D}^{\mathsf{O}}(k, y)$. The ideal world is similar to the real world except that $\mathsf{E}(k, \cdot)$ and $\mathsf{D}(k, \cdot)$ are replaced by a random permutation P and its inverse. To exclude trivial attacks, we do not allow decryption of ciphertexts that were obtained from the encryption oracle and such queries are answered by $\perp$ in both worlds. (Otherwise the key can be recovered by decrypting the encryption of $\phi(k)$ if ϕ is easily invertible.) The real and ideal world are formally defined in Fig. 2 (ignore the additional world pw for now). The KDM-CCA advantage of an adversary $\mathcal{A}$ against BC with respect to Φ is defined as

$$\mathbf{Adv}_{\mathrm{BC}^{\mathsf{O}}}^{\mathrm{kdm\text{-}cca}}(\mathcal{A}, \Phi) := \mathbf{Adv}_{\mathrm{iw,rw}}(\mathcal{A}) .$$

Without loss of generality we assume throughout the paper that the adversary does not place repeat queries to its oracles. This is indeed without loss of generality since all oracles are deterministic and repeat queries can be handled by keeping track of queries made so far.

3.2 A Generic Lemma

In order to allow a convenient application of the H-coefficient technique when proving the KDM security of a block cipher BC^{O}, we introduce an intermediate world, called the perfect world (pw), defined in Fig. 2. Note that this world does not involve any key. The encryption and decryption oracles lazily sample two independent random permutations stored respectively in tables $\mathsf{T}_{\mathrm{enc}}$ and $\mathsf{T}_{\mathrm{dec}}$, except that consistency is ensured for constant functions $\phi \in \Phi_{\mathcal{M}}$: when a decryption query DEC(y) is made with $y \notin \mathsf{Dom}(\mathsf{T}_{\mathrm{dec}})$, a plaintext x is sampled from $\mathcal{M} \backslash \mathsf{Rng}(\mathsf{T}_{\mathrm{dec}})$ and the world assigns $\mathsf{T}_{\mathrm{dec}}(y) := x$ and $\mathsf{T}_{\mathrm{enc}}(\phi) := y$, where ϕ is the constant function $k \mapsto x$.

The following lemma upper-bounds the distinguishing advantage between the ideal and the perfect worlds. It does not depend on the block cipher at hand (neither the ideal nor the perfect world depends on it) nor on the oracle O (since neither in the ideal nor in the perfect world the encryption and decryption oracles depend on it). For specific block ciphers, this allows us to focus on the distinguishing advantage between the perfect and the real worlds, since by the triangular inequality

$$\mathbf{Adv}_{\mathrm{iw,rw}}(\mathcal{A}) \leq \mathbf{Adv}_{\mathrm{iw,pw}}(\mathcal{A}) + \mathbf{Adv}_{\mathrm{pw,rw}}(\mathcal{A}) . \tag{1}$$

Lemma 3.1. *Let Φ be a KDM set for key space $\mathcal{K}$ and message space $\mathcal{M}$. Let $\mathcal{A}$ be an adversary making at most q queries to KDENC or DEC. Then*

$$\mathbf{Adv}_{\mathrm{iw,pw}}(\mathcal{A}) \leq q^2 \cdot \mathbf{cf}(\Phi) + \frac{q^2}{|\mathcal{M}| - q} .$$

Game rw   // real

$O \twoheadleftarrow \mathsf{OSp}$
$k \twoheadleftarrow \mathsf{K}$
$L \leftarrow []$

Proc. KDENC(ϕ)

if $\phi \notin \Phi$ **return** $\bot$
$x \leftarrow \phi(k)$
$L \leftarrow L : \{\mathsf{E}^{\mathsf{O}}(k, x)\}$
return $\mathsf{E}^{\mathsf{O}}(k, x)$

Proc. DEC(y)

if $y \in L$ **return** $\bot$
else return $\mathsf{D}^{\mathsf{O}}(k, y)$

Proc. O(x)

return $\mathsf{O}(x)$

Game pw   // perfect

$O \twoheadleftarrow \mathsf{OSp}$
$T_{\mathsf{enc}} \leftarrow []; T_{\mathsf{dec}} \leftarrow []$

Proc. KDENC(ϕ)

if $\phi \notin \Phi$ **return** $\bot$
if $\phi \notin \mathsf{Dom}(T_{\mathsf{enc}})$ **then**
  $T_{\mathsf{enc}}(\phi) \twoheadleftarrow \mathcal{M} \setminus \mathsf{Rng}(T_{\mathsf{enc}})$
return $T_{\mathsf{enc}}(\phi)$

Proc. DEC(y)

if $y \in \mathsf{Rng}(T_{\mathsf{enc}})$ **return** $\bot$
if $y \notin \mathsf{Dom}(T_{\mathsf{dec}})$ **then**
  $x \twoheadleftarrow \mathcal{M} \setminus \mathsf{Rng}(T_{\mathsf{dec}})$
  $T_{\mathsf{dec}}(y) \leftarrow x$
  $T_{\mathsf{enc}}(\phi : k \mapsto x) \leftarrow y$
return $T_{\mathsf{dec}}(y)$

Proc. O(x)

return $\mathsf{O}(x)$

Game iw   // ideal

$O \twoheadleftarrow \mathsf{OSp}$
$k \twoheadleftarrow \mathsf{K}; L \leftarrow []$
$P \twoheadleftarrow \mathsf{Perm}(\mathcal{M})$

Proc. KDENC(ϕ)

if $\phi \notin \Phi$ **return** $\bot$
$x \leftarrow \phi(k)$
$L \leftarrow L : \{\mathsf{P}(x)\}$
return $\mathsf{P}(x)$

Proc. DEC(y)

if $y \in L$ **return** $\bot$
else return $\mathsf{P}^{-1}(y)$

Proc. O(x)

return $\mathsf{O}(x)$

Fig. 2. The real world rw (left) and the ideal world iw (right) defining KDM-CCA security. The intermediate perfect world pw (middle) is used in Lemma 3.1. Here K denotes a key-generation algorithm.

Proof. We apply the H-coefficient technique with $\mathsf{w}_0 := \mathsf{pw}$ and $\mathsf{w}_1 := \mathsf{iw}$. Fix a, without loss of generality, deterministic distinguisher $\mathcal{A}$ making at most q encryption or decryption queries. We assume, without loss of generality, that

- the adversary never repeats a query;
- the adversary never queries the constant function $\phi : k \mapsto x$ to KDENC if it has received x as answer to some query DEC(y) before (since in both worlds such a query would be answered by y); and
- the adversary never queries y to DEC if it has received y as answer to some query KDENC(ϕ) before (since in both worlds such a query would be answered by $\bot$).

We will refer to this as the *no-pointless-query* assumption.

We record the queries of the adversary to oracles KDENC or DEC in a list $\mathcal{Q}_{BC}$: it contains all tuples $(+, \phi, y)$ such that $\mathcal{A}$ queried KDENC(ϕ) and received answer y, and all tuples $(-, x, y)$ such that $\mathcal{A}$ queried DEC(y) and received answer x. The queries of the adversary to oracle O are recorded in a list $\mathcal{Q}_O$. After the adversary has finished querying the oracles, we reveal the key k in case the adversary interacts with the ideal world, while in the perfect world we reveal a uniformly random key independent of the oracle answers. Hence, a transcript is a triple $(\mathcal{Q}_{BC}, \mathcal{Q}_O, k)$.

Let $\mathcal{T}$ be the set of attainable transcripts for $\mathcal{A}$ and pw. An attainable transcript $\tau = (\mathcal{Q}_{BC}, \mathcal{Q}_O, k)$ is said to be *bad* iff any of the following holds.

(C-1) there exist $(+, \phi, y) \neq (+, \phi', y') \in \mathcal{Q}_{BC}$ such that
    (a) $\phi(k) = \phi'(k)$ or
    (b) $y = y'$;
(C-2) there exist $(+, \phi, y), (-, x, y') \in \mathcal{Q}_{BC}$ such that
    (a) $\phi(k) = x$ or
    (b) $y = y'$;
(C-3) there exist $(-x, y) \neq (-, x', y') \in \mathcal{Q}_{BC}$ such that
    (a) $x = x'$ or
    (b) $y = y'$.

Let $\mathcal{T}_{bad}$ denote the set of bad transcripts and let $\mathcal{T}_{good} := \mathcal{T} \setminus \mathcal{T}_{bad}$. We first upper bound the probability of getting a bad transcript in the perfect world.

Claim. $\Pr[X_{\mathcal{A},pw} \in \mathcal{T}_{bad}] \leq q^2 \cdot \mathbf{cf}(\Phi) + q^2/(|\mathcal{M}| - q)$.

Proof. We consider the probability of each condition in turn. Recall that in the perfect world, the key k is drawn at random independently of the oracle answers.

(C-1) Fix two queries $(+, \phi, y) \neq (+, \phi', y') \in \mathcal{Q}_{BC}$.
    (a) By Definition 3.1, $\phi(k) = \phi'(k)$ with probability at most $\mathbf{cf}(\Phi)$ over the choice of a random key k.
    (b) By the no-pointless-queries assumption, $\phi \neq \phi'$ and hence necessarily $y \neq y'$.
Summing over all possible pairs, (C-1) happens with probability at most $q^2/2 \cdot \mathbf{cf}(\Phi)$.

(C-2) Fix two queries $(+, \phi, y), (-, x, y') \in \mathcal{Q}_{BC}$.
    (a) If query $(+, \phi, y)$ came first, then x is uniformly random in a set of size at least $|\mathcal{M}| - q$ and independent of $\phi(k)$. Hence $\phi(k) = x$ with probability at most $1/(|\mathcal{M}| - q)$. If query $(-, x, y')$ came first, then by the no-pointless-query assumption, $\phi \neq (k \mapsto x)$, so that $\phi(k) = x$ with probability at most $\mathbf{cf}(\Phi)$ (otherwise it would constitute a claw with the constant function). All in all, $\phi(k) = x$ with probability at most $1/(|\mathcal{M}| - q) + \mathbf{cf}(\Phi)$.
    (b) If query $(+, \phi, y)$ came first, then by the no-pointless-query assumption $y' \neq y$. If query $(-, x, y')$ came first, then y is uniformly random in a set of size at least $|\mathcal{M}| - q$ and independent of y'. Hence $y = y'$ with probability at most $1/(|\mathcal{M}| - q)$.

Summing over all possible pairs of queries, (C-2) happens with probability at most $q^2/2 \cdot (2/(|\mathcal{M}| - q) + \mathbf{cf}(\Phi))$.

(C-3) Fix two queries $(-, x, y) \neq (-, x', y') \in \mathcal{Q}_{\mathrm{BC}}$. Then, by the no-pointless-queries assumption, $y \neq y'$ and hence $x \neq x'$, so that condition (C-3) cannot hold.

The result follows by applying the union bound.

Claim. Fix a good transcript $\tau = (\mathcal{Q}_{\mathrm{BC}}, \mathcal{Q}_{\mathrm{O}}, k)$. Then

$$\frac{\Pr[X_{\mathcal{A},\mathrm{iw}} = \tau]}{\Pr[X_{\mathcal{A},\mathrm{pw}} = \tau]} \geq 1 \ .$$

Proof. Let q_{enc}, resp. q_{dec}, denote the number of queries to KDENC, resp. DEC, in $\mathcal{Q}_{\mathrm{BC}}$ (with $q_{\mathrm{enc}} + q_{\mathrm{dec}} = q$). In the perfect world, queries to KDENC and DEC are answered by lazily sampling two independent injections $\mathsf{I}_{\mathrm{enc}} \colon [q_{\mathrm{enc}}] \to \mathcal{M}$ and $\mathsf{I}_{\mathrm{dec}} \colon [q_{\mathrm{dec}}] \to \mathcal{M}$. This follows from the no-pointless-queries assumption which implies that for any query KDENC(ϕ) we have $\phi \notin \mathsf{Dom}(\mathsf{T}_{\mathrm{enc}})$ and for any query DEC(y) we have $y \notin \mathsf{Dom}(\mathsf{T}_{\mathrm{dec}})$. Hence, letting $\mathcal{Q}_{\mathrm{enc}}$ and $\mathcal{Q}_{\mathrm{dec}}$ respectively denote the set of encryption and decryption queries in $\mathcal{Q}_{\mathrm{BC}}$ and K the key-generation algorithm we have

$$\Pr[X_{\mathcal{A},\mathrm{pw}} = \tau] = \Pr_{k' \leftarrow\!\shortmid \mathsf{K}}[k' = k] \cdot \Pr_{\mathsf{O} \leftarrow\!\shortmid \mathsf{OSp}}[\mathsf{O} \vdash \mathcal{Q}_{\mathrm{O}}] \cdot \Pr_{\mathsf{I}_{\mathrm{enc}}}[\mathsf{I}_{\mathrm{enc}} \vdash \mathcal{Q}_{\mathrm{enc}}] \cdot \Pr_{\mathsf{I}_{\mathrm{dec}}}[\mathsf{I}_{\mathrm{dec}} \vdash \mathcal{Q}_{\mathrm{dec}}]$$

$$= \Pr_{k' \leftarrow\!\shortmid \mathsf{K}}[k' = k] \cdot \Pr_{\mathsf{O} \leftarrow\!\shortmid \mathsf{OSp}}[\mathsf{O} \vdash \mathcal{Q}_{\mathrm{O}}] \cdot \frac{1}{(|\mathcal{M}|)_{q_{\mathrm{enc}}} \cdot (|\mathcal{M}|)_{q_{\mathrm{dec}}}} \ .$$

We now compute the probability of obtaining a good transcript τ in the ideal world. Consider the modified transcript $\mathcal{Q}'_{\mathrm{BC}}$ containing pairs $(x, y) \in \mathcal{M}^2$ constructed from $\mathcal{Q}_{\mathrm{BC}}$ as follows. For each triplet $(+, \phi, y) \in \mathcal{Q}_{\mathrm{BC}}$, append $(\phi(k), y)$ to $\mathcal{Q}'_{\mathrm{BC}}$ and for each $(-, x, y) \in \mathcal{Q}_{\mathrm{BC}}$, append (x, y) to $\mathcal{Q}'_{\mathrm{BC}}$. Then, for any $(x, y) \neq (x', y') \in \mathcal{Q}'_{\mathrm{BC}}$, we have $x \neq x'$ (as otherwise condition (C-1a), (C-2a), or (C-3a) would be met) and $y \neq y'$ (as otherwise condition (C-1b), (C-2b), or (C-3b) would be met). Hence,

$$\Pr[X_{\mathcal{A},\mathrm{iw}} = \tau] = \Pr_{k' \leftarrow\!\shortmid \mathsf{K}}[k' = k] \cdot \Pr_{\mathsf{O} \leftarrow\!\shortmid \mathsf{OSp}}[\mathsf{O} \vdash \mathcal{Q}_{\mathrm{O}}] \cdot \Pr_{\mathsf{P} \leftarrow\!\shortmid \mathsf{Perm}(\mathcal{M})}[\mathsf{P} \vdash \mathcal{Q}'_{\mathrm{BC}}]$$

$$= \Pr_{k' \leftarrow\!\shortmid \mathsf{K}}[k' = k] \cdot \Pr_{\mathsf{O} \leftarrow\!\shortmid \mathsf{OSp}}[\mathsf{O} \vdash \mathcal{Q}_{\mathrm{O}}] \cdot \frac{1}{(|\mathcal{M}|)_q} \ .$$

Thus,

$$\frac{\Pr[X_{\mathcal{A},\mathrm{iw}} = \tau]}{\Pr[X_{\mathcal{A},\mathrm{pw}} = \tau]} = \frac{(|\mathcal{M}|)_{q_{\mathrm{enc}}} \cdot (|\mathcal{M}|)_{q_{\mathrm{dec}}}}{(|\mathcal{M}|)_q} \geq 1 \ ,$$

where the inequality follows from $q_{\mathrm{enc}} + q_{\mathrm{dec}} = q$.

Lemma 3.1 follows by combining the above two claims with Lemma 2.1.

4   Four-Round KAF

In this section we study the 4-round KAF cipher with a single round function
$\mathsf{F}\colon \{0,1\}^n \to \{0,1\}^n$ and key $\mathbf{k} = (k_1, k_2, k_3, k_4) \in (\{0,1\}^n)^4$ where k_1 and
k_4 are uniformly random. Our results do not rely on any assumptions on the
distributions of k_2 and k_3 (which could be, for example, both set to 0). Given a
KDM function ϕ with range $\{0,1\}^{2n}$, we let ϕ_L and ϕ_R to respectively denote
the functions that return the n leftmost and the n rightmost bits of ϕ. Given a
KDM set Φ for message space $\mathcal{M} = \{0,1\}^{2n}$, we define $\Phi_L := \{\phi_L : \phi \in \Phi\}$ and
$\Phi_R := \{\phi_R : \phi \in \Phi\}$.

The theorem below states that the 4-round KAF with the same round function and uniformly random round keys k_1 and k_4 is KDM-CCA secure if the set
Φ of key-dependent functions has negligible claw-freeness (cf. Definition 3.1) and
Φ_R has negligible offset-freeness and offset-xor-freeness (cf. Definition 3.2 and
Definition 3.3).

Theorem 4.1. *Let $\mathsf{KAF}_{\mathbf{k}}^{\mathsf{F}}$ be the 4-round key-alternating Feistel cipher based on
a single round function $\mathsf{F}\colon \{0,1\}^n \to \{0,1\}^n$ where the key $\mathbf{k} = (k_1, k_2, k_3, k_4)$
is such that k_1 and k_4 are uniformly random and independent. Let $\mathcal{A}$ be an
adversary making at most $q \leq 2^n$ queries to KDEnc or Dec and at most q_{f}
queries to F, which is modeled as a random oracle. Then,*

$$\mathbf{Adv}_{\mathsf{KAF}_{\mathbf{k}}^{\mathsf{F}}}^{\mathrm{kdm\text{-}cca}}(\mathcal{A}, \Phi) \leq q^2 \cdot (2 \cdot \mathbf{cf}(\Phi) + 3/2 \cdot \mathbf{oxf}(\Phi_R) + 22/2^n) + qq_{\mathsf{f}} \cdot (\mathbf{of}(\Phi_R) + 7/2^n) \ .$$

Proof. Fix an adversary $\mathcal{A}$ attempting to distinguish the real and ideal worlds
defined in Fig. 2, where $\mathsf{OSp} := \mathsf{Func}(n)$ and $\mathrm{BC} = \mathsf{KAF}^{\mathsf{F}}$. Assume that $\mathcal{A}$ makes
at most $q \leq 2^n$ queries to KDEnc or Dec and q_{f} queries to F. By Eq. 1 and
Lemma 3.1, we have

$$\mathbf{Adv}_{\mathsf{KAF}_{\mathbf{k}}^{\mathsf{F}}}^{\mathrm{kdm\text{-}cca}}(\mathcal{A}, \Phi) \leq q^2 \cdot \mathbf{cf}(\Phi) + q^2/(|\mathcal{M}| - q) + \mathbf{Adv}_{\mathsf{pw,rw}}(\mathcal{A})$$

$$\leq q^2 \cdot \mathbf{cf}(\Phi) + q^2/2^n + \mathbf{Adv}_{\mathsf{pw,rw}}(\mathcal{A}) \ ,$$

where we used that $|\mathcal{M}| = 2^{2n}$ and $1/(2^{2n} - q) \leq 1/2^n$. Hence, it remains to
upper bound $\mathbf{Adv}_{\mathsf{pw,rw}}(\mathcal{A})$. We prove below that

$$\mathbf{Adv}_{\mathsf{pw,rw}}(\mathcal{A}) \leq q^2 \cdot (\mathbf{cf}(\Phi) + 3/2 \cdot \mathbf{oxf}(\Phi_R) + 21/2^n) + qq_{\mathsf{f}} \cdot (\mathbf{of}(\Phi_R) + 7/2^n) \ , \tag{2}$$

from which the result follows.

The remainder of this section is devoted to the proof of Eq. 2. Without loss
of generality, we make the same no-pointless-query assumption that we made
in the proof of Lemma 3.1. Our proof will use the H-coefficient technique. A
transcript τ is a tuple $(\mathcal{Q}_{\mathrm{BC}}, \mathcal{Q}_{\mathsf{F}}, \mathbf{k})$, where $\mathcal{Q}_{\mathrm{BC}}$ is the list of all forward queries
$(+, \phi, ST)$, with $\phi \in \Phi$ the query to KDEnc and ST the corresponding answer,
together with all backward queries $(-, L'R', S'T')$ with $L'R', S'T' \in (\{0,1\}^n)^2$
and $L'R'$ the answer of Dec when called on $S'T'$. List $\mathcal{Q}_{\mathsf{F}}$ contains queries
$(u, v) \in (\{0,1\}^n)^2$ to the public function F, where v is the answer of the oracle

F when called on input u. The key $\mathbf{k}$ is only revealed to the adversary after it has finished its queries, and is drawn independently of the oracle answers in the perfect world using the key-generation algorithm K (whose first and fourth components are uniform but not necessarily its second or third components).

We first define bad transcripts and upper bound the probability of obtaining such a transcript in the perfect world. Informally, a transcript is said to be bad if an unexpected collision occurs in the set of all inputs to the *first* or the *fourth* round functions. Note that the adversary can let some inputs collide with probability 1, for example by querying $\mathrm{DEC}(ST)$ and $\mathrm{DEC}(ST')$; bad transcripts only capture collisions that happen "by chance." We formalize this next.

Definition 4.1. *A transcript* $\tau = (\mathcal{Q}_{\mathrm{BC}}, \mathcal{Q}_{\mathsf{F}}, \mathbf{k})$ *with* $\mathbf{k} = (k_1, k_2, k_3, k_4)$ *in the perfect world is said to be* bad *iff any of the following holds.*

(C-1) *there exist* $(+, \phi, ST) \in \mathcal{Q}_{\mathrm{BC}}$ *and* $(u, v) \in \mathcal{Q}_{\mathsf{F}}$ *such that*
   (a) $\phi_R(\mathbf{k}) \oplus k_1 = u$ *or*
   (b) $S \oplus k_4 = u;$
(C-2) *there exist* $(-, LR, ST) \in \mathcal{Q}_{\mathrm{BC}}$ *and* $(u, v) \in \mathcal{Q}_{\mathsf{F}}$ *such that*
   (a) $R \oplus k_1 = u$ *or*
   (b) $S \oplus k_4 = u;$
(C-3) *there exist* $(+, \phi, ST) \neq (+, \phi', S'T') \in \mathcal{Q}_{\mathrm{BC}}$ *such that*
   (a) $\phi(\mathbf{k}) = \phi'(\mathbf{k})$ *or*
   (b) $S = S';$
(C-4) *there exist* $(+, \phi, ST), (+, \phi', S'T') \in \mathcal{Q}_{\mathrm{BC}}$ *(not necessarily distinct) such that* $\phi_R(\mathbf{k}) \oplus k_1 = S' \oplus k_4;$
(C-5) *there exist* $(-, LR, ST) \neq (-, L'R', S'T') \in \mathcal{Q}_{\mathrm{BC}}$ *such that* $R = R';$
(C-6 *there exist* $(-, LR, ST), (-, L'R', S'T') \in \mathcal{Q}_{\mathrm{BC}}$ *(not necessarily distinct) such that* $R \oplus k_1 = S' \oplus k_4;$
(C-7) *there exist* $(+, \phi, ST), (-, L'R', S'T') \in \mathcal{Q}_{\mathrm{BC}}$ *such that*
   (a) $\phi(\mathbf{k}) = L'R'$ *or*
   (b) $ST = S'T'$ *or*
   (c) $\phi_R(\mathbf{k}) \oplus k_1 = S' \oplus k_4$ *or*
   (d) $S \oplus k_4 = R' \oplus k_1.$

Let $\mathcal{T}_{\mathrm{bad}}$ *denote the set of bad transcripts and let* $\mathcal{T}_{\mathrm{good}} := \mathcal{T} \setminus \mathcal{T}_{\mathrm{bad}}$.

Lemma 4.1. *Let* $\mathcal{A}$ *be a distinguisher making at most* $q \leq 2^n$ *queries to* KDENC *or* DEC *and* q_{f} *queries to* F. *With* $\mathcal{T}_{\mathrm{bad}}$ *defined as above,*

$$\Pr[X_{\mathcal{A}, \mathsf{pw}} \in \mathcal{T}_{\mathrm{bad}}] \leq q^2 \cdot (\mathbf{cf}(\Phi) + 3/2 \cdot \mathbf{oxf}(\Phi_R) + 6/2^n) + qq_{\mathsf{f}} \cdot (\mathbf{of}(\Phi_R) + 3/2^n) .$$

Proof. We compute the probability of each condition in turn. Recall that in pw, the key $\mathbf{k} = (k_1, k_2, k_3, k_4)$ is drawn at random and independently of all oracle answers at the end.

(C-1) Fix an encryption query $(+, \phi, ST) \in \mathcal{Q}_{\mathrm{BC}}$ and a query to the public function $(u, v) \in \mathcal{Q}_{\mathsf{F}}$.
   (a) By Definition 3.2, $\phi_R(\mathbf{k}) = k_1 \oplus u$ with probability at most $\mathbf{of}(\Phi_R)$;

(b) Since k_4 is uniformly random and independent of the query transcript, $k_4 = S \oplus u$ with probability at most $1/2^n$.

Summing over all possible pairs, condition (C-1) happens with probability at most $qq_{\mathsf{f}}(\mathbf{of}(\Phi_R) + 1/2^n)$.

(C-2) Fix a decryption query $(-, LR, ST) \in \mathcal{Q}_{\mathrm{BC}}$ and a query to F $(u, v) \in \mathcal{Q}_{\mathsf{F}}$.

(a) Since k_1 is uniformly random and independent of the query transcript, $R \oplus u = k_1$ with probability at most $1/2^n$.

(b) Since k_4 is uniformly random and independent of the query transcript, $S \oplus u = k_4$ with probability at most $1/2^n$.

Summing over all possible pairs, condition (C-2) happens with probability at most $2qq_{\mathsf{f}}/2^n$.

(C-3) Fix two queries $(+, \phi, ST) \neq (+, \phi', S'T') \in \mathcal{Q}_{\mathrm{BC}}$. Since the adversary never repeats queries, we have $\phi \neq \phi'$.

(a) By Definition 3.1, $\phi(\mathbf{k}) = \phi'(\mathbf{k})$ with probability at most $\mathbf{cf}(\Phi)$ over the choice of a random $\mathbf{k}$.

(b) Since $\phi \neq \phi'$, the output $S'T'$ is sampled uniformly at random in a set of size at least $2^{2n} - q$ and independently of ST. Thus $S = S'$ with probability at most $2^n/(2^{2n} - q) \leq 1/(2^n - 1) \leq 2/2^n$.

Summing over all possible distinct pairs, condition (C-3) happens with probability at most $q^2/2 \cdot (\mathbf{cf}(\Phi) + 4/2^n)$.

(C-4) Fix two queries $(+, \phi, ST), (+, \phi', S'T') \in \mathcal{Q}_{\mathrm{BC}}$. By Definition 3.3, $\phi_R(\mathbf{k}) = S' \oplus k_1 \oplus k_4$ with probability at most $\mathbf{oxf}(\Phi_R)$ over the choice of $\mathbf{k}$. Summing over all possible pairs, condition (C-4) happens with probability at most $q^2 \cdot \mathbf{oxf}(\Phi_R)$.

(C-5) Fix two decryption queries $(-, LR, ST) \neq (-, L'R', S'T') \in \mathcal{Q}_{\mathrm{BC}}$. The value $L'R'$ is sampled uniformly at random in a set of size at least $2^{2n} - q$ and independently of LR. Thus, $R = R'$ with probability at most $2^n/(2^{2n} - q) \leq 1/(2^n - 1) \leq 2/2^n$. Summing over all possible distinct pairs, condition (C-5) happens with probability at most $q^2/2^n$.

(C-6) Fix two decryption queries $(-, LR, ST), (-, L'R', S'T') \in \mathcal{Q}_{\mathrm{BC}}$. As k_1 and k_4 are randomly sampled, $R \oplus S' = k_1 \oplus k_4$ with probability at most $1/2^n$. Summing over all possible distinct pairs, condition (C-6) happens with probability at most $q^2/2^n$.

(C-7) Fix an encryption query $(+, \phi, ST) \in \mathcal{Q}_{\mathrm{BC}}$ and a decryption query $(-, L'R', S'T') \in \mathcal{Q}_{\mathrm{BC}}$.

(a) By Definition 3.1, $\phi(\mathbf{k}) = L'R'$ with probability at most $\mathbf{cf}(\Phi)$.

(b) We distinguish two cases. If the encryption query occurs before the decryption query, then necessarily $ST \neq S'T'$ due to the no-pointless-query assumption (the adversary cannot ask Dec to decrypt a value that was received as an answer to the KDEnc oracle). If the decryption query occurs before the encryption query, then ST is uniformly random in a set of size at least $2^{2n} - q$ and independent of $S'T'$. Hence, the condition occurs with probability at most $1/(2^{2n} - q) \leq 1/2^n$.

(c) By Definition 3.3, $\phi_R(\mathbf{k}) = S' \oplus k_1 \oplus k_4$ with probability at most $\mathbf{oxf}(\Phi_R)$ over the choice of $\mathbf{k}$.

(d) Since k_1 and k_4 are drawn uniformly at random and independently of the query transcript, the probability that $k_1 \oplus k_4 = S \oplus R'$ is at most $1/2^n$.

Summing over all possible distinct pairs, condition (C-7) happens with probability at most $q^2/2 \cdot (\mathbf{cf}(\Phi) + \mathbf{oxf}(\Phi_R) + 4/2^n)$.

The result follows by applying the union bound over conditions (C-1) to (C-7).

We now lower bound $\Pr[X_{\mathcal{A},\mathsf{rw}} = \tau]/\Pr[X_{\mathcal{A},\mathsf{pw}} = \tau]$ for a good transcript τ. To this end, we introduce the following definition of a *bad function* F with respect to a good τ. Informally, this definition states that there is a collision among the set of all inputs to the second or third-round functions (conditions (C'-3), (C'-5), and (C'-7)) or among these and direct, first-round, or second-round queries (conditions (C'-1) and (C'-2)).

Definition 4.2. *Fix a good transcript* $\tau = (\mathcal{Q}_{\mathrm{BC}}, \mathcal{Q}_{\mathsf{F}}, \mathbf{k})$. *Let*

$$\mathsf{Dom}(\mathsf{F}) := \{ u \in \{0,1\}^n : \exists (u, v) \in \mathcal{Q}_{\mathsf{F}} \}, \quad and$$

$$\mathsf{Dom}'(\mathsf{F}) := \left\{ u \in \{0,1\}^n : \begin{array}{l} \exists (+, \phi, ST) \in \mathcal{Q}_{\mathrm{BC}}, u = \phi_R(\mathbf{k}) \oplus k_1 \vee \\ \exists (+, \phi, ST) \in \mathcal{Q}_{\mathrm{BC}}, u = S \oplus k_4 \vee \\ \exists (-, LR, ST) \in \mathcal{Q}_{\mathrm{BC}}, u = R \oplus k_1 \vee \\ \exists (-, LR, ST) \in \mathcal{Q}_{\mathrm{BC}}, u = S \oplus k_4 \end{array} \right\}.$$

A function F *is said to be* bad *with respect to* τ, *denoted* $\mathsf{Bad}(\mathsf{F}, \tau)$, *iff any of the following holds.*

(C'-1) there exists $(+, \phi, ST) \in \mathcal{Q}_{\mathrm{BC}}$ *such that*
  (a) $\phi_L(\mathbf{k}) \oplus \mathsf{F}(\phi_R(\mathbf{k}) \oplus k_1) \oplus k_2 \in \mathsf{Dom}(\mathsf{F}) \cup \mathsf{Dom}'(\mathsf{F})$ *or*
  (b) $T \oplus \mathsf{F}(S \oplus k_4) \oplus k_3 \in \mathsf{Dom}(\mathsf{F}) \cup \mathsf{Dom}'(\mathsf{F})$;
(C'-2) there exists $(-, LR, ST) \in \mathcal{Q}_{\mathrm{BC}}$ *such that*
  (a) $L \oplus \mathsf{F}(R \oplus k_1) \oplus k_2 \in \mathsf{Dom}(\mathsf{F}) \cup \mathsf{Dom}'(\mathsf{F})$ *or*
  (b) $T \oplus \mathsf{F}(S \oplus k_4) \oplus k_3 \in \mathsf{Dom}(\mathsf{F}) \cup \mathsf{Dom}'(\mathsf{F})$;
(C'-3) there exist $(+, \phi, ST) \neq (+, \phi', S'T') \in \mathcal{Q}_{\mathrm{BC}}$ *such that*
  (a) $\phi_L(\mathbf{k}) \oplus \mathsf{F}(\phi_R(\mathbf{k}) \oplus k_1) = \phi'_L(\mathbf{k}) \oplus \mathsf{F}(\phi'_R(\mathbf{k}) \oplus k_1)$ *or*
  (b) $T \oplus \mathsf{F}(S \oplus k_4) = T' \oplus \mathsf{F}(S' \oplus k_4)$;
(C'-4) there exist $(+, \phi, ST), (+, \phi', S'T') \in \mathcal{Q}_{\mathrm{BC}}$ *(not necessarily distinct) such that* $\phi_L(\mathbf{k}) \oplus \mathsf{F}(\phi_R(\mathbf{k}) \oplus k_1) \oplus k_2 = T' \oplus \mathsf{F}(S' \oplus k_4) \oplus k_3$;
(C'-5) there exist $(-, LR, ST) \neq (-, L'R', S'T') \in \mathcal{Q}_{\mathrm{BC}}$ *such that*
  (a) $L \oplus \mathsf{F}(R \oplus k_1) = L' \oplus \mathsf{F}(R' \oplus k_1)$ *or*
  (b) $T \oplus \mathsf{F}(S \oplus k_4) = T' \oplus \mathsf{F}(S' \oplus k_4)$;
(C'-6) there exist $(-, LR, ST), (-, L'R', S'T') \in \mathcal{Q}_{\mathrm{BC}}$ *(not necessarily distinct) such that* $L \oplus \mathsf{F}(R \oplus k_1) \oplus k_2 = T' \oplus \mathsf{F}(S' \oplus k_4) \oplus k_3$;
(C'-7) there exist $(+, \phi, ST), (-, L'R', S'T') \in \mathcal{Q}_{\mathrm{BC}}$ *such that*
  (a) $\phi_L(\mathbf{k}) \oplus \mathsf{F}(\phi_R(\mathbf{k}) \oplus k_1) = L' \oplus \mathsf{F}(R' \oplus k_1)$ *or*
  (b) $T \oplus \mathsf{F}(S \oplus k_4) = T' \oplus \mathsf{F}(S' \oplus k_4)$ *or*
  (c) $\phi_L(\mathbf{k}) \oplus \mathsf{F}(\phi_R(\mathbf{k}) \oplus k_1) \oplus k_2 = T' \oplus \mathsf{F}(S' \oplus k_4) \oplus k_3$ *or*
  (d) $T \oplus \mathsf{F}(S \oplus k_4) \oplus k_3 = L' \oplus \mathsf{F}(R' \oplus k_1) \oplus k_2$.

Lemma 4.2. *Fix a good transcript $\tau = (\mathcal{Q}_{\mathsf{BC}}, \mathcal{Q}_{\mathsf{F}}, \mathbf{k})$. Then*

$$\Pr_{\mathsf{F} \leftarrow \mathsf{Func}(n)} [\mathsf{Bad}(\mathsf{F}, \tau) \mid \mathsf{F} \vdash \mathcal{Q}_{\mathsf{F}}] \leq 4 \cdot q q_{\mathsf{f}} / 2^n + 14 \cdot q^2 / 2^n .$$

Proof. First, note that $|\mathsf{Dom}(\mathsf{F})| = q_{\mathsf{f}}$ and $|\mathsf{Dom}'(\mathsf{F})| \leq 2q$. We now consider each condition in turn.[1]

(C'-1) Fix an encryption query $(+, \phi, ST) \in \mathcal{Q}_{\mathsf{BC}}$.

   (a) By $\neg$(C-1a), $\phi_R(\mathbf{k}) \oplus k_1$ is a fresh input for the function F and hence $\mathsf{F}(\phi_R(\mathbf{k}) \oplus k_1)$ is uniformly random. Thus, $\phi_L(\mathbf{k}) \oplus \mathsf{F}(\phi_R(\mathbf{k}) \oplus k_1) \oplus k_2 \in \mathsf{Dom}(\mathsf{F}) \cup \mathsf{Dom}'(\mathsf{F})$ with probability at most $(q_{\mathsf{f}} + 2q)/2^n$.

   (b) By $\neg$(C-1b), $S \oplus k_4$ is a fresh input for the function F and hence $\mathsf{F}(S \oplus k_4)$ is uniformly random. Thus, $T \oplus \mathsf{F}(S \oplus k_4) \oplus k_3 \in \mathsf{Dom}(\mathsf{F}) \cup \mathsf{Dom}'(\mathsf{F})$ with probability at most $(q_{\mathsf{f}} + 2q)/2^n$.

Summing over all encryption queries, condition (C'-1) happens with probability at most $2q(q_{\mathsf{f}} + 2q)/2^n$.

(C'-2) Fix a decryption query $(-, LR, ST) \in \mathcal{Q}_{\mathsf{BC}}$.

   (a) By $\neg$(C-2a), $R \oplus k_1$ is a fresh input for the function F and hence $\mathsf{F}(R \oplus k_1)$ is uniformly random. Thus, $L \oplus \mathsf{F}(R \oplus k_1) \oplus k_2 \in \mathsf{Dom}(\mathsf{F}) \cup \mathsf{Dom}'(\mathsf{F})$ with probability at most $(q_{\mathsf{f}} + 2q)/2^n$.

   (b) By $\neg$(C-2b), $S \oplus k_4$ is a fresh value for the function F and hence $T \oplus \mathsf{F}(S \oplus k_4) \oplus k_3 \in \mathsf{Dom}(\mathsf{F}) \cup \mathsf{Dom}'(\mathsf{F})$ with probability at most $(q_{\mathsf{f}} + 2q)/2^n$.

Summing over all decryption queries, condition (C'-2) happens with probability at most $2q(q_{\mathsf{f}} + 2q)/2^n$.

(C'-3) Fix $(+, \phi, ST) \neq (+, \phi', S'T') \in \mathcal{Q}_{\mathsf{BC}}$.

   (a) By $\neg$(C-1a), we have $\phi_R(\mathbf{k}) \oplus k_1 \notin \mathsf{Dom}(\mathsf{F})$ and $\phi'_R(\mathbf{k}) \oplus k_1 \notin \mathsf{Dom}(\mathsf{F})$. Moreover, by $\neg$(C-3a), we have that $\phi(\mathbf{k}) \neq \phi'(\mathbf{k})$. We distinguish two cases. If $\phi_R(\mathbf{k}) \neq \phi'_R(\mathbf{k})$, then $\mathsf{F}(\phi_R(\mathbf{k}) \oplus k_1)$ and $\mathsf{F}(\phi'_R(\mathbf{k}) \oplus k_1)$ are uniformly random and independent, so that $\phi_L(\mathbf{k}) \oplus \mathsf{F}(\phi_R(\mathbf{k}) \oplus k_1) = \phi'_L(\mathbf{k}) \oplus \mathsf{F}(\phi'_R(\mathbf{k}) \oplus k_1)$ with probability $1/2^n$. If $\phi_R(\mathbf{k}) = \phi'_R(\mathbf{k})$, then necessarily $\phi_L(\mathbf{k}) \neq \phi'_L(\mathbf{k})$, so that the condition cannot hold. Hence, this condition holds with probability at most $1/2^n$.

   (b) By $\neg$(C-1b), $S \oplus k_4 \notin \mathsf{Dom}(\mathsf{F})$ and $S' \oplus k_4 \notin \mathsf{Dom}(\mathsf{F})$; moreover, by $\neg$(C-3b), $S \neq S'$, so that $\mathsf{F}(S \oplus k_4)$ and $\mathsf{F}(S' \oplus k_4)$ are uniformly random and independent; hence, $T \oplus \mathsf{F}(S \oplus k_4) = T' \oplus \mathsf{F}(S' \oplus k_4)$ with probability at most $1/2^n$.

Summing over all possible pairs of distinct encryption queries, condition (C'-3) happens with probability at most $q^2/2^n$.

(C'-4) Fix two (possibly equal) encryption queries $(+, \phi, ST), (+, \phi', S'T') \in \mathcal{Q}_{\mathsf{BC}}$. By $\neg$(C-1a), $\phi_R(\mathbf{k}) \oplus k_1 \notin \mathsf{Dom}(\mathsf{F})$ and by $\neg$(C-1b), $S' \oplus k_4 \notin \mathsf{Dom}(\mathsf{F})$; moreover, by $\neg$(C-4), we have $\phi_R(\mathbf{k}) \oplus k_1 \neq S' \oplus k_4$, so that $\mathsf{F}(\phi_R(\mathbf{k}) \oplus k_1)$ and $\mathsf{F}(S' \oplus k_4)$ are uniformly random and independent; hence, $\phi_L(\mathbf{k}) \oplus \mathsf{F}(\phi_R(\mathbf{k}) \oplus k_1) \oplus k_2 = T' \oplus \mathsf{F}(S' \oplus k_4) \oplus k_3$ with probability at most $1/2^n$. Summing over all possible pairs, condition (C'-4) happens with probability at most $q^2/2^n$.

---

[1] In what follows, we will argue using the fact that the transcript is good by referring to which specific condition defining a bad transcript would hold, saying e.g., "By $\neg$(C-*ix*), …".

(C'-5) Fix two decryption queries $(-, LR, ST) \neq (-, L'R', S'T') \in \mathcal{Q}_{\mathrm{BC}}$.
   (a) By $\neg$(C-2a), $R \oplus k_1 \notin \mathsf{Dom}(\mathsf{F})$ and $R' \oplus k_1 \notin \mathsf{Dom}(\mathsf{F})$; moreover, by $\neg$(C-5), $R \neq R'$ so that $\mathsf{F}(R \oplus k_1)$ and $\mathsf{F}(R' \oplus k_1)$ are uniformly random and independent. Hence, $L \oplus \mathsf{F}(R \oplus k_1) = L' \oplus \mathsf{F}(R' \oplus k_1)$ with probability at most $1/2^n$.
   (b) By $\neg$(C-2b), $S \oplus k_4 \notin \mathsf{Dom}(\mathsf{F})$ and $S' \oplus k_4 \notin \mathsf{Dom}(\mathsf{F})$. We distinguish two cases. If $S \neq S'$ then $\mathsf{F}(S \oplus k_4)$ and $\mathsf{F}(S' \oplus k_4)$ are uniformly random and independent and hence $T \oplus \mathsf{F}(S \oplus k_4) = T' \oplus \mathsf{F}(S' \oplus k_4)$ with probability at most $1/2^n$. If $S = S'$ then necessarily $T \neq T'$ since the adversary does not repeat queries and hence the condition cannot hold. In all cases, the conditions hold with probability at most $1/2^n$.
By summing over all possible pairs of distinct decryption queries, condition (C'-5) happens with probability at most $q^2/2^n$.

   (C'-6)   Fix   two   (possibly equal) decryption queries $(-, LR, ST), (-, L'R', S'T') \in \mathcal{Q}_{\mathrm{BC}}$. By $\neg$(C-2a), $R \oplus k_1 \notin \mathsf{Dom}(\mathsf{F})$ and by $\neg$(C-2b), $S' \oplus k_4 \notin \mathsf{Dom}(\mathsf{F})$; moreover, by $\neg$(C-6), $R \oplus k_1 \neq S' \oplus k_4$ so that $\mathsf{F}(R \oplus k_1)$ and $\mathsf{F}(S' \oplus k_4)$ are uniformly random and independent; hence, $L \oplus \mathsf{F}(R \oplus k_1) \oplus k_2 = T' \oplus \mathsf{F}(S' \oplus k_4) \oplus k_3$ with probability at most $1/2^n$. Summing over all possible pairs, condition (C'-6) happens with probability at most $q^2/2^n$.
(C'-7) Fix an encryption query $(+, \phi, ST) \in \mathcal{Q}_{\mathrm{BC}}$ and a decryption query $(-, L'R', S'T') \in \mathcal{Q}_{\mathrm{BC}}$. By respectively $\neg$(C-1a), $\neg$(C-1b), $\neg$(C-2a), and $\neg$(C-2b), $\phi_R(\mathbf{k}) \oplus k_1$, $S \oplus k_4$, $R' \oplus k_1$, and $S' \oplus k_4$ are all fresh input values to F.
   (a) By $\neg$(C-7a), $\phi(\mathbf{k}) \neq L'R'$. We distinguish two cases. If $\phi_R(\mathbf{k}) \neq R'$, then $\mathsf{F}(\phi_R(\mathbf{k}) \oplus k_1)$ and $\mathsf{F}(R' \oplus k_1)$ are uniformly random and independent and thus $\phi_L(\mathbf{k}) \oplus \mathsf{F}(\phi_R(\mathbf{k}) \oplus k_1) = L' \oplus \mathsf{F}(R' \oplus k_1)$ with probability at most $1/2^n$. If $\phi_R(\mathbf{k}) = R'$, then necessarily $\phi_L(\mathbf{k}) \neq L'$ and hence the condition cannot hold. In all cases, the condition holds with probability at most $1/2^n$.
   (b) By $\neg$(C-7b), $ST \neq S'T'$. If $S \neq S'$, then $\mathsf{F}(S \oplus k_4)$ and $\mathsf{F}(S' \oplus k_4)$ are uniformly random and independent and hence $T \oplus \mathsf{F}(S \oplus k_4) = T' \oplus \mathsf{F}(S' \oplus k_4)$ with probability at most $1/2^n$. If $S = S'$, then necessarily $T \neq T'$ and the condition cannot hold. In all cases, the condition holds with probability at most $1/2^n$.
   (c) By $\neg$(C-7c), $\phi_R(\mathbf{k}) \oplus k_1 \neq S' \oplus k_4$ so that $\mathsf{F}(\phi_R(\mathbf{k}) \oplus k_1)$ and $\mathsf{F}(S' \oplus k_4)$ are uniformly random and independent and thus $\phi_L(\mathbf{k}) \oplus \mathsf{F}(\phi_R(\mathbf{k}) \oplus k_1) \oplus k_2 = T' \oplus \mathsf{F}(S' \oplus k_4) \oplus k_3$ with probability at most $1/2^n$.
   (d) By $\neg$(C-7d), $S \oplus k_4 \neq R' \oplus k_1$ so that $\mathsf{F}(S \oplus k_4)$ and $\mathsf{F}(R' \oplus k_1)$ are uniformly random and independent and thus $T \oplus \mathsf{F}(S \oplus k_4) \oplus k_3 = L' \oplus \mathsf{F}(R' \oplus k_1) \oplus k_2$ with probability at most $1/2^n$.
By summing over all possible pairs, condition (C'-7) happens with probability at most $2q^2/2^n$.

The result follows by applying the union bound over all conditions.

Lemma 4.3. *Fix a good transcript* $\tau = (\mathcal{Q}_{BC}, \mathcal{Q}_F, \mathbf{k})$. *Then*

$$\Pr_{F \leftarrow \mathrm{Func}(n)}[\mathsf{KAF}^F_{\mathbf{k}} \vdash \mathcal{Q}_{BC} \mid F \vdash \mathcal{Q}_F \wedge \neg \mathrm{Bad}(F, \tau)] = \frac{1}{(2^n)^{2q}} .$$

Proof. Let q_{enc} and q_{dec} respectively denote the number of queries to KDENC and DEC in $\mathcal{Q}_{BC}$ (with $q_{\mathrm{enc}} + q_{\mathrm{dec}} = q$). Using an arbitrary ordering, let

$$\mathcal{Q}_{BC} = [(+, \phi_1, S_1 T_1), \ldots, (+, \phi_{q_{\mathrm{enc}}}, S_{q_{\mathrm{enc}}} T_{q_{\mathrm{enc}}}),$$
$$(-, L_{q_{\mathrm{enc}}+1} R_{q_{\mathrm{enc}}+1}, S_{q_{\mathrm{enc}}+1} T_{q_{\mathrm{enc}}+1}), \ldots, (-, L_q R_q, S_q T_q)] .$$

For a given function F, let w_i and z_i be the i-th input to F in the second and third rounds respectively, i.e.,

$$\begin{aligned}
w_i &= \phi_{i,L}(\mathbf{k}) \oplus F(\phi_{i,R}(\mathbf{k}) \oplus k_1) \oplus k_2 & \text{for } 1 \le i \le q_{\mathrm{enc}} \\
&= L_i \oplus F(R_i \oplus k_1) \oplus k_2 & \text{for } q_{\mathrm{enc}} + 1 \le i \le q \\
z_i &= T_i \oplus F(S_i \oplus k_4) \oplus k_3 & \text{for } 1 \le i \le q .
\end{aligned}$$

Then event $\mathsf{KAF}^F_{\mathbf{k}} \vdash \mathcal{Q}_{BC}$ is equivalent to

$$\begin{cases} F(w_i) = \phi_{i,R}(\mathbf{k}) \oplus T_i \oplus F(S_i \oplus k_4) \\ F(z_i) = S_i \oplus \phi_{i,L}(\mathbf{k}) \oplus F(\phi_{i,R}(\mathbf{k}) \oplus k_1) \end{cases} \quad \text{for } 1 \le i \le q_{\mathrm{enc}} \quad (3)$$

$$\begin{cases} F(w_i) = R_i \oplus T_i \oplus F(S_i \oplus k_4) \\ F(z_i) = S_i \oplus L_i \oplus F(R_i \oplus k_1) \end{cases} \quad \text{for } q_{\mathrm{enc}} + 1 \le i \le q . \quad (4)$$

Conditioned on event $\neg \mathrm{Bad}(F, \tau)$, we have that $w_1, \ldots, w_q, z_1, \ldots, z_q$ are $2q$ distinct values as otherwise one of the conditions (C'-3)–(C'-7) would be fulfilled. Moreover, all these $2q$ values are distinct from values in $\mathrm{Dom}(F) \cup \mathrm{Dom}'(F)$, as otherwise condition (C'-1) or (C'-2) would be fulfilled. This implies that, even conditioned on $F \vdash \mathcal{Q}_F$, the $2q$ random values $F(w_1), \ldots, F(w_q), F(z_1), \ldots, F(z_q)$ are uniform and independent of $F(\phi_{i,R}(\mathbf{k}) \oplus k_1)$ for $1 \le i \le q_{\mathrm{enc}}$, $F(R_i \oplus k_1)$ for $q_{\mathrm{enc}} + 1 \le i \le q$, and $F(S_i \oplus k_4)$ for $1 \le i \le q$. Hence, Eqs. (3) and (4) hold with probability $(1/2^n)^{2q}$. $\qquad\blacksquare$

Lemma 4.4. *Fix a good transcript* $\tau = (\mathcal{Q}_{BC}, \mathcal{Q}_F, \mathbf{k})$. *Then,*

$$\frac{\Pr[X_{\mathcal{A}, \mathrm{rw}} = \tau]}{\Pr[X_{\mathcal{A}, \mathrm{pw}} = \tau]} \ge 1 - 4 \cdot q q_f / 2^n - 15 \cdot q^2 / 2^n .$$

Proof. Let $\tau = (\mathcal{Q}_{BC}, \mathcal{Q}_F, \mathbf{k})$ with $\mathbf{k} = (k_1, k_2, k_3, k_4)$ be a good transcript, and let q_{enc}, resp. q_{dec}, denote the number of queries to KDENC, resp. DEC, in $\mathcal{Q}_{BC}$, with $q_{\mathrm{enc}} + q_{\mathrm{dec}} = q$.

Exactly as in the proof of Lemma 3.1, one can show that

$$\Pr[X_{\mathcal{A}, \mathrm{pw}} = \tau] = \Pr_{\mathbf{k}' \leftarrow \mathsf{K}}[\mathbf{k}' = \mathbf{k}] \cdot \frac{1}{(2^n)^{q_f}} \cdot \frac{1}{(2^{2n})_{q_{\mathrm{enc}}}} \cdot \frac{1}{(2^{2n})_{q_{\mathrm{dec}}}} . \quad (5)$$

where K is the key-generation algorithm.

We now lower bound the probability that $X_{\mathcal{A},\mathrm{rw}} = \tau$.

$$\Pr[X_{\mathcal{A},\mathrm{rw}} = \tau] \tag{6}$$

$$= \Pr_{\mathbf{k}' \twoheadleftarrow \mathsf{K}}[\mathbf{k}' = \mathbf{k}] \cdot \Pr_{\mathsf{F} \twoheadleftarrow \mathsf{Func}(n)}[\mathsf{KAF}_{\mathbf{k}}^{\mathsf{F}} \vdash \mathcal{Q}_{\mathrm{BC}} \wedge \mathsf{F} \vdash \mathcal{Q}_{\mathsf{F}}]$$

$$= \Pr_{\mathbf{k}' \twoheadleftarrow \mathsf{K}}[\mathbf{k}' = \mathbf{k}] \cdot \Pr_{\mathsf{F} \twoheadleftarrow \mathsf{Func}(n)}[\mathsf{F} \vdash \mathcal{Q}_{\mathsf{F}}] \cdot \Pr_{\mathsf{F} \twoheadleftarrow \mathsf{Func}(n)}[\mathsf{KAF}_{\mathbf{k}}^{\mathsf{F}} \vdash \mathcal{Q}_{\mathrm{BC}} \mid \mathsf{F} \vdash \mathcal{Q}_{\mathsf{F}}]$$

$$= \Pr_{\mathbf{k}' \twoheadleftarrow \mathsf{K}}[\mathbf{k}' = \mathbf{k}] \cdot \frac{1}{(2^n)^{q_{\mathrm{f}}}} \cdot \Pr_{\mathsf{F} \twoheadleftarrow \mathsf{Func}(n)}[\mathsf{KAF}_{\mathbf{k}}^{\mathsf{F}} \vdash \mathcal{Q}_{\mathrm{BC}} \mid \mathsf{F} \vdash \mathcal{Q}_{\mathsf{F}}]$$

$$= \Pr_{\mathbf{k}' \twoheadleftarrow \mathsf{K}}[\mathbf{k}' = \mathbf{k}] \cdot \frac{1}{(2^n)^{q_{\mathrm{f}}}} \cdot \Pr_{\mathsf{F} \twoheadleftarrow \mathsf{Func}(n)}[\mathsf{KAF}_{\mathbf{k}}^{\mathsf{F}} \vdash \mathcal{Q}_{\mathrm{BC}} \mid \mathsf{F} \vdash \mathcal{Q}_{\mathsf{F}} \wedge \neg\mathsf{Bad}(\mathsf{F}, \tau)]$$

$$\cdot (1 - \Pr_{\mathsf{F} \twoheadleftarrow \mathsf{Func}(n)}[\mathsf{Bad}(\mathsf{F}, \tau) \mid \mathsf{F} \vdash \mathcal{Q}_{\mathsf{F}}]) . \tag{7}$$

Combining Eq. 7 and Eq. 5 we get

$$\frac{\Pr[X_{\mathcal{A},\mathrm{rw}} = \tau]}{\Pr[X_{\mathcal{A},\mathrm{pw}} = \tau]} = (2^{2n})_{q_{\mathrm{enc}}} \cdot (2^{2n})_{q_{\mathrm{dec}}} \cdot \Pr[\mathsf{KAF}_{\mathbf{k}}^{\mathsf{F}} \vdash \mathcal{Q}_{\mathrm{BC}} \mid \mathsf{F} \vdash \mathcal{Q}_{\mathsf{F}} \wedge \neg\mathsf{Bad}(\mathsf{F}, \tau)]$$

$$\cdot (1 - \Pr[\mathsf{Bad}(\mathsf{F}, \tau) \mid \mathsf{F} \vdash \mathcal{Q}_{\mathsf{F}}]) ,$$

where all probabilities are over $\mathsf{F} \twoheadleftarrow \mathsf{Func}(n)$. Using Lemma 4.3 and Lemma 4.2, we obtain

$$\frac{\Pr[X_{\mathcal{A},\mathrm{rw}} = \tau]}{\Pr[X_{\mathcal{A},\mathrm{pw}} = \tau]} \geq \frac{(2^{2n})_{q_{\mathrm{enc}}} \cdot (2^{2n})_{q_{\mathrm{dec}}}}{(2^n)^{2q}} \cdot \left(1 - \frac{4qq_{\mathrm{f}}}{2^n} - \frac{14q^2}{2^n}\right) \tag{8}$$

$$= \left(1 - \frac{4qq_{\mathrm{f}}}{2^n} - \frac{14q^2}{2^n}\right) \cdot \prod_{i=0}^{q_{\mathrm{enc}}-1}\left(1 - \frac{i}{2^{2n}}\right) \cdot \prod_{i=0}^{q_{\mathrm{dec}}-1}\left(1 - \frac{i}{2^{2n}}\right) \tag{9}$$

$$\geq \left(1 - \frac{4qq_{\mathrm{f}}}{2^n} - \frac{14q^2}{2^n}\right) \cdot \left(1 - \frac{q_{\mathrm{enc}}^2}{2 \cdot 2^{2n}}\right) \cdot \left(1 - \frac{q_{\mathrm{dec}}^2}{2 \cdot 2^{2n}}\right) \tag{10}$$

$$\geq 1 - \frac{4qq_{\mathrm{f}}}{2^n} - \frac{15q^2}{2^n} . \tag{11}$$

Combining Lemma 2.1 with Lemma 4.1 and Lemma 4.4, we finally obtain Eq. 2, which concludes the proof of Theorem 4.1.

5   Attacks

5.1   Necessity of Offset-Freeness

We start by showing that the condition that Φ_R is offset-free is necessary for the KDM-CPA security of 4-round KAF (with the same round function F and independent keys $\mathbf{k} = (k_1, k_2, k_3, k_4)$).[2] This attack takes advantage of a collision at the inputs to the third-round F within two encryption queries:

---

[2] Note that for a set Φ, if Φ_R is offset-free then so is Φ, but not necessary the other way round.

- Adversary $\mathcal{A}$ chooses two distinct values x and x' and obtains $\mathsf{F}(x)$, $\mathsf{F}(x')$, $\mathsf{F}^2(x)$ and $\mathsf{F}^2(x')$ and builds the values

$$\Delta_L := \mathsf{F}^2(x) \oplus x, \Delta_R := \mathsf{F}(x), \Delta'_L := \mathsf{F}^2(x') \oplus x', \Delta'_R := \mathsf{F}(x') .$$

- $\mathcal{A}$ then calls the KDEnc oracle twice on inputs $\phi = (\phi_L, \phi_R)$ and $\phi' = (\phi'_L, \phi'_R)$ where

$$\phi_L(\mathbf{k}) := k_2 \oplus \Delta_L \quad \text{and} \quad \phi_R(\mathbf{k}) := k_1 \oplus \Delta_R ,$$

$$\phi'_L(\mathbf{k}) := k_2 \oplus \Delta'_L \quad \text{and} \quad \phi'_R(\mathbf{k}) := k_1 \oplus \Delta'_R .$$

The adversary receives ST and $S'T'$ as the respective answers. Note that any set Φ_R containing both ϕ_R and ϕ'_R is not offset-free.
- $\mathcal{A}$ returns 1 iff $S \oplus S' = x \oplus x'$.

The adversary returns 1 with probability 1 in the real world whereas it returns 1 with probability $1/2^n$ in the ideal world. To see the former, note that the input $k_2 \oplus \mathsf{F}^2(x) \oplus x | k_1 \oplus \mathsf{F}(x)$ is processed though the first three rounds as follows:

$$k_2 \oplus \mathsf{F}^2(x) \oplus x | k_1 \oplus \mathsf{F}(x)$$
$$\downarrow$$
$$k_1 \oplus \mathsf{F}(x) | x \oplus k_2$$
$$\downarrow$$
$$x \oplus k_2 | k_1$$
$$\downarrow$$
$$k_1 | x \oplus k_2 \oplus \mathsf{F}(k_1 \oplus k_3).$$

Thus the left half of the output is $x \oplus k_2 \oplus \mathsf{F}(k_1 \oplus k_3)$. Hence the xor of the left halves of two encryptions with constants x and x' is $x \oplus x'$. Note that this attack triggers a collision in the third round function.

5.2   Sliding Attacks

We now analyze the most simple KAF configuration whereby all round functions and keys are identical. This construction is already known to be insecure in the CPA model for any number of rounds: using two encryption queries we have $\mathsf{KAF}(LR) = ST$ and $\mathsf{KAF}(TS) = LR$, which is unlikely for the ideal cipher. In the KDM model, however, we are able to give a stronger *key-recovery* attack using a single query. The adversary chooses an arbitrary value $\Delta \in \{0,1\}^n$ and calls KDEnc on function ϕ, where

$$\phi_R(k) := k \oplus \mathsf{F}(\Delta) \oplus \mathsf{F}\big(\mathsf{F}^2(\Delta) \oplus \Delta\big)$$
$$*\phi_L(k) := k \oplus \mathsf{F}^2(\Delta) \oplus \Delta \oplus \mathsf{F}\big(\mathsf{F}(\Delta) \oplus \mathsf{F}(\mathsf{F}^2(\Delta) \oplus \Delta)\big) .$$

It receives a value ST as the answer and returns T as its guess for the k. This attack is depicted in Fig. 4.

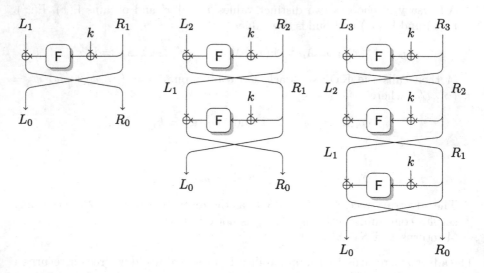

Fig. 3. Backwards construction of inputs leading to a particular output.

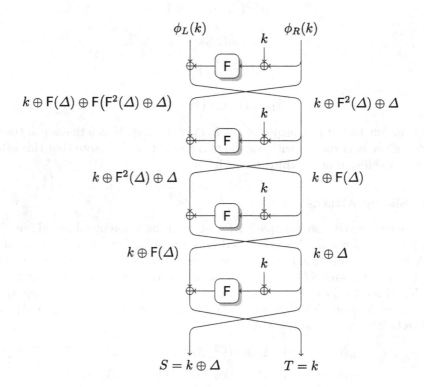

Fig. 4. Sliding attack on 4-round KAF with reuse of keys and round functions.

This attack can be generalized for any number of rounds. Instead of giving a direct expression for any number of rounds r (which we believe would be somewhat hard to read) we give a recursive definition based on Fig. 4. The idea is that we arrange an input $L_r|R_r$ to the r-round KAF so that its output $S|T$ is $L_0|R_0 = k \oplus \Delta|k$. To this end, following the decryption circuit (see Fig. 3), for $i > 0$ we define

$$L_{i+1} \mid R_{i+1} := \mathsf{F}(L_i \oplus k) \oplus R_i \mid L_i .$$

Observe that $L_r|R_r$ corresponds to the decryption of $L_0|R_0$ and hence an encryption of $L_r|R_r$ will result in $L_0|R_0$. We also let $L_0^* \mid R_0^* := \Delta \mid 0^n$ and similarly define

$$L_{i+1}^* \mid R_{i+1}^* := \mathsf{F}(L_i^*) \oplus R_i^* \mid L_i^* .$$

We claim that for any $i \geq 0$,

$$L_i \mid R_i = L_i^* \oplus k \mid R_i^* \oplus k .$$

Now since $L_{i+1}^*|R_{i+1}^*$ is independent of k, we can define two maps $\phi_L(k) := L_r^* \oplus k$ and $\phi_R(k) := R_r^* \oplus k$ that offset the key by constants. Next we query KDENC on (ϕ_L, ϕ_R), which corresponds to encrypting $L_r|R_r$, the result of which will be $L_0|R_0$, and from which the key k can be read off.

We now prove the claim inductively. The claim trivially holds for $i = 0$. Suppose now that the claim holds for i. We show that it holds for $i + 1$:

$$\begin{aligned}
L_{i+1} \mid R_{i+1} &= \mathsf{F}(L_i \oplus k) \oplus R_i \mid L_i \\
&= \mathsf{F}(L_i^* \oplus k \oplus k) \oplus R_i^* \oplus k \mid L_i^* \oplus k \\
&= \mathsf{F}(L_i^*) \oplus R_i^* \oplus k \mid L_i^* \oplus k \\
&= L_{i+1}^* \oplus k \mid R_{i+1}^* \oplus k .
\end{aligned}$$

In the above, the first equality is by the definition of $L_{i+1} \mid R_{i+1}$, the second by the induction hypothesis, and the last by the definition of $L_{i+1}^* \mid R_{i+1}^*$.

The attack generalizes further to r-round KAF where two keys k_1 and k_0 are alternatively used in odd and even-numbered rounds. We define $L_0 := k_{r \bmod 2} \oplus \Delta, R_0 := k_{r+1 \bmod 2}, L_0^* := \Delta$, and $R_0^* := 0^n$. Following the decryption circuit we set

$$\begin{aligned}
L_{i+1} \mid R_{i+1} &:= \mathsf{F}(L_i \oplus k_{i+r \bmod 2}) \oplus R_i \mid L_i, \quad \text{and} \\
L_{i+1}^* \mid R_{i+1}^* &:= \mathsf{F}(L_i^*) \oplus R_i^* \mid L_i^* .
\end{aligned}$$

Note, once again, that $L_{i+1}^* \mid R_{i+1}^*$ is independent of the key and the sequence can be computed via access to F. We prove inductively that

$$L_i \mid R_i = L_i^* \oplus k_{i+r \bmod 2} \mid R_i^* \oplus k_{i+r+1 \bmod 2} .$$

This is trivial when $i = 0$. Furthermore,

$$
\begin{aligned}
L_{i+1} \mid R_{i+1} &= \mathsf{F}(L_i \oplus k_{i+r \bmod 2}) \oplus R_i \mid L_i \\
&= \mathsf{F}(L_i^* \oplus k_{i+r \bmod 2} \oplus k_{i+r \bmod 2}) \oplus R_i^* \oplus k_{i+r+1 \bmod 2} \\
&\qquad\qquad\qquad\qquad\qquad\qquad\qquad\qquad \mid L_i^* \oplus k_{i+r \bmod 2} \\
&= \mathsf{F}(L_i^*) \oplus R_i^* \oplus k_{i+r+1 \bmod 2} \mid L_i^* \oplus k_{i+r \bmod 2} \\
&= L_{i+1}^* \oplus k_{(i+1)+r \bmod 2} \mid R_{i+1}^* \oplus k_{(i+1)+r+1 \bmod 2} \, .
\end{aligned}
$$

Hence keys k_1 and k_0 can be extracted by querying $\mathrm{KDENC}(\phi_L, \phi_R)$, where $\phi_L(k) := L_r^* \oplus k_0$ and $\phi_R(k) := R_r^* \oplus k_1$ as the response will be $L_0 \mid R_0 = k_{r \bmod 2} \oplus \Delta \mid k_{r+1 \bmod 2}$.

6   Discussion

We developed a generic proof strategy, based on the H-coefficient technique to analyze the KDM security of block ciphers. In the full version of the paper [12], we show that our technique can be applied in other settings and we revisit the KDM security of the basic Even–Mansour cipher with only a single round [13, Section 6.1]. We obtain another (arguably simpler) proof of the KDM security of the 1-round EM construction if the set of functions available to the attacker is claw-free and offset-free.

We studied the KDM-CCA security of the 4-round KAF cipher with a single round function if the set of key-dependent functions has negligible claw-freeness, offset-freeness and offset-xor-freeness. An important open problem is to find the minimal k such that the k-round KAF cipher with a single round function achieves KDM-CCA security assuming only that the set of key-dependent functions has (only) negligible claw-freeness. Our attack shows that necessarily $k \geq 5$. Our proof strategy does go through directly for $k \in \{5, 6, 7\}$ since an adversary can cause a collision in inputs to the first and third round function if it can use offsets as key-dependent functions. We do not claim that k-round KAF for $k \in \{5, 6, 7\}$ are KDM-CCA-insecure for some class of claw-free key-dependent functions but only that our technique cannot disprove it. It seems doable to prove the security of 8-round KAF in this setting using our technique but the proof would be much harder along lines we have considered.

References

1. Anderson, R., Biham, E.: Two practical and provably secure block ciphers: BEAR and LION. In: Gollmann, D. (ed.) FSE 1996. LNCS, vol. 1039, pp. 113–120. Springer, Heidelberg (1996). https://doi.org/10.1007/3-540-60865-6_48
2. Applebaum, B.: Key-dependent message security: generic amplification and completeness. In: Paterson, K.G. (ed.) EUROCRYPT 2011. LNCS, vol. 6632, pp. 527–546. Springer, Heidelberg (2011). https://doi.org/10.1007/978-3-642-20465-4_29
3. Barbosa, M., Farshim, P.: The related-key analysis of feistel constructions. In: Cid, C., Rechberger, C. (eds.) FSE 2014. LNCS, vol. 8540, pp. 265–284. Springer, Heidelberg (2015). https://doi.org/10.1007/978-3-662-46706-0_14

4. Beaulieu, R., Shors, D., Smith, J., Treatman-Clark, S., Weeks, B., Wingers, L.: The SIMON and SPECK families of lightweight block ciphers. Cryptology ePrint Archive, Report 2013/404, 2013 (2013). http://eprint.iacr.org/2013/404
5. Black, J., Rogaway, P., Shrimpton, T.: Encryption-scheme security in the presence of key-dependent messages. In: Nyberg, K., Heys, H. (eds.) SAC 2002. LNCS, vol. 2595, pp. 62–75. Springer, Heidelberg (2003). https://doi.org/10.1007/3-540-36492-7_6
6. Boneh, D., Halevi, S., Hamburg, M., Ostrovsky, R.: Circular-secure encryption from decision Diffie-Hellman. In: Wagner, D. (ed.) CRYPTO 2008. LNCS, vol. 5157, pp. 108–125. Springer, Heidelberg (2008). https://doi.org/10.1007/978-3-540-85174-5_7
7. Camenisch, J., Chandran, N., Shoup, V.: A public key encryption scheme secure against key dependent chosen plaintext and adaptive chosen ciphertext attacks. In: Joux, A. (ed.) EUROCRYPT 2009. LNCS, vol. 5479, pp. 351–368. Springer, Heidelberg (2009). https://doi.org/10.1007/978-3-642-01001-9_20
8. Chen, S., Lampe, R., Lee, J., Seurin, Y., Steinberger, J.: Minimizing the two-round even-Mansour cipher. In: Garay, J.A., Gennaro, R. (eds.) CRYPTO 2014. LNCS, vol. 8616, pp. 39–56. Springer, Heidelberg (2014). https://doi.org/10.1007/978-3-662-44371-2_3
9. Chen, S., Steinberger, J.: Tight security bounds for key-alternating ciphers. In: Nguyen, P.Q., Oswald, E. (eds.) EUROCRYPT 2014. LNCS, vol. 8441, pp. 327–350. Springer, Heidelberg (2014). https://doi.org/10.1007/978-3-642-55220-5_19
10. Dai, Y., Steinberger, J.: Indifferentiability of 8-round feistel networks. In: Robshaw, M., Katz, J. (eds.) CRYPTO 2016. LNCS, vol. 9814, pp. 95–120. Springer, Heidelberg (2016). https://doi.org/10.1007/978-3-662-53018-4_4
11. Even, S., Mansour, Y.: A construction of a cipher from a single pseudorandom permutation. In: Imai, H., Rivest, R.L., Matsumoto, T. (eds.) ASIACRYPT 1991. LNCS, vol. 739, pp. 210–224. Springer, Heidelberg (1993). https://doi.org/10.1007/3-540-57332-1_17
12. Farshim, P., Khati, L., Seurin, Y., Vergnaud, D.: The key-dependent message security of key-alternating Feistel ciphers 2021. IACR Cryptol. ePrint Arch (2021)
13. Farshim, P., Khati, L., Vergnaud, D.: Security of Even-Mansour ciphers under key-dependent messages. IACR Trans. Symm. Cryptol. 2017(2), 84–104 (2017)
14. Guo, C., Lin, D.: On the indifferentiability of key-alternating feistel ciphers with no key derivation. In: Dodis, Y., Nielsen, J.B. (eds.) TCC 2015. LNCS, vol. 9014, pp. 110–133. Springer, Heidelberg (2015). https://doi.org/10.1007/978-3-662-46494-6_6
15. Guo, C., Wang, L.: Revisiting key-alternating feistel ciphers for shorter keys and multi-user security. In: Peyrin, T., Galbraith, S. (eds.) ASIACRYPT 2018. LNCS, vol. 11272, pp. 213–243. Springer, Cham (2018). https://doi.org/10.1007/978-3-030-03326-2_8
16. Hoang, V.T., Rogaway, P.: On generalized feistel networks. In: Rabin, T. (ed.) CRYPTO 2010. LNCS, vol. 6223, pp. 613–630. Springer, Heidelberg (2010). https://doi.org/10.1007/978-3-642-14623-7_33
17. Iwata, T., Kurosawa, K.: On the pseudorandomness of the AES finalists - RC6 and Serpent. In: Schneier, B. (ed.) FSE 2000. LNCS, vol. 1978, pp. 231–243. Springer, Heidelberg (2001)
18. Khati, L., Mouha, N., Vergnaud, D.: Full disk encryption: bridging theory and practice. In: Handschuh, H. (ed.) CT-RSA 2017. LNCS, vol. 10159, pp. 241–257. Springer, Cham (2017). https://doi.org/10.1007/978-3-319-52153-4_14

19. Lampe, R., Seurin, Y.: Security analysis of key-alternating feistel ciphers. In: Cid, C., Rechberger, C. (eds.) FSE 2014. LNCS, vol. 8540, pp. 243–264. Springer, Heidelberg (2015). https://doi.org/10.1007/978-3-662-46706-0_13

20. Luby, M., Rackoff, C.: How to construct pseudo-random permutations from pseudorandom functions. In: Williams, H.C. (ed.) CRYPTO 1985. LNCS, vol. 218, pp. 447–447. Springer, Heidelberg (1986). https://doi.org/10.1007/3-540-39799-X_34

21. Matsui, M.: New block encryption algorithm MISTY. In: Biham, E. (ed.) FSE 1997. LNCS, vol. 1267, pp. 54–68. Springer, Heidelberg (1997). https://doi.org/10.1007/BFb0052334

22. Maurer, U.M.: A simplified and generalized treatment of Luby-Rackoff pseudorandom permutation generators. In: Rueppel, R.A. (ed.) EUROCRYPT 1992. LNCS, vol. 658, pp. 239–255. Springer, Heidelberg (1993). https://doi.org/10.1007/3-540-47555-9_21

23. Maurer, U., Pietrzak, K.: The security of many-round Luby-Rackoff pseudorandom permutations. In: Biham, E. (ed.) EUROCRYPT 2003. LNCS, vol. 2656, pp. 544–561. Springer, Heidelberg (2003). https://doi.org/10.1007/3-540-39200-9_34

24. Patarin, J.: Pseudorandom permutations based on the D.E.S. scheme. In: Cohen, G., Charpin, P. (eds.) EUROCODE 1990. LNCS, vol. 514, pp. 193–204. Springer, Heidelberg (1991). https://doi.org/10.1007/3-540-54303-1_131

25. Patarin, J.: New results on pseudorandom permutation generators based on the des scheme. In: Feigenbaum, J. (ed.) CRYPTO 1991. LNCS, vol. 576, pp. 301–312. Springer, Heidelberg (1992). https://doi.org/10.1007/3-540-46766-1_25

26. Patarin, J.: About feistel schemes with six (or more) rounds. In: Vaudenay, S. (ed.) FSE 1998. LNCS, vol. 1372, pp. 103–121. Springer, Heidelberg (1998). https://doi.org/10.1007/3-540-69710-1_8

27. Patarin, J.: Security of random feistel schemes with 5 or more rounds. In: Franklin, M. (ed.) CRYPTO 2004. LNCS, vol. 3152, pp. 106–122. Springer, Heidelberg (2004). https://doi.org/10.1007/978-3-540-28628-8_7

28. Patarin, J.: The "Coefficients H" technique (invited talk). In: Avanzi, R.M., Keliher, L., Sica, F. (eds.) SAC 2008. LNCS, vol. 5381, pp. 328–345. Springer, Heidelberg (2009). https://doi.org/10.1007/978-3-642-04159-4_21

29. Schwartz, J.T.: Fast probabilistic algorithms for verification of polynomial identities. J. ACM (JACM) 27(4), 701–717 (1980)

Mesh Messaging in Large-Scale Protests: Breaking Bridgefy

Martin R. Albrecht, Jorge Blasco, Rikke Bjerg Jensen, and Lenka Mareková[✉]

Royal Holloway, University of London, London, UK
{martin.albrecht,jorge.blascoalis,rikke.jensen,lenka.marekova}@rhul.ac.uk

Abstract. Mesh messaging applications allow users in relative proximity to communicate without the Internet. The most viable offering in this space, Bridgefy, has recently seen increased uptake in areas experiencing large-scale protests (Hong Kong, India, Iran, US, Zimbabwe, Belarus), suggesting its use in these protests. It is also being promoted as a communication tool for use in such situations by its developers and others. In this work, we report on a security analysis of Bridgefy. Our results show that Bridgefy, as analysed, permitted its users to be tracked, offered no authenticity, no effective confidentiality protections and lacked resilience against adversarially crafted messages. We verified these vulnerabilities by demonstrating a series of practical attacks on Bridgefy. Thus, if protesters relied on Bridgefy, an adversary could produce social graphs about them, read their messages, impersonate anyone to anyone and shut down the entire network with a single maliciously crafted message.

Keywords: Mesh messaging · Bridgefy · Security analysis

1 Introduction

Mesh messaging applications rely on wireless technologies such as Bluetooth Low Energy (BLE) to create communication networks that do not require Internet connectivity. These can be useful in scenarios where the cellular network may simply be overloaded, e.g. during mass gatherings, or when governments impose restrictions on Internet usage, up to a full blackout, to suppress civil unrest. While the functionality requirements of such networks may be the same in both of these scenarios – delivering messages from A to B – the security requirements for their users change dramatically.

In September 2019, Forbes reported "Hong Kong Protestors Using Mesh Messaging App China Can't Block: Usage Up 3685%" [45] in reference to an increase in downloads of a mesh messaging application, Bridgefy [1], in Hong Kong. Bridgefy is both an application and a platform for developers to create their own mesh network applications.[1] It uses BLE or Bluetooth Classic and is designed for use cases such as "music festivals, sports stadiums, rural communities, natural disasters, traveling abroad", as given by its Google Play store

---

[1] As we discuss in Sect. 2.4, alternatives to Bridgefy are scarce, making it the predominant example of such an application/framework.

© Springer Nature Switzerland AG 2021
K. G. Paterson (Ed.): CT-RSA 2021, LNCS 12704, pp. 375–398, 2021.
https://doi.org/10.1007/978-3-030-75539-3_16

description [20]. Other use cases mentioned on its webpage are ad distribution (including "before/during/after natural disasters" to "capitalize on those markets before anybody else" [1]) and turn-based games. The Bridgefy application has crossed 1.7 million downloads as of August 2020 [57].

Though it was advertised as "safe" [20] and "private" [18] and its creators claimed it was secured by end-to-end encryption [45,51,67], none of the aforementioned use cases can be considered as taking place in adversarial environments, such as situations of civil unrest where attempts to subvert the application's security are not merely possible, but to be expected, and where such attacks can have harsh consequences for its users. Despite this, the Bridgefy developers advertised the application for such scenarios [45,71,73,74] and media reports suggest the application is indeed relied upon.

Hong Kong. International news reports of Bridgefy being used in anti-extradition law protests in Hong Kong began around September 2019 [17,45,59,81], reporting a spike in downloads that was attributed to slow mobile Internet speeds caused by mass gatherings of protesters [22]. Around the same time, Bridgefy's CEO reported more than 60,000 installations of the application in a period of seven days, mostly from Hong Kong [59]. However, a Hong Kong based report available in English [15] gave a mixed evaluation of these claims: in the midst of a demonstration, not many protesters appeared to be using Bridgefy. The same report also attributes the spike in Bridgefy downloads to a DDoS attack against other popular communication means used in these protests: Telegram and the Reddit-like forum LIHKG.

India. The next reports to appear centred on the Citizenship Amendment Act protests in India [10] that occurred in December 2019. Here the rise in downloads was attributed to an Internet shutdown occurring during the same period [47,63]. It appears that the media narrative about Bridgefy's use in Hong Kong might have had an effect: "So, Mascarenhas and 15 organisers of the street protest decided to take a leaf out of the Hong Kong protesters' book and downloaded the Bridgefy app" [54]. The Bridgefy developers reported continued adoption in summer 2020 [75].

Iran. While press reports from Iran remain scarce, there is evidence to suggest that some people are trying to use Bridgefy during Internet shutdowns and restrictions: the rise of customer support queries coming from Iran and a claim by the Bridgefy CEO that it is being distributed via USB devices [48].

Lebanon. Bridgefy now appears among recommended applications to use during an Internet shutdown, e.g. in the list compiled by a Lebanese NGO during the October 2019 Lebanon protests [62]. A media report suggests adoption [67].

US. The Bridgefy developers reported uptake of Bridgefy during the Black Lives Matter protests across the US [74,76]. It is promoted for use in these protests by the developers and others on social media [68,69,74].

Zimbabwe. Media and social media reports advertised Bridgefy as a tool to counter a government-mandated Internet shutdown [46, 49] in summer 2020. The Bridgefy developers reported an uptick in adoption [77].

Belarus. Social media posts and the Bridgefy developers suggest adoption in light of a government-mandated Internet shutdown [78].

Thailand. Social media posts encouraged student protesters to install the Bridgefy application during August 2020 [70].

1.1 Contributions

We reverse engineered Bridgefy's messaging platform, giving an overview in Sect. 3, and in Sect. 4 report several vulnerabilities voiding both the security claims made by the Bridgefy developers and the security goals arising from its use in large-scale protests. In particular, we describe various avenues for tracking users of the Bridgefy application and for building social graphs of their interactions both in real time and after the fact. We then use the fact that Bridgefy implemented no effective authentication mechanism between users (nor a state machine) to impersonate arbitrary users. This attack is easily extended to an attacker-in-the-middle (MITM) attack for subverting public-key encryption. We also present variants of Bleichenbacher's attack [12] which break confidentiality using $\approx 2^{17}$ chosen ciphertexts. Our variants exploit the composition of PKCS#1 v1.5 encryption and Gzip compression in Bridgefy. Moreover, we utilise compression to undermine the advertised resilience of Bridgefy: using a single message "zip bomb" we could completely disable the mesh network, since clients would forward any payload before parsing it which then caused them to hang until a reinstallation of the application.

Overall, we conclude that using Bridgefy, as available prior to our work, represented a significant risk to participants of protests. In October 2020 and in response to this work, the Bridgefy developers published a revision of their framework and application adopting the Signal protocol. We discuss our findings and report on the disclosure process in Sect. 5.

2 Preliminaries

We denote concatenation of strings or bytes by ||. Strings of byte values are written in hexadecimal and prefixed with 0x, in big-endian order.

We analysed the Bridgefy apk version 2.1.28 dated January 2020 and available in the Google Play store. It includes the Bridgefy SDK version 1.0.6. In what follows, when we write "Bridgefy" we mean this apk and SDK versions, unless explicitly stated otherwise. As stated above, the Bridgefy developers released an update of both their apk and their SDK in response to a preliminary version of this work and our analysis does not apply as is to these updated versions (cf. Sect. 5).

2.1 Reverse Engineering

Since the Bridgefy source code was not available, we decompiled the apk to (obfuscated) Java classes using Jadx [61]. The initial deobfuscation was done automatically by Jadx, with the remaining classes and methods being done by hand using artefacts left in the code and by inspecting the application's execution.

This inspection was performed using Frida, a dynamic instrumentation toolkit [28], which allows for scripts to be injected into running processes, essentially treating them as black boxes but enabling a variety of operations on them. In the context of Android applications written in Java, these include tracing class instances and hooking specific functions to monitor their inputs/outputs or to modify their behaviour during runtime.

2.2 Primitives Used

Message Encoding. To encapsulate Bluetooth messages and their metadata, Bridgefy uses MessagePack [29], a binary serialisation format that is more compact than and advertised as an alternative to JSON.

It is then compressed using Gzip [39], which utilises the widely-used DEFLATE compressed data format [38]. The standard implementation found in the java.util.zip library is used in the application. A Gzip file begins with a 10-byte header, which consists of a fixed prefix 0x1f8b08 followed by a flags byte and six additional bytes which are usually set to 0. Depending on which flags are set, optional fields such as a comment field are placed between the header and the actual DEFLATE payload. A trailer at the end of the Gzip file consists of two 4-byte fields: a CRC32 and the length, both over the uncompressed data.

RSA PKCS#1 v1.5. Bridgefy uses the (now deprecated) PKCS#1 v1.5 [40] standard. This standard defines a method of using RSA encryption, in particular specifying how the plaintext should be padded before being encrypted. The format of the padded data that will be encrypted is 0x0002 || <*random non-zero bytes*> || 0x00 || <*message*>. If the size of the RSA modulus and hence the size of the encryption block is k bytes, then the maximum length of the message is $k - 11$ bytes to allow for at least 8 bytes of padding.

This padding format enables a well-known attack by Bleichenbacher [12] (for variants/improvements of Bleichenbacher's attack see e.g. [6,7,14,44]). The attack requires a padding oracle, i.e. the ability to obtain an answer to whether a given ciphertext decrypts to something that conforms to the padding format. Sending some number of ciphertexts, each chosen based on previous oracle responses, leads to full plaintext recovery. For RSA with $k = 128$, the number of chosen ciphertexts required has been shown to be between 2^{12} and 2^{16} [16].

In more detail, let c be the target ciphertext, n the public modulus, and (e, d) the public and private exponents, respectively. We have $\mathrm{pad}(m) = c^d \mod n$ for the target message m. The chosen ciphertexts will be of the form $c^* = s^e \cdot c \mod n$ for some s. If c^* has correct padding, we know the first two bytes of

$s \cdot \text{pad}(m)$, and hence a range for its possible values. The attack thus first finds small values of s which result in a positive answer from the oracle and for each of them computes a set of ranges for the value of $\text{pad}(m)$. Once there is only one possible range, larger values of s are tried in order to narrow this range down to only one value, which is the original message.

2.3   Related Work

Secure Messaging. Message layer security has received renewed attention in the last decade, with an effort to standardise a protocol – simply dubbed Messaging Layer Security (MLS) – now underway by the IETF [66], with several academic works proposing solutions or analysing security [4,5,23]. The use of secure messaging by "high-risk users" is considered in [26,34]. In particular, those works analyse interviews with human rights activists and secure messaging application developers to establish common and diverging concerns.

Compression in Security. The first compression side channels in the context of encryption were described by [43], based on the observation that the compression rate can reveal information about the plaintext. Since then, there have been practical attacks exploiting the compression rate "leakage" in TLS and HTTP, dubbed CRIME [25] and BREACH [32], which enabled the recovery of HTTP cookies and contents, respectively. Similarly, [31] uses Gzip as a format oracle in a CCA attack. Beyond cryptography, compression has also been utilised for denial of service attacks in the form of so-called "zip bombs" [27], where an attacker prepares a compressed payload that decompresses to a massive message.

Mesh Networking Security. Wireless mesh networks have a long history, but until recently they have been developed mainly in the context of improving or expanding Wi-Fi connectivity via various ad hoc routing protocols, where the mesh usually does not include client devices. Flood-based networks using Bluetooth started gaining traction with the introduction of BLE, which optimises for low power and low cost, and which has been part of the core specification [13] since Bluetooth 4.0. BLE hardware is integrated in all current major smartphone brands, and the specification has native support in all common operating systems.

Previous work on the security analysis of Bluetooth focused on finding vulnerabilities in the pairing process or showing the inadequacy of its security modes, some of which have been fixed in later versions of the specification (see [24,35] for surveys of attacks focusing on the classic version of Bluetooth). As a more recent addition, BLE has not received as much comprehensive analysis, but general as well as IoT-focused attacks exist [41,56,60,80]. Research on BLE-based tracking has looked into the usage of unique identifiers by applications and IoT devices [9,82]. The literature on security in the context of BLE-based mesh networks is scarce, though the Bluetooth Mesh Profile [58] developed by the Bluetooth SIG is now beginning to be studied [2,3].

2.4   Alternative Mesh Applications

We list various alternative chat applications that target scenarios where Internet connectivity is lacking, in particular paying attention to their potential use in a protest setting.

FireChat. FireChat [52] was a mobile application for secure wireless mesh networking meant for communication without an Internet connection. Though it was not built for protests, it became the tool of choice in various demonstrations since 2014, e.g. in Iraq, Hong Kong and Taiwan [8,11,42], and since then was also promoted as such by the creators of the application. However, it had not received any updates in 2019 and as of April 2020, it is no longer available on the Google Play store and its webpage has been removed, so it appears that its development has been discontinued.

BLE Mesh Networking. Bluetooth itself provides a specification for building mesh networks based on Bluetooth Low Energy that is referred to as the Bluetooth Mesh Profile [58]. While it defines a robust model for implementing a flood-based network for up to 32,000 participating nodes, its focus is not on messaging but rather connectivity of low-power IoT devices within smart homes or smart cities. As a result, it is more suitable for networks that are managed centrally and whose topology is stable over time, which is the opposite of the unpredictable and always-changing flow of a crowd during a mass protest. Further, it makes heavy use of the advertising bearer (a feature not widely available in smartphones), which imposes constraints on the bandwidth of the network – messages can have a maximum size of 384 bytes, and nodes are advised to not transmit more than 100 messages in any 10 s window. The profile makes use of cryptography for securing the network from outside observers as well as from outside interference, but it does expect participating nodes to be benign, which cannot be assumed in the messaging setting. From within the network, a malicious node can not only observe but also impersonate other nodes and deny them service.

HypeLabs. The Hype SDK offered by HypeLabs [37] sets out a similar goal as Bridgefy, which is to offer secure mesh networks for a variety of purposes when there is no Internet connection. Besides Bluetooth, it also utilises Wi-Fi, and supports a variety of platforms. Among its use cases, the Hype SDK whitepaper [36] lists connectivity between IoT devices, social networking and messaging, distributed storage as well as connectivity during catastrophes and emergency broadcasting. While an example chat application is available on Google Play (with only 100+ downloads), HypeLabs does not offer the end-user solutions for those use cases themselves, merely offering the SDK as a paid product for developers. There is no information available on what applications are using the SDK, if any.

Briar. Briar [55] describes itself as "secure messaging, anywhere" [55] and is referenced in online discussions on the use of mesh networking applications in protests [50]. However, Briar does not realise a mesh network. Instead it opens point-to-point sockets over a Bluetooth Classic (as opposed to Low Energy) channel to nearby nodes. Its reach is thus limited to one hop unless users manually forward messages.

Serval. Serval Mesh [30] is an Android application implementing a mesh network using Wi-Fi that sets its goal as enabling communication in places which lack infrastructure. Originally developed for natural disasters, the project includes special hardware Mesh Extenders that are supposed to enhance coverage. While the application is available for download, it cannot be accessed from Google Play because it targets an old version of Android to allow it to run on older devices such as the ones primarily used in rural communities. Work on the project is still ongoing, as it is not ready for deployment at scale. Hence its utility in large-scale protests where access to technology itself is not a barrier is currently limited.

Subnodes. The use of additional hardware devices enables a different approach to maintaining connectivity, which is taken by the open source project Subnodes [65]. It allows local area wireless networks to be set up on a Raspberry Pi, which then acts as a web server that can provide e.g. a chat room. Multiple devices can be connected in a mesh using the BATMAN routing protocol [53], which is meant for dynamic and unreliable networks. However, setting up and operating such a network requires technical knowledge. In the setting of a protest, even carrying the hardware device for one of the network's access points could put the operator at risk.

3 Bridgefy Architecture

In this section, we give an overview of the Bridgefy messaging architecture. The key feature of Bridgefy is that it exchanges data using Bluetooth when an Internet connection is not available. The application can send the following kinds of messages:

- one-to-one messages between two parties
  - sent over the Internet if both parties are online,
  - sent directly via Bluetooth if the parties are in physical range, or
  - sent over the Bluetooth mesh network, and
- Bluetooth broadcast messages that anyone can read in a special "Broadcast mode" room.

Note that the Bluetooth messages are handled separately from the ones exchanged over the Internet using the Bridgefy server, i.e. there is no support for communication between one user who is on the Internet and one who is on the mesh network.

3.1 Bluetooth Messages

Bridgefy supports connections over both BLE and Bluetooth Classic, but the latter is a legacy option for devices without BLE support, so we focus on BLE.

How the Generic Attribute Profile (GATT) protocol is configured is not relevant for our analysis, so we only consider message processing starting from and up to characteristic read and write requests. BLE packet data is received as an array of bytes, which is parsed according to the MessagePack format and processed further based on message type. At the topmost level, all messages are represented as a BleEntity which has a given entity type et. Table 1 matches the entity type to the type of its content ct and the class that implements it. Details of all classes representing messages can be found in the full version of this paper[2].

Table 1. Entity types.

BleEntity types		
et	content	class for ct
0	Handshake	BleHandshake
1	Direct message	BleEntityContent
3	Mesh message	ForwardTransaction
AppEntity types		
et	content	extending class
0	Encrypted handshake	AppEntityHandShake
1	Any message	AppEntityMessage
4	Receipt	AppEntitySignal

Encryption Scheme. One-to-one Bluetooth (mesh and direct) messages in Bridgefy, represented as MessagePacks, are first compressed using Gzip and then encrypted using RSA with PKCS#1 v1.5 padding. The key size is 2048 bits and the input is split into blocks of size up to 245 bytes and encrypted one-by-one in an ECB-like fashion using Java SE's "RSA/ECB/PKCS1Padding", producing output blocks of size 256 bytes. Decryption errors do not produce a user or network visible direct error message.

Direct Messages. Messages sent to a user who is in direct Bluetooth range have $et = 1$ and so ct is of type BleEntityContent. Upon reception, its payload is decrypted, decompressed and then used to construct the content of a Message object. Note that the receiver does not parse the sender ID from the message itself. Instead, it sets the sender to be the user ID which corresponds to the device from which it received the message. This link between user IDs and Bluetooth devices is determined during the initial handshake that we describe in Sect. 3.2.

The content of the Message object is parsed into an AppEntity, which also contains an entity type et that determines the final class of the message. A direct message has $et = 1$ here as well, so it is parsed as an AppEntityMessage. Afterwards, a delivery receipt for the message that was received is sent and the message is displayed to the user. Receipts take the format of AppEntitySignal: one is sent when a message is delivered as described above, and another one when the user views the chat containing the message.

---

[2] Available at https://eprint.iacr.org/2021/214.

Mesh Messages. Bridgefy implements a managed flood-based mesh network, preventing infinite loops using a time-to-live counter that is decremented whenever a packet is forwarded; when it reaches zero the packet is discarded. Messages that are transmitted using the mesh network, whether it is one-to-one messages encrypted to a user that is not in direct range, or unencrypted broadcast messages that anyone can read, have et = 3. Such a BleEntity may hold multiple mesh messages of either kind. We note that these contain the sender and the receiver of one-to-one messages in plaintext.

The received one-to-one mesh messages are processed depending on the receiver ID – if it matches the client's user ID, they will try to decrypt the message, triggering the same processing as in the case of direct messages, and also send a special "mesh reach" message that signals that the encrypted message has found its recipient over the mesh. If the receiver ID does not match, the packet is added to the set of packets that will be forwarded to the mesh.

The received broadcast messages are first sent to the mesh. Then the client constructs AppEntityMessages and processes them the same as one-to-one messages before displaying them.

3.2   Handshake Protocol

Clients establish a session by running a handshake protocol, whose messages follow the BleEntity form with et = 0. The content of the entity is parsed as a BleHandshake which contains a request type rq and response rp. The handshake protocol is best understood as an exchange of requests and responses such that each message consists of a response to the previous request bundled with the next request. There are three types of requests:

- rq = null: no request,
- rq = 0: general request for user's information,
- rq = 1: request for user's public key.

The first handshake message that is sent when a new BLE device is detected, regardless of whether they have communicated before, has rq = 0 and also contains the user's ID, supported versions of the SDK and the CRC32 of the user's public key. The processing of received handshake messages depends on whether the two users know each other's public keys (either because they have connected before, or because they are contacts and the server supplied the keys when they were connected to the Internet).

Key Exchange. In the case when the parties do not have each other's public keys, this exchange is illustrated in Fig. 1: Ivan is already online and scanning for other users when Ursula comes into range and initiates the handshake. The protocol can be understood to consist of two main parts, first the key exchange that occurs in plaintext, and second an encrypted "application handshake" which exchanges information such as usernames and phone numbers. Before the second part begins, the devices may also exchange recent mesh messages that the device that was offline may have missed.[3]

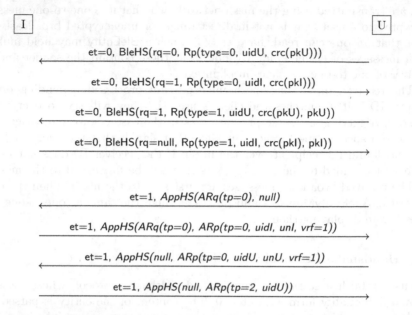

Fig. 1. Handshake protocol including key exchange between Ivan and Ursula. We abbreviate HandShake with HS. Here uidI, uidU are user IDs, pkI, pkU are the public keys and unI, unU are usernames of Ivan and Ursula, and crc(pkU) > crc(pkI). Messages in *italics* are encrypted.

In Fig. 1 some fields of the objects are omitted for clarity. Rp represents a response object (ResponseJson) while ARq and ARp are application requests and responses (AppRequestJson and AppResponseJson). The AppHandShake(rq, rp) object is wrapped in an AppEntityHandShake which forms the content of the Message that is actually compressed and encrypted. Note that the order of who initialises the BleHandshake depends on which user came online later, while the first AppHandShake is sent by the party whose CRC32 of their public key has a larger value. We are also only displaying the case when a user has not verified their phone number (which is the default behaviour in the application), i.e. vrf = 1. If they have, AppHandShake additionally includes a request and a response for the phone number.

---

[3] This is facilitated by the dump flag in ForwardTransaction, but we omit this exchange in the figure as it is not relevant to the actual handshake protocol.

Known Keys. In the case when both parties already know each other's public keys, there are only two BleHandshake messages exchanged, and both follow the format of the first message shown in Fig. 1, where rq = 0. The exchange of encrypted AppHandShake messages then continues unchanged.

Conditions. When two devices come into range, the handshake protocol is executed automatically and direct messages can only be sent after the handshake is complete. Only clients in physical range can execute the BleHandShake part of the protocol. Devices that are communicating via the mesh network do not perform the handshake at all, so they can only exchange messages if they already know each other's keys from the Bridgefy server or because they have been in range once before.

3.3   Routing via the Bridgefy Server

An Internet connection is required when a user first installs the application, which registers them with the Bridgefy server. All requests are done via HTTPS, the APIs for which are in the package me.bridgefy.backend.v3.

The BgfyUser class that models the information that is sent to the server during registration contains the user's chosen name, user ID, the list of users blocked by this user, and if they are "verified" then also their phone number. Afterwards, a contacts request is done every time an Internet connection is available (regardless of whether a user is verified or not) and the user refreshes the application. The phone numbers of the user's contacts are uploaded to the server to obtain a list of contacts that are also Bridgefy users. BgfyKeyApi then provides methods to store and retrieve the users' public keys from the server.

Messages sent between online users are of a simpler form than the Bluetooth messages: an instance of BgfyMessage contains the sender and receiver IDs, the RSA encryption of the text of the message and some metadata, such as a timestamp and the delivered/read status of the message in plaintext. The server will queue messages sent to users who are not currently online until they connect to the Internet again.

4   Attacks

In this section, we show that Bridgefy does not provide confidentiality of messages and also that it does not satisfy the additional security needs arising in a protest setting: privacy, authenticity and reliability in adversarial settings.

4.1   Privacy

Here, we discuss vulnerabilities in Bridgefy pertaining to user privacy in contrast to confidentiality of messages. We note that Bridgefy initially made no claim about anonymity in its marketing but disabled mandating phone number verification to address anonymity needs in 2019 [72].

Local User Tracking. To prevent tracking, Bluetooth-enabled devices may use "random" addresses which change over time (for details on the addressing scheme see [13, Section 10.8]). However, when a Bridgefy client sends BLE ADV_IND packets (something that is done continuously while the application is running), it transmits an identifier in the service data that is the CRC32 value of its user ID, encoded in 10 bytes as decimal digits. The user ID does not change unless the user reinstalls the application, so passive observation of the network is enough to enable tracking all users.

In addition, the automatic handshake protocol composed with public-key caching provides a mechanism to perform historical contact tracing. If the devices of two users have been in range before, they will not request each other's public keys, but they will do so automatically if that has not been the case.

Participant Discovery. Until December 2019 [72], Bridgefy required users to register with a phone number. Users still have the option to do so, but it is no longer the default. If the user gives the permission to the application to access the contacts stored on their phone, the application will check which of those contacts are already Bridgefy users based on phone numbers and display those contacts to the user. When Bridgefy is predominantly installed on phones of protesters, this allows the identification of participants by running contact discovery against all local phone numbers. While an adversary with significant control over the network, such as a state actor, might have alternative means to collect such information, this approach is also available to e.g. employers or activists supporting the other side.

Social Graph. All one-to-one messages sent over the mesh network contain the sender and receiver IDs in plaintext, so a passive adversary with physical presence can build a social graph of what IDs are communicating with whom. The adversary can further use the server's API to learn the usernames corresponding to those IDs (via the getUserById request in BgfyUserApi). In addition, since three receipts are sent when a message is received – "mesh reach" in clear, encrypted "delivery" receipt, encrypted "viewed" receipt – a passive attacker can also build an approximate, dynamic topology of the network, since users that are further away from each other will have a larger delay between a message and its receipts.

4.2 Authenticity

Bridgefy does not utilise cryptographic authentication mechanisms. As a result, an adversary can impersonate any user.

The initial handshake through which parties exchange their public keys or identify each other after coming in range relies on two pieces of information to establish the identities: a user ID and the lower-level Bluetooth device address. Neither of these is an actual authentication mechanism: the user ID is public information which can be learned from observing the network, while [56] shows that it is possible to broadcast with any BLE device address.

However, an attacker does not need to go to such lengths. Spoofing can be done by sending a handshake message which triggers the other side to overwrite the information it currently has associated with a given user. Suppose there are two users who have communicated with each other before, Ursula and Ivan, and the attacker wishes to impersonate Ivan to Ursula. When the attacker comes into range of Ursula, she will initiate the handshake. The attacker will send a response of type 1, simply replacing its own user ID, public key and the CRC of its public key with Ivan's, and also copies Ivan's username, as shown in Fig. 2.

This works because the processing of handshakes in Bridgefy is not stateful and parts of the handshake such as the request value rq and type of rp act as control messages. This handshake is enough for Ursula's application to merge the attacker and Ivan into one user, and therefore show messages from the attacker as if they came from Ivan. If the real Ivan comes in range at the time the attacker is connected to Ursula, he will be able to communicate with her and receive responses from her that the attacker will not be able to decrypt. However, he will not be able to see the attacker's presence. We implemented this attack and verified that it works, see Sect. 4.3.

The messages exchanged over the mesh network (when users are not in direct range) merely contain the user ID of the sender, so they can be spoofed with ease. We also note that although the handshake protocol is meant for parties in range, the second part of the handshake (i.e. AppHandshake) can also be sent over the mesh network. This means that users can be convinced to change the usernames and phone numbers associated with their Bridgefy contacts via the mesh network.

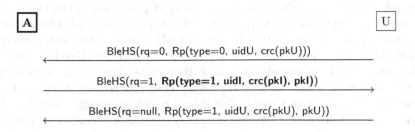

Fig. 2. Impersonation attack, with attacker modifications in **bold**.

4.3 Confidentiality

Confidentiality of message contents is both a security goal mentioned in Bridgefy's marketing material and relied upon by participants in protests. In this section, we show that the implemented protections are not sufficient to satisfy this goal.

IND-CPA. Bridgefy's encryption scheme only offers a security level of 2^{64} in a standard IND-CPA security game, i.e. a passive adversary can decide whether a message m_0 or m_1 of its choosing was encrypted as c. The adversary picks messages of length 245 bytes and tries all 255^8 possible values for PKCS#1 v1.5 padding until it finds a match for the challenge ciphertext c.

Plaintext File Sharing. Bridgefy allows its users to send direct messages composed of either just text or containing a location they want to share. The latter is processed as a special text message containing coordinates, and so these two types are encrypted, but the same is not true for any additional data such as image files. Only the payload of the BleEntityContent is encrypted, which does not include the byte array BleEntity.data that is used to transmit files. While the application itself does not currently offer the functionality to share images or other files, it is part of the SDK and receiving media files does work in the application. The fact that files are transmitted in plaintext is not stated in the documentation, so for developers using the SDK it would be easy to assume that files are shared privately when using this functionality.

MITM. This attack is an extension of the impersonation attack described in Sect. 4.2 where we convince the client to change the public key for any user ID it has already communicated with. Suppose that Ivan is out of range, and the attacker initiates a handshake with Ursula where rq = null, rp is of type 0 and contains the CRC of the attacker's key as well as Ivan's user ID as the sender ID (the user ID being replaced in all following handshake messages as well). The logic of the handshake processing in Ursula's client dictates that since the CRC does not match the CRC of Ivan's key that it has saved, it has to make a request of type 1, i.e. a request for an updated public key. Then the attacker only needs to supply its own key, which will get associated with Ivan's user ID, as shown in Fig. 3. Afterwards, whenever Ursula sends a Bluetooth message to Ivan, it will be encrypted under the attacker's key. Further, Ursula's client will display messages from the attacker as if they came from Ivan, so this attack also provides impersonation. If at this stage Ivan comes back in range, he will not be able to connect to Ursula. The attack is not persistent, though – if the attacker goes out of range, Ivan (when in range) can run a legitimate handshake and restore communication.

We verified this and the previous impersonation attack in a setup with four Android devices, where the attacker had two devices running Frida scripts that modified the relevant handshake messages. Two attacker devices were used to instantiate a full attacker in the middle attack, which is an artefact of us hot-patching the Bridgefy application using Frida scripts: one device to communicate with Ursula on behalf of Ivan and another with Ivan on behalf of Ursula.

We also note that since the Bridgefy server serves as a trusted database of users' public keys, if compromised, it would be trivial to mount an attacker in the middle attack on the communication of any two users. This would also impact users who are planning to only use the application offline since the server would only need to supply them the wrong keys during registration.

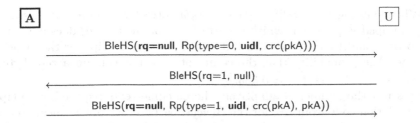

Fig. 3. One side of the MITM attack, with attacker modifications in **bold**.

Padding Oracle Attack. The following chosen ciphertext attack is enabled by the fact that all one-to-one messages use public-key encryption but no authentication, so we can construct valid ciphertexts as if coming from any sender. We can also track BLE packets and replay them at will, reordering or substituting ciphertext blocks.

We instantiate a variant of Bleichenbacher's attack [12] on RSA with PKCS#1 v1.5 padding using Bridgefy's delivery receipts. This attack relies on distinguishing whether a ciphertext was processed successfully or not. The receiver of a message sends a message status update when a message has been received and processed, i.e. decrypted, decompressed and parsed. If there was an error on the receiver's side, no message is sent. No other indication of successful delivery or (type of) error is sent. Since the sender of a Bridgefy message cannot distinguish between decryption errors or decompression errors merely from the information it gets from the receiver, we construct a padding oracle that circumvents this issue.

Suppose that Ivan sends a ciphertext c encrypting the message m to Ursula that we intercept. In the classical Bleichenbacher's attack, we would form a new ciphertext $c^* = s^e \cdot c \mod n$ for some s where n is the modulus and e is the exponent of Ursula's public key. Now suppose that c^* has a correct padding. Since messages are processed in blocks, we can prepend and append valid ciphertexts. These are guaranteed to pass the padding checks as they are honestly generated ciphertexts (we recall that there is no authentication). We will construct these blocks in such a way that decompression of the joint contents will succeed with non-negligible probability, and therefore enable us to get a delivery receipt which will instantiate our padding oracle.

The Gzip file format [39] specifies a number of optional flags. If the flag FLG.FCOMMENT is set, the header is followed by a number of "comment" bytes, terminated with a zero byte, that are essentially ignored. In particular, these bytes are not covered by the CRC32 checksum contained in the Gzip trailer. Thus, we let c_0 be the encryption of a 10-byte Gzip header with this flag set followed by up to 245 non-zero bytes, and let c_1 be the encryption of a zero byte followed by a valid compressed MessagePack payload (i.e. of a message from the attacker to Ursula) and Gzip trailer.

When put together, $c_0||c^*||c_1$ encrypts a correctly compressed message as long as unpad($s \cdot$ pad(m)) (which is part of the comment field) does not contain a zero byte, and therefore Ursula will send a delivery receipt for the attacker's message. The probability that the comment does not contain a zero byte for random s is $\geq \left(1 - \frac{1}{256}\right)^{245} \approx 0.383$.

To study the number of adaptively chosen ciphertexts required, we adapted the simulation code from [16] for the Bleichenbacher-style oracle encountered in this attack: a payload will pass the test if it has valid padding for messages of any valid length ("FFT" in [7] parlance) and if it does not contain a zero byte in the "message" part after splitting off the padding. We then ran a Bleichenbacher-style attack $4,096$ times (on 80 cores, taking about 12h in total) and recorded how often the oracle was called in each attack. We give a histogram of our data in Fig. 4. The median is $2^{16.75}$, the mean $2^{17.36}$. Our SageMath [64] script, based on Python code in [16], and the raw data for Fig. 4 are attached to the electronic version of this document.

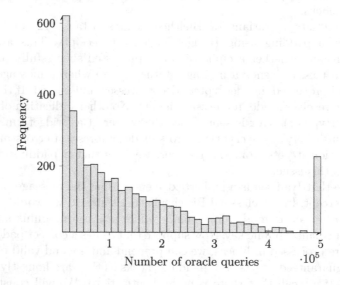

Fig. 4. Density distribution for number of ciphertexts required to mount a padding-oracle attack via Gzip comments.

We have verified the applicability of this attack in Bridgefy using ciphertexts c^* constructed to be PKCS#1 v1.5-conforming (i.e. where we set $s = $ pad(m)$^{-1} \cdot$ pad(r) mod n where r is 245 random bytes). We used Frida to run a script on the attacker's device that would send $c_0||c^*||c_1$ to the target Bridgefy user via Bluetooth, and record whether it gets a delivery receipt for the message contained in c_1 or not. The observed frequency of the receipts matched the probability given earlier. This oracle suffices to instantiate Bleichenbacher's original attack. In our preliminary experiments we were able to send a ciphertext every 450 ms, suggesting 50% of attacks complete in less than 14 h. We note, however, that our timings are based on us hotpatching Bridgefy to send the messages and that a higher throughput might be achievable.

Padding Oracles from a Timing Side-Channel. Our decompression oracle depends on the Bridgefy SDK processing three blocks as a joint ciphertext. While we verified that this behaviour is also exhibited by the Bridgefy application, the application itself never sends ciphertexts that span more than two blocks as it imposes a limit of 256 bytes on the size of the text of each message. Thus, a stopgap mitigation of our previous attack could be to disable the processing of more than two blocks of ciphertext jointly together.

We sketch an alternative attack that only requires two blocks of ciphertext per message. It is enabled by the fact that when a receiver processes an incorrect message, there is a difference in the time it takes to process it depending on what kind of error was encountered. This difference is clearly observable for ciphertexts that consist of at least two blocks, where the error occurs in the first block. We note that padding errors occurring in the second block can be observed by swapping the blocks, as they are decrypted individually.

Figure 5 (raw data is attached to the electronic version of this document) shows the differences for experiments run on the target device, measured using Frida. A script was injected into the Bridgefy application that would call the method responsible for extracting a message from a received BLE packet (including decryption and decompression) on given valid or invalid data. The execution time of this method was measured directly on the device using Java.

If multiple messages are received, they are processed sequentially, which enables the propagation of these timing differences to the network level. That is, the attacker sends two messages, one consisting of $c^* \| c'$ where $c^* = s^e \cdot c \mod n$ is the modified target ciphertext and c' is an arbitrary ciphertext block, and one consisting of some unrelated message, either as direct messages one after another or a mesh transaction containing both messages among its packets. The side-channel being considered is then simply the time it takes to receive the delivery receipt on the second valid message.

We leave exploring whether this could be instantiated in practice to future work, since our previous attacks do not require this timing channel. We note, though, that an adversary would likely need more precise control over the timing of when packets are released than that offered by stock Android devices in order to capture the correct difference in a BLE environment.

4.4   Denial of Service

Bridgefy's appeal to protesters to enable messaging in light of an Internet shutdown makes resilience to denial of service attacks a key concern. While a flood-based network can be resilient as a consequence of its simplicity, some particularities of the Bridgefy setup make it vulnerable.

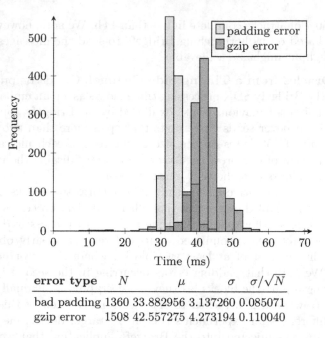

error type	N	μ	σ	$\sigma/\sqrt{N}$
bad padding	1360	33.882956	3.137260	0.085071
gzip error	1508	42.557275	4.273194	0.110040

Fig. 5. Execution time of ChunkUtils.stitchChunksToEntity for 2 ciphertext blocks in milliseconds. In the table, N is the number of samples in each experiment.

Broad DoS. Due to the use of compression, Bridgefy is vulnerable to "zip bomb" attacks. In particular, compressing a message of size 10 MB containing a repeated single character results in a payload of size 10 KB, which can be easily transmitted over the BLE mesh network. Then, when the client attempts to display this message, the application becomes unresponsive to the point of requiring reinstallation to make it usable again. Sending such a message to the broadcast chat provides a trivial way of disabling many clients at the same time, since clients will first forward the message further and only then start the processing to display it which causes them to hang. As a consequence, a single adversarially generated message can take down the entire network. We implemented this attack and tested it in practice on a number of Android devices.

Targeted DoS. A consequence of the MITM attack from Sect. 4.3 is that it provides a way to prevent given two users from connecting, even if they are in Bluetooth range, since the attacker's key becomes attached to one of the user ids.

5   Discussion

While our attacks reveal severe deficiencies in the security of both the Bridgefy application (v2.1.28) and the SDK (v1.0.6), it is natural to ask whether they are valid and what lessons can be drawn from them for cryptographic research.

Given that most of our attacks are variants of attacks known in the literature, it is worth asking why Bridgefy did not mitigate against them. A simple answer to this question might be that the application was not designed for adversarial settings and that therefore our attacks are out of scope, externally imposing security goals. However, such an account would fail to note that Bridgefy's security falls short also in settings where attacks are not expected to be the norm, i.e. Bridgefy does not satisfy standard privacy guarantees expected of any modern messaging application. In particular, prior to our work, Bridgefy developers advertised the app/SDK as "private" and as featuring end-to-end encryption; our attacks thus broke Bridgefy's own security claims.

More importantly, however, Bridgefy *is* used in highly adversarial settings where its security ought to stand up to powerful nation-state adversaries and the Bridgefy developers advertise their application for these contexts [45,71,73,74]. Technologies need to be evaluated under the conditions they are used in. Here, our attacks highlight the value of secure by design approaches to development. While designers might envision certain use cases, users, in the absence of alternatives, may reach for whatever solution is available.

Our work thus draws attention to this problem space. While it is difficult to assess the actual reliance of protesters on mesh communication, the *idea* of resilient communication in the face of a government-mandated Internet shutdown is present throughout protests across the globe [8,10,11,42,45,46,70,73,74,76,78]. Yet, these users are not well served by the existing solutions they rely on. Thus, it is a pressing topic for future work to design communication protocols and tools that cater to these needs. We note, though, that this requires understanding "these needs" to avoid a disconnect between what designers design for and what users in these settings require [26,34].

5.1 Responsible Disclosure

We disclosed the vulnerabilities described in this work to the Bridgefy developers on 27 April 2020 and they acknowledged receipt on the same day. We agreed on a public disclosure date of 24 August 2020. Starting from 1 June 2020, the Bridgefy team began informing their users that they should not expect confidentiality guarantees from the current version of the application [79]. On 8 July 2020, the developers informed us that they were implementing a switch to the Signal protocol to provide cryptographic assurances in their SDK. On 24 August 2020, we published an abridged[4] version of this paper in conjunction with a media article [33]. The Bridgefy team published a statement on the same day [19]. On 30 October 2020, an update finalising the switch to Signal was released [21]. If implemented correctly, it would rule out many of the attacks described in this work. Note, however, that we have not reviewed these changes and we recommend an independent security audit to verify they have been implemented correctly.

---

[4] We had omitted details of the Bridgefy architecture, as the attacks had not been mitigated at that point in time.

Acknowledgements. Part of this work was done while Albrecht was visiting the Simons Institute for the Theory of Computing. The research of Mareková was supported by the EPSRC and the UK Government as part of the Centre for Doctoral Training in Cyber Security at Royal Holloway, University of London (EP/P009301/1). We thank Kenny Paterson and Eamonn Postlethwaite for comments on an earlier version of this paper.

References

1. Bridgefy, April 2020. https://web.archive.org/web/20200411143157/www.bridgefy.me/
2. Adomnicai, A., Fournier, J.J.A., Masson, L.: Hardware security threats against Bluetooth mesh networks. In: 2018 IEEE Conference on Communications and Network Security, CNS 2018, Beijing, China, 30 May–1 June 2018, pp. 1–9. IEEE (2018). https://doi.org/10.1109/CNS.2018.8433184
3. Álvarez, F., Almon, L., Hahn, A., Hollick, M.: Toxic friends in your network: breaking the Bluetooth Mesh friendship concept. In: Mehrnezhad, M., van der Merwe, T., Hao, F. (eds.) Proceedings of the 5th ACM Workshop on Security Standardisation Research Workshop, London, UK, 11 November 2019, pp. 1–12. ACM (2019). https://doi.org/10.1145/3338500.3360334
4. Alwen, J., et al.: Keep the dirt: Tainted TreeKEM, an efficient and provably secure continuous group key agreement protocol. Cryptology ePrint Archive, Report 2019/1489 (2019). https://eprint.iacr.org/2019/1489
5. Alwen, J., Coretti, S., Dodis, Y., Tselekounis, Y.: Security analysis and improvements for the IETF MLS standard for group messaging. Cryptology ePrint Archive, Report 2019/1189 (2019). https://eprint.iacr.org/2019/1189
6. Aviram, N., et al.: DROWN: breaking TLS using SSLv2. In: Holz, T., Savage, S. (eds.): USENIX Security 2016, pp. 689–706. USENIX Association, August 2016
7. Bardou, R., Focardi, R., Kawamoto, Y., Simionato, L., Steel, G., Tsay, J.-K.: Efficient padding oracle attacks on cryptographic hardware. In: Safavi-Naini, R., Canetti, R. (eds.) CRYPTO 2012. LNCS, vol. 7417, pp. 608–625. Springer, Heidelberg (2012). https://doi.org/10.1007/978-3-642-32009-5_36
8. BBC News: Iraqis use FireChat messaging app to overcome net block, June 2014. http://web.archive.org/web/20190325080943/https://www.bbc.com/news/technology-27994309k
9. Becker, J.K., Li, D., Starobinski, D.: Tracking anonymized Bluetooth devices. In: Proceedings on Privacy Enhancing Technologies, vol. 2019, no. 3, pp. 50–65 (2019)
10. Bhavani, D.K.: Internet shutdown? Why Bridgefy app that enables offline messaging is trending in India, December 2019. http://web.archive.org/web/20200105053448/https://www.thehindu.com/sci-tech/technology/internet-shutdown-why-bridgefy-app-that-enables-offline-messaging-is-trending-in-india/article30336067.ece
11. Bland, A.: FireChat - the messaging app that's powering the Hong Kong protests, September 2014. http://web.archive.org/web/20200328142327/https://www.theguardian.com/world/2014/sep/29/firechat-messaging-app-powering-hong-kong-protests
12. Bleichenbacher, D.: Chosen ciphertext attacks against protocols based on the RSA encryption standard PKCS #1. In: Krawczyk, H. (ed.) CRYPTO 1998. LNCS, vol. 1462, pp. 1–12. Springer, Heidelberg (1998). https://doi.org/10.1007/BFb0055716

13. Bluetooth SIG: Core specification 5.1, January 2019. https://www.bluetooth.com/specifications/bluetooth-core-specification/
14. Böck, H., Somorovsky, J., Young, C.: Return of Bleichenbacher's oracle threat (ROBOT). In: Enck, W., Felt, A.P. (eds.) USENIX Security 2018, pp. 817–849. USENIX Association, August 2018
15. Borak, M.: We tested a messaging app used by Hong Kong protesters that works without an internet connection, September 2019. http://web.archive.org/web/20191206182048/https://www.abacusnews.com/digital-life/we-tested-messaging-app-used-hong-kong-protesters-works-without-internet-connection/article/3025661
16. Boyle, G.: 20 Years of Bleichenbacher attacks. Technical Reports RHUL-ISG-2019-1. Information Security Group, Royal Holloway University of London (2019)
17. Brewster, T.: Hong Kong protesters are using this 'mesh' messaging app–but should they trust it? September 2019. http://web.archive.org/web/20191219071731/https://www.forbes.com/sites/thomasbrewster/2019/09/04/hong-kong-protesters-are-using-this-mesh-messaging-app-but-should-they-trust-it/
18. Bridgefy: Developers (2018). https://blog.bridgefy.me/developers.html, https://archive.vn/yjg9f
19. Bridgefy: Bridgefy's commitment to privacy and security, August 2020. http://web.archive.org/web/20200826183604/https://bridgefy.me/bridgefys-commitment-to-privacy-and-security/
20. Bridgefy: Offline messaging, April 2020. https://web.archive.org/20200411143133/play.google.com/store/apps/details?id=me.bridgefy.main
21. Bridgefy: Technical article on our security updates, November 2020. http://web.archive.org/web/20201102093540/https://bridgefy.me/technical-article-on-our-security-updates/
22. Cortés, V.: Bridgefy sees massive spike in downloads during Hong Kong protests, August 2019. http://web.archive.org/web/20191013072633/www.contxto.com/en/mexico/mexican-bridgefy-sees-massive-spike-in-downloads-during-hong-kong-protests/
23. Cremers, C., Hale, B., Kohbrok, K.: Efficient post-compromise security beyond one group. Cryptology ePrint Archive, Report 2019/477 (2019). https://eprint.iacr.org/2019/477
24. Dunning, J.P.: Taming the blue beast: a survey of Bluetooth based threats. IEEE Secur. Priv. 8(2), 20–27 (2010). https://doi.org/10.1109/MSP.2010.3
25. Duong, T., Rizzo, J.: The CRIME attack. Presentation at Ekoparty Security Conference (2012)
26. Ermoshina, K., Halpin, H., Musiani, F.: Can Johnny build a protocol? Coordinating developer and user intentions for privacy-enhanced secure messaging protocols. In: 2nd IEEE European Symposium on Security and Privacy (EuroS&P 2017) (2017)
27. Fifield, D.: A better zip bomb. In: 13th USENIX Workshop on Offensive Technologies (WOOT 2019), Santa Clara. USENIX Association, August 2019
28. Frida: A dynamic instrumentation framework, v12.8.9, February 2020. https://frida.re/
29. Furuhashi, S.: MessagePack (2008). https://msgpack.org/
30. Gardner-Stephen, P.: The Serval Project (2017). http://www.servalproject.org/
31. Garman, C., Green, M., Kaptchuk, G., Miers, I., Rushanan, M.: Dancing on the lip of the volcano: chosen ciphertext attacks on Apple iMessage. In: Holz, T., Savage, S. (eds.): USENIX Security 2016, pp. 655–672. USENIX Association, August 2016

32. Gluck, Y., Harris, N., Prado, A.: BREACH: reviving the CRIME attack. Black Hat USA (2013)
33. Goodin, D.: Bridgefy, the messenger promoted for mass protests, is a privacy disaster, August 2020. https://arstechnica.com/features/2020/08/bridgefy-the-app-promoted-for-mass-protests-is-a-privacy-disaster/
34. Halpin, H., Ermoshina, K., Musiani, F.: Co-ordinating developers and high-risk users of privacy-enhanced secure messaging protocols. In: Cremers, C., Lehmann, A. (eds.) SSR 2018. LNCS, vol. 11322, pp. 56–75. Springer, Cham (2018). https://doi.org/10.1007/978-3-030-04762-7_4
35. Hassan, S.S., Bibon, S.D., Hossain, M.S., Atiquzzaman, M.: Security threats in Bluetooth technology. Comput. Secur. **74**, 308–322 (2018). https://doi.org/10.1016/j.cose.2017.03.008
36. HypeLabs: The Hype SDK: a technical overview (2019). https://hypelabs.io/documents/Hype-SDK.pdf
37. HypeLabs (2020). https://hypelabs.io
38. IETF: DEFLATE compressed data format specification version 1.3, May 1996. https://tools.ietf.org/html/rfc1951
39. IETF: GZIP file format specification version 4.3, May 1996. https://tools.ietf.org/html/rfc1952
40. IETF: PKCS #1: RSA encryption version 1.5, March 1998. https://tools.ietf.org/html/rfc2313
41. Jasek, S.: GATTacking Bluetooth smart devices (2016). https://github.com/securing/docs/raw/master/whitepaper.pdf
42. Josh Horwitz, T.i.A.: Unblockable? Unstoppable? FireChat messaging app unites China and Taiwan in free speech... and it's not pretty, March 2014. http://web.archive.org/web/20141027180653/https://www.techinasia.com/unblockable-unstoppable-firechat-messaging-app-unites-china-and-taiwan-in-free-speech-and-its-not-pretty/
43. Kelsey, J.: Compression and information leakage of plaintext. In: Daemen, J., Rijmen, V. (eds.) FSE 2002. LNCS, vol. 2365, pp. 263–276. Springer, Heidelberg (2002). https://doi.org/10.1007/3-540-45661-9_21
44. Klíma, V., Pokorný, O., Rosa, T.: Attacking RSA-based sessions in SSL/TLS. In: Walter, C.D., Koç, Ç.K., Paar, C. (eds.) CHES 2003. LNCS, vol. 2779, pp. 426–440. Springer, Heidelberg (2003). https://doi.org/10.1007/978-3-540-45238-6_33
45. Koetsier, J.: Hong Kong protestors using mesh messaging app China can't block: usage up 3685%, September 2019. https://web.archive.org/web/20200411154603/www.forbes.com/sites/johnkoetsier/2019/09/02/hong-kong-protestors-using-mesh-messaging-app-china-cant-block-usage-up-3685/
46. Magaisa, A.T.: https://twitter.com/wamagaisa/status/1288817111796797440. http://archive.today/DVRZf, July 2020
47. Mihindukulasuriya, R.: FireChat, Bridgefy see massive rise in downloads amid internet shutdowns during CAA protests, December 2019. http://web.archive.org/web/20200109212954/https://theprint.in/india/firechat-bridgefy-see-massive-rise-in-downloads-amid-internet-shutdowns-during-caa-protests/340058/
48. Mohan, P.: How the internet shutdown in Kashmir is splintering India's democracy, March 2020. http://web.archive.org/web/20200408111230/https://www.fastcompany.com/90470779/how-the-internet-shutdown-in-kashmir-is-splintering-indias-democracy

49. Mudzingwa, F.: This offline messenger that might keep you connected if the govt decides to shut down the internet, August 2020. https://web.archive.org/web/20200816101930/www.techzim.co.zw/2020/07/bridgefy-is-an-offline-messenger-that-might-keep-you-connected-if-the-govt-decides-to-shut-down-the-internet/

50. News, H.: Hong Kong protestors using Bridgefy's Bluetooth-based mesh network messaging app, August 2019. https://web.archive.org/web/20191016114954/news.ycombinator.com/item?id=20861948

51. Ng, B.: Bridgefy: a startup that enables messaging without internet, August 2019. http://archive.today/2020.06.07-120425/https://www.ejinsight.com/eji/article/id/2230121/20190826-bridgefy-a-startup-that-enables-messaging-without-internet

52. Open Garden: FireChat, October 2019. http://web.archive.org/web/20200111174316/https://www.opengarden.com/firechat/

53. Open Mesh: B.A.T.M.A.N. Advanced (2020). https://www.open-mesh.org/projects/batman-adv/wiki

54. Purohit, K.: Whatsapp to Bridgefy, what Hong Kong taught India's leaderless protesters, December 2019. http://web.archive.org/web/20200406103939/https://www.scmp.com/week-asia/politics/article/3042633/whatsapp-bridgefy-what-hong-kong-taught-indias-leaderless

55. Rogers, M., Saitta, E., Grote, T., Dehm, J., Wieder, B.: Briar, March 2018. https://web.archive.org/web/20191016114519/briarproject.org/

56. Ryan, M.: Bluetooth: with low energy comes low security. In: Proceedings of the 7th USENIX Conference on Offensive Technologies (WOOT 2013), p. 4. USENIX Association, USA (2013)

57. Schwartz, L.: The world's protest app of choice, August 2020. https://restofworld.org/2020/the-worlds-protest-app-of-choice/, http://archive.today/5kOhr

58. SIG, B.: Mesh profile specification 1.0.1, January 2019. https://www.bluetooth.com/specifications/mesh-specifications/

59. Silva, M.D.: Hong Kong protestors are once again using mesh networks to preempt an internet shutdown, September 2019. http://archive.today/2019.09.20-220517/https://qz.com/1701045/hong-kong-protestors-use-bridgefy-to-preempt-internet-shutdown/

60. Sivakumaran, P., Blasco, J.: A study of the feasibility of co-located app attacks against BLE and a large-scale analysis of the current application-layer security landscape. In: Heninger, N., Traynor, P. (eds.) USENIX Security 2019, pp. 1–18. USENIX Association, August 2019

61. Skylot: Jadx - Dex to Java decompiler, v1.1.0, December 2019. https://github.com/skylot/jadx

62. SMEX: Lebanon protests: how to communicate securely in case of a network disruption, October 2019. https://smex.org/lebanon-protests-how-to-communicate-securely-in-case-of-a-network-disruption-2/, http://archive.today/hx1lp

63. Software Freedom Law Centre, India: Internet shutdown tracker (2020). https://internetshutdowns.in/

64. Stein, W., et al.: Sage mathematics software version 9.0. The Sage Development Team (2019). http://www.sagemath.org

65. Subnodes: Subnodes (2018). http://subnodes.org/

66. Sullivan, N., Turner, S., Kaduk, B., Cohn-Gordon, K., et al.: Messaging Layer Security (MLS), November 2018. https://datatracker.ietf.org/wg/mls/about/

67. Teknologiia Lebanon: Lebanese protesters are using this 'Bridgefy' messaging app
    – what is it? January 2020. https://medium.com/@teknologiialb/lebanese-
    protesters-are-using-this-bridgefy-messaging-app-what-is-it-74614e169197,
    https://archive.vn/udqly
68. The Stranger: How to message people at protests even without internet access, June
    2020. https://www.thestranger.com/slog/2020/06/03/43829749/how-to-message-
    people-at-protests-even-without-internet-access, http://archive.is/8UrWQ
69. Twitter: Bridgefy search, June 2020. https://twitter.com/search?q=bridgefy,
    http://archive.today/hwklY
70. Twitter - B1O15J, August 2020. https://twitter.com/B1O15J/status/
    1294603355277336576, https://archive.vn/dkPqD
71. Twitter - Bridgefy, November 2019. https://twitter.com/bridgefy/status/
    1197191632665415686, http://archive.today/aNKQy
72. Twitter - Bridgefy, December 2019. https://twitter.com/bridgefy/status/
    1209924773486170113, http://archive.today/aQZDL
73. Twitter - Bridgefy, January 2020. https://twitter.com/bridgefy/status/
    1216473058753597453, http://archive.today/x1gG4
74. Twitter - Bridgefy, June 2020. https://twitter.com/bridgefy/status/
    1268905414248153089. http://archive.today/odSbW
75. Twitter - Bridgefy, July 2020. https://twitter.com/bridgefy/status/
    1287768436244983808, https://archive.vn/WQfZm
76. Twitter - Bridgefy, June 2020. https://twitter.com/bridgefy/status/
    1268015807252004864, http://archive.today/uKNRm
77. Twitter - Bridgefy, August 2020. https://twitter.com/bridgefy/status/
    1289576487004168197, https://archive.vn/zbxgR
78. Twitter - Bridgefy, August 2020. https://twitter.com/bridgefy/status/
    1292880821725036545, https://archive.vn/tKr0t
79. Twitter - Bridgefy, June 2020. https://twitter.com/bridgefy/status/
    1267469099266965506, http://archive.today/40pzC
80. Uher, J., Mennecke, R.G., Farroha, B.S.: Denial of sleep attacks in Bluetooth
    Low Energy wireless sensor networks. In: Brand, J., Valenti, M.C., Akinpelu, A.,
    Doshi, B.T., Gorsic, B.L. (eds.) 2016 IEEE Military Communications Conference,
    MILCOM 2016, Baltimore, MD, USA, 1–3 November 2016, pp. 1231–1236. IEEE
    (2016). https://doi.org/10.1109/MILCOM.2016.7795499
81. Wakefield, J.: Hong Kong protesters using Bluetooth Bridgefy app, Septem-
    ber 2019. http://web.archive.org/web/20200305062625/https://www.bbc.co.uk/
    news/technology-49565587
82. Zuo, C., Wen, H., Lin, Z., Zhang, Y.: Automatic fingerprinting of vulnerable BLE
    IoT devices with static UUIDs from mobile apps. In: Proceedings of the 2019 ACM
    SIGSAC Conference on Computer and Communications Security, pp. 1469–1483.
    ACM (2019)

Inverse-Sybil Attacks in Automated Contact Tracing

Benedikt Auerbach$^{(\boxtimes)}$ ⬤, Suvradip Chakraborty, Karen Klein,
Guillermo Pascual-Perez ⬤, Krzysztof Pietrzak, Michael Walter ⬤,
and Michelle Yeo

IST Austria, Klosterneuburg, Austria
{bauerbac,schakrab,kklein,gpascual,pietrzak,mwalter,myeo}@ist.ac.at

Abstract. Automated contract tracing aims at supporting manual contact tracing during pandemics by alerting users of encounters with infected people. There are currently many proposals for protocols (like the "decentralized" DP-3T and PACT or the "centralized" ROBERT and DESIRE) to be run on mobile phones, where the basic idea is to regularly broadcast (using low energy Bluetooth) some values, and at the same time store (a function of) incoming messages broadcasted by users in their proximity. In the existing proposals one can trigger false positives on a massive scale by an "inverse-Sybil" attack, where a large number of devices (malicious users or hacked phones) pretend to be the same user, such that later, just a single person needs to be diagnosed (and allowed to upload) to trigger an alert for all users who were in proximity to any of this large group of devices.

We propose the first protocols that do not succumb to such attacks assuming the devices involved in the attack do not constantly communicate, which we observe is a necessary assumption. The high level idea of the protocols is to derive the values to be broadcasted by a hash chain, so that two (or more) devices who want to launch an inverse-Sybil attack will not be able to connect their respective chains and thus only one of them will be able to upload. Our protocols also achieve security against replay, belated replay, and one of them even against relay attacks.

Keywords: Automated contact tracing · Replay attacks · Relay attacks · Inverse sybil attacks

1 Introduction

1.1 Automated Contact Tracing

One central element in managing the current Covid-19 pandemic is contact tracing, which aims at identifying individuals who were in contact with diagnosed

Guillermo Pascual-Perez and Michelle Yeo were funded by the European Union's Horizon 2020 research and innovation programme under the Marie Skłodowska–Curie Grant Agreement No. 665385; the remaining contributors to this project have received funding from the European Research Council (ERC) under the European Union's Horizon 2020 research and innovation programme (682815 - TOCNeT).

K. G. Paterson (Ed.): CT-RSA 2021, LNCS 12704, pp. 399–421, 2021.
https://doi.org/10.1007/978-3-030-75539-3_17

people so they can be warned and further spread can be prevented. While contact tracing is done mostly manually, there are many projects which develop automated contact tracing tools leveraging the fact that many people carry mobile phones around most of the time.

While some early tracing apps used GPS coordinates, most ongoing efforts bet on low energy Bluetooth to identify proximity of devices. Some of the larger projects include east [2,9] and west coast PACT [11], Covid Watch [1], DP-3T [16], Robert [5], its successor Desire [10] and Pepp-PT [3]. Google and Apple [4] released an API for Android and iOS phones which solves some issues earlier apps had (in particular, using Bluetooth in the background and synchronising Bluetooth MAC rotations with other key rotations). As this API is fairly specific its use is limited to basically the DP-3T protocol.

In typical contact-tracing schemes users broadcast messages to, and process messages received from other users in close proximity. If a user is diagnosed she prepares a report message and sends it to the backend server. The server uses the message to generate data which allows other users in combination with their current internal state to evaluate whether they were in contact with an infected person.

Coming up with a practical protocol is challenging. The protocol should be **simple** and **efficient** enough to be implemented in short time and using just low energy Bluetooth. As the usage of an app should be voluntarily, the app should provide strong **privacy** and **security** guarantees to not disincentivize people from using it.

1.2   False Positives

One important security aspect is preventing false positives, that is, having a user's device trigger an alert even though she was not in proximity with a diagnosed user. Triggering false positives cannot be completely prevented, a dedicated adversary will always be able to e.g. "borrow" the phone of a person who shows symptoms and bring it into proximity of users he wants to get alerted. What is more worrying are attacks which either are much easier to launch or that can easily be scaled. If such large scale attacks should happen they will likely undermine trust and thus deployment of the app. There are individuals and even some authoritarian states that actively try to undermine efforts to contain the epidemic, at this point mostly by disinformation,[1] but potential low-cost large-scale attacks on tracing apps would also make a worthy target.

Even more worrying, such attacks might not only affect the reputation and thus deployment of the app, but also external events like elections; Launching false alerts on a large scale could keep a particular electorate from voting.[2]

---

[1] https://www.aies.at/download/2020/AIES-Fokus-2020-03.pdf.

[2] https://www.forbes.com/sites/michaeldelcastillo/2020/08/27/google-and-apple-downplay-possible-election-threat-identified-in-their-covid-19-tracing-software.

Replay Attacks. One type of such attack are replay attacks, where an adversary simply records the message broadcasted by the device of a user Alice, and can later replay this broadcast (potentially after altering it) to some user Bob, such that Bob will be alerted should Alice report sick. Such an attack is clearly much easier to launch and scale than "borrowing" the device of Alice. One way to prevent replay attacks without compromising privacy but somewhat losing in efficiency and simplicity is by interaction [17] or at least non-interactive message exchange [7,10]. The Google-Apple API [4] implicitly stores and authenticates the epoch of each encounter (basically, the time rounded to 15 min) to achieve some security against replay attacks, thus giving up a lot in privacy to prevent replaying messages that are older than 15 min. This still leaves a lot of room for replays, in particular if combined with relaying messages as discussed next. A way to prevent replay attacks by authenticating the time of the exchange without ever storing this sensitive data, termed "delayed authentication", was suggested in [15]. Iovino et al. [14] show that the Google-Apple API also succumbs to so called belated replay attacks. That is, adversaries that are able to control the targeted device's internal clock can trigger false positives by replaying report messages already published by the server.

Relay Attacks. Even if replay attacks are not possible (e.g. because one uses message exchange [7,10,17] or a message can only trigger an alert if replayed right away [15]) existing schemes can still succumb to relay attacks, where the messages received by one device are sent to some other device far away, to be replayed there. This attack is more difficult to launch than a replay attack, but also more difficult to protect against. The only proposals we are aware of which aim at preventing them [13,15,17] require some kind of location dependent value like coarse GPS coordinates or cell tower IDs.

Inverse-Sybil Attacks. While replay and relay attacks on tracing apps have already received some attention, "inverse-Sybil" attacks seem at least as devastating but have attained little attention so far. In such attacks, many different devices pretend to be just one user, so that later it's sufficient that a single person is diagnosed and can upload its values in order to alert all users who were in proximity to any of the many devices. The devices involved in such an attack could belong to malicious covidiots, or to honest users whose phones got hacked. In this work we propose two protocols that do not succumb to inverse-Sybil attacks. Below we first shortly discuss how such attacks affect the various types of tracing protocols suggested, the discussion borrows from Vaudenay [18], where this attack is called a "terrorist attack". The attacks are illustrated in Fig. 1.

Decentralized. In so called decentralized schemes like DP-3T [16], devices regularly broadcast ephemeral IDs derived from some initial key K, and also store IDs broadcasted by other devices in their proximity. If diagnosed, the devices upload their keys K to a backend server. The devices daily download keys of infected users from the server and check if they have locally stored any of the IDs corresponding to those keys. If yes, the devices raise an alert.[3] It's particularly easy to launch an inverse-Sybil attack against decentralized schemes, one just needs to initialize the attacking devices with the same initial key K.

Centralized. Centralized schemes like Robert [5] and CleverParrot [8] are similar, but here an infected user uploads the received (not the broadcasted) IDs to the server, who then informs the senders of those broadcasts about their risk. To launch an inverse-Sybil attack against such schemes the attacking devices don't need to be initialized with the same key, in fact, they don't need to broadcast anything at all. Before uploading to the server, the attacker simply collects the messages received from any devices he gets his hands on, and uploads all of them.

As in centralized schemes the server learns the number of encounters, he can set an upper bound on the number of encounters a single diagnosed user can upload, which makes an inverse-Sybil attack much less scalable.

Non-interactive Exchange. Schemes including Desire [10] and Pronto-C2 [7] require the devices to exchange messages (say X and Y) at an encounter, and from these then compute a shared token $S = f(X, Y)$.[4]

In Desire and Pronto-C2 the token is derived by a non-interactive key exchange (NIKE), concretely, a Diffie-Hellman exchange $X = g^x, Y = g^y, S = g^{xy}$. The goal is to prevent a user who passively records the exchange to learn S.

Our first protocol also uses an exchange, but for a different goal, and for us it's sufficient to just use hashing $S = H(X, Y)$ to derive the token.

The inverse-Sybil attack as described above also can be launched against schemes that use a non-interactive exchange, but now the attack devices need to be active (i.e., broadcast, not just record) during the attack also for centralized schemes like Desire.

While recently formal models of integrity properties of contact tracing schemes have been proposed, they either do not consider inverse-Sybil attacks [12], or only do so in the limited sense of imposing upper bounds on the number of alerts a single report message to the server can trigger [8].

Modeling Inverse-Sybil Attacks. We first discuss a simple security notion for inverse-Sybil attacks that considers an adversary which consists of four parts $(\mathcal{A}_0, \mathcal{A}_1, \mathcal{A}_2, \mathcal{A}_3)$ where

---

[3] This oversimplifies things, in reality a risk score is computed based on the number, duration, signal strength etc., of the encounters, which then may or may not raise an alert. How the risk is computed is of course crucial, but not important for this work.

[4] In Desire it's called a "private encounter token" (PET), and is uploaded to the server for a risk assessment (so it's a more centralized scheme), while in Pronto-C2 only diagnosed users upload the tokens, which are then downloaded by all other devices to make the assessment on their phones (so a more decentralized scheme).

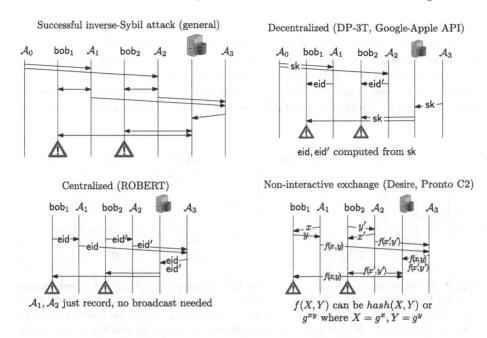

Fig. 1. (top left) Illustration of a successful inverse-Sybil attack: both bobs trigger an alert even though they interacted with different devices $\mathcal{A}_1, \mathcal{A}_2$. (rest) The attacks on the various protocol types outlined in Sect. 1.2.

- $\mathcal{A}_0$ chooses initial states for $\mathcal{A}_1, \mathcal{A}_2$.
- $\mathcal{A}_1$ and $\mathcal{A}_2$ interact with honest devices bob_1 and bob_2.
- $\mathcal{A}_1$ and $\mathcal{A}_2$ pass their state to $\mathcal{A}_3$.
- $\mathcal{A}_3$ is then allowed to upload some combined state to the backend server (like a diagnosed user).
- The adversary wins the game if both, bob_1 and bob_2, raise an alert after interacting with the backend server.

The notions we achieve for our actual protocols are a bit weaker, in particular, in Protocol 1 the adversary can combine a small number of received random beacons from two devices (basically the encounters in the first epoch) and in our Protocol 2 we need to assume that the locations of the devices in the future are not already known when the attack starts.

On the Assumption that Devices Can't Communicate. Let us stress that in the security game above we do not allow $\mathcal{A}_1$ and $\mathcal{A}_2$ to communicate. The reason is that a successful inverse-Sybil attack seems unavoidable (while preserving privacy) if such communication was allowed: $\mathcal{A}_1$ can simply send its entire state to $\mathcal{A}_2$ after interacting with bob_1, who then interacts with bob_2. The final state of $\mathcal{A}_2$ has the distribution of a single device $\mathcal{C}$ first interacting with bob_1 then with bob_2, and if this was the case we want both bobs to trigger an alert, this is illustrated in Fig. 2. Thus, without giving up on privacy (by e.g. storing location data and checking movement patterns), presumably the best we can hope for is a protocol which prevents an inverse-Sybil attack assuming the devices involved in the attack do not communicate. Such an assumption might be justified if one considers the case where the attack is launched by hacked devices, as such communication might be hard or at least easily detectable.

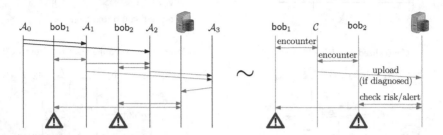

Fig. 2. If the attacking devices $\mathcal{A}_1, \mathcal{A}_2$ could communicate during the attack (arrow in red), they can emulate the transcript (shown in green) of a single honest device $\mathcal{C}$ interacting with $\mathsf{bob}_1, \mathsf{bob}_2$ and the server. As such a $\mathcal{C}$ can make both bobs trigger an alert by running the honest protocol, the adversary can always win the game. (Color figure online)

If we can't exclude communication, we note that the security of our schemes degrades gracefully with the frequency in which such communication is possible. Basically, in our first protocol, at every point in time at most one of the devices will be able to have interactions with other devices which later will trigger an alert, and moving this "token" from one device to another requires communication between the two devices. In our second protocol the token can only be passed once per epoch, but on the downside, several devices can be active at the same time as long as they are at the same location dependent coordinate.

Only under very strong additional assumptions, in particular if the devices run trusted hardware, inverse-Sybil attacks can be prevented in various ways, even if the devices can communicate.

Using Hash Chains to Prevent Inverse-Sybil Attacks. Below we outline the two proposed protocols which do not succumb to inverse-Sybil attacks. The basic idea is to force the devices to derive their broadcasted values from a hash chain. If diagnosed, a user will upload the chain to the server, who will then verify it's indeed a proper hash chain.

The main problem with this idea is that one needs to force the chains of different attacking devices to diverge, so later, when the adversary can upload a chain, only users who interacted with the device creating that particular chain will raise an alert. To enforce diverting chains, we will make the devices infuse unpredictable values to their chains. We propose two ways of doing this, both protocols are decentralized (i.e., the risk assessment is done on the devices), but it's straightforward to change them to centralized variants.

Protocol 1 (Sect. 2, decentralized, non-interactive exchange) The basic idea of our first proposal is to let devices exchange some randomness at an encounter, together with the heads of their hash chains. The received randomness must then be used to progress the hash chain. Should a user be diagnosed and her hash-chain is uploaded, the other device can verify that the randomness it chose was used to progress that chain from the head it received. A toy version of this protocol is illustrated in Fig. 3 (the encounter) and 4 (report and alert).

Protocol 2 (Sect. 4, decentralized, location based coordinate) Our second protocol is similar to simple protocols like the unlinkable DP-3T, but the broadcasted values are derived via a hash-chain (not sampled at random). We also need the device to measure some location dependent coordinate with every epoch which is then infused to the hash chain at the end of the epoch. Apart from the need of a location dependent coordinate, the scheme is basically as efficient as the unlinkable variant of DP-3T. In particular, no message exchanges are necessary and the upload by a diagnosed user is linear in the number of epochs, but independent of the number of encounters. This comes at the cost of weaker security against inverse-Sybil attacks compared to Protocol 1, since we need the location coordinate to be unpredictable for the protocol to be secure, cf. Fig. 10.

The Privacy Cost of Hash Chains. In our protocols diagnosed users must upload the hash chain to the backend server, that then checks if the uploaded values indeed form a hash chain. This immediately raises serious privacy concerns, but we'll argue that the privacy cost of our protocols is fairly minor; apart from the fact that the server can learn an ordering of the uploaded values (which then would give some extra information should the server collude with other users), the protocols provide the same privacy guarantees as their underlying protocols without the chaining (which do not provide security against inverse-Sybil attacks).

2 Protocol 1: Decentralized, Non-Interactive Exchange

In this section we describe our first contact tracing protocol using hash chains which does not succumb to inverse-Sybil attacks. To illustrate the main idea behind the protocol, in Sect. 2.1 we'll consider a toy version of the protocol which assumes a (unrealistic) restricted communication model. We will then describe and motivate the changes to the protocol required to make it private and correct in a general communication model.

Alice	Bob
// h_A current hash value	// h_B current hash value
$\rho_A \leftarrow_\$ \{0,1\}^r$	$\rho_B \leftarrow_\$ \{0,1\}^r$
	h_A, ρ_A
	$\longleftarrow$
	h_B, ρ_B
store (h_A, ρ_B) in L_A^{rep}	store (h_B, ρ_A) in L_B^{rep}
store (h_B, ρ_A) in L_A^{eval}	store (h_A, ρ_B) in L_B^{eval}
$h_A \leftarrow H(h_A, \rho_B)$	$h_B \leftarrow H(h_B, \rho_A)$

Fig. 3. Broadcast/receive phase of the toy protocol.

Alice	Server	Bob
// L^{rep} report list	// L^{ser} server list	// L^{eval} evaluation list

.... report infection ....

$$L^{\text{rep}} \longrightarrow$$

$$((h_1, \rho_1), \ldots, (h_n, \rho_n)) \leftarrow L^{\text{rep}}$$
$$\textbf{for } i \text{ in } \{1, \ldots, n-1\}$$
$$\quad \textbf{if } h_{i+1} \neq H(h_i, \rho_i)$$
$$\quad\quad \textbf{reject} \text{ report}$$
$$L^{\text{ser}} \leftarrow L^{\text{ser}} \cup L^{\text{rep}}$$

.... evaluate risk ....

$$L^{\text{ser}} \longrightarrow$$

$$\textbf{if } L^{\text{ser}} \cap L^{\text{eval}} \neq \emptyset$$
$$\quad \textbf{return} \text{ "contact"}$$
$$\textbf{return} \text{ "no contact"}$$

Fig. 4. Report/risk-evaluation phase of the toy protocol.

2.1 Toy Protocol

The description of our toy protocol is given below, its broadcast/receive phase is additionally depicted in Fig. 3, and its report/evaluate phase in Fig. 4. To analyze it, we'll make the (unrealistic) assumptions that all parties proceed in the protocol in a synchronized manner, i.e., messages between two parties are broadcast and received at the same time, and consider a setting where users meet in pairs: a broadcasted message from user A is received by at most one other user B, and in this case also A receives the message from B.

- (setup) Users sample a genesis hash value h_1 and set the current head of the hash chain to $h \leftarrow h_1$. Then they initialize empty lists L^{rep} and L^{eval} which are used to store information to be reported to the backend server in case of infection or used to evaluate whether contact with an infected person occurred, respectively.
- (broadcast) In regular intervals each user samples a random string $\rho \leftarrow_\$ \{0,1\}^r$ and broadcasts the message (h, ρ) where h is the current head of the hash chain.

- (receive broadcast message) When Alice with current hash value h_A receives a broadcast message (h_B, ρ_B) from Bob she proceeds as follows. She appends the pair (h_A, ρ_B) to L^{rep} and stores (h_B, ρ_A) in L^{eval}. Then she computes the new head of the hash chain as $h_A \leftarrow H(h_A, \rho_B)$.
- (report message to backend server) When diagnosed users upload the list $L^{\text{rep}} = ((h_1, \rho_1), \ldots, (h_n, \rho_n))$ to the server. The server verifies that the uploaded values indeed form a hash chain, i.e., that $h_{i+1} = H(h_i, \rho_i)$ for all $i \in \{1, \ldots, n-1\}$. If the uploaded values pass this check the server includes all elements of L^{rep} to the list L^{ser}.
- (evaluate infection risk) After downloading L^{ser} from the server users check whether L^{ser} contains any of the hash-randomness pairs stored in L^{eval}. If this is the case they assume that they were in contact with an infected party.

Security. The toy protocol does not succumb to inverse-Sibil attacks. In Sect. 3 we provide a formal security model for inverse-Sybil attacks and give a security proof for the full protocol described in Sect. 2.2.

Correctness. Assume that Alice and Bob met and simultaneously exchanged messages (h_A, ρ_A) and (h_B, ρ_B). Then the pair (h_A, ρ_B) is stored by Alice in L^{rep} and by Bob in L^{eval}. If Alice later is diagnosed and uploads L^{rep}, Bob will learn that he was in contact with an infected person.

This toy protocol cannot handle simultaneous encounters of more than two parties. For example, assume both, Bob and Charlie, received Alice's message (h_A, ρ_A) at the same time. Even if Alice records messages from both users, it's not clear how to process them. We could let Alice process both sequentially, say first Bob's message as $h'_A \leftarrow H(h_A, \rho_B)$, and then Charlie's $h''_A \leftarrow H(h'_A, \rho_C)$. Then later, should Alice be diagnosed and upload $(h_A, \rho_B), (h'_A, \rho_C)$, Charlie who stored (h_A, ρ_C) will get a false negative and not recognize the encounter.

Our full protocol overcomes this issue by advancing in epochs. The randomness broadcast by other parties is collected in a pool that at the end of the current epoch is used to extend the hash chain by one link.

Privacy. The toy protocol is a minimal solution to prevent inverse-Sybil attacks but has several weaknesses regarding privacy. Below, we discuss some privacy issues of the toy protocol, and how they are addressed in Protocol 1

(i) Problem (Reconstruction of chains): After learning the list L^{ser} from the server, a user Bob is able to reconstruct the hash chains contained in this list even if the tuples in L^{ser} are randomly permuted: check for each pair $(h, \rho), (h', \rho') \in L^{\text{ser}}$ if $h' = H(h, \rho)$ to identify all chain links. If a reconstructed chain can be linked to a user, this reveals how many encounters this user had. Moreover a user can determine the position in this chain where it had encounters with this person.
Solution (Keyed hash function): We use a keyed hash function so Bob can't evaluate the hash function. Let us stress that this will not improve privacy

against a malicious server because the server is given the hashing key as it must verify the uploaded values indeed form a chain. Leakage of the ordering of encounters to the server is the price we pay in privacy for preventing inverse-Sybil attacks.

(ii) Problem (Correlated uploads): Parallel encounters are not just a problem for correctness as we discussed above, but also privacy. If both Bob and Charlie met Alice at the same time, both will receive the same message (h_A, ρ_A). Bob will then store (h_B, ρ_A) and Charlie (h_C, ρ_A) in their L^{rep} list. This is bad for privacy, for example if both, Bob and Charlie, later are diagnosed and upload their L^{rep} lists, (at least) the server will see that they both uploaded the same ρ_A, and thus they must have been in proximity. Solution (Unique chaining values): The chaining value (σ_A in Fig. 5 below) in Protocol 1 is not just the received randomness as in the toy protocol, but a hash of the received randomness and the heads of the hash chains of both parties. This ensures that all the L^{rep} lists (containing the chains users will upload if diagnosed) simply look like random and independent hash chains.

2.2 Description of Protocol 1

We now describe our actual hash-chain based protocol. Unlike the toy protocol it proceeds in epochs. Users broadcast the same message during the full duration of an epoch and pool incoming messages in a set that is used to update the hash chain at the beginning of the next epoch. The protocol makes use of three hash functions H_1, H_2, and H_3. It is additionally parametrized by an integer γ that serves as an upper limit on the number of contacts that can be processed per epoch. Its formal description is given below. Its broadcast/receive phase is additionally depicted in Fig. 5, and its report/evaluate phase in Fig. 6.

- (setup) Alice samples a key k_A and a genesis hash value h_1. She sets the current head of the hash chain to $h \leftarrow h_1$. Then she initializes empty lists L^{rep} and L^{eval} which are used to store information to be reported to the backend server in case of infection or used to evaluate whether contact with an infected person occurred, respectively.
- (broadcast) At the beginning of every epoch Alice samples a random string $\rho_A \leftarrow_{\$} \{0,1\}^r$ and sets C to the empty set. She broadcasts the message (h_A, ρ_A) consisting of the current head of the hash chain and this randomness during the full duration of the epoch.
- (receive broadcast message) Let h_A denote her current head of the hash chain. Whenever she receives a broadcast message (h_B, ρ_B) from Bob she proceeds as follows. She computes $\sigma_A \leftarrow H_2(h_A, h_B, \rho_B)$ and adds σ_A to the set C. Then she computes the value $\sigma'_A \leftarrow H_3(h_B, h_A, \rho_A)$ and stores it in L^{eval}.
- (end of epoch) When the epoch ends (we discuss below when that should happen), Alice appends the tuple (h_A, C) to L^{rep} and updates the hash chain using C as $h_A \leftarrow H_1(k_A, h_A, C)$, but for efficiency reasons only if she received at least one broadcast, i.e., $C \neq \emptyset$.

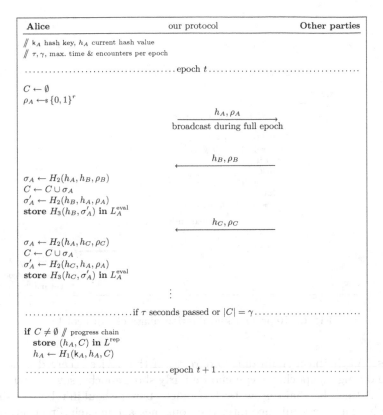

Fig. 5. Broadcast/receive phase of Protocol 1

- (report message to backend server) If diagnosed, Alice is allowed to upload her key k_A and the list $L^{\text{rep}} = ((h_1, C_1), \ldots, (h_n, C_n))$ to the server. The server verifies that the uploaded values indeed form a hash chain, i.e., that $h_{i+1} = H(k_A, h_i, C_i)$ for all $i \in \{1, \ldots, n-1\}$. If the uploaded values pass this check the server updates its list L^{ser} as follows. For every set C_i it adds the hash value $H_3(h_i, \sigma)$ to L^{ser} for all $\sigma \in C_i$.
- (evaluate infection risk) After downloading L^{ser} from the server a user Bob will check whether L^{ser} contains any of the pairs stored in L^{eval} (of the last two weeks say, older entries are deleted). If this is the case he assumes that he was in proximity to another infected user.

Efficiency. In Protocol 1 the amount of data a diagnosed user has to upload, and more importantly, every other user needs to download, is linear in the number of encounters a diagnosed user had. In the full version of this work [6] we describe a variant of Protocol 1 where the up and downloads are independent of the number of encounters, but which has weaker privacy properties.

Alice	Server	Bob
$/\!/$ L^{rep} report list	$/\!/$ L^{ser} server list	$/\!/$ L^{eval} evaluation list
$/\!/$ k private key		

....report infection...

Alice → Server: k, L^{rep}

$((h_1, C_1), \ldots, (h_n, C_n)) \leftarrow L^{rep}$
for i **in** $\{1, \ldots, n-1\}$
    if $h_{i+1} \neq H_1(k, h_i, C_i)$
        reject report $/\!/$ invalid chain
for i **in** $\{1, \ldots, n\}$
    if $|C_i| > \gamma$
        reject report $/\!/$ too many encounters
    for $\sigma \in C_i$
        store $H_3(h_i, \sigma)$ **in** L^{ser}

....evaluate risk...

Server → Bob: L^{ser}

if $L^{ser} \cap L^{eval} \neq \emptyset$
    return "contact"
return "no contact"

Fig. 6. Report/risk-evaluation phase of Protocol 1

Epochs. As the hash chain only progresses if the device received at least one message during an epoch, we can choose fairly short epochs, say $\tau = 60$ seconds, without letting the chain grow by too much, but it shouldn't be too short so that we have a successful encounter (i.e., one message in each direction) of close devices within each sufficiently overlapping epochs with good probability. Choosing a small τ also gives better security against replay attacks, which are only possible within an epoch. Another advantage of a smaller τ is that it makes tracing devices using passive recording more difficult as the broadcasts in consecutive epochs cannot be linked (except retroactively by the server after a user reports). We also bound the maximum number of contacts per epoch to some γ. We do this as otherwise an inverse-Sybil attack is possible by simply never letting the attacking devices progress the hash chain. With this bound we can guarantee that in a valid chain all but at most γ of the encounters must have been received by the same device.

Correctness. Consider two parties A and B who meet, and where B receives (h_A, ρ_A) from A, and A receives (h_B, ρ_B) from B. Then (by construction) B stores $H_3(h_A, \sigma) \in L^{eval}$ where $\sigma = H_2(h_A, h_B, \rho_B)$, while A stores $(h_A, C) \in L^{rep}$ where $\sigma \in C$. Should A be diagnosed and upload L^{rep}, B will get a L^{ser} which contains $H_3(h_A, \sigma)$, and thus B will raise a contact alert as this value is in its L^{eval} list.

Privacy. We briefly discuss the privacy of users in various cases (user diagnosed or not, server privacy breached or not).

Non-diagnosed user. As discussed in Sect. 2.1, as we use a keyed hash function a device just broadcasts (pseudo)random and unlinkable values. Thus, as long as the user isn't diagnosed and agrees to upload its L^{rep} list, the device gets hacked or is seized, there's no serious privacy risk.

Diagnosed user. We now discuss what happens to a diagnosed user who agrees to upload its L^{rep} list.

- Server view: As the chaining values are just randomized hashes, from the server's perspective the lists L^{rep} uploaded by diagnosed users just look like random and independent hash chains. In particular, the server will not see which chains belong to users who had a contact. What the chains do leak, is the number of epochs with non-zero encounters, and the number of encounters in each epoch.
- Other users' view: A user who gets the L^{ser} list from the server only learns the size of this list, and combined with its locally stored data this only leaks what it should: the size of the intersection of this list with his L^{eval} list, which is the number of exchanges with devices of later diagnosed users.
- Joint view of Server and other users: If the view of the server and the data on the device X is combined, one can additionally deduce where in an uploaded chain an encounter with X happened.

The above discussion assumes an honest but curious adversary,[5] once we consider active attacks, tracking devices, etc., privacy becomes a much more complex issue. Discussions on schemes similar to ours are in [7,10,18]. We will not go into this discussion and rather focus on the main goal of our schemes, namely robustness against false positives.

Security. As triggering an alert requires that the hash chain includes a value broadcasted by the alerted device, Protocol 1 does not succumb to replay attacks and belated replay attacks. In the next section we show that, most importantly, it also is secure against inverse-Sybil attacks.

3   Security of Protocol 1

We now discuss the security of Protocol 1 against inverse-Sybil attacks. As a first observation, note that two rogue devices could broadcast the same value (h, ρ) in the first epoch, and later combine their respective lists $(h, C_1), (h, C_2)$ for this epoch into a report list $L^{\text{rep}} = ((h, C = C_1 \cup C_2))$ and upload it. As it consists of a single link, L^{rep} will pass the server's verification of the hash chain. Thus, assuming that C_1 and C_2 jointly do not contain more than γ elements, all users who interacted with one of the devices will raise an alert.

Below we will show that this restricted attack is basically the only possible inverse-Sybil attack against Protocol 1. In more detail, consider an attack

---

[5] And some precautions we didn't explicitly mention, like the necessity to permute the L^{ser} list and let the devices store the L^{eval} list in a history independent datastructure.

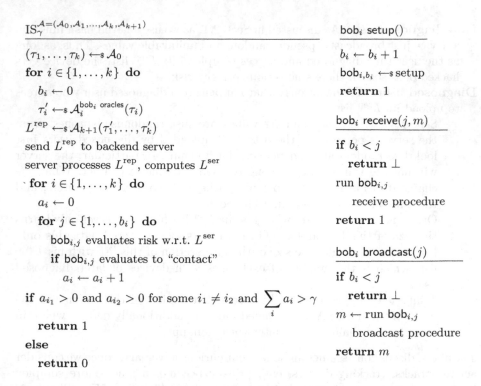

$IS_\gamma^{\mathcal{A}=(\mathcal{A}_0,\mathcal{A}_1,\dots,\mathcal{A}_k,\mathcal{A}_{k+1})}$

$(\tau_1,\dots,\tau_k) \leftarrow_{\$} \mathcal{A}_0$

for $i \in \{1,\dots,k\}$ **do**

   $b_i \leftarrow 0$

   $\tau_i' \leftarrow_{\$} \mathcal{A}_i^{\text{bob}_i \text{ oracles}}(\tau_i)$

$L^{\text{rep}} \leftarrow_{\$} \mathcal{A}_{k+1}(\tau_1',\dots,\tau_k')$

send L^{rep} to backend server

server processes L^{rep}, computes L^{ser}

for $i \in \{1,\dots,k\}$ **do**

   $a_i \leftarrow 0$

   for $j \in \{1,\dots,b_i\}$ **do**

     $\text{bob}_{i,j}$ evaluates risk w.r.t. L^{ser}

     if $\text{bob}_{i,j}$ evaluates to "contact"

       $a_i \leftarrow a_i + 1$

if $a_{i_1} > 0$ and $a_{i_2} > 0$ for some $i_1 \neq i_2$ and $\sum_i a_i > \gamma$

   return 1

else

   return 0

$\text{bob}_i \text{ setup}()$

$b_i \leftarrow b_i + 1$

$\text{bob}_{i,b_i} \leftarrow_{\$} \text{setup}$

return 1

$\text{bob}_i \text{ receive}(j,m)$

if $b_i < j$

   return $\bot$

run $\text{bob}_{i,j}$

   receive procedure

return 1

$\text{bob}_i \text{ broadcast}(j)$

if $b_i < j$

   return $\bot$

$m \leftarrow$ run $\text{bob}_{i,j}$

   broadcast procedure

return m

Fig. 7. Inverse-Sybil security game

where the adversary initiates a large number of devices (that cannot communicate during the attack), and later combines their states into a hash chain $L^{\text{rep}} = (h_1, C_1), (h_2, C_2), \dots, (h_n, C_n)$ to upload. Assume this upload later alerts users $\text{bob}_1, \text{bob}_2, \dots, \text{bob}_t$ because they had an encounter with one of the devices. Then, as we show below, with overwhelming probability one of two cases holds:

1. There was no inverse-Sybil attack, that is, all alerted bob's encountered the same device.
2. All the encounters of the bobs that trigger an alert are recorded in the same C_i and all other $C_j, j \neq i$ contain only values that cannot trigger an alert.

While the 2nd point means an inverse-Sybil attack is possible, it must be restricted to an upload which in total can only contain γ values that will actually raise an alert.

3.1   Security Game

We now give a formal description of the inverse-Sybil security game $IS_\gamma^{\mathcal{A}}$ against which Protocol 1 is secure. The game is given in Fig. 7. It is parameterized by an integer γ and defined with respect to adversary $\mathcal{A} = (\mathcal{A}_0, \mathcal{A}_1, \dots, \mathcal{A}_k, \mathcal{A}_{k+1})$, k

being the number of independently acting devices used in the attack. Adversary $\mathcal{A}_0$ sets up states to be used by these devices. More precisely, $\mathcal{A}_0$ for $i \in \{1, \ldots, k\}$ generates initial states τ_i. Then $\mathcal{A}_i$ is run on input τ_i. Each $\mathcal{A}_i$ has access to three oracles. The jth call to oracle bob_i setup sets up a user $\mathsf{bob}_{i,j}$. Oracle bob_i receive on input of index j and message m results in $\mathsf{bob}_{i,j}$ receiving and processing m. Finally, bob_i broadcast on input of index j runs $\mathsf{bob}_{i,j}$'s broadcast procedure and returns the corresponding message.

At the end of the game $\mathcal{A}_1, \ldots, \mathcal{A}_k$ output states, on input of which $\mathcal{A}_{k+1}$ generates a single report message L^{rep} which in turn is processed by the backend server. Then all $\mathsf{bob}_{i,j}$ evaluate their risks status with respect to the resulting L^{ser}. The attack is considered to have been successful if (a) at least two bobs that interacted with different $\mathcal{A}_i$ raise an alert and (b) the overall number of alerts raised exceeds γ.

3.2 Security of Protocol 1

We obtain the following.

Theorem 1. *If H_1, H_2, H_3 are modeled as random oracles with range $\{0,1\}^w$, any adversary $\mathcal{A}$ making at most a total of q queries to H_1, H_2, H_3 and having at most t interactions with the bobs in total, can win the $\mathrm{IS}_\gamma^{\mathcal{A}}$ game against Protocol 1 with probability at most $\frac{t^2+tq}{2^r} + \frac{2q^2+2qt+tq(q+t)}{2^w}$, where r is the length of the random values ρ broadcast during the protocol execution.*

Proof. Let $\mathcal{A} = (\mathcal{A}_0, \ldots, \mathcal{A}_{k+1})$ be an adversary that wins the $\mathrm{IS}_\gamma^{\mathcal{A}}$ game. Note that in order to win, the adversary must have initiated $\mathsf{bob}_{i,j}$ for at least $\gamma + 1$ different values (i,j) and made them raise an alert. Thus, for these (i,j) the report list $L^{\mathsf{rep}} = ((h_1, C_1), \ldots, (h_n, C_n))$ uploaded by $\mathcal{A}_{k+1}$ must contain $C_{\ell_{i,j}}$ and $\sigma_{\ell_{i,j}} \in C_{\ell_{i,j}}$ such that $H_3(h_{\ell_{i,j}}, \sigma_{\ell_{i,j}}) \in L^{\mathsf{eval}}_{\mathsf{bob}_{i,j}}$.

Next, we will show that with overwhelming probability all values stored in the evaluation lists $L^{\mathsf{eval}}_{\mathsf{bob}_{i,j}}$ are pairwise distinct. To this end, recall that the lists $L^{\mathsf{eval}}_{\mathsf{bob}_{i,j}}$ contain hash values of the form $H_3(h_A, H_2(h_A, h_B, \rho_B))$, where ρ_B is sampled uniformly at random from $\{0,1\}^r$. With probability at least $1 - t^2/2^r$ all ρ_B are distinct. Thus with probability at least $(1 - t^2/2^r)(1 - q^2/2^w)$ all values $H_2(h_A, h_B, \rho_B)$, are distinct and in turn with probability at least

$$(1 - t^2/2^r)(1 - q^2/2^w)^2 \geq 1 - t^2/2^r - 2q^2/2^w$$

all values in $\{L^{\mathsf{eval}}_{\mathsf{bob}_{i,j}}\}_{i,j}$ are distinct.

In turn, as the server when processing L^{rep} verifies that all C_ℓ satisfy $|C_\ell| \leq \gamma$, there must exist $\ell_1 < \ell_2$ such that C_{ℓ_1} and C_{ℓ_2} contain values resulting in an alert of some $\mathsf{bob}_{i,j}$. Further, $\mathcal{A}$ winning the inverse-Sybil game implies that the i values of at least two bobs raising an alert differ. So there exist $i_1 \neq i_2$, j_1, j_2 and $\sigma_{\ell_1} \in C_{\ell_1}$, $\sigma_{\ell_2} \in C_{\ell_2}$ such that

$$H_3(h_{\ell_1}, \sigma_{\ell_1}) \in L^{\mathsf{eval}}_{\mathsf{bob}_{i_1,j_1}} \quad \text{and} \quad H_3(h_{\ell_2}, \sigma_{\ell_2}) \in L^{\mathsf{eval}}_{\mathsf{bob}_{i_2,j_2}} .$$

Note that $H_3(h_{\ell_1}, \sigma_{\ell_1})$ depends on randomness ρ_{ℓ_1} that was generated by bob_{i_1, j_1} and hence is not known to adversary $\mathcal{A}_{i_2}$ who had to send the value h_{ℓ_2} to bob_{i_2, j_2} via oracle bob_{i_2} broadcast(j_2). Since the server verifies that L^{rep} forms indeed a hash chain under H_1, in order to win $\mathcal{A}_{k+1}$ needs to find inputs to a hash chain under H_1 from some $(\mathsf{k}, h_{\ell_1}, C_{\ell_1})$ to h_{ℓ_2}, where C_{ℓ_1} contains a value generated independently from h_{ℓ_2}. If H_1, H_2 and H_3 are random oracles, this is infeasible with polynomially many oracle calls, as we show next.

For $i \in \{0, \ldots, k+1\}$ let Q_i denote the queries of $\mathcal{A}_i$ to random oracles H_1, H_2, H_3 and $q_i = |Q_i|$. For $i \in \{1, \ldots, k\}$ let T_i be the values $h'_{\mathcal{A}_i}$ sent by $\mathcal{A}_i$ as part of a query bob_i receive$(j, (h'_{\mathcal{A}_i}, \rho'_{\mathcal{A}_i}))$ for some j, and let $t_i = |T_i|$. Finally, we define $I_j = \{0, \ldots, k\} \setminus \{j\}$ and

$$\overline{Q}_j = \bigcup_{i \in I_j} Q_i \; ,$$

i.e. $\overline{Q}_j$ contains all queries made by $\mathcal{A}$ except the ones by $\mathcal{A}_j$ and $\mathcal{A}_{k+1}$. We next argue that with overwhelming probability there is no query $(\mathsf{k}, h_{\ell_1}, C_{\ell_1})$ to H_1 in $\overline{Q}_{i_1}$. Recall that C_{ℓ_1} contains a value σ_{ℓ_1} such that $H_3(h_{\ell_1}, \sigma_{\ell_1}) = \sigma_B$ for some $\sigma_B = H_3(h_A, H_2(h_A, h_B, \rho_B)) \in L^{\mathrm{eval}}_{\mathsf{bob}_{i_1, j_1}}$, where ρ_B is sampled uniformly at random by bob_{i_1, j_1}. Since bob_{i_1, j_1} only interacts with $\mathcal{A}_{i_1}$, with probability at least $1 - q/2^r$ there is no query (h_A, h_B, ρ_B) to oracle H_2 in $\overline{Q}_{i_1}$. Conditioned on no such query being made, since H_2 is modeled as a random oracle, with probability at least $1 - q/2^w$ the set $\overline{Q}_{i_1}$ contains no query of the form $(h_A, H_2(h_A, h_B, \rho_B))$ to H_3. Finally, as H_3 is modeled as a random oracle, in this case σ_B looks uniformly random to all $\mathcal{A}_i$ with $i \in I_{i_1}$. Note that $\overline{Q}_{i_1}$ containing the query $(\mathsf{k}, h_{\ell_1}, C_{\ell_1})$ to H_1 implies that the adversary found a preimage of σ_B under H_3. Thus, the probability of this event is bounded by $q/2^w$. Summing up, the probability that $(\mathsf{k}, h_{\ell_1}, C_{\ell_1})$ is queried to H_1 in $\overline{Q}_{i_1}$ is at most $q/2^r + 2q/2^w$.

Assuming that no such query is made, since H_1 is modeled as a random oracle, the link h_{i_1+1} of the hash chain looks uniformly random to all adversaries $\mathcal{A}_i$ with $i \in I_{i_1}$ and in particular is independent from $h_{\ell_2} \in T_{i_2}$. So, to construct a hash chain from h_{ℓ_1+1} to h_{ℓ_2} it is necessary that some query in $Q_{i_1} \cup Q_{k+1} \setminus \overline{Q}_{i_1}$ for H_1 collides with one in T_{i_2} or any of the queries in $\overline{Q}_{i_1}$. The probability of this event is at most $q(q+t)/2^w$. Finally, we get another multiplicative factor of t by taking the union bound over all possible σ_{ℓ_2} resulting in an upper bound of

$$\frac{t^2}{2^r} + 2\frac{q^2}{2^w} + t \cdot \left(\frac{q}{2^r} + \frac{2q}{2^w} + \frac{q(q+t)}{2^w} \right)$$

on $\mathcal{A}$'s probability to win game $\mathrm{IS}^{\mathcal{A}}_{\gamma}$. $\square$

4   Protocol 2: Decentralized, Using Location for Chaining

In this section we describe our second protocol, which requires that the devices have access to some location based coordinate. This coordinate is infused into the hash-chain so chains of different devices (at different coordinates) will diverge, and thus prevent an inverse-Sybil attack. Possible coordinates are coarse grained GPS location, cell tower IDs or information from IP addresses.

The protocol progresses in epochs (say of $\tau = 60$ seconds), where at the beginning of an epoch the device samples randomness ρ and its coordinate ℓ. It then broadcasts ρ together with the head h of its hash chain. If during an epoch at least one message was received, the hash chain is extended by hashing the current head with a commitment of the location ℓ using randomness ρ.

4.1   Protocol Description

The protocol makes use of collision resistant hash functions H_1 to progress the chain, and a hash function H_2 which is basically used as a commitment scheme (and we use notation $H_2(m; \rho)$ to denote it's used as commitment for message m using randomness ρ), but we need H_2 to be hiding even if the same randomness is used for many messages. For this it's sufficient that H_2 is collision resistant (for binding), and for a random ρ, $H_2(\cdot; \rho)$ is a PRF with key ρ.

A formal description of Protocol 2 is given below. The broadcast/receive phase is additionally depicted in Fig. 8, and its report/evaluate phase in Fig. 9.

– (setup) Users sample a key k and a genesis hash value h_1, and set the current head of the hash chain to $h \leftarrow h_1$. Then they initialize empty lists L^{rep} and L^{eval} which are used to store information to be reported to the backend server in case of infection or used to evaluate whether contact with an infected person occurred, respectively.
– (epoch starts) An epoch starts every τ seconds, and the epoch number t is the number of epochs since some globally fixed timepoint (say Jan. 1st 2020, 12am CEST). At the beginning of every epoch the device samples a random string $\rho \leftarrow_{\$} \{0, 1\}^r$ and retrieves its current coordinate $\ell \leftarrow$ get Coordinate.
– (broadcast) During the epoch the device regularly broadcasts the head h of its current chain together with ρ.
– (receive broadcast message) Whenever the device receives a message (h_B, ρ_B) it computes a commitment to the current coordinate and time (i.e., epoch number t) using the received randomness $\sigma_B \leftarrow H_2(\ell, t; \rho_B)$, and stores the tuple (h_B, σ_B) in L^{eval}.
– (epoch ends) If at the end of the epoch there was at least one message received during this epoch (contact= 1), the device computes a commitment $\sigma \leftarrow H_2(\ell, t; \rho)$ to its coordinate and time using randomness ρ, it appends this σ and the head h of the chain to the list L^{rep} (of values to be reported in case of being diagnosed), and progresses its hash chain as $h \leftarrow H_1(k, h, \sigma)$.
– (report message to backend server) If diagnosed users upload their key k and the list $L^{\mathrm{rep}} = ((h_1, \sigma_1), \dots, (h_n, \sigma_n))$ to the server. The server verifies that the uploaded values indeed form a hash chain, i.e., that $h_{i+1} = H_1(k, h_i, \sigma_i)$ for all $i \in \{1, \dots, n-1\}$. If the uploaded values pass this check the server updates its list L^{ser} by adding L^{rep} to it.

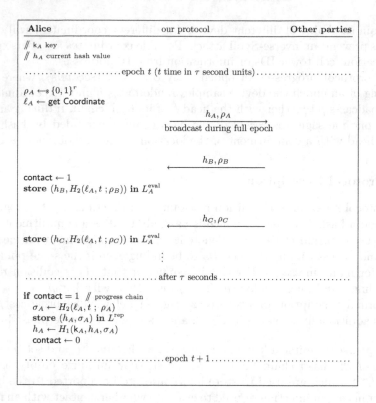

Fig. 8. Broadcast/receive phase of Protocol 2

- (evaluate risk) After downloading L^{ser} from the server users check whether L^{ser} contains any of the pairs stored in L^{eval}. If this is the case they assume that they were in contact with an infected party. As the user learns the size of the intersection, a more sophisticated risk evaluation is also possible.

4.2 Correctness, Privacy and Epochs

Correctness. Consider two devices A and B who measured locations ℓ_A and ℓ_B and are in epochs t_A and t_B, and where A receives (h_B, ρ_B) from B and thus stores $(h_B, \sigma = H_2(\ell_A, t_A; \rho_B))$ in L_A^{eval}. Assume B receives at least one message during this epoch, then it will store $(h_B, \sigma' = H_2(\ell_B, t_B; \rho_B))$ in its L_B^{rep} list.

If later B is diagnosed it uploads its L_B^{rep} list to the server. At its next risk evaluation A will receive L^{ser} (which now contains L_B^{rep}) from the server. It will report a contact if $L^{\mathrm{ser}} \cap L_A^{\mathrm{eval}} \neq \emptyset$ which holds if $\sigma' = \sigma$ or equivalently

$$(h_B, H_2(\ell_B, t_B; \rho_B)) = (h_B, H_2(\ell_A, t_A; \rho_B))$$

which is implied by $(\ell_A, t_A) = (\ell_B, t_B)$. Summing up, in the setting above A will correctly report a contact if

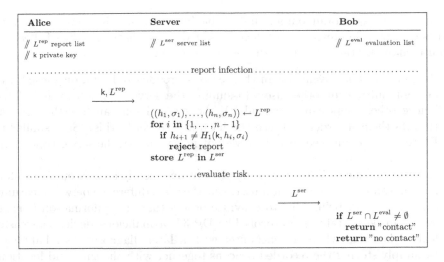

Fig. 9. Report/risk-evaluation phase of Protocol 2

1. A and B are synchronised, i.e., in the same epoch $t_A = t_B$.
2. B received at least one message during epoch t_B.
3. A and B were at the same locations (i.e., $\ell_A = \ell_B$) at the beginning of the epoch.

Condition 2. should be satisfied in most cases simply because the fact that A received a message from B means B should also have received a message from A. This condition only exists because we let the devices progress their chains only in epochs where encounters happened.[6]

Epochs. As epochs are synchronized, even if the coordinates of the devices change frequently because the devices are moving, two devices will still have the same coordinate as long as they were at the same coordinate at the beginning of an epoch, think of two passengers in a moving train. But we can have a mismatch (and thus false negative) if two devices meet that were at different coordinates at the beginning of an epoch, e.g., two people meet at a train station, where at the beginning of the epoch, one person was in the moving train, while the other was waiting at the platform. To address this problem one should keep the epochs sufficiently short, in particular, much shorter than the exposure time that would raise an alert.

Privacy. Our Protocol 2 is similar to the unlinkable variant of DP-3T, and thus has similar privacy properties. In particular, the only thing non-diagnosed users

---

[6] The reason for only progressing if there was an encounter is that this way the chain is shorter (thus there's less to up and download), the chain reveals less information (i.e., even the server can't tell where the empty epochs were) and tracing using passive recording devices becomes more difficult.

broadcast are pseudorandom and unlinkable beacons. But there are two privacy issues that arise in our protocol which DP-3T does not have. The first is because we use chaining, the second because we use coordinates:

1. (Server can link) Even though the beacons broadcasted by a diagnosed user are not linkable by other users (assuming the server permutes the L^{ser} list before other users can download it), the server itself can link the beacons (it gets them in order and also the hash key to verify this). So – similar to Protocol 1 – compared to DP-3T we put more trust in the server concerning this privacy aspect.
2. (Digital evidence) When discussing privacy, one mostly focuses on what information can be learned about a user. But there's a difference between learning something, and being able to convince others that this information is legit. While in decentralized protocols like DP-3T a malicious device can easily learn when and where an encounter with a later diagnosed user happened by simply storing the recorded beacons together with the time and location, it's not clear how the device would produce convincing evidence linking the uploaded beacon with this time and location.

In a protocol that uses time and location, like our Protocol 2, one can produce such evidence by basically time-stamping the entire transcript of an encounter (e.g. by posting a hash of it on a blockchain), and later, when a user is diagnosed and its encounter tokens become public, use this time-stamped data as evidence of the encounter. This problem already arises when one uses time to prevent replay attacks, and location to prevent relay attacks as discussed in [15] for details.

5   Security of Protocol 2

5.1   Security Against Replay and Relay Attacks

The protocol is secure against replay, belated replay, and relay attacks in the following sense: Assume Alice is at location ℓ_A and epoch t_A, broadcasts (h_A, ρ_A) and thus stores $(h_A, \sigma_A = H_2(\ell_A, t_A; \rho_A)) \in L^{\text{rep}}$. Now, assume an adversary replays the message with potentially changed randomness (h_A, ρ'_A) to user Bob who is at a different location and/or epoch $(\ell_B, t_B) \neq (\ell_A, t_A)$ than Alice was. Bob then stores $(h_A, \sigma_B = H_2(\ell_B, t_B; \rho'_A)) \in L^{\text{eval}}$. Should Alice later upload her L^{rep} list, then the replayed message will trigger a contact warning for Bob if $\sigma_A = \sigma_B$, i.e.,

$$H_2(\ell_A, t_A; \rho_A) = H_2(\ell_B, t_B; \rho'_A),$$

and this condition is necessary as long as L^{eval} does not contain a pair (h'_A, σ'_A) with $h'_A = h_A$ and $\sigma'_A \neq \sigma_A$. Since the latter happens only with negligible probability, this implies that Bob must break the binding property of the commitment scheme.

5.2   Security Against Inverse-Sybil Attacks

Protocol 2 achieves weaker security against inverse-Sybil attacks since there is less interaction: the randomness chosen by the users in Protocol 1 is replaced by location to defend somewhat against inverse-Sybil attacks. Accordingly, we need to weaken the model in order to prove security. In particular, we cannot let the adversary have control of the locations, otherwise it can trivially carry out an attack. So we assume that the locations of the encounters with the bobs follow some unpredictable distributions $\mathcal{P}_i$. The formal security game weak-$\mathrm{IS}^{\mathcal{A}}_{\mathcal{P}_1,\mathcal{P}_2}$ can be found in Fig. 10. We believe that whenever the location coordinates are not chosen too coarse, this still implies a meaningful security guarantee.

---

weak-$\mathrm{IS}^{\mathcal{A}=(\mathcal{A}_0,\mathcal{A}_1,\mathcal{A}_2,\mathcal{A}_3)}_{\mathcal{P}_1,\mathcal{P}_2}$

$\tau_1, \tau_2 \leftarrow_\$ \mathcal{A}_0$

for $i \in \{1,2\}$ **do**

   $\mathrm{bob}_i \leftarrow_\$ \mathrm{setup}$

   $\tau_i' \leftarrow_\$ \mathcal{A}_i^{\mathrm{bob}_i\ \mathrm{oracles}}(\tau_i)$

$L^{\mathrm{rep}} \leftarrow_\$ \mathcal{A}_3(\tau_1', \tau_2')$

send L^{rep} to backend server

server processes L^{rep}, computes L^{ser}

   for $i \in \{1,2\}$ **do**

      bob_i evaluates risk w.r.t. L^{ser}

if both bobs evaluate to "contact"

   return 1

else

   return 0

$\mathrm{bob}_i\ \mathrm{receive}(h_A, \rho_A)$

$\ell \leftarrow_\$ \mathcal{P}_i$

run bob_i receive procedure with coordinate ℓ

return ℓ

$\mathrm{bob}_i\ \mathrm{broadcast}$

$\ell \leftarrow_\$ \mathcal{P}_i$

run bob_i broadcast procedure with coordinate ℓ

return the result and ℓ

Fig. 10. Weak inverse-Sybil security game

For Protocol 2 we obtain the following theorem.

Theorem 2. *If H_1 is modeled as a random oracle, H_2 is ϵ-collision-resistant, and $\mathcal{P}_1, \mathcal{P}_2$ are independent and have min-entropy at least k, then any adversary $\mathcal{A}$ making at most q queries to $H_1 : \{0,1\}^* \to \{0,1\}^w$ and having at most t interactions with the bobs can win the weak-$\mathrm{IS}^{\mathcal{A}}_{\mathcal{P}_1,\mathcal{P}_2}$ game against Protocol 2 with probability at most $\frac{q+1}{2^k} + \frac{2q^2}{2^w} + \epsilon$.*

Proof. Let $\mathcal{A} = (\mathcal{A}_0, \mathcal{A}_1, \mathcal{A}_2, \mathcal{A}_3)$ be an adversary that wins the weak-$\mathrm{IS}^{\mathcal{A}}_{\mathcal{P}_1,\mathcal{P}_2}$ game with non-negligible advantage. We assume that the first samples from $\mathcal{P}_1$ and $\mathcal{P}_2$ are different, which happens with probability at least $1 - 2^{-k}$. Furthermore, since both bobs evaluate to "contact", we must have that for both of them $L^{\mathrm{ser}} \cap L^{\mathrm{eval}} \neq \emptyset$, i.e. L^{ser} contains pairs (h_{A_1}, σ_{A_1}) and (h_{A_2}, σ_{A_2}) such that during the game bob_j received h_{A_j} and ρ_{A_j} at epoch t_j and coordinate ℓ_j and it holds $\sigma_{A_j} = H_2(\ell_j, t_j; \rho_{A_j})$, where $j \in \{1,2\}$. Then, since the server verifies the hash chain, we must have that τ_3 consists of a key k and a list L of pairs (h_i, σ_i) such that $h_{i+1} = H_1(\mathsf{k}, h_i, \sigma_i)$ and $(h_{A_1}, \sigma_{A_1}), (h_{A_2}, \sigma_{A_2}) \in L$.

We consider two cases: First, assume case 1) $(h_{A_1}, \sigma_{A_1}) = (h_{A_2}, \sigma_{A_2})$. Since $h_{A_1} = h_{A_2}$, either exactly the same sequence of coordinates were infused into the hash chain to obtain h_{A_1} and h_{A_2}, or $\mathcal{A}$ found a collision for H_1 or H_2. Furthermore, since $\sigma_{A_1} = \sigma_{A_2}$ either the coordinates where the adversaries $\mathcal{A}_i$ meet the respective bob_i coincide as well, or $\mathcal{A}$ found a collision for H_2. Thus, either the location histories of $\mathcal{A}_1$ and $\mathcal{A}_2$ coincide, which happens with probability at most 2^{-k}, or $\mathcal{A}$ found a collision for H_1 or H_2, which happens with probability at most $\epsilon + q^2/2^w$.

Now, let's assume case 2) $(h_{A_1}, \sigma_{A_1}) \neq (h_{A_2}, \sigma_{A_2})$. We assume that $\mathcal{A}$ does not find a collision for H_2, since this case would already be covered by the upper bound for case 1. W.l.o.g. assume that (h_{A_1}, σ_{A_1}) appears before (h_{A_2}, σ_{A_2}) in L. Note that $\mathcal{A}_2$ outputs h_{A_2} without knowing (h_{A_1}, σ_{A_1}) and $\mathcal{P}_1$ has entropy k. So $\mathcal{A}_3$ needs to find inputs to a hash chain from (h_{A_1}, σ_{A_1}) that collides with h_{A_2}. Similar to the proof of Protocol 1, let Q_i be the queries of $\mathcal{A}_i$ to H_1 and $q_i = |Q_i|$. Furthermore, let $h = H_1(\mathsf{k}, h_{A_1}, \sigma_{A_1})$. Since (h_{A_1}, σ_{A_1}) is not known to $\mathcal{A}_2$, we have $(\mathsf{k}, h_{A_1}, \sigma_{A_1}) \notin Q_0 \cup Q_2$ except with probability $(q_0 + q_2)/2^k$. So except with this probability h looks uniformly random to $\mathcal{A}_0$ and $\mathcal{A}_2$, because H_1 is modeled as a RO. Accordingly, h is independent of any of the queries in $Q_0 \cup Q_2$. So constructing a hash chain between h and any of the values in $Q_0 \cup Q_2$ requires that the value of H_1 under some query in $Q_1 \cup Q_3$ collides with (the first entry of) any of the queries in $Q_0 \cup Q_2$. The probability of this event is less than $(q_1 + q_3) \cdot \frac{q_0 + q_2}{2^w}$. Thus, in case 2) the probability of τ_3 causing an alert for bob_1 and bob_2 is at most $\frac{q_0 + q_2}{2^k} + \frac{(q_1 + q_3)(q_0 + q_2)}{2^w}$. By setting $q = \sum_i q_i$ and combining the two cases, we get an upper bound of $\frac{q+1}{2^k} + \frac{2q^2}{2^w} + \epsilon$.   □

References

1. Covid watch (2020). https://www.covidwatch.org/
2. Pact: Private automated contact tracing (2020). https://pact.mit.edu/
3. Pepp-pt: Pan-european privacy-preserving proximity tracing (2020). https://github.com/pepp-pt
4. Privacy-preserving contact tracing (2020). https://www.apple.com/covid19/contacttracing
5. Robert: Robust and privacypreserving proximity tracing (2020). https://github.com/ROBERT-proximity-tracing
6. Auerbach, B., et al.: Inverse-sybil attacks in automated contact tracing. Cryptology ePrint Archive, Report 2020/670 (2020). https://eprint.iacr.org/2020/670
7. Avitabile, G., Botta, V., Iovino, V., Visconti, I.: Towards defeating mass surveillance and sars-cov-2: The pronto-c2 fully decentralized automatic contact tracing system. Cryptology ePrint Archive, Report 2020/493 (2020). https://eprint.iacr.org/2020/493
8. Canetti, R., et al.: Privacy-preserving automated exposure notification. Cryptology ePrint Archive, Report 2020/863 (2020). https://eprint.iacr.org/2020/863

9. Canetti, R., Trachtenberg, A., Varia, M.: Anonymous collocation discovery: taming the coronavirus while preserving privacy. CoRR ArXiv:abs/2003.13670 (2020). https://arxiv.org/abs/2003.13670

10. Castelluccia, C., et al.: DESIRE: a third way for a european exposure notification system leveraging the best of centralized and decentralized systems. CoRR ArXiv:abs/2008.01621 (2020). https://arxiv.org/abs/2008.01621

11. Chan, J., et al.: PACT: privacy sensitive protocols and mechanisms for mobile contact tracing. CoRR ArXiv:abs/2004.03544 (2020). https://arxiv.org/abs/2004.03544

12. Danz, N., Derwisch, O., Lehmann, A., Puenter, W., Stolle, M., Ziemann, J.: Security and privacy of decentralized cryptographic contact tracing. Cryptology ePrint Archive, Report 2020/1309 (2020). https://eprint.iacr.org/2020/1309

13. Gvili, Y.: Security analysis of the covid-19 contact tracing specifications by apple inc. and google inc. Cryptology ePrint Archive, Report 2020/428 (2020). https://eprint.iacr.org/2020/428

14. Iovino, V., Vaudenay, S., Vuagnoux, M.: On the effectiveness of time travel to inject covid-19 alerts. Cryptology ePrint Archive, Report 2020/1393 (2020). https://eprint.iacr.org/2020/1393

15. Pietrzak, K.: Delayed authentication: preventing replay and relay attacks in private contact tracing. In: Bhargavan, K., Oswald, E., Prabhakaran, M. (eds.) INDOCRYPT 2020. LNCS, vol. 12578, pp. 3–15. Springer, Cham (2020). https://doi.org/10.1007/978-3-030-65277-7_1

16. Troncoso, C., et al.: Dp3t: decentralized privacy-preserving proximity tracing (2020). https://github.com/DP-3T

17. Vaudenay, S.: Analysis of dp3t. Cryptology ePrint Archive, Report 2020/399 (2020).https://eprint.iacr.org/2020/399

18. Vaudenay, S.: Centralized or decentralized? the contact tracing dilemma. Cryptology ePrint Archive, Report 2020/531 (2020). https://eprint.iacr.org/2020/531

On the Effectiveness of Time Travel to Inject COVID-19 Alerts

Vincenzo Iovino[1], Serge Vaudenay[2(✉)], and Martin Vuagnoux[3]

[1] University of Salerno, Fisciano, Italy
[2] EPFL, Lausanne, Switzerland
serge.vaudenay@epfl.ch
[3] base23, Geneva, Switzerland

Abstract. Digital contact tracing apps allow to alert people who have been in contact with people who may be contagious. The Google/Apple Exposure Notification (GAEN) system is based on Bluetooth proximity estimation. It has been adopted by many countries around the world. However, many possible attacks are known. The goal of some of them is to inject a false alert on someone else's phone. This way, an adversary can eliminate a competitor in a sport event or a business in general. Political parties can also prevent people from voting.

In this report, we review several methods to inject false alerts. One of them requires to corrupt the clock of the smartphone of the victim. For that, we build a time-traveling machine to be able to remotely set up the clock on a smartphone and experiment our attack. We show how easy this can be done. We successfully tested several smartphones with either the Swiss or the Italian app (SwissCovid or Immuni). We confirm it also works on other GAEN-based apps: NHS COVID-19 (in England and Wales), Corona-Warn-App (in Germany), and Coronalert (Belgium).

The time-machine can also be used in active attack to identify smartphones. We can recognize smartphones that we have passively seen in the past. We can passively recognize in the future smartphones that we can see in present. We can also make smartphones identify themselves with a unique number.

Finally, we report a simpler attack which needs no time machine but relies on the existence of still-valid keys reported on the server. We observed the case in several countries. The attack is made trivial in Austria, Denmark, Spain, Italy, the Netherlands, Alabama, Delaware, Wyoming, Canada, and England & Wales. Other regions are affected by interoperability too.

1 Introduction

Google and Apple deployed together the Exposure Notification (GAEN) system as a tool to fight the pandemic [3]. The goal of an GAEN-based app is to alert

---

Videos are available on https://vimeo.com/477605525 (teaser) and https://vimeo.com/476901083. A full version of this paper is available on Eprint [19].

© Springer Nature Switzerland AG 2021
K. G. Paterson (Ed.): CT-RSA 2021, LNCS 12704, pp. 422–443, 2021.
https://doi.org/10.1007/978-3-030-75539-3_18

people who have been in close proximity for long enough with someone who was positively tested with COVID-19 and who volunteered to report. How a user responds to such alert is up to the user, but one would expect that such user would contact authorities and be put in quarantine for a few days. In Switzerland, the alerted user is eligible to have a free COVID-19 test but the result of the test would not change his quarantine status.

GAEN is provided by default in all recent Android or iOS smartphones which are equipped with Bluetooth (except Chinese ones due to US regulation). It is installed without the consent of the user. However, it remains inactive until the user activates it (and possibly install an app which depends on the region).[1]

Once activated, GAEN works silently. A user who is tested positive with COVID-19 is expected to contribute by reporting through GAEN. This may have the consequence of triggering an alert on the phones of the GAEN users whom the COVID-positive user met.

Assuming an alerted user is likely to self-quarantine, and possibly make a test and wait for the result, this alerted user may interrupt his activities for a few days. A malicious adversary could take advantage of making some phones raise an alert. In a sport competition (or any other competition), an alerted competitor would stay away for some time. Malicious false alert injections could be done at scale to disrupt the activities of a company or an organization. This could be done to deter people from voting [17].

False injection attacks have been well identified for long [24, 25]. It was sometimes called the *lazy student attack* where a lazy student was trying to escape from an exam by putting people in quarantine [15]. Nevertheless, the GAEN protocol was deployed without addressing those attacks.

In most of cases, those attacks require to exploit a backdoor in the system, or to corrupt the health authority infrastructure, or to corrupt a diagnosed user. Our goal is to show how easily and inexpensively we can make an attack which requires no such corruption.

Another important goal of GAEN is privacy preservation. Smartphones constantly broadcast random-looking numbers which are changing every few minutes. They are made to be unlinkable and unpredictable. It is already known that unlinkability is broken for positive cases who report, due to the so-called *paparazzi attack* [24]. Linkability is also sometimes harmed by that rotation of values and addresses is not well synchronized.[2] Another goal of our work it to be able to recognize that two broadcasts which were obtained at different time come from the same smartphone and also to identify smartphones, even though the user did not report.

Our Contribution. In this paper, we analyze possible false alert injection attacks. We focus on one which requires to corrupt the clock of the victim and to literally make it travel through time. By doing so, we can replay Bluetooth identifiers

---

[1] Throughout this paper, when we use *"GAEN"* as a noun, we mean a process which runs in the phone. Otherwise, we refer to the *"GAEN system"*, the *"GAEN infrastructure"*, or the *"GAEN protocol"* interchangeably.

[2] Little Thumb attack: https://vimeo.com/453948863.

which have just been publicly reported but that the victim did not see yet. We replay them by making the victim go to the time corresponding to the replayed identifier then coming back to present time. We show several ways to make a smartphone travel through time and to make it receive an alert when it comes back to present time.

In the easiest setting, we assume that the victim and the adversary are connected to the same Wi-Fi network. This network does not need be administrated by the adversary. Essentially, the network tells the current time to the phone. We report on our successful experiments.

Fig. 1. Raspberry Pi Zero W

In Sect. 6.1 we describe the equipment we used in the experiments: a Raspberry Pi Zero W (Fig. 1) and a home-assembled device endowed with an ESP32 chipset (Fig. 2), both available on the market for about 10$. It takes less than a minute to run the attack. In favorable cases (specifically, with the variant using a rogue base station), the attack duration can be reduced to one second. The attacks possibly works on all GAEN-based systems. We mostly tested it on the Swiss and Italian systems (SwissCovid and Immuni). We also verified on other apps. We conclude that such attacks are serious threats to society.

Fig. 2. Our ESP32-based device

Our attacks experimentally confirm the evidence that the GAEN infrastructure offers no protection even against (traditional) replay attacks. Switzerland reports 1 750 000 daily activations, which represents 20% of the population. There are millions of users in other countries too. Hence, many potential victims. They can be attacked from far away. Although the authorized Bluetooth maximum range is of 100 m, boosting it with a 10 kW amplifier in 2.4 GHz would enlarge the radius to many kilometers easily. Actually, commercial products are available [12].

Our technique can be also used to debug the notification mechanism of GAEN without directly involving infected individuals; this is a step forward in disclosing the GAEN's internals since GAEN is closed source and not even debuggable. (Precisely, to experiment with the GAEN system, you need a special authorization.)

In Sect. 7, we observe that several regions do post on their servers keys which are still valid and can be replayed with no time machine. This is the case of Austria, Denmark, Spain, Italy, the Netherlands. However, other regions like Canada and England & Wales post keys which have just expired and which are still accepted in replay attacks. In other regions, the existence of such keys in any interoperable region may be usable in a replay attack too.

In Sect. 8, we adapt the time-machine attack to break privacy. If an adversary has passively seen a smartphone in the past, it can recognize it in present using an active attack: namely, by making it replay the broadcast from the past. If an adversary wants to passively recognize a smartphone in the future, he can make it play the future broadcast immediately. Finally, by using a reference date in the far future and making the smartphone broadcast the key of this date, the adversary make smartphone identify themselves with a unique number.

Disclaimer. We did a responsible disclosure. We first reported and discussed the attack with the Italian Team of Immuni on September 24, 2020.[3] Few days after we received an answer from an account administrated by the team stating:

> *"thank you for reporting this replay attack. Unfortunately we believe that this is an attack against GAEN rather than Immuni and so it should be resolved by a protocol implementation update. Should you have suggestions for our own code base to prevent or mitigate the attack, please let us know and we will evaluate them."*

We reported the attack in Switzerland on October 5, 2020.[4] We received an acknowledgement on October 10 stating:

> *"The NCSC considers the risk in this case as acceptable. The risk assessment must also take into account whether there is a benefit and a ROI for*

---

[3] https://github.com/immuni-app/immuni-app-android/issues/278.

[4] Registered incident INR 8418 by the National Cyber Security Center (NCSC) https://www.ncsc.admin.ch/dam/ncsc/de/dokumente/2020/SwissCovid_Public_Security_Test_Current_Findings.pdf.download.pdf/SwissCovid_Public_Security_Test_Current_Findings.pdf.

someone who takes advantage of it. Especially since an attacker typically must be on site."

We also reported a detailed attack scenario to Google on October 8.[5] We received the following response:

"At first glance, this might not be severe enough to qualify for a reward, though the panel will take a look at the next meeting and we'll update you once we've got more information."

(They subsequently offered a \$500 bug bounty reward.) The attack was also mentioned in the Swiss press and in an official document by Italian authorities. In *24 Heures* on October 8[6], the representative of EPFL declared that the described attack is technically possible but would require too much resources and efforts.

The Italian "Garante della Privacy" (the national data protection officer)[7] commented that replay attacks with the purpose of generating fake notifications do not represent a serious vulnerability since they require the attacker to take possession of the victim's phone. Since both traditional replay attacks and the variants of replay attacks we show in this paper can be performed without taking possession of the victim's phone, we contacted the aforementioned Italian authorities to provide clarifications about replay attacks and to ask whether they are aware of the fact that replay attacks can be performed without taking possession of the victim's phone but at time of writing we did not receive any answer.

Contrary to the reports in the news, we show here that time-travel attacks are easy to perform and effective.

2   How GAEN Works

In short, GAEN selects every day a random key called TEK (as for *Temporary Exposure Key*). Given the daily TEK, it deterministically derives some ephemeral keys called RPI (as for *Rolling Proximity Identifier*). Each RPI is emitted over Bluetooth several times per second during several minutes. Additionally, GAEN scans Bluetooth signals every 3–5 min and stores all received RPIs coming from other phones. If the user is diagnosed, the local health authorities provide an access code (which is called a *covidcode* in Switzerland). This is a one-time access code which is valid for 24 h which can be used to *report*. If GAEN is instructed to report, it releases every TEK which was used in the last few days which the user allows to publish. At this point, a TEK is called a *diagnosis key*. The report and access code are sent to a server which publishes the diagnosis keys. Once a while, GAEN is also provided with the published diagnosis keys on the server. GAEN

---

[5] Reference 170394116 for component 310426.

[6] https://www.24heures.ch/les-quatre-failles-qui-continuent-de-miner-swisscovid-348144831017.

[7] https://www.garanteprivacy.it/home/docweb/-/docweb-display/docweb/9468919.

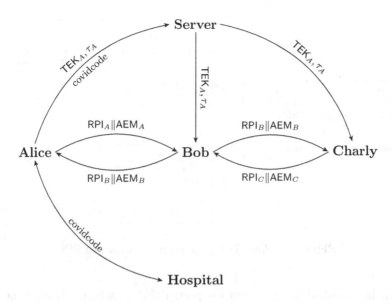

Fig. 3. Exposure notification infrastructure

re-derives the RPI from those diagnosis keys and compares with the stored RPI of encounters. Depending on how many are in common, an alert is raised.

In Fig. 3, we have three users with their smartphones: Alice, Bob, and Charly. Bob meets the two others but Alice and Charly do not meet each other. They exchange their RPI. After a while, Alice gets positive and receives a covidcode. She publishes her TEK using her covidcode. Other participants see the diagnosis key from Alice. They compare the derived RPI with what they have received. Only Bob finds a match and raises an alert. AEM and τ are defined below.

More precisely, we set

$$\mathsf{RPI} = f(\mathsf{TEK}, t)$$

where t is the time when RPI is used for the first time and f is a cryptographic function based on AES [3]. In the GAEN system, time is encoded with a 10-minute precision. Actually, the value of t is just incremented from one RPI to the next one, starting from the time when TEK is used for the first time. There is also an Associated Encrypted Metadata (AEM) which is derived by

$$\mathsf{AEM} = g(\mathsf{TEK}, \mathsf{RPI}) \oplus \mathsf{metadata}$$

where $\oplus$ denotes the bitwise exclusive OR operation, metadata encodes the power π used by the sender to emit the Bluetooth signal, and g is a similar cryptographic function.

We list below a few important details.

- What is sent over Bluetooth is the pair $(\mathsf{RPI}, \mathsf{AEM})$.
- Received $(\mathsf{RPI}, \mathsf{AEM})$ pairs are stored with the time of reception t and the power p of reception.

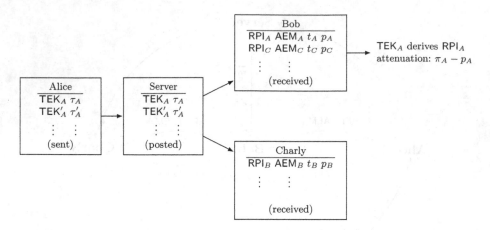

Fig. 4. Matching TEK from server to captured RPI

- What is published on the server are pairs (TEK, τ) where τ is the time when TEK was used for the first time. (See Fig. 4.)
- New (TEK, τ) pairs are posted on the server with a date of release (not shown on the picture). Since they are posted when the user reports, the posting date can be quite different from τ. This posting date is used to retrieve only newly uploaded pairs. Hence, the downloaded τ do not come in order.
- When GAEN gets the downloaded diagnosis key TEK and derives the RPI, the time is compared with what is stored with a tolerance of ± 2 h. If it matches, the receiver can decrypt AEM to recover the metadata, deduce the sending power π, then compare with the receiving power p to deduce the signal attenuation $\pi - p$.
- For Switzerland, the attenuation is compared with two thresholds which are denoted as t_1 and t_2 in the reference document [10]. If larger than t_2, it is considered as too far and ignored. If between t_1 and t_2, the duration is divided by two to account that the distance is not so close. If lower than t_1, the encounter is considered as very close and the duration is fully counted. SwissCovid was launched on June 25, 2020 and the sensibility of parameters has been increased twice. Since September 11, 2020, the parameters are $t_1 = 55$ dB, $t_2 = 63$ dB [10].

  With those parameters, in lab experimental settings [10], the probability to catch an encounter at various distances is as follows:

Distance of encounter	1.5 m	2 m	3 m
$\Pr[\text{attenuation} < t_1]$	57.3%	51.6%	45.6%
$\Pr[\text{attenuation} < t_2]$	89.6%	87.5%	84.2%

- For Italy, only one threshold of 73 dB is used [21]. The same lab experiment as above indicate probabilities of 100%. Since July 9, the unique threshold was changed to 63 dB.
- Every scan which spotted an encounter counts for the rounded number of minutes since the last scan with a maximum of 5 min (possibly divided by two as indicated above). The total sum is returned and compared to a threshold of 15 min.

3 Summary of Techniques for False Alert Injection

We list here several strategies to inject false alerts.

Injection with Real Encounters. The adversary encounters the victim normally and the victim records the sent RPI. If the adversary manages to fill a false report with his TEK, this will cause an alert for the victim [24]. Filling a false report can done

- either due to a bug in the system
- or by corrupting the health authority system
- or by corrupting a user who received the credentials to report.

Switzerland corrected one bug: the ability for the reporter to set verification algorithm to "none" in the query, instructing the server not to verify credentials [1]. This is actually a commonly known attack on implementations using JWT (JSON Web Tokens) which is based on a dangerous default configuration [22].

A corruption system was fully detailed and analyzed by Avitabile, Friolo, and Visconti [14]. Either positive people who receive a covidcode could sell it to buyers who would want to run the attack, or just-tested positive people could be paid for reporting a TEK provided by an attacker. The system could be made in such a way that buyers and sellers would never meet, their anonymity would be preserved, and their transaction would be secured. The infrastructure for this black business would collect a percentage on the payment. It would run with smart contracts and cryptocurrencies.

Injection with Simulated GAEN. We assume that the adversary uses a device (for instance, a laptop computer with a Bluetooth dongle) which mimics the behavior of the GAEN system. One difference is that this device sends Bluetooth signal with high power but announces them with a low power in AEM. This way, he can send the signal from far away and the computed attenuation will be low, like in a close proximity case. The victim can receive an RPI which is sent from the device and believe in a proximity. Reporting the TEK could be done like for the real encounter attack. The device can be attached to a running dog or a drone [15,18]. The attack can be done by a real infected person as a *trolling attack* [18].

A second advantage of this attack is that the sending device could be synchronized in its simulation with several other devices. (Synchronization would mean to use the same TEK.) This could be used by a group of adversaries (terrorists, activists, gang) to inject false alerts in many victims [25]. All members of the group would be considered as a single person by the GAEN system and all their encounters would receive the same keys. In this case, it could also make sense to have one member of the group (a kamikaze) to genuinely become positive and report. The goal of such attack would be to sabotage the digital contact tracing infrastructure, to lock ships in harbors (by targeting sailors), or to paralyze a city in quarantine [15].

Injection with Replay Attack. Another false encounter injection attack consists of replaying the RPI of someone else. Due to the GAEN infrastructure, the RPI is valid for about two hours. One strategy consists of capturing the RPI of people who are likely to be reported soon. It could be people going to a test center, or people who are known to have symptoms but who did not get their test results yet [24]. Capturing their RPI can be done from far away with a good Bluetooth receiver. The malleability of the metadata in AEM can also be exploited to decrease the announced sending power [16,26].

Injection with Belated Replay Attack. Another form of replay attack consists of replaying the RPI which are derived from the publicly posted diagnosis keys [24]. Because GAEN only tries to match new diagnosis keys, the adversary can try with recently updated TEKs which have not been downloaded yet by the victim. This is doable since the app checks only a few times for newly uploaded keys during the day. Those keys are however outdated and would normally be discarded when GAEN compares RPI with the ones derived from the diagnosis keys. However, we could send the phone of the victim in the past then send the outdated RPI to the phone. When the phone would be brought back to present, it would eventually raise an alert. Sending a phone in the past requires no time travel machine. It suffices to corrupt its internal clock.

A variant of this attack which surprisingly works uses no time machine but replays keys which are posted on the public server and *still valid*.

Attack Model. In the rest of the paper, we consider the following attack model. The adversary has the ability to control the clock of the victim (this ability will not be used in Sect. 7). We do not assume any other ability such as changing the clock on the server, forging covidcodes, or corrupting people. Except in Sect. 8, the goal is to inject an alert on the phone of the victim without the victim having encountered a contagious person. In Sect. 8, the goal is to defeat the unlinkability protection in the GAEN system and to infer if two phones which have been encountered are the same. Except in Sect. 7, we do not rely on any specific implementation of digital contact tracing. We use GAEN as it is specified and implemented in commonly available phones.

4   Time-Traveling Phones

Several techniques to corrupt the date and time of a smartphone have been identified (see Park et al. [23] for detailed information). In this section, we describe four of them. Modern smartphone operating systems use at boot time NTP (Network Time Protocol) if network access is provided. NITZ (Network Identity and Time Zone) may be optionally broadcasted by mobile operators. GNSS (Global Navigation Satellite System) such as GPS can also be used. Finally, the clock can be manually set. The priority of these clock sources depends on the smartphone vendors. Some of them can be disabled by default, but in general, the priority (which we deduced by experiment on our phones) is MANUAL > NITZ > NTP > GNSS.

4.1 Set Clock Manually

This is technically the easiest attack, but it requires a physical access to the smartphone.[8] An adversary picks a newly published TEK and computes one RPI for a date and time in the past. The adversary physically accesses the smartphone and sets the corresponding clock. Then, he replays the RPI for 15 min using a Bluetooth device such as a smartphone or a laptop. Finally, the adversary sets the time back to present. As soon as the smartphone updates the new TEK list, an alert is raised.

A single RPI is generally not supposed to be repeated during 15 min as its rotation time is shorter (typically: 10 min). It seems that implementations do not care if it is the case. However, we can also use two consecutive RPI from the same TEK and repeat them for their natural duration time.

Observe that in some circumstances the purpose of the attacker can be to send a fake notification to his own phone, in which case the assumption that the adversary has physical access to the phone of the victim makes perfect sense. This self-injection attack can be done to scare friends and family members, to get the permission of staying home from work, or to get priority for the COVID-19 test.[9] Furthermore, in the case of the Italian app Immuni, each risk notification is communicated to the Italian Ministry of Health: the Italian authorities keep a counter on how many risk notifications have been sent to Immuni's users.[10] Therefore, sending fake notifications even to phones controlled by the adversary represents a serious attack in itself since it allows the attacker to inflate the official counter arbitrarily.

The Italian's counter of risk notifications only takes into account notifications sent from phones endowed with the "hardware attestation" technology, a service offered by Google. So, our attacks show a way to bypass this trusted computing mechanism to manipulate the official counters.

---

[8] It can be done without this assumption by using a vulnerability of the phone allowing to execute a code remotely.

[9] Indeed, in Switzerland a risk notification has legal value in the sense that it gives priority for the COVID-19 test, a free test, and also subsidies when the employer does not give a salary to stay home without being sick.

[10] https://www.immuni.italia.it/dashboard.html.

4.2   Rogue NTP Server

If the smartphone is connected on the Internet on Wi-Fi, it may use NTP (Network Time Protocol) to synchronize clock information. If the adversary connects to the same Wi-Fi network of the victim, he may set an ARP-spoofing attack to redirect all NTP queries to a rogue server. Since NTP authentication is optional, the response from the rogue NTP server will be accepted and then, the adversary can remotely set the date and time of the smartphone.

If the adversary owns the Wi-Fi network (what we call a rogue Wi-Fi network), the attack is even simpler as it no longer requires any ARP-spoofing. Instead, the adversary sets up an NTP server and controls time.

If the mobile network has a priority over NTP, we may assume that the victim is not connected to the mobile network. Otherwise, the adversary may have to jam it.

Depending on the smartphone vendors, NTP is used permanently or only at the boot time, then every 24 h. Sometimes, third-party apps force constant NTP synchronization. The adversary may wait until an NTP request is sent to trigger the whole attack. Otherwise, the adversary must make the victim's smartphone reboot. Making a target to reboot can be done by social engineering (by convincing the victim to reboot). Another way is to use a Denial-of-Service attack. With DoS, the adversary can remotely reboot a smartphone.

4.3   Rogue Base Station

NITZ messages are sent by mobile operator to synchronize time and date when a smartphone is connected to a new mobile network. This is generally used to set new time zone when roaming on another country.

Since the adversary must be physically close to the victim to broadcast replayed RPI, he may also set up a rogue mobile network base station to send corrupt NITZ message. Thus, when the victim is connected to the rogue mobile network, the date and time is modified. Compared to previous techniques, the adversary can now modify clock information at any time by disconnecting and reconnecting the smartphone at will. Note that since the adversary also controls mobile data, he may block update or NTP Requests to avoid potential issues.

Making sure that the victim connects to the rogue base station may require to jam the signal of the one it uses and to impersonate the network it subscribed to. Since there is no authentication of the base station, this is easily done.

4.4   Rogue GNSS

The last technique is to send a fake GNSS signal to modify internal clock of smartphones. Open source tools are available to generate GPS signals [7]. This attack is less practical, since smartphones may not accept GNSS as trusted source clock by default. Moreover, NITZ and NTP take precedence over GNSS.

5   Master of Time Attack

A limitation of the attacks described above is the need to stay for at least 15 min close to the victim to replay RPI. However, GAEN is not continuously scanning Bluetooth broadcast (because of power consumption). Indeed, only 5 s of scan is performed regularly by the smartphone.[11] The duration between two scans is random but typically in the 3–5 min range. Since the adversary is able to modify the date and time at any time, we define an improvement, called *Master of Time*, to accelerate the alert injection process.

The goal of the improvement is to trigger the 5-s scans more quickly. The adversary first goes in the past to the corresponding time and date of the replayed RPI. This generally triggers a 5-s scan. After that, a random delay is selected by the phone. However, the adversary updates the time again, but to 5 min later. The phone realizes it missed to scan and this triggers an immediate opportunistic scan. After this new 5-s scan, the adversary updates the time to 5 min later again and a third scan is launched. Finally in 15 s, the adversary can trigger enough 5-s scans to simulate an exposure of more than 15 min. This improvement can be applied to all the techniques described above.

There is actually no need to wait for the entire duration of a scan. We can actually reduce the duration between time jumps to 200 ms but we should also increase the frequency of sending RPI. Hence, we broadcast over Bluetooth every 30 ms. Since the duration of a time jump using a rogue base station takes 100 ms, the entire attack takes less than one second in total.

6   Experiments

In this section, we give a detailed description of the Rogue NTP Server Attack and the Rogue Base Station Attack with threat model, experimental setup and results. We tested all options of the attack we mention. We should stress that attacks are not always stable (our success rate is at least 80%) but failure cases are often due to bugs in the phone (in the app, in GAEN, or in the operating system). We found workaround to increase the reliability. However, this technology is a living matter and so are the workarounds we found.

6.1   Rogue NTP Server

We list here a few assumptions.

- The adversary must be within the Bluetooth range of the victim.[12]
- The adversary must access to the same Wi-Fi network of the smartphone and redirect data traffic (by using ARP spoofing attack or rogue Wi-Fi network).

---

[11] Technically, the scan listens for 4 s but an extra second may be needed to activate the scan.

[12] This range could be enlarged using a 2.4 GHz amplifier.

- If NITZ has a priority over NTP, we assume that the victim is not connected to the mobile network. Otherwise, the adversary may have to jam it.
- Depending on the smartphone model, the adversary may need to force NTP as explained in Sect. 4.2.
- We also assume that the victim has not pulled yet the last updated TEK-list which is used by the adversary. (Otherwise, the victim will not try to match it and the attack fails.)

The hardware needed for this attack is relatively simple. Only Wi-Fi and Bluetooth are needed. We tested several smartphones (Motorola z2 force, Samsung Galaxy S6, Samsung Galaxy A5; in Sect. 6.3 we tested with a more recent phone.). We used a Raspberry Pi Zero W (Fig. 1) to host a rogue NTP server. We use a custom Python-based NTP server to deliver the date and time retrieved from the selected TEK.

We also tested using a different hardware platform. We used an home-assembled device endowed with an ESP32 chipset available on Amazon for about 10 Euros. Full fledged devices with the ESP32 chipset are available in different sizes, for instance in watches[13], and as such are easily concealable by an attacker.

In rogue Wi-Fi settings, we set up the device as a rogue Wi-Fi access point. Then, we redirect all UDP connections on port 123 to the rogue NTP server (hosted on the same device). We also configure the access point to block TEK-list queries by the smartphone to avoid potential issues. When using a genuine Wi-Fi network, we use ARP spoofing to redirect to the rogue NTP server and also to block Internet access to the victim's phone so as to prevent the download of the TEK-list during the critical phases of the attack.

The attack then works as follows.

1. The adversary retrieves the updated TEK-list (which is publicly available) from the official server.
2. He picks a new TEK and derives an RPI and AEM. The emission power in AEM is set to low to improve the chances for the RPI to be accepted.
3. The adversary waits for an NTP request from the smartphone[14]. He replies to NTP requests with the date and time of the RPI (i.e. in the past).
4. He sends for at least 15 min the RPI∥AEM using the Raspberry Pi Zero W and Bluez tools.
5. The active part of the attack can stop here. The adversary can wait for the smartphone to restore the date and time by itself, then update the TEK-list and raise an alert. Alternately, the adversary can set the clock back to normal then wait for the TEK-list update.

We tested all variants of the attacks described above with success. Sometimes the smartphone has issues to update the TEK-list and it may need up to 12 h to trigger the alert.

---

[13] https://www.banggood.com/it/LILYGO-TTGO-T-Watch-2020-ESP32-Main-Chip-1_54-Inch-Touch-Display-Programmable-Wearable-Environmental-Interaction-Watch-p-1671427.html.

[14] He can also trigger it with a Denial-of-Service attack to reboot the smartphone.

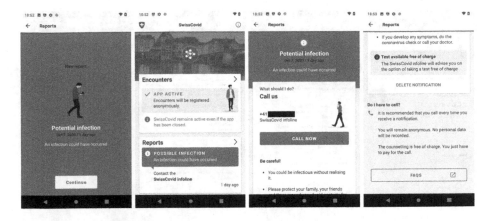

Fig. 5. Screen captures of SwissCovid raising an alert

The experiment was performed for SwissCovid and Immuni. Figure 5 shows screenshots of an alert on SwissCovid and Fig. 6 shows pictures of an alert on Immuni. Observe that while SwissCovid allows to take screenshots of alerts, Immuni prevents that for security reasons.

6.2 Rogue Base Station

We list here a few assumptions.

- The victim must be within the range of the adversary rogue base station and Bluetooth USB dongle (this range can be enlarged using amplifiers).
- The victim smartphone is registered to the rogue base station.
- We also assume that the victim has not pulled yet the last updated TEK-list which is used by the adversary. (Otherwise, the victim will not try to match it and the attack fails.)

For this attack we used a mini PC Fitlet2 (Intel J3455) with a Bluetooth USB dongle and the Software Defined Radio (SDR) USRP B200-mini (Fig. 7). We used several open source projects such as Osmocom suite [4], OpenBTS [8], YateBTS [11] and srsLTE [9]. We eventually setup a 2G rogue base station because of the lack of mutual authentication. Our tests were realized in a Faraday cage to comply with legal regulations. Since the rogue base station also manages network access, we block TEK-list updates and NTP requests. Note that the cost of the attack can be significantly reduced by using a modified Motorola C123 mobile phone as the SDR [5] or even a USB-to-VGA dongle [6]! Below we describe our attack with the Master of Time variant, Hence, the whole attack takes less than a second.

1. The adversary retrieves the updated TEK-list (which is publicly available) from the official server.

Fig. 6. Pictures of immuni raising an alert

2. He picks a new TEK and derives an RPI and AEM. The emission power is set to low to improve the chances for the RPI to be accepted.
3. Using NITZ message, the adversary sends the smartphone to the past at the corresponding date and time of the RPI.
4. He sends the RPI‖AEM using the Bluetooth USB dongle, following the Master of Time attack with NITZ. This requires less than a second.
5. The active part of the attack can stop here. The adversary can wait for the smartphone to restore date and time by disconnecting it from the rogue base station or sets the clock back to normal on the smartphone with a last NITZ message.
6. The app eventually updates the TEK-list. The replayed RPI will be considered as genuine since the exposure duration is more than 15 min, within the defined time frame and emitted with low power. Hence, an alert will be raised.

The attack using a 2G rogue base station is common. As all phones are compatible with 2G, it may only require to jam 3G/4G signals. Most likely, 2G will phase out from smartphones way later than the virus. If not, rogue 3G/4G base stations can be made too, but it would require to bypass authentication (at least, on phones which use it [23]).

6.3 Experimenting the Attack with a Journalist

A demo of the attack on the Immuni's app was carried out in presence of a journalist of the Italian television RAI who was seemingly interested in making the public aware of the danger of replay attacks in general. (The demo and the interview did not focus on time-traveling phones and the more sophisticated technicalities we show in this paper). For this, the journalist bought a new smartphone (Samsung Galaxy A21S) on October 16, 2020 and we used it as a target. At the end of the demo, the journalist saw an alert for a close contact which was supposed to have occurred on October 14, two days before the smartphone was

Fig. 7. Rogue base station USRP B200-Mini with a Fitlet2

bought! Every step, from the purchase of the phone to the display of the alert, was filmed by the journalist.[15]

6.4 Other GAEN-based Apps

We tried few other GAEN-based apps with success. With NHS COVID-19 (the app which is used in England and Wales), the app puts the user in quarantine and releases it after a few days (we used our time machine to check it). The app also shows at-risk areas (like BR1 which is in London). Figure 8 also shows Corona-Warn-App (the app in Germany) and Coronalert (Belgium).

7 KISS Attack

GAEN was developed with the *Keep It Stupid Simple* (KISS) principle. We can have false alert injection attacks following this principle too: by replaying keys which are publicly available.

7.1 Still-Valid Keys

The previous attack uses reported keys which are outdated and needs a time machine to replay them. Sometimes, as it is allowed by the GAEN infrastructure, diagnosed users also want to report on the server for some RPIs that they

---

[15] https://www.rai.it/programmi/report/.

Fig. 8. Screen captures of various GAEN-based apps raising an alert

have broadcasted in the last minutes. These are keys derived by the currently used TEK which is valid for the rest of the day. Hence, we sometimes find on the server some TEKs which are still active. It is a bit surprising because this potential attack was already mentioned in a report disclosed the 8th of April [24, Section 4.3].

Sometimes, regions are careful not to post still-valid keys but they publish just-expired ones which are still accepted due to the tolerance of GAEN with the validity period.

We monitored the existence of still-valid or just-expired keys in GAEN-based systems. During a few days, we regularly checked if the server were suggesting TEKs which were still active in many regions. Our results are as follows:

- Regions we tested (23): AT, BE, CA, CH, CZ, DE, DK, EE, ES, FI, GI, IE, IT, LV, MT, NL, PL, PT, USAL (Alabama), USDE (Delaware), USWY (Wyoming), UKEW (England & Wales), UKNI (North Ireland).
- Regions providing still-valid TEKs as we observed (8): AT, DK, ES, IT, NL, USAL (Alabama), USDE (Delaware), USWY (Wyoming).
- Regions providing just-expired TEKs as we observed (2): CA, UKEW (England & Wales).

In all regions with valid TEKs observed, we successfully injected false alerts without any time machine. More screen captures are shown on Fig. 9.

To monitor reported TEKs on servers, we used the information collected by the TACT project by Leith and Farrell [20] and some of the scripts they developed.[16]

---

[16] https://github.com/sftcd/tek_transparency/.

Fig. 9. Screen captures of more GAEN-based apps raising an alert

7.2 Consequences of Interoperability

The interoperability infrastructure in Europe is based on a *Federation Gateway Service*. As of 19 October 2020[17], the following regions in Europe are part of it:

Germany	Denmark
Ireland	Croatia
Italy	Poland
Republic of Latvia	The Netherlands
Spain	Cyprus

The system works as follows [2]: a user selects the regions he visited or he is visiting on his home app. In the case the user is diagnosed and reports, the

---

17 https://ec.europa.eu/health/sites/health/files/ehealth/docs/gateway_jointcontrolle rs_en.pdf.

app will indicate the regions visited by the user (as declared). His home server will forward to the Federation Gateway Service. Each server retrieves from this service the keys they are interested in. This could mean all keys. When the app wants to check exposure, it retrieves from its home server the keys of relevant regions. This is how the systems works with Immuni in Italy. Things could be a bit different in other countries.

When a still-valid key is discovered in any region A of the interoperable system, users of any other region B of the system may be subject to the attack if the key is transferred from A to B. For instance, we observed that still-valid keys are never transferred to Germany.

However, as soon as we observe a valid key in—say—Italy, we can start replaying it in any country and hope it will be transferred there. With a Bluetooth dongle, we can replay 100–200 different RPI during a 4-s Bluetooth scan. They will all count for a few minutes encounter. Hence, we can blindly try all the still-valid keys from any country and hope that one will appear on the server. During our monitoring period, we found from 200 to 500 still-valid keys every day in the indicated countries.

We list below the transfers of still-valid keys which we observed:

– Regions reporting transferred still-valid keys: DK, ES, IT, NL, LV, PL, IE.
– Region reporting transferred just-expired keys: DE.

8   My-Number Attack

On Android, GAEN cleans up its list of TEKs when they are older than 14 days. This operation is done once a while or when the smartphone is rebooted. However, TEKs are immediately generated as soon as they are needed, i.e. when the date is modified or at midnight. Interestingly, if a TEK has been already picked for this day, it will be reused, as well as the RPIs.

An adversary controlling the time can exploit these principles to identify smartphones. We list below several attacks which have been successfully tested.

To mitigate the attack, we can inspire from those verses:

> You don't have my number
> We don't need each other now
> *Foals — My Number*

Back to the Past. The adversary wants to recognize a smartphone which sent an RPI in the recent past (less than 14 days old) at a specific date and time. Alternately, a forensic attack on a smartphone wants to recognize its past encounters by the stored RPIs. The adversary wonders if the smartphone to recognize is currently around. He uses a time machine to send the surrounding smartphones to the specific date and time. Then, he compares collected RPIs. If the same RPI is received, the smartphone is identified. Clearly, this breaks the unlinkability claims of the GAEN protocol.

Back to the Future. The adversary wants to identify smartphones around him during a future event which will occur at a given date. For this, the adversary can identify smartphones in the present and send them to this future date to collect the RPIs they will use. Then, when the even occurs, these smartphones will repeat the collected RPIs and the adversary will associate them with an identity.

Back to the Far Future. To identify smartphones on request, the adversary can send them systematically to a specific date in the far future, such as 12.9.2021. By moving into a fixed date in the far future, GAEN will create a TEK for this date and it will stay in memory until 14 days after this date, which could practically mean "forever". Hence, every smartphone will advertise itself by broadcasting a unique RPI which will always be the same until 26.9.2021.

Note that we were able to create TEKs for the year of 2150, but the operating system became unstable. In particular, a value containing the number of days since epoch (coded with 2 bytes) was overflowed.

9   Countermeasures

Clearly, GAEN was developed under the assumption that phones have a reliable clock. Our attacks show that phones do *not* have a reliable clock, that it can be controlled by an adversary, and that it can be exploited to break GAEN.

As a countermeasure, we would urge operating systems developers to strengthen the security of the clock, or at least to implement detection of time-travel attacks. Clearly, a dirty quick fix could be to keep record of past clocks and to check that the clock value only increases. GAEN should not proceed if the clock is rewinded. However, this would open the door to denial-of-services attacks. Ideally, such monitoring should be done at the operating system level.

If there is no way to rely on a clock, the GAEN infrastructure should be revisited. Ideally, the server should not give information helping the adversary to replay beacons. To avoid more possible replay attacks, the encounter could rely on an interactive protocol which would make replay impossible. This would require to reopen the debate on centralized versus decentralized systems and about third ways in between [25]. Some alternate solutions exist such as Pronto-C2 [13].

As for the KISS attack, clearly, TEKs must be better filtered. Countries should never post a key which is still active or just expired. They should further monitor if countries in the same federation do so and filter the dangerous TEKs they would publish.

10   Conclusion

In this paper, we demonstrate that alert injections against the GAEN infrastructure of Google and Apple are easy to achieve even without collaboration or corruption of infected individual, Apple, Google, or health authorities. The attack requires little equipment, is fast, and can be done by anyone. It could be done at scale too.

Moreover, people can generate alert injections on their own phones motivated by different purposes: e.g., frightening their own family members or friends, showing the alert to their employers to be exempted by work, or simply to have priority to the COVID-19 test with the terrible side effect of congesting the health system. We point out that in Italy the Ministry of Health does receive a notification when a user is alerted and being such notifications anonymous is impossible for the authorities to distinguish genuine alerts from fake ones; terrorists and criminals could generate fake alerts on phones controlled by themselves to make the Italian health authorities believe that there are much more at-risk individuals, so to induce Italian authorities to take drastic political decisions.

The time machine can also be used to break privacy and identify smartphones. In an active attack, we can recognize smartphones from the past, smartphones in the future, or even make them identify with a unique number.

The time machine's techniques we describe in this work are also useful to test the GAEN system offline and to figure out details that are not public since GAEN is not open source and Google and Apple restrict access to the GAEN's API to health authorities.

Acknowledgements. The authors thank Biagio Pepe, Mario Ianulardo, and Shinjo Park for useful suggestions and technical advice. We also thank Doug Leith and Stephen Farrell for their script and help to test our attacks in some regions.

References

1. CVE-2020-15957. https://cve.mitre.org/cgi-bin/cvename.cgi?name=CVE-2020-15957
2. eHealth Network Guidelines to the EU Member States and the European Commission on Interoperability specifications for cross-border transmission chains between approved apps. Detailed interoperability elements between COVID+ Keys driven solutions. V1.0 16 June 2020. https://ec.europa.eu/health/sites/health/files/ehealth/docs/mobileapps_interoperabilitydetailedelements_en.pdf
3. Exposure Notification. Cryptography Specification. v1.2 April 2020. Apple & Google. https://www.google.com/covid19/exposurenotifications/
4. Osmocom Suite. https://osmocom.org/
5. OsmocomBB. https://projects.osmocom.org/projects/baseband
6. osmo-fl2k. https://osmocom.org/projects/osmo-fl2k
7. osqzss. https://github.com/osqzss/gps-sdr-sim
8. Range Networks. OpenBTS. http://openbts.org
9. srsLTE. https://www.srslte.com/
10. SwissCovid Exposure Score Calculation. Version of 11 September 2020. https://github.com/admin-ch/PT-System-Documents/blob/master/SwissCovid-ExposureScore.pdf
11. Yate. YateBTS. https://yatebts.com
12. Dallon Adams, R.: 20-mile Bluetooth beacon? Apptricity announces Ultra Long-Range device. TechRepublic 2020. https://www.techrepublic.com/article/20-mile-bluetooth-beacon-apptricity-announces-ultra-long-range-device/

13. Avitabile, G., Botta, V., Iovino, V., Visconti, I.: Towards defeating mass surveillance and SARS-CoV-2: The Pronto-C2 fully decentralized automatic contact tracing system. Cryptology ePrint Archive: Report 2020/493. IACR. http://eprint.iacr.org/2020/493

14. Avitabile, G., Friolo, D., Visconti, I.: TEnK-U: terrorist attacks for fake exposure notifications in contact tracing systems. Cryptology ePrint Archive: Report 2020/1150. IACR. http://eprint.iacr.org/2020/1150

15. Bonnetain, X., et al.: Le traçage anonyme, dangereux oxymore. Analyse de risques à destination des non-spécialistes. (English version: Anonymous Tracing, a Dangerous Oxymoron – A Risk Analysis for Non-Specialists.). https://risques-tracage.fr/

16. Dehaye, P.-O., Reardon, J.: SwissCovid: a critical analysis of risk assessment by Swiss authorities. Preprint arXiv:2006.10719 [cs.CR] (2020). https://arxiv.org/abs/2006.10719

17. Gennaro, R., Krellenstein, A., Krellenstein, J.: Exposure notification system may allow for large-scale voter suppression. https://static1.squarespace.com/static/5e937afbfd7a75746167b39c/t/5f47a87e58d3de0db3da91b2/1598531714869/Exposure_Notification.pdf

18. Gvili, Y.: Security Analysis of the COVID-19 Contact Tracing Specifications by Apple Inc. and Google Inc., Cryptology ePrint Archive: Report 2020/428. IACR. http://eprint.iacr.org/2020/428

19. Iovino, V., Vaudenay, S., Vuagnoux, M.: On the effectiveness of time travel to inject COVID-19 alerts. Cryptology ePrint Archive: Report 2020/1393. IACR. http://eprint.iacr.org/2020/1393

20. Leith, D.J., Farrell, S.: Testing Apps for COVID-19 Tracing (TACT). Research project. https://down.dsg.cs.tcd.ie/tact/

21. Leith, D.J., Farrell, S.: Measurement-based evaluation Of Google/Apple exposure notification API for proximity detection in a light-rail tram. PLoS ONE **15**(9) (2020). https://doi.org/10.1371/journal.pone.0239943

22. Li, V.: Hacking JSON Web Tokens (JWTs), 27 October 2019. https://medium.com/swlh/hacking-json-web-tokens-jwts-9122efe91e4a

23. Park, S., Shaik, A., Borgaonkar, R., Seifert, J.: White rabbit in mobile: effect of unsecured clock source in smartphones. In: Proceedings of the 6th Workshop on Security and Privacy in Smartphones and Mobile Devices, SPSM@CCS 2016, Vienna, Austria, 24 October 2016, pp. 13–21. ACM (2016.) https://doi.org/10.1145/2994459.2994465

24. Vaudenay, S.: Analysis of DP3T – between Scylla and Charybdis. Cryptology ePrint Archive: Report 2020/399. IACR. http://eprint.iacr.org/2020/399

25. Vaudenay, S.: Centralized or decentralized? The contact tracing dilemma. Cryptology ePrint Archive: Report 2020/531. IACR. http://eprint.iacr.org/2020/531

26. Vaudenay, S., Vuagnoux, M.: Analysis of SwissCovid. https://lasec.epfl.ch/people/vaudenay/swisscovid/swisscovid-ana.pdf

SoK: How (not) to Design and Implement Post-quantum Cryptography

James Howe[1], Thomas Prest[1]([⊠]), and Daniel Apon[2]

[1] PQShield, Oxford, UK
{james.howe,thomas.prest}@pqshield.com
[2] National Institute of Standards and Technology, Gaithersburg, USA
daniel.apon@nist.gov

Abstract. Post-quantum cryptography has known a Cambrian explosion in the last decade. What started as a very theoretical and mathematical area has now evolved into a sprawling research field, complete with side-channel resistant embedded implementations, large scale deployment tests and standardization efforts. This study systematizes the current state of knowledge on post-quantum cryptography. Compared to existing studies, we adopt a transversal point of view and center our study around three areas: (i) paradigms, (ii) implementation, (iii) deployment. Our point of view allows to cast almost all classical and post-quantum schemes into just a few paradigms. We highlight trends, common methodologies, and pitfalls to look for and recurrent challenges.

1 Introduction

Since Shor's discovery of polynomial-time quantum algorithms for the factoring and discrete logarithm problems, researchers have looked at ways to manage the potential advent of large-scale quantum computers, a prospect which has become much more tangible of late. The proposed solutions are cryptographic schemes based on problems assumed to be resistant to quantum computers, such as those related to lattices or hash functions. *Post-quantum cryptography* (PQC) is an umbrella term that encompasses the design, implementation, and integration of these schemes. This document is a Systematization of Knowledge (SoK) on this diverse and progressive topic.

We have made two editorial choices. First, an exhaustive SoK on PQC could span several books, so we limited our study to signatures and key-establishment schemes, as these are the backbone of the immense majority of protocols. This study will not cover more advanced functionalities such as homomorphic encryption schemes, threshold cryptography, etcetera.

Second, most surveys to-date are either (i) organized around each *family* [26] – (a) lattices, (b) codes, (c) multivariate equations, (d) isogenies, (e) hash and one-way functions – or (ii) focused on a single family [88,151]. Our study instead adopts a transversal approach, and is organized as follows: (a) paradigms, (b) implementation, and (c) deployment. We see several advantages to this approach:

© Springer Nature Switzerland AG 2021
K. G. Paterson (Ed.): CT-RSA 2021, LNCS 12704, pp. 444–477, 2021.
https://doi.org/10.1007/978-3-030-75539-3_19

- Compared to previous surveys, it provides a new point of view that abstracts away much of the mathematical complexity of each family, and instead emphasizes common paradigms, methodologies, and threat models.
- In practice, there are challenges that have been solved by one family of scheme and not another. This document's structure makes it easy to highlight *what* these problems are, and *how* they were solved. Consequently, it aims to provide specific direction for research; i.e., (i) problems to solve, and (ii) general methodologies to solve them.
- If a new family of hardness assumptions emerges – as isogeny-based cryptography recently has – we hope the guidelines in this document will provide a framework to safely design, implement, and deploy schemes based on it.

1.1 Our Findings

A first finding is that almost all post-quantum (PQ) schemes fit into one of four paradigms: Fiat-Shamir signatures, Hash-then-sign, Diffie-Hellman key-exchange, and encryption. Moreover, the same few properties (e.g., homomorphism) and folklore tricks are leveraged again and again.

Successful schemes do not hesitate to *bend* paradigms in order to preserve the security proof *and* the underlying assumption. In contrast, forcing an assumption into a paradigm may break the assumption, the security proof, or both.

Our second finding is that many PQ schemes fell short in secure, isochronous implementations which in turn lead to undeserved opinions on side-channel vulnerabilities. We also find some PQ schemes are significantly more amenable to implementations in hardware, software, their efficiencies with masking, which then translates into how performant they are in various use-cases.

Our last finding (see the full version [114]) is that all real-world efforts to deploy post-quantum cryptography will have to contend with new, unique problems. They may require a diverse combination of computational assumptions *woven together* into a single hybrid scheme. They may require special attention to *physical management* of sensitive state. And they have very unbalanced performance profiles, requiring different solutions for different application scenarios.

2 The Raw Material: Hard Problems

We first present the raw material from which cryptographic schemes are made of: hard problems. Although there exists a myriad of post-quantum hard problems, many of them share similarities that we will highlight.

2.1 Baseline: Problems that are not Post-quantum

We first present problems that are classically hard but quantumly easy. The first family of problems relates to the discrete logarithm in finite groups; that is, the Discrete Logarithm (DLOG) problem, the Decisional Diffie-Hellman (DDH), and the Computational Diffie-Hellman (CDH) problems.

Definition 1 (DLOG/DDH/CDH). *Let $\mathbb{G}$ be a cyclic group of generator g. The discrete logarithm problem (DLOG) and the decisional/computational Diffie-Hellman problems (DDH/CDH) are defined as follows:*

- *DLOG: Given g^a for a random $a \in |\mathbb{G}|$, find a.*
- *DDH: Given g^a, g^b and g^c for random $a, b \in |\mathbb{G}|$, determine if $c = ab$.*
- *CDH: Given g^a, g^b for random $a, b \in |\mathbb{G}|$, compute g^{ab}.*

In cryptography, $\mathbb{G}$ is usually the ring $\mathbb{Z}_p$ for a large prime p, or the group of rational points of an elliptic curve. The following algebraic relations are extremely useful to build cryptosystems, for example Schnorr signatures [173] use (1) and (2) whereas the Diffie-Hellman key-exchange [77] uses (2):

$$g^a \cdot g^b = g^{a+b}, \tag{1}$$

$$\left(g^a\right)^b = \left(g^b\right)^a = g^{ab}. \tag{2}$$

The second family of problems relates to factoring.

Definition 2 (RSA and Factoring). *Let p, q be large prime integers, $N = p \cdot q$ and e be an integer.*

- *Factoring: Given N, find p and q.*
- *RSA: Efficiently invert the following function over a non-negligible fraction of its inputs:*

$$x \in \mathbb{Z}_N \mapsto x^e \bmod N. \tag{3}$$

For adequate parameters, the problems in Definition 1 and 2 are believed hard to solve by classical computers. However, Shor has shown that they are solvable in polynomial time by a quantum computer [177]. As these problems underlie virtually all current public-key cryptosystems, Shor's discovery motivated the following research for alternative, quantum-safe problems.

2.2 Problems on Lattices

The most well-known problems based on lattices are Learning With Errors (LWE) [138, 163], Short Integer Solution (SIS) [3, 135] and "NTRU" [111].

Definition 3 (SIS, LWE, and NTRU). *Let $\mathcal{R} = \mathbb{Z}_q[x]/(\phi(x))$ be a ring, and $\mathbf{A} \in \mathcal{R}^{n \times m}$ be uniformly random. The Short Integer Solution (SIS) and Learning with Errors (LWE) problems are defined as follows:*

- *SIS: Find a short nonzero $\mathbf{v} \in \mathcal{R}^m$ such that $\mathbf{A}\mathbf{v} = 0$.*
- *LWE: Let $\mathbf{b} = \mathbf{A}^t\mathbf{s} + \mathbf{e}$, where $\mathbf{s} \in \mathcal{R}^n$ and $\mathbf{e} \in \mathcal{R}^m$ are sampled from the 'secret' distribution and 'error' distribution, respectively.*
  - *Decision: Distinguish $(\mathbf{A}, \mathbf{b})$ from uniform.*
  - *Search: Find $\mathbf{s}$.*
- *NTRU: Let $h = f/g \in \mathcal{R}$, where $f, g \in \mathcal{R}$ are 'short.' Given h, find f, g.*

SIS, LWE, and NTRU exist in many variants [135,138,155,163], obtained by changing $\mathcal{R}, n, m$, or the error distributions. To give a rough idea, a common choice is to take $\mathcal{R} = \mathbb{Z}_q[x]/(x^d + 1)$, with d a power-of-two, and n, m such that nd and md are in the order of magnitude of 1000. The versatility of SIS, LWE, and NTRU is a blessing and a curse for scheme designers, as it offers freedom but also makes it easy to select insecure parameters [153].

We are not aware of closed formulae for the hardness of SIS, LWE, and NTRU. However, the most common way to attack these problems is to interpret them as lattice problems, then run lattice reduction algorithms [7,9]. For example, the BKZ algorithm [174] with a blocksize $B \leq nd$ is estimated to solve these in time $\tilde{O}(2^{0.292 \cdot B})$ classically [21], and $\tilde{O}(2^{0.265 \cdot B})$ quantumly [132] via Grover's algorithm.

2.3 Problems on Codes

Error-correcting codes provide some of the oldest post-quantum cryptosystems. These usually rely on two problems:

- The Syndrome Decoding (SD) problem, see Definition 4.
- Hardness of distinguishing a code in a family $\mathcal{F}$ from a pseudorandom one.

We first present SD. Note that it is similar to SIS (Definition 3).

Definition 4 (SD). *Given a matrix $\mathbf{H} \in \mathbb{F}_2^{k \times n}$ and a syndrome $s \in \mathbb{F}_2^k$, the Syndrom Decoding (SD) problem is to find $e \in \mathbb{F}_2^n$ of Hamming weight w such that $\mathbf{H}e = s$.*

Since 1962, several algorithms have been presented to solve the SD problem, their complexity gradually improving from $2^{0.1207n}$ [160] to $2^{0.0885n}$ [42]. These algorithms share similarities in their designs and [182] recently showed that when $w = o(n)$, they all have the same asymptotic complexity $\approx 2^{w \log_2(n/k)}$. For many of these algorithms, quantum variants have been proposed. They achieve quantum complexities that are essentially square roots of the classical ones, by using either Grover or quantum walks.

The second problem is not as clearly defined, as it is rather a class of problems. Informally, it states that for a given family $\mathcal{C} = (C_i)_i$ of codes, a matrix $\mathbf{G}$ generating a code $C_i \in \mathcal{C}$ is hard to distinguish from a random matrix. For example, two variants of BIKE [11] assume that it is hard to distinguish from random either of these *quasi-cyclic codes* (or QC codes):

$$h_0/h_1 \tag{4}$$

$$g, g \cdot h_0 + h_1 \tag{5}$$

where $g, h_0, h_1 \in \mathbb{F}_2[x]/(x^r - 1)$, g is random and h_0, h_1 have small Hamming weight. Note that (4) and (5) are reminiscent of NTRU and (ring-)LWE, respectively (see Definition 3). Hence all the lattice problems we have defined have code counterparts, and reciprocally. Besides the QC codes of (4)–(5), another popular family of codes are Goppa codes [28,59,140].

2.4   Problems on Multivariate Systems

The third family of problems is based on multivariate systems. In practice, only multivariate *quadratics* (i.e., of degree 2) are used. They are the Multivariate Quadratic (MQ) and Extended Isomorphism of Polynomials (EIP) problems.

Definition 5 (MQ and EIP). *Let $\mathbb{F}$ be a finite field. Let $\mathbf{F} : \mathbb{F}^n \to \mathbb{F}^m$ of the form $\mathbf{F}(\mathbf{x}) = (f_1(\mathbf{x}), \dots, f_m(\mathbf{x}))$, where each $f_i : \mathbb{F}^n \to \mathbb{F}$ is a multivariate polynomial of degree at most 2 in the coefficients of $\mathbf{x}$.*

- *MQ: Given $\mathbf{y} \in \mathbb{F}^m$ and the map $\mathbf{F}$:*
  - **Decision:** *Is there an $\mathbf{x}$ such that $\mathbf{F}(\mathbf{x}) = \mathbf{y}$?*
  - **Search:** *Find $\mathbf{x}$ such that $\mathbf{F}(\mathbf{x}) = \mathbf{y}$.*
- *EIP: Let $\mathbf{S} : \mathbb{F}^n \to \mathbb{F}^n$ and $\mathbf{T} : \mathbb{F}^m \to \mathbb{F}^m$ be uniformly random affine maps. Given $\mathbf{P} = \mathbf{S} \circ \mathbf{F} \circ \mathbf{T}$ and the promise that the map $\mathbf{F}$ is in a publicly known set $\mathcal{F}$, find $\mathbf{F}$.*

Note that MQ is solvable in polynomial time for $m^2 = O(n)$ or $n^2 = O(m)$; therefore this problem is more interesting when $n = \Theta(m)$, which we assume henceforth. Also note that EIP can be parameterized by the set $\mathcal{F}$ to which the secret map $\mathbf{F}$ belongs. For example, the Unbalanced Oil and Vinegar (UOV) and Hidden Field Equation (HFEv) problems, used by Rainbow [79] and GeMSS [46] respectively, are instantiations of the EIP "framework".

Algorithms for solving MQ or EIP include F4/F5 [86], XL [60,76] or Cross-bred [126]. The best algorithms [33,126,186] combine algebraic techniques – e.g., solving Gröbner bases – with exhaustive search, which can be sped up using Grover's algorithm in the quantum setting, see [27] as an example. The asymptotic complexities of these algorithms are clearly exponential in n, but we did not find simple formulae to express them (either classically or quantumly), except for special cases ($q = 2$ and $n = m$) which do not accurately reflect concrete instantiations such as the signature schemes Rainbow [79] and MQDSS [171].

2.5   Problems on One-Way and Hash Functions

The most peculiar family of PQ problems relates to properties of (generic) one-way and hash functions. These problems are algebraically unstructured, which is desirable security-wise, but tends to imply more inefficient schemes.

Definition 6 (Problems on hash functions). *Let $H : X \to Y$ be a function, where $Y = 2^n$.*

- **Preimage:** *Given $y \in Y$, find $x \in X$ such that $H(x) = y$.*
- **Second preimage:** *Given $x_1 \in X$, find $x_2 \neq x_1$ such that $H(x_1) = H(x_2)$.*
- **Collision:** *Find $x_1 \neq x_2$ such that $H(x_1) = H(x_2)$.*

The best classical algorithm against (second) preimage is exhaustive search, hence a complexity $O(2^n)$. Grover's famous quantum algorithm [102] performs this search with a quadratic speed-up, hence a complexity $O(2^{n/2})$. Regarding collision, the best classical algorithm is the birthday attack with a complexity $O(2^{n/2})$, and (disputed) results place the complexity of the best quantum attack between $O(2^{2n/5})$ [51] and $\Theta(2^{n/3})$ [189].

2.6 Problems on Isogenies

Isogeny problems provide a higher-level twist on Definition 1. Elliptic curve cryptography posits that when given g and g^a, with g being a point on an elliptic curve E, it is hard to recover a. Similarly, isogeny-based cryptography posits that given elliptic curves E and E' over $\mathbb{F}_{p^2}$, it is hard to find a surjective group morphism (or *isogeny*, in this context) $\phi : E \to E'$.

Isogeny-based cryptography is a fast-moving field. Elliptic curves can be ordinary ($E[p] \simeq \mathbb{Z}_p$) or supersingular ($E[p] \simeq \{0\}$). Recall that the torsion subgroup $E[n]$ is the kernel of the map $P \in E \mapsto [n]P$. Most isogeny schemes work with supersingular curves, which parameters scale better. Two problems (or variations thereof) have emerged. Definition 7 provides simplified descriptions of them.

Definition 7 (Problems on isogenies). *We define the Supersingular Isogeny Diffie-Hellman (SIDH) and Commutative SIDH (CSIDH) problems as follows:*

- **SIDH:** *Given two elliptic curves E, E_A and the value of an isogeny $\phi : E \to E_A$ on $E[\ell^e]$, find ϕ.*
- **CSIDH:** *Given two elliptic curves E, E_A, find an efficiently computable isogeny $\phi \in \mathcal{Cl}(\mathcal{O})$ s.t. $E_A = \phi \cdot E$, where $\mathcal{Cl}(\mathcal{O})$ is the class group of $\mathcal{O} = \mathbb{Z}[\sqrt{-p}]$.*

Note that the CSIDH problem adapts DDH to the isogeny setting, and one can similarly adapt CDH (see Definition 1). Note that both problems are quantumly equivalent [94], whereas CDH and DDH are not known to be classically equivalent, except in special cases.

For SIDH, the best classical attack is via a claw-finding algorithm due to van Oorschot-Wiener [183]. Surprisingly, a recent result [124] shows that the best known quantum attack performs *worse* than [183]. The hardness of CSIDH reduces to solving a hidden shift problem, for which Kuperberg proposed quantum sub-exponential algorithms [130,131]. The actual quantum security of CSIDH is still being debated [40,152].

2.7 Summary of Problems

Figure 1 summarizes the classical and quantum hardness estimates of the problems we presented. Quantum estimates are particularly prone to change, notably due to (a) the lack of clear consensus on the cost of quantum memory, (b) the prospect of future algorithmic improvements.

3 Paradigms are Guidelines, not Panaceas

In the classical world, there are two paradigms for signing:

- Fiat-Shamir (FS) [90], proven in the random oracle model (ROM) by [158]. One example is Schnorr signatures and (EC)DSA.

Problem	Factoring /DLOG	SIS /LWE	SD	MQ	EIP	SIDH	CSIDH	(Second) Preimg.	Coll.
Classical	$e^{\tilde{O}((\log p)^{1/3})}$	$2^{0.292 \cdot B}$	$2^{0.0885 \cdot n}$	?	?	$O(p^{1/4})$	$O(p^{1/4})$	$O(2^n)$	$O(2^{n/2})$
Quantum	$\text{poly}(N)$	$2^{0.265 \cdot B}$	$2^{0.05804 \cdot n}$	?	?	$O(p^{1/4})$	$e^{\tilde{O}(\sqrt{\log p})}$	$O(2^{n/2})$	$\Theta(2^{n/3})$

Fig. 1. Classical and quantum hardness of some problems.

- Hash-then-sign. The most prominent formalization of this paradigm is the Full Domain Hash [24] (FDH), proven in the ROM by [25,58]. Numerous instantiations exist, such as RSA-PSS and Rabin signatures.

There are also two paradigms for key establishment:

- Public-key encryption, like El Gamal [83] or RSA [165].
- Diffie-Hellman (DH) key-exchange [77].

At a conceptual level, this section shows that most PQ signature or key establishment schemes can be cast under one of these four paradigms. This is summarized by Table 1, which also provides us with two open questions:

(Q1) Can we have isogeny-based Hash-then-sign schemes?
(Q2) Can we have multivariate key establishment schemes?

The prospect that we will have practical key establishment schemes based on symmetric primitives only seems unlikely, see [16]. For (Q1) and (Q2), we hope that the guidelines provided in this section will help to answer them.

Table 1. Correspondence between post-quantum schemes and problems.

	Signature		Key establishment	
	Hash-&-Sign	Fiat-Shamir	DH-style	PKE
Lattices	[54,161]	[39,139]	[154]	[67,175,190]
Codes	[73]	[179,185]	[1]	[11,28]
Isogenies	?	[36,69]	[48,70,122]	[123]
Multivariate	[46,79]	[171]	?	?
Symmetric	[120]	[35,188]	–	–

Our main takeaway is that scheme designers should treat paradigms as guidelines. In particular, a fruitful approach is to weaken some properties, as long as the final scheme achieves meaningful security notions. For example:

- Efficient PQ variants of the FDH framework discards trapdoor permutations for weakened definitions, which suffice for signatures, see Sect. 3.4.
- *Fiat-Shamir with Aborts* changes the protocol flow and may only prove knowledge of an approximate solution. This suffices for signatures, see Sect. 3.1

On the other hand, fitting a problem into a predefined paradigm is an interesting first step, but may result in impractical (if not broken) parameters, that are usually resolved by slight paradigm tweaks. Examples are rigid adaptations of:

- DH with lattices [107] and isogenies [70], see Sect. 3.5.
- FDH with codes [59] or lattices [112], see Sect. 3.4.

3.1 Schnorr Signatures over Lattices

Figure 2 recalls the structure of an identification scheme, or ID scheme. Any ID scheme can be converted into a signature via the Fiat-Shamir transform [90]. A efficient ID scheme is Schnorr's 3-move protocol [173]. It instantiates Fig. 2 with the parameters in Table 2 (column 2). It also requires additive and multiplicative properties similar to (1)–(2).

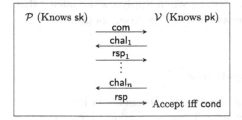
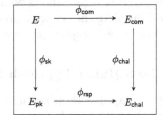

Fig. 2. A $(2n + 1)$-move ID scheme.   **Fig. 3.** SQISign.

Fortunately, lattice and code problems do have properties similar to (1)–(2). An early attempt to propose Schnorr lattice signatures is NSS [110], which was broken by statistical attacks [98]. The high-level explanation is that the ID scheme in NSS did not satisfy the *honest verifier zero-knowledge* (HVZK) property. Each transcript leaked a bit of information about sk, which [98] exploited to recover sk. This was fixed by Lyubashevsky's scheme [137], by giving the prover the possibility to abort the protocol with a probability chosen to factor out the dependency to sk from the signature. This changes the flow of the ID scheme, but allows to prove HVZK. It is also invisible to the verifier as the signer will simply restart the signing procedure in case of an abort. An example instantiation is shown in Table 2 (column 3).

On the other hand, properties of lattices enable specific tricks tailored to this setting. For example, for LWE, least significant bits (LSBs) do not really matter. Let $\lfloor \mathbf{u} \rfloor_b$ be a lossy representation of $\mathbf{u}$ that discards the b LSBs for each coefficient of $\mathbf{u}$. Finding a search-LWE solution $(\mathbf{s}_1, \mathbf{s}_2)$ for $(\mathbf{A}, \lfloor \mathbf{t} \rfloor_b)$ implies a solution $(\mathbf{s}_1, \mathbf{s}'_2)$ for $(\mathbf{A}, \mathbf{t})$, with $\|\mathbf{s}_2 - \mathbf{s}'_2\|_\infty \leq 2^b$. This indicates that, as long as b is not too large, LSBs are not too important for LWE.

This intuition was formalized by [15], who show that dropping $\mathbf{z}_2$ and checking only the high bits of com allowed to reduce the signature size by about 2,

Table 2. Instantiations of Schnorr Signatures.

Element	Schnorr	Lyubashevsky (w/ LWE)
sk	Uniform x	Short $(\mathbf{s}_1, \mathbf{s}_2)$
pk	$g, h = g^x$	$\mathbf{A}, \mathbf{t} = \mathbf{A} \cdot \mathbf{s}_1 + \mathbf{s}_2$
com	g^r for uniform r	$\mathbf{A} \cdot \mathbf{r}_1 + \mathbf{r}_2$ for short $(\mathbf{r}_1, \mathbf{r}_2)$
chal	Uniform c	Short c
rsp	$r - cx$	$(\mathbf{z}_1, \mathbf{z}_2) = (\mathbf{r}_1 - c\mathbf{s}_1, \mathbf{r}_2 - c\mathbf{s}_2)$
cond	$\mathsf{com} = g^{\mathsf{rsp}} \cdot h^c$	$(\mathsf{com} = \mathbf{A}\mathbf{z}_1 + \mathbf{z}_2 - c\mathbf{t}) \wedge ((\mathbf{z}_i)_i \text{ short})$
Abort?	No	Yes

for essentially the same (provable) security guarantees. Similarly, [103] applied this idea to reduce the public key size. The idea was refined by Dilithium [139]. However, qTESLA [39] shows what can go wrong when applying this idea without checking that the security proof is preserved (in this case, soundness), as it was shown to be completely insecure.

3.2   The SQISign Approach for Signatures

SQISign [71] applies the Fiat-Shamir transform to the ID scheme in Fig. 3. Given a public elliptic curve E, the private key is an isogeny $\phi_{\mathsf{sk}} : E \to E_{\mathsf{pk}}$ and the public key is E_{pk}. The prover commits to E_{com}, the challenge is a description of $\phi_{\mathsf{chal}} : E_{\mathsf{com}} \to E_{\mathsf{chal}}$ and the response is an isogeny $\phi_{\mathsf{rsp}} : E_{\mathsf{pk}} \to E_{\mathsf{chal}}$.

A valuable (and unique over isogeny-based signatures) feature of SQISign is the high soundness of each round, which makes it require only a single round. On the other hand, computing ϕ_{rsp} requires a lot of care in order for the HVZK property to hold, as shown by [71].

3.3   Beyond High Soundness Signatures

For the (vast majority of) problems that do not possess the (algebraic) properties needed to provide high soundness (thus few-rounds) signatures, there still exist several tricks that enable efficient FS signatures. Scheme designers need to consider two things:

- The soundness error ϵ of the ID protocol is often too large. For example, Stern's protocols [179] have $\epsilon \geq 1/2$. A solution is to repeat the protocol k times so that $\epsilon^k \leq 2^{-\lambda}$ for bit-security λ, but this is not a panacea.
- For some problems, a 3-move ID protocol may be less efficient than an n-move protocol with $n > 3$, or may even not be known.

We first elaborate on the first point. When the soundness ϵ of an ID protocol is too small, the protocol is repeated k times. Typically, all k iterations are performed in parallel (as opposed to sequentially). Parallel repetition is often *expected* by scheme designers to provide exponential soundness ϵ^k, however it is not the case in general; it is proven effective for 3-move *interactive* protocols, but counter-examples exist for higher-move protocols [23,127], see also Remark 1.

Next, we present 3-moves and 5-moves ID schemes. As long as the underlying problem admits some linearity properties, one can build an ID scheme on it [14]. It is the case of all the schemes presented below.

<u>PKP:</u> A 5-move protocol based on the Permuted Kernel Problem (PKP) was proposed in [176], with a soundness error of $\frac{p}{2p-2} \approx 1/2$, where p is the cardinal of the underlying ring. It was later instantiated by PKP-DSS [38].

<u>MQ:</u> The first ID schemes for MQ were proposed by [169]. A key idea of [169] was to use the polar form of $\mathbf{F}$: $\mathbf{G}(\mathbf{x}_1, \mathbf{x}_2) = \mathbf{F}(\mathbf{x}_1 + \mathbf{x}_2) - \mathbf{F}(\mathbf{x}_1) - \mathbf{F}(\mathbf{x}_2)$.

$\mathbf{G}$ is bilinear, and this was exploited to propose a 3-move protocol with soundness error $2/3$, and a 5-move one with soundness error $1/2 + 1/q \approx 1/2$. The latter protocol was instantiated by MQDSS [53,171] using the Fiat-Shamir transform.

<u>Codes:</u> Many code-based schemes derive from Stern's elegant protocols [179,180], which are based on the SD problem. Stern proposed a 3-move with soundness error $2/3$, and a 5-move protocol with soundness error $1/2$. The 3-move version was improved by Veron [185] using the generator matrix of a code instead of its parity check matrix, hence it is often seen as a dual of Stern's protocol. However, most derivatives of Stern's protocol are based on the 5-move variant.

<u>Isogenies:</u> The CSIDH problem has been used to propose an ID scheme that, interestingly, is very similar to the well-known proof of knowledge for graph isomorphism. A useful trick used by SeaSign [69] is to use n public keys; this improves the soundness error down to $\frac{1}{n+1}$. CSI-Fish [36] improved it to $\frac{1}{2n+1}$ by using symmetries specific to isogenies. Both schemes combine this with Merkle trees, which provides a trade-off between signing time and soundness error.

<u>Cut-and-Choose:</u> This *generic* technique [129] provides a trade-off between signing time and soundness error. It had been used by [34] to provide MQ-based and PKP-based signatures that are more compact than MQDSS and PKP-DSS.

Remark 1. [127] shows that for 5-round ID schemes with k parallel repetitions, the soundness error may be larger than ϵ^k, and provides a combinatorial attack against MQ-based schemes of [53,171] and the PKP-based scheme of [38]. It warns that it might apply on 5-round variants of Stern's protocol. This shows that "intuitive" properties may not always be taken for granted.

3.4 Full Domain Hash Signatures

Hash-then-sign schemes are among the most intuitive schemes at a high level. A standard way to construct them is via the *Full Domain Hash* (FDH) framework. We note $D(X)$ a distribution over a set X, $U(Y)$ the uniform distribution over a set Y and $\approx^s$ for statistical indistinguishability. Let $(\mathsf{sk}, \mathsf{pk})$ be an asymmetric keypair. Associate to it a pair $(f_{\mathsf{pk}}, g_{\mathsf{sk}})$ of efficiently computable functions $f_{\mathsf{pk}} : X \to Y$ (surjective) and $g_{\mathsf{sk}} : Y \to X$ (injective). Consider these properties:

(T1) Given only pk, f_{pk} is computationally hard to invert on (almost all of) Y.
(T2) $f_{pk} \circ g_{sk}$ is the identity over Y, and $X = Y$ (hence f_{pk}, g_{sk} are permutations).
(T3) There exists a distribution $D(X)$ over X such that for almost any $y \in Y$:
$\{x \leftarrow D(X), \text{conditioned on } f_{pk}(x) = y\} \approx^s \{x \leftarrow g_{sk}(y)\}$.
(T4) $\{(x, y)|x \leftarrow D(X), y \leftarrow f_{pk}(x)\} \approx^s \{(x, y)|y \leftarrow U(Y), x \leftarrow g_{sk}(y)\}$.

We say that (f_{pk}, g_{sk}) is:

– A trapdoor permutation (TP) if it satisfies (T1), (T2);
– A trapdoor preimage sampleable function (TPSF) if it satisfies (T1), (*T3*);
– An average TPSF if it satisfies (T1), (T4).

Note that since $(\textit{T2}) \Rightarrow (\textit{T3}) \Rightarrow (\textit{T4})^1$, we have the following relation:

$$\text{TP} \Rightarrow \text{TPSF} \Rightarrow \text{Average TPSF}.$$

The FDH framework [24,25] allows, in its original form, to build hash-then-sign schemes from a hash function and a TP family as in Fig. 4. Note that the function of (3) induces a RSA-based TP if one knows the factorization $N = p \cdot q$.

---

sign(msg, sk)

– Compute $H(\mathsf{msg}) = y \in Y$;
– Return $\mathsf{sig} \leftarrow f_{sk}^{-1}(y)$.

verify(msg, pk, sig)

– Accept iff $f_{pk}(\mathsf{sig}) = H(\mathsf{msg})$.

Fig. 4. The Full-Domain Hash (FDH) framework.

Notable efforts at transposing the FDH framework in a post-quantum setting are the code-based schemes CFS [59] and RankSign [93]. The bit-security of CFS scales logarithmically in its parameters, making the scheme impractical, and [87] showed that its security proof requires infeasible parameters. Similarly, [74] showed that RankSign's proposed parameters made the underlying problem easy, and that it required impractical parameters for the scheme to be secure. Both CFS and RankSign indicate that a rigid transposition of FDH framework (using TP) in a post-quantum setting seems highly non-trivial

Early lattice-based attempts such as GGHSign [100] and NTRUSign [112] instead chose to replace TPs with trapdoor one-way functions (with $|X| \gg |Y|$), that only satisfied (T1) and a *weakened* form of (T2) (dropping the requirement $X = Y$). In particular, this weaker form of (T2) no longer implied (T3). However, (T3) plays an important role in the original security proof of the FDH, which did no longer apply. More critically, each $y \in Y$ now admitted many $x_i \in X$ such that $f_{pk}(x_i) = y$, and the x_i picked by the signing algorithm depended of

---

[1] (T2) implies (T3) with $D(X) = U(X)$.

sk. This dependency was exploited by learning attacks [82,146] to recover the signing key.

For lattices, the first real progress was done by [97]. Its main contribution was to introduce TPSFs, to prove that they can be used to instantiate the FDH, and to propose provably secure lattice-based TPSFs. Several follow-up schemes have been proposed [81,142], including Falcon [161].

However, it is not known how to instantiate efficient TPSFs from code-based assumptions. Hence the work of [50,73] relaxed – again – this notion by proposing average TPSFs, showed that they suffice to instantiate the FDH framework, and proposed a signature scheme based on code-based average TPSFs, Wave [73]. Interestingly, this idea was proposed independently by [54], which show that lattice-based average TPSFs require milder parameters than TPSFs, hence improving upon the efficiency of some TPSF-based lattice signatures [32].

Multivariate schemes encountered and solved this problem independently. It was first noticed in [168] that some multivariate hash-then-sign schemes relied on a trapdoor function that only verified (T1) and a weak form of (T2). Hence [168] introduced of a salt during the signing procedure in order to satisfy (T3) and enable a FDH-style proof. This solution is used by GeMSS [46] and Rainbow [79].

3.5 Diffie-Hellman and El Gamal

The Diffie-Hellman (DH) key-exchange protocol [77] and the derived encryption scheme by El Gamal [83] are staples of classical public key cryptography. El Gamal has been notably easier to adapt to PQ assumptions than DH. Classically, DH relies on (2), which provides a simple way for two parties to agree on a shared secret g^{ab}, by instantiating Fig. 5 with Fig. 6 (column 2). Unfortunately, such a simple relation is harder to obtain with PQ assumptions, as we will see.

Isogenies over elliptic curves are natural candidates to instantiate Fig. 5, with Alice (resp. Bob) knowing a private isogeny $\phi_A : E \to E_A$ ($\phi_B : E \to E_B$) and sending E_A (resp. E_B) to the other party. Unfortunately, existing instantiations requires either ordinary curves [61,167] – which parameters don't scale well [70] –, or supersingular curves with a restricted class of isogenies like CSIDH [48] – which quantum security is debated [40,152]. SIDH [89,122] uses supersingular curves of smooth order, which security scales well but, unlike [48,61,70,167], don't provide a clean relation similar to (2).

For SIDH to work, Alice needs to transmit, in addition to E_A, the image $\phi_A(E_2)$ of its private isogeny $\phi_A : E \to E_A$ over the torsion subgroup $E_2 = E[2^{\ell_2}]$. Similarly, Bob applies ϕ_B to $E_3 = E[3^{\ell_3}]$. With this extra information, the two parties can agree on a common curve E_{AB}. A mild constraint of this solution is that, prior to the protocol, each party must "pick a side" by agreeing who picks E_2 or E_3. Alternatively, one can apply the protocol twice.

A straightforward adaptation of DH to codes and lattices is challenging as well, this time due to *noise*. For example, a rigid transposition with LWE gives:

$$(\mathbf{s}_a^t \cdot \mathbf{A} + \mathbf{e}_a^t)\mathbf{s}_b \approx \mathbf{s}_a^t(\mathbf{A} \cdot \mathbf{s}_b + \mathbf{e}_b) \tag{6}$$

	Alice			Bob
	Knows a			Knows b
		$A = a * G$		
		$B = G * b \, (+\, h)$		
	ssk $= f(a * B, h)$			ssk $= A * b$

	(EC)DH	SIDH	LWE
G	$g \in \mathbb{G}$	$(P_i, Q_i)_i$	$\mathbf{A} \in R_q^{k \times k}$
a	$a \in |\mathbb{G}|$	ϕ_A	$(\mathbf{s}_a, \mathbf{e}_a)$ short
A	g^a	$E_A, \phi_A(E_2)$	$\mathbf{s}_a^t \cdot \mathbf{A} + \mathbf{e}_a^t$
B	g^b	$E_B, \phi_B(E_3)$	$\mathbf{A} \cdot \mathbf{s}_b + \mathbf{e}_b$
h	-	-	Yes
Static?	Yes	No	No

Fig. 5. DH with reconciliation   **Fig. 6.** Instantiations of Fig. 5.

Both parties would end up with "noisy secrets" that differ on their lower bits, which is problematic. In a purely non-interactive setting, this approach does not seem to work, except if q is very large, say $q \geq 2^\lambda$, which is impractical [107]. This is resolved in [78,154] by having Bob send a hint indicating "how to round the noisy secret". Note that this solution seems to preclude non-interactivity, as h depends on what Alice sent to Bob.

Figure 6 summarizes the two approaches to achieve "post-quantum DH" (besides CSIDH). These solutions cannot be used with static key shares, as it would enable key-recovery attacks [91,95]. The last one is also interactive. Thus they cannot be used as drop-in replacements to (non-interactive) (semi-)static DH.

Many desirable properties of classical DH are lost in translation when transposing it to a PQ setting. As such, most practical schemes take El Gamal as a starting point instead, replacing DLOG with LWE [145,175], LWR [67], or SIDH [123]. Schemes that rely on "trapdoors" – like McEliece [28,140] or BIKE-2 [11] – are more akin to RSA encryption, though this analogy is a weaker one.

4   Return of Symmetric Cryptography

Another takeaway is that, despite PQC being mostly a public-key matter, symmetric cryptography plays a surprisingly important role and should not be neglected. In particular, two families of signatures based on one-way and hash functions have emerged, with two radically different philosophies:

- Hash-based signatures treat hash functions as *black boxes* and build signatures using only generic data structures and combinatorial tricks, see Sect. 4.1.
- Signatures based on zero-knowledge proofs treat one-way functions as *white boxes* and leverage knowledge of their internal structure to maximize their efficiency, see Sect. 4.2.

Interestingly, some techniques developed by these schemes have also benefited more "standard" schemes. Examples are Merkle trees, used by multivariate [37] and isogeny-based [36,69] schemes, or the *cut-and-choose* technique [129].

4.1   Hash-Based Signatures

Hash-based signatures (HBS) are a peculiar family of schemes for two reasons; (a) they rely solely on the hardness properties of hash functions, (b) they follow a paradigm of their own. At a high level:

- The public key pk commits secret values using one or more hash functions.
- Each signature reveals (intermediate) secret values that allow to recompute pk and convince the verifier that the signer does indeed know sk.

Lamport's HBS [134] epitomizes this idea. In its simplest form, the public key is: $\mathsf{pk} = (\mathsf{pk}_{i,0}, \mathsf{pk}_{i,1})_{i \in [\lambda]} = (H(\mathsf{sk}_{i,0}), H(\mathsf{sk}_{i,1}))_{i \in [\lambda]}$, and the signature of a message $\mathsf{msg} = (b_i)_i \in \{0,1\}^\lambda$ is $\mathsf{sig} = (\mathsf{sk}_{i,b_i})_i$. The verifier can then hash sig componentwise and check it against pk. It is easily shown that Lamport's signature scheme is secure under the preimage resistance of H. However, there are two caveats:

- pk and sig require $O(\lambda^2)$ bits, which is rather large.
- It is a one-time signature (OTS), meaning it is only secure as long as it performs no more than one signature.

For four decades, several tricks have been proposed to mitigate these caveats. Because of the unstructured nature of hash functions, these tricks typically rely on combinatorics and/or generic data structures.

<u>Generic Structures:</u> One line of research proposes efficient data structures that use OTS as building blocks. By hashing public keys into a tree, Merkle trees [141] allow to improve efficiency and sign more than one message. Goldreich trees [99] use trees' leaves to sign other trees' roots. Both ideas can be combined, as done by SPHINCS($^+$) [30,31,120]. Finally, efficient Merkle tree traversal algorithms were proposed [181].

<u>OTS:</u> Another line of research proposed more efficient OTS. The most efficient one so far is a variant of Winternitz's OTS (see [45,141]), called WOTS+ [119], which uses bitmasks to rely on second-preimage resistance – instead of collision resistance for the original scheme. Stateless few-time signatures (FTS) were also proposed, such as BiBa [156], HORS (Hash to Obtain Random Subsets) [164], a HORS variant with trees, HORST [30], one with PRNGs, PORS [13], and another one with forests, FORS [31,120]. These can be used to build *stateless* signatures, discussed below.

These tools allow to build hash-based *stateful* and *stateless* signatures.

Stateful schemes require the signer to maintain an internal state in order to keep track of the key material used. This encompasses XMSS, its multi-tree variant XMSS^{MT} and LMS, all recently standardized by NIST [56]. Stateful schemes can be efficient but their statefulness is often an undesirable property.

Stateless signatures set their parameters so that, even without maintaining a state, signing many messages will preserve security with overwhelming probability. As a result, they are less efficient than their stateful counterparts, but more flexible. For example, SPHINCS$^+$ [31,120] combines Merkle and Goldreich trees with WOTS+ as an OTS, FORS as a FTS, plus a few other tricks.

4.2 Signatures Based on ZKPs and OWFs

Signatures based on zero-knowledge proofs (ZKPs) and one-way functions (OWFs) leverage this principle:

- The public key is $pk = F(sk)$, where F is a OWF.
- A signature is a ZKP that $pk = F(sk)$; using the MPC-in-the-head [121].

Note that all Fiat-Shamir signatures can already be interpreted as ZKP that $pk = F(sk)$, however they usually leverage algebraic structure to gain efficiency, and as a result rely on assumptions that are algebraic in nature.

The protocols discussed here are fully generic as they work with any OWF. This is done by leveraging the *MPC-in-the-head* technique [121]. This technique creates non-interactive proofs for an arbitrary circuit (Boolean or arithmetic), by simulating the execution of an MPC (*multiparty computation*) protocol, committing to the execution, and revealing the state of a subset of the parties in order to let the verifier (partially) check correctness of the execution. Two parallel yet connected lines of research turned this abstract idea into a reality.

Protocols: The first line of research provides protocols for generic statements. These have only recently become practical, see ZKB++ [52] and KKW [129]. For bit-security λ and a circuit with $|C|$ AND gates, total proof sizes are $O(\lambda|C|)$, for ZKB++, and $O(\lambda|C|/\log n)$, for KKW, respectively, where the *cut-and-choose* approach of KKW allows a trade-off between signing and signature size, via the parameter n. For boolean (resp. arithmetic) circuits of cryptographic sizes, these two schemes (resp. the sacrificing method [19]) are the current state of the art.

Circuits: The second line of research provides circuits with low multiplicative complexity. Because of their unusual constraints, their internal structure is typically very different from classical symmetric primitives and they require new approaches to be studied. Prominent examples are LowMC [8], which has been extensively studied [80,125,136], or the Legendre PRF [63,101]. Note that these primitives have applications that go far beyond PQC; for example, the Legendre PRF is used by the Ethereum 2.0 protocol.

Combining these two lines of research, one obtain signature schemes. For example, Picnic [188] combines LowMC with either ZKB++ or KKW, and LegRoast [35] combines the Legendre PRF with the sacrificing method [19]. Due to the novely of this approach, it is likely that we will see many more schemes based on it in the future. Two works instantiate F with AES: BBQ [72] uses KKW, and Banquet [20] improves efficiency via amortization techniques.

5 The Implementation Challenges in PQC

This section discusses the implementation challenges in PQC; specifically discussing attacks via implementation pitfalls and side-channels, countermeasures, and finally the jungle of embedded devices and use-cases for PQC schemes. We somewhat focus on NIST PQC candidates due to similarities in the operations each PQC family requires.

5.1   Decryption Failures and Reaction Attacks

Attacks based on decryption failures – also known as reaction attacks – were first discovered about 20 years ago, with an attack [108] on the McEliece [140] and Ajtai-Dwork [4] cryptosystems, and another [117] on NTRU [111]. They were forgotten for more than a decade before being recently rediscovered. It is clear by now that designers of noisy cryptosystems, such as lattice-based and code-based, need to take these into account. We explain how reaction attacks work and how to thwart them. At a high level, *all* lattice-based and code-based encryption schemes follow this high-level description: $\mathsf{ct} = \mathsf{pk} \cdot \mathbf{e} + \mathbf{e}' + \mathsf{Encode}(\mathsf{msg})$, where $\mathsf{Encode}(\mathsf{msg})$ is an encoding of msg and $(\mathbf{e}, \mathbf{e}')$ is a noisy error vector. The decryption key sk is used to obtain $\mathsf{Encode}(\mathsf{msg})$ plus some noise, then recover msg. However, this may fail for a small portion of the admissible $(\mathbf{e}, \mathbf{e}')$, and this portion depends on sk. The high-level strategy of reaction attacks uses:

- **Precomputation.** Precompute "toxic" errors $(\mathbf{e}, \mathbf{e}')$ that have a high probability of leading to decryption failures;
- **Query.** Use these toxic errors to send ciphertexts to the target; observe decryption failures.
- **Reconstruction.** Deduce sk from the decryption failures.

Note that reaction attacks are CCA attacks. In CCA schemes, $(\mathbf{e}, \mathbf{e}')$ is generated by passing msg and/or pk into a pseudo-random generator (PRG), so adversaries have to find toxic vectors through exhaustive search. Hence precomputation is often the most computationally intensive phase.

Reaction attacks have been proposed against code-based schemes in the Hamming metric [105], in the rank metric [170], and for lattice-based schemes [65, 66, 106]. Interestingly, attacks against schemes that use lattices or the Hamming metric are very geometric (learning the geometry of the private key), whereas those that target rank metric schemes learn algebraic relations.

For lattice-based schemes, *directional failure boosting* [64] allows, once a toxic error $(\mathbf{e}, \mathbf{e}')$ has been found, to find many more at little cost. Therefore, lattice schemes *must* keep their failure probability negligible, as they are otherwise directly vulnerable to reaction attacks. No such conclusion has been made for code-based schemes yet, but we recommend scheme designers to err on the safe side. Scheme designers need to consider two things with respect to reaction attacks. First, the probability of decryption failures should be negligible.

- This can be achieved by selecting the parameters accordingly, as done by Kyber [175], Saber [67], and FrodoKEM [145]. One may even eliminate them completely like NTRU [190] and NTRU Prime [29], but this may result in slightly larger parameters.
- Another solution is to use redundancy; KEMs need to encapsulate a symmetric key of λ bits, however schemes can often encrypt a much larger message msg. One can use the extra bits to embed an error-correcting code (ECC). However, this solution has two caveats. First, the ECC should be constant-time (e.g., XEf [190] and Melas codes [109]), as timing attacks have been

observed when that was not the case [68]. Second, this requires to perform a tedious analysis of the noise distribution; incorrect analyses have led to theoretical attacks [65, 106].

Second, schemes with decryption failures – even negligible – should use CCA transforms that take these into account. In effect, most PQ KEMs in this situation use variants of the transforms described [113], which do handle them.

5.2   Implementation Attacks in PQC

Isochrony: Before NIST began their PQC standardization effort, many PQC schemes were susceptible to implementation attacks; meaning that due to bad coding practices, some attack vectors were found which led to successful attacks. Definition 5 in [115] provides a fairly formal definition for isochronous algorithms (i.e., an algorithm with no timing leakage) which allows us to differentiate between these initial implementation attacks, of which many did not qualify. Good programming practices exist for ensuring timing analysis resilience and have been well discussed before[1]. These practices cover much more low-level instances of isochronous designs; as conditional jumps, data-dependent branching, and memory accesses of secret information can also lead to detrimental attacks. Some tools such as `ctgrind`, `ctverif`, and `flow-tracker` exist to check whether functions are isochronous, however with operations in PQC such as rejection sampling it is not clear how effective these tools will be. Thus, it would also be prudent to check post-compilation code of the sensitive operations within an implementation.

Implementation Attacks: The first types of implementation attacks on PQC were mainly on the BLISS signature scheme and exploited the cache-timing leakages from the Gaussian samplers, as they mostly operate by accessing pre-computed values stored in memory [44, 157]. The attacks use the FLUSH+RELOAD [187] technique and exploit cache access patterns in the samplers to gain access to some coefficients of values that are added during the signature's calculation. However, optimisations to the Gaussian samplers, such as using guide-tables, and non-isochronous table access enabled these attacks. More leakage sources and implementation attacks against the StrongSwan implementation of BLISS were also found [84], which range from data dependent branches present in the Gaussian sampling algorithm to using branch tracing in the signature's rejection step. These attacks can be mitigated by bypassing conditional branches; that is, using a consistent access pattern (e.g., using linear searching of the table) and having isochronous runtime. In particular, making Gaussian samplers provably secure and statistically proficient have been researched [115] and thus should be followed for secure implementations of lattice-based schemes such as Falcon and FrodoKEM or more advanced primitives such as IBE and FHE.

Sensitive Modules: Although these attacks are on a scheme's implementation, rather than something inherently insecure in its algorithm, they have acted as a

---

[1] See for example https://www.bearssl.org/constanttime.html.

cautionary note for how some schemes have operations, which do not use secret information, but could be described as *sensitive* as if they are implemented incorrectly, they can lead to a successful attack. A clear example of this is for Gaussian samplers, which is why they were not used in Dilithium. Once an attacker finds the error vector, $\mathbf{e}$, using these side-channels from a LWE equation of the form $\mathbf{b} = \mathbf{A} \times \mathbf{s} + \mathbf{e} \bmod q$, then gaining the secret can be achieved using Gaussian elimination. Moreover, it is not always necessary to find the entire secret, as was the case in the past for RSA [57], and side-channels can be combined with lattice reduction algorithms efficiently to significantly improve attacks on post-quantum schemes. This has been built into a framework [62], which builds in side information into lattice reduction algorithms in order to predict the performance of lattice attacks and estimate the security loss for given side-channel information.

Attacks on Sparse Multipliers: Some of the timing leakage found in Strong Swan's BLISS implementation [84] exploited the sparseness of one of the polynomials in the multiplication. The NIST PQC candidate HQC [2] was also susceptible to a similar attack during decryption. At one point in time they proposed a sparse-dense multiplier to improve the performance, however the multiplication would only access the secret-key polynomial h times, for a secret-key containing only h 1's. To shield this algorithm they then proposed to permute on the memory-access locations, however the secret can also be recovered by observing the memory cells.

FO Transform Attacks: A sensitive component that can potentially affect all PQC candidates is in the Fujisaki-Okamoto (FO) transformation, required in most PQ KEMs in order to covert the CPA-secure part into an IND-CCA secure scheme. However, it has been shown that this operation is also sensitive to timing attacks, even though the operations do not use any secret information. This attack [104] was shown on FrodoKEM, and was enabled due to its use of non-isochronous `memcmp` in the implementation of the ciphertext comparison step, which allows recovery of the secret key with about 2^{30} decapsulation calls. This attack is directly applied to FrodoKEM, but is likely that other PQC candidates such as BIKE, HQC, and SIKE are also susceptible. Initial fixes of this were also shown to be vulnerable in FrodoKEM[2] and SIKE[3].

A component of the FO transform is Keccak (more specifically SHAKE) which was standardized by NIST in FIPS-202 for SHA-3 and is used extensively within NIST PQC candidates for so-called seed-expansion and computation of the shared secret. This symmetric operation is also sensitive to side-channels and could potentially lead to recovery of the shared-secret generated in the KEM. In particular, a single trace attack was demonstrated on the Keccak permutation in the ephemeral key setting [128], but seemingly realistic only on 8-bit devices.

Decryption in BIKE: The BIKE decryption algorithm is designed to proceed in a repetitive sequence of steps, whereby an increase in repetitions increases

---

[2] See https://groups.google.com/a/list.nist.gov/g/pqc-forum/c/kSUKzDNc5ME.
[3] See https://groups.google.com/a/list.nist.gov/g/pqc-forum/c/QvhRo7T2OL8.

the likelihood of proper decryption. This makes the procedure inherently non-isochronous, unlikely other NIST PQC candidates. Thus, it was proposed to artificially truncate this procedure at some fixed number. Experimentally, a round-count as small as 10 is sufficient to guarantee proper decryption. However, unlike lattice-based KEMs, there is no mathematical guarantee that this is sufficient to reduce the decryption failure rate below 2^λ, where $\lambda \in \{128, 192, 256\}$ is the concrete security parameter.[4] Thus, despite BIKE being designed as CPA scheme as well as a CPA-to-CCA scheme, they have only formally claimed CPA-security (ephemeral keys) for their construction, as opposed to CCA-security (long-term keys). It remains open to provide the proper analysis to solve this issue.

5.3 Side-Channels and Countermeasures

In the Status Report on the Second Round of the NIST Post-Quantum Cryptography Standardization Process [5] it is stated that:

> NIST hopes to see more and better data for performance in the third round. This performance data will hopefully include implementations that protect against side-channel attacks, such as timing attacks, power monitoring attacks, fault attacks, etc.

In their initial submission requirements [147] NIST also noted "schemes that can be made resistant to side-channel attacks at minimal cost are more desirable than those whose performance is severely hampered by any attempt to resist side-channel attacks". Thus, some of the remaining candidates have offered masked implementations, or this has been done by the research community. Also, see [10] for an extensive summary of attacks against NIST PQC third round candidates.

Masking Dilithium: Migliore et al. [143] demonstrate DPA weaknesses in the unmasked Dilithium implementation, and in addition to this provide a masking scheme using the ISW probing model following the previous techniques for masking GLP and BLISS [17,18]. Like the previous provably secure masking schemes, they alter some of the procedures in Dilithium by adding in efficient masking of its sensitive operations. Moreover, some parameters are changed to gain extra performance efficiencies in the masked design, such as making the prime modulus a power-of-two, which increases the performance by 7.3–9× compared to using the original prime modulus during masking. A power-of-two modulus means the optimised multiplication technique, the NTT multiplier, is no longer possible so they proposed Karatsuba multiplication. The results for key generation and signing are between 8–12× slower for order 2 masking and 13–28× slower for order 3 masking, compared to the reference implementations. This is also backed-up by experimental leakage tests on the masked designs.

Masking Saber: Verhulst [184] provides DPA on Saber, as well as developing a masking scheme for its decryption protocol, which is later extended in [22]. The masking schemes only use additive first-order masking which thus makes it only

---

[4] Known, formal analyses guarantees are closer to 2^{-40} at 128-bit security.

2-2.5x slower than being unprotected. However it is probably still vulnerable to template attacks [148]. Saber lends itself to practical masking due to its use of LWR, as opposed to other KEMs using (M-)LWE. However, Saber uses a less efficient multiplication method (a combination of Toom-Cook, Karatsuba, and schoolbook multiplication) compared to schemes which use NTT; thus it is an interesting open question as to whether NTT is the most practical multiplication method (due to its conflict with efficient masking) and how these masked PQC schemes practically compare, particularly with the recent research improving the performance of Saber and others using NTTs [55].

DPA on Multiplication: NTRU and NTRU Prime can both use a combination of Toom-Cook and Karatsuba to speed-up their polynomial multiplication, thus whether they can reuse techniques from Saber's masked implementation is an important research question. NTRU Prime in particular requires masking since some power analysis attacks can read off the secret key with the naked eye [118]. Attacks on these multiplication methods, which are in the time-domain, are likely to be simpler than those in the NTT or FFT domains as there is only one multiplication per coefficient of the secret, which thus makes protection of this multipliers more urgent. A single-trace power analysis attack on FrodoKEM exploits the fact that the secret matrix is used multiple times during the matrix multiplication operation, enabling horizontal differential power analysis [41].

Correlation power analysis and algebraic key recovery attacks have also been shown on the schemes Rainbow and UOV [149] by targeting the secret maps within the MQ signature schemes, during the matrix-vector computations. This attack is relevant for many MQ schemes that use the affine-substitution quadratic-affine (ASA) structure. They also discuss countermeasures to SPA and DPA attacks by using standard methods seen before such as shuffling of the indices or adding a pseudo-random matrix (i.e., additive masking).

Attacks on Syndrome Decoding: A variant of McEliece PKE, QcBits, was shown to be susceptible to DPA [166]. The attack partially recovers the secret key during the syndrome computation of the decoding phase. They also propose a simple countermeasure for the syndrome calculation stage, which exploits the fact that since QC-MDPC codes are linear, the XOR of two codewords is another codeword. Thus, a codeword can be masked by XORing it with another random codeword before the syndrome calculation.

This attack was then extended [178] to recover the *full* secret of QcBits, with more accuracy, using a multi-trace attack. Moreover, using the DPA counter-measures proposed in [166] and in the ephemeral key setting, they provide a single-trace attack on QcBits. Lastly and most interestingly, they describe how these attacks can be applied to BIKE, by targetting the private syndrome decoding computation stage where long-term keys are utilized. For ephemeral keys, the multi-target attacks are not applicable, however the single-trace attack can be applied to recover the private key and also the secret message.

Classic McEliece is also not immune from side-channel attacks targeting this operation. A reaction attack [133] using iterative chunking and information set decoding can enable recovery of the values of the error vector using a single decryption oracle request. A recent attack has also shown vulnerabilities in Classic McEliece's syndrome computation to fault attacks [49].

Masking Matrix Multiplication: Masking schemes which use matrix multiplication have the potential to be efficiently masked using affine masking (i.e., a combination of additive and multiplicative masking) similarly used in AES [92]. First-order additive masking has already been proposed for FrodoKEM [116]. Warnings for side-channel protection were also seen in Picnic, where the attack was able to recover the shared secret and the secret key, by targetting the MPC-LowMC block cipher, a core component to the signature scheme [96].

Cold-Boot Attacks: PQC schemes have also been shown to be susceptible to cold-boot attacks [6,159], which was previously shown on NTRU [150]. Cold-boot attacks exploit the fact that secret data can remain in a computer's memory (DRAM) after it is powered down and supposedly deleted. Albrecht et al. [6] describe how to achieve this by attacking the secret-keys stored for use in the NTT multiplier in Kyber and NewHope, and after some post-processing using lattice reductions, is able to retrieve the secret-key.

Fault Attacks: Fault attacks have also been investigated for PQC schemes. One of the most famous (microarchitectural) fault attacks is the Rowhammer exploit (CVE-2015-0565), which allows unprivileged attackers to corrupt or change data stored in certain, vulnerable memory chips, and has been extended to other exploits such as RAMBleed (CVE-2019-0174). QuantumHammer [144] utilises this exploit to recover secret key bits on LUOV, a second round NIST PQC candidate for multivariate-quadratic signatures. The attack does somewhat exploit the 'lifted' algebraic structure that is present in LUOV, so whether this attack could be applied to other PQC schemes is an open question.

Determinism in signatures is generally considered preferable from a security perspective, as attacks are possible on randomly generated nonces (e.g., [85]). This prompted EdDSA, which uses deterministically generated nonces. NIST [5] noted the potential for nonce reuse in PQC schemes such as Kyber. Indeed, fault attacks which exploit the scheme's determinism have been demonstrated on SPHINCS+ [47] and Dilithium [43,162], with EdDSA also showing susceptibility to DPA [172]. As such, some PQC candidates offer an optional non-deterministic variant, such as SPHINCS+ using OptRand, or random *salt* used in Dilithium, Falcon, GeMSS, Picnic, and Rainbow.

Hedging: An interesting alternative to mitigating these fault attacks (and randomness failures) is by using *hedging*, which creates a middle-ground between fully deterministic and fully probabilistic signatures, by deriving the per-signature randomness from a combination of the secret-key, message, and a nonce. This is formalized for Fiat-Shamir signatures and apply the results to hedged versions of XEdDSA, a variant of EdDSA used in the Signal messaging protocol, and to Picnic2, and show hedging mitigates many of the possible fault attacks [12].

Key Reuse: These attacks, which have been shown to cause issues for real-world implementations in EMV [75], are also applicable in PQC; such as lattice-based schemes [91], supersingular isogeny-based schemes [95], and potentially more.

We continue the practical discussions on PQC in the full version of this paper [114], focusing on embedded implementations and use cases, and then providing an overview of how PQC is being standardized, what new protocols are being designed, and any large scale experiments that have been conducted thus far.

References

1. Aguilar, C., Gaborit, P., Lacharme, P., Schrek, J., Zemor, G.: Noisy Diffie-Hellman protocols. Rump session of PQCrypto (2010). https://www.yumpu.com/en/document/view/53051354/noisy-diffie-hellman-protocols
2. Melchor, C.A., et al.: HQC. Technical report, National Institute of Standards and Technology (2019). https://csrc.nist.gov/projects/post-quantum-cryptography/round-2-submissions
3. Ajtai, M.: Generating hard instances of lattice problems (extended abstract). In: 28th ACM STOC, pp. 99–108. ACM Press, May 1996. https://doi.org/10.1145/237814.237838
4. Ajtai, M., Dwork, C.: A public-key cryptosystem with worst-case/average-case equivalence. In: 29th ACM STOC, pp. 284–293. ACM Press, May 1997. https://doi.org/10.1145/258533.258604
5. Alagic, G., et al.: status report on the second round of the NIST post-quantum cryptography standardization process. Technical report, NIST (2020)
6. Albrecht, M.R., Deo, A., Paterson, K.G.: Cold boot attacks on ring and module LWE keys under the NTT. IACR TCHES 2018(3), 173–213 (2018). https://doi.org/10.13154/tches.v2018.i3.173-213. https://tches.iacr.org/index.php/TCHES/article/view/7273. ISSN 2569–2925
7. Albrecht, M.R., Player, R., Scott, S.: On the concrete hardness of learning with errors. J. Math. Cryptol. 9(3), 169–203 (2015). http://www.degruyter.com/view/j/jmc.2015.9.issue-3/jmc-2015-0016/jmc-2015-0016.xml
8. Albrecht, M.R., Rechberger, C., Schneider, T., Tiessen, T., Zohner, M.: Ciphers for MPC and FHE. In: Oswald, E., Fischlin, M. (eds.) EUROCRYPT 2015. LNCS, vol. 9056, pp. 430–454. Springer, Heidelberg (2015). https://doi.org/10.1007/978-3-662-46800-5_17
9. Albrecht, M.R., et al.: Estimate all the LWE, NTRU schemes!. In: Catalano, D., De Prisco, R. (eds.) SCN 2018. LNCS, vol. 11035, pp. 351–367. Springer, Cham (2018). https://doi.org/10.1007/978-3-319-98113-0_19
10. Apon, D., Howe, J.: Attacks on NIST PQC 3rd round candidates. In: IACR Real World Crypto Symposium, January 2021. https://iacr.org/submit/files/slides/2021/rwc/rwc2021/22/slides.pdf
11. Aragon, N., et al.: BIKE. Technical report, National Institute of Standards and Technology (2019). https://csrc.nist.gov/projects/post-quantum-cryptography/round-2-submissions
12. Aranha, D.F., Orlandi, C., Takahashi, A., Zaverucha, G.: Security of Hedged Fiat-Shamir signatures under fault attacks. In: Canteaut, A., Ishai, Y. (eds.) EUROCRYPT 2020. LNCS, vol. 12105, pp. 644–674. Springer, Cham (2020). https://doi.org/10.1007/978-3-030-45721-1_23

13. Aumasson, J.-P., Endignoux, G.: Improving stateless hash-based signatures. In: Smart, N.P. (ed.) CT-RSA 2018. LNCS, vol. 10808, pp. 219–242. Springer, Cham (2018). https://doi.org/10.1007/978-3-319-76953-0_12

14. Backendal, M., Bellare, M., Sorrell, J., Sun, J.: The Fiat-Shamir Zoo: relating the security of different signature variants. In: Gruschka, N. (ed.) NordSec 2018. LNCS, vol. 11252, pp. 154–170. Springer, Cham (2018). https://doi.org/10.1007/978-3-030-03638-6_10

15. Bai, S., Galbraith, S.D.: An improved compression technique for signatures based on learning with errors. In: Benaloh, J. (ed.) CT-RSA 2014. LNCS, vol. 8366, pp. 28–47. Springer, Cham (2014). https://doi.org/10.1007/978-3-319-04852-9_2

16. Barak, B., Mahmoody-Ghidary, M.: Merkle's key agreement protocol is optimal: an $O(n^2)$ attack on any key agreement from random oracles. J. Cryptol. **30**(3), 699–734 (2017). https://doi.org/10.1007/s00145-016-9233-9

17. Barthe, G., Belaïd, S., Espitau, T., Fouque, P.-A., Rossi, M., Tibouchi, M.: GALACTICS: Gaussian sampling for lattice-based constant-time implementation of cryptographic signatures, revisited. In: Cavallaro, L., Kinder, J., Wang, X., Katz, J. (eds.) ACM CCS, pp. 2147–2164. ACM Press, November 2019. https://doi.org/10.1145/3319535.3363223

18. Barthe, G., et al.: Masking the GLP lattice-based signature scheme at any order. In: Nielsen, J.B., Rijmen, V. (eds.) EUROCRYPT 2018. LNCS, vol. 10821, pp. 354–384. Springer, Cham (2018). https://doi.org/10.1007/978-3-319-78375-8_12

19. Baum, C., Nof, A.: Concretely-efficient zero-knowledge arguments for arithmetic circuits and their application to lattice-based cryptography. In: Kiayias, A., Kohlweiss, M., Wallden, P., Zikas, V. (eds.) PKC 2020. LNCS, vol. 12110, pp. 495–526. Springer, Cham (2020). https://doi.org/10.1007/978-3-030-45374-9_17

20. Baum, C., de Saint Guilhem, C.D., Kales, D., Orsini, E., Scholl, P., Zaverucha, G.: Banquet: short and fast signatures from AES. PKC (2021). https://eprint.iacr.org/2021/068

21. Becker, A., Ducas, L., Gama, N., Laarhoven, T.: New directions in nearest neighbor searching with applications to lattice sieving. In: Krauthgamer, R., (ed.) SODA, pp. 10–24. SIAM (2016). https://doi.org/10.1137/1.9781611974331.ch2. https://doi.org/10.1137/1.9781611974331.ch2

22. Van Beirendonck, M., D'Anvers, J.-P., Karmakar, A., Balasch, J., Verbauwhede, I.: A side-channel resistant implementation of SABER. Cryptology ePrint Archive, Report 2020/733 (2020). https://eprint.iacr.org/2020/733

23. Bellare, M., Impagliazzo, R., Naor, M.: Does parallel repetition lower the error in computationally sound protocols? In: 38th FOCS, pp. 374–383. IEEE Computer Society Press, October 1997. https://doi.org/10.1109/SFCS.1997.646126

24. Bellare, M., Rogaway, P.: Random oracles are practical: a paradigm for designing efficient protocols. In: Denning, D.E., Pyle, R., Ganesan, R., Sandhu, R.S., Ashby, V. (eds.) ACM CCS, vol. 93, pp. 62–73. ACM Press, November 1993. https://doi.org/10.1145/168588.168596

25. Bellare, M., Rogaway, P.: The exact security of digital signatures-how to sign with RSA and Rabin. In: Maurer, U. (ed.) EUROCRYPT 1996. LNCS, vol. 1070, pp. 399–416. Springer, Heidelberg (1996). https://doi.org/10.1007/3-540-68339-9_34

26. Bernstein, D.J., Buchmann, J., Dahmen, E. (eds.) Post-Quantum Cryptography (2009). https://doi.org/10.1007/978-3-540-88702-7

27. Bernstein, D.J., Yang, B.-Y.: Asymptotically faster quantum algorithms to solve multivariate quadratic equations. Cryptology ePrint Archive, Report 2017/1206 (2017). https://eprint.iacr.org/2017/1206

28. Bernstein, D.J., et al.: Classic McEliece. Technical report, National Institute of Standards and Technology (2019). https://csrc.nist.gov/projects/post-quantum-cryptography/round-2-submissions
29. Bernstein, D.J., Chuengsatiansup, C., Lange, T., van Vredendaal, C.: NTRU Prime. Technical report, National Institute of Standards and Technology (2019). https://csrc.nist.gov/projects/post-quantum-cryptography/round-2-submissions
30. Bernstein, D.J., et al.: SPHINCS: practical stateless hash-based signatures. In: Oswald, E., Fischlin, M. (eds.) EUROCRYPT 2015. LNCS, vol. 9056, pp. 368–397. Springer, Heidelberg (2015). https://doi.org/10.1007/978-3-662-46800-5_15
31. Bernstein, D.J., Hülsing, A., Kölbl, S., Niederhagen, R., Rijneveld, J., Schwabe, P.: The SPHINCS+ signature framework. In: Cavallaro, L., Kinder, J., Wang, X., Katz, J. (ed.) ACM CCS, pp. 2129–2146. ACM Press, November 2019. https://doi.org/10.1145/3319535.3363229
32. Bert, P., Fouque, P.-A., Roux-Langlois, A., Sabt, M.: Practical implementation of ring-SIS/LWE based signature and IBE. In: Lange, T., Steinwandt, R. (eds.) PQCrypto 2018. LNCS, vol. 10786, pp. 271–291. Springer, Cham (2018). https://doi.org/10.1007/978-3-319-79063-3_13
33. Bettale, L., Faugère, J.-C., Perret, L.: Solving polynomial systems over finite fields: improved analysis of the hybrid approach. In: ISSAC, pp. 67–74. ACM (2012)
34. Beullens, W.: Sigma protocols for MQ, PKP and SIS, and Fishy signature schemes. In: Canteaut, A., Ishai, Y. (eds.) EUROCRYPT 2020. LNCS, vol. 12107, pp. 183–211. Springer, Cham (2020). https://doi.org/10.1007/978-3-030-45727-3_7
35. Beullens, W., Delpech de Saint Guilhem, C.: LegRoast: efficient post-quantum signatures from the Legendre PRF. In: Ding, J., Tillich, J.-P. (eds.) PQCrypto 2020. LNCS, vol. 12100, pp. 130–150. Springer, Cham (2020). https://doi.org/10.1007/978-3-030-44223-1_8
36. Beullens, W., Kleinjung, T., Vercauteren, F.: CSI-FiSh: efficient isogeny based signatures through class group computations. In: Galbraith, S.D., Moriai, S. (eds.) ASIACRYPT 2019. LNCS, vol. 11921, pp. 227–247. Springer, Cham (2019). https://doi.org/10.1007/978-3-030-34578-5_9
37. Beullens, W., Preneel, B., Szepieniec, A.: Public key compression for constrained linear signature schemes. In: Cid, C., Jacobson Jr., M.J. (eds.) SAC. LNCS, vol. 11349, pp. 300–321. Springer, Heidelberg (2019). https://doi.org/10.1007/978-3-030-10970-7_14
38. Beullens, W., Faugère, J.-C., Koussa, E., Macario-Rat, G., Patarin, J., Perret, L.: PKP-based signature scheme. In: Hao, F., Ruj, S., Sen Gupta, S. (eds.) INDOCRYPT 2019. LNCS, vol. 11898, pp. 3–22. Springer, Cham (2019). https://doi.org/10.1007/978-3-030-35423-7_1
39. Bindel, N., et al.: qTESLA. Technical report, National Institute of Standards and Technology (2019). https://csrc.nist.gov/projects/post-quantum-cryptography/round-2-submissions
40. Bonnetain, X., Schrottenloher, A.: Quantum security analysis of CSIDH. In: Canteaut, A., Ishai, Y. (eds.) EUROCRYPT 2020. LNCS, vol. 12106, pp. 493–522. Springer, Cham (2020). https://doi.org/10.1007/978-3-030-45724-2_17
41. Bos, J.W., Friedberger, S., Martinoli, M., Oswald, E., Stam, M.: Assessing the feasibility of single trace power analysis of Frodo. In: Cid, C., Jacobson Jr., M.J. (eds.) SAC. LNCS, vol. 11349, pp. 216–234. Springer, Heidelberg (2019). https://doi.org/10.1007/978-3-030-10970-7_10

42. Both, L., May, A.: Decoding linear codes with high error rate and its impact for LPN security. In: Lange, T., Steinwandt, R. (eds.) PQCrypto 2018. LNCS, vol. 10786, pp. 25–46. Springer, Cham (2018). https://doi.org/10.1007/978-3-319-79063-3_2

43. Bruinderink, L.G., Pessl, P.: Differential fault attacks on deterministic lattice signatures. IACR TCHES 2018(3), 21–43 (2018). https://doi.org/10.13154/tches.v2018.i3.21-43.   https://tches.iacr.org/index.php/TCHES/article/view/7267. ISSN 2569–2925

44. Groot Bruinderink, L., Hülsing, A., Lange, T., Yarom, Y.: Flush, gauss, and reload - a cache attack on the BLISS lattice-based signature scheme. In: Gierlichs, B., Poschmann, A.Y. (eds.) CHES 2016. LNCS, vol. 9813, pp. 323–345. Springer, Heidelberg (2016). https://doi.org/10.1007/978-3-662-53140-2_16

45. Buchmann, J., Dahmen, E., Ereth, S., Hülsing, A., Rückert, M.: On the security of the Winternitz one-time signature scheme. In: Nitaj, A., Pointcheval, D. (eds.) AFRICACRYPT 11. LNCS, vol. 6737, pp. 363–378. Springer, Heidelberg (2011). https://doi.org/10.1007/978-3-642-21969-6_23

46. Casanova, A., Faugère, J.-C., Macario-Rat, G., Patarin, J., Perret, L., Ryckeghem, J.: GeMSS. Technical report, National Institute of Standards and Technology (2019). https://csrc.nist.gov/projects/post-quantum-cryptography/round-2-submissions

47. Castelnovi, L., Martinelli, A., Prest, T.: Grafting trees: a fault attack against the SPHINCS framework. In: Lange, T., Steinwandt, R. (eds.) PQCrypto 2018. LNCS, vol. 10786, pp. 165–184. Springer, Cham (2018). https://doi.org/10.1007/978-3-319-79063-3_8

48. Castryck, W., Lange, T., Martindale, C., Panny, L., Renes, J.: CSIDH: an efficient post-quantum commutative group action. In: Peyrin, T., Galbraith, S. (eds.) ASIACRYPT 2018. LNCS, vol. 11274, pp. 395–427. Springer, Cham (2018). https://doi.org/10.1007/978-3-030-03332-3_15

49. Cayrel, P.-L., Colombier, B., Dragoi, V.-F., Menu, A., Bossuet, L.: Message-recovery laser fault injection attack on the classic Mceliece cryptosystem. In: EUROCRYPT (2021)

50. Chailloux, A., Debris-Alazard, T.: Tight and optimal reductions for signatures based on average trapdoor preimage sampleable functions and applications to code-based signatures. In: Kiayias, A., Kohlweiss, M., Wallden, P., Zikas, V. (eds.) PKC 2020. LNCS, vol. 12111, pp. 453–479. Springer, Cham (2020). https://doi.org/10.1007/978-3-030-45388-6_16

51. Chailloux, A., Naya-Plasencia, M., Schrottenloher, A.: An efficient quantum collision search algorithm and implications on symmetric cryptography. In: Takagi, T., Peyrin, T. (eds.) ASIACRYPT 2017. LNCS, vol. 10625, pp. 211–240. Springer, Cham (2017). https://doi.org/10.1007/978-3-319-70697-9_8

52. Chase, M., et al.: Post-quantum zero-knowledge and signatures from symmetric-key primitives. In: Thuraisingham, B.M., Evans, D., Malkin, T., Xu, D. (eds.) ACM CCS, pp. 1825–1842. ACM Press, October/November 2017. https://doi.org/10.1145/3133956.3133997

53. Chen, M.-S., Hülsing, A., Rijneveld, J., Samardjiska, S., Schwabe, P.: From 5-Pass $\mathcal{MQ}$-based identification to $\mathcal{MQ}$-based signatures. In: Cheon, J.H., Takagi, T. (eds.) ASIACRYPT 2016. LNCS, vol. 10032, pp. 135–165. Springer, Heidelberg (2016). https://doi.org/10.1007/978-3-662-53890-6_5

54. Chen, Y., Genise, N., Mukherjee, P.: Approximate trapdoors for lattices and smaller hash-and-sign signatures. In: Galbraith, S.D., Moriai, S. (eds.) ASI-

ACRYPT 2019. LNCS, vol. 11923, pp. 3–32. Springer, Cham (2019). https://doi.org/10.1007/978-3-030-34618-8_1

55. Chung, C.-M.M., Hwang, V., Kannwischer, M.J., G., Seiler, M.J., Shih, C.-J., Yang, B.-Y.: NTT multiplication for NTT-unfriendly rings. Cryptology ePrint Archive, Report 2020/1397 (2020). https://eprint.iacr.org/2020/1397

56. Cooper, D., Apon, D., Dang, Q., Davidson, M., Dworkin, M., Miller, C.: Recommendation for stateful hash-based signature schemes (2020). https://doi.org/10.6028/NIST.SP.800-208

57. Coppersmith, D.: Small solutions to polynomial equations, and low exponent RSA vulnerabilities. J. Cryptol. **10**(4), 233–260 (1997). https://doi.org/10.1007/s001459900030

58. Coron, J.-S.: On the exact security of full domain hash. In: Bellare, M. (ed.) CRYPTO 2000. LNCS, vol. 1880, pp. 229–235. Springer, Heidelberg (2000). https://doi.org/10.1007/3-540-44598-6_14

59. Courtois, N.T., Finiasz, M., Sendrier, N.: How to achieve a McEliece-based digital signature scheme. In: Boyd, C. (ed.) ASIACRYPT 2001. LNCS, vol. 2248, pp. 157–174. Springer, Heidelberg (2001). https://doi.org/10.1007/3-540-45682-1_10

60. Courtois, N., Klimov, A., Patarin, J., Shamir, A.: Efficient algorithms for solving overdefined systems of multivariate polynomial equations. In: Preneel, B. (ed.) EUROCRYPT 2000. LNCS, vol. 1807, pp. 392–407. Springer, Heidelberg (2000). https://doi.org/10.1007/3-540-45539-6_27

61. Couveignes, J.-M.: Hard homogeneous spaces. Cryptology ePrint Archive, Report 2006/291 (2006). http://eprint.iacr.org/2006/291

62. Dachman-Soled, D., Ducas, L., Gong, H., Rossi, M.: LWE with side information: attacks and concrete security estimation. In: Micciancio, D., Ristenpart, T. (eds.) CRYPTO 2020. LNCS, vol. 12171, pp. 329–358. Springer, Cham (2020). https://doi.org/10.1007/978-3-030-56880-1_12

63. Damgård, I.B.: On the randomness of Legendre and Jacobi sequences. In: Goldwasser, S. (ed.) CRYPTO 1988. LNCS, vol. 403, pp. 163–172. Springer, New York (1990). https://doi.org/10.1007/0-387-34799-2_13

64. D'Anvers, J.-P., Rossi, M., Virdia, F.: (One) failure is not an option: bootstrapping the search for failures in lattice-based encryption schemes. In: Canteaut, A., Ishai, Y. (eds.) EUROCRYPT 2020. LNCS, vol. 12107, pp. 3–33. Springer, Cham (2020). https://doi.org/10.1007/978-3-030-45727-3_1

65. D'Anvers, J.-P., Vercauteren, F., Verbauwhede, I.: The impact of error dependencies on ring/Mod-LWE/LWR based schemes. In: Ding, J., Steinwandt, R. (eds.) PQCrypto 2019. LNCS, vol. 11505, pp. 103–115. Springer, Cham (2019). https://doi.org/10.1007/978-3-030-25510-7_6

66. D'Anvers, J.-P., Guo, Q., Johansson, T., Nilsson, A., Vercauteren, F., Verbauwhede, I.: Decryption failure attacks on IND-CCA secure lattice-based schemes. In: Lin, D., Sako, K. (eds.) PKC 2019. LNCS, vol. 11443, pp. 565–598. Springer, Cham (2019). https://doi.org/10.1007/978-3-030-17259-6_19

67. D'Anvers, J.-P., Karmakar, A., Roy, S.S., Vercauteren, F.: SABER. Technical report, National Institute of Standards and Technology (2019). https://csrc.nist.gov/projects/post-quantum-cryptography/round-2-submissions

68. D'Anvers, J.-P., Tiepelt, M., Vercauteren, F., Verbauwhede, I.: Timing attacks on error correcting codes in post-quantum schemes. In: Bilgin, B., Petkova-Nikova, S., Rijmen, V. (eds.) TIS@CCS, pp. 2–9. ACM (2019). https://doi.org/10.1145/3338467.3358948. https://doi.org/10.1145/3338467.3358948

69. De Feo, L., Galbraith, S.D.: SeaSign: compact isogeny signatures from class group actions. In: Ishai, Y., Rijmen, V. (eds.) EUROCRYPT 2019. LNCS, vol. 11478, pp. 759–789. Springer, Cham (2019). https://doi.org/10.1007/978-3-030-17659-4_26

70. De Feo, L., Kieffer, J., Smith, B.: Towards practical key exchange from ordinary isogeny graphs. In: Peyrin, T., Galbraith, S. (eds.) ASIACRYPT 2018. LNCS, vol. 11274, pp. 365–394. Springer, Cham (2018). https://doi.org/10.1007/978-3-030-03332-3_14

71. De Feo, L., Kohel, D., Leroux, A., Petit, C., Wesolowski, B.: SQISign: compact post-quantum signatures from quaternions and isogenies. In: Moriai, S., Wang, H. (eds.) ASIACRYPT 2020. LNCS, vol. 12491, pp. 64–93. Springer, Cham (2020). https://doi.org/10.1007/978-3-030-64837-4_3

72. de Saint Guilhem, C.D., De Meyer, L., Orsini, E., Smart, N.P.: BBQ: using AES in picnic signatures. In: Paterson, K.G., Stebila, D. (eds.) SAC 2019. LNCS, vol. 11959, pp. 669–692. Springer, Cham (2020). https://doi.org/10.1007/978-3-030-38471-5_27

73. Debris-Alazard, T., Sendrier, N., Tillich, J.-P.: Wave: a new family of trapdoor one-way preimage sampleable functions based on codes. In: Galbraith, S.D., Moriai, S. (eds.) ASIACRYPT 2019. LNCS, vol. 11921, pp. 21–51. Springer, Cham (2019). https://doi.org/10.1007/978-3-030-34578-5_2

74. Debris-Alazard, T., Tillich, J.-P.: Two attacks on rank metric code-based schemes: RankSign and an IBE scheme. In: Peyrin, T., Galbraith, S. (eds.) ASIACRYPT 2018. LNCS, vol. 11272, pp. 62–92. Springer, Cham (2018). https://doi.org/10.1007/978-3-030-03326-2_3

75. Degabriele, J.P., Lehmann, A., Paterson, K.G., Smart, N.P., Strefler, M.: On the joint security of encryption and signature in EMV. In: Dunkelman, O. (ed.) CT-RSA 2012. LNCS, vol. 7178, pp. 116–135. Springer, Heidelberg (2012). https://doi.org/10.1007/978-3-642-27954-6_8

76. Diem, C.: The XL-algorithm and a conjecture from commutative algebra. In: Lee, P.J. (ed.) ASIACRYPT 2004. LNCS, vol. 3329, pp. 323–337. Springer, Heidelberg (2004). https://doi.org/10.1007/978-3-540-30539-2_23

77. Diffie, W., Hellman, M.E.: New directions in cryptography. IEEE Trans. Inf. Theory **22**(6), 644–654 (1976)

78. Ding, J., Xie, X., Lin, X.: A simple provably secure key exchange scheme based on the learning with errors problem. Cryptology ePrint Archive, Report 2012/688 (2012). http://eprint.iacr.org/2012/688

79. Ding, J., Chen, M.-S., Petzoldt, A., Schmidt, D., Yang, B.-Y.: Rainbow. Technical report, National Institute of Standards and Technology (2019). https://csrc.nist.gov/projects/post-quantum-cryptography/round-2-submissions

80. Dinur, I., Kales, D., Promitzer, A., Ramacher, S., Rechberger, C.: Linear equivalence of block ciphers with partial non-linear layers: application to LowMC. In: Ishai, Y., Rijmen, V. (eds.) EUROCRYPT 2019. LNCS, vol. 11476, pp. 343–372. Springer, Cham (2019). https://doi.org/10.1007/978-3-030-17653-2_12

81. Ducas, L., Lyubashevsky, V., Prest, T.: Efficient identity-based encryption over NTRU lattices. In: Sarkar, P., Iwata, T. (eds.) ASIACRYPT 2014. LNCS, vol. 8874, pp. 22–41. Springer, Heidelberg (2014). https://doi.org/10.1007/978-3-662-45608-8_2

82. Ducas, L., Nguyen, P.Q.: Learning a zonotope and more: cryptanalysis of NTRUSign countermeasures. In: Wang, X., Sako, K. (eds.) ASIACRYPT 2012. LNCS, vol. 7658, pp. 433–450. Springer, Heidelberg (2012). https://doi.org/10.1007/978-3-642-34961-4_27

83. ElGamal, T.: A public key cryptosystem and a signature scheme based on discrete logarithms. IEEE Trans. Inf. Theory **31**, 469–472 (1985)
84. Espitau, T., Fouque, P.-A., Gérard, B., Tibouchi, M.: Side-channel attacks on BLISS lattice-based signatures: exploiting branch tracing against strongSwan and electromagnetic emanations in microcontrollers. In: Thuraisingham, B.M., Evans, D., Malkin, T., Xu, D. (eds.) ACM CCS, pp. 1857–1874. ACM Press, October/November 2017. https://doi.org/10.1145/3133956.3134028
85. fail0verflow. Console Hacking 2010: PS3 Epic Fail. In: 27th Chaos Communications Congress (2010)
86. Faugère, J.C.: A new efficient algorithm for computing gröbner bases without reduction to zero (f5). In: ISSAC 2002, pp. 75–83. Association for Computing Machinery, New York (2002). ISBN 1581134843. https://doi.org/10.1145/780506. 780516
87. Faugère, J.-C., Gauthier-Umaña, V., Otmani, A., Perret, L., Tillich, J.-P.: A distinguisher for high-rate Mceliece cryptosystems. IEEE Trans. Inf. Theory **59**(10), 6830–6844 (2013)
88. Feo, L.D.: Mathematics of isogeny based cryptography (2017)
89. De Feo, L., Jao, D., Plût, J.: Towards quantum-resistant cryptosystems from supersingular elliptic curve isogenies. J. Math. Cryptol. **8**(3), 209–247 (2014)
90. Fiat, A., Shamir, A.: How to prove yourself: practical solutions to identification and signature problems. In: Odlyzko, A.M. (ed.) CRYPTO 1986. LNCS, vol. 263, pp. 186–194. Springer, Heidelberg (1987). https://doi.org/10.1007/3-540-47721-7_12
91. Fluhrer, S.: Cryptanalysis of ring-LWE based key exchange with key share reuse. Cryptology ePrint Archive, Report 2016/085 (2016). http://eprint.iacr.org/2016/085
92. Fumaroli, G., Martinelli, A., Prouff, E., Rivain, M.: Affine masking against higher-order side channel analysis. In: Biryukov, A., Gong, G., Stinson, D.R. (eds.) SAC 2010. LNCS, vol. 6544, pp. 262–280. Springer, Heidelberg (2011). https://doi.org/10.1007/978-3-642-19574-7_18
93. Gaborit, P., Ruatta, O., Schrek, J., Zémor, G.: RankSign: an efficient signature algorithm based on the rank metric. In: Mosca, M. (ed.) PQCrypto 2014. LNCS, vol. 8772, pp. 88–107. Springer, Cham (2014). https://doi.org/10.1007/978-3-319-11659-4_6
94. Galbraith, S., Panny, L., Smith, B., Vercauteren, F.: Quantum equivalence of the DLP and CDHP for group actions. Cryptology ePrint Archive, Report 2018/1199 (2018). https://eprint.iacr.org/2018/1199
95. Galbraith, S.D., Petit, C., Shani, B., Ti, Y.B.: On the security of supersingular isogeny cryptosystems. In: Cheon, J.H., Takagi, T. (eds.) ASIACRYPT 2016. LNCS, vol. 10031, pp. 63–91. Springer, Heidelberg (2016). https://doi.org/10.1007/978-3-662-53887-6_3
96. Gellersen, T., Seker, O., Eisenbarth, T.: Differential power analysis of the picnic signature scheme. Cryptology ePrint Archive, Report 2020/267 (2020). https://eprint.iacr.org/2020/267
97. Gentry, C., Peikert, C., Vaikuntanathan, V.: Trapdoors for hard lattices and new cryptographic constructions. In: Ladner, R.E., Dwork, C. (eds.) 40th ACM STOC, pp. 197–206. ACM Press, May 2008. https://doi.org/10.1145/1374376.1374407
98. Gentry, C., Jonsson, J., Stern, J., Szydlo, M.: Cryptanalysis of the NTRU signature scheme (NSS) from Eurocrypt 2001. In: Boyd, C. (ed.) ASIACRYPT 2001. LNCS, vol. 2248, pp. 1–20. Springer, Heidelberg (2001). https://doi.org/10.1007/3-540-45682-1_1

99. Goldreich, O.: Two remarks concerning the Goldwasser-Micali-Rivest signature scheme. In: Odlyzko, A.M. (ed.) CRYPTO 1986. LNCS, vol. 263, pp. 104–110. Springer, Heidelberg (1987). https://doi.org/10.1007/3-540-47721-7_8

100. Goldreich, O., Goldwasser, S., Halevi, S.: Public-key cryptosystems from lattice reduction problems. In: Kaliski, B.S. (ed.) CRYPTO 1997. LNCS, vol. 1294, pp. 112–131. Springer, Heidelberg (1997). https://doi.org/10.1007/BFb0052231

101. Grassi, L., Rechberger, C., Rotaru, D., Scholl, P., Smart, N.P.: MPC-friendly symmetric key primitives. In: Weippl, E.R., Katzenbeisser, S., Kruegel, C., Myers, A.C., Halevi, S. (eds.) ACM CCS, pp. 430–443. ACM Press, October 2016. https://doi.org/10.1145/2976749.2978332

102. Grover, L.K.: A fast quantum mechanical algorithm for database search. In: 28th ACM STOC, pp. 212–219. ACM Press, May 1996. https://doi.org/10.1145/237814.237866

103. Güneysu, T., Lyubashevsky, V., Pöppelmann, T.: Practical lattice-based cryptography: a signature scheme for embedded systems. In: Prouff, E., Schaumont, P. (eds.) CHES 2012. LNCS, vol. 7428, pp. 530–547. Springer, Heidelberg (2012). https://doi.org/10.1007/978-3-642-33027-8_31

104. Guo, Q., Johansson, T., Nilsson, A.: A key-recovery timing attack on post-quantum primitives using the Fujisaki-Okamoto transformation and its application on FrodoKEM. In: Micciancio, D., Ristenpart, T. (eds.) CRYPTO 2020. LNCS, vol. 12171, pp. 359–386. Springer, Cham (2020). https://doi.org/10.1007/978-3-030-56880-1_13

105. Guo, Q., Johansson, T., Stankovski, P.: A key recovery attack on MDPC with CCA security using decoding errors. In: Cheon, J.H., Takagi, T. (eds.) ASIACRYPT 2016. LNCS, vol. 10031, pp. 789–815. Springer, Heidelberg (2016). https://doi.org/10.1007/978-3-662-53887-6_29

106. Guo, Q., Johansson, T., Yang, J.: A novel CCA attack using decryption errors against LAC. In: Galbraith, S.D., Moriai, S. (eds.) ASIACRYPT 2019. LNCS, vol. 11921, pp. 82–111. Springer, Cham (2019). https://doi.org/10.1007/978-3-030-34578-5_4

107. Guo, S., Kamath, P., Rosen, A., Sotiraki, K.: Limits on the efficiency of (Ring) LWE based non-interactive key exchange. In: Kiayias, A., Kohlweiss, M., Wallden, P., Zikas, V. (eds.) PKC 2020. LNCS, vol. 12110, pp. 374–395. Springer, Cham (2020). https://doi.org/10.1007/978-3-030-45374-9_13

108. Hall, C., Goldberg, I., Schneier, B.: Reaction attacks against several public-key cryptosystems. In: Varadharajan, V., Yi, M. (eds.) ICICS 99. LNCS, vol. 1726, pp. 2–12. Springer, Heidelberg (1999)

109. Hamburg, M.: Three Bears. Technical report, National Institute of Standards and Technology (2019). https://csrc.nist.gov/projects/post-quantum-cryptography/round-2-submissions

110. Hoffstein, J., Pipher, J., Silverman, J.H.: NSS: An NTRU lattice-based signature scheme. In: Pfitzmann, B. (ed.) EUROCRYPT 2001. LNCS, vol. 2045, pp. 211–228. Springer, Heidelberg (2001). https://doi.org/10.1007/3-540-44987-6_14

111. Hoffstein, J., Pipher, J., Silverman, J.H.: NTRU: A ring-based public key cryptosystem. In: Buhler, J.P. (ed.) ANTS 1998. LNCS, vol. 1423, pp. 267–288. Springer, Heidelberg (1998). https://doi.org/10.1007/BFb0054868

112. Hoffstein, J., Howgrave-Graham, N., Pipher, J., Silverman, J.H., Whyte, W.: NTRUSign: digital signatures using the NTRU lattice. In: Joye, M. (ed.) CT-RSA 2003. LNCS, vol. 2612, pp. 122–140. Springer, Heidelberg (2003). https://doi.org/10.1007/3-540-36563-X_9

113. Hofheinz, D., Hövelmanns, K., Kiltz, E.: A modular analysis of the Fujisaki-Okamoto transformation. In: Kalai, Y., Reyzin, L. (eds.) TCC 2017. LNCS, vol. 10677, pp. 341–371. Springer, Cham (2017). https://doi.org/10.1007/978-3-319-70500-2_12

114. Howe, J., Prest, T., Apon, D.: SOK: how (not) to design and implement post-quantum cryptography. Cryptology ePrint Archive, Report 2021 (2021). https://eprint.iacr.org/2021/

115. Paquin, C., Stebila, D., Tamvada, G.: Benchmarking post-quantum cryptography in TLS. In: Ding, J., Tillich, J.-P. (eds.) PQCrypto 2020. LNCS, vol. 12100, pp. 72–91. Springer, Cham (2020). https://doi.org/10.1007/978-3-030-44223-1_5

116. Howe, J., Martinoli, M., Oswald, E., Regazzoni, F.: Optimised Lattice-Based Key Encapsulation in Hardware. In: NIST's Second PQC Standardization Conference (2019)

117. Howgrave-Graham, N., et al.: The impact of decryption failures on the security of NTRU encryption. In: Boneh, D. (ed.) CRYPTO 2003. LNCS, vol. 2729, pp. 226–246. Springer, Heidelberg (2003). https://doi.org/10.1007/978-3-540-45146-4_14

118. Huang, W.-L., Chen, J.-P., Yang, B.-Y.: Power Analysis on NTRU Prime. IACR TCHES 2020(1) (2020). ISSN 2569–2925

119. Hülsing, A.: W-OTS+ - shorter signatures for hash-based signature schemes. In: Youssef, A., Nitaj, A., Hassanien, A.E. (eds.) AFRICACRYPT 2013. LNCS, vol. 7918, pp. 173–188. Springer, Heidelberg (2013). https://doi.org/10.1007/978-3-642-38553-7_10

120. Hulsing, A., et al.: SPHINCS+. Technical report, National Institute of Standards and Technology (2019). https://csrc.nist.gov/projects/post-quantum-cryptography/round-2-submissions

121. Ishai, Y., Kushilevitz, E., Ostrovsky, R., Sahai, A.: Zero-knowledge from secure multiparty computation. In: Johnson, D.S., Feige, U. (eds.) 39th ACM STOC, pp. 21–30. ACM Press, June 2007. https://doi.org/10.1145/1250790.1250794

122. Jao, D., De Feo, L.: Towards quantum-resistant cryptosystems from supersingular elliptic curve isogenies. In: Yang, B.-Y. (ed.) PQCrypto 2011. LNCS, vol. 7071, pp. 19–34. Springer, Heidelberg (2011). https://doi.org/10.1007/978-3-642-25405-5_2

123. Jao, D., et al.: SIKE. Technical report, National Institute of Standards and Technology (2019). https://csrc.nist.gov/projects/post-quantum-cryptography/round-2-submissions

124. Jaques, S., Schanck, J.M.: Quantum cryptanalysis in the RAM model: claw-finding attacks on SIKE. In: Boldyreva, A., Micciancio, D. (eds.) CRYPTO 2019. LNCS, vol. 11692, pp. 32–61. Springer, Cham (2019). https://doi.org/10.1007/978-3-030-26948-7_2

125. Jaques, S., Naehrig, M., Roetteler, M., Virdia, F.: Implementing grover oracles for quantum key search on AES and LowMC. In: Canteaut, A., Ishai, Y. (eds.) EUROCRYPT 2020. LNCS, vol. 12106, pp. 280–310. Springer, Cham (2020). https://doi.org/10.1007/978-3-030-45724-2_10

126. Joux, A., Vitse, V.: A crossbred algorithm for solving Boolean polynomial systems. Cryptology ePrint Archive, Report 2017/372 (2017). http://eprint.iacr.org/2017/372

127. Kales, D., Zaverucha, G.: An attack on some signature schemes constructed from five-pass identification schemes. Cryptology ePrint Archive, Report 2020/837 (2020). https://eprint.iacr.org/2020/837

128. Kannwischer, M.J., Pessl, P., Primas, R.: Single-trace attacks on Keccak. IACR TCHES 2020(3), 243–268 (2020). https://doi.org/10.13154/tches.v2020.i3.243-268. https://tches.iacr.org/index.php/TCHES/article/view/8590. ISSN 2569-2925

129. Katz, J., Kolesnikov, V., Wang, X.: Improved non-interactive zero knowledge with applications to post-quantum signatures. In: Lie, D., Mannan, M., Backes, M., Wang, X. (eds.) ACM CCS, pp. 525–537. ACM Press, October 2018. https://doi.org/10.1145/3243734.3243805

130. Kuperberg, G.: A subexponential-time quantum algorithm for the dihedral hidden subgroup problem. SIAM J. Comput. **35**(1), 170–188 (2005). https://doi.org/10.1137/S0097539703436345

131. Kuperberg, G.: Another subexponential-time quantum algorithm for the dihedral hidden subgroup problem. In: Severini, S., Brandão, F.G.S.L. (eds.) TQC, volume 22 of LIPIcs, pp. 20–34. Schloss Dagstuhl - Leibniz-Zentrum für Informatik (2013). https://doi.org/10.4230/LIPIcs.TQC.2013.20

132. Laarhoven, T., Mosca, M., van de Pol, J.: Finding shortest lattice vectors faster using quantum search. Des. Codes Cryptogr. **77**(2–3), 375–400 (2015). https://doi.org/10.1007/s10623-015-0067-5. https://doi.org/10.1007/s10623-015-0067-5

133. Lahr, N., Niederhagen, R., Petri, R., Samardjiska, S.: Side channel information set decoding using iterative chunking. In: Moriai, S., Wang, H. (eds.) ASIACRYPT 2020. LNCS, vol. 12491, pp. 881–910. Springer, Cham (2020). https://doi.org/10.1007/978-3-030-64837-4_29

134. Lamport, L.: Constructing digital signatures from a one-way function. Technical report SRI-CSL-98, SRI International Computer Science Laboratory, October 1979

135. Langlois, A., Stehlé, D.: Worst-case to average-case reductions for module lattices. Des. Codes Cryptogr. **75**(3), 565–599 (2015). https://doi.org/10.1007/s10623-014-9938-4. https://doi.org/10.1007/s10623-014-9938-4

136. Liu, F., Isobe, T., Meier, W. Cryptanalysis of full LowMC and LowMC-M with algebraic techniques. Cryptology ePrint Archive, Report 2020/1034 (2020). https://eprint.iacr.org/2020/1034

137. Lyubashevsky, V.: Fiat-Shamir with aborts: applications to lattice and factoring-based signatures. In: Matsui, M. (ed.) ASIACRYPT 2009. LNCS, vol. 5912, pp. 598–616. Springer, Heidelberg (2009). https://doi.org/10.1007/978-3-642-10366-7_35

138. Lyubashevsky, V., Peikert, C., Regev, O.: On ideal lattices and learning with errors over rings. In: Gilbert, H. (ed.) EUROCRYPT 2010. LNCS, vol. 6110, pp. 1–23. Springer, Heidelberg (2010). https://doi.org/10.1007/978-3-642-13190-5_1

139. Lyubashevsky, V., Ducas, L., Kiltz, E., Lepoint, T., Schwabe, P., Seiler, G., Stehlé, D.: CRYSTALS-DILITHIUM. Technical report, National Institute of Standards and Technology (2019). https://csrc.nist.gov/projects/post-quantum-cryptography/round-2-submissions

140. McEliece, R.J.: A public-key cryptosystem based on algebraic coding theory. JPL DSN Progress Report **44**, 05 (1978)

141. Merkle, R.C.: A certified digital signature. In: Brassard, G. (ed.) CRYPTO 1989. LNCS, vol. 435, pp. 218–238. Springer, New York (1990). https://doi.org/10.1007/0-387-34805-0_21

142. Micciancio, D., Peikert, C.: Trapdoors for lattices: simpler, tighter, faster, smaller. In: Pointcheval, D., Johansson, T. (eds.) EUROCRYPT 2012. LNCS, vol. 7237, pp. 700–718. Springer, Heidelberg (2012). https://doi.org/10.1007/978-3-642-29011-4_41

143. Migliore, V., Gérard, B., Tibouchi, M., Fouque, P.-A.: Masking dilithium. In: Deng, R.H., Gauthier-Umaña, V., Ochoa, M., Yung, M. (eds.) ACNS 2019. LNCS, vol. 11464, pp. 344–362. Springer, Cham (2019). https://doi.org/10.1007/978-3-030-21568-2_17

144. Mus, K., Islam, S., Sunar, B.: QuantumHammer: a practical hybrid attack on the LUOV signature scheme. In: Ligatti, J., Ou, X., Katz, J., Vigna, G. (eds.) ACM CCS 2020, pp. 1071–1084. ACM Press, November 2020. https://doi.org/10.1145/3372297.3417272

145. Naehrig, M., et al.: FrodoKEM. Technical report, National Institute of Standards and Technology (2019). https://csrc.nist.gov/projects/post-quantum-cryptography/round-2-submissions

146. Nguyen, P.Q., Regev, O.: Learning a parallelepiped: cryptanalysis of GGH and NTRU signatures. In: Vaudenay, S. (ed.) EUROCRYPT 2006. LNCS, vol. 4004, pp. 271–288. Springer, Heidelberg (2006). https://doi.org/10.1007/11761679_17

147. NIST: Submission requirements and evaluation criteria for the post-quantum cryptography standardization process (2016). https://csrc.nist.gov/CSRC/media/Projects/Post-Quantum-Cryptography/documents/call-for-proposals-final-dec-2016.pdf

148. Oswald, E., Mangard, S.: Template attacks on masking–resistance is futile. In: Abe, M. (ed.) CT-RSA 2007. LNCS, vol. 4377, pp. 243–256. Springer, Heidelberg (2006). https://doi.org/10.1007/11967668_16

149. Park, A., Shim, K.-A., Koo, N., Han, D.-G.: Side-channel attacks on post-quantum signature schemes based on multivariate quadratic equations. IACR TCHES 2018(3), 500–523 (2018). https://doi.org/10.13154/tches.v2018.i3.500-523. https://tches.iacr.org/index.php/TCHES/article/view/7284. ISSN 2569-2925

150. Paterson, K.G., Villanueva-Polanco, R.: Cold boot attacks on NTRU. In: Patra, A., Smart, N.P. (eds.) INDOCRYPT 2017. LNCS, vol. 10698, pp. 107–125. Springer, Cham (2017). https://doi.org/10.1007/978-3-319-71667-1_6

151. Peikert, C.: A decade of lattice cryptography. Cryptology ePrint Archive, Report 2015/939 (2015). http://eprint.iacr.org/2015/939

152. Peikert, C.: He gives C-sieves on the CSIDH. In: Canteaut, A., Ishai, Y. (eds.) EUROCRYPT 2020. LNCS, vol. 12106, pp. 463–492. Springer, Cham (2020). https://doi.org/10.1007/978-3-030-45724-2_16

153. Peikert, C.: How (Not) to instantiate ring-LWE. In: Zikas, V., De Prisco, R. (eds.) SCN 2016. LNCS, vol. 9841, pp. 411–430. Springer, Cham (2016). https://doi.org/10.1007/978-3-319-44618-9_22

154. Peikert, C.: Lattice cryptography for the internet. In: Mosca, M. (ed.) PQCrypto 2014. LNCS, vol. 8772, pp. 197–219. Springer, Cham (2014). https://doi.org/10.1007/978-3-319-11659-4_12

155. Peikert, C., Pepin, Z.: Algebraically structured LWE, revisited. In: Hofheinz, D., Rosen, A. (eds.) TCC 2019. LNCS, vol. 11891, pp. 1–23. Springer, Cham (2019). https://doi.org/10.1007/978-3-030-36030-6_1

156. Perrig, A.: The BiBa one-time signature and broadcast authentication protocol. In: Reiter, M.K., Samarati, P. (eds.) ACM CCS, pp. 28–37. ACM Press, November 2001. https://doi.org/10.1145/501983.501988

157. Pessl, P., Bruinderink, L.G., Yarom, Y.: To BLISS-B or not to be: attacking strongSwan's implementation of post-quantum signatures. In: Thuraisingham, B.M., Evans, D., Malkin, T., Xu, D. (eds.) ACM CCS, pp. 1843–1855. ACM Press, October/November 2017. https://doi.org/10.1145/3133956.3134023

158. Pointcheval, D., Stern, J.: Security proofs for signature schemes. In: Maurer, U. (ed.) EUROCRYPT 1996. LNCS, vol. 1070, pp. 387–398. Springer, Heidelberg (1996). https://doi.org/10.1007/3-540-68339-9_33

159. Polanco, R.L.V.: Cold Boot Attacks on Post-Quantum Schemes. Ph.D. thesis, Royal Holloway, University of London (2018)

160. Prange, E.: The use of information sets in decoding cyclic codes. IRE Trans. Inf. Theory **8**(5), 5–9 (1962). https://doi.org/10.1109/TIT.1962.1057777

161. Prest, T., et al.: FALCON. Technical report, National Institute of Standards and Technology (2019). https://csrc.nist.gov/projects/post-quantum-cryptography/round-2-submissions

162. Ravi, P., Jhanwar, M.P., Howe, J., Chattopadhyay, A., Bhasin, S.: Exploiting determinism in lattice-based signatures: practical fault attacks on PQM4 implementations of nist candidates. In: AsiaCCS, pp. 427–440 (2019)

163. Regev, O.: On lattices, learning with errors, random linear codes, and cryptography. In: Gabow, H.N., Fagin, R. (eds.) 37th ACM STOC, pp. 84–93. ACM Press, May 2005. https://doi.org/10.1145/1060590.1060603

164. Reyzin, L., Reyzin, N.: Better than BiBa: short one-time signatures with fast signing and verifying. In: Batten, L., Seberry, J. (eds.) ACISP 2002. LNCS, vol. 2384, pp. 144–153. Springer, Heidelberg (2002). https://doi.org/10.1007/3-540-45450-0_11

165. Rivest, R.L., Shamir, A., Adleman, L.M.: A method for obtaining digital signatures and public-key cryptosystems. Commun. Assoc. Comput. Machinery **21**(2), 120–126 (1978)

166. Rossi, M., Hamburg, M., Hutter, M., Marson, M.E.: A side-channel assisted cryptanalytic attack against QcBits. In: Fischer, W., Homma, N. (eds.) CHES 2017. LNCS, vol. 10529, pp. 3–23. Springer, Cham (2017). https://doi.org/10.1007/978-3-319-66787-4_1

167. Rostovtsev, A., Stolbunov, A.: Public-Key Cryptosystem Based On Isogenies. Cryptology ePrint Archive, Report 2006/145 (2006). http://eprint.iacr.org/2006/145

168. Sakumoto, K., Shirai, T., Hiwatari, H.: On provable security of UOV and HFE signature schemes against chosen-message attack. In: Yang, B.-Y. (ed.) PQCrypto 2011. LNCS, vol. 7071, pp. 68–82. Springer, Heidelberg (2011). https://doi.org/10.1007/978-3-642-25405-5_5

169. Sakumoto, K., Shirai, T., Hiwatari, H.: Public-key identification schemes based on multivariate quadratic polynomials. In: Rogaway, P. (ed.) CRYPTO 2011. LNCS, vol. 6841, pp. 706–723. Springer, Heidelberg (2011). https://doi.org/10.1007/978-3-642-22792-9_40

170. Samardjiska, S., Santini, P., Persichetti, E., Banegas, G.: A reaction attack against cryptosystems based on LRPC codes. In: Schwabe, P., Thériault, N. (eds.) LATINCRYPT 2019. LNCS, vol. 11774, pp. 197–216. Springer, Cham (2019). https://doi.org/10.1007/978-3-030-30530-7_10

171. Samardjiska, S., Chen, M.-S., Hulsing, A., Rijneveld, J., Schwabe, P.: MQDSS. Technical report, National Institute of Standards and Technology (2019). https://csrc.nist.gov/projects/post-quantum-cryptography/round-2-submissions

172. Samwel, N., Batina, L., Bertoni, G., Daemen, J., Susella, R.: Breaking Ed25519 in WolfSSL. In: Smart, N.P. (ed.) CT-RSA 2018. LNCS, vol. 10808, pp. 1–20. Springer, Cham (2018). https://doi.org/10.1007/978-3-319-76953-0_1

173. Schnorr, C.P.: Efficient identification and signatures for smart cards. In: Brassard, G. (ed.) CRYPTO 1989. LNCS, vol. 435, pp. 239–252. Springer, New York (1990). https://doi.org/10.1007/0-387-34805-0_22

174. Schnorr, C.-P., Euchner, M.: Lattice basis reduction: improved practical algorithms and solving subset sum problems. Math. Program. **66**, 181–199 (1994). https://doi.org/10.1007/BF01581144. https://doi.org/10.1007/BF01581144
175. Schwabe, P., et al.: CRYSTALS-KYBER. Technical report, National Institute of Standards and Technology (2019). https://csrc.nist.gov/projects/post-quantum-cryptography/round-2-submissions
176. Shamir, A.: An efficient identification scheme based on permuted kernels (extended abstract). In: Brassard, G. (ed.) CRYPTO 1989. LNCS, vol. 435, pp. 606–609. Springer, New York (1990). https://doi.org/10.1007/0-387-34805-0_54
177. Shor, P.W.: Algorithms for quantum computation: discrete logarithms and factoring. In: 35th FOCS, pp. 124–134. IEEE Computer Society Press, November 1994. https://doi.org/10.1109/SFCS.1994.365700
178. Sim, B.-Y., Kwon, J., Choi, K.Y., Cho, J., Park, A., Han, D.-G.: Novel side-channel attacks on quasi-cyclic code-based cryptography. IACR TCHES 2019(4), 180–212 (2019). https://doi.org/10.13154/tches.v2019.i4.180-212. https://tches.iacr.org/index.php/TCHES/article/view/8349. ISSN 2569–2925
179. Stern, J.: A new identification scheme based on syndrome decoding. In: Stinson, D.R. (ed.) CRYPTO 1993. LNCS, vol. 773, pp. 13–21. Springer, Heidelberg (1994). https://doi.org/10.1007/3-540-48329-2_2
180. Stern, J.: A new paradigm for public key identification. IEEE Trans. Inf. Theory **42**(6), 1757–1768 (1996). https://doi.org/10.1109/18.556672. https://doi.org/10.1109/18.556672
181. Szydlo, M.: Merkle tree traversal in log space and time. In: Cachin, C., Camenisch, J.L. (eds.) EUROCRYPT 2004. LNCS, vol. 3027, pp. 541–554. Springer, Heidelberg (2004). https://doi.org/10.1007/978-3-540-24676-3_32
182. Canto Torres, R., Sendrier, N.: Analysis of information set decoding for a sublinear error weight. In: Takagi, T. (ed.) PQCrypto 2016. LNCS, vol. 9606, pp. 144–161. Springer, Cham (2016). https://doi.org/10.1007/978-3-319-29360-8_10
183. van Oorschot, P.C., Wiener, M.J.: Parallel collision search with cryptanalytic applications. J. Cryptol. **12**(1), 1–28 (1999). https://doi.org/10.1007/PL00003816
184. Verhulst, K.: Power Analysis and Masking of Saber. Master's thesis, KU Leuven, Belgium (2019)
185. Véron, P.: Improved identification schemes based on error-correcting codes. Appl. Algebra Eng. Commun. Comput. **8**(1), 57–69 (1996). https://doi.org/10.1007/s002000050053. https://doi.org/10.1007/s002000050053
186. Yang, B.-Y., Chen, J.-M.: All in the XL family: theory and practice. In: Park, C., Chee, S. (eds.) ICISC 2004. LNCS, vol. 3506, pp. 67–86. Springer, Heidelberg (2005). https://doi.org/10.1007/11496618_7
187. Yarom, Y., Falkner, K., FLUSH+RELOAD: a high resolution, low noise, L3 cache side-channel attack. In: Fu, K., Jung, J. (eds.) USENIX Security, pp. 719–732. USENIX Association, August 2014
188. Zaverucha, G., et al.: Picnic. Technical report, National Institute of Standards and Technology (2019). https://csrc.nist.gov/projects/post-quantum-cryptography/round-2-submissions
189. Zhandry, M.: A note on the quantum collision and set equality problems. Quantum Inf. Comput. **15**(7&8), 557–567 (2015)
190. Zhang, Z., et al.: NTRUEncrypt. Technical report, National Institute of Standards and Technology (2019). https://csrc.nist.gov/projects/post-quantum-cryptography/round-2-submissions

Dual Lattice Attacks for Closest Vector Problems (with Preprocessing)

Thijs Laarhoven[1] and Michael Walter[2]

[1] Eindhoven University of Technology, Eindhoven, The Netherlands
[2] Institute of Science and Technology Austria, Klosterneuburg, Austria
michael.walter@ist.ac.at

Abstract. The dual attack has long been considered a relevant attack on lattice-based cryptographic schemes relying on the hardness of learning with errors (LWE) and its structured variants. As solving LWE corresponds to finding a nearest point on a lattice, one may naturally wonder how efficient this dual approach is for solving more general closest vector problems, such as the classical closest vector problem (CVP), the variants bounded distance decoding (BDD) and approximate CVP, and preprocessing versions of these problems. While primal, sieving-based solutions to these problems (with preprocessing) were recently studied in a series of works on approximate Voronoi cells [Laa16b, DLdW19, Laa20, DLvW20], for the dual attack no such overview exists, especially for problems with preprocessing. With one of the take-away messages of the approximate Voronoi cell line of work being that primal attacks work well for approximate CVP(P) but scale poorly for BDD(P), one may further wonder if the dual attack suffers the same drawbacks, or if it is perhaps a better solution when trying to solve BDD(P).

In this work we provide an overview of cost estimates for dual algorithms for solving these "classical" closest lattice vector problems. Heuristically we expect to solve the search version of average-case CVPP in time and space $2^{0.293d+o(d)}$ in the single-target model. The distinguishing version of average-case CVPP, where we wish to distinguish between random targets and targets planted at distance (say) $0.99 \cdot g_d$ from the lattice, has the same complexity in the single-target model, but can be solved in time and space $2^{0.195d+o(d)}$ in the multi-target setting, when given a large number of targets from either target distribution. This suggests an inequivalence between distinguishing and searching, as we do not expect a similar improvement in the multi-target setting to hold for search-CVPP. We analyze three slightly different decoders, both for distinguishing and searching, and experimentally obtain concrete cost estimates for the dual attack in dimensions 50 to 80, which confirm

Thijs Laarhoven and Michael Walter—TL is supported by an NWO Veni grant (016.Veni.192.005). MW is supported by the European Research Council, ERC consolidator grant (682815 – TOCNeT). Part of this work was done while both authors were visiting the Simons Institute for the Theory of Computing at the University of California, Berkeley.

© Springer Nature Switzerland AG 2021
K. G. Paterson (Ed.): CT-RSA 2021, LNCS 12704, pp. 478–502, 2021.
https://doi.org/10.1007/978-3-030-75539-3_20

our heuristic assumptions, and show that the hidden order terms in the asymptotic estimates are quite small.

Our main take-away message is that the dual attack appears to mirror the approximate Voronoi cell line of work – whereas using approximate Voronoi cells works well for approximate CVP(P) but scales poorly for BDD(P), the dual approach scales well for BDD(P) instances but performs poorly on approximate CVP(P).

Keywords: Lattice-based cryptography · Lattice algorithms · Primal/dual attacks · Closest vector problem (CVP) · Bounded distance decoding (BDD)

1   Introduction

Post-Quantum Cryptography. Ever since the breakthrough work of Shor in the 1990s [Sho94], revealing how quantum computers pose a major threat to currently deployed cryptographic primitives, researchers have been studying alternative approaches which have the potential to be resistant against quantum attacks. Over the past few decades, the field of "post-quantum cryptography" [BBD09] has gained in popularity, and the recent NIST standardization process [oSN17] has further focused the attention of the cryptographic community on preparing for a future where large-scale quantum computers are a reality.

Lattice-Based Cryptography. Out of all proposed alternatives for "classical" cryptography, lattice-based cryptography has emerged as a prime candidate for secure and efficient cryptography in the post-quantum era. Many basic primitives are simple and efficient to realize with e.g. learning with errors (LWE) and its ring variants [Reg05, SSTX09, Reg10], while more advanced cryptographic primitives (such as fully homomorphic encryption [Gen09]) can also be constructed using lattices. By far the most schemes submitted to the NIST competition base their security on the hardness of hard lattice problems.

Closest Vector Problems. Various hard lattice problems have been considered over time, with the two classical hard problems being the shortest vector problem (SVP) and the closest vector problem (CVP). The latter problem asks to find a nearest lattice point to an arbitrary target, and is arguably the hardest. CVP algorithms appear in various cryptographic contexts, both directly and indirectly (as a subroutine within another algorithm). Closely related to CVP are easier variants, such as bounded distance decoding (BDD) and approximate CVP, preprocessing versions of these problems, and modern related variants such as learning with errors (LWE) and structured variants.

Primal Attacks. For solving CVP and its variants, various approaches have been studied to date. Lattice enumeration [Kan83, MW15, AN17] was long considered the most practical, with a low memory requirement and fast heuristics.

Babai's polynomial time algorithms for the easiest CVP variants [Bab86] can be viewed as based on enumeration as well. Lattice sieving methods [AKS01, MV10, BDGL16, DLdW19, Laa20, DLvW20] make use of so-called approximate Voronoi cells, and achieve a superior asymptotic scaling of the time complexity. With recent advances in sieving [BDGL16, ADH+19, DSvW21, svp20] this likely is the method of choice when assessing the hardness of these problems in cryptographically relevant dimensions. The line of work on approximate Voronoi cells showed that while results for preprocessing problems are promising both for average-case CVPP and approximate CVPP, the results were somewhat disappointing for BDDP. An open question was raised whether this is inherent to the primal approach, and if other approaches were more suitable for BDDP.

Dual Attacks. An alternative approach for solving hard lattice problems (and in particular closest vector problems) is based on the dual lattice [AR04]. Using short vectors from the dual lattice, and computing dot products with a target vector, one can obtain probabilistic evidence indicating whether the target vector lies close to the lattice. Using many dual vectors, one can then construct both distinguishers and search algorithms using a gradient ascent approach [LLM06, DRS14]. The dual attack has mostly been considered in the context of LWE and BDD [LP11, APS15, HKM18, ADH+19], which suggests the dual approach may work better for the BDD regime and worse for the approximate CVP regime. To this date several open questions remain however, such as a thorough heuristic overview of the costs of the dual attack for classical lattice problems (i.e. not LWE), as well as an experimental assessment of the practicality of the dual attack for solving such closest vector problems. Moreover, the preprocessing setting has not yet been studied from a heuristic point of view, in the way that the approximate Voronoi cell approach has been studied recently.

1.1   Contributions

Revisiting the Dual Attack. In this work we give a thorough, but practical overview of the strengths and weaknesses of the dual attack for solving most closest vector problems. Starting from a generalized model which covers most variants of CVP(P) (Sect. 2.4), we study algorithms both for distinguishing and searching for nearby vectors in high-dimensional lattices (Sect. 3). We provide a heuristic complexity analysis of these algorithms, both with and without free preprocessing (Sect. 4), and we verified the heuristics and obtain more concrete cost estimates with experimental results (Sect. 5).

Decoders. Concretely, in terms of algorithms we provide three different *decoders* for combining dot products of different dual vectors with the target vector. The Aharonov–Regev decoder was presented in [AR04] and finds its motivation in approximating Gaussians over the lattice via the Fourier transform. Our Neyman–Pearson decoder follows from applying the celebrated Neyman–Pearson lemma [NP33] to the considered problem, and results in a slightly different, but asymptotically equivalent decoder. The third decoder is a simpler alternative to the previous two decoders, which conveniently requires no knowledge of the estimated distance from the lattice, and which appears to perform reasonably well in practice.

Algorithms. For our search algorithm we use the classical gradient ascent approach, previously studied in [LLM06, DRS14], but here instantiated in a more practical manner. We implemented this search algorithm (as well as distinguishers) in dimensions 50 to 80, showing that the actual performance closely matches theoretical predictions, with fast convergence for most BDD instances. To the best of our knowledge this is the first time concrete experimental results are reported for the dual attack for finding closest vectors in moderate dimensions.

Asymptotics. Theoretically, we show optimality of the Neyman–Pearson decoder within our model, thereby showing optimality of the associated heuristics using the proposed decoders. For preprocessing problems, we can solve BDDP with radius $r \cdot g_d$ (with g_d the Gaussian heuristic) in time $e^{dr^2(1+o(1))/e^2}$ for small r. For r close to 1, distinguishing many targets as either BDD samples or random vectors can be done in time $e^{d(1+o(1))/e^2} \approx 2^{0.195d+o(d)}$, while finding a nearest vector or distinguishing based on only few target vectors requires time $2^{0.293d+o(d)}$. The results for the preprocessing setting are shown in Figs. 1a–1b. For the setting where preprocessing is not free, taking into account basis reduction costs leads to Figs. 1c–1d. These sketch the same picture as the preprocessing results: the dual attack seems complementary to the primal attack, with the dual attack scaling well for $r \leq 1$ and the primal attack scaling well for $r \geq 1$.

Experiments. To validate the heuristic, theoretical claims, as well as to get an idea how well the dual attack really works for solving these problems in practice, we implemented and tested our algorithms as well, focusing on the BDD(P) regime with radius slightly below the Gaussian heuristic. The performance of the distinguishers and search algorithms is remarkably close to our theoretical predictions, even when the preprocessing simply consists of a lattice sieve.

Take-Away Message. Summarizing, in practice the dual attack seems to perform as good as can be expected from the theoretical estimates. Whereas a primal approach works better for approximate CVP(P), the dual attack is arguably the right solution for solving BDD(P). With the approximate Voronoi cell approach and the dual attack working well in disjoint regimes, one could say the dual attack is a complementary solution to the primal attack.

Open Problems. Recently, algorithms for CVP(P) have found further applications, besides for studying the hardness of lattice problems [BKV19, PMHS19]. One application that may be of interest is in a hybrid with lattice enumeration [DLdW20]. Within the enumeration tree, various CVP instances appear on the same lattice, one of which leads to the solution. Rather than solving CVP for each of these targets, a distinguisher may be sufficient for discarding the majority of targets. We leave a study of this hybrid for future work.

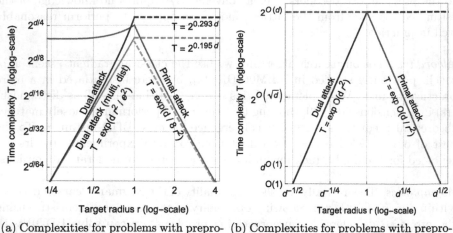

(a) Complexities for problems with prepro-cessing for small radii $r = O(1)$.

(b) Complexities for problems with prepro-cessing, for medium radii $r = d^{\pm O(1)}$.

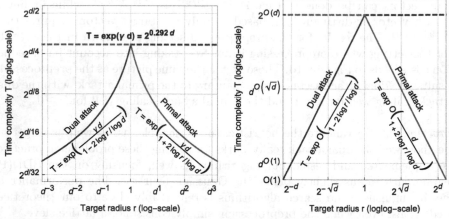

(c) Complexities for problems without pre-processing for medium radii $r = d^{\pm O(1)}$.

(d) Complexities for problems without pre-processing, for large radii $r = 2^{d^{\pm O(1)}}$.

Fig. 1. Asymptotic complexities for primal and dual attacks, with (a, b) and without preprocessing (c, d), in the regimes of exponential (a, c) and arbitrary time complexity scalings (b, d). The radius r denotes the multiplicative factor in front of the Gaussian heuristic for the distance from the target to the planted nearby lattice point. The dual attack (blue) represents distinguishing and searching costs for one target. The primal attack (red) covers approaches based on approximate Voronoi cells. When distinguishing a large number of targets, and using only one dual vector, we obtain slightly improved results for the preprocessing regime (cyan). The dual attack works well for BDD(P) (the regime $r \leq 1$), while the primal attack works well for approximate CVP(P) (the regime $r \geq 1$). The dual attack for BDDP becomes polynomial-time for radius $r \cdot g_d$ when $r = O(\sqrt{\log d/d})$. The primal attack for approximate CVPP becomes polynomial-time when $r = O(\sqrt{d/\log d})$. (Color figure online)

2   Preliminaries

Notation. Reals and integers are denoted by lower case letters and distributions by upper case letter. Bold letters are reserved for vectors (lower case) and matrices (upper case). The i-th entry of a vector $\boldsymbol{v}$ is denoted by v_i and the j-th column vector of a matrix $\mathbf{B}$ by $\boldsymbol{b}_j$. We denote the d-dimensional ball of radius r by $B_d(r)$ and the unit-sphere by $\mathcal{S}^{d-1}$, which are always centered at $\boldsymbol{0}$ unless stated otherwise. We may omit the dimension d if clear from context.

2.1   Lattices

Basics. Given a set $\mathbf{B} = \{\boldsymbol{b}_1, \ldots, \boldsymbol{b}_m\} \subset \mathbb{R}^d$ of linearly independent basis vectors (which can equivalently be represented as a matrix $\mathbf{B} \in \mathbb{R}^{d \times m}$ with the vectors $\boldsymbol{b}_i$ as columns), the lattice generated by $\mathbf{B}$ is defined as $\mathcal{L} = \mathcal{L}(\mathbf{B}) := \{\mathbf{B}\boldsymbol{x} : \boldsymbol{x} \in \mathbb{Z}^d\}$. In case $m = d$ we say the lattice is full-rank, and unless otherwise stated, throughout the paper we will implicitly assume $m = d$. We write $\mathrm{Vol}(\mathcal{L}) := \det(\mathbf{B}^T \mathbf{B})^{1/2}$ for the volume of a lattice $\mathcal{L}$, and w.l.o.g. throughout the paper we will assume that $\mathcal{L}$ is normalized to have volume one (i.e. by multiplying $\mathbf{B}$ by the appropriate scalar multiple). Given a basis $\mathbf{B}$, we write $\mathbf{B}^* = \{\boldsymbol{b}_1^*, \ldots, \boldsymbol{b}_m^*\}$ for its Gram–Schmidt orthogonalization. We write $D_{\boldsymbol{t}+\mathcal{L},s}$ for the discrete Gaussian distribution on $\boldsymbol{t} + \mathcal{L}$ with probability mass function satisfying $\Pr[\boldsymbol{X} = \boldsymbol{x}] \propto \rho_s(\boldsymbol{x}) := \exp(-\pi \|\boldsymbol{x}\|^2 / s^2)$, normalized such that $\sum_{\boldsymbol{x} \in \boldsymbol{t}+\mathcal{L}} \Pr[\boldsymbol{X} = \boldsymbol{x}] = 1$. We define $\lambda_1(\mathcal{L}) := \min_{\boldsymbol{v} \in \mathcal{L} \setminus \{\boldsymbol{0}\}} \|\boldsymbol{v}\|$ and for $\boldsymbol{t} \in \mathbb{R}^d$ we define $\mathrm{dist}(\boldsymbol{t}, \mathcal{L}) := \min_{\boldsymbol{v} \in \mathcal{L}} \|\boldsymbol{t} - \boldsymbol{v}\|$, where all norms are Euclidean norms.

Dual Lattices. Given a lattice $\mathcal{L}$, its dual lattice $\mathcal{L}^*$ contains all vectors $\boldsymbol{w} \in \mathbb{R}^d$ such that $\langle \boldsymbol{v}, \boldsymbol{w} \rangle \in \mathbb{Z}$ for all primal lattice vectors $\boldsymbol{v} \in \mathcal{L}$. This set of vectors again forms a lattice, and for full-rank primal lattices $\mathcal{L}$ a basis of this dual lattice is given by $\mathbf{B}^{-T}$. Since $\mathrm{Vol}(\mathcal{L}^*) = 1/\mathrm{Vol}(\mathcal{L})$, if $\mathcal{L}$ is normalized to have volume 1, then also $\mathcal{L}^*$ has volume 1. We commonly denote primal lattice vectors by $\boldsymbol{v}$, and dual vectors by $\boldsymbol{w}$.

Lattice Problems. Given a description of a lattice $\mathcal{L}$, the shortest vector problem (SVP) asks to find a shortest non-zero lattice vector $\boldsymbol{s} \in \mathcal{L}$, satisfying $\|\boldsymbol{s}\| = \lambda_1(\mathcal{L})$. For approximate versions of this problem (SVP$_r$ with $r \geq 1$), returning any non-zero lattice vector $\boldsymbol{v} \in \mathcal{L}$ of norm $\|\boldsymbol{v}\| \leq r \cdot \lambda_1(\mathcal{L})$ suffices as a solution. A different relaxation of SVP is unique SVP (uSVP$_r$ with $r \leq 1$), where one is tasked to find the shortest non-zero vector in a lattice with the guarantee that there is one particularly short vector $\boldsymbol{s}$ in the lattice: $\|\boldsymbol{s}\| \leq r \cdot \min_{\boldsymbol{v} \in \mathcal{L}, \boldsymbol{v} \neq \lambda \cdot \boldsymbol{s}} \|\boldsymbol{v}\|$. Given a description of a lattice $\mathcal{L}$ and a target vector $\boldsymbol{t} \in \mathbb{R}^d$, the closest vector problem (CVP) is to find a lattice vector $\boldsymbol{s} \in \mathcal{L}$ satisfying $\|\boldsymbol{t} - \boldsymbol{s}\| = \mathrm{dist}(\boldsymbol{t}, \mathcal{L})$. Similarly, we may define approximate CVP (CVP$_r$ with $r \geq 1$) as the approximate version of CVP, where any vector $\boldsymbol{s} \in \mathcal{L}$ with $\|\boldsymbol{t} - \boldsymbol{s}\| \leq \gamma \cdot \mathrm{dist}(\boldsymbol{t}, \mathcal{L})$ qualifies as a solution. The analogue of uSVP for the inhomogeneous setting is often called bounded distance decoding (BDD$_r$ with $r \leq 1$), where one is tasked to find the closest vector with the guarantee that it lies within radius $r \cdot \lambda_1(\mathcal{L})$ of the lattice.

2.2 Heuristic Assumptions

Before describing and analyzing dual lattice attacks, let us first describe the heuristic assumptions we will use to model the problems. Under this heuristic model we will be able to obtain sharp bounds on the costs of dual attacks, at the cost of no longer having a proof of correctness – for exotic, non-random lattices these bounds may well be too optimistic, and even for average-case lattices we can only "prove" the resulting complexities under these additional assumptions.

The Gaussian Heuristic. The determinant $\det(\mathcal{L}) = \mathrm{Vol}(\mathcal{L})$ describes the volume of the fundamental domain, as well as the density of lattice points in space. This metric indicates that if we have a random, large region $\mathcal{R} \subset \mathbb{R}^d$ of volume $\mathrm{Vol}(\mathcal{R})$, then the number of lattice points contained in $\mathcal{R}$ can be estimated as $\mathrm{Vol}(\mathcal{R})/\mathrm{Vol}(\mathcal{L})$. Since a ball of radius r has volume $\mathrm{Vol}\,B(r) = r^d V_d(1)$, with $V_d(1) = (2\pi e/d)^{d/2+o(d)}$ the volume of the ball with unit radius, we expect for any constant $\varepsilon > 0$ with overwhelming probability the ball of radius r around a point in space to contain no lattice points if $r < (1-\varepsilon)g_d$, and to contain many lattice points if $r > (1+\varepsilon)g_d$. Here, $g_d = \sqrt{d/(2\pi e)} \cdot \left(1 + O\left(\frac{1}{d}\right)\right)$ denotes the Gaussian heuristic in dimension d. Putting such a ball around the origin, we expect a shortest non-zero vector in the lattice to have norm $\lambda_1(\mathcal{L}) = g_d(1+o(1))$, and similarly for random target vectors $\boldsymbol{t} \in \mathbb{R}^d$ we expect the closest vector in the lattice to $\boldsymbol{t}$ to lie at distance $\mathrm{dist}(\boldsymbol{t}, \mathcal{L}) = g_d(1 + o(1))$.

Distributions of Lattice Points. Building upon the Gaussian heuristic, we further estimate the distribution of lattice points in space as follows: there is one lattice point $\boldsymbol{0}$ of norm 0, and for any $\alpha \geq 1$ we expect there to be $\alpha^{d+o(d)}$ lattice vectors of norm $\alpha g_d(1 + o(1))$. The Euclidean norm of the n-th shortest vector in a lattice of volume 1 can therefore be estimated as $n^{1/d} g_d(1 + o(1))$.

The Geometric Series Assumption. In the context of lattice basis reduction, we rely on the geometric series assumption [SE94], which states that the norms of the Gram–Schmidt vectors of a block reduced basis form a geometric sequence, i.e. $\|\boldsymbol{b}_i^*\| = \delta^{d-2i+1}$. Here, $\delta > 1$ indicates the quality of the basis: the smaller δ, the better the quality of the basis, and the harder these bases generally are to obtain. For block reduced bases with block size k, we obtain the commonly known estimate $\delta = \delta_k = g_k^{1/(k-1)} = 1 + O\left(\log k/k\right)$ (see e.g. [APS15, MW16]). This estimate is mostly accurate when $k \ll d$, as for $k \approx d$ the shape of the basis is expected to be an average-case HKZ-shape for which the Gram–Schmidt norms do not exactly follow a geometric sequence anymore.

2.3 Lattice Algorithms and Cost Models

The Cost of SVP. To solve SVP, several heuristic methods are known, and most belong to either the class of enumeration algorithms (running in super-exponential time and polynomial space) [Kan83, MW15, AN17] or sieving algorithms (running in $2^{O(d)}$ time and space) [AKS01, Laa16a, BDGL16]. As in our analysis we are interested in minimizing the asymptotic time complexity, we will model the cost of solving SVP by the cost of the best heuristic sieve in dimension d [BDGL16], which classically runs in time $T_{\text{SVP}}(d) = (3/2)^{d/2+o(d)} \approx 2^{0.292d+o(d)}$. Apart from solving SVP, sieving algorithms are actually expected to return all the $(4/3)^{d/2} \approx 2^{0.208d+o(d)}$ shortest non-zero vectors in the lattice; compared to the best sieving algorithms for finding only one short vector, the overhead in the time complexity is only a factor $2^{o(d)}$ [Duc18]. To find even more short lattice vectors, one may use a *relaxed sieve* [Laa16b, Algorithm 5].

The Cost of Approximate SVP. To approximate the shortest vector in a lattice and obtain a basis following the GSA, one commonly uses block reduction with the block size k determining the parameter $\delta = \delta_k$ [Sch87, SE94, GN08, MW16]. The cost of block reduction is usually modeled as the cost of solving SVP in dimension k, via $T_{\text{BKZ}}(k) = d^{O(1)} \cdot T_{\text{SVP}}(k)$, with some overhead which is polynomial in d. Together with the geometric series assumption, this describes a trade-off between the time complexity for the basis reduction and the quality of the reduced basis.

The Cost of BDD. To the best of our knowledge, the most efficient way to solve BDD is through Kannan's embedding [Kan87]. In the full version we briefly sketch the analysis and derive the following result using our heuristic assumptions. (We do not claim novelty; this is just for convenience of the reader.)

Corollary 1 (Solving BDD with sieving and BKZ). *Let $r = d^a$ be a radius for some constant $a < \frac{1}{2}$. Solving BDD with radius r using Kannan's embedding and lattice reduction with sieving has complexity $2^{\frac{0.292}{2(1-a)}d+o(d)}$ under suitable heuristics.*

The Cost of BDDP. The situation is less clear in the preprocessing setting. The above embedding approach is unlikely to be able to make much use of the free preprocessing. The obvious approach would be to strongly reduce the basis before embedding the target vector. But since the goal is to apply block reduction using sieving to the final basis, the preprocessing might as well directly precompute many short vectors for the individual blocks that will be considered during the reduction. Once the target is embedded, block reduction will successively pass it through the blocks and attempt to shorten it using the precomputed vectors. This is essentially an instance of the approximate Voronoi cell algorithm for which we know that its complexity does not scale well with the radius in the BDD parameter range (see Fig. 1a).

Another approach for BDDP is to strongly reduce the basis and perform enumeration to decode the target. While this might be an efficient way to tackle the problem for small instances in practice, it is asymptotically inefficient for the parameter ranges considered in this work. As shown by [HKM18], there is a very narrow range in the target distance parameter where the running time of enumeration switches from polynomial to super-exponential. (The analysis of enumeration in [HKM18] is in a somewhat different setting but carries to ours as well.) The parameters for which enumeration solves the problem in polynomial time are very small ($r = d^a$ for constant $a < 0$), which is outside the scope of this work for BDDP. Super-exponential running times are clearly asymptotically worse than what can already be achieved in the non-preprocessing setting.

The Cost of Approximate CVP(P). If sufficient amount of memory is available, the asymptotically most efficient methods to solve approximate CVP(P) are based on using a large database of short primal lattice vectors and applying a slicing procedure to move the target into the Voronoi cell defined by the vectors in the database. The more short vectors the database contains, the closer this Voronoi cell approximates the Voronoi cell of the lattice. If this approximation held with equality, this would solve CVP exactly (which corresponds to the adequately called Voronoi cell algorithm [MV10]). The coarser the approximation of the lattice's Voronoi cell is, the worse the approximation factor. Unfortunately, it is unclear how the approximate Voronoi cell algorithm might take advantage of a guarantee that the target vector is close to the lattice. For this reason, solving BDD(P) with this method is effectively as hard as solving CVP(P). See Fig. 1c and 1a for concrete complexities.

2.4   Model

We only summarize our model due to space constraints such that the remaining part of this work should be intelligible. For details and clarifications we refer to the full version. To formalize different versions of CVP we define two distributions: the *planted target distribution* and the *random target distribution*. Both are defined by choosing some lattice vector $v \in \mathcal{L}$ (the exact distribution for this is not important for this work, since all our algorithms are invariant under shifts of lattice vectors) and adding some noise $e \in \mathbb{R}^d$, to form a target vector $t = v + e$. In the case of the planted target, the noise e is chosen uniformly at random from the sphere $rg_d\mathcal{S}^{d-1}$, while in the random case the noise is chosen uniformly at random from the fundamental parallelepiped generated by the lattice basis. This also corresponds to the limit of the planted distribution for $r \to \infty$. We define the distinguishing version of our problems as distinguishing between samples (multi-target) or one sample (single target) from the two distributions. The search version in the single target (multi-target) setting is to recover a lattice point within distance rg_d given a sample (multiple samples, resp.) from the planted target distribution. For $r \ll 1$ we refer to these problems as BDD problems, for $r \approx 1$ as "average case" CVP, and for $r \gg 1$ as approximate CVP. We also consider the preprocessing versions of these problems: BDDP, "average case" CVPP and approximate CVPP, resp., where one is given the lattice basis ahead of time and is allowed arbitrary computation on the lattice for "free" before receiving the target(s). The complexity of an algorithm is then measured in the complexity of the query phase only.

3   Algorithms

In this section we will describe algorithms for solving closest vector problems using vectors from the dual lattice, both for distinguishing between a planted distribution and the random distribution, and for actually finding a nearby lattice vector to a (planted) target vector. The heuristic analysis of these algorithms will follow in Sect. 4, and results of experiments are reported in Sect. 5.

3.1   The Aharonov–Regev Decoder

We will start with the Fourier-based derivation of the dual attack, which naturally results in a decoder similar to the one described by Aharonov–Regev [AR04] (and later used in [LLM06, DRS14]). First, suppose we have a target vector t, and let c denote the closest lattice point to t. Then by using (asymptotic) properties of Gaussians, we can derive the following approximations for the mass of a discrete Gaussian at $c - t$:

$$\rho_s(c - t) \approx \sum_{v \in \mathcal{L}} \rho_s(v - t) \approx \sum_{v \in \mathcal{L}} \rho_s(v + t) \Big/ \sum_{v \in \mathcal{L}} \rho_s(v). \tag{1}$$

The first approximation relies on c being significantly closer to t than all other vectors, so that $\rho_s(c - t) \gg \rho_s(v - t)$ for all other lattice vectors $v \in \mathcal{L} \setminus \{c\}$. In that case the sum essentially collapses to the biggest term $\rho_s(c - t)$. The second approximation relies on $s \leq 1$ being sufficiently small, so that the sum in the denominator is approximately equal to 1.[1] Next, applying the Fourier transform [AR04], we translate the latter term to a function on the dual lattice:

$$\rho_s(c - t) \approx \sum_{w \in \mathcal{L}^*} \rho_{1/s}(w) \cos(2\pi \langle w, t \rangle) \Big/ \sum_{w \in \mathcal{L}^*} \rho_{1/s}(w). \tag{2}$$

Finally, we can approximate this infinite sum over dual vectors by only taking the sum over a set $\mathcal{W} \subset \mathcal{L}^*$ of short dual vectors (e.g. those of norm at most some radius R), which contribute the most to the numerator above. For this approximation to be accurate we require that the infinite sum over $w \in \mathcal{L}^*$ is well approximated by the finite sum over only vectors $w \in \mathcal{W}$:

$$\rho_s(c - t) \approx \frac{1}{M} \sum_{w \in \mathcal{W}} \rho_{1/s}(w) \cos(2\pi \langle w, t \rangle), \qquad M = \sum_{w \in \mathcal{L}^*} \rho_{1/s}(w). \tag{3}$$

Note that while the initial function $\rho_s(c-t)$ cannot be evaluated without knowledge of c, this last term is a finite sum over dot products of dual lattice vectors with the target vector, scaled with a constant M which does not depend on the target t. In particular, disregarding the scaling factor $1/M$, the finite sum can be seen as an indicator to the magnitude of $\rho_s(c - t)$, which itself is large if t

---

[1] For the method to work we only need the denominator to be constant in t.

lies close to the lattice (to c) and small if t lies far from the lattice. This finite sum can therefore be used to assess if t lies close to the lattice:

$$f_{\mathrm{AR}}^{(\mathcal{W})}(t) := \sum_{w \in W} \rho_{1/s}(w) \cos(2\pi \langle w, t \rangle). \tag{4}$$

This quantity can be seen as an instantiation of [AR04, Lemma 1.3] on $\mathcal{W} \subset \mathcal{L}^*$: sampling from a discrete Gaussian restricted to $\mathcal{W}$ and taking the sum of cosines is equivalent to sampling from a uniform distribution over $\mathcal{W}$ and weighing the terms with appropriate Gaussian weights. The above decoder computes the expected value of this sum exactly, as $f_{\mathrm{AR}}^{(\mathcal{W})}(t) = \mathbb{E}_{w \sim \mathcal{W}}[\rho_{1/s}(w) \cos(2\pi \langle w, t \rangle)]$.

Note that there is one unspecified parameter $s > 0$ above, which corresponds to both the width of the Gaussian over the primal lattice and the reciprocal of the width of the Gaussian over the dual lattice. For the series of approximations to hold, we need both s and $1/s$ to be small enough, so that in the primal lattice the mass of the entire sum over $v \in \mathcal{L}$ is concentrated around c, and the sum over all dual vectors is well approximated by the sum over only a finite subset $\mathcal{W} \subset \mathcal{L}^*$.

3.2 The Neyman–Pearson Decoder

While the above derivation of the Aharonov–Regev decoder is quite straightforward, it is unclear whether this decoder is actually optimal for trying to distinguish (or search) using dual lattice vectors. Furthermore, the role of the parameter s remains unclear; s should neither be too small nor too large, and finding the optimal value is not obvious. Both Aharonov–Regev [AR04] and Dadush–Regev–Stephens-Davidowitz [DRS14] fixed $s = 1$, but perhaps one can do better (in theory and in practice) with a better choice of s.

In the full version we prove the following lemma, showing that from a probabilistic point of view, the following Neyman–Pearson decoder is optimal.

Lemma 1 (Optimal decoder). *Let $r > 0$ be given. Suppose we wish to distinguish between samples from the random target distribution and samples from the planted target distribution with radius $r \cdot g_d$, given a set of dual vectors $\mathcal{W} \subset \mathcal{L}^*$, and based only on dot products $\langle w, t \rangle$ mod 1. Let $s > 0$ be defined as:*

$$s = r \cdot g_d \cdot \sqrt{\frac{2\pi}{d}}. \tag{5}$$

Then an optimal distinguisher consists of computing the following quantity and making a decision based on whether this quantity exceeds a threshold η:

$$f_{\mathrm{NP}}^{(\mathcal{W})}(t) := \sum_{w \in W} \ln \left(1 + 2 \sum_{k=1}^{\infty} \rho_{1/s}(kw) \cos(2\pi k \langle w, t \rangle) \right). \tag{6}$$

At first sight this decoder shares many similarities with the Aharonov–Regev decoder, in the form of the sum over Gaussian weights and cosines with dot products. The relation with the Aharonov-Regev decoder can be formalized (see full version) to show that, up to order terms, they are scalar multiples:

$$f_{\mathrm{NP}}^{(\mathcal{W})}(t) \sim 2 \cdot f_{\mathrm{AR}}^{(\mathcal{W})}(t). \tag{7}$$

In contrast to the Aharonov–Regev decoder however, the Neyman–Pearson decoder comes with a guarantee of optimality within the model described in Sect. 2.4. Moreover, this decoder comes with an explicit description of the optimal parameter s to use to achieve the best performance. We will later use this as a guideline for choosing a parameter s for the Aharonov–Regev decoder in practice.

Using the asymptotic (heuristic) relation $g_d \approx \sqrt{d/(2\pi e)}$, the above optimal parameter s is approximately $s \approx r/\sqrt{e}$. For BDD problems with radius close to the average-case CVP radius, we have $r \approx 1$ and $s \approx 1/\sqrt{e}$. As the BDD radius decreases, the optimal value s decreases linearly with r as well, and thus the width $1/s$ of the Gaussian in the dual increases and scales as $1/r$. As r decreases, the Gaussian over the dual becomes flatter and flatter, and most terms in the summations will roughly have equal weights. This suggests that at least for the easier BDD instances of small radius, using equal weights in the summation may be almost as good as using Gaussian weights.

3.3   The Simple Decoder

While the Neyman–Pearson decoder is in a sense a more complicated decoder than the Aharonov–Regev decoder, attempting to achieve a superior theoretical performance, the third decoder we consider favors simplicity over optimality.

In most applications, the set $\mathcal{W}$ will consist of short dual vectors, which will mostly have similar Euclidean norms. For instance, if $\mathcal{W}$ is the output of a sieve, we expect the ratio between the norm of the shortest and longest vectors in $\mathcal{W}$ to be approximately $\sqrt{4/3}$, i.e. at most a 16% difference in norms between the shortest and longest vectors in $\mathcal{W}$. As all norms are very similar anyway, one may attempt to simplify the decoder even further by removing this weighing factor, and using the following "simple" decoder instead:

$$f_{\mathrm{simple}}^{(\mathcal{W})}(t) := \sum_{w \in \mathcal{W}} \cos(2\pi\langle w, t\rangle). \tag{8}$$

From an alternative point of view, this simple decoder can be seen as the limiting case of the Aharonov–Regev decoder where we let $s \to 0^+$. For small s, the width of the dual Gaussian $1/s$ increases, and all vectors will essentially have the same probability mass after normalization. As the optimal parameter s decreases with the BDD radius r for the Neyman–Pearson decoder, this limiting case may be most relevant for BDD instances with small radius.

Although this decoder may not come with the same optimality guarantees as the Neyman–Pearson decoder, and only approximates it, this decoder does have one particularly convenient property: it can be computed without knowledge

---

Algorithm 1. A dual distinguisher

Require: A target $t \in \mathbb{R}^d$, a set of dual vectors $\mathcal{W} \subset \mathcal{L}^*$, a decoder f
Ensure: The boolean output estimates whether t lies close to the lattice or not
1: Choose a threshold $\eta > 0$
2: **return** $f^{(\mathcal{W})}(t) > \eta$

Algorithm 2. A dual search algorithm

Require: A target $t \in \mathbb{R}^d$, a set of dual vectors $\mathcal{W} \subset \mathcal{L}^*$, a decoder f
Ensure: The output vector is an estimate for the closest lattice vector to t
1: Choose a step size parameter $\delta > 0$
2: **while** $\|\mathrm{Babai}(t) - t\| > \frac{1}{2}\lambda_1(\mathcal{L})$ **do** $\triangleright$ any bound $0 < R \le \frac{1}{2}\lambda_1(\mathcal{L})$ works
3:     $t \leftarrow t + \delta \cdot \nabla f^{(\mathcal{W})}(t)$
4: **return** $\mathrm{Babai}(t)$

---

of r! Whereas the other decoders require knowledge of r to compute the optimal Gaussian width s, the simple decoder is a function only of $\mathcal{W}$ and t. This might make this decoder more useful in practice, as r may not be known.

3.4   Distinguishing Algorithms

As already described above, given any decoder f we can easily use this decoder as a distinguisher to decide if we are close to the lattice or not, by evaluating it at t and seeing whether the resulting value is small or large. Formally, this approach is depicted in Algorithm 1. Besides the decoder f and the set of dual vectors $\mathcal{W}$, the only parameter that needs to be chosen is the threshold η, which controls the trade-off between the false positive (deciding t lies close to the lattice when it does not) and false negative error probabilities. Increasing η decreases the false positive rate and increases the number of false negatives.

3.5   Search Algorithms

To actually find the closest vector to a target vector, we will use the classical gradient ascent approach, which was previously used in [LLM06, DRS14]. Recall that up to scaling, all decoders approximate a Gaussian mass at $c - t$:

$$\exp\left(-\frac{\pi}{s^2}\|c - t\|^2\right) = \rho_s(c - t) \approx C \cdot f^{(\mathcal{W})}(t). \tag{9}$$

Computing the gradient of the Gaussian as a function of t, we obtain the relation:

$$\frac{2\pi}{s^2}(c - t)\exp\left(-\frac{\pi}{s^2}\|c - t\|^2\right) = \nabla\rho_s(c - t) \approx C \cdot \nabla f^{(\mathcal{W})}(t). \tag{10}$$

For the exact Gaussian mass function we can isolate c, which then gives us an approximation for c in terms of f and its gradient:

$$c = t + \frac{s^2}{2\pi} \cdot \frac{\nabla\rho_s(c - t)}{\rho_s(c - t)} \approx t + \frac{s^2}{2\pi} \cdot \frac{\nabla f^{(\mathcal{W})}(t)}{f^{(\mathcal{W})}(t)}. \tag{11}$$

Here the direction $\nabla f^{(\mathcal{W})}(t)$ can be seen as an approximation to the direction we need to move in, starting from t, to move towards the closest vector c. The scalar $s^2/(2\pi f^{(\mathcal{W})}(t))$ controls the step size in this direction; this would be our best guess to get as close to c in one step as possible. In practice one may choose to use a smaller step size δ, and repeatedly iterate replacing t by $t' = t + \delta \cdot \nabla f^{(\mathcal{W})}(t)$ to slowly move towards c. Ideally, iterating this procedure a few times, our estimates will get more accurate, and t' will eventually lie close enough to c for polynomial-time closest vector algorithms (e.g. Babai's algorithms [Bab86]) to recover c. This is formalized in Algorithm 2.

For illustration, note that we can compute gradients for the decoders explicitly. For instance, for the Aharonov–Regev decoder we have:

$$\nabla f_{\mathrm{AR}}^{(\mathcal{W})}(t) = -2\pi \sum_{w \in \mathcal{W}} \rho_{1/s}(w) \sin(2\pi \langle w, t \rangle) \cdot w. \tag{12}$$

Our best guess for the nearest lattice point c, given t and $\mathcal{W}$, would be:

$$c_{\mathrm{AR}}^{(\mathcal{W})} = t - s^2 \cdot \frac{\sum_{w \in \mathcal{W}} \rho_{1/s}(w) \sin(2\pi \langle w, t \rangle) \cdot w}{\sum_{w \in \mathcal{W}} \rho_{1/s}(w) \cos(2\pi \langle w, t \rangle)}. \tag{13}$$

For the Neyman–Pearson decoder and simple decoder we can similarly derive explicit expressions for the gradient, and obtain preliminary estimates for c based on the provided evidence.

3.6   Choosing the Set of Dual Vectors $\mathcal{W}$

Although some long dual vectors may contribute more to the output of the decoders if they happen to be almost parallel to $t - c$, overall the largest contribution to the sums appearing in all three decoders comes from the shortest dual vectors. Some logical choices for $\mathcal{W}$ would therefore be:

1. $\mathcal{W} = \{s^*\}$, where s^* is a shortest non-zero vector of $\mathcal{L}^*$;
2. $\mathcal{W} = \mathcal{L}^* \cap B(R \cdot g_d)$, i.e. all dual lattice vectors of norm at most $R \cdot g_d$;
3. $\mathcal{W} = \mathrm{Sieve}(\mathcal{L}^*)$, i.e. the output of a lattice sieve applied to (a basis of) $\mathcal{L}^*$;
4. $\mathcal{W} = \mathrm{BKZSieve}(\mathcal{L}^*, k)$, i.e. running a sieving-based BKZ algorithm with block size k on a basis of $\mathcal{L}^*$, and outputting the database of short vectors found in the top block of the basis [ADH+19].

The first choice commonly does not suffice to actually distinguish for one target vector, but the distinguishing advantage per vector is maximized for this option (for more details we refer to the full version). This choice of $\mathcal{W}$ is often considered in cryptanalytic contexts when studying the performance of dual attacks on LWE. The second choice is a more realistic choice when we actually wish to distinguish or find a closest lattice point to a single target vector, rather than just maximizing the distinguishing advantage. Computing this set $\mathcal{W}$ may be costly (see [DLdW19] for a preprocessing method attempting to achieve this), but in preprocessing problems this is likely the best set $\mathcal{W}$ one can possibly use.

The third option is an approximation to the second approach, and may make more sense in practical contexts. The fourth option is a more sensible option when the costs of the preprocessing phase are taken into account as well, as then we commonly wish to balance the preprocessing costs and the costs of the dual attack via a suitable choice of the block size k.

4 Asymptotics

To study the performance of the algorithms from the previous section, we will first analyze the distributions of the output of the decoder, when the target is either planted or random. Then we will analyze how this can be used to assess the costs of distinguishing and searching for nearest vectors.

4.1 Output Distributions of the Decoders

From the definition of the planted target distribution with radius $r \cdot g_d$, the target is of the form $t = c + e$ where $c \in \mathcal{L}$ and e is sampled uniformly at random from the sphere of radius $r \cdot g_d$. All decoders consider dot products between the target and dual lattice vectors, for which we have:

$$\langle t, w \rangle = \langle c + e, w \rangle = \langle c, w \rangle + \langle e, w \rangle \in \langle e, w \rangle + \mathbb{Z}. \qquad (14)$$

Here $\langle c, w \rangle \in \mathbb{Z}$ since $c \in \mathcal{L}$ and $w \in \mathcal{L}^*$. As in all decoders the quantity $\langle t, w \rangle$ is the argument of a cosine, with multiplicative factor 2π, we are interested in the distribution of $\langle t, w \rangle \bmod 1$, which equals the distribution of $\langle e, w \rangle \bmod 1$.

Now, by assumption the distribution of e is independent from w. By either assuming the distribution of e is spherically symmetric or the distribution of w is spherically symmetric[2], we can rewrite the above as follows:

$$\langle e, w \rangle = \|e\| \cdot \|w\| \cdot \left\langle \frac{e}{\|e\|}, \frac{w}{\|w\|} \right\rangle \sim \|e\| \cdot \|w\| \cdot \langle r_1, r_2 \rangle, \quad r_1, r_2 \sim \mathcal{S}^{d-1}. \qquad (15)$$

Here r_1, r_2 are drawn uniformly at random from $\mathcal{S}^{d-1}$. Without loss of generality we may fix $r_1 = e_1$ as the first unit vector, so that the dot product is the first coordinate of the random unit vector r_2. In high dimensions the uniform distribution on the unit sphere is essentially equivalent to sampling each coordinate independently from a Gaussian with mean 0 and variance $1/d$ (and normalizing[3]), so up to order terms the distribution of the first coordinate of r_2 is equal to the Gaussian distribution with mean 0 and variance $1/d$. So focusing on the regime of large d, it follows that:

$$\langle e, w \rangle \sim \mathcal{N}\left(0, \tfrac{1}{d} \cdot \|w\|^2 \cdot \|e\|^2\right). \qquad (16)$$

---

[2] The following argument therefore holds not only if t is from the planted target distribution, but also if t is fixed and the distribution of the dual vectors is modeled via the Gaussian heuristic.

[3] For large d the squared norm of such a vector follows a chi-squared distribution, which is closely concentrated around 1.

For the original dot product, taken modulo 1, we thus obtain:

$$(\langle t, w \rangle \bmod 1) \sim \mathcal{N}\left(0, \tfrac{1}{d} \cdot \|w\|^2 \cdot \|e\|^2\right) \bmod 1. \tag{17}$$

This distribution is sketched in Fig. 2a.

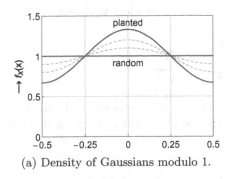

(a) Density of Gaussians modulo 1.

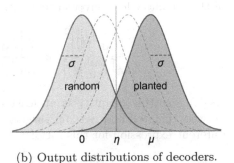

(b) Output distributions of decoders.

Fig. 2. A graphical sketch of Gaussian densities modulo 1, with varying planted target radii, and the output distributions of the three decoders. We wish to distinguish between Gaussians with similar standard deviations but different means.

In the full version, we further study the output distribution of each decoder by deriving the following expressions for the means μ and variances σ^2 for each of the decoders from the previous section, assuming that t was sampled from the planted target distribution for radius r. We remark that some of the analysis for μ_{simple} and σ_{simple} was also recently carried out in [EJK20] in the context of analyzing small secret LWE.

$$\mathbb{E}[f_{\text{AR}}^{(\mathcal{W})}(t)] \approx \sum_{w \in \mathcal{W}} \rho_{1/s}(w)^2, \qquad \text{Var}[f_{\text{AR}}^{(\mathcal{W})}(t)] \approx \tfrac{1}{2} \sum_{w \in \mathcal{W}} \rho_{1/s}(w)^2, \tag{18}$$

$$\mathbb{E}[f_{\text{NP}}^{(\mathcal{W})}(t)] \approx 2 \sum_{w \in \mathcal{W}} \rho_{1/s}(w)^2, \qquad \text{Var}[f_{\text{NP}}^{(\mathcal{W})}(t)] \approx 2 \sum_{w \in \mathcal{W}} \rho_{1/s}(w)^2, \tag{19}$$

$$\mathbb{E}[f_{\text{simple}}^{(\mathcal{W})}(t)] \approx \sum_{w \in \mathcal{W}} \rho_{1/s}(w), \qquad \text{Var}[f_{\text{simple}}^{(\mathcal{W})}(t)] \approx \tfrac{1}{2} \sum_{w \in \mathcal{W}} 1. \tag{20}$$

The above expressions are over the randomness of t drawn from the planted target distribution with radius r. If instead we consider targets r from the random target distribution, then for all three decoders we have $\mathbb{E}[f^{(\mathcal{W})}(r)] = 0$ and $\text{Var}[f^{(\mathcal{W})}(r)] \approx \text{Var}[f^{(\mathcal{W})}(t)]$ with t again from the planted distribution with radius r. Figure 2b thus illustrates the situation well, in that in both cases the output distribution follows a Gaussian with the same variance, but the mean depends on whether t was planted or random.

In all applications we try to distinguish/search for a closest vector using a large number of samples $\langle w, t \rangle$, either using many dual vectors w or many targets t, and taking appropriate sums as defined in the decoders. As the terms of the summation are approximately identically distributed[4], by the central limit theorem we expect the output of the decoder to be approximately Gaussian, with the above means and variances.

Assuming that the output distributions are perfectly Gaussian, as sketched in Fig. 2b, we can distinguish with constant errors iff μ/σ is at least constant, with the ratio implying the distinguishing advantage. Considering the squares of this quantity for convenience, for the AR and NP decoders we have:

$$\frac{\mathbb{E}\left[f_{\mathrm{AR}}^{(\mathcal{W})}(t)\right]^2}{\mathrm{Var}\left[f_{\mathrm{AR}}^{(\mathcal{W})}(t)\right]} \approx \frac{\mathbb{E}\left[f_{\mathrm{NP}}^{(\mathcal{W})}(t)\right]^2}{\mathrm{Var}\left[f_{\mathrm{NP}}^{(\mathcal{W})}(t)\right]} \approx 2 \sum_{w \in \mathcal{W}} \rho_{1/s}(w)^2. \tag{21}$$

As long as this quantity is at least constant, we can confidently distinguish between planted and random targets. For the simple decoder we get a slightly different expression for this ratio:

$$\frac{\mathbb{E}\left[f_{\mathrm{simple}}^{(\mathcal{W})}(t)\right]^2}{\mathrm{Var}\left[f_{\mathrm{simple}}^{(\mathcal{W})}(t)\right]} \approx \frac{2}{|\mathcal{W}|}\left(\sum_{w \in \mathcal{W}} \rho_{1/s}(w)\right)^2. \tag{22}$$

Observe that the Cauchy–Schwarz inequality applied to the $|\mathcal{W}|$-dimensional vectors $x = (1)_{w \in \mathcal{W}}$ and $y = (\rho_{1/s}(w))_{w \in \mathcal{W}}$ shows that this quantity for the simple decoder is never larger than for the other two decoders, with equality only iff the weights $\rho_{1/s}(w)$ are all the same. As we wish to maximize this ratio to maximize our distinguishing advantage, the simple decoder is not better than the other decoders, and is not much worse if vectors in $\mathcal{W}$ have similar norms.

A similar argument can be used to analyze the costs of the gradient ascent approach. To make progress, we need the gradient to point in the direction of c, starting from t: as long as the gradient is pointing in this direction, a small step in the direction of the gradient will bring us closer to c. Studying the associated random variable $\langle \nabla f^{(\mathcal{W})}(t), t - c \rangle$, we again see that by the central limit theorem this will be approximately Gaussian (see full version for details). Considering the ratio between the means and standard deviations, for the AR decoder this quantity scales as:

$$\frac{\mathbb{E}\left[\langle \nabla f_{\mathrm{AR}}^{(\mathcal{W})}(t), t - c \rangle\right]^2}{\mathrm{Var}\left[\langle \nabla f_{\mathrm{AR}}^{(\mathcal{W})}(t), t - c \rangle\right]} = 4\pi s^2 \sum_{w \in \mathcal{W}} \|w\|^2 \rho_{1/s}^2(w). \tag{23}$$

Up to polynomial factors in d (e.g. s^2 and $\|w\|^2$), this is equivalent to the condition for the distinguisher to succeed.

---

[4] For the simple decoder indeed the distribution of each term is identical. Due to the weighing factors $\rho_{1/s}(w)$ in the other two decoders, the terms are not quite identically distributed. However, in most cases of interest, the important contribution to the output distribution comes from a subset of vectors of $\mathcal{W}$ with almost equal norms.

4.2   Closest Vector Problems with Preprocessing

We study two separate applications: (i) we are given a large number of target vectors, and we wish to decide whether they come from the planted target distribution or from the random distribution; and (ii) we have only one target vector and we either want to distinguish correctly or find a closest lattice point to it. The former problem has a lower asymptotic complexity, as it allows us to reuse the shortest dual vector for different targets.

Lemma 2 (Multi-target distinguishing, with preprocessing). *Suppose an arbitrary number of targets $t_1, t_2, \ldots$ is given, which are either all from the random target distribution or all from the planted target distribution with given radius $r \cdot g_d$, for arbitrary $r > 0$. Let $w \in \mathcal{L}^*$ be the shortest dual vector of norm $\|w\| = g_d(1 + o(1))$, and suppose w is known. Then heuristically we can distinguish between these two cases using w in time:*

$$T = 2^{r^2(d+o(d))/(e^2 \ln 2)} \approx 2^{0.195 r^2 (d+o(d))}. \tag{24}$$

For $r = 1$ we need $2^{0.195d+o(d)}$ target vectors to distinguish planted targets from random. This only works when using many targets, as otherwise the dual vectors increase in length and increase the asymptotic complexity. Note that we do not claim to find a closest vector to any of the targets in this amount of time.

We stress that even for $r \gg 1$ we obtain a non-zero distinguishing advantage; as described in the full version, this is because even when planting a target at distance $10 \cdot \lambda_1(\mathcal{L})$, the resulting distribution is slightly different from the uniform distribution (modulo the fundamental domain). As expected, we do observe that for large r the distribution becomes almost indistinguishable from random.

Lemma 3 (Single-target distinguishing, with preprocessing). *Suppose we are given a single target t from either the random target distribution or the planted target distribution with radius $r \cdot g_d$, with $r > 0$ known. Let $w_1, w_2, \cdots \in \mathcal{L}^*$ be the (given) shortest vectors of the dual lattice, and suppose their norms follow the Gaussian heuristic prediction, $\|w_n\| = n^{1/d} g_d(1 + o(1))$. Then heuristically we can distinguish whether t is random or planted in time:*

$$T = \alpha^{d+o(d)}, \qquad (\text{with } \alpha := \min\{\beta : e^2 \ln \beta = \beta^2 r^2\}.) \tag{25}$$

For what approximately corresponds to average-case CVPP, substituting $r = 1$ leads to $\alpha \approx 1.2253$ and $T \approx 2^{0.293d+o(d)}$, where we stress that the constant $0.2931\ldots$ is *not* the same as the $\log_2(3/2)/2 \approx 0.2924\ldots$ exponent of sieving for SVP. For smaller radii the complexities decrease quickly, and similar to the multi-target distinguishing case the complexity scales as $\exp O(r^2 d)$, with the complexity for BDD with preprocessing becoming polynomial when $r = O(\sqrt{(\ln d)/d})$. This is depicted in Figs. 1a and 1b.

For finding closest vectors, Algorithm 2 gives a natural heuristic approach based on a gradient ascent. As argued above, the quantity $\langle \nabla f^{(\mathcal{W})}(t), t - c \rangle$ may be of particular interest. This quantity is sufficiently bounded away from 0 for similar parameters as for distinguishing to work, thereby suggesting that similar asymptotics likely hold for searching and distinguishing. After all, if we can use a distinguisher to correctly determine when we are close to the lattice or not, using it as a black box we can take small steps in well-chosen directions starting from t and determine if we are making progress or not. In the next section we will compare experimental results for searching and distinguishing to further strengthen the following claim.

Lemma 4 (Single-target searching, with preprocessing). *Heuristically we expect to be able to solve the planted closest vector problem with preprocessing with radii $r \cdot g_d$ for $r < 1$ with similar complexities as Lemma 3.*

Finally, while the above results cover distinguishing planted cases at arbitrary radii, and searching close vectors for radii $r < 1$, this does not give any insights how to solve the search version of approximate CVPP. Experimentally, as well as intuitively, it is unclear if any guarantees can be given on the quality of the output of such a gradient ascent method if the algorithm fails to find the nearest lattice point. This may be inherent to the dual approach, similar to how the poor performance for BDD with preprocessing may be inherent to the primal approximate Voronoi cell approach. Note however that we can always achieve the same complexities for approximate CVPP as for "average-case CVPP" (BDDP with radius approaching g_d) as indicated in Figs. 1a and 1b). We leave it as an open problem to study if the dual attack can be improved for approximate CVPP, compared to exact CVPP.

4.3 Closest Vector Problems Without Preprocessing

While the previous results focused on being given the short dual vectors, here we will take into account the costs for generating these dual vectors as well. We will focus on using some form of sieving based block reduction, which covers the most sensible, efficient choices of preprocessing before running the dual attack.

Lemma 5 (Single-target searching, without preprocessing). *Heuristically we expect to be able to solve the planted closest vector problem (without preprocessing) with target radius $r \cdot g_d$ for $r = d^\alpha$, $\alpha < 0$, in time T as follows:*

$$T = (3/2)^{(d+o(d))/(2-4\alpha)} \approx 2^{0.292(d+o(d))/(1-2\alpha)}. \tag{26}$$

As for the other results, a derivation can be found in the full version. The resulting trade-offs between the radius r and the time complexity T are depicted in Figs. 1c and 1d. These figures are similar to the plots for the preprocessing case, except that the x-axes have been stretched out significantly; to reduce the constant in the exponent one needs r to scale polynomially with d (as opposed to $r = O(1)$ for the preprocessing case), and to achieve polynomial time complexity one needs $r = 2^{-O(d)}$ (cf. $r = O(\sqrt{\log d/d})$ for the preprocessing case). Note that the latter regime matches what we intuitively expect; a BDD instance with exponentially small radius can also be solved in polynomial time using LLL basis reduction followed by one of Babai's algorithms.

Finally, similar to the preprocessing case we do not expect the dual approach to work well for solving approximate CVP. Finding a way to give better guarantees for approximate CVP(P), or showing that the dual attack is unable to solve this problem efficiently, is left as an open problem.

5 Experiments

5.1 Setup

To verify our assumptions and the heuristic estimates, we conducted the following experiments. We used G6K [ADH+19] to compute a large set of short vectors $\mathcal{W}_d$ for the SVP challenge lattice (seed 0) in dimension $d \in \{55, 60, 65, 70, 75, 80\}$ by extracting the vectors in the sieving database after a full sieve on these lattices. In the full version we give some more details on the databases we used. We treated the challenge lattices as the dual of the lattices we target to solve BDD for and created samples from the planted target distribution with parameter $r \cdot g_d$, where we arbitrarily fixed the closest lattice point to be $\mathbf{0}$.

5.2 Evaluating the Distinguishers

Our first experiment was targeted at verifying the heuristic complexity of the distinguishing algorithms and comparing the three different score functions. For this, we chose 1000 different targets of length rg_d for various $r \in [0.5, 0.9]$. For each of them, we computed the score functions f_j for $j \in \{\text{simple}, \text{AR}, \text{NP}\}$ using the i shortest vectors of $\mathcal{W}_d$. We denote the resulting set of scores as $f_j^i(\mathcal{W}_d, r)$. (For practicality reasons we only computed $f_j^i(\mathcal{W}_d, r)$ for i being multiples of 100.) Additionally, we computed the score functions $\hat{f}_j^i(\mathcal{W}_d, r)$ for targets from the random target distribution, i.e. we chose $\langle t, w \rangle$ uniformly at random from $[-0.5, 0.5]$ for all dual vectors w. We now evaluated how well the score functions can distinguish between targets at distance rg_d from the random target distribution. Let $p \in [0, 0.5)$ be a parameter. For each r we computed the minimal i such that $f_j^i(\mathcal{W}_d, r)$ and $\hat{f}_j^i(\mathcal{W}_d, r)$ overlap by at most a p-fraction. In other words, we computed the minimal i such that the p-percentile of $f_j^i(\mathcal{W}_d, r)$ is larger than the $(1-p)$-percentile of $\hat{f}_j^i(\mathcal{W}_d, r)$. Additionally, we computed two types of predictions for the distinguishing complexity. First, we used the vectors in $\mathcal{W}_d$ to predict the complexity of the f_{AR} distinguisher by assuming that the result of the score function under the planted and random target distributions was a perfect Gaussian. We call this the data dependent (d.d.) estimate. Second, we also estimated the complexity in a similar way, but by assuming that $\mathcal{W}_d$ contained all the shortest vectors in the dual lattice and that the lengths of these followed the distribution given by the Gaussian heuristic. We denote this by the data independent (d.i.) estimate. The results show that the estimates are very close to the experimental data, which in turn verifies the assumption that the result of the score function can indeed be well approximated by a Gaussian. For f_{simple} this was independently verified in [EJK20] in a similar setting.

Exemplary results are plotted in Figs. 3a and 3b, for varying radius and dimension, respectively, and $p = 0.1$. They represent typical examples from our data sets. We fitted models to the curves to evaluate the dependency of the practical complexity on r (d, resp.). Figure 1a suggests that at least for r not too close to 1, the dependency on r should be roughly quadratic. If all dual vectors in the database had length $\|\boldsymbol{w}\| = g_d$, we would expect a curve of the form $\exp((d/e^2)r^2) + O(1)$. However, there are longer vectors in our sets $\mathcal{W}_d$, and the vectors are used in increasing length. This has a progressively negative effect on the complexity, which explains the worse constants computed for the curves in Fig. 3a. On the other hand, the curves in Fig. 3b adhere very closely to the heuristic value computed in Lemma 3. The slight variances in the leading constant in the exponent can be easily explained with the small set of data points used to fit the curves. Finally, we see that the score functions all perform similarly well. Since f_{simple} is the fastest to compute, this will likely give the best results in practice for distinguishing.

5.3   Evaluating the Search Algorithms

In the second part of our experiments, we evaluated the decoding algorithm based on gradient ascent. During our experiments we noticed that f_{AR} and f_{simple} perform similarly well, so we arbitrarily choose to report the results for f_{AR}. We chose the step size such that the update corresponds to (13) as a sensible first guess. Otherwise, the methodology was similar to the previous set of experiments. We only performed one step of the gradient ascent algorithm and declared success if it resulted in a target closer to the lattice than the initial target. Intuitively, since after a successful first step the problem becomes easier, this should be a good proxy for the success probability of the full algorithm. Exemplary results are given in Figs. 3c and 3d again depending on r and the dimension d, respectively. The results are similar to the distinguishing case, with close adherence to the heuristic estimate of Lemma 3 w.r.t. the dependence on d. As expected, the success probability only affects constant factors in the complexity.

In the previous experiments, we only considered the gradient ascent method with a fixed step size given by the analysis in Sect. 3.5. Since we only compute an approximation of the true step, it stands to reason that in some cases a poor approximation may lead to failure of the algorithm, even though the computed update is roughly pointing in the right direction. One may hope to reduce the number of such cases by reducing the step size. This should give a trade-off between the success probability of the algorithm and the running time. In order to evaluate the potential of this approach, we repeated the above experiments, but we now deemed any trial successful where the first update $\boldsymbol{u}$ satisfied $\langle \boldsymbol{u}, \boldsymbol{e} \rangle < 0$, where $\boldsymbol{e}$ is the error vector of the target. If this is satisfied, this implies that there is a step size such that the update succeeds in reducing the distance to the lattice. The results are shown in Figs. 3e and 3f, analogously to the ones

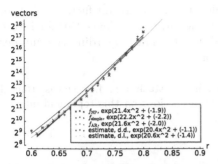

(a) Complexity of distinguishing the planted target distribution with radius $r \cdot g_d$ from the random target distribution with success probability 0.90 in dimension 80.

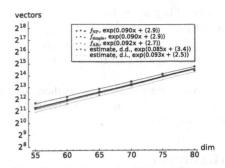

(b) Complexity of distinguishing a planted target with radius $0.75 \cdot g_d$ from a random target with success probability 0.90. The theoretical estimate from Lemma 3 is $\exp(0.0913d + o(d))$.

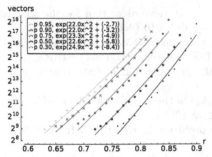

(c) Complexity of decoding a target at distance $r \cdot g_d$ with success probability p in dimension 80.

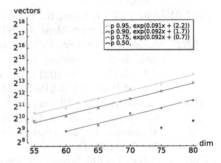

(d) Complexity of decoding a target with radius $0.75 \cdot g_d$ with success probability p. Lemma 4 predicts $\exp(0.0913d+o(d))$.

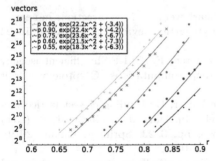

(e) "Lower bound" for complexity of decoding a target with radius $r \cdot g_d$ in dimension 80 with success probability p.

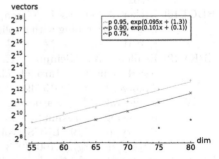

(f) "Lower bound" for complexity of decoding a target with radius $0.75 \cdot g_d$ with success probability p.

Fig. 3. Exemplary results, for distinguishing (a, b), decoding (c, d), and a "lower bound" (e, f). Left (a, c, e): $d = 80$ fixed, varying r. Right (b, d, f): $r = 0.75$ fixed, varying d.

above. They show that the results only differ in small constant factors ($\lesssim e$). In practice, it might be worth exploring this trade-off, but we leave this for future work. In the full version we give some additional results regarding the number of steps required to recover the target vector.

Acknowledgments. The authors thank Sauvik Bhattacharya, Léo Ducas, Rachel Player, and Christine van Vredendaal for early discussions on this topic and on preliminary results.

References

[ADH+19] Albrecht, M.R., Ducas, L., Herold, G., Kirshanova, E., Postlethwaite, E.W., Stevens, M.: The general sieve kernel and new records in lattice reduction. In: Ishai, Y., Rijmen, V. (eds.) EUROCRYPT 2019. LNCS, vol. 11477, pp. 717–746. Springer, Cham (2019). https://doi.org/10.1007/978-3-030-17656-3_25

[AKS01] Ajtai, M., Kumar, R., Sivakumar, D.: A sieve algorithm for the shortest lattice vector problem. In: STOC, pp. 601–610 (2001)

[AN17] Aono, Y., Nguyen, P.Q.: Random sampling revisited: lattice enumeration with discrete pruning. In: Coron, J.-S., Nielsen, J.B. (eds.) EUROCRYPT 2017. LNCS, vol. 10211, pp. 65–102. Springer, Cham (2017). https://doi.org/10.1007/978-3-319-56614-6_3

[APS15] Albrecht, M.R., Player, R., Scott, S.: On the concrete hardness of learning with errors. J. Math. Cryptol. **9**, 1–38 (2015)

[AR04] Aharonov, D., Regev, O.: Lattice problems in NP∩coNP. In: FOCS, pp. 362–371 (2004)

[Bab86] Babai, L.: On Lovasz lattice reduction and the nearest lattice point problem. Combinatorica **6**(1), 1–13 (1986)

[BBD09] Bernstein, D.J., Buchmann, J., Dahmen, E. (eds.): Post-quantum Cryptography. Springer, Heidelberg (2009). https://doi.org/10.1007/978-3-540-88702-7

[BDGL16] Becker, A., Ducas, L., Gama, N., Laarhoven, T.: New directions in nearest neighbor searching with applications to lattice sieving. In: SODA, pp. 10–24 (2016)

[BKV19] Beullens, W., Kleinjung, T., Vercauteren, F.: CSI-FiSh: efficient isogeny based signatures through class group computations. Cryptology ePrint Archive, Report 2019/498 (2019)

[DLdW19] Doulgerakis, E., Laarhoven, T., de Weger, B.: Finding closest lattice vectors using approximate Voronoi cells. In: Ding, J., Steinwandt, R. (eds.) PQCrypto 2019. LNCS, vol. 11505, pp. 3–22. Springer, Cham (2019). https://doi.org/10.1007/978-3-030-25510-7_1

[DLdW20] Doulgerakis, E., Laarhoven, T., de Weger, B.: Sieve, enumerate, slice, and lift: hybrid lattice algorithms for SVP via CVPP. In: Nitaj, A., Youssef, A. (eds.) AFRICACRYPT 2020. LNCS, vol. 12174, pp. 301–320. Springer, Cham (2020). https://doi.org/10.1007/978-3-030-51938-4_15

[DLvW20] Ducas, L., Laarhoven, T., van Woerden, W.P.J.: The randomized slicer for CVPP: sharper, faster, smaller, batchier. In: Kiayias, A., Kohlweiss, M., Wallden, P., Zikas, V. (eds.) PKC 2020. LNCS, vol. 12111, pp. 3–36. Springer, Cham (2020). https://doi.org/10.1007/978-3-030-45388-6_1

[DRS14] Dadush, D., Regev, O., Stephens-Davidowitz, N.: On the closest vector problem with a distance guarantee. In: CCC, pp. 98–109 (2014)

[DSvW21] Ducas, L., Stevens, M., van Woerden, W.: Advanced lattice sieving on GPUs, with tensor cores. Cryptology ePrint Archive, Report 2021/141 (2021). https://eprint.iacr.org/2021/141

[Duc18] Ducas, L.: Shortest vector from lattice sieving: a few dimensions for free. In: Nielsen, J.B., Rijmen, V. (eds.) EUROCRYPT 2018. LNCS, vol. 10820, pp. 125–145. Springer, Cham (2018). https://doi.org/10.1007/978-3-319-78381-9_5

[EJK20] Espitau, T., Joux, A., Kharchenko, N.: On a hybrid approach to solve small secret LWE. Cryptology ePrint Archive, Report 2020/515 (2020). https://eprint.iacr.org/2020/515

[Gen09] Gentry, C.: Fully homomorphic encryption using ideal lattices. In: STOC, pp. 169–178 (2009)

[GN08]   Gama, N., Nguyen, P.Q.: Finding short lattice vectors within mordell's inequality. In: STOC, pp. 207–216. ACM (2008)

[HKM18] Herold, G., Kirshanova, E., May, A.: On the asymptotic complexity of solving LWE. Des. Codes Crypt. **86**, 55–83 (2018)

[Kan83] Ravi Kannan. Improved algorithms for integer programming and related lattice problems. In: STOC, pp. 193–206 (1983)

[Kan87] Kannan, R.: Minkowski's convex body theorem and integer programming. Math. Oper. Res. **12**(3), 415–440 (1987)

[Laa16a] Laarhoven, T.: Search problems in cryptography. Ph.D. thesis, Eindhoven University of Technology (2016)

[Laa16b] Laarhoven, T.: Sieving for closest lattice vectors (with preprocessing). In: Avanzi, R., Heys, H. (eds.) SAC 2016. LNCS, vol. 10532, pp. 523–542. Springer, Cham (2017). https://doi.org/10.1007/978-3-319-69453-5_28

[Laa20] Laarhoven, T.: Approximate Voronoi cells for lattices, revisited. J. Math. Cryptol. **15**(1), 60–71 (2020)

[LLM06] Liu, Y.-K., Lyubashevsky, V., Micciancio, D.: On bounded distance decoding for general lattices. In: Díaz, J., Jansen, K., Rolim, J.D.P., Zwick, U. (eds.) APPROX/RANDOM -2006. LNCS, vol. 4110, pp. 450–461. Springer, Heidelberg (2006). https://doi.org/10.1007/11830924_41

[LP11]   Lindner, R., Peikert, C.: Better key sizes (and attacks) for LWE-based encryption. In: Kiayias, A. (ed.) CT-RSA 2011. LNCS, vol. 6558, pp. 319–339. Springer, Heidelberg (2011). https://doi.org/10.1007/978-3-642-19074-2_21

[MV10]   Micciancio, D., Voulgaris, P.: A deterministic single exponential time algorithm for most lattice problems based on Voronoi cell computations. In: STOC, pp. 351–358 (2010)

[MW15]   Micciancio, D., Walter, M.: Fast lattice point enumeration with minimal overhead. In: SODA, pp. 276–294 (2015)

[MW16]   Micciancio, D., Walter, M.: Practical, predictable lattice basis reduction. In: Fischlin, M., Coron, J.-S. (eds.) EUROCRYPT 2016. LNCS, vol. 9665, pp. 820–849. Springer, Heidelberg (2016). https://doi.org/10.1007/978-3-662-49890-3_31

[NP33]   Jerzy Neyman and Egon Sharpe Pearson: On the problem of the most efficient tests of statistical hypotheses. Phil. Trans. R. Soc. Lond. A **231**(694–706), 289–337 (1933)

[oSN17] The National Institute of Standards and Technology (NIST). Post-quantum cryptography (2017)

[PMHS19] Pellet-Mary, A., Hanrot, G., Stehlé, D.: Approx-SVP in ideal lattices with pre-processing. In: Ishai, Y., Rijmen, V. (eds.) EUROCRYPT 2019. LNCS, vol. 11477, pp. 685–716. Springer, Cham (2019). https://doi.org/10.1007/978-3-030-17656-3_24

[Reg05] Regev, O.: On lattices, learning with errors, random linear codes, and cryptography. In: STOC, pp. 84–93 (2005)

[Reg10] Regev, O.: The learning with errors problem (invited survey). In: CCC, pp. 191–204 (2010)

[Sch87] Schnorr, C.-P.: A hierarchy of polynomial time lattice basis reduction algorithms. Theoret. Comput. Sci. **53**(2–3), 201–224 (1987)

[SE94] Schnorr, C.-P., Euchner, M.: Lattice basis reduction: improved practical algorithms and solving subset sum problems. Math. Program. **66**(2–3), 181–199 (1994)

[Sho94] Shor, P.W.: Algorithms for quantum computation: discrete logarithms and factoring. In: FOCS, pp. 124–134 (1994)

[SSTX09] Stehlé, D., Steinfeld, R., Tanaka, K., Xagawa, K.: Efficient public key encryption based on ideal lattices. In: Matsui, M. (ed.) ASIACRYPT 2009. LNCS, vol. 5912, pp. 617–635. Springer, Heidelberg (2009). https://doi.org/10.1007/978-3-642-10366-7_36

[svp20] SVP challenge (2020). http://latticechallenge.org/svp-challenge/

On the Hardness of Module-LWE
with Binary Secret

Katharina Boudgoust[(✉)], Corentin Jeudy, Adeline Roux-Langlois,
and Weiqiang Wen

Univ Rennes, CNRS, IRISA, Rennes, France
katharina.boudgoust@irisa.fr

Abstract. We prove that the *Module Learning With Errors* (M-LWE)
problem with binary secrets and rank d is at least as hard as the standard version of M-LWE with uniform secret and rank k, where the rank
increases from k to $d \geq (k+1)\log_2 q + \omega(\log_2 n)$, and the Gaussian noise
from α to $\beta = \alpha \cdot \Theta(n^2\sqrt{d})$, where n is the ring degree and q the modulus. Our work improves on the recent work by Boudgoust et al. in 2020
by a factor of $\sqrt{md}$ in the Gaussian noise, where m is the number of
given M-LWE samples, when q fulfills some number-theoretic requirements. We use a different approach than Boudgoust et al. to achieve this
hardness result by adapting the previous work from Brakerski et al. in
2013 for the *Learning With Errors* problem to the module setting. The
proof applies to cyclotomic fields, but most results hold for a larger class
of number fields, and may be of independent interest.

Keywords: Lattice-based cryptography · Module learning with
errors · Binary secret

1 Introduction

Lattice-based cryptography has become more and more popular over the past
two decades as lattices offer a variety of presumed hard problems as security foundations for public-key cryptographic primitives. Lattices, which are discrete sub-
groups of the Euclidean space, provide several computational problems that are
conjectured to be hard to solve with respect to both classical and quantum computers. One central problem is the *Shortest Vector Problem* (SVP), which asks to
find a shortest non-zero vector from the given lattice. SVP also appears in a decisional variant (GapSVP), and its approximate counterpart (GapSVP$_\gamma$). The latter asks to decide if the norm of such a vector is less than a threshold r or greater
than γr for a factor $\gamma \geq 1$. The security of most lattice-based primitives are however based on average-case problems, such as the *Learning With Errors* (LWE)
problem introduced by Regev [Reg05, Reg09]. This problem emerges in two
versions: its *search* variant asks to find the secret $\mathbf{s} \in \mathbb{Z}_q^n$ given samples of
the form $(\mathbf{a}, q^{-1}\langle\mathbf{a}, \mathbf{s}\rangle + e)$, where $\mathbf{a}$ is uniform over $\mathbb{Z}_q^n$ and e a small error
over $\mathbb{T} = \mathbb{R}/\mathbb{Z}$. The *decisional* variant asks to distinguish between such samples

© Springer Nature Switzerland AG 2021
K. G. Paterson (Ed.): CT-RSA 2021, LNCS 12704, pp. 503–526, 2021.
https://doi.org/10.1007/978-3-030-75539-3_21

for a uniform $\mathbf{s} \in \mathbb{Z}_q^n$, and uniformly random samples in $\mathbb{Z}_q^n \times \mathbb{T}$. We use LWE to denote the latter. The error is usually sampled from a Gaussian distribution D_α of parameter $\alpha > 0$. The appeal of the LWE problem comes from its ties with well-known lattice problems like GapSVP_γ. It enjoys both quantum [Reg05] and classical [Pei09, BLP+13] worst-case to average-case reductions from GapSVP_γ, making it a firm candidate for cryptographic constructions. The LWE problem opened the way to a wide variety of simple to advanced cryptographic primitives ranging from public-key encryption [Reg05, GPV08, MP12], fully-homomorphic encryption [BGV12, BV14, DM15], recently to non-interactive zero-knowledge proofs [PS19], and many others.

Although LWE provides provably secure cryptosystems, all these schemes lack efficiency which motivates the research around structured variants. These variants gain in efficiency by considering the ring of integers of a number field (R-LWE) [LPR10, RSW18], a ring of polynomials (P-LWE) [SSTX09] or a module over a number field (M-LWE) [BGV12, LS15]. In this work, we focus on the latter as it offers a nice security-efficiency trade-off by bridging LWE and R-LWE. Let K be a number field of degree n and R its ring of integers. We use d to denote the module rank and q for the modulus. We also define the quotient ring $R_q = R/qR$, the real tensor field $K_\mathbb{R} = K \otimes_\mathbb{Q} \mathbb{R}$ and the torus $\mathbb{T}_{R^\vee} = K_\mathbb{R}/R^\vee$, where $R^\vee$ is the dual ideal of R. The secret is now chosen in $(R_q^\vee)^d$, and the error from a distribution ψ over $K_\mathbb{R}$. The *Search*-M-LWE problem asks to recover the secret $\mathbf{s} \in (R_q^\vee)^d$ from arbitrarily many samples $(\mathbf{a}, q^{-1}\langle \mathbf{a},\mathbf{s}\rangle + e \bmod R^\vee)$, for $\mathbf{a}$ uniformly random over R_q^d and e sampled from ψ. In this work, we only consider the decisional variant denoted by M-LWE, where one has to distinguish such samples for a uniformly random secret $\mathbf{s} \in (R_q^\vee)^d$, from uniformly random samples in $R_q^d \times \mathbb{T}_{R^\vee}$. It also benefits from a worst-case to average-case reduction, first shown by Langlois and Stehlé [LS15] through a quantum reduction, and recently by Boudgoust et al. [BJRW20] through a classical reduction for a module rank $d \geq 2n$, where n is the ring degree. The underlying lattice problems are though restricted to *module lattices*, which correspond to finitely generated R-modules, where R is the ring of integers of a number field.

In practice, the LWE problem is often used with a *small* secret, i.e., Gaussian (Hermite-Normal-Form-LWE) or even binary (bin-LWE). The latter corresponds to choosing the secret $\mathbf{s}$ in $\{0,1\}^n$, and it is particularly interesting as it simplifies computations and thus increases efficiency. Modulus-rank switching techniques [BLP+13, AD17, WW19] rely on using small secrets as it keeps the noise blowup to a minimum. The binary secret variant also happens to be essential for some FHE schemes as in [DM15]. First studied by Goldwasser et al. [GKPV10], it is later improved by Brakerski et al. [BLP+13] and Micciancio [Mic18] using more technical proofs. Recent work by Brakerski and Döttling [BD20] extends the hardness to more general secret distributions. The question of whether these hardness results for bin-LWE carry over to the module setting was left open. As part of the proof of the classical hardness of M-LWE, a first reduction was proposed from M-LWE to bin-M-LWE using the Rényi divergence by Boudgoust et al. [BJRW20]. The reduction increases the module rank from k to d by roughly a $\log_2 q$ factor, which allows to preserve the complexity of an exhaustive search, while increasing the noise by a factor $n^2 d\sqrt{m}$, where m is the number of samples, n the ring degree and d the final module rank. Another very recent paper by Lin et al. [LWW20] uses the noise lossiness argument from [BD20] to prove the hardness of M-LWE for general entropic distributions.

Our Contributions. In this paper, we give an alternative approach to prove the hardness of M-LWE with binary secrets over cyclotomic fields. The result is summarized in an informal way in the following. For a more formal statement, we refer to Theorem 2.

Theorem 1 (Informal). *For a cyclotomic field of degree n, the* bin-M-LWE *problem with rank d and Gaussian parameter less than β is at least as hard as* M-LWE *with rank k and Gaussian parameter α, if $d \geq (k+1)\log_2 q + \omega(\log_2 n)$ and $\beta/\alpha = \Theta(n^2\sqrt{d})$, where q is a modulus such that the cyclotomic polynomial has a specific splitting behavior in $\mathbb{Z}_q[x]$.*

Note that the increase in the noise does not depend on the number of provided bin-M-LWE samples, in contrast to [BJRW20]. In the hope of achieving better parameters than [BJRW20], which is inspired by the proof of [GKPV10], we follow the proof idea of Brakerski et al. [BLP+13] by introducing the two intermediate problems first-is-errorless M-LWE and ext-M-LWE. We first reduce M-LWE to the first-is-errorless M-LWE variant, where the first sample is not perturbed by an error. We then reduce the latter to ext-M-LWE, which can be seen as M-LWE with an extra information on the error vector $\mathbf{e}$ given by $\langle\mathbf{e},\mathbf{z}\rangle$ for a uniformly chosen $\mathbf{z}$ in the set of binary ring elements set $\mathcal{Z} = (R_2^\vee)^d$. In the work of Alperin-Sheriff and Apon [AA16] for their reduction from M-LWE to the deterministic variant Module Learning With Rounding, the authors introduce a variant of ext-M-LWE that gives $\mathrm{Tr}(\langle\mathbf{e},\mathbf{z}\rangle)$ to the attacker instead. This variant is not suited for our reduction due to our lossy argument in Lemma 17. The field trace does not provide enough information to reconstruct $\mathbf{N}^T\mathbf{z}$ from the hint, where $\mathbf{N}$ is our Gaussian matrix. We discuss further the differences in Sects. 3.2 and 3.3. We then use a lossy argument, relying on the newly derived ext-M-LWE hardness assumption and a ring version of the leftover hash lemma, to reduce ext-M-LWE to bin-M-LWE. An overview of the full reduction is provided in Fig. 1.

The main challenge is the use of matrices composed of ring elements. The proof in [BLP+13, Lemma 4.7] requires the construction of unimodular matrices which is not straightforward to adapt in the module setting because of invertibility issues. The construction in Lemma 15 relies on units of the quotient ring R/qR, which are much harder to describe than the units of $\mathbb{Z}/q\mathbb{Z}$ to say the least. This is the reason why we need to control the splitting structure of the cyclotomic polynomial modulo q. Lemma 2 [LS18, Theorem 1.1] solves this issue but requires q to satisfy certain number-theoretic properties and to be sufficiently large so that all the non-zero binary ring elements are units of R_q. The second complication comes from using both the coefficient embedding and

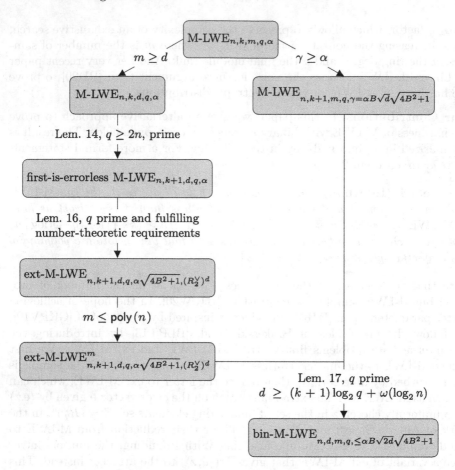

Fig. 1. Summary of the proof of Theorem 2, where $B = \max_{x \in R_2} \|\sigma(x)\|_\infty$ and σ is the canonical embedding. In cyclotomic fields, we have $B \leq n$. Note that Lemma 17 uses d samples from ext-M-LWE, where d is the module rank in bin-M-LWE. The assumptions on q concern the splitting behavior of the cyclotomic polynomial in $\mathbb{Z}_q[x]$, and are discussed in Sect. 3.3.

the canonical embedding. Even though some manipulations on Gaussian distributions require the use of the canonical embedding, we choose the secret to be binary in the coefficient embedding rather than the canonical embedding. As discussed in Sect. 3.1 for power-of-two cyclotomics, using the canonical embedding for binary secrets requires the rank d to be larger by a factor n than when using the coefficient embedding.

In the whole reduction, the ring degree n, number of samples m and modulus q are preserved, where m needs to be larger than d and q needs to be a prime satisfying certain number-theoretic properties. With the help of the modulus-switching technique of Langlois and Stehlé [LS15, Theorem 4.8], we can then relax the restriction on the modulus q to be any polynomially large modulus, at the expense of a loss in the Gaussian noise. The ranks must satisfy $d \geq (k+1)\log_2 q + \omega(\log_2 n)$, in the same manner as in [BJRW20]. However, our noise growth is smaller as our Gaussian parameter only increases by a factor $n\sqrt{2d}\sqrt{4n^2+1} = \Theta(n^2\sqrt{d})$ for cyclotomics. Our reduction removes the dependency in m in the noise ratio $n^2d\sqrt{m}$ present in [BJRW20], which is more advantageous as we usually take $m = O(n\log_2 n)$ samples, and also gains an extra factor $\sqrt{d}$. As we directly show the hardness of decision bin-M-LWE one does not need the extra search-to-decision step in [BJRW20] which overall improves their classical hardness proof. Our result implies the hardness of M-LWE with a small (with respect to coefficients) secret and a moderate rank (e.g., $\omega(\log_2 n)$), which holds even with arbitrarily many samples. For a flexible choice of parameters (allowing efficiency optimizations), NIST candidates [BDK+18, DKL+18] considered M-LWE variants with a small secret and also a small rank, while restricting the number of samples to be small (e.g., linear in n) for ruling out the BKW type of attacks [KF15]. It is difficult to compare our result to the work by Lin et al. [LWW20] as their reduction does not use the coefficient embedding for the entropic secret distribution. Additionally, when bridging to LWE, the noise ratio is improved to $\sqrt{10d}$ as our construction in Lemma 15 matches the one from [BLP+13, Claim 4.6]. Our work thus matches the results from Brakerski et al. [BLP+13] when we take the ring R to be of degree 1.

The entire reduction is so far limited to cyclotomic fields due to Lemmas 14 and 15. However, the other results are proven for a larger class of number fields, namely for the number fields $K = \mathbb{Q}(\zeta)$ such that their ring of integers is $R = \mathbb{Z}[\zeta]$, where ζ is an algebraic number. It ensures that R and its dual $R^\vee$ are linked by the equality $R^\vee = (f'(\zeta))^{-1}R$, where f is the minimal polynomial of ζ, and it also ensures the unique factorization of ideals. This class includes cyclotomic fields, quadratic fields $K = \mathbb{Q}(\sqrt{d})$ for square-free d with $d \neq 1 \bmod 4$, and number fields with f of square-free discriminant. These parts of the reduction can be extended to other number fields by using the quantity $B = \max_{x \in R_2} \|\sigma(x)\|_\infty$ introduced in Sect. 2.1, which we use throughout Sects. 3.3 and 3.4. The infinity norm here is simply the infinity norm over $\mathbb{C}^n$, and σ the canonical embedding. We discuss how to upper-bound B in Lemma 1, but in the case of cyclotomic fields we simply have $B \leq n$. Extending Lemmas 14 and 15 to this broader class of number fields may however require additional constraints.

Open Problems. In this paper, most of our results rely on the class of number fields $K = \mathbb{Q}(\zeta)$ where the ring of integers is $R = \mathbb{Z}[\zeta]$. Although this class includes all cyclotomic fields, we leave as an open problem to generalize these results to a larger class of number fields.

The leftover hash lemma used in the reduction of Lemma 17 requires the module rank d to be super-logarithmic in n. The proof of hardness of M-LWE with binary secret thus remains open for a lower module rank. In practice, a constant rank is used for increased efficiency, like the CRYSTALS-Kyber [BDK+18] candidate at the NIST standardization competition [NIS]. The interest in a lower module rank also stems from the extreme case $d = 1$ which corresponds to R-LWE. The hardness of bin-R-LWE remains an open problem.

The construction in Lemma 15 seems optimized in terms of its impact on the Gaussian parameter. However, its invertibility restricts the underlying number field, as well as the structure of the chosen modulus q. A better understanding of the unit group of R_q for general cyclotomic fields and other number fields might help relax the restrictions on the modulus q for the reduction to go through.

2   Preliminaries

Throughout the paper, q denotes a positive integer, $\mathbb{Z}_q$ denotes the ring of integers modulo q. In a ring R, we write (p) for the principal ideal generated by $p \in R$, and R_p for the quotient ring $R/(p) = R/pR$. For simplicity, we denote by $[n]$ the set $\{1, \ldots, n\}$ for any positive integer n. Vectors and matrices are written in bold and their transpose (resp. Hermitian) is denoted by superscript T (resp. $\dagger$). We denote the Euclidean norm and infinity norm of $\mathbb{C}^n$ by $\|\cdot\|_2$ and $\|\cdot\|_\infty$ respectively. We also define the *spectral norm* of any matrix $\mathbf{A} \in \mathbb{C}^{n \times m}$ by $\|\mathbf{A}\|_2 = \max_{\mathbf{x} \in \mathbb{C}^m \setminus \{0\}} \|\mathbf{A}\mathbf{x}\|_2 / \|\mathbf{x}\|_2$, and the *max norm* as $\|\mathbf{A}\|_{\max} = \max_{i \in [n], j \in [m]} |a_{i,j}|$. The statistical distance between two discrete distribution P and Q over a countable set S is defined by $\Delta(P, Q) = \frac{1}{2} \sum_{x \in S} |P(x) - Q(x)|$, with integration for continuous distributions. The uniform distribution over a finite set S is denoted by $U(S)$, and we use $x \hookleftarrow P$ to denote sampling x according to P.

2.1   Algebraic Number Theory Background

A complex number ζ is called an *algebraic number* if it is root of a polynomial over $\mathbb{Q}$. The monic polynomial f of minimal degree among such polynomials is called *the minimal polynomial* or *defining polynomial* of ζ, and is unique. If the minimal polynomial of ζ only has integer coefficients, then ζ is called an *algebraic integer*. A *number field* $K = \mathbb{Q}(\zeta)$ is the finite field extension of the rationals by adjoining the algebraic number ζ. Its degree is defined as the degree of the minimal polynomial of ζ. We define the tensor field $K_\mathbb{R} = K \otimes_\mathbb{Q} \mathbb{R}$ which can be seen as the finite field extension of the reals by adjoining ζ. The set of all algebraic integers in K is a ring called the *ring of integers*, and we denote it by R. We always have $\mathbb{Z}[\zeta] \subseteq R$, but only special classes of number fields verify $\mathbb{Z}[\zeta] = R$. Among them, there are cyclotomic fields, which correspond to number fields where ζ is a primitive ν-th root of unity, for an integer ν. The ν-th cyclotomic number field has degree $n = \varphi(\nu)$, where φ is Euler's totient function. In this case, the minimal polynomial is $f = \Phi_\nu = \prod_{j \in [n]} (x - \alpha_j)$, where the α_j are the distinct primitive ν-th roots of unity. For the power-of-two cyclotomic field where $\nu = 2^{\ell+1}$, it yields $n = \varphi(\nu) = 2^\ell$, and $\Phi_\nu = x^n + 1$.

The Space H. We use t_1 to denote the number of real roots of the minimal polynomial of the underlying number field, and t_2 the number of pairs of complex conjugate roots, which yields $n = t_1 + 2t_2$. The space $H \subseteq \mathbb{C}^n$ is defined by $H =$

$\left\{ \mathbf{x} \in \mathbb{R}^{t_1} \times \mathbb{C}^{2t_2} : \forall j \in [t_2], x_{t_1+t_2+j} = \overline{x_{t_1+j}} \right\}$. We can verify that H is a $\mathbb{R}$-vector space of dimension n with the columns of $\mathbf{H}$ as orthonormal basis, where

$$\mathbf{H} = \begin{bmatrix} \mathbf{I}_{t_1} & 0 & 0 \\ 0 & \frac{1}{\sqrt{2}}\mathbf{I}_{t_2} & \frac{i}{\sqrt{2}}\mathbf{I}_{t_2} \\ 0 & \frac{1}{\sqrt{2}}\mathbf{I}_{t_2} & \frac{-i}{\sqrt{2}}\mathbf{I}_{t_2} \end{bmatrix}, \text{ with } \mathbf{I}_k \text{ the identity matrix of size } k.$$

Coefficient Embedding. A number field $K = \mathbb{Q}(\zeta)$ of degree n can be seen as a $\mathbb{Q}$-vector space of dimension n with basis $\{1, \zeta, \ldots, \zeta^{n-1}\}$. Hence, every element $x \in K$ can be written as $x = \sum_{j=0}^{n-1} x_j \zeta^j$, with $x_j \in \mathbb{Q}$. The *coefficient embedding* is the isomorphism τ between K and $\mathbb{Q}^n$ that maps every $x \in K$ to its coefficient vector $\tau(x) = [x_0, \ldots, x_{n-1}]^T$. We also extend the coefficient embedding to $K_{\mathbb{R}}$, which yields an isomorphism between $K_{\mathbb{R}}$ and $\mathbb{R}^n$.

Canonical Embedding. All the following definitions extend to $K_{\mathbb{R}}$ in the obvious way. A number field $K = \mathbb{Q}(\zeta)$ with defining polynomial f of degree n has exactly n field homomorphisms $\sigma_i : K \to \mathbb{C}$ that map ζ to each of the distinct roots of the defining polynomial. We denote by $\sigma_1, \ldots, \sigma_{t_1}$ the real embeddings (i.e. the embeddings that map ζ to one of the real roots of f) and $\sigma_{t_1+1}, \ldots, \sigma_{t_1+2t_2}$ the complex ones. Since f is in $\mathbb{Q}[x]$, the fundamental theorem of algebra states that the complex roots come as conjugate pairs, and therefore $\sigma_{t_1+t_2+j} = \overline{\sigma_{t_1+j}}$ for all $j \in [t_2]$. The *canonical embedding* σ is the field homomorphism from K to $\mathbb{C}^n$ defined as $\sigma(x) = [\sigma_1(x), \ldots, \sigma_n(x)]^T$, where the addition and multiplication of vectors is performed component-wise. The range of σ is a subset of H, and therefore we can map any $x \in K$ to $\mathbb{R}^n$ via the map σ_H defined by $\sigma_H(x) = \mathbf{H}^{\dagger} \cdot \sigma(x)$ for all $x \in K$. We also mention that the extension of σ to $K_{\mathbb{R}}$ is an isomorphism from $K_{\mathbb{R}}$ to H. Multiplication is no longer component-wise with σ_H but it can be described by a left multiplication, namely $\sigma_H(x \cdot y) = \mathbf{H}^{\dagger} \cdot \text{diag}(\sigma(x)) \cdot \mathbf{H} \sigma_H(y)$, for any $x, y \in K$. Note that for any $x \in K$, $\mathbf{H}^{\dagger} \cdot \text{diag}(\sigma(x)) \cdot \mathbf{H} \in \mathbb{R}^{n \times n}$, and has the $|\sigma_j(x)|$ as singular values.

We define the trace $\text{Tr} : K \to \mathbb{Q}$ of K by $\text{Tr}(x) = \sum_{j \in [n]} \sigma_j(x)$ for any $x \in K$. We use it to define the *dual* of R as $R^{\vee} = \{x \in K : \text{Tr}(xR) \subseteq \mathbb{Z}\}$. For the class of number fields for which we have $R = \mathbb{Z}[\zeta]$, we have $R^{\vee} = \lambda^{-1} R$ where $\lambda = f'(\zeta) \in \mathbb{C}$. In particular, for power-of-two cyclotomics $\lambda = n$. We also define the norm $N : K \to \mathbb{Q}$ of K by $N(x) = \prod_{j \in [n]} \sigma_j(x)$ for any $x \in K$.

Distortion Between Embeddings. Both embeddings play important roles in this paper, and we recall how to go from one to the other. By applying σ to an element $x = \sum_{i=0}^{n-1} x_i \zeta^i \in K$, we see that $\sigma(x)$ and $\tau(x)$ are linked through a linear operator which is the Vandermonde matrix of the roots of the defining polynomial f. For $j \in [n]$, we let $\alpha_j = \sigma_j(\zeta)$ be the j-th root of f. Then, we obtain that $\sigma(x) = \mathbf{V}\tau(x)$, where $\mathbf{V} = \left[\alpha_i^{j-1}\right]_{i,j \in [n]}$. This transformation does not necessarily carry the structure from one embedding to the other, e.g., a binary vector in the coefficient embedding need not to be binary in the canonical embedding. Changing the embedding also impacts the norm, which is captured by the inequalities $\|\mathbf{V}^{-1}\|_2^{-1} \|\tau(x)\|_2 \leq \|\sigma(x)\|_2 \leq \|\mathbf{V}\|_2 \|\tau(x)\|_2$.

Hence, $\|\mathbf{V}\|_2$ and $\|\mathbf{V}^{-1}\|_2$ help approximating the distortion between both embeddings. Roşca et al. [RSW18] give additional insight on this distortion for specific number fields. Throughout this paper, we are interested in the parameter defined by $B = \max_{x \in R_2} \|\sigma(x)\|_\infty$ that is inherent to the ring. This parameter intervenes in the proof of Lemmas 15 and 17, where we need an upper-bound on $\|\sigma(x)\|_\infty$, for $x \in R_2$, that is independent of x. Recall that if x is in R_2, then its coefficient vector $\tau(x)$ is in $\{0,1\}^n$. Here, we provide an upper-bound on B, that is further simplified for cyclotomic number fields. The proof can be found in the full version [BJRW21].

Lemma 1. *Let K be a number field of degree n, and R its ring of integers. Let $\mathbf{V}$ be the transformation between both embeddings. Then, $B = \max_{x \in R_2} \|\sigma(x)\|_\infty \leq n\|\mathbf{V}\|_{\max}$. In particular, for cyclotomic fields, it yields $B \leq n$.*

Ideals and Units. An ideal $\mathcal{I}$ is *principal* if it is generated by a single element u, meaning $\mathcal{I} = uR = (u)$. We extend the field norm and define the norm of an ideal $N(\mathcal{I})$ as the index of $\mathcal{I}$ as an additive subgroup of R, which corresponds to $N(\mathcal{I}) = |R/\mathcal{I}|$. The norm is still multiplicative and verifies $N((a)) = |N(a)|$ for any $a \in K$. We also define the *dual* of an ideal $\mathcal{I}$ by $\mathcal{I}^\vee = \{x \in K : \mathrm{Tr}(x\mathcal{I}) \subseteq \mathbb{Z}\}$. In the construction of Lemma 15, we need a condition for binary elements of $R_2 = R/(2)$ to be invertible in R_q for a specific q. To do so, we rely on the small norm condition proven in [LS18, Theorem 1.1].

Lemma 2 (Theorem 1.1 [LS18]). *Let K be the ν-th cyclotomic field, with $\nu = \prod_i p_i^{e_i}$ be its prime-power factorization, with $e_i \geq 1$. We denote R the ring of integers of K. Also, let $\mu = \prod_i p_i^{f_i}$ for any $f_i \in [e_i]$. Let q be a prime such that $q = 1 \bmod \mu$, and $\mathrm{ord}_\nu(q) = \nu/\mu$, where ord_ν is the multiplicative order modulo ν. Then, any element y of $R_q = R/qR$ satisfying $0 < \|\tau(y)\|_\infty < q^{1/\varphi(\mu)}/\mathfrak{s}_1(\mu)$ is a unit in R_q, where $\mathfrak{s}_1(\mu)$ denotes the largest singular value of the Vandermonde matrix of the μ-th cyclotomic field.*

In the case where ν is a prime power, then so is μ and then [LPR13] states that $\mathfrak{s}_1(\mu) = \sqrt{\mu}$ if μ is odd, and $\mathfrak{s}_1(\mu) = \sqrt{\mu/2}$ otherwise. For more general cases, we refer to the discussions from Lyubashevsky and Seiler [LS18, Conj. 2.6]. We also refer to [LS18, Theorem 2.5] that establishes the density of such primes q for specific values of ν and μ.

We also recall two results from [WW19] that we need in the proof of Lemma 14 to construct a matrix of $\mathbf{U} \in R_q^{k \times k}$ that is invertible in R_q, i.e., such that there exists a matrix $\mathbf{U}^{-1} \in R_q^{k \times k}$ that verifies $\mathbf{U}\mathbf{U}^{-1} = \mathbf{I}_k \bmod qR = \mathbf{U}^{-1}\mathbf{U}$. This requires the prime q to be unramified in the cyclotomic field, which comes down to it not dividing the discriminant Δ_K. In cyclotomics, this is equivalent to q not dividing ν. The condition from Lemma 2 subsumes this one as $q = 1 \bmod \mu$ entails that q is not a prime factor of ν. We say that the vectors $\mathbf{a}_1, \ldots, \mathbf{a}_i \in R_q^k$ are R_q-linearly independent if for all $x_1, \ldots, x_i \in R_q$, $\sum_{j \in [i]} x_j \mathbf{a}_j = 0 \bmod qR$ implies $x_1 = \ldots = x_i = 0$.

Lemma 3 (Lemma 9 [WW19]). *Let K be the cyclotomic field of degree $n = \varphi(\nu)$, and R its ring of integers. Let q, k be positive integers such that q is a prime that verifies $q \geq n$ and $q \nmid \nu$. Then for any $i \in \{0, \ldots, k-1\}$ and R_q-linearly independent vectors $\mathbf{a}_1, \ldots, \mathbf{a}_i \in R_q^k$, the probability of sampling a vector $\mathbf{b} \hookleftarrow U(R_q^k)$ such that $\mathbf{a}_1, \ldots, \mathbf{a}_i, \mathbf{b}$ are R_q-linearly independent is at least $1 - \frac{n}{q}$.*

Lemma 4 (Lemma 18 [WW19]). *Let K be the cyclotomic field of degree $n = \varphi(\nu)$, and R its ring of integers. Let q, k be positive integers such that q is a prime that verifies $q \geq n$ and $q \nmid \nu$. Let $\mathbf{A} = [\mathbf{a}_1, \ldots, \mathbf{a}_k] \in R_q^{k \times k}$. Then, $\mathbf{A}$ is invertible modulo qR if and only if $\mathbf{a}_1, \ldots, \mathbf{a}_k$ are R_q-linearly independent.*

2.2 Lattices

A *lattice* Λ is the set of integer combinations of a basis $\mathbf{B} = [\mathbf{b}_i]_{i \in [r]} \in \mathbb{R}^{n \times r}$, i.e. $\Lambda = \sum_{i \in [r]} \mathbb{Z} \cdot \mathbf{b}_i$. In this work, we only consider *full-rank* lattices, namely lattices for which $r = n$. We define the *dual lattice* of a lattice Λ by $\Lambda^* = \{\mathbf{x} \in \text{Span}(\Lambda) : \forall \mathbf{y} \in \Lambda, \langle \mathbf{x}, \mathbf{y} \rangle \in \mathbb{Z}\}$. We denote by $\lambda_1^\infty(\Lambda)$ the *first minimum* of the lattice Λ with respect to the infinity norm, i.e., the infinity norm of a shortest non-zero vector of Λ. Any ideal $\mathcal{I}$ embeds into a lattice $\sigma(\mathcal{I})$ in H, and a lattice $\sigma_H(\mathcal{I})$ in $\mathbb{R}^n$, which we call *ideal lattices*. For an R-module $M \subseteq K^d$, $(\sigma, \ldots, \sigma)(M)$ is a lattice in H^d and $(\sigma_H, \ldots, \sigma_H)(M)$ is a lattice in $\mathbb{R}^{nd}$, both of which are called *module lattices*. The positive integer d is the module rank. To ease readability, we simply use $\mathcal{I}$ (resp. M) to denote the ideal lattice (resp. the module lattice). Note that the ideal lattice $\sigma(\mathcal{I}^\vee)$ corresponding to the dual ideal $\mathcal{I}$ is the same as the dual lattice up to complex conjugation, i.e., $\sigma(\mathcal{I}^\vee) = \overline{\sigma(\mathcal{I})^*}$. We also note that if $\mathcal{I}^d$ denotes $\mathcal{I} \times \ldots \times \mathcal{I}$, then $\lambda_1^\infty(\mathcal{I}^d) = \lambda_1^\infty(\mathcal{I})$. For a vector $\mathbf{x} \in K^d$, we define $\|\mathbf{x}\|_\infty = \max_{k \in [n], i \in [d]} |\sigma_k(x_i)|$, and $\|\mathbf{x}\|_{2,\infty} = \max_{k \in [n]} \sqrt{\sum_{i \in [d]} |\sigma_k(x_i)|^2}$.

2.3 Probabilities

Gaussian Measures. For a positive definite matrix $\mathbf{\Sigma} \in \mathbb{R}^n$, a vector $\mathbf{c} \in \mathbb{R}^n$, we define the Gaussian function by $\rho_{\mathbf{c}, \sqrt{\mathbf{\Sigma}}}(\mathbf{x}) = \exp(-\pi(\mathbf{x} - \mathbf{c})^T \mathbf{\Sigma}^{-1}(\mathbf{x} - \mathbf{c}))$ for all $\mathbf{x} \in \mathbb{R}^n$. We extend this definition to the degenerate case, i.e., positive semi-definite, by considering the generalized Moore-Penrose inverse. For convenience, we use the same notation as the standard inverse. We then define the continuous Gaussian probability distribution by its density $D_{\mathbf{c}, \sqrt{\mathbf{\Sigma}}}(\mathbf{x}) = (\det(\mathbf{\Sigma}))^{-1/2} \rho_{\mathbf{c}, \sqrt{\mathbf{\Sigma}}}(\mathbf{x})$. By abuse of notation, we call $\mathbf{\Sigma}$ the covariance matrix, even if in theory the covariance matrix of $D_{\mathbf{c}, \sqrt{\mathbf{\Sigma}}}$ is $\mathbf{\Sigma}/(2\pi)$. If $\mathbf{\Sigma}$ is diagonal with diagonal vector $\mathbf{r}^2 \in (\mathbb{R}^+)^n$, we simply write $D_{\mathbf{c}, \mathbf{r}}$, and if $\mathbf{c} = 0$, we omit it. When $\mathbf{\Sigma} = \alpha^2 \mathbf{I}_n$, we simplify further to $D_{\mathbf{c}, \alpha}$. We then define the discrete Gaussian distribution by conditioning $\mathbf{x}$ to be in a lattice Λ, i.e. $\mathcal{D}_{\Lambda, \mathbf{c}, \sqrt{\mathbf{\Sigma}}}(\mathbf{x}) = D_{\mathbf{c}, \sqrt{\mathbf{\Sigma}}}(\mathbf{x})/D_{\mathbf{c}, \sqrt{\mathbf{\Sigma}}}(\Lambda)$ for all $\mathbf{x} \in \Lambda$, and where $D_{\mathbf{c}, \sqrt{\mathbf{\Sigma}}}(\Lambda) = \sum_{\mathbf{y} \in \Lambda} D_{\mathbf{c}, \sqrt{\mathbf{\Sigma}}}(\mathbf{y})$.

The *smoothing parameter* of a lattice Λ denoted by $\eta_\varepsilon(\Lambda)$ for some $\varepsilon > 0$, introduced in [MR07], is the smallest $s > 0$ such that $\rho_{1/s}(\Lambda^* \setminus \{0\}) \leq \varepsilon$. It represents the smallest Gaussian parameter $s > 0$ such that the discrete Gaussian $\mathcal{D}_{\Lambda,\mathbf{c},s}$ behaves like a continuous Gaussian distribution. We recall the following bound on the smoothing parameter that we need throughout this paper.

Lemma 5 (Lemma 3.5 [Pei08]). *For an n-dimensional lattice Λ and $\varepsilon > 0$, we have $\eta_\varepsilon(\Lambda) \leq \sqrt{\ln(2n(1+1/\varepsilon))/\pi}/\lambda_1^\infty(\Lambda^*)$.*

Lemma 6 (Lemma 4.1 [MR07]). *Let Λ be an n-dimensional lattice, $\varepsilon > 0$, and $\alpha > \eta_\varepsilon(\Lambda)$. Then the distribution of the coset $\mathbf{e} + \Lambda$, where $\mathbf{e} \hookleftarrow D_\alpha$, is within statistical distance $\varepsilon/2$ of the uniform distribution over the cosets of Λ.*

We now extend a result on the sum of a continuous Gaussian and a discrete one to more general Gaussian distributions. In particular, the lemma works for two elliptical Gaussians, which we use in the proof of Lemma 11. The proof can be found in the full version [BJRW21].

Lemma 7 (Adapted from Lemma 2.8 [LS15] & Claim 3.9 [Reg09]). *Let Λ be an n-dimensional lattice, $\mathbf{a} \in \mathbb{R}^n$, $\mathbf{R}, \mathbf{S}$ two positive semi-definite matrices of $\mathbb{R}^{n \times n}$, and $\mathbf{T} = \mathbf{R} + \mathbf{S}$. We also define $\mathbf{U} = \left(\mathbf{R}^{-1} + \mathbf{S}^{-1}\right)^{-1}$, and we assume that $\rho_{\sqrt{\mathbf{U}^{-1}}}(\Lambda^* \setminus \{0\}) \leq \varepsilon$ for some $\varepsilon \in (0, 1/2)$. Consider the distribution Y on $\mathbb{R}^n$ obtained by adding a discrete sample from $\mathcal{D}_{\Lambda+\mathbf{a},\sqrt{\mathbf{R}}}$ and a continuous sample from $D_{\sqrt{\mathbf{S}}}$. Then we have $\Delta(Y, D_{\sqrt{\mathbf{T}}}) \leq 2\varepsilon$.*

Lemma 8 (Lemma 2.10 [BLP+13] & Theorem 3.1 [Pei10]). *Let Λ be an n-dimensional lattice, $\varepsilon \in (0, 1/2]$, and $\beta, r > 0$ such that $r \geq \eta_\varepsilon(\Lambda)$. Then the distribution of $\mathbf{x} + \mathbf{y}$, obtained by first sampling $\mathbf{x}$ from D_β, and then $\mathbf{y}$ sampled from $\mathcal{D}_{\Lambda,\mathbf{x},r}$, is within statistical distance 8ε of $\mathcal{D}_{\Lambda,\sqrt{\beta^2+r^2}}$.*

Module Gaussians. As introduced in [LPR10] for Gaussians over $K_\mathbb{R}$, we define general Gaussian distributions over $K_\mathbb{R}^d$ through their embedding to $\mathbb{R}^{nd}$. It is obtained by sampling $\mathbf{y}^{(H)} \in \mathbb{R}^{nd}$ according to $D_{\sqrt{\Sigma}}$ for some positive semi-definite matrix Σ in $\mathbb{R}^{nd \times nd}$ and then mapping it back to $K_\mathbb{R}^d$ by $\mathbf{y} = \sigma_H^{-1}(\mathbf{y}^{(H)})$. To ease readability, we denote the described distribution of $\mathbf{y} \in K_\mathbb{R}^d$ by $D_{\sqrt{\Sigma}}$. In the proof of Lemma 16, we also need the distribution of $\mathbf{y} = \mathbf{U}\mathbf{e}$ for an arbitrary matrix $\mathbf{U}$ and a Gaussian vector $\mathbf{e} \in K_\mathbb{R}^d$ with independent coefficients. To do so, we need the ring homomorphism $\theta : K_\mathbb{R}^{k \times \ell} \to \mathbb{C}^{nk \times n\ell}$ defined by

$$\theta(\mathbf{A}) = \begin{bmatrix} \mathbf{D}_{1,1} - \mathbf{D}_{1,\ell} \\ | \quad \diagdown \quad | \\ \mathbf{D}_{k,1} - \mathbf{D}_{k,\ell} \end{bmatrix}, \text{ with } \mathbf{D}_{i,j} = \mathrm{diag}(\sigma(a_{i,j})) \in \mathbb{C}^{n \times n}.$$

Lemma 9. *Let K be a number field of degree n, and d a positive integer. Let $\mathbb{S} \in \mathbb{R}^{nd \times nd}$ be a positive semi-definite matrix, and $\mathbf{U} \in K_\mathbb{R}^{d \times d}$. We denote $\Sigma = \left(\mathbb{H}^\dagger \theta(\mathbf{U}) \mathbb{H}\right) \mathbb{S} \left(\mathbb{H}^\dagger \theta(\mathbf{U}) \mathbb{H}\right)^\dagger \in \mathbb{R}^{nd \times nd}$, where $\mathbb{H} = \mathrm{diag}(\mathbf{H}, \ldots, \mathbf{H}) \in \mathbb{C}^{nd \times nd}$, with $\mathbf{H}$ the matrix form of the basis of the space H previously defined. Then, the distribution of $\mathbf{y} = \mathbf{U}\mathbf{e}$, where $\mathbf{e} \in K_\mathbb{R}^d$ is distributed according to $D_{\sqrt{\mathbb{S}}}$, is exactly $D_{\sqrt{\Sigma}}$.*

Proof. Let $\mathbf{e} = [e_i]_{i \in d} \in K_{\mathbb{R}}^d$ be a Gaussian vector distributed according to $D_{\sqrt{\mathbb{S}}}$. For all $i \in [d]$, we have $y_i = \sum_{j \in [d]} u_{i,j} e_j$ and thus $\sigma(y_i) = \sum_{j \in [d]} \sigma(u_{i,j}) \odot \sigma(e_j)$, where $\odot$ denotes the Hadamard product. The Hadamard product $\mathbf{a} \odot \mathbf{b}$ of two vectors $\mathbf{a}$ and $\mathbf{b}$ can also be expressed as the matrix-vector product $\mathrm{diag}(\mathbf{a}) \cdot \mathbf{b}$. It results in

$$\sigma(\mathbf{y}) = \begin{bmatrix} \sigma(y_1) \\ | \\ \sigma(y_d) \end{bmatrix} = \theta(\mathbf{U})\sigma(\mathbf{e}),$$

where $\theta(\mathbf{U})$ is the block matrix $[\mathrm{diag}(\sigma(u_{i,j}))]_{i,j \in [d]} \in \mathbb{C}^{nd \times nd}$. As we have seen before, we can decompose σ on the basis of H and get $\sigma(y_i) = \mathbf{H} y_i^{(H)}$ (respectively $\sigma(e_i) = \mathbf{H} e_i^{(H)}$) for all $i \in [d]$. By using the block matrix product, we end up with

$$\sigma(\mathbf{y}) = \begin{bmatrix} \mathbf{H} & \\ & \diagdown \\ & & \mathbf{H} \end{bmatrix} \begin{bmatrix} \mathbf{y}_1^{(H)} \\ | \\ \mathbf{y}_d^{(H)} \end{bmatrix} = \mathbb{H}\mathbf{y}^{(H)}.$$

Thus $\mathbb{H}\mathbf{y}^{(H)} = \theta(\mathbf{U})\mathbb{H}\mathbf{e}^{(H)}$, which leads to $\mathbf{y}^{(H)} = \mathbb{H}^\dagger \theta(\mathbf{U})\mathbb{H}\mathbf{e}^{(H)}$. Now notice that the blocks of $\mathbb{H}^\dagger \theta(\mathbf{U})\mathbb{H}$ are the $\mathbf{H}^\dagger \mathrm{diag}(\sigma(u_{i,j}))\mathbf{H}$ which correspond to the matrix form of the multiplication by $u_{i,j}$ in the basis of the space H and thus is in $\mathbb{R}^{n \times n}$. Hence $\mathbb{H}^\dagger \theta(\mathbf{U})\mathbb{H} \in \mathbb{R}^{nd \times nd}$.

By definition, $\mathbf{e}^{(H)}$ is distributed according to $D_{\sqrt{\mathbb{S}}}$. Thus $\mathbf{y}^{(H)}$ is also distributed along a 0-centered Gaussian over $\mathbb{R}^{nd}$, but with covariance matrix

$$\Sigma = \left(\mathbb{H}^\dagger \theta(\mathbf{U})\mathbb{H}\right) \mathbb{S} \left(\mathbb{H}^\dagger \theta(\mathbf{U})\mathbb{H}\right)^\dagger.$$

$\square$

In particular, when $\mathbb{S} = \mathrm{diag}(r_1^2, \ldots, r_1^2, \ldots, r_d^2, \ldots, r_d^2)$ for some positive reals $r_1, \ldots, r_d$, then $\sqrt{\mathbb{S}}$ commutes with $\mathbb{H}$ and the covariance simplifies to $\Sigma = \mathbb{H}^\dagger \widetilde{\mathbb{U}} \widetilde{\mathbb{U}}^\dagger \mathbb{H}$, with $\widetilde{\mathbb{U}} = [\mathrm{diag}(\sigma(r_j u_{i,j}))]_{i,j \in [d]}$. We also need two other lemmata related to the inner product of $K_{\mathbb{R}}^d$ (which results in an element of $K_{\mathbb{R}}$) between a Gaussian vector and an arbitrary one. In particular, we use Lemma 11 in the proof of Lemma 17 in order to decompose a Gaussian noise into an inner product.

Lemma 10 (Lem. 2.13 [LS15]). *Let $\mathbf{r} \in (\mathbb{R}^+)^n \cap H$, $\mathbf{z} \in K^d$ fixed and $\mathbf{e} \in K_{\mathbb{R}}^d$ sampled from $D_{\sqrt{\Sigma}}$, where $\sqrt{\Sigma} = [\delta_{i,j}\mathrm{diag}(\mathbf{r})]_{i,j \in [d]} \in \mathbb{R}^{nd \times nd}$. Then $\langle \mathbf{z}, \mathbf{e} \rangle = \sum_{i \in [d]} z_i e_i$ is distributed according to $D_{\mathbf{r}'}$ with $r_j' = r_j \sqrt{\sum_{i \in [d]} |\sigma_j(z_i)|^2}$.*

Lemma 11 (Adapted from Corollary 3.10 [Reg09]). *Let $M \subset K^d$ be an R-module (yielding a module lattice), let $\mathbf{u}, \mathbf{z} \in K^d$ be fixed, and let $\beta, \gamma > 0$. Assume that $(1/\beta^2 + \|\mathbf{z}\|_{2,\infty}^2/\gamma^2)^{-1/2} \geq \eta_\varepsilon(M)$ for some $\varepsilon \in (0, 1/2)$. Then the distribution of $\langle \mathbf{z}, \mathbf{v} \rangle + e$ where $\mathbf{v}$ is sampled from $\mathcal{D}_{M+\mathbf{u}, \beta}$ and $e \in K_{\mathbb{R}}$ is sampled from D_γ, is within statistical distance at most 2ε from the elliptical Gaussian $D_{\mathbf{r}}$ over $K_{\mathbb{R}}$, where $r_j = \sqrt{\beta^2 \sum_{i \in [d]} |\sigma_j(z_i)|^2 + \gamma^2}$ for $j \in [n]$.*

Proof. Consider $\mathbf{h} \in (K_{\mathbb{R}})^d$ distributed according to $D_{\mathbf{r}',\ldots,\mathbf{r}'}$, where $\mathbf{r}'$ is given by $r'_j = \gamma / \sqrt{\sum_{i \in [d]} |\sigma_j(z_i)|^2}$ for $j \in [n]$. Then by Lemma 10, $\langle \mathbf{z}, \mathbf{h} \rangle$ is distributed as D_γ and therefore $\Delta(\langle \mathbf{z}, \mathbf{v} \rangle + e, D_{\mathbf{r}}) = \Delta(\langle \mathbf{z}, \mathbf{v} + \mathbf{h} \rangle, D_{\mathbf{r}})$. Now, we denote $\mathbf{t}$ such that $t_j = \sqrt{\beta^2 + (r'_j)^2}$ for $j \in [n]$. Note that by assumption

$$\min_{j \in [n]} \beta r'_j / t_j = (1/\beta^2 + \max_{j \in [n]} \sum_{i \in [d]} |\sigma_j(z_i)|^2 / \gamma^2)^{-1/2}$$

$$= (1/\beta^2 + \|\mathbf{z}\|_{2,\infty}^2 / \gamma^2)^{-1/2} \geq \eta_\varepsilon(M).$$

Lemma 7 therefore applies and yields that $\mathbf{v} + \mathbf{h}$ is distributed as $D_{\mathbf{t},\ldots,\mathbf{t}}$, within statistical distance at most 2ε. By applying once more Lemma 10 and noticing that the statistical distance does not increase when applying a function (here the scalar product with $\mathbf{z}$), then we get that $\langle \mathbf{z}, \mathbf{v} + \mathbf{h} \rangle$ is distributed as $D_{\mathbf{r}}$ within statistical distance at most 2ε, where $r_j = t_j \sqrt{\sum_{i \in [d]} |\sigma_j(z_i)|^2} = \sqrt{\beta^2 \sum_{i \in [d]} |\sigma_j(z_i)|^2 + \gamma^2}$ for $j \in [n]$. □

2.4   Ring Leftover Hash Lemma

The proof of Lemma 17 also requires a leftover hash lemma over rings, where the vector contains binary polynomials. We use the following adaption of [Mic07] proven by Boudgoust et al. [BJRW20].

Lemma 12 (Lemma 7 [BJRW20]). *Let q be prime and n, k and d be positive integers. Further, let f be the defining polynomial of degree n of the number field $K \cong \mathbb{Q}[x]/(f)$ such that its ring of integers is given by $R = \mathbb{Z}[x]/(f)$. We set $R_q = R/qR$ and $R_2 = R/2R$. Then, $\Delta((\mathbf{C}, \mathbf{Cz}), (\mathbf{C}, \mathbf{s})) \leq \frac{1}{2} \sqrt{\left(1 + \frac{q^k}{2^d}\right)^n - 1}$, where $\mathbf{C} \hookleftarrow U((R_q)^{k \times d})$, $\mathbf{z} \hookleftarrow U((R_2)^d)$ and $\mathbf{s} \hookleftarrow U((R_q)^k)$.*

2.5   Module Learning with Errors

The LWE problem over modules was first defined by Brakerski et al. [BGV12] and studied at length by Langlois and Stehlé [LS15]. We consider a number field K of degree n, R its ring of integers, and let d denote the module rank. Let ψ be a distribution on $K_{\mathbb{R}}$ and $\mathbf{s} \in (R_q^\vee)^d$ be a vector. We let $A_{\mathbf{s},\psi}^{(R^d)}$ denote the distribution on $(R_q)^d \times \mathbb{T}_{R^\vee}$ obtained by choosing a vector $\mathbf{a} \hookleftarrow U((R_q)^d)$, an element $e \leftarrow \psi$ and returning $(\mathbf{a}, q^{-1}\langle \mathbf{a}, \mathbf{s} \rangle + e \mod R^\vee)$.

Definition 1. *Let q, d be positive integers with $q \geq 2$. Let Υ be a distribution on a family of distributions on $K_{\mathbb{R}}$. The problem M-LWE$_{n,d,q,\Upsilon}$ is as follows: Sample $\mathbf{s} \hookleftarrow U((R_q^\vee)^d)$ and $\psi \hookleftarrow \Upsilon$. The goal is to distinguish between arbitrarily many independent samples from $A_{\mathbf{s},\psi}^{(R^d)}$ and the same number of independent samples from $U((R_q)^d \times \mathbb{T}_{R^\vee})$. If the number of samples m is fixed, we denote it by M-LWE$_{n,d,m,q,\Upsilon}$.*

When the error distribution is a Gaussian distribution of parameter $\alpha > 0$, we write M-LWE$_{n,d,m,q,\alpha}$, and if the Gaussian is elliptical bounded by β, i.e., $D_{\mathbf{r}}$ for $\mathbf{r} \in (\mathbb{R}^+)^n$ such that $\|\mathbf{r}\|_\infty \leq \beta$, we write M-LWE$_{n,d,m,q,\leq\beta}$. The same goes for other variants of M-LWE. For the M-LWE problem and its variants that we introduce later, we denote by Adv$[\mathcal{A}]$ the advantage of an adversary $\mathcal{A}$ in distinguishing between the two distributions of the problem.

Binary Secret. Another possibility is to change the distribution of the secret. We focus on the case where the secret is chosen to be binary in the coefficient embedding. We thus define bin-M-LWE$_{n,d,m,q,\Upsilon}$ to be the M-LWE problem where the secret $\mathbf{s}$ is sampled uniformly in $(R_2^\vee)^d$. We justify this choice of embedding in Sect. 3.1.

3   Hardness of M-LWE with Binary Secret

In this section, we prove our main contribution which is a reduction from M-LWE with rank k to bin-M-LWE with rank d satisfying $d \geq (k+1)\log_2 q + \omega(\log_2 n)$, for cyclotomic fields. The reduction preserves the modulus q, that needs to be prime satisfying number-theoretic restrictions, the ring degree n and the number of samples m, but the noise is increased by a factor of $n\sqrt{2d}\sqrt{4n^2+1}$. Our proof follows the same idea as in [BLP+13] that we adapt over modules. The noise ratio is polynomial in n, but smaller than $n^2 d\sqrt{m}$ in [BJRW20]. Not only does it no longer depend on the number of samples m, which becomes more advantageous as the typical choice for m is $m = O(n\log_2 n)$, but we also gain a factor of $\sqrt{d}$. For the reduction, m also needs to be larger than the target module rank d, and at most polynomial in n because of the hybrid argument used for ext-M-LWE with multiple secrets. The reduction in Theorem 2 works for all cyclotomic fields, but most results apply for all number fields $K = \mathbb{Q}(\zeta)$ such that the ring of integers is $R = \mathbb{Z}[\zeta]$, the bottleneck being the construction in Lemma 15.

Theorem 2. Let $\nu = \prod_i p_i^{e_i}$, K be the cyclotomic field of degree $n = \varphi(\nu)$, and R its ring of integers. Let $\mu = \prod_i p_i$ and q be a prime number such that $q = 1 \bmod \mu$, $ord_\nu(q) = \nu/\mu$ and $q > \max(2n, \mathfrak{s}_1(\mu)^{\varphi(\mu)})$, where $\mathfrak{s}_1(\mu)$ denotes the largest singular value of the Vandermonde matrix of the μ-th cyclotomic field. Further, let k, d, m be three positive integers such that $d \geq (k+1)\log_2 q + \omega(\log_2 n)$, and $d \leq m \leq \text{poly}(n)$. Let $\alpha \geq q^{-1}\sqrt{\ln(2nd(1+1/\varepsilon))/\pi}$ and $\beta \geq \alpha \cdot n\sqrt{2d}\sqrt{4n^2+1}$. Then there is a reduction from M-LWE$_{n,k,m,q,\alpha}$ to bin-M-LWE$_{n,d,m,q,\leq\beta}$, such that if $\mathcal{A}$ solves the latter with advantage Adv$[\mathcal{A}]$, then there exists an algorithm $\mathcal{B}$ that solves the former with advantage

$$\text{Adv}[\mathcal{B}] \geq \frac{1}{3m}\left(\text{Adv}[\mathcal{A}] - \frac{1}{2}\sqrt{\left(1 + \frac{q^{k+1}}{2^d}\right)^n - 1}\right) - \frac{37\varepsilon}{2}.$$

The noise ratio β/α contains three main terms. The factor n encapsulates the norm distortion between the coefficient and the canonical embedding, as well as the actual length of the binary vectors. The second term $\sqrt{2d}$ stems from the masking of $\mathbf{z}$ when introduced in the first hybrid in the proof of Lemma 17. The last factor $\sqrt{4n^2 + 1}$ solely represents the impact of giving information on the error in the ext-M-LWE problem.

3.1 Choice of Embedding for Binary Secrets

As mentioned in the introduction, the variant of M-LWE using a binary secret requires the choice of an embedding in which the secret is binary. As praised in [LPR10, LPR13], the canonical embedding has nice algebraic and geometric properties that make it a good choice of embedding. However, in this section, we justify our choice of the coefficient embedding, by analyzing the set of secrets that are binary in the canonical embedding in the case of power-of-two cyclotomics. The conjugation symmetry of the canonical embedding first restricts the choice of secrets to $(\sigma^{-1}(\{0,1\}^n \cap H))^d$, where d denotes the module rank and the space H is the range of σ. In addition, the tightest worst-case to average-case reductions for M-LWE require $\mathbf{s}$ to be taken from $(R_q^\vee)^d$. However, σ^{-1} maps H to $K_\mathbb{R}$ but not necessarily to R or to $R^\vee$. We thus have to further restrict the set of secrets to $\mathcal{Z} = (R_q^\vee \cap \sigma^{-1}(\{0, \lambda^{-1}\}^n \cap H))^d$, where λ is such that $R^\vee = \lambda^{-1}R$. In the case of power-of-two cyclotomics, $\lambda = n$ is real and therefore yields $\lambda \mathcal{Z} = (R_q \cap \sigma^{-1}(\{0,1\}^n \cap H))^d$.

Lagrange Basis. As opposed to R_2 which corresponds to binary vectors in the coefficient embedding, the power basis is not adapted to describe the set $\lambda \mathcal{Z}$. We thus introduce the Lagrange basis. We denote by $\alpha_j = \sigma_j(\zeta)$ the j-th root of the defining polynomial f. Recall that we assume that α_j is real for $j \in [t_1]$, and that we have $\alpha_{t_1+j} = \overline{\alpha_{t_1+t_2+j}} \in \mathbb{C}$ for $j \in [t_2]$. Applying σ_j to an element $r = \sum_{i=0}^{n-1} r_i \zeta^i \in K_\mathbb{R}$ comes down to evaluating the polynomial $p_r = \sum_{i=0}^{n-1} r_i x^i$ at α_j. We use this polynomial interpretation to define elements of $K_\mathbb{R}$ that form a basis of $\sigma^{-1}(\{0,1\}^n \cap H)$.

Lagrange interpolation defines polynomials that map a set of distinct elements to 0 and 1. Since the α_j are distinct as f is irreducible, we can apply a similar method and define $L_k = \prod_{j \in [n] \setminus \{k\}} \frac{x - \alpha_j}{\alpha_k - \alpha_j}$ for $k \in [t_1]$, which is real due to the conjugation symmetry of the roots. For $k \in \{t_1 + 1, \ldots, t_1 + t_2\}$, we define $L_k = \prod_{j \in [n] \setminus \{k\}} \frac{x - \alpha_j}{\alpha_k - \alpha_j} + \prod_{j \in [n] \setminus \{k+t_2\}} \frac{x - \alpha_j}{\alpha_{k+t_2} - \alpha_j} = 2\Re\left(\prod_{j \in [n] \setminus \{k\}} \frac{x - \alpha_j}{\alpha_k - \alpha_j}\right)$. Hence the polynomials lie in $\mathbb{R}[x]$ and we have $L_k(\alpha_j) = \delta_{k,j}$ for $(k,j) \in [t_1] \times [n]$, and $L_k(\alpha_j) = \delta_{k,j} + \delta_{k+t_2,j}$ for $(k,j) \in \{t_1 + 1, \ldots, t_1 + t_2\} \times [n]$.

Therefore, by defining the Lagrange basis l with the corresponding $l_k \cong L_k(\zeta) \in K_\mathbb{R}$, we have linear independence and $\sigma^{-1}(\{0,1\}^n \cap H) = \sum_{k \in [t_1 + t_2]} \{0,1\} \cdot l_k$, because $\sigma(l_k) = \mathbf{e}_k$ if $k \in [t_1]$ and $\sigma(l_k) = \mathbf{e}_k + \mathbf{e}_{k+t_2}$ if $k \in \{t_1 + 1, \ldots, t_1 + t_2\}$. As far as we are aware, this is the first time that the Lagrange basis is used in the setting of structured lattice-based cryptography. We now need to determine which of these combinations lie in R_q in order to properly define the set of secrets.

Power-of-Two Cyclotomics. We now look at the Lagrange basis in the specific case where n is a power of two.

Lemma 13. *Let R be the cyclotomic ring of integers of degree $n = 2^\ell$. Then, for any integer $q \geq 1$, the set $R_q \cap \sigma^{-1}(\{0,1\}^n \cap H)$ contains only 0 and 1.*

Proof. Recall that in cyclotomic fields, we have $t_1 = 0$ and $t_2 = n/2$. We know that the defining polynomial is $x^n + 1$ and therefore we can re-index the roots as $\alpha_j = \exp(i(2j+1)\pi/n)$, j now ranging from 0 to $n-1$. We can therefore study the complex product. We look at the constant coefficient of L_k, i.e., $A_k = L_k(0) = 2\Re\left(\prod_{0 \leq j < n, j \neq k} \frac{-\alpha_j}{\alpha_k - \alpha_j}\right)$. To ease notation, we write $j \neq k$ instead of $j \in \{0, \ldots, n-1\} \setminus \{k\}$ for the product indexes. We first look at the product for a fixed $k \in \{0, \ldots, n/2 - 1\}$.

$$\prod_{j \neq k}(\alpha_k - \alpha_j) = \alpha_k^{n-1}\prod_{j \neq k}(1 - \alpha_j/\alpha_k) = -\alpha_k^{-1}\prod_{j \neq k}(1 - e^{i2\pi(j-k)/n})$$

$$= -\alpha_k^{-1}\prod_{l=1}^{n-1}(1 - e^{i2\pi l/n}),$$

using the fact that $\alpha_k^n + 1 = 0$ and the circularity of the complex exponential. Yet, we also have $\prod_{l=0}^{n-1}(x - e^{i2\pi l/n}) = x^n - 1 = (x-1)\sum_{l=0}^{n-1} x^l$. By simplifying both sides by $x-1$ and then evaluating at 1, we have $\prod_{l=1}^{n-1}(1 - e^{i2\pi l/n}) = \sum_{l=0}^{n-1} 1^l = n$. The product of the numerators in the definition of A_k is $(-1)^{n-1}\overline{\alpha_k}$ because we can pair all of the roots α_j with their conjugates, which gives $\alpha_j\overline{\alpha_j} = |\alpha_j|^2 = 1$, except for $\overline{\alpha_k}$. Hence, $A_k = 2\Re(-\overline{\alpha_k}/(-n/\alpha_k))$ because n is even, which yields $A_k = \frac{2}{n}$. Now we take a subset $S \subseteq \{0, \ldots, n/2-1\}$ and we study $\sum_{k \in S} L_k$. Note that the case of $S = \{0, \ldots, n/2-1\}$ corresponds to adding all the Lagrange basis elements which results in 1, and the case $S = \emptyset$ results in 0 by convention. So we now assume that $0 < |S| < n/2$. The constant coefficient of $\sum_{k \in S} L_k$ is $2|S|/n \in (0,1)$ and is therefore not an integer. Hence, $\sum_{k \in S} L_k \notin \mathbb{Z}[x]$ which means that the element $\sum_{k \in S} l_k$ is not in R nor R_q for any $q \geq 1$.

It proves that the only binary combination of the Lagrange basis that are in R are 0 and 1, and the same conclusion is valid for R_q for any $q \geq 1$. $\square$

Hence to preserve the complexity of a brute force attack when comparing the two embeddings, the module rank would have to be increased by a factor n in the case where we take the canonical embedding to represent binary secrets. In this case, the (dual of the) secrets are from $\{0,1\}^d$ and therefore discard most of the available ring structure as opposed to R_2^d. We remark that this issue hasn't been addressed by [LWW20]. It seems that for too narrow bounds on the entropic secret distribution, the number of available secrets is much smaller in the canonical embedding compared to the number with regard to the coefficient embedding.

3.2   First-is-Errorless M-LWE

We follow the same idea as Brakerski et al. [BLP+13] by gradually giving more information to the adversary while proving that this additional information does not increase the advantage too much. We define the module version of *first-is-errorless* LWE, from [BLP+13], where the first equation is given without error. A similar definition and reduction from M-LWE are given in [AA16]. The only difference between the two reductions comes from the pre-processing step, which is simplified in our case due to the further restrictions on q of our overall reduction.

Definition 2 (First-is-errorless M-LWE). *Let K be a number field of degree n and R its ring of integers. Let q, k be positive integers. We denote by $R_q = R/qR$, $K_{\mathbb{R}} = K \otimes_{\mathbb{Q}} \mathbb{R}$, and $\mathbb{T}_{R^{\vee}} = K_{\mathbb{R}}/R^{\vee}$ as usual.*

Let Υ be a distribution over a family of distributions over $K_{\mathbb{R}}$. The first-is-errorless variant of the M-LWE problem is to distinguish between the following cases. On the one hand, the first sample is uniform over $(R_q)^k \times q^{-1}R^{\vee}/R^{\vee}$ and the rest are uniform over $(R_q)^k \times \mathbb{T}_{R^{\vee}}$. On the other hand, there is some unknown $\mathbf{s}$ uniformly sampled over $(R_q^{\vee})^k$ and ψ sampled from Υ such that the first sample is from $A_{\mathbf{s},\{0\}}^{(R^k)}$ and the rest are distributed as $A_{\mathbf{s},\psi}^{(R^k)}$, where $\{0\}$ is the distribution that is deterministically 0.

We denote it by first-is-errorless M-LWE$_{n,k,q,\Upsilon}$ *or, when the number of samples m is fixed,* first-is-errorless M-LWE$_{n,k,m,q,\Upsilon}$.

Lemma 14 (Adapted from Lemma 4.3 [BLP+13]). *Let K be the cyclotomic field of degree $n = \varphi(\nu)$, and R its ring of integers. Let $q \geq 2n$ be a prime integer such that $q \nmid \nu$, k a positive integer, and Υ a distribution over a family of distributions over $K_{\mathbb{R}}$. There is a polynomial-time reduction from* M-LWE$_{n,k-1,q,\Upsilon}$ *to the variant* first-is-errorless M-LWE$_{n,k,q,\Upsilon}$.

Proof. The reduction first chooses $\mathbf{a}' \hookleftarrow U((R_q)^k)$ and then $\mathbf{b}_2, \ldots, \mathbf{b}_k$ i.i.d. from $U((R_q)^k)$ such that $\mathbf{a}', \mathbf{b}_2, \ldots, \mathbf{b}_k$ are R_q-linearly independent. Each time we draw a uniformly random column, the probability that the new column is R_q-linearly independent with the previous ones is at least $1 - n/q$ for $q \geq n$ by Lemma 3. Since we require $q \geq 2n$, this probability is at least $1/2$. Therefore, we only need a polynomial number of uniformly sampled columns in R_q^k to construct a matrix of $R_q^{k \times k}$ invertible modulo qR.

The preprocessing step results in a matrix $\mathbf{U} = [\mathbf{a}', \mathbf{b}_2, \ldots, \mathbf{b}_k] \in (R_q)^{k \times k}$ that is invertible modulo qR according to Lemma 4. Then, sample s_0 uniformly in $R_q^{\vee}$. The reduction is as follows. For the first sample, it outputs $(\mathbf{a}', q^{-1} \cdot s_0 \bmod R^{\vee}) \in (R_q)^k \times q^{-1}R^{\vee}/R^{\vee}$. The other samples are produced by taking $(\mathbf{a}, b) \in (R_q)^{k-1} \times \mathbb{T}_{R^{\vee}}$ from the M-LWE challenger, picking a fresh randomly chosen $a'' \in R_q$, and outputting $(\mathbf{U}(a''|\mathbf{a}), b + q^{-1}(s_0 \cdot a'') \bmod R^{\vee}) \in (R_q)^k \times \mathbb{T}_{R^{\vee}}$, with the vertical bar denoting concatenation. We now analyze correctness. First note that the first component is uniform over $(R_q)^k$. Indeed, $\mathbf{a}'$ is uniform over $(R_q)^k$ for the first sample, and since $\mathbf{a}$ is uniform over $(R_q)^{k-1}$, a'' is uniform over R_q, and $\mathbf{U}$ is invertible in $(R_q)^{k \times k}$, then $\mathbf{U}(a''|\mathbf{a})$ is uniform over $(R_q)^k$ as well.

If b is uniform, the first sample yields $q^{-1}s_0 \bmod R^{\vee}$ uniform over $q^{-1}R^{\vee}/R^{\vee}$. For the other samples, $b + q^{-1}(s_0 \cdot a'') \bmod R^{\vee}$ is uniform over $\mathbb{T}_{R^{\vee}}$ and independent of $\mathbf{U}(a''|\mathbf{a})$ but also independent from the first sample because b

masks $q^{-1}(s_0 \cdot a'')$. If $b = q^{-1}\langle \mathbf{a}, \mathbf{s} \rangle + e \bmod R^\vee$ for some uniform $\mathbf{s} \in (R_q^\vee)^{k-1}$ and $e \hookleftarrow \psi$ for some $\psi \hookleftarrow \Upsilon$, then $q^{-1}s_0 = q^{-1}\langle \mathbf{e}_1, (s_0|\mathbf{s}) \rangle = q^{-1}\langle \mathbf{U}\mathbf{e}_1, \mathbf{U}^{-T}(s_0|\mathbf{s}) \rangle = q^{-1}\langle \mathbf{a}', \mathbf{U}^{-T}(s_0|\mathbf{s}) \rangle$, where $\mathbf{e}_1 = [1, 0, \dots, 0]^T$. For the other samples, we have $b + q^{-1}(s_0 \cdot a'') \bmod R^\vee = q^{-1}\langle \mathbf{U}(a''|\mathbf{a}), \mathbf{U}^{-T}(s_0|\mathbf{s}) \rangle + e \bmod R^\vee$. Note that $(s_0|\mathbf{s})$ is uniform over $(R_q^\vee)^k$ so $\mathbf{U}^{-T}(s_0|\mathbf{s})$ is also uniform over $(R_q^\vee)^k$ because $\mathbf{U}^{-T}$ is invertible in R_q. Therefore the reduction outputs samples according to first-is-errorless M-LWE with secret $\mathbf{s}' = \mathbf{U}^{-T}(s_0|\mathbf{s})$. $\qquad\square$

3.3 Extended M-LWE

We now define the module version of the *Extended* LWE problem introduced in [BLP+13], where the adversary is allowed a hint on the errors. As opposed to [AA16], we allow for multiple secret and one single hint vector $\mathbf{z}$, as required by our final reduction of Lemma 17.

Definition 3 (Extended M-LWE). *Let K be a number field of degree n, and R its ring of integers. Let m, q, k, t be positive integers. Let $\mathcal{Z} \subseteq (R^\vee)^m$ and ψ a discrete distribution over $q^{-1}(R^\vee)^m$. The* Extended M-LWE *problem, denoted by* $\mathrm{ext\text{-}M\text{-}LWE}_{n,k,m,q,\psi,\mathcal{Z}}^t$, *is as follows. The algorithm first samples $\mathbf{z} \in \mathcal{Z}$ and then receives a tuple $(\mathbf{A}, (\mathbf{b}_i)_{i \in [t]}, (\langle \mathbf{e}_i, \mathbf{z} \rangle)_{i \in [t]})$, over $(R_q)^{k \times m} \times \left((q^{-1}R^\vee/R^\vee)^m\right)^t \times (q^{-1}R^\vee)^t$. Its goal is to distinguish between the following cases. On one side, $\mathbf{A}$ is sampled uniformly over $(R_q)^{k \times m}$, and for all $i \in [t], \mathbf{e}_i \in q^{-1}(R^\vee)^m$ are independent and identically distributed from ψ, and define $\mathbf{b}_i = q^{-1}\mathbf{A}^T\mathbf{s}_i + \mathbf{e}_i \bmod R^\vee$ for some uniformly chosen $\mathbf{s}_i \in (R_q^\vee)^k$. On the other side, everything is identical except that the $\mathbf{b}_i$ are sampled uniformly over $(q^{-1}R^\vee/R^\vee)^m$, independently from $\mathbf{A}$ and the error vectors.*

By a standard hybrid argument, $\mathrm{ext\text{-}M\text{-}LWE}^1$ reduces to $\mathrm{ext\text{-}M\text{-}LWE}^t$ while reducing the advantage by a factor t, for any polynomially bounded t, and choice of parameters n, k, m, q, ψ and $\mathcal{Z}$. For simplicity in what follows, for a matrix $\mathbf{A} \in R^{m \times m}$, we denote by $\mathbf{A}^\perp \in R^{m \times (m-1)}$ the submatrix of $\mathbf{A}$ obtained by removing the leftmost column. Our reduction from first-is-errorless M-LWE to ext-M-LWE in Lemma 16 requires the construction of a matrix $\mathbf{U}_\mathbf{z} \in R^{m \times m}$, for all vectors $\mathbf{z} \in \mathcal{Z} = (R_2^\vee)^m$, satisfying several properties. This matrix allows us to transform samples from a first-is-errorless M-LWE challenger into samples that we can give to an oracle for ext-M-LWE. The largest singular value of its submatrix $\mathbf{U}_\mathbf{z}^\perp$ (when embedded with θ), controls the increase in the Gaussian parameter. We propose a construction for which we bound the largest singular value above by a quantity independent on $\mathbf{z}$, as needed in the reduction.

Lemma 15. *Let $\nu = \prod_i p_i^{e_i}$, K be the cyclotomic field of degree $n = \varphi(\nu)$, and R its ring of integers. Let $\mu = \prod_i p_i$ and q be a prime number such that $q = 1 \bmod \mu$, $\mathrm{ord}_\nu(q) = \nu/\mu$ and $q > \mathfrak{s}_1(\mu)^{\varphi(\mu)}$, where $\mathfrak{s}_1(\mu)$ denotes the largest singular value of the Vandermonde matrix of the μ-th cyclotomic field. Finally, let m be a positive integer, and $\mathcal{Z} = (R_2^\vee)^m$, and we recall the ring parameter $B = \max_{x \in R_2} \|\sigma(x)\|_\infty$. For all $\mathbf{z} \in \mathcal{Z}$, there is an efficiently computable matrix $\mathbf{U}_\mathbf{z} \in$*

$R^{m \times m}$ *that is invertible modulo* qR *and that verifies the following:* $\mathbf{z}$ *is orthogonal to the columns of* $\mathbf{U}_{\mathbf{z}}^{\perp}$, *and the largest singular value of* $\theta(\mathbf{U}_{\mathbf{z}}^{\perp}) \in \mathbb{C}^{mn \times (m-1)n}$ *is at most* $\xi = 2B$.

Proof. Recall that for these number fields, we have $R_p^{\vee} = \lambda^{-1} R_p$ for any $p \in \mathbb{Z}$ with $\lambda = f'(\zeta)$. Let $\mathbf{z} \in \mathcal{Z}$ and denote $\widetilde{\mathbf{z}} = \lambda \mathbf{z} \in R_2^m$. First, we construct $\mathbf{U}_{\mathbf{z}}$ in the case where all the $\widetilde{z}_i$ are non-zero. To do so, we define the intermediate matrices $\mathbf{A}$, and $\mathbf{B}$ of $R^{m \times m}$, all unspecified entries being zeros:

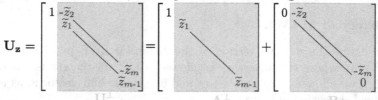

The matrix $\mathbf{U}_{\mathbf{z}}$ is invertible in modulo qR only if all the $\widetilde{z}_i$ (except $\widetilde{z}_m$) are in $R_q^{\times}$. Yet, since they are all non-zero binary polynomials (elements of R_2), we have that for all i in $[m]$, $\|\tau(\widetilde{z}_i)\|_{\infty} = 1$, where τ is the coefficient embedding. By Lemma 2, since q verifies the algebraic conditions taking all $f_i = 1$ and $q^{1/\varphi(\mu)}/\mathfrak{s}_1(\mu) > 1$, all the $\widetilde{z}_i$ are in $R_q^{\times}$.

By construction, the last $m - 1$ columns of $\mathbf{U}_{\mathbf{z}}$ are orthogonal to $\widetilde{\mathbf{z}}$. Let $\mathbf{U}_{\mathbf{z}}^{\perp}$ be the submatrix of $\mathbf{U}_{\mathbf{z}}$ obtained by removing the leftmost column as shown above. Since θ is a ring homomorphism, we have $\theta(\mathbf{U}_{\mathbf{z}}^{\perp}) = \theta(\mathbf{A}^{\perp}) + \theta(\mathbf{B}^{\perp})$. We now need to bound the spectral norm of these two matrices, and use the triangle inequality to conclude. For any vector $\mathbf{x} \in \mathbb{C}^{(m-1)n}$, we have that $\|\theta(\mathbf{A}^{\perp})\mathbf{x}\|_2 = \sqrt{\sum_{i \in [m-1]} \sum_{j \in [n]} |\sigma_j(\widetilde{z}_i)|^2 |x_{j+n(i-1)}|^2} \leq B\|\mathbf{x}\|_2$, because each $\widetilde{z}_i$ is in R_2. This yields $\|\theta(\mathbf{A}^{\perp})\|_2 \leq B$. A similar calculation on $\mathbf{B}^{\perp}$ leads to $\|\theta(\mathbf{B}^{\perp})\|_2 \leq B$, thus resulting in $\|\theta(\mathbf{U}_{\mathbf{z}}^{\perp})\|_2 \leq 2B$.

Now assume that $\widetilde{z}_{i_0}, \ldots, \widetilde{z}_m$ are zeros for some i_0 in $[m]$. If the zeros do not appear last in the vector $\widetilde{\mathbf{z}}$, we can replace $\widetilde{\mathbf{z}}$ with $\mathbf{S}\widetilde{\mathbf{z}}$, where $\mathbf{S} \in R^{m \times m}$ swaps the coordinates of $\widetilde{\mathbf{z}}$ so that the zeros appear last. Since $\mathbf{S}$ is unitary, it preserves the singular values as well as invertibility. Then, the construction remains the same except that the $\widetilde{z}_{i_0}, \ldots, \widetilde{z}_m$ on the diagonal are replaced by 1. The orthogonality is preserved, and $\|\theta(\mathbf{U}_{\mathbf{z}}^{\perp})\|_2$ can still be bounded above by $2B$. □

Notice that when the ring is of degree 1, the constructions in the different cases match the ones from [BLP+13, Claim 4.6]. So do the singular values as $B \leq n = 1$ by Lemma 1. Also, the construction differs from the notion of quality in [AA16] due to the discrepancies between the two definitions of ext-M-LWE.

Lemma 16 (Adapted from Lemma 4.7 [BLP+13]). *Let* $\nu = \prod_i p_i^{e_i}$, *K be the cyclotomic field of degree* $n = \varphi(\nu)$, *and R its ring of integers. Let* $\mu = \prod_i p_i$ *and q be a prime such that* $q = 1 \bmod \mu$, $ord_{\nu}(q) = \nu/\mu$ *and* $q > \mathfrak{s}_1(\mu)^{\varphi(\mu)}$, *where* $\mathfrak{s}_1(\mu)$ *denotes the largest singular value of the Vandermonde matrix of the μ-th cyclotomic field. Let m, k positive integers,* $\mathcal{Z} = (R_2^{\vee})^m$, $\varepsilon \in (0, 1/2)$ *and* $\alpha \geq q^{-1}\sqrt{\ln(2mn(1+1/\varepsilon))/\pi}$. *Then, there is a probabilistic reduction from* first-is-errorless M-LWE$_{n,k,m,q,\alpha}$ *to* ext-M-LWE$_{n,k,m,q,\alpha\sqrt{4B^2+1},\mathcal{Z}}$ *that reduces the advantage by at most* $33\varepsilon/2$, *where* $B = \max_{x \in R_2} \|\sigma(x)\|_\infty$.

Note that by the transference theorems, we have $\lambda_1^\infty(R) \geq N(R)^{1/n} = 1$. So, using the fact that $(q\Lambda)^* = q^{-1}\Lambda^*$, we have

$$\lambda_1^\infty((q^{-1}(R^\vee)^m)^*) = \lambda_1^\infty(q((R^\vee)^m)^*) = q\lambda_1^\infty(((R^\vee)^m)^*) = q\lambda_1^\infty(R) \geq q,$$

which together with Lemma 5 yields $q^{-1}\sqrt{\ln(2mn(1+1/\varepsilon))/\pi} \geq \eta_\varepsilon(q^{-1}(R^\vee)^m)$.

Proof. Assume we have access to an oracle $\mathcal{O}$ for ext-M-LWE$_{n,k,m,q,\alpha\sqrt{\xi^2+1},\mathcal{Z}}$. We take m samples from the first-is-errorless challenger, resulting in $(\mathbf{A}, \mathbf{b}) \in (R_q)^{k \times m} \times ((q^{-1}R^\vee/R^\vee) \times \mathbb{T}_{R^\vee}^{m-1})$. Assume we need to provide samples to $\mathcal{O}$ for some $\mathbf{z} \in \mathcal{Z}$. By Lemma 15 we can efficiently compute a matrix $\mathbf{U_z} \in R^{m \times m}$ that is invertible modulo qR, such that its submatrix $\mathbf{U_z^\perp}$ is orthogonal to $\mathbf{z}$, and that $\theta(\mathbf{U_z^\perp})$ has largest singular value less than $\xi = 2B$. The reduction first samples $\mathbf{f} \in K_\mathbb{R}^m$ from the continuous Gaussian distribution of covariance matrix $\alpha^2(\xi^2\mathbf{I}_{mn} - \mathbb{H}^\dagger\theta(\mathbf{U_z^\perp})\theta(\mathbf{U_z^\perp})^\dagger\mathbb{H}) \in \mathbb{R}^{mn \times mn}$, where $\mathbb{H}$ is defined as in Sect. 2.3. Note that $\mathbb{H}$ is unitary and therefore preserves the largest singular value. The reduction then computes $\mathbf{b}' = \mathbf{U_z}\mathbf{b} + \mathbf{f}$ and samples $\mathbf{c}$ from $\mathcal{D}_{q^{-1}(R^\vee)^m - \mathbf{b}',\alpha}$, and finally gives the following to $\mathcal{O}$

$$(\mathbf{A}' = \mathbf{A}\mathbf{U_z}^T, \mathbf{b}' + \mathbf{c} \bmod R^\vee, \langle \mathbf{z}, \mathbf{f} + \mathbf{c}\rangle).$$

Note that this tuple is in $(R_q)^{k \times m} \times (q^{-1}R^\vee/R^\vee)^m \times q^{-1}R^\vee$, as required. We now prove correctness. First, consider the case where $\mathbf{A}$ is uniformly random over $R_q^{k \times m}$ and $\mathbf{b} = q^{-1}\mathbf{A}^T\mathbf{s} + \mathbf{e} \bmod R^\vee$ for some uniform $\mathbf{s} \in (R_q^\vee)^k$, and $\mathbf{e}$ sampled from $\{0\} \times D_\alpha^{m-1}$ where $\{0\}$ denotes the distribution that is deterministically 0. Since $\mathbf{U_z}$ is invertible modulo qR, $\mathbf{A}' = \mathbf{A}\mathbf{U_z}^T$ is also uniform over $(R_q)^{k \times m}$ as required. From now on we condition on an arbitrary $\mathbf{A}'$ and analyze the distribution of the remaining components. We have $\mathbf{b}' = q^{-1}\mathbf{U_z}\mathbf{A}^T\mathbf{s} + \mathbf{U_z}\mathbf{e} + \mathbf{f} = q^{-1}(\mathbf{A}')^T\mathbf{s} + \mathbf{U_z}\mathbf{e} + \mathbf{f}$. Since the first coefficient of $\mathbf{e}$ is deterministically 0 the first column is ignored in the covariance matrix, and then $\mathbf{U_z}\mathbf{e}$ is distributed as the Gaussian over $K_\mathbb{R}^m$ of covariance matrix $\alpha^2\mathbb{H}^\dagger\theta(\mathbf{U_z^\perp})\theta(\mathbf{U_z^\perp})^\dagger\mathbb{H}$ by Lemma 9. Hence the vector $\mathbf{U_z}\mathbf{e} + \mathbf{f}$ is distributed as the Gaussian over $K_\mathbb{R}^m$ of covariance matrix $\alpha^2\mathbb{H}^\dagger\theta(\mathbf{U_z^\perp})\theta(\mathbf{U_z^\perp})^\dagger\mathbb{H} + \alpha^2(\xi^2\mathbf{I}_{mn} - \mathbb{H}^\dagger\theta(\mathbf{U_z^\perp})\theta(\mathbf{U_z^\perp})^\dagger\mathbb{H})$ which is identical to $D_{\alpha\xi}^m$. Since $q^{-1}(\mathbf{A}')^T\mathbf{s} \in q^{-1}(R^\vee)^m$, the coset $q^{-1}(R^\vee)^m - \mathbf{b}'$ is the same as $q^{-1}(R^\vee)^m - (\mathbf{U_z}\mathbf{e} + \mathbf{f})$, which yields that $\mathbf{c}$ can be seen as being sampled from $\mathcal{D}_{q^{-1}(R^\vee)^m - (\mathbf{U_z}\mathbf{e} + \mathbf{f}),\alpha}$. By the remark made before the proof, we have $\alpha \geq \eta_\varepsilon(q^{-1}(R^\vee)^m)$, so by Lemma 8, the distribution of $\mathbf{U_z}\mathbf{e} + \mathbf{f} + \mathbf{c}$ is within statistical distance 8ε of $\mathcal{D}_{q^{-1}(R^\vee)^m,\alpha\sqrt{\xi^2+1}}$, which shows that the second component is correctly distributed up to 8ε. Note that $\mathbf{U_z}\mathbf{e} = \sum_{i \in [m]} e_i \cdot \mathbf{u}_i$ is in the space spanned by the columns of $\mathbf{U_z^\perp}$ because $e_1 = 0$. This yields $\langle \mathbf{z}, \mathbf{U_z}\mathbf{e}\rangle = 0$ as $\mathbf{z}$ is orthogonal to the columns of $\mathbf{U_z^\perp}$. This proves that the third component equals $\langle \mathbf{z}, \mathbf{U_z}\mathbf{e} + \mathbf{f} + \mathbf{c}\rangle$ and is thus correctly distributed.

Now consider the case where both $\mathbf{A}$ and $\mathbf{b}$ are uniform. First, observe that $\alpha \geq \eta_\varepsilon(q^{-1}(R^\vee)^m)$ and therefore by Lemma 6, the distribution of $(\mathbf{A}, \mathbf{b})$ is within statistical distance $\varepsilon/2$ of the distribution of $(\mathbf{A}, \mathbf{e}'+\mathbf{e})$ where $\mathbf{e}' \in (q^{-1}R^\vee/R^\vee)^m$ is uniform and $\mathbf{e}$ is distributed from $\{0\} \times D_\alpha^{m-1}$. So we can assume our input is $(\mathbf{A}, \mathbf{e}' + \mathbf{e})$. $\mathbf{A}'$ is uniform as before, and clearly independent of the other two components. Moreover, since $\mathbf{b}' = \mathbf{U_z}\mathbf{e}' + \mathbf{U_z}\mathbf{e} + \mathbf{f}$ and $\mathbf{U_z}\mathbf{e}' \in q^{-1}(R^\vee)^m$, then the coset $q^{-1}(R^\vee)^m - \mathbf{b}'$ is identical to $q^{-1}(R^\vee)^m - (\mathbf{U_z}\mathbf{e} + \mathbf{f})$. For the same reasons as above, $\mathbf{U_z}\mathbf{e} + \mathbf{f} + \mathbf{c}$ is distributed as $\mathcal{D}_{q^{-1}(R^\vee)^m, \alpha\sqrt{\xi^2+1}}$ within statistical distance of at most 8ε, and in particular independent of $\mathbf{e}'$. So the third component is correctly distributed because once again $\langle \mathbf{z}, \mathbf{U_z}\mathbf{e} \rangle = 0$. Finally, since $\mathbf{e}'$ is independent of the first and third components, and that $\mathbf{U_z}\mathbf{e}'$ is uniform over $(q^{-1}R^\vee/R^\vee)^m$ as $\mathbf{U_z}$ is invertible modulo qR, it yields that the second component is uniform and independent of the other ones as required. $\square$

Instantiation in Power-of-Two Cyclotomics. The condition on the modulus q in Lemmas 15 and 16 stems from the invertibility result from Lyubashevsky and Seiler [LS18]. This result can be simplified in the power-of-two case [LS18, Corollary 1.2] where it is conditioned on the number $\kappa > 1$ of splitting factors of $x^n + 1$ in $\mathbb{Z}_q[x]$. Choosing κ as a power of two less than $n = 2^\ell$, q now has to be a prime congruent to $2\kappa + 1$ modulo 4κ. The invertibility condition then becomes $0 < \|\tau(y)\|_\infty < q^{1/\kappa}/\sqrt{\kappa}$ for any y in R_q. The upper bound is decreasing with κ so the smaller κ, the more invertible elements. The smallest choice for κ is $\kappa = 2$, which leads to choosing a prime $q = 5 \bmod 8$. In our context, having $q^{1/2}/\sqrt{2} > 1$ is sufficient as our elements have binary coefficients. This requires $q > 2$ which is subsumed by $q = 5 \bmod 8$.

3.4   Reduction to bin-M-LWE

We now provide the final step of the overall reduction, by reducing to the binary secret version of M-LWE using a sequence of hybrids. The idea is to use the set $\mathcal{Z}$ of the ext-M-LWE problem as our set of secrets. The problem ext-M-LWE$_{n,k,d,q,\alpha,\{0\}^d}^m$ mentioned in the lemma statement is trivially harder than ext-M-LWE$_{n,k,d,q,\alpha,(R_2^\vee)^d}^m$, that is also why it is not specified in Fig. 1.

Lemma 17 (Adapted from Lemma 4.9 [BLP+13]). *Let $K = \mathbb{Q}(\zeta)$ be a number field of degree n, such that its ring of integers is $R = \mathbb{Z}[\zeta]$, with defining polynomial f. Let q be a prime modulus. Let k, m, d be positive integers such that $d \geq k\log_2 q + \omega(\log_2 n)$ Further, let $\varepsilon \in (0, 1/2)$ and $\alpha, \gamma, \beta, \delta$ be positive reals such that $\alpha \geq q^{-1}\sqrt{2\ln(2nd(1+1/\varepsilon))/\pi}$, $\gamma = \alpha B\sqrt{d}$, $\beta = \alpha B\sqrt{2d}$, where $B = \max_{x\in R_2}\|\sigma(x)\|_\infty$, and $\delta = \frac{1}{2}\sqrt{(1 + q^k/2^d)^n - 1}$. Then there is a reduction from ext-M-LWE$_{n,k,d,q,\alpha,(R_2^\vee)^d}^m$, M-LWE$_{n,k,m,q,\gamma}$ and ext-M-LWE$_{n,k,d,q,\alpha,\{0\}^d}^m$ to bin-M-LWE$_{n,d,m,q,\leq\beta}$, such that if $\mathcal{B}_1$, $\mathcal{B}_2$ and $\mathcal{B}_3$ are the algorithms obtained by applying these hybrids to an algorithm $\mathcal{A}$, then*

$$\mathrm{Adv}[\mathcal{A}] \leq \mathrm{Adv}[\mathcal{B}_1] + \mathrm{Adv}[\mathcal{B}_2] + \mathrm{Adv}[\mathcal{B}_3] + 2m\varepsilon + \delta.$$

Proof. For $x \in R^\vee$, we denote $\widetilde{x} = \lambda x \in R$ as before, where $\lambda = f'(\zeta)$. We extend this notation to vectors and matrices in the obvious way. We consider $\mathbf{z} \hookleftarrow U((R_2^\vee)^d)$ and $\mathbf{e} \in K_\mathbb{R}^m$ sampled from the continuous Gaussian $D_\mathbf{r}^m$ with parameter vector $\mathbf{r}$ with $r_j^2 = \gamma^2 + \alpha^2 \sum_i |\sigma_j(\widetilde{z}_i)|^2$. Yet, we have $\|\mathbf{r}\|_\infty = \sqrt{\gamma^2 + \alpha^2 \|\widetilde{\mathbf{z}}\|_{2,\infty}^2}$, as well as $\|\widetilde{\mathbf{z}}\|_{2,\infty}^2 \leq \sum_{i \in [d]} \|\sigma(\widetilde{z}_i)\|_\infty^2$. Recalling the parameter $B = \max_{x \in R_2} \|\sigma(x)\|_\infty$, that can be bounded above by n for cyclotomics by Lemma 1, we get $\|\mathbf{r}\|_\infty \leq \sqrt{\gamma^2 + B^2 d\alpha^2} = B\sqrt{2d}\alpha = \beta$. In addition, we sample $\mathbf{A}$ uniformly over $(R_q)^{d \times m}$ and define $\mathbf{b} = q^{-1}\mathbf{A}^T \mathbf{z} + \mathbf{e} \bmod R^\vee$.

First hybrid. We denote by H_0 the distribution of $(\mathbf{A}, \mathbf{b})$ and H_1 the distribution of $(\mathbf{A}, q^{-1}\mathbf{A}^T\mathbf{z} - \lambda \mathbf{N}^T\mathbf{z} + \widehat{\mathbf{e}} \bmod R^\vee)$, where $\mathbf{N} \hookleftarrow \mathcal{D}_{q^{-1}R^\vee, \alpha}^{d \times m}$ and $\widehat{\mathbf{e}} \hookleftarrow D_\gamma^m$. By looking at each component of the vectors we claim that $\Delta([-\mathbf{N}^T\widetilde{\mathbf{z}} + \widehat{\mathbf{e}}]_i, \mathbf{e}_i) \leq 2\varepsilon$. Indeed, $(1/\alpha^2 + \|\widetilde{\mathbf{z}}\|_{2,\infty}^2/\gamma^2)^{-1/2} \geq \alpha/\sqrt{2}$ and $\alpha/\sqrt{2} \geq \eta_\varepsilon(q^{-1}(R^\vee)^d)$ as explained for Lemma 16. If $\mathbf{n}_i \in q^{-1}(R^\vee)^d$ denotes the i-th column of $\mathbf{N}$, Lemma 11 yields the claim as $[-\mathbf{N}^T\widetilde{\mathbf{z}} + \widehat{\mathbf{e}}]_i = \langle \mathbf{n}_i, -\widetilde{\mathbf{z}} \rangle + \widehat{e}_i$, thus giving $\Delta(-\mathbf{N}^T\widetilde{\mathbf{z}} + \widehat{\mathbf{e}}, \mathbf{e}) \leq 2m\varepsilon$.

$$|\Pr(\mathcal{A}(H_0)) - \Pr(\mathcal{A}(H_1))| \leq 2m\varepsilon. \tag{1}$$

Second Hybrid. We define H_2 to be the distribution of $(\widehat{\mathbf{A}}, q^{-1}\widehat{\mathbf{A}}^T\mathbf{z} - \lambda \mathbf{N}^T\mathbf{z} + \widehat{\mathbf{e}} \bmod R^\vee) = (\widehat{\mathbf{A}}, q^{-1}(\lambda \mathbf{B})^T\mathbf{Cz} + \widehat{\mathbf{e}} \bmod R^\vee)$ where $\mathbf{B}$ is uniformly sampled over $(R_q^\vee)^{k \times m}$, $\mathbf{C}$ uniformly sampled over $R_q^{k \times d}$ and $\widehat{\mathbf{A}} = \lambda q(q^{-1}\mathbf{C}^T\mathbf{B} + \mathbf{N} \bmod R^\vee)$. We argue that a distinguisher between H_1 and H_2 can be used to derive an adversary $\mathcal{B}_1$ for ext-M-LWE$_{n,k,d,q,\alpha,(R_2^\vee)^d}^m$ with the same advantage. To do so, $\mathcal{B}_1$ transforms the samples from the challenger of the ext-M-LWE problem to samples defined in H_1 or the ones in H_2 depending on whether or not the received samples are uniform. In the uniform case, $(\mathbf{C}, (\lambda q)^{-1}\mathbf{A}, \mathbf{N}^T\mathbf{z})$ can be efficiently transformed into a sample from H_1. Note that $(\lambda q)^{-1}\mathbf{A}$ indeed corresponds to the uniform case of ext-M-LWE, because $\mathbf{A}$ is uniform over R_q and $(\lambda q)^{-1}R_q$ can be seen as $q^{-1}R^\vee/R^\vee$. In the other case, if we apply the same transformation to the ext-M-LWE sample $(\mathbf{C}, q^{-1}\mathbf{C}^T\mathbf{B} + \mathbf{N} \bmod R^\vee, \mathbf{N}^T\mathbf{z})$, it leads to a sample from H_2. Hence, $\mathcal{B}_1$ is a distinguisher for ext-M-LWE$_{n,k,d,q,\alpha,(R_2^\vee)^d}^m$, and

$$|\Pr(\mathcal{A}(H_1)) - \Pr(\mathcal{A}(H_2))| = \mathrm{Adv}[\mathcal{B}_1]. \tag{2}$$

Third Hybrid. Next we define H_3 to be the distribution of $(\widehat{\mathbf{A}}, q^{-1}\widetilde{\mathbf{B}}^T\mathbf{s} + \widehat{\mathbf{e}} \bmod R^\vee)$, where $\widetilde{\mathbf{B}} = \lambda \mathbf{B} \in R_q^{k \times m}$, and $\mathbf{s}$ is uniform over $(R_q^\vee)^k$. By the Ring Leftover Hash Lemma stated in Lemma 12, we have that $(\mathbf{C}, \mathbf{C}\widetilde{\mathbf{z}})$ is within statistical distance at most δ from $(\mathbf{C}, \widetilde{\mathbf{s}})$. By multiplying by λ^{-1} and using the fact that a function does not increase the statistical distance, we have that $\Delta((\mathbf{C}, \mathbf{Cz}), (\mathbf{C}, \mathbf{s})) \leq \delta$. Note that the condition $d \geq k \log_2 q + \omega(\log_2 n)$ implies $\delta \leq n^{-\omega(1)}$. This yields

$$|\Pr(\mathcal{A}(H_2)) - \Pr(\mathcal{A}(H_3))| \leq \delta. \tag{3}$$

Fourth Hybrid. We then replace the second component by the uniform as we define H_4 to be the distribution of $(\widehat{\mathbf{A}}, \mathbf{u})$, with $\mathbf{u} \hookleftarrow U(\mathbb{T}_{R^\vee}^m)$. A distinguisher between H_3 and H_4 can be used to derive an adversary $\mathcal{B}_2$ for M-LWE$_{n,k,m,q,\gamma}$. For that, $\mathcal{B}_2$ applies the efficient transformation to the samples from the M-LWE challenger, which turns $(\widetilde{\mathbf{B}}, \mathbf{u})$ into a sample from H_4 in the uniform case, and $(\widetilde{\mathbf{B}}, q^{-1}\widetilde{\mathbf{B}}^T\mathbf{s}+\widehat{\mathbf{e}} \bmod R^\vee)$ into a sample from H_3 in the M-LWE case. Therefore, $\mathcal{B}_2$ is a distinguisher for M-LWE$_{n,k,m,q,\gamma}$ such that

$$|\Pr(\mathcal{A}(H_3)) - \Pr(\mathcal{A}(H_4))| = \mathrm{Adv}[\mathcal{B}_2]. \tag{4}$$

Last Hybrid. We now change $\widehat{\mathbf{A}}$ back to uniform by defining H_5 to be the distribution of $(\mathbf{A}, \mathbf{u})$. With the same argument as for the second hybrid, we can construct an adversary $\mathcal{B}_3$ for ext-M-LWE$_{n,k,d,q,\alpha,\{0\}^d}^m$ (which corresponds to multiple-secret M-LWE without additional information on the error) based on a distinguisher between H_4 and H_5. It transforms $(\mathbf{C}, (\lambda q)^{-1}\widehat{A}, \mathbf{N}^T\mathbf{0})$ into a sample from H_4 (M-LWE case) and $(\mathbf{C}, (\lambda q)^{-1}\mathbf{A}, \mathbf{N}^T\mathbf{0})$ into a sample from H_5 (uniform case). We then get

$$|\Pr(\mathcal{A}(H_4)) - \Pr(\mathcal{A}(H_5))| = \mathrm{Adv}[\mathcal{B}_3]. \tag{5}$$

Putting Eqs. 1, 2, 3, 4, 5 altogether yields the result. $\square$

Acknowledgments. This work was supported by the European Union PRO-METHEUS project (Horizon 2020 Research and Innovation Program, grant 780701). It has also received a French government support managed by the National Research Agency in the "Investing for the Future" program, under the national project RISQ P141580-2660001/DOS0044216. Katharina Boudgoust is funded by the Direction Générale de l'Armement (Pôle de Recherche CYBER). We thank our anonymous referees of Indocrypt 2020 and CT-RSA 2021 for their thorough proof reading and constructive feedback.

References

[AA16]   Alperin-Sheriff, J., Apon, D.: Dimension-preserving reductions from LWE to LWR. IACR Cryptology ePrint Archive 2016:589 (2016)

[AD17]   Albrecht, M.R., Deo, A.: Large modulus ring-LWE $\geq$ module-LWE. In: Takagi, T., Peyrin, T. (eds.) ASIACRYPT 2017. LNCS, vol. 10624, pp. 267–296. Springer, Cham (2017). https://doi.org/10.1007/978-3-319-70694-8_10

[BD20]   Brakerski, Z., Döttling, N.: Hardness of LWE on general entropic distributions. In: Canteaut, A., Ishai, Y. (eds.) EUROCRYPT 2020. LNCS, vol. 12106, pp. 551–575. Springer, Cham (2020). https://doi.org/10.1007/978-3-030-45724-2_19

[BDK+18] Bos, J.W., et al.: CRYSTALS - kyber: a CCA-secure module-lattice-based KEM. In: 2018 IEEE European Symposium on Security and Privacy, EuroS&P 2018, London, United Kingdom, 24–26 April 2018, pp. 353–367 (2018)

[BGV12]   Brakerski, Z., Gentry, C., Vaikuntanathan, V.: (Leveled) fully homomorphic encryption without bootstrapping. In: Innovations in Theoretical Computer Science 2012, Cambridge, MA, USA, 8–10 January 2012, pp. 309–325 (2012)

[BJRW20] Boudgoust, K., Jeudy, C., Roux-Langlois, A., Wen, W.: Towards classical hardness of module-LWE: the linear rank case. In: Moriai, S., Wang, H. (eds.) ASIACRYPT 2020. LNCS, vol. 12492, pp. 289–317. Springer, Cham (2020). https://doi.org/10.1007/978-3-030-64834-3_10

[BJRW21] Boudgoust, K., Jeudy, C., Roux-Langlois, A., Wen, W.: On the hardness of module-lwe with binary secrets. IACR Cryptology ePrint Archive 2021:265 (2021)

[BLP+13] Brakerski, Z., Langlois, A., Peikert, C., Regev, O., Stehlé, D.: Classical hardness of learning with errors. In: Symposium on Theory of Computing Conference, STOC 2013, Palo Alto, CA, USA, 1–4 June 2013, pp. 575–584 (2013)

[BV14] Brakerski, Z., Vaikuntanathan, V.: Efficient fully homomorphic encryption from (standard) LWE. SIAM J. Comput. **43**(2), 831–871 (2014)

[DKL+18] Ducas, L., et al.: Crystals-dilithium: a lattice-based digital signature scheme. IACR Trans. Cryptogr. Hardw. Embed. Syst. **2018**(1), 238–268 (2018)

[DM15] Ducas, L., Micciancio, D.: FHEW: bootstrapping homomorphic encryption in less than a second. In: Oswald, E., Fischlin, M. (eds.) EUROCRYPT 2015. LNCS, vol. 9056, pp. 617–640. Springer, Heidelberg (2015). https://doi.org/10.1007/978-3-662-46800-5_24

[GKPV10] Goldwasser, S., Kalai, Y.T., Peikert, C., Vaikuntanathan, V.: Robustness of the learning with errors assumption. In: Proceedings of the Innovations in Computer Science - ICS 2010, Tsinghua University, Beijing, China, 5–7 January 2010, pp. 230–240. Tsinghua University Press (2010)

[GPV08] Gentry, C., Peikert, C., Vaikuntanathan, V.: Trapdoors for hard lattices and new cryptographic constructions. In: Proceedings of the 40th Annual ACM Symposium on Theory of Computing, Victoria, British Columbia, Canada, 17–20 May 2008, pp. 197–206. ACM (2008)

[KF15] Kirchner, P., Fouque, P.-A.: An improved BKW algorithm for LWE with applications to cryptography and lattices. In: Gennaro, R., Robshaw, M. (eds.) CRYPTO 2015. LNCS, vol. 9215, pp. 43–62. Springer, Heidelberg (2015). https://doi.org/10.1007/978-3-662-47989-6_3

[LPR10] Lyubashevsky, V., Peikert, C., Regev, O.: On ideal lattices and learning with errors over rings. In: Gilbert, H. (ed.) EUROCRYPT 2010. LNCS, vol. 6110, pp. 1–23. Springer, Heidelberg (2010). https://doi.org/10.1007/978-3-642-13190-5_1

[LPR13] Lyubashevsky, V., Peikert, C., Regev, O.: On ideal lattices and learning with errors over rings. J. ACM **60**(6), 43:1–43:35 (2013)

[LS15] Langlois, A., Stehlé, D.: Worst-case to average-case reductions for module lattices. Des. Codes Crypt. **75**(3), 565–599 (2014). https://doi.org/10.1007/s10623-014-9938-4

[LS18] Lyubashevsky, V., Seiler, G.: Short, invertible elements in partially splitting cyclotomic rings and applications to lattice-based zero-knowledge proofs. In: Nielsen, J.B., Rijmen, V. (eds.) EUROCRYPT 2018. LNCS, vol. 10820, pp. 204–224. Springer, Cham (2018). https://doi.org/10.1007/978-3-319-78381-9_8

[LWW20] Lin, H., Wang, Y., Wang, M.: Hardness of module-LWE and ring-LWE on general entropic distributions. IACR Cryptology ePrint Archive 2020:1238 (2020)

[Mic07] Micciancio, D.: Generalized compact knapsacks, cyclic lattices, and efficient one-way functions. Comput. Complex. **16**(4), 365–411 (2007)

[Mic18] Micciancio, D.: On the hardness of learning with errors with binary secrets. Theory Comput. **14**(1), 1–17 (2018)

[MP12] Micciancio, D., Peikert, C.: Trapdoors for lattices: simpler, tighter, faster, smaller. In: Pointcheval, D., Johansson, T. (eds.) EUROCRYPT 2012. LNCS, vol. 7237, pp. 700–718. Springer, Heidelberg (2012). https://doi.org/10.1007/978-3-642-29011-4_41

[MR07] Micciancio, D., Regev, O.: Worst-case to average-case reductions based on Gaussian measures. SIAM J. Comput. **37**(1), 267–302 (2007)

[NIS] NIST. Post-quantum cryptography standardization. https://csrc.nist.gov/Projects/Post-Quantum-Cryptography/Post-Quantum-Cryptography-Standardization

[Pei08] Peikert, C.: Limits on the hardness of lattice problems in l_p norms. Comput. Complex. **17**(2), 300–351 (2008)

[Pei09] Peikert, C.: Public-key cryptosystems from the worst-case shortest vector problem: extended abstract. In: Proceedings of the 41st Annual ACM Symposium on Theory of Computing, STOC 2009, Bethesda, MD, USA, 31 May–2 June 2009, pp. 333–342 (2009)

[Pei10] Peikert, C.: An efficient and parallel Gaussian sampler for lattices. In: Rabin, T. (ed.) CRYPTO 2010. LNCS, vol. 6223, pp. 80–97. Springer, Heidelberg (2010). https://doi.org/10.1007/978-3-642-14623-7_5

[PS19] Peikert, C., Shiehian, S.: Noninteractive zero knowledge for NP from (plain) learning with errors. In: Boldyreva, A., Micciancio, D. (eds.) CRYPTO 2019. LNCS, vol. 11692, pp. 89–114. Springer, Cham (2019). https://doi.org/10.1007/978-3-030-26948-7_4

[Reg05] Regev, O.: On lattices, learning with errors, random linear codes, and cryptography. In: Proceedings of the 37th Annual ACM Symposium on Theory of Computing, Baltimore, MD, USA, 22–24 May 2005, pp. 84–93 (2005)

[Reg09] Regev, O.: On lattices, learning with errors, random linear codes, and cryptography. J. ACM **56**(6), 34:1–34:40 (2009)

[RSW18] Rosca, M., Stehlé, D., Wallet, A.: On the ring-LWE and polynomial-LWE problems. In: Nielsen, J.B., Rijmen, V. (eds.) EUROCRYPT 2018. LNCS, vol. 10820, pp. 146–173. Springer, Cham (2018). https://doi.org/10.1007/978-3-319-78381-9_6

[SSTX09] Stehlé, D., Steinfeld, R., Tanaka, K., Xagawa, K.: Efficient public key encryption based on ideal lattices. In: Matsui, M. (ed.) ASIACRYPT 2009. LNCS, vol. 5912, pp. 617–635. Springer, Heidelberg (2009). https://doi.org/10.1007/978-3-642-10366-7_36

[WW19] Wang, Y., Wang, M.: Module-LWE versus ring-LWE, revisited. IACR Cryptology ePrint Archive 2019:930 (2019)

Multi-party Revocation in Sovrin: Performance through Distributed Trust

Lukas Helminger[1,2], Daniel Kales[1], Sebastian Ramacher[3] (ID),
and Roman Walch[1,2(✉)]

[1] Graz University of Technology, Graz, Austria
{lukas.helminger,daniel.kales,roman.walch}@iaik.tugraz.at
[2] Know-Center GmbH, Graz, Austria
[3] AIT Austrian Institute of Technology, Vienna, Austria
sebastian.ramacher@ait.ac.at

Abstract. Accumulators provide compact representations of large sets and compact membership witnesses. Besides constant-size witnesses, public-key accumulators provide efficient updates of both the accumulator itself and the witness. However, bilinear group based accumulators come with drawbacks: they require a trusted setup and their performance is not practical for real-world applications with large sets.

In this paper, we introduce multi-party public-key accumulators dubbed *dynamic (threshold) secret-shared accumulators*. We present an instantiation using bilinear groups having access to more efficient witness generation and update algorithms that utilize the shares of the secret trapdoors sampled by the parties generating the public parameters. Specifically, for the q-SDH-based accumulators, we provide a maliciously-secure variant sped up by a secure multi-party computation (MPC) protocol (IMACC'19) built on top of SPDZ and a maliciously secure threshold variant built with Shamir secret sharing. For these schemes, a performant proof-of-concept implementation is provided, which substantiates the practicability of public-key accumulators in this setting.

We explore applications of dynamic (threshold) secret-shared accumulators to revocation schemes of group signatures and credentials system. In particular, we consider it as part of Sovrin's system for anonymous credentials where credentials are issued by the foundation of trusted nodes.

Keywords: Multiparty computation · Dynamic accumulators · Distributed trust · Threshold accumulators

1 Introduction

Digital identity management systems become an increasingly important corner stone of digital workflows. Self-sovereign identity (SSI) systems such as Sovrin[1]

---

[1] https://sovrin.org/.

The full version is available online at: https://eprint.iacr.org/2020/724

K. G. Paterson (Ed.): CT-RSA 2021, LNCS 12704, pp. 527–551, 2021.
https://doi.org/10.1007/978-3-030-75539-3_22

are of central interest as underlined by a recent push in the European Union for a cross-border SSI system.[2] But all these systems face a similar issue, namely that of efficient revocation. Regardless of whether they are built from signatures, group signatures or anonymous credentials, such systems have to consider mechanisms to revoke a user's identity information. Especially for identity management systems with a focus on privacy, revocation may threaten those privacy guarantees. As such various forms of privacy-preserving revocations have emerged in the literature including approaches based on various forms of deny- or allowlists including [3,13,31] among many others.

One promising approach regarding efficiency is based on denylists (or allowlists) via cryptographic accumulators which were introduced by Benaloh and de Mare [11]. They allow one to accumulate a finite set $\mathcal{X}$ into a succinct value called the accumulator. For every element in this set, one can efficiently compute a witness certifying its membership, and additionally, some accumulators also support efficient non-memberships witnesses. However, it should be computationally infeasible to find a membership witness for non-accumulated values and a non-membership witness for accumulated values, respectively. Accumulators facilitate privacy-preserving revocation mechanisms, which is especially relevant for privacy-friendly authentication mechanisms like group signatures and credentials. For a denylist approach, the issuing authority accumulates all revoked users and users prove in zero-knowledge that they know a non-membership witness for their credential. Alternatively, for a allowlist approach, the issuing authority accumulates all users and users then prove in zero-knowledge that they know a membership witness. As both approaches may involve large lists, efficient accumulator updates as well as efficient proofs are important for building an overall efficient system. For example, in Sovrin [37] and Hyperledger Indy[3] such an accumulator-based approach with allowlists following the ideas of [31] is used. Their credentials contain a unique revocation ID attribute, i_R, which are accumulated. Each user obtains a membership witness proving that their i_R is contained in the accumulator. Once a credential is revoked, the corresponding i_R gets removed from the accumulator and all users have to update their proofs accordingly. The revoked user is no longer able to prove knowledge of a verifying witness and thus verification fails.

Accumulators are an important primitive and building block in many cryptographic protocols. In particular, Merkle trees [44] have seen many applications in both the cryptographic literature but also in practice. For example, they have been used to implement Certificate Transparency (CT) [38] where all issued certificates are publicly logged, i.e., accumulated. Accumulators also find application in credentials [13], ring, and group signatures [26,39], anonymous cash [45], among many others. When looking at accumulators deployed in practice, many systems rely on Merkle trees. Most prominently we can observe this fact in CT. Even though new certificates are continuously added to the log,

---

[2] https://essif-lab.eu/.

[3] https://hyperledger-indy.readthedocs.io/projects/hipe/en/latest/text/0011-cred-revocation/README.html.

the system is designed around a Merkle tree that gets recomputed all the time instead of updating a dynamic public-key accumulator. The reason is two-fold: first, for dynamic accumulators to be efficiently computable, knowledge of the secret trapdoor used to generate the public parameters is required. Without this information, witness generation and accumulator updates are simply too slow for large sets (cf. [35]). Secondly, in this setting it is of paramount importance that the log servers do not have access to the secret trapdoor. Otherwise malicious servers would be able to present membership witnesses for every certificate even if it was not included in the log.

The latter issue can also be observed in other applications of public-key accumulators. The approaches due to Garman et al. [31] and the one used in Sovrin rely on the Strong-RSA and q-SDH accumulators, respectively. Both these accumulators have trapdoors: in the first case the factorization of the RSA modulus and in the second case a secret exponent. Therefore, the security of the system requires those trapdoors to stay secret. Hence, these protocols require to put significant trust in the parties generating the public parameters. If they would act maliciously and not delete the secret trapdoors, they would be able to break all these protocols in one way or another. To circumvent this problem, Sander [47] proposed a variant of an RSA-based accumulator from RSA moduli with unknown factorization. Alternatively, secure multi-party computation (MPC) protocols enable us to compute the public parameters and thereby replace the trusted third party. As long as a large enough subset of parties is honest, the secret trapdoor is not available to anyone. Over the years, efficient solutions for distributed parameter generation have emerged, e.g., for distributed RSA key generation [16,17,29], or distributed ECDSA key generation [41].

Based on the recent progress in efficient MPC protocols, we ask the following question: *what if the parties kept their shares of the secret trapdoor?* Are the algorithms of the public-key accumulators exploiting knowledge of the secret trapdoor faster if performed within an (maliciously-secure) MPC protocol than their variants relying only on the public parameters?

1.1   Our Techniques

We give a short overview of how our construction works which allows us to positively answer this question for accumulators in the discrete logarithm setting. Let us consider the accumulator based on the q-SDH assumption which is based on the fact that given powers $g^{s^i} \in \mathbb{G}$ for all i up to q where $s \in \mathbb{Z}_p$ is unknown, it is possible to evaluate polynomials $f \in \mathbb{Z}_p[X]$ up to degree q at s in the exponent, i.e., $g^{f(s)}$. This is done by taking the coefficients of the polynomial, i.e., $f = \sum_{i=0}^{q} a_i X^i$, and computing $g^{f(s)}$ as $\prod_{i=0}^{q} (g^{s^i})^{a_i}$. The accumulator is built by defining a polynomial with the elements as roots and evaluating this polynomial at s in the exponent. A witness is simply the corresponding factor canceled out, i.e., $g^{f(s)(s-x)^{-1}}$. Verification of the witness is performed by checking whether the corresponding factor and the witness match $g^{f(s)}$ using a pairing equation.

If s is known, all computations are more efficient: $f(s)$ can be directly evaluated in $\mathbb{Z}_p$ and the generation of the accumulator only requires one exponentiation in $\mathbb{G}$. The same is true for the computation of the witness. For the latter, the asymptotic runtime is thereby reduced from $\mathcal{O}(|\mathcal{X}|)$ to $\mathcal{O}(1)$. This improvement comes at a cost: if s is known, witnesses for non-members can be produced.

On the other hand, if multiple parties first produce s in an additively secret-shared fashion, these parties can cooperate in a secret-sharing based MPC protocol. Thereby, all the computations can still benefit from the knowledge of s. Indeed, the parties would compute their share of $g^{f(s)}$ and $g^{f(s)(s-x)^{-1}}$ respectively and thanks to the partial knowledge of s could still perform all operations – except the final exponentiation – in $\mathbb{Z}_p$. Furthermore, all involved computations are generic enough to be instantiated with MPC protocols with different trust assumptions. These include the dishonest majority protocol SPDZ [21,24] and honest majority threshold protocols based on Shamir secret sharing [48].

1.2 Our Contribution

Starting from the very recent treatment of accumulators in the UC model [15] by Baldimtsi et al. [4], we introduce the notion of *(threshold) secret-shared accumulators*. As the name suggests, it covers accumulators where the trapdoor is available in a (potentially full) threshold secret-shared fashion with multiple parties running the parameter generation as well as the algorithms that profit from the availability of the trapdoor. Since the MPC literature discusses security in the UC model, we also chose to do so for our accumulators.

Based on recent improvements on distributed key generation of discrete logarithms, we provide dynamic public-key accumulators without trusted setup. During the parameter generation, the involved parties keep their shares of the secret trapdoor. Consequently, we present MPC protocols secure in the semi-honest and the malicious security model, respectively, implementing the algorithms for accumulator generation, witness generation, and accumulator updates exploiting the shares of the secret trapdoor. Specifically, we give such protocols for q-SDH accumulators [25,46], which can be build from dishonest-majority full-threshold protocols (e.g., SPDZ [21,24]) and from honest-majority threshold MPC protocols (e.g., Shamir secret sharing [48]). In particular, our protocol enables updates to the accumulator independent of the size of the accumulated set. For increased efficiency, we consider this accumulator in bilinear groups of Type-3. Due to their structure, the construction nicely generalizes to any number of parties.

We provide a proof-of-concept implementation of our protocols in two MPC frameworks, MP-SPDZ [36] and FRESCO.[4] We evaluate the efficiency of our protocols and compare them to the performance of an implementation, having no access to the secret trapdoors as usual for the public-key accumulators. We evaluate our protocol in the LAN and WAN setting in the semi-honest and malicious security model for various choices of parties and accumulator sizes. For the latter, we choose sizes up to 2^{14}. Specifically, for the q-SDH accumulator, we observe the expected $\mathcal{O}(1)$ runtimes for witness creation and accumulator updates, which cannot be achieved without access to the trapdoor. Notably, for

---

[4] https://github.com/aicis/fresco.

the tested numbers of up to 5 parties, the MPC-enabled accumulator creation algorithms are faster for 2^{10} elements in the LAN setting than its non-MPC counterpart (without access to the secret trapdoor). For 2^{14} elements the algorithms are also faster in the WAN setting.

Finally, we discuss how our proposed MPC-based accumulators might impact revocation in distributed credential systems such as Sovrin [37]. In this scenario, the trust in the nodes run by the Sovrin foundation members can further be reduced. In addition, this approach generalizes to any accumulator-based revocation scheme and can be combined with threshold key management systems. We also discuss applications to CT and its privacy-preserving extension [35].

1.3 Related Work

When cryptographic protocols are deployed that require the setup of public parameters by a trusted third party, issues similar to those mentioned for public-key accumulators may arise. As discussed before, especially cryptocurrencies had to come up with ways to circumvent this problem for accumulators but also the common reference string (CRS) of zero-knowledge SNARKs [14]. Here, trust in the CRS is of paramount importance on the verifier side to prevent malicious provers from cheating. But also provers need to trust the CRS as otherwise zero-knowledge might not hold. We note that there are alternative approaches, namely subversion-resilient zk-SNARKS [9] to reduce the trust required in the CRS generator. Groth et al. [33] recently introduced the notion of an updatable CRS where first generic compilers [1] are available to lift any zk-SNARK to an updatable simulation sound extractable zk-SNARK. There the CRS can be updated and if the initial generation or one of the updates was done honestly, neither soundness nor zero-knowledge can be subverted. In the random oracle model (ROM), those considerations become less of a concern and the trust put into the CRS can be minimized, e.g., as done in the construction of STARKs [10].

Approaches that try to fix the issue directly in the formalization of accumulators and corresponding constructions have also been studied. For example, Lipmaa [42] proposed a modified model tailored to the hidden order group setting. In this model, the parameter setup is split into two algorithms, Setup and Gen where the adversary can control the trapdoors output by Setup, but can neither influence nor access the randomness used by Gen. However, constructions in this model so far have been provided using assumptions based on modules over Euclidean rings, and are not applicable to the efficient standard constructions we are interested in. More recently, Boneh et al. [12] revisited the RSA accumulator without trapdoor which allows the accumulator to be instantiated from unknown order groups without trusted setup such as class groups of quadratic imaginary orders [34] and hyperelliptic curves of genus 2 or 3 [27].

The area of secure multiparty computation has seen a lot of interest both in improving the MPC protocols itself to a wide range of practical applications. In particular, SPDZ [21,24] has seen a lot of interest, improvements and extensions. This interest also led to multiple MPC frameworks, e.g., MP-SPDZ [36],

FRESCO and SCALE-MAMBA,[5] enabling easy prototyping for researchers as well as developers. For practical applications of MPC, one can observe first MPC-based systems turned into products such as Unbound's virtual hardware security model (HSM).[6] For such a virtual HSM, one essentially wants to provide distributed key generation [29] together with threshold signatures [22] allowing to replace a physical HSM. Similar techniques are also interesting for securing wallets for the use in cryptocurrencies, where especially protocols for ECDSA [32,41] are of importance to secure the secret key material. Similarly, such protocols are also of interest for securing the secret key material of internet infrastructure such as DNSSEC [20]. Additionally, addressing privacy concerns in machine learning algorithms has become increasingly popular recently, with MPC protocols being one of the building blocks to achieve private classification and private model training as in [50] for example. Recent works [49] also started to generalize the algorithms that are used as parts of those protocols allowing group operations on elliptic curve groups with secret exponents or secret group elements.

2   Preliminaries

In this section, we introduce cryptographic primitives we use as building blocks. For notation and assumptions, we refer to the full version.

2.1   UC Security and ABB

In this paper, we mainly work in the UC model first introduced by Canetti [15]. The success of the UC model stems from its universal composition theorem, which, informally speaking, states that it is safe to use a secure protocol as a sub-protocol in a more complex one. This strong statement enables one to analyze and proof the security of involved protocols in a modular way, allowing us to build upon work that was already proven to be secure in the UC model.

The importance of the UC model for secure multiparty computation stems from the arithmetic black box (ABB) [23]. The ABB models a secure general-purpose computer in the UC model. It allows performing arithmetic operations on private inputs provided by the parties. The result of these operations is then revealed to all parties. Working with the ABB provides us with a tool of abstracting arithmetic operations, including addition and multiplication in fields.

2.2   SPDZ, Shamir, and Derived Protocols

Our protocols build upon SPDZ [21,24] and Shamir secret sharing [48], concrete implementations of the abstract ABB. SPDZ itself is based on an additive secret-sharing over a finite field $\mathbb{F}_p$ with information-theoretic MACs making the protocol statistically UC secure against an active adversary corrupting all

---

[5] https://homes.esat.kuleuven.be/~nsmart/SCALE/.
[6] https://www.unboundtech.com/usecase/virtual-hsm/.

but one player. On the other hand, Shamir secret sharing is a threshold sharing scheme where $k \leq n$ out of n parties are enough to evaluate the protocol correctly. Therefore, it is naturally robust against parties dropping out during the computation; however, it assumes an honest-majority amongst all parties for security. Shamir secret sharing can be made maliciously UC secure in the honest-majority setting using techniques from [18] or [40].

We will denote the ideal functionality of the online protocol of SPDZ and Shamir secret sharing by $\mathcal{F}_{\text{Abb}}$. For an easy use of these protocols later in our accumulators, we give a high-level description of the functionality together with an intuitive notation. We assume that the computations are performed by n (or k) parties and we denote by $\langle s \rangle \in \mathbb{F}_p$ a secret-shared value between the parties in a finite field with p elements, where p is prime. The ideal functionality $\mathcal{F}_{\text{Abb}}$ provides us with the following basis operations: Addition $\langle a + b \rangle \leftarrow \langle a \rangle + \langle b \rangle$ (can be computed locally), multiplication $\langle ab \rangle \leftarrow \langle a \rangle \cdot \langle b \rangle$ (interactive 1-round protocol), sampling $\langle r \rangle \xleftarrow{R} \mathbb{F}_p$, and opening a share $\langle a \rangle$. For convenience, we assume that we have also access to the inverse function $\langle a^{-1} \rangle$. Computation of the inverse can be efficiently implemented using a standard form of masking as first done in [5]. Given an opening of $\langle z \rangle = \langle r \cdot a \rangle$, the inverse of $\langle a \rangle$ is then equal to $z^{-1} \langle r \rangle$. However, there is a small failure probability if either a or r is zero. In our case, the field size is large enough that the probability of a random element being zero is negligible.

There is one additional sub-protocol which we will often need. Recent work [49] introduced protocols – in particular based on SPDZ – for group operations of elliptic curve groups supporting secret exponents and secret group elements. For this work, we only need the protocol for exponentiation of a public point with a secret exponent. Let $\mathbb{G}$ be a cyclic group of prime order p and $g \in \mathbb{G}$. Further, let $\langle a \rangle \in \mathbb{F}_p$ be a secret-shared exponent.

$\text{Exp}_{\mathbb{G}}(\langle a \rangle, g)$: The parties locally compute $\langle g^a \rangle \leftarrow g^{\langle a \rangle}$.

Since the security proof of this sub-protocol in [49] does not use any exclusive property of an elliptic curve group, it applies to any cyclic group of prime order.

All protocols discussed so far are secure in the UC model, making them safe to use in our accumulators as sub-protocols. Therefore, we will refer to their ideal functionality as $\mathcal{F}_{\text{ABB+}}$. As a result, our protocols become secure in the UC model as long as we do not reveal any intermediate values.

2.3 Accumulators

We rely on the formalization of accumulators by Derler et al. [25]. We recall definitions of static and dynamic accumulators in the full version.

2.4 Pairing-Based Accumulator

We recall the q-SDH-based accumulator from [25], which is based on the accumulator by Nguyen [46]. The idea here is to encode the accumulated elements in a

---

$\underline{\mathsf{Gen}(1^\kappa, q)}$: Let $\mathsf{BG} = (p, \mathbb{G}_1, \mathbb{G}_2, \mathbb{G}_T, e, g_1, g_2) \leftarrow \mathsf{BGen}(\kappa)$. Choose $s \overset{R}{\leftarrow} \mathbb{Z}_p^*$ and
return $\mathsf{sk}_\Lambda \leftarrow s$ and $\mathsf{pk}_\Lambda \leftarrow (\mathsf{BG}, (g_1^{s^i})_{i=1}^q, g_2^s)$.

$\underline{\mathsf{Eval}((\mathsf{sk}_\Lambda, \mathsf{pk}_\Lambda), \mathcal{X})}$: Parse $\mathcal{X} \subset \mathbb{Z}_p^*$. Choose $r \overset{R}{\leftarrow} \mathbb{Z}_p^*$. If $\mathsf{sk}_\Lambda \neq \emptyset$, compute $\Lambda_\mathcal{X} \leftarrow$
$g_1^{r \prod_{x \in \mathcal{X}}(x+s)}$. Otherwise, expand the polynomial $\prod_{x \in \mathcal{X}}(x + X) = \sum_{i=0}^n a_i X^i$,
and compute $\Lambda_\mathcal{X} \leftarrow ((\prod_{i=0}^n g_1^{s^i})^{a_i})^r$. Return $\Lambda_\mathcal{X}$ and $\mathsf{aux} \leftarrow (\mathsf{add} \leftarrow 0, r, \mathcal{X})$.

$\underline{\mathsf{WitCreate}((\mathsf{sk}_\Lambda, \mathsf{pk}_\Lambda), \Lambda_\mathcal{X}, \mathsf{aux}, x)}$: Parse aux as $(r, \mathcal{X})$. If $x \notin \mathcal{X}$, return $\perp$. If
$\mathsf{sk}_\Lambda \neq \emptyset$, compute and return $\mathsf{wit}_x \leftarrow \Lambda_\mathcal{X}^{(x+s)^{-1}}$. Otherwise, run $(\mathsf{wit}_x, \dots) \leftarrow$
$\mathsf{Eval}((\mathsf{sk}_\Lambda, \mathsf{pk}_\Lambda), \mathcal{X} \setminus \{x\}; r)$, and return wit_x.

$\underline{\mathsf{Verify}(\mathsf{pk}_\Lambda, \Lambda_\mathcal{X}, \mathsf{wit}_x, x)}$: Return 1 if $e(\Lambda_\mathcal{X}, g_2) = e(\mathsf{wit}_x, g_2^x \cdot g_2^s)$, otherwise return
0.

$\underline{\mathsf{Add}((\mathsf{sk}_\Lambda, \mathsf{pk}_\Lambda), \Lambda_\mathcal{X}, \mathsf{aux}, x)}$: Parse aux as $(r, \mathcal{X})$. If $x \in \mathcal{X}$, return $\perp$. Set $\mathcal{X}' \leftarrow$
$\mathcal{X} \cup \{x\}$. If $\mathsf{sk}_\Lambda \neq \emptyset$, compute and return $\Lambda_{\mathcal{X}'} \leftarrow \Lambda_\mathcal{X}^{x+s}$ and $\mathsf{aux}' \leftarrow (r, \mathcal{X}', \mathsf{add} \leftarrow$
$1, \Lambda_\mathcal{X}, \Lambda_{\mathcal{X}'})$. Otherwise, return $\mathsf{Eval}((\mathsf{sk}_\Lambda, \mathsf{pk}_\Lambda), \mathcal{X}'; r)$ with aux extended with
$(\mathsf{add} \leftarrow 1, \Lambda_\mathcal{X}, \Lambda_{\mathcal{X}'})$.

$\underline{\mathsf{Delete}((\mathsf{sk}_\Lambda, \mathsf{pk}_\Lambda), \Lambda_\mathcal{X}, \mathsf{aux}, x)}$: Parse aux as $(r, \mathcal{X})$. If $x \notin \mathcal{X}$, return $\perp$. Set $\mathcal{X}' \leftarrow \mathcal{X} \setminus$
$\{x\}$. If $\mathsf{sk}_\Lambda \neq \emptyset$, compute and return $\Lambda_{\mathcal{X}'} \leftarrow \Lambda_\mathcal{X}^{(x+s)^{-1}}$ and $\mathsf{aux}' \leftarrow (r, \mathcal{X}', \mathsf{add} \leftarrow$
$-1, \Lambda_\mathcal{X}, \Lambda_{\mathcal{X}'})$. Otherwise, return $\mathsf{Eval}((\mathsf{sk}_\Lambda, \mathsf{pk}_\Lambda), \mathcal{X}'; r)$ with aux extended with
$(\mathsf{add} \leftarrow 0, \Lambda_\mathcal{X}, \Lambda_{\mathcal{X}'})$.

$\underline{\mathsf{WitUpdate}((\mathsf{sk}_\Lambda, \mathsf{pk}_\Lambda), \mathsf{wit}_{x_i}, \mathsf{aux}, x)}$: Parse aux as $(\perp, \perp, \mathsf{add}, \Lambda_\mathcal{X}, \Lambda_{\mathcal{X}'})$. If $\mathsf{add} =$
0, return $\perp$. Return $\Lambda_\mathcal{X} \cdot \mathsf{wit}_{x_i}^{x-x_i}$ if $\mathsf{add} = 1$. If instead $\mathsf{add} = -1$, return
$(\Lambda_{\mathcal{X}'}^{-1} \cdot \mathsf{wit}_{x_i})^{(x-x_i)^{-1}}$. In the last two cases in addition return $\mathsf{aux} \leftarrow (\mathsf{add} \leftarrow 0)$.

Scheme 1: q-SDH-based accumulator in the Type-3 setting.

polynomial. This polynomial is then evaluated for a fixed element and the result
is randomized to obtain the accumulator. A witness consists of the evaluation
of the same polynomial with the term corresponding to the respective element
cancelled out. For verification, a pairing evaluation is used to check whether the
polynomial encoded in the witness is a factor of the one encoded in the accumulator. As it is typically more efficient to work with bilinear groups of Type-3 [30],
we state the accumulator as depicted in Scheme 1 in this setting. Correctness
is clear, except for the $\mathsf{WitUpdate}$ subroutine: To update witness wit_{x_i} of the
element x_i after the element x was added to the accumulator $\Lambda_\mathcal{X}$ to create the
new accumulator $\Lambda_{\mathcal{X}'} = \Lambda_\mathcal{X}^{(x+s)}$, one computes:

$$\Lambda_\mathcal{X} \cdot \mathsf{wit}_{x_i}^{(x-x_i)} = \Lambda_\mathcal{X}^{(x_i+s) \cdot (x_i+s)^{-1}} \cdot \Lambda_\mathcal{X}^{(x-x_i) \cdot (x_i+s)^{-1}}$$
$$= \Lambda_\mathcal{X}^{(x+s) \cdot (x_i+s)^{-1}} = \Lambda_{\mathcal{X}'}^{(x_i+s)^{-1}}$$

which results in the desired updated witness. Similar, if the element x gets
removed instead, one computes the following to get the desired witness:

$$(\Lambda_{\mathcal{X}'}^{-1} \cdot \mathsf{wit}_{x_i})^{(x-x_i)^{-1}} = \Lambda_{\mathcal{X}'}^{-(x_i+s) \cdot (x_i+s)^{-1} \cdot (x-x_i)^{-1}} \cdot \Lambda_{\mathcal{X}'}^{(x+s) \cdot (x_i+s)^{-1} \cdot (x-x_i)^{-1}}$$
$$= \Lambda_{\mathcal{X}'}^{(x_i+s)^{-1} \cdot (x-x_i)^{-1} \cdot (x-x_i+s-s)} = \Lambda_{\mathcal{X}'}^{(x_i+s)^{-1}}$$

The proof of collision freeness follows from the q-SDH assumption. For completeness, we still restate the theorem from [25] adopted to the Type-3 setting. For the proof, we refer to the full version.

Theorem 1. *If the q-SDH assumption holds, then Scheme 1 is collision-free.*

Remark 1. Note that for support of arbitrary accumulation domains, the accumulator requires a suitable hash function mapping to $\mathbb{Z}_p^*$. For the MPC-based accumulators that we will define later, it is clear that the hash function can be evaluated in public. For simplicity, we omit the hash function in our discussion.

2.5   UC Secure Accumulators

Only recently, Baldimtsi et al. [4] formalized the security of accumulators in the UC framework. Interestingly, they showed, that any correct and collision-free standard accumulator is automatically UC secure. We, however, want to note, that their definitions of accumulators are slightly different then the framework by Derler et al. (which we are using). Hence, we adapt the ideal functionality $\mathcal{F}_{\mathrm{Acc}}$ from [4] to match our setting: First our ideal functionality $\mathcal{F}_{\mathrm{Acc}}$ consists of two more sub-functionalities. This is due to a separation of the algorithms responsible for the evaluation, addition, and deletion. Secondly, our $\mathcal{F}_{\mathrm{Acc}}$ is simplified to our purpose, whereas $\mathcal{F}_{\mathrm{Acc}}$ from Baldimtsi et al. is in their words "an entire menu of functionalities covering all different types of accumulators". Thirdly, we added identity checks to sub-functionalities (where necessary) to be consistent with the given definitions of accumulators.

The resulting ideal functionality can be found in the full version. Note that the ideal functionality has up to three parties. First, the party which holds the set $\mathcal{X}$ is the accumulator manager $\mathcal{AM}$, responsible for the algorithms Gen, Eval, WitCreate, Add and Delete. The second party $\mathcal{H}$ owns a witness and is interested in keeping it updated and for this reason, performs the algorithm WitUpdate. The last party $\mathcal{V}$ can be seen as an external party. $\mathcal{V}$ is only able to use Verify to check the membership of an element in the accumulated set.

In the following theorem we adapt the proof from [4] to our setting:

Theorem 2. *If $\Pi_{Acc} = (\mathsf{Gen}, \mathsf{Eval}, \mathsf{WitCreate}, \mathsf{Verify}, \mathsf{Add}, \mathsf{Delete}, \mathsf{WitUpdate})$ is a correct and collision-free dynamic accumulator with deterministic* Verify*, then Π_{Acc} UC emulates $\mathcal{F}_{Acc}$.*

For the proof we refer to the full version. As a direct consequence of Theorems 1 and 2, the accumulator from Scheme 1 is also secure in the UC model of [4] since it is correct and collision-free:

Corollary 1. *Scheme 1 emulates $\mathcal{F}_{Acc}$ in the UC model.*

3   Multi-Party Public-Key Accumulators

With the building blocks in place, we are now able to go into the details of our construction. We first present the formal notion of (threshold) secret-shared accumulators, their ideal functionality, and then present our constructions.

For the syntax of the MPC-based accumulator, which we dub *(threshold)* *secret-shared accumulator*, we use the bracket notation $\langle s \rangle$ from Sect. 2.2 to denote a secret shared value. If we want to explicitly highlight the different shares, we write $\langle s \rangle = (s_1, \ldots, s_n)$, where the share s_i belongs to a party P_i. We base the definition on the framework of Derler et al. [25], where our algorithms behave in the same way, but instead of taking an optional secret trapdoor, the algorithms are given shares of the secret as input. Consequently, Gen outputs shares of the secret trapdoor instead of the secret key. The static version of the accumulator is defined as follows:

Definition 1 (Static (Threshold) Secret-Shared Accumulator). *Let us assume that we have a (threshold) secret sharing-scheme. A static (threshold) secret-shared accumulator for $n \in \mathbb{N}$ parties $P_1, \ldots, P_n$ is a tuple of PPT algorithms* (Gen, Eval, WitCreate, Verify) *which are defined as follows:*

Gen$(1^\kappa, q)$: *This algorithm takes a security parameter κ and a parameter q. If $q \neq \infty$, then q is an upper bound on the number of elements to be accumulated. It returns a key pair $(\mathsf{sk}_\Lambda^i, \mathsf{pk}_\Lambda)$ to each party P_i such that $\mathsf{sk}_\Lambda = \mathsf{Open}(\mathsf{sk}_\Lambda^1, \ldots, \mathsf{sk}_\Lambda^n)$, denoted by $\langle \mathsf{sk}_\Lambda \rangle$. We assume that the accumulator public key pk_Λ implicitly defines the accumulation domain D_Λ.*

Eval$(((\langle \mathsf{sk}_\Lambda \rangle, \mathsf{pk}_\Lambda), \mathcal{X})$: *This algorithm takes a secret-shared private key $\langle \mathsf{sk}_\Lambda \rangle$ a public key pk_Λ and a set $\mathcal{X}$ to be accumulated and returns an accumulator $\Lambda_\mathcal{X}$ together with some auxiliary information* aux *to every party P_i.*

WitCreate$(((\langle \mathsf{sk}_\Lambda \rangle, \mathsf{pk}_\Lambda), \Lambda_\mathcal{X}, \mathsf{aux}, x)$: *This algorithm takes a secret-shared private key $\langle \mathsf{sk}_\Lambda \rangle$ a public key pk_Λ, an accumulator $\Lambda_\mathcal{X}$, auxiliary information* aux *and a value x. It returns $\bot$, if $x \notin \mathcal{X}$, and a witness* wit_x *for x otherwise to every party P_i.*

Verify$(\mathsf{pk}_\Lambda, \Lambda_\mathcal{X}, \mathsf{wit}_x, x)$: *This algorithm takes a public key pk_Λ, an accumulator $\Lambda_\mathcal{X}$, a witness* wit_x *and a value x. It returns 1 if* wit_x *is a witness for $x \in \mathcal{X}$ and 0 otherwise.*

In analogy to the non-interactive case, dynamic accumulators provide additional algorithms to add elements to the accumulator and remove elements from it, respectively, and update already existing witnesses accordingly.

Definition 2 (Dynamic (Threshold) Secret-Shared Accumulator). *A dynamic (threshold) secret-shared accumulator is a static (threshold) secret-shared accumulator with an additional tuple of PPT algorithms* (Add, Delete, WitUpdate) *which are defined as follows:*

Add$(((\langle \mathsf{sk}_\Lambda \rangle, \mathsf{pk}_\Lambda), \Lambda_\mathcal{X}, \mathsf{aux}, x)$: *This algorithm takes a secret-shared private key $\langle \mathsf{sk}_\Lambda \rangle$ a public key pk_Λ, an accumulator $\Lambda_\mathcal{X}$, auxiliary information* aux, *as well as an element x to be added. If $x \in \mathcal{X}$, it returns $\bot$ to every party P_i. Otherwise, it returns the updated accumulator $\Lambda_{\mathcal{X}'}$ with $\mathcal{X}' \leftarrow \mathcal{X} \cup \{x\}$ and updated auxiliary information* aux' *to every party P_i.*

Delete$(((\langle \mathsf{sk}_\Lambda \rangle, \mathsf{pk}_\Lambda), \Lambda_\mathcal{X}, \mathsf{aux}, x)$: *This algorithm takes a secret-shared private key $\langle \mathsf{sk}_\Lambda \rangle$ a public key pk_Λ, an accumulator $\Lambda_\mathcal{X}$, auxiliary information* aux, *as well as an element x to be added. If $x \notin \mathcal{X}$, it returns $\bot$ to every party P_i.*

Otherwise, it returns the updated accumulator $\Lambda_{\mathcal{X}'}$ with $\mathcal{X}' \leftarrow \mathcal{X} \setminus \{x\}$ and updated auxiliary information aux$'$ to every party P_i.

WitUpdate$((\langle sk_\Lambda \rangle, pk_\Lambda), wit_{x_i}, aux, x)$: *This algorithm takes a secret-shared private key $\langle sk_\Lambda \rangle$ a public key pk_Λ, a witness wit_{x_i} to be updated, auxiliary information aux and an element x which was added to/deleted from the accumulator, where aux indicates addition or deletion. It returns an updated witness wit'_{x_i} on success and $\perp$ otherwise to every party P_i.*

Correctness and collision-freeness naturally translate from the non-interactive accumulators to the (threshold) secret-shared ones.

For our case, the ideal functionality for (threshold) secret-shared accumulators, dubbed $\mathcal{F}_{\mathrm{MPC\text{-}Acc}}$ is more interesting. $\mathcal{F}_{\mathrm{MPC\text{-}Acc}}$ is very similar to $\mathcal{F}_{\mathrm{Acc}}$ and can be found in the full version. The only difference in describing the ideal functionality for accumulators in the MPC setting arises from the fact that we now have not only one accumulator manager but n, denoted by $\mathcal{AM}_1, \ldots, \mathcal{AM}_n$. More concretely, whenever a sub-functionality of $\mathcal{F}_{\mathrm{MPC\text{-}Acc}}$ – that makes use of the secret key – gets a request from a manager identity $\mathcal{AM}_i$, it now also gets a participation message from the other managers identities A_j for $j \neq i$. Furthermore, the accumulator managers take the role of the witness holder. The party $\mathcal{V}$, however, stays unchanged.

3.1 Dynamic (Threshold) Secret-Shared Accumulator from the q-SDH Assumption

For the generation of public parameters Gen, we can rely on already established methods to produce ECDSA key pairs and exponentiations with secret exponents, respectively. These methods can directly be applied to the accumulators. Taking the q-SDH accumulator as an example, the first step is to sample the secret scalar $s \in \mathbb{Z}_p$. Intuitively, each party samples its own share s_i and the secret trapdoor s would then be $s = \mathsf{Open}(s_1, \ldots, s_n)$. The next step, the calculation of the basis elements g^{s^j} for $j = 1, \ldots, q$, is optional, but can be performed to provide public parameters, that are useful even to parties without knowledge of s. All of these elements can be computed using $\mathsf{Exp}_{\mathbb{G}}$ and the secret-shared s, respectively its powers. For the accumulator evaluation, Eval, the parties first sample their shares of r. Then, they jointly compute shares of $r \cdot f(s)$ using their shares of r and s. The so-obtained exponent and $\mathsf{Exp}_{\mathbb{G}}$ produce the final result.

For witness creation, WitCreate, it gets more interesting. Of course, one could simply run Eval again with one element removed from the set. In this case, we can do better, though. The difference between the accumulator and a witness is that in the latter, one factor of the polynomial is canceled. Since s is available, it is thus possible to cancel this factor without recomputing the polynomial from the start. Indeed, to compute the witness for an element x, we can compute $(s+x)^{-1}$ and then apply that inverse using $\mathsf{Exp}_{\mathbb{G}}$ to the accumulator to get the witness. Note though, that before the parties perform this step, they need to check if x is actually contained in $\mathcal{X}$. Otherwise, they would produce a membership witness for a non-member. In that case, the verification would check whether

$f(s)(s+x)^{-1}(s+x)$ matches $f(s)$, which of course also holds even if $s+x$ is not a factor of $f(s)$. In contrast, when performing Eval with only the publicly available information, this issue does not occur since there the witness will not verify. Add and Delete can be implemented in a similar manner. When adding an element to the accumulator, the polynomial is extended by one factor. Removal of an element requires that one factor is canceled. Both operations can be performed by first computing the factor using the shares of s and then running $\mathsf{Exp}_{\mathbb{G}}$.

Now, we present the MPC version of the q-SDH accumulator in Scheme 2 following the intuition outlined above. Note, that the algorithm for WitUpdate is unlikely to be faster than its non-MPC version from Scheme 1. Indeed, the non-MPC version requires only exponentiations in $\mathbb{G}_1$ and a multiplication without the knowledge of the secret trapdoor. We provide the version using the trapdoor for completeness but will use the non-MPC version of the algorithm in practical implementations. Note further that we let Gen choose the bilinear group BG, but this group can already be fixed a priori.

$\mathsf{Gen}(1^\kappa, q)$: $\mathsf{BG} = (p, \mathbb{G}_1, \mathbb{G}_2, \mathbb{G}_T, e, g_1, g_2) \leftarrow \mathsf{BGen}(\kappa)$. Compute $\langle \mathsf{sk}_\Lambda \rangle \leftarrow$ $\mathsf{sRand}(\mathbb{Z}_p^*)$. Compute $h \leftarrow \mathsf{Open}(g_2^{\langle \mathsf{sk}_\Lambda \rangle})$. Return $\mathsf{pk}_\Lambda \leftarrow (\mathsf{BG}, h)$.

$\mathsf{Eval}(((\langle \mathsf{sk}_\Lambda \rangle, \mathsf{pk}_\Lambda), \mathcal{X})$: Parse pk_Λ as (BG, h) and $\mathcal{X}$ as subset of $\mathbb{Z}_p^*$. Choose $\langle r \rangle \leftarrow$ $\mathsf{sRand}(\mathbb{Z}_p^*)$. Compute $\langle q \rangle \leftarrow \prod_{x \in \mathcal{X}} (x + \langle \mathsf{sk}_\Lambda \rangle) \in \mathbb{Z}_p^*$ and $\langle t \rangle \leftarrow \langle q \rangle \cdot \langle r \rangle$. The algorithm returns $\Lambda_\mathcal{X} \leftarrow \mathsf{Open}(g_1^{\langle t \rangle})$ and $\mathsf{aux} \leftarrow (\mathsf{add} \leftarrow 0, \mathcal{X})$.

$\mathsf{WitCreate}(((\langle \mathsf{sk}_\Lambda \rangle, \mathsf{pk}_\Lambda), \Lambda_\mathcal{X}, \mathsf{aux}, x)$: Returns $\bot$ if $x \notin \mathcal{X}$. Otherwise, $\langle z \rangle \leftarrow \langle (x + \langle \mathsf{sk}_\Lambda \rangle)^{-1} \rangle$. Return $\mathsf{wit}_x \leftarrow \mathsf{Open}(\Lambda_\mathcal{X}^{\langle z \rangle})$.

$\mathsf{Verify}(\mathsf{pk}_\Lambda, \Lambda_\mathcal{X}, \mathsf{wit}_x, x)$: Parse pk_Λ as (BG, h). If $e(\Lambda_\mathcal{X}, g_2) = e(\mathsf{wit}_x, g_2^x \cdot h)$ holds, return 1, otherwise return 0.

$\mathsf{Add}(((\langle \mathsf{sk}_\Lambda \rangle, \mathsf{pk}_\Lambda), \Lambda_\mathcal{X}, \mathsf{aux}, x)$: Returns $\bot$ if $x \in \mathcal{X}$. Otherwise set $\mathcal{X}' \leftarrow \mathcal{X} \cup \{x\}$. Return $\Lambda_{\mathcal{X}'} \leftarrow \Lambda_\mathcal{X}^x \cdot \mathsf{Open}(\Lambda_\mathcal{X}^{\langle \mathsf{sk}_\Lambda \rangle})$ and $\mathsf{aux} \leftarrow (\mathsf{add} \leftarrow 1, \mathcal{X}')$.

$\mathsf{Delete}(((\langle \mathsf{sk}_\Lambda \rangle, \mathsf{pk}_\Lambda), \Lambda_\mathcal{X}, \mathsf{aux}, x)$: If $x \notin \mathcal{X}$, return $\bot$. Otherwise set $\mathcal{X}' \leftarrow \mathcal{X} \setminus \{x\}$, and compute $\langle y \rangle \leftarrow \langle (x + \langle \mathsf{sk}_\Lambda \rangle)^{-1} \rangle$. Return $\Lambda_{\mathcal{X}'} \leftarrow \mathsf{Open}(\Lambda_\mathcal{X}^{\langle y \rangle})$ and $\mathsf{aux} \leftarrow (\mathsf{add} \leftarrow -1, \mathcal{X}')$.

$\mathsf{WitUpdate}(((\langle \mathsf{sk}_\Lambda \rangle, \mathsf{pk}_\Lambda), \mathsf{wit}_{x_i}, \mathsf{aux}, x)$: Parse aux as $(\mathsf{add}, \mathcal{X})$. Return $\bot$ if $\mathsf{add} = 0$ or $x_i \notin \mathcal{X}$. In case $\mathsf{add} = 1$, return $\mathsf{wit}_{x_i} \leftarrow \mathsf{wit}_{x_i}^x \cdot \mathsf{Open}(\mathsf{wit}_{x_i}^{\langle \mathsf{sk}_\Lambda \rangle})$ and $\mathsf{aux} \leftarrow (\mathsf{add} \leftarrow 0, \mathcal{X})$. If instead $\mathsf{add} = -1$, it compute $\langle y \rangle \leftarrow \langle (x + \langle \mathsf{sk}_\Lambda \rangle)^{-1} \rangle$. Return $\mathsf{wit}_{x_i} \leftarrow \mathsf{Open}(\mathsf{wit}_{x_i}^{\langle y \rangle})$ and $\mathsf{aux} \leftarrow (\mathsf{add} \leftarrow 0, \mathcal{X})$.

Scheme 2: MPC-q-SDH: Dynamic (threshold) secret-shared accumulator from q-SDH for $n \geq 2$ parties.

Theorem 3. *Scheme 2 UC emulates* $\mathcal{F}_{Acc\text{-}MPC}$ *in the* $\mathcal{F}_{ABB+}$*-hybrid model.*

Proof. At this point, we make use of the UC model. Informally speaking, accumulators are UC secure, and SPDZ, Shamir secret sharing, and the derived operations UC emulate $\mathcal{F}_{ABB+}$. Therefore, according to the universal composition theorem, the use of these MPC protocols in the accumulator Scheme 2 can be done without losing UC security. For a better understanding, we begin by showing the desired accumulator properties for Scheme 2.

The proof of the correctness follows directly from the correctness proof from Scheme 1 for the case where the secret key is known. Collision-freeness is also derived from the non-interactive q-SDH accumulator. (It is true that now each party has a share of the trapdoor, but without the other shares no party can create a valid witness.) Since Verify is obviously deterministic, Scheme 2 fulfills all necessary assumption of Theorem 2. After applying Theorem 2, we get a simulator $\mathcal{S}_{Acc}$ interacting with the ideal functionality $\mathcal{F}_{Acc}$. Since we now also have to simulate the non-interactive sub-protocols, we have to extend $\mathcal{S}_{Acc}$. We construct $\mathcal{S}_{Acc\text{-}MPC}$ by building upon $\mathcal{S}_{Acc}$ and in addition internally simulate $\mathcal{F}_{ABB+}$. As described in Sect. 2.2, the MPC protocols used in the above algorithms are all secure in the UC model. Since we do not open any secret-shared values besides uniformly random elements and the output or values that can be immediately derived from the output, the algorithms are secure due to the universal composition theorem.   □

Remark 2. In Gen of Scheme 2 we explicitly do not compute $h_i \leftarrow g_1^{s^i}$. Hence, using Eval without access to s is not possible. But the public key is significantly smaller and so is the runtime of the Gen algorithm. If, however, these values are needed to support a non-secret-shared Eval, one can modify Gen to also compute the necessary values enabling trade-offs between an efficient Eval and an inefficient Gen. Updates to this accumulator then still profit from the efficiency of the secret shared trapdoor. Additionally, q gives an upper bound on the size of the accumulated sets, and thus needs to be considered in the selection of the curves even though the powers of g_1 are not placed in the public key.

3.2   SPDZ vs. Shamir Secret Sharing

In this section, we want to compare two MPC protocols on which our MPC-q-SDH Accumulator can be based on, namely SPDZ and Shamir secret sharing. Both protocols allow us to keep shares of the secret trapdoor and improve performance compared to the keyless q-SDH Accumulator. However, in relying on these protocols for security, the trust assumptions of the MPC-q-SDH Accumulator also have to include the underlying protocols' trust-assumptions.

SPDZ is a full-threshold dishonest-majority protocol that protects against $n - 1$ corrupted parties. Therefore, an honest party will always detect malicious behavior. However, full-threshold schemes are not robust; if one party fails to supply its shares, the computation always fails.

On the contrary, Shamir secret sharing is an honest-majority threshold protocol. It is more robust than SPDZ since it allows $k \leq \frac{n-1}{2}$ corrupted parties while still being capable of providing correct results. This also means, if some parties ($k \leq \frac{n-1}{2}$) fail to provide their shares, the other parties can still compute the correct results without them. Thus, no accumulator manager on its own is a single point of failure. However, if more than k parties are corrupted, the adversaries can reconstruct the secret trapdoor and, therefore, compromise the security of our MPC-q-SDH Accumulator.

Table 1. Performance of the accumulator algorithms without access to the secret trapdoors. Time in milliseconds averaged over 100 executions.

Accu.	$|\mathcal{X}|$	Gen	Eval	WitCreate	Add	WitUpdate	Delete	WitUpdate
Scheme 1	2^{10}	649	1 117	1 116	1 116	0.6	1 120	0.7
	2^{14}	9 062	116 031	115 870	115 575	0.6	116 154	0.7
Merkle-Tree	2^{10}	–	1.12	0.05[a]	1.12	0.05[a]	1.12	0.05[a]
	2^{14}	–	15.53	0.83[a]	15.53	0.83[a]	15.53	0.83[a]

[a] Assuming that the full Merkle-tree is known as auxiliary data.

4   Implementation and Performance Evaluation

We implemented the proposed dynamic (threshold) secret-shared accumulator from q-SDH and evaluated it against small to large sets.[7] Our primary implementations are based on SPDZ with OT-based preprocessing and Shamir secret sharing in the MP-SPDZ [36][8] framework. However, to demonstrate the usability of our accumulator, we additionally build an implementation in the malicious security setting with dishonest-majority based on the FRESCO framework. We discuss the benchmarks for the MP-SPDZ implementation in this section. For a discussion of the FRESCO benchmarks we refer the reader to the full version.

Remark 3. We want to note, that in our benchmarks we test the performance of the MPC variant of WitUpdate from Scheme 2, even though in practice the non-MPC variant from Scheme 1 should be used.

MP-SPDZ implements the SPDZ protocol with various extensions, as well as semi-honest and malicious variants of Shamir secret sharing [18,19,40]. For pairing and elliptic curve group operations, we rely on relic[9] and integrate $\mathsf{Exp_G}$, Output-$\mathbb{G}$, and the corresponding operations to update the MAC described in [49] into MP-SPDZ. We use the pairing friendly BLS12-381 curve [7], which provides around 120 bit of security following recent estimates [6]. For completeness, we also implemented the q-SDH accumulator from Scheme 1 and a Merkle-tree accumulator using SHA-256. This enables us to compare the performance in cases where the secret trapdoors are available in the MPC case and when they are not. In Table 1, we present the numbers for various sizes of accumulated sets.

The evaluation of the MPC protocols was performed on a cluster with a Xeon E5-4669v4 CPU, where each party was assigned only 1 core. The hosts were connected via a 1 Gbit/s LAN network, and an average round-trip time of <1 ms. For the WAN setting, a network with a round-trip time of 100 ms and a bandwidth of 100 Mbit/s was simulated. We provide benchmarks for both preprocessing and online phases of the MPC protocols, where the cost of the preprocessing phase is determined by the number of shared multiplications, whereas the performance of the online phase is proportional to the multiplicative depth of the circuit and the number of openings.

---

[7] The source code is available at https://github.com/IAIK/MPC-Accumulator.
[8] https://github.com/data61/MP-SPDZ.
[9] https://github.com/relic-toolkit/relic.

Table 2. Number of Beaver triples, shared random values, and opening rounds required by MPC-q-SDH.

	Gen	Eval	WitCreate	Add	WitUpdate	Delete	WitUpdate
Beaver triples[a]	0	$\|\mathcal{X}\|$	1	0	0	1	1
Random values	1	1	1	0	0	1	1
Opening rounds	1	$\lceil \log_2(\|\mathcal{X}\| + 1) \rceil + 1$	3	1	1	3	3

[a]Note, semi-honest Shamir secret sharing does not require Beaver triples.

4.1   Evaluation of MPC-q-SDH

In the offline phase of the implemented MPC protocols, the required Beaver triples [8] for shared multiplication and the pre-shared random values are generated. A shared inverse operation requires one multiplication and one shared random value. In Table 2, we list the number of triples required for each operation for the MPC-q-SDH accumulator. Except for Eval they require a constant number of multiplications and inverse operations and, therefore, a constant number of Beaver triples and shared random elements. In Eval, the number of required Beaver triples is determined by $|\mathcal{X}|$. Furthermore, Table 2 lists the number of opening rounds (including openings in multiplications, excluding MAC-checks) of the online phase of the MPC-q-SDH accumulator allowing one to calculate the number of communication rounds for different sharing schemes.

As discussed in Remark 2, Gen is not producing the public parameters h_i. If Eval without MPC is desired, the time and communication of Eval for the respective set sizes should be added to the time and communication of Gen to obtain an estimate of its performance.

Dishonest-Majority Based on SPDZ. Table 3 compares the offline performance of the MPC-q-SDH accumulator based on SPDZ in different settings. We give both timings for the accumulation of $|\mathcal{X}|$ elements in Eval and the necessary pre-computation for a single inversion, which is used in several other operations (e.g., WitCreate). Additionally we also give the time for pre-computing a single random element, which is required to generate the authenticated share of the secret-key in Eval. Further note that batching the generation of many triples together like for the Eval phase is more efficient in practice than producing a single triple and as these triples are not dependent on the input, all parties can continuously generate triples in the background for later use in the online phase.

In Table 4, we present the online performance of our MPC-q-SDH accumulator based on SPDZ for different set sizes, parties, security settings, and network settings. It can clearly be seen, that – except for the Eval operation – the runtime of each operation is independent of the set size. In other words, after an initial accumulation of a given set, every other operation has constant time. In comparison, the runtime of the non-MPC accumulators without access to the secret trapdoor, as depicted in Table 1, depends on the size of the accumulated set. Our MPC-accumulator outperforms the non-MPC q-SDH accumulators the larger the accumulated set gets. In the LAN setting MPC-q-SDH's Eval is faster

Table 3. Offline phase performance of different steps of the MPC-q-SDH accumulator with access to the secret trapdoor based on MP-SPDZ. Time in milliseconds.

	Operation	$|\mathcal{X}|$	LAN setting				WAN setting			
			$n = 2$	3	4	5	2	3	4	5
Semi-honest	BaseOTs	$2^{10}, 2^{14}$	0.03	0.08	0.14	0.23	0.14	0.31	0.56	0.84
	Inverse	$2^{10}, 2^{14}$	0.78	1.72	3.06	4.03	209.9	227.5	322.8	331.0
	Gen	$2^{10}, 2^{14}$	0.44	1.21	1.76	3.01	207.7	223.6	325.9	332.0
	Eval	2^{10}	189	397	706	959	4 695	8 215	13 680	25 725
		2^{14}	4000	8 308	14 380	17 928	55 542	109 720	214 585	356 330
Malicious	Inverse	$2^{10}, 2^{14}$	4.34	7.93	11.5	15.3	840.5	1 262	1 538	1 914
	Gen	$2^{10}, 2^{14}$	2.56	4.23	6.80	9.32	841.3	1 235	1 540	1 856
	Eval	2^{10}	1 601	2 849	4 345	6 227	25 737	45 254	87 328	141 181
		2^{14}	31 099	62 978	89 132	145 574	412 747	682 033	1 364 660	2 236 860

than the non-MPC version for all benchmarked players, even in the WAN settings it outperforms the non-MPC version in the two player case. For 2^{14} elements, it is even faster for all benchmarked players in all settings, including the WAN setting. In any case, the witnesses have constant size contrary to the $\log_2(|\mathcal{X}|)$ sized witnesses of the Merkle-tree accumulator.

The numbers for the evaluation of the online phase in the WAN setting are also presented in Table 4. The overhead that can be observed compared to the LAN setting is influenced by the communication cost. Since our implementation implements all multiplications in Eval in a depth-optimized tree-like fashion, the overhead from switching to a WAN setting is not too severe.

On the first look, one can observe an irregularity in our benchmarks. More specifically, notice that for four or more parties, the maliciously secure evaluation of the Eval online phase is consistently faster than the semi-honest evaluation of the same phase. However, this is a direct consequence of a difference in how MP-SPDZ handles the communication in those security models, where communication is handled in a non-synchronized send-to-all approach in the malicious setting and a synchronized broadcast approach in the semi-honest setting. The synchronization in the latter case scales worse for more parties and, therefore, introduces some additional delays.

Finally, Table 5 depicts the size of the communication between the parties for both offline and online phases. The communication of Eval has to account for a number of multiplications dependent on $\mathcal{X}$ and therefore scales linearly with its size. As we already observed for the runtime of MPC-q-SDH, also the communication of WitCreate, Add, Delete and WitUpdate is independent of the size of the accumulated set, and additionally less than 200 kB for all algorithms. Combined with the analysis of the runtime, we conclude that the performance of the operations that might be performed multiple times per accumulator is very efficient in both runtime and communication. When compared to the performance of the non-MPC accumulators in Table 1, we see that the performance of operations that benefit from access to the secret trapdoor are multiple orders of magnitude faster in the MPC accumulators and, in the LAN setting, even come close to the

Table 4. Online phase performance of the MPC-q-SDH accumulator with access to the secret trapdoor based on SPDZ implemented in MP-SPDZ, for both the LAN and WAN settings with n parties. Time in milliseconds averaged over 50 executions.

Operation	$|\mathcal{X}|$	Semi-honest								Malicious							
		LAN setting				WAN setting				LAN setting				WAN setting			
		$n=2$	3	4	5	2	3	4	5	2	3	4	5	2	3	4	5
Gen	2^{10}	4	4	7	19	53	110	170	219	11	13	25	37	169	278	395	505
	2^{14}	4	4	9	20	56	111	172	220	11	13	28	48	179	280	396	506
Eval	2^{10}	3	13	58	231	635	1277	1916	2558	10	17	50	131	966	1327	1669	1995
	2^{14}	26	47	117	315	949	1948	3166	4571	89	94	174	225	1297	1979	2830	3872
WitCreate	2^{10}	2	2	32	39	168	320	482	645	5	10	35	75	372	606	823	1050
	2^{14}	2	2	28	51	168	320	473	638	5	6	28	80	365	606	835	1052
Add	2^{10}	2	2	8	17	47	107	166	213	5	5	17	31	170	273	388	499
	2^{14}	2	2	5	14	50	108	170	214	5	5	17	42	173	271	383	491
WitUpdate$_{\text{Add}}$	2^{10}	2	2	5	30	60	108	154	214	5	7	12	34	159	276	390	495
	2^{14}	2	2	3	20	60	107	152	217	5	6	10	54	154	275	390	500
Delete	2^{10}	2	2	21	58	156	319	488	639	5	10	47	78	379	598	818	1034
	2^{14}	2	2	23	55	158	318	489	642	5	6	38	87	385	603	822	1033
WitUpdate$_{\text{Delete}}$	2^{10}	2	2	52	47	165	320	475	643	5	10	26	100	374	604	828	1044
	2^{14}	2	4	43	57	162	323	475	639	5	10	35	74	365	599	827	1048

Table 5. Communication cost (in kB per party) of the MPC-q-SDH accumulator with access to the secret trapdoor based on SPDZ implemented in MP-SPDZ.

Operations	$|\mathcal{X}|$	Semi-honest		Malicious	
		Offline[a]	Online	Offline[a]	Online
Gen	$2^{10}, 2^{14}$	20	0.10	86	0.24
Eval	2^{10}	12571	66	79549	66
	2^{14}	200823	1049	1271484	1049
WitCreate, Delete, WitUpdate$_{\text{Delete}}$	$2^{10}, 2^{14}$	33	0.15	164	0.37
Add, WitUpdate$_{\text{Add}}$	$2^{10}, 2^{14}$	4	0.05	4	0.14

[a]Includes BaseOTs for a new connection

performance of the standard Merkle-tree accumulator, for both the semi-honest and malicious variant.

Honest-Majority Threshold Sharing based on Shamir Secret Sharing. In this section, we discuss the benchmarks of our implementation based on Shamir secret sharing. MP-SPDZ implements semi-honest Shamir secret sharing based on [19] and a maliciously secure variant following [40][10]. In Table 6, we present the offline phase runtime, in Table 7 we show the runtime of the online phase, and in Table 8 we depict the size of the communication between the parties for the 3-party case.

---

[10] A newer version of MP-SPDZ now implements maliciously secure Shamir secret sharing following [18].

Table 6. Offline phase performance of different steps of the MPC-q-SDH accumulator with access to the secret trapdoor in the semi-honest (SH) and malicious threshold setting implemented in MP-SPDZ. Time in milliseconds.

	Operation	$|\mathcal{X}|$	LAN setting			WAN setting		
			$n =$ 3	4	5	3	4	5
SH	Inverse	$2^{10}, 2^{14}$	6	9	14	473	585	998
Malicious	Inverse	$2^{10}, 2^{14}$	7	9	17	1 036	1 231	2 136
	Gen	$2^{10}, 2^{14}$	6	11	17	1 008	1 256	2 233
	Eval	2^{10}	20	29	48	1 232	2 089	2 629
		2^{14}	218	245	510	3 431	8 130	8 519

The most expensive part of the SPDZ offline phase is creating the Beaver triples required for the Eval operation. As Table 6 shows, this step is several orders of magnitudes cheaper in the Shamir-based implementation. This is especially true in the semi-honest setting, in which no Beaver triples are required in the Shamir-based implementation. The offline runtime of the other operations is similar to the SPDZ-based implementations.

The Shamir-based implementation's online runtime is slightly cheaper than the runtime of the SPDZ-based implementation, except for the Eval operation. However, the difference in runtime of the Eval operation is also not significant, especially when considering the trade for the much cheaper offline phase.

Similar behavior can be seen for the communication cost, as depicted in Table 8. Offline communication is several orders of magnitude smaller in the

Table 7. Online phase performance of the MPC-q-SDH accumulator with access to the secret trapdoor in the threshold setting implemented in MP-SPDZ, for both the LAN and WAN settings with n parties. Time in milliseconds averaged over 50 executions.

Operation	$|\mathcal{X}|$	Semi-honest						Malicious					
		LAN setting			WAN setting			LAN setting			WAN setting		
		$n =$ 3	4	5	3	4	5	3	4	5	3	4	5
Gen	2^{10}	5	5	7	109	111	118	7	7	14	112	119	228
	2^{14}	5	5	7	110	111	120	7	7	14	113	120	230
Eval	2^{10}	5	6	9	1 278	1 314	2 474	9	9	16	1 285	1 422	2 578
	2^{14}	33	40	77	1 788	2 776	3 831	80	84	161	2 018	3 938	4 636
WitCreate	2^{10}	2	2	3	317	319	440	3	3	5	324	336	648
	2^{14}	2	2	3	318	321	443	3	3	5	323	332	642
Add	2^{10}	2	2	3	109	108	114	3	3	5	109	111	215
	2^{14}	2	2	3	107	108	113	3	3	5	110	112	220
WitUpdate$_{Add}$	2^{10}	2	2	3	107	107	112	3	3	5	107	112	217
	2^{14}	2	2	3	107	108	114	3	3	5	108	114	220
Delete	2^{10}	2	2	3	320	321	438	3	3	5	320	332	642
	2^{14}	2	2	3	317	321	439	3	3	5	321	331	642
WitUpdate$_{Delete}$	2^{10}	2	2	3	320	321	441	3	3	5	321	333	647
	2^{14}	2	2	3	316	320	441	3	3	5	320	332	645

Shamir-based implementation than in SPDZ, while online communication is similar to the SPDZ based version. Only the Eval operation requires about twice as much online communication in the Shamir-based implementation. To summarize, our honest-majority threshold implementation based on Shamir secret sharing provides much better offline phase performance, with similar online performance compared to our dishonest majority full-threshold implementation.

4.2 Further Improvement

The maliciously secure MPC protocols we use in this work delay the MAC check to the output phase after executing the Open subroutine. This means, it is possible for intermediate results to be wrong due to tampering of an attacker; however, since honest parties only reveal randomized values during the openings in a multiplication, no information about secret values can be gained by attackers.

Similar to threshold signature schemes [20,28,32], the protocols can be optimized by skipping the MAC checks at the end of WitCreate, Add, Delete, and WitUpdate and use the Verify step of the accumulator to check for correctness instead. The only feasible attack on this optimization is to produce invalid accumulators/witnesses without leaking information on the secret trapdoor; however, false output values can be detected during verification. Therefore, we can execute the semi-honest online phase and call Verify at the end, while still protecting against malicious parties. This trades the extra round of communication in the MAC check for an evaluation of a bilinear pairing ($\approx 10\,\mathrm{ms}$ on our benchmark platform) which results in a further speedup, especially in the WAN-setting.

5 Applications

5.1 Credential Revocation in Distributed Credential Systems

As first application of MPC-based accumulators, we focus on distributed credential systems [31], and in particular, on the implementation in Sovrin [37]. In general, anonymous credentials provide a mechanism for making identity assertions while maintaining privacy, yet, in classical, non-distributed systems require

Table 8. Communication cost (in kB per party) of the MPC-q-SDH accumulator in the 3-party threshold setting implemented in MP-SPDZ.

Operation	$|\mathcal{X}|$	Semi-honest		Malicious	
		Offline	Online	Offline	Online
Gen	2^{10}, 2^{14}	0.26	0.20	0.65	0.20
Eval	2^{10}	0.26	66	459	131
	2^{14}	0.26	1 049	7 340	2 097
WitCreate, Delete, WitUpdate$_{\text{Delete}}$	2^{10}, 2^{14}	0.26	0.23	1.1	0.3
Add, WitUpdate$_{\text{Add}}$	2^{10}, 2^{14}	0	0.11	0	0.11

a trusted credential issuer. This central issuer, however, is both a single point of failure and a target for compromise and can make it challenging to deploy such a system. In a distributed credential system, on the other hand, this trusted credential issuer is eliminated, e.g., by using distributed ledgers.

We shortly recall how Sovrin implements revocation. When issuing a credential, every user gets a unique revocation identifier i_R. All valid revocation IDs are accumulated using a q-SDH accumulator which is published. Additionally, the users obtains a witness certifying membership of its i_R in the accumulator. Whenever a user shows their credential, they have to prove that they know this witness for their i_R with respect to the published accumulator. When a new user joins, the accumulator has to be updated. Consequently, all the witnesses have to be updated as well, as otherwise they would no longer be able to provide a valid proof. Similar, in the case that a user is revoked and thus removed from the accumulator, all other users have to update their witnesses accordingly. Also, the verifiers always have to check for updated accumulators.

Now, recall that the q-SDH accumulator supports all required operations without needing access to the trapdoor. Hence, all operations can be performed and, especially, the users can update their witnesses on their own if the corresponding i_Rs are published on the ledger. While functionality-wise all operations are supported, performance-wise a large number of users becomes an issue. With potentially millions to billions of users, adding and deleting members from the accumulator becomes increasingly expensive (cf. Table 1). Hence, at a certain size, having access to the trapdoor would be beneficial. But, on the other side, generating membership witnesses for non-members would then become possible.

The latter is also an issue during the setup of the system. Trusting one third party to generate the public parameters of the accumulator might be undesired in a distributed system as in this case. The special structure of the Sovrin ecosystem with their semi-trusted foundation members, however, naturally fits to our multi-party accumulator. First, the foundation members can setup the public parameters in a distributed manner. Secondly, as all of them have shares of the trapdoor, they can also run the updates of the accumulator using the MPC-q-SDH-accumulator. Additionally, using a threshold secret sharing scheme can add robustness against foundation members failing to provide their shares for computations. The change to this accumulator is completely transparent to the clients and verifiers and no changes are required there. Furthermore, the Verify step of the MPC-q-SDH-accumulator is equal to the Verify operation of the non-MPC q-SDH-accumulator. Therefore, the same efficient zero-knowledge proofs [2] can be used to prove knowledge of a witness without revealing it. These proofs are significantly more efficient then proving witnesses of a Merkle-Tree-accumulator, even when SNARK-friendly hash functions are used.

5.2 Privacy-Preserving Certificate-Transparency Logs

We finally look at the application of accumulators in the CT ecosystem. Certificate Authorities request the inclusion of certificates in the log whenever they sign a new certificate. Once the certificate was included in the log, auditors can check the consistency of this log. Additionally, TLS clients also verify whether all certificates that they obtain were actually logged, thereby ensuring that log servers do not hand out promises of certificate inclusion without following through. Technically, the CT log is realized as a Merkle-tree accumulator containing all certificates. As certificates need to be added continuously, it is made dynamic by simply recalculating the root hash and all the proofs. Functionality wise, dynamic accumulators would perfectly fit this use-case. However, their real-world performance without secret trapdoors is not good enough – recalculating hash trees is just more efficient. Knowledge of the secret trapdoors would however be catastrophic for this application, as the guarantees of the whole system break down: log servers could produce witnesses for any certificate they get queried on, even if it was never submitted to the log servers for inclusion.

In the CT ecosystem, the clients need to contact the log servers for the inclusion proof, and therefore verifying certificates has negative privacy implications, as this query reveals the browsing behavior of the client to the log server. Based on previous work by Lueks and Goldberg [43], Kales et al. [35] proposed to rethink retrieval of the inclusion proofs by employing multi-server private information retrieval (PIR) to query the proofs. To further improve performance, the accumulator is split into sub-accumulators based on, e.g., time periods. All sub-accumulators are then accumulated in a top-level accumulator. Consequently, the witnesses with respect to the sub-accumulator stay constant and can be embedded in the server's certificate and only the membership-proofs of the sub-accumulators need to be updated when new certificates are added to the log. Only these top-level proofs have to be queried using PIR, thus greatly improving the overall performance, as smaller databases are more efficient to query.

However, one drawback of this solution is the increase in certificate size if one were to include this static membership witness for the sub-accumulator in the certificate itself. Kales et al. [35] propose to build sub-accumulators per hour, which would result in sub-accumulators that hold about 2^{16} certificates. A Merkle-tree membership proof for these sub-accumulators is 512 bytes in size when using SHA-256. In contrast, a membership proof for the q-SDH accumulator is only 48 bytes in size (with the curve used in our implementation). A typical DER-encoded X509 certificate using RSA-2048 as used in TLS is about 1–2 KB in size, meaning inclusion of the Merkle-tree sub-accumulator membership proof would increase the certificate size by 25–50%, whereas the q-SDH sub-accumulator membership proof only increases the size by 2.5–5%.

We can now leverage the fact that their solution already requires two non-colluding servers for the multi-server PIR. These servers hold copies of the Merkle-tree accumulator and answer private membership queries for the top-level accumulator. Switching the used accumulators to our MPC-q-SDH accumulator would give the benefit of small, constant size membership proofs, while still being performant enough to accumulate and produce witnesses for all elements of a sub-accumulator in one hour.

Acknowledgments. This work was supported by EU's Horizon 2020 project under grant agreement n°825225 (Safe-DEED) and n°871473 (KRAKEN), and EU's Horizon 2020 ECSEL Joint Undertaking grant agreement n°783119 (SECREDAS), and by the "DDAI" COMET Module within the COMET – Competence Centers for Excellent Technologies Programme, funded by the Austrian Federal Ministry for Transport, Innovation and Technology (bmvit), the Austrian Federal Ministry for Digital and Economic Affairs (bmdw), the Austrian Research Promotion Agency (FFG), the province of Styria (SFG) and partners from industry and academia. The COMET Programme is managed by FFG.

References

1. Abdolmaleki, B., Ramacher, S., Slamanig, D.: Lift-and-shift: obtaining simulation extractable subversion and updatable snarks generically. In: CCS, pp. 1987–2005. ACM (2020)
2. Acar, T., Chow, S.S.M., Nguyen, L.: Accumulators and U-prove revocation. In: Sadeghi, A.-R. (ed.) FC 2013. LNCS, vol. 7859, pp. 189–196. Springer, Heidelberg (2013). https://doi.org/10.1007/978-3-642-39884-1_15
3. Baldimtsi, F., et al.: Accumulators with applications to anonymity-preserving revocation. In: EuroS&P, pp. 301–315. IEEE (2017)
4. Badimtsi, F., Canetti, R., Yakoubov, S.: Universally composable accumulators. In: Jarecki, S. (ed.) CT-RSA 2020. LNCS, vol. 12006, pp. 638–666. Springer, Cham (2020). https://doi.org/10.1007/978-3-030-40186-3_27
5. Bar-Ilan, J., Beaver, D.: Non-cryptographic fault-tolerant computing in constant number of rounds of interaction. In: PODC, pp. 201–209. ACM (1989)
6. Barbulescu, R., Duquesne, S.: Updating key size estimations for pairings. J. Cryptol. **32**(4), 1298–1336 (2019)
7. Barreto, P.S.L.M., Lynn, B., Scott, M.: Constructing elliptic curves with prescribed embedding degrees. In: Cimato, S., Persiano, G., Galdi, C. (eds.) SCN 2002. LNCS, vol. 2576, pp. 257–267. Springer, Heidelberg (2003). https://doi.org/10.1007/3-540-36413-7_19
8. Beaver, D.: Efficient multiparty protocols using circuit randomization. In: Feigenbaum, J. (ed.) CRYPTO 1991. LNCS, vol. 576, pp. 420–432. Springer, Heidelberg (1992). https://doi.org/10.1007/3-540-46766-1_34
9. Bellare, M., Fuchsbauer, G., Scafuro, A.: NIZKs with an untrusted CRS: security in the face of parameter subversion. In: Cheon, J.H., Takagi, T. (eds.) ASIACRYPT 2016. LNCS, vol. 10032, pp. 777–804. Springer, Heidelberg (2016). https://doi.org/10.1007/978-3-662-53890-6_26
10. Ben-Sasson, E., Bentov, I., Horesh, Y., Riabzev, M.: Scalable zero knowledge with no trusted setup. In: Boldyreva, A., Micciancio, D. (eds.) CRYPTO 2019. LNCS, vol. 11694, pp. 701–732. Springer, Cham (2019). https://doi.org/10.1007/978-3-030-26954-8_23
11. Benaloh, J., de Mare, M.: One-way accumulators: a decentralized alternative to digital signatures. In: Helleseth, T. (ed.) EUROCRYPT 1993. LNCS, vol. 765, pp. 274–285. Springer, Heidelberg (1994). https://doi.org/10.1007/3-540-48285-7_24
12. Boneh, D., Bünz, B., Fisch, B.: Batching techniques for accumulators with applications to IOPs and stateless blockchains. In: Boldyreva, A., Micciancio, D. (eds.) CRYPTO 2019. LNCS, vol. 11692, pp. 561–586. Springer, Cham (2019). https://doi.org/10.1007/978-3-030-26948-7_20

13. Camenisch, J., Lysyanskaya, A.: Dynamic accumulators and application to efficient revocation of anonymous credentials. In: Yung, M. (ed.) CRYPTO 2002. LNCS, vol. 2442, pp. 61–76. Springer, Heidelberg (2002). https://doi.org/10.1007/3-540-45708-9_5

14. Campanelli, M., Gennaro, R., Goldfeder, S., Nizzardo, L.: Zero-knowledge contingent payments revisited: attacks and payments for services. In: ACM CCS, pp. 229–243. ACM (2017)

15. Canetti, R.: Universally composable security: a new paradigm for cryptographic protocols. In: FOCS, pp. 136–145. IEEE (2001)

16. Chen, M., et al.: Multiparty generation of an RSA modulus. In: Micciancio, D., Ristenpart, T. (eds.) CRYPTO 2020. LNCS, vol. 12172, pp. 64–93. Springer, Cham (2020). https://doi.org/10.1007/978-3-030-56877-1_3

17. Chen, M., et al.: Diogenes: lightweight scalable RSA modulus generation with a dishonest majority. IACR Cryptol. ePrint Arch. **2020**, 374 (2020)

18. Chida, K., et al.: Fast large-scale honest-majority MPC for malicious adversaries. In: Shacham, H., Boldyreva, A. (eds.) CRYPTO 2018. LNCS, vol. 10993, pp. 34–64. Springer, Cham (2018). https://doi.org/10.1007/978-3-319-96878-0_2

19. Cramer, R., Damgård, I., Maurer, U.: General secure multi-party computation from any linear secret-sharing scheme. In: Preneel, B. (ed.) EUROCRYPT 2000. LNCS, vol. 1807, pp. 316–334. Springer, Heidelberg (2000). https://doi.org/10.1007/3-540-45539-6_22

20. Dalskov, A., Orlandi, C., Keller, M., Shrishak, K., Shulman, H.: Securing DNSSEC keys via threshold ECDSA from generic MPC. In: Chen, L., Li, N., Liang, K., Schneider, S. (eds.) ESORICS 2020. LNCS, vol. 12309, pp. 654–673. Springer, Cham (2020). https://doi.org/10.1007/978-3-030-59013-0_32

21. Damgård, I., Keller, M., Larraia, E., Pastro, V., Scholl, P., Smart, N.P.: Practical covertly secure MPC for dishonest majority – or: breaking the SPDZ limits. In: Crampton, J., Jajodia, S., Mayes, K. (eds.) ESORICS 2013. LNCS, vol. 8134, pp. 1–18. Springer, Heidelberg (2013). https://doi.org/10.1007/978-3-642-40203-6_1

22. Damgård, I., Koprowski, M.: Practical threshold RSA signatures without a trusted dealer. In: Pfitzmann, B. (ed.) EUROCRYPT 2001. LNCS, vol. 2045, pp. 152–165. Springer, Heidelberg (2001). https://doi.org/10.1007/3-540-44987-6_10

23. Damgård, I., Nielsen, J.B.: Universally composable efficient multiparty computation from threshold homomorphic encryption. In: Boneh, D. (ed.) CRYPTO 2003. LNCS, vol. 2729, pp. 247–264. Springer, Heidelberg (2003). https://doi.org/10.1007/978-3-540-45146-4_15

24. Damgård, I., Pastro, V., Smart, N., Zakarias, S.: Multiparty computation from somewhat homomorphic encryption. In: Safavi-Naini, R., Canetti, R. (eds.) CRYPTO 2012. LNCS, vol. 7417, pp. 643–662. Springer, Heidelberg (2012). https://doi.org/10.1007/978-3-642-32009-5_38

25. Derler, D., Hanser, C., Slamanig, D.: Revisiting cryptographic accumulators, additional properties and relations to other primitives. In: Nyberg, K. (ed.) CT-RSA 2015. LNCS, vol. 9048, pp. 127–144. Springer, Cham (2015). https://doi.org/10.1007/978-3-319-16715-2_7

26. Derler, D., Ramacher, S., Slamanig, D.: Post-quantum zero-knowledge proofs for accumulators with applications to ring signatures from symmetric-key primitives. In: Lange, T., Steinwandt, R. (eds.) PQCrypto 2018. LNCS, vol. 10786, pp. 419–440. Springer, Cham (2018). https://doi.org/10.1007/978-3-319-79063-3_20

27. Dobson, S., Galbraith, S.D.: Trustless groups of unknown order with hyperelliptic curves. IACR ePrint **2020**, 196 (2020)

28. Doerner, J., Kondi, Y., Lee, E., Shelat, A.: Threshold ECDSA from ECDSA assumptions: the multiparty case. In: IEEE S&P, pp. 1051–1066. IEEE (2019)
29. Frederiksen, T.K., Lindell, Y., Osheter, V., Pinkas, B.: Fast distributed RSA key generation for semi-honest and malicious adversaries. In: Shacham, H., Boldyreva, A. (eds.) CRYPTO 2018. LNCS, vol. 10992, pp. 331–361. Springer, Cham (2018). https://doi.org/10.1007/978-3-319-96881-0_12
30. Galbraith, S.D., Paterson, K.G., Smart, N.P.: Pairings for cryptographers. Discret. Appl. Math. **156**(16), 3113–3121 (2008)
31. Garman, C., Green, M., Miers, I.: Decentralized anonymous credentials. In: NDSS. The Internet Society (2014)
32. Gennaro, R., Goldfeder, S.: Fast multiparty threshold ECDSA with fast trustless setup. In: ACM CCS, pp. 1179–1194. ACM (2018)
33. Groth, J., Kohlweiss, M., Maller, M., Meiklejohn, S., Miers, I.: Updatable and universal common reference strings with applications to zk-SNARKs. In: Shacham, H., Boldyreva, A. (eds.) CRYPTO 2018. LNCS, vol. 10993, pp. 698–728. Springer, Cham (2018). https://doi.org/10.1007/978-3-319-96878-0_24
34. Hamdy, S., Möller, B.: Security of cryptosystems based on class groups of imaginary quadratic orders. In: Okamoto, T. (ed.) ASIACRYPT 2000. LNCS, vol. 1976, pp. 234–247. Springer, Heidelberg (2000). https://doi.org/10.1007/3-540-44448-3_18
35. Kales, D., Omolola, O., Ramacher, S.: Revisiting user privacy for certificate transparency. In: EuroS&P, pp. 432–447. IEEE (2019)
36. Keller, M.: MP-SPDZ: a versatile framework for multi-party computation. In: CCS, pp. 1575–1590. ACM (2020)
37. Khovratovich, D., Law, J.: Sovrin: digitial signatures in the blockchain area (2016). https://sovrin.org/wp-content/uploads/AnonCred-RWC.pdf
38. Laurie, B.: Certificate transparency. ACM Queue **12**(8), 10–19 (2014)
39. Libert, B., Ling, S., Nguyen, K., Wang, H.: Zero-knowledge arguments for lattice-based accumulators: logarithmic-size ring signatures and group signatures without trapdoors. In: Fischlin, M., Coron, J.-S. (eds.) EUROCRYPT 2016. LNCS, vol. 9666, pp. 1–31. Springer, Heidelberg (2016). https://doi.org/10.1007/978-3-662-49896-5_1
40. Lindell, Y., Nof, A.: A framework for constructing fast MPC over arithmetic circuits with malicious adversaries and an honest-majority. In: CCS, pp. 259–276. ACM (2017)
41. Lindell, Y., Nof, A.: Fast secure multiparty ECDSA with practical distributed key generation and applications to cryptocurrency custody. In: ACM CCS, pp. 1837–1854. ACM (2018)
42. Lipmaa, H.: Secure accumulators from Euclidean rings without trusted setup. In: Bao, F., Samarati, P., Zhou, J. (eds.) ACNS 2012. LNCS, vol. 7341, pp. 224–240. Springer, Heidelberg (2012). https://doi.org/10.1007/978-3-642-31284-7_14
43. Lueks, W., Goldberg, I.: Sublinear scaling for multi-client private information retrieval. In: Böhme, R., Okamoto, T. (eds.) FC 2015. LNCS, vol. 8975, pp. 168–186. Springer, Heidelberg (2015). https://doi.org/10.1007/978-3-662-47854-7_10
44. Merkle, R.C.: A certified digital signature. In: Brassard, G. (ed.) CRYPTO 1989. LNCS, vol. 435, pp. 218–238. Springer, New York (1990). https://doi.org/10.1007/0-387-34805-0_21
45. Miers, I., Garman, C., Green, M., Rubin, A.D.: Zerocoin: anonymous distributed e-cash from bitcoin. In: IEEE S&P, pp. 397–411. IEEE (2013)
46. Nguyen, L.: Accumulators from bilinear pairings and applications. In: Menezes, A. (ed.) CT-RSA 2005. LNCS, vol. 3376, pp. 275–292. Springer, Heidelberg (2005). https://doi.org/10.1007/978-3-540-30574-3_19

47. Sander, T.: Efficient accumulators without trapdoor extended abstract. In: Varad-harajan, V., Mu, Y. (eds.) ICICS 1999. LNCS, vol. 1726, pp. 252–262. Springer, Heidelberg (1999). https://doi.org/10.1007/978-3-540-47942-0_21
48. Shamir, A.: How to share a secret. Commun. ACM **22**(11), 612–613 (1979)
49. Smart, N.P., Talibi Alaoui, Y.: Distributing any elliptic curve based protocol. In: Albrecht, M. (ed.) IMACC 2019. LNCS, vol. 11929, pp. 342–366. Springer, Cham (2019). https://doi.org/10.1007/978-3-030-35199-1_17
50. Wagh, S., Gupta, D., Chandran, N.: SecureNN: 3-party secure computation for neural network training. PoPETs **2019**(3), 26–49 (2019)

Balancing Privacy and Accountability in Blockchain Identity Management

Ivan Damgård[1], Chaya Ganesh[2], Hamidreza Khoshakhlagh[1(✉)],
Claudio Orlandi[1], and Luisa Siniscalchi[1]

[1] Concordium Blockchain Research Center, Aarhus University, Aarhus, Denmark
hamidreza@cs.au.dk
[2] Indian Institute of Science, Bangalore, Bangalore, India

Abstract. The lack of privacy in the first generation of cryptocurrencies such as Bitcoin, Ethereum, etc. is a well known problem in cryptocurrency research. To overcome this problem, several new cryptocurrencies were designed to guarantee transaction privacy and anonymity for their users (examples include ZCash, Monero, etc.).

However, the anonymity provided by such systems appears to be fundamentally problematic in current business and legislation settings: banks and other financial institutions must follow rules such as "Know Your Customer" (KYC), "Anti Money Laundering" (AML), etc. It is also well known that the (alleged or real) anonymity guarantees provided by cryptocurrencies have attracted ill-intentioned individuals to this space, who look at cryptocurrencies as a way of facilitating illegal activities (tax-evasion, ransom-ware, trading of illegal substances, etc.).

The fact that current cryptocurrencies do not comply with such regulations can in part explain why traditional financial institutions have so far been very sceptical of the ongoing cryptocurrency and Blockchain revolution.

In this paper, we propose a novel design principle for identity management in Blockchains. The goal of our design is to maintain privacy, while still allowing compliance with current regulations and preventing exploitations of Blockchain technology for purposes which are incompatible with the social good.

1 Introduction

Early applications of blockchain to payment systems such as Bitcoin do not guarantee privacy. In the Bitcoin blockchain, blocks posted on the public ledger consist of transactions, making Bitcoin transparent – transactions are there for

Research supported by: the Concordium Blockchain Research Center (COBRA), Aarhus University, Denmark; the Carlsberg Foundation under the Semper Ardens Research Project CF18-112 (BCM); the European Research Council (ERC) under the European Unions's Horizon 2020 research and innovation programme under grant agreement No. 669255 (MPCPRO); the European Research Council (ERC) under the European Unions's Horizon 2020 research and innovation programme under grant agreement No. 803096 (SPEC).

K. G. Paterson (Ed.): CT-RSA 2021, LNCS 12704, pp. 552–576, 2021.
https://doi.org/10.1007/978-3-030-75539-3_23

everybody to see. However, the identities are pseudonymous, and not tied to real world identities. Consequently, Bitcoin has the property that while the ownership of money is implicitly anonymous, the flow of money is globally visible. While this was perceived to be truly anonymous early on, there have been several works that deanonymize Bitcoin flow by analysing the payment graph [30]. To overcome the problem of lack of privacy in the first generation of cryptocurrencies such as Bitcoin, Ethereum, etc., new systems were designed to guarantee transaction privacy and anonymity for their users [6,24,35]. Systems like Zerocash [6] fully hide both the value inside a transaction, and the sender and receiver identities. Most blockchain use-cases, however, are hindered by complete privacy as they need *accountability* and *identity management*. Privacy-preserving systems like ZCash are not designed with accountability in mind[1]. In order to conform with regulations like "Know your customer" (KYC) and "Anti-money laundering" (AML), a legal authority should be able to learn the value and identities of the parties involved in any transaction; this requirement seems to be at odds with privacy. The seemingly contradictory requirements of transaction privacy & user anonymity, and regulatory requirements such as KYC/AML imposed on financial and banking institutions is a major hurdle in widespread adoption of the blockchain.

Our Contribution. In this work, we address the problem of balancing accountability with privacy in blockchain-based systems. We propose a new architectural design of an "identity layer" that will provide privacy for its users – that is, no one, observing the network transactions and the status of the Blockchain should be able to learn about the identity of the owner of any account in the system. At the same time, the identity layer achieves accountability in the sense that in the presence of a reasonable suspicion, law-enforcement agencies (or other authorized parties), will be able to access the transaction history of a given user and/or block its funds, in a way similar to what is guaranteed today by traditional financial institutions. We develop cryptographic mechanisms that enhance accountability measures against misuse of the blockchain, while still providing privacy. Towards this end, we employ cryptographic techniques to design provably secure protocols, with both privacy and accountability guarantees. We prove the security of our constructions in the Universal Composability (UC) framework. We provide a high-level overview of the design of the system, and then discuss the techniques and cryptographic tools used. We believe that such an identity layer design will make Blockchain and cryptocurrencies more attractive for regulators, public institutions and traditional businesses which are interested in complying with existing legislation. In fact, the identity layer of Concordium[2], an upcoming major Blockchain project, is based on the design presented in this paper.

Overview of the System. In the proposed system, the identity and credentials of each participant in the network are initially verified and stored by authorized

---

[1] Zcash considers solutions to implement AML and KYC controls [1], however this solution requires trust on a single party.

[2] concordium.com.

parties called *Identity Providers* (IPs). Each user can open a limited number of accounts where an account has an identifier that is derived from a PRF applied to a value that is between 1 and the maximal number of accounts, say n. The PRF key K is held by the user. When a user registers with an IP, K is encrypted through a threshold encryption scheme, and this ciphertext is stored with the IP. This is set up such that an appropriate number of *Anonymity Revokers* (ARs) would be able to decrypt. Standard anonymous credentials are used to certify additional attributes of the user.

When a user creates an account, they prepare some data to be published on the blockchain. This includes a threshold encryption of the account holder's public key (that was also stored with the IP at registration time). It also includes zero-knowledge proofs that the attributes the user chooses to publish in the account have been signed by the IP, and that the account identifier has been correctly computed. Thus, an account may contain complete identification of the account holder, if the user chooses to include it, or it may reveal less information, for instance the citizenship and age of the account holder.

Finally, an account includes various account specific public keys. Using the corresponding secret keys, the account holder can then perform transactions anonymously in the network. Depending on the key material included in accounts, several different ways to do transactions can be realized – this is a problem orthogonal to that of implementing the identity layer, and we give some informal examples of how this could be done in the full version [18].

If it is suspected that an account is used for fraudulent purposes, the encrypted account information can be decrypted by a qualified set of the ARs, and an anonymous account can be linked (via the public key) to an id provided by the IP. On the other hand, if a particular user is suspected of fraud, the IP can provide its record for this user, and a qualified set of ARs can decrypt the information to learn the PRF key K. Now, they can generate the set of all values $\mathsf{PRF}_\mathsf{K}(x)$ for $x = 1, \ldots, n$ which are all the possible values for an account identifier. One can then identify all accounts of the user by searching the blockchain for accounts with these identifiers. Privacy is therefore guaranteed for all users, except those whose anonymity is revoked by a sufficient number of ARs.

Note that the above also implies that we have a mechanism for preventing a user from opening an unbounded number of accounts using a single certificate from the IP: if this were possible, it would open the door for attacks where an individual registers with an IP and then allow other individuals to open accounts in their name, perhaps after payment of a small sum of money. On the other hand, we do not want the account holder to have to interact with the IP for every new account it wants to create, as this would affect efficiency. While the concrete number of accounts allowed per user is an implementation dependent parameter, our technique allows to achieve a reasonable tradeoff. The zero-knowledge proofs force the user to compute the account id's correctly, which only allows n different id's. Thus, if one attempts to open more accounts than allowed, this must result in a pre-existing account identifier, and the Blockchain will reject it.

We prove security of the system when either any number of account holders are actively corrupt, or when the identity providers are semi-honest corrupt. Note that, similar to certification authorities in standard PKI, we need some trust in the IPs: a malicious identity provider (equivalently, a malicious account holder colluding with a semi-honest IP and therefore learning the key), could produce certificates containing false identities, therefore undermining the system. Finally, depending on which properties we want to emphasize, we could tolerate different corruption levels among the anonymity revokers. Thus our system is secure in the presence of actively corrupt users and a threshold number of passively corrupt anonymity revokers; or, in the presence of passively corrupt identity-provider and a threshold number of passively corrupt anonymity revokers. In our design it is paramount that the service provided by the anonymity revokers to be available, and we want to emphasize privacy. Thus, we opt for assuming a majority of semi-honest ARs. Using standard methods, we could instead tolerate a minority of actively corrupted ARs.

Overview of Technical Ideas. We use cryptographic schemes such as Pedersen commitments [34], Dodis-Yampolskiy PRF [21], Pointcheval-Sanders (PS) signature scheme [36], CL encryption scheme [12]. We use zkSNARKs in combination with commitments and signatures in the spirit of [2,10]: the PS blind signature we use is defined using groups of a certain prime order, and when a user proves knowledge of a signature, the message that is signed is committed to using a Pedersen-type commitment in such a group. Now, we can use standard sigma-protocols to provide commitments to individual attributes of the user in the same group, and finally use SNARKs on committed messages to show statements such as "the age attribute of the user is a number greater than 18". In this way, we only need to use SNARKs on rather small circuits, and we can achieve much greater efficiency than if we had to convert large statements involving, e.g., group operations into a Boolean circuit to be evaluated inside the SNARK. In this way, creating an account requires a constant number of exponentiations (i.e., independent of the security parameter), and likewise, the number of group elements in an account is constant.

We provide a generic lifting transformation for Fiat Shamir NIZKs for DL-languages into UC NIZKs. While such a transformation by encrypting the witness under a key that is part of the CRS (and the secret key part of the CRS trapdoor) is folklore [20], using the CL encryption scheme allows us to efficiently prove statements about values in the exponent, which is novel to the best of our knowledge.

Related Work. The cryptographic tools used in building our solution, like commitment schemes, blind signatures, zero-knowledge proofs, and threshold encryption are based on anonymous credentials technology. Anonymous credentials [14] allow a party to prove to a verifier that one has a set of credentials without revealing anything beyond this fact. Revocable anonymity [9,28] allows a trusted third party to discover the identity of all otherwise anonymous participants. Conditional anonymity requires that a user's transactions remain anonymous until certain conditions are violated [7,8,17]. In [17], an unclonable identification scheme is introduced, that is, roughly, an identification scheme where honest users can identify themselves anonymously as members of a group, but where clones of users can be detected and have their identities revealed if they identify themselves simultaneously. This was extended from one-time authentication to n-times anonymous authentication in [7] where a certain number of unlinkable accounts are derived that can later be efficiently traced. The works of [4,32,40,41] addressed related problems of allowing a user to show a credential anonymously and unlinkably up to n times to a particular verifier. The potential for abuse of unconditional anonymity by misbehaving users has been articulated in the context of group signatures. In a group signature scheme, each group member can sign a message on behalf of a group such that anyone can verify that the group signature is produced by someone in the group, but not who exactly. Our idea for identifying all accounts of a user in case of revocation by using a PRF to generate account identifiers is reminiscent of the work of traceable signatures [15] that enable a tracing agent to identify all signatures produced by a particular member. The idea of deriving a certain number of unlinkable accounts that can later be efficiently traced has been used in various forms in the anonymous credential literature [5,7,15] for the purposes of balancing accountability and anonymity.

Unfortunately none of the previous works seem to fit our intended use case, which motivated us to design the system described in this paper. Moreover, the toolbox of efficient tools available to the protocol designer has grown in recent years (e.g., the CL encryption scheme, advances in SNARKs, etc.), which also motivates exploring new designs.

The zkLedger protocol [31] is an asset transfer scheme that hides transaction amounts and sender-receiver relationship, and supports auditing. The protocol is for a setting where the transacting parties are banks, and requires the participation of the banks for an audit to take place. The work of [3] presents a privacy-preserving token management system that supports auditing in permissioned blockchains. The system of [3] is in the UTXO framework, where users own tokens that are certified, and prove ownership of tokens in a privacy-preserving manner. In contrast, we work in the account-based model; and our design is modular – the identity layer is separate from the transaction layer. One main difference of our work from the works of [31] and [3] is that while both these works assume that the entire system is permissioned, again our design is more modular: our ID layer obviously assumes that IPs and ARs are known (and trusted to some extent) and is therefore in some sense permissioned. However, the ID layer can work on top of the consensus mechanism of a permissionless blockchain, i.e., any blockchain that can be abstracted using the ledger functionality, that we define of our full version.

Finally, Solidus [13] is a privacy-preserving system that allows customers of financial institutions (e.g., banks) to transfer assets and ensures that only the banks of the sender and receiver learn the transaction details. While there is no explicit audit functionality in Solidus, banks can reveal the content of a suspicious transaction to the authorized auditors. However this approach requires to trust a single party (i.e., the bank).

2 Preliminaries and Building Blocks

2.1 Notation

For any positive integer n, $[n]$ denotes the set $\{1,\ldots,n\}$. We write $f(\lambda) \approx_\lambda g(\lambda)$ if the difference between f and g is negligible in λ. We use DPT (resp. PPT) to mean a deterministic (resp. probabilistic) polynomial time algorithm. We denote by $Y \leftarrow_\$ \mathsf{F}(X)$ a probabilistic algorithm F that on input X outputs Y. Similarly, notation $Y \leftarrow \mathsf{F}(X)$ is used for a deterministic algorithm with input X and output Y. All adversaries will be stateful. We use the identifier AH for account holder, IP for identity provider and AR for anonymity revoker. By an identifier, we mean an arbitrary string that uniquely identifies a party. Throughout the paper, $\mathbb{F}_q$ will denote the field with q elements.

2.2 Pseudorandom Functions

We define a weak notion of PRF robustness, meaning that is should be hard to find a key that produce collisions with the PRF evaluation of an honest user. Our definition is similar to the one in [22], but here one of the two keys is chosen honestly.

Definition 2.1 (Weakly Robust PRF). *A PRF is weakly robust if:*

$$\Pr[\mathsf{K} \leftarrow_\$ \mathsf{Gen}(1^\lambda), (x^*, \mathsf{K}^*) \leftarrow_\$ \mathcal{A}^{PRF_\mathsf{K}(\cdot)}(1^\lambda) : \exists (x, y) \in \mathcal{Q}, PRF_{\mathsf{K}^*}(x^*) = y] \approx_\lambda 0$$

where $\mathcal{Q}$ is the set of inputs/outputs of the oracle available to the adversary.

Instantiation with Dodis-Yampolskiy PRF. We use the PRF of Dodis and Yampolskiy [21] that operates in a group $\mathbb{G}$ of order q with generator g. On input x and the PRF key $\mathsf{K} \leftarrow_\$ \mathbb{F}_q$, $PRF_\mathsf{K}(x) = g^{1/\mathsf{K}+x}$. This is shown to be pseudorandom under the Decisional Diffie-Hellman Inversion assumption in group $\mathbb{G}$. Note that the security holds only for small domains, namely inputs that are slightly superlogarithmic in the security parameter, but this is sufficient for our work, as the maximum number of accounts a user can open is less than a constant $\mathsf{Max}_{\mathsf{ACC}}$. It can also be easily shown that the Dodis-Yampolskiy PRF is weakly robust: using the PRF assumption, we can replace the output of the PRF oracle with random group elements. If the adversary outputs an input x^* and key K^* that are compatible with one of the output of the oracles, we can compute the discrete logarithm of that element as $1/(\mathsf{K}^* + x^*)$.

2.3 Blind Signature Schemes

We adapt the notation of [38] to two-round blind signature schemes.

Definition 2.2 (Blind Signature Schemes). *An interactive signature scheme between a signer S and user U consists of a tuple of efficient algorithms* $\mathsf{BS} = (\mathsf{Setup}, \mathsf{KeyGen}, \mathsf{Sign}_1, \mathsf{Sign}_2, \mathsf{Unblind}, \mathsf{VerifySig})$ *where*

- $\mathsf{Setup}(1^\lambda)$, *on input the security parameter* 1^λ *outputs* pp, *which is given implicitly as input to all other algorithms, even when omitted.*
- $\mathsf{KeyGen}(\mathsf{pp})$, *on input the public parameter* pp *generates a key pair* $(\mathsf{sk}, \mathsf{pk})$ *for security parameter* λ.
- $\mathsf{Sign}_1(\mathsf{pk}, m)$, *which is run by* U, *takes as input* pk *and a message* $m \in \{0,1\}^*$ *and outputs* sign_1 *and* ω *(wlog* ω *can be thought of as the randomness used to run* Sign_1).
- $\mathsf{Sign}_2(\mathsf{sk}, \mathsf{sign}_1)$, *which is run by* S, *takes as input* sk *and* sign_1 *and outputs* sign_2.
- $\mathsf{Unblind}(\mathsf{sign}_2, \omega)$, *which is run by* U, *takes as input* sign_2, ω *and outputs* σ.
- $\mathsf{VerifySig}(\mathsf{pk}, m, \sigma)$ *outputs a bit.*

Remark 2.1. Note that a blind signature scheme implicitly defines a normal signature scheme as well, where the signing algorithm $\mathsf{Sign}(\mathsf{sk}, m)$ simply emulates a blind signature protocol and outputs the resulting signature σ.

The correctness property of the scheme requires that the following holds: for any $(\mathsf{pp}) \leftarrow_\$ \mathsf{Setup}(1^\lambda)$, $(\mathsf{sk}, \mathsf{pk}) \leftarrow_\$ \mathsf{KeyGen}(\mathsf{pp})$, any message $m \in \{0,1\}^*$, if $(\mathsf{sign}_1, \omega) \leftarrow_\$ \mathsf{Sign}_1(\mathsf{pk}, m)$, $\mathsf{sign}_2 \leftarrow_\$ \mathsf{Sign}_2(\mathsf{sk}, \mathsf{sign}_1)$, $\sigma = \mathsf{Unblind}(\mathsf{sign}_2, \omega)$ then $\mathsf{VerifySig}(\mathsf{pk}, m, \sigma) = 1$ with overwhelming probability over $\lambda \in \mathbb{N}$.

We require the standard notion of *existential unforgeability under chosen message attacks* (EUF-CMA) [27]. The blind signature scheme we use should additionally satisfy two properties, namely *Blindness* and *simulatability*, where the second is an ad-hoc definition required for our UC proof of security that ensures the existence of an additional simulation algorithm Sim that can simulate sign_2. The formal definition of these properties can be found in the full version [18].

2.4 (Ad-Hoc) Threshold Encryption Scheme

Definition 2.3. *A* (n, d)-*threshold encryption scheme* $\mathsf{TE} = (\mathsf{TKeyGen}, \mathsf{TEnc}, \mathsf{ShareDec}, \mathsf{TCombine})$ *over message space M consists of the following algorithms:*

- $\mathsf{TKeyGen}(1^\lambda)$ *is a randomized key generation algorithm that takes the security parameter λ as input and returns a private-public key pair* $(\mathsf{sk}, \mathsf{pk})$.
- $\mathsf{TEnc}^{\mathsf{n,d}}_{\mathsf{pk}_R}(m)$, *a probabilistic encryption algorithm that encrypts a message* $m \in M$ *to a set of public keys* $\mathsf{pk}_R = \{\mathsf{pk}_i\}_{i \in R}$ *in such a way that any size* $\mathsf{d} + 1$ *subset of the recipient set should jointly be able to decrypt. We sometimes write* $\mathsf{TEnc}^{\mathsf{n,d}}_{\mathsf{pk}_R}(m; r)$ *when we want to be able to fix the value of the randomness r to a specific value.*

- $\mathsf{ShareDec}^{n,d}_{pk_R,sk_i}(ct)$, *on input a ciphertext ct and a secret key* sk_i, *outputs a decryption share* μ_i.
- $\mathsf{TCombine}^{n,d}_{pk_R}(ct, \{\mu_i\}_{i \in I})$, *a deterministic algorithm that takes a subset* $I \subset [n]$ *with size* $\mathsf{d}+1$ *of decryption shares* $\{\mu_i\}_{i \in I}$ *and outputs either a message* $m \in M$ *or* $\perp$.

We use the static security definition of Reyzin et al. [37] for threshold encryption schemes which requires two properties, namely *static semantic security* and *partial decryption simulatability* as defined in appendix of the full version [18].

For the definitions of Commitments scheme, Secret Sharing and Zero-Knowledge proofs, we refer the reader to the full version [18].

3   System Design

We give a high-level overview of the design of the identity layer in terms of the entities involved, data objects and protocols between the entities.

Entities Involved. The following entities are involved in our design:

- Account Holders (AH): those are individuals who hold accounts on the block-chain. We assume AHs possess some mean for performing legal identification (e.g., a passport), in the country where they live. They are interested in opening accounts and performing transactions on the blockchain but, before doing so, they have to register with an Identity Provider (IP).
- Identity Provider (IP): an identity provider is an entity that, as the name suggests, can provide a digital identity to an AH. The identity provider "authorizes" a user to open accounts on the blockchain, and therefore to perform transactions. Jumping ahead, when observing transactions on the blockchain, it should not be possible to find out the identity of an AH (not even for the IP itself), while everyone should be able to see which IP has authorized a given account, thus creating trust in the account.
- Anonymity Revoker (AR): anonymity revokers are parties which are involved in case where law-enforcement or other authorized entities need to be able to extract the identity of the owner of some account on the blockchain. We can make threshold assumptions on the AR and e.g., require that at least $\mathsf{d}+1$ ARs must give an approval before the anonymity of a user is revoked.

Data Objects. We now describe the data objects that are held by the entities.

Account Holder Certificate (AHC). After an account holder registers with an identity provider, the AH obtains a certificate containing:

- A public identity credential $\mathsf{IDcred}_{\mathsf{PUB}}$ and a secret identity credential $\mathsf{IDcred}_{\mathsf{SEC}}$.
- A key K for a pseudorandom function PRF.
- One or more attribute lists AL such as some identifier, age, citizenship, expiration date, etc.

- A signature on $(\mathsf{IDcred}_{\mathsf{SEC}}, \mathsf{K}, \mathsf{AL})$ that can be checked using $\mathsf{pk}_{\mathsf{IP}}$. A valid signature proves that an AH with attributes as in AL has registered with IP and has proved knowledge of $\mathsf{IDcred}_{\mathsf{SEC}}$ corresponding to $\mathsf{IDcred}_{\mathsf{PUB}}$.

Account Creation Information (ACI). Given an AHC, an account holder can create new accounts and post the corresponding ACI on the ledger, containing:

- $\mathsf{RegID}_{\mathsf{ACC}}$, an account registration ID. This is defined to be $\mathsf{RegID}_{\mathsf{ACC}} = \mathsf{PRF}_{\mathsf{K}}(x)$ where K is a key held by AH and signed by the IP, and where the account in question is the x'th account opened by the AH based on a given AHC. If AH behaves honestly, then $\mathsf{RegID}_{\mathsf{ACC}}$ is unique for the account, and $x \leq \mathsf{Max}_{\mathsf{ACC}}$. The latter condition is enforced by the proof below, the former can be checked publicly.
- Anonymity revocation data: this is a threshold encryption $\mathsf{E}_{\mathsf{ID}} = \mathsf{TEnc}^{n,d}_{\mathsf{PK}_{\mathsf{AR}}}(\mathsf{IDcred}_{\mathsf{PUB}})$, where any subset of size $d+1$ of anonymity revokers are able to decrypt E_{ID} and obtain $\mathsf{IDcred}_{\mathsf{PUB}}$.
- The identity IP of the identity provider who did the signature in the AHC used for this account.
- An account specific public key $\mathsf{pk}_{\mathsf{ACC}}$. It will be used, for instance, to verify transactions related to the account.
- A policy P, which asserts some information about the attribute list AL.
- A proof π that can be checked using $\mathsf{pk}_{\mathsf{IP}}$ and verifies that ACI can only be created by an AH that has obtained an AHC from IP, such that $\mathsf{P}(\mathsf{AL}) = \top$, where AH knows the secret keys corresponding to $\mathsf{pk}_{\mathsf{ACC}}$, as well as $\mathsf{IDcred}_{\mathsf{SEC}}$ corresponding to the $\mathsf{IDcred}_{\mathsf{PUB}}$ that was presented to the IP, and where $\mathsf{RegID}_{\mathsf{ACC}}$, E_{ID} and $\mathsf{E}_{\mathsf{RegID}} = \mathsf{TEnc}^{n,d}_{\mathsf{PK}_{\mathsf{AR}}}(\mathsf{K})$ are correctly generated.

Identity Provider's information on Account Holder (IPIAH). This is the data record that the IP stores after an AH has registered. It contains:

- The name AH of the account holder and its public identity credential $\mathsf{IDcred}_{\mathsf{PUB}}$.
- A set of anonymity revokers $\mathsf{AR}_1, ..., \mathsf{AR}_n$ with public keys $\mathsf{PK}_{\mathsf{AR}}$ and an encryption $\mathsf{E}_{\mathsf{RegID}} = \mathsf{TEnc}^{n,d}_{\mathsf{PK}_{\mathsf{AR}}}(\mathsf{K})$. Here, K is the PRF key chosen by the AH at registration time.

Protocols. The following are the main protocols in our design.

Account Holder Registration. The protocol takes place between an IP and an AH who owns a key pair $(\mathsf{IDcred}_{\mathsf{SEC}}, \mathsf{IDcred}_{\mathsf{PUB}})$ and an attribute list AL. At the end of the protocol, the AH receives an AHC and the IP obtains a IPIAH as described above. The AH sends their attribute list AL to IP and proves (via non-cryptographic means) their identity to IP. More concretely, this means that the IP must verify that the entity it is talking to indeed has the name AH and hence it received AL from the correct entity. It should also verify that the attributes in AL are correct w.r.t. the AH. The AH also sends to IP their public key $\mathsf{IDcred}_{\mathsf{PUB}}$

and an encryption $E_{RegID} = TEnc_{PK_{AR}}^{n,d}(K)$ where K is a PRF key. Next, AH and IP engage in a blind signature scheme, which allows AH to receive a signature on $(IDcred_{SEC}, K, AL)$ that is generated under the secret key sk_{IP} of the IP. In addition, AH proves (cryptographically, in ZK) that they know $IDcred_{SEC}$ corresponding to $IDcred_{PUB}$, that the same $IDcred_{SEC}$ was input to the blind signature, and that the encryption contains the same K that was input to the blind signature scheme. IP stores $IPIAH = (ID_{AH}, IDcred_{PUB}, AL, E_{RegID}, AR_1, \ldots, AR_n)$.

Create New Account. An account holder AH wants to create an account that satisfies some policy P (e.g., above 18, resident in country X, etc.). They take as input an AHC, a policy P and the public key pk_{AR} of one (or more) anonymity revoker(s) with name AR. At the end, AH produces some ACI that can be posted to the blockchain. They also need to store secret key sk_{ACC} that is specific to the account. The protocol works as follows: AH generates an account key pair (pk_{ACC}, sk_{ACC}) and an encryption of their public identity credential $IDcred_{PUB}$ under the public key of the anonymity revokers' PK_{AR}, i.e., $E_{ID} = TEnc_{PK_{AR}}^{n,d}(IDcred_{PUB})$. Next, AH calculates $RegID_{ACC} = PRF_K(x)$, where we assume this is the x'th account that is opened using the AHC that is input. At last, AH produces a non-interactive zero-knowledge (NIZK) proof of knowledge proving that everything was computed correctly e.g., the predicate satisfies the attributes, the signature, keys, and encryptions are valid, and x is below Max_{ACC}.

Revoke Anonymity of Account. Revocation of the anonymity of an account can be done by at least $d + 1$ of the n ARs involved in the set-up of the account, working together with the IP with whom the AH registered. The input is an account identifier $RegID_{ACC}$ and the output is the name AH of the account holder. The protocol proceeds as follows: Given an account $RegID_{ACC}$ whose anonymity needs to be revoked, the ARs find the ACI containing $RegID_{ACC}$ on the blockchain, collaborate to decrypt E_{ID} and learn $IDcred_{PUB}$. The registration information also contains the public name IP of the identity provider who registered $IDcred_{PUB}$. The AR's contact this IP who then locates the $IPIAH = (AH, IDcred_{PUB}, AL, E_{RegID}, AR_1, \ldots, AR_n)$ record that contains the $IDcred_{PUB}$ that was decrypted. This record also includes AH, thus IP and the set of ARs have now identified the AH.

Trace Accounts of User. If a user with a given name AH is suspected of engaging in illegal activities, the IP and a set of at least $d + 1$ ARs can identify all accounts of that user. The IP searches its database to locate the $IPIAH = (AH, IDcred_{PUB}, AL, E_{RegID}, AR_1, \ldots, AR_n)$ containing the relevant AH. This record also contains the names of the relevant AR's. A qualified set of these could decrypt the E_{RegID} to learn the PRF key K and generate all values $PRF_K(x)$ for $x = 1, \ldots, Max_{ACC}$ in public. However, due to technicalities in the security reduction, this would require the PRF to satisfy some form of "selective opening attack" security. Instead, we let the AR's decrypt the ciphertext and evaluate the PRF on $x = 1, \ldots, Max_{ACC}$ inside an MPC protocol, so that K is never revealed to anyone. Either way, the produced values are all the possible values for $RegID_{ACC}$ that the AH could have used to form valid accounts, so one can now search the blockchain for accounts with these registration IDs.

Informal Analysis of the Design. If an AH misbehaves and opens more accounts than they are allowed to, this must result in two or more accounts with the same $\mathsf{RegID}_{\mathsf{ACC}}$. This can be publicly detected by the blockchain, and the second account will be discarded. We note that for this to work, we assume that incentives have been created so that some parties will indeed observe the duplicates and alert the relevant entities. Moreover, the construction satisfies *revocability* and *traceability*, meaning a malicious AH cannot create a valid account such that the anonymity revokers together with the identity provider are unable to revoke its anonymity or trace it. This follows from the soundness of the underlying zero-knowledge proofs which imply $\mathsf{E}_{\mathsf{ID}} = \mathsf{TEnc}^{n,d}_{\mathsf{PK}_{\mathsf{AR}}}(\mathsf{IDcred}_{\mathsf{PUB}})$ and $\mathsf{E}_{\mathsf{RegID}} = \mathsf{TEnc}^{n,d}_{\mathsf{PK}_{\mathsf{AR}}}(\mathsf{K})$. Thus, any subset of size $d + 1$ of anonymity revokers can decrypt E_{ID} (resp. $\mathsf{E}_{\mathsf{RegID}}$) and revoke the AH's anonymity (resp. trace all the AH's accounts). Lastly, due to the security of the underlying PRF and the threshold encryption scheme and also the ZK property of the proof $\pi \in \mathsf{ACI}$, our design supports *anonymity* of the account holders, in the sense that a malicious identity provider even by cooperating with d anonymity revokers and other dishonest account holders cannot link a valid account to an account holder. Since we are using a Blockchain e.g., an imperfect bulletin board, we also need to worry that a malicious AH cannot "rush" and steal an honest user account number by maliciously choosing a PRF key K which "hits" some of the account numbers of the honest users which have not yet been finalized by the Blockchain. In order to do this, we define and use a *weakly robust* PRF.

4   ID-Layer Formalization

We use the UC-security [11] framework with static corruption. In the following, the reader is assumed to be familiar with the basic concepts of UC security and is referred to [11] for a more detailed description.

In the rest of the section we describe the main ideal functionalities in our construction. We defer other (standard) ideal functionalities used by our protocol to the full version [18].

4.1   The ID Layer Functionality

The functionality $\mathcal{F}_{\mathsf{id\text{-}layer}}$ captures the security properties offered by the design of our identity layer while hiding the implementation details. After the functionality is initialized, it allows identity providers IP to issue credentials to account holders AH based on their attribute lists AL. At the level of the ideal functionality, a credential is just a pointer to a record storing the tuple $(\mathsf{AH}, \mathsf{IP}, \mathsf{AL})$. Armed with a credential, an AH can create up to $\mathsf{Max}_{\mathsf{ACC}}$ accounts. When creating an account, the AH can choose a predicate P of their attributes to be made public (e.g., "I am over 18, I am resident of country X" etc.) which, together with the IP who authorized this account, are the only information which are made public. We capture this by having the functionality leak only the fact that an account was created and not the identity of the AH.[3] Moreover, when creating an account, the AH also registers a key-pair associated to this account. The functionality is parametrized by any key-pair relation, which allows our ideal functionality to be used as a building block in more complex protocols, where the AH then can use those keys for authentication, encryption, etc. Our functionality also exposes some of the details about the underlying ledger on top of which it is implemented, thus new accounts are added to a buffer which can be permuted by the adversary before becoming finalized. This is inevitable as we run this on top of a ledger which has the same properties. The final two commands of the ideal functionality, revoke and trace, allow a qualified set of anonymity revokers AR and an IP to respectively disclose the AH behind a given account, or to find all accounts belonging to a certain AH.

Functionality Identity layer $\mathcal{F}_{\text{id-layer}}$

We assume that $\{\mathsf{IP}_1, \ldots, \mathsf{IP}_m, \mathsf{AR}_1, \ldots, \mathsf{AR}_n\}$ is the set of identifiers for identity providers and anonymity revokers. The functionality is parameterized by values m, n and threshold d, together with an NP (key-pair) relation $\mathcal{R}_{\mathsf{ACC}}$ such that when parties input CreateACC, they also specify a key-pair and the functionality verifies if the key-pair satisfies $\mathcal{R}_{\mathsf{ACC}}$. Moreover, the functionality maintains the following initially empty records: Count, where Count[cid] counts the number of accounts created by certificate cid, and two records Cert and ACC, respectively for keeping track of certificates and accounts and a list L of public account information.

Initialize
    On (INITIALIZE) from party $P \in \{\mathsf{IP}_1, \ldots, \mathsf{IP}_m, \mathsf{AR}_1, \ldots, \mathsf{AR}_n\}$, output to $\mathcal{A}$ (INITIALIZED, P).
    If all parties have been initialized, store (READY).
Issue
    On (ISSUE, IP, AL) from an honest account holder AH (or the adversary in the name of corrupted account holder AH) and input (ISSUE, AH) from identity provider IP:
    – If not (READY), then ignore.

---

[3] Note that the environment provides all inputs and sees all outputs. It can therefore observe that an account is created right after it instructed an account holder to create an account, and can make the connection between the two. This corresponds to the fact that in a real application an adversary may know that in a long time interval, only one user creates an account, and so the next account that shows up on chain must belong to that user. Of course, our system cannot prevent this - the best we can do is to make sure that the account itself is anonymous. This follows in our model because the ideal adversary - the simulator - will not learn the identity of the holder and will still have to produce account information which are indistinguishable from the real protocol, thus proving that the account information leaks no information about its holder.

- If there is already a cid with $\mathsf{Cert}[\mathsf{cid}] = (\mathsf{AH}, \mathsf{IP}, \cdot, \cdot)$, then abort; otherwise, if IP is honest (resp. corrupt), then send $(\mathtt{ISSUE})$ (resp. $(\mathtt{ISSUE}, \mathsf{AH}, \mathsf{IP}, \mathsf{AL}))$ to $\mathcal{A}$.
- Upon receiving $(\mathsf{cid}, \mathtt{ISSUE})$ from $\mathcal{A}$, if $\mathsf{cid} = \bot$ (in the case of corrupt IP) or if there already exists cid s.t. $\mathsf{Cert}[\mathsf{cid}] \neq \bot$, then abort. Otherwise, set $\mathsf{Cert}[\mathsf{cid}] \leftarrow (\mathsf{AH}, \mathsf{IP}, \mathsf{AL})$ and output $(\mathtt{ISSUED}, \mathsf{cid})$ to AH.

Account Creation

Upon inputs $(\mathtt{CreateACC}, \mathsf{cid}, \mathsf{P}, (\mathsf{sk}_{\mathsf{ACC}}, \mathsf{pk}_{\mathsf{ACC}}))$ from honest account holders AH (or the adversary in the name of corrupted account holder AH), if not $(\mathtt{READY})$, then ignore. Else, proceed as follows:

- If $\mathsf{Cert}[\mathsf{cid}] = \bot$ then abort, else retrieve $(\mathsf{AH}', \mathsf{IP}, \mathsf{AL}) \leftarrow \mathsf{Cert}[\mathsf{cid}]$.
- Check if $\mathsf{AH}' = \mathsf{AH}$ and $\mathsf{Count}[\mathsf{cid}] < \mathsf{Max}_{\mathsf{ACC}}$ and that AL satisfies the policy P.
- Verify that the key pair $(\mathsf{sk}_{\mathsf{ACC}}, \mathsf{pk}_{\mathsf{ACC}})$ satisfies the relation $\mathcal{R}_{\mathsf{ACC}}$ and abort otherwise.
- Output $(\mathtt{CreateACC}, \mathsf{P}, \mathsf{pk}_{\mathsf{ACC}}, \mathsf{IP})$ to $\mathcal{A}$.
- Receiving a response $(\mathtt{CreateACC}, \mathsf{aid})$ from $\mathcal{A}$, if $\mathsf{aid} = \bot$ or $\mathsf{ACC}[\mathsf{aid}] \neq \bot$, then abort, else do the followings:
  - set $\mathsf{ACC}[\mathsf{aid}] \leftarrow (\mathsf{cid}, \mathsf{P}, \mathsf{sk}_{\mathsf{ACC}})$.
  - set $\mathsf{Count}[\mathsf{cid}] \leftarrow \mathsf{Count}[\mathsf{cid}] + 1$.
  - add the tuple $(\mathsf{aid}, \mathsf{P}, \mathsf{pk}_{\mathsf{ACC}}, \mathsf{IP})$ to the account buffer.
- Return $(\mathtt{Created}, \mathsf{aid})$ to AH.

Account Buffer Release

Upon input $(\mathtt{RELEASE}, \Pi)$ from the adversary $\mathcal{A}$, remove all tuples from the account buffer and add the permuted tuples $(\mathsf{aid}, \mathsf{P}, \mathsf{pk}_{\mathsf{ACC}}, \mathsf{IP})$ of accounts to the account list L.

Accounts Retrieve

On $(\mathtt{RETRIEVE})$ from an account holder or party $P \in \{\mathsf{IP}_1, \ldots, \mathsf{IP}_m, \mathsf{AR}_1, \ldots, \mathsf{AR}_n\}$, output a list including all existing tuples $(\mathsf{aid}, \mathsf{P}, \mathsf{pk}_{\mathsf{ACC}}, \mathsf{IP})$ in the account list L.

Revoke

Upon input $(\mathtt{REVOKE}, \mathsf{aid})$ from a (possibly corrupt) identity provider IP and a set of (possibly corrupt) anonymity revokers $\{\mathsf{AR}_i\}_{i \in I \subseteq [n]}$, proceed as follows:

- If $\mathsf{ACC}[\mathsf{aid}] = \bot$ then return $\bot$. Otherwise, retrieve $(\mathsf{cid}, \mathsf{P}, \mathsf{sk}_{\mathsf{ACC}}) \leftarrow \mathsf{ACC}[\mathsf{aid}]$.
- If IP is the same as the identity provider in $\mathsf{Cert}[\mathsf{cid}]$ and $|I| > d$, then return $(\mathsf{aid}, \mathsf{AH})$ to the IP and $\{\mathsf{AR}_i\}_{i \in I}$. Otherwise, return $\bot$. Moreover, if the identity provider or at least one anonymity revoker is corrupt, output $(\mathsf{aid}, \mathsf{AH})$ to $\mathcal{A}$ as well.

Trace

Upon input $(\mathtt{TRACE}, \mathsf{AH})$ from a (possibly corrupt) identity provider IP and a set of (possibly corrupt) anonymity revokers $\{\mathsf{AR}_i\}_{i \in I}$, proceed as follows:

- If there is no record $(\mathsf{AH}, \mathsf{IP}, \cdot, \cdot)$ in Cert, then return $\perp$. Otherwise, retrieve $(\mathsf{AH}, \mathsf{IP}, \cdot) \leftarrow \mathsf{Cert}[\mathsf{cid}]$.
- If $|I| > \mathsf{d}$, return to IP and $\{\mathsf{AR}_i\}_{i \in I}$ the list of all aid's such that $\mathsf{ACC}[\mathsf{aid}] = (\mathsf{cid}, \cdot, \cdot)$. Moreover, if the identity provider or at least one anonymity revoker is corrupt, return the list to $\mathcal{A}$ as well.

4.2 Issuing Credentials – The Functionality

We describe here $\mathcal{F}_{\mathsf{issue}}$, an ideal functionality capturing the desired properties of the issue protocol, which allows an identity provider to issue credentials to account holders. Note that the functionality can be seen as an augmented blind signature functionality: the account holder receives a signature (under the secret key of the identity provider) on a secret message m (as in blind signatures) but also on some public auxiliary information aux and on a secret key chosen by the account holder. The identity provider is not supposed to learn m (as in blind signatures), but in addition the identity provider learns a ciphertext which is guaranteed to contain an encryption of m and the public key corresponding to the secret key which is being signed.

Functionality Issue $\mathcal{F}_{\mathsf{issue}}^{\mathcal{R}, \mathsf{TE}, \mathsf{SIG}}$

The functionality is parametrized by an NP relation $\mathcal{R}$ corresponding to the account holders key pair, a signature scheme $\mathsf{SIG} = (\mathsf{Setup}, \mathsf{KeyGen}, \mathsf{Sign}, \mathsf{VerifySig})$ and a (n, d)-threshold encryption scheme $\mathsf{TE} = (\mathsf{TKeyGen}, \mathsf{TEnc}, \mathsf{TDec})$. We assume that $\{\mathsf{IP}_1, \ldots, \mathsf{IP}_m\}$ is the set of identifiers for identity providers.

Setup
- Upon input (SETUP) from any party, and only once, run $\mathsf{pp} \leftarrow_{\$} \mathsf{Setup}(1^{\lambda})$ and return (SETUPREADY, pp) to all parties.

Initialize
- Upon input (INITIALIZE, $(\mathsf{sk}_{\mathsf{IP}}, \mathsf{pk}_{\mathsf{IP}})$) from identity provider IP, ignore if the party is already initialized or if SETUPREADY has not been returned yet. Otherwise, if $(\mathsf{sk}_{\mathsf{IP}}, \mathsf{pk}_{\mathsf{IP}})$ is a valid key pair according to the relation defined by $\mathsf{KeyGen}(\mathsf{pp})$, store $(\mathsf{sk}_{\mathsf{IP}}, \mathsf{pk}_{\mathsf{IP}})$ for this party and output (INITIALIZED, $\mathsf{pk}_{\mathsf{IP}}, \mathsf{IP}$) to $\mathcal{A}$.
- If all parties have been initialized, store (READY).

Issue
On input $\Big(\mathsf{ISSUE}, (ct, m, r, \mathsf{pk}_{\mathsf{AR}}), \mathsf{aux}, (\mathsf{sk}_{\mathsf{AH}}, \mathsf{pk}_{\mathsf{AH}}), \mathsf{IP}\Big)$ from account holder AH and input (ISSUE, $\mathsf{AH}, \mathsf{pk}_{\mathsf{AR}}$) from identity provider IP:
- If not (READY), then ignore.
- If $(\mathsf{sk}_{\mathsf{AH}}, \mathsf{pk}_{\mathsf{AH}}) \notin \mathcal{R}$ or $ct \neq \mathsf{TEnc}_{\mathsf{PK}_{\mathsf{AR}}}^{\mathsf{n}, \mathsf{d}}(m; r)$ then abort.
- Otherwise compute $\sigma \leftarrow_{\$} \mathsf{Sign}((\mathsf{sk}_{\mathsf{AH}}, m, \mathsf{aux}), \mathsf{sk}_{\mathsf{IP}})$.
- Output σ to AH and $(\mathsf{pk}_{\mathsf{AH}}, \mathsf{aux}, ct)$ to IP.

5   Formal Protocols Specifications

5.1   Identity Layer Protocol

The protocol $\Pi_{\text{id-layer}}$ is run by parties interacting with ideal functionalities $\mathcal{F}_{\text{reg}}, \mathcal{F}_{\text{issue}}, \mathcal{F}_{\text{nizk}}, \mathcal{F}_{\text{crs}}, \mathcal{F}_{\text{ledger}}$ and $\mathcal{F}_{\text{mpc-prf}}$. Let $\mathcal{R}$ and $\mathcal{R}_{\text{ACC}}$ be NP relations corresponding to the account holders' key-pair and accounts' key-pair, respectively. Let $\mathsf{TE} = (\mathsf{TKeyGen}, \mathsf{TEnc}, \mathsf{TDec})$ denote a threshold encryption scheme, PRF a pseudorandom function and $\mathsf{SIG} = (\mathsf{KeyGen}, \mathsf{Sign}, \mathsf{VerifySig})$ a signature scheme. Protocol $\Pi_{\text{id-layer}}$ proceeds as follows.

Protocol Identity layer $\Pi_{\text{id-layer}}$

Parameters for ideal functionalities.

- We use a $\mathcal{F}_{\text{ledger}}$ that implements the following VALIDATE predicate: the predicate accepts if the NIZK proof π is valid and if $\mathsf{RegID}_{\text{ACC}}$ has not been seen before.
- We use a $\mathcal{F}_{\text{crs}}$ functionality that outputs the public parameters for the signature scheme and the threshold encryption scheme.

The protocol description for an account holder AH.

- On input $(\mathsf{ISSUE}, \mathsf{IP}, \mathsf{AL})$, retrieve the public key PK_{IP} of identity provider IP and the vector PK_{AR} of all public keys of the anonymity revokers via $\mathcal{F}_{\text{reg}}$ and proceed as follows:
  - Generate a key pair $(\mathsf{IDcred}_{\text{SEC}}, \mathsf{IDcred}_{\text{PUB}})$ satisfying $\mathcal{R}$.
  - Choose a random key K for PRF and compute the encryption $\mathsf{E}_{\text{RegID}} = \mathsf{TEnc}_{\text{PK}_{\text{AR}}}^{n,d}(\mathsf{K}; r)$ with randomness r.
  - Call $\mathcal{F}_{\text{issue}}^{\mathcal{R}, \mathsf{TE}, \mathsf{BS}}$ on input $\Big(\mathsf{ISSUE}, (\mathsf{E}_{\text{RegID}}, \mathsf{K}, r, \mathsf{PK}_{\text{AR}}), \mathsf{AL}, (\mathsf{IDcred}_{\text{SEC}},$ $\mathsf{IDcred}_{\text{PUB}}), \mathsf{IP}\Big)$. After receiving the response σ from $\mathcal{F}_{\text{issue}}^{\mathcal{R}, \mathsf{TE}, \mathsf{BS}}$, set $\mathsf{cid} = (\mathsf{IP}, \mathsf{AL}, \mathsf{IDcred}_{\text{SEC}}, \sigma, \mathsf{K})$.
- On input $(\mathsf{CreateACC}, \mathsf{cid}, \mathsf{P})$, proceed as follows
  - If there is no record $\mathsf{cid} = (\mathsf{IP}, \mathsf{AL}, \mathsf{IDcred}_{\text{SEC}}, \sigma, \mathsf{K})$, then abort.
  - Generate an account key pair $(\mathsf{pk}_{\text{ACC}}, \mathsf{sk}_{\text{ACC}})$ satisfying $\mathcal{R}_{\text{ACC}}$.
  - Compute $\mathsf{E}_{\text{ID}} = \mathsf{TEnc}_{\text{PK}_{\text{AR}}}^{n,d}(\mathsf{IDcred}_{\text{PUB}}; r')$.
  - Compute $\mathsf{RegID}_{\text{ACC}} = \mathsf{PRF}_{\text{K}}(x)$, where this is x'th account that is created using cid.
  - Produce a NIZK π by calling $\mathcal{F}_{\text{nizk}}$ for statement

$$st = (\mathsf{P}, \mathsf{E}_{\text{ID}}, \mathsf{RegID}_{\text{ACC}}, \mathsf{IP}, \mathsf{pk}_{\text{ACC}})$$

  using secret witness

$$w = (\sigma, x, r', \mathsf{IDcred}_{\text{SEC}}, \mathsf{K}, \mathsf{AL}, \mathsf{sk}_{\text{ACC}}, \mathsf{IDcred}_{\text{PUB}})$$

  for the relation $\mathcal{R}(st, w)$ that outputs $\top$ if:

1. The signature σ is valid for $(\mathsf{IDcred}_{\mathsf{SEC}}, \mathsf{K}, \mathsf{AL})$ under $\mathsf{pk}_{\mathsf{IP}}$.
2. AL satisfies the policy i.e., $P(\mathsf{AL}) = \top$.
3. $\mathsf{RegID}_{\mathsf{ACC}} = \mathsf{PRF}_{\mathsf{K}}(x)$ for some $0 < x \leq \mathsf{Max}_{\mathsf{ACC}}$.
4. $\mathsf{E}_{\mathsf{ID}} = \mathsf{TEnc}^{\mathsf{n,d}}_{\mathsf{PK}_{\mathsf{AR}}}(\mathsf{IDcred}_{\mathsf{PUB}}; \mathsf{r}')$.
5. $(\mathsf{pk}_{\mathsf{ACC}}, \mathsf{sk}_{\mathsf{ACC}})$ is a valid key pair according to $\mathcal{R}_{\mathsf{ACC}}$.
6. $(\mathsf{IDcred}_{\mathsf{SEC}}, \mathsf{IDcred}_{\mathsf{PUB}})$ is a valid key pair according to $\mathcal{R}$

- Let $\mathsf{ACI} = (\mathsf{RegID}_{\mathsf{ACC}}, \mathsf{E}_{\mathsf{ID}}, \mathsf{IP}, \mathsf{pk}_{\mathsf{ACC}}, \mathsf{P}, st, \pi)$ and $\mathsf{SI}_{\mathsf{ACC}} = \mathsf{sk}_{\mathsf{ACC}}$. Send the input $(\mathtt{APPEND}, \mathsf{ACI})$ to $\mathcal{F}_{\mathsf{ledger}}$.
- Store tuple $(\mathsf{ACI}, \mathsf{SI}_{\mathsf{ACC}})$ internally and return $(\mathtt{Created}, \mathsf{RegID}_{\mathsf{ACC}})$.
- On input $(\mathtt{RETRIEVE})$, call $\mathcal{F}_{\mathsf{ledger}}$ on input $\mathtt{RETRIEVE}$. After receiving $(\mathtt{RETRIEVE}, L)$ from $\mathcal{F}_{\mathsf{ledger}}$, output L.

The protocol description for identity providers and anonymity revokers.

- On input $\mathtt{INITIALIZE}$ from $P \in \{\mathsf{IP}_1, \ldots, \mathsf{IP}_m\}$, obtain crs from $\mathcal{F}_{\mathsf{crs}}$, generate key pair $(\mathsf{sk}_{\mathsf{IP}}, \mathsf{pk}_{\mathsf{IP}}) \leftarrow_{\$} \mathsf{KeyGen}(1^\lambda)$ and input $(\mathtt{INITIALIZE}, (\mathsf{sk}_{\mathsf{IP}}, \mathsf{pk}_{\mathsf{IP}}))$ to $\mathcal{F}^{\mathcal{R}, \mathsf{TE}, \mathsf{SIG}}_{\mathsf{issue}}$.
- On input $\mathtt{INITIALIZE}$ from $P \in \{\mathsf{AR}_1, \ldots, \mathsf{AR}_n\}$, obtain crs from $\mathcal{F}_{\mathsf{crs}}$, generate key pair $(\mathsf{sk}_{\mathsf{AR}}, \mathsf{pk}_{\mathsf{AR}}) \leftarrow_{\$} \mathsf{TKeyGen}(1^\lambda)$ and input $(\mathtt{REGISTER}, \mathsf{sk}_{\mathsf{AR}}, \mathsf{pk}_{\mathsf{AR}})$ to $\mathcal{F}_{\mathsf{reg}}$.
- On input $(\mathtt{ISSUE}, \mathsf{AH})$ from identity provider IP, call $\mathcal{F}^{\mathcal{R}, \mathsf{TE}, \mathsf{SIG}}_{\mathsf{issue}}$ with input $(\mathtt{ISSUE}, \mathsf{AH}, \mathsf{pk}_{\mathsf{AR}})$. After receiving the response $(\mathsf{IDcred}_{\mathsf{PUB}}, \mathsf{AL}, \mathsf{E}_{\mathsf{RegID}})$ from $\mathcal{F}^{\mathcal{R}, \mathsf{TE}, \mathsf{SIG}}_{\mathsf{issue}}$, set $\mathsf{IPIAH} = (\mathsf{AH}, \mathsf{IDcred}_{\mathsf{PUB}}, \mathsf{AL}, \mathsf{E}_{\mathsf{RegID}})$.
- On input $(\mathtt{RETRIEVE})$, call $\mathcal{F}_{\mathsf{ledger}}$ on input $\mathtt{RETRIEVE}$. After receiving $(\mathtt{RETRIEVE}, L)$ from $\mathcal{F}_{\mathsf{ledger}}$, output L.
- On input $(\mathtt{REVOKE}, \mathsf{RegID}_{\mathsf{ACC}})$ from an identity provider IP and a set of anonymity revokers $\{\mathsf{AR}_i\}_{i \in I \subseteq [n]}$, proceed as follows:
  - Anonymity revokers call $\mathcal{F}_{\mathsf{ledger}}$ on input $\mathtt{RETRIEVE}$. After receiving $(\mathtt{RETRIEVE}, L)$ from $\mathcal{F}_{\mathsf{ledger}}$, they first look up ACI in L that contains $\mathsf{RegID}_{\mathsf{ACC}}$. Next, each AR_i decrypts the E_{ID} of the ACI by computing $\mu_i = \mathsf{ShareDec}^{\mathsf{n,d}}_{pk_I, \mathsf{sk}_i}(\mathsf{E}_{\mathsf{ID}})$. Finally, all anonymity revokers combine their shares and compute $\mathsf{IDcred}_{\mathsf{PUB}} = \mathsf{TCombine}^{\mathsf{n,d}}_{pk_I}(\mathsf{E}_{\mathsf{ID}}, \{\mu_i\}_{i \in I})$ and return $\mathsf{IDcred}_{\mathsf{PUB}}$ to the IP.
  - The ACI contains the public name IP of the identity provider who registered $\mathsf{IDcred}_{\mathsf{PUB}}$. If IP is different from the requester, then ignore. Else, the IP locates the $\mathsf{IPIAH} = (\mathsf{AH}, \mathsf{IDcred}_{\mathsf{PUB}}, \mathsf{AL}, \mathsf{E}_{\mathsf{RegID}})$ record, containing the $\mathsf{IDcred}_{\mathsf{PUB}}$ that was decrypted and outputs AH.
- On input $(\mathtt{TRACE}, \mathsf{AH})$ from an identity provider IP and a set of anonymity revokers $\{\mathsf{AR}_i\}_{i \in I \subseteq [n]}$, proceed as follows:
  - IP searches the database to locate the $\mathsf{IPIAH} = (\mathsf{AH}, \mathsf{IDcred}_{\mathsf{PUB}}, \mathsf{AL}, \mathsf{E}_{\mathsf{RegID}})$ containing the relevant AH and sends $\mathsf{E}_{\mathsf{RegID}}$ via $\mathcal{F}_{\mathsf{smt}}$ to the set of anonymity revokers.

- Each AR_i computes $K_i = \mathsf{ShareDec}^{n,d}_{pk_I, sk_i}(E_{\mathsf{RegID}})$. Then, they call $\mathcal{F}_{\mathsf{mpc\text{-}prf}}$ on input $(\mathtt{COMPUTE}, K_i)$ and receive all values $\mathsf{PRF}_K(x)$ for $x = 1, \ldots, \mathsf{Max}_{\mathsf{ACC}}$. These values are all the possible values for $\mathsf{RegID}_{\mathsf{ACC}}$ that the AH could have used to form valid accounts.

5.2   Proof of Security for Identity Layer

Tolerated Corruptions. We prove security in two separate cases: with arbitrarily many malicious AHs and up to threshold semi-honest ARs, or with semi honest IP and up to threshold semi-honest ARs. Note that for technical reasons we cannot let the IP be corrupt (even if only semi-honest) at the same time with a malicious AH, since in this case the (monolithic) adversary would learn the secret key of the corrupt IP and would be able to forge invalid credentials for the corrupt AH's.

Assumptions on the Environment. We consider executions with restricted adversaries and environments, that only input attribute lists AL in the ISSUE command which are valid with respect to the account holder. This restriction captures the fact that an honest IP in the real world is trusted to check (by non-cryptographic means) that an account holder AH actually satisfies the claimed attribute list AL.

Theorem 5.1. *Suppose that* TE *is a* (n, d)-*threshold encryption scheme,* PRF *is a weakly robust pseudorandom function,* $\mathcal{R}$ *a hard relation, and* SIG $=$ (KeyGen, Sign, VerifySig) *is a EUF-CMA signature scheme, then* $\Pi_{\mathsf{id\text{-}layer}}$, *for all restricted environment (as defined above), securely implements* $\mathcal{F}_{\mathsf{id\text{-}layer}}$ *in the* $\{\mathcal{F}_{\mathsf{crs}}, \mathcal{F}_{\mathsf{reg}}, \mathcal{F}_{\mathsf{nizk}}, \mathcal{F}_{\mathsf{smt}}, \mathcal{F}^{\mathcal{R},\mathsf{TE},\mathsf{SIG}}_{\mathsf{issue}}, \mathcal{F}_{\mathsf{ledger}}, \mathcal{F}_{\mathsf{mpc\text{-}prf}}\}$-*hybrid model in the presence of an actively corrupted* AH, *and* d *semi-honest anonymity revokers* $AR_1, \ldots, AR_d$, *or semi-honest* IP *and* d *semi-honest anonymity revokers* $AR_1, \ldots, AR_d$.

The simulator Sim emulates internally functionalities $\mathcal{F}_{\mathsf{crs}}, \mathcal{F}_{\mathsf{reg}}, \mathcal{F}_{\mathsf{nizk}}, \mathcal{F}_{\mathsf{smt}}, \mathcal{F}^{\mathcal{R},\mathsf{TE},\mathsf{SIG}}_{\mathsf{issue}}, \mathcal{F}_{\mathsf{ledger}}, \mathcal{F}_{\mathsf{mpc\text{-}prf}}$. At the start Sim initializes empty lists $\mathsf{list}_{\mathsf{issue}}$, $\mathsf{list}_{\mathsf{acc}}$, $\mathsf{list}_{\mathsf{ledger}}$, $\mathsf{list}_{\mathsf{h\text{-}aid}}$, $\mathsf{list}_{\mathsf{h\text{-}pk}}$, $\mathsf{list}_{\mathsf{h\text{-}sig}}$. Here is the description of the simulator:

- Command INITIALIZE. Sim emulates $\mathcal{F}_{\mathsf{crs}}$ and generates public parameters for the signature scheme and threshold encryption scheme. Every time an honest or semi-honest IP or AR invokes the initialize command, the simulator generates a key-pair for them.
- Command ISSUE. *Passively corrupted* IP, *honest* AH. The simulator receives $(\mathtt{ISSUE}, \mathsf{AH}, \mathsf{IP}, \mathsf{AL})$ in case of corrupt IP from the ideal functionality $\mathcal{F}_{\mathsf{id\text{-}layer}}$, and has to produce a view indistinguishable from the protocol which is consistent with this. The simulator does so by emulating the output $\mathcal{F}_{\mathsf{issue}}$ for IP namely $(\mathsf{IDcred}_{\mathsf{PUB}}, \mathsf{AL}, E_{\mathsf{RegID}})$ to IP where the simulator encrypts a dummy

value for E_{RegID} and $IDcred_{PUB}$ is generated according to $\mathcal{R}$. The simulator adds E_{RegID} to $list_{h\text{-}ct}$ and $IDcred_{PUB}$ to $list_{h\text{-}pk}$. Sim adds to $list_{issue}$ the entry $\langle (AH, AL, IP); (E_{RegID}, IDcred_{PUB}, AL) \rangle$.

Malicious AH, *honest* IP. When a corrupt AH invokes $\mathcal{F}_{issue}^{\mathcal{R}, TE, SIG}$ on command $\big(ISSUE, (E_{RegID}, K, r, PK_{AR}), AL, (IDcred_{SEC}, IDcred_{PUB}), IP \big)$, Sim aborts if E_{RegID} is not an encryption of K or if $(IDcred_{SEC}, IDcred_{PUB})$ is not a valid keypair; Sim outputs `fail` if $E_{RegID} \in list_{h\text{-}ct}$ or if $IDcred_{PUB} \in list_{h\text{-}pk}$. Otherwise, Sim calls command ISSUE of the functionality on input (IP, AL) and returns cid $= (IP, AL, IDcred_{SEC}, \sigma, K)$ to AH where σ is a signature computed by Sim using Sign of SIG (since the simulator is internally emulating the honest IP w.r.t. the corrupt account holder AH). Sim adds $(\sigma; (IDcred_{SEC}, K, AL); IP)$ to $list_{h\text{-}sig}$.

- Command `CreateACC`. *Malicious* AH. When a corrupt AH invokes $\mathcal{F}_{ledger}$ on input $ACI = (st, \pi)$ (where $st = (P, E_{ID}, RegID_{ACC}, IP, pk_{ACC}))$, the simulator Sim uses $\mathcal{F}_{nizk}$ to extract the witness $w = (\sigma, x, r', IDcred_{SEC}, K, AL, sk_{ACC}, IDcred_{PUB})$ (or abort if the proof doesn't verify). If the simulator sees a repeated account $(RegID_{ACC}, E_{ID}, IP, pk_{ACC}, P, \pi) \in list_{acc}$. Otherwise, the simulator outputs `fail` if one of the following condition holds: $(\sigma; (IDcred_{SEC}, K, AL); IP) \notin list_{h\text{-}sig}$, if $IDcred_{PUB} \in list_{h\text{-}pk}$, if $E_{ID} \in list_{h\text{-}ct}$, if $RegID_{ACC} \in list_{h\text{-}aid}$, or if $x > Max_{ACC}$. Otherwise the simulator inputs the $CreateACC(cid, P, (sk_{ACC}, pk_{ACC}))$ command to the ideal functionality and, when asked, inputs aid $= RegID_{ACC}$ to the ideal functionality.

  Honest AH. For an honest AH, the simulator upon receiving $(CreateACC, P, pk_{ACC}, IP)$ from the ideal functionality, picks a random aid in the domain of the PRF and forwards it to the functionality (also adds it into $list_{h\text{-}aid}$). Then, the simulator prepares $st = (P, E_{ID}, RegID_{ACC} = aid, IP, pk_{ACC})$ where E_{ID} is an encryption of a dummy value (and is added to $list_{h\text{-}ct}$), simulates a proof π via $\mathcal{F}_{nizk}$ and appends (st, π) to the buffer of the ledger. Add entry $(RegID_{ACC}, E_{ID}, IP, pk_{ACC}, P, \pi)$ in $list_{acc}$.

- Command `RELEASE`. the simulator simulates these commands directly simulating the calls to $\mathcal{F}_{ledger}$ e.g., when the adversary invokes $(RELEASE, \Pi)$ adds the permuted buffer to the list $list_{ledger}$ and then resets the buffer.

- Command `RETRIEVE`. Sim emulates the retrieve command in $\mathcal{F}_{ledger}$ and gives as output $list_{ledger}$.

- Command `REVOKE`. *Semi-honest* IP *and up to* d AR, *honest* AH. When the IP and a qualified set of AR (of which up to d are corrupt) invoke REVOKE, the simulator Sim obtains $RegID_{ACC} = aid$ and AH from the input/output of the functionality $\mathcal{F}_{id\text{-}layer}$. Now Sim, using $RegID_{ACC}$, searches $list_{acc}$ and retrieves the corresponding E_{ID}. Similarly, using (AH, IP), searches $list_{issue}$ and retrieves the corresponding $IDcred_{PUB}$. Then the simulator Sim equivocates the decryption of E_{ID} to $IDcred_{PUB}$ using SimShare (defined in the simulatability property of the threshold encryption scheme).

  Malicious AH *and up to* d AR. The simulator receives $(RegID_{ACC}, AH)$ from the ideal functionality, looks up the ciphertext E_{ID} corresponding to $RegID_{ACC}$ and runs the threshold decryption protocol as honest parties would do.

– Command TRACE. *Semi-honest* IP *and up to* d AR, *honest* AH. When the IP and a qualified set of AR (of which up to d are corrupt) invoke TRACE, the simulator Sim receives AH and a list $\text{list}_{\text{RegID}_{\text{ACC}}}$ of aid's from the input/output of the functionality $\mathcal{F}_{\text{id-layer}}$. Now Sim recovers the ciphertext E_{RegID}. Finally Sim programs the output of $\mathcal{F}_{\text{mpc-prf}}$ to be consistent with $\text{list}_{\text{RegID}_{\text{ACC}}}$.
Malicious AH *and up to* d AR. The simulator receives AH and a list of accounts $\{\text{RegID}_{\text{ACC}}\}$ from the ideal functionality. The simulator looks up the ciphertext E_{RegID} corresponding to AH and emulates $\mathcal{F}_{\text{mpc-prf}}$ to output the list $\{\text{RegID}_{\text{ACC}}\}$.

We show in the full version [18] that the view of the environment in the real world and in the ideal world with the simulator described above are indistinguishable via a series of hybrids. The main idea is the following: we start by arguing that the probability that the simulator outputs `fail` is negligible, since this immediately leads to an attack on one of the underlying primitives. (Essentially ruling out `fail` rules out all ways in which a malicious AH can open an invalid account). We then change the way in which the simulator produces accounts for the honest AH piece by piece, and at every step we argue that indistinguishability follows from the security of one of the underlying primitives, until we reach the distribution of the real protocol.

5.3   Credential Issue Protocol

The issue protocol Π_{issue} uses as its main ingredient a two-round blind signature scheme (as defined in Sect. 2.3), augmented with a NIZK that proves that the input to the blind-signature protocol is consistent with the ciphertext and the public-key that the account holder sends to the identity provider.

Protocol Issue Π_{issue}

The protocol operates in the $\{\mathcal{F}_{\text{crs}}, \mathcal{F}_{\text{reg}}, \mathcal{F}_{\text{nizk}}, \mathcal{F}_{\text{smt}}\}$-hybrid model. Let BS $=$ (Setup, KeyGen, Sign$_1$, Sign$_2$, Unblind, VerifySig) be a blind signature scheme and TE $=$ (TKeyGen, TEnc, TDec) be a (n, d)-threshold encryption scheme, and $\mathcal{R}$ an NP relation corresponding to the account holder's key pair.

– Upon input (SETUP), use $\mathcal{F}_{\text{crs}}^{\text{Setup}}$ to generate pp $\leftarrow_s$ Setup(1^λ) and publicize it to all parties.
– Upon input (INITIALIZE, (sk$_{\text{IP}}$, pk$_{\text{IP}}$)), the identity provider IP checks if the key pair has a correct distribution with respect to the KeyGen(pp). If yes, stores (sk$_{\text{IP}}$, pk$_{\text{IP}}$) and sends (REGISTER, sk$_{\text{IP}}$, pk$_{\text{IP}}$) to $\mathcal{F}_{\text{reg}}$.
– Upon an input $\big(\text{ISSUE}, (ct, m, r, \text{pk}_{\text{AR}}), \text{aux}, (\text{sk}_{\text{AH}}, \text{pk}_{\text{AH}}), \text{IP}\big)$ to the account holder AH and an input (ISSUE, AH, pk$_{\text{AR}}$) to an identity provider IP, proceed as follows:
   1. AH retrieves pk$_{\text{IP}}$ from $\mathcal{F}_{\text{reg}}$, computes sign$_1$ = Sign$_1$(pk$_{\text{IP}}$, (sk$_{\text{AH}}$, m, aux), pp; r') and sends (PROVE, st, w) to $\mathcal{F}_{\text{nizk}}$ for statement $st =$

$(\mathsf{pk}_{\mathsf{AH}}, \mathsf{sign}_1, ct, \mathsf{aux}, \mathsf{pp})$ using secret witness $w = (\mathsf{sk}_{\mathsf{AH}}, m, r', r)$ for the relation $\mathcal{R}_1(st, w)$ that outputs $\top$ if:

(a) $(\mathsf{sk}_{\mathsf{AH}}, \mathsf{pk}_{\mathsf{AH}}) \in \mathcal{R}$.

(b) $\mathsf{sign}_1 = \mathsf{Sign}_1(\mathsf{pk}_{\mathsf{IP}}, (\mathsf{sk}_{\mathsf{AH}}, m, \mathsf{aux}), \mathsf{pp}; r')$.

(c) $ct = \mathsf{TEnc}^{\mathsf{n},\mathsf{d}}_{\mathsf{PK}_{\mathsf{AR}}}(m; r)$

2. Upon receiving the proof π, AH sends $(\mathsf{SEND}, \mathsf{IP}, (st, \pi))$ to $\mathcal{F}_{\mathsf{smt}}$.

3. Upon receiving $(\mathsf{SENT}, \mathsf{AH}, (st, \pi))$ from $\mathcal{F}_{\mathsf{smt}}$, IP inputs $(\mathsf{VERIFY}, st, \pi)$ (for relation $\mathcal{R}_1$) to $\mathcal{F}_{\mathsf{nizk}}$. If they pass, IP computes and sends (through $\mathcal{F}_{\mathsf{smt}}$) $\mathsf{sign}_2 \leftarrow \mathsf{Sign}_2(\mathsf{sk}_{\mathsf{IP}}, \mathsf{sign}_1)$. AH runs $\mathsf{Unblind}(\mathsf{sign}_2, r')$ and obtains a signature σ on $(\mathsf{sk}_{\mathsf{AH}}, m, \mathsf{aux})$.

5.4 Proof of Security for Issue Protocol

Theorem 5.2. *Assume that* $\mathsf{BS} = (\mathsf{Setup}, \mathsf{KeyGen}, \mathsf{Sign}_1, \mathsf{Sign}_2, \mathsf{Unblind}, \mathsf{VerifySig})$ *is a blind signature scheme. Then,* Π_{issue} *securely implements* $\mathcal{F}_{\mathsf{issue}}$ *in the* $\{\mathcal{F}_{\mathsf{crs}}, \mathcal{F}_{\mathsf{reg}}, \mathcal{F}_{\mathsf{nizk}}, \mathcal{F}_{\mathsf{smt}}\}$-*hybrid model in the presence of an actively corrupted* AH *or a passively corrupted* IP.

Security follows from the properties of the blind signature scheme: when the AR is corrupt the simulator extracts the adversary's secret values and randomness from the NIZK, submits them to the ideal functionality and then simulates sign_2 using the simulatability of the blind signature, which is therefore indistinguishable; when IP is corrupt the simulator learns its inputs/outputs from the ideal functionality, computes sign_1 on dummy inputs (which is indistinguishable thanks to the blindness property), and "simulates" the NIZK (which is trivial in the hybrid model). We defer the proof to the full version [18].

6   Putting Everything Together

We presented all components of the system in a modular way. We now describe how to instantiate each of the components needed in the ID-layer.

UC-NIZK. We use two different types of non-interactive zero knowledge proofs in our implementation. One is based on Σ-protocols made non-interactive with the Fiat-Shamir (FS) transform [25], and the other is preprocessing-based zkSNARKs [26,33] in the crs model. Unfortunately, known instantiations of both types of NIZKs do not satisfy UC-security.

In order to lift SNARK to be UC-secure we use the transformation of Kosba et al. [29]. At a high level, the transformation works having the prover prove an augmented relation $\mathcal{R}_{\mathcal{L}'}$ that is given in appendix of the full version [18]. A pair of one-time signing/verification keys are generated for each proof. The prover is additionally required to show that a ciphertext encrypts the witness of the underlying relation $\mathcal{R}_{\mathcal{L}}$, or the PRF was correctly evaluated on the signature key under a committed key. Then the prover is required to sign the statement together with the proof of $\mathcal{L}'$. Since our goal is to use SNARKs on small circuits for the purposes of prover efficiency, we treat the augmented relation $\mathcal{R}_{\mathcal{L}'}$ as a composite statement [2,10] and use a combination of SNARKs and sigma protocols to prove the augmented relation of the transformation. We use the CL scheme [12] for encryption, and $f_k : x \rightarrow H(x)^k$, for $k \in \mathbb{Z}_q$ as the PRF where H maps bit strings to group elements. This PRF can be shown to be secure under the DDH assumption where H is modeled as a random oracle. We can use a sigma protocol to prove correct evaluation of the PRF given public input, public output, and committed key g^k. A standard sigma protocol proof of equality of discrete logarithms can be used to prove equality of CL encrypted and Pedersen committed messages. The composition theorem from [2] can be invoked to argue security of the NIZK for the composite statement formed as the AND of the statements of the lifting transformation.

As shown in the full version [18], a simulation-sound NIZK (such as Fiat-Shamir as shown in [23]) and a perfectly correct CPA-secure encryption scheme are sufficient to instantiate a simulation-extractable NIZK by transforming the relation to include a ciphertext encrypting the witness. While this lifting technique for transforming a (sound) NIZK to a knowledge-sound NIZK is folklore, the use of CL encryption scheme [12] for this goal is novel up to our knowledge. Our choice of the CL encryption scheme in the transformation means that we can at the same time encrypt messages in the same plaintext space as the commitment schemes (thus allowing for efficient proofs of equality of discrete logarithms), and guarantee efficient decryption by the extractor. This is as opposed to using e.g., Pailler (where we could have efficient decryption but would need range proofs to prove equality of exponents in different groups) or ElGamal "in the exponent" (where the group order could be the same but efficient decryption can only be achieved by encrypting the witness in short chunks).

Implementation of Π_{issue}. We instantiate the blind signature scheme BS by the Pointcheval-Sanders (PS) signature scheme [36]. We recall the PS scheme in the full version [18], and prove that it satisfies the definitions of Blindness (here we prove a stronger variant than what given in the original paper) and Simulatability (which we define, as it is needed for proving UC security of the overall construction). We adopt the threshold encryption TE scheme described in [19] which follows the share and encrypt paradigm. We use the CL encryption scheme [12] to encrypt. Once again, our choice of CL encryption scheme means that we can at the same time encrypt messages in the same plaintext space as the commitment schemes (for efficient equality proofs) and guarantee efficient decryption when needed in the TRACE command by the ARs.

We now describe the Σ-protocols we use to prove relation $\mathcal{R}_1$ in Π_{issue}. We let $\mathcal{R}$ be the discrete log relation where $\mathsf{pk} = g^{\mathsf{sk}}$. Then, we can prove that public keys and secret keys satisfy $\mathcal{R}$ using standard Σ-protocols. The message output by Sign_1 in the PS blind signature is essentially a Pedersen commitment for vectors. So we prove that Sign_1 was executed correctly using a Sigma protocol (note that due to the homomorphic nature of Pedersen commitment we don't need to prove that the values in the AL which are leaked to the IP are correct, since both parties can add those to the commitment "in public"). Finally, we use a sigma protocol for proving that the ciphertext encrypts the right value, and use standard "AND" composition of Σ-protocols to assert that the values appearing in different proofs are consistent.

Implementation of $\Pi_{\text{id-layer}}$. We instantiate the weakly robust PRF scheme (Definition 2.1) with Dodis-Yampolskiy PRF [21]. In this case we use ElGamal as the base encryption scheme for the "share-and-encrypt" ad-hoc threshold encryption scheme TE (Definition 2.4). This is because we are encrypting the public key as a group element, which can also be seen as an encryption of the secret key for "ElGamal in the exponent". Note that this allows to both easily prove knowledge of the secret key, and to make sure that the ARs will only learn the AH public key when decrypting. Due to the algebraic nature of the DY PRF, we can efficiently evaluate it inside an MPC protocol as required to implement $\mathcal{F}_{\text{mpc-prf}}$ using techniques described in [16,39].

When creating a new account, we use both SNARKs and Sigma protocols for proving a single composite statement consisting of a circuit-part and an algebraic part using the technique of [2] to obtain SNARK on algebraically committed input. This commitment is used to tie the witness of the Sigma protocol to the witness used in the SNARK. We describe briefly how we use a combination of Σ-protocols and SNARKs in order to prove relation $\mathcal{R}$ in $\Pi_{\text{id-layer}}$. We use SNARKs on committed input to prove that account holder's attribute list satisfies a certain policy, and for proving that $x \leq \text{Max}_{\text{ACC}}$ for committed x and public Max_{ACC}. Note that all the Σ-protocol proofs are made non-interactive using Fiat-Shamir. All the sigma protocols above are described in the full version [18].

Implementation of a Transaction Layer. We include a high-level description of a method for transferring money on the ledger in the accounts-based model in the full version of the paper [18].

Acknowledgements. The authors would like to thank all members of the Concordium Blockchain Research Center and the Concordium AG for useful feedback, and in particular: Matthias Hall-Andersen, Jesper Buus Nielsen, Torben Pedersen, Daniel Tschudi.

References

1. Zcash Regulatory and Compliance Brief. https://z.cash/wp-content/uploads/2020/07/Zcash-Regulatory-Brief-062020.pdf. Accessed 01 June 2020
2. Agrawal, S., Ganesh, C., Mohassel, P.: Non-interactive zero-knowledge proofs for composite statements. In: Shacham, H., Boldyreva, A. (eds.) CRYPTO 2018. LNCS, vol. 10993, pp. 643–673. Springer, Cham (2018). https://doi.org/10.1007/978-3-319-96878-0_22

3. Androulaki, E., Camenisch, J., Caro, A.D., Dubovitskaya, M., Elkhiyaoui, K., Tackmann, B.: Privacy-preserving auditable token payments in a permissioned blockchain system. In: Proceedings of the 2nd ACM Conference on Advances in Financial Technologies, pp. 255–267 (2020)

4. Au, M.H., Susilo, W., Mu, Y.: Constant-size dynamic k-TAA. In: De Prisco, R., Yung, M. (eds.) SCN 2006. LNCS, vol. 4116, pp. 111–125. Springer, Heidelberg (2006). https://doi.org/10.1007/11832072_8

5. Au, M.H., Susilo, W., Mu, Y., Chow, S.S.: Constant-size dynamic k-times anonymous authentication. IEEE Syst. J. **7**(2), 249–261 (2012)

6. Ben-Sasson, E., et al.: Zerocash: decentralized anonymous payments from bitcoin. In: 2014 IEEE Symposium on Security and Privacy. IEEE Computer Society Press (May 2014)

7. Camenisch, J., Hohenberger, S., Kohlweiss, M., Lysyanskaya, A., Meyerovich, M.: How to win the clonewars: efficient periodic n-times anonymous authentication. In: ACM CCS 2006. ACM Press (October/November 2006)

8. Camenisch, J., Hohenberger, S., Lysyanskaya, A.: Compact e-cash. In: Cramer, R. (ed.) EUROCRYPT 2005. LNCS, vol. 3494, pp. 302–321. Springer, Heidelberg (2005). https://doi.org/10.1007/11426639_18

9. Camenisch, J., Maurer, U., Stadler, M.: Digital payment systems with passive anonymity-revoking trustees. In: Bertino, E., Kurth, H., Martella, G., Montolivo, E. (eds.) ESORICS 1996. LNCS, vol. 1146, pp. 33–43. Springer, Heidelberg (1996). https://doi.org/10.1007/3-540-61770-1_26

10. Campanelli, M., Fiore, D., Querol, A.: LegoSNARK: modular design and composition of succinct zero-knowledge proofs. In: ACM CCS 2019. ACM Press (November 2019)

11. Canetti, R.: Universally composable security: a new paradigm for cryptographic protocols. In: 42nd FOCS. IEEE Computer Society Press (October 2001)

12. Das, P., Jacobson, M.J., Scheidler, R.: Improved efficiency of a linearly homomorphic cryptosystem. In: Carlet, C., Guilley, S., Nitaj, A., Souidi, E.M. (eds.) C2SI 2019. LNCS, vol. 11445, pp. 349–368. Springer, Cham (2019). https://doi.org/10.1007/978-3-030-16458-4_20

13. Cecchetti, E., Zhang, F., Ji, Y., Kosba, A.E., Juels, A., Shi, E.: Solidus: confidential distributed ledger transactions via PVORM. In: ACM CCS 2017. ACM Press (October/November 2017)

14. Chaum, D.: Blind signature system. In: CRYPTO 1983. Plenum Press, New York (1983)

15. Chow, S.S.M.: Real traceable signatures. In: Jacobson, M.J., Rijmen, V., Safavi-Naini, R. (eds.) SAC 2009. LNCS, vol. 5867, pp. 92–107. Springer, Heidelberg (2009). https://doi.org/10.1007/978-3-642-05445-7_6

16. Dalskov, A., Orlandi, C., Keller, M., Shrishak, K., Shulman, H.: Securing DNSSEC keys via threshold ECDSA from generic MPC. In: Chen, L., Li, N., Liang, K., Schneider, S. (eds.) ESORICS 2020. LNCS, vol. 12309, pp. 654–673. Springer, Cham (2020). https://doi.org/10.1007/978-3-030-59013-0_32

17. Damgård, I., Dupont, K., Pedersen, M.Ø.: Unclonable group identification. In: Vaudenay, S. (ed.) EUROCRYPT 2006. LNCS, vol. 4004, pp. 555–572. Springer, Heidelberg (2006). https://doi.org/10.1007/11761679_33

18. Damgård, I., Ganesh, C., Khoshakhlagh, H., Orlandi, C., Siniscalchi, L.: Balancing privacy and accountability in blockchain identity management. IACR Cryptol. ePrint Arch. 2020, vol. 1511 (2020). https://eprint.iacr.org/2020/1511

19. Daza, V., Herranz, J., Morillo, P., Ràfols, C.: CCA2-secure threshold broadcast encryption with shorter ciphertexts. In: Susilo, W., Liu, J.K., Mu, Y. (eds.) ProvSec 2007. LNCS, vol. 4784, pp. 35–50. Springer, Heidelberg (2007). https://doi.org/10.1007/978-3-540-75670-5_3

20. De Santis, A., Persiano, G.: Zero-knowledge proofs of knowledge without interaction (extended abstract). In: 33rd FOCS. IEEE Computer Society Press (October 1992)

21. Dodis, Y., Yampolskiy, A.: A verifiable random function with short proofs and keys. In: Vaudenay, S. (ed.) PKC 2005. LNCS, vol. 3386, pp. 416–431. Springer, Heidelberg (2005). https://doi.org/10.1007/978-3-540-30580-4_28

22. Farshim, P., Orlandi, C., Roşie, R.: Security of symmetric primitives under incorrect usage of keys. IACR Trans. Symm. Cryptol. 2017(1), 449–473 (2017)

23. Faust, S., Kohlweiss, M., Marson, G.A., Venturi, D.: On the non-malleability of the Fiat-Shamir transform. In: Galbraith, S., Nandi, M. (eds.) INDOCRYPT 2012. LNCS, vol. 7668, pp. 60–79. Springer, Heidelberg (2012). https://doi.org/10.1007/978-3-642-34931-7_5

24. Fauzi, P., Meiklejohn, S., Mercer, R., Orlandi, C.: Quisquis: a new design for anonymous cryptocurrencies. In: Galbraith, S.D., Moriai, S. (eds.) ASIACRYPT 2019. LNCS, vol. 11921, pp. 649–678. Springer, Cham (2019). https://doi.org/10.1007/978-3-030-34578-5_23

25. Fiat, A., Shamir, A.: How to prove yourself: practical solutions to identification and signature problems. In: Odlyzko, A.M. (ed.) CRYPTO 1986. LNCS, vol. 263, pp. 186–194. Springer, Heidelberg (1987). https://doi.org/10.1007/3-540-47721-7_12

26. Gennaro, R., Gentry, C., Parno, B., Raykova, M.: Quadratic span programs and succinct NIZKs without PCPs. In: Johansson, T., Nguyen, P.Q. (eds.) EUROCRYPT 2013. LNCS, vol. 7881, pp. 626–645. Springer, Heidelberg (2013). https://doi.org/10.1007/978-3-642-38348-9_37

27. Goldwasser, S., Micali, S., Rivest, R.L.: A digital signature scheme secure against adaptive chosen-message attacks. SIAM J. Comput. 17(2), 281–308 (1988)

28. Kiayias, A., Tsiounis, Y., Yung, M.: Traceable signatures. In: Cachin, C., Camenisch, J.L. (eds.) EUROCRYPT 2004. LNCS, vol. 3027, pp. 571–589. Springer, Heidelberg (2004). https://doi.org/10.1007/978-3-540-24676-3_34

29. Kosba, A., et al.: How to use SNARKs in universally composable protocols. Cryptology ePrint Archive, Report 2015/1093 (2015). http://eprint.iacr.org/2015/1093

30. Meiklejohn, S., et al.: A fistful of bitcoins: characterizing payments among men with no names. In: Proceedings of the 2013 Conference on Internet Measurement Conference, pp. 127–140 (2013)

31. Narula, N., Vasquez, W., Virza, M.: zkLedger: privacy-preserving auditing for distributed ledgers. Cryptology ePrint Archive, Report 2018/241 (2018). https://eprint.iacr.org/2018/241

32. Nguyen, L., Safavi-Naini, R.: Dynamic k-times anonymous authentication. In: Ioannidis, J., Keromytis, A., Yung, M. (eds.) ACNS 2005. LNCS, vol. 3531, pp. 318–333. Springer, Heidelberg (2005). https://doi.org/10.1007/11496137_22

33. Parno, B., Howell, J., Gentry, C., Raykova, M.: Pinocchio: nearly practical verifiable computation. In: 2013 IEEE Symposium on Security and Privacy. IEEE Computer Society Press (May 2013)

34. Pedersen, T.P.: Non-interactive and information-theoretic secure verifiable secret sharing. In: Feigenbaum, J. (ed.) CRYPTO 1991. LNCS, vol. 576, pp. 129–140. Springer, Heidelberg (1992). https://doi.org/10.1007/3-540-46766-1_9

35. Poelstra, A., Back, A., Friedenbach, M., Maxwell, G., Wuille, P.: Confidential assets. In: Zohar, A., et al. (eds.) FC 2018. LNCS, vol. 10958, pp. 43–63. Springer, Heidelberg (2019). https://doi.org/10.1007/978-3-662-58820-8_4

36. Pointcheval, D., Sanders, O.: Short randomizable signatures. In: Sako, K. (ed.) CT-RSA 2016. LNCS, vol. 9610, pp. 111–126. Springer, Cham (2016). https://doi.org/10.1007/978-3-319-29485-8_7

37. Reyzin, L., Smith, A., Yakoubov, S.: Turning HATE into LOVE: homomorphic ad hoc threshold encryption for scalable MPC. Cryptology ePrint Archive, Report 2018/997 (2018). https://eprint.iacr.org/2018/997

38. Schröder, D., Unruh, D.: Security of blind signatures revisited. In: Fischlin, M., Buchmann, J., Manulis, M. (eds.) PKC 2012. LNCS, vol. 7293, pp. 662–679. Springer, Heidelberg (2012). https://doi.org/10.1007/978-3-642-30057-8_39

39. Smart, N.P., Talibi Alaoui, Y.: Distributing any elliptic curve based protocol. In: Albrecht, M. (ed.) IMACC 2019. LNCS, vol. 11929, pp. 342–366. Springer, Cham (2019). https://doi.org/10.1007/978-3-030-35199-1_17

40. Teranishi, I., Furukawa, J., Sako, K.: k-times anonymous authentication (extended abstract). In: Lee, P.J. (ed.) ASIACRYPT 2004. LNCS, vol. 3329, pp. 308–322. Springer, Heidelberg (2004). https://doi.org/10.1007/978-3-540-30539-2_22

41. Teranishi, I., Sako, K.: k-times anonymous authentication with a constant proving cost. In: Yung, M., Dodis, Y., Kiayias, A., Malkin, T. (eds.) PKC 2006. LNCS, vol. 3958, pp. 525–542. Springer, Heidelberg (2006). https://doi.org/10.1007/11745853_34

Non-interactive Half-Aggregation
of EdDSA and Variants
# of Schnorr Signatures

Konstantinos Chalkias[1]([✉]), François Garillot[1], Yashvanth Kondi[2],
and Valeria Nikolaenko[1]

[1] Novi/Facebook, Menlo Park, USA
[2] Northeastern University, Boston, USA

Abstract. Schnorr's signature scheme provides an elegant method to
derive signatures with security rooted in the hardness of the discrete logarithm problem, which is a well-studied assumption and conducive to efficient cryptography. However, unlike pairing-based schemes which allow
arbitrarily many signatures to be aggregated to a single *constant* sized
signature, achieving significant non-interactive compression for Schnorr
signatures and their variants has remained elusive. This work shows how
to compress a set of independent EdDSA/Schnorr signatures to roughly
half their naive size. Our technique does not employ generic succinct
proofs; it is agnostic to both the hash function as well as the specific
representation of the group used to instantiate the signature scheme.
We demonstrate via an implementation that our aggregation scheme
is indeed practical. Additionally, we give strong evidence that achieving better compression would imply proving statements specific to the
hash function in Schnorr's scheme, which would entail significant effort
for standardized schemes such as SHA2 in EdDSA. Among the others, our solution has direct applications to compressing Ed25519-based
blockchain blocks because transactions are independent and normally
users do not interact with each other.

Keywords: Schnorr · EdDSA · Signatures · Aggregation

1 Introduction

Schnorr's signature scheme [57] is an elegant digital signature scheme whose
security is rooted in the hardness of computing discrete logarithms in a given
group. Elliptic curve groups in particular have found favour in practical instantiations of Schnorr as they are secured by conservative well-studied assumptions,
while simultaneously allowing for fast arithmetic. One such instantiation is the
EdDSA signature scheme [10], which is deployed widely across the internet (in
such protocols as TLS 1.3, SSH, Tor, GnuPGP, Signal and more).

Y. Kondi—did part of this work during an internship at Novi Financial/Facebook
Research.

K. G. Paterson (Ed.): CT-RSA 2021, LNCS 12704, pp. 577–608, 2021.
https://doi.org/10.1007/978-3-030-75539-3_24

However, the downside of cryptography based on older assumptions is that it lacks the functionality of modern tools. In this work, we are concerned with the ability to *aggregate* signatures without any prior interaction between the signers. Informally speaking, an aggregate signature scheme allows a set of signatures to be compressed into a smaller representative unit, which verifies only if all of the signatures used in its generation were valid. Importantly, this aggregation operation must not require any secret key material, so that any observer of a set of signatures may aggregate them. Quite famously, pairing-based signatures [12,14] support compression of an arbitrary number of signatures into a constant sized aggregate. Thus far, it has remained unclear how to achieve any sort of non-trivial non-interactive compression for Schnorr signatures without relying on generic tools such as SNARKs.

In order to make headway in studying how to compress Schnorr signatures, we loosely cast this problem as an issue of *information optimality*. We first recap the structure of such a signature in order to frame the problem.

Structure of Schnorr signatures. Assume that we instantiate Schnorr's signature scheme in a group $(\mathbb{G}, +)$ with generator $B \in \mathbb{G}$ of prime order q. A signer possesses a secret key $\mathsf{sk} \in \mathbb{Z}_q$ for which the corresponding public key is $\mathsf{pk} = \mathsf{sk} \cdot B$. In order to sign a message m, the signer samples $r \leftarrow \mathbb{Z}_q$, and computes $R = r \cdot B$ and $S = \mathsf{sk} \cdot H(R, \mathsf{pk}, m) + r$. The signature itself is $\sigma = (R, S)$. This format of Schnorr signature is employed in EdDSA [10]. The original form of Schnorr signatures are slightly different: $\sigma = (H(R, \mathsf{pk}, m), S)$, the verification rederives R and verifies the hash. Schnorr signatures of this format can be shortened by a quarter via halving the output of the hash function [48,57], but this format does not allow for half-aggregation, *thus we are focusing on the Schnorr-type signatures in the (R, S) format.* We enumerate most of the popular Schnorr variants in Appendix A.3 discussing compatibility with our aggregation approach.

In practice, the groups that are used to instantiate Schnorr signatures are elliptic curves which are believed to be 'optimally hard', i.e. no attacks better than generic ones are known for computing discrete logarithms in these curves groups. As an example, the Ed25519 curve which requires 256 bits to represent a curve point is believed to instantiate an optimal 128-bit security level. Consequently, elliptic curve based Schnorr signatures are quite compact: at a λ-bit security level, instantiation with a 2λ-bit curve yields signatures that comprise only 4λ bits. Note that we ignore the few bits of overhead/security loss due to the specific representation of the curve.

Schnorr Signatures are Not Information Optimal. Given a fixed public key, a fresh Schnorr signature carries only 2λ bits of information. Indeed for a 2λ-bit curve, there are only $2^{2\lambda}$ pairs of accepting (R, S) tuples. It seems unlikely that we can achieve an information-optimal representation for a single signature[1].

---

[1] Even for shortened Schnorr signatures $\sigma = (H(R, \mathsf{pk}, m), S)$, where the output of the hash function is halved, signatures are at least 3λ bits, i.e. 50% larger than the amount of information they carry.

However we can not rule out this possibility when transmitting a larger number of signatures. Transmitting n Schnorr signatures at a λ-bit security level naively requires $4n\lambda$ bits, whereas they only convey $2n\lambda$ bits of information. Therefore we ask:

> How much information do we need to transmit in order to aggregate the effect of n Schnorr signatures?

We specify that we are only interested in aggregation methods that are agnostic to the curve and the hash function used for Schnorr - in particular aggregation must only make oracle use of these objects. This is not merely a theoretical concern, as proving statements that depend on the curve or code of the hash function can be quite involved in practice.

Related work is covered in Appendix A where we discuss existing security proofs for Schnorr signatures, multi-signatures, other variants of Schnorr and prior work on non-interactive aggregation of signatures.

1.1 Our Contributions

This works advances the study of non-interactive compression of Schnorr signatures.

Simple Half-Aggregation. We give an elegant construction to aggregate n Schnorr signatures over 2λ bit curves by transmitting only $2(n + 1)\lambda$ bits of information - i.e. only *half* the size of a naive transmission. This effectively cuts down nearly all of the redundancies in naively transmitting Schnorr signatures. Our construction relies on the Forking Lemma for provable security and consequently suffers from a quadratic security loss similar to Schnorr signatures themselves. Fortunately, this gap between provably secure and actually used parameters in practice has thus far not been known to induce any attacks. We also show how this aggregation method leads to a deterministic way of verifying a batch of Schnorr signatures.

Almost Half-Aggregation with Provable Guarantees. In light of the lossy proof of our half-aggregation construction, we give a different aggregation scheme that permits a *tight* reduction to the unforgeability of Schnorr signatures. However this comes at higher cost, specifically $2(n+\epsilon)\lambda$ bits to aggregate n signatures where $\epsilon \in O(\lambda/\log\lambda)$ is independent of n. This construction is based on Fischlin's transformation [28], and gives an uncompromising answer to the security question while still retaining reasonable practical efficiency. More concretely the compression rate of this construction passes 40% as soon as we aggregate 128 signatures, and tends towards the optimal 50% as n increases.

Implementations. We implement and comprehensively benchmark both constructions. We demonstrate that the simple half-aggregation construction is already practical for wide adoption, and we study the performance of our almost half-aggregation construction in order to better understand the overhead of provable security in this setting.

A Lower Bound. Finally, we give strong evidence that it is not possible to achieve non-trivial compression beyond $2n\lambda$ bits without substantially higher computation costs, i.e. our half-aggregation construction is essentially optimal as far as generic methods go. In particular, we show that aggregating Schnorr signatures from different users (for which no special distribution is fixed ahead of time) at a rate non-trivially better than 50% must necessarily be non-blackbox in the hash function used to instantiate the scheme.

In summary, we propose a lightweight half-aggregation scheme for Schnorr signatures, a slightly worse performing scheme which settles the underlying theoretical question uncompromisingly, and finally strong evidence that achieving a better compression rate is likely to be substantially more computationally expensive.

2   Proof-of-knowledge for a Collection of Signatures

In this section we first briefly recall the Schnorr and EdDSA signatures. We then construct a three-move protocol for the proof of knowledge of a collection signatures, we then discuss two ways to make it non-interactive with different security/efficiency trade-offs.

2.1   Schnorr/EdDSA Signatures

We explore Schnorr signatures in the form that generalizes the EdDSA signatures [10]. We use EdDSA, in particular Ed25519, for the purpose of benchmarks as it is the most widely deployed variant of Schnorr today. The exact algorithm for EdDSA signatures can be found in the original paper or in the Appendix B. Appendix A provides more information on other forms of Schnorr signatures.

We assume the scheme to be defined for a group $\mathbb{G}$ where the discrete log is hard with the scalar field $\mathbb{Z}_q$, we will denote the designated base point of order q to be $B \in \mathbb{G}$. We will use additive notation to represent the group operation.

Algorithm 1. Schnorr in (R, S)-format and EdDSA signatures

KeyGen(): sample a random scalar $s \xleftarrow{\$} \mathbb{Z}_q$, output a secret key $sk = s$ and a public key $pk = s \cdot B$.

Sign(sk, m): sample a random scalar $r \xleftarrow{\$} \mathbb{Z}_q$ (in EdDSA r is deduced from the secret key and the message), compute $R = r \cdot B$ and $S = r + H_0(R, A, m) \cdot s$, output $\sigma = (R, S)$.

Verify(m, pk, σ): for $\sigma = (R, S)$ and pk $= A$ accept if $S \cdot B = R + H_0(R, A, m) \cdot A$.

2.2 Three-Move (Sigma) Protocol

The construction takes inspiration from the batching of Sigma protocols for Schnorr's identification scheme [33].

A Sigma protocol is a three-move protocol run by a prover P and a verifier V for some relation $R = \{(x, w)\}$, for $(x, w) \in R$, x is called an *instance* and w is called a witness. $R \subseteq \{0, 1\}^* \times \{0, 1\}^*$, where there exists a polynomial p such that for any $(x, w) \in R$, the length of the witness is bounded $|w| \leq p(|x|)$. Often-times, x is a computational problem and w is a solution to that problem. In the Sigma protocol the prover convinces the verifier that it knows a witness of an instance x known to both of them. The protocol produces a transcript of the form (a, e, z) which consists of (in the order of exchanged messages): the *commitment* a sent by P, the *challenge* e sent by V and the *response* z sent by P. The verifier accepts or rejects the transcript. A Sigma protocol for the relation R with n-special soundness guarantees the existence of an extractor Ext which when given valid transcripts (accepted by the verifier) with different challenges $(a, e_1, z_1), (a, e_2, z_2), \ldots (a, e_n, z_n)$ for an instance x, produces (with certainty) a witness w for the statement, s.t. $(x, w) \in R$. We will not be concerned with the zero-knowledge property of the protocol for our application.

For a group $\mathbb{G}$ with generator $B \in \mathbb{G}$ of order $q \in \mathbb{Z}$, define the relation $R_{\mathsf{DL}} = \{(\mathsf{pk}, \mathsf{sk}) \in (\mathbb{G}, \mathbb{Z}_q) : \mathsf{pk} = \mathsf{sk} \cdot B\}$. Schnorr's identification protocol [57] is a two-special sound Sigma protocol for the relation R_{DL}: given two transcripts with the same commitment and different challenges, the secret key (discrete logarithm of pk) can be extracted. It is known how to compress n instances of Schnorr's protocol to produce an n-special sound Sigma protocol at essentially the same cost [33], we use similar ideas to derive a Sigma protocol for the aggregation of Schnorr signatures, i.e. for the following relation (with hash function H_0):

$$
\begin{aligned}
R_{\mathsf{aggr}} = \{(x, w) \mid & x = (\mathsf{pk}_1, m_1, \ldots, \mathsf{pk}_n, m_n), w = (\sigma_1, \ldots, \sigma_n), \\
& \mathsf{Verify}(m_i, \mathsf{pk}_i, \sigma_i) = \mathsf{true} \text{ for } \forall i \in [n]\} = \\
= \{(x, w) \mid & x = (A_1, m_1, \ldots, A_n, m_n), w = (R_1, S_1, \ldots, R_n, S_n), \\
& S_i \cdot B = R_i + H_0(R_i, A_i, m_i) \cdot A_i \text{ for } i = 1..n\}
\end{aligned}
$$

Theorem 1. *Protocol 2 is an n-special sound Sigma protocol for R_{aggr}.*

Proof. Completeness is easy to verify. Extraction is always successful due to the following: let $F \in \mathbb{G}[X]$ be the degree $n - 1$ polynomial where the coefficient of x^{i-1} is given by $R_i + H(R_i, \mathsf{pk}_i, m_i) \cdot \mathsf{pk}_i$ for each $i \in [n]$. Define $f \in \mathbb{Z}_q[X]$ as the isomorphic degree $n - 1$ polynomial over $\mathbb{Z}_q$ such that the coefficient of x^{i-1} in f is S_i (the discrete logarithm of the corresponding coefficient in F). Observe that $f(x) \cdot B = F(x)$ for each $x \in \mathbb{Z}_q$. Given a transcript (a, e, z), V_{Σ} accepts iff $z \cdot B = F(e)$, which is true iff $z = f(e)$. Therefore n valid transcripts $(a, e_1, z_1), \ldots, (a, e_n, z_n)$ define n distinct evaluations of f (which has degree $n - 1$) allowing for recovery of coefficients $[S_i]_{i \in [n]}$ efficiently. This is precisely

Protocol 2. Sigma protocol for a collection of signatures R_{aggr}

For instance $x = \{(\mathsf{pk}_i = A_i, m_i)\}_{i=1}^n$ and witness $w = \{\sigma_i = (R_i, S_i)\}_{i=1}^n$
Prover $P_\Sigma(x, w)$:
   1. **Commitment:** $a = [R_1, \ldots, R_n]$
   2. **Challenge:** $e \xleftarrow{\$} \mathbb{Z}_q^*$
   3. **Response:** $z = \sum_{i \in [n]} S_i \cdot e^{i-1}$
Verifier $V_\Sigma(x, (a, e, z))$: Output 1 iff $z \cdot B = \sum_{i \in [n]} e^{i-1}(R_i + H_0(R_i, A_i, m_i) \cdot A_i)$
Extractor $\mathsf{Ext}_\Sigma((a, e_1, z_1), \ldots, (a, e_n, z_n))$: Define the $n \times n$ matrix $E = [e_i^j]_{i,j \in [n]}$ and
   the column vector $Z = ([z_i]_{i \in [n]})^T$. Output $[S_1, \ldots, S_n] = (E^{-1}Z)^T$.

---

the operation carried out by Ext_Σ, expressed as a product of matrices. Note that $E = [e_i^j]_{i,j \in [n]}$ is always invertible; each e_i is known to be distinct, and so E is always a Vandermonde matrix. □

2.3 Proof-of-knowledge

A proof-of-knowledge for a relation $R = \{(x, w)\}$ is a protocol that realizes the following functionality:

$$\mathcal{F}^R((x, w), x) = (\emptyset, R(x, w))$$

i.e. the prover and verifier have inputs (x, w) and x respectively, and receive outputs $\emptyset$ and $R(x, w)$ respectively. This definition is taken from Hazay and Lindell [35, 36] who show it to be equivalent to the original definition of Bellare and Goldreich [5]. We additionally let a corrupt verifier learn $\mathsf{aux}(w)$ for some auxiliary information function aux. As we do not care about zero-knowledge at all (only compression) this can simply be the identity function, i.e. $\mathsf{aux}(w) = w$.

Proofs-of-knowledge allow for the drop-in replacement mechanism that we desire: instead of an instruction of the form "A sends n signatures to B" in a higher level protocol, one can simply specify that "A sends n signatures to $\mathcal{F}^R$, and B checks that its output from $\mathcal{F}^R$ is 1".

Among the several landmark transformations of a Sigma protocol into a non-interactive proof [27, 28, 51], the most commonly used is the Fiat-Shamir transform [27]: for a relation R a valid transcript of the form (a, e, z) can be transformed into a proof by hashing the commitment to generate the challenge non-interactively: $\mathsf{proof} = (a, e = H_1(a, x), z)$. Unfortunately, this transformation induces a security loss, applied directly to the n-sound Sigma protocol for the relation R_{aggr} from the previous section (Protocol 2), the prover will have to be rewinded n times to extract the witness. This transformation however gives a more efficient construction for non-interactive aggregation of signatures that we discuss in Sect. 3.

To achieve tighter security reduction, we look into the literature on proof-of-knowledge with online extractions [51]. There extractors can output the witness immediately without rewinding, in addition to the instance and the proof the extractors are given all the hash queries the prover made. We achieve a proof-of-knowledge for the relation R_{aggr} which immediately gives an aggregate signature scheme whose security can be *tightly* reduced to unforgeability of Schnorr's signatures as we discuss in Sect. 3.3. We present both protocols in this Section.

Protocol 3. Non-interactive proof-of-knowledge for R_{aggr}

Parameters: A curve group G with generator $B \in G$ of order $q \in \mathbb{Z}$. For instance $x = \{(\mathsf{pk}_i = A_i, m_i)\}_{i=1}^n$ and witness $w = \{\sigma_i = (S_i, R_i)\}_{i=1}^n$ we define three algorithms. Hash function H_1 modeled as a Random-Oracle.

Prover $P(x, w) \to$ proof:

    1. Compute the scalar $e = H_1(R_1, A_1, m_1, \ldots, R_n, A_n, m_n)$
    2. Compute the scalar $S_{\text{aggr}} = \sum_{i=1}^n e^{i-1} \cdot S_i$.
    3. Output the proof $\sigma_{\text{aggr}} = [R_1, \ldots, R_n, S_{\text{aggr}}]$.

Verifier $V_{\mathsf{RO}}(x, \mathsf{proof} = [R_1, \ldots, R_n, S_{\text{aggr}}]) \leftarrow 0/1$:

    1. Compute the scalar $e = H_1(R_1, A_1, m_1, \ldots, R_n, A_n, m_n)$.
    2. If $\sum_{i=1}^n e^{i-1} (R_i + H_0(R_i, A_i, m_i) \cdot A_i) = S_{\text{aggr}} \cdot B$, output *true*,
    3. otherwise output *false*.

2.3.1 Fiat-Shamir Transformation

Theorem 2. *For every prover P that produces an accepting proof with probability ϵ and runtime T having made a list of queries $\mathcal{Q}$ to* RO, *there is an extractor* Ext *that outputs a valid signature for each* $\mathsf{pk}_i \in \mathsf{pk}_{\text{aggr}}$ *in time* $nT + \mathsf{poly}(\lambda)$, *with probability at least* $\epsilon - (n \cdot \mathcal{Q})^2 / 2^{h+1}$, *where h is the bit-length of the H_1's output. It follows that the scheme* (P, V, Ext) *is a non-interactive proof-of-knowledge for the relation* R_{aggr} *in the random oracle model.*

Proof. The extractor Ext runs the adversary n times programming the random oracle to output fresh random values on each run, giving n proofs that can be used to obtain n accepting transcripts (a, e_i, z_i) for $i \in [n]$ and invokes Ext_Σ once they are found. Ext runs in time nT, and additionally $poly(\kappa)$ to run Ext_Σ. The extractor fails in case not all of the e_i are distinct which happens with probability at most $(n \cdot \mathcal{Q})^2 / 2^{h+1}$ by the birthday bound when we estimate the probability of at least one hash-collision between the queries of n runs of the adversary. $\qquad\square$

Another form of the protocol with the challenges derived with independent hashes allows for extraction of any single signature with a single rewinding. This protocol is a foundation for the half-aggregation construction for Schnorr signatures described in Sect. 3.3. To construct an extractor we use a variant of the Forking Lemma. Originally the Forking Lemma was introduced in the work of Pointcheval and Stern [53]. We use a generalized version described in [7].

Protocol 4. Non-interactive proof-of-knowledge for R_{aggr}

Parameters: A curve group G with generator $B \in G$ of order $q \in \mathbb{Z}$. For instance $x = \{(\text{pk}_i = A_i, m_i)\}_{i=1}^n$ and witness $w = \{\sigma_i = (S_i, R_i)\}_{i=1}^n$ we define three algorithms. Hash function H_1 modeled as a Random-Oracle.

Prover $P(x, w) \rightarrow$ proof:

 1. For $i \in [n]$ compute the scalars $e_i = H_1(R_1, A_1, m_1, \ldots, R_n, A_n, m_n, i)$
 2. Compute the scalar $S_{aggr} = \sum_{i=1}^n e_i \cdot S_i$.
 3. Output the proof $\sigma_{aggr} = [R_1, \ldots, R_n, S_{aggr}]$.

Verifier $V_{RO}(x, \text{proof} = [R_1, \ldots, R_n, S_{aggr}]) \leftarrow 0/1$:

 1. For $i \in [n]$ compute the scalars $e_i = H_1(R_1, A_1, m_1, \ldots, R_n, A_n, m_n, i)$.
 2. If $\sum_{i=1}^n e_i (R_i + H_0(R_i, A_i, m_i) \cdot A_i) = S_{aggr} \cdot B$, output *true*,
 3. otherwise output *false*.

---

[7] **Generalized Forking Lemma.** *Fix an integer $q \geq 1$ and a set H of size $h \geq 2$. Let $\mathcal{A}$ be a randomized algorithm. The algorithm $\mathcal{A}$ is given an input $in = (\text{pk}, h_1, \ldots, h_q)$ and randomness y, it returns a pair, the first element of which is an integer I and the second element of which is a side output* proof:

$$(I, \text{proof}) \leftarrow \mathcal{A}(in; y).$$

We say that the algorithm $\mathcal{A}$ succeeds if $I \geq 1$ and fails if $I = 0$. Let IG be a randomized input generator algorithm. We define the success probability of $\mathcal{A}$ as:

$$acc = \Pr[I \geq 1; \text{input} \xleftarrow{\$} \text{IG}; (h_1, \ldots, h_q) \xleftarrow{\$} H; (I, \text{proof}) \xleftarrow{\$} \mathcal{A}(\text{input}, h_1, \ldots, h_q)].$$

We define a randomized generalized forking algorithm $F_{\mathcal{A}}$ that depends on $\mathcal{A}$:

$F_{\mathcal{A}}(\text{input})$ *forking algorithm:*

1. *Pick coins y for $\mathcal{A}$ at random*
2. $h_1, \ldots, h_q \xleftarrow{\$} H$
3. $(I, \text{proof}) := \mathcal{A}(x, i, h_1, \ldots, h_q; y)$
4. *If $I = 0$ then return $(0, \perp, \perp)$*
5. $h'_1, \ldots, h'_q \xleftarrow{\$} H$
6. $(I', \text{proof}') := \mathcal{A}(x, i, h_1, \ldots, h_{I-1}, h'_I, \ldots, h'_q; y)$
7. *If $(I = I'$ and $h_I \neq h'_I)$ then return $(1, \text{proof}, \text{proof}')$*
8. *Else return $(0, \perp, \perp)$.*

Let $frk = \Pr[b = 1; \text{input} \xleftarrow{\$} \text{IG}; (b, \text{proof}, \text{proof}') \xleftarrow{\$} F_{\mathcal{A}}(i, x)]$.

Then $frk \geq acc \cdot \left(\frac{acc}{q} - \frac{1}{h} \right)$.

Theorem 3. *For every prover P that produces an accepting proof for a collection of n signatures with probability ϵ and runtime T having made a list of queries $\mathcal{Q}$ to RO (H_1), there is an extractor Ext that given $i^* \in [n]$ outputs an*

i^*-th signature that is valid under pk_{i^*} for message m_{i^*} in time $2T \cdot n$, with probability at least $\epsilon \cdot (\epsilon/(n \cdot Q) - 1/2^h)$, where h is the bit-length of the H_1's output.

Proof. The extractor will run the prover P for the same input twice to obtain two proofs that differ on the last component:

$$\mathsf{proof} = [R_1, \ldots, R_n, S_{\mathsf{aggr}}] \text{ and } \mathsf{proof}' = [R_1, \ldots, R_n, S'_{\mathsf{aggr}}]$$

it will then be able to extract a signature on pk_{i^*}.

We first wrap the prover P into an algorithm $\mathcal{A}$ to be used in the Forking Lemma. The algorithm $\mathcal{A}$ takes input $in = (\{(\mathsf{pk}_i, m_i)\}_{i=1}^n, i^*, h_1, \ldots, h_q)$, for $q = (Q + 1) \cdot n$, and a random tape y, it runs the prover P and programs its H_1 random oracle outputs as follows: on the input that was already queried before, output the same value (we record all the past H_1 queries). In case the query can not be parsed as $(R_1, A_1, m_1, \ldots, R_n, A_n, m_n, j) \in (G \times G \times \{0,1\}^*)^n \times [n]$ or in case the public key A_{i^*} does not match the one in the input: $A_{i^*} \neq \mathsf{pk}_{i^*}$, program the oracle to the next unused value of y. Otherwise, if $A_{i^*} = \mathsf{pk}_{i^*}$ and the query is of the form $(R_1, A_1, m_1, \ldots, R_n, A_n, m_n, j) \in (G \times G \times \{0,1\}^*)^n \times [n]$, do the following: (1) for each $i \in [n] \backslash i^*$ program the oracle on index i, i.e. on input $(R_1, A_1, m_1, \ldots, R_n, A_n, m_n, i)$, to the next unused value of y, (2) program the oracle on index i^*, i.e. on input $(R_1, A_1, m_1, \ldots, R_n, A_n, m_n, i^*)$, to the next unused value of h: h_t and (3) record the index into the table $T[R_1, A_1, m_1, \ldots, R_n, A_n, m_n, i^*] := t$.

Note that when the oracle is queried on some $(R_1, A_1, m_1, \ldots, R_n, A_n, m_n, j)$, all the related n queries are determined, those are queries of the form $(R_1, A_1, m_1, \ldots, R_n, A_n, m_n, i)$ for $i \in [n]$, so we program all those n queries ahead of time, when a fresh tuple $(R_1, A_1, m_1, \ldots, R_n, A_n, m_n)$ is queried to the H_1 oracle (i.e. on one real query, we program n related queries). The index t recorded in the table T is the potential forking point, so we program the queries $(R_1, A_1, m_1, \ldots, R_n, A_n, m_n, i)$ for $i \in [n] \backslash i^*$ first, to the values of y, making sure that those values of y [2] are read before the forking point (the positions of y that are used here are therefore the same between rewindings), we finally program $(R_1, A_1, m_1, \ldots, R_n, A_n, m_n, i^*)$ to the next value of h (the potential forking point, therefore an oracle query at this value may differ between rewindings). Note also that in the process of programming we ignore the index j where the real query has been asked, it is only being used to give back the correct programmed value.

When the prover outputs a $\mathsf{proof} = [R_1, \ldots, R_n, S_{\mathsf{aggr}}]$, the algorithm $\mathcal{A}$ performs additional queries $H_1(R_1, A_1, m_1, \ldots, R_n, A_n, m_n, j)$ for all $j \in [n]$, making sure those are defined, and if the proof is valid, it outputs $I = T[R_1, A_1, m_1, \ldots, R_n, A_n, m_n, i^*]$ and proof, otherwise it outputs $(0, \perp)$.

Next we use the forking lemma to construct an algorithm $F_{\mathcal{A}}$ that produces two valid proofs proof and proof' and an index I. Since the same randomness and the same oracle values were used until index I, it must be the case that two proofs satisfy:

---

[2] An anonymous reviewer suggested a PRF could be used to derive the values of y from a single seed in order to save space for an implementation of the reduction.

$$\text{proof} = [R_1, \ldots, R_n, S_{\text{aggr}}], \quad \sum_{i=1}^{n} e_i \left(R_i + H_0(R_i, A_i, m_i) \cdot A_i \right) = S_{\text{aggr}} \cdot B, \quad (1)$$

$$\text{proof}' = [R_1, \ldots, R_n, S'_{\text{aggr}}], \quad \sum_{i=1}^{n} e'_i \left(R_i + H_0(R_i, A_i, m_i) \cdot A_i \right) = S'_{\text{aggr}} \cdot B,$$

where $e_{i^*} \neq e'_{i^*}$ and for $\forall i \neq i^* e_i = e'_i$,

since the latter are programmed before the forking point I. $\hspace{2cm}$ (2)

Subtracting the two equations (Eq. 1 and Eq. 2) we extracted a signature $(S = S_{\text{aggr}} - S'_{\text{aggr}}, R_i)$ on message m_i under the public key A_i.

The success probability of $\mathcal{A}$ is ϵ, hence the probability of successful extraction according to the Forking Lemma is $\epsilon \cdot (\epsilon/(n \cdot Q) - 1/2^h)$. The extractor runs the prover twice and on each one random oracle query programs at most $n - 1$ additional random oracle queries. $\hspace{2cm}$ □

Note that Ext extracts a single signature at a specified position. To extract all of the n signatures, the prover needs to be rewinded n times.

Corollary 1. *For every prover P that produces an accepting proof with probability ϵ and runtime T having made a list of queries Q to RO, there is an extractor Ext that outputs a full witness (i.e. all valid signatures for all $pk_i \in pk_{\text{aggr}}$) in time $(n + 1)Tn$, with probability at least $\left(\epsilon \cdot (\epsilon/(n \cdot Q) - 1/2^h) \right)^n$, where h is the bit-length of the H_1's output. It follows that the scheme (P, V, Ext) is a non-interactive proof-of-knowledge for the relation R_{aggr} in the random oracle model.*

2.3.2 Fischlin's Transformation

Pass [51] was the first to formalize the online extraction problem in the random oracle model and give a generic transformation from any 2-special sound sigma protocol to a non-interactive proof-of-knowledge with online extraction. Intuitively, Pass's transformation is a cut-and-choose protocol where each challenge is limited to a logarithmic number of bits. The prover can therefore compute transcripts for all of the challenges (since there are a polynomial number of them), put the transcripts as leaves of the Merkle tree and compute the Merkle root. The extractor will see all of the transcripts on the leaves since it can examine random-oracle queries. The prover may construct an actual challenge by hashing the root of the tree and the original commitment, map the result to one of the leaves and reveal the Merkle path as a proof of correctness which induces a logarithmic communication overhead. Fischlin's transformation [28] implements essentially the same idea (albeit for a specific class of Sigma protocols) where the transcripts for opening the cut-and-choose are selected at *constant* communication overhead, however at the expense of at least twice the number of hash queries in expectation. Roughly, the selection process works by repeatedly querying (a, e_i, z_i) to RO until one that satisfies $RO(a, e_i, z_i) = 0^\ell$ is found.

A proof-of-knowledge that permits an online extractor is very easy to use in a larger protocol; it essentially implements an oracle that outputs 1 to the verifier iff the prover gives it a valid witness. A reduction that makes use of an adversary for a larger protocol simply receives the witness on behalf of this oracle, while incurring only an additive loss of security corresponding to the extraction error. This is the design principle of Universal Composability [17] and permits modular analysis for higher level protocols, which in this case means that invoking the aggregated proof oracle is "almost equivalent" to simply sending the signatures in the clear.

We construct a non-interactive version of our aggregation protocol with ideas inspired by Fischlin's transformation, so that proofs produced by our protocol will permit online extraction. There are various subtle differences from Fischlin's context, such as different soundness levels for the underlying and compiled protocols to permit compression, and the lack of zero-knowledge, and so we specify the non-interactive protocol directly in its entirety below, and prove it secure from scratch.

Protocol 5. Non-interactive proof-of-knowledge for R_{aggr}

Prover $P_{\mathsf{RO}}(x, w) \rightarrow$ proof:

1. Initialize an array of curve points, $\mathbf{a} = [R_1, \ldots, R_n]$.
2. Initialize empty arrays of scalars: $\mathbf{e} = [\perp]^r$ and $\mathbf{z} = [\perp]^r$; $\mathbf{e}, \mathbf{z} \in (\mathbb{Z}_q \cup \perp)^r$.
3. Set ind $= 1$, $e = 1$.
4. While ind $\leq r$, do:
   (a) Compute $z = \sum_{i \in [n]} S_i \cdot e^{i-1}$.
   (b) If $\mathsf{RO}(\mathbf{a}, \mathsf{ind}, e, z) \stackrel{?}{=} 0^\ell$:
       - Set $\mathbf{e}_{\mathsf{ind}} = e$ and $\mathbf{z}_{\mathsf{ind}} = z$
       - Increment the ind counter and reset $e = 1$
   (c) Else: increment e
5. Output the proof $(\mathbf{a}, \mathbf{e}, \mathbf{z})$

Verifier $V_{\mathsf{RO}}(x, \mathsf{proof} = (\mathbf{a}, \mathbf{e}, \mathbf{z})) \leftarrow 0/1$:

1. Output 1 (accept) if both of the following equalities hold for every ind $\in [r]$:

$$\mathsf{RO}(\mathbf{a}, \mathsf{ind}, \mathbf{e}_{\mathsf{ind}}, \mathbf{z}_{\mathsf{ind}}) = 0^\ell \bigwedge \mathbf{z}_{\mathsf{ind}} \cdot G = \sum_{i \in [n]} \mathbf{e}_{\mathsf{ind}}^{i-1}(R_i + H(R_i, \mathsf{pk}_i, m_i) \cdot \mathsf{pk}_i)$$

2. Output 0 (reject) if even one test does not pass.

The parameters ℓ, r are set to achieve λ bits of security, and adjusted as a tradeoff between computation and communication cost. In particular, the scheme achieves $r(\ell - \log_2(n)) = \lambda$ bits of security, proofs are of size n curve points and r field elements, and take $r \cdot 2^\ell$ hash queries to produce (in expectation).

Theorem 4. *The scheme (P, V, Ext) is a non-interactive proof-of-knowledge for the relation R_{aggr} in the random oracle model. Furthermore for every prover P^* that produces an accepting proof with probability ϵ and runtime T having made a list of queries Q to RO, the extractor Ext given Q outputs a valid signature for each $\mathsf{pk}_i \in \mathsf{pk}_{\mathsf{aggr}}$ in time $T + \mathrm{poly}(\lambda)$, with probability at least $\epsilon - T \cdot 2^{-\lambda}$.*

Proof.
Completeness. It is easy to verify that when P terminates by outputting a proof, V accepts this proof string. P terminates once it has found r independent pre-images of 0^ℓ per RO; in expectation, this takes $r \cdot 2^\ell$ queries, which is polynomial in λ as $\ell \in O(\log \lambda)$ and $r \in O(\mathsf{poly}(\lambda))$. The prover therefore runs in expected polynomial time.

Proof of Knowledge. The extractor Ext works by inspecting queries to RO to find n accepting transcripts (a, e_i, z_i) and invoking Ext_Σ once they are found. First note that Ext runs in at most $|\mathcal{Q}| \leq T$ steps to inspect queries to RO, and additionally $\mathsf{poly}(\lambda)$ to run Ext_Σ. We now focus on bounding the extraction error. As Ext_Σ works with certainty when given $(a, e_1, z_1), \ldots, (a, e_n, z_n)$, it only remains to quantify the probability with which Ext will succeed in finding at least n accepting transcripts in the list of RO queries. The event that the extractor fails is equivalent to the event that P^* is able to output an accepting proof despite querying fewer than n valid transcripts (prefixed by the same a) to RO; call this event fail. Define the event fail_a as the event that P^* is able to output an accepting proof $(a, \mathbf{e}, \mathbf{z})$ despite querying fewer than n valid transcripts (prefixed specifically by a) to RO. Define $\mathsf{fail}_{a,\mathsf{ind}}$ as the event that P^* queries fewer than n valid transcripts to RO prefixed specifically by a, ind, for each $\mathsf{ind} \in [r]$. Let $Q_{\mathsf{ind},1}, \ldots, Q_{\mathsf{ind},m}$ index the valid transcripts queried to RO with prefix a, ind. The event $\mathsf{fail}_{a,\mathsf{ind}}$ occurs only when $m < n$, and so the probability that $\mathsf{fail}_{a,\mathsf{ind}}$ occurs for a given ind can therefore be computed as follows:

$$\Pr[\mathsf{fail}_{a,\mathsf{ind}}] = \Pr[\mathsf{RO}(Q_{\mathsf{ind},1}) = 0^\ell \vee \cdots \vee \mathsf{RO}(Q_{\mathsf{ind},m}) = 0^\ell] \leq \sum_{j \in [m]} \Pr[\mathsf{RO}(Q_{\mathsf{ind},j}) = 0^\ell]$$

$$\leq \sum_{j \in [n]} \Pr[\mathsf{RO}(Q_{\mathsf{ind},j}) = 0^\ell] = \sum_{j \in [n]} \frac{1}{2^\ell} = \frac{n}{2^\ell} = \frac{1}{2^{\ell - \log_2(n)}}$$

Subsequently to bound fail_a itself, we make the following observations:

- For fail_a to occur, it must be the case that $\mathsf{fail}_{a,\mathsf{ind}}$ occurs for every $\mathsf{ind} \in [r]$. This follows easily, because every transcript prefixed by a, ind is of course prefixed by a.
- Each event $\mathsf{fail}_{a,\mathsf{ind}}$ is independent as the sets of queries they consider are prefixed by different ind values and so are completely disjoint.

The probability that fail_a occurs can hence be bounded as follows:

$$\Pr[\mathsf{fail}_a] \leq \Pr[\mathsf{fail}_{a,1} \wedge \cdots \wedge \mathsf{fail}_{a,r}] = \prod_{i \in [r]} \Pr[\mathsf{fail}_{a,i}] \leq \prod_{i \in [r]} \frac{1}{2^{\ell - \log(n)}} = 2^{-r(\ell - \log(n))}$$

The parameters r, ℓ are set so that $r(\ell - \log(n)) \geq \lambda$ and so the above probability simplifies to $2^{-\lambda}$. As P^* runs in time T, in order to derive the overall probability of the extractor's failure (i.e. event fail) we take a union bound over potentially T unique a values, finally giving us $\Pr[\mathsf{fail}] \leq T \cdot 2^{-\lambda}$ which proves the theorem. $\qquad\square$

3 Non-interactive Half-Aggregation of Schnorr/EdDSA Signatures

Following the definition of Boneh et al. [12], we say that a signature scheme supports aggregation if given n signatures on n messages from n public keys (that can be different or repeating) it is possible to compress all these signatures into a shorter signature non-interactively. Aggregate signatures are related to non-interactive multisignatures [38, 46] with independent key generations. In multisignatures, a set of signers collectively sign the same message, producing a single signature, while here we focus on compressing the signatures on distinct messages. Our aggregation could be used to compress certificate chains, signatures on transactions or consensus messages of a blockchain, and everywhere where a batch of signatures needs to be stored efficiently or transmitted over a low-bandwidth channel. The aggregation that we present here can in practice be done by any third-party, the party does not have to be trusted, it needs access to the messages, the public keys of the users and the signatures, but it does not need to have access to users' secret keys.

The aggregate signature scheme consists of five algorithms: KeyGen, Sign, Verify, AggregateSig, AggregateVerify. The first three algorithms are the same as in the ordinary signature scheme:

KeyGen(1^λ): given a security parameter output a secret-public key pair (sk, pk).

Sign(sk, m): given a secret key and a message output a signature σ.

Verify(m, pk, σ): given a message, a public key and a signature output accept or reject.

AggregateSig((m_1, pk_1, σ_1), ..., (m_n, pk_n, σ_n)) $\to \sigma_{aggr}$: for an input set of n triplets –message, public key, signature, output an aggregate signature σ_{aggr}.

AggregateVerify((m_1, pk_1), ..., (m_n, pk_n), σ_{aggr}) $\to$ {**accept**/**reject**}: for an input set of n pairs –message, public key– and an aggregate signature, output accept or reject.

Some schemes may allow an aggregation of the public keys as well, AggregatePK, but we do not focus on such schemes here.

We recall the EUF-CMA security and Strong Binding Security (SBS) of the single signature scheme in Appendix C. Intuitively, EUF-CMA (existential unforgeability under chosen message attacks) guarantees that any efficient adversary who has the public key pk of the signer and received an arbitrary number of signatures on messages of its choice: $\{m_i, \sigma_i\}_{i=1}^N$, cannot output a valid signature σ^* for a new message $m^* \notin \{m_i\}_{i=1}^N$ (except with negligible probability). An SBS guarantees that the signature is binding both to the message and to the public key, e.g. no efficient adversary may produce two public keys pk, pk', two signatures m, m', s.t. (pk, m) $\neq$ (pk', m') and a signature σ that verifies successfully under (pk, m) and (pk', m').

3.1 Aggregate Signature Security

Intuitively, the aggregate signature scheme is secure if no adversary can produce new aggregate signatures on a sequence of chosen keys where at least one of the keys is honest. We follow the definition of [12], the attacker's goal is to produce an existential forgery for an aggregate signature given access to the signing oracle on the honest key. An attacker $\mathcal{A}$ plays the following game parameterized by n, that we call chosen-key aggregate existential forgery under chosen-message attacks (CK-AEUF-CMA).

$\underline{G_{\mathcal{A}}^{\text{CK-AEUF-CMA}}(n)}$ security game:

1. $(\text{pk}^*, \text{sk}^*) \leftarrow \text{KeyGen}()$
2. $((m_1, \text{pk}_1), \ldots, (m_n, \text{pk}_n), \sigma_{\text{aggr}}) \leftarrow \mathcal{A}^{O_{\text{Sign}(\text{sk}^*, \cdot)}}(\text{pk}^*)$,
3. accept if $\exists i \in [n]$ s.t. $\text{pk}^* = \text{pk}_i$, and $m_i \notin \mathcal{L}_{\text{Sign}}$, and AggregateVerify$((m_1, \text{pk}_1), \ldots, (m_n, \text{pk}_n), \sigma_{\text{aggr}})$

$\underline{O_{\text{Sign}(\text{sk}^*, m)}}$ constructs the set $\mathcal{L}_{\text{Sign}}$:

$\quad \sigma \leftarrow \text{Sign}(\text{sk}^*, m); \; \mathcal{L}_{\text{Sign}} \leftarrow \mathcal{L}_{\text{Sign}} \cup m; \; \text{return } \sigma$

In this game an attacker is given an honestly generated challenge public key pk^*, he can choose all of the rest public keys, except the challenge public key, and may ask any number of chosen message queries for signatures on this key, at the end the adversary should output a sequence of n public keys (including the challenge public key), a sequence of n messages and an aggregate signature where the message corresponding to the public key pk^* did not appear in the signing queries done by the adversary. The adversary wins if the forgery successfully verifies.

Definition 1. *An attacker $\mathcal{A}$, (t, ϵ)-breaks a CK-AEUF-CMA security of aggregate signature scheme if $\mathcal{A}$ runs in time at most t and wins the CK-AEUF-CMA game with probability ϵ. An aggregate signature scheme is (t, ϵ)-CK-AEUF-CMA-secure if no forger (t, ϵ)-breaks it.*

More broadly, we say that an aggregate signature scheme is CK-AEUF-CMA-secure if no polynomial-time (in the security parameter) adversary may break the scheme other than with the negligible probability. Nonetheless, to instantiate the scheme with some concrete parameters, we will use a more rigid definition stated above. If the scheme is (t, ϵ)-CK-AEUF-CMA-secure, we say that it provides $\log_2(t/\epsilon)$-bits of security.

Note that the adversary has the ability to derive the rest of the public keys from the honest key pk^* in hope to cancel out the unknown components in the aggregate verification. Our constructions naturally prevent these attacks, otherwise generic methods of proving the knowledge of the secret keys could be used [46]. Note also that the original definition of Boneh et al. [12] places the honest public key as the first key in the forged sequence, since their scheme is agnostic to the ordering of the keys, our case is different and thus we give an adversary the ability to choose the position for the honest public key in the sequence.

In our constructions of aggregate Schnorr signatures we show that a valid single-signature forgery can be extracted from any adversary on the aggregate scheme.

The SBS definition translates to the aggregate signature defined as follows. $G_{\mathcal{A}}^{\text{CK-ASBS}}(n)$ security game:

1. $((m_1, \mathsf{pk}_1), \ldots, (m_n, \mathsf{pk}_n), (m_1', \mathsf{pk}_1'), \ldots, (m_n', \mathsf{pk}_n'), \sigma_{\text{aggr}}) \leftarrow \mathcal{A}(n),$
2. accept if $[(m_1, \mathsf{pk}_1), \ldots, (m_n, \mathsf{pk}_n)] \neq [(m_1', \mathsf{pk}_1'), \ldots, (m_n', \mathsf{pk}_n')] \wedge$
   AggregateVerify$((m_1, \mathsf{pk}_1), \ldots, (m_n, \mathsf{pk}_n), \sigma_{\text{aggr}}) \wedge$
   AggregateVerify$((m_1', \mathsf{pk}_1'), \ldots, (m_n', \mathsf{pk}_n'), \sigma_{\text{aggr}})$

Definition 2. *An attacker* $\mathcal{A}$, (t, ϵ)*-breaks a CK-ASBS security of aggregate signature scheme if* $\mathcal{A}$ *runs in time at most* t *and wins the CK-ASBS game with probability* ϵ. *An aggregate signature scheme is* (t, ϵ)*-CK-ASBS-secure if no forger* (t, ϵ)*-breaks it.*

3.2 Half-Aggregation

The half-aggregation scheme for Schnorr's/EdDSA signatures runs the proof-of-knowledge protocol (Protocol 4 from Sect. 2) to obtain a proof that would serve as an aggregate signature. We present the construction for completeness here in Algorithm 6.

Algorithm 6. Half-aggregation of EdDSA signatures

AggregateSig$((m_1, \mathsf{pk}_1, \sigma_1), \ldots, (m_n, \mathsf{pk}_n, \sigma_n)) \rightarrow \sigma_{\text{aggr}}$:
1: Parse the signature as the group element and the scalar: $\sigma_i = (R_i, S_i)$.
2: Parse the public key as a group element: $\mathsf{pk}_i = A_i$.
3: For $i \in 1..n$ compute the scalars $e_i \leftarrow H_1(R_1, A_1, m_1, \ldots, R_n, A_n, m_n, i)$.
4: Compute an aggregate scalar $S_{\text{aggr}} = \sum_{i=1}^{n} e_i \cdot S_i$.
5: Output an aggregate signature $\sigma_{\text{aggr}} = [R_1, \ldots, R_n, S_{\text{aggr}}]$.

AggregateVerify$((m_1, \mathsf{pk}_1), \ldots, (m_n, \mathsf{pk}_n), \sigma_{\text{aggr}}) \rightarrow 0/1$:
1: Parse the aggregate signature as $\sigma_{\text{aggr}} = [R_1, \ldots, R_n, S_{\text{aggr}}]$.
2: Parse each public key as a group element $\mathsf{pk}_i = A_i$.
3: Compute $e_i \leftarrow H_1(R_1, A_1, m_1, \ldots, R_n, A_n, m_n, i)$ for $i \in 1..n$
4: If $\sum_{i=1}^{n} e_i (R_i + H_0(R_i, A_i, m_i) \cdot A_i) = S_{\text{aggr}} \cdot B$, output *true*,
5: otherwise output *false*.

Note that the scheme of Algorithm 6 compresses n signatures by a factor of $2 + O(1/n)$: it takes n signatures, where each of them is one group element and one scalar, it compresses the scalars into a single scalar, therefore the resulting aggregate signature is comprised of one scalar and n group elements, compared to n scalar and n group elements before aggregation.

Note that the set of R-s can be pre-published as part of the public key or part of previously signed messages, the aggregate signature becomes constant size, but signatures become stateful, as it should be recorded which R-s have already been used. Reuse of R leads to a complete leak of the secret key. Even small biasis in R weakens the security of the scheme [1]. This approach departs from the deterministic nature of deriving nonces in EdDSA, loosing its potential security benefits, though it will go unnoticed for the verifier.

Note also that for large messages the following optimized aggregation could be used to speed-up the verifier: each e_i could be computed as $e_i = H_1(H_0(R_1, A_1, m_1), \ldots, H_0(R_n, A_n, m_n), i)$, since the verifier computes $H_0(R_i, A_i, m_i)$ anyway, it can reuse those values to compute the coefficients for the aggregation, thus making the length of the input to H_1 smaller. Though this optimization will only work for the form of Schnorr signature where the public key, A_i, is hashed.

Theorem 5. *If there is an adversary* Adv_1 *that can* (t, ϵ)-break the CK-AEUF-CMA security of the aggregate signature scheme in Algorithm 6, then this adversary can be transformed into an adversary Adv_2 that can $(2tn, \epsilon \cdot (\epsilon/(nt) - 1/2^h))$-break the EUF-CMA security of the underlying signature scheme, where h is the bit-length of the H_1's output.

The proof of this Theorem is very similar to the proof of Theorem 3 and can be found in the full-version of this paper. The only caveat here is that to apply the extractor from Theorem 3, it is required to know the index of pk* in a list of public keys, but this index can be obtained from examining the position of pk* in the random oracle queries to H_1.

Theorem 6. *No adversary running in time* t *may break the CK-ASBS security of the aggregate signature scheme described in Algorithm 6, other than with probability at most* $t^2/2^{2\lambda+1}$.

The proof of this Theorem can be found in Appendix D

Parameter selection and benchmarks. Theorem 5 has a quadratic security loss in its time-to-success ratio: assuming that EUF-CMA provides 128-bits of security (which is the case for example for Ed25519 signature scheme) the theorem guarantees only 64-bits security for CK-AEUF-CMA with 128-bits H_1-hashes; and assuming that EUF-CMA provides 224-bits of security (which is the case for example for Ed448 signature scheme) the theorem guarantees 112-bits security for CK-AEUF-CMA with 256-bits H_1-hashes[3]. A similar loss in the reduction from single Schnorr/EdDSA signature security to a discrete logarithm problem was not deemed to require the increase in the hardness of the underlying problems (i.e. the discrete logarithm problem). The proof that reduces security of Schnorr/EdDSA to the discrete logarithm problem also uses the Forking Lemma, but no attacks were found to exploit the loss suggested by such proof. Research suggests that the loss given by the Forking Lemma is inevitable for the proof of security of Schnorr/EdDSA signatures [29,58], whether it is likewise inevitable for non-interactive half-aggregation of Schnorr/EdDSA signatures remains an open question.

---

[3] Note that additionally $2\log_2(n) + 1$ bits of security will be lost due to n.

Table 1. For n individual signatures we compare batch-verification, aggregate-verification and aggregation with 128,256,512-bits output for H_1, for Ed25519 signatures. SHA-256 cropped to 128-bits used for 128-bits H_1, SHA-256 used for 256-bits H_1, SHA-512 used for 512-bits H_1. The benchmarks are run using the ed25519-dalek library.

n	Sequential verification	Batch verification	AggregateVerify			AggregateSig		
			128	256	512	128	256	512
16	0.8 ms	0.39 ms	0.37 ms	0.43 ms	0.44 ms	9.75 μs	10.6 μs	16.98 μs
32	1.6 ms	0.75 ms	0.68 ms	0.79 ms	0.83 ms	19.25 μs	21.5 μs	33.02 μs
64	3.2 ms	1.39 ms	1.35 ms	1.52 ms	1.58 ms	39.35 μs	41.4 μs	67.63 μs
128	6.4 ms	2.73 ms	2.61 ms	2.95 ms	3.04 ms	78.6 μs	84.9 μs	134.44 μs
256	12.8 ms	4.86 ms	4.69 ms	5.41 ms	5.54 ms	151.6 μs	165.6 μs	260.36 μs
512	25.7 ms	8.92 ms	8.00 ms	9.86 ms	9.54 ms	316.1 μs	341.7 μs	526.50 μs
1024	51.5 ms	16.15 ms	15.25 ms	17.46 ms	18.31 ms	613.5 μs	657.9 μs	1088.0 μs
131072	6.59 s	1.98 s	1.71 s	2.11 s	2.09 s	80.21 ms	84.60 ms	133.96 ms

We benchmark [18] the scheme to understand the effect of using 128-bits of H_1 output vs. 256-bits of H_1 output and present the results in Table 1.[4] Note that the performance loss in aggregate signature's verification between the two approaches is only about 15%, which might not justify the a use of smaller hashes. We also benchmark the use of 512-bits hashes of H_1, same-size scalar are used in the EdDSA signature scheme, the advantage of this approach is that the scalars generated this way are distributed uniformly at random (within negligible statistical distance from uniform).

3.3 Half+ε-Aggregation

The half+ε-aggregation scheme for EdDSA/Schnorr's signatures runs the proof-of-knowledge protocol (Protocol 5 from Sect. 2) to obtain a proof that would serve as an aggregate signature. For completeness we present the constructions in Algorithm 7.

Theorem 7. *If there is an adversary* Adv_1 *that can* (t, ϵ)*-break the CK-AEUF-CMA security of the aggregate signature scheme defined in Algorithm 7 making* Q *oracle queries to* H_1, *then this adversary can be transformed into an adversary* Adv_2 *that can* $(t + \mathsf{poly}(\lambda), \epsilon - t \cdot 2^{-\lambda})$*-break the EUF-CMA security of the underlying signature scheme.*

The theorem is a simple corollary of Theorem 4.

---

[4] The 'curve25519-dalek' and 'ed25519-dalek' libraries were used for the benchmark of this entire section, which ran on a AMD Ryzen 9 3950X 16-Core CPU. We used the scalar u64 backend of the dalek suite of libraries, to offer comparable results across a wide range of architectures, and the implementation does make use of Pippenger's bucketization algorithm for multi-exponentiation.

Algorithm 7. Almost-half-aggregation of EdDSA signatures

$\mathsf{AggregateSig}((m_1, \mathsf{pk}_1, \sigma_1), \ldots, (m_n, \mathsf{pk}_n, \sigma_n)) \to \sigma_{\mathsf{aggr}}$:
1: Let $\sigma_i = (R_i, S_i)$.
2: Compute the hash $h_a = H_2(R_1, \cdots, R_n)$.
3: Set the empty arrays of scalars $\mathbf{e} := [\bot]^r$ and $\mathbf{z} := [\bot]^r$; $\mathbf{e}, \mathbf{z} \in (\mathbb{Z}_q \cup \bot)^r$.
4: Set the counter $j := 1$.
5: Set the scalar $e := 1$.
6: **while** $j \le r$ **do**
7:     Compute $z := \sum_{i=1}^{n} S_i \cdot e^{i-1}$.
8:     **if** $H_1(h_a, j, e, z) = 0^\ell$ **then**
9:         Set $\mathbf{e}_j := e$; set $\mathbf{z}_j := z$; increment the counter j; reset the scalar $e = 1$.
10:    **else**
11:        Increment the scalar e.
12: Output the aggregate signature $\sigma_{\mathsf{aggr}} = ([R_1, \cdots, R_n], \mathbf{e}, \mathbf{z})$.

$\mathsf{AggregateVerify}((m_1, \mathsf{pk}_1), \ldots, (m_n, \mathsf{pk}_n), \sigma_{\mathsf{aggr}}) \to 0/1$:
1: Let $\sigma_{\mathsf{aggr}} = ([R_1, \cdots, R_n], \mathbf{e}, \mathbf{z})$.
2: Compute $h_a = H_2(R_1, \cdots, R_n)$.
3: Output 1 (accept) if both of the following equalities hold for every $j \in 1..r$:

$$H_1(h_a, j, \mathbf{e}_j, \mathbf{z}_j) = 0^\ell \text{ and } \mathbf{z}_j \cdot G = \sum_{i=1}^{n} \mathbf{e}_j^{i-1}(R_i + H_0(R_i, \mathsf{pk}_i, m_i) \cdot \mathsf{pk}_i)$$

4: Output 0 (reject) if the test does not pass for some j.

Theorem 8. *If there is an adversary Adv_1 that can (t, ϵ)-break the CK-ASBS-CMA security of the aggregate signature scheme defined in Algorithm 7 making Q oracle queries to H_1, then this adversary can be transformed into an adversary Adv_2 that can $(t + \mathsf{poly}(\lambda), (\epsilon - t \cdot 2^{-\lambda})^2)$-break the EUF-CMA security of the underlying signature scheme.*

The proof can be found in Appendix E

The security loss in this construction is much smaller, for example, the security remains at 128-bits for 128-bits output H_1-hash for Ed25519 signature scheme, and at 224-bits for 256-bits output H_1 for Ed448 signature scheme. But the compression rate for this aggregate signature scheme here is worse than for the previous scheme: the aggregated signature has n group elements, r full scalars and r small scalars of length ℓ in expectation, therefore the size of the signature is n group elements plus $r \cdot \lambda + r \cdot \ell$ bits. If we set λ and r to be constants and increase n, set $\ell = \log_2(n) + \lambda/r$, the size of the aggregate signature will be n group elements plus $O(log(n))$ bits, therefore the compression of the aggregation approaches 50% as n grows.

In Appendix F we explain a methodology for picking parameters to optimize for aggregator's time. Table 2 shows a selection of values across different trade-offs. Note that despite the aggregation time being rather slow, as the aggregator has to do many oracle-queries, it is highly parallelizable which is not reflected in our benchmarks: given $M \leq r2^{\ell}$ processors it is straightforward to parallelize aggregation into M threads.

4 Deterministic Batch Verification of Schnorr Signatures

As another application of the proof-of-knowledge techniques we present *deterministic* batch verification. Batch verification is a technique that allows to verify a batch of signatures faster than verifying signatures one-by-one. Not all of the Schnorr's signatures' variants support batch verification, only those that transmit R instead of the hash $H(..)$ do.

Bernstein et al. [10] built and benchmarked an optimized variant for batch verification for EdDSA signatures utilizing the state-of-the-art methods for scalar-multiplication methods. To batch-verify a set of signatures (R_i, S_i) for $i = 1..n$ corresponding to the set of messages $\{m_i\}_{i=1..n}$ and the set of public keys A_i, they propose to choose "independent uniform random 128-bit integers z_i" and verify the equation

$$(-\sum_i z_i S_i \bmod \ell)B + \sum_i z_i R_i + \sum_i (z_i H_0(R_i, A_i, m_i) \bmod \ell)A_i = 0. \qquad (3)$$

As we explain in the next paragraph with many real-world examples, it is often dangerous to rely on randomness in cryptographic implementations, particularly so for deployments on a cloud. It would thus be desirable to

Table 2. The compression rate, the computation cost (for aggregation and aggregate-verification) for aggregating n Ed25519 signatures with SHA-256 hash function used for H_1. The ℓ is set to be $\ell = \log_2(n) + 128/r$. The benchmarks are run using the ed25519-dalek library.

Compression	n	r	AggregateVerify	AggregateSig
0.52	512	16	134.11 ms	197.89 s
	1024	32	516.55 ms	76.857 s
0.53	256	16	74.449 ms	62.649 s
	512	32	291.04 ms	25.272 s
0.57	128	16	41.565 ms	12.007 s
	256	32	147.48 ms	6.1843 s
0.63	32	8	5.7735 ms	46.330 s
	64	16	23.007 ms	4.2622 s
	128	32	82.235 ms	1.3073 s
0.77	16	8	2.9823 ms	12.455 s
	32	16	10.377 ms	1.2994 s
	64	32	42.807 ms	403.55 ms

make protocols not utilize randomness in secure-critical components, such as signature-verifications. We note that batch verification (Eq. 3) is a probabilistic version of the Algorithm 6 for verification of half-aggregation of EdDSA signatures. From the security proof of half-aggregation it therefore follows that batch verification can be made deterministic by deriving scalars with hashes as $z_i = H_1(R_1, A_1, m_1, \ldots, R_n, A_n, m_n, i)$.

Note that particularly for Ed25519 signature scheme it is advised [19] to multiply by a cofactor 8 in single- and batch- verification equations (when batch verification is intended to be used).

Determinism's Value in Blockchains The history of the flaws of widely-deployed, modern pseudo-random number generator (PRNG) has shown enough variety in root causes to warrant caution, exhibiting bugs [47,61], probable tampering [20], and poor boot seeding [37]. Yet more recent work has observed correlated low entropy events in public block chains [15,21], and attributed classes of these events to PRNG seeding.

When juxtaposed with the convenience of deployment afforded by public clouds, often used in the deployment of blockchains, this presents a new challenge. Indeed, deploying a cryptographic algorithm on cloud infrastructure often entails that its components will run as guest processes in a virtualized environment of some sort. Existing literature shows that such guests have a lower rate of acquiring entropy [26,42], that their PRNG behaves deterministically on boot and reset [25,55], and that they show coupled entropy in multi-tenancy situations [40].

We suspect the cloud's virtualized deployment context worsen the biases observed in PRNG, and hence recommend the consideration of deterministic variants of both batch verification and aggregation.

The kind of aggregated signature verification in this paper may also be available to deterministic runtimes, which by design disable access to random generator apis. One such example is DJVM [22], where a special Java ClassLoader ensures that loaded classes cannot be influenced by factors such as hardware random number generators, system clocks, network packets or the contents of the local filesystem. Those runtimes are relevant for blockchains, which despise non-determinism including RNG invocations to avoid accidental or malicious misuse in smart contracts that would break consensus. Nonetheless, all blockchains support signature verification. A deterministic batch verifier would hence be very useful in these settings, especially as it applies to batching signatures on different messages too (i.e., independent blockchain transactions).

5   Impossibility of Non-interactive Compression by More Than a Half

Given that we have shown that it is possible to compress Schnorr signatures by a constant factor, it is natural to ask if we can do better. Indeed, the existence of succinct proof systems where the proofs are smaller than the witnesses themselves indicates that this is possible, even without extra assumptions or trusted setup if one were to use Bulletproofs [16] or IOP based proofs [8,9] for instance. This rules out proving any non-trivial lower bound on the communication complexity of aggregating Schnorr's signatures. However, one may wonder what overhead is incurred in using such generic SNARKs, given their excellent compression. Here we make progress towards answering this question, in particular we show that non-trivially improving on our aggregation scheme must rely on the hash function used in the instantiation of Schnorr's signature scheme.

We show in Theorem 9 that if the hash function used by Schnorr's signature scheme is modeled as a random oracle, then the verifier must query the nonces associated with each of the signatures to the random oracle. Given that each nonce has 2λ bits of entropy, it is unlikely that an aggregate signature non-trivially smaller than $2n\lambda$ can reliably induce the verifier to query all n nonces.

The implication is that an aggregation scheme that transmits fewer than $2n\lambda$ bits must not be making oracle use of the hash function; in particular it depends on the code of the hash function used to instantiate Schnorr's scheme. To our knowledge, there are no hash functions that are believed to securely instantiate Schnorr's signature scheme while simultaneously allowing for succinct proofs better than applying generic SNARKs to their circuit representations. Note that the hash function must have powerful properties in order for Schnorr's scheme to be proven secure, either believed to be instantiating a random oracle [54] or having strong concrete hardness [48]. Given that the only known techniques for making use of the code of the hash function in this context is by using SNARKs generically, we take this to be an indication that compressing Schnorr signatures with a rate better than 50% will incur the overhead of proving statements about complex hash functions. For instance compressing n Ed25519 signatures at a rate better than 50% may require proving n instances of SHA-512 via SNARKs.

For "self-verifying" objects such as signatures (aggregate or otherwise) one can generically achieve some notion of compression by simply omitting $O(\log \lambda)$ bits of the signature string, and have the verifier try all possible assignments of these omitted bits along with the transmitted string, and accept if any of them verify. Conversely, one may instruct the signer to generate a signature such that the trailing $O(\log \lambda)$ bits are always zero (similarly to blockchain mining) and need not be transmitted (this is achieved by repeatedly signing with different random tapes). There are two avenues to apply these optimizations:

1. **Aggregating optimized Schnorr signatures.** One could apply these optimizations to the underlying Schnorr signature itself, so that aggregating them even with our scheme produces an aggregate signature of size $2n(\lambda - O(\log \lambda))$ which in practice is considerably better than $2n\lambda$ as n scales. In the rest of this section we only consider the aggregation of Schnorr signatures that are produced by the regular unoptimized signing algorithm, i.e. where nonces have the full $2n\lambda$ bits of entropy. This quantifies the baseline for the most common use case, and has the benefit of a simpler proof. However, it is simple to adapt our proof technique to show that aggregation with compression rate

non-trivially greater than 50% is infeasible with this optimized Schnorr as the baseline as well.

2. **Aggregating unoptimized Schnorr signatures**. One could apply this optimization to save $O(\log \lambda)$ bits overall in the aggregated signature. In this case, $O(\log \lambda)$ is an additive term in the aggregated signature size and its effect disappears as n increases, and so we categorize this a trivial improvement.

Proof Intuition. Our argument hinges on the fact that the verifier of a Fiat-Shamir transformed proof must query the random oracle on the 'first message' of the underlying sigma protocol. In Schnorr's signature scheme, this represents that the nonce R must be queried by the verifier to the random oracle. It then follows that omitting this R value for a single signature in the aggregate signature with noticeable probability will directly result in an attack on unforgeability of the aggregate signature.

We give this question a formal treatment in Appendix G.

Acknowledgement. The authors would like to thank Payman Mohassel (Novi/ Facebook) and Isis Lovecruft for insightful discussions at the early stages of this work; and all anonymous reviewers of this paper for comments and suggestions that greatly improved the quality of this paper.

Appendix A   Related work

Appendix A.1   Security Proofs

Schnorr signatures were proposed by Claus Schnorr [57], and in the original paper a compact version was proposed, which outputted signatures of size 3λ, where λ is the provided security level (i.e. 128). In 1996, Pointcheval and Stern [53] applied their newly introduced Forking Lemma to provide the first formal security for a 2λ-bit ideal hash assuming the underlying discrete logarithm is hard. In [59] the first proof of Schnorr's ID against active attacks is provided in the GGM (Generic Group Model), but without focus on Fiat-Shamir constructions.

A significant contribution from Neven et al. [48] was to apply the GGM and other results of [7] to prove security using a λ-bit hash function. Briefly, in their proof, hash functions are not handled as random oracles, but they should offer specific properties, such as variants of preimage and second preimage resistance; but not collision resistance. However, as we mention in Section A.3, most of the real world applications do not assume honest signers, and thus non-repudiation is an important property, which unfortunately requires a collision resistant H_0.

Finally, the works from Backendal et al. [2] clarified the relation between the UF-security of different Schnorr variants, while in [31] a *tight* reduction of the UF-security of Schnorr signatures to *discrete log* in the Algebraic Group Model [30] (AGM)+ROM was presented.

Appendix A.2   Multi-signatures

One of the main advantages of Schnorr signatures compared to ECDSA is its linearity which allows to add two (or more) Schnorr signatures together and get a valid compact aggregated output indistinguishable from a single signature. The concept of multi-signature is to allow co-signing on the same message. Even if the messages are different, there are techniques using indexed Merkle tree accumulators to agree on a common tree root and then everyone signs that root. However, just adding Schnorr signatures is not secure as the requirement to protect against rogue key and other similar attacks is essential, especially in blockchain systems.

There is indeed a number of practical proposals that require two or three rounds of interaction until co-signers agree on a common R and public key A value [3,7,11,23,41,43,45,49,50,56,60]. One of the most recent is the compact two-round Musig2 [49] which also supports pre-processing (before co-signers learn the message to be signed) of all but the first round, effectively enabling a non-interactive signing process. Musig2 security is proven in the AGM+ROM model and it relies on the hardness of the OMDL problem.

Another promising two-round protocol is FROST [41] which has a similar logic with Musig2, but it utilizes verifiable random functions (VRFs) and mostly considers a threshold signature setting.

Note that even with pre-processing, Musig2 requires an initial setup with broadcasting and maintaining state. Compared to half-aggregation which can work with zero interaction between signers, Musig2 and FROST have a huge potential for controlled environments (i.e., validator sets in blockchains), but might not be ideal in settings where the co-signers do not know each other in advance or when public keys and group formation are rotated/updated very often.

Appendix A.3   Schnorr signature variants

There exist multiple variants of the original Schnorr scheme and the majority of them are incompatible between each other. Some of the most notable differences include:

- H_0 is not binding to the public key and thus it's computed as $H_0(R||m)$ instead of $H_0(R||A||m)$ [32,57]. Note that these signatures are malleable as shown in the EdDSA paper (page 7, Malleability paragraph) [10].
- H_0 changing the order of inputs in H_0, such as $H_0(m||R)$. Note that protocols in which m is the first input to the hash function require collision resistant hash functions, as a malicious message submitter (who doesn't know R), can try to find two messages m_0 and m_1 where $H_0(m_0) = H_0(m_1)$. This is the main reason for which the Pure EdDSA RFC 8032 [39] suggests $H_0(R||A||m)$ versus any other combination.
- H_0 takes as inputs only the x-coordinate of R, such as the EC-SDSA-opt in [32] and BIP-Schnorr [52].

– send the scalar H_0 instead of the point R. This variation (often referred to as *compact*) was proposed in the original Schnorr paper [57] and avoids the minor complexity of encoding the R point in the signature, while it allows for potentially shorter signatures by 25%. The idea is that only half of the H_0 bytes suffice to provide SUF-CMA security at the target security level of 128 bits. While this allows 48-byte signatures, there are two major caveats:

- according to Bellare et al. [6] (page 39), the (R, S) version (mentioned as BNN in that paper) achieves semi-strong unforgeability, while the original 48-byte Schnorr only normal unforgeability. In short, because finding collisions in a short hash function is easy, a malicious signer can break message binding (non-repudiation) by finding two messages m_0 and m_1 where $truncated(H(R||A||m_0)) == truncated(H(R||A||m_1))$
- as mentioned, collisions in 128-bit truncated H_0 require a 64-bit effort. But because the SUF-CMA model assumes honest signers, in multi-sig scenarios where potentially distrusting signers co-sign, some malicious coalition can try to obtain a valid signature on a message that an honest co-signer did not intend to sign.

Due to the above, and because compact signatures do not seem to support non-interactive aggregation or batch verification, it is clear that *this work is compatible with most of the (R, S) Schnorr signature variants*, EdDSA being one of them. Also note that half-aggregation achieves an asymptotic 50% size reduction and compares favorably against multiple *compact* Schnorr signatures.

Appendix A.4   Non-Schnorr schemes

Some of the best applications of non-interactive signature aggregation include shortening certificate chains and blockchain blocks. Putting Schnorr variants aside, there is a plethora of popular signature schemes used in real world applications including ECDSA, RSA, BLS and some newer post-quantum schemes i.e., based on hash functions or lattices. Regarding ECDSA, although there exist interactive threshold schemes, to the best of our knowledge there is no work around non-interactive aggregation, mainly due to the modular inversion involved [44]. Similarly, in RSA two users cannot share the same modulus N, which makes interactivity essential; however there exist sequential aggregate RSA signatures which however imply interaction [13]. Along the same lines, we are not aware of efficient multi-sig constructions for Lamport-based post-quantum schemes.

On the other hand, BLS is considered the most aggregation and blockchain friendly signature scheme, which by design allows for deriving a single signature from multiple outputs without any prior interaction and without proving knowledge or possession of secret keys [11]. The main practicality drawback of BLS schemes is that they are based on pairing-friendly curves and hashing to point functions for which there are on-going standardization efforts and limited HSM support. Also, the verification function of a rogue-key secure BLS scheme is still more expensive than Schnorr (aggregated or not) mainly due to the slower pairing computations.

Appendix A.5   Schnorr batching and aggregation

Similar approaches to generating linear combinations of signatures have been used for batch verification in the past as shown in Sect. 4. The original idea of operating on a group of signatures by means of a random linear combination of their members is due to Bellare et al. [4]. Other approaches consider an aggregated signature from public keys owned by the same user, which removes the requirement for rogue key resistance. For instance, in [33] an interactive batching technique is provided resulting to faster verification using higher degree polynomials.

Half-aggregation has already been proposed in the past, but either in its simple form without random linear combinations [24] (which is prone to rogue key attacks) or using non-standard Schnorr variants that are not compatible with EdDSA. Γ-signatures [62] are the closest prior work to our approach, also achieving half aggregation, but with a significantly modified and slightly slower Schnorr scheme. Additionally, their security is based on the custom *non-malleable* discrete logarithm (NMDL) assumption, although the authors claim that it could easily be proven secure against the stronger *explicit* knowledge-of-exponent assumption EKEA. On the other hand, we believe that our security guarantees are much more powerful as they are actually a proof of knowledge of signatures, which means that they can be used as a drop-in replacement in any protocol (where having the exact original signature strings is not important), without changing any underlying assumptions; and therefore be compliant with the standards.

Appendix B   EdDSA signatures

EdDSA signature [10] is originally defined over Curve25519 in its twisted Edwards form and is often called Ed25519. The scheme provides ~ 128 bits of security. The general name, EdDSA, refers to instantiation of the scheme over any compatible elliptic curve. Another notable instantiation is Ed448 [34, 39] offering ~ 224 bits of security. A concrete instantiation of the scheme would depend on the elliptic curve and the security level. The Algorithm 8 is given in the most general form.

Algorithm 8. EdDSA Algorithm

KeyGen(1^λ): Sample uniformly random sk $\xleftarrow{\$} \{0,1\}^{2\lambda}$. Expand the secret with a hash function that gives 4λ-bits outputs: $(s, k) \leftarrow H_1(\mathsf{sk})$. Interpreting s as a scalar, compute the public key pk $= A$, where $A = s \cdot B$.

Sign($(s, k), m$): Generate a pseudorandom secret scalar $r := H_2(k, m)$, compute a curve point: $R := r \cdot B$. Compute the scalar $S := (r + H_0(R, A, M) \cdot s)$ and output $\sigma = (R, S)$.

Verify($m, \mathsf{pk}, \sigma = (R, S)$): Accept if $S \cdot B = R + H_0(R, A, M) \cdot A$.

Appendix C   Single signature security

An attacker $\mathcal{A}$ plays the following game:
$G_{\mathcal{A}}^{\mathsf{EUF\text{-}CMA}}()$ security game:

1. $(\mathsf{pk}^*, \mathsf{sk}^*) \leftarrow \mathsf{KeyGen}()$
2. $(m, \sigma) \leftarrow \mathcal{A}^{O_{\mathsf{Sign}(\mathsf{sk}^*, \cdot)}}(\mathsf{pk}^*)$
3. accept if
   $m_i \notin \mathcal{L}_{\mathsf{Sign}} \ \wedge \ \mathsf{Verify}(m, \mathsf{pk}^*, \sigma)$

$O_{\mathsf{Sign}(\mathsf{sk}^*, \cdot)}$, the signing oracle, constructs the set $\mathcal{L}_{\mathsf{Sign}}$:

1. On input m, compute $\sigma \leftarrow \mathsf{Sign}(\mathsf{sk}^*, m)$
2. $\mathcal{L}_{\mathsf{Sign}} \leftarrow \mathcal{L}_{\mathsf{Sign}} \cup m$
3. return σ

Definition 3. *An attacker $\mathcal{A}$, (t, ϵ)-breaks a EUF-CMA security of the signature scheme if $\mathcal{A}$ runs in time at most t and wins the EUF-CMA game with probability ϵ. A signature scheme is (t, ϵ)-EUF-CMA-secure if no forger (t, ϵ)-breaks it.*

Likewise, if the scheme is (t, ϵ)-EUF-CMA-secure, we say that it achieves $\log_2(t/\epsilon)$-bits *security level.*

Note also that there is an additional requirement on single signature security which becomes increasingly important especially in blockchain applications is Strong Binding [19], it prevents a malicious signer from constructing a signature that is valid against different public keys and/or different messages. We define the associated game:
$G_{\mathcal{A}}^{\mathsf{SBS}}()$ security game:

1. $(\mathsf{pk}, m, \mathsf{pk}', m', \sigma) \leftarrow \mathcal{A}()$
2. accept if $(\mathsf{pk}, m) \neq (\mathsf{pk}', m') \ \wedge \ \mathsf{Verify}(m, \mathsf{pk}, \sigma) \ \wedge \ \mathsf{Verify}(m', \mathsf{pk}', \sigma)$

Definition 4. *An attacker $\mathcal{A}$, (t, ϵ)-breaks SBS security of the signature scheme if $\mathcal{A}$ runs in time at most t and wins the SBS game with probability ϵ. A signature scheme is (t, ϵ)-SBS-secure if no forger (t, ϵ)-breaks it.*

Appendix D   Proof of Theorem 6

Proof. By statistical argument we show that the adversary may only produce an SBS forgery with negligible probability. For a successful forgery $((A_1, m_1), \ldots, (A_n, m_n), \sigma_{\mathsf{aggr}}) \neq ((A_1', m_1'), \ldots (A_2', m_2'), \sigma_{\mathsf{aggr}})$, all $2n$ underlying signatures can be extracted: $\sigma_1, \ldots, \sigma_n, \sigma_1', \ldots, \sigma_n'$. All of those signatures have the same R components (since those are part of σ_{aggr}), but possibly different S components. When a query is made to the random oracle $H_1(R_1, A_1, m_1, \ldots, R_n, A_n, m_n, i)$, denote the output by h_i^j, where j is the incrementing counter for the unique tuples $(R_1, A_1, m_1, \ldots, R_n, A_n, m_n)$ queried to the random oracle. Denote by s_i^j the discrete log of $R_1 + H_0(R_i, A_i, m_i)A_i$ (here we work under the assumption that the discrete log can always be uniquely determined). Without loss of generality we assume that the adversary verifies the forgery, therefore for some two indices j' and j'' (that correspond to the SBS forgery output by the adversary) it must hold that the linear combination of the $\{s_i^{j'}\}_{i=1}^n$'s with coefficients $\{h_i^{j'}\}_{i=1}^n$ is equal to the linear combination of $\{s_i^{j''}\}_{i=1}^n$'s with coefficients $\{h_i^{j''}\}_{i=1}^n$. Having that in the RO-model, we can assume that the values $\{h_i^{j'}\}_{i=1}^n$ and $\{h_i^{j''}\}_{i=1}^n$ are programmed to uniformly random independent values after the s's values are determined. Each h randomizes the non-zero value of s to an exponent indistinguishable from random, therefore creating a random element as a result of a linear combination. Therefore the probability of a successful forgery for the adversary must be bounded by the collision probability $Q^2/(2 \cdot |\mathbb{G}|)$, where $Q \leq t$ is the number of H_1-queries and $|\mathbb{G}|$ is the size of the group (for prime order groups, or an order of a base point). $\qquad\square$

Appendix E   Proof of Theorem 8

Proof. From the forgery produced by the adversary Adv_1: $((m_1, \mathsf{pk}_1), \dots, (m_n, \mathsf{pk}_n), (m_1', \mathsf{pk}_1'), \dots, (m'g_n, \mathsf{pk}_n'), \sigma_{\mathsf{aggr}})$, we extract two sets of signatures by running the extractor of Theorem 4: $(\sigma_1, \dots, \sigma_n)$ and $(\sigma_1', \dots, \sigma_n')$. Those signatures have the same R-components $(R_1, \dots, R_n)$, but possibly different S-components $(S_1, S_1', \dots, S_n, S_n')$ when aggregated those components produce the same signature σ, therefore for some random $e \neq e'$, it holds that $\sum_{i=1}^n S_i \cdot e^{i-1} = \sum_{i=1}^n S_i' \cdot e'^{i-1}$ which may happen with probability at most 2^λ when $(S_1, \dots, S_n) \neq (S_1', \dots, S_n')$. Assuming that $(S_1, \dots, S_n) = (S_1', \dots, S_n')$, but $[(m_1, \mathsf{pk}_1), \dots, (m_n, \mathsf{pk}_n)] \neq [(m_1', \mathsf{pk}_1'), \dots, (m_n', \mathsf{pk}_n')]$, as required for the forgery of Adv_1 to be successful, it follows that at some position $i \in [n]$ where the equality breaks, a successful single SBS-forgery can be constructed: $(m_i, \mathsf{pk}_i, m_i', \mathsf{pk}_i', \sigma = (R_i, S_i))$. $\qquad\square$

Appendix F   Parameter selection for almost-half-aggregation

In this section we explain a methodology of picking parameters for aggregation scheme described in Algorithm 7.

However, as we explain next, it is more efficient to do the aggregation in batches, i.e. aggregate some fixed constant number of signatures, choosing this number to achieve a desired trade-off between compression rate, aggregation time and verification time. The computational complexity of the aggregator is $O(r \cdot n \cdot 2^\ell)$ and of the verifier is $O(n \cdot r)$. In fact, in this scheme the verifier is about $r/2 > 1$ times less efficient than verifying signatures iteratively one-by-one, therefore this compression scheme will always sacrifice verifier's computational efficiency for compressed storage or network bandwidth for transmission of signatures. The aggregator's complexity is by far greater than the verifier's, we approximate it next through compression rate c and batch size n. The compression rate can be approximated as

$$c = (256 \cdot n + r \cdot 256 + r \cdot \ell)/(512 \cdot n) \approx (n + r)/(2n).$$

We can estimate the aggregator's time through $r = n(2c - 1)$ as $O(n^3 \cdot (2c - 1) \cdot 2^{\lambda/n/(2c-1)})$. For a fixed compression rate c it achieves minimum at a batch-size n shown on Fig. 1 for $\lambda = 128$. The verifier's time can be estimated through compression rate as $O(n^2(2c-1))$, it is therefore most optimal to select an upper bound on the batch size according to Fig. 1 and lower the batch-size to trade-off between aggregator's and verifier's runtime. We report optimal aggregation times for the given compression rate in Fig. 2 for Ed25519 signature scheme. Amortized verification per signature is constant for constant r, amortized optimal aggregation per signature is linear in the batch size n.

Appendix G   Formal analysis for the impossibility of non-interactive compression by more than a half

This section expands on the impossibility of non-interactive compression by more than half and extends Sect. 5. We first fix the exact distribution of signatures that must be aggregated, and then reason about the output of any given aggregation scheme on this input.
$\mathsf{GenSigs}(n, 1^\lambda)$:

1. For each $i \in [n]$, sample $(\mathsf{pk}_i, \mathsf{sk}_i) \leftarrow \mathsf{KeyGen}(1^\lambda)$ and $r_i \leftarrow F_s$, and compute $R_i = r_i \cdot B$ and $\sigma_i = \mathsf{sk}_i \cdot \mathsf{RO}(\mathsf{pk}_i, R_i, 0) + r_i$
2. Output $(\mathsf{pk}_i, R_i, \sigma_i)_{i \in [n]}$

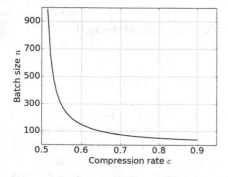

c	n	AggregateVerify amortized	AggregateSig amortized
0.55	296	500 µs	39.7 ms
0.6	148	562 µs	16.9 ms
0.65	98	609 µs	9.4 ms
0.7	74	582 µs	12.7 ms
0.75	59	562 µs	4.2 ms

Fig. 1. Optimal batch size to achieve the minimum aggregation time.

Fig. 2. Aggregation and verification time amortized per signature. Parameters n, r are set to achieve the smallest aggregation time: n is chosen from Fig. 1, $r = 30$.

The GenSigs algorithm simply creates n uniformly sampled signatures on the message '0'.

Theorem 9. *Let* (AggregateSig, AggregateVerify) *characterize an aggregate signature scheme for* KeyGen, Sign, Verify *as per Schnorr with group* $(\mathbb{G}, B, q)$ *such that* $|q| = 2\lambda$. *Let* $\mathcal{Q}_V$ *be the list of queries made to* RO *by*

$$\text{AggregateVerify}^{\text{RO}}(\text{AggregateSig}^{\text{RO}}(\{pk_i, R_i, \sigma_i\}_{i \in [n]}))$$

where $(pk_i, R_i, \sigma_i)_{i \in [n]} \leftarrow \text{GenSigs}(n, 1^\lambda)$. *Then for any* n, $\max((\Pr[(pk_i, R_i, 0) \notin \mathcal{Q}_V])_{i \in [n]})$ *is negligible in* λ.

Proof. Let $\varepsilon = \max((\Pr[(pk_i, R_i, 0) \notin \mathcal{Q}_V])_{i \in [n]})$, and let $j \in [n]$ be the corresponding index. We now define an alternative signature generation algorithm as follows,
GenSigs$^*(n, j, pk_j, 1^\lambda)$:

1. For each $i \in [n] \setminus j$, sample $(pk_i, sk_i) \leftarrow \text{KeyGen}(1^\lambda)$ and $r_i \leftarrow F_s$, and compute $R_i = r_i \cdot B$ and $\sigma_i = sk_i \cdot \text{RO}(pk_i, R_i, 0) + r_i$
2. Sample $\sigma_j \leftarrow F_s$ and $e_j \leftarrow F_s$
3. Set $R_j = \sigma_i \cdot B - e_j \cdot pk_j$
4. Output $(pk_i, R_i, \sigma_i)_{i \in [n]}$

Observe the following two facts about GenSigs*: (1) it does not use sk_j, and (2) the distributions of GenSigs and GenSigs* appear identical to any algorithm that does not query $(pk_i, R_i, 0)$ to RO. The first fact directly makes GenSigs* conducive to an adversary in the aggregated signature game: given challenge public key pk, simply invoke GenSigs* with $pk_j = pk$ to produce $(pk_i, R_i, \sigma_i)_{i \in [n]}$ and then feed these to AggregateSig[5]. The advantage this simple adversary is given by the probability that the verifier does not notice that that GenSigs* did not supply a valid signature under pk^* to AggregateSig, and we can quantify this using the second fact as follows:

$$\Pr[\text{AggregateVerify}^{\text{RO}}(\text{AggregateSig}^{\text{RO}}(\text{GenSigs}^*(n, j, pk_j, 1^\lambda))) = 1]$$
$$= \Pr[\text{AggregateVerify}^{\text{RO}}(\text{AggregateSig}^{\text{RO}}(\text{GenSigs}(n, 1^\lambda))) = 1] - \Pr[(pk_i, R_i, 0) \in \mathcal{Q}_V]$$
$$= 1 - \Pr[(pk_i, R_i, 0) \in \mathcal{Q}_V]$$
$$= 1 - (1 - \varepsilon) = \varepsilon$$

Assuming unforgeability of the aggregated signature scheme, ε must be negligible. $\qquad \square$

References

1. Aranha, D.F., Orlandi, C., Takahashi, A., Zaverucha, G.: Security of hedged fiat-shamir signatures under fault attacks. In: Eurocrypt (2020)

---

[5] If necessary, intercept $(pk_j, R_j, 0)$ queried by AggregateSig to RO, and respond with e_j as set by GenSigs*.

2. Backendal, M., Bellare, M., Sorrell, J., Sun, J.: The fiat-shamir zoo: relating the security of different signature variants. In: Nordic Conference on Secure IT Systems, pp. 154–170. Springer (2018)
3. Bagherzandi, A., Cheon, J.-H., Jarecki, S.: Multisignatures secure under the discrete logarithm assumption and a generalized forking lemma. In: ACM CCS (2008)
4. Bellare, M., Garay, J.A., Rabin, T.: Fast batch verification for modular exponentiation and digital signatures. In: Nyberg, K. (ed.) EUROCRYPT 1998. LNCS, vol. 1403, pp. 236–250. Springer, Heidelberg (1998). https://doi.org/10.1007/BFb0054130
5. Bellare, M., Goldreich, O.: On defining proofs of knowledge. In: Brickell, E.F. (ed.) Advances in Cryptology - CRYPTO'92. Lecture Notes in Computer Science, vol. 740, pp. 390–420. Springer, Heidelberg (1993)
6. Bellare, M., Namprempre, C., Neven, G.: Security proofs for identity-based identification and signature schemes. J. Cryptol. **22**(1), 1–61 (2009)
7. Bellare, M., Neven, G.: Multi-signatures in the plain public-key model and a general forking lemma. In: ACM CCS (2006)
8. Ben-Sasson, E., Bentov, I., Horesh, Y., Riabzev, M.: Scalable, transparent, and post-quantum secure computational integrity. Cryptology ePrint Archive, Report 2018/046 (2018). https://eprint.iacr.org/2018/046
9. Ben-Sasson, E., Chiesa, A., Riabzev, M., Spooner, N., Virza, M., Ward, N.P.: Aurora: transparent succinct arguments for R1CS. In: Eurocrypt (2019)
10. Bernstein, D.J., Duif, N., Lange, T., Schwabe, P., Yang, B.-Y.: High-speed high-security signatures. In: CHES (2011)
11. Boneh, D., Drijvers, M., Neven, G.: Compact multi-signatures for smaller blockchains. In: Asiacrypt (2018)
12. Boneh, D., Gentry, C., Lynn, B., Shacham, H.: Aggregate and verifiably encrypted signatures from bilinear maps. In: Eurocrypt (2003)
13. Boneh, D., Gentry, C., Shacham, H., et al.: A survey of two signature aggregation techniques, Ben Lynn (2003)
14. Boneh, D., Lynn, B., Shacham, H.: Short signatures from the Weil pairing. In: Asiacrypt (2001)
15. Breitner, J., Heninger, N.: Biased nonce sense: Lattice attacks against weak ECDSA signatures in cryptocurrencies. In: International Conference on Financial Cryptography and Data Security, pp. 3–20. Springer (2019)
16. Bünz, B., Bootle, J., Boneh, D., Poelstra, A., Wuille, P., Maxwell, G.: Bulletproofs: short proofs for confidential transactions and more. In: IEEE S&P, pp. 315–334 (2018)
17. Canetti, R.: Universally composable security: a new paradigm for cryptographic protocols. In: FOCS (2001)
18. Chalkias, K., Garillot, F., Kondi, Y., Nikolaenko, V.: ed25519-dalek-fiat, branch:half-aggregation (2021). https://github.com/novifinancial/ed25519-dalek-fiat/tree/half-aggregation
19. Chalkias, K., Garillot, F., Nikolaenko, V.: Taming the many EDDSAS. Technical Report, Cryptology ePrint Archive, Report 2020/1244 (2020). https://eprint.iacr.org/2020/1244
20. Checkoway, S., et al.: A systematic analysis of the juniper dual EC incident. In: ACM CCS (2016)
21. Courtois, N.T., Emirdag, P., Valsorda, F.: Private key recovery combination attacks: on extreme fragility of popular bitcoin key management, wallet and cold storage solutions in presence of poor RNG events (2014)

22. Djvm - the deterministic JVM library (2020)
23. Drijvers, M., et al.: On the security of two-round multi-signatures. In: 2019 IEEE Symposium on Security and Privacy (SP), pp. 1084–1101. IEEE (2019)
24. Dryja, T.: Per-block non-interactive Schnorr signature aggregation (2017)
25. Everspaugh, A., Zhai, Y., Jellinek, R., Ristenpart, T., Swift, M.: Not-So-Random numbers in virtualized linux and the whirlwind RNG. In: 2014 IEEE Symposium on Security and Privacy, pp. 559–574. IEEE (May 2014)
26. Fernandes, D.A.B., Soares, L.F.B., Freire, M.M., Inacio, P.R.M.: Randomness in virtual machines. In: 2013 IEEE/ACM 6th International Conference on Utility and Cloud Computing, pp. 282–286. IEEE (Dec 2013)
27. Fiat, A., Shamir, A.: How to prove yourself: practical solutions to identification and signature problems. In: Crypto (1987)
28. Fischlin, M.: Communication-efficient non-interactive proofs of knowledge with online extractors. In: Crypto (2005)
29. Fleischhacker, N., Jager, T., Schröder, D.: On tight security proofs for Schnorr signatures. J. Cryptol. $32(2)$, 566–599 (2019)
30. Fuchsbauer, G., Kiltz, E., Loss, J.: The algebraic group model and its applications. In: Crypto (2018)
31. Fuchsbauer, G., Plouviez, A., Seurin, Y.: Blind Schnorr signatures and signed elgamal encryption in the algebraic group model. In: Eurocrypt (2020)
32. Bundesamt für Sicherheit in der Informationstechnik (BSI). Elliptic curve cryptography, Technical Guideline TR-03111 (2009)
33. Gennaro, R., Leigh, D., Sundaram, R., Yerazunis, W.S.: Batching Schnorr identification scheme with applications to privacy-preserving authorization and low-bandwidth communication devices. In: Asiacrypt (2004)
34. Hamburg, M.: Ed448-goldilocks, a new elliptic curve. Cryptology ePrint Archive, Report 2015/625 (2015). http://eprint.iacr.org/2015/625
35. Hazay, C., Lindell, Y.: Efficient Secure Two-Party Protocols: Techniques and Constructions, 1st edn. Springer-Verlag, Berlin (2010)
36. Hazay, C., Lindell, Y.: A note on zero-knowledge proofs of knowledge and the ZKPOK ideal functionality. IACR Cryptol. ePrint Arch. 2010, 552 (2010)
37. Heninger, N., Durumeric, Z., Wustrow, E., Halderman, J.A.: Mining your PS and QS: detection of widespread weak keys in network devices. In: USENIX Security Symposium (2012)
38. Itakura, K., Nakamura, K.: A public-key cryptosystem suitable for digital multisignatures. In: NEC Research & Development (1983)
39. Josefsson, S., Liusvaara, I.: Edwards-curve digital signature algorithm (EdDSA) (2017)
40. Kerrigan, B., Chen, Yu.: A study of entropy sources in cloud computers: random number generation on cloud hosts. In: Kotenko, I., Skormin, V. (eds.) MMM-ACNS 2012. LNCS, vol. 7531, pp. 286–298. Springer, Heidelberg (2012). https://doi.org/10.1007/978-3-642-33704-8_24
41. Komlo, C., Goldberg, I.: Frost: flexible round-optimized Schnorr threshold signatures. IACR Cryptol. ePrint Arch (2020)
42. Kumari, R., Alimomeni, M., Safavi-Naini, R.: Performance analysis of linux RNG in virtualized environments. In: ACM Workshop on Cloud Computing Security Workshop (2015)
43. Ma, C., Weng, J., Li, Y., Deng, R.: Efficient discrete logarithm based multisignature scheme in the plain public key model. Designs Codes Cryptograph. $54(2)$, 121–133 (2010)

44. Maxwell, G., Poelstra, A., Seurin, Y., Wuille, P.: Simple Schnorr multi-signatures with applications to bitcoin. Cryptology ePrint Archive, Report 2018/068 (2018). https://eprint.iacr.org/2018/068
45. Maxwell, G., Poelstra, A., Seurin, Y., Wuille, P.: Simple Schnorr multi-signatures with applications to bitcoin. Designs Codes Cryptograph. **87**(9), 2139–2164 (2019)
46. Micali, S., Ohta, K., Reyzin, L.: Accountable-subgroup multisignatures. In: ACM CCS (2001)
47. Michaelis, Kai., Meyer, Christopher, Schwenk, Jörg: Randomly failed! the state of randomness in current java implementations. In: Dawson, Ed (ed.) CT-RSA 2013. LNCS, vol. 7779, pp. 129–144. Springer, Heidelberg (2013). https://doi.org/10.1007/978-3-642-36095-4_9
48. Neven, G., Smart, N.P., Warinschi, B.: Hash function requirements for Schnorr signatures. J. Math. Cryptol. **3**(1), 69–87 (2009)
49. Nick, J., Ruffing, T., Seurin, Y.: Musig2: Simple two-round Schnorr multi-signatures. IACR Cryptol. ePrint Arch. Technical Report (2020)
50. Nick, J., Ruffing, T., Seurin, Y., Wuille, P.: Musig-dn: Schnorr multi-signatures with verifiably deterministic nonces. In: ACM CCS (2020)
51. Pass, R.: On deniability in the common reference string and random oracle model. In: Crypto (2003)
52. Pieter, W., Jonas, N., Tim.: BIP: 340, Schnorr signatures for secp256k1 (2020)
53. Pointcheval, D., Stern, J.: Security proofs for signature schemes. In: Eurocrypt (1996)
54. Pointcheval, D., Stern, J.: Security arguments for digital signatures and blind signatures. J. Cryptol. **13**(3), 361–396 (2000)
55. Ristenpart, T., Yilek, S.: When good randomness goes bad: virtual machine reset vulnerabilities and hedging deployed cryptography. In: NDSS (2010)
56. Ristenpart, T., Yilek, S.: The power of proofs-of-possession: securing multiparty signatures against rogue-key attacks. In: Eurocrypt (2007)
57. Schnorr, C.-P.: Efficient signature generation by smart cards. J. Cryptol. **4**(3), 161–174 (1991)
58. Seurin, Y.: On the exact security of Schnorr-type signatures in the random oracle model. In: Eurocrypt (2012)
59. Shoup, V.: Lower bounds for discrete logarithms and related problems. In: Eurocrypt (1997)
60. Syta, E.: Keeping authorities "honest or bust" with decentralized witness cosigning. In: IEEE S&P (2016)
61. Yilek, S., Rescorla, E., Shacham, H., Enright, B., Savage, S.: When private keys are public: Results from the 2008 Debian OpenSSL vulnerability. In: ACM SIGCOMM Internet Measurement Conference IMC (2009)
62. Zhao, Y.: Aggregation of gamma-signatures and applications to bitcoin. IACR Cryptol. ePrint Arch. **2018**, 414 (2018)

A Framework to Optimize Implementations of Matrices

Da Lin, Zejun Xiang$^{(\boxtimes)}$, Xiangyong Zeng, and Shasha Zhang

Faculty of Mathematics and Statistics, Hubei Key Laboratory of Applied
Mathematics, Hubei University, Wuhan, China
linda@stu.hubu.edu.cn, {xiangzejun,xzeng}@hubu.edu.cn

Abstract. In this paper, we propose several reduction rules to optimize the given implementation of a binary matrix over $\mathbb{F}_2$. Moreover, we design a top-layer framework which can make use of the existing search algorithms for solving SLP problems as well as our proposed reduction rules. Thus, efficient implementations of matrices with fewer XOR gates can be expected with the framework. Our framework outperforms algorithms such as Paar1, RPaar1, BP, BFI, RNBP, A1 and A2 when tested on random matrices with various densities and those matrices designed in recent literature. Notably, we find an implementation of AES MixColumns using only 91 XORs, which is currently the shortest implementation to the best of our knowledge.

Keywords: Binary matrix · SLP · XOR gate · AES MixColumns

1 Introduction

As the main role to provide diffusion, which is proposed by Shannon [33] as one of the fundamental design principles of cryptographic primitives, the linear layer has been widely concerned and designed elaborately. The linear layer of a cipher can be generally represented by a linear function from $\mathbb{F}_2^n$ to $\mathbb{F}_2^m$, which takes $(x_0, x_1, \cdots, x_{n-1})$ as the input and $(y_0, y_1, \cdots, y_{m-1})$ as the output.

A linear layer with good cryptographic properties can help to resist some well-known attacks, such as differential attack [8] and linear attack [24]. Following the wide trail design strategy, a maximum distance separable (MDS for short) matrix is adopted by AES [13] to provide optimal resistance to differential attack and linear attack. Meanwhile, lightweight cryptography has received a lot of attention in the past decade as the resource constrained devices have been used in a wide range. The software or hardware or both of them need to be considered in the design of lightweight cryptographic primitives. Thus, this has inspired the design of lightweight components, which could be used to design lightweight ciphers [14, 17, 20–23]. On the other hand, optimizing the implementation of various components already used in standard ciphers is another line of research, which could largely reduce the cost of a cipher and is of much practical significance [2, 19, 40].

© Springer Nature Switzerland AG 2021
K. G. Paterson (Ed.): CT-RSA 2021, LNCS 12704, pp. 609–632, 2021.
https://doi.org/10.1007/978-3-030-75539-3_25

Owing to the comprehensive researches on S-box, there are some tools or platforms [3,7,15,17,27,36] can be used to search for optimized implementation of S-box focusing on various criteria, for instance, bitslice gate complexity, gate equivalent complexity, multiplicative complexity and depth complexity. Gate equivalent complexity and depth complexity have also been discussed in linear layers. In order to optimize the gate equivalent complexity of a matrix, one should consider the implementation of this matrix with the smallest XOR-gate count. However, if the depth complexity is considered, the longest path connecting the input and the output should be minimized.

The problem of finding the implementation of a matrix with the fewest XOR gates is NP-hard [9,10]. Thus, the SAT-based method [36] and LIGHTER [17] can provide optimal implementation for small matrices but may fail for large domain size. However, there are still many heuristics that could give quite good implementations. The two mostly used heuristics were proposed in [28] and [11]. It is worth noting that Paar's algorithms [28] are *cancellation-free*, which means the operands in the gates sharing no common variable. Besides, Boyar-Peralta's (BP) algorithm [11] would be time-consuming when the matrix is dense. To remedy this, Visconti *et al.* computed the targets by creating a complement instance of the given matrix and generating a "common path" [38]. This improvement of BP algorithm is based on the fact that the complement of a dense matrix is sparse. There are many other variants of BP algorithm which differ in the tie-breaking phase [2,21,26,29,37]. In [29], three algorithms named Improved-BP, Shortest-Dist-First and Focused-Search were proposed. With the attention paid to the construction of lightweight involutory MDS matrices, Li *et al.* introduced the depth into BP algorithm to search implementations with limited depth in [21]. The constraint on circuit depth has also been discussed in [26], where Maximov and Ekdahl required that each input or output bit has its own delay. Given a matrix M, a new method based on BP algorithm that left-multiplying and right-multiplying M with randomly generated permutation matrices was introduced in [2] by Banik *et al.*, the best result will be kept after running the algorithm multiple times. In the following, we will use BFI to denote Banik *et al.*'s method for short. In CHES-2020 [37], Tan and Peyrin presented several improved BP algorithms (RNBP, A1 and A2) by inducing randomisation or focusing on the nearest target in a way different from Shortest-Dist-First algorithm proposed in [29]. Recently, a quite different heuristic based on the decomposition of matrix was proposed in [40]. The cost of a matrix is equivalently treated as the number of type-3 elementary matrices, thus, optimizing a matrix is to find a matrix decomposition with fewest type-3 elementary matrices. Similar to BFI, we will denote Xiang *et al.*'s heuristic by XZLBZ in this paper. In addition to those heuristics focusing on 2-input XOR gates, there are also researches take the 3-input XOR gates into consideration [1,2]. Besides BFI algorithm, Banik *et al.* also proposed a graph based heuristic in [2] to find a circuit occupies less area, the implementation produced in this way is constructed by using both 2-input and 3-input XOR gates. Not long afterward, Baski *et al.* introduced 3-input XOR into BP algorithm in [1] and improved the implementation of AES MixColumns based on the algorithms RNBP and BFI.

Contributions. In this paper we propose a top-layer framework for searching optimized implementation of matrices. Our framework consists of two building blocks, one of which is the combination of several mostly used heuristics for optimizing matrix implementation. Another building block is a reduction procedure we proposed to further reduce the cost of a given matrix implementation. These two building blocks are combined in an interactive way such that it could produce better implementation in a wide range compared with previous results. Specifically, we first generate an implementation of a given matrix by one of the heuristics embedded in our framework, then our reduction procedure is performed to further reduce the cost. These two steps will be executed iteratively in a way that part of the implementation is replaced by an equivalent one using again one of the heuristics embedded in our framework. Note that we can choose different heuristics each time when necessary within the search process. Thus, one of the advantages of this framework is that it can inherently inherit the merits of all heuristics. Moreover, due to the modular design of our framework, it enjoys the extra advantage that other heuristics for optimizing matrix implementation can be easily incorporated into our framework, even for heuristics that might be proposed in the future.

In order to prove the effectiveness of our reduction procedure, we fix the heuristic and use our framework to search for further improvements of the implementations provided by RNBP, A1 and A2. The experimental results shown in Fig. 1 reveal that even though RNBP, A1 or A2 can provide quite good implementations, XOR count can still be reduced by the reduction procedure of our framework. Moreover, we test the whole framework on these matrices with the same running time as in [37]. The results show that our framework can find the best implementation with an overwhelming percentage, especially for small matrices (i.e., 15×15 and 16×16). The results are shown in Table 4. We also test our framework on those recently proposed matrices. Compared with the implementations of [2,19,40], the results in Table 5 show that our framework can further reduce the cost in most cases. For most matrices from [14], our framework outperforms BP, Paar2, RSDF, RNBP, A1 and A2 in most cases (20 out of 24 matrices). Finally, the framework is used to implement the matrices used in block ciphers or hash functions and the results are given in Table 7. Even though the AES MixColumns has been widely optimized, it can still be improved by our framework. As a new record, an implementation of AES MixColumns requiring only 91 XORs (beating all previous records) is first reported in this paper (shown in Table 8).

Organization. The rest of the paper is organized as follows. Section 2 presents some notations and several heuristics in the open literature. In Sect. 3, a reduction procedure for optimizing a given matrix implementation is proposed. In Sect. 4, we present our general search framework. We present the applications of this framework on various matrices in Sect. 5. Finally, Sect. 6 concludes the paper.

2   Preliminaries

2.1   Notations

Let $\mathbb{F}_2$ denote the finite field with two elements 0 and 1, and $\mathbb{F}_2^n$ denote the n-dimensional vector space over $\mathbb{F}_2$. Let $X = (x_0, x_1, \cdots, x_{n-1}) \in \mathbb{F}_2^n$ denote an n-bit vector, where x_i is the ith coordinate of X. We use $\mathbb{F}_{2^s}$ to denote the finite field with 2^s elements. $M_{m \times n}$ denotes an $m \times n$ matrix over $\mathbb{F}_2$. We use $\oplus$ and $\&$ to represent XOR and AND operations over $\mathbb{F}_2$. The Hamming weight of a matrix M is denoted by $wt(M)$, which counts the number of 1's contained in M.

2.2   Existing Heuristics for Optimizing Matrix Implementation

We give a brief overview in this subsection of several open heuristics for searching optimized matrix implementation under different metrics. The g-XOR metric of a matrix counts the number of operations $x_i = x_j \oplus x_k$ ($0 \leq j, k < i$ and $i = n, n+1, \cdots, t-1$) that implement the corresponding linear transformation, and the s-XOR metric of a matrix counts the number of operations $x_i = x_i \oplus x_j$ ($0 \leq i, j < n - 1$ that implement the corresponding linear transformation.

Paar's Algorithm. In [28], Paar studied how to find efficient arithmetic for Reed-Solomon encoders which were based on feed-back shift registers. Two algorithms were proposed to optimize the multiplication with a constant in $\mathbb{F}_{2^n}$.

Given a binary matrix over $\mathbb{F}_2$, the first algorithm, known as Paar1, precompute the bitwise AND of all possible pairs of column c_i and c_j, where $i \neq j$ and $i, j \in \{0, 1, \cdots, n-1\}$. The product of $c_i \& c_j$ with the maximal Hamming weight will be kept as a new column and be added to the right of the matrix, and the columns c_i and c_j are updated as $c_i \oplus (c_i \& c_j)$ and $c_j \oplus (c_i \& c_j)$ respectively. Then the above steps are repeated on this new matrix until the Hamming weight of each row equals 1.

However, there might be multiple pairs of columns such that whose bitwise AND have the same maximal Hamming weight. If this situation occurs, Paar1 will select the one appears first while the second algorithm Paar2 will try all candidate pairs. As a result, Paar2 is more time-consuming than Paar1 but may yield an implementation with a lower cost. However, as mentioned in [37], Paar2 may not be efficient as the dimension of the matrices increases due to the exhaustive search. Therefore, we consider the randomised version of the Paar1 (i.e., RPaar1 in [37], which takes the candidates leading to the same maximal Hamming weight with equal possibility) rather than Paar2 in this paper.

BP Algorithm. Boyar and Peralta proposed a new heuristic in [11] for minimizing the number of XOR gates needed to implement a matrix.

Denote $x_0, x_1, \cdots, x_{n-1}$ and $y_0, y_1, \cdots, y_{m-1}$ the n input bits and the m output bits of an $m \times n$ matrix M. Thus, y_i's can be expressed as linear Boolean functions over x_j's. Boyar and Peralta's heuristic defined two parameters. One parameter is the base S which records the set of known variables (or expressions). Another parameter is the distance vector $Dist[]$, and

$Dist = (\delta(S, y_0), \delta(S, y_1), \cdots, \delta(S, y_{m-1}))$, where $\delta(S, y_i)$ indicates the minimum number of XORs required that can obtain y_i from S.

Initially, the heuristic first include all input variables $x_0, x_1, \cdots, x_{n-1}$ into the base S, and the distance vector $Dist[\,]$ is initialized as the Hamming weight of each row minus one, i.e., $Dist[i] = \delta(S, y_i) = wt(M_i) - 1$, $i \in [0, m-1]$, where M_i denotes the ith row of M. Then the heuristic picks two variables from S and denotes the sum of these two variables by a new variable, such that if this new variable is added into S, the sum of the new distance vector can be minimized. BP algorithm performs the above steps until all elements of $Dist[\,]$ are zero. In each step when choosing a new base element, if there are more than one candidates that can minimize the sum of the new distance vector, the Euclidean Norm will be utilized to resolve ties, only the one that maximizes the Euclidean Norm of the updated vector $Dist[\,]$ can be added to S.

BP algorithm is not that efficient as Paar1, since the process of picking new base element is time-consuming. The strategy of *pre-emptive*, which usually improves running time without increasing the cost, is given in [11] that the XOR of two base element $S[i]$ and $S[j]$ will be picked directly if $S[i] \oplus S[j]$ is equal to an output bit.

Banik *et al.*'s Algorithm. Banik *et al.* proposed a new idea based on BP algorithm in [2]. For a given matrix M, Banik *et al.* first randomly generated two permutation matrices P and Q. Then, they computed $M_R = P \cdot M \cdot Q$ and took M_R as the input of BP algorithm. In order to find an implementation with fewer XOR gates, the algorithm will be run multiple times with new randomly generated permutation matrices each time.

BFI algorithm is based on the fact that the order of rows/columns does no change the underlying linear system, thus the cost for implementing matrices M and M_R are the same. More specifically, left-multiplying a permutation matrix P is equivalent to rearranging the rows of M, while right-multiplying a permutation Q is equivalent to rearranging the columns of M. These operations only change the orders of the inputs and the outputs of matrix M, but may influence the implementation given by BP algorithm.

Tan and Peyrin's Algorithm. Tan and Peyrin proposed three modified non-deterministic global heuristics in [37] to find optimized implementation of matrices: RNBP, A1 and A2, which are variants of BP heuristic.

The RNBP (Randomised-Normal-BP) differs in the tie-breaking phase with BP algorithm. In the original BP algorithm, if there are multiple candidates which all minimize the sum of the distance vector, one should compute the Euclidean Norm of these distance vectors and choose the candidate with the maximal Euclidean Norm. However, if there are still more than one candidates with the same maximal Euclidean Norm, BP algorithm will choose the first candidate or use some randomisation. Boyar and Peralta introduced randomisation in this phase in [11], where the first appeared candidate is chosen (or discarded) with probability $1/2$, and process the second candidate in a similar way if the first candidate is discarded. However, this leads to an unequal probability of choosing these equally good candidates. For this reason, RNBP treats these candidates equally and each one is chosen with a same probability.

The A1 algorithm is performed in four steps: Filtering, Selecting, Tie-breaker and Randomisation. In the Filtering step, the candidates that can reduce at least one of the nearest targets (whose corresponding value in $Dist$ vector is minimal and non-zero) are kept. Then, select the candidates in selecting phase that minimize the sum of distance vectors from those passing the filtering phase. If more than one candidates pass the first two steps, the Euclidean Norm will be used as a tie-breaker (i.e., choose the one with a maximal Euclidean Norm). If the tie-breaker fails to resolve the tie, the remaining candidates will be randomly picked with equal probability.

Algorithm A1 and A2 are approximately the same with the only difference that the Tie-breaker step is skipped in A2. A2 seems to provide more randomisation compared with A1, this may explain why A2 can get better results than A1 in most cases.

Xiang *et al.*'s Algorithm. In [40], Xiang *et al.* proposed a quite different heuristic based on matrix decomposition to search optimized implementation of invertible matrices. The authors first decomposed a given invertible matrix as a product of elementary matrices, and they showed that the implementation cost of the matrix is only related to the number of type-3 elementary matrices within the matrix decomposition if s-XOR metric is considered. Note that a type-3 elementary matrix in $\mathbb{F}_2$ is a matrix produced by adding a row (column) of the identity matrix to another row (column). Based on this observation, the authors converted the problem of optimizing matrix implementation to the problem of finding a matrix decomposition with as fewer type-3 elementary matrices as possible. Thus, the authors presented three strategies to decompose a matrix based on the theory of linear algebra. Moreover, the authors also presented seven rules of elementary matrix multiplication over $\mathbb{F}_2$ in order to further reduce the number of type-3 elementary matrices. Combined with these seven rules, the new heuristic can be roughly divided into two steps. The first step is to decompose the given matrix into a product of elementary matrices, and the second step is to build a lot of equivalent decompositions to be optimized by using the seven rules. However, this heuristic can be only applied to invertible matrices since only invertible matrices can be decomposed as a product of elementary matrices.

2.3 Techniques for Optimizing a Given Implementation

Although searching an optimized implementation of a matrix has been studied extensively (see Sect. 2.2), however, there is still room for further improvements by directly optimizing a given matrix implementation.

Tan and Peyrin introduced two local optimization techniques in [37]. The first technique called *swapping orders* is to identify and rearrange the operations within a special part of an implementation aiming at finding some repeat operations as well as reducing the gate depth. In the second technique, an implementation is represented by a tree, and each XOR operation is stored in a binary tree with three nodes. Then, an exhaustive search is performed on a partial tree. Note that the tree structure of a matrix implementation is usually too large to perform exhaustive search on the whole tree.

In order to derive all the potential reduction rules in the *swapping orders* technique, we list in the following table all possible cases after *swapping orders* technique under different constraints on depth based on the sequence given in [37].

Table 1. Three possible sequences after *swapping orders*.

Given *seq*	Case 1		Case 2	Case 3
	if *depth(e)*<*max*{*depth(b)*, *depth(c)*}			if *depth(e)* ≥ *max*{*depth(b)*, *depth(c)*}
	if *depth(b)*<*depth(c)*	if *depth(b)* ≥ *depth(c)*		Remain unchanged
...	...		...	...
$a = b \oplus c$	$a = e \oplus b$		$a = e \oplus c$	$a = b \oplus c$
$d = a \oplus e$	$d = a \oplus c$		$d = a \oplus b$	$d = a \oplus e$
$f = b \oplus e$	$f = b \oplus e$		$f = b \oplus e$	$f = b \oplus e$
...	...		...	...

3   New Reduction for a Given Matrix Implementation

In this section, we first introduce several reduction rules to reduce the cost of a given implementation. Then, we present a reduction procedure based on these rules. For an $m \times n$ matrix M over $\mathbb{F}_2$, an implementation of M (in terms of g-XOR metric) is a sequence of l operations $t_i = t_j \oplus t_k$, $(i = n, n+1, \cdots, n+l-1$ and $j, k < i)$, where t_i are the n input bits for $i = 0, 1, \cdots, n-1$ and each of the m output bits equals to some t_i for $i = 0, 1, \cdots, n+l-1$. To simplify the representation, we will denote $t_i = t_j \oplus t_k$ by $t_{i,j,k}$ for short. Thus, an implementation of a matrix $M_{m \times n}$ can be represented as $seq = t_{n,j_0,k_0}, t_{n+1,j_1,k_1}, \cdots, t_{n+l-1,j_{l-1},k_{l-1}}$.

Reduction Rules. Given an implementation *seq* of matrix $M_{m \times n}$ with l XOR gates. Let $t_u, t_v, t_w, t_a, t_b, t_c$ be registers used for implementing $M_{m \times n}$, where $n \leqslant u < v < w \leqslant n + l - 1$ and $a \neq b \neq c$. Then the following reduction rules hold.

1. If operations $t_{u,a,b}$ and $t_{v,a,u}$ are contained in *seq*, then the values stored in t_v and t_b are identical, since $t_v = t_a \oplus t_u = t_a \oplus (t_a \oplus t_b) = t_b$. Thus $t_{v,a,u}$ can be removed and therefore reducing one XOR in *seq*. We would like to emphasis that before we delete $t_{v,a,u}$, we need to scrutinize all the operations besides $t_{u,a,b}$ and $t_{v,a,u}$ in *seq*, and replace t_v by t_b. Moreover, if t_u is only used in $t_{v,a,u}$, we can further reduce the implementation cost by removing $t_{u,a,b}$. The corresponding reduction rules are listed as R1 and R2 in Table 2.

2. If operations $t_{u,a,b}$, $t_{v,c,u}$ and $t_{w,a,c}$ are contained in *seq*. We can observe that the value stored in t_v can also be obtained by $t_b \oplus t_w$ with the condition that t_w has to be generated before t_v (Note that this is always true, since t_a, t_c are generated before t_v). If t_u is only used in $t_{v,c,u}$, we can remove t_u and replace $t_{v,c,u}$ by $t_{v,b,w}$, which leads to the reduction of one XOR gate as show with R3 in Table 2.

3. If operations $t_{u,a,b}$, $t_{v,a,c}$ and $t_{w,c,u}$ are contained in *seq*. The value stored in t_w can also be obtained by $t_b \oplus t_v$. If t_u is only used in $t_{w,c,u}$, one XOR can be saved by removing t_u and replacing $t_{w,c,u}$ by $t_{w,b,v}$. The procedure is shown in Table 2 with R4.

4. If operations $t_{u,a,b}$, $t_{v,a,c}$ and $t_{w,b,v}$ are contained in *seq*. Note that t_w can also be generated by $t_c \oplus t_u$. We can remove t_v and replace $t_{w,b,v}$ by $t_{w,c,u}$ if t_v is only used in $t_{w,b,v}$. The reduction rule is listed as R5 in Table 2.

5. If operations $t_{u,a,b}$, $t_{v,c,u}$ and $t_{w,a,v}$ are contained in *seq*. The value stored in t_w is equal to $t_b \oplus t_c$, and we can replace $t_{w,a,v}$ by $t_{w,b,c}$. Clearly, we can remove t_v if t_v is only used in $t_{w,a,v}$ (see R6 in Table 2). Otherwise, t_v should be kept. However, we can utilize t_w to generate t_v by $t_v = t_a \oplus t_w$. In this case, the order of generating t_v and t_w is changed, and this requires the condition t_w has to be generated before t_v. This may make us achieve an possible improvement by removing t_u if t_u is only used in $t_{v,c,u}$ and replacing $t_{v,c,u}$ by $t_{v,a,w}$ (R7 in Table 2). Specially, if both t_u and t_v are only used once (i.e. t_u is only used in $t_{v,c,u}$ and t_v is only used in $t_{w,a,v}$), we can delete both of them, thus reduce the implementation cost by 2 XORs (R8 in Table 2).

6. If operations $t_{u,a,b}$, $t_{v,a,c}$ and $t_{w,u,v}$ are contained in *seq*, clearly we have $t_w = t_b \oplus t_c$. If t_u is only used in $t_{w,u,v}$, one XOR can be saved by removing t_u and replacing $t_{w,u,v}$ by $t_{w,b,c}$ (R9 in Table 2). If t_v is only used in $t_{w,u,v}$, we can remove t_v and replace $t_{w,u,v}$ by $t_{w,b,c}$ to save one XOR (R10 in Table 2). Specially, if both t_u and t_v are only used once, it will save 2 XORs by removing t_u and t_v (R11 in Table 2).

Note that the prerequisite that these reduction rules hold is the output of each deleted XOR operation cannot be the output of the matrix. The core idea of the reduction rules is that XORing the same value will cancel each other in $\mathbb{F}_2$. Note that the order of operations might be changed within several rules, such as R3 and R7, which rearrange the order of t_v and t_w. This is based on the fact that the newly generated value can never be used before. Thus, we can safely move it forward if the two operands on the right have been obtained. Take R3 as an example, the original value stored in t_v is $t_c \oplus t_u$, which means t_c has been generated before t_v. Similarly, t_a has been generated before t_u. Thus, it is available to use t_a and t_c to obtain t_w right before t_v.

Meanwhile, the order of operations may affect the reduction. Indeed, our proposed rules have taken the order of operations into consideration. We can notice that the three operations in R3 and R4 are similar except the order, both of them can help to reduce one XOR but produce different resulting implementations.

Reduction Rules Derived from [37]. Given the sequence as in Table 1, we can find that our proposed rule R3 will provide the same sequence as *swapping orders*

Table 2. The reduction rules to reduce gate count.

Xor Gates	R1	R2	R3	R4
original	... $t_u = t_a \oplus t_b$ ... $t_v = t_a \oplus t_u$ ...	... $t_u = t_a \oplus t_b$ ... $t_v = t_a \oplus t_u$ ...	... $t_u = t_a \oplus t_b$ ... $t_v = t_c \oplus t_u$ ... $t_w = t_a \oplus t_c$ ...	... $t_u = t_a \oplus t_b$ ... $t_v = t_a \oplus t_c$ ... $t_w = t_c \oplus t_u$ ...
reduced	... $t_u = t_a \oplus t_b$ ... ~~$t_v = t_a \oplus t_u$~~ $t_v = t_b$ ...	... ~~$t_u = t_a \oplus t_b$~~ ... ~~$t_v = t_a \oplus t_u$~~ $t_v = t_b$ ...	... ~~$t_u = t_a \oplus t_b$~~ $t_w = t_a \oplus t_c$ ~~$t_v = t_c \oplus t_u$~~ $t_v = t_b \oplus t_w$ ... ~~$t_w = t_a \oplus t_c$~~ ...	... ~~$t_u = t_a \oplus t_b$~~ ... $t_v = t_a \oplus t_c$ ... ~~$t_w = t_c \oplus t_u$~~ $t_w = t_b \oplus t_v$ ...
condition	none	t_u is only used in $t_{v,a,u}$	t_u is only used in $t_{v,c,u}$	t_u is only used in $t_{w,c,u}$

Xor Gates	R5	R6	R7	R8
original	... $t_u = t_a \oplus t_b$ ... $t_v = t_a \oplus t_c$ ... $t_w = t_b \oplus t_v$ ...	... $t_u = t_a \oplus t_b$ ... $t_v = t_c \oplus t_u$ ... $t_w = t_a \oplus t_v$ ...	... $t_u = t_a \oplus t_b$ ... $t_v = t_c \oplus t_u$ ... $t_w = t_a \oplus t_v$ ...	... $t_u = t_a \oplus t_b$ ... $t_v = t_c \oplus t_u$ ... $t_w = t_a \oplus t_v$ ...
reduced	... $t_u = t_a \oplus t_b$ ... ~~$t_v = t_a \oplus t_c$~~ ... ~~$t_w = t_b \oplus t_v$~~ $t_w = t_c \oplus t_u$ ...	... $t_u = t_a \oplus t_b$ ... ~~$t_v = t_c \oplus t_u$~~ ... ~~$t_w = t_a \oplus t_v$~~ $t_w = t_b \oplus t_c$ ...	... ~~$t_u = t_a \oplus t_b$~~ ... $t_w = t_b \oplus t_c$ ~~$t_v = t_c \oplus t_u$~~ $t_v = t_a \oplus t_w$ ... ~~$t_w = t_a \oplus t_v$~~	... ~~$t_u = t_a \oplus t_b$~~ ... ~~$t_v = t_c \oplus t_u$~~ ... ~~$t_w = t_a \oplus t_v$~~ $t_w = t_b \oplus t_c$ ...
condition	t_v is only used in $t_{w,b,v}$	t_v is only used in $t_{w,a,v}$	t_u is only used in $t_{v,c,u}$	t_u is only used in $t_{v,c,u}$ t_v is only used in $t_{w,a,v}$

Xor Gates	R9	R10	R11	
original	... $t_u = t_a \oplus t_b$ ... $t_v = t_a \oplus t_c$ ... $t_w = t_u \oplus t_v$ ...	... $t_u = t_a \oplus t_b$ ... $t_v = t_a \oplus t_c$ ... $t_w = t_u \oplus t_v$ ...	... $t_u = t_a \oplus t_b$ ... $t_v = t_a \oplus t_c$ ... $t_w = t_u \oplus t_v$ ...	
reduced	... ~~$t_u = t_a \oplus t_b$~~ ... $t_v = t_a \oplus t_c$ ... ~~$t_w = t_u \oplus t_v$~~ $t_w = t_b \oplus t_c$ ...	... $t_u = t_a \oplus t_b$ ... ~~$t_v = t_a \oplus t_c$~~ ... ~~$t_w = t_u \oplus t_v$~~ $t_w = t_b \oplus t_c$ ...	... ~~$t_u = t_a \oplus t_b$~~ ... ~~$t_v = t_a \oplus t_c$~~ ... ~~$t_w = t_u \oplus t_v$~~ $t_w = t_b \oplus t_c$ ...	
condition	t_u is only used in $t_{w,u,v}$	t_v is only used in $t_{w,u,v}$	t_u is only used in $t_{w,u,v}$ t_v is only used in $t_{w,u,v}$	

under the condition $depth(b)<depth(c)$ and $depth(e)<max\{depth(b),depth(c)\}$ (as case 1 shown in Table 1). In this case, our rule R3 is the same as the *swapping orders* technique. Besides, as mentioned in [37], the *swapping orders* technique focus on the gate depth, which means the reduction procedure shown in Table 1 are based on the condition that $depth(e)<max\{depth(b),depth(c)\}$, but if $depth(e) \geq max\{depth(b),depth(c)\}$, the given sequence will remain unchanged, and *swapping orders* will cause no reduction (see case 3 in Table 1). Since we focus only on the XOR count, R3 will reduce one XOR in any case, i.e. we do not consider the depth. Therefore, R3 is a variant of *swapping orders* but more general. As well as R4 and R5, for the reason that they can be seen as containing the same gates with R3 but only differ in gate order. The rest rules listed in Table 2 can help to reduce the cost in a way different from the *swapping orders* technique, which can be verified in a similar way as above.

Reduction Procedure. We present in Algorithm 1 a reduction procedure which exploits the reduction rules listed in Table 2 to optimize a given implementation.

A toy example is listed here to illustrate the usage of Algorithm 1.

Example 1. Given a matrix M,

$$M = \begin{bmatrix} 1 & 1 & 0 & 0 \\ 0 & 1 & 1 & 0 \\ 1 & 0 & 1 & 1 \\ 0 & 1 & 0 & 1 \end{bmatrix}$$

and its implementation *seq* which is shown in the column "Given *seq*" of Table 3, we have $seq = t_{4,2,3}, t_{5,1,3}, t_{6,0,3}, t_{7,4,5}, t_{8,4,6}, t_{9,4,7}, t_{10,3,7}, t_{11,7,8}, t_{12,10,11}$ initially. Algorithm 1 will perform the loop to find reductions and update *seq* as follows:

- The operation tuple $(t_{4,2,3}, t_{5,1,3}, t_{7,4,5})$ satisfies R10. Thus, we can remove t_5, and replace $t_{7,4,5}$ by $t_{7,1,2}$. *seq* is updated as $seq = t_{4,2,3}, t_{6,0,3}, t_{7,1,2}, t_{8,4,6}, t_{9,4,7}, t_{10,3,7}, t_{11,7,8}, t_{12,10,11}$;
- The operation tuple $(t_{4,2,3}, t_{6,0,3}, t_{8,4,6})$ satisfies R10, and we can remove t_6 and replace $t_{8,4,6}$ by $t_{8,0,2}$. *seq* is updated as $seq = t_{4,2,3}, t_{7,1,2}, t_{8,0,2}, t_{9,4,7}, t_{10,3,7}, t_{11,7,8}, t_{12,10,11}$;
- The operation tuple $(t_{4,2,3}, t_{7,1,2}, t_{9,4,7})$ satisfies R9. We can remove t_4 and replace $t_{9,4,7}$ by $t_{9,1,3}$. *seq* is updated as $seq = t_{7,1,2}, t_{8,0,2}, t_{9,1,3}, t_{10,3,7}, t_{11,7,8}, t_{12,10,11}$;
- The operation tuple $(t_{7,1,2}, t_{8,0,2}, t_{11,7,8})$ satisfies R10. We can remove t_8, and replace $t_{11,7,8}$ by $t_{11,0,1}$. *seq* is updated as $seq = t_{7,1,2}, t_{9,1,3}, t_{10,3,7}, t_{11,0,1}, t_{12,10,11}$;

There is no longer any tuple satisfying R1–R11 at this point, thus, the optimized implementation of M is shown in the column "Optimized *seq*" of Table 3.

Table 3. The implementation of M.

No.	Given seq	Optimized seq	No.	Given seq	Optimized seq
1	$t_4 = t_2 \oplus t_3$	Removed	6	$t_9 = t_4 \oplus t_7\,[y_3]$	$t_9 = t_1 \oplus t_3\,[y_3]$
2	$t_5 = t_1 \oplus t_3$	Removed	7	$t_{10} = t_3 \oplus t_7$	$t_{10} = t_3 \oplus t_7$
3	$t_6 = t_0 \oplus t_3$	Removed	8	$t_{11} = t_7 \oplus t_8\,[y_0]$	$t_{11} = t_0 \oplus t_1\,[y_0]$
4	$t_7 = t_4 \oplus t_5\,[y_1]$	$t_7 = t_1 \oplus t_2\,[y_1]$	9	$t_{12} = t_{10} \oplus t_{11}\,[y_2]$	$t_{12} = t_{10} \oplus t_{11}\,[y_2]$
5	$t_8 = t_4 \oplus t_6$	Removed			

Algorithm 1. Cost Reduction for a Given Matrix Implementation

---

Input: The implementation $seq = t_{n,j_0,k_0}, t_{n+1,j_1,k_1}, \cdots, t_{n+l-1,j_{l-1},k_{l-1}}$ for a given $m \times n$
   matrix M;
Output: Reduced implementation **Reduce**(seq) of M;
1: $flag \leftarrow True$;
2: $l \leftarrow |seq|$;   ▷ XOR count of seq
3: **while** $flag$ **do**
4:     $flag \leftarrow False$;
5:     **for** $u = n, n+l-2$ **do**
6:         **for** $v = u+1, n+l-1$ **do**
7:             **if** the operations in t_u and t_v match R1 or R2 in Section 3 **then**
8:                 reduce seq and update seq;
9:                 $l \leftarrow |seq|$;
10:                $flag \leftarrow True$;
11:                break;
12:            **end if**
13:            **for** $w = v+1, n+l-1$ **do**
14:                **if** the operations in t_u, t_v, t_w match one of R3-R11 in Section 3 **then**
15:                    reduce seq and update seq;
16:                    $l \leftarrow |seq|$;
17:                    $flag \leftarrow True$;
18:                    break;
19:                **end if**
20:            **end for**
21:            **if** $flag$ **then**
22:                break;
23:            **end if**
24:        **end for**
25:        **if** $flag$ **then**
26:            break;
27:        **end if**
28:    **end for**
29: **end while**
       return seq;

---

4   A General Framework of Optimization

Algorithm 1 presented in Sect. 3 can be used to possibly reduce the cost of any given implementation of matrices. However, if we only apply Algorithm 1 to the resulting implementations of existing heuristics (i.e., Paar1, RPaar1, BP, BFI,

RNBP, A1, A2 and Xiang *et al.*'s heuristic), the optimization effect may not be very satisfactory. There are two reasons for this. Since there are seven heuristics available for us, we can only apply Algorithm 1 to at most seven (Xiang *et al.*'s heuristic cannot be used if the matrix considered is not invertible) instances of implementation of a given matrix, and it is likely that there are not so many reductions with such a few instances. Another reason is due to the inherent optimization of those heuristics. For example, the A1 algorithm may run the procedure multiple times and return the best one. This optimized implementation is hard for us to further reduce the cost. Thus, we present a framework in this section which is able to combine the existing heuristics and generate a sufficiently large number of implementations of a given matrix. Then, we apply Algorithm 1 to those implementations and keep the best record. It should be noted that BFI algorithm shuffles the rows and columns of the target matrix, and then applies BP algorithm (Paar's algorithms for large matrices) to find a better solution. In fact, we can take the product matrix obtained by left-mutiplying and right-multiplying random permutation matrices with the target matrix as the input of any other heuristics introduced in Sect. 2.2. Therefore, in this paper we modify BFI algorithm, and combine their method with all the other heuristics.

Note that Xiang *et al.*'s heuristic has used the idea of generating a lot of decompositions of a given matrix. The authors achieved this idea by picking out a segment from the decomposition and replacing this part by another one which was considered as the equivalent decomposition of the chosen segment. Clearly, due to the feature of their heuristic by using s-XOR metric and matrix decomposition, the product of any selected segment is an invertible matrix with the same size of the original matrix. In the following, we extend this technique in a more general and elaborate way.

Given an $m \times n$ matrix M and its implementation with l XOR operations $seq = t_{n,j_0,k_0}, t_{n+1,j_1,k_1}, \cdots, t_{n+l-1,j_{l-1},k_{l-1}}$, which is generated by using one of the heuristics introduced in Sect. 2.2. We pick a set of consecutive XOR operations of seq with length g and denote those picked XOR operations t_{n+i,j_i,k_i}, $t_{n+i+1,j_{i+1},k_{i+1}}, \cdots, t_{n+i+g-1,j_{i+g-1},k_{i+g-1}}$ as seq', where $0 \leqslant i \leqslant l - g$. It is clear that such a sequence of XOR operations can define a matrix M'. It is worth noting that such a matrix M' is not necessary an invertible matrix, nor even a square matrix. With this recovered matrix M', we can use again one of the heuristics to find an implementation of M' which is then inserted into the original implementation sequence seq. Thus, an equivalent implementation of the original matrix M is generated. Since we can pick an arbitrary number (less than the total length of seq) of consecutive XOR operations from any part of seq, we can generate sufficiently many implementations from which it may yield a good one by applying Algorithm 1. We illustrate in Algorithm 2 our general framework, where **Imp**(M) returns an implementation of M using one of the heuristics, and **Recover**(seq) returns a matrix defined by seq.

Issues of Recovering M'. Intuitively, for any XOR operation $x_i = x_j \oplus x_k$ within seq', the two operands on the right side of the XOR operation is the inputs of

---

Algorithm 2. Search Optimized Matrix Implementation

Input: An $m \times n$ matrix M or

      An implementation $seq = t_{n,j_0,k_0}, t_{n+1,j_1,k_1}, \cdots, t_{n+l-1,j_{l-1},k_{l-1}}$ of a matrix;

Output: Optimized implementation;

1: **if** M is the input **then**

2:     $seq \leftarrow \mathbf{Imp}(M)$;   ▷ by Paar1 or RPaar1 or BP or BFI or RNBP or A1 or A2

3: **end if**

4: $seq \leftarrow \mathbf{Reduce}(seq)$;   ▷ Algorithm 1

5: $l \leftarrow |seq|$;   ▷ XOR count of seq

6: $g \leftarrow l$;

7: **while** $g \geq 2$ **do**

8:     $g = g - 1$;

9:     **for** $i = 0, l - g$ **do**

10:         $seq_1 = t_{n,j_0,k_0}, t_{n+1,j_1,k_1}, \cdots, t_{n+i-1,j_{i-1},k_{i-1}}$;

11:         $seq_2 = t_{n+i,j_i,k_i}, t_{n+i+1,j_{i+1},k_{i+1}}, \cdots, t_{n+i+g-1,j_{i+g-1},k_{i+g-1}}$;

12:         $seq_3 = t_{n+i+g,j_{i+g},k_{i+g}}, t_{n+i+g+1,j_{i+g+1},k_{i+g+1}}, \cdots, t_{n+l-1,j_{l-1},k_{l-1}}$;

13:         $M' = \mathbf{Recover}(seq_2)$;

14:         $seq_2' = \mathbf{Imp}(M')$; ▷ by Paar1 or RPaar1 or BP or BFI or RNBP or A1 or A2

15:         $seq' = seq_1 + seq_2' + seq_3$;

16:         $seq* \leftarrow \mathbf{Reduce}(seq')$ ▷ Algorithm 1

17:         **if** $|seq| > |seq*|$ **then**

18:             $seq = seq*$;

19:             $l = |seq*|$;

20:             $g \leftarrow l$;

21:             break;

22:         **end if**

23:     **end for**

24: **end while**

    return seq;

M', and the operand on the left side is the output of M'. However, we will show that it is a quite tricky process to identify the *real* inputs and the *real* outputs of M'. We first initialize two empty sets S_i and S_o. Then all the operands on the left side of the XOR operations within seq' are added to S_o. To identify the *real* outputs, we have to check each operand in S_o whether it is equal to some output bit of M or it is used anywhere in seq while outside seq', we can remove it from S_o if neither of these happens. After this process, S_o contains all the *real* outputs. Then, for each operand in S_o, we compute its linear expression over the inputs of the original matrix M by tracing backward according to seq and add the variables in the expression to S_i, i.e., the *real* inputs for a picked segment are a subset of the input of matrix M. Once the *real* inputs and the *real* outputs are identified, each operand in the *real* output set S_o can be expressed as a linear combination of the operands in S_i.

To elaborate the procedure of recovering the matrix M', we take the implementation of the matrix listed in Table 3 as an example.

Example 2. Let's consider the implementation listed in the column "Given *seq*" of Table 3, and we choose $t_{5,1,3}, t_{6,0,3}, t_{7,4,5}, t_{8,4,6}$ as a consecutive segment. Firstly we initialize $S_o = \{t_5, t_6, t_7, t_8\}$. Then, we keep t_7 as a *real* output since it stores the value of the output bit y_1. t_5 and t_6 should be removed because they are only used to generate t_7 and t_8 respectively, and never be used outside the segment. Thus the *real* outputs are $S_o = \{t_7, t_8\}$. Note that $t_7 = t_4 \oplus t_5$, where $t_4 = t_2 \oplus t_3$ and $t_5 = t_1 \oplus t_3$ are intermediate values. Thus, t_7 can be iteratively expressed as $t_7 = t_2 \oplus t_3 \oplus t_1 \oplus t_3 = t_1 \oplus t_2$, which indicates that t_1, t_2 should be included in the *real* inputs. Similarly, $t_8 = t_2 \oplus t_3 \oplus t_0 \oplus t_3 = t_0 \oplus t_2$. Therefore the *real* inputs are $S_i = \{t_1, t_2\} \cup \{t_0, t_2\} = \{t_0, t_1, t_2\}$, and the temporary matrix M' is

$$\begin{bmatrix} 0 & 1 & 1 \\ 1 & 0 & 1 \end{bmatrix}.$$

The equivalent matrix recovered in Example 2 verifies that we cannot always obtain an invertible matrix (nor even a square matrix), which restricts ourselves to Paar1, RPaar1, BP, BFI, RNBP, A1 and A2 for finding an implementation for the recovered matrix M'.

Note that each heuristic adopts randomisation within itself, thus it will generate different implementations for different calls even for the same matrix. Therefore, each time when Algorithm 2 is called it may obtain different results. Thus, we can run the procedure several times and keep the best one.

Advantage. Our framework is a unified framework to search optimized implementation of matrices. All heuristics are used as sub-modules in our framework, this makes our framework enjoy the advantage that anyone can easily incorporate his own heuristic into our framework as a sub-module, and make use of the reduction procedure (Algorithm 1) and our iterative search idea to further reduce the cost. In addition, our framework provides a lot of flexibility within itself. We do not fix which heuristic is used when necessary. For instance, one can use a fixed heuristic each time when it needed in our framework to get an implementation of a matrix. This situation is necessary when someone wants to compare the optimization effect of different heuristics. Besides, we can use this framework by randomly choosing a heuristic each time. Since each heuristic has its own advantages, this hybrid and combinatorial usage of random choices of heuristics may utilize the advantages of all heuristics.

The Implementation of Our Framework. Our framework is constructed based on the existing heuristics proposed in [2,11,28,37] and we use some openly available implementations for these heuristics. For BP and Paar1 algorithms, we use the implementations that are provided in the GitHub repository stated in [19]. RPaar1, which takes a candidate with equal possibility, is implemented by a slight tweaking of Paar1. As to RNBP, A1 and A2, we use the implementations given by Tan and Peyrin as they mentioned in [37]. In order to implement BFI algorithm, we generate two permutation matrices randomly and use them as the authors did in [2].

All the source codes of our framework are available at: https://github.com/DaLin10512/framework.

5   Applications

In this section, we apply our framework to a large number of matrices and compare the results with various search algorithms. We first introduce the following three functionalities that our framework can provide, which are based on the tweakable features described in Sect. 4.

1. **Direct Optimization** - Given a matrix, our framework can provide implementations with good performance in terms of XOR count using one of the heuristics embedded in our framework. This is a direct reapplication of the previous heuristics presented in [2, 11, 28, 37];
2. **Further Reduction** - Any given implementation can be loaded to Algorithm 2 as an input, thus, our framework can be used to search possible improvements of the given implementation;
3. **Iterative Optimization** - This functionality is almost the same as **Further Reduction**, the only difference is that the matrix is taken as the input of Algorithm 2 in this method.

Our framework can be used to search possible better implementations by running Algorithm 2 multiple times. Therefore, the approaches **Further Reduction** and **Iterative Optimization** may cost more time than the first method but a potentially better implementation can be expected in some situations.

5.1   Applications to Random Matrices

Tan and Peyrin tested their heuristics on a large number of random square matrices in [37]. More specifically, for a given size (range from 15 to 20) and density (range from 0.1 to 0.9), 10 matrices were randomly generated and then tested. The authors run their procedure multiple times in a given time.

We first evaluate the effectiveness of our proposed reduction procedure and apply the framework on random matrices used in [37] by using **Further Reduction** functionality. To this end, we try to optimize the implementations provided by RNBP, A1 and A2 given in [37] and evaluate the average cost that saved comparing with the BP heuristic. In order to have a fair comparison, we use the same fixed heuristic in our framework when optimizing the implementations given by different heuristics, i.e., we only use RNBP (A1, A2) to search the implementation of recovered matrices (generated in the framework) when optimizing the implementations provided by RNBP (A1, A2). It is worth mentioning that the implementations given by RNBP, A1 and A2 are obtained by running the algorithms for a given time. We allocate our framework the same time for the given matrix as in [37] and keep RNBP (A1, A2) running during the phase that our framework is being used for further reduction. The results are shown in Fig. 1, where RNBP (A1, A2) denotes the results obtained by using the corresponding algorithms proposed in [37] and RNBP-Opt (A1-Opt, A2-Opt) denotes the results returned by our framework when taking the optimized implementation of RNBP (A1, A2) as the input. As show in Fig. 1, even though Tan and Peyrin's heuristics can get better implementation compared with BP heuristic, the costs can still be reduced by our general framework.

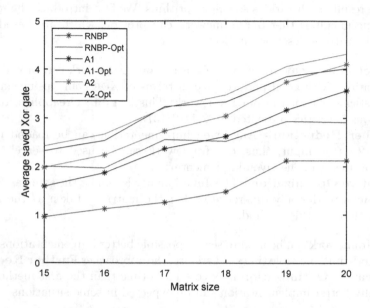

Fig. 1. Average XOR count saved for various algorithms compared with BP.

In addition, we apply our framework with random choices of heuristics to these random matrices by using **Iterative Reduction** functionality, and compare the results with Paar1, RPaar1, BP, BFI, RNBP, A1 and A2. All the matrices are allocated the same running time given in [37] except Paar1, RPaar1 and BP. As in [37], we run RPaar1 10000 times for each matrix due to its efficiency and pick the best implementation. The percentages of the best implementation given by different methods are shown in Table 4. The experiment results show that our framework has an overwhelming advantage.

5.2   Applications to Cipher Matrices

We tested our general framework on some recently designed matrices which have been optimized in [2,19,37,40]. Note that [40] reported several best implementations on those matrices, however, the optimizing algorithm can only apply to invertible matrices, thus it is not applicable to those intermediately recovered matrices in our framework. We can only use the **Further Reduction** functionality of our framework to try to further reduce the cost of the implementations

Table 4. Percentage of the best implementation produced by various algorithms for various square matrix sizes.

Matrix size	Paar1 [28]	RPaar1 [37]	BP [11]	BFI [2]	RNBP [37]	A1 [37]	A2 [37]	Our framework Sect. 4
15	13.33	13.33	14.44	18.89	23.33	32.22	44.44	100.00
16	11.11	14.44	17.78	22.22	22.22	27.78	37.78	96.67
17	8.89	10.00	12.22	21.11	14.44	26.67	26.67	93.33
18	10.00	11.11	11.11	13.33	13.33	25.56	38.89	96.67
19	7.78	7.78	14.44	15.56	22.22	34.44	54.44	86.67
20	8.89	10.00	13.33	15.56	18.89	36.67	58.89	73.33

given by [40]. Moreover, we also applied the **Iterative Optimization** functionality to these matrices. The experiment results show that most matrices can be further optimized by our framework. The details are listed in the columns "FurOpt" and "IterOpt" in Table 5. In order to obtain the implementations given by different heuristics, we allocated various times from several hours to several days for those tested matrices. It should be noted that for 8×8 matrices over $GL(8, F_2)$, only [19] (use Paar1 and BP) and [2] (use BFI) have reported implementations of these six matrices ([40] have reported an implementation of one matrix, which is designed by [35]). Thus, we only list the results on matrices of size 16×16 and 32×32 in Table 5 for better comparison.

Besides, we also applied our framework to those MDS matrices constructed specially in [14] with functionality **Iterative Optimization**. As Tan and Peyrin did in [37], we allocated 15000 s for each of the 12 matrices with size 16×16 and 5 days for each of the 12 matrices with size 32×32 tested in this paper. The results are shown in Table 6. What we need to emphasize here is that the authors in [14] applied Yosys synthesis tool [39] and the authors in [37] applied **LocalOpt & Yosys** technique to improve their optimized implementation. However, neither Yosys synthesis tool nor **LocalOpt & Yosys** technique is applied to the implementations returned by our framework, thus we only compare the results before Yosys synthesis tool and **LocalOpt & Yosys** technique are used for further optimization. Nevertheless, further optimization may be expected if they are applied to our results. Comparing the costs of these 24 matrices under various global optimization algorithms (BP, Paar2, RSDF, RNBP, A1 and A2), our framework can find better implementations for 20 matrices. Furthermore, we note that the costs given in [14] for implementing these MDS matrices, which are generated along with the construction for their optimized implementation, have been improved to a certain extend as listed in the column "Const." of Table 6, our framework can still find better implementations than [14] for 10 matrices.

Our general framework has also been applied to matrices used in several block ciphers and hash functions as did in [2,19,40]. Since our framework can independently call different heuristics to optimize a matrix implementation, it will be never worse than previous results. [2,19,40] tested 24 matrices, our framework can find better implementations for 6 matrices of all the 24 matrices, and Table 7 list the corresponding results. The improvement achieved by our framework is not that significant in this case. Although the reason for this is not clear, this might be caused by the fact that matrices used in block ciphers and hash functions are denser than those newly designed matrices. Thus, limited by the solution speed of BP algorithm and its variants for large/dense matrices, the improvement of our framework on these matrices might be affected. Nevertheless, our framework can still return an implementation of AES MixColumns with only 91 XORs, which beats all records, and its implementation details can be found in Table 8.

Table 5. Implementation cost of newly designed matrices.

Matrix	Paar1 [28]	Paar2 [28]	BP [11]	BFI [2]	XZLBZ [40]	RNBP [37]	A1 [37]	A2 [37]	FurOpt[†]	IterOpt[†]
4 × 4 matrices over GL (4, F_2)										
[35]	50	48	48	46	44	46	46	46	–	44/7
[23]	49	46	44	44	44	43	43	43	–	43/4
[22]	48	47	44	44	44	43	44	43	43/4	43/4
[6]	48	47	42	42	41	40	41	40	40/5	40/7
[30]	46	45	43	42	41	41	41	41	–	40/7
[17]	48	47	43	42	41	42	41	40	40/7	40/6
[35]*	52	48	48	47	44	46	45	44	–	43/8
[22]*	51	48	48	46	44	47	45	45	–	43/8
[30]*	50	48	42	40	38	39	39	38	–	37/7
[17]*	51	47	47	46	41	45	43	43	–	41/10
4 × 4 matrices over GL (8, F_2)										
[35]	100	98	100	94	90	94	92	93	–	91/7
[23]	116	116	112	110	121	108	108	109	108/8	107/6
[22]	102	102	102	102	104	99	99	99	99/4	99/5
[6]	116	112	110	108	114	106	106	106	105/8	105/7
[30]	110	108	107	104	114	103	102	102	101/11	100/9
[17]	96	95	86	86	82	84	82	82	80/7	80/6
[35]*	104	101	100	94	91	92	92	92	–	89/8
[22]*	101	97	91	90	87	89	89	88	–	86/9
[30]*	110	109	100	98	93	97	99	97	92/8	95/7
[17]*	102	100	91	92	83	89	86	86	–	84/6
8 × 8 matrices over GL (4, F_2)										
[35]	210	209	194	192	170	176	–	–	169/20	172/10
[31]	205	205	201	203	183	180	–	–	178/10	177/10
[35]*	222	222	217	212	185	182	–	–	178/17	172/22

* Involutory matrix.
† We only present depths in these columns, since the results given in [2,19,40] only list XOR count.

Table 6. Implementation costs (XOR/depth) of matrices of size 16×16 and 32×32 in [14].

Matrix	Instantiation (α, β, γ)	Const.*[14]	BP [14]	Paar2 [14]	RSDF [37]	RNBP [37]	A1 [37]	A2 [37]	Our framework Sect. 4
$M_{4,5}^{9,3}$	$(A_4, -, -)$	39/5	38/7	45/5	38/8	38/7	39/9	38/8	35/9
$M_{4,5}^{9,3}$	$(A_4^{-1}, -, -)$	39/5	40/4	46/4	39/9	39/7	38/6	36/6	35/6
$M_{4,6}^{8,3}$	$(A_4, -, -)$	35/5	38/7	45/5	39/8	38/8	39/10	38/6	35/9
$M_{4,6}^{8,3}$	$(A_4^{-1}, -, -)$	35/6	40/4	46/4	37/9	39/7	38/5	36/6	35/6
$M_{4,5}^{8,3}$	$(A_4^{-1}, A_4, A_4^{-2})$	36/6	40/6	47/4	40/17	39/7	39/11	39/9	36/9
$M_{4,4}^{9,4}$	$(A_4, -, -)$	40/4	41/9	47/5	42/14	40/10	39/9	39/9	38/7
$M_{4,4}^{9,3}$	(A_4, A_4^{-1}, A_4^2)	40/4	40/7	43/4	40/10	39/7	42/10	41/7	38/7
$M_{4,4}^{8,4}$	$(A_4, -, -)$	38/4	40/7	43/5	41/10	39/8	40/7	40/7	38/6
$M_{4,4}^{8,4'}$	$(A_4, -, -)$	38/4	43/6	41/4	40/6	42/6	41/7	40/6	38/5
$M_{4,4}^{8,4''}$	$(A_4, -, -)$	37/4	40/5	43/5	41/12	40/6	40/6	39/7	37/6
$M_{4,3}^{9,5}$	$(A_4, -, -)$	41/3	40/4	43/4	43/7	40/5	41/7	40/5	39/5
$M_{4,3}^{9,5}$	$(A_4^{-1}, -, -)$	41/3	43/5	44/3	44/10	41/6	41/7	40/6	40/5
$M_{4,5}^{9,3}$	$(A_8, -, -)$	75/5	74/5	88/4	82/12	69/6	79/9	70/6	67/5
$M_{4,5}^{9,3}$	$(A_8^{-1}, -, -)$	75/5	71/6	89/5	89/15	69/6	80/7	68/7	67/5
$M_{4,6}^{8,3}$	$(A_8, -, -)$	67/5	74/5	88/4	85/18	68/6	79/8	71/8	67/5
$M_{4,6}^{8,3}$	$(A_8^{-1}, -, -)$	67/5	71/6	89/5	85/15	69/6	80/7	68/7	67/6
$M_{4,5}^{8,3}$	$(A_8^{-1}, A_8, A_8^{-2})$	68/5	75/6	77/4	84/16	75/6	74/8	71/6	68/6
$M_{4,4}^{9,4}$	$(A_8, -, -)$	76/4	77/6	92/4	89/14	76/6	76/7	77/7	76/5
$M_{4,4}^{9,3}$	(A_8, A_8^{-1}, A_8^2)	76/4	76/6	83/6	85/16	75/8	78/8	76/8	74/8
$M_{4,4}^{8,4}$	$(A_8, -, -)$	70/4	72/5	74/4	90/17	70/6	70/7	70/7	70/7
$M_{4,4}^{8,4'}$	$(A_8, -, -)$	70/4	81/7	79/5	89/10	79/6	75/8	74/6	72/7
$M_{4,4}^{8,4''}$	$(A_8, -, -)$	69/4	72/6	85/5	90/14	70/6	77/6	70/6	69/6
$M_{4,3}^{9,5}$	$(A_8, -, -)$	77/3	76/7	86/4	87/10	76/6	77/7	76/6	75/5
$M_{4,3}^{9,5}$	$(A_8^{-1}, -, -)$	77/3	79/5	86/4	91/14	77/6	77/7	77/5	77/6

* This column presents the results listed in the column "Ours" of Table 5 in [14].

Table 7. Implementation costs of cipher matrices.

Cipher	Paar1 [28]	Paar2 [28]	BP [11]	BFI [2]	XZLBZ [40]	RNBP [37]	A1 [37]	A2 [37]	FurOpt[†]	IterOpt[†]
AES [13]	108	108	97	95	92	95	95	94	91/7	93/6
ANUBIS [5]	121	121	106	102	98	100	103	105	96/11	97/12
CLEFIA M_0 [34]	121	121	106	102	98	100	103	105	96/11	97/12
CLEFIA M_1 [34]	121	121	111	110	103	108	108	109	–	108/7
FOX MU4 [18]	144	143	137	131	136	132	135	135	130/9	131/9
TWOFISH [32]	151	149	129	125	111	124	122	–	–	121/14
JOLTIK [16]	52	48	48	47	44	46	45	44	–	43/8
SMALLSCALE AES [12]	54	54	47	45	43	46	44	45	–	43/5
WHIRLWIND M_0 [4]	218	218	212	210	183	188	–	–	–	183/16
WHIRLWIND M_1 [4]	246	244	235	234	190	188	–	–	–	180/17

† We only present depths in these columns, since the results given in [2,19,40] only list XOR count.

Table 8. An implementation of AES MixColumns with 91 XORs, where x_0, x_1, $\cdots$, x_{31} are the 32 input bits, y_0, y_1, $\cdots$, y_{31} are the 32 output bits.

$t_{32} = x_{23} + x_{31}$	$t_{51} = x_2 + t_{42}$	$t_{70} = t_{32} + t_{40}$	$t_{89} = x_{29} + t_{38}$	$t_{108} = t_{102} + t_{107}[y_3]$
$t_{33} = x_{15} + x_{31}$	$t_{52} = x_{25} + t_{47}$	$t_{71} = x_8 + t_{70}[y_{16}]$	$t_{90} = t_{87} + t_{89}[y_{29}]$	$t_{109} = t_{61} + t_{52}$
$t_{34} = x_4 + x_{12}$	$t_{53} = t_{41} + t_{47}[y_0]$	$t_{72} = t_{46} + t_{70}[y_8]$	$t_{91} = t_{78} + t_{89}[y_{13}]$	$t_{110} = t_{53} + t_{55}[y_{24}]$
$t_{35} = x_{13} + x_{21}$	$t_{54} = t_{32} + t_{41}$	$t_{73} = t_{41} + t_{69}$	$t_{92} = x_2 + t_{48}$	$t_{111} = t_{109} + t_{110}[y_{25}]$
$t_{36} = x_9 + x_{17}$	$t_{55} = t_{33} + t_{40}$	$t_{74} = t_{66} + t_{73}[y_{28}]$	$t_{93} = t_{36} + t_{92}[y_{10}]$	$t_{112} = t_{51} + t_{63}[y_{18}]$
$t_{37} = x_{11} + x_{27}$	$t_{56} = t_{32} + t_{45}$	$t_{75} = x_{29} + t_{35}$	$t_{94} = t_{33} + t_{49}$	$t_{113} = t_{52} + t_{97}[y_{17}]$
$t_{38} = x_4 + x_{28}$	$t_{57} = x_7 + t_{43}$	$t_{76} = t_{34} + t_{75}[y_5]$	$t_{95} = x_7 + t_{94}[y_{23}]$	$t_{114} = t_{54} + t_{57}[y_7]$
$t_{39} = x_5 + x_{21}$	$t_{58} = t_{39} + t_{49}$	$t_{77} = x_{28} + t_{69}$	$t_{96} = t_{40} + t_{71}$	$t_{115} = t_{56} + t_{57}[y_{15}]$
$t_{40} = x_0 + x_{24}$	$t_{59} = x_3 + x_{27}$	$t_{78} = t_{39} + t_{77}$	$t_{97} = t_{42} + t_{96}$	$t_{116} = t_{88} + t_{106}[y_{22}]$
$t_{41} = x_7 + x_{15}$	$t_{60} = x_{25} + t_{36}$	$t_{79} = t_{76} + t_{78}[y_{21}]$	$t_{98} = x_{10} + t_{92}$	$t_{117} = t_{97} + t_{62}[y_9]$
$t_{42} = x_1 + x_9$	$t_{61} = x_1 + t_{60}$	$t_{80} = t_{33} + t_{37}$	$t_{99} = t_{51} + t_{98}[y_2]$	$t_{118} = t_{56} + t_{95}[y_{31}]$
$t_{43} = x_6 + x_{14}$	$t_{62} = t_{46} + t_{60}$	$t_{81} = t_{38} + t_{80}$	$t_{100} = t_{48} + t_{68}$	$t_{119} = t_{93} + t_{63}[y_{26}]$
$t_{44} = x_{16} + x_{24}$	$t_{63} = t_{50} + t_{61}$	$t_{82} = t_{74} + t_{81}[y_4]$	$t_{101} = t_{67} + t_{100}[y_{11}]$	$t_{120} = t_{58} + t_{116}[y_{30}]$
$t_{45} = x_6 + x_{22}$	$t_{64} = t_{35} + t_{45}$	$t_{83} = x_{27} + t_{68}$	$t_{102} = t_{37} + t_{100}$	$t_{121} = t_{62} + t_{110}[y_1]$
$t_{46} = x_{16} + t_{33}$	$t_{65} = x_{30} + t_{64}[y_{14}]$	$t_{84} = x_{20} + t_{83}$	$t_{103} = x_{19} + t_{102}$	$t_{122} = t_{108} + t_{67}[y_{27}]$
$t_{47} = x_8 + t_{44}$	$t_{66} = t_{33} + t_{59}$	$t_{85} = t_{77} + t_{84}[y_{20}]$	$t_{104} = x_3 + t_{103}[y_{19}]$	
$t_{48} = x_{18} + x_{26}$	$t_{67} = t_{50} + t_{66}$	$t_{86} = t_{81} + t_{84}[y_{12}]$	$t_{105} = t_{39} + t_{65}$	
$t_{49} = x_{22} + x_{30}$	$t_{68} = x_{19} + t_{32}$	$t_{87} = x_5 + t_{75}$	$t_{106} = t_{43} + t_{105}[y_6]$	
$t_{50} = x_{10} + x_{26}$	$t_{69} = x_{20} + t_{34}$	$t_{88} = t_{45} + t_{87}$	$t_{107} = t_{54} + t_{98}$	

6   Conclusion and Future Work

In this work, we proposed several reduction rules for reducing the cost of a matrix implementation. Different from the reduction rules proposed in [40], we do not require that the operations that meet our rules must be adjacent. Based on these rules we designed a framework which combines several state-of-the-art heuristics and our proposed reduction procedure. Thus, our framework can expect better implementations compared with previous search algorithms. Our experimental results on a large range of matrices verify that, our framework performs better on average, especially for small and (or) sparse matrices. Moreover, our framework provides a lot of tweakable features that one can easily handle to meet his own need. As an application, our framework finds an implementation of AES MixColumns with only 91 g-XOR operations for the first time. In the following, we discuss several possible directions for future researches.

Dense Matrices. Being embedded with the heuristics of BP, BFI, RNBP, A1 and A2, our framework is time-consuming for large dense matrices, even though it can give shorter implementations than previous works in most cases. However, Paar's algorithm can make up for this to some extend. Thus, we can for example fix a bound for the density and/or size of matrices, and use Paar's algorithms to find the implementation of a matrix if its density and/or size is beyond this bound.

Depth Complexity. In this paper, we do not focus on depth complexity. But as a main parameter determining the circuit delay, the depth of an implementation cannot be neglected. The focus of the reduction procedure is the XOR count, however, it might be possible to take the depth into consideration, such as in [21,26]. Although our framework focuses on XOR count, the depth of the implementation for implementing AES MixColumns given in Table 8 is 7, which is a little higher than the results with depth 6 given in [25,40] but lower than the implementation with depth 9 given in [37].

3-input XOR. Even though a 3-input XOR gate can be realized by two 2-input XOR gates, the hardware cost of one 3-input XOR gate is much lower than two 2-input XOR gates. Whether the reduction rules given in Sect. 3 can be extended to 3-input XOR gates is a possible direction for further researches, as well as new reduction rules for 3-input XOR gates.

Acknowledgments. We would like to thank the anonymous reviewers for their helpful comments and suggestions. This work was supported by the Application Foundation Frontier Project of Wuhan Science and Technology Bureau (Grant No. 2020010601012189) and the National Natural Science Foundation of China (Grant No. 61802119).

References

1. Baksi, A., Karmakar, B., Dasu, V.A., Saha, D., Chattopadhyay, A.: Further insights on implementation of the linear layer. https://www.esat.kuleuven.be/cosic/events/silc2020/wp-content/uploads/sites/4/2020/10/Submission1.pdf
2. Banik, S., Funabiki, Y., Isobe, T.: More results on shortest linear programs. In: Attrapadung, N., Yagi, T. (eds.) IWSEC 2019. LNCS, vol. 11689, pp. 109–128. Springer, Cham (2019). https://doi.org/10.1007/978-3-030-26834-3_7
3. Bao, Z., Guo, J., Ling, S., Sasaki, Y.: PEIGEN - a platform for evaluation, implementation, and generation of S-boxes. IACR Trans. Symmetric Cryptol. **2019**(1), 330–394 (2019). https://doi.org/10.13154/tosc.v2019.i1.330-394

4. Barreto, P.S.L.M., Nikov, V., Nikova, S., Rijmen, V., Tischhauser, E.: Whirlwind: a new cryptographic hash function. Des. Codes Cryptogr. **56**(2–3), 141–162 (2010). https://doi.org/10.1007/s10623-010-9391-y
5. Barreto, P.S., Rijmen, V.: The ANUBIS block cipher. In: First Open NESSIE Workshop (2000)
6. Beierle, C., Kranz, T., Leander, G.: Lightweight multiplication in $GF(2^n)$ with applications to MDS matrices. In: Robshaw, M., Katz, J. (eds.) CRYPTO 2016. LNCS, vol. 9814, pp. 625–653. Springer, Heidelberg (2016). https://doi.org/10.1007/978-3-662-53018-4_23
7. Biham, E.: A fast new DES implementation in software. In: Biham, E. (ed.) FSE 1997. LNCS, vol. 1267, pp. 260–272. Springer, Heidelberg (1997). https://doi.org/10.1007/BFb0052352
8. Biham, E., Shamir, A.: Differential cryptanalysis of DES-like cryptosystems. J. Cryptol. **4**(1), 3–72 (1991). https://doi.org/10.1007/BF00630563
9. Boyar, J., Matthews, P., Peralta, R.: On the shortest linear straight-line program for computing linear forms. In: Ochmański, E., Tyszkiewicz, J. (eds.) MFCS 2008. LNCS, vol. 5162, pp. 168–179. Springer, Heidelberg (2008). https://doi.org/10.1007/978-3-540-85238-4_13
10. Boyar, J., Matthews, P., Peralta, R.: Logic minimization techniques with applications to cryptology. J. Cryptol. **26**(2), 280–312 (2012). https://doi.org/10.1007/s00145-012-9124-7
11. Boyar, J., Peralta, R.: A new combinational logic minimization technique with applications to cryptology. In: Festa, P. (ed.) SEA 2010. LNCS, vol. 6049, pp. 178–189. Springer, Heidelberg (2010). https://doi.org/10.1007/978-3-642-13193-6_16
12. Cid, C., Murphy, S., Robshaw, M.J.B.: Small scale variants of the AES. In: Gilbert, H., Handschuh, H. (eds.) FSE 2005. LNCS, vol. 3557, pp. 145–162. Springer, Heidelberg (2005). https://doi.org/10.1007/11502760_10
13. Daemen, J., Rijmen, V.: The Design of Rijndael: AES - The Advanced Encryption Standard. Information Security and Cryptography, Springer, Heidelberg (2002). https://doi.org/10.1007/978-3-662-04722-4
14. Duval, S., Leurent, G.: MDS matrices with lightweight circuits. IACR Trans. Symmetric Cryptol. **2018**(2), 48–78 (2018). https://doi.org/10.13154/tosc.v2018.i2.48-78
15. Guo, J., Jean, J., Nikolic, I., Qiao, K., Sasaki, Y., Sim, S.M.: Invariant subspace attack against midori64 and the resistance criteria for S-box designs. IACR Trans. Symmetric Cryptol. **2016**(1), 33–56 (2016). https://doi.org/10.13154/tosc.v2016.i1.33-56
16. Jean, J., Nikolić, I., Peyrin, T.: Joltik. Submission to the CAESAR competition (2014)
17. Jean, J., Peyrin, T., Sim, S.M., Tourteaux, J.: Optimizing implementations of lightweight building blocks. IACR Trans. Symmetric Cryptol. **2017**(4), 130–168 (2017). https://doi.org/10.13154/tosc.v2017.i4.130-168
18. Junod, P., Vaudenay, S.: FOX: a new family of block ciphers. In: Handschuh, H., Hasan, M.A. (eds.) SAC 2004. LNCS, vol. 3357, pp. 114–129. Springer, Heidelberg (2004). https://doi.org/10.1007/978-3-540-30564-4_8
19. Kranz, T., Leander, G., Stoffelen, K., Wiemer, F.: Shorter linear straight-line programs for MDS matrices. IACR Trans. Symmetric Cryptol. **2017**(4), 188–211 (2017). https://doi.org/10.13154/tosc.v2017.i4.188-211
20. Li, C., Wang, Q.: Design of lightweight linear diffusion layers from near-MDS matrices. IACR Trans. Symmetric Cryptol. **2017**(1), 129–155 (2017). https://doi.org/10.13154/tosc.v2017.i1.129-155

21. Li, S., Sun, S., Li, C., Wei, Z., Hu, L.: Constructing low-latency involutory MDS matrices with lightweight circuits. IACR Trans. Symmetric Cryptol. **2019**(1), 84–117 (2019). https://doi.org/10.13154/tosc.v2019.i1.84-117

22. Li, Y., Wang, M.: On the construction of lightweight circulant involutory MDS matrices. In: Peyrin, T. (ed.) FSE 2016. LNCS, vol. 9783, pp. 121–139. Springer, Heidelberg (2016). https://doi.org/10.1007/978-3-662-52993-5_7

23. Liu, M., Sim, S.M.: Lightweight MDS generalized circulant matrices. In: Peyrin, T. (ed.) FSE 2016. LNCS, vol. 9783, pp. 101–120. Springer, Heidelberg (2016). https://doi.org/10.1007/978-3-662-52993-5_6

24. Matsui, M.: Linear cryptanalysis method for DES cipher. In: Helleseth, T. (ed.) EUROCRYPT 1993. LNCS, vol. 765, pp. 386–397. Springer, Heidelberg (1994). https://doi.org/10.1007/3-540-48285-7_33

25. Maximov, A.: AES MixColumn with 92 XOR gates. IACR Cryptol. ePrint Arch. **2019**, 833 (2019). https://eprint.iacr.org/2019/833

26. Maximov, A., Ekdahl, P.: New circuit minimization techniques for smaller and faster AES SBoxes. IACR Trans. Cryptogr. Hardw. Embed. Syst. **2019**(4), 91–125 (2019). https://doi.org/10.13154/tches.v2019.i4.91-125

27. Osvik, D.A.: Speeding up serpent. In: The Third Advanced Encryption Standard Candidate Conference, New York, USA, 13–14 April 2000, pp. 317–329. National Institute of Standards and Technology (2000)

28. Paar, C.: Optimized arithmetic for Reed-Solomon encoders. In: IEEE International Symposium on Information Theory, p. 250 (1997)

29. Reyhani-Masoleh, A., Taha, M.M.I., Ashmawy, D.: Smashing the implementation records of AES S-box. IACR Trans. Cryptogr. Hardw. Embed. Syst. **2018**(2), 298–336 (2018). https://doi.org/10.13154/tches.v2018.i2.298-336

30. Sarkar, S., Syed, H.: Lightweight diffusion layer: importance of toeplitz matrices. IACR Trans. Symmetric Cryptol. **2016**(1), 95–113 (2016). https://doi.org/10.13154/tosc.v2016.i1.95-113

31. Sarkar, S., Syed, H.: Analysis of toeplitz MDS matrices. In: Pieprzyk, J., Suriadi, S. (eds.) ACISP 2017. LNCS, vol. 10343, pp. 3–18. Springer, Cham (2017). https://doi.org/10.1007/978-3-319-59870-3_1

32. Schneier, B., Kelsey, J., Whiting, D., Wagner, D., Hall, C., Ferguson, N.: Twofish: a 128-bit block cipher (1998)

33. Shannon, C.E.: Communication theory of secrecy systems. Bell Syst. Tech. J. **28**(4), 656–715 (1949). https://doi.org/10.1002/j.1538-7305.1949.tb00928.x

34. Shirai, T., Shibutani, K., Akishita, T., Moriai, S., Iwata, T.: The 128-bit blockcipher CLEFIA (extended abstract). In: Biryukov, A. (ed.) FSE 2007. LNCS, vol. 4593, pp. 181–195. Springer, Heidelberg (2007). https://doi.org/10.1007/978-3-540-74619-5_12

35. Sim, S.M., Khoo, K., Oggier, F., Peyrin, T.: Lightweight MDS involution matrices. In: Leander, G. (ed.) FSE 2015. LNCS, vol. 9054, pp. 471–493. Springer, Heidelberg (2015). https://doi.org/10.1007/978-3-662-48116-5_23

36. Stoffelen, K.: Optimizing S-box implementations for several criteria using SAT solvers. In: Peyrin, T. (ed.) FSE 2016. LNCS, vol. 9783, pp. 140–160. Springer, Heidelberg (2016). https://doi.org/10.1007/978-3-662-52993-5_8

37. Tan, Q.Q., Peyrin, T.: Improved heuristics for short linear programs. IACR Trans. Cryptogr. Hardw. Embed. Syst. **2020**(1), 203–230 (2020). https://doi.org/10.13154/tches.v2020.i1.203-230

38. Visconti, A., Schiavo, C.V., Peralta, R.: Improved upper bounds for the expected circuit complexity of dense systems of linear equations over GF(2). Inf. Process. Lett. **137**, 1–5 (2018). https://doi.org/10.1016/j.ipl.2018.04.010

39. Wolf, C.: Yosys open synthesis suite. http://www.clifford.at/yosys
40. Xiang, Z., Zeng, X., Lin, D., Bao, Z., Zhang, S.: Optimizing implementations of linear layers. IACR Trans. Symmetric Cryptol. **2020**(2), 120–145 (2020). https://doi.org/10.13154/tosc.v2020.i2.120-145

Improvements to RSA Key Generation and CRT on Embedded Devices

Mike Hamburg[✉], Mike Tunstall, and Qinglai Xiao

Rambus, Inc., San Jose, USA
{mhamburg,mtunstall,qxiao}@rambus.com

Abstract. RSA key generation requires devices to generate large prime numbers. The naïve approach is to generate candidates at random, and then test each one for (probable) primality. However, it is faster to use a *sieve* method, where the candidates are chosen so as not to be divisible by a list of small prime numbers $\{p_i\}$.

Sieve methods can be somewhat complex and time-consuming, at least by the standards of embedded and hardware implementations, and they can be tricky to defend against side-channel analysis. Here we describe an improvement on Joye et al.'s sieve based on the Chinese Remainder Theorem (CRT). We also describe a new sieve method using quadratic residuosity which is simpler and faster than previously known methods, and which can produce values in desired RSA parameter ranges such as $(2^{n-1/2}, 2^n)$ with minimal additional work. The same methods can be used to generate strong primes and DSA moduli.

We also demonstrate a technique for RSA private key operations using the Chinese Remainder Theorem (RSA-CRT) without $q^{-1} \bmod p$. This technique also leads to inversion-free batch RSA and inversion-free RSA $\bmod p^k q$.

We demonstrate how an embedded device can use our key generation and RSA-CRT techniques to perform RSA efficiently without storing the private key itself: only a symmetric seed and one or two short hints are required.

Keywords: RSA · Prime generation

1 Introduction

To generate private keys for the RSA cryptosystem [RSA78], devices must choose random, secret prime numbers. Prime number generation is also required for finite-field Diffie-Hellman (DH) and DSA parameter generation [DH76,KG13]. DH and DSA parameter generation has become a more common requirement since the Logjam attack [ABD+15], which allows multiple DH and DSA keys to be attacked together if they use the same parameter set.

Prime generation algorithms may use sieving techniques to reduce the number of candidates that must be tested. [JPV00] describes two sieving methods: one based on the Chinese Remainder Theorem (CRT) and one based on

© Springer Nature Switzerland AG 2021
K. G. Paterson (Ed.): CT-RSA 2021, LNCS 12704, pp. 633–656, 2021.
https://doi.org/10.1007/978-3-030-75539-3_26

Carmichael's λ function; the latter is improved in [JP06]. Here we describe an improvement to the CRT sieve to mitigate its largest downside, namely a large precomputed table of CRT coefficients. We also describe a novel sieving algorithm based on quadratic residuosity, which may be more resistant to side-channel attack than a CRT-based sieve.

Our improved sieving algorithms work well with the other known techniques for generating RSA keys, DSA keys and strong primes on embedded devices [JPV00, JP03]. With some modification, our CRT-based sieve can be used to efficiently generate safe primes as well.

The RSA private operation is also often implemented using the CRT, which quarters the computation time. The CRT requires an extra value, $q^{-1} \bmod p$, which is typically computed during key generation and stored with the private key. We show how to modify a side-channel countermeasure to perform RSA-CRT efficiently without this value, simplifying key generation and storage. The technique generalizes trivially to multi-prime RSA. Less trivially, it generalizes to inverse-free RSA modulo $p^k q$ [Tak98, Tak04], which previously required inversion not only of $q \bmod p$ but also of the public encryption exponent $e \bmod p$.

In fact, these are instances of a more general batching technique [Ham12] which we briefly recap in Sect. 3.2. This generalized batching technique has previously been applied to elliptic curves, but not to RSA. It can also be used to implement batch RSA [Fia90] without inversion.

For embedded devices whose nonvolatile memory consists only of fuses, the cost of storing an RSA private key is significant. It would be preferable if the private key could be expanded from a secret seed—perhaps even a PUF key—instead of being stored. RSA key generation is slow, but can be skipped by using one or two short (16-bit) hints which are recorded in nonvolatile memory. With previous techniques, compressing the keys this way would result in a large performance loss. But with our new key generation and RSA-CRT techniques, it only incurs a few percent performance loss, at least for larger RSA keys.

For brevity, this conference version omits the proof of Theorem 1. It is found in Appendix A of the full version, to be found at https://eprint.iacr.org/2020/1507.

1.1   Notation

Let $\mathbb{R}$ denote the real numbers. Let $\mathbb{Z}$ and $\mathbb{Z}/n$ denote the integers and the ring of integers mod an integer n, respectively. Let $\mathbb{F}_{p^e}$ denote the Galois field of p^e elements. Call two integers (m, n) *coprime* if their greatest common divisor is 1. Let $(\mathbb{Z}/n)^*$ be the multiplicative group of $\mathbb{Z}/n$, which contains the elements $m \in \mathbb{Z}/n$ which are coprime to n.

For positive integers (p, e, n), let $p|n$ or $p \nmid n$ mean that p divides or does not divide n, respectively, and let $p^e || n$ mean that p^e divides n but p^{e+1} does not. In all cases where this notation is used, p is a prime number. For brevity we sometimes omit that qualification in notations such as "for all $p^e || n$".

Let $\phi(n)$ and $\lambda(n)$ denote the Euler and Carmichael totient functions, respectively:

$$\phi(n) := \prod_{p^e||n} p^{e-1} \cdot (p-1) \quad \text{and} \quad \lambda(n) := \text{LCM} \{p^{e-1} \cdot (p-1) \text{ for all } p^e||n\}$$

For all $x \in (\mathbb{Z}/n)^*, x^{\phi(n)} = x^{\lambda(n)} = 1$.

For integers (x, p), we say that x is a *quadratic residue* (resp *quadratic non-residue*) mod p if there exists (resp does not exist) an integer y such that $x \equiv y^2$ mod p. We will only consider quadratic (non)residues modulo prime p.

For any ring R, and any group G with group operation $\odot$, and any functions $F_1, F_2 : G \to R$, their convolution $F_1 * F_2$ is defined as:

$$(F_1 * F_2)(x) := \sum_{x_1 \odot x_2 = x} F_1(x_1) \cdot F_2(x_2).$$

The power-convolution F_1^{*k} is defined as the convolution $F_1 * F_1 * \ldots * F_1$ of k copies of F_1.

A probability distribution $\mathcal{D}$ on a finite set S may be seen as a *stochastic function* $S \to \mathbb{R}$, meaning a function such that $\mathcal{D}(x) \geqslant 0$ for each $x \in S$, and $\sum_{x \in S} \mathcal{D}(x) = 1$. If S is a group, then this allows us to convolve distributions. This gives the distribution of the product of two samples:

$$\mathcal{D}_1 * \mathcal{D}_2 = \{x_1 \odot x_2 : x_1 \leftarrow \mathcal{D}_1, x_2 \leftarrow \mathcal{D}_2\}.$$

The notation $x \xleftarrow{\$} S$ means to choose an element uniformly at random from a set S. The notation $[A, B]$ means the interval from A to B, inclusive.

The Montgomery reduction [Mon85] of x mod N is x/R mod N for some fixed value $R > N$ which is coprime to N. This is usually implemented for N odd and R a power of 2, in which case it is typically more efficient than ordinary reduction (implemented using, e.g., Barrett's reduction algorithm [Bar87]). The operation taking $(x, y) \to xy/R$ mod N is called Montgomery multiplication.

2 Generating Prime Numbers

2.1 Naïve Algorithm

Generating random prime numbers is, in some sense, simple. There are well-established probabilistic primality tests[1] [Rab80, PSW80, AM93] that work for large numbers, and an approximately $1/(n \ln 2)$ fraction of the numbers less than 2^n are prime. So we can just choose random numbers and test them for (probable)

---

[1] Most of these algorithms exhibit false positives in rare cases. That is, when given a prime number they always say that it is prime, but they may accept a composite number as prime with some tiny probability. The present work does not address this issue.

primality. If a 1024-bit prime is desired, it will take about $1024 \cdot \ln 2 \approx 710$ tries in expectation, but may take much longer if the generator is unlucky.

This naïve algorithm is shown in Algorithm 1. However, typically the test "if p is prime" is somewhat slow, requiring an exponentiation in the case of a Fermat or Miller-Rabin test. The primality test may be sped up somewhat by using trial division by several small primes $\{p_i\}$ before testing, but this is not especially fast either. Furthermore, it risks revealing information about p mod p_i via a side-channel such as power consumption.

Algorithm 1. Naïve prime generation

1: **procedure** PRIMEGEN(L, H, t)   ▷ Try t times to generate a prime in $[L, H]$
2:     **for** $i = 1$ to t **do**
3:         $p \xleftarrow{\$} [L, H]$
4:         **if** p is prime **then return** p
5:     **end for**
6:     **return** Failure
7: **end procedure**

2.2   Sieving Algorithms

The naïve algorithm's performance can be improved by choosing p in a way that is guaranteed not to be divisible by small primes; for example, we might choose $x \in (\mathbb{Z}/M)^*$, for a constant M which is divisible by many small primes. Since we wish to generate primes in a certain range—an interval $[L, H]$—we can then adjust x to be in that range without changing its value mod M. This sieving method is shown in Algorithm 2, which is a variant of Joye et al.'s sieving algorithm [JPV00, Fig. 6]. This algorithm samples from the slightly narrower interval $\left[L, L + \lfloor \frac{H-L}{M} \rfloor \cdot M \right]$. If this is close enough to H, it may be acceptable; otherwise we can instead sample from the slightly wider interval $\left[L, L + \lceil \frac{H-L}{M} \rceil \cdot M \right]$ and reject candidates that are greater than H.

Algorithm 2. Prime generation using sieve [JPV00]

1: **procedure** PRIMEGEN(L, H, t)   ▷ Try t times to generate a prime in $[L, H]$
2:     Let M be a product of small primes.
3:     $x \xleftarrow{\$} (\mathbb{Z}/M)^*$ ▷ This step is tricky
4:     **for** $i = 1$ to t **do**
5:         $\alpha \xleftarrow{\$} [0, \lfloor (H - L)/M \rfloor - 1]$
6:         $p \leftarrow L + (x - L \bmod M) + \alpha M$ ▷ Choose $p \equiv x \bmod M$
7:         **if** p is prime **then return** p
8:         $x \leftarrow \text{NEXT}(x)$ ▷ May just be $x \xleftarrow{\$} (\mathbb{Z}/M)^*$ again
9:     **end for**
10:     **return** Failure
11: **end procedure**

This sieving algorithm provides a considerable speedup, of approximately $M/\phi(M)$. For example, by taking M the 1019-bit product of the first 131 primes, this is a factor of ≈ 11.8, improving 1024-bit prime generation from 710 tries to 60 tries in expectation.

To increase performance, the sieving algorithm does not necessarily repeat the sampling procedure for each candidate p. Instead, it updates the sample $x \leftarrow \text{NEXT}(x)$, where NEXT is some (possibly randomized) update function. Joye et al. take $\text{NEXT}(x) := 2 \cdot x \bmod M$. This forces them to take M odd; to avoid running the primality test on even p, they add M if p is even. The choice of a deterministic update function is problematic, because it allows side-channel attackers to accumulate information about x across several iterations [CC07]. It also reduces the entropy of the resulting primes, because the algorithm is more likely to choose primes p such that $p/2^i \bmod M$ is composite for the first few i.

The difficulty remains in sampling efficiently from $(\mathbb{Z}/M)^*$. The samples should be nearly uniform[2] in $(\mathbb{Z}/M)^*$. Rejection sampling would work, but it is slow for large M, and calculating $\text{GCD}(x, M)$ to test coprimality has side-channel concerns [AGTB19, CAB20].

Joye-Paillier-Vaudenay CRT Sieve. Joye, Paillier and Vaudenay suggest to sample $(\mathbb{Z}/M)^*$ using the Chinese Remainder Theorem [JPV00, Fig. 3]. Let $[\![M_i]\!]_{i=1}^n$ be a sequence of mutually coprime integers – Joye et al. take them to be prime powers. Let $M := \prod_i M_i$, and precompute a sequence $[\![\theta_i]\!]_{i=1}^n$ where $\theta_i \equiv 1$ mod M_i and $\theta_i \equiv 0 \bmod M_j$ for all $j \neq i$. Then one can sample $x \xleftarrow{\$} (\mathbb{Z}/M)^*$ as

$$x \leftarrow \left(\sum x_i \cdot \theta_i \right) \quad \bmod M \quad \text{where each} \quad x_i \xleftarrow{\$} (\mathbb{Z}/M_i)^*.$$

Here sampling from $(\mathbb{Z}/M_i)^*$ may be much faster and simpler than sampling from $(\mathbb{Z}/M)^*$. If M_i is a prime power q^e, we just need to choose a sample that is not divisible by q. For M_i of other forms, sampling algorithms will still be simpler and faster with short M_i (e.g. one machine word) than with long ones. The simplest approach is just to sample at random and then reject if $\text{GCD}(M_i, x_i) \neq 1$.

However, this method has a significant disadvantage: it requires precomputing and storing a list of large numbers $[\![\theta_i]\!]_{i=1}^n$. We are also concerned that the use of small secrets x_i may be vulnerable to template attacks.

Improved CRT Sieve. However, we observe that it is not required to take $\theta_i \equiv 1 \bmod M_i$. Indeed, it is only required that θ_i is coprime to M_i, and divisible by each M_j for $j \neq i$. So we can instead take $\theta_i := M/M_i$, avoiding the need to store it. That is, we can take

$$x \leftarrow \left(\sum x_i \cdot (M/M_i) \right) \quad \bmod M \quad \text{where each} \quad x_i \xleftarrow{\$} (\mathbb{Z}/M_i)^*.$$

---

[2] They need not be cryptographically indistinguishable from uniform. In practice, a wide variety of not-quite-uniform distributions are used [SNS+16]. This seems to be sufficient so long as (p, q) are close enough to uniform and are uncorrelated [NSS+17].

In fact, we can avoid the division by computing the sum iteratively, as shown in Algorithm 3. This novel algorithm is at least as fast as the Joye-Paillier-Vaudenay version, but does not require storage of $[\![\theta_i]\!]_{i=1}^n$.

Algorithm 3. Improved sampling from $(\mathbb{Z}/M)^*$ using CRT (new)

```
1: procedure SAMPLE([[Mi]]i=1^n)
2:     x ← 0
3:     M ← 1
4:     for i = 1 to n do
5:         xi ←$ (Z/Mi)*
6:         x ← (x · Mi + xi · M) mod (M · Mi)
7:         M ← M · Mi
8:     end for
9:     return x
10: end procedure
```

We can use a similar technique to improve the NEXT algorithm, so that it is randomized to deter side-channel attacks. We can do this by choosing a random M_i, sampling $y_i \xleftarrow{\$} (\mathbb{Z}/M_i)^*$, and returning

$$x \cdot (y_i \cdot (M/M_i) + M_i) \bmod M.$$

This works because the factor $y_i \cdot (M/M_i) + M_i$ is always coprime to M:

- It is congruent to $y_i \cdot (M/M_i) \bmod M_i$, and this value is coprime to M_i by construction.
- It is congruent to $M_i \bmod M_j$ for $j \neq i$, and again M_i is coprime to M_j.

Joye-Paillier sieve with Carmichael's λ. However, we are still concerned that the small domain of x_i may lead to template attacks. It would be preferable to implement a sieve that uses only large random numbers.

Joye and Paillier suggest to sample from $(\mathbb{Z}/M)^*$ as shown in [JP06, Fig. 4], reproduced in Algorithm 4. This algorithm is based on Carmichael's observation that for each prime $q^e | M$,

$$x^{\lambda(M)} \bmod q^e = \begin{cases} 0 \text{ if } q | x \\ 1 \text{ otherwise} \end{cases}$$

So the update $x \leftarrow x + r \cdot (1 - x^{\lambda(M)})$ only affects $x \bmod q^e$ if $q | x$.

The sampling algorithm is somewhat slow: 2.15 iterations are required in expectation, and each iteration requires an exponentiation mod M. If M is again the 1019-bit product of the first 131 primes, then $\lambda(M)$ has 276 bits. Therefore overall sampling from $(\mathbb{Z}/M)^*$ is about 58% as expensive as a Fermat or Miller-Rabin primality test of the same size, so sampling independently before every primality test would cause a noticeable slowdown. Because the performance decreases as $\lambda(M)$ increases, this method works best if M has only small prime factors; or at least if for all primes $q | M, q - 1$ has only small prime factors.

Algorithm 4. Sampling from $(\mathbb{Z}/M)^*$ using Carmichael's λ [JP06]

1: **procedure** SAMPLE$(M, \lambda(M))$
2:    $x \xleftarrow{\$} \mathbb{Z}/M$
3:    $z \leftarrow 1 - x^{\lambda(M)} \bmod M$
4:    **while** $z \neq 0$ **do**
5:       $r \xleftarrow{\$} \mathbb{Z}/M$
6:       $x \leftarrow x + rz$
7:       $z \leftarrow 1 - x^{\lambda(M)} \bmod M$
8:    **end while**
9:    **return** x
10: **end procedure**

2.3 New Sampling Algorithm with Quadratic Residuosity

Here we describe a novel sieving algorithm using quadratic residuosity. We expect this method to resist side-channel attacks because it performs only a few calculations, and all intermediate values have high entropy.

Let M be an odd number; a good choice is the product of the first n odd primes, but we can use any odd number of known factorization. Let u be chosen such that $-u$ is a quadratic nonresidue mod each prime $q|M$. Call such a u "valid" mod M. If the factorization of M is known, then it is straightforward to find valid u using the Chinese Remainder Theorem, as we will soon describe. The values (M, u) can be precomputed, and stored in read-only memory (ROM) on the device that needs to generate primes, or they can be calculated on the fly to save ROM.

Then for all $r \in \mathbb{Z}$, by definition $r^2 \not\equiv -u \bmod$ each $q|M$. So $r^2 + u$ is not divisible by any $q|M$: it is coprime to M. With (M, u) precomputed, the prime generation algorithm can very easily sample from $(\mathbb{Z}/M)^*$, simply by choosing r at random and computing $r^2 + u \bmod M$. The same technique could be used with any other polynomial function that does not have a root modulo any $q|M$, such as $ur^2 + 1$, but $r^2 + u$ is simple and requires only one multiplication.

These samples are not uniformly random: in particular, they cover only about half of $(\mathbb{Z}/q^e)^*$ for each $q^e||M$. So if M is divisible by n distinct primes, the range is only slightly more than a 2^{-n} fraction of $(\mathbb{Z}/M)^*$. But we will show that the product of several independent samples approaches a uniformly random distribution on $(\mathbb{Z}/M)^*$. Since prime generation algorithms usually do not require perfectly uniform output, a product of between 4 and 10 such samples will be close enough to uniform for most practical purposes, as shown in Fig. 1. We suggest using 6 samples, which loses less than 0.11 bits of min-entropy for all M.

If a system is equipped with a fast random number generator, then the new sieving technique is fast enough (11 multiplies mod M for 6 samples, compared to several hundred for Algorithm 4) that we do not need to use an update function NEXT(x). We can just choose a fresh sample x every time. However, if the random number generator is somewhat slow, we can set NEXT$(x) = x \cdot (y^2 + u) \bmod M$, where y is a fresh random sample. This improves on $\text{NEXT}(x) = 2x \bmod M$: it is more uniform, and it mitigates side-channel leakage related to x. This version is shown in Algorithm 5. Note that Line 6 guarantees that p is odd and coprime to M, and that $p \in [L \cdot 2s, L \cdot 2s + 2M - 1]$.

Algorithm 5. Prime generation with novel sieving algorithm (new)

1: **procedure** $\text{PRIMEGEN}(L, H, s, t)$ $\qquad \triangleright$ Generate a nearly random prime in $[L \cdot 2s, H \cdot 2s]$
2: $\quad$ Let M be odd of known factorization, such that $M < H - L$ but only slightly.
3: $\quad$ Choose u so that $-u$ is a QNR mod all odd primes dividing M.
4: $\quad x \leftarrow \prod_{j=1}^{6}(r_j^2 + u) \bmod M$, where each $r_j \xleftarrow{\$} \mathbb{Z}/M$.
5: $\quad$ **for** $i = 1$ to t **do**
6: $\quad\quad p \leftarrow L \cdot 2s + (2x + M - L \cdot 2s \bmod 2M)$
7: $\quad\quad \alpha \xleftarrow{\$} [0, s-1]$
8: $\quad\quad p \leftarrow p + 2M\alpha$
9: $\quad\quad$ **if** p is prime **then return** p
10: $\quad\quad r \xleftarrow{\$} \mathbb{Z}/M$
11: $\quad\quad x \leftarrow x \cdot (r^2 + u) \bmod M$
12: $\quad$ **end for**
13: $\quad$ **return** Failure
14: **end procedure**

Note also that it is easy to sample $r \leftarrow \mathbb{Z}/M$ with a high degree of uniformity. Simply set R to be a power of 2 (or of the machine's word size) such that $R > 2^{64} \cdot M$ (or an even larger bound); choose $r \xleftarrow{\$} [0, R-1]$; and then reduce r mod M.

Variants. With M odd, this approach works with no modifications when using power-of-2 Montgomery multiplication and Montgomery reduction mod M: if x is coprime to M, then so is $\text{MONTREDUCE}(x)$. Before primality testing, x can be made odd, or 3 mod 4 for easier Miller-Rabin implementation, by adding a suitable multiple of M.

On systems where modular multiplication does not use Montgomery reduction, the modulus $2M$ can be used instead, and the candidates can then be guaranteed to be odd. Specifically, we can sample candidate primes in the residue class

$$\prod_{i=1}^{k}(2(r_i^2 + u) + M) \bmod 2M.$$

Likewise, x can be constrained to be 3 mod 4. Constrain u to be 1 mod 4, and sample candidate primes in the residue class

$$-\prod_{i=1}^{k}((2r_i)^2 + u) \bmod 4M.$$

Or again, we can sample x from $(\mathbb{Z}/M)^*$ as usual and then test $(4x + cM) \bmod 4M$ for primality, where $c \in \{1, 3\}$ is chosen such that $cM \equiv 3 \bmod 4$. The same techniques can be used to ensure that $x \equiv 2 \bmod 3$, which is required for RSA with $e = 3$.

Uniformity mod M. Algorithm 5 draws samples from the distribution

$$\mathcal{D}_{M,k,u} := \prod_{i=1}^{k} (x_i^2 + u) \bmod M : x_i \xleftarrow{\$} [0, M).$$

How close is $\mathcal{D}_{M,k,u}$ to the uniform distribution $\mathcal{U}_M$ on $(\mathbb{Z}/M)^*$? We will bound the maximum difference in probability to sample each x mod a prime power:

$$\|\mathcal{D}_{q^e,k,u} - \mathcal{U}_{q^e}\|_\infty := \max_{x \in (\mathbb{Z}/q^e)^*} |\Pr[\mathcal{D}_{q^e,k,u} = x] - \Pr[\mathcal{U}_{q^e} = x]|$$

This in turn will allow us to bound the L_1 distance

$$\|\mathcal{D}_{M,k,u} - \mathcal{U}_M\|_1 := \sum_{x \in (\mathbb{Z}/M)^*} |\Pr[\mathcal{D}_{M,k,u} = x] - \Pr[\mathcal{U}_M = x]|$$

$$\leqslant \sum_{q^e \| M} \phi(q^e) \cdot \|\mathcal{D}_{q^e,k,u} - \mathcal{U}_{q^e}\|_\infty$$

and the min-entropy loss

$$\delta H_\infty := \max_{x \in (\mathbb{Z}/M)^*} \frac{\Pr[\mathcal{D}_{M,k,u} = x]}{\Pr[\mathcal{U}_M = x]}$$

$$\leqslant \sum_{q^e \| M} \frac{\phi(q^e) \cdot \|\mathcal{D}_{q^e,k,u} - \mathcal{U}_{q^e}\|_\infty}{\ln 2}$$

These three measures do not depend on which u is chosen, so long as it is valid mod M. In practice, min-entropy loss is probably the most relevant: if the adversary can break a single RSA key with probability ϵ when $p \leftarrow \mathcal{U}_M$, then it will succeed with probability at most $\epsilon \cdot 2^{\delta H_\infty}$ when $p \leftarrow \mathcal{D}_{M,k,u}$.

We can bound the L_1 distance using the following theorem, which we prove in the full version:

Theorem 1 (Uniformity of $\mathcal{D}_{M,k,u}$). *Let M be a positive odd integer, let u be valid mod M, and let $k \geqslant 4$. Let $\mathcal{U}_M$ be the uniform distribution on $(\mathbb{Z}/M)^*$. Let*

$$\epsilon_{M,k} := \sum_{\text{prime } q | M} \left(\frac{2}{\sqrt{q}}\right)^{\lfloor k/2 \rfloor}.$$

Then

$$\|\mathcal{D}_{M,k,u} - \mathcal{U}_M\|_1 < \epsilon_{M,k} \quad and \quad \delta H_\infty < \frac{\epsilon_{M,k}}{\ln 2}.$$

Note that for $k > 6$, the sum converges for all primes q, so it allows us to prove a bound that does not depend on M.

For concrete (M, k) this theorem is somewhat loose, so we also took an empirical approach to calculate the L_∞ distance. For this approach, we calculated the distribution $\mathcal{D}_{M,k,u}$ for $k \in \{1, 2\}$ with M the product of the first 200 or 1000 odd primes. Then for $3 \leqslant k \leqslant 10$, we were additionally able to extend the bound to powers of those primes using an equation from the proof of Theorem 1 (found in the full version of this paper); the bound from this equation does not converge for $k \leqslant 2$. Theorem 1 itself then bounds the maximum additional distance that can be seen with even larger M. The result is shown in Fig. 1.

	First 200 odd primes		First 1000 odd primes		All larger primes	
k	L_1	δH_∞	L_1	δH_∞	L_1	δH_∞
1	2	197.3305	2	996.9990	-	-
2	1.4362	29.1962	1.6889	65.6709	-	-
3	2	4.6741	2	5.6428	-	-
4	0.5510	0.7963	0.5659	0.8164	-	-
5	0.1252	0.1806	0.1255	0.1810	-	-
6	0.0453	0.0653	0.0453	0.0653	0.02989	0.04312
7	0.0157	0.0226	0.0157	0.0226	-	-
8	0.0058	0.0084	0.0058	0.0084	0.00022	0.00031
9	0.0023	0.0033	0.0023	0.0033	-	-
10	0.0010	0.0015	0.0010	0.0015	$3.1 \cdot 10^{-6}$	$4.5 \cdot 10^{-6}$

Fig. 1. Bounds on L_1 distance and min-entropy loss between $\mathcal{D}_{M,k,u}$ and $\mathcal{U}_M$. For $k \geqslant 3$, this includes any power of the given primes, but for $k \in \{1, 2\}$ it only includes the first power. The "all larger primes" column is a bound for $M = \prod q_i^{e_i}$ where all the prime factors q_i are beyond the first thousand odd primes; the bound in Theorem 1 converges for even $k \geqslant 6$. Note that the L_1 distance cannot be greater than 2.

Choosing M. The value of M is relatively unconstrained, beyond being odd and of known factorization. If p is random in some range and is coprime to M, then it is prime with probability about $M/(\phi(M)\ln p)$, or twice that if M is odd and p is made odd before testing. For efficiency, M should be chosen as a multiple of the first several odd primes, so that $M/\phi(M)$ is as large as possible. But suppose we wish to generate primes in an interval $[L, H]$. We could generate M by first taking, say, $M_1 < (H - L)/2^{32}$ as a product of the first n odd primes, and then calculating

$$M = M_1 \cdot \left\lfloor \frac{H - L}{2M_1} \right\rfloor.$$

This would result in an M very close to $(H - L)/2$, so that adding $2M \cdot \alpha$ can be skipped, and the distribution would still be close to uniform on $[L, H]$. Or we could choose M such that $(H - L)/(2M)$ is very nearly a power of 2, so that at least sampling α is easier. This improvement is incorporated into Algorithm 5. The flexibility in M is an improvement on the Joye-Paillier sieve, where M should be chosen smooth so that $\lambda(M)$ is small.

Another option is to follow Joye-Paillier by setting M somewhat smaller than $(H - L)/2$, and then adjust L and H to be multiples of M. In that case, α is not typically chosen from a power-of-2 range, but subtracting $2L \bmod M$ can be skipped.

When generating RSA keys, the range is usually chosen as

$$[L, H] = [2^{(b-1)/2}, 2^{b/2} - 1]$$

for some even integer b. That way, if $L \leqslant p, q \leqslant H$, then $2^{b-1} \leqslant p \cdot q < 2^b$; that is, $N = pq$ has exactly b bits. To support this case, we can set M to slightly less than $(H - L)/2$ for the lowest supported value of b. For higher values, $H - L$ is very nearly a power of 2 times M. This makes the sieve efficient in both cases. This technique is similar to [JP06, Fig. 5].

Choosing u. We must choose a valid u, meaning one such that $-u$ is a quadratic nonresidue mod each prime $q|M$. This can be performed by finding such a u_q mod each q, and then combining these using the CRT. However, we do not need the full CRT, because we do not care exactly what u is mod q. It is sufficient to calculate

$$u = \sum_{q^e || M} u_p \cdot (M/q^e)^2 \quad \bmod M$$

where each u_q is a quadratic nonresidue mod q. Then for each $q|M$,

$$-u \equiv -u_p \cdot k_p^2 \quad \bmod q \text{ for some nonzero } k_q,$$

so u is also a quadratic nonresidue mod q. This u may also be calculated iteratively, much as in Algorithm 3. For each $q \equiv 3 \bmod 4$, we can take $u_q = 1$.

It is also an interesting question to choose u as small as possible. This issue is discussed in Appendix B.

Supporting Multiple Parameter Sets with Less Storage. If a device supports key generation for multiple sizes, it is preferable (but not necessary) to use a specific M for each size. That is, use larger values of M to generate larger primes, so that more small divisors can be sieved out. The parameters could be stored separately for each M, but there is an opportunity to save space as the larger M values should be (at least nearly) divisible by the smaller ones. So we can sample mod M_1 for the smallest supported parameter size, mod $M_1 \cdot M_2$ for the next size, and in general mod $M = \prod_{i=1}^{n} M_i$ for the nth smallest size or tier of sizes.

There are a few different options for how to do this. The simplest is to store a u which is valid mod all the M_i, and thus mod their product. The u value can be (Montgomery) reduced modulo M before use. It is also possible to store a separate u_i (or reduce u separately) mod each M_i; we could then sample separately mod each M_i and combine them into one sample mod M using Sect. 2.2. This is likely faster for the first sample due to smaller multiplications, but slower for the Next function if it is used.

Or we could combine the parameters as

$$M := \prod_{i=1}^{n} M_i, \quad u := \sum_{i=1}^{n} u_i \cdot (M/M_i)^2 \bmod M$$

and then sample using only the QR sieve mod M.

2.4   Applications

Generating Primes for RSA Keys. Our new sieve simplifies finding primes in a particular range such as $[2^{(b-1)/2}, 2^b]$, which is the slowest step in RSA key generation. Previous work discusses efficient generation of RSA keys once the prime generation step is done [JP03].

One additional issue with RSA key generation is that we must have $e \nmid p - 1$. When $e = 3$ this means that $p \equiv 2 \bmod 3$, which can be accommodated as discussed in Sect. 2.3. Otherwise it can be accomplished by rejection sampling. Or if e is coprime to M, one could sample $x \leftarrow (\mathbb{Z}/M)^*$ and $y \leftarrow \mathbb{Z}/e$ such that both y and $yM - 1$ are coprime to e; and then set the candidate prime to $p \leftarrow x \cdot e + y \cdot M$.

Generating DSA Moduli, Safe Primes and Strong Primes. Some standards require generation of primes with specific properties, such as "strong primes" where $p + 1$ and/or $p - 1$ have large prime factors. Either of our sieve methods can be used to replace the **g** function in [JPV00, Figs. 8 and 12] to generate DSA moduli and strong primes respectively. These both require sampling candidate primes which are congruent to $a \bmod m$ for certain (a, m) with m coprime to M. In particular, DSA moduli are congruent to $1 \bmod 2q$. We can proceed by computing $\bar{m} = am^{-1} \bmod M$, and then to sample values $x \bmod M$. We can then compute candidate primes $p \equiv (x - \bar{m})m + a \bmod Mb$. By construction, these are congruent to $a \bmod m$, and to $xm \bmod M$. If m and M are coprime, then xm is uniformly random in $(\mathbb{Z}/M)^*$.

Generating "safe primes" $p = 2q + 1$, for which q is also prime, is more difficult if we wish to sieve both p and q. However, our CRT-based sieve can be adapted easily enough to match [JPV00, Fig. 10]. Joye et al. solve the CRT equations $x \equiv x_i \bmod M_i$ as

$$x \leftarrow \sum_{i=1}^{n} x_i \cdot \theta_i \quad \text{where} \quad \theta_i \bmod M_j = \begin{cases} 1 \text{ if } i = j \\ 0 \text{ if } i \neq j \end{cases}$$

Joye et al. rejection sample each x_i such that x_i and $2x_i + 1$ are both in $(\mathbb{Z}/M_i)^*$. We instead compute

$$x \leftarrow \sum_{i=1}^{n} x_i \cdot \theta_i \quad \text{where} \quad \theta_i = \prod_{j \neq i} M_j$$

so we need x_i and $2(x_i \cdot \theta_i) + 1$ both to be in $(\mathbb{Z}/M_i)^*$.

Blinding Inversions mod M. The sieve can be used for techniques other than prime generation. For example, if for some algorithm we must invert a value x modulo a public constant M, we can use this technique to generate a nearly-uniform r which is coprime to M. We can then compute $x^{-1} \equiv r \cdot (rx)^{-1}$ mod M to mitigate side-channel attacks on the inversion process.

3   RSA-CRT Without q^{-1} Mod p

Let (N, e) be an RSA public key. The RSA private permutation computes $m = x^d$ mod N, where $d \equiv e^{-1}$ mod $\lambda(N)$. However, since the party with the private key also knows the factorization $N = pq$, it is more efficient to compute $m_p = x^{d_p}$ mod p, where $d_p \equiv e^{-1}$ mod $p - 1$, and likewise with q. This information may be combined using the Chinese Remainder Theorem (CRT):

$$m = ((m_p - m_q) \cdot q^{-1} \quad \mathrm{mod}\ p) \cdot q + m_q.$$

This technique is called RSA-CRT. The RSA-CRT computation requires q^{-1} mod p, which is typically stored as part of the private key; it can also be computed when the key is loaded, but this has performance and potentially side-channel problems [CAB20].

CRT could also be performed as

$$m \equiv (m_p \cdot q^{-1} \quad \mathrm{mod}\ p) \cdot q \ + \ (m_q \cdot p^{-1} \quad \mathrm{mod}\ q) \cdot p \quad \mathrm{mod}\ N$$

but this appears to require even more information. However, there is a trick to compute $m_p \cdot q^{-1}$ mod p without knowing q^{-1} mod p, which is based on the multiplicative masking in [EL10]. Choose any $y \in (\mathbb{Z}/p)^*$ and let

$$\alpha := (xy)^{e-1} \quad \mathrm{mod}\ p$$
$$\beta := (\alpha \cdot y)^{p-1-d_p} \equiv (\alpha \cdot y)^{-1/e} \quad \mathrm{mod}\ p$$
$$m_{p,y} := \beta \cdot x \equiv x^{1/e} \cdot y^{-1} \quad \mathrm{mod}\ p \tag{1}$$

This computes $m_{p,y}$ using one long exponentiation and one short one, and three multiplications. Setting $y = q$ gives a way to compute RSA-CRT without any inversions.

For multiplicative masking we can instead set $y = rq$ where $r \xleftarrow{\$} (\mathbb{Z}/N)^*$, so that:[3]

$$m_{p,rq} \equiv x^d \cdot (rq)^{-1} \quad \mathrm{mod}\ p.$$

We can compute $m_{q,rp}$ analogously, and combine to calculate mr^{-1} mod N. That is,

$$m \equiv r \cdot (m_{p,rq} \cdot q + m_{q,rp} \cdot p) \quad \mathrm{mod}\ N.$$

---

[3] A random $r \xleftarrow{\$} \mathbb{Z}/N$ will be coprime to N with overwhelming probability. But if we wanted to be sure then we could reuse one of our sieve techniques.

This allows us to compute RSA-CRT decryption with message blinding, using only (p, q, e, d_p, d_q). The technique is compatible with other blinding techniques for (p, q, d_p, d_q), such as [EL10], and for techniques which skip the step of converting to Montgomery form.

Our technique generalizes to multi-prime with $N = \prod p_i$, where the reconstruction equation is

$$ m \equiv \sum \left(m_{p_i} \cdot \left(\frac{N}{p_i} \right)^{-1} \mod p_i \right) \cdot \frac{N}{p_i} \mod N. $$

The inner term $m_{p_i} \cdot (N/p_i)^{-1} \mod p_i$ can be computed using our blinding and inversion technique. Here N/p_i is perhaps better written as $\prod_{j \neq i} p_j$.

3.1   Inverse-Free RSA Mod $p^k q$

Another fast variant of RSA uses $N = p^k q$ [Tak98]. Our inversion-free CRT technique applies here as well, apparently trivially: we can use Eq. (1) to compute $x^{d \mod \phi(p^k)} \cdot (qr)^{-1} \mod p^k$, and combine this with $x^{d \mod \phi(q)} \cdot (p^k r)^{-1} \mod q$.

However, the point of RSA mod $p^k q$ is that $x^d \mod p^k$ can be accelerated. Instead of computing x^d directly mod p^k, the technique is to calculate $x^{d_p} \mod p$, where $d_p \equiv e^{-1} \mod p - 1$. This gives a solution to the equation

$$ m_1^e \equiv x \mod p^1, $$

which can then be iteratively lifted to a solution $m_k^e \equiv x \mod p^k$ using Hensel's lemma. This means that the trivial application of our technique will perform poorly, and we still need to compute $e^{-1} \mod p$ [Tak04].

We will instead compute $x^d \cdot y^{-1}$, by solving the equation

$$ (ym)^e \equiv x \mod p^k, $$

again with Hensel lifting. Given a nonzero solution $m_\ell \mod p^\ell$, we can lift it to a solution $m_{\ell+1} \mod p^{\ell+1}$ using the Hensel iteration

$$ m_{\ell+1} \equiv m_\ell + \frac{x - (ym)_\ell^e}{e \cdot y^e \cdot m_1^{e-1} \mod p} \mod p^{\ell+1}, $$

whose denominator $\delta := e \cdot y^e \cdot m_1^{e-1} \mod p$ is the derivative of $(ym)^e$ with respect to m. We can do this in an inverse-free manner given $m_1 = x^d \cdot y^{-1} \mod p$ and $\delta^{-1} \mod p$, where

$$ \delta^{-1} \equiv (e \cdot y^e \cdot m_1^{e-1})^{-1} \mod p $$
$$ \equiv (ym)^{1-e} \cdot (ye)^{-1} \mod p $$
$$ \equiv x^{d \cdot (1-e)} \cdot (ye)^{-1} \mod p $$
$$ \equiv x^{d-1} \cdot (ye)^{-1} \equiv x^d \cdot (yex)^{-1} \mod p $$

This value $\delta^{-1} \equiv x^d \cdot (yex)^{-1} \bmod p$ can be computed using the blinding and inversion method from Eq. (1), and from it we can compute $m_1 \equiv x^d \cdot y^{-1} \equiv \delta^{-1} \cdot ex \bmod p$. As before, we can do this with $y := qr$ for random r, to achieve a blinded, inverse-free CRT algorithm.

Thus, we can extend our technique to inverse-free RSA modulo general products of powers of primes.

3.2 Generalized Batching

Our inverse-free CRT technique was inspired by side-channel countermeasures, but it is a special case of a framework for inversion and root calculations [Ham12] including

$$(x, y) \to (x^{1/e}, y^{-1}) \quad \bmod p$$

when x and y are nonzero. We can do this by calculating

$$\alpha := (xy)^{e-1}$$
$$\beta := (\alpha \cdot y)^{-1/e} \equiv x^{1/e-1} \cdot y^{-1} \quad \bmod p$$
$$x^{1/e} \equiv \beta \cdot xy \quad \bmod p$$
$$y^{-1} \equiv \alpha \cdot \beta^e \quad \bmod p$$

This technique was proposed for elliptic curves, and to our knowledge has not been applied to RSA before. The principle is to consider the exponential lattice $\mathcal{L}$ of expressions the form $x^a \cdot y^b$ for $a, b \in \mathbb{Z}$. For more inputs, a higher-dimensional lattice may be used. The target expression(s) such as $\{x^{1/e}, y^{-1}\}$ lie in a superlattice $\mathcal{L}'$ of volume $1/e$. If (as in this example) $\mathcal{L}'/\mathcal{L}$ is one-dimensional, then we can find an element $z \in \mathcal{L}'$, such that $\{x, y, z\}$ span $\mathcal{L}'$, the coefficients of z are either all positive or all negative, and the target element is spanned by $\{x, y, z\}$ with (small) non-negative coefficients. Typically this is best done by giving z strictly negative coefficients, so that non-negative linear combinations of $\{x, y, z\}$ cover all of $\mathcal{L}'$.

Then z can be computed by calculating $\pm ez$ as a non-negative integer combination of $\{x, y\}$, and then applying the $\pm 1/e$ map (or more generally, using the $\pm k/e$ map for some integer k coprime to e) at the cost of a single large exponentiation. Since now $\{x, y, z\}$ span the target expressions with small non-negative coefficients, these targets can be calculated using only multiplications and small exponentiations.

This principle generalizes batch RSA [Fia90], Montgomery's batched inversion, and batch inversion and square root [Ham12]. It directly provides an inversion-free variant of batch RSA: for example, batching a message $m_3 = x_3^{1/3}$ and $m_5 = x_5^{1/5}$ can be calculated as:

$$z := (x_3^5 \cdot x_5^3)^{-1/15} = x_3^{-1/3} \cdot x_5^{-1/5}; \qquad m_3 = z^5 \cdot x_3^2 \cdot x_5; \qquad m_5 = z^9 \cdot x_3^3 \cdot x_5^2.$$

This can be further optimized with an appropriate addition chain, and possibly by choosing a different generator z of the lattice.

These techniques can batch multiple small roots and/or inverses using one large exponentiation if and only if the roots are of relatively prime degrees. Otherwise the quotient $\mathcal{L}'/\mathcal{L}$ has multiple generators, so while a batching technique might provide a speedup in some cases, it will require more than one large exponentiation.

We note that batching techniques can also be used to avoid conversions to Montgomery form. The Montgomery form of a number x is $x \cdot R \bmod p$ for some R. Multiplication and exponentiation are typically faster when the inputs are given in Montgomery form. Division by $R \bmod p$ is fast: it is Montgomery reduction. But multiplication by $R \bmod p$ requires Barrett reduction, which is slower and more complex in hardware. However, consider that x is itself the Montgomery form of another number $\hat{x} := x/R \bmod p$. So we can compute

$$x^{1/e} = (\hat{x} \cdot R)^{1/e} = (\hat{x}^{e-1}/R)^{-1/e} \cdot \hat{x}$$

where the input $\hat{x}$ is given by its Montgomery form x, and now we are only dividing by R instead of multiplying by it. This technique may not be worthwhile by itself, because it requires an extra short exponentiation, but it is essentially free if batching is already in use. As a special case of this, random blinding values can be assumed to already be in Montgomery form.

4   RSA with Compressed Private Keys

Our new sieving and RSA-CRT algorithms give an interesting improvement to *compressed* RSA private keys for devices with limited nonvolatile storage. This can be done easily enough just by replacing the random numbers in the usual RSA key generation algorithm with a pseudorandom generator, and storing only the secret seed for that generator. The private key can then be regenerated from the seed whenever it is needed. But RSA key generation is notoriously slow, so this compression mechanism is usually unacceptable. However, if we record hints indicating on which iterations h_p resp h_q we found p resp q, then p and q can be reconstructed very quickly, skipping all the primality tests. This is easiest if each iteration samples an independent candidate p, so that only the h_pth and h_qth iterations must be performed to reconstruct (p, q).

This technique could have been used with other RSA key generation algorithms, but at a significant cost in efficiency. Algorithm 1 would suffer from long key generation time. The Joye-Paillier-Vaudenay CRT sieve requires large ROM storage, whereas their Carmichael λ sieve requires extra large exponentiations in order to use the key. But with our Algorithms 3 or 5, the performance penalty to generating and to use the key is very small. With previous techniques, we also would have needed to avoid RSA-CRT or else compute $q^{-1} \bmod p$, but with inverse-free RSA-CRT we can also mitigate that performance cost. The other nontrivial step, computing d from e, has a shortcut for small prime e [JP03].

We work through the details with Algorithm 5. In the key generation algorithm we can replace the random number generator with a pseudorandom function $F_k(i, h, j;\ R)$. Its arguments are:

- the secret seed k;
- a flag $i \in \{0, 1\}$ indicating whether we're generating p or q (or from a larger domain for multi-prime RSA);
- a hint $h \in [0, t - 1]$ where t is the maximum number of attempts to find a prime in key generation (e.g. $t = \ln \frac{\phi(M)}{\epsilon \cdot M} \cdot \ln p$ for a failure rate near ϵ);
- a counter $j \in [0, m]$ where m is the number of samples required for uniformity (e.g. $m = 6$);
- and the size R of the desired range.

F_k should return a uniformly pseudorandom integer in $[0, R - 1]$. This enables us to sample pseudorandom integers in $[L \cdot 2s, H \cdot 2s]$ which are coprime to M using the SIEVESAMPLE routine shown in Algorithm 6.

The secret primes (p, q) can then be represented by the parameters (L, H, s, e), the secret seed k and the hints h_p and h_q. The private key can be reconstructed by calling SIEVESAMPLE:

$$p = \text{SIEVESAMPLE}(L, H, s, k, 0, h_p) \quad \text{and} \quad q = \text{SIEVESAMPLE}(L, H, s, k, 1, h_q).$$

The other values in the private key, $d \bmod p - 1$ and $\bmod q - 1$, can be reconstructed efficiently using Arazi's lemma and Hensel's lemma as shown in [JP03], reproduced as DMOD. A complete compressed RSA algorithm is shown in Algorithm 6. If the negligible probability of failure from line 37 is unacceptable, we can instead generate $(p, q) \equiv 3 \bmod 4$, and implement that line using Algorithm 5 with $u = 1$.

Suppose we wish to generate 1536-bit primes for RSA-3072, roughly corresponding to 128-bit security. If M is divisible by the first 180 primes so that $\phi(M)/M \approx 0.08$, then each candidate will be prime with probability

$$\text{Pr}[\text{prime}] \approx \frac{M}{1536 \cdot \phi(M) \cdot \ln 2} \approx \frac{1}{85}.$$

If we set $t = 2^{16}$, then COMPRESSEDRSA will fail to find a suitable p or q with probability about $2 \cdot e^{-t \cdot \text{Pr}[\text{prime}]} < 2^{-1111}$. So a 3072-bit private RSA key may be compressed to 160 bits with no loss of security: a 128-bit key and two 16-bit hints.

To prevent mistakes, it may also be useful to store (s, e), or to make the pseudorandom function F depend on them, or both. In hardware deployed to a hostile environment, it is also worth adding fault countermeasures, for example a checksum on (p, q, d_p, d_q), to prevent fault attacks [ABF+03].

If k is derived—for example from hardware constants, a master key or a PUF—then only h_p and h_q need to be stored. If k can be chosen by the generator (i.e. it is not a derived key), then storage requirements can be further reduced by removing h_p, and instead re-randomizing k in the first loop. Various other arrangements can be used to trade hint size for key generation performance, such as using a shorter hint h_q and incrementing h_p if no prime q can be found.

Combining the new RSA-CRT technique with Algorithm 6, we can implement RSA efficiently with compressed private keys. For RSA-3072 with $e = 65537$, the calculations of (p, q, d_p, d_q) and the recovery of the final m costs:

Algorithm 6. RSA with compressed private keys

1: **procedure** SIEVESAMPLE(L, H, s, k, i, h) ▷ Sample a value in $[L \cdot 2s, H \cdot 2s]$ using $F_k(i, h, \cdot)$
2:    Let M be a multiple of many small primes, such that $M < H - L$ but only slightly.
3:    Let u be odd such that $-u$ is a QNR mod all odd primes dividing M.
4:    $x \leftarrow \prod_{j=1}^{6} \left(F_k(i, h, j;\ M)^2 + u \right) \bmod M$.
5:    $\alpha \xleftarrow{\$} F_k(i, h, 0;\ s)$
6:    **return** $p \leftarrow L \cdot 2s + (2x + M - L \cdot 2s \bmod 2M) + 2\alpha M$
7: **end procedure**

8: **procedure** COMPRESSEDRSAKEYGEN(L, H, s, e, t, k)
9:    **for** $h_p = 0$ to $t - 1$ **do**
10:        $p \leftarrow$ SIEVESAMPLE($L, H, s, k, 0, h_p$)
11:        **if** $e \nmid p - 1$ and p is prime **then goto** line 14
12:    **end for**
13:    **return** Failure
14:
15:    **for** $h_q = 0$ to $t - 1$ **do**
16:        $q \leftarrow$ SIEVESAMPLE($L, H, s, k, 1, h_q$)
17:        **if** $e \nmid q - 1$ and q is prime **then goto** line 20
18:    **end for**
19:    **return** Failure
20:
21:    **return** public key $(p \cdot q, e)$ and compressed private key $(L, H, s, e;\ k, h_p, h_q)$
22: **end procedure**

23: **procedure** DMOD(e, ϕ, H)   ▷ Computes $e^{-1} \bmod \phi < H$ if e is prime and $e \nmid \phi$
24:    $R \leftarrow 2^{\lceil \lg H \rceil}$
25:    $\bar{e} \leftarrow 1$
26:    **for** $i = 1$ to $\lceil \lg \lg R \rceil$ **do**   ▷ Compute $\bar{e} \leftarrow e^{-1} \bmod R$
27:        $\bar{e} \leftarrow \bar{e} \cdot (2 - e \cdot \bar{e}) \bmod 2^{2^i}$
28:    **end for**   ▷ In practice, share $\bar{e}$ for the two calls
29:    **return** $(1 + (-\phi^{e-2} \bmod e) \cdot \phi) \cdot \bar{e} \bmod R$ ▷ Arazi's lemma
30: **end procedure**

31: **procedure** COMPRESSEDRSAPRIVATE($(L, H, s, e;\ k, h_p, h_q),\ x$))
32:    $p \leftarrow$ SIEVESAMPLE($L, H, s, k, 0, h_p$)
33:    $q \leftarrow$ SIEVESAMPLE($L, H, s, k, 1, h_q$)
34:    $d_p \leftarrow$ DMOD($e, p - 1, H \cdot 2s$)
35:    $d_q \leftarrow$ DMOD($e, q - 1, H \cdot 2s$)
36:    $N \leftarrow pq$
37:    $r \xleftarrow{\$} (\mathbb{Z}/N)^*$ ▷ Or $r \xleftarrow{\$} \mathbb{Z}/N$ works with overwhelming probability
38:    $\alpha_p \leftarrow (qrx)^{e-1} \bmod p$
39:    $m_p \leftarrow (qr \cdot \alpha_p)^{p-1-d_p} \bmod p$
40:    $\alpha_q \leftarrow (prx)^{e-1} \bmod q$
41:    $m_q \leftarrow (pr \cdot \alpha_q)^{q-1-d_q} \bmod q$
42:    **return** $rx \cdot (m_p \cdot q + m_q \cdot p) \bmod N$ ▷ Returns $x^{1/e} \bmod N$
43: **end procedure**

- 11 multiplications mod M to sample p, and as many for q.
- 4 multiplications mod R, and several smaller ones, to compute d_p and d_q.
- 19 multiplications mod p, plus one long exponentiation mod p, to compute $q \cdot r$, $\alpha_p \leftarrow (x \cdot qr)^{e-1}$ and $m_p = (qr \cdot \alpha_p)^{p-1-d_p}$; and the same to compute m_q.
- 2 integer multiplications and two multiplications mod N to calculate the final output $m \equiv x \cdot r \cdot (m_p \cdot q + m_q \cdot p) \bmod N$.

Counting the wider multiplications mod N as four, the additional cost of private key compression and blinding together is around 72 large multiplications (mostly squarings) plus a few smaller ones. The exponentiations mod p and q collectively cost some 12882 or 3715 multiplications with the Montgomery ladder and sliding window approaches, respectively, meaning that the additional cost is between 0.6% and 3% of the total runtime.

The same techniques generalize naturally to multi-prime RSA and RSA mod $p^k q$.

5   Performance

We tested our new techniques by modifying OpenSSL 1.1.1j to support the Joye-Paillier sieve, the quadratic residuosity sieve, inversion-free RSA and compressed private keys. We tested on a 2.3 GHz Intel Core i3-6100U processor at 2.3 GHz; this processor is convenient for benchmarks because it does not use TurboBoost. The OpenSSL big number API does not exactly match our algorithms, and we adjusted our algorithms to match its API. In particular, we didn't use Hensel lifting, and we were not able to avoid many conversions into and out of Montgomery form. The results are shown in Table 1. Note that prime generation is a Poisson process, so those timings have an enormous variance and the difference between the Carmichael sieve and the new QR sieve is not significant.

Table 1. Performance comparison of new techniques; timings in thousands or millions of cycles (k or M). Prime generation is averaged over 2000 trials. Signatures are averaged over 100,000 trials: 1000 trials for each of 100 different keys, without outliers more than twice the mean removed. The same 100 keys are used for the standard, inverse-free and compressed versions.

Operation	1024-bit	2048-bit	3072-bit	4096-bit
Primegen OpenSSL standard	26 M	143 M	400 M	950 M
Primegen Carmichael sieve [JP06]	6 M	60 M	257 M	802 M
Primegen new QR sieve	6 M	58 M	251 M	731 M
RSA-CRT sign standard	305 k	2077 k	6161 k	13992 k
RSA-CRT sign inverse-free	412 k	2248 k	6420 k	14376 k
RSA-CRT sign compressed	532 k	2403 k	6622 k	14644 k

5.1 Discussion

OpenSSL's standard key generation uses trial division and not sieving, so a large performance increase is expected. As expected, Joye-Paillier sieve and quadratic residuosity sieve have similar performance.

The overhead from inverse-free and compressed signatures is larger than we expected, amounting to 4% and 7.5% respectively for RSA-3072. Part of this is due to adjusting our algorithms to the OpenSSL APIs, so the overhead might be smaller (or larger!) in an embedded environment. Even at 7.5% it might be worthwhile if nonvolatile memory is limited.

6 Future Work

We leave to future work the task of evaluating the embedded performance, side-channel resistance and fault resistance of these methods, as well as any application to post-quantum RSA [BHLV17,Sch18].

Acknowledgements. Special thanks to Denis Pochuev for feedback on RSA with $p^k \cdot q$.

Intellectual Property Disclosure. Some of these techniques may be covered by US and/or international patents.

A Proof of Theorem 1

We prove this theorem in the extended version, at https://eprint.iacr.org/2020/1507.

B Minimizing u

We say that u is "valid" mod M if $\left(\frac{-u}{p}\right) = -1$ for all primes $p|M$. If M's factorization is known, then it is easy to find a valid u_p modulo each $p|M$ (e.g. by checking the Jacobi symbol $\left(\frac{-u_p}{p}\right)$ until a valid u_p is found), and to combine them using the Chinese Remainder Theorem. But what is the minimum valid u? Using a smaller u could allow the same u to be used for several values of M, or could reduce memory usage and compute time, but mostly it is a mathematically interesting question. For simplicity, we assume here that M is square-free.

If there are n primes dividing M, then a random element of $(\mathbb{Z}/M)^*$ is valid with probability 2^{-n}, so we expect the minimum valid u to be around $u_{\text{minexp}} := 2^n \cdot M/\phi(M)$. A brute-force strategy would require about u_{minexp} work, which is infeasible past the first 50 primes or so. But this work can be reduced somewhat, particularly if we settle for a small but not minimal u.

B.1   Sparse Solutions to Linear Equations

The most effective method we found was to search for valid u of the form $u = q_1 \cdot q_2 \cdots q_m$ where the q_i's are in some set Q. The validity criterion is that:

$$\text{for each prime } p | M, \quad \left(\frac{-u}{p}\right) = \left(\frac{-1}{p}\right) \cdot \left(\frac{q_1}{p}\right) \cdots \left(\frac{q_m}{p}\right) \tag{2}$$

If each q_i is coprime to M, then the Jacobi symbols are all either -1 or 1; mapping these to 1 and 0 respectively translates the validity criterion to a system of affine equations over $\mathbb{F}_2$. This allows us to solve for u with xor-list or sparse solution techniques, such as:

- A birthday attack or stronger collision technique [VOW99] for $m = 2$ and Q a large set (e.g. $|Q| \approx 2^{32}$).
- Wagner's xor-list algorithm [Wag02] for m small and Q a large set.
- Information set decoding for large m and a relatively small set Q (e.g. the first 1000 primes not dividing M).

Using a birthday attack, we discovered that the 59-bit value

$$u = \texttt{0x4b0555d761f3f52}$$

is valid mod the 383-bit product of the first 59 odd primes. We also used Wagner's algorithm to search for u a product of four 32-bit odd numbers, requiring it to be valid mod at least the first 72 odd primes. We ran the algorithm for a day on a 64-core Amazon EC2 Graviton2 instance, producing some 5 million results. Notably,

$$u = \texttt{0xe3b0f73b0050ab294417001ad1e63d}$$

is valid mod the 729-bit product of the first 99 odd primes. Our search was tuned to find u relatively close to u_{minexp}; tuning it differently would have been faster or found valid u mod more primes, but the resulting u would be significantly larger.

It isn't necessary to choose M before u. One could start with a small u which is valid mod the first several primes, and then choose further primes $p | M$ so that u is valid. This sacrifices some performance, because discarding small primes reduces $M/\phi(M)$. Our search using Wagner's algorithm found that

$$u = \texttt{0x23e9ee9bd621b0b248e8b59a4c80bb55}$$

performs well across a range of bit sizes, losing about 0.5% of performance compared to an unconstrained (M, u) at 1024 bits and 3% at 2048 bits.

The quality of results from Wagner's algorithm should fall off exponentially with the number of primes dividing M, because at each step the algorithm multiplies two intermediate values to produce another intermediate that solves b more equations, for some block size b. So while it performs well for the first 100 primes, ISD appears to perform better for the first 400 primes.

B.2   Multiple u

Instead of using linear equations to search for a single u, we could choose a few small u such that at least one of them is valid for every $p|M$. For example, for each of the first 133 odd primes, at least one of $u \in U := \{1, 2, 5, 19\}$ is valid. We could factor M into $\prod_{u \in U} M_u$ such that u is valid mod the corresponding M_u. Then we could sample values $x_u \xleftarrow{\$} (\mathbb{Z}/M_u)^*$ and combine them as in Sect. 2.2.

B.3   Quadratic Minimization

Two other techniques are based on finding small values of quadratic functions over the integers. One is to factor M as $M_1 \cdot M_3$ where M_1 contains the 1-mod-4 factors and M_3 contains the 3-mod-4 factors of M. Valid u are of the form $u \equiv x^2$ mod M_3 for some x coprime to M_3. We may plug in $x = \lfloor \sqrt{kM_3} \rfloor + \ell$ for small positive integers k, ℓ as a more efficient brute force technique. This technique gives many candidate values of u which are around $\sqrt{M_3} \approx \sqrt[4]{M}$, but it still takes exponential time as M increases.

The second approach is to choose small, coprime, square-free positive integers (α, β), and then partition M as $M_0 \cdot M_1$, such that

$$u = \alpha M_0 - \beta M_1$$

is valid. This will be true if:

1. For all primes $p|M$, if $p|\alpha$ then $p|M_0$ and likewise if $p|\beta$ then $p|M_1$.
2. For all other primes $p|M_0$, $\left(\frac{\beta}{p}\right) \cdot \prod_{q|M_1} \left(\frac{q}{p}\right) = -1$ and vice versa.

These equations are actually affine: switching a prime p from M_0 to M_1 or back has the same effect on all the equations regardless of where the other primes are assigned. They can therefore be solved efficiently for a given (α, β) with probability about $(1 - \frac{1}{2}) \cdot (1 - \frac{1}{4}) \cdots \approx 0.29$.

To further reduce u, we make two improvements. First, we extend the equation to $u = \alpha M_0 x^2 - \beta M_1 y^2$ where x is coprime to $\beta M_1 y^2$ and vice versa. By setting x/y as convergents to $\sqrt{\beta M_1/(\alpha M_0)}$, we can find many valid values of $u \approx \sqrt{\alpha \cdot \beta \cdot M_0 \cdot M_1}$. Furthermore, we don't need to set $M = M_0 \cdot M_1$ exactly: it suffices to instead choose $M_2|M$ upfront and set $M = M_0 \cdot M_1 \cdot M_2$. This method produces many u which are valid mod $M_0 \cdot M_1$, and we can continue until by chance we find one which is also valid mod M_2. Overall, this approach finds u which are slightly smaller than $\sqrt{M}$, as does ISD, but ISD seems to work better in practice.

References

[ABD+15] Adrian, D., et al.: Imperfect forward secrecy: how Diffie-Hellman fails in practice. In: Ray, I., Li, N., Kruegel, C. (eds.) ACM CCS 2015, pp. 5–17. ACM Press (2015)

[ABF+03] Aumüller, C., Bier, P., Fischer, W., Hofreiter, P., Seifert, J.-P.: Fault attacks on RSA with CRT: concrete results and practical countermeasures. In: Kaliski, B.S., Koç, K., Paar, C. (eds.) CHES 2002. LNCS, vol. 2523, pp. 260–275. Springer, Heidelberg (2003). https://doi.org/10.1007/3-540-36400-5_20

[AGTB19] Aldaya A.C., García, C.P., Tapia, L.M.A., Brumley, B.B.: Cache-timing attacks on RSA key generation. IACR TCHES 2019(4), 213–242 (2019). https://tches.iacr.org/index.php/TCHES/article/view/8350

[AM93] Atkin, A.O.L., Morain, F.: Elliptic curves and primality proving. Math. Comput. 61(203), 29–68 (1993)

[Bar87] Barrett, P.: Implementing the Rivest Shamir and Adleman public key encryption algorithm on a standard digital signal processor. In: Odlyzko, A.M. (ed.) CRYPTO 1986. LNCS, vol. 263, pp. 311–323. Springer, Heidelberg (1987). https://doi.org/10.1007/3-540-47721-7_24

[BHLV17] Bernstein, D.J., Heninger, N., Lou, P., Valenta, L.: Post-quantum RSA. In: Lange, T., Takagi, T. (eds.) PQCrypto 2017. LNCS, vol. 10346, pp. 311–329. Springer, Cham (2017). https://doi.org/10.1007/978-3-319-59879-6_18

[CAB20] Aldaya, A.C., Brumley, B.: When one vulnerable primitive turns viral: novel single-trace attacks on ECDSA and RSA. In: CHES 2020, p. 03 (2020)

[CC07] Clavier, C., Coron, J.-S.: On the implementation of a fast prime generation algorithm. In: Paillier, P., Verbauwhede, I. (eds.) CHES 2007. LNCS, vol. 4727, pp. 443–449. Springer, Heidelberg (2007). https://doi.org/10.1007/978-3-540-74735-2_30

[DH76] Diffie, W., Hellman, M.E.: New directions in cryptography. IEEE Trans. Inf. Theory 22(6), 644–654 (1976)

[EL10] Ebeid, N.M., Lambert, R.: A new CRT-RSA algorithm resistant to powerful fault attacks. In: WESS 2010, p. 8. ACM (2010)

[Fia90] Fiat, A.: Batch RSA. In: Brassard, G. (ed.) CRYPTO 1989. LNCS, vol. 435, pp. 175–185. Springer, New York (1990). https://doi.org/10.1007/0-387-34805-0_17

[Ham12] Hamburg, M.: Fast and compact elliptic-curve cryptography. Cryptology ePrint Archive, Report 2012/309 (2012). http://eprint.iacr.org/2012/309

[JP03] Joye, M., Paillier, P.: GCD-free algorithms for computing modular inverses. In: Walter, C.D., Koç, Ç.K., Paar, C. (eds.) CHES 2003. LNCS, vol. 2779, pp. 243–253. Springer, Heidelberg (2003). https://doi.org/10.1007/978-3-540-45238-6_20

[JP06] Joye, M., Paillier, P.: Fast generation of prime numbers on portable devices: an update. In: Goubin, L., Matsui, M. (eds.) CHES 2006. LNCS, vol. 4249, pp. 160–173. Springer, Heidelberg (2006). https://doi.org/10.1007/11894063_13

[JPV00] Joye, M., Paillier, P., Vaudenay, S.: Efficient generation of prime numbers. In: Koç, Ç.K., Paar, C. (eds.) CHES 2000. LNCS, vol. 1965, pp. 340–354. Springer, Heidelberg (2000). https://doi.org/10.1007/3-540-44499-8_27

[KG13] Kerry, C.F., Gallagher, P.D.: Digital signature standard (DSS). FIPS Pub 186-4 (2013). https://doi.org/10.6028/NIST.FIPS.186-4

[Mon85] Montgomery, P.L.: Modular multiplication without trial division. Math. Comput. 44(170), 519–521 (1985)

[NSS+17] Nemec, M., Sýs, M., Svenda, P., Klinec, D., Matyas, V.: The return of Coppersmith's attack: practical factorization o f widely used RSA moduli.

In: Thuraisingham, B.M., Evans, D., Malkin, T., Xu, D. (eds.) ACM CCS 2017, pp. 1631–1648. ACM Press (2017)

[PSW80] Pomerance, C., Selfridge, J.L., Wagstaff, S.S.: The pseudoprimes to $25 \cdot 10^9$. Math. Comput. **35**(151), 1003–1026 (1980)

[Rab80] Rabin, M.O.: Probabilistic algorithm for testing primality. J. Number Theory **12**(1), 128–138 (1980)

[RSA78] Rivest, R.L., Shamir, A., Adleman, L.M.: A method for obtaining digital signatures and public-key cryptosystems. Commun. Assoc. Comput. Mach. **21**(2), 120–126 (1978)

[Sch18] Schanck, J.M.: Multi-power post-quantum RSA. Cryptology ePrint Archive, Report 2018/325 (2018). https://eprint.iacr.org/2018/325

[SNS+16] Svenda, P., et al.: The million-key question - investigating the origins of RSA public keys. In: Holz, T., Savage, S. (ed.) USENIX Security 2016, pp. 893–910. USENIX Association (2016)

[Tak98] Takagi, T.: Fast RSA-type cryptosystem modulo $p^k q$. In: Krawczyk, H. (ed.) CRYPTO 1998. LNCS, vol. 1462, pp. 318–326. Springer, Heidelberg (1998). https://doi.org/10.1007/BFb0055738

[Tak04] Takagi, T.: A fast RSA-type public-key primitive modulo $p^k q$ using Hensel lifting. IEICE Trans. Fundam. Electron. Commun. Comput. Sci. **87**(1), 94–101 (2004)

[VOW99] Van Oorschot, P.C., Wiener, M.J.: Parallel collision search with cryptanalytic applications. J. Cryptol. **12**(1), 1–28 (1999)

[Wag02] Wagner, D.: A generalized birthday problem. In: Yung, M. (ed.) CRYPTO 2002. LNCS, vol. 2442, pp. 288–304. Springer, Heidelberg (2002). https://doi.org/10.1007/3-540-45708-9_19

On the Cost of ASIC Hardware Crackers: A SHA-1 Case Study

Anupam Chattopadhyay[1], Mustafa Khairallah[1,4], Gaëtan Leurent[2], Zakaria Najm[1,3], Thomas Peyrin[1,4(✉)], and Vesselin Velichkov[5]

[1] Nanyang Technological University, Nanyang, Singapore
{anupam,zakaria.najm,thomas.peyrin}@ntu.edu.sg,
mustafam001@e.ntu.edu.sg

[2] Inria, Paris, France
gaetan.leurent@inria.fr

[3] TU Delft, Delft, The Netherlands

[4] Temasek Labs @ NTU, Nanyang, Singapore

[5] University of Edinburgh, Edinburgh, UK
vvelichk@staffmail.ed.ac.uk

Abstract. In February 2017, the SHA-1 hashing algorithm was practically broken using an identical-prefix collision attack implemented on a GPU cluster, and in January 2020 a chosen-prefix collision was first computed with practical implications on various security protocols. These advances opened the door for several research questions, such as the minimal cost to perform these attacks in practice. In particular, one may wonder what is the best technology for software/hardware cryptanalysis of such primitives. In this paper, we address some of these questions by studying the challenges and costs of building an ASIC cluster for performing attacks against a hash function. Our study takes into account different scenarios and includes two cryptanalytic strategies that can be used to find such collisions: a classical generic birthday search, and a state-of-the-art differential attack using neutral bits for SHA-1.

We show that for generic attacks, GPU and ASIC poses a serious practical threat to primitives with security level ~ 64 bits, with rented GPU a good solution for a one-off attack, and ASICs more efficient if the attack has to be run a few times. ASICs also pose a non-negligible security risk for primitives with 80-bit security. For differential attacks, GPUs (purchased or rented) are often a very cost-effective choice, but ASIC provides an alternative for organizations that can afford the initial cost and look for a compact, energy-efficient, reusable solution. In the case of SHA-1, we show that an ASIC cluster costing a few millions would be able to generate chosen-prefix collisions in a day or even in a minute. This extends the attack surface to TLS and SSH, for which the chosen-prefix collision would need to be generated very quickly.

Keywords: SHA-1 · Cryptanalysis · ASIC · Birthday problem · Hash functions

© Springer Nature Switzerland AG 2021
K. G. Paterson (Ed.): CT-RSA 2021, LNCS 12704, pp. 657–681, 2021.
https://doi.org/10.1007/978-3-030-75539-3_27

1   Introduction

Hardware cryptanalysis has always been an important part of modern cryptography. It studies building application-specific electronic machines for performing cryptanalytic attacks. These machines can use different technologies, starting from mechanical computers during World War II, to FPGA, GPU or ASIC in the modern days. A full discussion of the history and state of the art of this field can be found in [11]. A widely held belief is that FPGAs and GPUs are suited for small-scale or low-budget computations, while ASIC is predicted to be better for heavy computational tasks or if the attacker has an important budget to spend. It is intuitive that a chip that is designed for a specific task is much more efficient than a general-purpose chip for the same task. However, since ASIC design has a huge non-recurring cost for fabrication, it is only competitive when a huge amount of chips is required. Besides, unlike the cryptographic algorithms themselves, which are usually optimized for hardware implementations, the cryptanalytic algorithms are usually designed for general-purpose computing machines. Hence, it is not necessarily true that ASIC implementations of such algorithms are more efficient. In other words, ASIC can always be at least as efficient as general-purpose CPUs or GPUS, as in the worst case the ASIC designer can simply design a circuit that is similar to the general-purpose one, but the gap in efficiency between the ASIC and the general-purpose circuit depends on the algorithm being implemented.

In general, ASIC provides an unfair advantage to players with bigger budgets. This has led to speculation that large intelligence entities may already possess ASIC hardware crackers that can break some of the widely used cryptographic schemes. In this paper, we address the question of the feasibility of such machines and whether it is more beneficial to use ASIC for cryptanalysis. The answer to this question is yes, but only for generic attacks of very large complexities, e.g. $> 2^{64}$. For low scale or more complicated cryptanalytic attacks, GPUs provide a very competitive option, due to re-usability, mass production and/or the possibility of renting them.

A relevant topic to our study is blockchain mining. As discussed earlier, big players can gain a huge advantage by using expensive ASICs. This has been a trend for Bitcoin specifically, where the introduction of a new ASIC machine lowers the profitability of older machines significantly. To maintain fairness of blockchain and cryptocurrency mining, memory-bound and ASIC-resistant hashing algorithms have been used, such as Ethash [23] for the Ethereum cryptocurrency and the X16R algorithm [24].

Related Work. COPACOBANA [12] was introduced in CHES 2006 as an FPGA cluster consisting on 120 FPGAs. It is considered to be the first publicly reported configurable platform built specifically for cryptanalysis. The design philosophy behind the architecture depends on three assumptions:

1. Cryptanalytic algorithms are parallelisable.
2. Different nodes need to communicate with each other only for a very limited amount of time.

3. Since the target algorithms are computationally intensive, the communication with the host is very limited compared to the time spent on the computational tasks.

These assumptions are satisfied by both brute force (generic) and a lot of cryptanalytic attacks. Hence, the COPACOBANA has been used to accelerate several attacks [6]. In our study we follow the same assumptions and add one more assumption:

4. Each node requires a constant/low amount of storage. The overall attack can be implemented using an almost memory-less algorithm.

This assumption needs to be satisfied by the attack algorithm in order to make sure that the efficiency due to parallelisation is not lost due to memory operations. For example, a naive approach to implementing a generic birthday collision search on m nodes, can lead to only $\sqrt{m}$ speed up compared to a single node if the algorithm doesn't satisfy this assumption.

Our Contributions. This paper is an attempt at answering three important research questions:

- *Can the cost of the collision attacks against* SHA-1 *be reduced?* There has been major breakthroughs in the cryptanalysis of SHA-1 over the past few years, with the first practical identical-prefix collision (IPC) found in February 2017 [17] and the first chosen-prefix collision (CPC) found in January 2020 [14]. While these attacks are practical on general-purpose GPUs, they still take a few months to generate one collision, by both academic and industrial entities. Interestingly, the authors of [14] remarked that TLS and SSH connections using SHA-1 signatures to authenticate the handshake could be attacked with the SLOTH attack [2] if the chosen-prefix collision can be generated quickly. Hence, we would like to check if ASIC can provide a better alternative to speed up the attacks, using larger budgets. We actually show that chosen-prefix collisions could be generated within a day or even a minute using an ASIC cluster costing a few dozen Million USD (the amortized cost per chosen-prefix collision is then much lower).
- *What is the difference between generic attacks and cryptanalytic attacks in terms of cost and implementation?* When analyzing a new cipher, any algorithm that has a theoretical time complexity lower than the generic attacks is considered a successful attack and the cipher is considered broken. For example, an n-bit hash function that is collision resistant up to the birthday bound is considered insecure if there is a cryptanalytic attack that requires less than $2^{0.9n/2}$ hash calls. Most of the time, researchers only measure time complexity in terms of function calls and ignore other operations required to perform the attack if they are much smaller. However, in practice, it can be a lot harder to implement a cryptanalytic attack compared to a generic attack, even with lower theoretical complexity. There are countless attacks published every year with a complexity very close to the generic one, but a natural example of such

scenarios is the biclique attack against AES [4], where the brute force complexity is reduced only by a small factor from 2^{128} to $2^{126.1}$. However, one can question if implementing the simple brute force attack would actually be much less complex in practice. In this paper, we compare the generic 64-bit birthday CPC attack over a 128-bit hash function to the cryptanalytic CPC attack against SHA-1 (which costs close to $2^{63.6}$ operations on GPUs, and of a lower complexity in theory) showing that in practice, the generic attack cost is more than 5 times cheaper than the ad-hoc CPC attack. Attacks like biclique or complex cryptanalysis are even more difficult to implement than the ad-hoc CPC attack and might require a huge memory, which probably makes the gap even larger. Hence, we argue that for a cryptanalytic attack to be competitive against a generic algorithm in practice, one must ensure a sufficiently large gap, at least of a factor 5, if not more (only an actual hardware implementation testing or estimation could give accurate bounds on that factor).

- *How secure is an 80-bit collision-resistant hash function?* In the NIST Lightweight Cryptography Workshop 2019, Tom Broström proposed an application for lightweight cryptography where the SIMON cipher [1] is used in the Davis-Meyer construction as a secure compression function which is collision-resistant at most up to 2^{64} computations [19]. Besides, it remains a common belief that SHA-1 is insecure due to the cryptanalytic attacks against it, but it would have still been acceptable otherwise. Actually, it is only since 2011 that 80-bit security is not recommended anymore by the NIST, and 80-bit security for data already encrypted with this level of protection is deemed acceptable as a legacy feature, accepting some inherent risk. Hence, we study the cost of implementing the generic 2^{80} birthday collision attack against SHA-1, showing that it is within our reach in the near future, costing ≈ 61 million USD to implement the attack in 1 month, which is not out of reach of large budget players, *e.g.* large government entities, and with the decreasing cost of ASICs, this will even be within reach of academic/industrial entities in the near future.

Finally, we argue that ASIC provides the most efficient technology for implementing high complexity and generic attacks, while GPU provides a competitive option for cryptanalytic and medium/low cost attacks.

2   Hash Functions and Cryptanalysis

Cryptographic hash functions are one of the main and most widely used primitives in symmetric key cryptography. One of their key applications is to provide data integrity by ensuring each message will lead to a seemingly random digital *fingerprint*. They are also used as building blocks of some digital signature and authentication schemes. A cryptographic hash function takes a message of arbitrary length as input and returns a fixed-size string, which is called the hash value/tag. In order for the function to be considered secure, it must be hard to find collisions, i.e. two or more different messages that have the same tag. More specifically, a n-bit cryptographically secure hash function must satisfy at least the security notion of collision resistance, *i.e.* finding a pair (M_1, M_2) of distinct messages, such that $H(M_1) = H(M_2)$ must require about $2^{n/2}$ computations.

2.1 SHA-1 and Related Attacks.

The SHA-1 hash function defines a generalized-Feistel-based compression function used inside the Merkle-Damgård (MD) algorithm. It was selected in 1995 as a replacement for the SHA-0 hash function after some weaknesses have been discovered in the latter. While the two functions are relatively similar, SHA-1 was considered collision resistant till 2005, when Wang *et al.* proposed the first cryptanalytic attack on SHA-1 [22]. Since then, a lot of efforts have been targeted towards making the attack more efficient. In 2015, the authors of [7] provided an estimation for finding near collisions on SHA-1, which is a critical step in the collision attacks. The authors provided a design of an Application-Specific Instruction-set Processor (ASIP), named Cracken, which executes specific parts of the attack. It was estimated that to execute the free-start collision and real collision attacks from [16], the attacks will take 46 and 65 d and cost 15 and 121 Million Euros respectively. At Eurocrypt 2019, Leurent and Peyrin [13] provided a chosen-prefix attacks which uses two parts: first a birthday search to reach an acceptable set of differences in the chaining variable, and then a differential cryptanalysis part that successively generate near-collision blocks to eventually reach the final collision. The attack was implemented on GPUs and a first chosen-prefix collision was published in January 2020 [14].

2.2 Birthday Search in Practice.

The efficient design of a collision search algorithm is not a trivial task, especially if the attacker wants to use parallelization over a set of computing machines. This issue is discussed in details in [21]. The collision search problem can be treated as a graph search problem, where the attacker is looking for two edges with the same endpoint but with different starting points. Pollard's rho method [15] helps finding a collision in the functional graph with a small memory requirement. The underlying idea is to start at any vertex and perform a random walk in the graph until a cycle is found. Unless the attacker is unlucky to have chosen a starting point that is part of the cycle, he ends up with a graph that resembles the Greek letter ρ and the collision is detected. Unfortunately, this method is not efficiently parallelizable, as it provides only $\mathcal{O}(\sqrt{m})$ speed-up when m cores are used. In [21], the authors proposed a method to achieve $\mathcal{O}(m)$ speed-up, using limited memory and communication requirements. This algorithm leads to very efficient parallel implementations, and is the basis for our study.

However, in the chosen-prefix collision attack against SHA-1, it is not applied directly to the compression function of SHA-1, but to a helper function. Let IV_i represent a chaining value to the compression function (reached after processing a prefix), x a message block, and $H(IV_i, x)$ the application of the SHA-1 compression function. The goal of the birthday phase of CPC attack is to find many solutions x_1 and x_2 such that $L(H(IV_1, x_1)) = L(H(IV_2, x_2))$, where $L(x)$ is a linear function applied to a word x, in order to select some of the output bits of the compression function. The helper function is defined as:

$$f(x) = \begin{cases} L(H(IV_1, x)), & \text{if } x = 1 \pmod 2 \\ L(H(IV_2, x)), & \text{otherwise.} \end{cases} \tag{1}$$

When a collision $f(x_1) = f(x_2)$ is found, we have $x_1 \neq x_2 \pmod 2$ with probability one half, and in this case we obtain $L(H(IV_1, x_1)) = L(H(IV_2, x_2))$.

2.3 Differential Cryptanalysis

In this section we briefly describe the algorithms involved in the second part of the chosen-prefix collision attack: the generation of successive near-collision blocks to reach the final collision. The details of this differential attack can be found in [10, 13, 14, 16–18, 22]. For each new near-collision block, the attacker has to go through three main steps:

1. Preparing a fully defined differential path for the SHA-1 compression function (in particular a non-linear part has to be generated for the first few steps of the SHA-1 compression function)
2. Find base solutions for the first few steps of this differential path (a base solution is simply two messages inputs that verify the planned differential path in the internal state up to the starting step of the neutral bits).
3. Expand those solutions into many solutions using what is known as neutral bits (in order to amortize the cost of the base solution), and check whether any of these solutions verify the differential path until the output of the compression function.

A neutral bit for a step i is a bit (or a combination of bits) of the message such that when its value is flipped on a base solution valid until step i, the differential path is still satisfied with high probability until step i. Most of the time, a neutral bit is a single bit, but it can sometimes be composed of a combination of bits. A neutral bit for a step i allows to amortize the cost of finding a solution to the differential path until step i.

The hardware cluster we consider consists of one master node and many slave nodes. The master builds a proper differential path for the compression function steps, based on the incoming chaining values, and generates base solutions based on this path. The slave is then required to expand these base solutions into a wider set of potential solutions and find out which of them satisfy the differential path until a certain step r (we selected $r = 40$ for ASIC for implementation efficiency purposes, but we remark that $r = 61$ was selected for GPU even though it does not have much impact) in the SHA-1 compression function. The master then aggregates all the solutions that are valid up to step r and exhaustively search for solutions that are valid up to step 80. This is repeated several times until a valid solution for the differential path is found. Consequently, we define a slave as a dedicated core that is responsible for extending a base solution found by the master into a set of potential solutions by traversing the tree of solutions defined by the neutral bits.

Unfortunately, this attack is not hardware-friendly and needs a lot of control logic. The master has to send to the slave:

1. A base solution, which consists of two message blocks M_1 and M_2.
2. A set $[DP]$ of differential specifications for the slave to check conformance.
3. A group of neutral bit sets N_i, where the neutral bits in N_i are supposed to be neutral up to step i.

Combining a base solution (M_1, M_2) valid at step i and the set N_i, we get about $2^{|N_i|}$ new solutions that are valid up to step i, simply by trying all the possible combinations of the neutral bits in the set. In a naive approach, each of these partial solutions is expended to $2^{|N_{i+1}|}$ by applying combinations of the next set. Eventually, we would end up with $2^{\sum_i N_i}$ partial solutions, organised in a tree as shown in Fig. 1. However, the neutral bits N_{i+1} are defined such that they don't impact the path up to step $i+1$. Therefore, if the partial solution does *not* satisfy the conditions at step $i+1$, there is no need to apply the neutral bits N_{i+1}, and we can instead cut the corresponding branch from the tree. Indeed, there is a certain probability that a solution valid at step i will be valid at step $i + 1$, according to the SHA-1 differential path selected. With the parameters used in SHA-1 collision attacks, most subtrees fail.

We can generate the partial solutions using a graph search algorithm to start navigating the tree from its root, and neglect complete subtrees that are failing. In this paper we choose Depth-First Search (DFS) graph search, with some modifications to suit our specific problems, in order to satisfy our assumptions for the cryptanalytic algorithm, as DFS has low memory requirements.

Our Attack Scenarios. In this paper we consider three attack scenarios:

1. A plain 2^{64} birthday search: a generic birthday attack against a 128-bit hash function, constructed by selecting only 128 bits out of the 160 output bits of the SHA-1 compression function.
2. A plain 2^{80} birthday search: a generic birthday search over the full space of the SHA-1 compression function.
3. The chosen-prefix collision attack on SHA-1 from Leurent and Peyrin [13,14].

These three scenarios cover two generic attacks against two security levels used in practice and one cryptanalytic attack.

3   Hardware Birthday Cluster

In this section, we describe the hardware core that handles the birthday attack. First, we define the nodes used in the proposed cluster. Then, we describe the design of the slave nodes and the communication requirements.

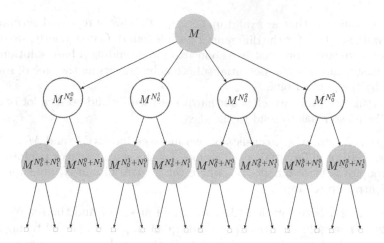

Fig. 1. Building partial solutions with neutral bits

3.1   Cluster Nodes

The cluster used to apply the parallel birthday search attack consists of two types of nodes:

1. *Master*: a software-based CPU that manages the attack from high level and performs some jobs including choosing the initial prefixes, distributing the attack loads among slaves, sorting of the outputs and identifying colliding traces.
2. *Birthday Slaves*: dedicated cores that can perform different parts of the parallel birthday search. Specifically, it compute traces in the functional graph of the function in question, and once the master has identified colliding traces, the core also can locate the exact collision in these traces.

3.2   Hardware Design of Birthday Slaves

The design of the proposed birthday slave is shown in Fig. 2. It's main role is to iterate the helper function of Eq. 1. It consists of a reconfigurable ROM, where the initial trace value x_0, IV_1 and IV_2 are loaded, a logic SHA-1 core which performs the step function of SHA-1, a comparator to compute $L(x)$, x (mod 2) and check whether a given x is a distinguished point (see [21]) or not, a memory to store distinguished points and a control unit to handle the communications with the master, and measure the lengths of different traces.

In order to estimate the cost of the proposed core, the area and speed are compared to a single, step-based SHA-1 core, which is a standard practice in estimating the cost of SHA-1 cryptanalytic attacks. We have implemented a full SHA-1 core and it has an area of 6.2 KGE and 0.21 ns critical path. The implementation of the core in Fig. 2 using a step-based SHA-1 core requires at least twice this area. Moreover, its critical path is dominated by the memory and

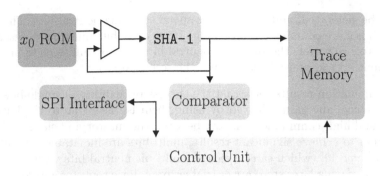

Fig. 2. Birthday slave for the parallel collision algorithm

counters in the control logic. Besides, it is not expected that a huge ASIC cluster will run at a speed higher than 1 GHz, due to the power consumption. Hence, in order to regain the efficiency lost due to the extra control logic and memories, it is a good approach to try to use this logic with as many SHA-1 steps as possible. Given these experiments and the huge cost of the control overhead, we increase the efficiency by cascading 4 SHA-1 steps instead of one in the SHA-1 core. This makes the critical path around 1ns, but a full SHA-1 computations takes only 20 cycles instead of 80, and the overhead 25% instead of 100%.

4 Verification

We have verified the attack by finding collisions on a small number of bits using functional simulation of the hardware implementations. Specifically, we found collisions on $20 \sim 330$ bits of the output. We have also generated traces for larger number of bits and compared them to traces generated using software implementations.

5 Hardware Differential Attack Cluster Design

In this section we discuss the challenges and different trade-offs when implementing the neutral bit search algorithm in ASIC and give a description of the circuit. The cluster architecture uses 3 types of nodes: master nodes, birthday slaves (BC), and neutral bit slaves (NB).

5.1 Neutral Bits

One of the trade-offs when implementing the attack is whether to consider neutral bits as only single-bits or to use the more general sets of multi-bits. The first approach leads to a very small circuit, but it strongly limits the number of usable neutral bits. This increases the overall work load, as more base solutions need to be generated, and more time is spend applying neutral bits. The second approach is more complex, because multi-bit neutral bits must be represented by a bit-vector. However, the single-bit neutral bits are not sufficient to implement an efficient attack, and we have to use the second option:

1. Our simulation results show that the success probability of single-bits is very low. Hence, any gain achieved by using them is offset due to the huge work load and high communication cost between the master and slave.
2. In order to achieve significant results, multi-bits are inevitable. In particular, *boomerangs* [9] (which can be seen as multi-bit neutral bits with extra conditions to reach a later step) are crucial cryptanalytic tools for a low-complexity attack against SHA-1. Hence, avoiding multi-bits can lead to a drastic loss in terms of attack efficiency.

5.2   Storage

Each multi-bit neutral bit is represented by a 512-bit vector, which indicates the location of the involved bits in the message block (a SHA-1 message block is indeed 512-bit long). However, we noticed that almost all the neutral bits involve bits only in the last 6 32-bit words of the message block. Therefore, we reduced the representation to only 192 bits. Yet, since the original chosen-prefix collision attack against SHA-1 uses ~ 60 neutral bits, including boomerangs, this requires a representation of $\sim 11,520$ bits. Besides, the last few levels of the tree requires 320 bits per neutral bits as the boomerangs can be located as early as step 6. In addition, for each level of the tree search we need a counter to trace which node we are testing. The tree used in the attack has ~ 10 levels, and our experiments show that the maximum number of neutral bits in one level is ~ 26 bits. Hence, the overall size of the counters is ~ 260 bits. In order to design the circuit that handles this tree search algorithm, we tried out four different approaches:

1. Generic approach: we assume that each tree level can have ~ 28 neutral bits (slightly higher than our experiments for tolerance). Also, assume that these levels can be related to any step of the SHA-1 compression function between 10 and 26, i.e. 16 possible steps. In total, this requires $\sim 63,670$ memory locations (Flip-Flops).
2. Statistical approach: from the software experiments and simulations, we identified an average number of neutral bits per level. In the design, we use the maximum number of neutral bits we observe for each level (in addition to two extra bits for tolerance). We observed that only the first few levels require such a huge storage, while the later levels usually have $3 \sim 7$ bits per level. In addition, boomerangs are usually $3 \sim 4$ per level. This reduces the memory requirement by about 50%. However, it remains a huge requirement.
3. Configurable approach: our experiments showed that not only the number of neutral bits per level can be predicted, but also the values of these bits. In other words, very few bits have different values for different blocks. Hence, we can fix each neutral bit to two or three choices and use flip-flops to configure

which choice is selected during execution. This reduces the cost significantly. However, the cost is still high as a multiplexer has an area only $\sim 50\%$ of a flip-flop. Besides, we still need flip-flops for configuring these multiplexers.

4. Another approach is to reduce the cost by fixing the neutral bit values to a set of statistically dominant values. Indeed, [14] reports using the same neutral bits for each near-collision bloc. This eliminates the need to store the neutral-bit reference values.

At the end, we chose the third approach, since our analysis shows that it captures the reality, while allowing some level of freedom for the attacker to adjust the attack parameters after fabrication.

5.3   Architecture

Figure 3 shows the architecture of the neutral-bit slave. It consists of a register file to store the differential path for comparison, a configurable ROM to store the base solution, a unit to enumerate the different neutral bit patterns and maintains the tree level for the graph search algorithm, and the SHA-1 step logic.

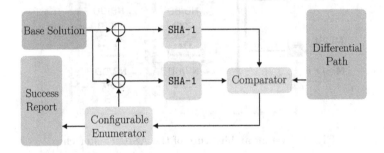

Fig. 3. Neutral-bit slave hardware architecture

6   Chip Design

In this section, we describe our process for simulating the proposed chips and the results in terms of power, area and performance for each.

6.1   Chip Architecture

A challenge when designing this cluster is the communication overhead between the master and the slaves. A 100 MHz SPI bus interface is used as a one-to-one communication interface with the attack server. A set of ASICs can also be daisy-chained, thanks to this interface, in such a way to lower the number

of interconnects with the master. It provides enough bandwidth to handle the
data exchanges between the BD/NB slave cluster and the attack server. The
CU (Control Unit) is responsible for dispatching the 32-bit de-serialized packets
sent by the attack sever to configure the BD/NB slaves. It is also responsible
for daisy-chaining and demultiplexing the output traces of the different BD/NB
slaves to the SPI bus interface before the serialization. Each ASIC also outputs
an asynchronous interrupt signal. The interrupt signal is 1 when at least one
BD/NB slave is done, and an output trace is available. Those interrupt signals
are managed by a set of ZYNQ board cluster interfaces.

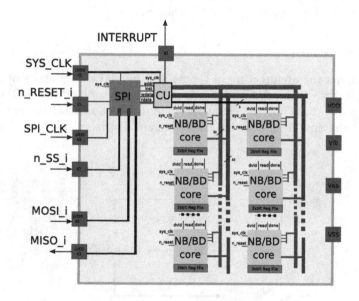

Fig. 4. System architecture of the ASIC cluster chip

6.2 ASIC Fabrication and Running Cost

Estimating the cost of fabricating and running an ASIC cluster can be challenging as many parameters are confidential to the fabs. In order to estimate
the costs of the attacks considered, we developed a methodology based on the
information available publicly. We considered the FD-SOI 28 nm technology from
ST-Microelectronics. For small scale academic projects, the price of a small batch
of up to 100 die, the fabrication cost in US$ can be estimated by:

$$p_{100} = \begin{cases} 125400 + (A - 12) * 7700, & \text{if } A > 12 \text{ mm}^2 \\ 20900 + (A - 2) * 9900, & \text{if } 2 \text{ mm}^2 \leq A \leq 12 \text{ mm}^2 \end{cases}$$

where A is the die area in mm^2 and p_{100} is the price of the first 100 die in US$s (USD). For small scale projects with more than 100 die, the price for a lot of 100 extra die is between 21,120 and 38,500 USD depending on the die area and the number of reticules in a wafer. MPW runs uses Multi Layer Reticule technic to reduce the overall cost of the mask and additional dies. For our purposes, we consider a small scale project to be a project with at most 25 wafers [20]. For large scale projects, a market study published at the FDSOI Forum in 2018 showed that the die manufacturing cost per 40 mm^2 is 0.9 USD for the 28 nm technology [8]. Hence, our methodology for estimating the costs consists of the three parts we explained. In reality, a more accurate methodology is probably available for the fabs to fill in the gaps. However, we believe that the overall cost will be in the same range.

On top of the fabrication cost, we need to consider the running cost of the ASIC cluster, which includes the energy consumption and cooling. We have performed post-layout extraction and simulation in order to estimate the power consumption of the different chips. In order to simplify the cost analysis, we use a figure of 18 cents/KWh, which is higher than the electricity consumption price in most countries [5]. Hence, we only consider the energy consumption of the chips and not the cooling cost or other factors that will be added after fabrication. The performances and power result are provided in Table 1.

6.3   Results

Two different architectures of SHA-1 crackers are compared here. The first architecture is based on 2 separate ASIC slaves that handle the two parts of the attack, $i.e.$, the birthday search (BD) and the neutral bits part (NB). The two phases are performed sequentially. Figure 5 depicts the overall cost required to build the machine and find the first chosen-prefix collision depending on the time ratio between the two phases. For ASIC, the overall minimum cost is not perfectly at 50% ratio. Hence, we consider a two-stage pipeline architecture at the cost of slightly more hardware to balance the birthday and neutral-bit parts.

Our birthday (BD) core uses 16927.1 gate equivalents (GEs) per SHA-1 rounds., while our neutral-bit core (NB) uses 170442.7 GEs. Our best implementation is a 4-round SHA-1 unrolled compression function that can be clocked at 900 MHz at $V_{core} = 0.92$V and $V_{fbb} = 0$V. Using body biasing and LVT transistors for the critical path, we can further decrease the threshold voltage and increase the running frequency. With $V_{fbb} = +2.0$V we can increase the running frequency of our fastest core by 40%, reaching 1262 MHz with a 2% increase in dissipated power. The chip can be further over-clocked by increasing V_{core} but at the cost of a quadratic increase in the dissipated power, so a more costly cooling system. The results of our implementations are shown in Table 1. As shown in Fig. 19, a BD slave contains up to ~ 15 BD cores per mm^2 while an NB slave contains ~ 1.5 NB cores per mm^2.

In our study, the overall cost is calculated without the cooling and infrastructure. Note that as shown in Fig. 6, the total cost required to build an ASIC-based cracker greatly depends on the die size. This is due to the fact that the initial

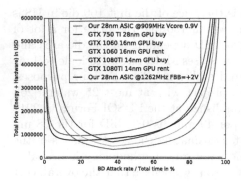

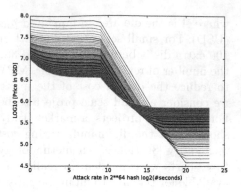

Fig. 5. Impact of the BD/NB time ratio on the cost

Fig. 6. Impact of the die size and latency on the HW cost (4 to 100 mm^2 28 nm FD-SOI). The top left line in blue represents 4 mm^2 and the bottom left is 100 mm^2.

Table 1. ASIC implementation performances for 2 corners cases: high performance at 900 MHz and high performance with FBB at 1262 MHz.

Version	900 MHz $V_{fbb}=$ 0V		1262 MHz $V_{fbb}=$ +2V	
	BD	NB	BD	NB
Power (in mW)	71.1	289	72.6	294
CP delay (in ps)	1110	1110	792	792
Area (in mm^2)	0.0650	0.6545	0.0650	0.6545

cost is predominant when the die size is large. The overall hardware cost tends to the same for any die size when the attack is fast.

6.4   Attack Rates and Execution Time

As shown in Table 2, a single NB slave of 16 mm^2 contains up to 24 NB cores and can generate up to 976 solutions up to step 40 of SHA-1 per second. Each solution A_{40} requires 31 Million cycles, on average. A single BD slave of 16 mm^2 contains up to 245 BD cores and provides a hash rate of 20.6 GH/s for the fastest version of our design. As a comparison, as shown in Table 3 and taken from [14], a single GTX 1060 GPU provides a hash rate of 4.0 GH/s and can generate 2000 A_{40} solutions per second. If we take the birthday part of the attack as a reference, the neutral bit part is ten time less efficient in hardware than on GPU.

The second architecture is based on GPU. For GPU, it is cost-wise more interesting to take advantage of its reconfigurability to minimize the cost. Hence, we consider in our cost analysis that the chosen-prefix collision is performed serially by reusing the same GPU for the two attack phases. In Table 4, the cost

Table 2. Our best 16 mm^2 ASIC implementation performances for 2 corners

Parameter	900 MHz	1262 MHz
SHA-1/core/sec	$2^{25.8}$	$2^{26.3}$
SHA-1/core/month	$2^{47.1}$	$2^{47.6}$
SHA-1/chip/month	$2^{55.1}$	$2^{55.6}$
A_{40} Solutions/core/sec	$2^{4.9}$	$2^{5.3}$
A_{40} Solutions/core/month	$2^{26.1}$	$2^{26.7}$
A_{40} Solutions/chip/month	$2^{30.8}$	$2^{31.2}$

Table 3. SHA-1 hash rate from hashcat for various GPU models, as well as measured rate of solutions at step 33 (A_{33}-solutions). Data taken from [14].

GPU	arch	Hash Rate	A_{33} rate	A_{40} rate	Price	Power	Rental
GTX 750 Ti	Maxwell	0.9 GH/s	62 k/s	250 k/s	$144	60W	
GTX 1060	Pascal	4.0 GH/s	470 k/s	2 k/s	$300	120W	$35/month
GTX 1080 Ti	Pascal	12.8 GH/s	1500 k/s	6.2 k/s	$1300	250W	

of the three attack scenarios is provided. We give in this table the cost to build the ASIC- and GPU-based clusters for 3 different speeds, *i.e.*, one attack per month, one attack per day and one attack per minute. The latency corresponds to the delay to get the first collision. For instance, a two-stage ASIC-based machine able to generate one SHA-1 collision every months, will generate the first collision in two months. A GPU-based machine generates the first collision in one month for the same attack rate. Our ASIC-based two stage pipelined architecture has twice the latency of a sequential GPU-based machine for the same attack rate. Our benchmark (Figs. 15 and 16) provides a comparison between our ASIC cluster and two of the most widely spread GPU based machines, *i.e.*, the GTX 1080TI (CMOS 14 nm) and the GTX 1060 (CMOS 16 nm) for different attack rates. The numbers for the GTX 750 TI (CMOS 28 nm technology) are also added to the benchmark as it provides an idea of the performance obtained with a GPU based on a similar technology node as our ASIC.

Note on the use of FPGAs. Our ASIC design have been tested on FPGA platform. FPGA can be considered as a good alternative to ASIC thanks to its reconfigurability property. However, one of the largest FPGAs from Xilinx, namely the Virtex 7 xc7vx330t-3ffg1157 can fit only 20 instances of the Birthday core running at 135 MHz in one chip. The same FPGA can fit only 16 instances of the Neutral Bit core running at 133 MHz. In order to do the 2^{64} generic birthday search, we need $2^{36.6}$ FPGA-seconds, *i.e.*, in order to do it in one month we need $2^{15.3}$ FPGAs. As a single FPGA costs around 8000 USD, this attack would cost around 319 Million USD. This is more than one thousand times the cost of the same attack on ASIC and 440 times the cost on GPU, making it irrelevant for the purpose of analyzing SHA-1. Even if FPGAs can be rented, a similar factor is expected compared to renting GPUs. It is worth mentioning that FPGA-based

Table 4. Comparison of attack costs with various parameters. Costs are given in USD (k stands for thousand, M for Million, B for Billion, T for Trillion, Q for Quadrillion). Amortized cost is the cost per attack assuming that the hardware is used continuously during three years. Note that it is possible to get slightly more energy efficient platforms and implementations at the cost of more expensive hardware. We list the cheapest platform after one attack, energy included.

Platform	ASIC			GPU rent			GPU buy		
Attack	64	CPC	80	64	CPC	80	64	CPC	80
Energy Cost	$776	$1.6k	$50.9M	-	-	-	$18k	$12k	$1.2B
Cluster for 1 attack per month									
Latency (month)	1	2	1	1	1	1	1	1	1
Hardware Cost	$257k	$1.1M	$11M	-	-	-	$715k	$490k	$47B
First Attack Cost	$257k	$1.1M	$61.9M	$61k	$43k	$4B	$733k	$502k	$48B
Amortized Cost	$7.9k	$32.1k	$51.2M	$61k	$43k	$4B	$38k	$26k	$2.5B
Cluster for 1 attack per day									
Latency (day)	1	2	1	1	1	1	1	1	1
Hardware Cost	$1.4M	$3.7M	$218M	-	-	-	$22M	$15M	$1.4T
First Attack Cost	$1.4M	$3.7M	$269M	$61k	$43k	$4B	$22M	$15M	$1.4T
Amortized Cost	$2k	$5k	$51.1M	$61k	$43k	$4B	$38k	$26k	$2.5B
Cluster for 1 attack per minute									
Latency (minute)	1	2	1	1	1	1	1	1	1
Hardware Cost	$8.5M	$48M	$263B	-	-	-	$31B	$21B	$2Q
First Attack Cost	$8.5M	$48M	$263B	$61k	$43k	$4B	$31B	$21B	$2Q
Amortized Cost	$781	$1.6k	$51M	$61k	$43k	$4B	$38k	$26k	$2.5B

clusters, such as COPACABANA, use cheaper FPGAs. However, they are usually used for smaller projects and will face the same challenge to scale up to the level of attacks awe are considering.

7   Cost Analysis and Comparisons

As explained throughout the paper, we have performed several experiments to identify the different implementation trade-offs for the attack scenarios we consider. In this section, we analyze the cost estimates of implementing these attacks in ASIC vs. consumer GPU. We consider three attack scenarios that fall into two categories: generic birthday attacks and differential cryptanalysis of SHA-1. Before discussing the analysis in more details, here are a few general conclusions that we reached through our experiments, which can be helpful for building future hardware crackers:

1. The cost of implementing memoryless generic attacks, such as the parallel collision search of [21], in hardware can range from 20% to 50% of the overall ASIC implementation, while the rest is dedicated to the attacked primitive, e.g. the SHA-1 hash function.
2. For iterative cryptographic algorithms, such as hash functions and block ciphers, a way to reduce the attack cost is to use unrolling. This approach is similar to using memoryless algorithms. Instead of computing one step of

the function every clock cycle, we compute several steps in the same cycle. This amortizes the costs of the attack logic among several steps. For example, implementing the birthday attack using a single-step iterative SHA-1 core leads to a circuits where only 20% of the area is used by the SHA-1 logic and 80% of the area is due to the attack logic, registers and comparisons. On the other hand, using a core that computes 4 steps every clock cycles leads to a circuit with a 50%/50% ratio. While this technique may increase the critical path of the circuit and reduce the frequency, it also reduces the overall number of cycles, so the overall time to compute a single SHA-1 per core is almost constant.

3. For cryptanalytic attacks, the cost is dominated by the attack logic, which may include a huge number of comparisons, modifications and registers. These extra operations are usually different from one step to another, so they consume a huge area. Besides, the state machine of these attacks can be very costly. In such scenarios, the advantage of using ASICs becomes diminished compared to consumer GPUs, except for very high budgets, especially as the GPUs are reusable and can be rented.

7.1 2^{64} Birthday Attack

The first attack scenario we consider is attacking a hash function with 2^{64} birthday collision complexity. The hash function used is the SHA-1 compression function reduced to only 128 output bits, as explained in Sect. 2. A single ASIC core is described in Sect. 3. The time to finish such an attack depends on the number of chips fabricated and the size of each chip. A single ASIC core running at 1262 MHz contributes $2^{26.33}$ SHA-1 computations per second. The attack costs $2^{37.67}$ core-seconds. To reach this complexity, Fig. 6 shows the price required vs. the estimated time needed to finish the attack, including the fabrication cost of chips of different sizes and the energy consumption.

To put these numbers into perspective, the NVIDIA GeForce GTX 1080 TI GPU (14nm technology) can do about $2^{33.6}$ SHA-1 computations per second, so implementing the attack on GPU would require $2^{30.4}$ GPU-seconds. In order to implement this attack in one month, we need to buy around 550 GPUs costing around 715k USD and around 18k USD in energy. As shown in Fig. 7, a GTX 1060-based machine is a bit less expensive, costing 525k USD but consuming around 28k in energy for the same job (using 1750 GPUs).

Besides, as shown in Fig. 7, for any attack rate it is cheaper to buy an ASIC cluster than a GPU-based cluster. The difference reaches 1 order of magnitude from a rate of 1 attack per week. Furthermore, the ASIC-based cluster consumes 1 to 2 order of magnitude less energy than any GPU-based solution. As shown in Table 4, the minimum cost in energy per attack on ASIC is as low as 776 USD. An ASIC-based cracker able to generate one collision per month would cost 257k USD. For an attack rate of 1 attack per minute, it would cost 8.5 million USD.

An alternative option is to rent the GPUs. This would cost around $61k per attack, assuming a rental price of $209/month for a machine with 6 GTX 1060 GPUs. This makes the GPU rental very competitive for a single attack, around 4

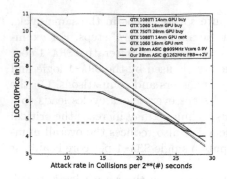

Fig. 7. 2^{64} BD machine price for different attack rates: ASIC vs GPU

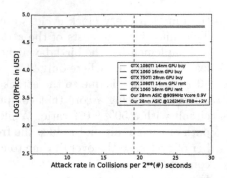

Fig. 8. Energy cost per 2^{64} BD attack: ASIC vs GPU

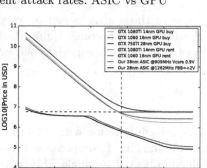

Fig. 9. Total cost (HW+E) for 100 2^{64} BD attack at a given attack rate: ASIC vs GPU

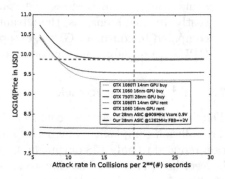

Fig. 10. Total cost (HW+E) for 100k 2^{64} BD attack at a given attack rate: ASIC vs GPU

times cheaper than an ASIC cluster. However, the ASIC cluster quickly become much more cost effective when the attack is repeated (see Fig. 9).

7.2 2^{80} Birthday Attack

In this section, we look at the cost of implementing a generic birthday collision search for the full SHA-1 output, which requires around 2^{80} SHA-1 computations. The algorithm is the same as the previous attack, except that we use the full output of the SHA-1 compression function. Since a single ASIC core performs $2^{26.33}$ SHA-1 computations per second, the birthday collision search costs $2^{53.67}$ core-seconds, or around 454 million years on a single core. Fortunately, for a powerful attacker with enough money, the cost for producing ASICs grows slowly for large number of chips. The fabrication cost of a hardware cluster to perform the attack in one month costs only 11 million USD, as opposed to around 34 billion USD for GTX 1060. Hence in this case, for any attack rate as shown in Graphs 13 and 14 the only realistic option is to build an ASIC cluster.

Running the attack costs around 50.9 million USD in energy, which matches the order of magnitude estimated from the bitcoin network: the network currently computes about $2^{70.2}$ SHA-256 every ten minutes, for a reward of 12.5 bitcoin, or roughly \$85k at the time of writing. This would price a 2^{80} computation at 75 million USD.

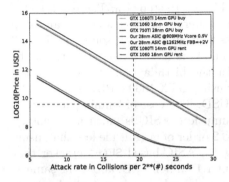

Fig. 11. 2^{80} BD machine price for different attack rates: ASIC vs GPU

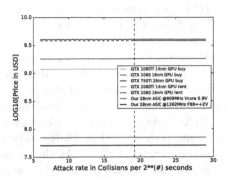

Fig. 12. Energy cost per 2^{80} BD attack: ASIC vs GPU

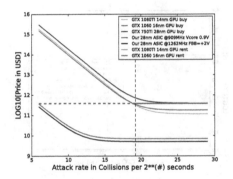

Fig. 13. Total cost (HW+E) for 100 2^{80} BD attack at a given attack rate: ASIC vs GPU

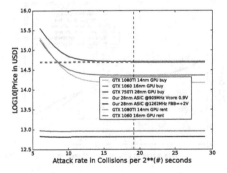

Fig. 14. Total cost (HW+E) for 100k 2^{80} attack at a given attack rate: ASIC vs GPU

7.3   Chosen Prefix Differential Collision Attack

The chosen-prefix collision attack proposed by Leurent and Peyrin [14] consists of two main parts: a birthday search attack, and a differential collision attack. The authors provide different trade-offs between the complexity of the two parts. In their paper, the number of solutions required for the neutral bits up to step

33 is provided. This number of solutions corresponds to the number of solutions required to get a valid solution with high probability. Step 33 is chosen because there is a zero difference at this state, so there is a single path at this step, and solutions are generated fast enough to measure the rate easily. This configuration requires to generate about $2^{62.05}$ SHA-1 computations for the birthday part and $2^{49.78}$ solutions up to step 33. In this paper, it is cost-wise more interesting for ASIC to generate solutions for the neutral bits up to step A_{40}. There is a factor $2^{7.91}$ difference in the number of solutions to generate between step A_{33} and step A_{40}. Hence a chosen-prefix collision requires to generate $2^{41.87}$ solutions. Table 3 provides the hash rates and solution rates numbers used in our estimate for the cost on GPU. This gives 38 GPU-years for the birthday, and 65 years for the neutral bits. The estimated cost per attack using GTX 1060 GPU, assuming 209 USD per month for 6 GPU is about 43k USD. The cost of running the attack in GPU is dominated by the energy consumption. ASIC is much more energy efficient, as shown in Fig. 16. It can be up to 2 order of magnitude less than using common consumer GPU. As shown in Fig. 15, ASIC-based SHA-1 cracker that generate one collision per month, costs about 1.1 million USD, about the same as the cheapest GPU-based cracker from our benchmark. However, a single attack on GPU costs about 19000 USD in energy. Hence from 100 attacks as shown in Figs. 17 and 18 as well as for attack rates greater than 1 attack per week, an ASIC-based SHA-1 cracker is the only realistic option.

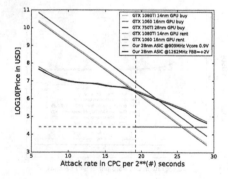
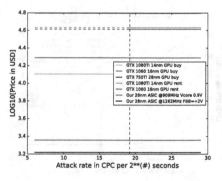

Fig. 15. CPC machine price for different attack rates: ASIC vs GPU

Fig. 16. Energy cost per CPC attack: ASIC vs GPU

7.4   Limitations

While we did our best to estimate the price of the attacks as accurately as possible, our figures should only be considered as orders of magnitude because the pricing of hardware and energy can vary significantly. ASIC pricing is not completely public, and energy prices depend on the country. Moreover, our estimate only include hardware cost and energy, neglecting other operating costs such as

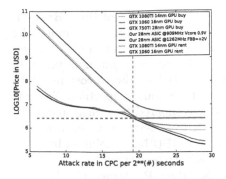
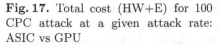

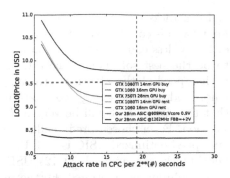

Fig. 17. Total cost (HW+E) for 100 CPC attack at a given attack rate: ASIC vs GPU

Fig. 18. Total cost (HW+E) for 100k CPC attack at a given attack rate: ASIC vs GPU

cooling and servers to control the cluster (however, the energy price we use is somewhat high, so it can be considered as including some operating costs).

Another caveat is that we only consider the computation part of the attacks. In reality, there is some need for communication between the nodes, and some steps of the attacks must be done sequentially. Concretely, the generic birthday attacks must sort the data after computing all the chains, and the CPC attack must compute several near-collision blocks sequentially. This will likely add some latency to the computation, and running the attack in one minute will be a huge challenge, even when the required computational power is available.

8   Conclusion

Our paper provides a precise comparison between ASIC-based and GPU-based solutions for cryptanalysis, with a case study on generic birthday search and a case study on the recent chosen-prefix collision on SHA-1. For the former, we show that generic birthday attacks can be performed very easily with ASICs against a 128-bit hash function, and that even a 160-bit hash function would not stand against a huge, yet potentially affordable, ASIC cluster. For the latter, we created two independent ASICs that handle the two parts separately. Our comparisons with GPU-based solutions show a clear advantage of ASIC-based solutions. In particular, we remark that the chosen-prefix collisions for SHA-1 can be generated in under a minute, with an ASIC cluster that costs a few dozen Millions dollars. Such ability would allow an attacker to apply the SLOTH attack [2] on TLS or SSH connections using SHA-1. In the introduction, we posed three research questions; the first question is related to the cost of attacks on SHA-1. Our study showed that ASIC is clearly the best choice for very high complexities attacks, or for attacks that need to be performed in a short amount of time. However, for proof-of- concept or cryptographic research in general, where complexities of 2^{64} or less can be computed in a month or so, renting a set of GPUs seems to be the best solution. If the attack needs to be repeated multiple times, or if the speed of the attack is critical, then the initial hardware cost might be amortized and the energy cost per attack might become important. We note that the energy cost will be very high on GPU compared to a dedicated ASIC solution. For a chosen-prefix collision on SHA-1, the energy cost per attack for our speed-optimized ASIC is 1.6k USD. The best GPU based solution from our benchmarks consumes about 12k USD per attack. Hence, the cost of the ASIC-based solution is amortized. Furthermore, when the CPC attack rate becomes higher than 100 attacks per month, the ASIC solution is cheaper than any GPU-based solution in our benchmarks. In this case, the cost of the GPU rent is prohibitive and the ASIC is the only realistic threat. In the second question, we target the comparison between generic attacks and cryptanalytic attacks for similar theoretical level of numeric complexity. In our study, we show that for a similar level of $\sim 2^{64}$ computations, it is $\sim 75 \sim 82\%$ cheaper to implement a generic birthday search, compared to the differential CPC attack on SHA-1. This means that for these two attacks, the generic attack has an advantage of 5×. One can study more advanced brute force attacks, such as the biclique technique, in order to compare with generic ones. A preliminary study have been published on this topic [3], where the authors compare the cost of building a brute force machine for AES vs. implementing the biclique. They find that the cost of implementing the biclique attack is cheaper than brute force, but slightly worse than what is theoretically expected. However, they only consider one extreme architecture for the brute force machine, and we believe that this can be optimized bringing the cost of brute force down to lower than the biclique attack. However, we leave this hypothesis for future work. Last but not least, the third question is whether the 80-bit security level is still adequate for practical use in less demanding applications. Our study is a warning, showing that not only SHA-1 is indeed practically fully broken, but also that search-based and memory-less generic attacks with complexity $\leq 2^{80}$ are within practical reach.

Acknowledgements. The authors would like to thank the anonymous reviewers for their helpful comments. The authors are supported by a Temasek Labs grant (DSOCL16194).

A   Chip layout

(a) NB Slave ASIC CMOS 28nm FD-SOI layout.

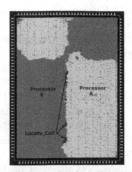

(b) Layout Birthday core.

(c) Sample $1mm^2$. asic layout with 1 NB core.

(d) Sample $1mm^2$ ASIC layout with 12 BD core.

Fig. 19. SHA-1 cryptanalysis accelerator ASIC Layouts

References

1. Beaulieu, R., Shors, D., Smith, J., Treatman-Clark, S., Weeks, B., Wingers, L.: The simon and speck lightweight block ciphers. In: Proceedings of the 52nd Annual Design Automation Conference. DAC 2015, Association for Computing Machinery, New York, NY, USA (2015). https://doi.org/10.1145/2744769.2747946
2. Bhargavan, K., Leurent, G.: Transcript collision attacks: breaking authentication in TLS, IKE and SSH. In: NDSS 2016. The Internet Society (2016)
3. Bogdanov, A., Kavun, E., Paar, C., Rechberger, C., Yalcin, T.: Better than brute-force–optimized hardware architecture for efficient biclique attacks on aes-128. In: ECRYPT Workshop, SHARCS-Special Purpose Hardware for Attacking Cryptographic Systems (2012)
4. Bogdanov, A., Khovratovich, D., Rechberger, C.: Biclique cryptanalysis of the full AES. In: Lee, D.H., Wang, X. (eds.) Advances in Cryptology - ASIACRYPT 2011, pp. 344–371. Springer, Heidelberg (2011)
5. globalpetrolprices.com: https://www.globalpetrolprices.com

6. Güneysu, T., Kasper, T., Novotnỳ, M., Paar, C., Rupp, A.: Cryptanalysis with COPACOBANA. IEEE Trans. Comput. **57**(11), 1498–1513 (2008)
7. Hassan, M., Khalid, A., Chattopadhyay, A., Rechberger, C., Güneysu, T., Paar, C.: New asic/fpga cost estimates for sha-1 collisions. In: Digital System Design (DSD), 2015 Euromicro Conference on, pp. 669–676. IEEE (2015)
8. Jones, H.: FINFET and FD SOI: market and cost analysis. FDSOI Forum 2018. http://soiconsortium.eu/wp-content/uploads/2018/08/MS-FDSOI9.1818-cr.pdf (2018)
9. Joux, A., Peyrin, T.: Hash functions and the (amplified) boomerang attack. In: Menezes, A. (ed.) CRYPTO 2007. LNCS, vol. 4622, pp. 244–263. Springer, Heidelberg (2007). https://doi.org/10.1007/978-3-540-74143-5_14
10. Karpman, P., Peyrin, T., Stevens, M.: Practical free-start collision attacks on 76-step SHA-1. In: Gennaro, R., Robshaw, M. (eds.) CRYPTO 2015. LNCS, vol. 9215, pp. 623–642. Springer, Heidelberg (2015). https://doi.org/10.1007/978-3-662-47989-6_30
11. Khairallah, M., Najm, Z., Chattopadhyay, A., Peyrin, T.: Crack me if you can: Hardware acceleration bridging the gap between practical and theoretical cryptanalysis?: a survey. In: Proceedings of the 18th International Conference on Embedded Computer Systems: Architectures, Modeling, and Simulation. pp. 167–172. SAMOS 2018, ACM, New York, NY, USA (2018). http://doi.acm.org/10.1145/3229631.3239366
12. Kumar, S., Paar, C., Pelzl, J., Pfeiffer, G., Schimmler, M.: Breaking ciphers with COPACOBANA –a cost-optimized parallel code breaker. In: Goubin, L., Matsui, M. (eds.) CHES 2006. LNCS, vol. 4249, pp. 101–118. Springer, Heidelberg (2006). https://doi.org/10.1007/11894063_9
13. Leurent, G., Peyrin, T.: From collisions to chosen-prefix collisions application to full SHA-1. In: Ishai, Y., Rijmen, V. (eds.) EUROCRYPT 2019. LNCS, vol. 11478, pp. 527–555. Springer, Cham (2019). https://doi.org/10.1007/978-3-030-17659-4_18
14. Leurent, G., Peyrin, T.: Sha-1 is a shambles - first chosen-prefix collision on sha-1 and application to the pgp web of trust. Cryptology ePrint Archive, Report 2020/014 (2020), https://eprint.iacr.org/2020/014
15. Pollard, J.M.: Monte carlo methods for index computation. Math. Comput. **32**(143), 918–924 (1978)
16. Stevens, M.: New collision attacks on SHA-1 based on optimal joint local-collision analysis. In: Johansson, T., Nguyen, P.Q. (eds.) EUROCRYPT 2013. LNCS, vol. 7881, pp. 245–261. Springer, Heidelberg (2013). https://doi.org/10.1007/978-3-642-38348-9_15
17. Stevens, M., Bursztein, E., Karpman, P., Albertini, A., Markov, Y.: The first collision for full SHA-1. In: Katz, J., Shacham, H. (eds.) CRYPTO 2017. LNCS, vol. 10401, pp. 570–596. Springer, Cham (2017). https://doi.org/10.1007/978-3-319-63688-7_19
18. Stevens, M., Karpman, P., Peyrin, T.: Freestart collision for full SHA-1. In: Fischlin, M., Coron, J.-S. (eds.) EUROCRYPT 2016. LNCS, vol. 9665, pp. 459–483. Springer, Heidelberg (2016). https://doi.org/10.1007/978-3-662-49890-3_18
19. BroStöm, T.: Lightweight trusted computing. https://www.nist.gov/news-events/events/2019/11/lightweight-cryptography-workshop-2019 (2019)
20. Tu, Y.M., Lu, C.W.: The influence of lot size on production performance in wafer fabrication based on simulation. In: Procedia Engineering, 13th Global Congress on Manufacturing and Management Zhengzhou, China 28–30 November, 2016, vol. 174, pp. 135–144 (2017). http://www.sciencedirect.com/science/article/pii/S1877705817301807,

21. Van Oorschot, P.C., Wiener, M.J.: Parallel collision search with cryptanalytic applications. J. Cryptol. **12**(1), 1–28 (1999)
22. Wang, X., Yao, A.C., Yao, F.: Cryptanalysis on sha-1. In: Cryptographic Hash Workshop hosted by NIST (2005)
23. Wiki, E.: Ethash. GitHub Ethereum Wiki. https://github.com/ethereum/wiki/wiki/Ethash (2017)
24. X16R: https://en.bitcoinwiki.org/wiki/X16R

Author Index

Abram, Damiano 51
Alaoui, Younes Talibi 1
Albrecht, Martin R. 375
Alpár, Greg 100
Apon, Daniel 444
Aranha, Diego F. 227
Auerbach, Benedikt 399

Baghery, Karim 26
Baum, Carsten 227
Biryukov, Alex 276
Blasco, Jorge 375
Boudgoust, Katharina 503

Chakraborty, Suvradip 399
Chalkias, Konstantinos 577
Chattopadhyay, Anupam 657
Cozzo, Daniele 1

Damgård, Ivan 51, 552
Du, Shaoyu 299

Farshim, Pooya 351
Feng, Dengguo 299

Ganesh, Chaya 552
Garillot, François 577
Gjøsteen, Kristian 227
Gong, Xinxin 299
Guilhem, Cyprien Delpech de Saint 26
Guo, Chun 326

Hamburg, Mike 633
Hao, Yonglin 299
Helminger, Lukas 527
Howe, James 444

Iovino, Vincenzo 422

Jensen, Rikke Bjerg 375
Jeudy, Corentin 503
Jiao, Lin 299

Kales, Daniel 527
Khairallah, Mustafa 657

Khati, Louiza 351
Khoshakhlagh, Hamidreza 552
Klein, Karen 399
Kondi, Yashvanth 577
Krips, Toomas 252

Laarhoven, Thijs 478
Leurent, Gaëtan 657
Li, Muzhou 126
Lin, Da 609
Lipmaa, Helger 252

Mareková, Lenka 375
May, Alexander 75

Najm, Zakaria 657
Nikolaenko, Valeria 577
Niu, Chao 126

Orlandi, Claudio 552
Orsini, Emmanuela 26

Pan, Jiaxin 201
Pascual-Perez, Guillermo 399
Peyrin, Thomas 657
Pietrzak, Krzysztof 399
Poettering, Bertram 148
Prest, Thomas 444

Qian, Chen 201

Ramacher, Sebastian 527
Ringerud, Magnus 201
Rösler, Paul 148
Roux-Langlois, Adeline 503

Sanders, Olivier 177
Schlieper, Lars 75
Scholl, Peter 51
Schwenk, Jörg 148
Schwinger, Jonathan 75
Seurin, Yannick 351
Silde, Tjerand 227
Siniscalchi, Luisa 552
Smart, Nigel P. 1, 26

Stebila, Douglas   148
Sun, Siwei   126

Tanguy, Titouan   26
Traoré, Jacques   177
Trieflinger, Sven   51
Tunge, Thor   227
Tunstall, Mike   633

Udovenko, Aleksei   276

Vaudenay, Serge   422
Velichkov, Vesselin   657
Venema, Marloes   100
Vergnaud, Damien   351

Vitto, Giuseppe   276
Vuagnoux, Martin   422

Walch, Roman   527
Walter, Michael   399, 478
Wang, Meiqin   126
Wen, Weiqiang   503

Xiang, Zejun   609
Xiao, Qinglai   633

Yeo, Michelle   399
Yu, Wenqi   326

Zeng, Xiangyong   609
Zhang, Shasha   609
Zhao, Yuqing   326

Printed in the United States
by Baker & Taylor Publisher Services

Printed in the United States
by Baker & Taylor Publisher Services